^{THE}Java^{TM} Developers
ALMANAC 1.4
Volume 1

The Java™ Series

Lisa Friendly, Series Editor
Tim Lindholm, Technical Editor
Ken Arnold, Technical Editor of The Jini™ Technology Series
Jim Inscore, Technical Editor of The Java™ Series, Enterprise Edition

http://www.javaseries.com

THE Java™ Developers ALMANAC 1.4

Volume 1

Examples and Quick Reference

Patrick Chan

✦Addison-Wesley

Boston • San Francisco • New York • Toronto • Montreal
London • Munich • Paris • Madrid
Capetown • Sydney • Tokyo • Singapore • Mexico City

Pearson Education Corporate Sales Division
201 W. 103rd Street
Indianapolis, IN 46290
(800) 428-5331
corpsales@pearsoned.com

Visit AW on the Web: www.aw.com/cseng/

Library of Congress Control Number: 2002102591

Pearson Education, Inc.
Rights and Contracts Department
75 Arlington Street, Suite 300
Boston, MA 02116
Fax: (617) 848-7047

ISBN 0-201-75280-8
Text printed on recycled paper
1 2 3 4 5 6 7 8 9 10—CRS—0605040302
First printing, March 2002

To Kevin and Melissa
For the things that really matter.

Contents

Preface

Welcome to the fourth edition of *The Java™ Developers Almanac*.

There was a time when I intimately knew *all* of the Java class libraries. I knew how it all worked and exactly how everything fit together. I knew what subclassed what, what overrode what, and so on (of course, it helped that I was one of the original developers :-). But aside from the occasional inability to remember which argument of `Vector.insertElementAt()` is the index, I rarely had to refer to any reference documentation.

Version 1.1 added 250 classes and my mastery of the Java class libraries was reduced to half. This left me feeling a little disoriented since I no longer knew my way around, and the increased size of the libraries exceeded my ability to recall the details of the signatures.

Since I make my living writing Java code, it was important that I find an efficient way of "navigating" the new libraries. What I wanted was a quick overview of all of the libraries; something that covered every class and briefly showed their relationships; something that would allow me to explore and quickly learn about new packages. This need led to this book.

The Java™ Developers Almanac is like a map of the Java class libraries. It's a compact and portable tool that covers almost all[1] of the libraries, if only from a bird's-eye view. It's great for reminding you of things like method names and parameters. With today's class count at 3000, you're bound to forget a few details now and again. The almanac is great for discovering the relationships between the classes, such as determining all methods that return an image. It's also great for quickly exploring a new package.

While this book is comprehensive, the libraries are so vast that there simply isn't enough room to provide equally comprehensive documentation. So if you're working with a package that is new to you, you'll probably also need a tutorial book such as *The Java Tutorial, Second Edition* (Campione and Walrath, Addison-Wesley, 1998), a detailed reference such as *The Java Class Libraries, Volumes 1 and 2* (Chan, Lee, and Kramer, Addison-Wesley, 1998), and/or the on-line documentation at *http://java.sun.com/docs*.

---

1. Due to size constraints, the `javax.swing.plaf.*` packages are left out of Volume 2.

The book is divided into four parts, briefly described next.

Part 1: Packages

This part covers each package in alphabetical order: a brief description of the package, a description of each class and interface in the package, and a hierarchy diagram showing the relationship between the classes and interfaces in the package. This part is useful when you need an overview of a package or want to see what other related classes are available in a package.

Most packages provide a number of examples demonstrating common usage of classes in the package. The examples are designed to demonstrate a particular task using the smallest amount of code possible. Their main purpose is to show you which classes are involved in the described task and generally how they interact with each other.

Part 2: Classes

This part contains 500 pages of class tables, one for each class in all the covered packages. Each class table includes a class tree that shows the ancestry of the class and a list of every member in the class. Also included in the member lists are inherited members from superclasses. Thus you have a complete view of all members made available by a class. This part is useful when you're already working with a particular class and want a quick reference to all of the members in the class. New for this edition are example numbers on some of the members. This number refers to an example that demonstrates the use of the member (or a related member).

Part 3: Topics

This part is a set of quick-reference tables on miscellaneous topics. For example, the topic title "Java 1.4" contains a detailed analysis of the API differences between Java 1.3 and Java 1.4.

Part 4: Cross-Reference

This part is a cross-reference of all of the Java classes and interfaces covered in this book. This part is useful when you have questions such as What methods return an `Image` object? or What are all the descendents of `java.io.InputStream`?

Updates

As the title suggests, this book is intended to be updated whenever a new major version of the Java class libraries is released. Since it is designed for you to use in your everyday programming-related work, I would love to hear how I could improve it for the next version or simply what you thought about it. Although I'm afraid I probably won't be able to reply, I promise to read and consider each suggestion I receive. You can reach me at the following e-mail address:

almanac14@xeo.com

Acknowledgments

First and foremost, I thank Mike Hendrickson, who spent a great deal of time collaborating with me on this project. He helped me hone the ideas in this book and then supported me all of the way. It's been tremendous fun working with him.

Arthur Ogawa (*ogawa@teleport.com*), TeX master extraordinaire, provided me with TeX macros without which this book would have been impossible. Thanks for working with me in the wee hours of the morning trying to get everything just right.

I want to thank Lisa Friendly, the series editor, for all sorts of help getting this book off the ground and for getting me all of the support I needed.

Thanks to Lananh Dang who complained about my java.sql examples and ended up writing the java.sql examples for this edition.

Special thanks to Rosanna, my wife, who helped me with writing examples and many other parts of the book.

Many people gave me feedback or provided some other assistance in the making of this book. Thanks to Jens Alfke, Ken Arnold, Joshua Bloch, Paul Bommarito, David Brownell, Michael Bundschuh, Bartley Calder, Casey Cameron, Norman Chin, Mark Drumm, Robert Field, Janice Heiss, Jeff Jackson, Doug Kramer, Sheng Liang, Tim Lindholm, Hans Muller, John Pampuch, Rob Posadas, Mark Reinhold, Dan Rudman, Georges Saab, Bill Shannon, Ann Sunhachawee, Joanne Stewart-Taylor, Laurence Vanhelsuwe, Bruce Wallace, Kathy Walrath, and Tony Welch.

Finally, I want to thank the wonderful people at Addison-Wesley who made this project a lot of fun: Jacquelyn Doucette, Tracy Russ, and Sarah Weaver.

Patrick Chan
February 2002

Part 1

PACKAGES

This part contains information about each package covered in this book. For each there is a description of the package, a description of each class and interface in that package, and a hierarchy diagram showing the relationships between the classes and interfaces in the packages. The following legend describes each of these pieces.

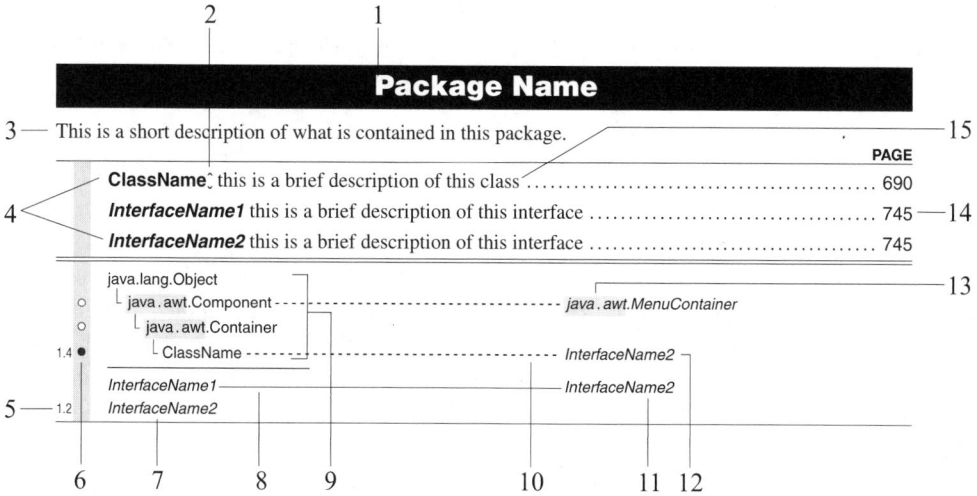

1. The name of the package
2. Has subclass or superclass
   The down-arrow indicator signifies that the class has one or more subclasses. In the case of an interface, it signifies that the interface is extended by one or more interfaces. The up-arrow indicator signifies that the class has a superclass other than `Exception`, `Error`, `Object`, or `RuntimeException`.
3. A brief description of the package
4. A complete list of classes and interfaces (interface names are italicized) in this package
5. The version of Java in which this class or interface was introduced
   You need the specified version of Java or higher in order to use the class. If the field is blank, the class or interface was introduced in Java 1.0. If the field contains an X, the class or interface belongs to an extension package. If the field contains a D, the class is deprecated.

6. A symbolic representation of a class's modifier set:

    ○ An abstract class

    ● A final class
7. The interfaces in the current package
8. Solid line signifying "extends"
9. The classes in the current package, arranged by inheritence
    A subclass appears below a superclass.
10. Dashed line signifying "implements"
11. Interfaces that are extended by the interfaces on the left
12. Interfaces that are implemented by the classes on the left
13. The shaded background behind a package name indicates that the details of this class is covered in another volume
14. The number of the page on which you will find more information about the class or interface
15. A brief description of a class or interface

Note: The class and interface descriptions were derived from Java Software's online documentation and so some of them may be missing since they have not yet been updated.

Examples

Most packages provide a number of examples demonstrating common usage of classes in the package. The examples are designed to illustrate a particular task using the smallest amount of code possible. Their main purpose is to show you which classes are involved in the described task and generally how they interact with each other. Italicized text in an example indicates the parts that should be replaced if you use it in your program. In some cases, an example may have sufficient detail for you to use directly; in other cases, you may have to look up the involved classes in another reference book for more information.

If the code of an example throws a checked exception, the code is surrounded by a `try`/`catch` statement. However, to reduce space and distraction, the catch clause is left blank. Such catch clauses should always handle the exception in some way and should never be left blank. At the very least, you should include a call to `e.printStackTrace()` to display the exception on the console.

An example is designated a number, for example e123. You will find these example numbers next to members in the "Classes" part of the book. A member with an example number indicates that the example uses the member.

Packages

Packages

Examples

Packages

Packages

Packages

9

Packages

java.util.prefs

java.util.regex

Packages

Packages

Permuted Index of Examples

Packages

Packages

27

Packages

Packages

Packages

33

Packages

Packages

Packages

Packages

Packages

Packages

Packages

java.beans

This package contains classes related to JavaBeans development. Some classes in this package are used by beans while they run in an application. These include the property and vetoable change event and listener classes. Most of the other classes in this package are meant to be used by a bean editor (that is, a development environment for customizing and putting together beans to create an application). These classes help the bean editor create a user interface that the user can use to customize the bean. Information (descriptors) about a bean is obtained both explicitly via bean-infos, and implicitly via introspection. This information includes the events fired by a bean, its public methods and parameters, its properties, and so on.

Packages

java.beans

java.lang.Object

1.1	├ Beans
1.4	├ Encoder
1.4	│ └ XMLEncoder
1.4	├ EventHandler - *java.lang.reflect.InvocationHandler*
1.1	├ FeatureDescriptor
1.1	│ ├ BeanDescriptor
1.1	│ ├ EventSetDescriptor
1.1	│ ├ MethodDescriptor
1.1	│ ├ ParameterDescriptor
1.1	│ └ PropertyDescriptor
1.1	│ └ IndexedPropertyDescriptor
1.1	├ Introspector
1.4 ○	├ PersistenceDelegate
1.4	│ └ DefaultPersistenceDelegate
1.1	├ PropertyChangeSupport - *java.io.Serializable*
1.1	├ PropertyEditorManager
1.1	├ PropertyEditorSupport - *PropertyEditor*
1.1	├ SimpleBeanInfo - *BeanInfo*
1.4	├ Statement
1.4	│ └ Expression
1.1	├ VetoableChangeSupport - *java.io.Serializable*
1.4	├ XMLDecoder
1.4 ○	├ java.util.EventListenerProxy - *java.util.EventListener*
1.4	│ ├ PropertyChangeListenerProxy - - - - - - - - - - - - - - - - *PropertyChangeListener*ˆ
1.4	│ └ VetoableChangeListenerProxy - - - - - - - - - - - - - - - - *VetoableChangeListener*ˆ

Class   *Interface*   —extends   - - -implements   ○ abstract   ● final   ˆ—has superclass   —has subclass   package—see other volume

```
        java.lang.Object
1.1       ├ java.util.EventObject---------------------------------,--java.io.Serializable
1.1       │   └ PropertyChangeEvent
          └ java.lang.Throwable-----------------------------------'
              └ java.lang.Exception
1.1                 ├ IntrospectionException
1.1                 └ PropertyVetoException
```

1.2	*AppletInitializer*
1.1	*BeanInfo*
1.1	*Customizer*
1.2	*DesignMode*
1.4	*ExceptionListener*
1.1	*PropertyChangeListener* ——————————————— *java.util.EventListener*
1.1	*PropertyEditor*
1.1	*VetoableChangeListener* ———————————
1.1	*Visibility*

ε1. The Quintessential Bean

This example bean has a single property called property. If the property were not a boolean, it would not have an isX() method. Also, if the property were read-only, it would not have a setX() method.

```java
import java.io.Serializable;

public class BasicBean implements Serializable {
    boolean property;
    public BasicBean() {
    }
    public boolean getProperty() {
        return property;
    }
    public boolean isProperty() {
        return property;
    }
    public void setProperty(boolean newValue) {
        property = newValue;
    }
}
```

ε2. Implementing a Bound Property

A bound property fires a PropertyChangeEvent whenever its value is changed. This example bean implements a single bound integer property called myProperty.

```java
int myProperty;
public int getMyProperty() {
    return myProperty;
}
public void setMyProperty(int newValue) {
    int oldValue = myProperty;
    myProperty = newValue;
    pceListeners.firePropertyChange("myProperty", new Integer(oldValue), new Integer(newValue));
}

// Create the listener list.
PropertyChangeSupport pceListeners = new PropertyChangeSupport(this);

// The listener list wrapper methods.
```

```
        public synchronized void addPropertyChangeListener(PropertyChangeListener listener) {
            pceListeners.addPropertyChangeListener(listener);
        }
        public synchronized void removePropertyChangeListener(PropertyChangeListener listener) {
            pceListeners.removePropertyChangeListener(listener);
        }
```

ε3. Implementing a Constrained Property

A constrained property fires a PropertyChangeEvent whenever its value is about to be changed. Any listener can veto the event, thereby preventing the change. This example bean implements a single constrained integer property called myProperty.

```
        int myProperty;
        public int getMyProperty() {
            return myProperty;
        }
        public void setMyProperty(int newValue) throws PropertyVetoException {
            try {
                vceListeners.fireVetoableChange(
                    "myProperty", new Integer(myProperty), new Integer(newValue));
                myProperty = newValue;
            } catch (PropertyVetoException e) {
                throw e;
            }
        }

        // Create the listener list.
        VetoableChangeSupport vceListeners = new VetoableChangeSupport(this);

        // The listener list wrapper methods.
        public synchronized void addVetoableChangeListener(VetoableChangeListener listener) {
            vceListeners.addVetoableChangeListener(listener);
        }
        public synchronized void removeVetoableChangeListener(VetoableChangeListener listener) {
            vceListeners.removeVetoableChangeListener(listener);
        }
```

ε4. Instantiating a Bean

```
        try {
            MyBean bean = (MyBean)Beans.instantiate(ClassLoader.getSystemClassLoader(), "MyBean");
        } catch (ClassNotFoundException e) {
        } catch (IOException e) {
        }
```

ε5. Listing the Property Names of a Bean

This example determines the properties of a bean with the type MyBean.

```
        try {
            BeanInfo bi = Introspector.getBeanInfo(MyBean.class);
            PropertyDescriptor[] pds = bi.getPropertyDescriptors();
            for (int i=0; i<pds.length; i++) {
                // Get property name
                String propName = pds[i].getName();
            }
            // class, prop1, prop2, PROP3
```

Class *Interface* —extends - - -implements   O abstract   ● final   ^—has superclass   ͺ—has subclass   package—see other volume

```
    } catch (java.beans.IntrospectionException e) {
    }
    public class MyBean {
        // Property prop1
        public String getProp1() {
            return null;
        }
        public void setProp1(String s) {
        }

        // Property prop2
        public int getProp2() {
            return 0;
        }
        public void setProp2(int i) {
        }

        // Property PROP
        public byte[] getPROP3() {
            return null;
        }
        public void setPROP3(byte[] bytes) {
        }
    }
```

ε6. Getting and Setting a Property of a Bean

This example demonstrates how to get and set the value of a property in a bean using Expression and Statement. The example gets and sets three types of properties, an Object, a primitive type, and an array. Both these classes use the name of the method that gets or sets the property.

```
Object o = new MyBean();
try {
    // Get the value of prop1
    Expression expr = new Expression(o, "getProp1", new Object[0]);
    expr.execute();
    String s = (String)expr.getValue();

    // Set the value of prop1
    Statement stmt = new Statement(o, "setProp1", new Object[]{"new string"});
    stmt.execute();

    // Get the value of prop2
    expr = new Expression(o, "getProp2", new Object[0]);
    expr.execute();
    int i = ((Integer)expr.getValue()).intValue();

    // Set the value of prop2
    stmt = new Statement(o, "setProp2", new Object[]{new Integer(123)});
    stmt.execute();

    // Get the value of prop1
    expr = new Expression(o, "getProp3", new Object[0]);
    expr.execute();
    byte[] bytes = (byte[])expr.getValue();

    // Set the value of prop1
    stmt = new Statement(o, "setProp3", new Object[]{new byte[]{0x12, 0x23}});
    stmt.execute();
} catch (Exception e) {
```

```
        }
    public class MyBean {
        // Property prop1
        String prop1;
        public String getProp1() {
            return prop1;
        }
        public void setProp1(String s) {
            prop1 = s;
        }

        // Property prop2
        int prop2;
        public int getProp2() {
            return prop2;
        }
        public void setProp2(int i) {
            prop2 = i;
        }

        // Property prop3
        byte[] prop3;
        public byte[] getProp3() {
            return prop3;
        }
        public void setProp3(byte[] bytes) {
            prop3 = bytes;
        }
    }
```

Serialization

ε7. Serializing a Bean to XML

The XMLEncoder class serializes an object in similar fashion to java.io.ObjectOutput. However, unlike ObjectOutput, which persists all non-transient private and public data, the XMLEncoder only persists the value of public properties. In particular, for every public property, XMLEncoder calls its getter method and persists the returned value. In deserialization, a newly created object is initialized with these persisted property values. Therefore, any private state that is not associated with a property will, by default, not be persisted.

See also "ε8. Deserializing a Bean from XML".

```
    // Create an object and set properties
    MyClass o = new MyClass();
    o.setProp(1);
    o.setProps(new int[]{1, 2, 3});

    try {
        // Serialize object into XML
        XMLEncoder encoder = new XMLEncoder(new BufferedOutputStream(
            new FileOutputStream("outfilename.xml")));
        encoder.writeObject(o);
        encoder.close();
    } catch (FileNotFoundException e) {
    }
```

Class   *Interface*   —extends   - - -implements   ○ abstract   ● final   ^—has superclass   ⌐—has subclass   package—see other volume

```
// This class defines two properties - prop and props
public class MyClass {
    // The prop property
    int i;
    public int getProp() {
        return i;
    }
    public void setProp(int i) {
        this.i = i;
    }

    // The props property
    int[] iarray = new int[0];
    public int[] getProps() {
        return iarray;
    }
    public void setProps(int[] iarray) {
        this.iarray = iarray;
    }
}
```

Here is the XML data:

```
<?xml version="1.0" encoding="UTF-8"?>
<java version="1.4.0" class="java.beans.XMLDecoder">
    <object class="MyClass">
        <void property="prop">
            <int>1</int>
        </void>
        <void property="props">
            <array class="int" length="3">
                <void index="0">
                    <int>1</int>
                </void>
                <void index="1">
                    <int>2</int>
                </void>
                <void index="2">
                    <int>3</int>
                </void>
            </array>
        </void>
    </object>
</java>
```

ε8. Deserializing a Bean from XML

See also "ε7. Serializing a Bean to XML".

```
// Deserialize an object
try {
    XMLDecoder decoder = new XMLDecoder(new BufferedInputStream(
        new FileInputStream("infilename.xml")));

    // MyClass is declared in "ε7. Serializing a Bean to XML"
    MyClass o = (MyClass)decoder.readObject();
    decoder.close();

    // Use the object
    int prop = o.getProp(); // 1
```

```
        int[] props = o.getProps(); // [1, 2, 3]
    } catch (FileNotFoundException e) {
    }
```

Here is the XML data being deserialized:

```xml
<?xml version="1.0" encoding="UTF-8"?>
<java version="1.4.0" class="java.beans.XMLDecoder">
    <object class="MyClass">
        <void property="prop">
            <int>1</int>
        </void>
        <void property="props">
            <array class="int" length="3">
                <void index="0">
                    <int>1</int>
                </void>
                <void index="1">
                    <int>2</int>
                </void>
                <void index="2">
                    <int>3</int>
                </void>
            </array>
        </void>
    </object>
</java>
```

ε9. Preventing a Bean Property from Being Serialized to XML

By default, when serializing an object into XML, the current value of all public properties is persisted (if they don't equal the default value). This example demonstrates how to prevent a public property from being persisted.

See also "ε8. Deserializing a Bean from XML".

```java
// Create an object and set properties
MyClass2 o = new MyClass2();
o.setProp(1);
o.setProps(new int[]{1, 2, 3});

try {
    // Serialize object into XML.
    // props is transient so it will not be persisted.
    XMLEncoder encoder = new XMLEncoder(new BufferedOutputStream(
        new FileOutputStream("outfilename.xml")));
    encoder.writeObject(o);
    encoder.close();
} catch (FileNotFoundException e) {
}

// This class defines two properties - prop and props.
// The props property is marked transient so that it will not
// be persisted if serialized into XML.
import java.beans.*;
public class MyClass2 {
    // The prop property
    int i;
```

```
        public int getProp() {
            return i;
        }
        public void setProp(int i) {
            this.i = i;
        }

        // The props property
        int[] iarray = new int[0];
        public int[] getProps() {
            return iarray;
        }
        public void setProps(int[] iarray) {
            this.iarray = iarray;
        }

        static {
            try {
                // Make the props property transient
                BeanInfo info = Introspector.getBeanInfo(MyClass2.class);
                PropertyDescriptor[] propertyDescriptors = info.getPropertyDescriptors();
                for (int i = 0; i < propertyDescriptors.length; ++i) {
                    PropertyDescriptor pd = propertyDescriptors[i];
                    if (pd.getName().equals("props")) {
                        pd.setValue("transient", Boolean.TRUE);
                    }
                }
            } catch (IntrospectionException e) {
            }
        }
    }
```

Here is the XML data:

```
    <?xml version="1.0" encoding="UTF-8"?>
    <java version="1.4.0" class="java.beans.XMLDecoder">
        <object class="MyClass2">
            <void property="prop">
                <int>1</int>
            </void>
        </object>
    </java>
```

ε10. Serializing an Immutable Bean Property to XML

An immutable property is one where the value is supplied to the constructor rather than through a setter method. By default, immutable properties are not persisted. This example demonstrates how to persist an immutable property called prop.

```
    // Create an object with an immutable property and set the value
    // of the immutable property in the constructor
    MyClass3 o = new MyClass3(123);

    try {
        // Create the encoder
        XMLEncoder encoder = new XMLEncoder(new BufferedOutputStream(
            new FileOutputStream("outfilename.xml")));

        // Specify to the encoder, the name of the property that is associated
        // with the constructor's parameter(s)
```

```
                String[] propertyNames = new String[]{"prop"};
                encoder.setPersistenceDelegate(MyClass3.class,
                    new DefaultPersistenceDelegate(propertyNames);

                // Serialize the object into XML
                encoder.writeObject(o);
                encoder.close();
            } catch (FileNotFoundException e) {
            }

        // This class defines an immutable property called prop.
        // The value of the immutable property is initialized
        import java.beans.*;
        public class MyClass3 {
            int prop;
            // The constructor that initializes the immutable property prop
            public MyClass3(int prop) {
                this.prop = prop;
            }

            // The immutable property
            public int getProp() {
                return prop;
            }
        }
```

Here is the XML data:

```
        <?xml version="1.0" encoding="UTF-8"?>
        <java version="1.4.0" class="java.beans.XMLDecoder">
            <object class="MyClass3">
                <int>123</int>
            </object>
        </java>
```

Events

ε11. Listening for a Property Change Event

A property change event is fired when a bound property is changed.

```
        // Register for property change events on the bean
        bean.addPropertyChangeListener(new MyPropertyChangeListener());

        class MyPropertyChangeListener implements PropertyChangeListener {
            // This method is called every time the property value is changed
            public void propertyChange(PropertyChangeEvent evt) {
                // Get the old value of the property
                Object oldValue = evt.getOldValue();

                // Get the new value of the property
                Object newValue = evt.getNewValue();
            }
        }
```

ε12. Listening for a Vetoable Property Change Event

A vetoable property change event is fired when a constrained property is changed. A listener can veto the change by throwing PropertyVetoException and preventing the change.

Class   *Interface*   —extends   - - -implements   ○ abstract   ● final   ˆ—has superclass   ˌ—has subclass   package—see other volume

```
// Register for property change events on the bean
bean.addVetoableChangeListener(new MyVetoableChangeListener());

class MyVetoableChangeListener implements VetoableChangeListener {
    // This method is called every time the property value is changed
    public void vetoableChange(PropertyChangeEvent evt) throws PropertyVetoException {
        // Get the old value of the property
        Object oldValue = evt.getOldValue();

        // Get the new value of the property
        Object newValue = evt.getNewValue();

        // Determine if the change should be vetoed, thereby preventing the change
        boolean veto = false;
        if (veto) {
            throw new PropertyVetoException("the reason for the veto", evt);
        }
    }
}
```

java.beans.beancontext

This package contains classes and interfaces relating to bean context. A bean context is a container for beans and defines the execution environment for the beans it contains. There can be several beans in a single bean context, and a bean context can be nested within another bean context. This package also contains events and listener interface for beans being added and removed from a bean context.

Packages

java.beans.beancontext

```
       java.lang.Object
1.2      ├ BeanContextChildSupport - - - - - - - - - - - - - - - - - - - - - - - - BeanContextChild ◌,
         │                                                                        BeanContextServicesListener ◌,
         │                                                                        java.io.Serializable ◌
1.2      │  └ BeanContextSupport - - - - - - - - - - - - - - - - - - - - - - - - BeanContext ◌, java.beans←
         │                                                                        .PropertyChangeListener ^,
         │                                                                        java.beans.VetoableChangeListener ^,
         │                                                                        java.io.Serializable ◌
1.2      │     └ BeanContextServicesSupport - - - - - - - - - - - - - - - - - BeanContextServices ^
1.2      ├ BeanContextServicesSupport.BCSSProxyServiceProvider - - - - BeanContextServiceProvider,
         │                                                                        BeanContextServiceRevokedListener ◌
1.2      ├ BeanContextServicesSupport.BCSSServiceProvider - - - - - -- java.io.Serializable ◌
1.2      ├ BeanContextSupport.BCSChild - - - - - - - - - - - - - - - - - - - - - - - ┘
1.2      │  └ BeanContextServicesSupport.BCSSChild
1.2  ●   ├ BeanContextSupport.BCSIterator - - - - - - - - - - - - - - - - - - - java.util.Iterator ◌
1.1      └ java.util.EventObject - - - - - - - - - - - - - - - - - - - - - - - - - - java.io.Serializable ◌
1.2  ○      └ BeanContextEvent
1.2         ├ BeanContextMembershipEvent
1.2         ├ BeanContextServiceAvailableEvent
1.2         └ BeanContextServiceRevokedEvent
```

```
1.2  BeanContext ◌ ──────────────────────────────────── BeanContextChild, java.beans.DesignMode,
                                                             java.beans.Visibility, java.util.Collection
1.2  BeanContextChild ◌
1.2  BeanContextChildComponentProxy
1.2  BeanContextContainerProxy
1.2  BeanContextMembershipListener ──────────────────── java.util.EventListener
1.2  BeanContextProxy
1.2  BeanContextServiceProvider
1.2  BeanContextServiceProviderBeanInfo ─────────────── java.beans.BeanInfo
1.2  BeanContextServiceRevokedListener ◌ ────────────── java.util.EventListener
1.2  BeanContextServices ────────────────────────────── BeanContext ^, BeanContextServicesListener ^
1.2  BeanContextServicesListener ◌ ──────────────────── BeanContextServiceRevokedListener ^
```

Class   *Interface*   —extends   - - -implements   ○ abstract   ● final   ^—has superclass   ◌—has subclass   package—see other volume

java.io

This package contains three main groups of classes and interfaces. The first group is for building data streams. A data stream is either an input stream for reading bytes or characters, or an output stream for writing bytes or characters. The second group contains classes and interfaces for object serialization. Object serialization is the process of converting an object's state into a byte stream in such a way that the byte stream can be re-converted back into a copy of the object. The last group is for dealing with the file system.

java.io

Class   *Interface*   —extends   - - -implements   ○ abstract   ● final   ˆ—has superclass   ˍ—has subclass   package—see other volume

```
      java.lang.Object
      ├ File - - - - - - - - - - - - - - - - - - - - - - - - - - - - - - - - Serializable,, java.lang.Comparable
  ●   ├ FileDescriptor
  ○   ├ InputStream
      │   ├ ByteArrayInputStream
      │   ├ FileInputStream
      │   ├ FilterInputStream
      │   │   ├ BufferedInputStream
      │   │   ├ DataInputStream - - - - - - - - - - - - - - - - - - - - - - - - - - - DataInput,
  D   │   │   ├ LineNumberInputStream
      │   │   └ PushbackInputStream
 1.1  │   ├ ObjectInputStream - - - - - - - - - - - - - - - - - - - - - - - - ObjectInput^, ObjectStreamConstants
      │   ├ PipedInputStream
      │   ├ SequenceInputStream
  D   │   └ StringBufferInputStream
1.2 ○ ├ ObjectInputStream.GetField
1.2 ○ ├ ObjectOutputStream.PutField
 1.1  ├ ObjectStreamClass - - - - - - - - - - - - - - - - - - - - - - - - - - Serializable,
 1.2  ├ ObjectStreamField - - - - - - - - - - - - - - - - - - - - - - - - - - java.lang.Comparable
  ○   ├ OutputStream
      │   ├ ByteArrayOutputStream
      │   ├ FileOutputStream
      │   ├ FilterOutputStream
      │   │   ├ BufferedOutputStream
      │   │   ├ DataOutputStream - - - - - - - - - - - - - - - - - - - - - - - DataOutput,
      │   │   └ PrintStream,
 1.1  │   ├ ObjectOutputStream - - - - - - - - - - - - - - - - - - - - - - - ObjectOutput^, ObjectStreamConstants
      │   └ PipedOutputStream
      ├ RandomAccessFile - - - - - - - - - - - - - - - - - - - - - - - - - - DataInput,, DataOutput,
```

Packages

java.io

java.lang.Object

1.1 ○	— Reader	
1.1		— BufferedReader
1.1		└ LineNumberReader
1.1		— CharArrayReader
1.1 ○		— FilterReader
1.1		└ PushbackReader
1.1		— InputStreamReader
1.1		└ FileReader
1.1		— PipedReader
1.1		└ StringReader
	— StreamTokenizer	
1.1 ○	— Writer	
1.1		— BufferedWriter
1.1		— CharArrayWriter
1.1 ○		— FilterWriter
1.1		— OutputStreamWriter
1.1		└ FileWriter
1.1		— PipedWriter
1.1		— PrintWriter
1.1		└ StringWriter

1.2 ○ — java.security.Permission ----------------------------- *Serializable* , *java.security.Guard*
1.2 ● | — FilePermission ---------------------------------- *Serializable*
1.2 ○ | └ java.security.BasicPermission ---------------------┐
1.2 ● | └ SerializablePermission |
        └ java.lang.Throwable - - - - - - - - - - - - - - - - ┘
            └ java.lang.Exception
                └ IOException

1.1	— CharConversionException
	— EOFException
	— FileNotFoundException
	— InterruptedIOException
1.1 ○	— ObjectStreamException
1.1		— InvalidClassException
1.1		— InvalidObjectException
1.1		— NotActiveException
1.1		— NotSerializableException
1.1		— OptionalDataException
1.1		— StreamCorruptedException
1.1		└ WriteAbortedException
1.1	— SyncFailedException
	— UTFDataFormatException
1.1	└ UnsupportedEncodingException

	DataInput	
	DataOutput	
1.1	*Externalizable* —————————————— *Serializable*
1.2	*FileFilter*	
	FilenameFilter	
1.1	*ObjectInput* —————————————————— *DataInput*
1.1	*ObjectInputValidation*	

Class   *Interface*   —extends   - - -implements   ○ abstract   ● final   ^—has superclass   ͺ—has subclass   package—see other volume

70

Filenames and Pathnames

ε13. Constructing a Filename Path

A File object is used to represent a filename. Creating the File object has no effect on the file system; the filename need not exist nor is it created.

On Windows, this example creates the path \a\b. On Unix, the path would be /a/b.

```
String path = File.separator + "a" + File.separator + "b";
```

ε14. Converting Between a Filename Path and a URL

```
// Create a file object
File file = new File("filename");

// Convert the file object to a URL
URL url = null;
try {
    // The file need not exist. It is made into an absolute path
    // by prefixing the current working directory
    url = file.toURL(); // file:/d:/almanac1.4/java.io/filename
} catch (MalformedURLException e) {
}

// Convert the URL to a file object
file = new File(url.getFile()); // d:/almanac1.4/java.io/filename

// Read the file contents using the URL
try {
    // Open an input stream
    InputStream is = url.openStream();

    // Read from is

    is.close();
} catch (IOException e) {
    // Could not open the file
}
```

ε15. Getting an Absolute Filename Path from a Relative Filename Path

```
File file = new File("filename.txt");
file = file.getAbsoluteFile(); // c:\temp\filename.txt

file = new File("dir"+File.separatorChar+"filename.txt");
file = file.getAbsoluteFile(); // c:\temp\dir\filename.txt

file = new File(".."+File.separatorChar+"filename.txt");
file = file.getAbsoluteFile(); // c:\temp\..\filename.txt

// Note that filename.txt does not need to exist
```

ε16. Determining If Two Filename Paths Refer to the Same File

A filename path may include redundant names such as '.' or '..' or symbolic links (on UNIX platforms). File.getCanonicalFile() converts a filename path to a unique canonical form suitable for comparisons.

```
File file1 = new File("./filename");
```

Packages

```
File file2 = new File("filename");

// Filename paths are not equal
boolean b = file1.equals(file2); // false

// Normalize the paths
try {
    file1 = file1.getCanonicalFile(); // c:\almanac1.4\filename
    file2 = file2.getCanonicalFile(); // c:\almanac1.4\filename
} catch (IOException e) {
}

// Filename paths are now equal
b = file1.equals(file2); // true
```

ε17. Getting the Parents of a Filename Path

```
// Get the parent of a relative filename path
File file = new File("Ex1.java");
String parentPath = file.getParent(); // null
File parentDir = file.getParentFile(); // null

// Get the parents of an absolute filename path
file = new File("D:\\almanac\\Ex1.java");
parentPath = file.getParent(); // D:\almanac
parentDir = file.getParentFile(); // D:\almanac

parentPath = parentDir.getParent(); // D:\
parentDir = parentDir.getParentFile(); // D:\

parentPath = parentDir.getParent(); // null
parentDir = parentDir.getParentFile(); // null
```

ε18. Determining If a Filename Path Is a File or a Directory

```
File dir = new File("directoryName");

boolean isDir = dir.isDirectory();
if (isDir) {
    // dir is a directory
} else {
    // dir is a file
}
```

Files

ε19. Determining If a File or Directory Exists

```
boolean exists = (new File("filename")).exists();
if (exists) {
    // File or directory exists
} else {
    // File or directory does not exist
}
```

ε20. Creating a File

```
try {
    File file = new File("filename");
```

Class   *Interface*   —extends   - - -implements   ○ abstract   ● final   ˆ—has superclass   ˯—has subclass   package—see other volume

```
        // Create file if it does not exist
        boolean success = file.createNewFile();
        if (success) {
            // File did not exist and was created
        } else {
            // File already exists
        }
    } catch (IOException e) {
    }
```

ε21. Getting the Size of a File

```
File file = new File("infilename");

// Get the number of bytes in the file
long length = file.length();
```

ε22. Deleting a File

```
boolean success = (new File("filename")).delete();
if (!success) {
    // Deletion failed
}
```

ε23. Creating a Temporary File

```
try {
    // Create temp file.
    File temp = File.createTempFile("pattern", ".suffix");

    // Delete temp file when program exits.
    temp.deleteOnExit();

    // Write to temp file
    BufferedWriter out = new BufferedWriter(new FileWriter(temp));
    out.write("aString");
    out.close();
} catch (IOException e) {
}
```

ε24. Renaming a File or Directory

```
// File (or directory) with old name
File file = new File("oldname");

// File (or directory) with new name
File file2 = new File("newname");

// Rename file (or directory)
boolean success = file.renameTo(file2);
if (!success) {
    // File was not successfully renamed
}
```

ε25. Moving a File or Directory to Another Directory

```
// File (or directory) to be moved
File file = new File("filename");

// Destination directory
File dir = new File("directoryname");

// Move file to new directory
```

```
    boolean success = file.renameTo(new File(dir, file.getName()));
    if (!success) {
        // File was not successfully moved
    }
```

ε26. Getting and Setting the Modification Time of a File or Directory

This example gets the last modified time of a file or directory and then sets it to the current time.

```
File file = new File("filename");

// Get the last modified time
long modifiedTime = file.lastModified();
// 0L is returned if the file does not exist

// Set the last modified time
long newModifiedTime = System.currentTimeMillis();
boolean success = file.setLastModified(newModifiedTime);
if (!success) {
    // operation failed.
}
```

ε27. Forcing Updates to a File to the Disk

In some applications, such as transaction processing, it is necessary to ensure that an update has been made to the disk. FileDescriptor.sync() blocks until all changes to a file are written to disk.

```
try {
    // Open or create the output file
    FileOutputStream os = new FileOutputStream("outfilename");
    FileDescriptor fd = os.getFD();

    // Write some data to the stream
    byte[] data = new byte[]{(byte)0xCA, (byte)0xFE, (byte)0xBA, (byte)0xBE};
    os.write(data);

    // Flush the data from the streams and writers into system buffers.
    // The data may or may not be written to disk.
    os.flush();

    // Block until the system buffers have been written to disk.
    // After this method returns, the data is guaranteed to have
    // been written to disk.
    fd.sync();
} catch (IOException e) {
}
```

Directories

ε28. Getting the Current Working Directory

The working directory is the location in the file system from where the java command was invoked.

```
String curDir = System.getProperty("user.dir");
```

ε29. Creating a Directory

```
// Create a directory; all ancestor directories must exist
boolean success = (new File("directoryName")).mkdir();
if (!success) {
```

Class *Interface* —extends - - -implements O abstract ● final ^—has superclass ˍ—has subclass package—see other volume

```
        // Directory creation failed
    }

    // Create a directory; all non-existent ancestor directories are
    // automatically created
    success = (new File("directoryName")).mkdirs();
    if (!success) {
        // Directory creation failed
    }
```

ε30. Deleting a Directory

```
    // Delete an empty directory
    boolean success = (new File("directoryName")).delete();
    if (!success) {
        // Deletion failed
    }
```

If the directory is not empty, it is necessary to first recursively delete all files and subdirectories in the directory. Here is a method that will delete a non-empty directory.

```
    // Deletes all files and subdirectories under dir.
    // Returns true if all deletions were successful.
    // If a deletion fails, the method stops attempting to delete and returns false.
    public static boolean deleteDir(File dir) {
        if (dir.isDirectory()) {
            String[] children = dir.list();
            for (int i=0; i<children.length; i++) {
                boolean success = deleteDir(new File(dir, children[i]));
                if (!success) {
                    return false;
                }
            }
        }

        // The directory is now empty so delete it
        return dir.delete();
    }
```

ε31. Listing the Files or Subdirectories in a Directory

```
    File dir = new File("directoryName");

    String[] children = dir.list();
    if (children == null) {
        // Either dir does not exist or is not a directory
    } else {
        for (int i=0; i<children.length; i++) {
            // Get filename of file or directory
            String filename = children[i];
        }
    }

    // It is also possible to filter the list of returned files.
    // This example does not return any files that start with '.'.
    FilenameFilter filter = new FilenameFilter() {
        public boolean accept(File dir, String name) {
            return !name.startsWith(".");
        }
    };
```

```
children = dir.list(filter);

// The list of files can also be retrieved as File objects
File[] files = dir.listFiles();

// This filter only returns directories
FileFilter fileFilter = new FileFilter() {
    public boolean accept(File file) {
        return file.isDirectory();
    }
};
files = dir.listFiles(fileFilter);
```

ε32. Listing the File System Roots

UNIX file systems have a single root, '/'. On Windows, each drive is a root. For example the C drive is represented by the root C:\.

```
File[] roots = File.listRoots();
for (int i=0; i<roots.length; i++) {
    process(roots[i]);
}
```

ε33. Traversing a Directory

```
public static void traverse(File dir) {
    process(dir);

    if (dir.isDirectory()) {
        String[] children = dir.list();
        for (int i=0; i<children.length; i++) {
            traverse(new File(dir, children[i]));
        }
    }
}
```

Reading and Writing

ε34. Reading Text from Standard Input

```
try {
    BufferedReader in = new BufferedReader(new InputStreamReader(System.in));
    String str = "";
    while (str != null) {
        System.out.print("> prompt ");
        str = in.readLine();
        process(str);
    }
} catch (IOException e) {
}
```

ε35. Reading Text from a File

```
try {
    BufferedReader in = new BufferedReader(new FileReader("infilename"));
    String str;
    while ((str = in.readLine()) != null) {
```

Class   *Interface*   —extends   - - -implements   ○ abstract   ● final   ^—has superclass   ‿—has subclass   package—see other volume

```
        process(str);
    }
    in.close();
} catch (IOException e) {
}
```

ε36. Reading a File into a Byte Array

This example implements a method that reads the entire contents of a file into a byte array.

```
// Returns the contents of the file in a byte array.
public static byte[] getBytesFromFile(File file) throws IOException {
    InputStream is = new FileInputStream(file);

    // Get the size of the file
    long length = file.length();

    // You cannot create an array using a long type.
    // It needs to be an int type.
    // Before converting to an int type, check
    // to ensure that file is not larger than Integer.MAX_VALUE.
    if (length > Integer.MAX_VALUE) {
        // File is too large
    }

    // Create the byte array to hold the data
    byte[] bytes = new byte[(int)length];

    // Read in the bytes
    int offset = 0;
    int numRead = 0;
    while (offset < bytes.length
            && (numRead=is.read(bytes, offset, bytes.length-offset)) >= 0) {
        offset += numRead;
    }

    // Ensure all the bytes have been read in
    if (offset < bytes.length) {
        throw new IOException("Could not completely read file "+file.getName());
    }

    // Close the input stream and return bytes
    is.close();
    return bytes;
}
```

ε37. Writing to a File

If the file does not already exist, it is automatically created.

```
try {
    BufferedWriter out = new BufferedWriter(new FileWriter("outfilename"));
    out.write("aString");
    out.close();
} catch (IOException e) {
}
```

ε38. Appending to a File

```
try {
    BufferedWriter out = new BufferedWriter(new FileWriter("filename", true));
    out.write("aString");
```

```
            out.close();
        } catch (IOException e) {
        }
```

ε39. Using a Random Access File

```
        try {
            File f = new File("filename");
            RandomAccessFile raf = new RandomAccessFile(f, "rw");

            // Read a character
            char ch = raf.readChar();

            // Seek to end of file
            raf.seek(f.length());

            // Append to the end
            raf.writeChars("aString");
            raf.close();
        } catch (IOException e) {
        }
```

Encodings

ε40. Reading UTF-8 Encoded Data

```
        try {
            BufferedReader in = new BufferedReader(
                new InputStreamReader(new FileInputStream("infilename"), "UTF8"));
            String str = in.readLine();
        } catch (UnsupportedEncodingException e) {
        } catch (IOException e) {
        }
```

ε41. Writing UTF-8 Encoded Data

```
        try {
            Writer out = new BufferedWriter(new OutputStreamWriter(
                new FileOutputStream("outfilename"), "UTF8"));
            out.write(aString);
            out.close();
        } catch (UnsupportedEncodingException e) {
        } catch (IOException e) {
        }
```

ε42. Reading ISO Latin-1 Encoded Data

```
        try {
            BufferedReader in = new BufferedReader(
                new InputStreamReader(new FileInputStream("infilename"), "8859_1"));
            String str = in.readLine();
        } catch (UnsupportedEncodingException e) {
        } catch (IOException e) {
        }
```

ε43. Writing ISO Latin-1 Encoded Data

```
        try {
```

Class *Interface* —extends - - -implements ○ abstract ● final ⌐—has superclass ⌐—has subclass package —see other volume

```
    Writer out = new BufferedWriter(
        new OutputStreamWriter(new FileOutputStream("outfilename"), "8859_1"));
    out.write(aString);
    out.close();
} catch (UnsupportedEncodingException e) {
} catch (IOException e) {
}
```

Serialization

ε44. Serializing an Object

The object to be serialized must implement java.io.Serializable. This example serializes a javax.swing.JButton object.

See also "ε45. Deserializing an Object".

```
Object object = new javax.swing.JButton("push me");

try {
    // Serialize to a file
    ObjectOutput out = new ObjectOutputStream(new FileOutputStream("filename.ser"));
    out.writeObject(object);
    out.close();

    // Serialize to a byte array
    ByteArrayOutputStream bos = new ByteArrayOutputStream() ;
    out = new ObjectOutputStream(bos) ;
    out.writeObject(object);
    out.close();

    // Get the bytes of the serialized object
    byte[] buf = bos.toByteArray();
} catch (IOException e) {
}
```

ε45. Deserializing an Object

This example deserializes a javax.swing.JButton object.

See also "ε44. Serializing an Object".

```
try {
    // Deserialize from a file
    File file = new File("filename.ser");
    ObjectInputStream in = new ObjectInputStream(new FileInputStream(file));
    // Deserialize the object
    javax.swing.JButton button = (javax.swing.JButton) in.readObject();
    in.close();

    // Get some byte array data
    byte[] bytes = getBytesFromFile(file);
    // see "ε36. Reading a File into a Byte Array" for the implementation of this method

    // Deserialize from a byte array
    in = new ObjectInputStream(new ByteArrayInputStream(bytes));
    button = (javax.swing.JButton) in.readObject();
    in.close();
} catch (ClassNotFoundException e) {
} catch (IOException e) {
}
```

ε46. Implementing a Serializable Singleton

By default, the deserialization process creates new instances of classes. This example demonstrates how to customize the deserialization process of a singleton to avoid creating new instances of the singleton.

```java
public class MySingleton implements Serializable {
    static MySingleton singleton = new MySingleton();

    private MySingleton() {
    }

    // This method is called immediately after an object of this class is deserialized.
    // This method returns the singleton instance.
    protected Object readResolve() {
        return singleton;
    }
}
```

Parsing

ε47. Tokenizing Java Source Code

The StreamTokenizer can be used for simple parsing of a Java source file into tokens. The tokenizer can be aware of Java-style comments and ignore them. It is also aware of Java quoting and escaping rules.

```java
try {
    // Create the tokenizer to read from a file
    FileReader rd = new FileReader("filename.java");
    StreamTokenizer st = new StreamTokenizer(rd);

    // Prepare the tokenizer for Java-style tokenizing rules
    st.parseNumbers();
    st.wordChars('_', '_');
    st.eolIsSignificant(true);

    // If whitespace is not to be discarded, make this call
    st.ordinaryChars(0, ' ');

    // These calls caused comments to be discarded
    st.slashSlashComments(true);
    st.slashStarComments(true);

    // Parse the file
    int token = st.nextToken();
    while (token != StreamTokenizer.TT_EOF) {
        token = st.nextToken();
        switch (token) {
        case StreamTokenizer.TT_NUMBER:
            // A number was found; the value is in nval
            double num = st.nval;
            break;
        case StreamTokenizer.TT_WORD:
            // A word was found; the value is in sval
            String word = st.sval;
            break;
        case '"':
            // A double-quoted string was found; sval contains the contents
            String dquoteVal = st.sval;
            break;
```

Class   *Interface*   —extends   - - -implements   ○ abstract   ● final   ˆ—has superclass   ˍ—has subclass   package—see other volume

```
            case '\":
                // A single-quoted string was found; sval contains the contents
                String squoteVal = st.sval;
                break;
            case StreamTokenizer.TT_EOL:
                // End of line character found
                break;
            case StreamTokenizer.TT_EOF:
                // End of file has been reached
                break;
            default:
                // A regular character was found; the value is the token itself
                char ch = (char)st.ttype;
                break;
            }
        }
        rd.close();
    } catch (IOException e) {
    }
```

java.lang

This package contains classes and interfaces that are an integral part of the Java language. These include Object, Throwable, String and Thread. All errors and exceptions that can be thrown by the Java virtual machine appear in this package. Also included are classes for accessing system resources, primitive type object wrappers, and a math class.

Packages

java.lang

Class *Interface* —extends - - -implements ○ abstract ● final ^—has superclass ⌣—has subclass package—see other volume

Packages

java.lang

```
       Object
  ●     ├ Boolean ------------------------------------------------ java.io.Serializable⌄
  ●     ├ Character ---------------------------------------------- Comparable, java.io.Serializable⌄
1.2     ├ Character.Subset
1.2 ●   │  └ Character.UnicodeBlock
  ●     ├ Class -------------------------------------------------- java.io.Serializable⌄
  ○     ├ ClassLoader⌄
  ●     ├ Compiler
  ●     ├ Math
  ○     ├ Number ------------------------------------------------ Comparable
1.1 ●   │  ├ Byte ----------------------------------------------
  ●     │  ├ Double -------------------------------------------
  ●     │  ├ Float --------------------------------------------
  ●     │  ├ Integer ------------------------------------------
  ●     │  ├ Long ---------------------------------------------
1.1 ●   │  └ Short --------------------------------------------
1.2     ├ Package
  ○     ├ Process
        ├ Runtime
        ├ SecurityManager⌄
1.4 ●   ├ StackTraceElement ------------------------------------ java.io.Serializable⌄
1.3 ●   ├ StrictMath
  ●     ├ String ------------------------------------------------ CharSequence, Comparable, java.io.Serializable⌄
  ●     ├ StringBuffer ------------------------------------------ CharSequence, java.io.Serializable⌄
  ●     ├ System
        ├ Thread ------------------------------------------------ Runnable
        ├ ThreadGroup
1.2     ├ ThreadLocal
1.2     │  └ InheritableThreadLocal
1.1 ●   ├ Void
1.2 ○   ├ java.security.Permission ------------------------------ java.io.Serializable⌄, java.security.Guard
1.2 ○   │  └ java.security.BasicPermission ---------------------- java.io.Serializable⌄
1.2 ●   │     └ RuntimePermission
        └ Throwable --------------------------------------------
          ├ Error
1.4       │ ├ AssertionError
```

Class *Interface* —extends - - -implements ○ abstract ● final ^—has superclass ⌄—has subclass package—see other volume

```
Object
  └ Throwable - - - - - - - - - - - - - - - - - - - - - - - - - - - - - - - - - - - - - - - - - - -⌐- - java.io.Serializable ⌣
        ├ Error
        │   ├ LinkageError
        │   │   ├ ClassCircularityError
        │   │   ├ ClassFormatError
  1.2   │   │   │   └ UnsupportedClassVersionError
  1.1   │   │   ├ ExceptionInInitializerError
        │   │   ├ IncompatibleClassChangeError
        │   │   │   ├ AbstractMethodError
        │   │   │   ├ IllegalAccessError
        │   │   │   ├ InstantiationError
        │   │   │   ├ NoSuchFieldError
        │   │   │   └ NoSuchMethodError
        │   │   ├ NoClassDefFoundError
        │   │   ├ UnsatisfiedLinkError
        │   │   └ VerifyError
        │   ├ ThreadDeath
        │   └ VirtualMachineError
        │       ├ InternalError
        │       ├ OutOfMemoryError
        │       ├ StackOverflowError
        │       └ UnknownError
        └ Exception
            ├ ClassNotFoundException
            ├ CloneNotSupportedException ⌣
            ├ IllegalAccessException
            ├ InstantiationException
            ├ InterruptedException
  1.1       ├ NoSuchFieldException
            ├ NoSuchMethodException
            └ RuntimeException
                ├ ArithmeticException
                ├ ArrayStoreException
                ├ ClassCastException
                ├ IllegalArgumentException
                │   ├ IllegalThreadStateException
                │   └ NumberFormatException
                ├ IllegalMonitorStateException
  1.1           ├ IllegalStateException ⌣
                ├ IndexOutOfBoundsException
                │   ├ ArrayIndexOutOfBoundsException
                │   └ StringIndexOutOfBoundsException
                ├ NegativeArraySizeException
                ├ NullPointerException
                ├ SecurityException ⌣
  1.2           └ UnsupportedOperationException ⌣
```

1.4 *CharSequence*

Cloneable ⌣

1.2 *Comparable*

Runnable

ε48. The Quintessential Java Application

The parameters to the application are made available in args.

```java
public class BasicApp {
    public static void main(String[] args) {
        for (int i=0; i<args.length; i++) {
            // process args[i];
        }
    }
}
```

This is the command to run the program:

```
> java BasicApp param1 param2 ...
```

ε49. Terminating the Application

```java
// No errors
int errorCode = 0;

// An error occurred
errorCode = -1;

// Terminate
System.exit(errorCode);
```

ε50. Determining When the Application Is About to Exit

When an application is terminated normally, the application first starts any registered "shutdown threads", waits for them to complete and then finally exits. Normal termination can be caused by a call to System.exit(), the completion of the last non-daemon thread, or the interruption of the application (control-C) by the user. Abnormal termination (which does not cause the shutdown threads to be started) is caused some major fault in the Java virtual machine or native library.

```java
// Register a shutdown thread
Runtime.getRuntime().addShutdownHook(new Thread() {
    // This method is called during shutdown
    public void run() {
        // Do shutdown work ...
    }
});
```

ε51. Computing Elapsed Time

```java
// Get current time
long start = System.currentTimeMillis();

// Do something ...

// Get elapsed time in milliseconds
long elapsedTimeMillis = System.currentTimeMillis()-start;

// Get elapsed time in seconds
float elapsedTimeSec = elapsedTimeMillis/1000F;

// Get elapsed time in minutes
float elapsedTimeMin = elapsedTimeMillis/(60*1000F);

// Get elapsed time in hours
float elapsedTimeHour = elapsedTimeMillis/(60*60*1000F);
```

Class *Interface* ——extends - - -implements ○ abstract ● final ^—has superclass ˷—has subclass package—see other volume

```
// Get elapsed time in days
float elapsedTimeDay = elapsedTimeMillis/(24*60*60*1000F);
```

ε52. Loading Native Code

On Windows, loadLibrary("s") loads s.dll. On Solaris, it loads s.so.

```
System.loadLibrary("libraryName");
```

ε53. Implementing a Class That Can Be Sorted

In order for a class to be used in a sorted collection such as a SortedTree or for it to be sortable by Collections.sort(), the class must implement Comparable.

```
public class MyClass implements Comparable {
    public int compareTo(Object o) {
        // If this < o, return a negative value
        // If this = o, return 0
        // If this > o, return a positive value
    }
}
```

ε54. Redirecting Standard Output, and Error

This example replaces standard output and error with a print stream that copies its output to both the console and to a file.

```
// All writes to this print stream are copied to two print streams
public class TeeStream extends PrintStream {
    PrintStream out;
    public TeeStream(PrintStream out1, PrintStream out2) {
        super(out1);
        this.out = out2;
    }
    public void write(byte buf[], int off, int len) {
        try {
            super.write(buf, off, len);
            out.write(buf, off, len);
        } catch (Exception e) {
        }
    }
    public void flush() {
        super.flush();
        out.flush();
    }
}
```

Here's an example that uses the class:

```
try {
    // Tee standard output
    PrintStream out = new PrintStream(new FileOutputStream("out.log"));
    PrintStream tee = new TeeStream(System.out, out);

    System.setOut(tee);

    // Tee standard error
    PrintStream err = new PrintStream(new FileOutputStream("err.log"));
    tee = new TeeStream(System.err, err);

    System.setErr(tee);
} catch (FileNotFoundException e) {
```

Packages

```
}
// Write to standard output and error and the log files
System.out.println("welcome");
System.err.println("error");
```

ε55. Getting the Size of the Heap

The heap is the area in memory in which objects are created.

```
// Get current size of heap in bytes
long heapSize = Runtime.getRuntime().totalMemory();

// Get maximum size of heap in bytes. The heap cannot grow beyond this size.
// Any attempt will result in an OutOfMemoryException.
long heapMaxSize = Runtime.getRuntime().maxMemory();

// Get amount of free memory within the heap in bytes. This size will increase
// after garbage collection and decrease as new objects are created.
long heapFreeSize = Runtime.getRuntime().freeMemory();
```

Objects

ε56. Cloning an Object

```
class MyClass implements Cloneable {
    public MyClass() {
    }
    public Object clone() {
        Cloneable theClone = new MyClass();
        // Initialize theClone.
        return theClone;
    }
}
```

Here's some code to create a clone.

```
MyClass myObject = new MyClass();
MyClass myObjectClone = (MyClass)myObject.clone();
```

Arrays are automatically cloneable:

```
int[] ints = new int[]{123, 234};
int[] intsClone = (int[])ints.clone();
```

ε57. Comparing Object Values Using Hash Codes

The hash code of an object is an integer value that's computed using the value of the object. For example, for a String object, the characters of the string are used to compute the hash code. For an Integer object, the integer value is used to compute the hash code.

Hash codes are typically used as an efficient way of comparing the values of two objects. For example, if the hash code of the string 'hello' is 33, another String object with the same contents would also a hash code of 33.

If the hash codes of two object values are different, the object values are guaranteed to be different. However, if the hash codes of two object values are the same, the object values are *not* guaranteed to be the same. An additional call to Object.equals() must be made to confirm that the object values are the same. A good hash code algorithm will minimize the chance of two different values having the same hash code.

Class   *Interface*   —extends   - - -implements   ○ abstract   ● final   ^—has superclass   ‿—has subclass   package —see other volume

The '==' operator is the most efficient way to determine if two objects (rather than object values) are the same. However, in very limited applications, it may be necessary to get the hash code of an object (called the identity hash code) rather than of the object value. For example, a hash table of objects requires the use of the identity hash code.

```
File file1 = new File("a");
File file2 = new File("a");
File file3 = new File("b");

// Get the hash codes
int hc1 = file1.hashCode(); // 1234416
int hc2 = file2.hashCode(); // 1234416
int hc3 = file3.hashCode(); // 1234419

// Check if two object values are the same
if (hc1 == hc2 && file1.equals(file2)) {
        // They are the same
}

// Get the identity hash codes
int ihc1 = System.identityHashCode(file1); // 1027049
int ihc2 = System.identityHashCode(file2); // 14642381
int ihc3 = System.identityHashCode(file3); // 6298545
```

ε58. Wrapping a Primitive Type in a Wrapper Object

In the Java language, the eight primitive types — boolean, byte, char, short, int, long, float, double — are not objects. However, in certain situations, objects are required. For example, collection classes such as Map and Set only work with objects. This issue is addressed by wrapping a primitive type in a "wrapper object." There is a wrapper object for each primitive type.

This example demonstrates how to wrap the value of a primitive type in a wrapper object and then subsequently retrieve the value of the primitive type.

```
// Create wrapper object for each primitive type
Boolean refBoolean = new Boolean(true);
Byte refByte = new Byte((byte)123);
Character refChar = new Character('x');
Short refShort = new Short((short)123);
Integer refInt = new Integer(123);
Long refLong = new Long(123L);
Float refFloat = new Float(12.3F);
Double refDouble = new Double(12.3D);

// Retrieving the value in a wrapper object
boolean bool = refBoolean.booleanValue();
byte b = refByte.byteValue();
char c = refChar.charValue();
short s = refShort.shortValue();
int i = refInt.intValue();
long l = refLong.longValue();
float f = refFloat.floatValue();
double d = refDouble.doubleValue();
```

Packages

Classes

ε59. Getting a Class Object

There are three ways to retrieve a Class object.

```
// By way of an object
Class cls = object.getClass();

// By way of a string
try {
    cls = Class.forName("java.lang.String");
} catch (ClassNotFoundException e) {
}

// By way of .class
cls = java.lang.String.class;
```

ε60. Getting the Name of a Class Object

```
// Get the fully-qualified name of a class
Class cls = java.lang.String.class;
String name = cls.getName(); // java.lang.String

// Get the fully-qualified name of a inner class
cls = java.util.Map.Entry.class;
name = cls.getName(); // java.util.Map$Entry

// Get the unqualified name of a class
cls = java.util.Map.Entry.class;
name = cls.getName();
if (name.lastIndexOf('.') > 0) {
    name = name.substring(name.lastIndexOf('.')+1); // Map$Entry
}
// The $ can be converted to a .
name = name.replace('$', '.'); // Map.Entry


// Get the name of a primitive type
name = int.class.getName(); // int

// Get the name of an array
name = boolean[].class.getName(); // [Z
name = byte[].class.getName(); // [B
name = char[].class.getName(); // [C
name = short[].class.getName(); // [S
name = int[].class.getName(); // [I
name = long[].class.getName(); // [J
name = float[].class.getName(); // [F
name = double[].class.getName(); // [D
name = String[].class.getName(); // [Ljava.lang.String;
name = int[][].class.getName(); // [[I

// Get the name of void
cls = Void.TYPE;
name = cls.getName(); // void
```

ε61. Determining If a Class Object Represents a Class or Interface

```
Class cls = java.lang.String.class;
boolean isClass = !cls.isInterface(); // true

cls = java.lang.Cloneable.class;
isClass = !cls.isInterface(); // false
```

Class *Interface* —extends - - -implements ○ abstract ● final ˆ—has superclass ˬ—has subclass package—see other volume

ε62. Getting the Superclass of an Object

```
Object o = new String();
Class sup = o.getClass().getSuperclass(); // java.lang.Object

// Superclass of Object is null
o = new Object();
sup = o.getClass().getSuperclass(); // null

// Although the type of o2 is an interface, getSuperclass() returns the object's superclass
Runnable o2 = new Runnable() {
    public void run() {
    }
};
sup = o2.getClass().getSuperclass(); // java.lang.Object
```

ε63. Getting the Superclass of a Class Object

```
Class cls = java.lang.String.class;
Class sup = cls.getSuperclass(); // java.lang.Object

cls = java.lang.Object.class;
sup = cls.getSuperclass(); // null

// The superclass of interfaces is always null
cls = java.lang.Cloneable.class;
sup = cls.getSuperclass(); // null

// The superclass of primitive types is always null
cls = int.class;
sup = cls.getSuperclass(); // null
```

ε64. Listing the Interfaces That a Class Implements

```
Class cls = java.lang.String.class;
Class[] intfs = cls.getInterfaces();
// [java.lang.Comparable, java.lang.CharSequence, java.io.Serializable]

// The interfaces for a primitive type is an empty array
cls = int.class;
intfs = cls.getInterfaces(); // []
```

ε65. Listing the Interfaces That an Interface Extends

```
Class cls = java.util.List.class;
Class[] intfs = cls.getInterfaces(); // java.util.Collection
```

ε66. Getting the Package of a Class

```
Class cls = java.lang.String.class;
Package pkg = cls.getPackage();
String name = pkg.getName(); // java.lang

// getPackage() returns null for a class in the unnamed package
cls = MyClass.class;
pkg = cls.getPackage(); // null

// getPackage() returns null for a primitive type or array
pkg = int.class.getPackage(); // null
pkg = int[].class.getPackage(); // null
```

ε67. Determining from Where a Class Was Loaded

```
// Get the location of this class
```

```
Class cls = this.getClass();
ProtectionDomain pDomain = cls.getProtectionDomain();
CodeSource cSource = pDomain.getCodeSource();
URL loc = cSource.getLocation(); // file:/c:/almanac14/examples/
```

It is not possible to determine the location of classes loaded by the system class loader in the same way since the class' code source is null. The only other method is to use the -verbose option on the java command. This causes the Java virtual machine to print a message every time a class is loaded.

```
> java -verbose MyApp
```

Here's a sample of the output:

```
[Opened c:\jdk1.4\jre\lib\rt.jar]
[Opened c:\jdk1.4\jre\lib\sunrsasign.jar]
[Opened c:\jdk1.4\jre\lib\jsse.jar]
[Opened c:\jdk1.4\jre\lib\jce.jar]
[Opened c:\jdk1.4\jre\lib\charsets.jar]
[Loaded java.lang.Object from c:\jdk1.4\jre\lib\rt.jar]
[Loaded java.io.Serializable from c:\jdk1.4\jre\lib\rt.jar]
[Loaded java.lang.Comparable from c:\jdk1.4\jre\lib\rt.jar]
[Loaded java.lang.CharSequence from c:\jdk1.4\jre\lib\rt.jar]
[Loaded java.lang.String from c:\jdk1.4\jre\lib\rt.jar]
[Loaded java.lang.Class from c:\jdk1.4\jre\lib\rt.jar]
[Loaded java.lang.Cloneable from c:\jdk1.4\jre\lib\rt.jar]
[Loaded java.lang.ClassLoader from c:\jdk1.4\jre\lib\rt.jar]
[Loaded java.lang.System from c:\jdk1.4\jre\lib\rt.jar]
[Loaded java.lang.Throwable from c:\jdk1.4\jre\lib\rt.jar]
```

ε68. Loading a Class That Is Not on the Classpath

A URLClassLoader can be used to load classes in any directory.

```
// Create a File object on the root of the directory containing the class file
File file = new File("c:\\myclasses\\");

try {
    // Convert File to a URL
    URL url = file.toURL(); // file:/c:/myclasses/
    URL[] urls = new URL[]{url};

    // Create a new class loader with the directory
    ClassLoader cl = new URLClassLoader(urls);

    // Load in the class; MyClass.class should be located in
    // the directory file:/c:/myclasses/com/mycompany
    Class cls = cl.loadClass("com.mycompany.MyClass");
} catch (MalformedURLException e) {
} catch (ClassNotFoundException e) {
}
```

ε69. Dynamically Reloading a Modified Class

This example demonstrates how to reload a modified class without restarting the application. The technique involves loading the "reloadable" class with a separate class loader. Each time the class needs to be reloaded, it is loaded using a new class loader and the previous class loader (with the old class) is abandoned.

It is important that the reloadable class not be on the classpath. Otherwise, the class will be loaded by some parent of the new class loader rather than by the new class loader itself. Once this happens, the class cannot be reloaded.

Since the class cannot be on the classpath, it is not possible to use the class name directly in the code (otherwise a ClassNotFoundException would be thrown during start up). To circumvent this problem, the reloadable class must be made to implement an interface and the interface name is used in the code.

This example places the reloadable class in a subdirectory called dir, which is not on the classpath. Here is the reloadable class:

```
public class MyReloadableClassImpl implements MyReloadableClass {
    public String myMethod() {
        return "a message";
    }
}
```

To compile this class, it is necessary to tell the compiler the location of MyReloadableClass. Since, for this example, it is located in the parent directory, the following command will compile this class:

```
> java -classpath .. MyReloadableClass
```

Here's the code that reloads the reloadable class:

```
// Get the directory (URL) of the reloadable class
URL[] urls = null;
try {
    // Convert the file object to a URL
    File dir = new File(System.getProperty("user.dir")
        +File.separator+"dir"+File.separator);
    URL url = dir.toURL(); // file:/c:/almanac1.4/examples/
    urls = new URL[]{url};
} catch (MalformedURLException e) {
}

try {
    // Create a new class loader with the directory
    ClassLoader cl = new URLClassLoader(urls);

    // Load in the class
    Class cls = cl.loadClass("MyReloadableClassImpl");

    // Create a new instance of the new class
    myObj = (MyReloadableClass)cls.newInstance();
} catch (IllegalAccessException e) {
} catch (InstantiationException e) {
} catch (ClassNotFoundException e) {
}
```

Here's some code that tests the reloadable class (a more realistic routine would periodically check the timestamp on the file). After the example is started, change the string returned by myMethod() and recompile.

```
try {
    while (true) {
        reloadMyReloadedClass();
        System.out.println(myObj.myMethod());
        Thread.sleep(5000);
    }
} catch (Exception e) {
}
```

Strings

ε70. Constructing a String

If you are constructing a string with several appends, it may be more efficient to construct it using a StringBuffer and then convert it to an immutable String object.

```
StringBuffer buf = new StringBuffer("Java");

// Append
buf.append(" Almanac v1/"); // Java Almanac v1/
buf.append(3); // Java Almanac v1/3

// Set
int index = 15;
buf.setCharAt(index, '.'); // Java Almanac v1.3

// Insert
index = 5;
buf.insert(index, "Developers ");// Java Developers Almanac v1.3

// Replace
int start = 27;
int end = 28;
buf.replace(start, end, "4"); // Java Developers Almanac v1.4

// Delete
start = 24;
end = 25;
buf.delete(start, end); // Java Developers Almanac 1.4

// Convert to string
String s = buf.toString();
```

ε71. Comparing Strings

See also "ε306. Comparing Strings in a Locale-Independent Way".

```
String s1 = "a";
String s2 = "A";
String s3 = "B";

// Check if identical
boolean b = s1.equals(s2); // false

// Check if identical ignoring case
b = s1.equalsIgnoreCase(s2); // true

// Check order of two strings
int i = s1.compareTo(s2); // 32; lowercase follows uppercase
if (i < 0) {
    // s1 precedes s2
} else if (i > 0) {
    // s1 follows s2
} else {
    // s1 equals s2
}

// Check order of two strings ignoring case
i = s1.compareToIgnoreCase(s3); // -1
if (i < 0) {
    // s1 precedes s3
```

Class *Interface* —extends - - -implements ○ abstract ● final ^—has superclass ⌐—has subclass package—see other volume

```
    } else if (i > 0) {
        // s1 follows s3
    } else {
        // s1 equals s3
    }

    // A string can also be compared with a StringBuffer;
    // see "ε70. Constructing a String"
    StringBuffer sbuf = new StringBuffer("a");
    b = s1.contentEquals(sbuf); // true
```

ε72. Determining If a String Contains a Substring

See also "ε423. Quintessential Regular Expression Search Program".

```
    String string = "Madam, I am Adam";

    // Starts with
    boolean b = string.startsWith("Mad"); // true

    // Ends with
    b = string.endsWith("dam"); // true

    // Anywhere
    b = string.indexOf("I am") > 0; // true

    // To ignore case, regular expressions must be used

    // Starts with
    b = string.matches("(?i)mad.*");

    // Ends with
    b = string.matches("(?i).*adam");

    // Anywhere
    b = string.matches("(?i).*i am.*");
```

ε73. Getting a Substring from a String

```
    int start = 1;
    int end = 4;
    String substr = "aString".substring(start, end); // Str
```

ε74. Searching a String for a Character or a Substring

See also "ε423. Quintessential Regular Expression Search Program".

```
    String string = "madam, i am Adam";

    // Characters

        // First occurrence of a c
        int index = string.indexOf('a'); // 1

        // Last occurrence
        index = string.lastIndexOf('a'); // 14

        // Not found
        index = string.lastIndexOf('z'); // -1

    // Substrings

        // First occurrence
        index = string.indexOf("dam"); // 1

        // Last occurrence
        index = string.lastIndexOf("dam"); // 13
```

```
                    // Not found
                    index = string.lastIndexOf("z"); // -1
```

ε75. Replacing Characters in a String

Since strings are immutable, the replace() method creates a new string with the replaced characters.

```
        // Replace all occurrences of 'a' with 'o'
        String newString = string.replace('a', 'o');
```

ε76. Replacing Substrings in a String

See also "ε429. Quintessential Regular Expression Search and Replace Program".

```
        static String replace(String str, String pattern, String replace) {
            int s = 0;
            int e = 0;
            StringBuffer result = new StringBuffer();

            while ((e = str.indexOf(pattern, s)) >= 0) {
                result.append(str.substring(s, e));
                result.append(replace);
                s = e+pattern.length();
            }
            result.append(str.substring(s));
            return result.toString();
        }
```

ε77. Converting a String to Upper or Lower Case

```
        // Convert to upper case
        String upper = string.toUpperCase();

        // Convert to lower case
        String lower = string.toLowerCase();
```

ε78. Converting a Primitive Type Value to a String

There are two ways to convert a primitive type value into a string. The explicit way is to call String.valueOf(). The implicit way is to use the string concatenation operator '+'.

```
        // Use String.valueOf()
        String s = String.valueOf(true); // true
        s = String.valueOf((byte)0x12); // 18
        s = String.valueOf((byte)0xFF); // -1
        s = String.valueOf('a'); // a
        s = String.valueOf((short)123); // 123
        s = String.valueOf(123); // 123
        s = String.valueOf(123L); // 123
        s = String.valueOf(1.23F); // 1.23
        s = String.valueOf(1.23D); // 1.23

        // Use +
        s = ""+true; // true
        s = ""+((byte)0x12); // 18
        s = ""+((byte)0xFF); // -1
        s = ""+'a'; // a
        s = ""+((short)123); // 123
        s = ""+123; // 123
        s = ""+123L; // 123
```

```
s = ""+1.23F; // 1.23
s = ""+1.23D; // 1.23
```

ε79. Converting Between Unicode and UTF-8

```
try {
    // Convert from Unicode to UTF-8
    String string = "abc\u5639\u563b";
    byte[] utf8 = string.getBytes("UTF-8");

    // Convert from UTF-8 to Unicode
    string = new String(utf8, "UTF-8");
} catch (UnsupportedEncodingException e) {
}
```

ε80. Determining a Character's Unicode Block

```
char ch = '\u5639';
Character.UnicodeBlock block = Character.UnicodeBlock.of(ch);
```

ε81. Determining If a String Is a Legal Java Identifier

Briefly, a valid Java identifier must start with a Unicode letter, underscore, or dollar sign ($). The other characters, if any, can be a Unicode letter, underscore, dollar sign, or digit.

For more details, see http://java.sun.com/docs/books/jls/second_edition/html/lexical.doc.html.

```
// Returns true if s is a legal Java identifier.
public static boolean isJavaIdentifier(String s) {
    if (s.length() == 0 || !Character.isJavaIdentifierStart(s.charAt(0))) {
        return false;
    }
    for (int i=1; i<s.length(); i++) {
        if (!Character.isJavaIdentifierPart(s.charAt(i))) {
            return false;
        }
    }
    return true;
}

// Some examples
boolean b = isJavaIdentifier("my_var"); // true
b = isJavaIdentifier("my_var.1"); // false
b = isJavaIdentifier("$my_var"); // true
b = isJavaIdentifier("\u0391var"); // true
b = isJavaIdentifier("_"); // true
b = isJavaIdentifier("$"); // true
b = isJavaIdentifier("1$my_var"); // false
```

Numbers

ε82. Converting a String to a Number

```
byte b = Byte.parseByte("123");
short s = Short.parseShort("123");
int i = Integer.parseInt("123");
long l = Long.parseLong("123");
float f = Float.parseFloat("123.4");
double d = Double.parseDouble("123.4e10");
```

ε83. Parsing and Formatting a Number into Binary, Octal, and Hexadecimal

```
int i = 1023;

// Parse and format to binary
i = Integer.parseInt("1111111111", 2); // 1023
String s = Integer.toString(i, 2); // 1111111111

// Parse and format to octal
i = Integer.parseInt("1777", 8); // 1023
s = Integer.toString(i, 8); // 1777

// Parse and format to decimal
i = Integer.parseInt("1023"); // 1023
s = Integer.toString(i); // 1023

// Parse and format to hexadecimal
i = Integer.parseInt("3ff", 16); // 1023
s = Integer.toString(i, 16); // 3ff

// Parse and format to arbitrary radix <= Character.MAX_RADIX
int radix = 32;
i = Integer.parseInt("vv", radix); // 1023
s = Integer.toString(i, radix); // vv
```

Arrays

ε84. Shifting Elements in an Array

```
// Shift all elements right by one
System.arraycopy(array, 0, array, 1, array.length-1);

// Shift all elements left by one
System.arraycopy(array, 1, array, 0, array.length-1);
```

ε85. Copying Elements from One Array to Another

```
System.arraycopy(src, 0, dst, 0, Math.min(src.length, dst.length));
```

System Properties

ε86. Getting and Setting the Value of a System Property

```
// Get a system property
String dir = System.getProperty("user.dir");

// Set a system property
String previousValue = System.setProperty("application.property", "newValue");
```

ε87. Setting the Value of a System Property from the Command Line

A system property can be set or overridden by specifying the -D option to the java command when running your program.

```
java -Dmy.prop="my value" MyApp

// Get the value of the system property
String prop = System.getProperty("my.prop");
// my value
```

Class   *Interface*   —extends   - - -implements   ○ abstract   ● final   ⌃—has superclass   ⌄—has subclass   package—see other volume

ε88. Listing All System Properties

```
// Get all system properties
Properties props = System.getProperties();

// Enumerate all system properties
Enumeration enum = props.propertyNames();
for (; enum.hasMoreElements(); ) {
    // Get property name
    String propName = (String)enum.nextElement();

    // Get property value
    String propValue = (String)props.get(propName);
}
```

Commands

ε89. Executing a Command

```
try {
    String command = "ls";
    Process child = Runtime.getRuntime().exec(command);
} catch (IOException e) {
}
```

ε90. Reading Output from a Command

```
try {
    // Execute command
    String command = "ls";
    Process child = Runtime.getRuntime().exec(command);

    // Get input stream to read from it
    InputStream in = child.getInputStream();
    int c;
    while ((c = in.read()) != -1) {
        process((char)c);
    }
    in.close();
} catch (IOException e) {
}
```

ε91. Sending Input to a Command

```
try {
    // Execute command
    String command = "cat";
    Process child = Runtime.getRuntime().exec(command);

    // Get output stream to write from it
    OutputStream out = child.getOutputStream();

    out.write("some text".getBytes());
    out.close();
} catch (IOException e) {
}
```

Threads

ε92. Creating a Thread

When a thread is created, it must be permanently bound to an object with a run() method. When the thread is started, it will invoke the object's run() method. More specifically, the object must implement the Runnable interface.

There are two ways to create a thread. The first is to declare a class that extends Thread. When the class is instantiated, the thread and object are created together and the object is automatically bound to the thread. By calling the object's start() method, the thread is started and immediately calls the object's run() method. Here is some code to demonstrate this method.

```
// This class extends Thread
class BasicThread1 extends Thread {
    // This method is called when the thread runs
    public void run() {
    }
}

// Create and start the thread
Thread thread = new BasicThread1();
thread.start();
```

The second way is to create the thread and supply it an object with a run() method. This object will be permanently associated with the thread. The object's run() method will be invoked when the thread is started. This method of thread creation is useful if you want many threads sharing an object. Here is an example that creates a Runnable object and then creates a thread with the object.

```
class BasicThread2 implements Runnable {
    // This method is called when the thread runs
    public void run() {
    }
}

// Create the object with the run() method
Runnable runnable = new BasicThread2();

// Create the thread supplying it with the runnable object
Thread thread = new Thread(runnable);

// Start the thread
thread.start();
```

ε93. Stopping a Thread

The proper way to stop a running thread is to set a variable that the thread checks occasionally. When the thread detects that the variable is set, it should return from the run() method.

Note: Thread.suspend() and Thread.stop() provide asynchronous methods of stopping a thread. However, these methods have been deprecated because they are very unsafe. Using them often results in deadlocks and incorrect resource cleanup.

```
// Create and start the thread
MyThread thread = new MyThread();
thread.start();

// Do work...

// Stop the thread
thread.allDone = true;
```

Class   *Interface*   —extends   - - -implements   ○ abstract   ● final   ^—has superclass   ⌄—has subclass   package—see other volume

```
class MyThread extends Thread {
    boolean allDone = false;

    // This method is called when the thread runs
    public void run() {
        while (true) {
            // Do work...

            if (allDone) {
                return;
            }

            // Do work...
        }
    }
}
```

ε94. Determining When a Thread Has Finished

This example demonstrates a few ways to determine whether or not a thread has returned from its run() method.

```
// Create and start a thread
Thread thread = new MyThread();
thread.start();

// Check if the thread has finished in a non-blocking way
if (thread.isAlive()) {
    // Thread has not finished
} else {
    // Finished
}

// Wait for the thread to finish but don't wait longer than a
// specified time
long delayMillis = 5000; // 5 seconds
try {
    thread.join(delayMillis);

    if (thread.isAlive()) {
        // Timeout occurred; thread has not finished
    } else {
        // Finished
    }
} catch (InterruptedException e) {
    // Thread was interrupted
}

// Wait indefinitely for the thread to finish
try {
    thread.join();
    // Finished
} catch (InterruptedException e) {
    // Thread was interrupted
}
```

ε95. Pausing the Current Thread

This example demonstrates how a thread can temporarily stop execution.

See also "ε96. Pausing a Thread"

```
    try {
```

```
        long numMillisecondsToSleep = 5000; // 5 seconds
        Thread.sleep(numMillisecondsToSleep);
    } catch (InterruptedException e) {
    }
```

ε96. Pausing a Thread

The proper way to temporarily pause the execution of another thread is to set a variable that the target thread checks occasionally. When the target thread detects that the variable is set, it calls Object.wait(). The paused thread can then be woken up by calling its Object.notify() method.

Note: Thread.suspend() and Thread.resume() provide methods for pausing a thread. However, these methods have been deprecated because they are very unsafe. Using them often results in deadlocks. With the approach above, the target thread can ensure that it will be paused in an appropriate place.

```
// Create and start the thread
MyThread thread = new MyThread();
thread.start();

while (true) {
    // Do work

    // Pause the thread
    synchronized (thread) {
        thread.pleaseWait = true;
    }

    // Do work

    // Resume the thread
    synchronized (thread) {
        thread.pleaseWait = false;
        thread.notify();
    }

    // Do work
}

class MyThread extends Thread {
    boolean pleaseWait = false;

    // This method is called when the thread runs
    public void run() {
        while (true) {
            // Do work

            // Check if should wait
            synchronized (this) {
                while (pleaseWait) {
                    try {
                        wait();
                    } catch (Exception e) {
                    }
                }
            }

            // Do work
        }
    }
}
```

ε97. Determining If the Current Thread Is Holding a Synchronized Lock

A thread can determine if it is holding the synchronized lock of a particular object.

```
public synchronized void myMethod() {
    boolean hasLock = false;
    Object o = new Object();

    // Determine if current thread has lock for o
    hasLock = Thread.holdsLock(o); // false
    synchronized (o) {
        hasLock = Thread.holdsLock(o); // true
    }

    // Check if current thread has lock for current object
    hasLock = Thread.holdsLock(this); // true
}
```

ε98. Allowing an Application with Live Threads to Exit

An application will automatically exit when there are no "non-daemon" threads running. In other words, a live daemon thread does not prevent an application from exiting.

A thread must be marked as a daemon thread before it is started. It cannot become a daemon thread after it is started. This means that you could not implement, for example, a thread pool where the threads become daemon threads only when inactive.

```
// This class extends Thread
class MyThread extends Thread {
    MyThread() {
        // Thread can be set as a daemon thread in the constructor
        setDaemon(true);
    }

    // This method is called when the thread runs
    public void run() {
        // Determine if this thread is a daemon thread
        boolean isDaemon = isDaemon();
    }
}

// Create the thread
Thread thread = new MyThread();

// Thread can be set as daemon by the creator
thread.setDaemon(true);

// Start the thread
thread.start();
```

ε99. Listing All Running Threads

A thread exists in a thread group and a thread group can contain other thread groups. This example visits all threads in all thread groups.

```
// Find the root thread group
ThreadGroup root = Thread.currentThread().getThreadGroup().getParent();
while (root.getParent() != null) {
    root = root.getParent();
}

// Visit each thread group
visit(root, 0);
```

```
    // This method recursively visits all thread groups under 'group'.
    public static void visit(ThreadGroup group, int level) {
        // Get threads in 'group'
        int numThreads = group.activeCount();
        Thread[] threads = new Thread[numThreads*2];
        numThreads = group.enumerate(threads, false);

        // Enumerate each thread in 'group'
        for (int i=0; i<numThreads; i++) {
            // Get thread
            Thread thread = threads[i];
        }

        // Get thread subgroups of 'group'
        int numGroups = group.activeGroupCount();
        ThreadGroup[] groups = new ThreadGroup[numGroups*2];
        numGroups = group.enumerate(groups, false);

        // Recursively visit each subgroup
        for (int i=0; i<numGroups; i++) {
            visit(groups[i], level+1);
        }
    }
```

Here's an example of some thread groups that contain some threads:

```
java.lang.ThreadGroup[name=system,maxpri=10]
    Thread[Reference Handler,10,system]
    Thread[Finalizer,8,system]
    Thread[Signal Dispatcher,10,system]
    Thread[CompileThread0,10,system]
    java.lang.ThreadGroup[name=main,maxpri=10]
        Thread[main,5,main]
        Thread[Thread-1,5,main]
```

ε100. Using a Thread-local Variable

```
static ThreadLocal tlData = new ThreadLocal();

public void aMethod() {
    // Retrieve value.
    Object o = tlData.get();

    // Set value.
    tlData.set(o);
}
```

ε101. Getting the Stack Trace of an Exception

```
try {
    // My code
} catch (Throwable e) {
    // Get the stack trace
    StackTraceElement stack[] = e.getStackTrace();

    // stack[0] contains the method that created the exception.
    // stack[stack.length-1] contains the oldest method call.
    // Enumerate each stack element.
    for (int i=0; i<stack.length; i++) {
        String filename = stack[i].getFileName();
```

Class *Interface* —extends - - -implements ⭕ abstract ● final ^—has superclass ‿—has subclass package—see other volume

```
        if (filename == null) {
            // The source filename is not available
        }
        String className = stack[i].getClassName();
        String methodName = stack[i].getMethodName();
        boolean isNativeMethod = stack[i].isNativeMethod();
        int line = stack[i].getLineNumber();
    }
}
```

ε102. Implementing a Work Queue

The work queue is thread-safe so that multiple threads can simultaneously add and remove objects from it.

```
class WorkQueue {
    LinkedList queue = new LinkedList();
    public synchronized void addWork(Object o) {
        queue.addLast(o);
        notify();
    }
    public synchronized Object getWork() throws InterruptedException {
        while (queue.isEmpty()) {
            wait();
        }
        return queue.removeFirst();
    }
}
```

Assertions

ε103. Compiling a Program with Assertions

To compile a program with assertions, you must add the command line option -source 1.4 to javac.

```
public class CompileAssert {
    public static void main(String[] args) {
        assert args.length > 0;
    }
}
```

This is the command to compile the program:

```
>javac -source 1.4 CompileAssert.java
```

ε104. Enabling Assertions from the Command Line

The command line options -ea and -da allow you to enable and disable assertion in a package subtree or in a class. Here are several examples of the switches.

Enable assertions in all non-system classes:

```
java -ea MyApp
```

Enable assertions in all classes in the unnamed package:

```
java -ea:... MyApp
```

Enable assertions in all classes in a package subtree:

```
java -ea:com.mycompany... MyApp
```

Enable assertions in a particular class:

Packages

java -ea:*com.mycompany.MyCompany MyApp*

Disable assertions in all classes in a package subtree:

java -da:*com.mycompany... MyApp*

Disable assertions in a particular class:

java -da:*com.mycompany.MyClass MyApp*

Multiple assertion switches on the command line are processed from left to right. Enable assertions in all classes in a package subtree except for one class:

java -ea:*com.mycompany... -da:com.mycompany.MyClass MyApp*

ε105. Handling an Assertion Error

When an assertion fails, AssertionError is thrown. Handling an assertion failure is rarely done. A situation in which you might handle an assertion failure is in the top-level loop of a high-availability server.

```
try {
    assert args.length > 0;
} catch (AssertionError e) {
    // In this case, the message is null
    String message = e.getMessage();
}

try {
    assert args.length > 0 : "my message";
} catch (AssertionError e) {
    // In this case, the message is a string
    String message = e.getMessage();
}
```

java.lang.ref

This package provides classes for obtaining information about references in the Java programming language. Reference objects are analogous to Class objects being used to represent a class. There are different types of references depending on their reachability. You can use a Reference in order to obtain information about the reference without hindering its corresponding object's eligibility for garbage-collection. References are useful for programs that cache objects.

	java.lang.Object
1.2 ○	├ Reference
1.2	│ ├ PhantomReference
1.2	│ ├ SoftReference
1.2	│ └ WeakReference
1.2	└ ReferenceQueue

Class *Interface* —extends - - -implements ○ abstract ● final ^—has superclass ‿—has subclass package—see other volume

ε106. Holding onto an Object Until Memory Becomes Low

A soft reference holds onto its referent until memory becomes low.

```
// Create up the soft reference.
SoftReference sr = new SoftReference(object);

// Use the soft reference.
Object o = sr.get();
if (o != null) {
    process(o);
} else {
    // The object is being collected or has been reclaimed.
}
```

ε107. Determining When an Object Is No Longer Used

A weak reference is used to determine when an object is no longer being referenced.

```
// Create the weak reference.
ReferenceQueue rq = new ReferenceQueue();
WeakReference wr = new WeakReference(object, rq);

// Wait for all the references to the object.
try {
    while (true) {
        Reference r = rq.remove();
        if (r == wr) {
            // Object is no longer referenced.
        }
    }
} catch (InterruptedException e) {
}
```

ε108. Determining When an Object Will Be Reclaimed

A phantom reference is used to determine when an object is just about to be reclaimed. Phantom references are safer to use than finalization because once an object is phantom reachable, it cannot be resurrected.

```
// Create the phantom reference.
ReferenceQueue rq = new ReferenceQueue();
PhantomReference pr = new PhantomReference(object, rq);

// Wait until the object is about to be reclaimed.
try {
    while (true) {
        Reference r = rq.remove();
        if (r == pr) {
            // The object is about to be reclaimed.
            // Clear the referent so that it can be reclaimed.
            r.clear();
        }
    }
} catch (InterruptedException e) {
}
```

Packages

java.lang.reflect

This package provides classes and interfaces for obtaining reflective information about classes and objects. Reflective information includes information about the members a class has, the signatures of a class's constructors and methods, and the types of its fields. You can create new objects, access and change an object's fields, and invoke the object's methods. This package is typically used by programs such as debuggers, interpreters, object inspectors, class browsers, and by Java runtime services such as Object Serialization and JavaBeans.

```
        java.lang.Object
1.2       ├ AccessibleObject
1.1 ●     │ ┌ Constructor --------------------------------------┬- Member
1.1 ●     │ ├ Field ------------------------------------------┐│
1.1 ●     │ └ Method -----------------------------------------┘│
1.1 ●     ├ Array
1.1       ├ Modifier
1.3       ├ Proxy ----------------------------------------------- java.io.Serializable⌣
1.2 ○     ├ java.security.Permission ---------------------------- java.io.Serializable⌣, java.security.Guard
1.2 ○     │ └ java.security.BasicPermission --------------------┬- java.io.Serializable⌣
1.2 ●     │     └ ReflectPermission                             │
          └ java.lang.Throwable ------------------------------┘
              └ java.lang.Exception
1.1             ├ InvocationTargetException
                └ java.lang.RuntimeException
1.3                 └ UndeclaredThrowableException

1.3       InvocationHandler
1.1       Member
```

ε109. Getting the Name of a Member Object

This example shows how to get the fully-qualified and non-fully-qualified name of a reflected object. See also "ε60. Getting the Name of a Class Object".

Class *Interface* —extends - - -implements ○ abstract ● final ˆ—has superclass ⌣—has subclass package—see other volume

```
Class cls = java.lang.String.class;
Method method = cls.getMethods()[0];
Field field = cls.getFields()[0];
Constructor constructor = cls.getConstructors()[0];
String name;

// Fully-qualified names
name = cls.getName(); // java.lang.String
name = cls.getName()+"."+field.getName(); // java.lang.String.CASE_INSENSITIVE_ORDER
name = constructor.getName(); // java.lang.String
name = cls.getName()+"."+method.getName(); // java.lang.String.hashCode

// Unqualified names
name = cls.getName().substring(cls.getPackage().getName().length()+1); // String
name = field.getName(); // CASE_INSENSITIVE_ORDER
name = constructor.getName().substring(cls.getPackage().getName().length()+1); // String
name = method.getName(); // hashCode
```

ε110. Overriding Default Access

By default, a reflected object enforces the access as defined by the Java language. For example, by default you cannot retrieve the value from a Field object if the Field object represents a private field. To bypass these access checks, you call setAccessible() on the reflected object. However, the program may not have permission to call setAccessible(), in which case SecurityException is thrown.

```
field.setAccessible(true);
constructor.setAccessible(true);
method.setAccessible(true);
```

ε111. Creating a Proxy Object

```
public interface MyInterface {
    void method();
}

public class MyInterfaceImpl implements MyInterface {
    public void method() {
    }
}

public class ProxyClass implements InvocationHandler {
    Object obj;
    public ProxyClass(Object o) {
        obj = o;
    }

    public Object invoke(Object proxy, Method m, Object[] args) throws Throwable {
        Object result = null;
        try {
            // Do something before the method is called ...
            result = m.invoke(obj, args);
        } catch (InvocationTargetException e) {
        } catch (Exception eBj) {
        } finally {
            // Do something after the method is called ...
        }
        return result;
    }
}

// This fragment creates a proxy for a MyInterface object.
```

Packages

```
MyInterface myintf = (MyInterface)Proxy.newProxyInstance(
    MyInterface.class.getClassLoader(),
    new Class[]{MyInterface.class},
    new ProxyClass(new MyInterfaceImpl()));

// Invoke the method
myintf.method();
```

Modifiers

ε112. Listing the Modifiers of a Class Object

```
int mods = cls.getModifiers();
if (Modifier.isPublic(mods)) {
    // class is public
}
```

ε113. Listing the Modifiers of a Member Object

Field, Constructor, and Method are all subclasses of Member.

```
// Modifiers from a field.
int mods = member.getModifiers();
if (Modifier.isPublic(mods)) {
    // member is public
}
```

Fields

ε114. Getting the Field Objects of a Class Object

There are three ways of obtaining a Field object from a Class object.

```
Class cls = java.awt.Point.class;

// By obtaining a list of all declared fields.
Field[] fields = cls.getDeclaredFields();

// By obtaining a list of all public fields, both declared and inherited.
fields = cls.getFields();
for (int i=0; i<fields.length; i++) {
    Class type = fields[i].getType();
    process(fields[i]);
}

// By obtaining a particular Field object.
// This example retrieves java.awt.Point.x.
try {
    Field field = cls.getField("x");
    process(field);
} catch (NoSuchFieldException e) {
}
```

ε115. Getting and Setting the Value of a Field

This example assumes that the field has the type int.

```
try {
    // Get value
```

Class *Interface* —extends - - -implements ○ abstract ● final ^—has superclass ‿—has subclass package—see other volume

```
    field.getInt(object);

    // Set value
    field.setInt(object, 123);

    // Get value of a static field
    field.getInt(null);

    // Set value of a static field
    field.setInt(null, 123);
} catch (IllegalAccessException e) {
}
```

Constructors

ε116. Getting a Constructor of a Class Object

There are two ways of obtaining a Constructor object from a Class object.

```
// By obtaining a list of all Constructors object.
Constructor[] cons = cls.getDeclaredConstructors();
for (int i=0; i<cons.length; i++) {
    Class[] paramTypes = cons[i].getParameterTypes();
    process(cons[i]);
}

// By obtaining a particular Constructor object.
// This example retrieves java.awt.Point(int, int).
try {
    Constructor con = java.awt.Point.class.getConstructor(new Class[]{int.class, int.class});
    process(con);
} catch (NoSuchMethodException e) {
}
```

ε117. Creating an Object Using a Constructor Object

This example creates a new Point object from the constructor Point(int,int).

```
try {
    java.awt.Point obj = (java.awt.Point)con.newInstance(
        new Object[]{new Integer(123), new Integer(123)});
} catch (InstantiationException e) {
} catch (IllegalAccessException e) {
} catch (InvocationTargetException e) {
}
```

Methods

ε118. Getting the Methods of a Class Object

There are three ways of obtaining a Method object from a Class object.

```
Class cls = java.lang.String.class;

// By obtaining a list of all declared methods.
Method[] methods = cls.getDeclaredMethods();

// By obtaining a list of all public methods, both declared and inherited.
methods = cls.getMethods();
for (int i=0; i<methods.length; i++) {
    Class returnType = methods[i].getReturnType();
```

Packages

```
        Class[] paramTypes = methods[i].getParameterTypes();
        process(methods[i]);
    }

    // By obtaining a particular Method object.
    // This example retrieves String.substring(int).
    try {
        Method method = cls.getMethod("substring", new Class[] {int.class});
        process(method);
    } catch (NoSuchMethodException e) {
    }
```

ε119. Invoking a Method Using a Method Object

```
    try {
        Object result = method.invoke(object, new Object[] {param1, param2, ..., paramN});
    } catch (IllegalAccessException e) {
    } catch (InvocationTargetException e) {
    }
```

Arrays

ε120. Determining If an Object Is an Array

```
    boolean b = object.getClass().isArray();
    if (b) {
        // object is an array
    }
```

ε121. Getting the Length and Dimensions of an Array Object

The length of an array is the number of elements of the array. The dimensions of an array type of int[][][] is three.

```
    Object o = new int[1][2][3];

    // Get length
    int len = Array.getLength(o); // 1

    // Get dimension
    int dim = getDim(o); // 3

    // If 'array' is an array object returns its dimensions; otherwise returns 0
    public static int getDim(Object array) {
        int dim = 0;
        Class cls = array.getClass();
        while (cls.isArray()) {
            dim++;
            cls = cls.getComponentType();
        }
        return dim;
    }
```

ε122. Getting the Component Type of an Array Object

The component type of an array is the type of an array's elements. For example, the component type of int[] is int. The component type of int[][] is int[].

```
    object.getClass().getComponentType();
```

ε123. Creating an Array

```
// An array of 10 ints.
int[] ints = (int[])Array.newInstance(int.class, 10);

// An array of 10 int-arrays.
int[][] ints2 = (int[][])Array.newInstance(int[].class, 10);

// A 10x20 2-dimenional int array.
ints2 = (int[][])Array.newInstance(int.class, new int[]{10, 20});
```

ε124. Expanding an Array

The length of an array cannot be changed. The closest thing to expanding an array is to create a larger one of the same type and copy the contents from the old array.

```
Object newArray = Array.newInstance(array.getClass().getComponentType(), Array.getLength(array)*2);
System.arraycopy(array, 0, newArray, 0, Array.getLength(array));
```

ε125. Getting and Setting the Value of an Element in an Array Object

```
// Get the value of the third element.
Object o = Array.get(array, 2);

// Set the value of the third element.
Array.set(array, 2, newValue);
```

java.math

This package contains classes for performing arithmetic and bit manipulation on arbitrary precision decimal and integer numbers. BigInteger and BigDecimal are analogous to the primitive types long and double except that BigInteger and BigDecimal support arbitrary precision, and therefore operations on them do not overflow or lose precision.

```
      java.lang.Object
 ○    └ java.lang.Number - - - - - - - - - - - - - - - - - - - - - - - - - - - - - - - - - - java.io.Serializable
1.1       ├ BigDecimal - - - - - - - - - - - - - - - - - - - - - - - - - - - - - - - - - - java.lang.Comparable
1.1       └ BigInteger - - - - - - - - - - - - - - - - - - - - - - - - - - - - - - - -
```

ε126. Operating with Big Integer Values

```
// Create via a string
BigInteger bi1 = new BigInteger("1234567890123456890");

// Create via a long
BigInteger bi2 = BigInteger.valueOf(123L);

bi1 = bi1.add(bi2);
bi1 = bi1.multiply(bi2);
bi1 = bi1.subtract(bi2);
bi1 = bi1.divide(bi2);
bi1 = bi1.negate();
int exponent = 2;
bi1 = bi1.pow(exponent);
```

ε127. Operating with Big Decimal Values

```java
// Create via a string
BigDecimal bd1 = new BigDecimal("123456789.0123456890");

// Create via a long
BigDecimal bd2 = BigDecimal.valueOf(123L);

bd1 = bd1.add(bd2);
bd1 = bd1.multiply(bd2);
bd1 = bd1.subtract(bd2);
bd1 = bd1.divide(bd2, BigDecimal.ROUND_UP);
bd1 = bd1.negate();
```

ε128. Setting the Decimal Place of a Big Decimal Value

```java
int decimalPlaces = 2;

// Truncates the big decimal value.
bd = bd.setScale(decimalPlaces, BigDecimal.ROUND_DOWN);
String string = bd.toString();
```

ε129. Performing Bitwise Operations with BigInteger

A BigInteger object is immutable. For a mutable object that supports bitwise operations, see "ε363. Performing Bitwise Operations on a Bit Vector".

```java
// Create via an array of bytes in twos-complement form.
// The byte-ordering is big-endian which means the most significant bit is in element 0.

// A negative value
byte[] bytes = new byte[]{(byte)0xFF, 0x00, 0x00}; // -65536

// A positive value
bytes = new byte[]{0x1, 0x00, 0x00}; // 65536
BigInteger bi = new BigInteger(bytes);

// Get the value of a bit
boolean b = bi.testBit(3); // 0
b = bi.testBit(16); // 1

// Set a bit
bi = bi.setBit(3);

// Clear a bit
bi = bi.clearBit(3);

// Flip a bit
bi = bi.flipBit(3);

// Shift the bits
bi = bi.shiftLeft(3);
bi = bi.shiftRight(1);

// Other bitwise operations
bi = bi.xor(bi);
bi = bi.and(bi);
bi = bi.not();
bi = bi.or(bi);
bi = bi.andNot(bi);

// Retrieve the current bits in a byte array in twos-complement form.
// The byte-ordering is big-endian which means the most significant bit is in element 0.
```

Class   *Interface*   —extends   - - -implements   ○ abstract   ● final   ˆ—has superclass   ‿—has subclass   package —see other volume

```
bytes = bi.toByteArray();
```

ε130. Parsing and Formatting a Big Integer into Binary, Octal, and Hexadecimal

```
BigInteger bi = new BigInteger("1023");

// Parse and format to binary
bi = new BigInteger("1111111111", 2); // 1023
String s = bi.toString(2); // 1111111111

// Parse and format to octal
bi = new BigInteger("1777", 8); // 1023
s = bi.toString(8); // 1777

// Parse and format to decimal
bi = new BigInteger("1023"); // 1023
s = bi.toString(); // 1023

// Parse and format to hexadecimal
bi = new BigInteger("3ff", 16); // 1023
s = bi.toString(16); // 3ff

// Parse and format to arbitrary radix <= Character.MAX_RADIX
int radix = 32;
bi = new BigInteger("vv", radix); // 1023
s = bi.toString(radix); // vv
```

ε131. Parsing and Formatting a Byte Array into Binary, Octal, and Hexadecimal

This example uses a BigInteger to convert a byte array to a string of binary, octal, or hexadecimal values.

```
// Get a byte array
byte[] bytes = new byte[]{(byte)0x12, (byte)0x0F, (byte)0xF0};

// Create a BigInteger using the byte array
BigInteger bi = new BigInteger(bytes);

// Format to binary
String s = bi.toString(2); // 100100000111111110000

// Format to octal
s = bi.toString(8); // 4407760

// Format to decimal
s = bi.toString(); // 1183728

// Format to hexadecimal
s = bi.toString(16); // 120ff0
if (s.length() % 2 != 0) {
    // Pad with 0
    s = "0"+s;
}


// Parse binary string
bi = new BigInteger("100100000111111110000", 2);

// Parse octal string
bi = new BigInteger("4407760", 8);

// Parse decimal string
bi = new BigInteger("1183728");

// Parse hexadecimal string
bi = new BigInteger("120ff0", 16);
```

Packages

```
// Get byte array
bytes = bi.toByteArray();
```

java.net

This package contains classes for implementing networking applications. Using these classes, you can communicate with any server on the Internet or implement your own Internet server, within the restrictions placed by the security manager with respect to the servers to which the application can connect. A number of classes are provided to make it convenient to use URLs to retrieve data on the Internet.

Class   *Interface*   —extends   - - -implements   ○ abstract   ● final   ^—has superclass   ͵—has subclass   package—see other volume

```
java.lang.Object
1.2 ○   - Authenticator
    ○   - ContentHandler
    ●   - DatagramPacket
        - DatagramSocket
1.1         └ MulticastSocket
1.1 ○   - DatagramSocketImpl - - - - - - - - - - - - - - - - - - - SocketOptions
        - InetAddress - - - - - - - - - - - - - - - - - - - - - - java.io.Serializable
1.4 ●       ├ Inet4Address
1.4 ●       └ Inet6Address
1.4 ●   - NetworkInterface
1.2 ●   - PasswordAuthentication
        - ServerSocket
        - Socket
1.4 ○   - SocketAddress - - - - - - - - - - - - - - - - - - - - -
1.4         └ InetSocketAddress
    ○   - SocketImpl - - - - - - - - - - - - - - - - - - - - - - SocketOptions
1.4 ●   - URI - - - - - - - - - - - - - - - - - - - - - - - - - java.io.Serializable, java.lang.Comparable
    ●   - URL - - - - - - - - - - - - - - - - - - - - - - - - - java.io.Serializable
    ○   - URLConnection
1.1 ○       ├ HttpURLConnection
1.2 ○       └ JarURLConnection
1.2     - URLDecoder
        - URLEncoder
    ○   - URLStreamHandler
```

Packages

```
        java.lang.Object
   O    ├ java.lang.ClassLoader
1.2     │    └ java.security.SecureClassLoader
1.2     │         └ URLClassLoader
1.2 O   ├ java.security.Permission ---------------------------- java.io.Serializable , java.security.Guard
1.2 ●   │    ├ SocketPermission ------------------------------ java.io.Serializable
1.2 O   │    └ java.security.BasicPermission---------------------┐
1.2 ●   │         └ NetPermission                               ┆
        └ java.lang.Throwable - - - - - - - - - - - - - - - - - ┘
             └ java.lang.Exception
1.4            ├ URISyntaxException
               └ java.io.IOException
                   ├ MalformedURLException
                   ├ ProtocolException
                   ├ SocketException
1.1                │    ├ BindException
1.1                │    ├ ConnectException
1.1                │    ├ NoRouteToHostException
1.4                │    └ PortUnreachableException
                   ├ UnknownHostException
                   ├ UnknownServiceException
                   └ java.io.InterruptedIOException
1.4                     └ SocketTimeoutException
```

	ContentHandlerFactory
1.3	*DatagramSocketImplFactory*
1.1	*FileNameMap*
	SocketImplFactory
1.2	*SocketOptions*
	URLStreamHandlerFactory

URLs

ε132. Creating a URL

```
try {
    // With components.
    URL url = new URL("http", "hostname", 80, "index.html");

    // With a single string.
    url = new URL("http://hostname:80/index.html");
} catch (MalformedURLException e) {
}
```

ε133. Converting Between a URL and a URI

```
URI uri = null;
URL url = null;

// Create a URI
try {
    uri = new URI("file://D:/almanac1.4/Ex1.java");
} catch (URISyntaxException e) {
}
```

Class *Interface* —extends - - -implements O abstract ● final ⌐—has superclass ⌐—has subclass package—see other volume

```
// Convert an absolute URI to a URL
try {
    url = uri.toURL();
} catch (IllegalArgumentException e) {
    // URI was not absolute
} catch (MalformedURLException e) {
}

// Convert a URL to a URI
try {
    uri = new URI(url.toString());
} catch (URISyntaxException e) {
}
```

ε134. Parsing a URL

```
try {
    URL url = new URL("http://hostname:80/index.html#_top_");

    String protocol = url.getProtocol(); // http
    String host = url.getHost(); // hostname
    int port = url.getPort(); // 80
    String file = url.getFile(); // index.html
    String ref = url.getRef(); // _top_
} catch (MalformedURLException e) {
}
```

ε135. Calling a CGI Using the POST Method

```
try {
    // Construct data
    String line = URLEncoder.encode("key1", "UTF-8") + "=" + URLEncoder.encode("value1", "UTF-8");
    line += "&" + URLEncoder.encode("key2", "UTF-8") + "=" + URLEncoder.encode("value2", "UTF-8");

    // Send data
    URL url = new URL("http://hostname:80/cgi");
    URLConnection conn = url.openConnection();
    conn.setDoOutput(true);
    OutputStreamWriter wr = new OutputStreamWriter(conn.getOutputStream());
    wr.write(line);
    wr.flush();
    wr.close();

    // Read lines from cgi-script
    BufferedReader rd = new BufferedReader(new InputStreamReader(conn.getInputStream()));
    while ((line = rd.readLine()) != null) {
        process(line);
    }
    rd.close();
} catch (Exception e) {
}
```

ε136. Getting Text from a URL

```
try {
    // Create a URL for the desired page
    URL url = new URL("http://hostname:80/index.html");

    // Read all the text returned by the server
    BufferedReader in = new BufferedReader(new InputStreamReader(url.openStream()));
    String str;
```

Packages

```
        while ((str = in.readLine()) != null) {
            // str is one line of text; readLine() strips the newline character(s)
        }
        in.close();
    } catch (MalformedURLException e) {
    } catch (IOException e) {
    }
```

ε137. Getting an Image from a URL

```
    try {
        // Create a URL for the image's location
        URL url = new URL("http://hostname:80/image.gif");

        // Get the image
        java.awt.Image image = java.awt.Toolkit.getDefaultToolkit().getDefaultToolkit().createImage(url);
    } catch (MalformedURLException e) {
    } catch (IOException e) {
    }
```

ε138. Getting a Jar File Using a URL

```
    try {
        // Create a URL that refers to a jar file on the net
        URL url = new URL("jar:http://hostname/my.jar!/");

        // Create a URL that refers to a jar file in the file system
        url = new URL("jar:file:/c:/almanac/my.jar!/");

        // Get the jar file
        JarURLConnection conn = (JarURLConnection)url.openConnection();
        JarFile jarfile = conn.getJarFile();

        // When no entry is specified on the URL, the entry name is null
        String entryName = conn.getEntryName(); // null


        // Create a URL that refers to an entry in the jar file
        url = new URL("jar:file:/c:/almanac/my.jar!/com/mycompany/MyClass.class");

        // Get the jar file
        conn = (JarURLConnection)url.openConnection();
        jarfile = conn.getJarFile();

        // Get the entry name; it should be the same as specified on URL
        entryName = conn.getEntryName();

        // Get the jar entry
        JarEntry jarEntry = conn.getJarEntry();
    } catch (MalformedURLException e) {
    } catch (IOException e) {
    }
```

ε139. Accessing a Password-Protected URL

```
    // Install the custom authenticator
    Authenticator.setDefault(new MyAuthenticator());

    // Access the page
    try {
        // Create a URL for the desired page
```

Class *Interface* —extends - - -implements ○ abstract ● final ⌐—has superclass ⌐—has subclass package—see other volume

```
        URL url = new URL("http://hostname:80/index.html");

        // Read all the text returned by the server
        BufferedReader in = new BufferedReader(new InputStreamReader(url.openStream()));
        String str;
        while ((str = in.readLine()) != null) {
            // str is one line of text; readLine() strips the newline character(s)
        }
        in.close();
    } catch (MalformedURLException e) {
    } catch (IOException e) {
    }

    public class MyAuthenticator extends Authenticator {
        // This method is called when a password-protected URL is accessed
        protected PasswordAuthentication getPasswordAuthentication() {
            // Get information about the request
            String promptString = getRequestingPrompt();
            String hostname = getRequestingHost();
            InetAddress ipaddr = getRequestingSite();
            int port = getRequestingPort();

            // Get the username from the user...
            String username = "myusername";

            // Get the password from the user...
            String password = "mypassword";

            // Return the information
            return new PasswordAuthentication(username, password.toCharArray());
        }
    }
```

HTTP

ε140. Getting the Response Headers from an HTTP Connection

```
    try {
        // Create a URLConnection object for a URL
        URL url = new URL("http://hostname:80");
        URLConnection conn = url.openConnection();

        // List all the response headers from the server.
        // Note: The first call to getHeaderFieldKey() will implicit send
        // the HTTP request to the server.
        for (int i=0; ; i++) {
            String headerName = conn.getHeaderFieldKey(i);
            String headerValue = conn.getHeaderField(i);

            if (headerName == null && headerValue == null) {
                // No more headers
                break;
            }
            if (headerName == null) {
                // The header value contains the server's HTTP version
            }
        }
    } catch (Exception e) {
    }
```

java.net

Here's a sample of headers from a website:

```
Key=Value

null=HTTP/1.1 200 OK
Server=Netscape-Enterprise/4.1
Date=Mon, 11 Feb 2002 09:23:26 GMT
Cache-control=public
Content-type=text/html
Etag="9fa67d2a-58-71-3bbdad3283"
Last-modified=Fri, 05 Oct 2001 12:53:06 GMT
Content-length=115
Accept-ranges=bytes
Connection=close
```

ε141. Getting the Cookies from an HTTP Connection

When the server wants to set a cookie in the client, it includes a response header of the form

Set-Cookie: *cookie-value*; expires=*date*; path=*path*; domain=*domain-name*; secure

cookie-value is some arbitrary string data that should be returned to the server in future URL requests. The life time of the cookie is specified by expires. If expires is not specified, the cookie expires at the end of the session. When a URL request is made, the cookie should be sent along only if domain-name matches the end of the fully-qualified host name of the URL request and path matches the beginning of the path of the URL request. If secure is specified, the cookie should be sent to the server only through HTTPS.

```java
try {
    // Create a URLConnection object for a URL
    URL url = new URL("http://hostname:80");
    URLConnection conn = url.openConnection();

    // Get all cookies from the server.
    // Note: The first call to getHeaderFieldKey() will implicit send
    // the HTTP request to the server.
    for (int i=0; ; i++) {
        String headerName = conn.getHeaderFieldKey(i);
        String headerValue = conn.getHeaderField(i);

        if (headerName == null && headerValue == null) {
            // No more headers
            break;
        }
        if ("Set-Cookie".equalsIgnoreCase(headerName)) {
            // Parse cookie
            String[] fields = headerValue.split(";\\s*");

            String cookieValue = fields[0];
            String expires = null;
            String path = null;
            String domain = null;
            boolean secure = false;

            // Parse each field
            for (int j=1; j<fields.length; j++) {
                if ("secure".equalsIgnoreCase(fields[j])) {
                    secure = true;
                } else if (fields[j].indexOf('=') > 0) {
                    String[] f = fields[j].split("=");
```

```
                    if ("expires".equalsIgnoreCase(f[0])) {
                        expires = f[1];
                    } else if ("domain".equalsIgnoreCase(f[0])) {
                        domain = f[1];
                    } else if ("path".equalsIgnoreCase(f[0])) {
                        path = f[1];
                    }
                }
            }
                // Save the cookie...
            }
        }
    } catch (MalformedURLException e) {
    } catch (IOException e) {
    }
```

Here's a sample of cookies from two websites:

```
B=a43ka6gu6f4n4&b=2; expires=Thu, 15 Apr 2010 20:00:00 GMT;
    path=/; domain=.yahoo.com

PREF=ID=e51:TM=686:LM=86:S=BL-w0; domain=.google.com; path=/;
    expires=Sun, 17-Jan-2038 19:14:07 GMT
```

ε142. Sending a Cookie to an HTTP Server

```
try {
    // Create a URLConnection object for a URL
    URL url = new URL("http://hostname:80");
    URLConnection conn = url.openConnection();

    // Set the cookie value to send
    conn.setRequestProperty("Cookie", "name1=value1; name2=value2");

    // Send the request to the server
    conn.connect();
} catch (MalformedURLException e) {
} catch (IOException e) {
}
```

ε143. Preventing Automatic Redirects in a HTTP Connection

By default, when you make an HTTP connection using URLConnection, the system automatically follows redirects until it reaches the final destination. This example demonstrates how to prevent automatic redirection.

```
// Disable automatic redirects for all HTTP requests
HttpURLConnection.setFollowRedirects(false);

// Disable automatic redirects for a particular connection
try {
    // Create a URLConnection object for a URL
    URL url = new URL("http://hostname:80");
    URLConnection conn = url.openConnection();

    // Disable automatic redirects just for this connection
    HttpURLConnection httpConn = (HttpURLConnection)conn;
    httpConn.setInstanceFollowRedirects(false);

    // Send the request to the server
    conn.connect();
```

```
    } catch (MalformedURLException e) {
    } catch (IOException e) {
    }
```

Hostnames and IP Addresses

ε144. Getting the IP Address of a Hostname

```
try {
    InetAddress addr = InetAddress.getByName("javaalmanac.com");
    byte[] ipAddr = addr.getAddress();

    // Convert to dot representation
    String ipAddrStr = "";
    for (int i=0; i<ipAddr.length; i++) {
        if (i > 0) {
            ipAddrStr += ".";
        }
        ipAddrStr += ipAddr[i]&0xFF;
    }
} catch (UnknownHostException e) {
}
```

ε145. Getting the Hostname of an IP Address

This example attempts to retrieve the hostname for an IP address. Note that getHostName() may not succeed, in which case it simply returns the IP address.

```
try {
    // Get hostname by textual representation of IP address
    InetAddress addr = InetAddress.getByName("127.0.0.1");

    // Get hostname by a byte array containing the IP address
    byte[] ipAddr = new byte[]{127, 0, 0, 1};
    addr = InetAddress.getByAddress(ipAddr);

    // Get the host name
    String hostname = addr.getHostName();

    // Get canonical host name
    String hostnameCanonical = addr.getCanonicalHostName();
} catch (UnknownHostException e) {
}
```

ε146. Getting the IP Address and Hostname of the Local Machine

```
try {
    InetAddress addr = InetAddress.getLocalHost();

    // Get IP Address
    byte[] ipAddr = addr.getAddress();

    // Get hostname
    String hostname = addr.getHostName();
} catch (UnknownHostException e) {
}
```

Class   *Interface*   —extends   - - -implements   O abstract   ● final   ˆ—has superclass   ⌐—has subclass   package—see other volume

Sockets

ε147. Creating a Client Socket

```
// Create a socket without a timeout
try {
    InetAddress addr = InetAddress.getByName("java.sun.com");
    int port = 80;

    // This constructor will block until the connection succeeds
    Socket socket = new Socket(addr, port);
} catch (UnknownHostException e) {
} catch (IOException e) {
}

// Create a socket with a timeout
try {
    InetAddress addr = InetAddress.getByName("java.sun.com");
    int port = 80;
    SocketAddress sockaddr = new InetSocketAddress(addr, port);

    // Create an unbound socket
    Socket sock = new Socket();

    // This method will block no more than timeoutMs.
    // If the timeout occurs, SocketTimeoutException is thrown.
    int timeoutMs = 2000; // 2 seconds
    sock.connect(sockaddr, timeoutMs);
} catch (UnknownHostException e) {
} catch (SocketTimeoutException e) {
} catch (IOException e) {
}
```

ε148. Creating a Server Socket

```
try {
    int port = 2000;
    ServerSocket srv = new ServerSocket(port);

    // Wait for connection from client.
    Socket socket = srv.accept();
} catch (IOException e) {
}
```

ε149. Reading Text from a Socket

```
try {
    BufferedReader rd = new BufferedReader(new InputStreamReader(socket.getInputStream()));

    String str;
    while ((str = rd.readLine()) != null) {
        process(str);
    }
    rd.close();
} catch (IOException e) {
}
```

ε150. Writing Text to a Socket

```
try {
    BufferedWriter wr = new BufferedWriter(new OutputStreamWriter(socket.getOutputStream()));
    wr.write("aString");
```

```
        wr.flush();
    } catch (IOException e) {
    }
```

Datagram

ε151. Sending a Datagram

```java
public static void send(InetAddress dst, int port, byte[] outbuf, int len) {
    try {
        DatagramPacket request = new DatagramPacket(outbuf, len, dst, port);
        DatagramSocket socket = new DatagramSocket();
        socket.send(request);
    } catch (SocketException e) {
    } catch (IOException e) {
    }
}
```

ε152. Receiving a Datagram

```java
try {
    byte[] inbuf = new byte[256]; // default size
    DatagramSocket socket = new DatagramSocket();

    // Wait for packet
    DatagramPacket packet = new DatagramPacket(inbuf, inbuf.length);
    socket.receive(packet);

    // Data is now in inbuf
    int numBytesReceived = packet.getLength();
} catch (SocketException e) {
} catch (IOException e) {
}
```

Multicast

ε153. Joining a Multicast Group

```java
public void join(String groupName, int port) {
    try {
        MulticastSocket msocket = new MulticastSocket(port);
        group = InetAddress.getByName(groupName);
        msocket.joinGroup(group);
    } catch (IOException e) {
    }
}
```

ε154. Receiving from a Multicast Group

Once you've created a multicast socket and joined the group, all datagrams sent to its corresponding multicast address will be available to be read from the socket. You can read from the socket just like you would from a unicast socket.

```java
public void read(MulticastSocket msocket, byte[] inbuf) {
    try {
        DatagramPacket packet = new DatagramPacket(inbuf, inbuf.length);
```

```
        // Wait for packet
        msocket.receive(packet);

        // Data is now in inbuf
        int numBytesReceived = packet.getLength();
    } catch (IOException e) {
    }
}
```

ε155. Sending to a Multicast Group

You can send to a multicast socket using either a DatagramSocket or a MulticastSocket. What makes it multicast is the address that is in the datagram. If the address is a multicast address, the datagram will reach the multicast members in the group. You only need to use MulticastSocket if you want to control the time-to-live of the datagram.

```
byte[] outbuf = new byte[1024];
int port = 1234;
try {
    DatagramSocket socket = new DatagramSocket();
    InetAddress groupAddr = InetAddress.getByName("228.1.2.3");
    DatagramPacket packet = new DatagramPacket(outbuf, outbuf.length, groupAddr, port);
    socket.send(packet);
} catch (SocketException e) {
} catch (IOException e) {
}
```

Encodings

ε156. Converting Between a Byte Array and Base64

This example uses non-standard classes in the sun.misc package to convert to and from Base64. These classes may change in the future.

```
try {
    // Convert a byte array to base64 string
    byte[] buf = new byte[]{0x12, 0x23};
    String s = new sun.misc.BASE64Encoder().encode(buf);

    // Convert base64 string to a byte array
    buf = new sun.misc.BASE64Decoder().decodeBuffer(s);
} catch (IOException e) {
}
```

ε157. Converting x-www-form-urlencoded Data

Name/value pairs that are formatted using the x-www-form-urlencoded specification appear as:

```
name1=value1&name2=value2
```

where nameN and valueN must be escaped. For example, 'a+b' will appear as 'a%2Bb' when escaped. The URLEncoder and URLDecoder classes are used to escape the names and values.

```
try {
    // Construct a x-www-form-urlencoded string
    String line = URLEncoder.encode("name1", "UTF-8") + "=" + URLEncoder.encode("value1", "UTF-8");
    line += "&" + URLEncoder.encode("name2", "UTF-8") + "=" + URLEncoder.encode("value2", "UTF-8");

    // Parse a x-www-form-urlencoded string
    String[] pairs = line.split("\\&");
    for (int i=0; i<pairs.length; i++) {
```

Packages

```
            String[] fields = pairs[i].split("=");
            String name = URLDecoder.decode(fields[0], "UTF-8");
            String value = URLDecoder.decode(fields[1], "UTF-8");
        }
    } catch (UnsupportedEncodingException e) {
    }
```

java.nio

This package defines the different types of buffers (containers of data) that are used throughout the New I/O (NIO) APIs.

```
         java.lang.Object
1.4 ○    ├ Buffer
1.4 ○    │   ├ ByteBuffer - - - - - - - - - - - - - - - - - - - - - - - - java.lang.Comparable
1.4 ○    │   │    └ MappedByteBuffer
1.4 ○    │   ├ CharBuffer - - - - - - - - - - - - - - - - - - - - - - - java.lang.CharSequence, java.lang.Comparable
1.4 ○    │   ├ DoubleBuffer - - - - - - - - - - - - - - - - - - - - - - java.lang.Comparable
1.4 ○    │   ├ FloatBuffer - - - - - - - - - - - - - - - - - - - - - - ┐
1.4 ○    │   ├ IntBuffer - - - - - - - - - - - - - - - - - - - - - - - │
1.4 ○    │   ├ LongBuffer - - - - - - - - - - - - - - - - - - - - - - - │
1.4 ○    │   └ ShortBuffer - - - - - - - - - - - - - - - - - - - - - - ┘
1.4 ●    ├ ByteOrder
         └ java.lang.Throwable - - - - - - - - - - - - - - - - - - - - java.io.Serializable
              └ java.lang.Exception
                   └ java.lang.RuntimeException
1.4                     ├ BufferOverflowException
1.4                     ├ BufferUnderflowException
1.1                     ├ java.lang.IllegalStateException
1.4                     │    └ InvalidMarkException
```

Class *Interface* —extends - - -implements ○ abstract ● final ^—has superclass —has subclass package—see other volume

```
java.lang.Object
  └ java.lang.Throwable - - - - - - - - - - - - - - - - - - - - - - - - - - - - - - - - - - - java.io.Serializable
      └ java.lang.Exception
          └ java.lang.RuntimeException
              └ java.lang.UnsupportedOperationException
1.2
1.4                 └ ReadOnlyBufferException
```

Byte Buffers

ε158. Creating a ByteBuffer

A ByteBuffer is a fixed-capacity buffer that holds byte values. This example demonstrates a number of ways to create a ByteBuffer.

See also "ε159. Getting Bytes from a ByteBuffer" and "ε160. Putting Bytes into a ByteBuffer".

```
// Create a ByteBuffer using a byte array
byte[] bytes = new byte[10];
ByteBuffer buf = ByteBuffer.wrap(bytes);

// Create a non-direct ByteBuffer with a 10 byte capacity
// The underlying storage is a byte array.
buf = ByteBuffer.allocate(10);

// Create a direct (memory-mapped) ByteBuffer with a 10 byte capacity.
buf = ByteBuffer.allocateDirect(10);

// To create a ByteBuffer for a memory-mapped file,
// see "ε166. Creating a Memory-Mapped File"
```

ε159. Getting Bytes from a ByteBuffer

A ByteBuffer has a capacity that determines how many bytes it contains. This capacity can never change. Any byte in the buffer can be retrieved using the absolute version of get(), which takes an index in the range [0..capacity-1].

The bytes in a ByteBuffer can also be retrieved using the relative version of get(), which uses the position and limit properties of the buffer. In particular, this version of get() retrieves the byte at the position and advances the position by one. get() cannot retrieve bytes past the limit (even though the limit might be less than the capacity). The position is always <= limit and limit is always <= capacity.

```
// Create an empty ByteBuffer with a 10 byte capacity
ByteBuffer bbuf = ByteBuffer.allocate(10);

// Get the ByteBuffer's capacity
int capacity = bbuf.capacity(); // 10

// Use the absolute get().
// This method does not affect the position.
byte b = bbuf.get(5); // position=0

// Set the position
bbuf.position(5);

// Use the relative get()
b = bbuf.get();

// Get the new position
int pos = bbuf.position(); // 6

// Get remaining byte count
int rem = bbuf.remaining(); // 4
```

```
// Set the limit
bbuf.limit(7); // remaining=1

// This convenience method sets the position to 0
bbuf.rewind(); // remaining=7
```

ε160. Putting Bytes into a ByteBuffer

A ByteBuffer has a capacity which determines how many bytes it contains. This capacity can never change. Any byte in the ByteBuffer can be modified using the absolute version of put(), which takes an index in the range [0..capacity-1].

The bytes in a ByteBuffer can also be set using the relative version of put(), which uses the position and limit properties of the buffer. In particular, this version of put() sets the byte at the position and advances the position by one. put() cannot set bytes past the limit (even though limit might be less than the capacity). The position is always <= limit and limit is always <= capacity.

```
// Create an empty ByteBuffer with a 10 byte capacity
ByteBuffer bbuf = ByteBuffer.allocate(10);

// Get the buffer's capacity
int capacity = bbuf.capacity(); // 10

// Use the absolute put().
// This method does not affect the position.
bbuf.put((byte)0xFF); // position=0

// Set the position
bbuf.position(5);

// Use the relative put()
bbuf.put((byte)0xFF);

// Get the new position
int pos = bbuf.position(); // 6

// Get remaining byte count
int rem = bbuf.remaining(); // 4

// Set the limit
bbuf.limit(7); // remaining=1

// This convenience method sets the position to 0
bbuf.rewind(); // remaining=7
```

ε161. Converting Between a ByteBuffer an a Byte Array

```
// Create a ByteBuffer from a byte array
byte[] bytes = new byte[10];
ByteBuffer buf = ByteBuffer.wrap(bytes);

// Retrieve bytes between the position and limit
// (see "ε160. Putting Bytes into a ByteBuffer")
bytes = new byte[buf.remaining()];
buf.get(bytes, 0, bytes.length);

// Retrieve all bytes in the buffer
buf.clear();
bytes = new byte[buf.capacity()];
buf.get(bytes, 0, bytes.length);
```

Class *Interface* —extends - - -implements ○ abstract ● final ^—has superclass ⌐—has subclass package—see other volume

ε162. Getting and Setting Non-Byte Java Types in a ByteBuffer

The ByteBuffer class provides convenience methods for getting and putting other multibyte Java primitive types. There are two issues to be aware of when using these methods. First, ensure that values will be stored using the desired byte ordering; see "ε165. Setting the Byte Ordering for a ByteBuffer" for more information.

Second, the hasRemaining() method cannot be used to determine if the buffer has room for a multibyte put. If your application needs to know this information, see "ε163. Creating a Non-Byte Java Type Buffer on a ByteBuffer" for an example that can provide this information.

```java
// Obtain a ByteBuffer; see also "ε158. Creating a ByteBuffer"
ByteBuffer buf = ByteBuffer.allocate(100);

// Put values of different types
buf.putChar((char)123);
buf.putShort((short)123);
buf.putInt(123);
buf.putLong(123L);
buf.putFloat(12.3F);
buf.putDouble(12.3D);

// Reset position for reading
buf.flip();

// Retrieve the values
char c = buf.getChar();
short s = buf.getShort();
int i = buf.getInt();
long l = buf.getLong();
float f = buf.getFloat();
double d = buf.getDouble();
```

ε163. Creating a Non-Byte Java Type Buffer on a ByteBuffer

You can create "views" on a ByteBuffer to support buffers of other Java primitive types. For example, by creating a character view on a ByteBuffer, you treat the ByteBuffer like a buffer of characters. The character buffer supports strings directly. Also, hasRemaining() properly works with characters rather than with bytes.

When you create a typed view, it is important to be aware that it is created on top of the bytes between position and limit. That is, the capacity of the new view is (limit - position). The limit of the new view may be reduced so that the capacity is an integral value based on the size of the type. Finally, the view shares the same storage as the underlying ByteBuffer, so any changes to the byte buffer will be seen by the view and visa versa. However, changes to a view's position or limit do not affect the ByteBuffer's properties and visa versa.

```java
// Obtain a ByteBuffer; see also "ε158. Creating a ByteBuffer"
ByteBuffer buf = ByteBuffer.allocate(15);
// remaining = 15

// Create a character ByteBuffer
CharBuffer cbuf = buf.asCharBuffer();
// remaining = 7

// Create a short ByteBuffer
ShortBuffer sbuf = buf.asShortBuffer();
// remaining = 7

// Create an integer ByteBuffer
IntBuffer ibuf = buf.asIntBuffer();
// remaining = 3
```

```
// Create a long ByteBuffer
LongBuffer lbuf = buf.asLongBuffer();
// remaining = 1

// Create a float ByteBuffer
FloatBuffer fbuf = buf.asFloatBuffer();
// remaining = 3

// Create a double ByteBuffer
DoubleBuffer dbuf = buf.asDoubleBuffer();
// remaining = 1
```

ε164. Using a ByteBuffer to Store Strings

This example demonstrates how to use a ByteBuffer to store characters. For example, an application may want to store strings in a file to avoid the conversion to and from bytes. The example creates a character view on the ByteBuffer that provides methods for reading and writing strings.

This example does not convert characters and bytes. For an example on how to convert characters to and from bytes, see "ε186. Converting Between Strings (Unicode) and Other Character Set Encodings".

```
// Obtain a ByteBuffer; see also "ε158. Creating a ByteBuffer"
ByteBuffer buf = ByteBuffer.allocate(100);

// Create a character ByteBuffer
CharBuffer cbuf = buf.asCharBuffer();

// Write a string
cbuf.put("a string");

// Convert character ByteBuffer to a string.
// Uses characters between current position and limit so flip it first
cbuf.flip();
String s = cbuf.toString(); // a string
// Does not affect position

// Get a substring
int start = 2; // start is relative to cbuf's current position
int end = 5;
CharSequence sub = cbuf.subSequence(start, end); // str
```

ε165. Setting the Byte Ordering for a ByteBuffer

By default, the byte ordering for a ByteBuffer is ByteOrder.BIG_ENDIAN. This means that if you put a multibyte value into the buffer, the most significant byte is written out first. With LITTLE_ENDIAN, the least significant byte is written out first.

```
// Obtain a ByteBuffer; see also "ε158. Creating a ByteBuffer"
ByteBuffer buf = ByteBuffer.allocate(10);

// Get default byte ordering
ByteOrder order = buf.order(); // ByteOrder.BIG_ENDIAN

// Put a multibyte value
buf.putShort(0, (short)123);
buf.get(0); // 0
buf.get(1); // 123

// Set to little endian
buf.order(ByteOrder.LITTLE_ENDIAN);

// Put a multibyte value
```

Class   *Interface*   —extends   - - -implements   O abstract   ● final   ˆ—has superclass   ‿—has subclass   package—see other volume

```
buf.putShort(0, (short)123);
buf.get(0); // 123
buf.get(1); // 0
```

ε166. Creating a Memory-Mapped File

Mapping a file in memory results in a ByteArray object. To access the byte array, see "ε159. Getting Bytes from a ByteBuffer" and "ε160. Putting Bytes into a ByteBuffer".

```
try {
    File file = new File("filename");

    // Create a read-only memory-mapped file
    FileChannel roChannel = new RandomAccessFile(file, "r").getChannel();
    ByteBuffer roBuf = roChannel.map(FileChannel.MapMode.READ_ONLY, 0, (int)roChannel.size());

    // Create a read-write memory-mapped file
    FileChannel rwChannel = new RandomAccessFile(file, "rw").getChannel();
    ByteBuffer wrBuf = rwChannel.map(FileChannel.MapMode.READ_WRITE, 0, (int)rwChannel.size());

    // Create a private (copy-on-write) memory-mapped file.
    // Any write to this channel results in a private copy of the data.
    FileChannel pvChannel = new RandomAccessFile(file, "rw").getChannel();
    ByteBuffer pvBuf = roChannel.map(FileChannel.MapMode.READ_WRITE, 0, (int)rwChannel.size());
} catch (IOException e) {
}
```

ε167. Persisting Changes to a Memory-Mapped ByteBuffer

Changes to a memory-mapped ByteBuffer are not necessarily sent immediately to the underlying storage device. In some applications, such as with a memory-mapped register, the change should be sent immediately. The MappedByteBuffer.force() method is used to force all changes to the underlying storage device immediately.

```
try {
    // Create a ByteBuffer on a memory-mapped file
    File file = new File("filename");
    FileChannel channel = new RandomAccessFile(file, "rw").getChannel();
    MappedByteBuffer buf = channel.map(FileChannel.MapMode.READ_WRITE, 0, (int)channel.size());

    // Make a change to the ByteBuffer
    buf.put(0, (byte)0xFF);

    // Force the change to the file system
    buf.force();

    // Close the file
    channel.close();
} catch (IOException e) {
}
```

ε168. Determining If a ByteBuffer Is Direct

A non-direct ByteBuffer is one where the contents are stored in the normal memory. A direct ByteBuffer is one where the contents are stored in some I/O device such as a disk drive or video board.

See also "ε158. Creating a ByteBuffer".

```
ByteBuffer bbuf = ByteBuffer.wrap(new byte[10]);
boolean isDirect = bbuf.isDirect(); // false
```

Packages

```
bbuf = ByteBuffer.allocate(10);
isDirect = bbuf.isDirect(); // false

bbuf = ByteBuffer.allocateDirect(10);
isDirect = bbuf.isDirect(); // true
```

ε169. Reading from a Channel with a ByteBuffer

This example uses a ByteBuffer to read from a channel. The tricky part of this operation is to remember to properly set the buffer's position before and after a read.

```
try {
    // Obtain a channel
    ReadableByteChannel channel = new FileInputStream("infile").getChannel();

    // Create a direct ByteBuffer; see also "ε158. Creating a ByteBuffer"
    ByteBuffer buf = ByteBuffer.allocateDirect(10);

    int numRead = 0;
    while (numRead >= 0) {
        // read() places read bytes at the buffer's position so the
        // position should always be properly set before calling read()
        // This method sets the position to 0
        buf.rewind();

        // Read bytes from the channel
        numRead = channel.read(buf);

        // The read() method also moves the position so in order to
        // read the new bytes, the buffer's position must be set back to 0
        buf.rewind();

        // Read bytes from ByteBuffer; see also
        // "ε159. Getting Bytes from a ByteBuffer"
        for (int i=0; i<numRead; i++) {
            byte b = buf.get();
        }
    }
} catch (Exception e) {
}
```

ε170. Writing to a Channel with a ByteBuffer

It is necessary to use a ByteBuffer to write to a channel. This example retrieves bytes from an input stream and writes them to a channel using a ByteBuffer. The tricky part of this operation is to remember to properly set the buffer's position before and after a write.

```
try {
    // Obtain a channel
    WritableByteChannel channel = new FileOutputStream("outfilename").getChannel();

    // Create a direct ByteBuffer;
    // see also "ε158. Creating a ByteBuffer"
    ByteBuffer buf = ByteBuffer.allocateDirect(10);

    byte[] bytes = new byte[1024];
    int count = 0;
    int index = 0;

    // Continue writing bytes until there are no more
    while (count >= 0) {
```

```
            if (index == count) {
                count = inputStream.read(bytes);
                index = 0;
            }
            // Fill ByteBuffer
            while (index < count && buf.hasRemaining()) {
                buf.put(bytes[index++]);
            }

            // Set the limit to the current position and the position to 0
            // making the new bytes visible for write()
            buf.flip();

            // Write the bytes to the channel
            int numWritten = channel.write(buf);

            // Check if all bytes were written
            if (buf.hasRemaining()) {
                // If not all bytes were written, move the unwritten bytes
                // to the beginning and set position just after the last
                // unwritten byte; also set limit to the capacity
                buf.compact();
            } else {
                // Set the position to 0 and the limit to capacity
                buf.clear();
            }
        }

        // Close the file
        channel.close();
    } catch (Exception e) {
    }
```

ε171. Writing and Appending a ByteBuffer to a File

If you have one or more ByteBuffers to dump to a file, use a FileChannel.

```
    // Write bbuf to filename
    ByteBuffer bbuf = getMyData();
    File file = new File("filename");

    // Set to true if the bytes should be appended to the file;
    // set to false if the bytes should replace current bytes
    // (if the file exists)
    boolean append = false;

    try {
        // Create a writable file channel
        FileChannel wChannel = new FileOutputStream(file, append).getChannel();

        // Write the ByteBuffer contents; the bytes between the ByteBuffer's
        // position and the limit is written to the file
        wChannel.write(bbuf);

        // Close the file
        wChannel.close();
    } catch (IOException e) {
    }
```

ε172. Copying One File to Another

```
    try {
```

```
                // Create channel on the source
                FileChannel srcChannel = new FileInputStream("srcFilename").getChannel();

                // Create channel on the destination
                FileChannel dstChannel = new FileOutputStream("dstFilename").getChannel();

                // Copy file contents from source to destination
                dstChannel.transferFrom(srcChannel, 0, srcChannel.size());

                // Close the channels
                srcChannel.close();
                dstChannel.close();
            } catch (IOException e) {
            }
```

Sockets

ε173. Creating a Non-Blocking Socket

This example shows how to create a non-blocking socket. A non-blocking socket requires a socket channel.

See also "ε176. Using a Selector to Manage Non-Blocking Sockets".

```
        // Creates a non-blocking socket channel for the specified host name and port.
        // connect() is called on the new channel before it is returned.
        public static SocketChannel createSocketChannel(String hostName, int port) throws IOException {
            // Create a non-blocking socket channel
            SocketChannel sChannel = SocketChannel.open();
            sChannel.configureBlocking(false);

            // Send a connection request to the server; this method is non-blocking
            sChannel.connect(new InetSocketAddress(hostName, port));
            return sChannel;
        }

        // Create a non-blocking socket and check for connections
        try {
            // Create a non-blocking socket channel on port 80
            SocketChannel sChannel = createSocketChannel("hostname.com", 80);

            // Before the socket is usable, the connection must be completed
            // by calling finishConnect(), which is non-blocking
            while (!sChannel.finishConnect()) {
                // Do something else
            }
            // Socket channel is now ready to use
        } catch (IOException e) {
        }
```

ε174. Reading from a SocketChannel

See also "ε173. Creating a Non-Blocking Socket".

```
        // Create a direct buffer to get bytes from socket.
        // Direct buffers should be long-lived and be reused as much as possible.
        ByteBuffer buf = ByteBuffer.allocateDirect(1024);

        try {
            // Clear the buffer and read bytes from socket
            buf.clear();
```

```
        int numBytesRead = socketChannel.read(buf);

        if (numBytesRead == -1) {
            // No more bytes can be read from the channel
            socketChannel.close();
        } else {
            // To read the bytes, flip the buffer
            buf.flip();

            // Read the bytes from the buffer ...;
            // see "ε159. Getting Bytes from a ByteBuffer"
        }
    } catch (IOException e) {
        // Connection may have been closed
    }
```

ε175. Writing to a SocketChannel

See also "ε173. Creating a Non-Blocking Socket".

```
    // Create a direct buffer to get bytes from socket.
    // Direct buffers should be long-lived and be reused as much as possible.
    ByteBuffer buf = ByteBuffer.allocateDirect(1024);

    try {
        // Fill the buffer with the bytes to write;
        // see "ε160. Putting Bytes into a ByteBuffer"
        buf.put((byte)0xFF);

        // Prepare the buffer for reading by the socket
        buf.flip();

        // Write bytes
        int numBytesWritten = socketChannel.write(buf);
    } catch (IOException e) {
        // Connection may have been closed
    }
```

ε176. Using a Selector to Manage Non-Blocking Sockets

Although you could poll each non-blocking socket for events, a more convenient and efficient method is to use a selector to manage the channels. The selector efficiently monitors the channels for changes and reports the events through a single method call.

The first step is to register a channel with a selector. The registration process yields an object called a "selection key" which identifies the selector/socket channel pair (a channel could be registered with another selector for different events). When an event occurs on a channel, the selector returns the selection key for that channel. The selection key also contains the type of event that occurred.

This example creates two sockets and registers them with a selector. The example then uses the selector to listen for events.

See also "ε179. Using a Selector to Manage Non-Blocking Server Sockets".

```
    // Create a selector and register two socket channels
    Selector selector = null;
    try {
        // Create the selector
        selector = Selector.open();

        // Create two non-blocking sockets. This method is implemented in
        // "ε173. Creating a Non-Blocking Socket".
```

Packages

```
            SocketChannel sChannel1 = createSocketChannel("hostname.com", 80);
            SocketChannel sChannel2 = createSocketChannel("hostname.com", 80);

            // Register the channel with selector, listening for all events
            sChannel1.register(selector, sChannel1.validOps());
            sChannel2.register(selector, sChannel1.validOps());
        } catch (IOException e) {
        }

        // Wait for events
        while (true) {
            try {
                // Wait for an event
                selector.select();
            } catch (IOException e) {
                // Handle error with selector
                break;
            }

            // Get list of selection keys with pending events
            Iterator it = selector.selectedKeys().iterator();

            // Process each key at a time
            while (it.hasNext()) {
                // Get the selection key
                SelectionKey selKey = (SelectionKey)it.next();

                // Remove it from the list to indicate that it is being processed
                it.remove();

                try {
                    processSelectionKey(selKey);
                } catch (IOException e) {
                    // Handle error with channel and unregister
                    selKey.cancel();
                }
            }
        }

    public void processSelectionKey(SelectionKey selKey) throws IOException {
        // Since the ready operations are cumulative,
        // need to check readiness for each operation
        if (selKey.isValid() && selKey.isConnectable()) {
            // Get channel with connection request
            SocketChannel sChannel = (SocketChannel)selKey.channel();

            boolean success = sChannel.finishConnect();
            if (!success) {
                // An error occurred; handle it

                // Unregister the channel with this selector
                selKey.cancel();
            }
        }
        if (selKey.isValid() && selKey.isReadable()) {
            // Get channel with bytes to read
            SocketChannel sChannel = (SocketChannel)selKey.channel();

            // See "ε174. Reading from a SocketChannel"
        }
```

Class *Interface* —extends - - -implements   ○ abstract   ● final   ^—has superclass   ‿—has subclass   package—see other volume

```
    if (selKey.isValid() && selKey.isWritable()) {
        // Get channel that's ready for more bytes
        SocketChannel sChannel = (SocketChannel)selKey.channel();

        // See "ε175. Writing to a SocketChannel"
    }
}
```

ε177. Creating a Non-Blocking Server Socket

This example shows how to create a non-blocking server socket. A non-blocking server socket requires a server socket channel.

See also "ε179. Using a Selector to Manage Non-Blocking Server Sockets".

```
// Create a non-blocking server socket and check for connections
try {
    // Create a non-blocking server socket channel on port 80
    ServerSocketChannel ssChannel = ServerSocketChannel.open();
    ssChannel.configureBlocking(false);
    int port = 80;
    ssChannel.socket().bind(new InetSocketAddress(port));

    // See "ε178. Accepting a Connection on a ServerSocketChannel"
    // for an example of accepting a connection request
} catch (IOException e) {
}
```

ε178. Accepting a Connection on a ServerSocketChannel

To create a ServerSocketChannel, see "ε177. Creating a Non-Blocking Server Socket".

```
// Get port that received the connection request; this information
// might be useful in determining how to handle the connection
int localPort = serverSocketChannel.socket().getLocalPort();

try {
    // Accept the connection request.
    // If serverSocketChannel is blocking, this method blocks.
    // The returned channel is in blocking mode.
    SocketChannel sChannel = serverSocketChannel.accept();

    // If serverSocketChannel is non-blocking, sChannel may be null
    if (sChannel == null) {
        // There were no pending connection requests; try again later.
        // To be notified of connection requests,
        // see "ε179. Using a Selector to Manage Non-Blocking Server Sockets".
    } else {
        // Use the socket channel to communicate with the client
        // See "ε176. Using a Selector to Manage Non-Blocking Sockets".
    }
} catch (IOException e) {
}
```

ε179. Using a Selector to Manage Non-Blocking Server Sockets

For more information about selectors, see "ε176. Using a Selector to Manage Non-Blocking Sockets".

This example creates two server sockets and registers them with a selector. The example then uses the selector to listen for events.

```
try {
    // Create the selector
```

```
            Selector selector = Selector.open();

            // Create two non-blocking server sockets on 80 and 81
            ServerSocketChannel ssChannel1 = ServerSocketChannel.open();
            ssChannel1.configureBlocking(false);
            ssChannel1.socket().bind(new InetSocketAddress(80));

            ServerSocketChannel ssChannel2 = ServerSocketChannel.open();
            ssChannel2.configureBlocking(false);
            ssChannel2.socket().bind(new InetSocketAddress(81));

            // Register both channels with selector
            ssChannel1.register(selector, SelectionKey.OP_ACCEPT);
            ssChannel2.register(selector, SelectionKey.OP_ACCEPT);

            while (true) {
                // Wait for an event
                selector.select();

                // Get list of selection keys with pending events
                Iterator it = selector.selectedKeys().iterator();

                // Process each key
                while (it.hasNext()) {
                    // Get the selection key
                    SelectionKey selKey = (SelectionKey)it.next();

                    // Remove it from the list to indicate that it is being processed
                    it.remove();

                    // Check if it's a connection request
                    if (selKey.isAcceptable()) {
                        // Get channel with connection request
                        ServerSocketChannel ssChannel = (ServerSocketChannel)selKey.channel();

                        // See "ε178. Accepting a Connection on a ServerSocketChannel"
                        // for an example of accepting a connection request
                    }
                }
            }
        } catch (IOException e) {
        }
```

ε180. Detecting When a Non-Blocking Socket Is Closed by the Remote Host

The only way to detect that the remote host has closed the connection is to attempt to read or write from the connection. If the remote host properly closed the connection, read() will return -1. If the connection was not terminated normally, read() and write() will throw an exception.

When using a selector to process events from a non-blocking socket, the selector will try to return an OP_READ or OP_WRITE event if the remote host has closed the socket.

```
        try {
            // Read from socket
            int numBytesRead = socketChannel.read(buf);

            if (numBytesRead == -1) {
                // No more bytes can be read from the channel
                socketChannel.close();
            } else {
                // Read the bytes from the buffer
```

Class *Interface* —extends - - -implements ○ abstract ● final ⌐—has superclass ⌐—has subclass package—see other volume

```
        }
    } catch (IOException e) {
        // Connection may have been closed
    }

    try {
        // Write to socket
        int numBytesWritten = socketChannel.write(buf);
    } catch (IOException e) {
        // Connection may have been closed
    }
```

File Locking

ε181. Creating a File Lock on a File

The behavior of the file lock is platform-dependent. On some platforms, the file lock is advisory, which means that unless an application checks for a file lock, it will not be prevented from accessing the file. On other platforms, the file lock is mandatory, which means that a file lock prevents any application from accessing the file.

```
    try {
        // Get a file channel for the file
        File file = new File("filename");
        FileChannel channel = new RandomAccessFile(file, "rw").getChannel();

        // Use the file channel to create a lock on the file.
        // This method blocks until it can retrieve the lock.
        FileLock lock = channel.lock();

        // Try acquiring the lock without blocking. This method returns
        // null or throws an exception if the file is already locked.
        try {
            lock = channel.tryLock();
        } catch (OverlappingFileLockException e) {
            // File is already locked in this thread or virtual machine
        }

        // Release the lock
        lock.release();

        // Close the file
        channel.close();
    } catch (Exception e) {
    }
```

ε182. Creating a Shared File Lock on a File

By default, a file lock is exclusive, which means that once acquired, no other access is permitted. A shared file lock allows other shared locks on the file (but no exclusive locks).

Note: Some platforms do not support shared locks, in which case the lock is automatically made into an exclusive lock. Use FileLock.isShared() to determine the type of the lock.

```
    try {
        // Obtain a file channel
        File file = new File("filename");
        FileChannel channel = new RandomAccessFile(file, "rw").getChannel();

        // Create a shared lock on the file.
        // This method blocks until it can retrieve the lock.
```

```
        FileLock lock = channel.lock(0, Long.MAX_VALUE, true);

        // Try acquiring a shared lock without blocking. This method returns
        // null or throws an exception if the file is already exclusively locked.
        try {
            lock = channel.tryLock(0, Long.MAX_VALUE, true);
        } catch (OverlappingFileLockException e) {
            // File is already locked in this thread or virtual machine
        }

        // Determine the type of the lock
        boolean isShared = lock.isShared();

        // Release the lock
        lock.release();

        // Close the file
        channel.close();
    } catch (Exception e) {
    }
```

Streams

ε183. Creating a Stream from a Channel

This example uses methods from Channels.newOutputStream() and Channels.newInputStream() to create streams on a file channel. Note: If the example had created a direct ByteBuffer from the file channel (see "ε166. Creating a Memory-Mapped File"), any reads or writes to the streams would appear in the direct ByteBuffer.

```
    try {
        // Create a read/writeable file channel
        File file = new File("filename");
        FileChannel channel = new RandomAccessFile(file, "rw").getChannel();

        // Create an output stream on the channel
        OutputStream os = Channels.newOutputStream(channel);

        // Create an inputstream on the channel
        InputStream is = Channels.newInputStream(channel);

        // Close the channel
        is.close();
    } catch (IOException e) {
    }
```

ε184. Creating a Stream on a ByteBuffer

This example implements methods for creating an input or output stream on a ByteBuffer.

```
    // Obtain a ByteBuffer; see "ε158. Creating a ByteBuffer".
    ByteBuffer buf = ByteBuffer.allocate(10);

    // Create an output stream on the ByteBuffer
    OutputStream os = newOutputStream(buf);

    // Create an input stream on the ByteBuffer
    InputStream is = newInputStream(buf);

    // Returns an output stream for a ByteBuffer.
    // The write() methods use the relative ByteBuffer put() methods.
```

Class   *Interface*   —extends   - - -implements   ○ abstract   ● final   ˆ—has superclass   ˌ—has subclass   package—see other volume

```
public static OutputStream newOutputStream(final ByteBuffer buf) {
    return new OutputStream() {
        public synchronized void write(int b) throws IOException {
            buf.put((byte)b);
        }

        public synchronized void write(byte[] bytes, int off, int len) throws IOException {
            buf.put(bytes, off, len);
        }
    };
}

// Returns an input stream for a ByteBuffer.
// The read() methods use the relative ByteBuffer get() methods.
public static InputStream newInputStream(final ByteBuffer buf) {
    return new InputStream() {
        public synchronized int read() throws IOException {
            if (!buf.hasRemaining()) {
                return -1;
            }
            return buf.get();
        }

        public synchronized int read(byte[] bytes, int off, int len) throws IOException {
            // Read only what's left
            len = Math.min(len, buf.remaining());
            buf.get(bytes, off, len);
            return len;
        }
    };
}
```

java.nio.channels

This package defines channels, which represent connections to entities that are capable of performing I/O operations, such as files and sockets. It also defines selectors, which are used for multiplexed, non-blocking I/O operations.

Packages

java.nio.channels

java.lang.Object

1.4 ●	├ Channels
1.4	├ FileChannel.MapMode
1.4 ○	├ FileLock
1.4 ○	├ Pipe
1.4 ○	├ SelectionKey

Class   *Interface*   —extends   - - -implements   ○ abstract   ● final   ˆ—has superclass   ˏ—has subclass   package—see other volume

```
       java.lang.Object
1.4 ○    ├ Selector
1.4 ○    ├ java.nio.channels.spi.AbstractInterruptibleChannel - - - - - - - - - - Channel, InterruptibleChannel^
1.4 ○    │   ├ FileChannel - - - - - - - - - - - - - - - - - - - - - - - - - - - - - ByteChannel^, GatheringByteChannel^,
                                                                                      ScatteringByteChannel^
1.4 ○    │   └ SelectableChannel - - - - - - - - - - - - - - - - - - - - - - - - - Channel
1.4 ○    │       └ java.nio.channels.spi.AbstractSelectableChannel
1.4 ○    │           ├ DatagramChannel - - - - - - - - - - - - - - - - - - - - - - ByteChannel^, GatheringByteChannel^,
                                                                                      ScatteringByteChannel^
1.4 ○    │           ├ Pipe.SinkChannel - - - - - - - - - - - - - - - - - - - - - - GatheringByteChannel^, WritableByteChannel
1.4 ○    │           ├ Pipe.SourceChannel - - - - - - - - - - - - - - - - - - - - - ReadableByteChannel, ScatteringByteChannel^
1.4 ○    │           ├ ServerSocketChannel
1.4 ○    │           └ SocketChannel - - - - - - - - - - - - - - - - - - - - - - - - ByteChannel^, GatheringByteChannel^,
                                                                                      ScatteringByteChannel^
         ├ java.lang.Throwable - - - - - - - - - - - - - - - - - - - - - - - - - - - java.io.Serializable
         │   └ java.lang.Exception
         │       ├ java.io.IOException
1.4      │       │   ├ ClosedChannelException
1.4      │       │   │   └ AsynchronousCloseException
1.4      │       │   │       └ ClosedByInterruptException
1.4      │       │   └ FileLockInterruptionException
         │       └ java.lang.RuntimeException
         │           ├ java.lang.IllegalArgumentException
1.4      │           │   ├ IllegalSelectorException
1.4      │           │   ├ UnresolvedAddressException
1.4      │           │   └ UnsupportedAddressTypeException
1.1      │           └ java.lang.IllegalStateException
1.4      │               ├ AlreadyConnectedException
1.4      │               ├ CancelledKeyException
1.4      │               ├ ClosedSelectorException
1.4      │               ├ ConnectionPendingException
1.4      │               ├ IllegalBlockingModeException
1.4      │               ├ NoConnectionPendingException
1.4      │               ├ NonReadableChannelException
1.4      │               ├ NonWritableChannelException
1.4      │               ├ NotYetBoundException
1.4      │               ├ NotYetConnectedException
1.4      │               └ OverlappingFileLockException

1.4      ByteChannel ─────────────────────────────────── ReadableByteChannel^, WritableByteChannel^
1.4      Channel
1.4      GatheringByteChannel ──────────────────────────── WritableByteChannel^
1.4      InterruptibleChannel ──────────────────────────── Channel
1.4      ReadableByteChannel ─────────────────────────────┐
1.4      ScatteringByteChannel ─────────────────────────── ReadableByteChannel^
1.4      WritableByteChannel ───────────────────────────── Channel
```

This package defines service-provider classes for the java.nio.channels package.

PAGE

1.4 ○ **AbstractInterruptibleChannel** is the base implementation class for interruptible channels 427

java.nio.channels.spi

```
         java.lang.Object
1.4 ○    ├ AbstractInterruptibleChannel - - - - - - - - - - - - - - - - - - - - - - - - - - java.nio.channels.Channel,
         │                                                                  java.nio.channels.InterruptibleChannel^
1.4 ○    └ java.nio.channels.SelectableChannel - - - - - - - - - - - - - - - - - java.nio.channels.Channel
1.4 ○         └ AbstractSelectableChannel,
1.4 ○    ├ SelectorProvider
1.4 ○    ├ java.nio.channels.SelectionKey
1.4 ○    │    └ AbstractSelectionKey
1.4 ○    └ java.nio.channels.Selector
1.4 ○         └ AbstractSelector
```

java.nio.charset

This package defines classes for manipulating character sets. It contains decoders and encoders for translating between bytes and Unicode characters.

```
         java.lang.Object
1.4 ○    ├ Charset - - - - - - - - - - - - - - - - - - - - - - - - - - - - - - - java.lang.Comparable
1.4 ○    ├ CharsetDecoder
1.4 ○    ├ CharsetEncoder
1.4      ├ CoderResult
1.4      ├ CodingErrorAction
         └ java.lang.Throwable - - - - - - - - - - - - - - - - - - - - - - - - - java.io.Serializable,
              ├ java.lang.Error
1.4           └ CoderMalfunctionError
```

Class   *Interface*   —extends   - - -implements   ○ abstract   ● final   ^—has superclass   ,—has subclass   package—see other volume

```
java.lang.Object
  └ java.lang.Throwable - - - - - - - - - - - - - - - - - - - - - - - - - - - - - - - - - java.io.Serializable
     └ java.lang.Exception
        ├ java.io.IOException
1.4        └ CharacterCodingException
1.4          ├ MalformedInputException
1.4          └ UnmappableCharacterException
        └ java.lang.RuntimeException
           └ java.lang.IllegalArgumentException
1.4           ├ IllegalCharsetNameException
1.4           └ UnsupportedCharsetException
```

ε185. Listing All Available Unicode to Character Set Converters

```
Map map = Charset.availableCharsets();
Iterator it = map.keySet().iterator();
while (it.hasNext()) {
    // Get charset name
    String charsetName = (String)it.next();

    // Get charset
    Charset charset = Charset.forName(charsetName);
}
```

Here's a sample of the output:

```
ISO-8859-1
ISO-8859-15
US-ASCII
UTF-16
UTF-16BE
UTF-16LE
UTF-8
windows-1252
```

ε186. Converting Between Strings (Unicode) and Other Character Set Encodings

Many network protocols and files store their characters with a byte-oriented character set such as ISO-8859-1 (ISO-Latin-1). However, Java's native character encoding is Unicode.

This example demonstrates how to convert ISO-8859-1 encoded bytes in a ByteBuffer to a string in a CharBuffer and visa versa.

```
// Create the encoder and decoder for ISO-8859-1
Charset charset = Charset.forName("ISO-8859-1");
CharsetDecoder decoder = charset.newDecoder();
CharsetEncoder encoder = charset.newEncoder();

try {
    // Convert a string to ISO-LATIN-1 bytes in a ByteBuffer
    // The new ByteBuffer is ready to be read.
    ByteBuffer bbuf = encoder.encode(CharBuffer.wrap("a string"));

    // Convert ISO-LATIN-1 bytes in a ByteBuffer to a character ByteBuffer and then to a string.
    // The new ByteBuffer is ready to be read.
    CharBuffer cbuf = decoder.decode(bbuf);
    String s = cbuf.toString();
} catch (CharacterCodingException e) {
}
```

Packages

java.nio.charset

In the example above, the encoding and decoding methods created new ByteBuffers into which to encode or decoding the data. Moreover, the newly allocated ByteBuffers are non-direct ("ε168. Determining If a ByteBuffer Is Direct"). The encoder and decoder provide methods that use a supplied ByteBuffer rather than create one. Here's an example that uses these methods:

```
// Create a direct ByteBuffer.
// This buffer will be used to send and recieve data from channels.
ByteBuffer bbuf = ByteBuffer.allocateDirect(1024);

// Create a non-direct character ByteBuffer
CharBuffer cbuf = CharBuffer.allocate(1024);

// Convert characters in cbuf to bbuf
encoder.encode(cbuf, bbuf, false);

// flip bbuf before reading from it
bbuf.flip();

// Convert bytes in bbuf to cbuf
decoder.decode(bbuf, cbuf, false);

// flip cbuf before reading from it
cbuf.flip();
```

java.nio.charset.spi

This package defines service-provider classes for the java.nio.charset package.

java.rmi

This is the RMI package. RMI is Remote Method Invocation. It is a mechanism that enables an object on one Java virtual machine to invoke methods on an object in another Java virtual machine. Any object that can be invoked this way must implement the Remote interface. When such an object is invoked, its arguments are "marshalled" and sent from the local virtual machine to the remote one, where the arguments are "unmarshalled." When the method terminates, the results are marshalled from the remote machine and sent to the caller's virtual machine. If the method invocation results in an exception being thrown, the exception is indicated to the caller.

Class *Interface* —extends - - -implements ○ abstract ● final ^—has superclass ⌐—has subclass package—see other volume

```
       java.lang.Object
1.2 ●   ├ MarshalledObject - - - - - - - - - - - - - - - - - - - - - - - - - java.io.Serializable
1.1 ●   ├ Naming
        ├ java.lang.SecurityManager
1.1     │  └ RMISecurityManager
        └ java.lang.Throwable - - - - - - - - - - - - - - - - - - - - - -
           └ java.lang.Exception
1.1          ├ AlreadyBoundException
1.1          ├ NotBoundException
             ├ java.io.IOException
1.1          │  └ RemoteException
1.1          │     ├ AccessException
1.1          │     ├ ConnectException
1.1          │     ├ ConnectIOException
1.1          │     ├ MarshalException
1.1          │     ├ NoSuchObjectException
1.1          │     ├ ServerError
1.1          │     ├ ServerException
D            │     ├ ServerRuntimeException
1.1          │     ├ StubNotFoundException
1.1          │     ├ UnexpectedException
1.1          │     ├ UnknownHostException
1.1          │     └ UnmarshalException
             └ java.lang.RuntimeException
                └ java.lang.SecurityException
D                  └ RMISecurityException
```

Packages

ε187. Starting the RMI Registry

Starting up the RMI registry allows you to create and export remote objects.

```
> rmiregistry
```

ε188. Defining and Exporting a Remote Object

1. Define the remote interface.

```java
import java.rmi.*;

public interface RObject extends Remote {
    void aMethod() throws RemoteException;
}
```

2. Define the remote object implementation.

```java
import java.rmi.*;
import java.rmi.server.UnicastRemoteObject;

public class RObjectImpl extends UnicastRemoteObject implements RObject {
    public RObjectImpl() throws RemoteException {
        super();
    }
    // All remote methods must throw RemoteException
    public void aMethod() throws RemoteException {
    }
}
```

3. Compile the remote object implementation.

```
> javac RObject.java RObjectImpl.java
```

4. Generate the skeletons and stubs.

```
> rmic RObjectImpl
```

5. Create an instance of the remote object and bind it to the RMI registry.

```java
try {
    RObject robj = new RObjectImpl();
    Naming.rebind("//localhost/RObjectServer", robj);
} catch (MalformedURLException e) {
} catch (UnknownHostException e) {
} catch (RemoteException e) {
}
```

ε189. Looking Up a Remote Object and Invoking a Method

```java
try {
    // Look up remote object
    RObject robj = (RObject) Naming.lookup("//localhost/RObjectServer");

    // Invoke method on remote object
    robj.aMethod();
} catch (MalformedURLException e) {
} catch (UnknownHostException e) {
} catch (NotBoundException e) {
} catch (RemoteException e) {
```

Class   *Interface*   —extends   - - -implements   ○ abstract   ● final   ⌐—has superclass   ⌐—has subclass   package—see other volume

```
}
```

ε190. Passing Parameters to a Remote Method

Arguments to remote methods must be primitive, serializable, or implement Remote. This example demonstrates the declaration and use of all three parameter types.

1. Define the remote interface.

```java
import java.rmi.*;

public interface RObject extends Remote {
    // This parameter is primitive.
    void primitiveArg(int num) throws RemoteException;

    // This parameter implements Serializable.
    void byValueArg(Integer num) throws RemoteException;

    // This parameter implements Remote.
    void byRefArg(ArgObject arg) throws RemoteException;
}

public interface ArgObject extends Remote {
    int aMethod() throws RemoteException;
}
```

2. Define the remote object implementation.

```java
import java.rmi.*;
import java.rmi.server.UnicastRemoteObject;

public class RObjectImpl extends UnicastRemoteObject implements RObject {
    public RObjectImpl() throws RemoteException {
        super();
    }
    public void primitiveArg(int num) throws RemoteException {
    }
    public void byValueArg(Integer num) throws RemoteException {
    }
    public void byRefArg(ArgObject arg) throws RemoteException {
    }
}
```

3. Compile the remote object implementation.

```
> javac RObject.java RObjectImpl.java
```

4. Generate the skeletons and stubs.

```
> rmic RObjectImpl
```

5. Create an instance of the remote object and bind it to the RMI registry.

```java
try {
    RObject robj = new RObjectImpl();
    Naming.rebind("//localhost/RObjectServer", robj);
} catch (MalformedURLException e) {
} catch (UnknownHostException e) {
} catch (RemoteException e) {
}
```

6. Look up the remote object and pass the parameters.

```java
try {
    // Look up the remote object
```

```
        RObject robj = (RObject) Naming.lookup("///localhost/RObjectServer");

        // Pass a primitive value as argument
        robj.primitiveArg(1998);

        // Pass a serializable object as argument
        robj.byValueArg(new Integer(9));

        // Pass a Remote object as argument
        robj.byRefArg(new ArgObjectImpl());
    } catch (MalformedURLException e) {
    } catch (UnknownHostException e) {
    } catch (NotBoundException e) {
    } catch (RemoteException e) {
    }
```

ε191. Returning Values from a Remote Method

Return values from remote methods must be primitive, serializable, or implement Remote. This example demonstrates the declaration and use of all three return types.

1. Define the remote interface.

```
import java.rmi.*;

public interface RObject extends Remote {
    // This return value is primitive.
    int primitiveRet() throws RemoteException;

    // This return value implements Serializable.
    Integer byValueRet() throws RemoteException;

    // This return value implements Remote.
    ArgObject byRefRet() throws RemoteException;
}
public interface ArgObject extends Remote {
    int aMethod() throws RemoteException;
}
```

2. Define the remote object implementation.

```
import java.rmi.*;
import java.rmi.server.UnicastRemoteObject;

public class RObjectImpl extends UnicastRemoteObject implements RObject {
    public RObjectImpl() throws RemoteException {
        super();
    }
    public int primitiveRet() throws RemoteException {
        return 3000;
    }
    public Integer byValueRet() throws RemoteException {
        return new Integer(2000);
    }
    public ArgObject byRefRet() throws RemoteException {
        return new ArgObjectImpl();
    }
}
```

3. Compile the remote object implementation.

Class   *Interface*   —extends   - - -implements   ○ abstract   ● final   ^—has superclass   ͺ—has subclass   package—see other volume

```
    > javac RObject.java RObjectImpl.java
```

4. Generate the skeletons and stubs.

```
    > rmic RObjectImpl
```

5. Create an instance of the remote object and bind it to the RMI Registry.

```
    try {
        RObject robj = new RObjectImpl();
        Naming.rebind("//localhost/RObjectServer", robj);
    } catch (MalformedURLException e) {
    } catch (UnknownHostException e) {
    } catch (RemoteException e) {
    }
```

6. Look up the remote object, invoke the methods, and receive the return values.

```
    try {
        // Look up the remote object
        RObject robj = (RObject) Naming.lookup("//localhost/RObjectServer");

        // Receive the primitive value as return value
        int r1 = robj.primitiveRet();

        // Receive the serializable object as return value
        Integer r2 = robj.byValueRet();

        // Receive the Remote Object as return value
        ArgObject aobj = robj.byRefRet();
    } catch (MalformedURLException e) {
    } catch (UnknownHostException e) {
    } catch (NotBoundException e) {
    } catch (RemoteException e) {
    }
```

ε192. Throwing an Exception from a Remote Method

1. Define the remote interface.

```
    import java.rmi.*;

    public interface RObject extends Remote {
        void aMethod() throws RemoteException;
    }
```

2. Define the remote object implementation.

```
    import java.rmi.*;
    import java.rmi.server.UnicastRemoteObject;

    public class RObjectImpl extends UnicastRemoteObject implements RObject {
        public RObjectImpl() throws RemoteException {
            super();
        }
        public void aMethod() throws RemoteException {
            // The actual exception must be wrapped in a RemoteException
            throw new RemoteException("message", new FileNotFoundException("message"));
        }
    }
```

3. Compile the remote object implementation.

```
    > javac RObject.java RObjectImpl.java
```

4. Generate the skeletons and stubs.

```
> rmic RObjectImpl
```

5. Create an instance of the remote object and bind it to the RMI registry.

```
try {
        RObject robj = new RObjectImpl();
        Naming.rebind("//localhost/RObjectServer", robj);
} catch (MalformedURLException e) {
} catch (UnknownHostException e) {
} catch (RemoteException e) {
}
```

6. Look up the remote object, invoke the method, and catch the exception.

```
try {
        // Look up the remote object.
        RObject robj = (RObject) Naming.lookup("//localhost/RObjectServer");

        // Invoke the method.
        robj.aMethod();
} catch (MalformedURLException e) {
} catch (UnknownHostException e) {
} catch (NotBoundException e) {
} catch (RemoteException e) {
        // Get the actual exception that was thrown.
        Throwable realException = e.detail;
}
```

java.rmi.activation

This package provides support for RMI Object Activation. A remote object's reference can be made "persistent" and later activated into a "live" object using the RMI activation mechanism.

Class   *Interface*   —extends   - - -implements   ○ abstract   ● final   ˆ—has superclass   ˌ—has subclass   package —see other volume

```
      java.lang.Object
1.2 ● │ ├ ActivationDesc --------------------------------------,-- java.io.Serializable˛
1.2 ● │ ├ ActivationGroupDesc -----------------------------------¦
1.2   │ ├ ActivationGroupDesc.CommandEnvironment ------------¦
1.2   │ ├ ActivationGroupID --------------------------------------¦
1.2   │ ├ ActivationID ---------------------------------------------¦
1.1 ○ │ ├ java.rmi.server.RemoteObject --------------------------- java.io.Serializable˛, java.rmi.Remote˛
1.1 ○ │ │ ├ java.rmi.server.RemoteServer
1.2 ○ │ │ │ ├ Activatable
1.1   │ │ │ └ java.rmi.server.UnicastRemoteObject
1.2 ○ │ │ │   └ ActivationGroup ----------------------------- ActivationInstantiator^
1.1 ○ │ │ └ java.rmi.server.RemoteStub
1.2 ● │ │   └ ActivationGroup_Stub ------------------------- ActivationInstantiator^, java.rmi.Remote˛
      │ ├ java.lang.Throwable ----------------------------------- java.io.Serializable˛
      │ │ └ java.lang.Exception
1.2   │ │ ├ ActivationException
1.2   │ │ │ ├ UnknownGroupException
1.2   │ │ │ └ UnknownObjectException
      │ │ └ java.io.IOException
1.1   │ │   └ java.rmi.RemoteException
1.2   │ │     └ ActivateFailedException

1.2   │ ActivationInstantiator ───────────────────────── java.rmi.Remote
1.2   │ ActivationMonitor ──────────────
1.2   │ ActivationSystem ─────────────
1.2   │ Activator ──────────
```

Packages

java.rmi.dgc

This package contains classes and interfaces for RMI distributed garbage-collection (DGC). When the RMI server returns an object to its client (caller of the remote method), it tracks the remote object's usage in the client. When there are no more references to the remote object on the client, or if the reference's "lease" expires and not renewed, the server garbage-collects the remote object.

```
      java.lang.Object
1.1 ● │ ├ Lease -------------------------------------------,-- java.io.Serializable˛
1.1 ● │ └ VMID --------------------------------------------¦
```

1.1   *DGC* ─── *java.rmi.Remote*

---

java.rmi.registry

This package contains a class and two interfaces for the RMI registry. A registry is a remote object that maps names to remote objects. A server registers its remote objects with the registry so that they can be looked up. When an object wants to invoke a method on a remote object, it must first look up the remote object using its name. The registry returns to the calling object a reference to the remote object, using which a remote method can be invoked.

java.lang.Object

1.1 ●   └ LocateRegistry

1.1   *Registry* ─────────────────────────────────── *java.rmi.Remote*

D   *RegistryHandler*

---

java.rmi.server

This package contains classes and interfaces for supporting the server side of RMI. A group of classes are used by the stubs and skeletons generated by the rmic stub compiler. Another group of classes implements the RMI Transport protocol and HTTP tunneling.

Class   *Interface*   —extends   - - -implements   ○ abstract   ● final   ^has superclass   ˬhas subclass   package—see other volume

```
        java.lang.Object
1.1 ●    ├─ ObjID ─────────────────────────────────── java.io.Serializable
D        ├─ Operation
1.1      ├─ RMIClassLoader
1.4 ○    ├─ RMIClassLoaderSpi
1.1 ○    ├─ RMISocketFactory ──────────────────── RMIClientSocketFactory, RMIServerSocketFactory
1.1 ○    ├─ RemoteObject ──────────────────────── java.io.Serializable, java.rmi.Remote
1.1 ○    │   ├─ RemoteServer
1.1      │   │   └─ UnicastRemoteObject
1.1 ○    │   └─ RemoteStub
1.1 ●    ├─ UID ──────────────────────────────── java.io.Serializable
○        ├─ java.io.OutputStream
         │   └─ java.io.FilterOutputStream
         │       └─ java.io.PrintStream
D        │           └─ LogStream
         └─ java.lang.Throwable ─────────────────────
             └─ java.lang.Exception
1.1              ├─ ServerNotActiveException
                 ├─ java.io.IOException
1.1              │   └─ java.rmi.RemoteException
1.1              │       ├─ ExportException
1.1              │       │   └─ SocketSecurityException
D                │       ├─ SkeletonMismatchException
D                │       └─ SkeletonNotFoundException
                 └─ java.lang.CloneNotSupportedException
1.1                  └─ ServerCloneException
```

D   *LoaderHandler*

1.2   *RMIClientSocketFactory*

Packages

java.security

This package contains the classes and interfaces for the security framework. The security framework supports the use of certificates, public and private keys, message digests, secure class-loading, object signing, and policy-based fine-grained access control. These features are supported in an algorithm-independent way. For example, you can use the same interfaces but different algorithms for creating the message digest of a stream of data.

Class *Interface* —extends - - -implements ○ abstract ● final ^—has superclass —has subclass package—see other volume

Packages

java.security

java.lang.Object

1.2 ●	AccessControlContext	
1.2 ●	AccessController	
1.2	AlgorithmParameterGenerator	
1.2 ○	AlgorithmParameterGeneratorSpi	
1.2	AlgorithmParameters	
1.2 ○	AlgorithmParametersSpi	
1.2	CodeSource	*java.io.Serializable*⌄
1.2	GuardedObject	
D ○	Identity	*Principal*⌄, *java.io.Serializable*⌄
D ○	IdentityScope	
D ○	Signer	
1.2	KeyFactory	
1.2 ○	KeyFactorySpi	
1.1 ●	KeyPair	*java.io.Serializable*⌄
1.2 ○	KeyPairGeneratorSpi	
1.1 ○	KeyPairGenerator	
1.2	KeyStore	
1.2 ○	KeyStoreSpi	
1.2 ○	MessageDigestSpi	
1.1 ○	MessageDigest	
1.2 ○	Permission	*Guard, java.io.Serializable*⌄
1.2 ●	AllPermission	

Class *Interface* —extends - - -implements ○ abstract ● final ˆ—has superclass ⌄—has subclass package—see other volume

	java.lang.Object	
1.2 ○	├ Permission - *Guard, java.io.Serializable* ⌄
1.2 ○	│ ├ BasicPermission - *java.io.Serializable* ⌄
1.2 ●	│ │ └ SecurityPermission
1.2 ●	│ └ UnresolvedPermission -
1.2 ○	├ PermissionCollection -
1.2 ●	│ └ Permissions -
1.2 ○	├ Policy
1.2	├ ProtectionDomain
1.2 ○	├ SecureRandomSpi -
1.1 ●	├ Security
1.2 ○	├ SignatureSpi
1.1 ○	│ └ Signature
1.2 ●	├ SignedObject -
○	├ java.io.InputStream
	│ └ java.io.FilterInputStream
1.1	│ └ DigestInputStream
○	├ java.io.OutputStream
	│ └ java.io.FilterOutputStream
1.1	│ └ DigestOutputStream
○	├ java.lang.ClassLoader
1.2	│ └ SecureClassLoader ⌄
○	├ java.util.Dictionary
	│ └ java.util.Hashtable - *java.io.Serializable* ⌄, *java.lang.Cloneable* ⌄,
	│ │ *java.util.Map* ⌄
	│ └ java.util.Properties
1.1 ○	│ └ Provider
	├ java.util.Random -·- - *java.io.Serializable* ⌄
1.1	│ └ SecureRandom
	└ java.lang.Throwable -
	│ └ java.lang.Exception
1.2	│ ├ GeneralSecurityException
1.1	│ │ ├ DigestException
1.2	│ │ ├ InvalidAlgorithmParameterException
1.1	│ │ ├ KeyException
1.1	│ │ │ ├ InvalidKeyException
1.1	│ │ │ └ KeyManagementException
1.2	│ │ ├ KeyStoreException
1.1	│ │ ├ NoSuchAlgorithmException
1.1	│ │ ├ NoSuchProviderException
1.1	│ │ ├ SignatureException
1.2	│ │ └ UnrecoverableKeyException
1.2	│ ├ PrivilegedActionException
	│ └ java.lang.RuntimeException
1.1	│ ├ ProviderException
	│ ├ java.lang.IllegalArgumentException
1.1	│ │ └ InvalidParameterException
	│ └ java.lang.SecurityException
1.2	│ └ AccessControlException
D	*Certificate*
1.3	*DomainCombiner*

Packages

java.security

ε193. Printing Security System Trace Messages

By setting the system property java.security.debug to all, the security system will print details of security related calls. The value all prints all available debugging information. For finer control of what is printed, see:

> http://java.sun.com/j2se/1.4/docs/guide/plugin/developer_guide/debugger.html#jsdp

Here's an example of setting the system property on the command line:

> java -Djava.security.debug=all *MyApp*

Here's a sample of trace messages:

```
access: access allowed (java.io.FilePermission c:\file1 read)
access: access allowed (java.io.FilePermission c:\file2 write)
access: access denied (java.util.PropertyPermission user.home read)
Exception in thread "main" java.security.AccessControlException: access denied (
java.util.PropertyPermission user.home read)
        at java.security.AccessControlContext.checkPermission(AccessControlContext.java:270)
        at java.security.AccessController.checkPermission(AccessController.java:401)
        at java.lang.SecurityManager.checkPermission(SecurityManager.java:542)
        at java.lang.SecurityManager.checkPropertyAccess(SecurityManager.java:1291)
        at java.lang.System.getProperty(System.java:572)
        at MyApp.main(MyApp.java:50)
```

ε194. Listing All Available Cryptographic Services

The providers of cryptographic services such as key generation algorithms, register their services with the Security class. A service is represented by a name of the form:

> *service-type.service-implementation*

An example of a service entry is SecureRandom.SHA1PRNG.

```
// This method returns all available services types
public static String[] getServiceTypes() {
    Set result = new HashSet();

    // All all providers
    Provider[] providers = Security.getProviders();
    for (int i=0; i<providers.length; i++) {
        // Get services provided by each provider
        Set keys = providers[i].keySet();
        for (Iterator it=keys.iterator(); it.hasNext(); ) {
            String key = (String)it.next();
            key = key.split(" ")[0];

            if (key.startsWith("Alg.Alias.")) {
                // Strip the alias
                key = key.substring(10);
```

Class *Interface* ——extends - - -implements ○ abstract ● final ^—has superclass ˏ—has subclass package—see other volume

```
            }
            int ix = key.indexOf('.');
            result.add(key.substring(0, ix));
        }
    }
    return (String[])result.toArray(new String[result.size()]);
}

// This method returns the available implementations for a service type
public static String[] getCryptoImpls(String serviceType) {
    Set result = new HashSet();

    // All all providers
    Provider[] providers = Security.getProviders();
    for (int i=0; i<providers.length; i++) {
        // Get services provided by each provider
        Set keys = providers[i].keySet();
        for (Iterator it=keys.iterator(); it.hasNext(); ) {
            String key = (String)it.next();
            key = key.split(" ")[0];

            if (key.startsWith(serviceType+".")) {
                result.add(key.substring(serviceType.length()+1));
            } else if (key.startsWith("Alg.Alias."+serviceType+".")) {
                // This is an alias
                result.add(key.substring(serviceType.length()+11));
            }
        }
    }
    return (String[])result.toArray(new String[result.size()]);
}
```

Here's a sample list of service types:

```
AlgorithmParameterGenerator
AlgorithmParameters
CertPathBuilder
CertPathValidator
CertStore
CertificateFactory
Cipher
GssApiMechanism
KeyAgreement
KeyFactory
KeyGenerator
KeyManagerFactory
KeyPairGenerator
KeyStore
Mac
MessageDigest
SSLContext
SecretKeyFactory
SecureRandom
Signature
TrustManagerFactory
```

Packages

ε195. Listing All Available Secure Random Number Generators

A secure random number generator can seed itself with unpredictable values and produce cryptographically strong pseudo-random numbers suitable for generating cryptographic keys.

Retrieving the list of available secure random number generators requires checking the services provided by all registered providers. The retrieved list of names can be used in creating a SecureRandom object.

```
// This method is implemented in "ε194. Listing All Available Cryptographic Services"
String[] names = getCryptoImpls("SecureRandom");
```

An example of the output:

```
SHA1PRNG
```

ε196. Generating a Secure Random Number

This example creates a random number using a secure random number generator: See also "ε195. Listing All Available Secure Random Number Generators".

```
try {
    // Create a secure random number generator
    SecureRandom sr = SecureRandom.getInstance("SHA1PRNG");

    // Get 1024 random bits
    byte[] bytes = new byte[1024/8];
    sr.nextBytes(bytes);

    // Create two secure number generators with the same seed
    int seedByteCount = 10;
    byte[] seed = sr.generateSeed(seedByteCount);

    sr = SecureRandom.getInstance("SHA1PRNG");
    sr.setSeed(seed);
    SecureRandom sr2 = SecureRandom.getInstance("SHA1PRNG");
    sr2.setSeed(seed);
} catch (NoSuchAlgorithmException e) {
}
```

Public and Private Keys

ε197. Listing All Available Public/Private Key Generators

Retrieving the list of available key generators requires checking the services provided by all registered providers. The retrieved list of names can be used in creating a KeyPairGenerator object.

```
// This method is implemented in "ε194. Listing All Available Cryptographic Services"
String[] names = getCryptoImpls("KeyPairGenerator");
```

An example of the output:

```
OID.1.2.840.10040.4.1
DiffieHellman
1.3.14.3.2.12
DH
1.2.840.10040.4.1
DSA
RSA
```

ε198. Generating a Public/Private Key Pair

This example generates a key pair for various public/private key algorithms. See also "ε197. Listing All Available Public/Private Key Generators".

```
try {
    // Generate a 1024-bit Digital Signature Algorithm (DSA) key pair
    KeyPairGenerator keyGen = KeyPairGenerator.getInstance("DSA");
    keyGen.initialize(1024);
    KeyPair keypair = keyGen.genKeyPair();
    PrivateKey privateKey = keypair.getPrivate();
    PublicKey publicKey = keypair.getPublic();

    // Generate a 576-bit DH key pair
    keyGen = KeyPairGenerator.getInstance("DH");
    keyGen.initialize(576);
    keypair = keyGen.genKeyPair();
    privateKey = keypair.getPrivate();
    publicKey = keypair.getPublic();

    // Generate a 1024-bit RSA key pair
    keyGen = KeyPairGenerator.getInstance("RSA");
    keyGen.initialize(1024);
    keypair = keyGen.genKeyPair();
    privateKey = keypair.getPrivate();
    publicKey = keypair.getPublic();
} catch (java.security.NoSuchAlgorithmException e) {
}
```

ε199. Getting the Bytes of a Generated Key Pair

```
try {
    String algorithm = "DSA"; // or RSA, DH, etc.

    // Generate a 1024-bit Digital Signature Algorithm (DSA) key pair
    KeyPairGenerator keyGen = KeyPairGenerator.getInstance(algorithm);
    keyGen.initialize(1024);
    KeyPair keypair = keyGen.genKeyPair();
    PrivateKey privateKey = keypair.getPrivate();
    PublicKey publicKey = keypair.getPublic();

    // Get the bytes of the public and private keys
    byte[] privateKeyBytes = privateKey.getEncoded();
    byte[] publicKeyBytes = publicKey.getEncoded();

    // Get the formats of the encoded bytes
    String format = privateKey.getFormat(); // PKCS#8
    format = publicKey.getFormat(); // X.509


    // The bytes can be converted back to public and private key objects
    KeyFactory keyFactory = KeyFactory.getInstance(algorithm);
    EncodedKeySpec privateKeySpec = new PKCS8EncodedKeySpec(privateKeyBytes);
    PrivateKey privateKey2 = keyFactory.generatePrivate(privateKeySpec);

    EncodedKeySpec publicKeySpec = new X509EncodedKeySpec(publicKeyBytes);
    PublicKey publicKey2 = keyFactory.generatePublic(publicKeySpec);

    // The orginal and new keys are the same
    boolean same = privateKey.equals(privateKey2); // true
    same = publicKey.equals(publicKey2); // true
} catch (InvalidKeySpecException e) {
```

Packages

```
        } catch (NoSuchAlgorithmException e) {
        }
```

ε200. Getting the Digital Signature Algorithm (DSA) Parameters of a Key Pair

The DSA requires three parameters to create a key pair — the prime (P), the subprime (Q), and the base (G). These three values are used to create a private key (called X) and a public key (called Y).

This example creates a DSA key pair with provider-supplied default values for P, Q, and G, and then retrieves the default values.

```
    try {
        // Generate a 1024-bit Digital Signature Algorithm (DSA) key pair
        KeyPairGenerator keyGen = KeyPairGenerator.getInstance("DSA");
        keyGen.initialize(1024);
        KeyPair keypair = keyGen.genKeyPair();
        DSAPrivateKey privateKey = (DSAPrivateKey)keypair.getPrivate();
        DSAPublicKey publicKey = (DSAPublicKey)keypair.getPublic();

        // Get p, q, g; they are the same for both private and public keys
        DSAParams dsaParams = privateKey.getParams();
        BigInteger p = dsaParams.getP();
        BigInteger q = dsaParams.getQ();
        BigInteger g = dsaParams.getG();

        // Get the private key's X
        BigInteger x = privateKey.getX();

        // Get the public key's Y
        BigInteger y = publicKey.getY();
    } catch (NoSuchAlgorithmException e) {
    }
```

ε201. Creating Key Objects from a Set of Digital Signature Algorithm (DSA) Parameters

The DSA requires three parameters to create a key pair - the prime (P), the subprime (Q), and the base (G). These three values are used to create a private key (called X) and a public key (called Y).

This example creates a PrivateKey and PublicKey from a set of DSA parameters.

```
    try {
        // Obtain the DSA parameters;
        // see "ε200. Getting the Digital Signature Algorithm (DSA) Parameters of a Key Pair"
        BigInteger p = ...;
        BigInteger q = ...;
        BigInteger g = ...;
        BigInteger x = ...;
        BigInteger y = ...;

        // Create the DSA key factory
        KeyFactory keyFactory = KeyFactory.getInstance("DSA");

        // Create the DSA private key
        KeySpec privateKeySpec = new DSAPrivateKeySpec(x, p, q, g);
        PrivateKey privateKey = keyFactory.generatePrivate(privateKeySpec);

        // Create the DSA public key
        KeySpec publicKeySpec = new DSAPublicKeySpec(y, p, q, g);
        PublicKey publicKey = keyFactory.generatePublic(publicKeySpec);
    } catch (InvalidKeySpecException e) {
    } catch (NoSuchAlgorithmException e) {
```

Class *Interface* —extends - - -implements ○ abstract ● final ^—has superclass ⌐—has subclass package—see other volume

}

ε202. Listing All Available Signature Algorithms

Retrieving the list of available signature algorithms requires checking the services provided by all registered providers. The retrieved list of names can be used in creating a Signature object.

```
// This method is implemented in "ε194. Listing All Available Cryptographic Services"
String[] names = getCryptoImpls("Signature");
```

An example of the output:

```
MD2withRSA
1.3.14.3.2.27
SHA/DSA
DSAWithSHA1
MD5withRSA
1.3.14.3.2.13
SHA1/DSA
SHA1withDSA
SHA1withRSA
1.2.840.10040.4.3
DSS
SHA-1/DSA
DSA
OID.1.2.840.10040.4.3
SHAwithDSA
```

ε203. Creating a Signature

See also "ε198. Generating a Public/Private Key Pair" and "ε202. Listing All Available Signature Algorithms".

```
// Returns the signature for the given buffer of bytes using the private key.
public static byte[] createSignature(PrivateKey key, byte[] buffer) {
    try {
        Signature sig = Signature.getInstance(key.getAlgorithm());
        sig.initSign(key);
        sig.update(buffer, 0, buffer.length);
        return sig.sign();
    } catch (SignatureException e) {
    } catch (InvalidKeyException e) {
    } catch (NoSuchAlgorithmException e) {
    }
    return null;
}
```

ε204. Verifying a Signature

See also "ε198. Generating a Public/Private Key Pair" and "ε202. Listing All Available Signature Algorithms".

```
// Verifies the signature for the given buffer of bytes using the public key.
public static boolean verifySignature(PublicKey key, byte[] buffer, byte[] signature) {
    try {
        Signature sig = Signature.getInstance(key.getAlgorithm());
        sig.initVerify(key);
```

Packages

```
                sig.update(buffer, 0, buffer.length);
                return sig.verify(signature);
        } catch (SignatureException e) {
        } catch (InvalidKeyException e) {
        } catch (NoSuchAlgorithmException e) {
        }
        return false;
    }
```

ε205. Signing a Java Object

A signed object makes a copy of a serializable object and signs it with a private key. Since the signed object makes a copy of the original object, any further modifications to the original object do not affect the signed object.

```
// Create a public and private key
PublicKey publicKey = null;
PrivateKey privateKey = null;
try {
    // Generate a 1024-bit Digital Signature Algorithm (DSA) key pair
    KeyPairGenerator keyGen = KeyPairGenerator.getInstance("DSA");
    keyGen.initialize(1024);
    KeyPair keypair = keyGen.genKeyPair();
    privateKey = keypair.getPrivate();
    publicKey = keypair.getPublic();
} catch (NoSuchAlgorithmException e) {
}

// Create the signed object
SignedObject so = null;
try {
    Serializable o = new MyClass();
    Signature sig = Signature.getInstance(privateKey.getAlgorithm());
    so = new SignedObject(o, privateKey, sig);
} catch (NoSuchAlgorithmException e) {
} catch (SignatureException e) {
} catch (InvalidKeyException e) {
} catch (IOException e) {
}

// Verify the signed object
try {
    Signature sig = Signature.getInstance(publicKey.getAlgorithm());
    // Verify the signed object
    boolean b = so.verify(publicKey, sig);

    // Retrieve the object
    MyClass o = (MyClass)so.getObject();
} catch (SignatureException e) {
} catch (InvalidKeyException e) {
} catch (NoSuchAlgorithmException e) {
} catch (ClassNotFoundException e) {
} catch (IOException e) {
}

public class MyClass implements Serializable {
    String s = "my string";
    int i = 123;
```

```
}
```

Message Digests

ε206. Listing All Available Message Digest Algorithms

Retrieving the list of available message digest algorithms requires checking the services provided by all registered providers. The retrieved list of names can be used in creating a MessageDigest object.

```
// This method is implemented in "ε194. Listing All Available Cryptographic Services"
String[] names = getCryptoImpls("MessageDigest");
```

An example of the output:

```
MD5
SHA
SHA1
SHA-1
```

ε207. Creating a Keyed Digest Using MD5

A "keyed" digest is one in which a secret key is used to create a digest for a buffer of bytes. You can use different keys to create different digests for the same buffer of bytes.

```
public static byte[] getKeyedDigest(byte[] buffer, byte[] key) {
    try {
        MessageDigest md5 = MessageDigest.getInstance("MD5");
        md5.update(buffer);
        return md5.digest(key);
    } catch (NoSuchAlgorithmException e) {
    }
    return null;
}
```

Key Store

ε208. Listing the Aliases in a Key Store

A key store is a collection of keys and certificates. Each key or certificate has a unique "alias" used to identify that key or certificate in the key store. This example lists all the aliases in a key store.

```
try {
    // Load the keystore in the user's home directory
    File file = new File(System.getProperty("user.home") + File.separatorChar + ".keystore");
    FileInputStream is = new FileInputStream(file);
    KeyStore keystore = KeyStore.getInstance(KeyStore.getDefaultType());
    String password = "my-keystore-password";
    keystore.load(is, password.toCharArray());

    // List the aliases
    Enumeration enum = keystore.aliases();
    for (; enum.hasMoreElements(); ) {
        String alias = (String)enum.nextElement();

        // Does alias refer to a private key?
        boolean b = keystore.isKeyEntry(alias);

        // Does alias refer to a trusted certificate?
        b = keystore.isCertificateEntry(alias);
    }
```

Packages

```
            is.close();
      } catch (java.security.cert.CertificateException e) {
      } catch (NoSuchAlgorithmException e) {
      } catch (FileNotFoundException e) {
            // Keystore does not exist
      } catch (KeyStoreException e) {
      } catch (IOException e) {
      }
```

The aliases can also be listed using keytool:

```
      > keytool -list -storepass my-keystore-password
```

ε209. Retrieving a Certificate from a Key Store

```
      try {
            // Load the keystore in the user's home directory
            FileInputStream is = new FileInputStream(System.getProperty("user.home")
                  + File.separatorChar + ".keystore");

            KeyStore keystore = KeyStore.getInstance(KeyStore.getDefaultType());
            keystore.load(is, "my-keystore-password".toCharArray());

            // Get certificate
            java.security.cert.Certificate cert = keystore.getCertificate("myalias");
      } catch (KeyStoreException e) {
      } catch (java.security.cert.CertificateException e) {
      } catch (NoSuchAlgorithmException e) {
      } catch (java.io.IOException e) {
      }
```

ε210. Retrieving a Key Pair from a Key Store

This example retrieves from a keystore, the private and public key associated with an alias. To load a keystore, see "ε208. Listing the Aliases in a Key Store".

```
      public KeyPair getPrivateKey(KeyStore keystore, String alias, char[] password) {
            try {
                  // Get private key
                  Key key = keystore.getKey(alias, password);
                  if (key instanceof PrivateKey) {
                        // Get certificate of public key
                        java.security.cert.Certificate cert = keystore.getCertificate(alias);

                        // Get public key
                        PublicKey publicKey = cert.getPublicKey();

                        // Return a key pair
                        return new KeyPair(publicKey, (PrivateKey)key);
                  }
            } catch (UnrecoverableKeyException e) {
            } catch (NoSuchAlgorithmException e) {
            } catch (KeyStoreException e) {
            }
            return null;
      }
```

ε211. Adding a Certificate to a Key Store

```
      // This method adds a certificate with the specified alias to the specified keystore file.
```

Class *Interface* —extends - - -implements ○ abstract ● final ^—has superclass ‿—has subclass package—see other volume

```
public static void addToKeyStore(File keystoreFile, char[] keystorePassword,
        String alias, java.security.cert.Certificate cert) {
    try {
        // Create an empty keystore object
        KeyStore keystore = KeyStore.getInstance(KeyStore.getDefaultType());

        // Load the keystore contents
        FileInputStream in = new FileInputStream(keystoreFile);
        keystore.load(in, keystorePassword);
        in.close();

        // Add the certificate
        keystore.setCertificateEntry(alias, cert);

        // Save the new keystore contents
        FileOutputStream out = new FileOutputStream(keystoreFile);
        keystore.store(out, keystorePassword);
        out.close();
    } catch (java.security.cert.CertificateException e) {
    } catch (NoSuchAlgorithmException e) {
    } catch (FileNotFoundException e) {
        // Keystore does not exist
    } catch (KeyStoreException e) {
    } catch (IOException e) {
    }
}
```

Permissions

ε212. Enabling the Security Manager

By default, no security manager is enabled which means that all security checks to protected resources and operations are disabled. To enable security checks, the security manager must be enabled.

Once enabled, policy files determine the type of access an entity has on a resource. For more details, see "ε220. Managing Policy Files".

This example enables the security manager.

```
// Before the security manager is enabled, this call is possible
System.setProperty("java.version", "malicious data");

try {
    // Enable the security manager
    SecurityManager sm = new SecurityManager();
    System.setSecurityManager(sm);
} catch (SecurityException se) {
    // SecurityManager already set
}

// This call is no longer possible; an AccessControlException is thrown
System.setProperty("java.version", "malicious data");
```

The security manager can also be installed from the command line:

```
> java -Djava.security.manager MyApp
```

ε213. Checking Read/Write Permission for a Directory

```
try {
    AccessController.checkPermission(new FilePermission("/tmp/*", "read,write"));
```

```
        // Has permission
    } catch (SecurityException e) {
        // Does not have permission
    }
```

ε214. Determining If One Permission Implies Another

```
    Permission perm1 = new FilePermission("/tmp/*", "read,write");
    Permission perm2 = new FilePermission("/tmp/abc", "read");

    if (perm1.implies(perm2)) {
        // perm1 implies perm2
    }
```

ε215. Creating a Custom Permission

This example creates a permission that controls access to pages of a book. The permission name consists of a book id, a colon, and a set of allowable pages. The set of allowable pages is specified as a comma-separated list of page ranges. For example, '88:1,3-4' specifies that pages 1, 3, and 4 are accessible in the book whose id is 88.

```java
    import java.io.*;
    import java.security.*;
    import java.util.*;

    public class BookPermission extends BasicPermission implements Serializable {
        String bookid = null;
        BitSet pages = new BitSet();

        public BookPermission(String perm) {
            super(perm);
            String[] fields = perm.split(":");

            // Get book id
            bookid = fields[0];

            // Get page ranges and set pages
            String[] ranges = fields[1].split(",");
            for (int i=0; i<ranges.length; i++) {
                // Get the start and end of the range
                String[] range = ranges[i].split("-");
                int start = Integer.parseInt(range[0]);
                int end = start;
                if (range.length > 1) {
                    end = Integer.parseInt(range[1]);
                }

                // Set the pages in the bitset
                pages.set(start, end+1);
            }
        }

        public boolean implies(Permission permission) {
            BookPermission bp = (BookPermission)permission;

            // Check book id
            if (!bookid.equals(bp.bookid)) {
                return false;
            }

            // Clone other pages bitset
```

Class *Interface* —extends - - -implements ○ abstract ● final ‾—has superclass ‗—has subclass package—see other volume

```
            BitSet pgs = (BitSet)bp.pages.clone();

            // OR both bitsets
            pgs.or(pages);

            // Return true if this bitset contains all the bits in the other bitset
            return pages.equals(pgs);
        }
        public String getActions() {
            return "";
        }
        public int hashCode() {
            return bookid.hashCode() ^pages.hashCode();
        }
        public boolean equals(Object obj) {
            if (!(obj instanceof BookPermission)) {
                return false;
            }
            BookPermission bp = (BookPermission)obj;
            return pages.equals(bp.pages) && bookid.equals(bp.bookid);
        }
    }
```

Here's some examples that use BookPermission:

```
    Permission p1 = new BookPermission("123:1-3,5,7-10");

    Permission p2 = new BookPermission("123:2");
    boolean b = p1.implies(p2); // false

    p2 = new BookPermission("123:3");
    b = p1.implies(p2); // true

    p2 = new BookPermission("1234:3");
    b = p1.implies(p2); // false

    p2 = new BookPermission("123:3,8-9");
    b = p1.implies(p2); // true

    p2 = new BookPermission("123:3-5");
    b = p1.implies(p2); // false
```

ε216. Controlling Access to an Object

This example demonstrates how to protect access to an object using a permission. Only threads with the required permission can access the object.

```
    // Create the object that requires protection
    String secretObj = "my secret";

    // Create the required permission that will protect the object
    Guard guard = new PropertyPermission("java.home", "read");

    // Create the guard
    GuardedObject gobj = new GuardedObject(secretObj, guard);

    // Get the guarded object
    try {
        Object o = gobj.getObject();
    } catch (AccessControlException e) {
        // Cannot access the object
    }
```

ε217. Listing All Permissions Granted to a Loaded Class

This example retrieves all the permissions granted to a particular class. These permissions are effective only if a security manager is installed (see "ε212. Enabling the Security Manager"). However, with a security manager installed, a class will require permission to execute Class.getProtectionDomain() and Policy.getPermissions().

```
// Get the protection domain for the class
ProtectionDomain domain = this.getClass().getProtectionDomain();

// With the protection domain, get all the permissions from the Policy object
PermissionCollection pcoll = Policy.getPolicy().getPermissions(domain);

// View each permission in the permission collection
Enumeration enum = pcoll.elements();
for (; enum.hasMoreElements(); ) {
    Permission p = (Permission)enum.nextElement();
}
```

Here's the list of permissions for a class under the default policy file:

```
(java.lang.RuntimePermission exitVM)
(java.lang.RuntimePermission stopThread)
(java.util.PropertyPermission java.specification.vendor read)
(java.util.PropertyPermission java.vm.specification.vendor read)
(java.util.PropertyPermission path.separator read)
(java.util.PropertyPermission java.vm.name read)
(java.util.PropertyPermission java.class.version read)
(java.util.PropertyPermission os.name read)
(java.util.PropertyPermission java.vendor.url read)
(java.util.PropertyPermission java.vendor read)
(java.util.PropertyPermission java.vm.vendor read)
(java.util.PropertyPermission file.separator read)
(java.util.PropertyPermission os.version read)
(java.util.PropertyPermission java.vm.version read)
(java.util.PropertyPermission java.version read)
(java.util.PropertyPermission line.separator read)
(java.util.PropertyPermission java.vm.specification.version read)
(java.util.PropertyPermission java.specification.name read)
(java.util.PropertyPermission java.vm.specification.name read)
(java.util.PropertyPermission java.specification.version read)
(java.util.PropertyPermission os.arch read)
(java.net.SocketPermission localhost:1024- listen,resolve)
(java.io.FilePermission \C:\users\almanac\- read)
```

Here's the list of permissions for the java.lang.String class which is loaded with the system class loader:

```
(java.security.AllPermission <all permissions> <all actions>)
```

ε218. Listing All Permissions Granted to Classes Loaded from a URL or Directory

A "code base" is a location of class or jar files specified using a URL. The URL may refer to a location on the Internet or a directory in the local file system. This example retrieves all the permissions granted to a particular class that's been loaded from a code base.

These permissions are effective only if the security manager is installed (see "ε212. Enabling the Security Manager"). However, with a security manager installed, a class will require permission to execute Class.getProtectionDomain() and Policy.getPermissions().

Class   *Interface*   —extends   - - -implements   ○ abstract   ● final   ^—has superclass   _—has subclass   package—see other volume

```
URL codebase = null;
try {
    // Get permissions for a URL
    codebase = new URL("http://java.sun.com/");

    // Get permissions for a directory
    codebase = new File("c:\\users\\almanac\\").toURL();
    codebase = new File(System.getProperty("user.home")).toURL();
} catch (MalformedURLException e) {
} catch (IOException e) {
}

// Construct a code source with the code base
CodeSource cs = new CodeSource(codebase, null);

// Get all granted permissions
PermissionCollection pcoll = Policy.getPolicy().getPermissions(cs);

// View each permission in the permission collection
Enumeration enum = pcoll.elements();
for (; enum.hasMoreElements(); ) {
    Permission p = (Permission)enum.nextElement();
}
```

When the above example is run with the following policy file:

```
grant codeBase "http://java.sun.com/-" {
    // Give permission to read all system properties
    permission java.util.PropertyPermission "*", "read";
};

grant codeBase "file:${user.home}/*" {
    // Give permission to execute all runtime-protected methods
    permission java.lang.RuntimePermission "*";
};
```

using the following command:

```
java -Djava.security.policy==my.policy MyApp
```

the permissions for the URL http://java.sun.com/ are:

```
(java.util.PropertyPermission * read)
```

and the permissions for the directory System.getProperty("user.home") are:

```
(java.lang.RuntimePermission *)
```

Policy Files

ε219. Creating a New Policy File

Use policytool to create or edit an existing policy file. This is an example of a policy file created using policytool. It grants two permissions. It grants code signed by Duke permission to read files located in the user's home directory. It also grants code from the location http://someserver/myjar.jar (regardless of who signed it) to read the file.encoding system property.

```
> policytool -file .policy

keystore ".keystore";
grant signedBy "Duke" {
    permission java.io.FilePermission "${user.dir}/-", "read";
};
```

```
grant codeBase "http://someserver/myjar.jar" {
    permission java.util.PropertyPermission "file.encoding", "read";
}
```

ε220. Managing Policy Files

By default, the JDK uses the policy files located in

```
file:${java.home}/lib/security/java.policy
file:${user.home}/.java.policy
```

These policy files are specified in the default security file:

```
${java.home}/lib/security/java.security
```

The final policy is the union of all granted permissions in all policy files. To specify an additional policy file, you can set the java.security.policy system property at the command line:

```
> java -Djava.security.manager -Djava.security.policy=someURL MyApp
or
> appletviewer -J-Djava.security.policy=someURL HTMLfile
```

To ignore the policies in the java.security file, and only use the specified policy, use '==' instead of '=':

```
> java -Djava.security.manager -Djava.security.policy==someURL MyApp
```

Additional policy files can also be added to the java.security file. For more information on policy files, see

```
http://java.sun.com/j2se/1.4/docs/guide/security/PolicyFiles.html
```

ε221. Protecting Files

Access to files is controlled with a policy file (see "ε220. Managing Policy Files"). Here are examples of policy file entries for controlling access to the system.

```
// grant all classes loaded from h1.com ability to read \temp\myfile
grant codeBase "http://h1.com/-" {
    permission java.io.FilePermission "c:\\temp\\myfile", "read";
};

// grant ability to create and write c:\temp\myfile
// Note: if \temp\myfile does not exist, it could be created as a directory
grant codeBase "http://h2.com/-" {
    permission java.io.FilePermission "c:\\temp\\myfile", "write";
};

// grant ability to list files in the user's home directory
grant codeBase "http://h3.com/-" {
    permission java.io.FilePermission "${user.home}", "read";
};

// grant ability to read any file or directory under c:\temp
// Note: does not grant ability to read c:\temp itself, i.e. no permission
// to call File.list() on c:\temp
grant codeBase "http://h4.com/-" {
    permission java.io.FilePermission "c:\\temp\\-", "read";
};

// grant ability to delete any file or directory in c:\temp\mydir
// Note: does not grant ability to delete c:\temp\mydir itself
grant codeBase "http://h5.com/*" {
    permission java.io.FilePermission "c:\\temp\\mydir\*", "delete";
```

```
    };

    // grant ability to execute (see Runtime.exec()) the file c:\java.exe
    grant codeBase "http://h6.com/-" {
        permission java.io.FilePermission "c:\\java.exe", "execute";
    };

    // grant ability to read and write any file in current directory
    // Note: this is equivalent to ${user.dir}/*
    grant codeBase "http://h7.com/-" {
        permission java.io.FilePermission "*", "read,write";
    };

    // grant ability to read any file under current directory
    // Note: this is equivalent to ${user.dir}/-
    grant codeBase "http://h8.com/-" {
        permission java.io.FilePermission "-", "read";
    };

    // grant ability to read any file
    grant codeBase "http://h9.com/-" {
        permission java.io.FilePermission "«ALL FILES»", "read";
    };
```

ε222. Protecting System Properties

Access to system properties (System.getProperty()) is controlled with a policy file (see "ε220. Managing Policy Files"). Here are examples of policy file entries for controlling access to system properties.

```
    // grant all classes loaded from h1.com ability to read the 'myprop' system properties
    grant codeBase "http://h1.com/-" {
        permission java.util.PropertyPermission "myprop", "read";
    };

    // grant ability to write the 'myprop' system properties
    grant codeBase "http://h2.com/-" {
        permission java.util.PropertyPermission "myprop", "write";
    };

    // grant ability to read and write the 'myprop' system properties
    grant codeBase "http://h3.com/-" {
        permission java.util.PropertyPermission "myprop", "read,write";
    };

    // grant ability to read all properties that start with 'myprops.'
    grant codeBase "http://h4.com/-" {
        permission java.util.PropertyPermission "myprops.*", "read";
    };

    // grant ability to read all system properties
    grant codeBase "http://h5.com/-" {
        permission java.util.PropertyPermission "*", "read";
    };

    // grant ability to write all system properties
    grant codeBase "http://h6.com/-" {
        permission java.util.PropertyPermission "*", "write";
    };

    // grant ability to read and write all system properties
    grant codeBase "http://h7.com/-" {
        permission java.util.PropertyPermission "*", "read,write";
```

```
};
```

java.security.acl

The classes and interfaces in this package have been superseded by classes in the java.security package. See java.security.Permission for details.

```
java.lang.Object
  └ java.lang.Throwable - - - - - - - - - - - - - - - - - - - - - - - - - - - - - - - - - java.io.Serializable
      └ java.lang.Exception
1.1        ├ AclNotFoundException
1.1        ├ LastOwnerException
1.1        └ NotOwnerException

1.1   Acl ─────────────────────────────────────── Owner
1.1   AclEntry ───────────────────────────────── java.lang.Cloneable
1.1   Group ──────────────────────────────────── java.security.Principal
1.1   Owner
1.1   Permission
```

java.security.cert

This package contains classes and interfaces for parsing and managing certifications. It contains support for X509 v3 certificates.

Class *Interface* —extends - - -implements ○ abstract ● final ^—has superclass ˎ—has subclass package—see other volume

Packages

java.security.cert

```
                java.lang.Object
1.2  ○          ├ CRL
1.2  ○          │ └ X509CRL - - - - - - - - - - - - - - - - - - - - - - - - - - - - - - - - - X509Extension
1.4             ├ CertPath - - - - - - - - - - - - - - - - - - - - - - - - - - - - - - ┌ - java.io.Serializable ⌄
1.4             ├ CertPath.CertPathRep - - - - - - - - - - - - - - - - - - - - - - ┐ │
1.4             ├ CertPathBuilder                                                  │ │
1.4  ○          ├ CertPathBuilderSpi                                               │ │
1.4             ├ CertPathValidator                                                │ │
1.4  ○          ├ CertPathValidatorSpi                                             │ │
1.4             ├ CertStore                                                        │ │
1.4  ○          ├ CertStoreSpi                                                     │ │
1.2  ○          ├ Certificate - - - - - - - - - - - - - - - - - - - - - - - - - - -┘ │
1.2  ○          │ └ X509Certificate - - - - - - - - - - - - - - - - - - - - - - - - - X509Extension
1.3             ├ Certificate.CertificateRep - - - - - - - - - - - - - - - - - - - - - java.io.Serializable ⌄
1.2             ├ CertificateFactory
1.2  ○          ├ CertificateFactorySpi
1.4             ├ CollectionCertStoreParameters - - - - - - - - - - - - - - - - ┌ - - CertStoreParameters ˆ
1.4             ├ LDAPCertStoreParameters - - - - - - - - - - - - - - - - - - - ┘
1.4  ○          ├ PKIXCertPathChecker - - - - - - - - - - - - - - - - - - - - - - - - - java.lang.Cloneable ⌄
1.4             ├ PKIXCertPathValidatorResult - - - - - - - - - - - - - - - - - - - - - CertPathValidatorResult ˆ
1.4             │ └ PKIXCertPathBuilderResult - - - - - - - - - - - - - - - - - - - - - CertPathBuilderResult ˆ
1.4             ├ PKIXParameters - - - - - - - - - - - - - - - - - - - - - - - - - - - CertPathParameters ˆ
1.4             │ └ PKIXBuilderParameters
1.4  ●          ├ PolicyQualifierInfo
1.4             ├ TrustAnchor
1.2  ○          ├ X509CRLEntry - - - - - - - - - - - - - - - - - - - - - - - - - - - - X509Extension
1.4             ├ X509CRLSelector - - - - - - - - - - - - - - - - - - - - - - - - - - - CRLSelector ˆ
1.4             ├ X509CertSelector - - - - - - - - - - - - - - - - - - - - - - - - - - - CertSelector ˆ
                └ java.lang.Throwable - - - - - - - - - - - - - - - - - - - - - - - - - java.io.Serializable ⌄
                  └ java.lang.Exception
1.2               └ java.security.GeneralSecurityException
1.2                 ├ CRLException
1.4                 ├ CertPathBuilderException
1.4                 ├ CertPathValidatorException
1.4                 ├ CertStoreException
1.2                 └ CertificateException
1.2                   ├ CertificateEncodingException
1.2                   ├ CertificateExpiredException
1.2                   ├ CertificateNotYetValidException
1.2                   └ CertificateParsingException

1.4    CRLSelector ─────────────────────────────────────────┐ java.lang.Cloneable
1.4    CertPathBuilderResult ───────────────────────────────┤
1.4    CertPathParameters ──────────────────────────────────┤
1.4    CertPathValidatorResult ─────────────────────────────┤
1.4    CertSelector ────────────────────────────────────────┤
1.4    CertStoreParameters ─────────────────────────────────┘
1.4    PolicyNode
1.2    X509Extension
```

Class   *Interface*   —extends   - - -implements   ○ abstract   ● final   ˆ—has superclass   ⌄—has subclass   package—see other volume

Certificates

ε223. Creating a New Key Pair and Self-signed Certificate Using keytool

This example uses the keytool program to create a new key pair and self-signed certificate for the principal Duke. The example generates a 1024-bit Digital Signature Algorithm (DSA) key pair.

```
> keytool -genkey -alias alias -keystore .keystore
Enter keystore password: password
What is your first and last name?
[Unknown]: Duke
What is the name of your organizational unit?
[Unknown]: JavaSoft
What is the name of your organization?
[Unknown]: Sun
What is the name of your City or Locality?
[Unknown]: Cupertino
What is the name of your State or Province?
[Unknown]: CA
What is the two-letter country code for this unit?
[Unknown]: US
Is <CN=Duke, OU=JavaSoft, O=Sun, L=Cupertino, ST=CA, C=US> correct?
[no]: yes
```

To create a 1024-bit RSA key:

```
> keytool -genkey -keyalg RSA -keysize 1024 -alias alias -keystore .keystore
```

ε224. Exporting a Certificate to a File

See also "ε225. Importing a Certificate from a File".

```java
// This method writes a certificate to a file. If binary is false, the
// certificate is base64 encoded.
public static void export(java.security.cert.Certificate cert, File file, boolean binary) {
    try {
        // Get the encoded form which is suitable for exporting
        byte[] buf = cert.getEncoded();

        FileOutputStream os = new FileOutputStream(file);
        if (binary) {
            // Write in binary form
            os.write(buf);
        } else {
            // Write in text form
            Writer wr = new OutputStreamWriter(os, Charset.forName("UTF-8"));
            wr.write("——BEGIN CERTIFICATE——\n");
            wr.write(new sun.misc.BASE64Encoder().encode(buf));
            wr.write("\n——END CERTIFICATE——\n");
            wr.flush();
        }
        os.close();
    } catch (CertificateEncodingException e) {
    } catch (IOException e) {
    }
}
```

If the certificate is in the key store, it can exported using keytool:

```
// Export in binary
> keytool -storepass my-keystore-password -alias myalias -export -file outfilename.cer
```

Packages

```
// Export in text format
> keytool -storepass my-keystore-password -alias myalias -export -rfc -file outfilename.cer
```

Here's an example of the text form of an exported certificate:

```
——BEGIN CERTIFICATE——
MIIC6TCCAqcCBDxgu/IwCwYHKoZIzjgEAwUAMFoxCzAJBgNVBAYTAIVTMQswCQYDVQQIEwJDQTES
MBAGA1UEBxMJUGFsbyBBbHRvMQowCAYDVQQKEwFJMQswCQYDVQQLEwJNZTERMA8GA1UEAxMIUG
IENoYW4wHhcNMDIwMjA2MDUxNTMwWhcNMDIwNTA3MDUxNTMwWjBaMQswCQYDVQQGEwJVUzELMAk
A1UECBMCQ0ExEjAQBgNVBAcTCVBhbG8gQWx0bzEKMAgGA1UEChMBSTELMAkGA1UECxMCTWUxETA
BgNVBAMTCFBhdCBDaGFuMIIBuDCCASwGByqGSM44BAEwggEfAoGBAP1/U4EddRIpUt9KnC7s5Of2
EbdSPO9EAMMeP4C2USZpRV1AllH7WT2NWPq/xfW6MPbLm1Vs14E7gB00b/JmYLdrmVClpJ+f6AR7
ECLCT7up1/63xhv4O1fnxqimFQ8E+4P208Uewwl1VBNaFpEy9nXzrith1yrv8ilDGZ3RSAHHAhUA
l2BQjxUjC8yykrmCouuEC/BYHPUCgYEA9+GghdabPd7LvKtcNrhXuXmUr7v6OuqC+VdMCz0HgmdR
WVeOutRZT+ZxBxCBgLRJFnEj6EwoFhO3zwkyjMim4TwWeotUfl0o4KOuHiuzpnWRbqN/C/ohNWLx
+2J6ASQ7zKTxvqhRklmog9/hWuWfBpKLZl6Ae1UlZAFMO/7PSSoDgYUAAoGBAPyx9uQ1PKBYO/2G
RPzbW4y6pphNRmObJQWbjY/ERuCQwLRrpREh9sgMnptZjRzLVpWdzxNa9bFMFXAYMgoTUIgAZ9yN
WPjp/JiFfzdlq3CY0CEey42M3mbD3pWsF9x4SSsJTpDobX/pm5XgtkhZXBZYtBk813Xv2LxyZ3OI
W1JnMAsGByqGSM44BAMFAAMvADAsAhQ5wayd5cpEo/vHmF7G5gVQ9cMKKAIUMfk2ZYxNdhe6oNmH
nR0AhnEHILE=
——END CERTIFICATE——
```

ε225. Importing a Certificate from a File

See also "ε224. Exporting a Certificate to a File".

```
// This method reads a certificate to a file. The certificate can be either
// binary or base64 encoded.
public static java.security.cert.Certificate importCertificate(File file) {
    try {
        FileInputStream is = new FileInputStream(file);

        CertificateFactory cf = CertificateFactory.getInstance("X.509");
        java.security.cert.Certificate cert = cf.generateCertificate(is);
        return cert;
    } catch (CertificateException e) {
    } catch (IOException e) {
    }
    return null;
}
```

A certificate can be imported into a keystore using keytool:

```
> keytool -storepass my-keystore-password -alias myalias -import -file infilename.cer
```

ε226. Listing All Available Certificate Formats

Retrieving the list of available certificate formats requires checking the services provided by all registered providers. The retrieved list of names can be used in creating a Certificate or CertPath object with CertificateFactory.

```
// This method is implemented in "ε194. Listing All Available Cryptographic Services"
String[] names = getCryptoImpls("CertificateFactory");
```

An example of the output:

```
X.509
X509
```

Class   *Interface*   —extends   - - -implements   O abstract   ● final   ⌐—has superclass   —has subclass   package—see other volume

ε227. Getting the Subject and Issuer Distinguished Names of an X509 Certificate

This example lists the subject and issuer distinguished names of the certificates in a keystore. To load a keystore, see "ε208. Listing the Aliases in a Key Store".

```
try {
    // List the aliases
    Enumeration enum = keystore.aliases();
    for (; enum.hasMoreElements(); ) {
        String alias = (String)enum.nextElement();

        java.security.cert.Certificate cert = keystore.getCertificate(alias);
        if (cert instanceof X509Certificate) {
            X509Certificate x509cert = (X509Certificate)cert;

            // Get subject
            Principal principal = x509cert.getSubjectDN();
            String subjectDn = principal.getName();

            // Get issuer
            principal = x509cert.getIssuerDN();
            String issuerDn = principal.getName();
        }
    }
} catch (KeyStoreException e) {
}
```

Certification Paths

ε228. Listing All Available Certification Path Validation Algorithms

Retrieving the list of available certification path validation algorithms requires checking the services provided by all registered providers. The retrieved list of names can be used in creating a CertPathValidator object.

```
// This method is implemented in "ε194. Listing All Available Cryptographic Services"
String[] names = getCryptoImpls("CertPathValidator");
```

An example of the output:

```
PKIX
```

ε229. Creating a Certification Path

This example demonstrates how to create a CertPath object from an list of certificates.

```
// The CA's certificate should be the last element in the array
public static CertPath createCertPath(java.security.cert.Certificate[] certs) {
    try {
        CertificateFactory certFact = CertificateFactory.getInstance("X.509");
        CertPath path = certFact.generateCertPath(Arrays.asList(certs));
        return path;
    } catch (java.security.cert.CertificateEncodingException e) {
    } catch (CertificateException e) {
    }
    return null;
}
```

Packages

ε230. Listing the Most-Trusted Certificate Authorities (CA) in a Key Store

This example lists the most-trusted CAs in the JDK's cacerts file. The most-trusted CAs are used to validate certification paths.

```java
try {
    // Load the JDK's cacerts keystore file
    String filename = System.getProperty("java.home")
        + "/lib/security/cacerts".replace('/', File.separatorChar);
    FileInputStream is = new FileInputStream(filename);
    KeyStore keystore = KeyStore.getInstance(KeyStore.getDefaultType());
    String password = "changeit";
    keystore.load(is, password.toCharArray());

    // This class retrieves the most-trusted CAs from the keystore
    PKIXParameters params = new PKIXParameters(keystore);

    // Get the set of trust anchors, which contain the most-trusted CA certificates
    Iterator it = params.getTrustAnchors().iterator();
    for (; it.hasNext(); ) {
        TrustAnchor ta = (TrustAnchor)it.next();

        // Get certificate
        X509Certificate cert = ta.getTrustedCert();
    }
} catch (CertificateException e) {
} catch (KeyStoreException e) {
} catch (NoSuchAlgorithmException e) {
} catch (InvalidAlgorithmParameterException e) {
} catch (IOException e) {
}
```

ε231. Validating a Certification Path

This example validates a chain of certificates using the most-trusted CAs in the JDK's cacerts file.

```java
try {
    // Load the JDK's cacerts keystore file
    String filename = System.getProperty("java.home")
        + "/lib/security/cacerts".replace('/', File.separatorChar);
    FileInputStream is = new FileInputStream(filename);
    KeyStore keystore = KeyStore.getInstance(KeyStore.getDefaultType());
    String password = "changeit";
    keystore.load(is, password.toCharArray());

    // Create the parameters for the validator
    PKIXParameters params = new PKIXParameters(keystore);

    // Disable CRL checking since we are not supplying any CRLs
    params.setRevocationEnabled(false);

    // Create the validator and validate the path
    // To create a path, see "ε229. Creating a Certification Path"
    CertPathValidator certPathValidator
        = CertPathValidator.getInstance(CertPathValidator.getDefaultType());
    CertPathValidatorResult result = certPathValidator.validate(certPath, params);

    // Get the CA used to validate this path
    PKIXCertPathValidatorResult pkixResult = (PKIXCertPathValidatorResult)result;
    TrustAnchor ta = pkixResult.getTrustAnchor();
```

Class *Interface* —extends - - -implements ○ abstract ● final ^—has superclass ‿—has subclass package—see other volume

```
        X509Certificate cert = ta.getTrustedCert();
    } catch (CertificateException e) {
    } catch (KeyStoreException e) {
    } catch (NoSuchAlgorithmException e) {
    } catch (InvalidAlgorithmParameterException e) {
    } catch (CertPathValidatorException e) {
        // Validation failed
    }
```

java.security.interfaces

This package contains interfaces for generating DSA (Digital Signature Algorithm) keys as defined in NIST's FIPS-186.

1.1	*DSAKey*	
1.1	*DSAKeyPairGenerator*	
1.1	*DSAParams*	
1.1	*DSAPrivateKey* ————————————— *DSAKey, java.security.PrivateKey*^	
1.1	*DSAPublicKey* ————————————— *DSAKey, java.security.PublicKey*^	
1.3	*RSAKey*	
1.4	*RSAMultiPrimePrivateCrtKey* —————— *RSAPrivateKey*^	
1.2	*RSAPrivateCrtKey* ———————	
1.2	*RSAPrivateKey* ————————————— *RSAKey, java.security.PrivateKey*^	
1.2	*RSAPublicKey* ————————————— *RSAKey, java.security.PublicKey*^	

java.security.spec

This package contains classes and interfaces for key specifications. Key specifications are transparent representations of the key material that constitutes a key. A key may be specified in either an algorithm-dependent way or an algorithm-independent way. This package contains key specifications for DSA public and private keys, PKCS #8 private keys in DER encoded format, and X509 public and private keys in DER encoded format.

java.security.spec

```
java.lang.Object
1.2     ├ DSAParameterSpec - - - - - - - - - - - - - - - - - - - - - - - - - - - - - - - - - AlgorithmParameterSpec,
                                                                                           java.security.interfaces.DSAParams
1.2     ├ DSAPrivateKeySpec - - - - - - - - - - - - - - - - - - - - - - - - - - - - - ┬ KeySpec
1.2     ├ DSAPublicKeySpec - - - - - - - - - - - - - - - - - - - - - - - - - - - - - ┐ ┊
1.2 ○   ├ EncodedKeySpec - - - - - - - - - - - - - - - - - - - - - - - - - - - - - - ┘ ┊
1.2     │  ├ PKCS8EncodedKeySpec
1.2     │  └ X509EncodedKeySpec
1.4     ├ PSSParameterSpec - - - - - - - - - - - - - - - - - - - - - - - - - - - - ┬ AlgorithmParameterSpec
1.3     ├ RSAKeyGenParameterSpec - - - - - - - - - - - - - - - - - - - - - - - ┘
1.4     ├ RSAOtherPrimeInfo
1.2     ├ RSAPrivateKeySpec - - - - - - - - - - - - - - - - - - - - - - - - - - - ┬ KeySpec
1.4     │  ├ RSAMultiPrimePrivateCrtKeySpec
1.2     │  └ RSAPrivateCrtKeySpec
1.2     ├ RSAPublicKeySpec - - - - - - - - - - - - - - - - - - - - - - - - - - - - ┘
        └ java.lang.Throwable - - - - - - - - - - - - - - - - - - - - - - - - - - - java.io.Serializable
           └ java.lang.Exception
1.2        └ java.security.GeneralSecurityException
1.2              ├ InvalidKeySpecException
1.2              └ InvalidParameterSpecException

1.2     AlgorithmParameterSpec
1.2     KeySpec
```

java.sql

This is the JDBC package. JDBC is a standard API for executing SQL statements. It contains classes and interfaces for creating SQL statements, and retrieving the results of executing those statements against

Class   *Interface*   —extends   - - -implements   ○ abstract   ● final   ^-has superclass   —has subclass   package—see other volume

relational databases. JDBC has a framework whereby different "drivers" can be installed dynamically to access different databases.

```
java.lang.Object
```
1.1	`├ DriverManager`
1.1	`├ DriverPropertyInfo`
1.1	`├ Types`
1.2 ○	`├ java.security.Permission` - *java.io.Serializable*, *java.security.Guard*
1.2 ○	`└ java.security.BasicPermission` - *java.io.Serializable*
1.3 ●	`└ SQLPermission`

java.sql

```
          java.lang.Object
          ├─ java.util.Date - - - - - - - - - - - - - - - - - - - - - - - - - - - - - - - java.io.Serializable., java.lang.Cloneable.,
          │                                                                                        java.lang.Comparable
1.1       │   ├─ Date
1.1       │   ├─ Time
1.1       │   └─ Timestamp
          └─ java.lang.Throwable - - - - - - - - - - - - - - - - - - - - - - - - - - - java.io.Serializable.
              └─ java.lang.Exception
1.1           └─ SQLException
1.2               ├─ BatchUpdateException
1.1               └─ SQLWarning
1.1                   └─ DataTruncation
```

1.2	*Array*
1.2	*Blob*
1.1	*CallableStatement* ─────────────────────── *PreparedStatement^*
1.2	*Clob*
1.1	*Connection*
1.1	*DatabaseMetaData*
1.1	*Driver*
1.4	*ParameterMetaData*
1.1	*PreparedStatement.* ────────────────────── *Statement*
1.2	*Ref*
1.1	*ResultSet.*
1.1	*ResultSetMetaData.*
1.2	*SQLData*
1.2	*SQLInput*
1.2	*SQLOutput*
1.4	*Savepoint*
1.1	*Statement.*
1.2	*Struct*

Drivers

ε232. Getting JDBC Drivers for a Database

Many of the new features in java.sql and javax.sql for J2SE 1.4 require JDBC 2.0 drivers. Information about available JDBC drivers for various databases is available at

> http://java.sun.com/products/jdbc

For an Oracle database, download and installation instructions are available at:

> http://otn.oracle.com/software/content.html

For a MySQL database, download and installation instructions are available at:

> http://mmMySQL.sourceforge.net

For a SQL Server database, there are many JDBC drivers available. Here are some:

> NetDirect: http://www.j-netdirect.com
> DataDirect: http://www.datadirect-technologies.com
> FreeTDS: http://www.freetds.org

Class *Interface* —extends - - -implements ○ abstract ● final ^—has superclass .—has subclass package—see other volume

ε233. Loading a JDBC Driver

Before a connection to a database can be established, the JDBC driver for that database must be loaded. Drivers automatically register themselves with the JDBC system when loaded. There are two ways to load a JDBC driver. The first is to specify the driver or colon-separated list of drivers on the command line:

```
> java -Djdbc.drivers=com.company1.Driver:com.company2.Driver MyApp
```

The second, and recommended method, is to call Class.forName() within the code:

```
try {
    // Load the JDBC driver
    String driverName = "org.gjt.mm.mysql.Driver";
    Class.forName(driverName);
} catch (ClassNotFoundException e) {
    // Could not find the driver
}
```

ε234. Listing All Loaded JDBC Drivers

This example lists all loaded JDBC drivers and gets information about each one.

```
List drivers = Collections.list(DriverManager.getDrivers());
for (int i=0; i<drivers.size(); i++) {
    Driver driver = (Driver)drivers.get(i);

    // Get name of driver
    String name = driver.getClass().getName();

    // Get version info
    int majorVersion = driver.getMajorVersion();
    int minorVersion = driver.getMinorVersion();
    boolean isJdbcCompliant = driver.jdbcCompliant();
}
```

Connections

ε235. Connecting to an Oracle Database

This example uses an Oracle JDBC driver to connect to an Oracle database instance located at 128.0.0.0:1521 with an sid called mydatabase.

```
Connection connection = null;
try {
    // Load the JDBC driver
    String driverName = "oracle.jdbc.driver.OracleDriver";
    Class.forName(driverName);

    // Create a connection to the database
    String serverName = "127.0.0.1";
    String portNumber = "1521";
    String sid = "mydatabase";
    String url = "jdbc:oracle:thin:@" + serverName + ":" + portNumber + ":" + sid;
    String username = "username";
    String password = "password";
    connection = DriverManager.getConnection(url, username, password);
} catch (ClassNotFoundException e) {
    // Could not find the database driver
} catch (SQLException e) {
    // Could not connect to the database
}
```

java.sql

ε236. Connecting to a MySQL Database

This example connects to a MySQL database using the MM JDBC driver for MySQL. You need to have an account in MySQL database to run this example. To create an account, you can connect to MySQL database on your platform as root, and run the following command:

```
mysql> GRANT ALL PRIVILEGES ON *.* TO username@localhost
IDENTIFIED BY 'password' WITH GRANT OPTION;

Connection connection = null;
try {
    // Load the JDBC driver
    String driverName = "org.gjt.mm.mysql.Driver"; // MySQL MM JDBC driver
    Class.forName(driverName);

    // Create a connection to the database
    String serverName = "localhost";
    String mydatabase = "mydatabase";
    String url = "jdbc:mysql://" + serverName + "/" + mydatabase; // a JDBC url
    String username = "username";
    String password = "password";
    connection = DriverManager.getConnection(url, username, password);
} catch (ClassNotFoundException e) {
    // Could not find the database driver
} catch (SQLException e) {
    // Could not connect to the database
}
```

ε237. Connecting to a SQLServer Database

This example connects to a SQLServer database using the NetDirect JDBC driver. For information about this driver, see "ε232. Getting JDBC Drivers for a Database".

```
Connection connection = null;
try {
    String driverName = "com.jnetdirect.jsql.JSQLDriver"; // NetDirect JDBC driver
    String serverName = "127.0.0.1";
    String portNumber = "1433";
    String mydatabase = serverName + ":" + portNumber;
    String url = "jdbc:JSQLConnect://" + mydatabase; // a JDBC url
    String username = "username";
    String password = "password";

    // Load the JDBC driver
    Class.forName(driverName);

    // Create a connection to the database
    connection = DriverManager.getConnection(url, username, password);
} catch (ClassNotFoundException e) {
    // Could not find the database driver
} catch (SQLException e) {
    // Could not connect to the database
}
```

ε238. Listing All Available Parameters for Creating a JDBC Connection

Driver.getPropertyInfo() returns a list of all available properties that can be supplied when using the driver to create a JDBC connection. This list can be displayed to the user.

```
try {
```

```
    // Load the driver
    String driverName = "org.gjt.mm.mysql.Driver"; // MySQL MM JDBC driver
    Class.forName(driverName);

    // Get the Driver instance
    String url = "jdbc:mysql://a/b";
    Driver driver = DriverManager.getDriver(url);

    // Get available properties
    DriverPropertyInfo[] info = driver.getPropertyInfo(url, null);
    for (int i=0; i<info.length; i++) {
        // Get name of property
        String name = info[i].name;

        // Is property value required?
        boolean isRequired = info[i].required;

        // Get current value
        String value = info[i].value;

        // Get description of property
        String desc = info[i].description;

        // Get possible choices for property; if null, value can be any string
        String[] choices = info[i].choices;
    }
} catch (ClassNotFoundException e) {
// Could not find the database driver
} catch (SQLException e) {
}
```

Here's the property values for the MySql driver:

```
Name(isRequired): Description
    default: default value
    choices: ...

HOST(true): Hostname of MySQL Server
    default: a

PORT(false): Port number of MySQL Server
    default: 3306

DBNAME(false): Database name
    default: b

user(true): Username to authenticate as
    default: null

password(true): Password to use for authentication
    default: null

autoReconnect(false): Should the driver try to re-establish bad connections?
    default: false
    choices: true, false

maxReconnects(false): Maximum number of reconnects to attempt if autoReconnect is true
    default: 3

initialTimeout(false): Initial timeout (seconds) to wait between failed connections
    default: 2
```

ε239. Determining If a Database Supports Transactions

```
try {
```

```
        DatabaseMetaData dmd = connection.getMetaData();
        if (dmd.supportsTransactions()) {
            // Transactions are supported
        } else {
            // Transactions are not supported
        }
    } catch (SQLException e) {
    }
```

ε240. Committing and Rolling Back Updates to a Database

By default, a connection commits all updates to the database immediately and automatically. For example, executing an UPDATE SQL query immediately commits the change. This example shows how to disable auto-commits and explicitly commit.

```
    try {
        // Disable auto commit
        connection.setAutoCommit(false);

        // Do SQL updates...

        // Commit updates
        connection.commit();
    } catch (SQLException e) {
        // Rollback update
        connection.rollback();
    }
```

ε241. Handling a SQL Exception

This example demonstrates how to retrieve the information in a SQLException.

```
    try {
        // Execute SQL statements...
    } catch (SQLException e) {
        while (e != null) {
            // Retrieve a human-readable message identifying the reason for the exception
            String message = e.getMessage();

            // This vendor-independent string contains a code that identifies
            // the reason for the exception.
            // The code follows the Open Group SQL conventions.
            String sqlState = e.getSQLState();

            // Retrieve a vendor-specific code identifying the reason for the exception.
            int errorCode = e.getErrorCode();

            // If it is necessary to execute code based on this error code,
            // you should ensure that the expected driver is being
            // used before using the error code.

            // Get driver name
            String driverName = connection.getMetaData().getDriverName();
            if (driverName.equals("Oracle JDBC Driver") && errorCode == 123) {
                // Process error...
            }

            // The exception may have been chained; process the next chained exception
            e = e.getNextException();
        }
```

Class   *Interface*   —extends   - - -implements   ○ abstract   ● final   ˆ—has superclass   ˬ—has subclass   package—see other volume

}

ε242. Determining If a SQL Warning Occurred

Some database operations can cause a warning which is not handled by an exception. These warning must be explicitly checked for. An example of a warning is a data truncation error during a read operation (see the DataTruncation class).

There are three places to check for a warning — on a Connection object, a Statement object, and a ResultSet object. This example demonstrates how to check for warning on each of these objects.

```
try {
    // Get warnings on Connection object
    SQLWarning warning = connection.getWarnings();
    while (warning != null) {
        // Process connection warning
        // For information on these values, see "ε241. Handling a SQL Exception"
        String message = warning.getMessage();
        String sqlState = warning.getSQLState();
        int errorCode = warning.getErrorCode();
        warning = warning.getNextWarning();
    }

    // Create a statement
    Statement stmt = connection.createStatement();

    // Use the statement...

    // Get warnings on Statement object
    warning = stmt.getWarnings();
    if (warning != null) {
        // Process statement warnings...
    }

    // Get a result set
    ResultSet resultSet = stmt.executeQuery("SELECT * FROM my_table");
    while (resultSet.next()) {
        // Use result set

        // Get warnings on the current row of the ResultSet object
        warning = resultSet.getWarnings();
        if (warning != null) {
            // Process result set warnings...
        }
    }
} catch (SQLException e) {
}
```

ε243. Getting the Driver of a Connection

Given a connection, it is not possible to determine the driver that created the connection. Although the connection can return a driver name, the returned name cannot be used to find the driver. For example,

```
try {
    DatabaseMetaData dmd = connection.getMetaData();
    String driverName = dmd.getDriverName(); // Mark Matthew's MySQL Driver
} catch (SQLException e) {
}
```

The best you can do is to use the URL used to create the connection:

```
try {
```

Packages

```
        // Create connection from URL
        Connection conn = DriverManager.getConnection(url, username, password);

        // Get driver from URL
        Driver driver = DriverManager.getDriver(url);
    } catch (SQLException e) {
    }
```

ε244. Setting the Number of Rows to Prefetch When Executing a SQL Query

When a SQL query is executed, the number of rows of data that a driver physically copies from the database to the client is called the "fetch size". If you are performance-tuning a particular query, you might be able to improve performance by adjusting the fetch size to better match the use of the query.

The fetch size can be set on a statement, in which case, all result sets created from that statement will use that fetch size. The fetch size can also be set on a result set at any time. In this case, the next time data needs to be fetched from the database, the driver will copy over as many rows as is specified by the current fetch size.

```
    try {
        // Get the fetch size of a statement
        Statement stmt = connection.createStatement ();
        int fetchSize = stmt.getFetchSize();

        // Set the fetch size on the statement
        stmt.setFetchSize(100);

        // Create a result set
        ResultSet resultSet = stmt.executeQuery("SELECT * FROM my_table");

        // Change the fetch size on the result set
        resultSet.setFetchSize(100);
    } catch (SQLException e) {
    }
```

Tables

ε245. Creating a Database Table

This example creates a table called my_table with one column, col_string, which holds strings.

```
    try {
        Statement stmt = connection.createStatement();

        // Create table called 'my_table'
        String sql = "CREATE TABLE my_table(col_string VARCHAR(254))";

        stmt.executeUpdate(sql);
    } catch (SQLException e) {
    }
```

ε246. Deleting a Database Table

This example deletes a table called my_table from a database.

```
    try {
        Statement stmt = connection.createStatement();
        stmt.executeUpdate("DROP TABLE my_table");
    } catch (SQLException e) {
    }
```

Class   *Interface*   —extends   - - -implements   ○ abstract   ● final   ^—has superclass   ‿—has subclass   package—see other volume

ε247. Listing All Table Names in a Database

```
try {
    // Gets the database metadata
    DatabaseMetaData dbmd = connection.getMetaData();

    // Specify the type of object; in this case we want tables
    String[] types = {"TABLE"};
    ResultSet resultSet = dbmd.getTables(null, null, "%", types);

    // Get the table names
    while (resultSet.next()) {
        // Get the table name
        String tableName = resultSet.getString(3);

        // Get the table's catalog and schema names (if any)
        String tableCatalog = resultSet.getString(1);
        String tableSchema = resultSet.getString(2);
    }
} catch (SQLException e) {
}
```

ε248. Creating a MySQL Table to Store Java Types

This example creates a MySQL table called mysql_all_table to store Java types.

```
try {
    Statement stmt = connection.createStatement();

    String sql = "CREATE TABLE mysql_all_table("
        + "col_boolean BOOL, " // boolean
        + "col_byte TINYINT, " // byte
        + "col_short SMALLINT, " // short
        + "col_int INTEGER, " // int
        + "col_long BIGINT, " // long
        + "col_float FLOAT, " // float
        + "col_double DOUBLE PRECISION, " // double
        + "col_bigdecimal DECIMAL(13,0), " // BigDecimal
        + "col_string VARCHAR(254), " // String
        + "col_date DATE, " // Date
        + "col_time TIME, " // Time
        + "col_timestamp TIMESTAMP, " // Timestamp
        + "col_asciistream TEXT, " // AsciiStream (< 2^16 bytes)
        + "col_binarystream LONGBLOB, " // BinaryStream (< 2^32 bytes)
        + "col_blob BLOB)"; // Blob (< 2^16 bytes)

    stmt.executeUpdate(sql);
} catch (SQLException e) {
}
```

ε249. Creating an Oracle Table to Store Java Types

This example creates an Oracle table called oracle_all_table to store Java types.

Oracle does not support the boolean Java type directly. A typical workaround is to use the Oracle CHAR(1) type and convert the boolean value to and from a string. Typically, false is converted to F and true is converted to T.

```
try {
    Statement stmt = connection.createStatement();

    // Create a VARRAY type; see "ε301. Creating a VARRAY Type in an Oracle Database"
    stmt.execute("CREATE TYPE number_varray AS VARRAY(10) OF NUMBER(12, 2)");
```

```
        // Create an OBJECT type; "ε296. Creating an OBJECT Type in an Oracle Database"
        stmt.execute ("CREATE TYPE my_object AS OBJECT(col_string2 VARCHAR(30), col_int2 INTE-
    GER)");

        // Note that Oracle database only allows at most one column of LONG type in a table.
        // Column Name Oracle Type Java Type
        String sql = "CREATE TABLE oracle_all_table("
            + "col_short SMALLINT, " // short
            + "col_int INTEGER, " // int
            + "col_float REAL, " // float; can also be NUMBER
            + "col_double DOUBLE PRECISION, " // double; can also be FLOAT or NUMBER
            + "col_bigdecimal DECIMAL(13,0), " // BigDecimal
            + "col_string VARCHAR2(254), " // String; can also be CHAR(n)
            + "col_characterstream LONG, " // CharacterStream or AsciiStream
            + "col_bytes RAW(2000), " // byte[]; can also be LONG RAW(n)
            + "col_binarystream RAW(2000), " // BinaryStream; can also be LONG RAW(n)
            + "col_timestamp DATE, " // Timestamp
            + "col_clob CLOB, " // Clob
            + "col_blob BLOB, " // Blob; can also be BFILE
            + "col_array number_varray, " // oracle.sql.ARRAY
            + "col_object my_object)"; // oracle.sql.OBJECT

        stmt.executeUpdate(sql);
    } catch (SQLException e) {
    }
```

ε250. Creating a SQLServer Table to Store Java Types

This example creates a SQLServer table called sqlserver_all_table to store Java types.

```
    try {
        Statement stmt = connection.createStatement();

        // Column Name SQLServer Type Java Type
        String sql = "CREATE TABLE sqlserver_all_table("
            + "col_boolean BIT, " // boolean
            + "col_byte TINYINT, " // byte
            + "col_short SMALLINT, " // short
            + "col_int INTEGER, " // int
            + "col_float REAL, " // float
            + "col_double DOUBLE PRECISION, " // double
            + "col_bigdecimal DECIMAL(13,0), " // BigDecimal; can also be NUMERIC(p,s)
            + "col_string VARCHAR(254), " // String
            + "col_date DATETIME, " // Date
            + "col_time DATETIME, " // Time
            + "col_timestamp TIMESTAMP, " // Timestamp
            + "col_characterstream TEXT, " // CharacterStream or AsciiStream (< 2 GBytes)
            + "col_binarystream IMAGE)"; // BinaryStream (< 2 GBytes)

        stmt.executeUpdate(sql);
    } catch (SQLException e) {
    }
```

ε251. Getting Rows from a Database Table

A SQL SELECT query is used to get data from a table. The results of the select query is called a result set. This example executes a SQL SELECT query and creates a result set.

See also "ε252. Getting Data from a Result Set".

```
try {
    // Create a result set containing all data from 'my_table'
    Statement stmt = connection.createStatement();
    ResultSet rs = stmt.executeQuery("SELECT * FROM my_table");
} catch (SQLException e) {
}
```

ε252. Getting Data from a Result Set

A result set contains the results of a SQL query. The results are kept in a set of "rows", one of which is designated the current row. A row must be made current before data can be retrieved from it. The result set maintains a reference to the current row called the "cursor".

The cursor is positioned before the first row when a result set is created. When a result set's next() method is called, the cursor moves to the first row of the result set and that row becomes the current row.

There are two ways to retrieve the data from the current row. The first uses a column index starting from 1. The second uses a column name. For example, with the query 'SELECT col1, col2 FROM table', the value for col2 can be retrieved using a column index of 2 or with the column name col2. This example demonstrates both methods.

```
try {
    // Create a result set containing all data from 'my_table'
    Statement stmt = connection.createStatement();
    ResultSet rs = stmt.executeQuery("SELECT * FROM my_table");

    // Fetch each row from the result set
    while (rs.next()) {
        // Get the data from the row using the column index
        String s = rs.getString(1);

        // Get the data from the row using the column name
        s = rs.getString("col_string");
    }
} catch (SQLException e) {
}
```

Here is another example of retrieving data from a result that uses the various getXXX() methods. This example uses the table created in "ε248. Creating a MySQL Table to Store Java Types".

```
try {
    // Create a result set containing all data from 'mysql_all_table'
    Statement stmt = connection.createStatement();
    ResultSet rs = stmt.executeQuery("SELECT * FROM mysql_all_table");

    // Fetch each row from the result set
    while (rs.next()) {
        boolean bool = rs.getBoolean("col_boolean");
        byte b = rs.getByte("col_byte");
        short s = rs.getShort("col_short");
        int i = rs.getInt("col_int");
        long l = rs.getLong("col_long");
```

Packages

```
                float f = rs.getFloat("col_float");
                double d = rs.getDouble("col_double");
                BigDecimal bd = rs.getBigDecimal("col_bigdecimal");
                String str = rs.getString("col_string");
                Date date = rs.getDate("col_date");
                Time t = rs.getTime("col_time");
                Timestamp ts = rs.getTimestamp("col_timestamp");
                InputStream ais = rs.getAsciiStream("col_asciistream");
                InputStream bis = rs.getBinaryStream("col_binarystream");
                Blob blob = rs.getBlob("col_blob");
            }
        } catch (SQLException e) {
        }
```

ε253. Determining If a Fetched Value Is NULL

When a ResultSet.getXXX() method encounters a NULL in the database, it will convert it to a default value. For example, if NULL was encountered in a NUMBER field, ResultSet.getInt() will return 0. In order to determine whether or not the actual value is a NULL, wasNull() must be called. This method must be called immediately after the value is fetched from the result set.

```
        // Fetch each row from the result set
        while (resultSet.next()) {
```

ε254. Getting the Column Names in a Result Set

```
        try {
            // Create a result set
            Statement stmt = connection.createStatement();
            ResultSet rs = stmt.executeQuery("SELECT * FROM my_table");

            // Get result set meta data
            ResultSetMetaData rsmd = rs.getMetaData();
            int numColumns = rsmd.getColumnCount();

            // Get the column names; column indices start from 1
            for (int i=1; i<numColumns+1; i++) {
                String columnName = rsmd.getColumnName(i);

                // Get the name of the column's table name
                String tableName = rsmd.getTableName(i);
            }
        } catch (SQLException e) {
        }
```

ε255. Getting the Number of Rows in a Database Table

This example gets the number of rows in a table using the SQL statement 'SELECT COUNT(*)'.

```
        try {
            // Select the number of rows in the table
            Statement stmt = connection.createStatement();
            ResultSet resultSet = stmt.executeQuery("SELECT COUNT(*) FROM my_table");

            // Get the number of rows from the result set
            resultSet.next();
            int rowcount = resultSet.getInt(1);
        } catch (SQLException e) {
        }
```

Class   *Interface*   —extends   - - -implements   ◯ abstract   ● final   ^—has superclass   ‿—has subclass   package—see other volume

ε256. Getting BLOB Data from a Database Table

A BLOB is a reference to data in a database. This example demonstrates how to retrieves bytes from a BLOB.

```java
try {
    Statement stmt = connection.createStatement();
    ResultSet rs = stmt.executeQuery("SELECT col_blob FROM mysql_all_table");

    if (rs.next()) {
        // Get the BLOB from the result set
        Blob blob = rs.getBlob("col_blob");

        // Get the number bytes in the BLOB
        long blobLength = blob.length();

        // Get bytes from the BLOB in a byte array
        int pos = 1; // position is 1-based
        int len = 10;
        byte[] bytes = blob.getBytes(pos, len);

        // Get bytes from the BLOB using a stream
        InputStream is = blob.getBinaryStream();
        int b = is.read();
    }
} catch (IOException e) {
} catch (SQLException e) {
}
```

ε257. Matching with Wildcards in a SQL Statement

SQL provides wildcard matching of text using the LIKE clause. Here is a SQL statement that uses a LIKE clause and a wildcard character. This SQL statement will find all rows with names that start with 'Pat'.

```
SELECT * FROM my_table WHERE name LIKE 'Pat%'
```

There are two wildcard characters available. The underscore (_) matches any character. The percent sign (%) matches zero or more characters.

```java
try {
    // Create a statement
    Statement stmt = connection.createStatement();

    // Select the row if col_string contains the word pat
    String sql = "SELECT * FROM my_table WHERE col_string LIKE '%pat%'";

    // Select the row if col_string ends with the word pat
    sql = "SELECT * FROM my_table WHERE col_string LIKE 'pat%'";

    // Select the row if col_string starts with abc and ends with xyz
    sql = "SELECT * FROM my_table WHERE col_string LIKE 'abc%xyz'";

    // Select the row if col_string equals the word pat%
    sql = "SELECT * FROM my_table WHERE col_string LIKE 'pat\\%'";

    // Select the row if col_string has 3 characters and starts with p and ends with t
    sql = "SELECT * FROM my_table WHERE col_string LIKE 'p_t'";

    // Select the row if col_string equals p_t
    sql = "SELECT * FROM my_table WHERE col_string LIKE 'p\\_t'";

    // Execute the query
    ResultSet resultSet = stmt.executeQuery(sql);
} catch (SQLException e) {
}
```

Inserting and Updating Data

ε258. Inserting a Row into a Database Table

```
try {
    Statement stmt = connection.createStatement();

    // Prepare a statement to insert a record
    String sql = "INSERT INTO my_table (col_string) VALUES('a string')";

    // Execute the insert statement
    stmt.executeUpdate(sql);
} catch (SQLException e) {
}
```

ε259. Inserting a Row into a Database Table Using a Prepared Statement

If you have a SQL statement that needs to be executed many times but with different values, a prepared statement can be used to improve performance. For example, if you have a website that looks up product information with a product id using the same query each time, a prepared statement should be used. A prepared statement is a precompiled SQL statement and its use saves the database from repeatedly having to compile the SQL statement each time it is executed.

A query in a prepared statement contains placeholders (represented by the '?' character) instead of explicit values. You set values for these placeholders and then execute the prepared statement.

```
try {
    // Prepare a statement to insert a record
    String sql = "INSERT INTO my_table (col_string) VALUES(?)";
    PreparedStatement pstmt = connection.prepareStatement(sql);

    // Insert 10 rows
    for (int i=0; i<10; i++) {
        // Set the value
        pstmt.setString(1, "row "+i);

        // Insert the row
        pstmt.executeUpdate();
    }
} catch (SQLException e) {
}
```

Here is another example of inserting with a prepared statement that uses the various setXXX() methods. This example uses the table created in "ε248. Creating a MySQL Table to Store Java Types".

```
try {
    // Prepare a statement to insert a record
    String sql = "INSERT INTO mysql_all_table("
        + "col_boolean,"
        + "col_byte,"
        + "col_short,"
        + "col_int,"
        + "col_long,"
        + "col_float,"
        + "col_double,"
        + "col_bigdecimal,"
        + "col_string,"
        + "col_date,"
        + "col_time,"
```

Class   *Interface*   —extends   - - -implements   ○ abstract   ● final   ⌐—has superclass   ⌐—has subclass   package—see other volume

```
                + "col_timestamp,"
                + "col_asciistream,"
                + "col_binarystream,"
                + "col_blob) "
                + "VALUES(?,?,?,?,?,?,?,?,?,?,?,?,?,?,?)";
        PreparedStatement pstmt = connection.prepareStatement(sql);

        // Set the values
        pstmt.setBoolean(1, true);
        pstmt.setByte(2, (byte)123);
        pstmt.setShort(3, (short)123);
        pstmt.setInt(4, 123);
        pstmt.setLong(5, 123L);
        pstmt.setFloat(6, 1.23F);
        pstmt.setDouble(7, 1.23D);
        pstmt.setBigDecimal(8, new BigDecimal(1.23));
        pstmt.setString(9, "a string");
        pstmt.setDate(10, new java.sql.Date(System.currentTimeMillis()));
        pstmt.setTime(11, new Time(System.currentTimeMillis()));
        pstmt.setTimestamp(12, new Timestamp(System.currentTimeMillis()));

        // Set the ascii stream
        File file = new File("infilename1");
        FileInputStream is = new FileInputStream(file);
        pstmt.setAsciiStream(13, is, (int)file.length());

        // Set the binary stream
        file = new File("infilename2");
        is = new FileInputStream(file);
        pstmt.setBinaryStream(14, is, (int)file.length());

        // Set the blob
        file = new File("infilename3");
        is = new FileInputStream(file);
        pstmt.setBinaryStream(15, is, (int)file.length());

        // Insert the row
        pstmt.executeUpdate();
    } catch (SQLException e) {
    } catch (FileNotFoundException e) {
    }
```

ε260. Getting and Inserting Binary Data into an Database Table

This example inserts and retrieves binary data into the table created in "ε248. Creating a MySQL Table to Store Java Types".

```
    try {
        // Prepare a statement to insert binary data
        String sql = "INSERT INTO mysql_all_table (col_binarystream) VALUES(?)";
        PreparedStatement pstmt = connection.prepareStatement(sql);

        // Create some binary data
        byte[] buffer = "some data".getBytes();

        // Set value for the prepared statement
        pstmt.setBytes(1, buffer);

        // Insert the data
        pstmt.executeUpdate();
        pstmt.close();
```

```
        // Select records from the table
        Statement stmt = connection.createStatement();
        ResultSet resultSet = stmt.executeQuery("SELECT * FROM mysql_all_table");
        while (resultSet.next()) {
            // Get data from the binary column
            byte[] bytes = resultSet.getBytes("col_binarystream");
        }
    } catch (SQLException e) {
    }
```

ε261. Updating a Row in a Database Table

This example updates a row in a table.

```
    try {
        Statement stmt = connection.createStatement();

        // Prepare a statement to update a record
        String sql = "UPDATE my_table SET col_string='a new string' WHERE col_string = 'a string'";

        // Execute the insert statement
        int updateCount = stmt.executeUpdate(sql);
        // updateCount contains the number of updated rows
    } catch (SQLException e) {
    }
```

Deleting Data

ε262. Deleting a Row from a Database Table

```
    try {
        // Create a statement
        Statement stmt = connection.createStatement();

        // Prepare a statement to insert a record
        String sql = "DELETE FROM my_table WHERE col_string='a string'";

        // Execute the delete statement
        int deleteCount = stmt.executeUpdate(sql);
        // deleteCount contains the number of deleted rows

        // Use a prepared statement to delete

        // Prepare a statement to delete a record
        sql = "DELETE FROM my_table WHERE col_string=?";
        PreparedStatement pstmt = connection.prepareStatement(sql);
        // Set the value
        pstmt.setString(1, "a string");
        deleteCount = pstmt.executeUpdate();
        System.err.println(e.getMessage());
```

ε263. Deleting All Rows from a Database Table

All the rows in a table can be deleted either by using the TRUNCATE or DELETE SQL statement. TRUNCATE is faster than DELETE since it does not generate rollback information, does not fire any delete trigger, and does not record any information.

This example deletes all the rows from a database table called my_table.

Class *Interface* —extends - - -implements ◯ abstract ● final ^—has superclass ‿—has subclass package—see other volume

```
try {
    Statement stmt = connection.createStatement();

    // Use TRUNCATE
    String sql = "TRUNCATE my_table";

    // Use DELETE
    sql = "DELETE FROM my_table";

    // Execute deletion
    stmt.executeUpdate(sql);
} catch (SQLException e) {
}
```

Batching

ε264. Determining If a Database Supports Batching

With batch updating, a set of SQL statements is assembled and then sent altogether to the database for execution. Batch updating can improve performance.

```
try {
    DatabaseMetaData dmd = connection.getMetaData();
    if (dmd.supportsBatchUpdates()) {
        // Batching is supported
    } else {
        // Batching is not supported
    }
} catch (SQLException e) {
}
```

ε265. Executing a Batch of SQL Statements in a Database

With batch updating, a set of SQL statements is assembled and then sent altogether to the database for execution. Batch updating can improve performance.

This example creates a batch of insert statements. Auto-commit is disabled so that you have the choice of committing or not in the event of an exception.

```
try {
    // Disable auto-commit
    connection.setAutoCommit(false);

    // Create a prepared statement
    String sql = "INSERT INTO my_table VALUES(?)";
    PreparedStatement pstmt = connection.prepareStatement(sql);

    // Insert 10 rows of data
    for (int i=0; i<10; i++) {
        pstmt.setString(1, ""+i);
        pstmt.addBatch();
    }

    // Execute the batch
    int [] updateCounts = pstmt.executeBatch();

    // All statements were successfully executed.
    // updateCounts contains one element for each batched statement.
    // updateCounts[i] contains the number of rows affected by that statement.
    processUpdateCounts(updateCounts);

    // Since there were no errors, commit
```

Packages

```
            connection.commit();
    } catch (BatchUpdateException e) {
        // Not all of the statements were successfully executed
        int[] updateCounts = e.getUpdateCounts();

        // Some databases will continue to execute after one fails.
        // If so, updateCounts.length will equal the number of batched statements.
        // If not, updateCounts.length will equal the number of successfully executed statements
        processUpdateCounts(updateCounts);

        // Either commit the successfully executed statements or rollback the entire batch
        connection.rollback();
    } catch (SQLException e) {
    }

    public static void processUpdateCounts(int[] updateCounts) {
        for (int i=0; i<updateCounts.length; i++) {
            if (updateCounts[i] >= 0) {
                // Successfully executed; the number represents number of affected rows
            } else if (updateCounts[i] == Statement.SUCCESS_NO_INFO) {
                // Successfully executed; number of affected rows not available
            } else if (updateCounts[i] == Statement.EXECUTE_FAILED) {
                // Failed to execute
            }
        }
    }
}
```

Scrollable Result Sets

ε266. Determining If a Database Supports Scrollable Result Sets

A scrollable result set allows the cursor to be moved to any row in the result set. This capability is useful for GUI tools that browse result sets.

There are two types of scrollable result sets. An "insensitive" scrollable result set is one where the values captured in the result set never change, even if changes are made to the table from which the data was retrieved. A "sensitive" scrollable result set is one where the current values in the table are reflected in the result set. So if a change is made to a row in the table, the result set will show the new data when the cursor is moved to that row.

```
    try {
        DatabaseMetaData dmd = connection.getMetaData();
        if (dmd.supportsResultSetType(ResultSet.TYPE_SCROLL_INSENSITIVE)) {
            // Insensitive scrollable result sets are supported
        }
        if (dmd.supportsResultSetType(ResultSet.TYPE_SCROLL_SENSITIVE)) {
            // Sensitive scrollable result sets are supported
        }
        if (!dmd.supportsResultSetType(ResultSet.TYPE_SCROLL_INSENSITIVE)
                && !dmd.supportsResultSetType(ResultSet.TYPE_SCROLL_SENSITIVE)) {
            // Updatable result sets are not supported
        }
    } catch (SQLException e) {
    }
```

Class   *Interface*   —extends   - - -implements   ○ abstract   ● final   ⌐has superclass   ⌐has subclass   package —see other volume

ε267. Creating a Scrollable Result Set

A scrollable result set allows the cursor to be moved to any row in the result set. This capability is useful for GUI tools for browsing result sets.

See also "ε266. Determining If a Database Supports Scrollable Result Sets".

```
try {
    // Create an insensitive scrollable result set
    Statement stmt = connection.createStatement(
        ResultSet.TYPE_SCROLL_INSENSITIVE, ResultSet.CONCUR_READ_ONLY);

    // Create a sensitive scrollable result set
    stmt = connection.createStatement(
        ResultSet.TYPE_SCROLL_SENSITIVE, ResultSet.CONCUR_READ_ONLY);
} catch (SQLException e) {
}
```

ε268. Determining If a Result Set Is Scrollable

See also "ε267. Creating a Scrollable Result Set".

```
try {
    // Get type of the result set
    int type = resultSet.getType();

    if (type == ResultSet.TYPE_SCROLL_INSENSITIVE
        || type == ResultSet.TYPE_SCROLL_SENSITIVE) {
        // Result set is scrollable
    } else {
        // Result set is not scrollable
    }
} catch (SQLException e) {
}
```

ε269. Moving the Cursor in a Scrollable Result Set

This example demonstrates the various methods for moving the cursor in a scrollable result set.

```
try {
    // Create a scrollable result set
    Statement stmt = connection.createStatement(
        ResultSet.TYPE_SCROLL_INSENSITIVE, ResultSet.CONCUR_READ_ONLY);
    ResultSet resultSet = stmt.executeQuery("SELECT * FROM my_table");

    // Move cursor forward
    while (resultSet.next()) {
        // Get data at cursor
        String s = resultSet.getString(1);
    }

    // Move cursor backward
    while (resultSet.previous()) {
        // Get data at cursor
        String s = resultSet.getString(1);
    }

    // Move cursor to the first row
    resultSet.first();

    // Move cursor to the last row
    resultSet.last();

    // Move cursor to the end, after the last row
```

```
            resultSet.afterLast();

            // Move cursor to the beginning, before the first row.
            // cursor position is 0.
            resultSet.beforeFirst();

            // Move cursor to the second row
            resultSet.absolute(2);

            // Move cursor to the last row
            resultSet.absolute(-1);

            // Move cursor to the second last row
            resultSet.absolute(-2);

            // Move cursor down 5 rows from the current row. If this moves
            // cursor beyond the last row, cursor is put after the last row
            resultSet.relative(5);

            // Move cursor up 3 rows from the current row. If this moves
            // cursor beyond the first row, cursor is put before the first row
            resultSet.relative(-3);
        } catch (SQLException e) {
        }
```

ε270. Getting the Cursor Position in a Scrollable Result Set

```
        try {
            // Create a scrollable result set
            Statement stmt = connection.createStatement(
                ResultSet.TYPE_SCROLL_INSENSITIVE, ResultSet.CONCUR_READ_ONLY);
            ResultSet resultSet = stmt.executeQuery("SELECT * FROM my_table");

            // Get cursor position
            int pos = resultSet.getRow(); // 0
            boolean b = resultSet.isBeforeFirst(); // true

            // Move cursor to the first row
            resultSet.next();

            // Get cursor position
            pos = resultSet.getRow(); // 1
            b = resultSet.isFirst(); // true

            // Move cursor to the last row
            resultSet.last();

            // Get cursor position
            pos = resultSet.getRow(); // If table has 10 rows, value would be 10
            b = resultSet.isLast(); // true

            // Move cursor past last row
            resultSet.afterLast();

            // Get cursor position
            pos = resultSet.getRow(); // If table has 10 rows, value would be 11
            b = resultSet.isAfterLast(); // true
        } catch (SQLException e) {
        }
```

ε271. Getting the Number of Rows in a Table Using a Scrollable Result Set

This example gets the number of rows in a scrollable result set by moving the cursor to the last row of the result set and then calling ResultSet.getRow().

```
try {
    // Create a scrollable result set
    Statement stmt = connection.createStatement(
        ResultSet.TYPE_SCROLL_INSENSITIVE, ResultSet.CONCUR_READ_ONLY);
    ResultSet resultSet = stmt.executeQuery("SELECT * FROM my_table");

    // Move to the end of the result set
    resultSet.last();

    // Get the row number of the last row which is also the row count
    int rowCount = resultSet.getRow();
} catch (SQLException e) {
}
```

Updatable Result Sets

ε272. Determining If a Database Supports Updatable Result Sets

An updatable result set allows modification to data in a table through the result set.

```
try {
    DatabaseMetaData dmd = connection.getMetaData();
    if (dmd.supportsResultSetConcurrency(
        ResultSet.TYPE_FORWARD_ONLY, ResultSet.CONCUR_UPDATABLE)) {
        // Updatable result sets are supported
    } else {
        // Updatable result sets are not supported
    }
} catch (SQLException e) {
}
```

ε273. Creating an Updatable Result Set

An updatable result set allows modification to data in a table through the result set. If the database does not support updatable result sets, the result sets returned from executeQuery() will be read-only. To get updatable results, the Statement object used to create the result sets must have the concurrency type ResultSet.CONCUR_UPDATABLE.

The query of an updatable result set must specify the primary key as one of the selected columns and select from only one table. For some drivers, 'SELECT * FROM my_table' will return a read-only result set, so make sure that you specify the column names.

See also "ε272. Determining If a Database Supports Updatable Result Sets".

```
try {
    // Create a statement that will return updatable result sets
    Statement stmt = connection.createStatement(
        ResultSet.TYPE_SCROLL_SENSITIVE, ResultSet.CONCUR_UPDATABLE);

    // Primary key col_string must be specified so that the result set is updatable
    ResultSet resultSet = stmt.executeQuery("SELECT col_string FROM my_table");
} catch (SQLException e) {
}
```

Packages

ε274. Determining If a Result Set Is Updatable

See also "ε273. Creating an Updatable Result Set".

```
try {
    // Get concurrency of the result set
    int concurrency = resultSet.getConcurrency();

    if (concurrency == ResultSet.CONCUR_UPDATABLE) {
        // Result set is updatable
    } else {
        // Result set is not updatable
    }
} catch (SQLException e) {
}
```

ε275. Updating a Row in a Database Table Using an Updatable Result Set

Updating the current row of an updatable result set involves calling ResultSet.updateXXX() methods followed by a call to updateRow().

See also "ε273. Creating an Updatable Result Set".

```
try {
    // Create an updatable result set
    Statement stmt = connection.createStatement(
        ResultSet.TYPE_SCROLL_SENSITIVE, ResultSet.CONCUR_UPDATABLE);
    ResultSet resultSet = stmt.executeQuery("SELECT * FROM my_table");

    // Move cursor to the row to update
    resultSet.first();

    // Update the value of column col_string on that row
    resultSet.updateString("col_string", "new data");

    // Update the row; if auto-commit is enabled, update is committed
    resultSet.updateRow();
} catch (SQLException e) {
}
```

ε276. Cancelling Updates to an Updatable Result Set

The effects of calling Result.updateXXX() methods can be cancelled by calling cancelRowUpdates(). However, updates cannot be cancelled after updateRow() has been called.

```
try {
    // Create an updatable result set
    Statement stmt = connection.createStatement(
        ResultSet.TYPE_SCROLL_SENSITIVE, ResultSet.CONCUR_UPDATABLE);
    ResultSet resultSet = stmt.executeQuery("SELECT * FROM my_table");

    // Move cursor to the row to update
    resultSet.first();

    // Update the value of column col_string on that row
    resultSet.updateString("col_string", "new data");

    // Discard the update to the row
    resultSet.cancelRowUpdates();
} catch (SQLException e) {
}
```

ε277. Inserting a Row into a Database Table Using an Updatable Result Set

An updatable result supports a row called the "insert row". It is a buffer for holding the values of a new row. After the fields in the "insert row" are filled, the new row can be inserted into the database using Result.insertRow().

```
try {
    // Create an updatable result set
    Statement stmt = connection.createStatement(
        ResultSet.TYPE_SCROLL_SENSITIVE, ResultSet.CONCUR_UPDATABLE);
    ResultSet resultSet = stmt.executeQuery("SELECT * FROM my_table");

    // Move cursor to the "insert row"
    resultSet.moveToInsertRow();

    // Set values for the new row.
    resultSet.updateString("col_string", "new data");

    // Insert the row
    resultSet.insertRow();
} catch (SQLException e) {
}
```

ε278. Deleting a Row from a Database Table Using an Updatable Result Set

```
try {
    // Create an updatable result set
    Statement stmt = connection.createStatement(
        ResultSet.TYPE_SCROLL_SENSITIVE, ResultSet.CONCUR_UPDATABLE);
    ResultSet resultSet = stmt.executeQuery("SELECT * FROM my_table");

    // Delete the first row
    resultSet.first();
    resultSet.deleteRow();
} catch (SQLException e) {
}
```

ε279. Refreshing a Row in an Updatable Result Set

```
try {
    // Create an updatable result set
    Statement stmt = connection.createStatement(
        ResultSet.TYPE_SCROLL_SENSITIVE, ResultSet.CONCUR_UPDATABLE);
    ResultSet resultSet = stmt.executeQuery("SELECT * FROM my_table");

    // Use the result set...

    // Retrieve the current values of the row from the database
    resultSet.refreshRow();
} catch(SQLException e) {
}
```

Procedures and Functions

ε280. Getting the Stored Procedure Names in a Database

This example retrieves the names of all stored procedures in a database.

```
try {
    // Get database metadata
    DatabaseMetaData dbmd = connection.getMetaData();
```

```
        // Get all stored procedures in any schema and catalog
        ResultSet resultSet = dbmd.getProcedures(null, null, "%");

        // Get stored procedure names from the result set
        while (resultSet.next()) {
            String procName = resultSet.getString(3);
        }
    } catch (SQLException e) {
    }
```

ε281. Calling a Stored Procedure in a Database

This example demonstrates how to call stored procedures with IN, OUT, and IN/OUT parameters.

```
    CallableStatement cs;
    try {
    // Call a procedure with no parameters
        cs = connection.prepareCall("{call myproc}");
        cs.execute();

    // Call a procedure with one IN parameter
        cs = connection.prepareCall("{call myprocin(?)}");

        // Set the value for the IN parameter
        cs.setString(1, "a string");

        // Execute the stored procedure
        cs.execute();

    // Call a procedure with one OUT parameter
        cs = connection.prepareCall("{call myprocout(?)}");

        // Register the type of the OUT parameter
        cs.registerOutParameter(1, Types.VARCHAR);

        // Execute the stored procedure and retrieve the OUT value
        cs.execute();
        String outParam = cs.getString(1); // OUT parameter

    // Call a procedure with one IN/OUT parameter
        cs = connection.prepareCall("{call myprocinout(?)}");

        // Register the type of the IN/OUT parameter
        cs.registerOutParameter(1, Types.VARCHAR);

        // Set the value for the IN/OUT parameter
        cs.setString(1, "a string");

        // Execute the stored procedure and retrieve the IN/OUT value
        cs.execute();
        outParam = cs.getString(1); // OUT parameter
    } catch (SQLException e) {
    }
```

ε282. Calling a Function in a Database

A function is essentially a stored procedure that returns a result. This example demonstrates how to call functions with IN, OUT, and IN/OUT parameters.

```
    CallableStatement cs;
    try {
    // Call a function with no parameters; the function returns a VARCHAR
```

```
    // Prepare the callable statement
    cs = connection.prepareCall("{? = call myfunc}");

    // Register the type of the return value
    cs.registerOutParameter(1, i);

    // Execute and retrieve the returned value
    cs.execute();
    String retValue = cs.getString(1);

// Call a function with one IN parameter; the function returns a VARCHAR
    cs = connection.prepareCall("{? = call myfuncin(?)}");

    // Register the type of the return value
    cs.registerOutParameter(1, Types.VARCHAR);

    // Set the value for the IN parameter
    cs.setString(2, "a string");

    // Execute and retrieve the returned value
    cs.execute();
    retValue = cs.getString(1);

// Call a function with one OUT parameter; the function returns a VARCHAR
    cs = connection.prepareCall("{? = call myfuncout(?)}");

    // Register the types of the return value and OUT parameter
    cs.registerOutParameter(1, Types.VARCHAR);
    cs.registerOutParameter(2, Types.VARCHAR);

    // Execute and retrieve the returned values
    cs.execute();
    retValue = cs.getString(1); // return value
    String outParam = cs.getString(2); // OUT parameter

// Call a function with one IN/OUT parameter; the function returns a VARCHAR
    cs = connection.prepareCall("{? = call myfuncinout(?)}");

    // Register the types of the return value and OUT parameter
    cs.registerOutParameter(1, Types.VARCHAR);
    cs.registerOutParameter(2, Types.VARCHAR);

    // Set the value for the IN/OUT parameter
    cs.setString(2, "a string");

    // Execute and retrieve the returned values
    cs.execute();
    retValue = cs.getString(1); // return value
    outParam = cs.getString(2); // IN/OUT parameter
} catch (SQLException e) {
}
```

ε283. Creating a Stored Procedure or Function in an Oracle Database

A stored procedure or function can be created with no parameters, IN parameters, OUT parameters, or IN/OUT parameters. There can be many parameters per stored procedure or function.

An IN parameter is a parameter whose value is passed into a stored procedure/function module. The value of an IN parameter is a constant; it can't be changed or reassigned within the module.

An OUT parameter is a parameter whose value is passed out of the stored procedure/function module, back to the calling PL/SQL block. An OUT parameter must be a variable, not a constant. It can be found only on the left-hand side of an assignment in the module. You cannot assign a default value to an OUT parameter outside of the module's body. In other words, an OUT parameter functions like an uninitialized variable.

java.sql

An IN/OUT parameter is a parameter that functions as an IN or an OUT parameter or both. The value of the IN/OUT parameter is passed into the stored procedure/function and a new value can be assigned to the parameter and passed out of the module. An IN/OUT parameter must be a variable, not a constant. However, it can be found on both sides of an assignment. In other words, an IN/OUT parameter functions like an initialized variable.

This example demonstrates the creation of a stored procedure called myproc with no parameter, myprocin with an IN parameter, myprocout with OUT parameter, and myprocinout with an IN/OUT parameter in an Oracle database.

This example also demonstrates the creation of a function called myfunc with no parameter, myfuncin with an IN parameter, myfuncout with OUT parameter, and myfuncinout with an IN/OUT parameter in an Oracle database. The function returns a VARCHAR.

```
try {
        Statement stmt = connection.createStatement();

        // Create procedure myproc with no parameters
        String procedure =
            "CREATE OR REPLACE PROCEDURE myproc IS "
            + "BEGIN "
            + "INSERT INTO oracle_table VALUES('string 1'); "
            + "END;";
        stmt.executeUpdate(procedure);

        // Create procedure myprocin with an IN parameter named x.
        // IN is the default mode for parameter, so both 'x VARCHAR' and 'x IN VARCHAR' are valid
        procedure =
            "CREATE OR REPLACE PROCEDURE myprocin(x VARCHAR) IS "
            + "BEGIN "
            + "INSERT INTO oracle_table VALUES(x); "
            + "END;";
        stmt.executeUpdate(procedure);

        // Create procedure myprocout with an OUT parameter named x
        procedure =
            "CREATE OR REPLACE PROCEDURE myprocout(x OUT VARCHAR) IS "
            + "BEGIN "
            + "INSERT INTO oracle_table VALUES('string 2'); "
            + "x := 'outvalue'; " // Assign a value to x
            + "END;";
        stmt.executeUpdate(procedure);

        // Create procedure myprocinout with an IN/OUT parameter named x.
        // x functions as an IN parameter and also as an OUT parameter.
        procedure =
            "CREATE OR REPLACE PROCEDURE myprocinout(x IN OUT VARCHAR) IS "
            + "BEGIN "
            + "INSERT INTO oracle_table VALUES(x); " // Use x as IN parameter
            + "x := 'outvalue'; " // Use x as OUT parameter
            + "END;";
        stmt.executeUpdate(procedure);

        // Create a function named 'myfunc' which returns a VARCHAR value 'a returned string'.
        // The function has no parameter.
        String function =
            "CREATE OR REPLACE FUNCTION myfunc RETURN VARCHAR IS "
            + "BEGIN "
```

```
        + "RETURN 'a returned string'; "
        + "END;";
    stmt.executeUpdate(function);

    // Create a function named 'myfuncin' which returns a VARCHAR value 'a returned string'.
    // The function has an IN parameter named x.
    function =
        "CREATE OR REPLACE FUNCTION myfuncin(x VARCHAR) RETURN VARCHAR IS "
        + "BEGIN "
        + "RETURN 'a return string'||x; "
        + "END;";
    stmt.executeUpdate(function);

    // Create a function named 'myfuncout' which returns a VARCHAR value 'a returned string'.
    // The function has an OUT parameter named x whose value 'outvalue' is also
    // returned to the calling PL/SQL block when the execution of the function ends.
    function =
        "CREATE OR REPLACE FUNCTION myfuncout(x OUT VARCHAR) RETURN VARCHAR IS "
        + "BEGIN "
        + "x:= 'outvalue'; "
        + "RETURN 'a returned string'; "
        + "END;";
    stmt.executeUpdate(function);

    // Create a function named 'myfuncinout' that returns a VARCHAR value 'a returned string'.
    // The function has an IN/OUT parameter named x. As an IN parameter, the value of x is
    // defined in the calling PL/SQL block before it is passed in 'myfuncinout'
    // function. As an OUT parameter, the new value of x, 'x value||outvalue', is also
    // returned to the calling PL/SQL block when the execution of the function ends.
    function =
        "CREATE OR REPLACE FUNCTION myfuncinout(x IN OUT VARCHAR) RETURN VARCHAR IS
"
        + "BEGIN "
        + "x:= x||'outvalue'; "
        + "RETURN 'a returned string'; "
        + "END;";
    stmt.executeUpdate(function);
} catch (SQLException e) {
}
```

Database Meta Data

ε284. Listing All Non-SQL92 Keywords Used by a Database

A keyword is a reserved word used by the database. Database objects such as tables or columns cannot be named with a keyword.

This example retrieves a list of keywords for a database. The keyword list from getSQLKeywords() is a comma separated list.

```
try {
    DatabaseMetaData dbmd = connection.getMetaData();

    // Get a list of keywords
    String[] keywords = dbmd.getSQLKeywords().split(",\\s*");
} catch (SQLException e) {
}
```

Examples in an Oracle database include:

ACCESS, ADD, ALTER, AUDIT, CLUSTER, COLUMN, COMMENT, COMPRESS, CONNECT, DATE, DROP, EXCLUSIVE, FILE, IDENTIFIED, IMMEDIATE, INCREMENT, INDEX, INITIAL, INTERSECT, LEVEL, LOCK, LONG, MAXEXTENTS, MINUS, MODE, NOAUDIT, NOCOMPRESS, NOWAIT, NUMBER, OFFLINE, ONLINE, PCTFREE, PRIOR, all_PL_SQL_reserved_ words

Examples in a MySQL database include:

AUTO_INCREMENT,BINARY,BLOB,ENUM,INFILE,LOAD,MEDIUMINT,OPTION,OUTFILE,REPLACE, SET,TEXT,UNSIGNED,ZEROFILL

ε285. Listing the String Functions Supported by a Database

This example retrieves a list of string functions that a database supports.

```
try {
    DatabaseMetaData dbmd = connection.getMetaData();

    // Get the list of string functions
    String[] stringFunctions = dbmd.getStringFunctions().split(",\\s*");
} catch (SQLException e) {
}
```

Examples in an Oracle database include:

CHR, INITCAP, LOWER, LPAD, LTRIM, NLS,_INITCAP, NLS,_LOWER, NLS,_UPPER, REPLACE, RPAD, RTRIM, SOUNDEX, SUBSTR, SUBSTRB, TRANSLATE, UPPER, ASCII, INSTR, INSTRB, LENGTH, LENGTHB, NLSSORT, CHARTOROWID, CONVERT, HEXTORAW, RAWTOHEX, ROWIDTOCHAR, TO_CHAR, TO_DATE, TO_LABEL, TO_MULTI_BYTE, TO_NUMBER, TO_SINGLE_BYTE

Examples in a MySQL database include:

ACII,CHAR,CHAR_LENGTH,CHARACTER_LENGTH,CONCAT,ELT,FIELD,FIND_IN_SET, INSERT,INSTR,INTERVAL,LCASE,LEFT,LENGTH,LOCATE,LOWER,LTRIM,MID,POSITION, OCTET_LENGTH,REPEAT,REPLACE,REVERSE,RIGHT,RTRIM,SPACE,SOUNDEX,SUBSTRING, SUBSTRING_INDEX,TRIM,UCASE,UPPER

ε286. Listing the Numeric Functions Supported by a Database

This example gets a list of numeric functions that a database supports.

```
try {
    DatabaseMetaData dbmd = connection.getMetaData();

    // Get the list of numeric functions
    String[] numericFunctions = dbmd.getNumericFunctions().split(",\\s*");
} catch (SQLException e) {
}
```

Examples in an Oracle database include:

ABS, CEIL, COS, COSH, EXP, FLOOR, LN, LOG, MOD, POWER, ROUND, SIGN, SIN, SINH, SQRT, TAN, TANH, TRUNC, AVG, COUNT, GLB, LUB, MAX, MIN, STDDEV, SUM, VARIANCE

Examples in a MySQL database include:

ABS,ACOS,ASIN,ATAN,ATAN2,BIT_COUNT,CEILING,COS,COT,DEGREES,EXP, FLOOR,LOG,LOG10,MAX,MIN,MOD,PI,POW,POWER,RADIANS,RAND,ROUND,SIN, SQRT,TAN,TRUNCATE

ε287. Listing the System Functions Supported by a Database

This example gets a list of system functions that a database supports.

```
try {
    DatabaseMetaData dbmd = connection.getMetaData();

    // Get the list of system functions
    String[] systemFunctions = dbmd.getSystemFunctions().split(",\\s*");
} catch (SQLException e) {
}
```

Examples in an Oracle database include:

DUMP, GREATEST, GREATEST_LB, LEAST, LEAST_UB, NVL, UID, USER, USERENV, VSIZE

Examples in a MySQL database include:

DUMP, GREATEST, GREATEST_LB, LEAST, LEAST_UB, NVL, UID, USER, USERENV, VSIZE

ε288. Listing the Time and Date Functions Supported by a Database

This example gets a list of time and date functions that a database supports.

```
try {
    DatabaseMetaData dbmd = connection.getMetaData();

    // Get the list of time and date functions
    String timedateFunctions[] = dbmd.getTimeDateFunctions().split(",\\s*");
} catch (SQLException e) {
}
```

Examples in an Oracle database include:

ADD_MONTHS, LAST_DAY, MONTHS_BETWEEN, NEW_TIME, NEXT_DAY, ROUND, SYSDATE, TRUNC

Examples in a MySQL database include:

DAYOFWEEK,WEEKDAY,DAYOFMONTH,DAYOFYEAR,MONTH,DAYNAME,MONTHNAME,QUARTER, WEEK,YEAR,HOUR,MINUTE,SECOND,PERIOD_ADD,PERIOD_DIFF,TO_DAYS,FROM_DAYS, DATE_FORMAT,TIME_FORMAT,CURDATE,CURRENT_DATE,CURTIME,CURRENT_TIME,NOW, SYSDATE,CURRENT_TIMESTAMP,UNIX_TIMESTAMP,FROM_UNIXTIME,SEC_TO_TIME, TIME_TO_SEC

ε289. Getting the Maximum Table Name Length in a Database

This example gets the maximum number of characters allowed in a table name.

```
try {
    // Gets database metadata
    DatabaseMetaData dbmd = connection.getMetaData();

    // Get max table name length
    int length = dbmd.getMaxTableNameLength();
} catch (SQLException e) {
}
```

ε290. Listing Available SQL Types Used by a Database

This example retrieves the SQL data types supported by a database and driver.

```
try {
    // Get database meta data
    DatabaseMetaData dbmd = connection.getMetaData();

    // Get type info
    ResultSet resultSet = dbmd.getTypeInfo();
```

```
        // Retrieve type info from the result set
        while (resultSet.next()) {
            // Get the database-specific type name
            String typeName = resultSet.getString("TYPE_NAME");

            // Get the java.sql.Types type to which this database-specific type is mapped
            short dataType = resultSet.getShort("DATA_TYPE");

            // Get the name of the java.sql.Types value.
            // This method is implemented in "ε291. Getting the Name of a JDBC Type"
            String jdbcTypeName = getJdbcTypeName(dataType);
        }
    } catch (SQLException e) {
    }
```

Here's an example of output for the MySQL database:

```
MySQL Type Name, JDBC Type Name

TINYINT, TINYINT
BIGINT, BIGINT
MEDIUMBLOB, LONGVARBINARY
MEDIUMTEXT, LONGVARBINARY
LONGBLOB, LONGVARBINARY
LONGTEXT, LONGVARBINARY
BLOB, LONGVARBINARY
TEXT, LONGVARBINARY
TINYBLOB, VARBINARY
TINYTEXT, VARBINARY
CHAR, CHAR
NUMERIC, NUMERIC
DECIMAL, DECIMAL
INT, INTEGER
MEDIUMINT, INTEGER
SMALLINT, SMALLINT
FLOAT, FLOAT
DOUBLE, DOUBLE
DOUBLE PRECISION, DOUBLE
REAL, DOUBLE
VARCHAR, VARCHAR
ENUM, VARCHAR
SET, VARCHAR
DATE, DATE
TIME, TIME
DATETIME, TIMESTAMP
TIMESTAMP, TIMESTAMP
```

ε291. Getting the Name of a JDBC Type

This example implements a convenient method for converting a java.sql.Types integer value into a printable name. This method is useful for debugging. The method uses reflection to get all the field names from java.sql.Types. It then retrieves their values and creates a map of values to names.

```
    // This method returns the name of a JDBC type.
    // Returns null if jdbcType is not recognized.
    public static String getJdbcTypeName(int jdbcType) {
        // Use reflection to populate a map of int values to names
        if (map == null) {
```

Class *Interface* —extends - - -implements ○ abstract ● final ^—has superclass ⌄—has subclass package—see other volume

```
        map = new HashMap();

        // Get all field in java.sql.Types
        Field[] fields = java.sql.Types.class.getFields();
        for (int i=0; i<fields.length; i++) {
            try {
                // Get field name
                String name = fields[i].getName();

                // Get field value
                Integer value = (Integer)fields[i].get(null);

                // Add to map
                map.put(value, name);
            } catch (IllegalAccessException e) {
            }
        }
    }

    // Return the JDBC type name
    return (String)map.get(new Integer(jdbcType));
}
static Map map;
```

ε292. Loading a Flat File to a MySQL Table

The default format of a file to load into a MySQL table is as follows: the fields must be separated by tabs, the input lines terminated by '\n', and backslashes(\), newlines (\n), and tabs (\t) escaped by a backslash. The MySQL documentation explains how to change these defaults.

This example loads a flat file called infile.txt to a MySQL table named mysql_2_table with an INT and a VARCHAR(20) column.

```
try {
    // Create the statement
    Statement stmt = connection.createStatement();

    // Load the data
    String filename = "c:\\\\temp\\\\infile.txt";
    String tablename = "mysql_2_table";
    stmt.executeUpdate("LOAD DATA INFILE \"" + filename + "\" INTO TABLE " + tablename);

    // If the file is comma-separated, use this statement
    stmt.executeUpdate("LOAD DATA INFILE \"" + filename + "\" INTO TABLE "
            + tablename + " FIELDS TERMINATED BY ','");

    // If the file is terminated by \r\n, use this statement
    stmt.executeUpdate("LOAD DATA INFILE \"" + filename + "\" INTO TABLE "
            + tablename + " LINES TERMINATED BY '\\r\\n'");
} catch (SQLException e) {
}
```

An example of the contents of infile.txt (\t represents an invisible tab character):

```
123\tString1
234\tString2
```

ε293. Exporting an Oracle Table to a Flat File

This example saves the output from a SELECT statement to a flat file named outfile.txt.

java.sql

To save to a file, turn on the spooler by typing 'spool outfile.txt' at the SQL prompt, execute the SELECT statement, then turn the spooler off by typing 'spool off' at the SQL prompt:

```
SQL> spool outfile.txt
SQL> select * from oracle_2_table;
SQL> spool off
```

You can also create a SQL script to turn on and off the spooler and format the output the way you want:

```
SQL> get_data.sql
```

The contents of get_data.sql are:

```
set term off; // Suppress the display so that you can spool output without seeing the output on the screen.
set heading off; // Turn off heading
set linesize 400; // Set the number of characters per line to 400. Adjust this number to 0 or something for
your real data.
set feedback off; // Turn off feedback
spool outfile.txt; // Spool the output to a file named 'outfile.txt'
select col1 ||','|| col2
from oracle_2_table; // Select each column from table oracle_2_table, delimiting by a comma
spool off;
```

ε294. Loading a Flat File to an Oracle Table

When loading a flat file into Oracle, the fields in the flat file should be separated by delimiters such as tabs or commas. The delimiter can be specified in the control file. The loader will map the fields in the file to the columns in the table. The first field is stored in the first column; the second field is stored in the second column, etc. If there are more fields than columns in the table, the remaining fields will be ignored. If there are less fields than columns in the table, the missing fields will be inserted as null values in the associated columns.

This example loads a flat file called infile.dat to an Oracle table named oracle_2_table with two columns of type INTEGER and VARCHAR(20). To load, run the sqlldr command from the shell as follows:

```
shell> sqlldr userid=userid@sid, control=ctrl_file.txt, log=log, errors=100
123\tString1
234\tString2
```

The contents of the control file ctrl_file.txt are:

```
load data
infile 'infile'
append into table oracle_2_table
fields terminated by ' '
trailing nullcols
(col1 decimal(13,0),
col2 varchar(40))
```

To specify a different terminator, such as a comma, change the fourth line above to:

```
fields terminated by ','
If oracle_2_table is already defined, you can use the following syntax for
the control file ctrl_file.txt:

load data
infile 'infile'
append into table oracle_2_table
fields terminated by ' '
trailing nullcols
```

```
(col1,
col2)
```

ε295. Exporting a MySQL Table to a Flat File

The default format of a file exported from MySQL is as follows: the fields are separated by tabs, the lines terminated by '\n', and backslashes(\), newlines (\n), and tabs (\t) escaped by a backslash. NULL is exported as \N.

This example exports the data in a table called mysql_table2 to a file named outfile.txt.

```
try {
    // Create the statement
    Statement stmt = connection.createStatement();

    // Export the data
    String filename = "c:\\\\temp\\\\outfile.txt";
    String tablename = "mysql_2_table";
    stmt.executeUpdate("SELECT * INTO OUTFILE \"" + filename + "\" FROM " + tablename);
} catch (SQLException e) {
}
```

Oracle OBJECTs

ε296. Creating an OBJECT Type in an Oracle Database

In Oracle, you can define a composite data structure called an OBJECT, which consists of one or more basic types. For example, you could define an object called book with a title (VARCHAR) and an price (NUMBER). An OBJECT can also contain other OBJECTs.

This example creates two OBJECT types. object2 contains two fields — a string and a number while object1 also contains two fields — a string and a value of type object2.

The example also creates a table to hold object1 values. See also "ε297. Inserting an OBJECT Value into an Oracle Table".

```
try {
    // Create a statement
    Statement stmt = connection.createStatement();

    // Create the 'object2' type
    stmt.execute("CREATE TYPE object2 AS OBJECT"
        + "(col_string2 VARCHAR(30), col_integer2 NUMBER)");

    // Create the 'object1' type
    stmt.execute("CREATE TYPE object1 AS OBJECT"
        + "(col_string1 VARCHAR(30), col_integer2 object2)");

    // Create a table with a column to hold a number and the new object1 type
    stmt.execute("CREATE TABLE object1_table(col_integer NUMBER, col_object1 object1)");
} catch (SQLException e) {
}
```

ε297. Inserting an OBJECT Value into an Oracle Table

This example inserts a row into a table with a column that contains an OBJECT type. The example uses the table and types created in "ε296. Creating an OBJECT Type in an Oracle Database".

```
try {
    // Create a statement
    Statement stmt = connection.createStatement();
```

```
        // Insert a row with values for both the object1 and object2 types
        stmt.execute("INSERT INTO object1_table VALUES(1, object1('str1', object2('obj2str1', 123)))");
    } catch (SQLException e) {
    }
```

ε298. Inserting an OBJECT Value into an Oracle Table Using a Prepared Statement

This example inserts Oracle OBJECTs into an Oracle table using a prepared statement. The example uses the OBJECT types and table created in "ε296. Creating an OBJECT Type in an Oracle Database".

```
    try {
        // Create an oracle.sql.STRUCT object to hold the values for 'object2'
        Object[] object2Values = new Object[]{"str", new BigDecimal(123)};
        oracle.sql.StructDescriptor structDesc =
            oracle.sql.StructDescriptor.createDescriptor("OBJECT2", connection);
        oracle.sql.STRUCT object2 =
            new oracle.sql.STRUCT(structDesc, connection, object2Values);

        // Create an oracle.sql.STRUCT object to hold the values for 'object1'
        Object[] object1Values = new Object[]{"str", object2};
        structDesc = oracle.sql.StructDescriptor.createDescriptor("OBJECT1", connection);
        oracle.sql.STRUCT object1 =
            new oracle.sql.STRUCT(structDesc, connection, object1Values);

        // Create a prepared statement for insertion into 'object1_table'
        PreparedStatement ps =
            connection.prepareStatement("INSERT INTO object1_table VALUES(?,?)");

        // Set the values to insert
        ps.setInt(1, 123);
        ps.setObject(2, object1);

        // Insert the new row
        ps.execute();
    } catch (SQLException e) {
    }
```

ε299. Getting an OBJECT Value from an Oracle Table

This example retrieves values contained in an Oracle OBJECT type. The example uses the table and types created in "ε296. Creating an OBJECT Type in an Oracle Database".

```
    try {
        // Create a statement
        Statement stmt = connection.createStatement();

        // Select rows from object1_table
        ResultSet resultSet = stmt.executeQuery("SELECT * FROM object1_table");

        // Get the OBJECT values from each row
        while (resultSet.next()) {
            // Get the integer from the first column 'col_integer' of the row
            int i = resultSet.getInt(1);

            // Get the object1 value from the second column 'col_object1'
            oracle.sql.STRUCT object1 = (oracle.sql.STRUCT)resultSet.getObject(2);

            // Get the object1 values from each row
            Object[] object1Values = object1.getAttributes();

            // Get the first value of object1, which is a string
```

```
            String str = (String)object1Values[0];

            // Get the second value of object1, which is of the type object2
            oracle.sql.STRUCT object2 = (oracle.sql.STRUCT)object1Values[1];

            // Get the values of object2
            Object object2Values[] = object2.getAttributes();
            str = (String)object2Values[0];
            BigDecimal num = (BigDecimal)object2Values[1];
        }
    } catch (SQLException e) {
    }
```

ε300. Deleting an OBJECT Type from an Oracle Table

This example deletes the OBJECTs and tables created in "ε296. Creating an OBJECT Type in an Oracle Database".

```
    try {
        // Create a statement
        Statement stmt = connection.createStatement();

        // Drop table object1_table and types object1 and object2
        stmt.execute("DROP TABLE object1_table");
        stmt.execute("DROP TYPE object1 FORCE");
        stmt.execute("DROP TYPE object2 FORCE");
    } catch (SQLException e) {
        // A drop statement will throw an exception if the table or type does not exist
    }
```

Oracle VARRAYs

ε301. Creating a VARRAY Type in an Oracle Database

A VARRAY is a variable-length ordered list of values of one type. This example creates a VARRAY that can hold up to ten NUMBER values.

```
    try {
        Statement stmt = connection.createStatement();

        // Create a 10-element VARRAY of NUMBERs
        stmt.execute("CREATE TYPE number_varray AS VARRAY(10) OF NUMBER(12, 2)");

        // Create a table with a column to hold the new VARRAY type
        stmt.execute("CREATE TABLE VARRAY_TABLE(col_number_array number_varray)");
    } catch (SQLException e) {
    }
```

ε302. Inserting a VARRAY Value into an Oracle Table

This example inserts a row with a VARRAY as defined in "ε301. Creating a VARRAY Type in an Oracle Database".

```
    try {
        // Create a statement
        Statement stmt = connection.createStatement();

        // Insert a row with an array of two values
        stmt.execute ("INSERT INTO varray_table VALUES(number_varray(123, 234))");
    } catch (SQLException e) {
    }
```

ε303. Inserting a VARRAY Value into an Oracle Table Using a Prepared Statement

This example inserts a row with a VARRAY of numbers as defined in "ε301. Creating a VARRAY Type in an Oracle Database". This example uses a prepared statement.

```
try {
    // Create an oracle.sql.ARRAY object to hold the values
    oracle.sql.ArrayDescriptor arrayDesc =
        oracle.sql.ArrayDescriptor.createDescriptor("number_varray", connection);
    int arrayValues[] = {123, 234};
    oracle.sql.ARRAY array = new oracle.sql.ARRAY(arrayDesc, connection, arrayValues);

    // Create a prepared statement for insertion into 'varray_table'
    PreparedStatement ps =
        connection.prepareStatement("INSERT INTO varray_table VALUES(?)");

    // Set the values to insert
    ((oracle.jdbc.driver.OraclePreparedStatement)ps).setARRAY(1, array);

    // Insert the new row
    ps.execute();
} catch (SQLException e) {
}
```

ε304. Getting a VARRAY Value from an Oracle Table

This example retrieves values contained in an Oracle VARRAY type. The example uses the table and array type created in "ε301. Creating a VARRAY Type in an Oracle Database".

```
try {
    // Create a statement
    Statement stmt = connection.createStatement();

    // Select rows from varray_table
    ResultSet resultSet = stmt.executeQuery("SELECT * FROM varray_table");

    // Get the VARRAY values from each row
    while (resultSet.next()) {
        // Get the VARRAY value in the first column
        oracle.sql.ARRAY array = ((oracle.jdbc.driver.OracleResultSet)resultSet).getARRAY(1);

        // Get the VARRAY elements; values.length is the number of values in the VARRAY
        java.math.BigDecimal[] values = (java.math.BigDecimal[])array.getArray();
    }
} catch (SQLException e) {
}
```

java.text

This package contains classes and interfaces for handling text, dates, numbers and messages in a manner independent of natural language. This means your main application or applet can be written to be language-independent and to call upon separate, dynamically linked localized resources. This allows the flexibility of adding localization for new languages at any time. This package contains three groups of classes. The first group is for formatting dates, numbers, and messages. The second group is for parsing, searching, and sorting strings. The last group is for iterating over characters, words, sentences, and line breaks.

Class *Interface* —extends - - -implements ○ abstract ● final ⌐has superclass ⌐has subclass package—see other volume

Packages

java.lang.Object
1.2   ├ Annotation
1.2   ├ AttributedCharacterIterator.Attribute - *java.io.Serializable*ˇ
1.4   │ └ Format.Field
1.4   │   ├ DateFormat.Field

```
         java.lang.Object
1.2        AttributedCharacterIterator.Attribute --------------------- java.io.Serializable
1.4          └ Format.Field
1.4              ├ MessageFormat.Field
1.4              └ NumberFormat.Field
1.2        AttributedString
1.4 ●      Bidi
1.1 ○      BreakIterator ------------------------------------------- java.lang.Cloneable
1.1 ●      CollationElementIterator
1.1 ●      CollationKey ------------------------------------------- java.lang.Comparable
1.1 ○      Collator ---------------------------------------------- java.lang.Cloneable, java.util.Comparator
1.1          └ RuleBasedCollator
1.1        DateFormatSymbols ------------------------------------- java.io.Serializable, java.lang.Cloneable
1.1 ●      DecimalFormatSymbols ------------------------------
1.1        FieldPosition
1.1 ○      Format ------------------------------------------
1.1 ○        DateFormat
1.1            └ SimpleDateFormat
1.1          MessageFormat
1.1 ○        └ NumberFormat
1.1            ├ ChoiceFormat
1.1            └ DecimalFormat
1.1        ParsePosition
1.1 ●      StringCharacterIterator ------------------------------ CharacterIterator
           java.lang.Throwable ------------------------------ java.io.Serializable
             └ java.lang.Exception
1.1            └ ParseException

1.2      AttributedCharacterIterator ——————————————— CharacterIterator
1.1      CharacterIterator —————————————————————— java.lang.Cloneable
```

ε305. Determining the Type of a Character

You should use the methods in the class Character to determine the properties of a character. These methods work for the entire Unicode character set.

```
char ch = 'a';
if (Character.isLetter(ch)) { // true
}
if (Character.isDigit(ch)) { // false
}
if (Character.isLowerCase(ch)) { // true
}
if (Character.isUpperCase(ch)) { // false
}
// See Character for more methods.
```

ε306. Comparing Strings in a Locale-Independent Way

```
Collator collator = Collator.getInstance(Locale.CANADA);
int compare = collator.compare(aString1, aString2);
if (compare < 0) {
    // aString1 < aString2
} else if (compare > 1) {
```

```
    // aString1 > aString2
} else {
    // aString1 = aString2
}
```

ε307. Iterating the Characters of a String

```
CharacterIterator it = new StringCharacterIterator("abcd");

// Iterate over the characters in the forward direction
for (char ch=it.first(); ch != CharacterIterator.DONE; ch=it.next()) {
    // Use ch ...
}

// Iterate over the characters in the backward direction
for (char ch=it.last(); ch != CharacterIterator.DONE; ch=it.previous()) {
    // Use ch ...
}

// Other methods
char ch = it.first(); // a
ch = it.current(); // a
ch = it.next(); // b
ch = it.current(); // b
ch = it.last(); // d
int pos = it.getIndex(); // 3
ch = it.next(); // DONE
pos = it.getIndex(); // 4
ch = it.previous(); // d
ch = it.setIndex(1); // b

// Change the characters
((StringCharacterIterator)it).setText("efgh");
ch = it.current(); // e

// Create an iterator on a substring (efgh)
int begin = 5;
int end = 9;
pos = 6;
it = new StringCharacterIterator("abcd efgh ijkl", begin, end, pos);
ch = it.current(); // f
ch = it.last(); // h
```

ε308. Adding an Attribute to a String

Some applications need to mark a range of characters in a string with an attribute, such as a color. The AttributedString class is a wrapper for a string that provides support for marking ranges of characters with an attribute. An attribute consists of a name, a value, and a contiguous range of characters on which the attribute applies.

This example marks a word in a string with the attribute called color and the value red.

```
// Declare an attribute name.
// An attribute name is an object that extends AttributedCharacterIterator.Attribute.
// Author's note: A more appropriate name would be AttributedCharacterIterator.AttributeName
static final AttributedCharacterIterator.Attribute COLOR
    = new AttributedCharacterIterator.Attribute("color") {
    };

// Create the attributed string
AttributedString astr = new AttributedString("the hot pot");
```

Packages

```
// Add the COLOR attribute on the word 'hot'
astr.addAttribute(COLOR, "Red", 4, 7);
```

ε309. Incrementing a Double by the Smallest Possible Amount

```
double d = 1.2;
```

```
// Get the largest double less than d
double d1 = ChoiceFormat.previousDouble(d); // 1.1999999999999997
```

```
// Get the smallest double greater than d
double d2 = ChoiceFormat.nextDouble(d); // 1.2000000000000002
```

ε310. Localizing Messages

Messages and text string should be localized in a "resource bundle". There are several types of resource bundles. This example demonstrates how to use a property-file type resource bundle. Here are two examples of resource files:

MyResources_en.properties:

```
hello=Hello
bye=Goodbye
```

MyResources_fr.properties:

```
hello=Bonjour
bye=Au Revoir
```

When loading a property-file resource bundle, a "base name" and desired locale is specified. The system then looks in the classpath for a file whose name matches one of the following patterns in order:

```
basename_locale.properties
basename.properties
basename_defaultLocale.properties
```

For example, given the base name MyResources, a locale of fr, and a default locale of en, the system first looks for

```
MyResources_fr.properties
MyResources.properties
MyResources_en.properties
```

Here's an example that loads a resource bundle:

```
String baseName = "MyResources";
try {
    // Get the resource bundle for the default locale
    ResourceBundle rb = ResourceBundle.getBundle(baseName);

    String key = "hello";
    String s = rb.getString(key); // Hello
    key = "bye";
    s = rb.getString(key); // Goodbye

    // Get the resource bundle for a specific locale
    rb = ResourceBundle.getBundle(baseName, Locale.FRENCH);

    key = "hello";
    s = rb.getString(key); // Bonjour
    key = "bye";
    s = rb.getString(key); // Au Revoir
```

Class   *Interface*   —extends   - - -implements   ○ abstract   ● final   ^—has superclass   ‿—has subclass   package—see other volume

```
} catch (MissingResourceException e) {
    // The resource bundle cannot be found or
    // the key does not exist in the resource bundle
}
```

ε311. Formatting a Number Using a Custom Format

A pattern of special characters is used to specify the format of the number. This example demonstrates some of the characters. For a complete listing, see the javadoc documentation for the DecimalFormat class.

There is no symbol that either displays a digit or a blank if no digit present. Hence, it is not possible to format a number so that it will have a specific width. To achieve a specific width, you must manually pad the formatted number.

```
// The 0 symbol shows a digit or 0 if no digit present
NumberFormat formatter = new DecimalFormat("000000");
String s = formatter.format(-1234.567); // -001235
// notice that the number was rounded up

// The # symbol shows a digit or nothing if no digit present
formatter = new DecimalFormat("##");
s = formatter.format(-1234.567); // -1235
s = formatter.format(0); // 0
formatter = new DecimalFormat("##00");
s = formatter.format(0); // 00


// The . symbol indicates the decimal point
formatter = new DecimalFormat(".00");
s = formatter.format(-.567); // -.57
formatter = new DecimalFormat("0.00");
s = formatter.format(-.567); // -0.57
formatter = new DecimalFormat("#.#");
s = formatter.format(-1234.567); // -1234.6
formatter = new DecimalFormat("#.######");
s = formatter.format(-1234.567); // -1234.567
formatter = new DecimalFormat(".######");
s = formatter.format(-1234.567); // -1234.567
formatter = new DecimalFormat("#.000000");
s = formatter.format(-1234.567); // -1234.567000


// The , symbol is used to group numbers
formatter = new DecimalFormat("#,###,###");
s = formatter.format(-1234.567); // -1,235
s = formatter.format(-1234567.890); // -1,234,568

// The ; symbol is used to specify an alternate pattern for negative values
formatter = new DecimalFormat("#;(#)");
s = formatter.format(-1234.567); // (1235)

// The ' symbol is used to quote literal symbols
formatter = new DecimalFormat("'#'#");
s = formatter.format(-1234.567); // -#1235
formatter = new DecimalFormat("'abc'#");
s = formatter.format(-1234.567); // -abc1235
```

ε312. Formatting and Parsing a Number for a Locale

A formatted number consists of locale-specific symbols such as the decimal point. For example, a Canadian decimal point is a dot while a German decimal point is a comma. This example demonstrates how to format a number for a particular locale.

```java
// Format for CANADA locale
Locale locale = Locale.CANADA;
String string = NumberFormat.getNumberInstance(locale).format(-1234.56); // -1,234.56

// Format for GERMAN locale
locale = Locale.GERMAN;
string = NumberFormat.getNumberInstance(locale).format(-1234.56); // -1.234,56

// Format for the default locale
string = NumberFormat.getNumberInstance().format(-1234.56);


// Parse a GERMAN number
try {
    Number number = NumberFormat.getNumberInstance(locale.GERMAN).parse("-1.234,56");
    if (number instanceof Long) {
        // Long value
    } else {
        // Double value
    }
} catch (ParseException e) {
}
```

ε313. Formatting a Number in Exponential Notation

The 'E' symbol specifies that a number should be formatted in exponential notation. The symbol also separates the mantissa from the exponent. The symbol must be followed by one or more '0' symbols. The number of '0' symbols specifies the minimum number of digits used to display the exponent.

```java
// Using only 0's to the left of E forces no decimal point
NumberFormat formatter = new DecimalFormat("0E0");
String s = formatter.format(-1234.567); // -1E3

formatter = new DecimalFormat("00E00");
s = formatter.format(-1234.567); // -12E02

formatter = new DecimalFormat("000E00");
s = formatter.format(-1234.567); // -123E01

formatter = new DecimalFormat("0000000000E0");
s = formatter.format(-1234.567); // -1234567000E-6


// Force minimum number of digits to left and right of decimal point
formatter = new DecimalFormat("0.0E0");
s = formatter.format(-1234.567); // -1.2E3

formatter = new DecimalFormat("00.00E0");
s = formatter.format(-1234.567); // -12.35E2
s = formatter.format(-.1234567); // -12.35E-2


// The number of #'s to the left of the decimal point (if any) specifies
// the multiple of the exponent. The total number of #'s (left and right)
// of the decimal point) specifies, the maximum number of digits to display
```

```
formatter = new DecimalFormat("#E0"); // exponent can be any value
s = formatter.format(-1234.567); // -.1E4
s = formatter.format(-.1234567); // -.1E0

formatter = new DecimalFormat("##E0"); // exponent must be multiple of 2
s = formatter.format(-1234.567); // -12E2
s = formatter.format(-123.4567); // -1.2E2
s = formatter.format(-12.34567); // -12E0

formatter = new DecimalFormat("###E0"); // exponent must be multiple of 3
s = formatter.format(-1234.567); // -1.23E3
s = formatter.format(-123.4567); // -123E0
s = formatter.format(-12.34567); // -12.3E0
s = formatter.format(-1.234567); // -12.3E0
s = formatter.format(-.1234567); // -123E-3
```

ε314. Formatting and Parsing Locale-specific Currency

```
// Format
Locale locale = Locale.GERMANY;
String string = NumberFormat.getCurrencyInstance(locale).format(123.45);
// 123,45 DM

locale = Locale.CANADA;
string = NumberFormat.getCurrencyInstance(locale).format(123.45);
// $123.45

// Parse
try {
    Number number = NumberFormat.getCurrencyInstance(locale).parse("$123.45");
    // 123.45
    if (number instanceof Long) {
        // Long value
    } else {
        // Double value
    }
} catch (ParseException e) {
}
```

ε315. Formatting and Parsing a Locale-specific Percentage

```
// Format
Locale locale = Locale.CANADA;
String string = NumberFormat.getPercentInstance(locale).format(123.45);
// 12,345%

// Parse
try {
    Number number = NumberFormat.getPercentInstance(locale).parse("123.45%");
    // 1.2345
    if (number instanceof Long) {
        // Long value
    } else {
        // Double value
    }
} catch (ParseException e) {
}
```

Packages

229

Times

ε316. Formatting the Time Using a Custom Format

A pattern of special characters is used to specify the format of the time. This example demonstrates some of the characters. For a complete listing, see the javadoc documentation for the SimpleDateFormat class.

Note: This example formats dates using the default locale (which, in the author's case, is Locale.ENGLISH). If the example is run in a different locale, the text (e.g., month names) will not be the same.

```
Format formatter;

// The hour (1-12)
formatter = new SimpleDateFormat("h"); // 8
formatter = new SimpleDateFormat("hh"); // 08

// The hour (0-23)
formatter = new SimpleDateFormat("H"); // 8
formatter = new SimpleDateFormat("HH"); // 08

// The minutes
formatter = new SimpleDateFormat("m"); // 7
formatter = new SimpleDateFormat("mm"); // 07

// The seconds
formatter = new SimpleDateFormat("s"); // 3
formatter = new SimpleDateFormat("ss"); // 03

// The am/pm marker
formatter = new SimpleDateFormat("a"); // AM

// The time zone
formatter = new SimpleDateFormat("z"); // PST
formatter = new SimpleDateFormat("zzzz"); // Pacific Standard Time
formatter = new SimpleDateFormat("Z"); // -0800

// Get today's date
Date date = new Date();

// Some examples
formatter = new SimpleDateFormat("hh:mm:ss a");
String s = formatter.format(date);
// 01:12:53 AM

formatter = new SimpleDateFormat("HH.mm.ss");
s = formatter.format(date);
// 14.36.33
```

ε317. Parsing the Time Using a Custom Format

A pattern of special characters is used to specify the format of the time to parse. The same set of pattern characters are used to parse times. See "ε316. Formatting the Time Using a Custom Format" for a listing of some pattern characters.

Note: This example formats dates using the default locale (which, in the author's case, is Locale.ENGLISH). If the example is run in a different locale, the text (e.g., month names) will not be the same.

```
try {
    // Some examples
    DateFormat formatter = new SimpleDateFormat("hh.mm.ss a");
    Date date = (Date)formatter.parse("02.36.33 PM");
```

Class *Interface* —extends - - -implements ○ abstract ● final ⌐—has superclass ⌐—has subclass package—see other volume

```
    formatter = new SimpleDateFormat("HH:mm:ss Z");
    date = (Date)formatter.parse("22:14:02 -0500");
} catch (ParseException e) {
}
```

ε318. Formatting and Parsing a Time for a Locale Using Default Formats

Every locale has four default formats for formatting and parsing times. They are called SHORT, MEDIUM, LONG, and FULL. The SHORT format consists entirely of numbers while the FULL format contains most of the time components. There is also a default format called DEFAULT and is the same as MEDIUM.

Note: This example formats dates using the default locale (which, in the author's case, is Locale.ENGLISH). If the example is run in a different locale, the text (e.g., month names) will not be the same.

```
// Format
Locale locale = Locale.ITALIAN;
Date date = new Date();

String s = DateFormat.getTimeInstance(DateFormat.SHORT, locale).format(date);
// 22.33

s = DateFormat.getTimeInstance(DateFormat.MEDIUM, locale).format(date);
// 22.33.03

s = DateFormat.getTimeInstance(DateFormat.LONG, locale).format(date);
// 22.33.03 PST

s = DateFormat.getTimeInstance(DateFormat.FULL, locale).format(date);
// 22.33.03 PST

s = DateFormat.getTimeInstance(DateFormat.DEFAULT, locale).format(date);
// 22.33.03

// Parse
try {
    date = DateFormat.getTimeInstance(
        DateFormat.DEFAULT, locale).parse("22.33.03");
} catch (ParseException e) {
}
```

ε319. Formatting and Parsing a Time for a Locale

To format and parse in a particular locale, specify the locale when creating the SimpleDateFormat object.

```
Locale locale = Locale.FRENCH;

// Format with a custom format
DateFormat formatter = new SimpleDateFormat("HH:mm:ss zzzz", locale);
String s = formatter.format(new Date());
// 21:44:07 Heure normale du Pacifique

// Format with a default format
s = DateFormat.getTimeInstance(DateFormat.MEDIUM, locale).format(new Date());
// 21:44:07

try {
    // Parse with a custom format
    formatter = new SimpleDateFormat("HH:mm:ss Z", locale);
    Date date = (Date)formatter.parse("21:44:07 Heure normale du Pacifique");

    // Parse with a default format
    date = DateFormat.getTimeInstance(DateFormat.MEDIUM, locale).parse("21:44:07");
} catch (ParseException e) {
```

```
    }
```

Dates

ε320. Formatting a Date Using a Custom Format

A pattern of special characters is used to specify the format of the date. This example demonstrates some of the characters. For a complete listing, see the javadoc documentation for the SimpleDateFormat class.

Note: This example formats dates using the default locale (which, in the author's case, is Locale.ENGLISH). If the example is run in a different locale, the text (e.g., month names) will not be the same.

```
Format formatter;

// The year
formatter = new SimpleDateFormat("yy"); // 02
formatter = new SimpleDateFormat("yyyy"); // 2002

// The month
formatter = new SimpleDateFormat("M"); // 1
formatter = new SimpleDateFormat("MM"); // 01
formatter = new SimpleDateFormat("MMM"); // Jan
formatter = new SimpleDateFormat("MMMM"); // January

// The day
formatter = new SimpleDateFormat("d"); // 29
formatter = new SimpleDateFormat("dd"); // 29

// The day in week
formatter = new SimpleDateFormat("E"); // Wed
formatter = new SimpleDateFormat("EEEE"); // Wednesday

// Get today's date
Date date = new Date();

// Some examples
formatter = new SimpleDateFormat("MM/dd/yy");
String s = formatter.format(date);
// 01/29/02

formatter = new SimpleDateFormat("dd-MMM-yy");
s = formatter.format(date);
// 29-Jan-02

// Examples with date and time; see also
// "ε316. Formatting the Time Using a Custom Format"
formatter = new SimpleDateFormat("yyyy.MM.dd.HH.mm.ss");
s = formatter.format(date);
// 2002.01.29.08.36.33

formatter = new SimpleDateFormat("E, dd MMM yyyy HH:mm:ss Z");
s = formatter.format(date);
// Tue, 29 Jan 2002 22:14:02 -0500
```

ε321. Parsing a Date Using a Custom Format

A pattern of special characters is used to specify the format of the date to parse. The same set of pattern characters are used to format and to parse dates. See "ε320. Formatting a Date Using a Custom Format" for a listing of some pattern characters.

Class   *Interface*   —extends   - - -implements   O abstract   ● final   ^—has superclass   ‿—has subclass   package—see other volume

Note: This example parses dates using the default locale (which, in the author's case, is Locale.ENGLISH). If the example is run in a different locale, the text (e.g., month names) will not be the same.

```
try {
    // Some examples
    DateFormat formatter = new SimpleDateFormat("MM/dd/yy");
    Date date = (Date)formatter.parse("01/29/02");

    formatter = new SimpleDateFormat("dd-MMM-yy");
    date = (Date)formatter.parse("29-Jan-02");

    // Parse a date and time; see also
    // "ε317. Parsing the Time Using a Custom Format"
    formatter = new SimpleDateFormat("yyyy.MM.dd.HH.mm.ss");
    date = (Date)formatter.parse("2002.01.29.08.36.33");

    formatter = new SimpleDateFormat("E, dd MMM yyyy HH:mm:ss Z");
    date = (Date)formatter.parse("Tue, 29 Jan 2002 22:14:02 -0500");
} catch (ParseException e) {
}
```

ε322. Formatting and Parsing a Date Using Default Formats

Every locale has four default formats for formatting and parsing dates. They are called SHORT, MEDIUM, LONG, and FULL. The SHORT format consists entirely of numbers while the FULL format contains most of the date components. There is also a default format called DEFAULT and is the same as MEDIUM.

Note: This example formats dates using the default locale (which, in the author's case, is Locale.ENGLISH). If the example is run in a different locale, the text (e.g., month names) will not be the same.

```
// Format
Date date = new Date();

String s = DateFormat.getDateInstance(DateFormat.SHORT).format(date);
// 2/16/02

s = DateFormat.getDateInstance(DateFormat.MEDIUM).format(date);
// Feb 16, 2002

s = DateFormat.getDateInstance(DateFormat.LONG).format(date);
// February 16, 2002

s = DateFormat.getDateInstance(DateFormat.FULL).format(date);
// Saturday, February 16, 2002

s = DateFormat.getDateInstance(DateFormat.DEFAULT).format(date);
// 29.01.2002

// Parse
try {
    date = DateFormat.getDateInstance(DateFormat.DEFAULT).parse("Feb 16, 2002");
} catch (ParseException e) {
}
```

ε323. Formatting and Parsing a Date for a Locale

To format and parse in a particular locale, specify the locale when creating the SimpleDateFormat object.

```
Locale locale = Locale.FRENCH;

// Format with a custom format
DateFormat formatter = new SimpleDateFormat("E, dd MMM yyyy", locale);
String s = formatter.format(new Date());
// mar., 29 janv. 2002
```

Packages

233

```
// Format with a default format
s = DateFormat.getDateInstance(DateFormat.MEDIUM, locale).format(new Date());
// 29 janv. 2002

try {
    // Parse with a custom format
    formatter = new SimpleDateFormat("E, dd MMM yyyy", locale);
    Date date = (Date)formatter.parse("mar., 29 janv. 2002");

    // Parse with a default format
    date = DateFormat.getDateInstance(DateFormat.MEDIUM, locale).parse("29 janv. 2002");
} catch (ParseException e) {
}
```

Messsages

ε324. Formatting a Message Containing a Number

```
Object[] params = new Object[]{new Integer(123), new Integer(1234)};
String msg = MessageFormat.format("There are {0} a"s and {1} b"s", params);
// There are 123 a's and 1,234 b's

msg = MessageFormat.format("There are {0,number} a"s and {1,number} b"s", params);
// There are 123 a's and 1,234 b's

// Use a custom format; see "ε311. Formatting a Number Using a Custom Format"
msg = MessageFormat.format("There are {0,number,#} a"s and {1,number,#} b"s", params);
// There are 123 a's and 1234 b's

// Floating point numbers
params = new Object[]{new Double(123.45), new Double(1234.56)};
msg = MessageFormat.format("There are {0,number,#.#} a"s and {1,number,#.#} b"s", params);
// There are 123.4 a's and 1234.6 b's

// Currency
msg = MessageFormat.format("There are {0,number,currency} a"s and {1,number,currency} b"s", params);
// There are $123.00 a's and $1,234.00 b's

// Percent
msg = MessageFormat.format("There are {0,number,percent} a"s and {1,number,percent} b"s", params);
// There are 12,345% a's and 123,456% b's
```

ε325. Formatting a Message Containing a Time

```
Object[] params = new Object[]{new Date(), new Date(0)};
String msg = MessageFormat.format("The time is {0} and UTC of 0 is {1}", params);
// The time is 2/27/02 2:08 PM and UTC of 0 is 12/31/69 4:00 PM

msg = MessageFormat.format("The time is {0,time} and UTC of 0 is {1,time}", params);
// The time is 2:08:48 PM and UTC of 0 is 4:00:00 PM

msg = MessageFormat.format("The time is {0,time,short} and UTC of 0 is {1,time,short}", params);
// The time is 2:08 PM and UTC of 0 is 4:00 PM

msg = MessageFormat.format("The time is {0,time,medium} and UTC of 0 is {1,time,medium}", params);
// The time is 2:08:48 PM and UTC of 0 is 4:00:00 PM

msg = MessageFormat.format("The time is {0,time,long} and UTC of 0 is {1,time,long}", params);
// The time is 2:08:48 PM PST and UTC of 0 is 4:00:00 PM PST
```

```
msg = MessageFormat.format("The time is {0,time,full} and UTC of 0 is {1,time,full}", params);
// The time is 2:08:48 PM PST and UTC of 0 is 4:00:00 PM PST
```

```
// Use a custom format; see "ε316. Formatting the Time Using a Custom Format"
msg = MessageFormat.format("The time is {0,time,HH-mm-ss} and UTC of 0 is {1,time,HH-mm-ss}",
params);
// The time is 14-11-41 and UTC of 0 is 16-00-00
```

ε326. Formatting a Message Containing a Date

```
Object[] params = new Object[]{new Date(), new Date(0)};
String msg = MessageFormat.format("Today is {0} and UTC of 0 is {1}", params);
// Today is 2/27/02 2:00 PM and UTC of 0 is 12/31/69 4:00 PM
```

```
msg = MessageFormat.format("Today is {0,date} and UTC of 0 is {1,date}", params);
// Today is Feb 27, 2002 and UTC of 0 is Dec 31, 1969
```

```
msg = MessageFormat.format("Today is {0,date,short} and UTC of 0 is {1,date,short}", params);
// Today is 2/27/02 and UTC of 0 is 12/31/69
```

```
msg = MessageFormat.format("Today is {0,date,medium} and UTC of 0 is {1,date,medium}", params);
// Today is Feb 27, 2002 and UTC of 0 is Dec 31, 1969
```

```
msg = MessageFormat.format("Today is {0,date,long} and UTC of 0 is {1,date,long}", params);
// Today is February 27, 2002 and UTC of 0 is December 31, 1969
```

```
msg = MessageFormat.format("Today is {0,date,full} and UTC of 0 is {1,date,full}", params);
// Today is Wednesday, February 27, 2002 and UTC of 0 is Wednesday, December 31, 1969
```

```
// Use a custom format; see "ε320. Formatting a Date Using a Custom Format"
msg = MessageFormat.format("Today is {0,date,MMM d} and UTC of 0 is {1,date,MMM d}", params);
// Today is Feb 27 and UTC of 0 is Dec 31
```

Words and Sentences

ε327. Determining the Character Boundaries in a Unicode String

```
BreakIterator iterator = BreakIterator.getCharacterInstance(Locale.CANADA);
iterator.setText("aString");
for (int index=iterator.first(); index != BreakIterator.DONE; index=iterator.next()) {
    process(index);
}
```

ε328. Determining the Word Boundaries in a Unicode String

The word break iterator finds both the beginning and end of words.

```
BreakIterator iterator = BreakIterator.getWordInstance(Locale.CANADA);
iterator.setText("a sentence");
for (int index=iterator.first(); index != BreakIterator.DONE; index=iterator.next()) {
    process(index);
}
```

ε329. Determining the Sentence Boundaries in a Unicode String

```
BreakIterator iterator = BreakIterator.getSentenceInstance(Locale.CANADA);
iterator.setText("A sentence. Another sentence.");
for (int index=iterator.first(); index != BreakIterator.DONE; index=iterator.next()) {
    process(index);
}
```

Packages

ε330. Determining Potential Line Breaks in a Unicode String

```
BreakIterator iterator = BreakIterator.getLineInstance(Locale.CANADA);
iterator.setText("line1\nline2");
for (int index=iterator.first(); index != BreakIterator.DONE; index=iterator.next()) {
    process(index);
}
```

java.util

This package contains a number of utility classes that are useful in typical Java applications. These include classes that implement useful data structures (the Collections framework), date- and time-related classes, locale, root interfaces for events, and miscellaneous classes including a simple string tokenizer and pseudorandom-number generator.

Class   *Interface*   —extends   - - -implements   ○ abstract   ● final   ⌃—has superclass   ⌄—has subclass   package—see other volume

Packages

java.util

java.lang.Object

1.2 ○	├ AbstractCollection -	*Collection* ‿
1.2 ○	├ AbstractList -	*List*^
1.2 ○	├ AbstractSequentialList	
1.2	└ LinkedList -	*List*^, *java.io.Serializable* ‿, *java.lang.Cloneable* ‿
1.2	├ ArrayList - ‐	*List*^, *RandomAccess*, *java.io.Serializable* ‿, *java.lang.Cloneable* ‿
	└ Vector -	
	└ Stack	
1.2 ○	└ AbstractSet -	*Set* ‿
1.2	├ HashSet - ‐	*Set* ‿, *java.io.Serializable* ‿, *java.lang.Cloneable* ‿
1.4	└ LinkedHashSet -	
1.2	└ TreeSet -	*SortedSet*^, *java.io.Serializable* ‿, *java.lang.Cloneable* ‿
1.2 ○	├ AbstractMap -	*Map* ‿
1.2	├ HashMap - ‐	*Map* ‿, *java.io.Serializable* ‿, *java.lang.Cloneable* ‿
1.4	└ LinkedHashMap	
1.4	├ IdentityHashMap -	
1.2	├ TreeMap -	*SortedMap*^, *java.io.Serializable* ‿, *java.lang.Cloneable* ‿
1.2	└ WeakHashMap -	*Map* ‿
1.2	├ Arrays	
1.2	├ BitSet - ‐	*java.io.Serializable* ‿, *java.lang.Cloneable* ‿
1.1 ○	├ Calendar - ‐	
1.1	└ GregorianCalendar	
1.2	├ Collections	
1.4 ●	├ Currency -	*java.io.Serializable* ‿
	├ Date ‿ -	*java.io.Serializable* ‿, *java.lang.Cloneable* ‿, *java.lang.Comparable*
○	├ Dictionary	
	└ Hashtable -	*Map* ‿, *java.io.Serializable* ‿, *java.lang.Cloneable* ‿
	└ Properties ‿	
1.4 ○	├ EventListenerProxy ‿ -	*EventListener* ‿
1.1	├ EventObject ‿ -	*java.io.Serializable* ‿
1.1 ●	├ Locale -	*java.io.Serializable* ‿, *java.lang.Cloneable* ‿
	├ Observable	
	├ Random ‿ -	*java.io.Serializable* ‿
1.1 ○	├ ResourceBundle	
1.1 ○	├ ListResourceBundle ‿	
1.1	└ PropertyResourceBundle	
	├ StringTokenizer -	*Enumeration* ‿
1.1 ○	├ TimeZone -	*java.io.Serializable* ‿, *java.lang.Cloneable* ‿
1.1	└ SimpleTimeZone	
1.3	├ Timer	
1.3 ○	├ TimerTask -	*java.lang.Runnable*
1.2 ○	├ java.security.Permission -	*java.io.Serializable* ‿, *java.security.Guard*
1.2 ○	└ java.security.BasicPermission - ‐	*java.io.Serializable* ‿
1.2 ●	└ PropertyPermission	

Class   *Interface*   —extends   - - -implements   ○ abstract   ● final   ^—has superclass   ‿—has subclass   package—see other volume

```
         java.lang.Object                                    ,- java.io.Serializable,
           └ java.lang.Throwable - - - - - - - - - - - - - - - - - - - - - - - - - - - - - - - - :
             └ java.lang.Exception
1.1              ├ TooManyListenersException
               └ java.lang.RuntimeException
1.2                ├ ConcurrentModificationException
                   ├ EmptyStackException
1.1                ├ MissingResourceException
                   └ NoSuchElementException
```

1.2	*Collection,*	
1.2	*Comparator*	
	Enumeration,	
1.1	*EventListener,*	
1.2	*Iterator,*	
1.2	*List* ——————————————————— *Collection*
1.2	*ListIterator* ————————————————— *Iterator*
1.2	*Map,*	
1.2	*Map.Entry*	
	Observer	
1.4	*RandomAccess*	
1.2	*Set,* ——————————————————— *Collection*
1.2	*SortedMap* ————————————————— *Map*
1.2	*SortedSet* ————————————————— *Set^*

ε331. Generating a Random Number

```
Random rand = new Random();

// Random integers
int i = rand.nextInt();
// Continually call nextInt() for more random integers ...

// Random integers that range from from 0 to n
int n = 10;
i = rand.nextInt(n+1);

// Random bytes
byte[] bytes = new byte[5];
rand.nextBytes(bytes);

// Other primitive types
boolean b = rand.nextBoolean();
long l = rand.nextLong();
float f = rand.nextFloat(); // 0.0 <= f < 1.0
double d = rand.nextDouble(); // 0.0 <= d < 1.0


// Create two random number generators with the same seed
long seed = rand.nextLong();
rand = new Random(seed);
Random rand2 = new Random(seed);
```

ε332. Breaking a String into Words

```
String aString = "word1 word2 word3";
StringTokenizer parser = new StringTokenizer(aString);
while (parser.hasMoreTokens()) {
```

```
        processWord(parser.nextToken());
    }
```

ε333. Creating a Custom Event

A new custom event must extends EventObject. Moreover, an event listener interface must be declared to allow objects to receive the new custom event. All listeners must extend from EventListener.

This example demonstrates all the steps necessary to create a new custom event.

```java
// Declare the event. It must extend EventObject.
public class MyEvent extends EventObject {
    public MyEvent(Object source) {
        super(source);
    }
}

// Declare the listener class. It must extend EventListener.
// A class must implement this interface to get MyEvents.
public interface MyEventListener extends EventListener {
    public void myEventOccurred(MyEvent evt);
}

// Add the event registration and notification code to a class.
public class MyClass {
    // Create the listener list
    protected javax.swing.event.EventListenerList listenerList =
        new javax.swing.event.EventListenerList();

    // This methods allows classes to register for MyEvents
    public void addMyEventListener(MyEventListener listener) {
        listenerList.add(MyEventListener.class, listener);
    }

    // This methods allows classes to unregister for MyEvents
    public void removeMyEventListener(MyEventListener listener) {
        listenerList.remove(MyEventListener.class, listener);
    }

    // This private class is used to fire MyEvents
    void fireMyEvent(MyEvent evt) {
        Object[] listeners = listenerList.getListenerList();
        // Each listener occupies two elements - the first is the listener class
        // and the second is the listener instance
        for (int i=0; i<listeners.length; i+=2) {
            if (listeners[i]==MyEventListener.class) {
                ((MyEventListener)listeners[i+1]).myEventOccurred(evt);
            }
        }
    }
}
```

Here's an example of how to register for MyEvents.

```java
MyClass c = new MyClass();

// Register for MyEvents from c
c.addMyEventListener(new MyEventListener() {
    public void myEventOccurred(MyEvent evt) {
        // MyEvent was fired
```

Class *Interface* —extends - - -implements ○ abstract ● final ^—has superclass ⌐—has subclass package—see other volume

```
        }
    });
```

ε334. Implementing a Simple Event Notifier

The Observer and Observable classes are superseded by a more elaborate event framework (see "ε333. Creating a Custom Event"). However, these two classes can still be useful for implementing a simple event notifier.

```
// Declare the model
class MyModel extends Observable {
    // The setChanged() protected method must overridden to make it public
    public synchronized void setChanged() {
        super.setChanged();
    }
}

// Create the model
MyModel model = new MyModel();

// Register for events
model.addObserver(new Observer() {
    public void update(Observable o, Object arg) {
    }
});

// Indicate that the model has changed
model.setChanged();

// Fire an event to all the views
Object arg = "some information about the event";
model.notifyObservers(arg);
```

ε335. Listing All Available Locales

```
Locale[] locales = Locale.getAvailableLocales();

for (int i=0; i<locales.length; i++) {
    // Get the 2-letter language code
    String language = locales[i].getLanguage();

    // Get the 2-letter country code; may be equal to ""
    String country = locales[i].getCountry();

    // Get localized name suitable for display to the user
    String locName = locales[i].getDisplayName();
}
```

Here's a sample of output using a default locale of Locale.ENGLISH:

```
Language Code, Country Code, Localized Name
ar, , Arabic
ar, AE, Arabic (United Arab Emirates)
ar, BH, Arabic (Bahrain)
ar, DZ, Arabic (Algeria)
ar, EG, Arabic (Egypt)
ar, IQ, Arabic (Iraq)
ar, JO, Arabic (Jordan)
ar, KW, Arabic (Kuwait)
ar, LB, Arabic (Lebanon)
```

Here's a sample of output using a default locale of Locale.FRENCH:

> Language Code, Country Code, Localized Name
> ar, , arabe
> ar, AE, arabe (Emirats Arabes Unis)
> ar, EG, arabe (Egypte)
> ar, IQ, arabe (Irak)
> ar, JO, arabe (Jordanie)
> ar, KW, arabe (Koweit)
> ar, LB, arabe (Liban)

ε336. Setting the Default Locale

There are two ways to change the default locale. The first is to set it on the command line:

> > java -Duser.language=*2-char-language-code* -Duser.region=*2-char-country-code MyApp*

```
// Set only language code
> java -Duser.language=fr -Duser.region= MyApp
// Set language and country code
> java -Duser.language=fr -Duser.region=CA MyApp
```

The second way to change the default locale is to call Locale.setDefault():

```
// Get default locale
Locale locale = Locale.getDefault();

// Set the default locale to pre-defined locale
Locale.setDefault(Locale.FRENCH);

// Set the default locale to custom locale
locale = new Locale("fr", "CA");
Locale.setDefault(locale);
```

ε337. Associating a Value with an Object

This example demonstrates how to associate a value with an arbitrary object. The technique involves saving the object and the associated value as a key/value pair in an IdentityHashMap. A HashMap cannot be used for this purpose since if two objects happen to equal via the Object.equals() method, one of the objects will not be stored.

```
// Create the map
Map objMap = new IdentityHashMap();

// Add the object and value pair to the map
Object o1 = new Integer(123);
Object o2 = new Integer(123);
objMap.put(o1, "first");
objMap.put(o2, "second");

// Retrieve the value associated with the objects
Object v1 = objMap.get(o1); // first
Object v2 = objMap.get(o2); // second
```

Arrays

ε338. Comparing Arrays

```
// null arrays are equal
boolean[] bArr1 = null;
boolean[] bArr2 = null;
boolean b = Arrays.equals(bArr1, bArr2); // true
```

Class   *Interface*   —extends   - - -implements   O abstract   ● final   ˆ—has superclass   ˬ—has subclass   package—see other volume

```
// Compare two boolean arrays
bArr1 = new boolean[]{true, false};
bArr2 = new boolean[]{true, false};
b = Arrays.equals(bArr1, null); // false
b = Arrays.equals(bArr1, bArr2); // true

// There are equals() methods for all eight primitive types
b = Arrays.equals(new byte[]{0}, new byte[]{0}); // true
b = Arrays.equals(new char[]{'a'}, new char[]{'a'}); // true
b = Arrays.equals(new short[]{0}, new short[]{0}); // true
b = Arrays.equals(new int[]{0}, new int[]{0}); // true
b = Arrays.equals(new long[]{0L}, new long[]{0L}); // true
b = Arrays.equals(new float[]{0F}, new float[]{0F}); // true
b = Arrays.equals(new double[]{0D}, new double[]{0D}); // true

// When comparing Object arrays, null elements are equals.
// If the elements are not null, Object.equals() is used.
b = Arrays.equals(new String[]{"a"}, new String[]{"a"}); // true
b = Arrays.equals(new String[]{null}, new String[]{null}); // true
```

ε339. Shuffling the Elements of a List or Array

Use Collections.shuffle() to randomly reorder the elements in a list.

```
// Create a list
List list = new ArrayList();

// Add elements to list

// Shuffle the elements in the list
Collections.shuffle(list);

// Create an array
String[] array = new String[]{"a", "b", "c"};

// Shuffle the elements in the array
Collections.shuffle(Arrays.asList(array));
```

ε340. Converting a Collection to an Array

```
// Create an array containing the elements in a list
Object[] objectArray = list.toArray();
MyClass[] array = (MyClass[])list.toArray(new MyClass[list.size()]);

// Create an array containing the elements in a set
objectArray = set.toArray();
array = (MyClass[])set.toArray(new MyClass[set.size()]);

// Create an array containing the keys in a map
objectArray = map.keySet().toArray();
array = (MyClass[])map.keySet().toArray(new MyClass[set.size()]);

// Create an array containing the values in a map
objectArray = map.values().toArray();
array = (MyClass[])map.values().toArray(new MyClass[set.size()]);
```

ε341. Converting an Array to a Collection

```
// Fixed-size list
List list = Arrays.asList(array);

// Growable list
list = new LinkedList(Arrays.asList(array));
```

```
// Duplicate elements are discarded
Set set = new HashSet(Arrays.asList(array));
```

Collections

ε342. Implementing a Queue

```
LinkedList queue = new LinkedList();

// Add to end of queue
queue.add(object);

// Get head of queue
Object o = queue.removeFirst();

// If the queue is to be used by multiple threads,
// the queue must be wrapped with code to synchronize the methods
queue = (LinkedList)Collections.synchronizedList(queue);
```

ε343. Implementing a Stack

```
LinkedList stack = new LinkedList();

// Push on top of stack
stack.addFirst(object);

// Pop off top of stack
Object o = stack.getFirst();

// If the queue is to be used by multiple threads,
// the queue must be wrapped with code to synchronize the methods
stack = (LinkedList)Collections.synchronizedList(stack);
```

ε344. Implementing a Least-Recently-Used (LRU) Cache

```
// Create cache
final int MAX_ENTRIES = 100;
Map cache = new LinkedHashMap(MAX_ENTRIES+1, .75F, true) {
    // This method is called just after a new entry has been added
    public boolean removeEldestEntry(Map.Entry eldest) {
        return size() > MAX_ENTRIES;
    }
};

// Add to cache
Object key = "key";
cache.put(key, object);

// Get object
Object o = cache.get(key);
if (o == null && !cache.containsKey(key)) {
    // Object not in cache. If null is not a possible value in the cache,
    // the call to cache.contains(key) is not needed
}

// If the cache is to be used by multiple threads,
// the cache must be wrapped with code to synchronize the methods
cache = (Map)Collections.synchronizedMap(cache);
```

Class   *Interface*   —extends   - - -implements   ○ abstract   ● final   ˆ—has superclass   ‿—has subclass   package—see other volume

ε345. Listing the Elements of a Collection

This example demonstrates how to iterate over the elements of various types of collections.

```
// For a set or list
for (Iterator it=collection.iterator(); it.hasNext(); ) {
    Object element = it.next();
}

// For keys of a map
for (Iterator it=map.keySet().iterator(); it.hasNext(); ) {
    Object key = it.next();
}

// For values of a map
for (Iterator it=map.values().iterator(); it.hasNext(); ) {
    Object value = it.next();
}

// For both the keys and values of a map
for (Iterator it=map.entrySet().iterator(); it.hasNext(); ) {
    Map.Entry entry = (Map.Entry)it.next();
    Object key = entry.getKey();
    Object value = entry.getValue();
}
```

ε346. Storing Primitive Types in a Collection

Collections can only store objects, not primitive types like int and double. Primitive types must be placed in a "wrapper" object before they can be placed in a collection. This example demonstrates the storing of int values in a Map.

See also: "ε58. Wrapping a Primitive Type in a Wrapper Object".

```
// Create map
Map map = new HashMap();

// Create int wrapper object
Integer refInt = new Integer(123);

// Store int in map
map.put("key", refInt);

// Get int value from map
refInt = (Integer)map.get("key");

// Get the integer value from wrapper object
int i = refInt.intValue();
```

ε347. Creating a Copy of a Collection

These examples create a shallow copy of a collection. That is, the new collection contains references to same objects as the source collection; the objects are not cloned.

```
List stuff = Arrays.asList(new String[]{"a", "b"});

// Make a copy of a list
List list = new ArrayList(stuff);
List list2 = new LinkedList(list);

// Make a copy of a set
Set set = new HashSet(stuff);
Set set2 = new TreeSet(set);

// Make a copy of a map
```

```
Map map = new HashMap();
// Add key/value pairs ...
Map map2 = new TreeMap(map);
```

ε348. Making a Collection Read-Only

Making a collection read-only involves wrapping the collection in another object whose mutation methods all throw UnsupportedOperationException.

```
List stuff = Arrays.asList(new String[]{"a", "b"});

// Make a list read-only
List list = new ArrayList(stuff);
list = Collections.unmodifiableList(list);

try {
    // Try modifying the list
    list.set(0, "new value");
} catch (UnsupportedOperationException e) {
    // Can't modify
}

// Make a set read-only
Set set = new HashSet(stuff);
set = Collections.unmodifiableSet(set);

// Make a map read-only
Map map = new HashMap();
// Add key/value pairs ...
map = Collections.unmodifiableMap(map);
```

Lists

ε349. Creating a List

```
// Create the list
List list = new LinkedList(); // Doubly-linked list
list = new ArrayList(); // List implemented as growable array

// Append an element to the list
list.add("a");

// Insert an element at the head of the list
list.add(0, "b");

// Get the number of elements in the list
int size = list.size(); // 2

// Retrieving the element at the end of the list
Object element = list.get(list.size()-1); // a

// Retrieving the element at the head of the list
element = list.get(0); // b

// Remove the first occurrence of an element
boolean b = list.remove("b"); // true
b = list.remove("b"); // false

// Remove the element at a particular index
element = list.remove(0); // a
```

Class   *Interface*   —extends   - - -implements   ○ abstract   ● final   ^—has superclass   ⌄—has subclass   package—see other volume

ε350. Sorting a List

```
// Create a list
String[] strArray = new String[] {"z", "a", "C"};
List list = Arrays.asList(strArray);

// Sort
Collections.sort(list);
// C, a, z

// Case-insensitive sort
Collections.sort(list, String.CASE_INSENSITIVE_ORDER);
// a, C, z

// Reverse-order sort
Collections.sort(list, Collections.reverseOrder());
// z, a, C

// Case-insensitive reverse-order sort
Collections.sort(list, String.CASE_INSENSITIVE_ORDER);
Collections.reverse(list);
// z, C, a
```

ε351. Operating on Lists

See also "ε349. Creating a List".

```
// Create the lists
List list1 = new ArrayList();
List list2 = new ArrayList();

// Add elements to the lists ...

// Copy all the elements from list2 to list1 (list1 += list2)
// list1 becomes the union of list1 and list2
list1.addAll(list2);

// Remove all the elements in list1 from list2 (list1 -= list2)
// list1 becomes the asymmetric difference of list1 and list2
list1.removeAll(list2);

// Get the intersection of list1 and list2
// list1 becomes the intersection of list1 and list2
list1.retainAll(list2);

// Remove all elements from a list
list1.clear();

// Truncate the list
int newSize = 2;
list1.subList(newSize, list1.size()).clear();
```

Sets

ε352. Creating a Set

A set is a collection that holds unique values. Adding a value that's already in the set has no effect.

```
// Create the set
Set set = new HashSet();

// Add elements to the set
set.add("a");
set.add("b");
```

```
    set.add("c");

    // Remove elements from the set
    set.remove("c");

    // Get number of elements in set
    int size = set.size(); // 2

    // Adding an element that already exists in the set has no effect
    set.add("a");
    size = set.size(); // 2

    // Determining if an element is in the set
    boolean b = set.contains("a"); // true
    b = set.contains("c"); // false

    // Iterating over the elements in the set
    Iterator it = set.iterator();
    while (it.hasNext()) {
        // Get element
        Object element = it.next();
    }

    // Create an array containing the elements in the set (in this case a String array)
    String[] array = (String[])set.toArray(new String[set.size()]);
```

ε353. Operating on Sets

See also "ε352. Creating a Set".

```
    // Create the sets
    Set set1 = new HashSet();
    Set set2 = new HashSet();

    // Add elements to the sets ...

    // Copy all the elements from set2 to set1 (set1 += set2)
    // set1 becomes the union of set1 and set2
    set1.addAll(set2);

    // Remove all the elements in set1 from set2 (set1 -= set2)
    // set1 becomes the asymmetric difference of set1 and set2
    set1.removeAll(set2);

    // Get the intersection of set1 and set2
    // set1 becomes the intersection of set1 and set2
    set1.retainAll(set2);

    // Remove all elements from a set
    set1.clear();
```

ε354. Creating a Set That Retains Order-of-Insertion

```
    Set set = new LinkedHashSet();

    // Add some elements
    set.add("1");
    set.add("2");
    set.add("3");
    set.add("2");

    // List the elements
    for (Iterator it=set.iterator(); it.hasNext(); ) {
```

Class *Interface* —extends - - -implements ○ abstract ● final ^—has superclass ‿—has subclass package —see other volume

```
        Object o = it.next();
    }
    // [1, 2, 3]
```

ε355. Creating a Hash Table

A hash table, or "map", holds key/value pairs.

```
// Create a hash table
Map map = new HashMap(); // hash table
map = new TreeMap(); // sorted map

// Add key/value pairs to the map
map.put("a", new Integer(1));
map.put("b", new Integer(2));
map.put("c", new Integer(3));

// Get number of entries in map
int size = map.size(); // 2

// Adding an entry whose key exists in the map causes
// the new value to replace the old value
Object oldValue = map.put("a", new Integer(9)); // 1

// Remove an entry from the map and return the value of the removed entry
oldValue = map.remove("c"); // 3

// Iterate over the keys in the map
Iterator it = map.keySet().iterator();
while (it.hasNext()) {
    // Get key
    Object key = it.next();
}

// Iterate over the values in the map
it = map.values().iterator();
while (it.hasNext()) {
    // Get value
    Object value = it.next();
}
```

ε356. Creating a Map That Retains Order-of-Insertion

```
Map map = new LinkedHashMap();

// Add some elements
map.put("1", "value1");
map.put("2", "value2");
map.put("3", "value3");
map.put("2", "value4");

// List the entries
for (Iterator it=map.keySet().iterator(); it.hasNext(); ) {
    Object key = it.next();
    Object value = map.get(key);
}
// [1=value1, 2=value4, 3=value3]
```

Packages

ε357. Automatically Removing an Unreferenced Element from a Hash Table

When a key is added to a map, the map will prevent the key from being garbage-collected. However, a "weak map" will automatically remove a key if the key is not being referenced by any other object. An example where this type of map might be useful is a registry where a registrant is automatically removed after it is garbage-collected.

```
// Create the weak map
Map weakMap = new WeakHashMap();

// Add a key to the weak map
weakMap.put(keyObject, valueObject);

// Get all keys that are still being referenced
Iterator it = weakMap.keySet().iterator();
while (it.hasNext()) {
    // Get key
    Object key = it.next();
}
```

The weak map does not automatically release the value if it is no longer used. To enable automatically release of the value, the value must be wrapped in a WeakReference object:

```
WeakReference weakValue = new WeakReference(valueObject);
weakMap.put(keyObject, weakValue);

// Get all keys that are still being referenced and check whether
// or not the value has been garbage-collected
it = weakMap.keySet().iterator();
while (it.hasNext()) {
    // Get key
    Object key = it.next();

    weakValue = (WeakReference)weakMap.get(key);
    if (weakValue == null) {
        // Value has been garbage-collected
    } else {
        // Get value
        valueObject = weakValue.get();
    }
}
```

Sorted Collections

ε358. Creating a Sorted Set

A sorted set is a set that maintains its elements in a sorted order. Inserts and retrievals are more expensive in a sorted set but iterations over the set is always in order.

See also "ε352. Creating a Set".

```
// Create the sorted set
SortedSet set = new TreeSet();

// Add elements to the set
set.add("b");
set.add("c");
set.add("a");

// Iterating over the elements in the set
```

```
Iterator it = set.iterator();
while (it.hasNext()) {
    // Get element
    Object element = it.next();
}
// The elements are iterated in order: a, b, c

// Create an array containing the elements in a set (in this case a String array).
// The elements in the array are in order.
String[] array = (String[])set.toArray(new String[set.size()]);
```

ε359. Sorting an Array

```
int[] intArray = new int[] {4, 1, 3, -23};
Arrays.sort(intArray);
// [-23, 1, 3, 4]

String[] strArray = new String[] {"z", "a", "C"};
Arrays.sort(strArray);
// [C, a, z]

// Case-insensitive sort
Arrays.sort(strArray, String.CASE_INSENSITIVE_ORDER);
// [a, C, z]

// Reverse-order sort
Arrays.sort(strArray, Collections.reverseOrder());
// [z, a, C]

// Case-insensitive reverse-order sort
Arrays.sort(strArray, String.CASE_INSENSITIVE_ORDER);
Collections.reverse(Arrays.asList(strArray));
// [z, C, a]
```

ε360. Finding an Element in a Sorted Array

This example also works if the object is a primitive type.

```
int index = Arrays.binarySearch(sortedArray, object);
if (index < 0) {
    // not found
}
```

ε361. Finding an Element in a Sorted List

```
int index = Collections.binarySearch(sortedList, object);
if (index < 0) {
    // not found
}
```

ε362. Inserting an Element into a Sorted List

```
int index = Collections.binarySearch(sortedList, object);
if (index < 0) {
    sortedList.add(-index-1, object);
}
```

Packages

Bits

ε363. Performing Bitwise Operations on a Bit Vector

The BitSet class implements a bit-vector of an arbitrary size. It automatically grows dynamically. This example demonstrates how to create and use a BitSet.

The BigInteger class also support bitwise operations (see "ε129. Performing Bitwise Operations with Big-Integer"). However, a BigInteger object is immutable where a BitSet is mutable.

```
// Create the bitset
BitSet bits = new BitSet();

// Set a bit on
bits.set(2); // 100 = decimal 4

// Retrieving the value of a bit
boolean b = bits.get(0); // false
b = bits.get(2); // true

// Clear a bit
bits.clear(1);

// Setting a range of bits
BitSet bits2 = new BitSet();
bits2.set(1, 4); // 1110

// And'ing two bitsets
bits.and(bits2); // 0100

// Xor'ing two bitsets
bits.xor(bits2); // 1010

// Flip all bits in the bitset
bits.flip(0, bits.length()); // 0101

// Andnot'ing two bitsets
bits.andNot(bits2); // 0001

// Or'ing two bitsets
bits.or(bits2); // 1111
```

ε364. Converting Between a BitSet and a Byte Array

There are no default methods for converting a BitSet to and from a byte array. This example implements two methods to do the conversion. These methods make it possible to easily work with both BitSet and BigInteger and take advantage of their capabilities when needed.

```
// Returns a bitset containing the values in bytes.
// The byte-ordering of bytes must be big-endian which means the most significant bit is in element 0.
public static BitSet fromByteArray(byte[] bytes) {
    BitSet bits = new BitSet();
    for (int i=0; i<bytes.length*8; i++) {
        if ((bytes[bytes.length-i/8-1]&(1<<(i%8))) > 0) {
            bits.set(i);
        }
    }
    return bits;
}

// Returns a byte array of at least length 1.
// The most significant bit in the result is guaranteed not to be a 1
```

Class *Interface* —extends - - -implements ○ abstract ● final ^—has superclass ⌐—has subclass package—see other volume

```
// (since BitSet does not support sign extension).
// The byte-ordering of the result is big-endian which means the most significant bit is in element 0.
// The bit at index 0 of the bit set is assumed to be the least significant bit.
public static byte[] toByteArray(BitSet bits) {
    byte[] bytes = new byte[bits.length()/8+1];
    for (int i=0; i<bits.length(); i++) {
        if (bits.get(i)) {
            bytes[bytes.length-i/8-1] |= 1«(i%8);
        }
    }
    return bytes;
}
```

Property Files

ε365. Reading and Writing a Properties File

```
// Read properties file.
Properties properties = new Properties();
try {
    properties.load(new FileInputStream("filename.properties"));
} catch (IOException e) {
}

// Write properties file.
try {
    properties.store(new FileOutputStream("filename.properties"), null);
} catch (IOException e) {
}
```

Here is an example of the contents of a properties file:

```
# a comment
! a comment

a = a string
b = a string with escape sequences \t \n \r \\\" \' \(space) \u0123
c = a string with a continuation line \
    continuation line
d.e.f = another string
```

ε366. Getting and Setting Properties

```
String string = properties.getProperty("a.b");
properties.setProperty("a.b", "new value");
```

Timers

ε367. Scheduling a Timer Task to Run at a Certain Time

```
int numberOfMillisecondsInTheFuture = 10000; // 10 sec
Date timeToRun = new Date(System.currentTimeMillis()+numberOfMillisecondsInTheFuture);
Timer timer = new Timer();

timer.schedule(new TimerTask() {
        public void run() {
            // Task here ...
        }
    }, timeToRun);
```

ε368. Scheduling a Timer Task to Run Repeatedly

```java
int delay = 5000; // delay for 5 sec.
int period = 1000; // repeat every sec.
Timer timer = new Timer();

timer.scheduleAtFixedRate(new TimerTask() {
        public void run() {
            // Task here ...
        }
    }, delay, period);
```

Time

ε369. Getting the Current Time

```java
Calendar cal = new GregorianCalendar();

// Get the components of the time
int hour12 = cal.get(Calendar.HOUR); // 0..11
int hour24 = cal.get(Calendar.HOUR_OF_DAY); // 0..23
int min = cal.get(Calendar.MINUTE); // 0..59
int sec = cal.get(Calendar.SECOND); // 0..59
int ms = cal.get(Calendar.MILLISECOND); // 0..999
int ampm = cal.get(Calendar.AM_PM); // 0=AM, 1=PM
```

ε370. Getting the Current Time in Another Time Zone

```java
// Get the current time in Hong Kong
Calendar cal = new GregorianCalendar(TimeZone.getTimeZone("Hongkong"));

int hour12 = cal.get(Calendar.HOUR); // 0..11
int minutes = cal.get(Calendar.MINUTE); // 0..59
int seconds = cal.get(Calendar.SECOND); // 0..59
boolean am = cal.get(Calendar.AM_PM) == Calendar.AM;

// Get the current hour-of-day at GMT
cal.setTimeZone(TimeZone.getTimeZone("GMT"));
int hour24 = cal.get(Calendar.HOUR_OF_DAY); // 0..23

// Get the current local hour-of-day
cal.setTimeZone(TimeZone.getDefault());
hour24 = cal.get(Calendar.HOUR_OF_DAY); // 0..23
```

ε371. Retrieving Information on All Available Time Zones

This example lists all time zones known by the JDK.

```java
Date today = new Date();

// Get all time zone ids
String[] zoneIds = TimeZone.getAvailableIDs();

// View every time zone
for (int i=0; i<zoneIds.length; i++) {
    // Get time zone by time zone id
    TimeZone tz = TimeZone.getTimeZone(zoneIds[i]);

    // Get the display name
    String shortName = tz.getDisplayName(tz.inDaylightTime(today), TimeZone.SHORT);
    String longName = tz.getDisplayName(tz.inDaylightTime(today), TimeZone.LONG);
```

```
    // Get the number of hours from GMT
    int rawOffset = tz.getRawOffset();
    int hour = rawOffset / (60*60*1000);
    int min = Math.abs(rawOffset / (60*1000)) % 60;

    // Does the time zone have a daylight savings time period?
    boolean hasDST = tz.useDaylightTime();

    // Is the time zone currently in a daylight savings time?
    boolean inDST = tz.inDaylightTime(today);
}
```

Here's a few time zone entries:

```
Id, Short Name, Long Name, Hour:Time from GMT

ACT, CST, Central Standard Time (Northern Territory) 9:30
AET, EST, Eastern Summer Time (New South Wales) 10:0
AGT, ART, Argentine Time -3:0
ART, EET, Eastern European Time 2:0
AST, AKST, Alaska Standard Time -9:0
Africa/Abidjan, GMT, Greenwich Mean Time 0:0
Africa/Accra, GMT, Greenwich Mean Time 0:0
Africa/Addis_Ababa, EAT, Eastern African Time 3:0
Africa/Algiers, CET, Central European Time 1:0
Africa/Asmera, EAT, Eastern African Time 3:0
Africa/Bamako, GMT, Greenwich Mean Time 0:0
Africa/Bangui, WAT, Western African Time 1:0
```

ε372. Converting Times Between Time Zones

There is a convenient setTimeZone() method in the Calendar object. However, it doesn't always return the correct results when used after a calendar field is set. This example demonstrates a more reliable way to convert a specific time from one time zone to another. It involves creating two Calendar instances and transfering the UTC (Coordinate Universal Time) from one to the other. The UTC is a representation of time and date that is independent of time zones.

```
    // Given a local time of 10am, get the time in Japan
    // Create a Calendar object with the local time zone
    Calendar local = new GregorianCalendar();
    local.set(Calendar.HOUR_OF_DAY, 10); // 0..23
    local.set(Calendar.MINUTE, 0);
    local.set(Calendar.SECOND, 0);

    // Create an instance using Japan's time zone and set it with the local UTC
    Calendar japanCal = new GregorianCalendar(TimeZone.getTimeZone("Japan"));
    japanCal.setTimeInMillis(local.getTimeInMillis());

    // Get the foreign time
    int hour = japanCal.get(Calendar.HOUR); // 3
    int minutes = japanCal.get(Calendar.MINUTE); // 0
    int seconds = japanCal.get(Calendar.SECOND); // 0
    boolean am = japanCal.get(Calendar.AM_PM) == Calendar.AM; //true


    // Given a time of 10am in Japan, get the local time
    japanCal = new GregorianCalendar(TimeZone.getTimeZone("Japan"));
    japanCal.set(Calendar.HOUR_OF_DAY, 10); // 0..23
    japanCal.set(Calendar.MINUTE, 0);
    japanCal.set(Calendar.SECOND, 0);
```

```
// Create a Calendar object with the local time zone and set
// the UTC from japanCal
local = new GregorianCalendar();
local.setTimeInMillis(japanCal.getTimeInMillis());

// Get the time in the local time zone
hour = local.get(Calendar.HOUR); // 5
minutes = local.get(Calendar.MINUTE); // 0
seconds = local.get(Calendar.SECOND); // 0
am = local.get(Calendar.AM_PM) == Calendar.AM; // false
```

Dates

ε373. Getting the Current Date

```
Calendar cal = new GregorianCalendar();

// Get the components of the date
int era = cal.get(Calendar.ERA); // 0=BC, 1=AD
int year = cal.get(Calendar.YEAR); // 2002
int month = cal.get(Calendar.MONTH); // 0=Jan, 1=Feb, ...
int day = cal.get(Calendar.DAY_OF_MONTH); // 1...
int dayOfWeek = cal.get(Calendar.DAY_OF_WEEK); // 1=Sunday, 2=Monday, ...
```

ε374. Creating a Date Object for a Particular Date

```
Calendar xmas = new GregorianCalendar(1998, Calendar.DECEMBER, 25);
Date date = xmas.getTime();
```

ε375. Determining the Number of Days in a Month

This example uses the Calendar class to determine the number of days in the month of a particular year.

```
// Create a calendar object of the desired month
Calendar cal = new GregorianCalendar(1999, Calendar.FEBRUARY, 1);

// Get the number of days in that month
int days = cal.getActualMaximum(Calendar.DAY_OF_MONTH); // 28

// Try month in a leap year
cal = new GregorianCalendar(2000, Calendar.FEBRUARY, 1);
days = cal.getActualMaximum(Calendar.DAY_OF_MONTH); // 29
```

ε376. Comparing Dates

```
Calendar xmas = new GregorianCalendar(1998, Calendar.DECEMBER, 25);

Calendar newyears = new GregorianCalendar(1999, Calendar.JANUARY, 1);

// Determine which is earlier
boolean b = xmas.after(newyears); // false
b = xmas.before(newyears); // true


// Get difference in milliseconds
long diffMillis = newyears.getTimeInMillis()-xmas.getTimeInMillis();

// Get difference in seconds
long diffSecs = diffMillis/(1000); // 604800

// Get difference in minutes
```

Class   *Interface*   —extends   - - -implements   ○ abstract   ● final   ^—has superclass   ‿—has subclass   package—see other volume

```
long diffMins = diffMillis/(60*1000); // 10080

// Get difference in hours
long diffHours = diffMillis/(60*60*1000); // 168

// Get difference in days
long diffDays = diffMillis/(24*60*60*1000); // 7
```

ε377. Determining a Person's Age

This example uses the Calendar class to compute a person's age.

```
// Create a calendar object with the date of birth
Calendar dateOfBirth = new GregorianCalendar(1972, Calendar.JANUARY, 27);

// Create a calendar object with today's date
Calendar today = Calendar.getInstance();

// Get age based on year
int age = today.get(Calendar.YEAR) - dateOfBirth.get(Calendar.YEAR);

// Add the tentative age to the date of birth to get this year's birthday
dateOfBirth.add(Calendar.YEAR, age);

// If this year's birthday has not happened yet, subtract one from age
if (today.before(dateOfBirth)) {
    age–;
}
```

ε378. Determining If a Year Is a Leap Year

```
GregorianCalendar cal = new GregorianCalendar();
boolean b = cal.isLeapYear(1998); // false
b = cal.isLeapYear(2000); // true
b = cal.isLeapYear(0); // true
```

ε379. Determining the Day-of-Week for a Particular Date

The day-of-week is an integer value where 1 is Sunday, 2 is Monday, ..., and 7 is Saturday

```
Calendar xmas = new GregorianCalendar(1998, Calendar.DECEMBER, 25);
int dayOfWeek = xmas.get(Calendar.DAY_OF_WEEK); // 6=Friday

Calendar cal = new GregorianCalendar(2003, Calendar.JANUARY, 1);
dayOfWeek = cal.get(Calendar.DAY_OF_WEEK); // 4=Wednesday
```

Packages

---

java.util.jar

This package contains classes for creating and reading JAR files. Its classes extend some of the classes in the java.util.zip package in order to support reading and storing meta-information about the JAR file contents in the form of a Manifest file.

```
java.lang.Object
1.2     ├ Attributes - - - - - - - - - - - - - - - - - - - - - - - - - - - - - - - - - - - - - - - - - java.lang.Cloneable ˎ, java.util.Map ˎ
1.2     ├ Attributes.Name
1.2     ├ Manifest - - - - - - - - - - - - - - - - - - - - - - - - - - - - - - - - - - - -ᵢ  java.lang.Cloneable ˎ
  ○     ├ java.io.InputStream
        │   └ java.io.FilterInputStream
1.1     │        └ java.util.zip.InflaterInputStream
1.1     │             └ java.util.zip.ZipInputStream
1.2     │                  └ JarInputStream
  ○     ├ java.io.OutputStream
        │   └ java.io.FilterOutputStream
1.1     │        └ java.util.zip.DeflaterOutputStream
1.1     │             └ java.util.zip.ZipOutputStream
1.2     │                  └ JarOutputStream
1.1     ├ java.util.zip.ZipEntry - - - - - - - - - - - - - - - - - - - - - -
1.2     │   └ JarEntry
1.1     ├ java.util.zip.ZipFile
1.2     │   └ JarFile
        └ java.lang.Throwable - - - - - - - - - - - - - - - - - - - - - - - - - - - java.io.Serializable ˎ
            └ java.lang.Exception
                └ java.io.IOException
1.1                  └ java.util.zip.ZipException
1.2                       └ JarException
```

ε380. Listing the Entries of a JAR File Manifest

```java
try {
    // Open the JAR file
    JarFile jarfile = new JarFile("filename.jar");

    // Get the manifest
    Manifest manifest = jarfile.getManifest();

    // Get the manifest entries
    Map map = manifest.getEntries();

    // Enumerate each entry
    for (Iterator it=map.keySet().iterator(); it.hasNext(); ) {
        // Get entry name
        String entryName = (String)it.next();

        // Get all attributes for the entry
        Attributes attrs = (Attributes)map.get(entryName);

        // Enumerate each attribute
        for (Iterator it2=attrs.keySet().iterator(); it2.hasNext(); ) {
            // Get attribute name
            Attributes.Name attrName = (Attributes.Name)it2.next();

            // Get attribute value
            String attrValue = attrs.getValue(attrName);
        }
    }
```

Class   *Interface*   —extends   - - -implements   ○ abstract   ● final   ˆ—has superclass   ˎ—has subclass   package—see other volume

```
    } catch (IOException e) {
    }
```

ε381. Listing the Main Attributes in a JAR File Manifest

The main attributes of a JAR file are values that are associated with the JAR file itself, not with any particular entry.

```
try {
    // Open the JAR file
    JarFile jarfile = new JarFile("filename.jar");

    // Get the manifest
    Manifest manifest = jarfile.getManifest();

    // Get the main attributes in the manifest
    Attributes attrs = (Attributes)manifest.getMainAttributes();

    // Enumerate each attribute
    for (Iterator it=attrs.keySet().iterator(); it.hasNext(); ) {
        // Get attribute name
        Attributes.Name attrName = (Attributes.Name)it.next();

        // Get attribute value
        String attrValue = attrs.getValue(attrName);
    }
} catch (IOException e) {
}
```

Here's an example of main attributes for a JAR file:

```
Attribute Name: Attribute Value

Specification-Title: Java Platform API Specification
Specification-Version: 1.4
Implementation-Title: Java Runtime Environment
Implementation-Version: 1.4.0-rc
Created-By: 1.4.0 (Sun Microsystems Inc.)
Manifest-Version: 1.0
Implementation-Vendor: Sun Microsystems, Inc.
Specification-Vendor: Sun Microsystems, Inc.
```

ε382. Creating a Manifest for a JAR File

A manifest for a JAR file can only be created from an input stream. This example creates a manifest from a file and from a constructed string. The format of a manifest is described in:

```
http://java.sun.com/products/jdk/1.2/docs/guide/jar/manifest.html
```

```
try {
    // Create a manifest from a file
    InputStream fis = new FileInputStream("manifestfile");
    Manifest manifest = new Manifest(fis);


    // Construct a string version of a manifest
    StringBuffer sbuf = new StringBuffer();
    sbuf.append("Manifest-Version: 1.0\n");
    sbuf.append("\n");
    sbuf.append("Name: javax/swing/JScrollPane.class\n");
    sbuf.append("Java-Bean: True\n");

    // Convert the string to a input stream
```

```
            InputStream is = new ByteArrayInputStream(sbuf.toString().getBytes("UTF-8"));

            // Create the manifest
            manifest = new Manifest(is);
    } catch (IOException e) {
    }
```

Here's an example of a manifest file:

```
    Manifest-Version: 1.0
    Specification-Title: Java Platform API Specification
    Specification-Version: 1.4
    Implementation-Title: Java Runtime Environment
    Implementation-Version: 1.4.0-rc
    Created-By: 1.4.0-rc (Sun Microsystems Inc.)
    Implementation-Vendor: Sun Microsystems, Inc.
    Specification-Vendor: Sun Microsystems, Inc.

    Name: javax/swing/JScrollPane.class
    Java-Bean: True

    Name: javax/swing/JCheckBoxMenuItem.class
    Java-Bean: True

    Name: javax/swing/JTabbedPane.class
    Java-Bean: True

    Name: javax/swing/JMenuItem.class
    Java-Bean: True

    Name: javax/swing/JTable.class
    Java-Bean: True
```

ε383. Writing a JAR File Manifest to a File

The format of a manifest file is described in:

http://java.sun.com/products/jdk/1.2/docs/guide/jar/manifest.html

This example retrieves the manifest from a JAR file and writes the manifest contents to a file.

```
    try {
        // Open the JAR file
        JarFile jarfile = new JarFile("filename.jar");

        // Get the manifest
        Manifest manifest = jarfile.getManifest();

        // Write the manifest to a file
        OutputStream fos = new FileOutputStream("manifest");
        jarfile.getManifest().write(fos);
        fos.close();
    } catch (IOException e) {
    }
```

Here's an example of a manifest file:

```
    Manifest-Version: 1.0
    Specification-Title: Java Platform API Specification
    Specification-Version: 1.4
    Implementation-Title: Java Runtime Environment
    Implementation-Version: 1.4.0-rc
```

Class   *Interface*   —extends   - - -implements   ○ abstract   ● final   ˆ—has superclass   ˳—has subclass   package—see other volume

Created-By: 1.4.0-rc (Sun Microsystems Inc.)
Implementation-Vendor: Sun Microsystems, Inc.
Specification-Vendor: Sun Microsystems, Inc.

Name: javax/swing/JScrollPane.class
Java-Bean: True

Name: javax/swing/JCheckBoxMenuItem.class
Java-Bean: True

Name: javax/swing/JTabbedPane.class
Java-Bean: True

Name: javax/swing/JMenuItem.class
Java-Bean: True

Name: javax/swing/JTable.class
Java-Bean: True

ε384. Creating and Signing a JAR File Using jarsigner

// Create the jar file
> jar cf *myjar.jar MyClass.class*

// Sign it with the certificate named *alias* in the keystore
> jarsigner -keystore *.keystore* -storepass *password myjar.jar alias*

java.util.logging

This package provides the classes and interfaces for performing logging. It allows software running on the Java platform to log messages at various levels of detail and allows the logged data to be exported to different types of destinations, including memory, output streams, consoles, files, and network sockets. The package also provides mechanisms for the logged data to be filtered and formatted.

java.lang.Object
1.4 ├ ErrorManager

```
        java.lang.Object
1.4 ○    ├ Formatter
1.4       ├ SimpleFormatter
1.4       └ XMLFormatter
1.4 ○    ├ Handler
1.4       ├ MemoryHandler
1.4       └ StreamHandler
1.4          ├ ConsoleHandler
1.4          ├ FileHandler
1.4          └ SocketHandler
1.4    ├ Level - - - - - - - - - - - - - - - - - - - - - - - - - - - ⌐ java.io.Serializable ˌ
1.4    ├ LogManager                                                   ⁝
1.4    ├ LogRecord - - - - - - - - - - - - - - - - - - - - - - - - - ⌙
1.4    ├ Logger
1.2 ○  └ java.security.Permission - - - - - - - - - - - - - - - - - java.io.Serializable ˌ, java.security.Guard
1.2 ○      └ java.security.BasicPermission - - - - - - - - - - - - - java.io.Serializable ˌ
1.4 ●          └ LoggingPermission
1.4    Filter
```

ε385. The Quintessential Logging Program

To log a message, you first need to obtain a Logger object and then use it to log the message. Loggers have names that resemble a fully qualified class name. Typically, log messages generated from a class would use a Logger with the same name as the class.

The logger contains one or more handlers that are responsible for processing the log records. A handler could write to a file or print to a console. Typically, the code that generates log records should not concern itself with where those log records end up. It only needs to decide the name of the logger to use.

This example logs a few messages to a logger. For examples of controlling the destination of the log messages, see "ε391. Writing Log Records to a Log File" and "ε392. Writing Log Records to Standard Error".

```java
import java.io.*;
import java.util.logging.*;

package com.mycompany;
public class BasicLogging {
    public static void main(String[] args) {
        // Get a logger; the logger is automatically created if
        // it doesn't already exist
        Logger logger = Logger.getLogger("com.mycompany.BasicLogging");

        // Log a few message at different severity levels
        logger.severe("my severe message");
        logger.warning("my warning message");
        logger.info("my info message");
        logger.config("my config message");
        logger.fine("my fine message");
        logger.finer("my finer message");
        logger.finest("my finest message");
    }
}
```

Class *Interface* —extends - - -implements ○ abstract ● final ^—has superclass ˌ—has subclass package—see other volume

ε386. Determining If a Message Will Be Logged

See also "ε389. Minimizing the Impact of Logging Code".

```
Logger logger = Logger.getLogger("com.mycompany.MyClass");

// Check if the message will be logged
if (logger.isLoggable(Level.FINEST)) {
    logger.finest("my finest message");
}
```

ε387. Logging a Method Call

The logger provides convenience methods Logger.entering() and Logger.exiting() for logging method calls. This example implements a method that logs the parameters upon entry and the result when returning.

See also "ε388. Logging an Exception".

```
package com.mycompany;
class MyClass {
    public boolean myMethod(int p1, Object p2) {
        // Log entry
        Logger logger = Logger.getLogger("com.mycompany.MyClass");
        if (logger.isLoggable(Level.FINER)) {
            logger.entering(this.getClass().getName(), "myMethod",
                            new Object[]{new Integer(p1), p2});
        }

        // Method body

        // Log exit
        boolean result = true;
        if (logger.isLoggable(Level.FINER)) {
            logger.exiting(this.getClass().getName(), "myMethod", new Boolean(result));

            // Use the following if the method does not return a value
            logger.exiting(this.getClass().getName(), "myMethod");
        }
        return result;
    }
}
```

Here is a sample of the output using a simple formatter and the following call:

```
new com.mycompany.MyClass().myMethod(123, "hello");

Jan 10, 2002 7:59:48 PM com.mycompany.MyClass myMethod
FINER: ENTRY 123 hello
Jan 10, 2002 7:59:49 PM com.mycompany.MyClass myMethod
FINER: RETURN true
Jan 10, 2002 7:59:49 PM com.mycompany.MyClass myMethod
FINER: RETURN
```

ε388. Logging an Exception

The logger method log() can be used to log an exception. Also, the convenience method Logger.throwing() can be used by a method about to throw an exception.

```
package com.mycompany;
class MyClass {
    public void myMethod() {
        Logger logger = Logger.getLogger("com.mycompany.MyClass");

        // This method should be used when an exception is encounted
```

```
        try {
            // Test with an exception
            throw new IOException();
        } catch (Throwable e){
            // Log the exception
            logger.log(Level.SEVERE, "Uncaught exception", e);
        }

        // When a method is throwing an exception, this method should be used
        Exception ex = new IllegalStateException();
        logger.throwing(this.getClass().getName(), "myMethod", ex);
    }
}
```

Here is a sample of the output generated by the example:

```
Jan 11, 2002 5:16:49 PM com.mycompany.MyClass myMethod
SEVERE: Uncaught exception
java.io.IOException
        at com.mycompany.MyClass.myMethod(com.mycompany.MyClass.java:32)
        at com.mycompany.MyClass.main(com.mycompany.MyClass.java:18)
Jan 11, 2002 5:16:50 PM com.mycompany.MyClass myMethod
FINER: THROW
java.lang.IllegalStateException
        at com.mycompany.MyClass.myMethod(com.mycompany.MyClass.java:25)
        at com.mycompany.MyClass.main(com.mycompany.MyClass.java:18)
```

ε389. Minimizing the Impact of Logging Code

It is good to add logging code to an application, but the logging code should minimize its impact on the application, especially if the logging is not enabled. In particular, if the message to be potentially logged needs to be constructed, the method call should be wrapped in a cheaper check. For example, the method call

```
int count = 123;
Logger logger = Logger.getLogger("com.mycompany.MyClass");
logger.finest("count: "+count);
```

will cause the count to be converted to a string and then concatenated to another string. This is a lot of wasted work if the message will not be logged. To avoid this overhead, use Logger.isLoggable() to check if the message would be logged before calling the logging method. For example,

```
if (logger.isLoggable(Level.FINEST)) {
    logger.finest("count: "+count);
}
```

ε390. Preventing a Logger from Forwarding Log Records to its Parent

By default, a logger sends a log record not only to its handlers but to all the handlers of ancestor loggers. If the effects of the parent handlers are not desired, it is necessary to prevent log records from being forwarded to the parent.

This example demonstrates how to stop a logger from sending log records to its parent.

Note: Although the level of a log record is tested against the logger's log level, this test is not done with any of the logger's parents. However, the log level of all handlers is still in effect.

```
// Get a logger
Logger logger = Logger.getLogger("com.mycompany");
```

```
// Stop forwarding log records to ancestor handlers
logger.setUseParentHandlers(false);

// Start forwarding log records to ancestor handlers
logger.setUseParentHandlers(true);
```

ε391. Writing Log Records to a Log File

To make a logger write log records to a file, you need to add a file handler to the logger.

```
try {
    // Create a file handler that write log record to a file called my.log
    FileHandler handler = new FileHandler("my.log");

    // Add to the desired logger
    Logger logger = Logger.getLogger("com.mycompany");
    logger.addHandler(handler);
} catch (IOException e) {
}
```

By default, a file handler overwrites the contents of the log file each time it is created. This example creates a file handler that appends.

```
try {
    // Create an appending file handler
    boolean append = true;
    FileHandler handler = new FileHandler("my.log", append);

    // Add to the desired logger
    Logger logger = Logger.getLogger("com.mycompany");
    logger.addHandler(handler);
} catch (IOException e) {
}
```

ε392. Writing Log Records to Standard Error

To make a logger print log records on standard error, you need to add a ConsoleHandler to the logger.

```
// Create a console handler
ConsoleHandler handler = new ConsoleHandler();

// Add to logger
Logger logger = Logger.getLogger("com.mycompany");
logger.addHandler(handler);
```

ε393. Writing Log Records Only After a Condition Occurs

Suppose you are trying to track down an infrequent bug on a production system with copious amounts of debug log messages. In most cases, when the bug occurs, it is not necessary to have the entire history of log messages; only a recent few are needed. To minimize the impact on the system, a MemoryHandler can be used to store a number of log records in memory and then dump them out only if the bug or other condition occurs.

```
try {
    // Create a memory handler with a memory of 100 records
    // and dumps the records into the file my.log when a
    // SEVERE message is logged
    FileHandler fhandler = new FileHandler("my.log");
    int numRec = 100;
    MemoryHandler mhandler = new MemoryHandler(fhandler, numRec, Level.SEVERE);

    // Add to the desired logger
```

```
            Logger logger = Logger.getLogger("com.mycompany");
            logger.addHandler(mhandler);
    } catch (IOException e) {
    }

    try {
            // Create a memory handler with a memory of 100 records
            // and dumps the records into the file my.log when a
            // some abitrary condition occurs
            FileHandler fhandler = new FileHandler("my.log");
            int numRec = 100;
            MemoryHandler mhandler = new MemoryHandler(fhandler, numRec, Level.OFF) {
                    public synchronized void publish(LogRecord record) {
                            // Log it before checking the condition
                            super.publish(record);

                            boolean condition = false;
                            if (condition) {
                                    // Condition occurred so dump buffered records
                                    push();
                            }
                    }
            };

            // Add to the desired logger
            Logger logger = Logger.getLogger("com.mycompany");
            logger.addHandler(mhandler);
    } catch (IOException e) {
    }
```

ε394. Setting a Filter on a Logger Handler

A handler automatically filters messages based on a log level. For other types of filtering, you can set your own custom filter on a handler.

```
    // Create a handler
    ConsoleHandler handler = new ConsoleHandler();

    // Set the filter
    handler.setFilter(new Filter() {
            public boolean isLoggable(LogRecord record) {
                    // return true if the record should be logged;
                    // false otherwise.
                    return true;
            }
    });
    // Add the handler to a logger
    Logger logger = Logger.getLogger("com.mycompany");
    logger.addHandler(handler);
```

Levels

ε395. Setting the Log Level of a Logger

The log level of a logger controls the severity of messages that it will log. In particular, a log record whose severity is greater than or equal to the logger's log level is logged.

Class   *Interface*   —extends   - - -implements   ○ abstract   ● final   ‾—has superclass   ͺ—has subclass   package—see other volume

A log level can be null, in which case the level is inherited from the logger's parent.

Note: Logger handlers also have a log level. A log record must first pass the logger's log level before it is compared to the handler's log level.

```
// Get a logger
Logger logger = Logger.getLogger("com.mycompany");

// Set the level to a particular level
logger.setLevel(Level.INFO);

// Set the level to that of its parent
logger.setLevel(null);

// Turn off all logging
logger.setLevel(Level.OFF);

// Turn on all logging
logger.setLevel(Level.ALL);
```

ε396. Getting the Log Level of a Logger

The log level of a logger controls how severe a log record must be before the logger accepts it. In particular, a log record whose level is greater than or equal to the logger's log level is logged.

A log level can be null, in which case the level is inherited from the logger's parent.

This example implements a method that returns the level of a logger. If the level is null, the method looks for an ancestor with a non-null level.

```
// Return the level of the specified logger.
// If the level of logger is null, the level of the closest
// ancestor with a non-null level is returned.
public static Level getLevel(Logger logger) {
    Level level = logger.getLevel();
    while (level == null && logger.getParent() != null) {
        logger = logger.getParent();
        level = logger.getLevel();
    }
    return level;
}
```

ε397. Comparing Log Levels

To compare the severity of two logging levels, use Level.intValue().

```
// Find the more severe log level
Level level1 = Level.INFO;
Level level2 = Level.CONFIG;

if (level1.intValue() > level2.intValue()) {
    // level1 is more severe
} else if (level1.intValue() < level2.intValue()) {
    // level2 is more severe
} else {
    // level1 == level2
}
```

ε398. Creating a Custom Log Level

To create a custom level, the Level class must be subclassed.

```
public class MyLevel extends Level {
    // Create the new level
```

Packages

```
                    public static final Level DISASTER = new MyLevel("DISASTER", Level.SEVERE.intValue()+1);

                    public MyLevel(String name, int value) {
                        super(name, value);
                    }
            }
```

An example that uses the custom level:

```
        // Use it directly
        Logger logger = Logger.getLogger("com.mycompany");
        logger.log(MyLevel.DISASTER, "my disaster message");

        // Retrieve by name
        Level disaster = Level.parse("DISASTER");
        logger.log(disaster, "my disaster message");
```

Formatters

ε399. Setting the Formatter of a Logger Handler

A logger's handler uses a formatter to write a log record out to the log file. Two formatters are available by default: SimpleFormatter and XMLFormatter. The simple formatter formats a log record to one or more lines of text. The XML formatter formats a log record to an XML entry, making it easier to reconstruct the log record later.

To create a custom formatter, see "ε400. Creating a Custom Formatter for a Logger Handler".

```
        class MyClass {
            public void myMethod() {
                // Get a logger
                Logger logger = Logger.getLogger("com.mycompany");

                // Create a new handler that uses the simple formatter
                try {
                    FileHandler fh = new FileHandler("mylog.txt");
                    fh.setFormatter(new SimpleFormatter());
                    logger.addHandler(fh);
                } catch (IOException e) {
                }

                // Create a new handler that uses the XML formatter
                try {
                    FileHandler fh = new FileHandler("mylog.xml");
                    fh.setFormatter(new XMLFormatter());
                    logger.addHandler(fh);
                } catch (IOException e) {
                }

                // Log a few messages
                logger.severe("my severe message");
                logger.warning("my warning message");
                logger.info("my info message");
                logger.config("my config message");
                logger.fine("my fine message");
                logger.finer("my finer message");
                logger.finest("my finest message");
            }
        }
```

Class *Interface* —extends - - -implements $\bigcirc$ abstract $\bullet$ final ^—has superclass ⌐—has subclass package—see other volume

Here is format generated by the simple formatter in mylog.txt:

```
Jan 11, 2002 10:05:21 AM MyClass myMethod
SEVERE: my severe message
Jan 11, 2002 10:05:22 AM MyClass myMethod
WARNING: my warning message
Jan 11, 2002 10:05:22 AM MyClass myMethod
INFO: my info message
Jan 11, 2002 10:05:22 AM MyClass myMethod
CONFIG: my config message
Jan 11, 2002 10:05:22 AM MyClass myMethod
FINE: my fine message
Jan 11, 2002 10:05:22 AM MyClass myMethod
FINER: my finer message
Jan 11, 2002 10:05:22 AM MyClass myMethod
FINEST: my finest message
```

Here is format generated by the XML formatter in mylog.xml:

```xml
<?xml version="1.0" encoding="windows-1252" standalone="no"?>
<!DOCTYPE log SYSTEM "logger.dtd">
<log>
<record>
    <date>2002-01-11T10:05:21</date>
    <millis>1010772321959</millis>
    <sequence>0</sequence>
    <logger>com.mycompany</logger>
    <level>SEVERE</level>
    <class>MyClass</class>
    <method>myMethod</method>
    <thread>10</thread>
    <message>my severe message</message>
</record>
<record>
    <date>2002-01-11T10:05:22</date>
    <millis>1010772322099</millis>
    <sequence>1</sequence>
    <logger>com.mycompany</logger>
    <level>WARNING</level>
    <class>MyClass</class>
    <method>myMethod</method>
    <thread>10</thread>
    <message>my warning message</message>
</record>
<record>
    <date>2002-01-11T10:05:22</date>
    <millis>1010772322099</millis>
    <sequence>2</sequence>
    <logger>com.mycompany</logger>
    <level>INFO</level>
    <class>MyClass</class>
    <method>myMethod</method>
    <thread>10</thread>
    <message>my info message</message>
</record>
<record>
    <date>2002-01-11T10:05:22</date>
    <millis>1010772322099</millis>
```

```
            <sequence>3</sequence>
            <logger>com.mycompany</logger>
            <level>CONFIG</level>
            <class>MyClass</class>
            <method>myMethod</method>
            <thread>10</thread>
            <message>my config message</message>
        </record>
        <record>
            <date>2002-01-11T10:05:22</date>
            <millis>1010772322109</millis>
            <sequence>4</sequence>
            <logger>com.mycompany</logger>
            <level>FINE</level>
            <class>MyClass</class>
            <method>myMethod</method>
            <thread>10</thread>
            <message>my fine message</message>
        </record>
        <record>
            <date>2002-01-11T10:05:22</date>
            <millis>1010772322109</millis>
            <sequence>5</sequence>
            <logger>com.mycompany</logger>
            <level>FINER</level>
            <class>MyClass</class>
            <method>myMethod</method>
            <thread>10</thread>
            <message>my finer message</message>
        </record>
        <record>
            <date>2002-01-11T10:05:22</date>
            <millis>1010772322119</millis>
            <sequence>6</sequence>
            <logger>com.mycompany</logger>
            <level>FINEST</level>
            <class>MyClass</class>
            <method>myMethod</method>
            <thread>10</thread>
            <message>my finest message</message>
        </record>
    </log>
```

ε400. Creating a Custom Formatter for a Logger Handler

A logger's handler uses a formatter to write a log record out to the log file. The java.util.logging package provides two formatters; see "ε399. Setting the Formatter of a Logger Handler" for more information. However, the logging package allows you to create custom formatters.

This example creates a custom formatter that prints one line for each log record and surrounds the log data with HTML tags.

```
// This custom formatter formats parts of a log record to a single line
class MyHtmlFormatter extends Formatter {
    // This method is called for every log records
    public String format(LogRecord rec) {
```

```
        StringBuffer buf = new StringBuffer(1000);
        // Bold any levels >= WARNING
        if (rec.getLevel().intValue() >= Level.WARNING.intValue()) {
            buf.append("<b>");
            buf.append(rec.getLevel());
            buf.append("</b>");
        } else {
            buf.append(rec.getLevel());
        }
        buf.append(' ');
        buf.append(rec.getMillis());
        buf.append(' ');
        buf.append(formatMessage(rec));
        buf.append('\n');
        return buf.toString();
    }

    // This method is called just after the handler using this
    // formatter is created
    public String getHead(Handler h) {
        return "<HTML><HEAD>"+(new Date())+"</HEAD><BODY><PRE>\n";
    }

    // This method is called just after the handler using this
    // formatter is closed
    public String getTail(Handler h) {
        return "</PRE></BODY></HTML>\n";
    }
}
```

Here's some code to use the custom formatter:

```
// Get the logger
Logger logger = Logger.getLogger("com.mycompany");
try {
    // Create a file handler that uses the custom formatter
    FileHandler fh = new FileHandler("mylog.html");
    fh.setFormatter(new MyHtmlFormatter());
    logger.addHandler(fh);
} catch (IOException e) {
}
// Log some messages
logger.setLevel(Level.ALL);
logger.severe("my severe message");
logger.info("my info message");
logger.entering(this.getClass().getName(), "myMethod", new Object[]{"para1", "para2"});
```

Here's the output from the example code above:

```
<HTML><HEAD>Fri Jan 11 13:32:57 PST 2002</HEAD><BODY><PRE>
<b>SEVERE</b> 1010784777240 my severe message
INFO 1010784777390 my info message
FINER 1010784777400 ENTRY para1 para2
</PRE></BODY></HTML>
```

ε401. Limiting the Size of a Log File

By default, a log file can grow without bound. It is possible to limit the size of the file by specifying the desired limit when creating a file handler. When a record is about to be logged and the file size is greater than the limit, the file is emptied before the record is logged. This example creates a file handler with a limit.

See also "ε402. Limiting the Size of a Log by Using a Rotating Sequence of Files".

```
try {
    // Create a file handler with a limit of 1 megabytes
    String pattern = "my.log";
    int limit = 1000000; // 1 Mb
    FileHandler fh = new FileHandler("my.log", limit, 1);

    // Add to logger
    Logger logger = Logger.getLogger("com.mycompany");
    logger.addHandler(fh);
} catch (IOException e) {
}
```

ε402. Limiting the Size of a Log by Using a Rotating Sequence of Files

The example "ε401. Limiting the Size of a Log File" shows how to limit the log file size by automatically emptying it when it reaches the limit. However, this approach has the disadvantage of discarding useful information even though the file size might be well within the limit. The FileHandler allows a more effective approach by allowing you to use a sequence of files to hold the log information. When a file fills up, the oldest file is emptied and logging resumes in that file.

More specifically, if there are N log files in the sequence, records are always dumped into logfile0. When logfile0 is filled, logfileN-2 is renamed to logfileN, logfileN-3 is renamed to logfileN-2, etc. Finally, logfile0 is renamed logfile1. A new logfile0 is created and logging resumes in the new logfile0. To read the log records in chronological order, you need to process the files from logfileN-1 to logfile0.

The logfile number is called the generation number and ranges from 0 to the number of logfiles - 1. When specifying the filename pattern to use for the logfiles, you need to include the location of the generation number using the '%g' placeholder. For example, using a filename pattern of 'my%g.log' with three log files will result in the files 'my0.log', 'my1.log', and 'my2.log'.

```
try {
    // Create a file handler that uses 3 logfiles, each with a limit of 1Mbyte
    String pattern = "my%g.log";
    int limit = 1000000; // 1 Mb
    int numLogFiles = 3;
    FileHandler fh = new FileHandler(pattern, limit, numLogFiles);

    // Add to logger
    Logger logger = Logger.getLogger("com.mycompany");
    logger.addHandler(fh);
} catch (IOException e) {
}
```

Class   *Interface*   —extends   - - -implements   ○ abstract   ● final   ^—has superclass   ⌐—has subclass   package—see other volume

Configuration

ε403. Configuring Logger Default Values with a Properties File

The default values for loggers and handlers can be set using a properties file. This example demonstrates a sample logging properties file.

For more information about logging properties, see the lib/logging.properties file in the JRE directory.

```
# Specify the handlers to create in the root logger
# (all loggers are children of the root logger)
# The following creates two handlers
handlers = java.util.logging.ConsoleHandler, java.util.logging.FileHandler

# Set the default logging level for the root logger
.level = ALL

# Set the default logging level for new ConsoleHandler instances
java.util.logging.ConsoleHandler.level = INFO

# Set the default logging level for new FileHandler instances
java.util.logging.FileHandler.level = ALL

# Set the default formatter for new ConsoleHandler instances
java.util.logging.ConsoleHandler.formatter = java.util.logging.SimpleFormatter

# Set the default logging level for the logger named com.mycompany
com.mycompany.level = ALL
```

The custom logging properties file is loaded by specifying a system property on the command line:

```
java -Djava.util.logging.config.file=mylogging.properties <class>
```

ε404. Determining When the Logging Configuration Properties are Reread

The original configuration properties file (see "ε403. Configuring Logger Default Values with a Properties File") can be reread using LogManager.readConfiguration(). This method fires a PropertyChangeEvent.

```
// Register for the event
LogManager.getLogManager().addPropertyChangeListener(
    new PropertyChangeListener() {
        // This method is called when configuration file is reread
        public void propertyChange(PropertyChangeEvent evt) {
            String propName = evt.getPropertyName();
            Object oldValue = evt.getOldValue();
            Object newValue = evt.getOldValue();
            // All values are null
        }
    });
```

java.util.prefs

This package allows applications to store and retrieve user and system preference and configuration data. This data is stored persistently in an implementation-dependent backing store. There are two separate trees of preference nodes, one for user preferences and one for system preferences.

```
       java.lang.Object
1.4 ○    ├ Preferences
1.4 ○    │   └ AbstractPreferences
1.1      ├ java.util.EventObject - - - - - - - - - - - - - - - - - - - - - - - - - - - -- - java.io.Serializable
1.4      │   ├ NodeChangeEvent
1.4      │   └ PreferenceChangeEvent
         └ java.lang.Throwable - - - - - - - - - - - - - - - - - - - - - - - - - -
             └ java.lang.Exception
1.4          ├ BackingStoreException
1.4          └ InvalidPreferencesFormatException

1.4      NodeChangeListener ——————————————————————— java.util.EventListener
1.4      PreferenceChangeListener ————————————
1.4      PreferencesFactory
```

ε405. Saving and Retrieving a Preference Value

Preference values are persistent key/value pairs. The key must be a string. Preference values are stored in a "preference node," which behaves much like a Map object. In order to get or set a preference value, the preference node containing that preference must first be retrieved.

By convention, a preference node is associated with a Java package. For example, if a class called com.mycompany.Foo needs to save some preferences, it would save them in the preference node associated with the package com.mycompany.

There are two types of preference nodes: a "system" type and a "user" type. A system node is shared by all users of a system. Any changes made to a system node are immediately visible to all users of the system. A user node is a node whose values are accessible only by the user using the application.

A preference node can be retrieved using a Class object or by a string. See "ε413. Retrieving a Preference Node" for an example.

This example retrieves the user preference node using a Class object and saves and retrieves a preference in the node.

```
// Retrieve the user preference node for the package com.mycompany
Preferences prefs = Preferences.userNodeForPackage(com.mycompany.MyClass.class);

// Preference key name
final String PREF_NAME = "name_of_preference";

// Set the value of the preference
String newValue = "a string";
prefs.put(PREF_NAME, newValue);
```

Class   *Interface*   —extends   - - -implements   ○ abstract   ● final   ^—has superclass   —has subclass   package—see other volume

```
// Get the value of the preference;
// default value is returned if the preference does not exist
String defaultValue = "default string";
String propertyValue = prefs.get(PREF_NAME, defaultValue); // "a string"
```

ε406. Determining If a Preference Node Contains a Specific Key

You cannot save null as a preference value. Therefore, if you retrieve a value using a default value of null, and null is returned, you can assume that the key is not present.

```
// Returns true if node contains the specified key; false otherwise.
public static boolean contains(Preferences node, String key) {
    return node.get(key, null) != null;
}
```

ε407. Determining If a Preference Node Contains a Specific Value

This example enumerates the key/value pairs in a preference node and checks each value for a match.

```
// Returns the key of a preference whose value matches the specified value;
// null is returned if no such key exists.
public static String containsValue(Preferences node, String value) {
    try {
        // Get all the keys
        String[] keys = node.keys();

        // Scan the keys
        for (int i=0; i<keys.length; i++) {
            if (value.equals(node.get(keys[i], null))) {
                return keys[i];
            }
        }
    } catch (BackingStoreException e) {
    }
    return null;
}
```

ε408. Removing a Preference from a Preference Node

```
// Get the user preference node for java.lang
Preferences prefs = Preferences.userNodeForPackage(String.class);

// Remove a preference in the node
final String PREF_NAME = "name_of_preference";
prefs.remove(PREF_NAME);

// Remove all preferences in the node
try {
    prefs.clear();
} catch (BackingStoreException e) {
}
```

ε409. Getting and Setting Java Type Values in a Preference

A preference node holds only string values. However, the Preferences class has convenience methods that will convert a number of basic Java types to and from strings. For example, Preferences.putByteArray() converts a byte array into a string and then saves the string value. Preferences.getByteArray() converts the string back into an array of bytes.

The types for which there are conversion methods are boolean, int, long, float, double, and byte[]. For all other types, serialization can be used to convert an arbitrary Java type into a byte array (see "ε44. Serializing an Object").

See also "ε410. Getting the Maximum Size of a Preference Key and Value".

```
// Retrieve the user preference node for the package com.mycompany
Preferences prefs = Preferences.userNodeForPackage(com.mycompany.MyClass.class);
```

```
// Preference key name
final String PREF_NAME = "name_of_preference";
```

```
// Save
prefs.put(PREF_NAME, "a string"); // String
prefs.putBoolean(PREF_NAME, true); // boolean
prefs.putInt(PREF_NAME, 123); // int
prefs.putLong(PREF_NAME, 123L); // long
prefs.putFloat(PREF_NAME, 12.3F); // float
prefs.putDouble(PREF_NAME, 12.3); // double
byte[] bytes = new byte[1024];
prefs.putByteArray(PREF_NAME, bytes); // byte[]
```

```
// Retrieve
String s = prefs.get(PREF_NAME, "a string"); // String
boolean b = prefs.getBoolean(PREF_NAME, true); // boolean
int i = prefs.getInt(PREF_NAME, 123); // int
long l = prefs.getLong(PREF_NAME, 123L); // long
float f = prefs.getFloat(PREF_NAME, 12.3F); // float
double d = prefs.getDouble(PREF_NAME, 12.3); // double
bytes = prefs.getByteArray(PREF_NAME, bytes); // byte[]
```

ε410. Getting the Maximum Size of a Preference Key and Value

```
// Get maximum key length
int keyMax = Preferences.MAX_KEY_LENGTH;
```

```
// Get maximum value length
int valueMax = Preferences.MAX_VALUE_LENGTH;
```

```
// Get maximum length of byte array values
int bytesMax = Preferences.MAX_VALUE_LENGTH * 3/4 ;
```

Nodes

ε411. Getting the Roots of the Preference Trees

There are two preference trees — the system tree and the user tree. The root of these trees is retrieved using Preferences.systemRoot() and Preferences.userRoot(). The roots are required when creating and retrieving preference nodes. See "ε413. Retrieving a Preference Node" for an example of retrieving preference nodes using a root.

```
// Get the system root
Preferences prefs = Preferences.systemRoot();
```

```
// Get the user root
prefs = Preferences.userRoot();
```

```
// The name of a root is ""
String name = prefs.name();
```

Class *Interface* —extends - - -implements ○ abstract ● final ^—has superclass ‿—has subclass package—see other volume

```
// The parent of a root is null
Preferences parent = prefs.parent();

// The absolute path of a root is "/"
String path = prefs.absolutePath();
```

ε412. Creating a Preference Node

The methods used to create a preference node are identical to the ones for retrieving a preference node. When retrieving a preference node, the preference node is automatically created if it doesn't exist. In fact, when you retrieve a node, you can't tell if it was just created or not.

See "ε413. Retrieving a Preference Node" for an example of retrieving preference nodes.

See also "ε415. Determining If a Preference Node Exists".

ε413. Retrieving a Preference Node

A preference node can be retrieved using a Class object or by a string. When using a Class object to retrieve a preference node, the package containing the Class object identifies the node.

It is important to note that these methods also automatically create the node if it doesn't exist. Since nodes take up resources, even when empty, you should avoid creating unnecessary nodes. See "ε415. Determining If a Preference Node Exists" for information on how to avoid creating nodes.

The string used to retrieve a preference node is called a path and resembles a file path. For example, the path for the preference node associated with the package com.mycompany is /com/mycompany.

Paths that begin with '/' are absolute paths. A relative path can be specified (one that does not begin with '/') and is treated relative to another preference node. For example, if you use the node at /javax/swing to retrieve another node with the path text/html, the node at /javax/swing/text/html is returned.

```
// System preference nodes

// Use a Class
Preferences prefs = Preferences.systemNodeForPackage(java.lang.String.class);

// Use an absolute path
prefs = Preferences.systemRoot().node("/java/lang/String");

// Use a relative path
prefs = Preferences.systemRoot().node("/javax/swing");
prefs = prefs.node("text/html");

// User preference nodes

// Use a class
prefs = Preferences.userNodeForPackage(com.mycompany.MyClass.class);

// Use an absolute path
prefs = Preferences.userRoot().node("/com/mycompany");

// Use a relative path
prefs = Preferences.userRoot().node("/javax/swing");
prefs = prefs.node("text/html");
```

ε414. Removing a Preference Node

Removing a preference node will remove all of the node's descendants.

See also "ε415. Determining If a Preference Node Exists".

```
try {
    // First check to see if the node is already removed;
    // otherwise, getting the node will automatically create it
```

```
            boolean exists = Preferences.userRoot().nodeExists("/foo"); // false

        if (!exists) {
            // Get the node
            Preferences prefs = Preferences.userRoot().node("/foo");

            // Remove the node
            prefs.removeNode();

            // Trying to remove it again would cause an IllegalStateException
            //prefs.removeNode();
        }

        // Create a node with a child
        Preferences prefs = Preferences.userRoot().node("/foo/child");
        exists = Preferences.userRoot().nodeExists("/foo"); // true
        exists = Preferences.userRoot().nodeExists("/foo/child"); // true

        // Remove the parent node
        Preferences.userRoot().node("/foo").removeNode();

        // Both parent and child are removed
        exists = Preferences.userRoot().nodeExists("/foo"); // false
        exists = Preferences.userRoot().nodeExists("/foo/child"); // false
    } catch (BackingStoreException e) {
    }
```

ε415. Determining If a Preference Node Exists

A preference node is automatically created whenever Preferences.node(), Preferences.userNodeForPackage(), or Preferences.systemNodeForPackage() is called. To avoid creating a node, you should first check to see if it exists.

```
    try {
        // Check if a node exists
        boolean exists = Preferences.userRoot().nodeExists("/foo"); // false

        // Get the node
        Preferences.userRoot().node("/foo");

        // Getting a non-existent node automatically creates it
        exists = Preferences.userRoot().nodeExists("/foo"); // true

        // Remove the node
        Preferences prefs = Preferences.userRoot().node("/foo");
        prefs.removeNode();

        // The following would cause an IllegalStateException
        //exists = prefs.nodeExists("/foo");

        // Use the following to determine if the node has been removed
        exists = prefs.nodeExists(""); // false
    } catch (BackingStoreException e) {
    }
```

ε416. Retrieving the Parent and Child Nodes of a Preference Node

```
    // Get a node
    Preferences prefs = Preferences.userNodeForPackage(java.lang.String.class);

    // Get the parent
    Preferences node = prefs.parent(); // /java
```

Class *Interface* —extends - - -implements ◯ abstract ● final ˆ—has superclass ⌐—has subclass package—see other volume

```
node = node.parent(); // null

// Get the names for nodes under java.lang
String[] names = null;
try {
    names = prefs.childrenNames();
} catch (BackingStoreException e) {
}

// Get the child nodes using the names
for (int i=0; i<names.length; i++) {
    node = prefs.node(names[i]);
}
```

ε417. Finding a Preference in a Preference Tree

There is no efficient method for finding a key in a preference node. All the nodes must be traversed and checked for the presence of the key. This example implements such a method.

This example can be modified to find nodes that matched values rather than keys by replacing contains() with containsValue(), as defined in "ε407. Determining If a Preference Node Contains a Specific Value".

```
// Find first occurrence
Preferences prefs = findNode(Preferences.userRoot(), null, "key");

// Find all occurrences
prefs = findNode(Preferences.userRoot(), null, "key");
while (prefs != null) {
    prefs = findNode(Preferences.userRoot(), prefs, "key");
}

// Traverses all the nodes from root depth-first.
// Returns the first node that contains the specified key.
// If start is non-null, the nodes are checked only after the
// start node is encountered.
// Returns null if not found.
public static Preferences findNode(Preferences root, Preferences start, String key) {
    // For the implementation of contains,
    // see "ε406. Determining If a Preference Node Contains a Specific Key"
    if (start == null && contains(root, key)) {
        // Found the key
        return root;
    }

    // The start node has been encountered so start checking from now on
    if (start != null && root.equals(start)) {
        start = null;
    }

    // Recursively check the child nodes
    try {
        String[] names = root.childrenNames();
        for (int i=0; i<names.length; i++) {
            Preferences n = findNode(root.node(names[i]), start, key);
            if (n != null) {
                // Found the key
                return n;
            }
        }
    } catch (BackingStoreException e) {
    }
```

Packages

279

```
                // Not found
                return null;
        }
```

Importing and Exporting

ε418. Importing Preferences

Preferences can be exported using Preferences.exportNode() (see "ε419. Exporting the Preferences in a Preference Node") and Preferences.exportSubtree() (see "ε420. Exporting the Preferences in a Subtree of Preference Nodes"). This exported data can be imported using Preferences.importPreferences().

Each preference in exported data contains the path of the node that held the preference. When the exported preference is later imported, it is added to the node with the same path.

This example demonstrates how to import a file of exported preference data.

```java
        // Create an input stream on a file
        InputStream is = null;
        try {
            is = new BufferedInputStream(new FileInputStream("output.xml"));
        } catch (FileNotFoundException e) {
        }

        // Import preference data
        try {
            Preferences.importPreferences(is);
        } catch (InvalidPreferencesFormatException e) {
        } catch (IOException e) {
        }
```

ε419. Exporting the Preferences in a Preference Node

This example demonstrates how to export the preferences in a preference node to a file. The exported values can be imported using Preferences.importPreferences() (see "ε418. Importing Preferences"). The format of the exported data is XML.

The exported data contains the path of the node that was exported. When the data is later imported, the preferences will be added to the node with exactly the same path.

```java
        // Retrieve the user preference node for the package java.lang
        Preferences prefs = Preferences.userNodeForPackage(String.class);

        // Save some values
        prefs.put("myString", "a string"); // String
        prefs.putBoolean("myBoolean", true); // boolean
        prefs.putInt("myInt", 123); // int
        prefs.putLong("myLong", 123L); // long
        prefs.putFloat("myFloat", 12.3F); // float
        prefs.putDouble("myDouble", 12.3); // double
        byte[] bytes = new byte[10];
        prefs.putByteArray("myByteArray", bytes); // byte[]

        try {
            // Export the node to a file
            prefs.exportNode(new FileOutputStream("output.xml"));
        } catch (IOException e) {
        } catch (BackingStoreException e) {
        }
```

Class *Interface* —extends - - -implements ○ abstract ● final ˄—has superclass ˅—has subclass package—see other volume

The code above generates the following XML data:

```
<?xml version="1.0" encoding="UTF-8"?>

<!DOCTYPE preferences SYSTEM 'http://java.sun.com/dtd/preferences.dtd'>

<preferences EXTERNAL_XML_VERSION="1.0">
<root type="user">
    <map />
    <node name="java">
    <map />
    <node name="lang">
        <map>
        <entry key="myString" value="a string" />
        <entry key="myBoolean" value="true" />
        <entry key="myInt" value="123" />
        <entry key="myLong" value="123" />
        <entry key="myFloat" value="12.3" />
        <entry key="myDouble" value="12.3" />
        <entry key="myByteArray" value="AAAAAAAAAAAAAA==" />
        </map>
    </node>
    </node>
</root>
</preferences>
```

ε420. Exporting the Preferences in a Subtree of Preference Nodes

This example demonstrates how to export the preferences of nodes in a subtree of preference nodes to a file. The export values can be imported using Preferences.importPreferences() (see "ε418. Importing Preferences"). The format of the exported data is XML.

For every node in the exported subtree, the path of the node and the preferences in that node are exported. When the data is later imported, the preferences are added to nodes with exactly the same paths.

```
// Retrieve the user preference node for the package java.lang
Preferences prefs = Preferences.userNodeForPackage(String.class);

// Save some values
prefs.put("myString", "a string"); // String
prefs.putBoolean("myBoolean", true); // boolean
prefs.putInt("myInt", 123); // int
prefs.putLong("myLong", 123L); // long

// Save some values in the parent node
prefs = prefs.parent();
prefs.putFloat("myFloat", 12.3F); // float
prefs.putDouble("myDouble", 12.3); // double
byte[] bytes = new byte[10];
prefs.putByteArray("myByteArray", bytes); // byte[]

try {
    prefs.exportSubtree(new FileOutputStream("output.xml"));
} catch (IOException e) {
} catch (BackingStoreException e) {
}
```

The code above generates the following XML data:

```
<?xml version="1.0" encoding="UTF-8"?>

<!DOCTYPE preferences SYSTEM 'http://java.sun.com/dtd/preferences.dtd'>
```

java.util.prefs

```xml
<preferences EXTERNAL_XML_VERSION="1.0">
<root type="user">
    <map />
    <node name="java">
    <map>
        <entry key="myFloat" value="12.3" />
        <entry key="myDouble" value="12.3" />
        <entry key="myByteArray" value="AAAAAAAAAAAAAA==" />
    </map>
    <node name="lang">
        <map>
        <entry key="myString" value="a string" />
        <entry key="myBoolean" value="true" />
        <entry key="myInt" value="123" />
        <entry key="myLong" value="123" />
        </map>
    </node>
    </node>
</root>
</preferences>
```

Events

ε421. Listening for Changes to Preference Values in a Preference Node

A PreferenceChangeEvent is fired when a preference is added, changed, or removed from a preference node. This event is only guaranteed to fire if the listener and modifier are in the same application. This event is not fired if the node is removed.

See also "ε422. Determining When a Preference Node Is Added or Removed".

```java
// Retrieve the user preference node for the package java.lang
Preferences prefs = Preferences.userNodeForPackage(String.class);

// Register the listener
prefs.addPreferenceChangeListener(new PreferenceChangeListener() {
    public void preferenceChange(PreferenceChangeEvent evt) {
        // Get the node that changed
        Preferences node = evt.getNode();

        // Get the affected key.
        // Note: it is not possible to tell if the key was new
        // or its value was changed.
        String key = evt.getKey();

        // Get the new value; if the new value is null,
        // the preference was removed
        String newValue = evt.getNewValue();
    }
});

// Add a preference
prefs.put("key", "a string");

// Modify the preference
prefs.put("key", "a new string");

// Remove the preference
```

```
prefs.remove("key");
```

ε422. Determining When a Preference Node Is Added or Removed

A NodeChangeEvent is fired when a preference node gets a new child node or loses a child node. This event is only guaranteed to fire if the listener and modifier are in the same application.

See also "ε421. Listening for Changes to Preference Values in a Preference Node".

```
// Retrieve the user preference node for the package java.lang
Preferences prefs = Preferences.userNodeForPackage(String.class);

// Register the listener
prefs.addNodeChangeListener(new NodeChangeListener() {
    public void childAdded(NodeChangeEvent evt) {
        // Get the node with the new child
        Preferences parent = evt.getParent();

        // Get the newly added child
        Preferences child = evt.getChild();
    }
    public void childRemoved(NodeChangeEvent evt) {
        // Get the node whose child was removed
        Preferences parent = evt.getParent();

        // Get the removed child
        Preferences child = evt.getChild();
    }
});

// Add a child preference node
Preferences child = prefs.node("new node");

try {
    // Remove the child preference node
    child.removeNode();

    // Remove current node; this does not fire a NodeChangeEvent
    prefs.removeNode();
} catch (BackingStoreException e) {
}
```

Packages

java.util.regex

This package provides support for matching character sequences against patterns specified by regular expressions.

```
java.lang.Object
```
1.4	●	├ Matcher
1.4	●	├ Pattern - ,- *java.io.Serializable* ˌ

```
java.lang.Object                                    ,- java.io.Serializable ,
  └ java.lang.Throwable - - - - - - - - - - - - - - - - - - - - - - - - -:
     └ java.lang.Exception
        └ java.lang.RuntimeException
           └ java.lang.IllegalArgumentException
              └ PatternSyntaxException
1.4
```

ε423. Quintessential Regular Expression Search Program

This example demonstrates how to use a regular expression to find matches in a string.

```java
import java.util.regex.*;

public class BasicMatch {
    public static void main(String[] args) {
        // Compile regular expression
        String patternStr = "b";
        Pattern pattern = Pattern.compile(patternStr);

        // Determine if pattern exists in input
        CharSequence inputStr = "a b c b";
        Matcher matcher = pattern.matcher(inputStr);
        boolean matchFound = matcher.find(); // true

        // Get matching string
        String match = matcher.group(); // b

        // Get indices of matching string
        int start = matcher.start(); // 2
        int end = matcher.end(); // 3
        // the end is index of the last matching character + 1

        // Find the next occurrence
        matchFound = matcher.find(); // true
    }
}
```

ε424. Determining If a String Matches a Pattern Exactly

There are two ways to determine if a string exactly matches a regular expression. The first is to add the boundary matcher '\A' to the beginning and '\z' to the end of the pattern. The other way is to use Matcher.matches(), which does not require changes to the pattern.

If the pattern only needs to match the beginning of the string, use Matcher.lookingAt().

```java
// Compile regular expression
String patternStr = "b";
Pattern pattern = Pattern.compile(patternStr);

// Determine if there is an exact match
CharSequence inputStr = "a b c";
Matcher matcher = pattern.matcher(inputStr);
boolean matchFound = matcher.matches(); // false

// Try a different input
matcher.reset("b");
matchFound = matcher.matches(); // true

// Determine if pattern matches beginning of input
matchFound = matcher.lookingAt(); // false
```

ε425. Applying Regular Expressions on the Contents of a File

The matching routines in java.util.regex require that the input be a CharSequence object. This example implements a method that efficiently returns the contents of a file in a CharSequence object.

```
// Converts the contents of a file into a CharSequence
// suitable for use by the regex package.
public CharSequence fromFile(String filename) throws IOException {
    FileInputStream fis = new FileInputStream(filename);
    FileChannel fc = fis.getChannel();

    // Create a read-only CharBuffer on the file
    ByteBuffer bbuf = fc.map(FileChannel.MapMode.READ_ONLY, 0, (int)fc.size());
    CharBuffer cbuf = Charset.forName("8859_1").newDecoder().decode(bbuf);
    return cbuf;
}
```

Here is sample code that uses the method:

```
try {
    // Create matcher on file
    Pattern pattern = Pattern.compile("pattern");
    Matcher matcher = pattern.matcher(fromFile("infile.txt"));

    // Find all matches
    while (matcher.find()) {
        // Get the matching string
        String match = matcher.group();
    }
} catch (IOException e) {
}
```

ε426. Removing Duplicate Whitespace in a String

```
// Returns a version of the input where all contiguous
// whitespace characters are replaced with a single
// space. Line terminators are treated like whitespace.
public static CharSequence removeDuplicateWhitespace(CharSequence inputStr) {
    String patternStr = "\\s+";
    String replaceStr = " ";
    Pattern pattern = Pattern.compile(patternStr);
    Matcher matcher = pattern.matcher(inputStr);
    return matcher.replaceAll(replaceStr);
}
```

ε427. Greedy and Nongreedy Matching in a Regular Expression

By default, pattern matching is greedy, which means that the matcher returns the longest match possible. For example, applying the pattern 'A.*c' to 'AbcAbcA' matches 'AbcAbc' rather than the shorter 'Abc'. To do nongreedy matching, a question mark must be added to the quantifier. For example, the pattern 'A.*?c' will find the shortest match possible.

```
// Greedy quantifiers
String match = find("A.*c", "AbcAbc"); // AbcAbc
match = find("A.+", "AbcAbc"); // AbcAbc

// Nongreedy quantifiers
match = find("A.*?c", "AbcAbc"); // Abc
match = find("A.+?", "AbcAbc"); // Abc

// Returns the first substring in input that matches the pattern.
```

```
    // Returns null if no match found.
    public static String find(String patternStr, CharSequence input) {
        Pattern pattern = Pattern.compile(patternStr);
        Matcher matcher = pattern.matcher(input);
        if (matcher.find()) {
            return matcher.group();
        }
        return null;
    }
```

ε428. Escaping Special Characters in a Pattern

Any nonalphanumeric character can be escaped with a backslash to remove it's special meaning (if any). This example implements a method that escapes all nonalphanumeric characters. This method is useful when the pattern is retrieved programmatically and it is necessary to search for the pattern literally.

Another method of escaping the characters in a pattern is to surround the pattern with \Q and \E. The only thing to watch out for is the presence of \E in the pattern, which would end the escaping of the pattern.

```
String patternStr = "i.e.";

boolean matchFound = Pattern.matches(patternStr, "i.e.");// true
matchFound = Pattern.matches(patternStr, "ibex"); // true

// Quote the pattern; i.e. surround with \Q and \E
matchFound = Pattern.matches("\\Q"+patternStr+"\\E", "i.e."); // true
matchFound = Pattern.matches("\\Q"+patternStr+"\\E", "ibex"); // false

// Escape the pattern
patternStr = escapeRE(patternStr); // i\.e\.

matchFound = Pattern.matches(patternStr, "i.e."); // true
matchFound = Pattern.matches(patternStr, "ibex"); // false

// Returns a pattern where all punctuation characters are escaped.
static Pattern escaper = Pattern.compile("([^a-zA-z0-9])");
public static String escapeRE(String str) {
    return escaper.matcher(str).replaceAll("\\\\$1");
}
```

Searching and Replacing

ε429. Quintessential Regular Expression Search and Replace Program

This program finds all matches to a regular expression pattern and replaces them with another string.

If the replacement is not a constant string, see "ε430. Searching and Replacing with Nonconstant Values Using a Regular Expression".

```
import java.util.regex.*;

public class BasicReplace {
    public static void main(String[] args) {
        CharSequence inputStr = "a b c a b c";
        String patternStr = "a";
        String replacementStr = "x";

        // Compile regular expression
        Pattern pattern = Pattern.compile(patternStr);

        // Replace all occurrences of pattern in input
```

Class *Interface* —extends - - -implements O abstract ● final ˆ—has superclass ˌ—has subclass package—see other volume

```
        Matcher matcher = pattern.matcher(inputStr);
        String output = matcher.replaceAll(replacementStr);
        // x b c x b c
    }
}
```

ε430. Searching and Replacing with Nonconstant Values Using a Regular Expression

The simplest way to replace all occurrences of a pattern in a CharSequence is to use Matcher.replaceAll(). However, this method is restricted to replacement values that are constant. If the replacement value is dynamic (e.g., converting the match to uppercase), Matcher.appendReplacement() must be used.

This example demonstrates the use of Matcher.appendReplacement() by converting all words that match '[a-zA-Z]+[0-9]+' to uppercase.

```
CharSequence inputStr = "ab12 cd efg34";
String patternStr = "([a-zA-Z]+[0-9]+)";

// Compile regular expression
Pattern pattern = Pattern.compile(patternStr);
Matcher matcher = pattern.matcher(inputStr);

// Replace all occurrences of pattern in input
StringBuffer buf = new StringBuffer();
boolean found = false;
while ((found = matcher.find())) {
    // Get the match result
    String replaceStr = matcher.group();

    // Convert to uppercase
    replaceStr = replaceStr.toUpperCase();

    // Insert replacement
    matcher.appendReplacement(buf, replaceStr);
}
matcher.appendTail(buf);

// Get result
String result = buf.toString();
// AB12 cd EFG34
```

Tokenizing

ε431. Parsing Character-Separated Data with a Regular Expression

A line from a flat-file is typically formatted using a separator character to separate the fields. If the separator is simply a comma, tab, or single character, the StringTokenizer class can be used to parse the line into fields. If the separator is more complex (e.g., a space after a comma), a regular expression is needed. String.split() conveniently parses a line using a regular expression to specify the separator.

String.split() returns only the nondelimiter strings. To obtain the delimiter strings, see "ε432. Parsing a String into Tokens Using a Regular Expression".

Note: The StringTokenizer does not conveniently handle empty fields properly. For example, given the line 'a„b', rather than return three fields (the second being empty), the StringTokenizer returns two fields, discarding the empty field. String.split() properly handles empty fields.

```
// Parse a comma-separated string
String inputStr = "a„b";
String patternStr = ",";
String[] fields = inputStr.split(patternStr);
```

```
// ["a", "", "b"]

// Parse a line whose separator is a comma followed by a space
inputStr = "a, b, c,d";
patternStr = ", ";
fields = inputStr.split(patternStr, -1);
// ["a", "b", "c,d"]

// Parse a line with and's and or's
inputStr = "a, b, and c";
patternStr = "[, ]+(and|or)*[, ]*";
fields = inputStr.split(patternStr, -1);
// ["a", "b", "c"]
```

ε432. Parsing a String into Tokens Using a Regular Expression

This example implements a tokenizer that uses regular expressions. The use of this tokenizer is similar to the StringTokenizer class in that you use it like an iterator to extract the tokens.

```
CharSequence inputStr = "a 1 2 b c 3 4";
String patternStr = "[a-z]";

// Set to false if only the tokens that match the pattern are to be returned.
// If true, the text between matching tokens are also returned.
boolean returnDelims = true;

// Create the tokenizer
Iterator tokenizer = new RETokenizer(inputStr, patternStr, returnDelims);

// Get the tokens (and delimiters)
for (; tokenizer.hasNext(); ) {
    String tokenOrDelim = (String)tokenizer.next();
}
// "", "a", " 1 2 ", "b", " ", "c"

class RETokenizer implements Iterator {
    // Holds the original input to search for tokens
    private CharSequence input;

    // Used to find tokens
    private Matcher matcher;

    // If true, the String between tokens are returned
    private boolean returnDelims;

    // The current delimiter value. If non-null, should be returned
    // at the next call to next()
    private String delim;

    // The current matched value. If non-null and delim=null,
    // should be returned at the next call to next()
    private String match;

    // The value of matcher.end() from the last successful match.
    private int lastEnd = 0;

    // patternStr is a regular expression pattern that identifies tokens.
    // If returnDelims delim is false, only those tokens that match the
    // pattern are returned. If returnDelims true, the text between
    // matching tokens are also returned. If returnDelims is true, the
    // tokens are returned in the following sequence - delimiter, token,
    // delimiter, token, etc. Tokens can never be empty but delimiters might
```

```
    // be empty (empty string).
    public RETokenizer(CharSequence input, String patternStr, boolean returnDelims) {
        // Save values
        this.input = input;
        this.returnDelims = returnDelims;

        // Compile pattern and prepare input
        Pattern pattern = Pattern.compile(patternStr);
        matcher = pattern.matcher(input);
    }

    // Returns true if there are more tokens or delimiters.
    public boolean hasNext() {
        if (matcher == null) {
            return false;
        }
        if (delim != null || match != null) {
            return true;
        }
        if (matcher.find()) {
            if (returnDelims) {
                delim = input.subSequence(lastEnd, matcher.start()).toString();
            }
            match = matcher.group();
            lastEnd = matcher.end();
        } else if (returnDelims && lastEnd < input.length()) {
            delim = input.subSequence(lastEnd, input.length()).toString();
            lastEnd = input.length();

            // Need to remove the matcher since it appears to automatically
            // reset itself once it reaches the end.
            matcher = null;
        }
        return delim != null || match != null;
    }

    // Returns the next token (or delimiter if returnDelims is true).
    public Object next() {
        String result = null;

        if (delim != null) {
            result = delim;
            delim = null;
        } else if (match != null) {
            result = match;
            match = null;
        }
        return result;
    }

    // Returns true if the call to next() will return a token rather
    // than a delimiter.
    public boolean isNextToken() {
        return delim == null && match != null;
    }

    // Not supported.
    public void remove() {
        throw new UnsupportedOperationException();
    }
```

```
}
```

ε433. Setting Case Sensitivity in a Regular Expression

By default, a pattern is case-sensitive. By adding a flag, a pattern can be made case-insensitive.

It is also possible to control case sensitivity within a pattern using the inline modifier '(?i)'. The inline modifier affects all characters to the right and in the same enclosing group, if any. For example, in the pattern 'a(b(?i)c)d', only 'c' is allowed to be case-insensitive. You can also force case sensitivity with '(?-i)'.

The inline modifier can also contain pattern characters using the form '(?i:abc)'. In this case, only those pattern characters inside the inline modifier's enclosing group are affected. This form does not capture text (see "ε436. Capturing Text in a Group in a Regular Expression").

```
CharSequence inputStr = "Abc";
String patternStr = "abc";

// Compile with case-insensitivity
Pattern pattern = Pattern.compile(patternStr, Pattern.CASE_INSENSITIVE);
Matcher matcher = pattern.matcher(inputStr);
boolean matchFound = matcher.matches(); // true

// Use an inline modifier
matchFound = pattern.matches("abc", "aBc"); // false
matchFound = pattern.matches("(?i)abc", "aBc"); // true
matchFound = pattern.matches("a(?i)bc", "aBc"); // true

// Use enclosing form
matchFound = pattern.matches("((?i)a)bc", "aBc"); // false
matchFound = pattern.matches("(?i:a)bc", "aBc"); // false
matchFound = pattern.matches("a((?i)b)c", "aBc"); // true
matchFound = pattern.matches("a(?i:b)c", "aBc"); // true

// Use a character set
matchFound = pattern.matches("[a-c]+", "aBc"); // false
matchFound = pattern.matches("(?i)[a-c]+", "aBc"); // true
```

ε434. Adding Comments to a Regular Expression

By default, whitespace in a regular expression is significant. By specifying the COMMENTS flag, whitespace can be ignored in a pattern. While in comment mode, a particular whitespace character can be matched using a character class (for example, [\ ] matches a space).

In comment mode, the '#' character and everything following it is ignored. This feature is useful when a pattern is read from a file. Comment mode allows the pattern to span multiple lines and be commented.

It is also possible to enable comments within a pattern using the inline modifier '(?x)'. The inline modifier affects all characters to the right and in the same enclosing group, if any. For example, in the pattern 'a(b(?x)c)d', only 'c' is allowed to have comments. You can also force no comments with '(?-x)'.

The inline modifier can also contain pattern characters using the form '(?x:abc)'. In this case, only those pattern characters inside the inline modifier's enclosing group are affected. This form does not capture text (see "ε436. Capturing Text in a Group in a Regular Expression").

```
CharSequence inputStr = "a b";
String patternStr = "a b";

// Compile without comments
```

```
Pattern pattern = Pattern.compile(patternStr);
Matcher matcher = pattern.matcher(inputStr);
boolean matchFound = matcher.matches(); // true

// Compile with comments
pattern = Pattern.compile(patternStr, Pattern.COMMENTS);
matcher = pattern.matcher(inputStr);
matchFound = matcher.matches(); // false

// Use COMMENTS but include a character class with a space
patternStr = "a [\] b";
pattern = Pattern.compile(patternStr, Pattern.COMMENTS);
matcher = pattern.matcher(inputStr);
matchFound = matcher.matches(); // true


// Use an inline modifier
matchFound = pattern.matches("a b", inputStr); // true
matchFound = pattern.matches("(?x)a b", inputStr); // false
matchFound = pattern.matches("(?x)a [\] b", inputStr); // true
matchFound = pattern.matches("(?x)a \\s b", inputStr); // true
matchFound = pattern.matches("a (?x: b )", inputStr); // true

// Tabs and newlines in the pattern are ignored as well
matchFound = pattern.matches("(?x)a \t\n \\s b", inputStr); // true

// Read pattern from file
try {
    File f = new File("pattern.txt");
    FileReader rd = new FileReader(f);
    char[] buf = new char[(int)f.length()];
    rd.read(buf);
    patternStr = new String(buf);

    matcher = pattern.matcher(inputStr);
    matchFound = matcher.matches(); // true
} catch (IOException e) {
}
```

Here are the contents of pattern.txt:

```
# This pattern matches "a b"
a # this is the first part
[\] # this is the second part
b # this is the third part
```


ε435. Compiling a Pattern with Multiple Flags

Multiple flags must be combined using the or operator (|).

```
CharSequence inputStr = "Abc\ndef";
String patternStr = "abc$";

// Compile with multiline and case-insensitive enabled
Pattern pattern = Pattern.compile(patternStr,
    Pattern.MULTILINE | Pattern.CASE_INSENSITIVE);
Matcher matcher = pattern.matcher(inputStr);
boolean matchFound = matcher.find(); // true
```

Groups

ε436. Capturing Text in a Group in a Regular Expression

A "group" is a pair of parentheses used to group subpatterns. For example, 'h(ali)t' matches 'hat' or 'hit'. A group also captures the matching text within the parentheses. For example,

```
input: abbc
pattern: a(b*)c
```

causes the substring 'bb' to be captured by the group '(b*)'. A pattern can have more than one group and the groups can be nested. For example,

```
pattern: (a(b*))+(c*)
```

contains three groups:

```
group 1: (a(b*))
group 2: (b*)
group 3: (c*)
```

The groups are numbered from left to right, outside to inside. There is an implicit group 0, which contains the entire match. Here is an example of what is captured in groups.

Notice that group 1 was applied twice, once to the input 'abb' and then to the input 'ab'. Only the most recent match is captured. Note that when using '*' on a group and the group matches zero times, the group will not be cleared. In particular, it will hold the most recently captured text. For example,

```
input: aba
pattern: (a(b)*)+
group 0: aba
group 1: a
group 2: b
```

Group 1 first matched 'ab' capturing 'b' in group 2. Group 1 then matched the 'a' with group 2 matching zero 'b's, therefore leaving intact the previously captured 'b'.

Note: If it is not necessary for a group to capture text, you should use a non-capturing group since it is more efficient. For more information, see "ε438. Using a Non-Capturing Group in a Regular Expression".

This example demonstrates how to retrieve the text in a group.

```
CharSequence inputStr = "abbabcd";
String patternStr = "(a(b*))+(c*)";

// Compile and use regular expression
Pattern pattern = Pattern.compile(patternStr);
Matcher matcher = pattern.matcher(inputStr);
boolean matchFound = matcher.find();

if (matchFound) {
    // Get all groups for this match
    for (int i=0; i<=matcher.groupCount(); i++) {
        String groupStr = matcher.group(i);
    }
}
```

ε437. Getting the Indices of a Matching Group in a Regular Expression

For more information about groups, see "ε436. Capturing Text in a Group in a Regular Expression".

```
CharSequence inputStr = "abbabcd";
```

```
String patternStr = "(a(b*))+(c*)";

// Compile and use regular expression
Pattern pattern = Pattern.compile(patternStr);
Matcher matcher = pattern.matcher(inputStr);
boolean matchFound = matcher.find();

if (matchFound) {
    // Get all groups for this match
    for (int i=0; i<=matcher.groupCount(); i++) {
        // Get the group's captured text
        String groupStr = matcher.group(i);

        // Get the group's indices
        int groupStart = matcher.start(i);
        int groupEnd = matcher.end(i);

        // groupStr is equivalent to
        inputStr.subSequence(groupStart, groupEnd);
    }
}
```

ε438. Using a Non-Capturing Group in a Regular Expression

By default, a group captures text (see "ε436. Capturing Text in a Group in a Regular Expression"). In some cases, a group is needed but there is no need to capture the text. A non-capturing group should be used to improve performance. A non-capturing group starts with '(?:'.

```
String inputStr = "abbabcd";
String patternStr = "(a(?:b*))+(c*)";
// (?:b*) is a non-capturing group

// Compile and use regular expression
Pattern pattern = Pattern.compile(patternStr);
Matcher matcher = pattern.matcher(inputStr);
boolean matchFound = matcher.find();

if (matchFound) {
    // Get all groups for this match
    for (int i=0; i<=matcher.groupCount(); i++) {
        String groupStr = matcher.group(i);
    }
    // group 0: abbabc
    // group 1: ab
    // group 2: c
}
```

ε439. Using the Captured Text of a Group within a Pattern

It is possible to use the value of a group within the same pattern. For example, suppose you're trying to extract the text between some XML tags and you don't know what the possible sets of tags are. However, you do know that the tag name appears in both the start and end tags. How do you take the dynamically matched tag name from the start tag and use it in the end tag?

Back references can be used in this scenario. A back reference refers to a capture group (see "ε436. Capturing Text in a Group in a Regular Expression") within the pattern. It has the form '\n' where n is a group number starting from 1. The back reference should not be contained in or precede the named group.

```
// Compile regular expression with a back reference to group 1
String patternStr = "<(\\S+?).*?>(.*?)</\\1>";
Pattern pattern = Pattern.compile(patternStr);
```

```
        Matcher matcher = pattern.matcher("");

        // Set the input
        matcher.reset("xx <tag a=b> yy </tag> zz");

        // Get tagname and contents of tag
        boolean matchFound = matcher.find(); // true
        String tagname = matcher.group(1); // tag
        String contents = matcher.group(2); // yy

        matcher.reset("xx <tag> yy </tag0>");
        matchFound = matcher.find(); // false
```

ε440. Using the Captured Text of a Group within a Replacement Pattern

Just as it is possible to use the value of a group within the same pattern (see "ε439. Using the Captured Text of a Group within a Pattern"), it is also possible to use a group value in the replacement pattern. Instead of a backslash, the form of the reference is '$n' where n is a group number starting from 0 (see "ε436. Capturing Text in a Group in a Regular Expression" for more information on groups).

```
        // Compile regular expression
        String patternStr = "\\((\\w+)\\)";
        String replaceStr = "<$1>";
        Pattern pattern = Pattern.compile(patternStr);

        // Replace all (\w+) with <$1>
        CharSequence inputStr = "a (b c) d (ef) g";
        Matcher matcher = pattern.matcher(inputStr);
        String output = matcher.replaceAll(replaceStr);
        // a (b c) d <ef> g
```

Lines

ε441. Using a Regular Expression to Filter Lines from a Reader

A common use of regular expressions is to find all lines that match a pattern, similar to the grep Unix command. This example reads lines using a BufferedReader and tests each line for a match.

```
    try {
        // Create the reader
        String filename = "infile.txt";
        String patternStr = "pattern";
        BufferedReader rd = new BufferedReader(new FileReader(filename));

        // Create the pattern
        Pattern pattern = Pattern.compile(patternStr);
        Matcher matcher = pattern.matcher("");

        // Retrieve all lines that match pattern
        String line = null;
        while ((line = rd.readLine()) != null) {
            matcher.reset(line);
            if (matcher.find()) {
                // line matches the pattern
            }
        }
    } catch (IOException e) {
    }
```

Class   *Interface*   —extends   - - -implements   ○ abstract   ● final   ˆ—has superclass   ‿—has subclass   package—see other volume

ε442. Implementing a FilterReader to Filter Lines Based on a Regular Expression

A common use of regular expressions is to find all lines that match a pattern, similar to the grep Unix command. This example implements a FilterReader that will filter an input stream based on a pattern.

```java
try {
    // Create the FilterReader
    String filename = "infile.txt";
    String pattern = "pattern";
    BufferedReader rd = new BufferedReader(new FileReader(filename));
    rd = new BufferedReader(new RegexReader(rd, pattern));

    // Retrieve all lines that match pattern
    String line = null;
    while ((line = rd.readLine()) != null) {
        // line matches the pattern
    }
} catch (IOException e) {
}

// This class takes a reader and a pattern and removes lines
// that don't match the pattern.
// Line terminators are converted to a \n.
public class RegexReader extends FilterReader {
    // This variable holds the current line.
    // If null and emitNewline is false, a newline must be fetched.
    String curLine;

    // This is the index of the first unread character in curLine.
    // If at any time curLineIx == curLine.length, curLine is set to null.
    int curLineIx;

    // If true, the newline at the end of curLine has not been returned.
    // It would have been more convenient to append the newline
    // onto freshly fetched lines. However, that would incur another
    // allocation and copy.
    boolean emitNewline;

    // Matcher used to test every line
    Matcher matcher;

    public RegexReader(BufferedReader in, String patternStr) {
        super(in);
        Pattern pattern = Pattern.compile(patternStr);
        matcher = pattern.matcher("");
    }

    // This overridden method fills cbuf with characters read from in.
    public int read(char cbuf[], int off, int len) throws IOException {
        // Fetch new line if necessary
        if (curLine == null && !emitNewline) {
            getNextLine();
        }

        // Return characters from current line
        if (curLine != null) {
            int num = Math.min(len, Math.min(cbuf.length-off,
                                        curLine.length()-curLineIx));
            // Copy characters from curLine to cbuf
            for (int i=0; i<num; i++) {
                cbuf[off++] = curLine.charAt(curLineIx++);
```

```
                }
                // No more characters in curLine
                if (curLineIx == curLine.length()) {
                    curLine = null;

                    // Is there room for the newline?
                    if (num < len && off < cbuf.length) {
                        cbuf[off++] = '\n';
                        emitNewline = false;
                        num++;
                    }
                }

                // Return number of character read
                return num;
            } else if (emitNewline && len > 0) {
                // Emit just the newline
                cbuf[off] = '\n';
                emitNewline = false;
                return 1;
            } else if (len > 0) {
                // No more characters left in input reader
                return -1;
            } else {
                // Client did not ask for any characters
                return 0;
            }
        }

        // Get next matching line
        private void getNextLine() throws IOException {
            curLine = ((BufferedReader)in).readLine();
            while (curLine != null) {
                matcher.reset(curLine);
                if (matcher.find()) {
                    emitNewline = true;
                    curLineIx = 0;
                    return;
                }
                curLine = ((BufferedReader)in).readLine();
            }
            return;
        }
        public boolean ready() throws IOException {
            return curLine != null || emitNewline || in.ready();
        }
        public boolean markSupported() {
            return false;
        }
    }
}
```

ε443. Matching Line Boundaries in a Regular Expression

By default, the beginning-of-line matcher (^) and end-of-line matcher ($) do not match at line boundaries. They match the beginning and end of the entire input sequence. For example, the pattern '^a' matches 'abc' but does not match 'def\nabc'. To enable '^' and '$' to match line boundaries, the pattern should be compiled with the multiline flag enabled.

It is also possible to enable multiline mode within a pattern using the inline modifier '(?m)'. For example, multiline mode is enabled in the pattern '(?m)^a'. Multiline mode can be disabled using '(?-m)'.

```
CharSequence inputStr = "abc\ndef";
String patternStr = "abc$";

// Compile with multiline enabled
Pattern pattern = Pattern.compile(patternStr, Pattern.MULTILINE);
Matcher matcher = pattern.matcher(inputStr);
boolean matchFound = matcher.find(); // true

// Use an inline modifier to enable multiline mode
matchFound = pattern.matches(".*abc$.*", "abc\r\ndef"); // false
matchFound = pattern.matches("(?m).*abc$.*", "abc\r\ndef"); // true
```

ε444. Matching Across Line Boundaries in a Regular Expression

By default, the any-character matcher (.) does not match line termination characters such as '\n' and '\r'. To allow dot (.) to match line termination characters, the pattern should be compiled with the dotall flag enabled.

It is also possible to enable dotall mode within a pattern using the inline modifier '(?s)'. For example, dotall mode is enabled in the pattern '(?s)a.*b'. Dotall mode can be disabled using '(?-s)'.

```
CharSequence inputStr = "abc\ndef";
String patternStr = ".*c.+d.*";

// Compile with dotall enabled
Pattern pattern = Pattern.compile(patternStr, Pattern.DOTALL);
Matcher matcher = pattern.matcher(inputStr);
boolean matchFound = matcher.matches(); // true

// Use an inline modifier to enable dotall mode
matchFound = pattern.matches(".*c.+d.*", "abc\r\ndef"); // false
matchFound = pattern.matches("(?s).*c.+d.*", "abc\r\ndef"); // true
```

ε445. Reading Lines from a String Using a Regular Expression

This example demonstrates how to read lines from a CharSequence. The lines can be terminated with any of the legal line termination character sequences: \r, \r\n, or \n.

```
CharSequence inputStr = "a\rb"; // Mac
inputStr = "a\r\nb"; // Windows
inputStr = "a\nb"; // Unix

// Compile the pattern
String patternStr = "^(.*)$";
Pattern pattern = Pattern.compile(patternStr, Pattern.MULTILINE);
Matcher matcher = pattern.matcher(inputStr);

// Read the lines
while (matcher.find()) {
    // Get the line with the line termination character sequence
    String lineWithTerminator = matcher.group(0);

    // Get the line without the line termination character sequence
    String lineWithoutTerminator = matcher.group(1);
}
```

ε446. Removing Line Termination Characters from a String

A line termination character sequence is a character or character pair from the set: \n, \r, \r\n, \u0085, \u2028, and \u2029.

Note: The character pair \n\r is considered a two-line terminator character and therefore will be replaced with two spaces.

```
// Returns a version of the input where all line terminators
// are replaced with a space.
public static CharSequence removeLineTerminators(CharSequence inputStr) {
    String patternStr = "(?m)$^|[\\r\\n]+\\z";
    String replaceStr = " ";
    Pattern pattern = Pattern.compile(patternStr);
    Matcher matcher = pattern.matcher(inputStr);
    return matcher.replaceAll(replaceStr);
}
```

Paragraphs

ε447. Reading Paragraphs from a String Using a Regular Expression

This example demonstrates how to read paragraphs from a CharSequence. A paragraph is a contiguous sequence of non-blank lines separated by one or more blank lines. The lines in a paragraph can be terminated with any of the legal line termination character sequences: \r, \r\n, or \n.

```
CharSequence inputStr = "a\r\rb"; // Mac
inputStr = "a\r\n\r\nb"; // Windows
inputStr = "a\n\nb"; // Unix

// Compile the pattern
String patternStr = "(^.*\\S+.*$)+";
Pattern pattern = Pattern.compile(patternStr, Pattern.MULTILINE);
Matcher matcher = pattern.matcher(inputStr);

// Read the paragraphs
while (matcher.find()) {
    // Get the paragraph
    String paragraph = matcher.group();
}
```

ε448. Parsing a String into Paragraphs Using a Regular Expression

This example demonstrates how to parse a CharSequence into an array of paragraphs. A paragraph is a contiguous sequence of non-blank lines separated by one or more blank lines. The lines in a paragraph can be terminated with any of the legal line termination character sequences: \r, \r\n, or \n.

```
CharSequence inputStr = "a\r\rb"; // Mac
inputStr = "a\r\n\r\nb"; // Windows
inputStr = "a\n\nb"; // Unix

String patternStr = "(?<=(\r\n|\r|\n))([ \\t]*$)+";

// Parse the input into paragraphs
String[] paras = Pattern.compile(patternStr, Pattern.MULTILINE).split(inputStr);

// Get paragraphs
for (int i=0; i<paras.length; i++) {
    String paragraph = paras[i];
}
```

Class *Interface* —extends   - - -implements   ○ abstract   ● final   ^—has superclass   ˌ—has subclass   package—see other volume

java.util.zip

This package contains classes for computing checksums of data, and for compressing and decompressing data using standard ZIP and GZIP formats.

```
       java.lang.Object
1.1    ├ Adler32 --------------------------------------------- Checksum
1.1    ├ CRC32 ---------------------------------------------┘
1.1    ├ Deflater
1.1    ├ Inflater
1.1    ├ ZipEntry --------------------------------------- java.lang.Cloneable
1.1    ├ ZipFile
   ○   ├ java.io.InputStream
           └ java.io.FilterInputStream
1.1            ├ CheckedInputStream
1.1            └ InflaterInputStream
1.1                ├ GZIPInputStream
1.1                └ ZipInputStream
   ○   ├ java.io.OutputStream
           └ java.io.FilterOutputStream
1.1            ├ CheckedOutputStream
1.1            └ DeflaterOutputStream
1.1                ├ GZIPOutputStream
1.1                └ ZipOutputStream
```

Packages

```
        java.lang.Object
          └ java.lang.Throwable - - - - - - - - - - - - - - - - - - - - - - - - - - - - - - - - - java.io.Serializable
            └ java.lang.Exception
1.1             ├ DataFormatException
              └ java.io.IOException
1.1              └ ZipException

1.1     Checksum
```

ε449. Compressing a Byte Array

See also "ε450. Decompressing a Byte Array".

```
byte[] input = "some some bytes to compress".getBytes();

// Create the compressor with highest level of compression
Deflater compressor = new Deflater();
compressor.setLevel(Deflater.BEST_COMPRESSION);

// Give the compressor the data to compress
compressor.setInput(input);
compressor.finish();

// Create an expandable byte array to hold the compressed data.
// You cannot use an array that's the same size as the orginal because
// there is no guarantee that the compressed data will be smaller than
// the uncompressed data.
ByteArrayOutputStream bos = new ByteArrayOutputStream(input.length);

// Compress the data
byte[] buf = new byte[1024];
while (!compressor.finished()) {
    int count = compressor.deflate(buf);
    bos.write(buf, 0, count);
}
try {
    bos.close();
} catch (IOException e) {
}

// Get the compressed data
byte[] compressedData = bos.toByteArray();
```

ε450. Decompressing a Byte Array

This example decompresses a byte array that was compressed using the Deflater class (see "ε449. Compressing a Byte Array").

```
// Create the decompressor and give it the data to compress
Inflater decompressor = new Inflater();
decompressor.setInput(compressedData);

// Create an expandable byte array to hold the decompressed data
ByteArrayOutputStream bos = new ByteArrayOutputStream(compressedData.length);

// Decompress the data
byte[] buf = new byte[1024];
while (!decompressor.finished()) {
    try {
        int count = decompressor.inflate(buf);
```

Class *Interface* —extends - - -implements ○ abstract ● final ‸—has superclass ⌄—has subclass package—see other volume

```
                bos.write(buf, 0, count);
            } catch (DataFormatException e) {
            }
    }
    try {
        bos.close();
    } catch (IOException e) {
    }

    // Get the decompressed data
    byte[] decompressedData = bos.toByteArray();
```

GZIP

ε451. Compressing a File in the GZIP Format

```
try {
    // Create the GZIP output stream
    String outFilename = "outfile.gzip";
    GZIPOutputStream out = new GZIPOutputStream(new FileOutputStream(outFilename));

    // Open the input file
    String inFilename = "infilename";
    FileInputStream in = new FileInputStream(inFilename);

    // Transfer bytes from the input file to the GZIP output stream
    byte[] buf = new byte[1024];
    int len;
    while ((len = in.read(buf)) > 0) {
        out.write(buf, 0, len);
    }
    in.close();

    // Complete the GZIP file
    out.finish();
    out.close();
} catch (IOException e) {
}
```

ε452. Uncompressing a File in the GZIP Format

```
try {
    // Open the compressed file
    String inFilename = "infile.gzip";
    GZIPInputStream in = new GZIPInputStream(new FileInputStream(inFilename));

    // Open the output file
    String outFilename = "outfile";
    OutputStream out = new FileOutputStream(outFilename);

    // Transfer bytes from the compressed file to the output file
    byte[] buf = new byte[1024];
    int len;
    while ((len = in.read(buf)) > 0) {
        out.write(buf, 0, len);
    }

    // Close the file and stream
    in.close();
    out.close();
```

```
    } catch (IOException e) {
    }
```

ZIP

ε453. Creating a ZIP File

```
// These are the files to include in the ZIP file
String[] filenames = new String[]{"filename1", "filename2"};

// Create a buffer for reading the files
byte[] buf = new byte[1024];

try {
    // Create the ZIP file
    String outFilename = "outfile.zip";
    ZipOutputStream out = new ZipOutputStream(new FileOutputStream(outFilename));

    // Compress the files
    for (int i=0; i<filenames.length; i++) {
        FileInputStream in = new FileInputStream(filenames[i]);

        // Add ZIP entry to output stream.
        out.putNextEntry(new ZipEntry(filenames[i]));

        // Transfer bytes from the file to the ZIP file
        int len;
        while ((len = in.read(buf)) > 0) {
            out.write(buf, 0, len);
        }

        // Complete the entry
        out.closeEntry();
        in.close();
    }

    // Complete the ZIP file
    out.close();
} catch (IOException e) {
}
```

ε454. Listing the Contents of a ZIP File

```
try {
    // Open the ZIP file
    ZipFile zf = new ZipFile("filename.zip");

    // Enumerate each entry
    for (Enumeration entries = zf.entries(); entries.hasMoreElements();) {
        // Get the entry name
        String zipEntryName = ((ZipEntry)entries.nextElement()).getName();
    }
} catch (IOException e) {
}
```

ε455. Retrieving a Compressed File from a ZIP File

This example reads a ZIP file and decompresses the first entry.

```
    try {
```

```
// Open the ZIP file
String inFilename = "infile.zip";
ZipInputStream in = new ZipInputStream(new FileInputStream(inFilename));

// Get the first entry
ZipEntry entry = in.getNextEntry();

// Open the output file
String outFilename = "o";
OutputStream out = new FileOutputStream(outFilename);

// Transfer bytes from the ZIP file to the output file
byte[] buf = new byte[1024];
int len;
while ((len = in.read(buf)) > 0) {
    out.write(buf, 0, len);
}

// Close the streams
out.close();
in.close();
} catch (IOException e) {
}
```

Checksums

ε456. Calculating the Checksum of a Byte Array

```
byte[] bytes = "some data".getBytes();

// Compute Adler-32 checksum
Checksum checksumEngine = new Adler32();
checksumEngine.update(bytes, 0, bytes.length);
long checksum = checksumEngine.getValue();

// Compute CRC-32 checksum
checksumEngine = new CRC32();
checksumEngine.update(bytes, 0, bytes.length);
checksum = checksumEngine.getValue();

// The checksum engine can be reused again for a different byte array by calling reset()
checksumEngine.reset();
```

ε457. Calculating the Checksum of a File

```
try {
    // Compute Adler-32 checksum
    CheckedInputStream cis = new CheckedInputStream(
        new FileInputStream("filename"), new Adler32());
    byte[] tempBuf = new byte[128];
    while (cis.read(tempBuf) >= 0) {
    }
    long checksum = cis.getChecksum().getValue();
} catch (IOException e) {
}
```

javax.crypto

This package provides the classes and interfaces for cryptographic operations. The cryptographic operations defined in this package include encryption, key generation and key agreement, and Message Authentication Code (MAC) generation.

```
      java.lang.Object
1.4      ├ Cipher
1.4      │  └ NullCipher
1.4      ├ CipherSpi
1.4      ├ EncryptedPrivateKeyInfo
1.4      ├ ExemptionMechanism
1.4      ├ ExemptionMechanismSpi
1.4      ├ KeyAgreement
1.4      ├ KeyAgreementSpi
1.4      ├ KeyGenerator
```

Class *Interface* —extends - - -implements ○ abstract ● final ^—has superclass —has subclass package—see other volume

```
       java.lang.Object
1.4 ○   ├ KeyGeneratorSpi
1.4     ├ Mac - - - - - - - - - - - - - - - - - - - - - - - - - - - java.lang.Cloneable﹀
1.4 ○   ├ MacSpi
1.4     ├ SealedObject - - - - - - - - - - - - - - - - - - - - - - ┌ java.io.Serializable﹀
1.4     ├ SecretKeyFactory                                        │
1.4 ○   ├ SecretKeyFactorySpi                                     │
    ○   ├ java.io.InputStream                                     │
        │  └ java.io.FilterInputStream                            │
1.4     │       └ CipherInputStream                               │
    ○   ├ java.io.OutputStream                                    │
        │  └ java.io.FilterOutputStream                           │
1.4     │       └ CipherOutputStream                              │
        └ java.lang.Throwable - - - - - - - - - - - - - - - - - - ┘
           └ java.lang.Exception
1.2          └ java.security.GeneralSecurityException
1.4             ├ BadPaddingException
1.4             ├ ExemptionMechanismException
1.4             ├ IllegalBlockSizeException
1.4             ├ NoSuchPaddingException
1.4             └ ShortBufferException

1.4  SecretKey﹀ ─────────────────────────── java.security.Key^
```

Symmetric Keys

ε458. Listing All Available Symmetric Key Generators

Retrieving the list of available key generators requires checking the services provided by all registered providers. The retrieved list of names can be used in creating a KeyGenerator object.

```
// This method is implemented in "ε194. Listing All Available Cryptographic Services"
String[] names = getCryptoImpls("KeyGenerator");
```

An example of the output:

```
HmacSHA1
Blowfish
HmacMD5
TripleDES
DESede
DES
```

ε459. Generating a Symmetric Key

This example generates a key for various symmetric cipher algorithms. See also "ε458. Listing All Available Symmetric Key Generators".

```
try {
    // Generate a DES key
    KeyGenerator keyGen = KeyGenerator.getInstance("DES");
    SecretKey key = keyGen.generateKey();

    // Generate a Blowfish key
    keyGen = KeyGenerator.getInstance("Blowfish");
    key = keyGen.generateKey();

    // Generate a triple DES key
```

```
        keyGen = KeyGenerator.getInstance("DESede");
        key = keyGen.generateKey();
    } catch (java.security.NoSuchAlgorithmException e) {
    }
```

ε460. Getting the Bytes of a Generated Symmetric Key

```
try {
    // Generate a key
    KeyGenerator keyGen = KeyGenerator.getInstance("DESede");
    SecretKey key = keyGen.generateKey();

    // Get the bytes of the key
    byte[] keyBytes = key.getEncoded();
    int numBytes = keyBytes.length;

    // The bytes can be converted back to a SecretKey
    SecretKey key2 = new SecretKeySpec(keyBytes, "DESede");
    boolean b = key.equals(key2); // true
} catch (NoSuchAlgorithmException e) {
}
```

Encrypting and Decrypting

ε461. Listing All Available Encryption and Decryption Algorithms

Retrieving the list of available encryption/decryption algorithms requires checking the services provided by all registered providers. The retrieved list of names can be used in creating a Cipher object.

```
// This method is implemented in "ε194. Listing All Available Cryptographic Services"
String[] names = getCryptoImpls("Cipher");
```

An example of the output:

```
Blowfish
DESede
PBEWithMD5AndTripleDES
TripleDES
DES
PBEWithMD5AndDES
```

ε462. Encrypting a String with DES

This example implements a class for encrypting and decrypting strings using DES. The class is created with a key and can be used repeatedly to encrypt and decrypt strings using that key.

```
public class DesEncrypter {
    Cipher ecipher;
    Cipher dcipher;

    DesEncrypter(SecretKey key) {
        try {
            ecipher = Cipher.getInstance("DES");
            dcipher = Cipher.getInstance("DES");
            ecipher.init(Cipher.ENCRYPT_MODE, key);
            dcipher.init(Cipher.DECRYPT_MODE, key);

        } catch (javax.crypto.NoSuchPaddingException e) {
        } catch (java.security.NoSuchAlgorithmException e) {
```

Class   *Interface*   —extends   - - -implements   O abstract   ● final   ^—has superclass   ‿—has subclass   package—see other volume

```
            } catch (java.security.InvalidKeyException e) {
            }
        }

        public String encrypt(String str) {
            try {
                // Encode the string into bytes using utf-8
                byte[] utf8 = str.getBytes("UTF8");

                // Encrypt
                byte[] enc = ecipher.doFinal(utf8);

                // Encode bytes to base64 to get a string
                return new sun.misc.BASE64Encoder().encode(enc);
            } catch (javax.crypto.BadPaddingException e) {
            } catch (IllegalBlockSizeException e) {
            } catch (UnsupportedEncodingException e) {
            } catch (java.io.IOException e) {
            }
            return null;
        }

        public String decrypt(String str) {
            try {
                // Decode base64 to get bytes
                byte[] dec = new sun.misc.BASE64Decoder().decodeBuffer(str);

                // Decrypt
                byte[] utf8 = dcipher.doFinal(dec);

                // Decode using utf-8
                return new String(utf8, "UTF8");
            } catch (javax.crypto.BadPaddingException e) {
            } catch (IllegalBlockSizeException e) {
            } catch (UnsupportedEncodingException e) {
            } catch (java.io.IOException e) {
            }
            return null;
        }
    }
```

Here's an example that uses the class:

```
try {
    // Generate a temporary key. In practice, you would save this key.
    // See also "ε464. Encrypting with DES Using a Pass Phrase".
    SecretKey key = KeyGenerator.getInstance("DES").generateKey();

    // Create encrypter/decrypter class
    DesEncrypter encrypter = new DesEncrypter(key);

    // Encrypt
    String encrypted = encrypter.encrypt("Don't tell anybody!");

    // Decrypt
    String decrypted = encrypter.decrypt(encrypted);
} catch (Exception e) {
}
```

ε463. Encrypting a File or Stream with DES

This example implements a class for encrypting and decrypting files or streams using DES. The class is created with a key and can be used repeatedly to encrypt and decrypt streams using that key.

```java
public class DesEncrypter {
    Cipher ecipher;
    Cipher dcipher;

    DesEncrypter(SecretKey key) {
        // Create an 8-byte initialization vector
        byte[] iv = new byte[]{
            (byte)0x8E, 0x12, 0x39, (byte)0x9C,
            0x07, 0x72, 0x6F, 0x5A
        };
        AlgorithmParameterSpec paramSpec = new IvParameterSpec(iv);
        try {
            ecipher = Cipher.getInstance("DES/CBC/PKCS5Padding");
            dcipher = Cipher.getInstance("DES/CBC/PKCS5Padding");

            // CBC requires an initialization vector
            ecipher.init(Cipher.ENCRYPT_MODE, key, paramSpec);
            dcipher.init(Cipher.DECRYPT_MODE, key, paramSpec);
        } catch (java.security.InvalidAlgorithmParameterException e) {
        } catch (javax.crypto.NoSuchPaddingException e) {
        } catch (java.security.NoSuchAlgorithmException e) {
        } catch (java.security.InvalidKeyException e) {
        }
    }

    // Buffer used to transport the bytes from one stream to another
    byte[] buf = new byte[1024];

    public void encrypt(InputStream in, OutputStream out) {
        try {
            // Bytes written to out will be encrypted
            out = new CipherOutputStream(out, ecipher);

            // Read in the cleartext bytes and write to out to encrypt
            int numRead = 0;
            while ((numRead = in.read(buf)) >= 0) {
                out.write(buf, 0, numRead);
            }
            out.close();
        } catch (java.io.IOException e) {
        }
    }

    public void decrypt(InputStream in, OutputStream out) {
        try {
            // Bytes read from in will be decrypted
            in = new CipherInputStream(in, dcipher);

            // Read in the decrypted bytes and write the cleartext to out
            int numRead = 0;
            while ((numRead = in.read(buf)) >= 0) {
                out.write(buf, 0, numRead);
            }
            out.close();
```

Class   *Interface*   —extends   - - -implements   ○ abstract   ● final   ˆ—has superclass   ˌ—has subclass   package —see other volume

308

```
        } catch (java.io.IOException e) {
        }
    }
}
```

Here's an example that uses the class:

```
try {
    // Generate a temporary key. In practice, you would save this key.
    // See also "ε464. Encrypting with DES Using a Pass Phrase".
    SecretKey key = KeyGenerator.getInstance("DES").generateKey();

    // Create encrypter/decrypter class
    DesEncrypter encrypter = new DesEncrypter(key);

    // Encrypt
    encrypter.encrypt(new FileInputStream("infilename"),
        new FileOutputStream("outfilename"));

    // Decrypt
    encrypter.decrypt(new FileInputStream("infilename"),
        new FileOutputStream("outfilename"));
} catch (Exception e) {
}
```

ε464. Encrypting with DES Using a Pass Phrase

This example demonstrates how to use a pass phrase (a string password of multiple words) for encryption.

```
public class DesEncrypter {
    Cipher ecipher;
    Cipher dcipher;

    // 8-byte Salt
    byte[] salt = {
        (byte)0xA9, (byte)0x9B, (byte)0xC8, (byte)0x32,
        (byte)0x56, (byte)0x35, (byte)0xE3, (byte)0x03
    };

    // Iteration count
    int iterationCount = 19;

    DesEncrypter(String passPhrase) {
        try {
            // Create the key
            KeySpec keySpec = new PBEKeySpec(passPhrase.toCharArray(), salt, iterationCount);
            SecretKey key = SecretKeyFactory.getInstance(
                "PBEWithMD5AndDES").generateSecret(keySpec);
            ecipher = Cipher.getInstance(key.getAlgorithm());
            dcipher = Cipher.getInstance(key.getAlgorithm());

            // Prepare the parameter to the ciphers
            AlgorithmParameterSpec paramSpec = new PBEParameterSpec(salt, iterationCount);

            // Create the ciphers
            ecipher.init(Cipher.ENCRYPT_MODE, key, paramSpec);
            dcipher.init(Cipher.DECRYPT_MODE, key, paramSpec);
        } catch (java.security.InvalidAlgorithmParameterException e) {
        } catch (java.security.spec.InvalidKeySpecException e) {
        } catch (javax.crypto.NoSuchPaddingException e) {
        } catch (java.security.NoSuchAlgorithmException e) {
        } catch (java.security.InvalidKeyException e) {
```

```
                }
            }

        public String encrypt(String str) {
            try {
                // Encode the string into bytes using utf-8
                byte[] utf8 = str.getBytes("UTF8");

                // Encrypt
                byte[] enc = ecipher.doFinal(utf8);

                // Encode bytes to base64 to get a string
                return new sun.misc.BASE64Encoder().encode(enc);
            } catch (javax.crypto.BadPaddingException e) {
            } catch (IllegalBlockSizeException e) {
            } catch (UnsupportedEncodingException e) {
            } catch (java.io.IOException e) {
            }
            return null;
        }

        public String decrypt(String str) {
            try {
                // Decode base64 to get bytes
                byte[] dec = new sun.misc.BASE64Decoder().decodeBuffer(str);

                // Decrypt
                byte[] utf8 = dcipher.doFinal(dec);

                // Decode using utf-8
                return new String(utf8, "UTF8");
            } catch (javax.crypto.BadPaddingException e) {
            } catch (IllegalBlockSizeException e) {
            } catch (UnsupportedEncodingException e) {
            } catch (java.io.IOException e) {
            }
            return null;
        }
    }

    // Here is an example that uses the class
    try {
        // Create encrypter/decrypter class
        DesEncrypter encrypter = new DesEncrypter("My Pass Phrase!");

        // Encrypt
        String encrypted = encrypter.encrypt("Don't tell anybody!");

        // Decrypt
        String decrypted = encrypter.decrypt(encrypted);
    } catch (Exception e) {
    }
```

ε465. Converting a 56-bit Value to a DES Key

The DES encrypter/decrypter requires a 64-bit key where only 56-bit are significant. The other 8-bit are parity bits used to ensure that the key has not been corrupted. To make the 64-bit key, the 56-bit value is broken up into 7-bit chunks. Each 7-bit chunk is moved into an 8-bit slot taking up the most significant bit

---

positions. The least significant bit (the parity bit) is set to either 1 or 0 in order to make the quantity of 1 bits in the byte an odd number.

This example implements a method to convert a 56-bit value into a valid DES key. Such a method could be used to convert a 7-character string password to a valid DES key.

See also "ε462. Encrypting a String with DES".

```
// Takes a 7-byte quantity and returns a valid 8-byte DES key.
// The input and output bytes are big-endian, where the most significant
// byte is in element 0.
public static byte[] addParity(byte[] in) {
    byte[] result = new byte[8];

    // Keeps track of the bit position in the result
    int resultIx = 1;

    // Used to keep track of the number of 1 bits in each 7-bit chunk
    int bitCount = 0;

    // Process each of the 56 bits
    for (int i=0; i<56; i++) {
        // Get the bit at bit position i
        boolean bit = (in[6-i/8]&(1«(i%8))) > 0;

        // If set, set the corresponding bit in the result
        if (bit) {
            result[7-resultIx/8] |= (1«(resultIx%8))&0xFF;
            bitCount++;
        }

        // Set the parity bit after every 7 bits
        if ((i+1) % 7 == 0) {
            if (bitCount % 2 == 0) {
                // Set low-order bit (parity bit) if bit count is even
                result[7-resultIx/8] |= 1;
            }
            resultIx++;
            bitCount = 0;
        }
        resultIx++;
    }
    return result;
}

// Get the 56-bit value
byte[] raw = new byte[]{0x01, 0x72, 0x43, 0x3E, 0x1C, 0x7A, 0x55};
byte[] keyBytes = addParity(raw);

// You can check that the parity has been set properly
try {
    boolean b = DESKeySpec.isParityAdjusted(keyBytes, 0);
} catch (java.security.InvalidKeyException e) {
    // The DES is invalid
}

// Convert the bytes into a SecretKey suitable for use by Cipher
SecretKey key = new SecretKeySpec(keyBytes, "DES");
```

ε466. Encrypting an Object with DES

This example demonstrates how to encrypt a serializable object.

```
try {
    // Generate a temporary key. In practice, you would save this key.
    // See also "ε464. Encrypting with DES Using a Pass Phrase".
    SecretKey key = KeyGenerator.getInstance("DES").generateKey();

    // Prepare the encrypter
    Cipher ecipher = Cipher.getInstance("DES");
    ecipher.init(Cipher.ENCRYPT_MODE, key);

    // Seal (encrypt) the object
    SealedObject so = new SealedObject(new MySecretClass(), ecipher);

    // Get the algorithm used to seal the object
    String algoName = so.getAlgorithm(); // DES

    // Prepare the decrypter
    Cipher dcipher = Cipher.getInstance("DES");
    dcipher.init(Cipher.DECRYPT_MODE, key);

    // Unseal (decrypt) the class
    MySecretClass o = (MySecretClass)so.getObject(dcipher);
} catch (java.io.IOException e) {
} catch (ClassNotFoundException e) {
} catch (javax.crypto.IllegalBlockSizeException e) {
} catch (javax.crypto.BadPaddingException e) {
} catch (javax.crypto.NoSuchPaddingException e) {
} catch (java.security.NoSuchAlgorithmException e) {
} catch (java.security.InvalidKeyException e) {
}

public class MySecretClass implements java.io.Serializable {
    String s = "the secret";
}
```

MAC

ε467. Listing All Available Message Authentication Code (MAC) Key Generators

Retrieving the list of available MAC algorithms requires checking the services provided by all registered providers.

```
// This method is implemented in "ε194. Listing All Available Cryptographic Services"
String[] names = getCryptoImpls("Mac");
```

An example of the output:

```
HmacSHA1
HmacMD5
```

ε468. Generating a Message Authentication Code (MAC) Key

For more information on a MAC, see RFC 2104. See also "ε467. Listing All Available Message Authentication Code (MAC) Key Generators".

```
try {
    // Generate a key for the HMAC-MD5 keyed-hashing algorithm
    KeyGenerator keyGen = KeyGenerator.getInstance("HmacMD5");
    SecretKey key = keyGen.generateKey();

    // Generate a key for the HMAC-SHA1 keyed-hashing algorithm
```

```
        keyGen = KeyGenerator.getInstance("HmacSHA1");
        key = keyGen.generateKey();
    } catch (java.security.NoSuchAlgorithmException e) {
    }
```

ε469. Generating a Message Authentication Code (MAC)

A MAC is like hash code for a sequence of bytes. Unlike a hash code, a MAC uses a secret key to generate the hash code, or more specifically, the "message digest". A MAC is generally used to check the integrity or validity of information based on a secret key.

```
    try {
        // Generate a key for the HMAC-MD5 keyed-hashing algorithm; see RFC 2104
        // In practice, you would save this key.
        KeyGenerator keyGen = KeyGenerator.getInstance("HmacMD5");
        SecretKey key = keyGen.generateKey();

        // Create a MAC object using HMAC-MD5 and initialize with key
        Mac mac = Mac.getInstance(key.getAlgorithm());
        mac.init(key);

        String str = "This message will be digested";

        // Encode the string into bytes using utf-8 and digest it
        byte[] utf8 = str.getBytes("UTF8");
        byte[] digest = mac.doFinal(utf8);

        // If desired, convert the digest into a string
        String digestB64 = new sun.misc.BASE64Encoder().encode(digest);
    } catch (InvalidKeyException e) {
    } catch (NoSuchAlgorithmException e) {
    } catch (UnsupportedEncodingException e) {
    }
```

Key Agreement

ε470. Generating a Parameter Set for the Diffie-Hellman Key Agreement Algorithm

Two parties use a "key agreement protocol" to generate identical secret keys for encryption without ever having to transmit the secret key. The protocol works by both parties agreeing on a set of values (a prime, a base, and a private value) which are used to generate a key pair. This example demonstrates how to generate the set of values.

The two parties then exchange the generated public keys and then use it to compute the secret encryption key. This is demonstrated in "ε471. Generating a Secret Key Using the Diffie-Hellman Key Agreement Algorithm".

```
    // Returns a comma-separated string of 3 values.
    // The first number is the prime modulus P.
    // The second number is the base generator G.
    // The third number is bit size of the random exponent L.
    public static String genDhParams() {
        try {
            // Create the parameter generator for a 1024-bit DH key pair
            AlgorithmParameterGenerator paramGen = AlgorithmParameterGenerator.getInstance("DH");
            paramGen.init(1024);

            // Generate the parameters
            AlgorithmParameters params = paramGen.generateParameters();
            DHParameterSpec dhSpec
```

Packages

```
                = (DHParameterSpec)params.getParameterSpec(DHParameterSpec.class);

        // Return the three values in a string
        return ""+dhSpec.getP()+","+dhSpec.getG()+","+dhSpec.getL();
    } catch (NoSuchAlgorithmException e) {
    } catch (InvalidParameterSpecException e) {
    }
    return null;
}
```

ε471. Generating a Secret Key Using the Diffie-Hellman Key Agreement Algorithm

Two parties use a "key agreement protocol" to generate identical secret keys for encryption without ever having to transmit the secret key. The protocol works by both parties agreeing on a set of values (a prime, a base, and a private value) which are used to generate a key pair. "ε470. Generating a Parameter Set for the Diffie-Hellman Key Agreement Algorithm" demonstrates how to generate the set of values.

This example uses the set of values and generates a key pair. The public key is then exchanged with the other party and the secret key is generated.

```
// Retrieve the prime, base, and private value for generating the key pair.
// If the values are encoded as in
// "ε470. Generating a Parameter Set for the Diffie-Hellman Key Agreement Algorithm",
// the following code will extract the values.
String[] values = valuesInStr.split(",");
BigInteger p = new BigInteger(values[0]);
BigInteger g = new BigInteger(values[1]);
int l = Integer.parseInt(values[2]);

try {
    // Use the values to generate a key pair
    KeyPairGenerator keyGen = KeyPairGenerator.getInstance("DH");
    DHParameterSpec dhSpec = new DHParameterSpec(p, g, l);
    keyGen.initialize(dhSpec);
    KeyPair keypair = keyGen.generateKeyPair();

    // Get the generated public and private keys
    PrivateKey privateKey = keypair.getPrivate();
    PublicKey publicKey = keypair.getPublic();

    // Send the public key bytes to the other party...
    byte[] publicKeyBytes = publicKey.getEncoded();

    // Retrieve the public key bytes of the other party
    publicKeyBytes = ...;

    // Convert the public key bytes into a PublicKey object
    X509EncodedKeySpec x509KeySpec = new X509EncodedKeySpec(publicKeyBytes);
    KeyFactory keyFact = KeyFactory.getInstance("DH");
    publicKey = keyFact.generatePublic(x509KeySpec);

    // Prepare to generate the secret key with the private key and public key of the other party
    KeyAgreement ka = KeyAgreement.getInstance("DH");
    ka.init(privateKey);
    ka.doPhase(publicKey, true);

    // Specify the type of key to generate;
    // see "ε458. Listing All Available Symmetric Key Generators"
    String algorithm = "DES";
```

Class *Interface* —extends - - -implements ○ abstract ● final ^—has superclass ⌐—has subclass package—see other volume

```
    // Generate the secret key
    SecretKey secretKey = ka.generateSecret(algorithm);

    // Use the secret key to encrypt/decrypt data;
    // see "ε462. Encrypting a String with DES"
} catch (java.security.InvalidKeyException e) {
} catch (java.security.spec.InvalidKeySpecException e) {
} catch (java.security.InvalidAlgorithmParameterException e) {
} catch (java.security.NoSuchAlgorithmException e) {
}
```

javax.crypto.interfaces

This package provides interfaces for Diffie-Hellman keys as defined in RSA Laboratories' PKCS #3.

javax.crypto.spec

This package provides classes and interfaces for key specifications and algorithm parameter specifications. A key specification is a transparent representation of the key material that constitutes a key. An algorithm parameter specification is a transparent representation of the sets of parameters used with an algorithm.

Packages

javax.crypto.spec

```
java.lang.Object
```

javax.naming

This package contains classes and interfaces for accessing naming services. JNDI is a naming and directory interface that is defined independent of any underlying service. Applications can use JNDI to access a variety of different naming and directory services. This package defines the notion of a context, which is the core interface for looking up, binding/unbinding, and renaming objects.

Class   *Interface*   —extends   - - -implements   ○ abstract   ● final   ˆ—has superclass   ˌ—has subclass   package—see other volume

```
     java.lang.Object
1.3   ├ CompositeName------------------------------------,--Nameˆ
1.3   ├ CompoundName-----------------------------------┘
1.3   ├ InitialContext,--------------------------------- Context,
1.3   ├ NameClassPair --------------------------------┬- java.io.Serializable,
1.3   │  └ Binding,                                   ┆
1.3 O ├ RefAddr---------------------------------------┘
1.3   │ ├ BinaryRefAddr
```

Packages

317

javax.naming

```
        java.lang.Object
1.3 ○   ├ RefAddr- - - - - - - - - - - - - - - - - - - - - - - - - - - - - - - - - - - - - ⌐- - java.io.Serializable⌐
1.3     │  └ StringRefAddr
1.3     ├ Reference- - - - - - - - - - - - - - - - - - - - - - - - - - - - - - java.io.Serializable⌐, java.lang.Cloneable⌐
1.3     │  └ LinkRef
        └ java.lang.Throwable- - - - - - - - - - - - - - - - - - - - - - - - java.io.Serializable⌐
            └ java.lang.Exception
1.3           └ NamingException
1.3             ├ CannotProceedException
1.3             ├ CommunicationException
1.3             ├ ConfigurationException
1.3             ├ ContextNotEmptyException
1.3             ├ InsufficientResourcesException
1.3             ├ InterruptedNamingException
1.3             ├ InvalidNameException
1.3             ├ LimitExceededException
1.3             │  ├ SizeLimitExceededException
1.3             │  └ TimeLimitExceededException
1.3             ├ LinkException
1.3             │  ├ LinkLoopException
1.3             │  └ MalformedLinkException
1.3             ├ NameAlreadyBoundException
1.3             ├ NameNotFoundException
1.3 ○           ├ NamingSecurityException
1.3             │  ├ AuthenticationException
1.3             │  ├ AuthenticationNotSupportedException
1.3             │  └ NoPermissionException
1.3             ├ NoInitialContextException
1.3             ├ NotContextException
1.3             ├ OperationNotSupportedException
1.3             ├ PartialResultException
1.3 ○           ├ ReferralException⌐
1.3             └ ServiceUnavailableException
```

```
1.3     Context⌐
1.3     Name ─────────────────────────────────── java.io.Serializable, java.lang.Cloneable
1.3     NameParser
1.3     NamingEnumeration ─────────────────────── java.util.Enumeration
1.3     Referenceable
```

ε472. Creating an Initial Context to the Naming Service

This example uses the JNDI/COS naming service provider to connect to the local tnameserv.

```
String url = "iiop://localhost/";
Hashtable env = new Hashtable();
env.put(Context.INITIAL_CONTEXT_FACTORY, "com.sun.jndi.cosnaming.CNCtxFactory");
env.put(Context.PROVIDER_URL, url);
try {
    Context ctx = new InitialContext(env);
} catch (NamingException e) {
}
```

ε473. Looking Up an Object from the Naming Service

This example looks up an object from the naming service.

```
try {
    Object obj = ctx.lookup("Sample");
} catch (NamingException e) {
}
```

ε474. Listing a Context in the Naming Service

This example lists a context in the naming service.

```
try {
    NamingEnumeration enum = ctx.list("child");
    while (enum.hasMore()) {
        NameClassPair entry = (NameClassPair)enum.next();
        process(entry);
    }
} catch (NamingException e) {
}
```

ε475. Adding, Replacing, Removing, and Renaming a Binding in the Naming Service

```
try {
    // Add a binding.
    ctx.bind("Name", new SampleObjectImpl());

    // Replace a binding.
    ctx.rebind("Name", new SampleObjectImpl());

    // Remove a binding.
    ctx.unbind("Name");

    // Rename a binding.
    ctx.rename("Name", "NewSample");
} catch (NamingException e) {
}
```

ε476. Creating and Destroying a Subcontext in the Naming Service

This example creates a subcontext in the naming service.

```
try {
    // Create a subcontext.
    Context childCtx = ctx.createSubcontext("child");

    // Destroy the subcontext.
    ctx.destroySubcontext("child");
} catch (NamingException e) {
}
```

ε477. Getting an Object's Fully Qualified Name

This example gets an object's fully qualified name in its own namespace.

```
try {
    Context obj = (Context)childCtx.lookup("grandChild");
    String fullname = obj.getNameInNamespace();
} catch (NamingException e) {
}
```

ε478. Using a URL as a Name to the Initial Context

This example looks up an object from the naming service by using a URL as a name.

```
try {
    Object obj = new InitialContext().lookup("iiop://localhost/Sample");
} catch (NamingException e) {
}
```

ε479. Parsing a JNDI Composite Name

In the composite name space, forward-slash (/) separates the composite components.

```
try {
    CompositeName composite = new CompositeName(
        "cn=John,o=hits/report/summary.txt");
    String first = composite.get(0); // cn=John,o=hits
    String last = composite.get(composite.size()-1); // summary.txt

    composite.add(0, "wiz.com"); // wiz.com/cn=John,o=hits/report/summary.txt
    composite.remove(2); // wiz.com/cn=John,o=hits/summary.txt
} catch (NamingException e) {
}
```

ε480. Parsing a JNDI Compound Name

This example parses a compound name using a parser from an LDAP service in which components are arranged from right to left, delimited by the comma character (,).

```
try {
    NameParser parser = ctx.getNameParser("");
    Name dn = parser.parse("cn=John, ou=People, o=JNDITutorial");

    dn.remove(1); // ou=People
    dn.add(0, "c=us"); // cn=John,o=JNDITutorial,c=us
    dn.add("cn=fs"); // cn=fs,cn=John,o=JNDITutorial,c=us
} catch (NamingException e) {
}
```

---

javax.naming.directory

This package extends the core javax.naming package to provide functionality for accessing directories in addition to naming services. This package allows applications to retrieves attributes associated with objects stored in the directory and to search for objects by using specified attributes.

Class   *Interface*   —extends   - - -implements   O abstract   ● final   ˆ—has superclass   ˘—has subclass   package—see other volume

```
java.lang.Object
1.3    ├ BasicAttribute ------------------------------------------- Attribute
1.3    ├ BasicAttributes ------------------------------------------ Attributes
1.3    ├ ModificationItem ---------------------------------- java.io.Serializable
1.3    ├ SearchControls ----------------------------------
1.3    ├ javax.naming.InitialContext ------------------------- javax.naming.Context
1.3    │    └ InitialDirContext --------------------------------- DirContext
1.3    ├ javax.naming.NameClassPair ----------------------- java.io.Serializable
1.3    │    └ javax.naming.Binding
1.3    │         └ SearchResult
1.3    └ java.lang.Throwable -------------------------------
              └ java.lang.Exception
1.3              └ javax.naming.NamingException
1.3                  ├ AttributeInUseException
1.3                  ├ AttributeModificationException
1.3                  ├ InvalidAttributeIdentifierException
1.3                  ├ InvalidAttributeValueException
1.3                  ├ InvalidAttributesException
1.3                  ├ InvalidSearchControlsException
1.3                  ├ InvalidSearchFilterException
1.3                  ├ NoSuchAttributeException
1.3                  └ SchemaViolationException

1.3    Attribute ————————————————————— java.io.Serializable, java.lang.Cloneable
1.3    Attributes ———————————————————
1.3    DirContext ————————————————————————— javax.naming.Context
```

ε481. Creating an Initial Context to a Directory

This example uses the JNDI/LDAP service provider to connect to an LDAP server on the local machine.

```
String url = "ldap://localhost/o=JNDITutorial";
Hashtable env = new Hashtable();
env.put(Context.INITIAL_CONTEXT_FACTORY, "com.sun.jndi.ldap.LdapCtxFactory");
env.put(Context.PROVIDER_URL, url);
```

```
    try {
        DirContext ctx = new InitialDirContext(env);
    } catch (NamingException e) {
    }
```

ε482. Reading an Object's Attributes from the Directory

This example reads some of an object's attributes from the directory.

```
    try {
        // Specify the ids of the attributes to return
        String[] attrIDs = {"sn", "telephonenumber", "golfhandicap", "mail"};

        // Get the attributes requested
        Attributes answer = ctx.getAttributes("cn=Ted Geisel, ou=People", attrIDs);

        NamingEnumeration enum = answer.getAll();
        while (enum.hasMore()) {
            Attribute attr = (Attribute)enum.next();
            process(attr);
        }
    } catch (NamingException e) {
    }
```

ε483. Modifying an Object's Attributes in the Directory

This example modifies some of an object's attributes from the directory.

```
    try {
        // Specify the changes to make
        ModificationItem[] mods = new ModificationItem[3];

        // Replace mail attribute with new value
        mods[0] = new ModificationItem(DirContext.REPLACE_ATTRIBUTE,
            new BasicAttribute("mail", "geisel@wizards.com"));

        // Add additional value to "telephonenumber"
        mods[1] = new ModificationItem(DirContext.ADD_ATTRIBUTE,
            new BasicAttribute("telephonenumber", "+1 555 555 5555"));

        // Remove jpegphoto
        mods[2] = new ModificationItem(DirContext.REMOVE_ATTRIBUTE,
            new BasicAttribute("jpegphoto"));

        // Perform requested modifications on named object
        ctx.modifyAttributes("cn=Ted Geisel, ou=People", mods);
    } catch (NamingException e) {
    }
```

ε484. Creating a Directory Entry

This example creates an entry in the directory.

```
    try {
        // Create attributes to be associated with the new entry
        Attributes attrs = new BasicAttributes(true); // case-ignore
        Attribute objclass = new BasicAttribute("objectclass");
        objclass.add("top");
        objclass.add("extensibleObject");
        attrs.put(objclass);

        // Create the context
```

Class *Interface* —extends - - -implements O abstract ● final ^—has superclass ⌐—has subclass package—see other volume

```
        Context entry = ctx.createSubcontext("cn=Sample", attrs);
    } catch (NamingException e) {
    }
```

ε485. Adding a Binding with Attributes to the Directory

This example adds a name-to-object binding along with attributes to the directory.

```
    try {
        // Create attributes to be associated with the new entry
        Attributes attrs = new BasicAttributes(true); // case-ignore
        Attribute objclass = new BasicAttribute("objectclass");
        objclass.add("top");
        objclass.add("extensibleObject");
        attrs.put(objclass);

        // Create the object to be bound
        Object obj = new SampleObjectImpl();

        // Create the context
        ctx.bind("cn=Sample", obj, attrs);
    } catch (NamingException e) {
    }
```

ε486. Performing a Basic Directory Search

This example searches the directory for objects that have certain specified attributes.

```
    try {
        // Specify the ids of the attributes to return
        String[] attrIDs = {"sn", "telephonenumber", "golfhandicap", "mail"};

        // Specify the attributes to match
        // Ask for objects that have attribute "sn" == Geisel and the "mail" attribute
        Attributes matchAttrs = new BasicAttributes(true); // ignore case
        matchAttrs.put(new BasicAttribute("sn", "Geisel"));
        matchAttrs.put(new BasicAttribute("mail"));

        // Search for objects with those matching attributes
        NamingEnumeration enum = ctx.search("ou=People", matchAttrs, attrIDs);

        while (enum.hasMore()) {
            SearchResult entry = (SearchResult)enum.next();
            process(entry);
        }
    } catch (NamingException e) {
    }
```

ε487. Searching the Directory by Using a Search Filter

This example searches the directory for objects by using a search filter.

```
    try {
        // Specify the ids of the attributes to return
        String[] attrIDs = {"sn", "telephonenumber", "golfhandicap", "mail"};

        SearchControls ctls = new SearchControls();
        ctls.setReturningAttributes(attrIDs);

        // Specify the search filter to match
        // Ask for objects that have attribute "sn" == Geisel and the "mail" attribute
        String filter = "(&(sn=Geisel)(mail=*))";

        // Search for objects using filter
```

```
                NamingEnumeration enum = ctx.search("ou=People", filter, ctls);

            while (enum.hasMore()) {
                SearchResult entry = (SearchResult)enum.next();
                process(entry);
            }
        } catch (NamingException e) {
        }
```

ε488. Searching a Subtree in the Directory

This example searches a subtree in the directory for objects by using a search filter.

```
        try {
            SearchControls ctls = new SearchControls();
            ctls.setSearchScope(SearchControls.SUBTREE_SCOPE);

            // Specify the search filter to match
            // Ask for objects that have attribute "sn" == Geisel and the "mail" attribute
            String filter = "(&(sn=Geisel)(mail=*))";

            // Search for objects using filter
            NamingEnumeration enum = ctx.search("", filter, ctls);

            while (enum.hasMore()) {
                SearchResult entry = (SearchResult)enum.next();
                process(entry);
            }
        } catch (NamingException e) {
        }
```

ε489. Cancelling a Directory Search

This example searches the directory for objects and abandons the search before it completes.

```
        try {
            // Specify the attributes to match
            // Ask for objects that have attribute "sn" == Geisel and the "mail" attribute
            Attributes matchAttrs = new BasicAttributes(true); // ignore case
            matchAttrs.put(new BasicAttribute("sn", "Geisel"));
            matchAttrs.put(new BasicAttribute("mail"));

            // Search for objects with those matching attributes
            NamingEnumeration enum = ctx.search("ou=People", matchAttrs);

            if (enum.hasMore()) {
                SearchResult entry = (SearchResult)enum.next();

                // Abandon rest of results
                enum.close();
            }
        } catch (NamingException e) {
        }
```

ε490. Getting an Object's Schema from the Directory

This example reads an object's schema from the directory.

```
        try {
            // Get context containing class definitions for cn=Ted Geisel entry
            DirContext tedClasses = ctx.getSchemaClassDefinition("cn=Ted Geisel, ou=People");
```

```
        // Enumerate class definitions
        NamingEnumeration enum = tedClasses.search("", null);
        while (enum.hasMore()) {
            DirContext entry = (DirContext)enum.next();
            process(entry);
        }
    } catch (NamingException e) {
    }
```

ε491. Getting an Attribute's Schema from the Directory

This example reads an attribute's schema from the directory.

```
    try {
        // Get an attribute of that type
        Attributes attrs = ctx.getAttributes("cn=Ted Geisel, ou=People", new String[]{"cn"});
        Attribute cnAttr = attrs.get("cn");

        // Get its attribute definition
        DirContext cnSchema = cnAttr.getAttributeDefinition();

        // Get cnSchema's attributes
        Attributes cnAttrs = cnSchema.getAttributes("");
    } catch (NamingException e) {
    }
```

ε492. Authenticating to the Directory

This example uses the JNDI/LDAP service provider to create an authenticated session to an LDAP server on the local machine, by using "simple" authentication.

```
    String url = "ldap://localhost/o=JNDITutorial";
    Hashtable env = new Hashtable();
    env.put(Context.INITIAL_CONTEXT_FACTORY, "com.sun.jndi.ldap.LdapCtxFactory");
    env.put(Context.PROVIDER_URL, url);
    env.put(Context.SECURITY_AUTHENTICATION, "simple");
    env.put(Context.SECURITY_PRINCIPAL, "userDN");
    env.put(Context.SECURITY_CREDENTIALS, "secret");
    try {
        DirContext ctx = new InitialDirContext(env);
    } catch (NamingException e) {
    }
```

Packages

javax.naming.event

This package defines the event notification operations of the JNDI.

```
        java.lang.Object
1.1       └ java.util.EventObject- - - - - - - - - - - - - - - - - - -:- - - - - - - - - - - - -java.io.Serializable
1.3            ├ NamingEvent
1.3            └ NamingExceptionEvent

1.3     EventContext ───────────────────────────────── javax.naming.Context
1.3     EventDirContext ──────────────────────────────── EventContext^, javax.naming.directory.DirContext^
1.3     NamespaceChangeListener ───────────────────────── NamingListener^
1.3     NamingListener ───────────────────────────────── java.util.EventListener
1.3     ObjectChangeListener ──────────────────────────── NamingListener^
```

ε493. Registering for Namespace Changes in the Directory

This example registers with the directory to receive notification when changes are made to the namespace.

```java
try {
    // Get event context for registering listener
    EventContext ctx = (EventContext)(new InitialContext(env).lookup("ou=People"));

    // Create listener
    NamingListener listener = new SampleNCListener();

    // Register listener for namespace change events
    ctx.addNamingListener("cn=John", EventContext.ONELEVEL_SCOPE, listener);
} catch (NamingException e) {
}
public class SampleNCListener implements NamespaceChangeListener {
    public SampleNCListener() {
    }
    public void objectAdded(NamingEvent evt) {
        process(evt.getNewBinding());
    }
    public void objectRemoved(NamingEvent evt) {
        process(evt.getOldBinding());
    }

    public void objectRenamed(NamingEvent evt) {
        process(evt.getOldBinding());
    }

    public void namingExceptionThrown(NamingExceptionEvent evt) {
        processException(evt.getException());
    }
}
```

ε494. Registering for Object Changes in the Directory

This example registers with the directory to receive notification when changes are made to objects that have certain attributes.

```java
try {
    // Get event context for registering listener
    EventDirContext ctx = (EventDirContext)(new InitialContext(env).lookup("ou=People"));

    // Create listener
    NamingListener listener = new SampleObjListener();
```

Class   *Interface*   —extends   - - -implements   ○ abstract   ● final   ^—has superclass   ‿—has subclass   package—see other volume

```
        // Specify to search the subtree
        SearchControls ctls = new SearchControls();
        ctls.setSearchScope(SearchControls.SUBTREE_SCOPE);

        // Specify the search filter of objects in which you're interested
        // Ask for objects that have "mail" attribute
        String filter = "(mail=*)";

        // Register listener for object change events
        ctx.addNamingListener("cn=John", filter, ctls, listener);
    } catch (NamingException e) {
    }
}
public class SampleObjListener implements ObjectChangeListener {
    public SampleObjListener() {
    }
    public void objectChanged(NamingEvent evt) {
        process(evt.getNewBinding());
        process(evt.getOldBinding());
    }
    public void namingExceptionThrown(NamingExceptionEvent evt) {
        processException(evt.getException());
    }
}
```

javax.naming.ldap

This package extends the directory operations of the JNDI. It is used by applications and service providers that deal with LDAP v3 "extended" operations and controls, as defined by RFC 2251. The core interface in this package is LdapContext, which defines methods on a context for performing "extended" operations and handling controls.

Packages

```
         java.lang.Object
1.3 O      ├ ControlFactory
1.4        ├ StartTlsRequest - - - - - - - - - - - - - - - - - - - - - - - - - - - - ExtendedRequest^
1.4 O      ├ StartTlsResponse - - - - - - - - - - - - - - - - - - - - - - - - - - - ExtendedResponse‿
1.1        ├ java.util.EventObject - - - - - - - - - - - - - - - - - - - - - - - java.io.Serializable‿
1.3        │   └ UnsolicitedNotificationEvent
1.3        ├ javax.naming.InitialContext - - - - - - - - - - - - - - - - - - - javax.naming.Context‿
1.3        │   └ javax.naming.directory.InitialDirContext - - - - - - - - - - - javax.naming.directory.DirContext‿
1.3        │       └ InitialLdapContext - - - - - - - - - - - - - - - - - - - - LdapContext^
1.3        └ java.lang.Throwable - - - - - - - - - - - - - - - - - - - - - - - - java.io.Serializable‿
               └ java.lang.Exception
1.3              └ javax.naming.NamingException
1.3 O              └ javax.naming.ReferralException
1.3 O                  └ LdapReferralException

1.3    Control ───────────────────────────────────────── java.io.Serializable
1.3    ExtendedRequest ─────────────────────────────────┐
1.3    ExtendedResponse‿ ───────────────────────────────┘
1.3    HasControls‿
1.3    LdapContext ─────────────────────────────────── javax.naming.directory.DirContext^
1.3    UnsolicitedNotification ─────────────────────── ExtendedResponse^, HasControls
1.3    UnsolicitedNotificationListener ─────────────── javax.naming.event.NamingListener^
```

ε495. Setting LDAP Connection Request Controls

This example uses the JNDI/LDAP service provider to connect to an LDAP server on the local machine and initializes its connection request controls.

```
try {
    // Create connection controls to use
    Control[] connectCtls = new Control[]{new SomeControl()};

    LdapContext ctx = new InitialLdapContext(env, connectCtls);
} catch (NamingException e) {
}
```

ε496. Setting LDAP Context Request Controls

This example uses the JNDI/LDAP service provider to connect to an LDAP server on the local machine. It sets the context's request controls to be a server-side Sort control and then performs a list(). The results of list() will be sorted.

```
try {
    LdapContext ctx = new InitialLdapContext(env, null);

    // Create critical Sort that sorts based on CN
    Control[] ctxCtls = new Control[]{
        new SortControl(new String[]{"cn"}, Control.CRITICAL)
    };

    // Sets context request controls; effect until unset
    ctx.setRequestControls(ctxCtls);

    // Perform list() with controls in effect
    NamingEnumeration answer = ctx.list("");

    // Enumerate answers
```

```
        while (answer.hasMore()) {
            NameClassPair item = (NameClassPair)answer.next();
        }
    } catch (NamingException e) {
    }
```

ε497. Getting LDAP Response Controls

This example uses the JNDI/LDAP service provider to connect to an LDAP server on the local machine. It then performs a search and looks for controls returned with the search responses.

```
    try {
        LdapContext ctx = new InitialLdapContext(env, null);

        // Perform search
        NamingEnumeration answer = ctx.search("ou=People", "(cn=*)", null);

        // Examine the response controls (if any)
        process(ctx.getResponseControls());

        // Enumerate answers
        while (answer.hasMore()) {
            SearchResult si = (SearchResult)answer.next();

            // Examine the response controls (if any)
            if (si instanceof HasControls) {
                process(((HasControls)si).getControls());
            }
        }
        // Examine the response controls (if any)
        process(ctx.getResponseControls());
    } catch (NamingException e) {
    }
```

ε498. Performing an LDAP "Extended" Operation

This example performs an "extended" operation on an LDAP context.

```
    try {
        LdapContext ctx = new InitialLdapContext(env, null);

        // Create "extended" operation to use
        ExtendedRequest req = new GetTimeRequest();

        // Perform the operation
        GetTimeResponse response = (GetTimeResponse) ctx.extendedOperation(req);
    } catch (NamingException e) {
    }
```

Packages

javax.naming.spi

This package defines the classes and interfaces that allow various directory and naming service providers to be dynamically plugged in beneath the JNDI API. This package also provides operations that allow different provider implementations to cooperate to complete client JNDI operations.

javax.naming.spi

```
         java.lang.Object
1.3       ├ DirStateFactory.Result
1.3       ├ NamingManager
1.3       │  └ DirectoryManager
1.3       └ ResolveResult - - - - - - - - - - - - - - - - - - - - - - - - - - - - - - -  java.io.Serializable⌄

1.3      DirObjectFactory ───────────────────────  ObjectFactory
1.3      DirStateFactory ───────────────────────  StateFactory
1.3      InitialContextFactory
1.3      InitialContextFactoryBuilder
1.3      ObjectFactory⌄
1.3      ObjectFactoryBuilder
1.3      Resolver
1.3      StateFactory⌄
```

javax.net

This package provides factory classes for creating sockets in an implementation-independent fashion.

```
         java.lang.Object
1.4 ○    ├ ServerSocketFactory⌄
1.4 ○    └ SocketFactory⌄
```

javax.net.ssl

This package provides support for secure sockets. It supports Secure Socket Layer (SSL) and related protocols for both client and server networking applications.

Class _Interface_ —extends - - -implements ○ abstract ● final ^—has superclass ⌄—has subclass package—see other volume

java.lang.Object

1.4 |- KeyManagerFactory

1.4 ○ |- KeyManagerFactorySpi

1.4 |- SSLContext

1.4 ○ |- SSLContextSpi

1.4 |- TrustManagerFactory

1.4 ○ |- TrustManagerFactorySpi

Packages

javax.net.ssl

```
         java.lang.Object
            ├ java.net.ServerSocket
1.4  ○         └ SSLServerSocket
            ├ java.net.Socket
1.4  ○         └ SSLSocket
     ○      ├ java.net.URLConnection
1.1  ○         └ java.net.HttpURLConnection
1.4  ○            └ HttpsURLConnection
1.2  ○      ├ java.security.Permission ---------------------------- java.io.Serializable˸, java.security.Guard
1.2  ○         └ java.security.BasicPermission --------------------˻- java.io.Serializable˸
1.4  ●            └ SSLPermission
1.1         ├ java.util.EventObject----------------------------
1.4         │ ├ HandshakeCompletedEvent
1.4         │ └ SSLSessionBindingEvent
1.4  ○      ├ javax.net.ServerSocketFactory
1.4  ○      │ └ SSLServerSocketFactory
1.4  ○      ├ javax.net.SocketFactory
1.4  ○      │ └ SSLSocketFactory
            └ java.lang.Throwable - - - - - - - - - - - - - - - - -
               └ java.lang.Exception
                  └ java.io.IOException
1.4                  └ SSLException
1.4                     ├ SSLHandshakeException
1.4                     ├ SSLKeyException
1.4                     ├ SSLPeerUnverifiedException
1.4                     └ SSLProtocolException

1.4   HandshakeCompletedListener ──────────────────────── java.util.EventListener
1.4   HostnameVerifier
1.4   KeyManager˸
1.4   ManagerFactoryParameters
1.4   SSLSession
1.4   SSLSessionBindingListener ──────────
1.4   SSLSessionContext
1.4   TrustManager˸
1.4   X509KeyManager ─────────────────────────── KeyManager
1.4   X509TrustManager ───────────────────────── TrustManager
```

ε499. Creating an SSL Client Socket

When an SSL client socket connects to an SSL server, it receives a certificate of authentication from the server. The client socket then validates the certificate against a set of certificates in its "trust store".

The default truststore is <java-home>/lib/security/cacerts. If the server's certificate cannot be validated with the certificates in the truststore, the server's certificate must be added to the truststore before the connection can be established.

```
try {
    int port = 443;
    String hostname = "hostname";
    SocketFactory socketFactory = SSLSocketFactory.getDefault();
    Socket socket = socketFactory.createSocket(hostname, port);

    // Create streams to securely send and receive data to the server
```

Class   *Interface*   —extends   - - -implements   ○ abstract   ● final   ˆ—has superclass   ˸—has subclass   package—see other volume

```
        InputStream in = socket.getInputStream();
        OutputStream out = socket.getOutputStream();

        // Read from in and write to out...

        // Close the socket
        in.close();
        out.close();
    } catch(IOException e) {
    }
```

A different truststore can be specified using the javax.net.ssl.trustStore system property. (If you are trying to set up an SSL client and server for testing purposes, you can set the truststore to the keystore that was created in "ε500. Creating an SSL Server Socket".)

```
> java -Djavax.net.ssl.trustStore=truststore -Djavax.net.ssl.trustStorePassword=123456 MyApp
```

ε500. Creating an SSL Server Socket

An SSL server socket requires certificates that it will send to clients for authentication. The certificates must be contained in a keystore whose location must be explicitly specified (there is no default). Following the example we describe how to create and specify a keystore for the SSL server socket to use.

```
    try {
        int port = 443;
        ServerSocketFactory ssocketFactory = SSLServerSocketFactory.getDefault();
        ServerSocket ssocket = ssocketFactory.createServerSocket(port);

        // Listen for connections
        Socket socket = ssocket.accept();

        // Create streams to securely send and receive data to the client
        InputStream in = socket.getInputStream();
        OutputStream out = socket.getOutputStream();

        // Read from in and write to out...

        // Close the socket
        in.close();
        out.close();
    } catch(IOException e) {
    }
```

Specify the keystore of certificates using the javax.net.ssl.keyStore system property:

```
> java -Djavax.net.ssl.keyStore=mySrvKeystore -Djavax.net.ssl.keyStorePassword=123456 MyServer
```

For testing purposes, you can create a keystore with a self-signed certificate, using the keytool command:

```
> keytool -keystore mySrvKeystore -keypasswd 123456 -genkey -keyalg RSA -alias mycert
```

ε501. Retrieving the Certification Path of an SSL Server

This example implements a client that connects to an SSL server and retrieves the server's certificates.
See also "ε211. Adding a Certificate to a Key Store".

```
    try {
        // Create the client socket
        int port = 443;
        String hostname = "hostname";
        SSLSocketFactory factory = HttpsURLConnection.getDefaultSSLSocketFactory();
        SSLSocket socket = (SSLSocket)factory.createSocket(hostname, port);

        // Connect to the server
```

Packages

```
        socket.startHandshake();

        // Retrieve the server's certificate chain
        java.security.cert.Certificate[] serverCerts =
            socket.getSession().getPeerCertificates();

        // Close the socket
        socket.close();
    } catch (SSLPeerUnverifiedException e) {
    } catch (IOException e) {
    } catch (java.security.cert.CertificateEncodingException e) {
    }
```

ε502. Disabling Certificate Validation in an HTTPS Connection

By default, accessing an HTTPS URL using the URL class results in an exception if the server's certificate chain cannot be validated has not previously been installed in the truststore. If you want to disable the validation of certificates for testing purposes, you need to override the default trust manager with one that trusts all certificates.

```
    // Create a trust manager that does not validate certificate chains
    TrustManager[] trustAllCerts = new TrustManager[]{
        new X509TrustManager() {
            public java.security.cert.X509Certificate[] getAcceptedIssuers() {
                return null;
            }
            public void checkClientTrusted(
                java.security.cert.X509Certificate[] certs, String authType) {
            }
            public void checkServerTrusted(
                java.security.cert.X509Certificate[] certs, String authType) {
            }
        }
    };

    // Install the all-trusting trust manager
    try {
        SSLContext sc = SSLContext.getInstance("SSL");
        sc.init(null, trustAllCerts, new java.security.SecureRandom());
        HttpsURLConnection.setDefaultSSLSocketFactory(sc.getSocketFactory());
    } catch (Exception e) {
    }

    // Now you can access an https URL without having the certificate in the truststore
    try {
        URL url = new URL("https://hostname/index.html");
    } catch (MalformedURLException e) {
    }
```

javax.rmi

This package contains classes and interfaces for building portable RMI applications that work over either IIOP or JRMP.

Class *Interface*   —extends   - - -implements   ○ abstract   ● final   ˆ—has superclass   ˌ—has subclass   package—see other volume

java.lang.Object
1.3   └ PortableRemoteObject

ε503. Starting the Name Server

If you are using RMI over the Java Remote Method Protocol (JRMP), start up the RMI registry so that you can create and export remote objects.

```
> rmiregistry
```

If you are using RMI over the Internet Inter-ORB Protocol (IIOP), start up the CORBA Common Object Services (COS) name server so that you can create and export remote objects.

```
> tnameserv
```

ε504. Defining and Exporting a Portable Remote Object

1. Define the remote interface.

```
import java.rmi.*;

public interface RObject extends Remote {
    void aMethod() throws RemoteException;
}
```

2. Define the portable remote object implementation.

```
import java.rmi.*;
import java.rmi.server.UnicastRemoteObject;

public class RObjectImpl extends UnicastRemoteObject implements RObject {
    public RObjectImpl() throws RemoteException {
        super();
    }
    // All remote methods must throw RemoteException
    public void aMethod() throws RemoteException {
    }
}
```

3. Compile the remote object implementation.

```
> javac RObject.java RObjectImpl.java
```

4. Generate the skeletons and stubs.

```
Using RMI over IIOP
> rmic -iiop RObjectImpl

Using RMI over JRMP
> rmic RObjectImpl
```

5. Create an instance of the remote object and bind it to a name service.

```
import javax.naming.*;
import java.rmi.RemoteException;


// JRMP: name = "rmi://localhost/RObjectServer";
// IIOP: name = "iiop://localhost/RObjectServer";
try {
```

Packages

```
        RObject robj = new RObjectImpl();
        new InitialContext().bind(name, robj);
    } catch (NamingException e) {
    } catch (RemoteException e) {
    }
```

ε505. Looking Up a Portable Remote Object and Invoking a Method

```
        import javax.naming.*;
        import java.rmi.RemoteException;
        import javax.rmi.PortableRemoteObject;


        // JRMP: name = "rmi://localhost/RObjectServer";
        // IIOP: name = "iiop://localhost/RObjectServer";
        try {
            // Look up remote object
            Object obj = new InitialContext().lookup(name);

            // Cast to the appropriate type
            RObject robj = (RObject)PortableRemoteObject.narrow(obj, RObject.class);

            // Invoke method on remote object
            robj.aMethod();
        } catch (NamingException e) {
        } catch (RemoteException e) {
        }
```

javax.rmi.CORBA

This package contains classes and interfaces for RMI over IIOP. They provide a standard interface between the generated stubs and ties and the RMI-IIOP runtime. They also allow third party ORBs to be used for RMI over IIOP as an alternative to the ORB supplied by Sun. They are not intended to be called directly from RMI-IIOP applications.

```
        java.lang.Object
1.3       ├ ClassDesc - - - - - - - - - - - - - - - - - - - - - - - - - - - - - - - java.io.Serializable
1.3       ├ Util
1.2  ○    └ org.omg.CORBA.portable.ObjectImpl - - - - - - - - - - - - - - - - org.omg.CORBA.Object
1.3  ○        └ org.omg.CORBA_2_3.portable.ObjectImpl
1.3  ○            └ Stub - - - - - - - - - - - - - - - - - - - - - - - - - - - - - java.io.Serializable
```

Class *Interface* —extends - - -implements ○ abstract ● final ^—has superclass ⌄—has subclass package—see other volume

javax.security.auth

This package provides a framework for authentication and authorization. The framework allows authentication to be performed in pluggable fashion. Different authentication modules can be plugged under an application without requiring modifications to the application itself. The authorization component allows specification of access controls based on code location, code signers, and code executors.

```
      java.lang.Object
D ○   ├ Policy
1.4 ● ├ Subject - - - - - - - - - - - - - - - - - - - - - - - - - - - - - - - - - - java.io.Serializable
1.4   ├ SubjectDomainCombiner - - - - - - - - - - - - - - - - - - - - - - - - java.security.DomainCombiner
1.2 ○ ├ java.security.Permission - - - - - - - - - - - - - - - - - - - - - - - - java.io.Serializable , java.security.Guard
1.4 ● │ ├ PrivateCredentialPermission
1.2 ○ │ ├ java.security.BasicPermission - - - - - - - - - - - - - - - - - - ┬ java.io.Serializable
1.4 ● │ │   └ AuthPermission                                      │
      └ java.lang.Throwable - - - - - - - - - - - - - - - - - - - - - - - - - - ┘
          └ java.lang.Exception
1.4         ├ DestroyFailedException
1.4         └ RefreshFailedException

1.4   Destroyable
1.4   Refreshable
```

javax.security.auth.callback

This package provides the classes necessary for services to interact with applications in order to retrieve information (such as usernames and passwords) or to display information (such as error and warning messages).

javax.security.auth.callback

```
     java.lang.Object
1.4   ├ ChoiceCallback ---------------------------------┬- Callback, java.io.Serializable ˌ
1.4   ├ ConfirmationCallback ---------------------------┊
1.4   ├ LanguageCallback -------------------------------┊
1.4   ├ NameCallback -----------------------------------┊
1.4   ├ PasswordCallback -------------------------------┊
1.4   ├ TextInputCallback ------------------------------┊
1.4   ├ TextOutputCallback-----------------------------┘
1.4   └ java.lang.Throwable ---------------------------- java.io.Serializable ˌ
         └ java.lang.Exception
1.4         └ UnsupportedCallbackException

1.4   Callback
1.4   CallbackHandler
```

javax.security.auth.kerberos

This package contains utility classes related to the Kerberos network authentication protocol. They include classes for representing Kerberos authentication information, including a Kerberos principal, a Kerberos key, and a Kerberos ticket. It also includes security permission classes for controlling access to the Kerberos service.

```
       java.lang.Object
1.4     ├ KerberosKey ------------------------------------ javax.crypto.SecretKeyˌ̂, javax.security.auth↵
                                                            .Destroyable
1.4 ●   ├ KerberosPrincipal------------------------------- java.io.Serializable ˌ, java.security.Principal ˌ
1.4     ├ KerberosTicket --------------------------------- java.io.Serializable ˌ, javax.security.auth↵
                                                            .Destroyable, javax.security.auth.Refreshable
1.2 ○   └ java.security.Permission ----------------------- java.io.Serializable ˌ, java.security.Guard
1.4 ●     ├ ServicePermission ----------------------------- java.io.Serializable ˌ
```

Class *Interface* —extends - - -implements ○ abstract ● final ^has superclass ˌhas subclass package—see other volume

```
           java.lang.Object
1.2 ○        └ java.security.Permission - - - - - - - - - - - - - - - - - - - - - - - - - - - - java.io.Serializable , java.security.Guard
                                                                            ┌─ java.io.Serializable
1.2 ○           └ java.security.BasicPermission - - - - - - - - - - - - - - - - - - - ┊
1.4 ●              └ DelegationPermission - - - - - - - - - - - - - - - - - - - - ┘
```

javax.security.auth.login

This package provides support for a pluggable authentication framework. It defines the classes that an application needs to configure and to perform authentication.

```
           java.lang.Object
1.4          ├ AppConfigurationEntry
1.4          ├ AppConfigurationEntry.LoginModuleControlFlag
1.4 ○        ├ Configuration
1.4          ├ LoginContext
             └ java.lang.Throwable - - - - - - - - - - - - - - - - - - - - - - - - - - - java.io.Serializable
                  └ java.lang.Exception
1.2                  └ java.security.GeneralSecurityException
1.4                     └ LoginException
1.4                        ├ AccountExpiredException
1.4                        ├ CredentialExpiredException
1.4                        └ FailedLoginException
```

ε507. Listing the Login Modules of an Entry in the Current Login Configuration

This example retrieves the login modules of a login-application entry in the current login configuration.

```java
Configuration config = Configuration.getConfiguration();

// Get the login modules
AppConfigurationEntry[] loginModuleEntries = config.getAppConfigurationEntry("AppName");
if (loginModuleEntries == null) {
    // There are no entries for the specified login-app name
}

// List the login modules
for (int i=0; i<loginModuleEntries.length; i++) {
    // Get login module name
    String name = loginModuleEntries[i].getLoginModuleName();

    // Get login module flag
    AppConfigurationEntry.LoginModuleControlFlag flag
```

Packages

```
                = loginModuleEntries[i].getControlFlag();

        if (flag == AppConfigurationEntry.LoginModuleControlFlag.OPTIONAL) {
            // The login module is not required to succeed.
            // Whether it succeeds or not, the next login module is invoked.
        } else if (flag == AppConfigurationEntry.LoginModuleControlFlag.REQUIRED) {
            // The login module is required to succeed.
            // Whether it succeeds or not, the next login module is invoked.
        } else if (flag == AppConfigurationEntry.LoginModuleControlFlag.REQUISITE) {
            // The login module is required to succeed. If it succeeds, the next
            // login module is invoked; otherwise, authentication fails and
            // no more login modules are invoked.
        } else if (flag == AppConfigurationEntry.LoginModuleControlFlag.SUFFICIENT) {
            // If this login module succeeds, authentication succeeds and no
            // more login modules are invoked
        }
    }
```

Here's a sample of a login configuration file:

```
AppName {
    com.sun.security.auth.module.NTLoginModule required;
    MyLoginModule1 requisite;
    MyLoginModule2 sufficient;
    MyLoginModule3 optional;
};
```

The login configuration file is specified at the command line:

```
> java -Djava.security.auth.login.config=myconfig.config MyApp
```

ε508. Getting the Login Name of the Currently Logged-In User

This example retrieves the login name of the user that is running the application.

```
try {
    String loginAppName = "GetLoginNameUnix";

    // If the application is run on NT rather than Unix, use this name
    loginAppName = "GetLoginNameNT";

    // Create login context
    LoginContext lc = new LoginContext(loginAppName,
        new com.sun.security.auth.callback.TextCallbackHandler());

    // Retrieve the information on the logged-in user
    lc.login();

    // Get the authenticated subject
    Subject subject = lc.getSubject();

    // Get the subject principals
    Principal principals[] = (Principal[])subject.getPrincipals().toArray(new Principal[0]);
    for (int i=0; i<principals.length; i++) {
        if (principals[i] instanceof com.sun.security.auth.NTUserPrincipal
                || principals[i] instanceof com.sun.security.auth.UnixPrincipal) {
            String loggedInUserName = principals[i].getName();
        }
    }
} catch (LoginException e) {
    // Login failed
```

Class   *Interface*   —extends   - - -implements   ○ abstract   ● final   ^—has superclass   _—has subclass   package—see other volume

```
    }
```

The example requires a login configuration file that specifies the login modules to execute when using a particular login-app name. This configuration file specifies two login-app names:

```
GetLoginNameNT {
    com.sun.security.auth.module.NTLoginModule required;
};
GetLoginNameUnix {
    com.sun.security.auth.module.UnixLoginModule required;
};
```

The login configuration file is specified at the command line:

```
> java -Djava.security.auth.login.config=myconfig.config MyApp
```

ε509. Handling the Callbacks from a Login Module

This example implements a class that handles a few types of callbacks from a login module.

```
// This login-module callback handler handles a few types of callbacks
public class MyCallbackHandler implements CallbackHandler {
    public void handle(Callback[] callbacks) throws IOException, UnsupportedCallbackException {
        for (int i=0; i<callbacks.length; i++) {
            if (callbacks[i] instanceof TextOutputCallback) {
                // This callback delivers messages from a login module
                TextOutputCallback toCb = (TextOutputCallback)callbacks[i];

                // Get message
                String msg = toCb.getMessage();

                // Get message type
                switch (toCb.getMessageType()) {
                case TextOutputCallback.INFORMATION:
                    break;
                case TextOutputCallback.ERROR:
                    break;
                case TextOutputCallback.WARNING:
                    break;
                }

                // Display message to the user ...
            } else if (callbacks[i] instanceof NameCallback) {
                // A login module is requesting the name of the user
                NameCallback nCb = (NameCallback)callbacks[i];

                // Get the prompt to display to the user
                String prompt = nCb.getPrompt();

                // Get the name ...

                // Set the name
                nCb.setName("username");
            } else if (callbacks[i] instanceof PasswordCallback) {
                // A login module is requesting the user's password
                PasswordCallback pCb = (PasswordCallback)callbacks[i];

                // Get the prompt to display to the user
                String prompt = pCb.getPrompt();

                // Get the password ...

                // Set the password
```

```
                    pCb.setPassword("password".toCharArray());
            } else if (callbacks[i] instanceof LanguageCallback) {
                // A login module is requesting the user's locale
                LanguageCallback lCb = (LanguageCallback)callbacks[i];

                // Get the locale ...

                // Set the locale
                lCb.setLocale(Locale.CHINESE);
            } else {
                throw new UnsupportedCallbackException(callbacks[i], "Unrecognized Callback");
            }
        }
    }
}
```

Here's an example that uses the callback handler:

```
try {
    // Create login context
    LoginContext lc = new LoginContext("LoginAppName",
        new MyCallbackHandler());
} catch (LoginException e) {
    // Login failed
}
```

javax.security.auth.spi

This package provides the interface to be used for implementing pluggable authentication modules.

javax.security.auth.x500

This package contains the classes for representing X500 authentication information, including an X500 principal and X500 private crendentials.

```
java.lang.Object
1.4 ●    ├ X500Principal------------------------------------------ java.io.Serializable, java.security.Principal
1.4 ●    └ X500PrivateCredential------------------------------------ javax.security.auth.Destroyable
```

Class *Interface* —extends - - -implements O abstract ● final ⌐has superclass ⌐has subclass package—see other volume

javax.security.cert

This package defines classes for representing public key certificates for use with the javax.net.ssl package. Use of this package is discouraged; instead, use the corresponding classes in the java.security.cert package.

```
java.lang.Object
1.4 O   ├ Certificate
1.4 O   │  └ X509Certificate
        ├ java.lang.Throwable - - - - - - - - - - - - - - - - - - - - - - - - - - - - - - - - - java.io.Serializable
        │  └ java.lang.Exception
1.4     │     └ CertificateException
1.4     │        ├ CertificateEncodingException
1.4     │        ├ CertificateExpiredException
1.4     │        ├ CertificateNotYetValidException
1.4     │        └ CertificateParsingException
```

ε506. Converting Between javax and java X509Certificates

Some methods in the javax.net.ssl package create certificate objects that are not compatible with the certificate objects in the java.security.cert package. This example implements two methods that convert between the two types of certificate objects.

```java
// Converts to java.security
public static java.security.cert.X509Certificate convert(javax.security.cert.X509Certificate cert) {
    try {
        byte[] encoded = cert.getEncoded();
        ByteArrayInputStream bis = new ByteArrayInputStream(encoded);
        java.security.cert.CertificateFactory cf
            = java.security.cert.CertificateFactory.getInstance("X.509");
        return (java.security.cert.X509Certificate)cf.generateCertificate(bis);
    } catch (java.security.cert.CertificateEncodingException e) {
    } catch (javax.security.cert.CertificateEncodingException e) {
    } catch (java.security.cert.CertificateException e) {
    }
    return null;
}

// Converts to javax.security
public static javax.security.cert.X509Certificate convert(java.security.cert.X509Certificate cert) {
    try {
        byte[] encoded = cert.getEncoded();
        return javax.security.cert.X509Certificate.getInstance(encoded);
    } catch (java.security.cert.CertificateEncodingException e) {
```

```
            } catch (javax.security.cert.CertificateEncodingException e) {
            } catch (javax.security.cert.CertificateException e) {
            }
            return null;
    }
```

javax.sql

This package supplements the java.sql package to provide APIs for server-side data source access and processing. It contains support for establishing connections to a database, connection pooling, distributed transactions, and rowsets.

```
       java.lang.Object
1.1      └ java.util.EventObject - - - - - - - - - - - - - - - - - - - - - - - - - - - - - - - java.io.Serializable
1.4         ├ ConnectionEvent
1.4         └ RowSetEvent

1.4      ConnectionEventListener ─────────────────────────── java.util.EventListener
1.4      ConnectionPoolDataSource
1.4      DataSource
1.4      PooledConnection
1.4      RowSet ───────────────────────────────────────── java.sql.ResultSet
1.4      RowSetInternal
1.4      RowSetListener ───────────────────────────────── java.util.EventListener
1.4      RowSetMetaData ──────────────────────────────── java.sql.ResultSetMetaData
1.4      RowSetReader
1.4      RowSetWriter
1.4      XAConnection ──────────────────────────────── PooledConnection
1.4      XADataSource
```

Class *Interface* —extends - - -implements   O abstract ● final ^—has superclass ⌄—has subclass package—see other volume

javax.transaction

This is a subset of the javax.transaction Standard Extension. These three exceptions are thrown by the ORB machinery during unmarshalling.

```
     java.lang.Object
       └ java.lang.Throwable - - - - - - - - - - - - - - - - - - - - - - - - - - - - - - - java.io.Serializable
           └ java.lang.Exception
               └ java.io.IOException
1.1                └ java.rmi.RemoteException
1.3                   ├ InvalidTransactionException
1.3                   ├ TransactionRequiredException
1.3                   └ TransactionRolledbackException
```

javax.transaction.xa

This package defines the contract between the transaction manager and the resource manager that allows the transaction manager to enlist and delist resource objects in transactions. The implementation of the interfaces defined in this package is provided by driver vendors.

```
     java.lang.Object
       └ java.lang.Throwable - - - - - - - - - - - - - - - - - - - - - - - - - - - - - - - java.io.Serializable
           └ java.lang.Exception
1.4            └ XAException

1.4  XAResource
1.4  Xid
```

javax.xml.parsers

This package provides classes for processing XML documents. It supports two types of parsers: Simple API for XML (SAX) and Document Object Model (DOM).

```
java.lang.Object
1.4 ○   ├ DocumentBuilder
1.4 ○   ├ DocumentBuilderFactory
1.4 ○   ├ SAXParser
1.4 ○   ├ SAXParserFactory
        └ java.lang.Throwable - - - - - - - - - - - - - - - - - - - - - - - - - - - - - - - - java.io.Serializable
            ├ java.lang.Error
1.4         │   └ FactoryConfigurationError
            └ java.lang.Exception
1.4             └ ParserConfigurationException
```

DOM

ε510. The Quintessential Program to Create a DOM Document from an XML File

```java
import java.io.*;
import javax.xml.parsers.*;
import org.w3c.dom.*;
import org.xml.sax.*;

public class BasicDom {
    public static void main(String[] args) {
        Document doc = parseXmlFile("infilename.xml", false);
    }

    // Parses an XML file and returns a DOM document.
    // If validating is true, the contents is validated against the DTD
    // specified in the file.
    public static Document parseXmlFile(String filename, boolean validating) {
        try {
            // Create a builder factory
            DocumentBuilderFactory factory = DocumentBuilderFactory.newInstance();
            factory.setValidating(validating);

            // Create the builder and parse the file
            Document doc = factory.newDocumentBuilder().parse(new File(filename));
            return doc;
        } catch (SAXException e) {
            // A parsing error occurred; the xml input is not valid
        } catch (ParserConfigurationException e) {
        } catch (IOException e) {
        }
        return null;
    }
}
```

ε511. Creating an Empty DOM Document

```java
public static Document createDomDocument() {
    try {
        DocumentBuilder builder = DocumentBuilderFactory.newInstance().newDocumentBuilder();
        Document doc = builder.newDocument();
```

```
            return doc;
        } catch (ParserConfigurationException e) {
        }
        return null;
    }
```

ε512. Converting an XML Fragment into a DOM Fragment

This example demonstrates how to parse an XML string fragment into a set of nodes suitable for insertion into a DOM document.

```
// Parses a string containing XML and returns a DocumentFragment
// containing the nodes of the parsed XML.
public static DocumentFragment parseXml(Document doc, String fragment) {
    // Wrap the fragment in an arbitrary element
    fragment = "<fragment>"+fragment+"</fragment>";
    try {
        // Create a DOM builder and parse the fragment
        DocumentBuilderFactory factory = DocumentBuilderFactory.newInstance();
        Document d = factory.newDocumentBuilder().parse(
            new InputSource(new StringReader(fragment)));

        // Import the nodes of the new document into doc so that they
        // will be compatible with doc
        Node node = doc.importNode(d.getDocumentElement(), true);

        // Create the document fragment node to hold the new nodes
        DocumentFragment docfrag = doc.createDocumentFragment();

        // Move the nodes into the fragment
        while (node.hasChildNodes()) {
            docfrag.appendChild(node.removeChild(node.getFirstChild()));
        }

        // Return the fragment
        return docfrag;
    } catch (SAXException e) {
        // A parsing error occurred; the xml input is not valid
    } catch (ParserConfigurationException e) {
    } catch (IOException e) {
    }
    return null;
}
```

Here's an example that uses the method:

```
// Obtain an XML document; this method is implemented in
// "ε510. The Quintessential Program to Create a DOM Document from an XML File"
Document doc = parseXmlFile("infilename.xml", false);

// Create a fragment
DocumentFragment frag = parseXml(doc, "hello <b>joe</b>");

// Append the new fragment to the end of the root element
Element element = doc.getDocumentElement();
element.appendChild(frag);
```

ε513. Handling Errors While Parsing an XML File

This example installs an error handler to a parser. The error handler logs error messages to a logger (see "ε385. The Quintessential Logging Program").

```
        // Create a builder
        DocumentBuilder builder = DocumentBuilderFactory.newInstance().newDocumentBuilder();

        // Set an error listener
        builder.setErrorHandler(new MyErrorHandler());

        // Use the builder to parse the file
        Document doc = builder.parse(new File("infilename.xml"));
    } catch (SAXException e) {
        // A parsing error occurred; the xml input is not valid.
        // This exception can still be thrown, even if an error handler is installed.
    } catch (ParserConfigurationException e) {
    } catch (IOException e) {
    }

    // This error handler uses a Logger to log error messages
    class MyErrorHandler implements ErrorHandler {
        // This method is called in the event of a recoverable error
        public void error(SAXParseException e) {
            log(Level.SEVERE, "Error", e);
        }

        // This method is called in the event of a non-recoverable error
        public void fatalError(SAXParseException e) {
            log(Level.SEVERE, "Fatal Error", e);
        }

        // This method is called in the event of a warning
        public void warning(SAXParseException e) {
            log(Level.WARNING, "Warning", e);
        }

        // Get logger to log errors
        private Logger logger = Logger.getLogger("com.mycompany");

        // Dump a log record to a logger
        private void log(Level level, String message, SAXParseException e) {
            // Get details
            int line = e.getLineNumber();
            int col = e.getColumnNumber();
            String publicId = e.getPublicId();
            String systemId = e.getSystemId();

            // Append details to message
            message = message + ": " + e.getMessage() + ": line="
                + line + ", col=" + col + ", PUBLIC="
                + publicId + ", SYSTEM=" + systemId;

            // Log the message
            logger.log(level, message);
        }
    }
```

Given the following input file, MyErrorHandler.fatalError() is called and parse() throws a SAXParseException as well.

```
    <!– invalid XML –>
    <root>
    <element>
    </root>
```

Class *Interface* —extends - - -implements ○ abstract ● final ^—has superclass ˏ—has subclass package—see other volume

DOM Parsing Options

ε514. Converting CDATA Nodes into Text Nodes While Parsing an XML File

By default, CDATA nodes in an XML file will be represented with CDATASection objects in a DOM document. This example demonstrates how to create a parser that converts CDATA nodes into text nodes.

```
try {
    // Create a builder factory
    DocumentBuilderFactory factory = DocumentBuilderFactory.newInstance();

    // Configure it to coalesce CDATA nodes
    factory.setCoalescing(true);

    // Create the builder and parse the file
    Document doc = factory.newDocumentBuilder().parse(new File("infilename.xml"));

    // doc will not contain any CDATA nodes
} catch (SAXException e) {
    // A parsing error occurred; the xml input is not valid
} catch (ParserConfigurationException e) {
} catch (IOException e) {
}
```

Here's some sample input:

```
<?xml version="1.0" encoding="UTF-8"?>
<root>
    Some pretext
    <![CDATA[Some text with lots of <"!@#$%'ˆ&*()> special characters]]>
    Some posttext
</root>
```

and output:

```
<?xml version="1.0" encoding="UTF-8"?>
<root>
    Some pretext
    Some text with lots of &lt;"!@#$%'ˆ&amp;*()&gt; special characters
    Some posttext
</root>
```

ε515. Ignoring Comments While Parsing an XML File

By default, Comment nodes are created for each comment in an XML file. If it is not necessary to preserve the comments, there is no need to create the nodes. This example demonstrates how to create a parser that ignores comments.

```
try {
    // Create a builder factory
    DocumentBuilderFactory factory = DocumentBuilderFactory.newInstance();

    // Configure it to ignore comments
    factory.setIgnoringComments(true);

    // Create the builder and parse the file
    Document doc = factory.newDocumentBuilder().parse(new File("infilename.xml"));

    // doc will not contain any Comment nodes
} catch (SAXException e) {
    // A parsing error occurred; the xml input is not valid
} catch (ParserConfigurationException e) {
} catch (IOException e) {
```

Packages

349

```
    }
```

Here's some sample input:

```
<?xml version="1.0" encoding="UTF-8"?>
<!– comment –>
<root>
    Some text
    <!– comment –>
    Some text
</root>
<!– comment –>
```

and output:

```
<?xml version="1.0" encoding="UTF-8"?>
<root>
    Some text

    Some text
</root>
```

ε516. Preventing Expansion of Entity References While Parsing an XML File

By default, entity references are expanded during parsing. This example demonstrates how to leave the entity references in the DOM document

Note: The default parser in J2SE 1.4 expands entity references in attribute values. There is no way to prevent this.

```
// Parses an XML file without expanding entity references and returns
// a DOM document. If validating is true, the contents is validated
// against the DTD specified in the file.
public static Document parseXmlFileNoExpandER(String filename, boolean validating) {
    try {
        // Create a builder factory
        DocumentBuilderFactory factory = DocumentBuilderFactory.newInstance();
        factory.setValidating(validating);

        // Prevent expansion of entity references
        factory.setExpandEntityReferences(false);

        // Create the builder and parse the file
        Document doc = factory.newDocumentBuilder().parse(new File(filename));
        return doc;
    } catch (SAXException e) {
        // A parsing error occurred; the xml input is not valid
    } catch (ParserConfigurationException e) {
    } catch (IOException e) {
    }
    return null;
}
```

SAX

ε517. The Quintessential Program to Parse an XML File Using SAX

```
import java.io.*;
import javax.xml.parsers.*;
```

```
import org.xml.sax.*;
import org.xml.sax.helpers.*;

public class BasicSax {
    public static void main(String[] args) {
        // Create a handler to handle the SAX events generated during parsing
        DefaultHandler handler = new MyHandler();

        // Parse the file using the handler
        parseXmlFile("infilename.xml", handler, false);
    }

    // DefaultHandler contain no-op implementations for all SAX events.
    // This class should override methods to capture the events of interest.
    static class MyHandler extends DefaultHandler {
    }

    // Parses an XML file using a SAX parser.
    // If validating is true, the contents is validated against the DTD
    // specified in the file.
    public static void parseXmlFile(String filename, DefaultHandler handler, boolean validating) {
        try {
            // Create a builder factory
            SAXParserFactory factory = SAXParserFactory.newInstance();
            factory.setValidating(validating);

            // Create the builder and parse the file
            factory.newSAXParser().parse(new File(filename), handler);
        } catch (SAXException e) {
            // A parsing error occurred; the xml input is not valid
        } catch (ParserConfigurationException e) {
        } catch (IOException e) {
        }
    }
}
```

javax.xml.transform

This package defines generic interfaces for transforming XML representations from a source to a result.

```
         java.lang.Object
1.4        ├ OutputKeys
1.4  O     ├ Transformer
1.4  O     ├ TransformerFactoryˎ
           └ java.lang.Throwable - - - - - - - - - - - - - - - - - - - - - - - - - - - java.io.Serializableˎ
             ├ java.lang.Error
1.4              └ TransformerFactoryConfigurationError
             └ java.lang.Exception
1.4              └ TransformerException
1.4                  └ TransformerConfigurationException

1.4      ErrorListener
1.4      Result
1.4      Source
1.4      SourceLocatorˎ
1.4      Templates
1.4      URIResolver
```

ε518. Writing a DOM Document to an XML File

```
// This method writes a DOM document to a file
public static void writeXmlFile(Document doc, String filename) {
    try {
        // Prepare the DOM document for writing
        Source source = new DOMSource(doc);

        // Prepare the output file
        File file = new File(filename);
        Result result = new StreamResult(file);

        // Write the DOM document to the file
        Transformer xformer = TransformerFactory.newInstance().newTransformer();
        xformer.transform(source, result);
    } catch (TransformerConfigurationException e) {
    } catch (TransformerException e) {
    }
}
```

ε519. Emitting a DOCTYPE Declaration When Writing an XML File from a DOM Document

By default, the DOCTYPE is not written when using a transformer to dump a DOM document to an XML file. This example demonstrates how to write a DOCTYPE with a public and system id. Unfortunately, it is not possible to write a DOCTYPE with an internal DTD.

```
// Create a document; this method is implemented in
// "ε510. The Quintessential Program to Create a DOM Document from an XML File"
Document doc = parseXmlFile("infilename.xml", false);

try {
    // Create a transformer
```

Class *Interface* —extends - - -implements O abstract ● final ˆ—has superclass ˎ—has subclass package—see other volume

```
Transformer xformer = TransformerFactory.newInstance().newTransformer();

    // Set the public and system id
    xformer.setOutputProperty(OutputKeys.DOCTYPE_PUBLIC, "publicId");
    xformer.setOutputProperty(OutputKeys.DOCTYPE_SYSTEM, "systemId");

    // Write the DOM document to a file
    Source source = new DOMSource(doc);
    Result result = new StreamResult(new File("outfilename.xml"));
    xformer.transform(source, result);
} catch (TransformerConfigurationException e) {
} catch (TransformerException e) {
}
```

This is the sample input for the example:

```
<?xml version="1.0" encoding="UTF-8"?>
<map>
    <entry key="key1" value="value1" />
    <entry key="key2" />
</map>
```

The resulting XML from running the example is:

```
<?xml version="1.0" encoding="UTF-8"?>
<!DOCTYPE map PUBLIC "publicId" "systemId">
<map>
    <entry key="key1" value="value1"/>
    <entry key="key2"/>
</map>
```

ε520. Writing Only the Text of a DOM Document

One of the three output methods of a transformer is text. With this output method, only the text in CharacterData nodes are written out. Comments are also written out since they are CharacterData nodes. To remove the comments, see "ε544. Removing a Node from a DOM Document".

```
// Create a document; this method is implemented in
// "ε510. The Quintessential Program to Create a DOM Document from an XML File"
Document doc = parseXmlFile("infilename.xml", false);

try {
    // Create a transformer
    Transformer xformer = TransformerFactory.newInstance().newTransformer();

    // Set the public and system id
    xformer.setOutputProperty(OutputKeys.METHOD, "text");

    // Write the DOM document to a file
    Source source = new DOMSource(doc);
    Result result = new StreamResult(new File("outfilename.xml"));
    xformer.transform(source, result);
} catch (TransformerConfigurationException e) {
} catch (TransformerException e) {
}
```

This is the sample input for the example:

```
<?xml version="1.0" encoding="UTF-8"?>
<root>
    <!– comment –>
    <?target instructions?>
```

```
            <elem1 attr="attrValue">
                cat &lt; <elem2> dog </elem2> rat
            </elem1>
            <![CDATA[cat < dog > rat]]>
        </root>
```

The resulting output from running the example is:

```
    <!– comment –>

        cat < dog rat

    cat < dog > rat
```

XSL

ε521. The Quintessential Program That Transforms an XML File with XSL

```java
import java.io.*;
import org.w3c.dom.*;
import org.xml.sax.*;
import javax.xml.parsers.*;
import javax.xml.transform.*;
import javax.xml.transform.dom.*;
import javax.xml.transform.stream.*;

public class BasicXsl {
    // This method applies the xslFilename to inFilename and writes
    // the output to outFilename.
    public static void xsl(String inFilename, String outFilename, String xslFilename) {
        try {
            // Create transformer factory
            TransformerFactory factory = TransformerFactory.newInstance();

            // Use the factory to create a template containing the xsl file
            Templates template = factory.newTemplates(new StreamSource(
                new FileInputStream(xslFilename)));

            // Use the template to create a transformer
            Transformer xformer = template.newTransformer();

            // Prepare the input and output files
            Source source = new StreamSource(new FileInputStream(inFilename));
            Result result = new StreamResult(new FileOutputStream(outFilename));

            // Apply the xsl file to the source file and write the result to the output file
            xformer.transform(source, result);
        } catch (FileNotFoundException e) {
        } catch (TransformerConfigurationException e) {
            // An error occurred in the XSL file
        } catch (TransformerException e) {
            // An error occurred while applying the XSL file
            // Get location of error in input file
            SourceLocator locator = e.getLocator();
            int col = locator.getColumnNumber();
            int line = locator.getLineNumber();
            String publicId = locator.getPublicId();
            String systemId = locator.getSystemId();
        }
```

Class   *Interface*   —extends   - - -implements   O abstract   ● final   ^—has superclass   ˌ—has subclass   package—see other volume

```
        }
    }
```

This is the sample input XML for the example:

```
<?xml version="1.0" encoding="UTF-8"?>
<map>
    <entry key="key1" value="value1" />
    <entry key="key2" />
</map>
```

This is the sample input XSL for the example. This XSL simply formats the key/value attributes in all entry elements into an HTML file.

```
<?xml version="1.0"?>
<xsl:stylesheet xmlns:xsl="http://www.w3.org/1999/XSL/Transform" version="1.0">
<xsl:output method="html" indent="yes"/>

<xsl:template match="map">
<HTML>
<HEAD>
<TITLE>Map</TITLE>
</HEAD>
<BODY>
    <xsl:apply-templates/>
</BODY>
</HTML>
</xsl:template>


<xsl:template match="entry">
    <xsl:value-of select="@key"/>=<xsl:value-of select="@value"/>
    <br></br>
</xsl:template>


</xsl:stylesheet>
```

The resulting HTML from running the example is:

```
<HTML>
<HEAD>
<META http-equiv="Content-Type" content="text/html; charset=UTF-8">
<TITLE>Map</TITLE>
</HEAD>
<BODY>
    key1=value1<br>
    key2=<br>

</BODY>
</HTML>
```

ε522. Transforming an XML File with XSL into a DOM Document

```
// This method applies the xslFilename to inFilename and
// returns DOM document containing the result.
public static Document parseXmlFile(String inFilename, String xslFilename) {
    try {
        // Create transformer factory
        TransformerFactory factory = TransformerFactory.newInstance();

        // Use the factory to create a template containing the xsl file
```

355

```
            Templates template = factory.newTemplates(new StreamSource(
                new FileInputStream(xslFilename)));

            // Use the template to create a transformer
            Transformer xformer = template.newTransformer();

            // Prepare the input file
            Source source = new StreamSource(new FileInputStream(inFilename));

            // Create a new document to hold the results
            DocumentBuilder builder = DocumentBuilderFactory.newInstance().newDocumentBuilder();
            Document doc = builder.newDocument();
            Result result = new DOMResult(doc);

            // Apply the xsl file to the source file and create the DOM tree
            xformer.transform(source, result);
            return doc;
        } catch (ParserConfigurationException e) {
            // An error occurred while creating an empty DOM document
        } catch (FileNotFoundException e) {
        } catch (TransformerConfigurationException e) {
            // An error occurred in the XSL file
        } catch (TransformerException e) {
            // An error occurred while applying the XSL file
        }
        return null;
    }
```

javax.xml.transform.dom

This package provides classes for using DOM nodes as source and and result of XML transformations.

```
    java.lang.Object
1.4   ├ DOMResult - - - - - - - - - - - - - - - - - - - - - - - - - - - - - - - - - javax.xml.transform.Result
1.4   └ DOMSource - - - - - - - - - - - - - - - - - - - - - - - - - - - - - - - - - javax.xml.transform.Source

1.4  DOMLocator ──────────────────────────────────── javax.xml.transform.SourceLocator
```

javax.xml.transform.sax

This package provides classes for using SAX events as source and result of XML transformations.

Class   *Interface*   —extends   - - -implements   ○ abstract   ● final   ^—has superclass   ⌐—has subclass   package—see other volume

```
java.lang.Object
1.4    ├ SAXResult ---------------------------------------- javax.xml.transform.Result
1.4    ├ SAXSource --------------------------------------- javax.xml.transform.Source
1.4 O  ├ javax.xml.transform.TransformerFactory
1.4 O       └ SAXTransformerFactory

1.4    TemplatesHandler ———————————————— org.xml.sax.ContentHandler
1.4    TransformerHandler ——————————————— org.xml.sax.ContentHandler,
                                                   org.xml.sax.DTDHandler,
                                                   org.xml.sax.ext.LexicalHandler
```

ε523. Generating SAX Parsing Events by Traversing a DOM Document

If you have developed a set of handlers for SAX events, it is possible to use these handlers on a source other than a file. This example demonstrates how to use the handlers on a DOM document.

```java
// Obtain a DOM document; this method is implemented in
// "ε510. The Quintessential Program to Create a DOM Document from an XML File"
Document doc = parseXmlFile("infilename.xml", false);

// Prepare the DOM source
Source source = new DOMSource(doc);

// Set the systemId of the source. This call is not strictly necessary
URI uri = new File("infilename.xml").toURI();
source.setSystemId(uri.toString());

// Create a handler to handle the SAX events
DefaultHandler handler = new MyHandler();

try {
    // Prepare the result
    SAXResult result = new SAXResult(handler);

    // Create a transformer
    Transformer xformer = TransformerFactory.newInstance().newTransformer();

    // Traverse the DOM tree
    xformer.transform(source, result);
} catch (TransformerConfigurationException e) {
} catch (TransformerException e) {
}

// DefaultHandler contain no-op implementations for all SAX events.
// This class should override methods to capture the events of interest.
class MyHandler extends DefaultHandler {
}
```

javax.xml.transform.stream

This package provides classes for using streams and Uniform Resource Identifiers (URIs) as source and result of XML transformations.

PAGE

Packages

javax.xml.transform.stream

java.lang.Object

1.4   ├ StreamResult - *javax.xml.transform.Result*

1.4   └ StreamSource - *javax.xml.transform.Source*

org.ietf.jgss

This package presents a framework that allows application developers to make use of security services such as authentication, data integrity, and data confidentiality from a variety of underlying security mechanisms like Kerberos, using a generic API. It is the Java language binding for the Generic Security Services API (GSS-API), as defined in 2853.

java.lang.Object

1.4   ├ ChannelBinding

1.4 ○   ├ GSSManager

1.4   ├ MessageProp

1.4   ├ Oid

       └ java.lang.Throwable - *java.io.Serializable*

          └ java.lang.Exception

1.4   └ GSSException

1.4   *GSSContext*

1.4   *GSSCredential* ———————————————————— *java.lang.Cloneable*

1.4   *GSSName*

org.omg.CORBA

This package contains classes and interfaces for use with programs that interact with CORBA services. CORBA is an object system that enables objects running on different platforms and possibly programmed using different programming languages to interoperate.

Class   *Interface*   —extends   - - -implements   ○ abstract   ● final   ^—has superclass   ˯—has subclass   package—see other volume

Packages

Class   *Interface*   —extends   - - -implements   ○ abstract   ● final   ˆ—has superclass   ˳—has subclass   package—see other volume

Packages

Class *Interface* —extends - - -implements ○ abstract ● final ^—has superclass —has subclass package—see other volume

	java.lang.Object	
1.2 ○	├ Any -	*org.omg.CORBA.portable.IDLEntity*^
1.2 ●	├ AnyHolder -,- -	*org.omg.CORBA.portable.Streamable* ˅
1.3 ○	├ AnySeqHelper	
1.3 ●	├ AnySeqHolder -	
1.2 ●	├ BooleanHolder -	
1.3 ○	├ BooleanSeqHelper	
1.3 ●	├ BooleanSeqHolder -	
1.2 ●	├ ByteHolder -	
1.2 ●	├ CharHolder -	
1.3 ○	├ CharSeqHelper	
1.3 ●	├ CharSeqHolder -	
1.2 ●	├ CompletionStatus -	*org.omg.CORBA.portable.IDLEntity*^
1.3 ○	├ CompletionStatusHelper	
1.2 ○	├ Context	
1.2 ○	├ ContextList	
1.3 ○	├ CurrentHelper	
1.3 ●	├ CurrentHolder -	*org.omg.CORBA.portable.Streamable* ˅
1.2	├ DefinitionKind -	*org.omg.CORBA.portable.IDLEntity*^
1.3 ○	├ DefinitionKindHelper	
1.2 ●	├ DoubleHolder -,-	*org.omg.CORBA.portable.Streamable* ˅
1.3 ○	├ DoubleSeqHelper	
1.3 ●	├ DoubleSeqHolder -	
1.2 ○	├ Environment	
1.2 ○	├ ExceptionList	
1.3 ○	├ FieldNameHelper	
1.2 ●	├ FixedHolder -	
1.2 ●	├ FloatHolder -	
1.3 ○	├ FloatSeqHelper	
1.3 ●	├ FloatSeqHolder -	
1.3 ○	├ IDLTypeHelper	

Packages

org.omg.CORBA

	java.lang.Object	·- *org.omg.CORBA.portable.Streamable* ⌄
1.3 ○	IdentifierHelper	
1.2 ●	IntHolder -	
1.4	LocalObject - *Object* ⌄	
1.2 ●	LongHolder - *org.omg.CORBA.portable.Streamable* ⌄	
1.3 ○	LongLongSeqHelper	
1.3 ●	LongLongSeqHolder -	
1.3 ○	LongSeqHelper	
1.3 ●	LongSeqHolder -	
1.2 ○	NVList	
1.2 ●	NameValuePair - *org.omg.CORBA.portable.IDLEntity* ⌃	
1.3 ○	NameValuePairHelper	
1.2 ○	NamedValue	
1.2 ○	ORB ⌄	
1.3 ○	ObjectHelper	
1.2 ●	ObjectHolder - ·- *org.omg.CORBA.portable.Streamable* ⌄	
1.3 ○	OctetSeqHelper	
1.3 ●	OctetSeqHolder -	
1.4	ParameterMode - *org.omg.CORBA.portable.IDLEntity* ⌃	
1.4 ○	ParameterModeHelper	
1.4 ●	ParameterModeHolder - *org.omg.CORBA.portable.Streamable* ⌄	
1.4 ○	PolicyErrorCodeHelper	
1.4 ○	PolicyErrorHelper	
1.4 ●	PolicyErrorHolder -	
1.3 ○	PolicyHelper	
1.3 ●	PolicyHolder -	
1.3 ○	PolicyListHelper	
1.3 ●	PolicyListHolder -	
1.3 ○	PolicyTypeHelper	
D	Principal	
D ●	PrincipalHolder -	
1.3 ○	RepositoryIdHelper	
1.2 ○	Request	
1.2 ○	ServerRequest	
1.2 ●	ServiceDetail -·- *org.omg.CORBA.portable.IDLEntity* ⌃	
1.2 ○	ServiceDetailHelper	
1.2 ●	ServiceInformation -	
1.2 ○	ServiceInformationHelper	
1.2 ●	ServiceInformationHolder - *org.omg.CORBA.portable.Streamable* ⌄	
1.2	SetOverrideType - *org.omg.CORBA.portable.IDLEntity* ⌃	
1.3 ○	SetOverrideTypeHelper	
1.2 ●	ShortHolder - *org.omg.CORBA.portable.Streamable* ⌄	
1.3 ○	ShortSeqHelper	
1.3 ●	ShortSeqHolder -	
1.2 ●	StringHolder -	
1.4 ○	StringSeqHelper	
1.4 ●	StringSeqHolder -	
1.3	StringValueHelper - *org.omg.CORBA.portable.BoxedValueHelper*	
1.2 ●	StructMember -·- *org.omg.CORBA.portable.IDLEntity* ⌃	
1.3 ○	StructMemberHelper	

Class   *Interface*   —extends   - - -implements   ○ abstract   ● final   ⌃—has superclass   ⌄—has subclass   package—see other volume

		java.lang.Object	– *org.omg.CORBA.portable.IDLEntity*↺
1.2		– TCKind	
1.2	○	– TypeCode -	
1.2	●	– TypeCodeHolder -	– *org.omg.CORBA.portable.Streamable*⌣
1.3	○	– ULongLongSeqHelper	
1.3	●	– ULongLongSeqHolder -	
1.3	○	– ULongSeqHelper	
1.3	●	– ULongSeqHolder -	
1.3	○	– UShortSeqHelper	
1.3	●	– UShortSeqHolder -	
1.2	●	– UnionMember -	*org.omg.CORBA.portable.IDLEntity*↺
1.3	○	– UnionMemberHelper	
1.4	○	– UnknownUserExceptionHelper	
1.4	●	– UnknownUserExceptionHolder - - - - - - - - - - - - - - - - -	– *org.omg.CORBA.portable.Streamable*⌣
1.3	○	– ValueBaseHelper	
1.3	●	– ValueBaseHolder -	
1.2	●	– ValueMember -	*org.omg.CORBA.portable.IDLEntity*↺
1.3	○	– ValueMemberHelper	
1.3	○	– VersionSpecHelper	
1.3	○	– VisibilityHelper	
1.3	○	– WCharSeqHelper	
1.3	●	– WCharSeqHolder -	– *org.omg.CORBA.portable.Streamable*⌣
1.4	○	– WStringSeqHelper	
1.4	●	– WStringSeqHolder -	
1.3		– WStringValueHelper -	*org.omg.CORBA.portable.BoxedValueHelper*
1.4	○	– WrongTransactionHelper	
1.4	●	– WrongTransactionHolder -	*org.omg.CORBA.portable.Streamable*⌣
1.2	○	– org.omg.CORBA.portable.ObjectImpl -	*Object*⌣
D		⌐ DynamicImplementation⌣	
1.3		⌐ _IDLTypeStub -	*IDLType*^
1.3		└ _PolicyStub -	*Policy*↺
		└ java.lang.Throwable -	*java.io.Serializable*⌣
		└ java.lang.Exception	
1.2	○	⌐ UserException -	*org.omg.CORBA.portable.IDLEntity*↺
1.2	●	⌐ Bounds	
1.2	●	⌐ PolicyError	
1.2	●	⌐ UnknownUserException	
1.2	●	└ WrongTransaction	
		└ java.lang.RuntimeException	
1.2	○	└ SystemException	
1.2	●	⌐ BAD_CONTEXT	
1.2	●	⌐ BAD_INV_ORDER	
1.2	●	⌐ BAD_OPERATION	
1.2	●	⌐ BAD_PARAM	
1.2	●	⌐ BAD_TYPECODE	
1.2	●	⌐ COMM_FAILURE	
1.2	●	⌐ DATA_CONVERSION	
1.2	●	⌐ FREE_MEM	
1.2	●	⌐ IMP_LIMIT	
1.2	●	⌐ INITIALIZE	
1.2	●	⌐ INTERNAL	

Packages

org.omg.CORBA

```
        java.lang.Object
          └ java.lang.Throwable ---------------------------------- java.io.Serializable ⌄
              └ java.lang.Exception
                  └ java.lang.RuntimeException
                      └ SystemException
```

1.2 ○	SystemException
1.2 ●	─ INTF_REPOS
1.2 ●	─ INVALID_TRANSACTION
1.2 ●	─ INV_FLAG
1.2 ●	─ INV_IDENT
1.2 ●	─ INV_OBJREF
1.2 ●	─ INV_POLICY
1.2 ●	─ MARSHAL
1.2 ●	─ NO_IMPLEMENT
1.2 ●	─ NO_MEMORY
1.2 ●	─ NO_PERMISSION
1.2 ●	─ NO_RESOURCES
1.2 ●	─ NO_RESPONSE
1.2 ●	─ OBJECT_NOT_EXIST
1.2 ●	─ OBJ_ADAPTER
1.2 ●	─ PERSIST_STORE
1.2 ●	─ TRANSACTION_REQUIRED
1.2 ●	─ TRANSACTION_ROLLEDBACK
1.2 ●	─ TRANSIENT
1.2 ●	└ UNKNOWN

1.2	*ARG_IN*	
1.2	*ARG_INOUT*	
1.2	*ARG_OUT*	
1.2	*BAD_POLICY*	
1.2	*BAD_POLICY_TYPE*	
1.2	*BAD_POLICY_VALUE*	
1.2	*CTX_RESTRICT_SCOPE*	
1.2	*Current* ⌄ ────────────────	*CurrentOperations, Object,*
		org.omg.CORBA.portable.IDLEntity ˆ
1.3	*CurrentOperations* ⌄	
1.3	*CustomMarshal* ⌄	
1.3	*DataInputStream* ───────────	*org.omg.CORBA.portable.ValueBase* ˆ
1.3	*DataOutputStream* ───────────	
1.2	*DomainManager* ─────────────	*DomainManagerOperations, Object,*
		org.omg.CORBA.portable.IDLEntity ˆ
1.3	*DomainManagerOperations* ⌄	
1.2	*DynAny* ⌄ ─────────────────	*Object*
1.2	*DynArray* ─────────────────	*DynAny* ˆ, *Object*
1.2	*DynEnum* ─────────────────	
1.2	*DynFixed* ─────────────────	
1.2	*DynSequence* ───────────────	
1.2	*DynStruct* ─────────────────	
1.2	*DynUnion* ─────────────────	
1.2	*DynValue* ─────────────────	
1.2	*IDLType* ─────────────────	*IDLTypeOperations* ˆ, *IRObject* ˆ,
		org.omg.CORBA.portable.IDLEntity ˆ

Class   *Interface*   ──extends   ‑‑‑implements   ○ abstract   ● final   ˆ—has superclass   ⌄—has subclass   package—see other volume

1.3	*IDLTypeOperations* ————————————————————	*IRObjectOperations*
1.2	*IRObject* ————————————————————	*IRObjectOperations, Object,*
		*org.omg.CORBA.portable.IDLEntity^*
1.3	*IRObjectOperations*	
1.3	*OMGVMCID*	
1.2	*Object*	
1.2	PRIVATE_MEMBER	
1.2	PUBLIC_MEMBER	
1.2	*Policy* ————————————————————	*Object, PolicyOperations, org.omg.CORBA↩*
		*.portable.IDLEntity^*
1.3	*PolicyOperations*	
1.2	UNSUPPORTED_POLICY	
1.2	UNSUPPORTED_POLICY_VALUE	
1.2	VM_ABSTRACT	
1.2	VM_CUSTOM	
1.2	VM_NONE	
1.2	VM_TRUNCATABLE	

---

org.omg.CORBA.DynAnyPackage

```
java.lang.Object
  └ java.lang.Throwable - - - - - - - - - - - - - - - - - - - - - - - - - - - - - - - java.io.Serializable
      └ java.lang.Exception
```
1.2 ○	└ org.omg.CORBA.UserException - org.omg.CORBA.portable.IDLEntity^
1.2 ●	├ Invalid
1.2 ●	├ InvalidSeq
1.2 ●	├ InvalidValue
1.2 ●	└ TypeMismatch

---

org.omg.CORBA.ORBPackage

This package contains a class for the CORBA InvalidName exception, which can be thrown by the ORB.resolve_initial_references() method.

org.omg.CORBA.ORBPackage

```
java.lang.Object
  └ java.lang.Throwable - - - - - - - - - - - - - - - - - - - - - - - - - - - - - - - - - java.io.Serializable
      └ java.lang.Exception
```

org.omg.CORBA.TypeCodePackage

This package contains classes for the CORBA exceptions that can be thrown by the CORBA TypeCode operations.

```
java.lang.Object
  └ java.lang.Throwable - - - - - - - - - - - - - - - - - - - - - - - - - - - - - - - - - java.io.Serializable
      └ java.lang.Exception
```

org.omg.CORBA.portable

This package contains classes and interfaces for developing ORB implementations.

Class   *Interface*   —extends   - - -implements   ○ abstract   ● final   ^—has superclass   —has subclass   package—see other volume

```
        java.lang.Object
1.2 O     ├ Delegate˘
1.2 O     ├ ObjectImpl˘ - - - - - - - - - - - - - - - - - - - - - - - - - - - - - - - - - org.omg.CORBA.Object˘
1.2       ├ ServantObject
    O     ├ java.io.InputStream
1.2 O     │  └ InputStream˘
    O     ├ java.io.OutputStream
1.2 O     │  └ OutputStream˘
          └ java.lang.Throwable - - - - - - - - - - - - - - - - - - - - - - - - - - - - java.io.Serializable˘
             └ java.lang.Exception
1.2          ├ ApplicationException
1.2 ●        ├ RemarshalException
             └ java.lang.RuntimeException
1.2 O           └ org.omg.CORBA.SystemException
1.3             ├ IndirectionException
1.3             └ UnknownException
```

1.3	*BoxedValueHelper*	
1.3	*CustomValue* ——————————————————	*ValueBase^, org.omg.CORBA.CustomMarshal*
1.2	*IDLEntity*˘ ——————————————————	*java.io.Serializable*
1.2	*InvokeHandler*˘	
1.2	*ResponseHandler*	
1.2	*Streamable*˘	
1.3	*StreamableValue* ——————————————————	*Streamable, ValueBase^*
1.3	*ValueBase*˘ ——————————————————	*IDLEntity^*
1.3	*ValueFactory*	

---

org.omg.CORBA_2_3

This package defines additions to interfaces in the org.omg.CORBA package. These additions conform to version 2.3 of the OMG CORBA specifications.

```
        java.lang.Object
1.2 O     └ org.omg.CORBA.ORB
1.3 O        └ ORB
```

---

org.omg.CORBA_2_3.portable

This package defines additions to interfaces in the org.omg.CORBA.portable package. These additions conform to version 2.3 of the OMG CORBA specifications.

```
       java.lang.Object
   ○     ├ java.io.InputStream
1.2 ○    │   └ org.omg.CORBA.portable.InputStream
1.3 ○    │       └ InputStream
   ○     ├ java.io.OutputStream
1.2 ○    │   └ org.omg.CORBA.portable.OutputStream
1.3 ○    │       └ OutputStream
1.2 ○    ├ org.omg.CORBA.portable.Delegate
1.3 ○    │   └ Delegate
1.2 ○    └ org.omg.CORBA.portable.ObjectImpl --------------------- org.omg.CORBA.Object¸
1.3 ○        └ ObjectImpl¸
```

org.omg.CosNaming

This package contains classes and interfaces for communicating with the COS naming server. The COS naming server provides a mapping of hierarchical names to CORBA object references.

Class   *Interface*   —extends   - - -implements   ○ abstract   ● final   ^—has superclass   ¸—has subclass   package—see other volume

		java.lang.Object	
1.2	●	├ Binding -	*org.omg.CORBA.portable.IDLEntity*⌒
1.2	○	├ BindingHelper	
1.2	●	├ BindingHolder -	*org.omg.CORBA.portable.Streamable*⌄
1.2	○	├ BindingIteratorHelper	
1.2	●	├ BindingIteratorHolder - ┐	
1.2	○	├ BindingListHelper	
1.2	●	├ BindingListHolder - ┘	
1.2		├ BindingType -	*org.omg.CORBA.portable.IDLEntity*⌒
1.2	○	├ BindingTypeHelper	
1.2	●	├ BindingTypeHolder -	*org.omg.CORBA.portable.Streamable*⌄
1.2	○	├ IstringHelper	
1.2	●	├ NameComponent -	*org.omg.CORBA.portable.IDLEntity*⌒
1.2	○	├ NameComponentHelper	
1.2	●	├ NameComponentHolder -	*org.omg.CORBA.portable.Streamable*⌄
1.2	○	├ NameHelper	
1.2	●	├ NameHolder - ┐	
1.4	○	├ NamingContextExtHelper	
1.4	●	├ NamingContextExtHolder - - - - - - - - - - - - - - - - - - ┤	
1.2	○	├ NamingContextHelper	
1.2	●	├ NamingContextHolder - ┘	
1.2	○	├ org.omg.CORBA.portable.ObjectImpl - - - - - - - - - - - - - - -	*org.omg.CORBA.Object*⌄
1.2		│ ├ _BindingIteratorStub -	*BindingIterator*^
1.4		│ ├ _NamingContextExtStub - - - - - - - - - - - - - - - - - -	*NamingContextExt*^
1.2		│ ├ _NamingContextStub -	*NamingContext*⌒
D		│ └ org.omg.CORBA.DynamicImplementation	
1.2	○	│ ├ _BindingIteratorImplBase - - - - - - - - - - - - - - - - - -	*BindingIterator*^
1.2	○	│ └ _NamingContextImplBase - - - - - - - - - - - - - - - - - -	*NamingContext*⌒
1.4	○	└ org.omg.PortableServer.Servant	
1.4	○	├ BindingIteratorPOA -	*BindingIteratorOperations*⌄,
			org.omg.CORBA.portable.InvokeHandler⌄
1.4	○	├ NamingContextExtPOA -	*NamingContextExtOperations*⌒,
			org.omg.CORBA.portable.InvokeHandler⌄
1.4	○	└ NamingContextPOA -	*NamingContextOperations*⌄,
			org.omg.CORBA.portable.InvokeHandler⌄

Packages

371

org.omg.CosNaming

org.omg.CosNaming.NamingContextExtPackage

org.omg.CosNaming.NamingContextPackage

This package contains helper and holder classes for CORBA exceptions that can be thrown by the COS naming server.

Class   *Interface*   —extends   - - -implements   ○ abstract   ● final   ^—has superclass   ‿—has subclass   package—see other volume

java.lang.Object

1.2	○	– AlreadyBoundHelper
1.2	●	– AlreadyBoundHolder - *org.omg.CORBA.portable.Streamable*˅
1.2	○	– CannotProceedHelper
1.2	●	– CannotProceedHolder -
1.2	○	– InvalidNameHelper
1.2	●	– InvalidNameHolder -
1.2	○	– NotEmptyHelper
1.2	●	– NotEmptyHolder -
1.2	○	– NotFoundHelper
1.2	●	– NotFoundHolder -
1.2		– NotFoundReason - *org.omg.CORBA.portable.IDLEntity*ˆ
1.2	○	– NotFoundReasonHelper
1.2	●	– NotFoundReasonHolder - *org.omg.CORBA.portable.Streamable*˅
		└ java.lang.Throwable - *java.io.Serializable*˅
		└ java.lang.Exception
1.2	○	└ org.omg.CORBA.UserException - - - - - - - - - - - - - - - - *org.omg.CORBA.portable.IDLEntity*ˆ
1.2	●	– AlreadyBound
1.2	●	– CannotProceed
1.2	●	– InvalidName
1.2	●	– NotEmpty
1.2	●	└ NotFound

org.omg.Dynamic

java.lang.Object

1.4	●	└ Parameter - *org.omg.CORBA.portable.IDLEntity*ˆ

org.omg.DynamicAny

org.omg.DynamicAny

java.lang.Object

1.4	○	⊢ AnySeqHelper
1.4	○	⊢ DynAnyFactoryHelper
1.4	○	⊢ DynAnyHelper
1.4	○	⊢ DynAnySeqHelper
1.4	○	⊢ DynArrayHelper

Class   *Interface*   —extends   - - -implements   ○ abstract   ● final   ^—has superclass   ⌐—has subclass   package—see other volume

```
        java.lang.Object
1.4 ○   ├ DynEnumHelper
1.4 ○   ├ DynFixedHelper
1.4 ○   ├ DynSequenceHelper
1.4 ○   ├ DynStructHelper
1.4 ○   ├ DynUnionHelper
1.4 ○   ├ DynValueHelper
1.4 ○   ├ FieldNameHelper
1.4 ●   ├ NameDynAnyPair - - - - - - - - - - - - - - - - - - - - - - - org.omg.CORBA.portable.IDLEntity
1.4 ○   ├ NameDynAnyPairHelper
1.4 ○   ├ NameDynAnyPairSeqHelper
1.4 ●   ├ NameValuePair - - - - - - - - - - - - - - - - - - - - - - -
1.4 ○   ├ NameValuePairHelper
1.4 ○   ├ NameValuePairSeqHelper
1.2 ○   └ org.omg.CORBA.portable.ObjectImpl - - - - - - - - - - - - - - - org.omg.CORBA.Object
1.4       ├ _DynAnyFactoryStub - - - - - - - - - - - - - - - - - - - - DynAnyFactory
1.4       ├ _DynAnyStub - - - - - - - - - - - - - - - - - - - - - - - - DynAny
1.4       ├ _DynArrayStub - - - - - - - - - - - - - - - - - - - - - - - DynArray
1.4       ├ _DynEnumStub - - - - - - - - - - - - - - - - - - - - - - - DynEnum
1.4       ├ _DynFixedStub - - - - - - - - - - - - - - - - - - - - - - - DynFixed
1.4       ├ _DynSequenceStub - - - - - - - - - - - - - - - - - - - - - DynSequence
1.4       ├ _DynStructStub - - - - - - - - - - - - - - - - - - - - - - DynStruct
1.4       ├ _DynUnionStub - - - - - - - - - - - - - - - - - - - - - - - DynUnion
1.4       └ _DynValueStub - - - - - - - - - - - - - - - - - - - - - - - DynValue
```

```
1.4  DynAny ————————————————— DynAnyOperations, org.omg.CORBA.Object,
                                org.omg.CORBA.portable.IDLEntity
1.4  DynAnyFactory ———————————— DynAnyFactoryOperations,
                                org.omg.CORBA.Object,
                                org.omg.CORBA.portable.IDLEntity
1.4  DynAnyFactoryOperations
1.4  DynAnyOperations
1.4  DynArray ————————————————— DynAny, DynArrayOperations,
                                org.omg.CORBA.portable.IDLEntity
1.4  DynArrayOperations ————————— DynAnyOperations
1.4  DynEnum ————————————————— DynAny, DynEnumOperations,
                                org.omg.CORBA.portable.IDLEntity
1.4  DynEnumOperations ————————— DynAnyOperations
1.4  DynFixed ————————————————— DynAny, DynFixedOperations,
                                org.omg.CORBA.portable.IDLEntity
1.4  DynFixedOperations ————————— DynAnyOperations
1.4  DynSequence ———————————— DynAny, DynSequenceOperations,
                                org.omg.CORBA.portable.IDLEntity
1.4  DynSequenceOperations ———— DynAnyOperations
1.4  DynStruct ————————————————— DynAny, DynStructOperations,
                                org.omg.CORBA.portable.IDLEntity
1.4  DynStructOperations ————————— DynAnyOperations
1.4  DynUnion ————————————————— DynAny, DynUnionOperations,
                                org.omg.CORBA.portable.IDLEntity
1.4  DynUnionOperations ————————— DynAnyOperations
1.4  DynValue ————————————————— DynValueCommon, DynValueOperations,
                                org.omg.CORBA.portable.IDLEntity
1.4  DynValueBox ———————————— DynValueBoxOperations, DynValueCommon,
                                org.omg.CORBA.portable.IDLEntity
1.4  DynValueBoxOperations ———— DynValueCommonOperations
```

Packages

org.omg.DynamicAny

1.4	*DynValueCommon* ───────────────────	*DynAny^, DynValueCommonOperations^, org.omg.CORBA.portable.IDLEntity^*
1.4	*DynValueCommonOperations* ───────────────	*DynAnyOperations*
1.4	*DynValueOperations* ─────────────────	*DynValueCommonOperations^*

org.omg.DynamicAny.DynAnyFactoryPackage

```
java.lang.Object
1.4 ○   ├ InconsistentTypeCodeHelper
        └ java.lang.Throwable - - - - - - - - - - - - - - - - - - - - - - - - - - - - - java.io.Serializable
            └ java.lang.Exception
1.2 ○           └ org.omg.CORBA.UserException - - - - - - - - - - - - - - - - - org.omg.CORBA.portable.IDLEntity^
1.4 ●               └ InconsistentTypeCode
```

org.omg.DynamicAny.DynAnyPackage

```
java.lang.Object
1.4 ○   ├ InvalidValueHelper
1.4 ○   ├ TypeMismatchHelper
        └ java.lang.Throwable - - - - - - - - - - - - - - - - - - - - - - - - - - - - - java.io.Serializable
            └ java.lang.Exception
1.2 ○           └ org.omg.CORBA.UserException - - - - - - - - - - - - - - - - - org.omg.CORBA.portable.IDLEntity^
1.4 ●               ├ InvalidValue
1.4 ●               └ TypeMismatch
```

org.omg.IOP

Class *Interface* ──extends   - - -implements   ○ abstract   ● final   ^─has superclass   ─has subclass   package─see other volume

java.lang.Object

1.4 ○	CodecFactoryHelper
1.4 ○	ComponentIdHelper
1.4 ●	Encoding -- *org.omg.CORBA.portable.IDLEntity*
1.4 ●	IOR -:
1.4 ○	IORHelper
1.4 ●	IORHolder -- - *org.omg.CORBA.portable.Streamable*
1.4 ○	MultipleComponentProfileHelper
1.4 ●	MultipleComponentProfileHolder -:
1.4 ○	ProfileIdHelper
1.4 ●	ServiceContext - *org.omg.CORBA.portable.IDLEntity*
1.4 ○	ServiceContextHelper
1.4 ●	ServiceContextHolder -- - *org.omg.CORBA.portable.Streamable*
1.4 ○	ServiceContextListHelper
1.4 ●	ServiceContextListHolder -:
1.4 ○	ServiceIdHelper
1.4 ●	TaggedComponent - *org.omg.CORBA.portable.IDLEntity*
1.4 ○	TaggedComponentHelper
1.4 ●	TaggedComponentHolder - *org.omg.CORBA.portable.Streamable*
1.4 ●	TaggedProfile - *org.omg.CORBA.portable.IDLEntity*
1.4 ○	TaggedProfileHelper
1.4 ●	TaggedProfileHolder - *org.omg.CORBA.portable.Streamable*

Packages

org.omg.IOP

org.omg.IOP.CodecFactoryPackage

```
       java.lang.Object
1.4 ○   ├ UnknownEncodingHelper
        └ java.lang.Throwable - - - - - - - - - - - - - - - - - - - - - - - - - - java.io.Serializable
           └ java.lang.Exception
1.2 ○        └ org.omg.CORBA.UserException - - - - - - - - - - - - - - - org.omg.CORBA.portable.IDLEntity^
1.4 ●           └ UnknownEncoding
```

org.omg.IOP.CodecPackage

```
       java.lang.Object
1.4 ○   ├ FormatMismatchHelper
1.4 ○   ├ InvalidTypeForEncodingHelper
1.4 ○   ├ TypeMismatchHelper
```

Class *Interface* —extends - - -implements ○ abstract ● final ^—has superclass ˌ—has subclass package—see other volume

```
      java.lang.Object
        └ java.lang.Throwable - - - - - - - - - - - - - - - - - - - - - - - - - - - - - - - java.io.Serializable
            └ java.lang.Exception
1.2 ○        └ org.omg.CORBA.UserException - - - - - - - - - - - - - - - - org.omg.CORBA.portable.IDLEntity
1.4 ●            ├ FormatMismatch
1.4 ●            ├ InvalidTypeForEncoding
1.4 ●            └ TypeMismatch
```

org.omg.Messaging

```
      java.lang.Object
1.4 ○   └ SyncScopeHelper
```

1.4   *SYNC_WITH_TRANSPORT*

org.omg.PortableInterceptor

Packages

org.omg.PortableInterceptor

```
        java.lang.Object
1.4 ○    ├ CurrentHelper
1.4 ○    ├ ForwardRequestHelper
1.4 ○    ├ InvalidSlotHelper
        └ java.lang.Throwable --------------------------------- java.io.Serializable,
            └ java.lang.Exception
1.2 ○         └ org.omg.CORBA.UserException ------------------- org.omg.CORBA.portable.IDLEntity^
1.4 ●            ├ ForwardRequest
1.4 ●            └ InvalidSlot
```

1.4	*ClientRequestInfo* ────────────────	*ClientRequestInfoOperations*^, *RequestInfo*^, org.omg.CORBA.portable.IDLEntity^
1.4	*ClientRequestInfoOperations*, ─────────	*RequestInfoOperations*
1.4	*ClientRequestInterceptor* ─────────────	*ClientRequestInterceptorOperations*^, *Interceptor*^, org.omg.CORBA.portable.IDLEntity^
1.4	*ClientRequestInterceptorOperations*, ────	*InterceptorOperations*
1.4	*Current* ────────────────────	*CurrentOperations*^, org.omg.CORBA.Current^, org.omg.CORBA.portable.IDLEntity^
1.4	*CurrentOperations*, ────────────	org.omg.CORBA.CurrentOperations
1.4	*IORInfo* ────────────────────	*IORInfoOperations*, org.omg.CORBA.Object, org.omg.CORBA.portable.IDLEntity^
1.4	*IORInfoOperations*,	
1.4	*IORInterceptor* ─────────────────	*IORInterceptorOperations*^, *Interceptor*^, org.omg.CORBA.portable.IDLEntity^
1.4	*IORInterceptorOperations*, ────────────	*InterceptorOperations*
1.4	*Interceptor*, ──────────────────	*InterceptorOperations*, org.omg.CORBA.Object, org.omg.CORBA.portable.IDLEntity^
1.4	*InterceptorOperations*,	
1.4	*LOCATION_FORWARD*	
1.4	*ORBInitInfo* ────────────────────	*ORBInitInfoOperations*, org.omg.CORBA.Object, org.omg.CORBA.portable.IDLEntity^
1.4	*ORBInitInfoOperations*,	
1.4	*ORBInitializer* ────────────────	*ORBInitializerOperations*, org.omg.CORBA.Object, org.omg.CORBA.portable.IDLEntity^
1.4	*ORBInitializerOperations*,	
1.4	*PolicyFactory* ────────────────	*PolicyFactoryOperations*, org.omg.CORBA.Object, org.omg.CORBA.portable.IDLEntity^
1.4	*PolicyFactoryOperations*,	
1.4	*RequestInfo*, ────────────────	*RequestInfoOperations*, org.omg.CORBA.Object, org.omg.CORBA.portable.IDLEntity^
1.4	*RequestInfoOperations*,	

Class *Interface* ──extends - - -implements ○ abstract ● final ^—has superclass ,—has subclass package—see other volume

org.omg.PortableInterceptor.ORBInitInfoPackage

org.omg.PortableServer

Packages

org.omg.PortableServer

java.lang.Object

1.4 ○   ├ CurrentHelper

1.4 ○   ├ ForwardRequestHelper

1.4   ├ IdAssignmentPolicyValue - *org.omg.CORBA.portable.IDLEntity*ˇ

1.4   ├ IdUniquenessPolicyValue - ┊

1.4   ├ ImplicitActivationPolicyValue - ┊

Class   *Interface*   —extends   - - -implements   ○ abstract   ● final   ^—has superclass   ˇ—has subclass   package—see other volume

```
      java.lang.Object                                        .- org.omg.CORBA.portable.IDLEntity˜
1.4    ├ LifespanPolicyValue - - - - - - - - - - - - - - - - - - - - - ┐
1.4 ○  ├ POAHelper                                                    ┆
1.4    ├ RequestProcessingPolicyValue - - - - - - - - - - - - - - - ┘
1.4 ○  ├ Servant
1.4 ○  │  ├ DynamicImplementation
1.4 ○  │  ├ ServantActivatorPOA - - - - - - - - - - - - - - - - - - - ServantActivatorOperations˜,
                                                                      org.omg.CORBA.portable.InvokeHandler˅
1.4 ○  │  └ ServantLocatorPOA - - - - - - - - - - - - - - - - - - - - ServantLocatorOperations˜,
                                                                      org.omg.CORBA.portable.InvokeHandler˅
1.4 ○  ├ ServantActivatorHelper
1.4 ○  ├ ServantLocatorHelper
1.4    ├ ServantRetentionPolicyValue - - - - - - - - - - - - - - - ┬ - org.omg.CORBA.portable.IDLEntity˜
1.4    ├ ThreadPolicyValue - - - - - - - - - - - - - - - - - - - - - ┘
1.2 ○  ├ org.omg.CORBA.portable.ObjectImpl - - - - - - - - - - - - - org.omg.CORBA.Object˅
1.4    │  ├ _ServantActivatorStub - - - - - - - - - - - - - - - - - - ServantActivator^
1.4    │  └ _ServantLocatorStub - - - - - - - - - - - - - - - - - - - ServantLocator^
       └ java.lang.Throwable - - - - - - - - - - - - - - - - - - - - java.io.Serializable˅
          └ java.lang.Exception
1.2 ○        └ org.omg.CORBA.UserException - - - - - - - - - - - - - org.omg.CORBA.portable.IDLEntity˜
1.4 ●           └ ForwardRequest
          ─────────────────────────────
1.4    AdapterActivator ─────────────────────────────────────────── AdapterActivatorOperations,
                                                                      org.omg.CORBA.Object,
                                                                      org.omg.CORBA.portable.IDLEntity^
1.4    AdapterActivatorOperations˅
1.4    Current ──────────────────────────────────────────────────── CurrentOperations^, org.omg.CORBA.Current^,
                                                                      org.omg.CORBA.portable.IDLEntity^
1.4    CurrentOperations˅ ────────────────────────────────────────── org.omg.CORBA.CurrentOperations
1.4    ID_ASSIGNMENT_POLICY_ID
1.4    ID_UNIQUENESS_POLICY_ID
1.4    IMPLICIT_ACTIVATION_POLICY_ID
1.4    IdAssignmentPolicy ──────────────────────────────────────── IdAssignmentPolicyOperations^,
                                                                      org.omg.CORBA.Policy^,
                                                                      org.omg.CORBA.portable.IDLEntity^
1.4    IdAssignmentPolicyOperations˅ ──────────────────────────────── org.omg.CORBA.PolicyOperations
1.4    IdUniquenessPolicy ──────────────────────────────────────── IdUniquenessPolicyOperations^,
                                                                      org.omg.CORBA.Policy^,
                                                                      org.omg.CORBA.portable.IDLEntity^
1.4    IdUniquenessPolicyOperations˅ ─────────────────────────────── org.omg.CORBA.PolicyOperations
1.4    ImplicitActivationPolicy ─────────────────────────────────── ImplicitActivationPolicyOperations^,
                                                                      org.omg.CORBA.Policy^,
                                                                      org.omg.CORBA.portable.IDLEntity^
1.4    ImplicitActivationPolicyOperations˅ ───────────────────────── org.omg.CORBA.PolicyOperations
1.4    LIFESPAN_POLICY_ID
1.4    LifespanPolicy ──────────────────────────────────────────── LifespanPolicyOperations^,
                                                                      org.omg.CORBA.Policy^,
                                                                      org.omg.CORBA.portable.IDLEntity^
1.4    LifespanPolicyOperations˅ ──────────────────────────────────── org.omg.CORBA.PolicyOperations
1.4    POA ──────────────────────────────────────────────────────── POAOperations, org.omg.CORBA.Object,
                                                                      org.omg.CORBA.portable.IDLEntity^
1.4    POAManager ──────────────────────────────────────────────── POAManagerOperations, org.omg.CORBA.Object,
                                                                      org.omg.CORBA.portable.IDLEntity^
1.4    POAManagerOperations˅
1.4    POAOperations˅
1.4    REQUEST_PROCESSING_POLICY_ID
```

Packages

org.omg.PortableServer

org.omg.PortableServer.CurrentPackage

```
          java.lang.Object
1.4 ○      ├ NoContextHelper
           └ java.lang.Throwable - - - - - - - - - - - - - - - - - - - - - - - java.io.Serializable˅
              └ java.lang.Exception
1.2 ○            └ org.omg.CORBA.UserException - - - - - - - - - - - - - - - org.omg.CORBA.portable.IDLEntity^
1.4 ●              └ NoContext
```

org.omg.PortableServer.POAManagerPackage

```
          java.lang.Object
1.4 ○      ├ AdapterInactiveHelper
1.4        ├ State - - - - - - - - - - - - - - - - - - - - - - - - - - - - - org.omg.CORBA.portable.IDLEntity^
```

Class   *Interface*   —extends   - - -implements   ○ abstract   ● final   ^—has superclass   ˅—has subclass   package—see other volume

```
java.lang.Object
  └ java.lang.Throwable - - - - - - - - - - - - - - - - - - - - - - - - - - - - - - - - java.io.Serializable
      └ java.lang.Exception
```
1.2 ○   └ org.omg.CORBA.UserException - - - - - - - - - - - - - - - - - - - org.omg.CORBA.portable.IDLEntity
1.4 ●   └ AdapterInactive

---

org.omg.PortableServer.POAPackage

```
java.lang.Object
```
1.4 ○   ├ AdapterAlreadyExistsHelper
1.4 ○   ├ AdapterNonExistentHelper
1.4 ○   ├ InvalidPolicyHelper
1.4 ○   ├ NoServantHelper
1.4 ○   ├ ObjectAlreadyActiveHelper
1.4 ○   ├ ObjectNotActiveHelper
1.4 ○   ├ ServantAlreadyActiveHelper
1.4 ○   ├ ServantNotActiveHelper
1.4 ○   ├ WrongAdapterHelper
1.4 ○   ├ WrongPolicyHelper
```
  └ java.lang.Throwable - - - - - - - - - - - - - - - - - - - - - - - - - - - - - - - - java.io.Serializable
      └ java.lang.Exception
```
1.2 ○   └ org.omg.CORBA.UserException - - - - - - - - - - - - - - - - - - - org.omg.CORBA.portable.IDLEntity
1.4 ●   ├ AdapterAlreadyExists
1.4 ●   ├ AdapterNonExistent
1.4 ●   ├ InvalidPolicy
1.4 ●   ├ NoServant
1.4 ●   ├ ObjectAlreadyActive
1.4 ●   ├ ObjectNotActive
1.4 ●   ├ ServantAlreadyActive

Packages

org.omg.PortableServer.POAPackage

```
java.lang.Object
  └ java.lang.Throwable - - - - - - - - - - - - - - - - - - - - - - - - - - - - - - - java.io.Serializable
      └ java.lang.Exception
1.2 ○       └ org.omg.CORBA.UserException - - - - - - - - - - - - - - - - - - - org.omg.CORBA.portable.IDLEntity
1.4 ●         ├ ServantNotActive
1.4 ●         ├ WrongAdapter
1.4 ●         └ WrongPolicy
```

org.omg.PortableServer.ServantLocatorPackage

```
java.lang.Object
1.4 ●  └ CookieHolder - - - - - - - - - - - - - - - - - - - - - - - - - - - - - - - - - - org.omg.CORBA.portable.Streamable
```

org.omg.PortableServer.portable

```
1.4   Delegate
```

org.omg.SendingContext

```
1.3   RunTime─────────────────────────────── RunTimeOperations, org.omg.CORBA.Object,
                                              org.omg.CORBA.portable.IDLEntityˆ
1.3   RunTimeOperations
```

org.omg.stub.java.rmi

```
java.lang.Object
1.2 ○  └ org.omg.CORBA.portable.ObjectImpl - - - - - - - - - - - - - - - - - org.omg.CORBA.Object
1.3 ○     └ org.omg.CORBA_2_3.portable.ObjectImpl
1.3 ○        └ javax.rmi.CORBA.Stub - - - - - - - - - - - - - - - - - - - - java.io.Serializable
1.3 ●           └ _Remote_Stub - - - - - - - - - - - - - - - - - - - - - - - java.rmi.Remote
```

Class   *Interface*   ──extends   - - -implements   ○ abstract   ● final   ˆ—has superclass   —has subclass   package—see other volume

This package provides the interfaces for the Document Object Model (DOM) Level 2 Core API. This package allows programs to dynamically access and update the content and structure of XML documents.

```
java.lang.Object
  └ java.lang.Throwable - - - - - - - - - - - - - - - - - - - - - - - - - - - - - - - - java.io.Serializable ˎ
      └ java.lang.Exception
          └ java.lang.RuntimeException
              └ DOMException
```

1.4

1.4   Attr ——————————————————————— Node

1.4   CDATASection ——————————————————— Textˆ

1.4   CharacterData ˎ ——————————————————— Node

1.4   Comment ——————————————————————— CharacterDataˆ

1.4   DOMImplementation

1.4   Document ——————————————————————— Node

1.4   DocumentFragment ————————————————

1.4   DocumentType ——————————————————

1.4   Element ————————————————————————

1.4   Entity ——————————————————————————

1.4   EntityReference ————————————————————

1.4   NamedNodeMap

1.4   Node ˎ

ε524. Visiting All the Nodes in a DOM Document

```
// Obtain an DOM document; this method is implemented in
// "ε510. The Quintessential Program to Create a DOM Document from an XML File"
Document doc = parseXmlFile("infilename.xml", true);

visit(doc, 0);

// This method visits all the nodes in a DOM tree
public static void visit(Node node, int level) {
    // Process node

    // If there are any children, visit each one
    NodeList list = node.getChildNodes();
    for (int i=0; i<list.getLength(); i++) {
        // Get child node
        Node childNode = list.item(i);

        // Visit child node
        visit(childNode, level+1);
    }
}
```

ε525. Copying a Subtree of Nodes in a DOM Document

```
// Obtain an element; the following method is implemented in
// "ε510. The Quintessential Program to Create a DOM Document from an XML File"
Document doc = parseXmlFile("infilename.xml", false);
NodeList list = doc.getElementsByTagName("entry");
Element element = (Element)list.item(0);

// Make a copy of the element, including any child nodes
Element dup = (Element)element.cloneNode(true);

// Insert the copy immediately after the cloned element
element.getParentNode().insertBefore(dup, element.getNextSibling());
```

This is the sample input for the example:

```
<root>
    <entry attr="value">
        a<i>b</i>c
    </entry>
</root>
```

This is the resulting XML:

```
<?xml version="1.0" encoding="UTF-8"?>
<root>
    <entry attr="value">
        a<i>b</i>c
    </entry><entry attr="value">
        a<i>b</i>c
    </entry>
```

</root>

ε526. Copying a Subtree of Nodes from One DOM Document to Another

When copying a subtree of nodes from one document to another, cloning the subtree and then inserting it into the other document will result in a "wrong document" exception. The subtree of nodes must be "imported" into the other document using importNode().

```
// Obtain an element in one document; the following method is implemented in
// "ε510. The Quintessential Program to Create a DOM Document from an XML File"
Document doc1 = parseXmlFile("infilename1.xml", false);
NodeList list = doc1.getElementsByTagName("entry");
Element element = (Element)list.item(0);

// Create another document
Document doc2 = parseXmlFile("infilename2.xml", false);

// Make a copy of the element subtree suitable for inserting into doc2
Node dup = doc2.importNode(element, true);

// Insert the copy into doc2
doc2.getDocumentElement().appendChild(dup);
```

Getting Nodes

ε527. Getting a Node Relative to Another Node in a DOM Document

This example demonstrates the various methods for using a node to retrieve related nodes — parent, child, etc.

```
// Get the parent
Node parent = node.getParentNode();

// Get children
NodeList children = node.getChildNodes();

// Get first child; null if no children
Node child = node.getFirstChild();

// Get last child; null if no children
child = node.getLastChild();

// Get next sibling; null if node is last child
Node sibling = node.getNextSibling();

// Get previous sibling; null if node is first child
sibling = node.getPreviousSibling();

// Get first sibling
sibling = node.getParentNode().getFirstChild();

// Get last sibling
sibling = node.getParentNode().getLastChild();
```

ε528. Getting the Notations in a DOM Document

The notations declared in the DTD of an XML document are available in the DocumentType object of a DOM document.

```
// Obtain a document; the following method is implemented in
// "ε510. The Quintessential Program to Create a DOM Document from an XML File"
Document doc = parseXmlFile("infilename.xml", false);

// Get list of notations
```

Packages

389

```
NamedNodeMap notations = doc.getDoctype().getNotations();
for (int i=0; i<notations.getLength(); i++) {
    // Get notation node
    Notation notation = (Notation)notations.item(i);

    // Get details in notation node
    String notationName = notation.getNodeName();
    String notationPublicId = notation.getPublicId();
    String notationSystemId = notation.getSystemId();
}
```

This is the sample input for the example:

```
<?xml version="1.0" encoding="UTF-8"?>
<!DOCTYPE root [
    <!NOTATION not1 PUBLIC "publicId" "systemId1">
    <!NOTATION not2 SYSTEM "systemId2">
    <!NOTATION not3 SYSTEM "http://hostname.com/systemid">
    <!NOTATION not4 SYSTEM "">
]>
<root>
</root>
```

This is the data in the Notation nodes from the above input file. Note that the system ids are converted to absolute URIs.

```
Name, PublicId, SystemId

not1, publicId, file:D:/almanac/1.4/egs/org.w3c.dom/systemId1
not2, null, file:D:/almanac/1.4/egs/org.w3c.dom/systemId2
not3, null, http://hostname.com/systemid
not4, null, file:D:/almanac/1.4/egs/org.w3c.dom/.
```

ε529. Getting the Declared Entities in a DOM Document

The entities declared in the DTD of an XML document are available in the DOM document. Unfortunately, with J2SE 1.4's default parser, only the names, not the values, are available. In order to obtain the values, you must parse the file without expanding entity references and then scan the DOM document for the unexpanded entity references. The unexpanded entity references contain the values.

Note: By default, a parser expands entity references while constructing the DOM tree. See "ε516. Preventing Expansion of Entity References While Parsing an XML File" to prevent expansion. The default parser in J2SE 1.4 expands entity references in attribute values. There is no way to prevent this.

```
// Obtain a document; this method is implemented in
// "ε516. Preventing Expansion of Entity References While Parsing an XML File"
Document doc = parseXmlFileNoExpandER("infilename.xml", true);

// Scan the document for entity references and get their values.
// The values are stored in the map using the entity name as the key.
Map entityValues = new HashMap();
getEntityValues(doc, entityValues);

// Get list of declared entities
NamedNodeMap entities = doc.getDoctype().getEntities();
for (int i=0; i<entities.getLength(); i++) {
    Entity entity = (Entity)entities.item(i);
    String entityName = entity.getNodeName();
    String entityPublicId = entity.getPublicId();
```

```
            String entitySystemId = entity.getSystemId();

            // Get the value of the entity, which is its set of child nodes
            Node entityValue = (Node)entityValues.get(entityName);
    }

    // This method walks the document looking for entity references.
    // When one is found, this method adds the entity reference node
    // to 'map' using the name as the key.
    public static void getEntityValues(Node node, Map map) {
        if (node instanceof EntityReference) {
            map.put(node.getNodeName(), node);
        }

        // Visit the children
        NodeList list = node.getChildNodes();
        for (int i=0; i<list.getLength(); i++) {
            getEntityValues(list.item(i), map);
        }
    }
```

This is the sample input for the example:

```
<?xml version="1.0" encoding="UTF-8"?>
<!DOCTYPE root [
    <!ENTITY entity1 "an internal entity">

    <!-- This is a parameter entity; it will not appear in the DOM document -->
    <!ENTITY % entity2 "a | b">

    <!-- This is an external text entity -->
    <!ENTITY entity3 SYSTEM "External.xml">

    <!-- This is an external parameter entity; it includes DTD from
         another file. It will not appear in the DOM document. However,
         any non-parameter entities declared in the file will be included. -->
    <!ENTITY % entity4 SYSTEM "More.dtd">
    %entity4;

    <!-- entity5 is an unparsed entity; it can only appear as an attribute value -->
    <!ENTITY entity5 SYSTEM "pic.jpg" NDATA NOTA1>
    <!NOTATION NOTA1 SYSTEM "jpgviewer.exe">
    <!ELEMENT elem2 EMPTY>
    <!ATTLIST elem2 attr ENTITY #REQUIRED>
]>
<root a="&entity1;">
    &entity1;
    &entity3;
    &ent1;
    &ent2;
    <elem2 attr="entity5"/>
</root>
```

External.xml:

```
<!-- a file with XML markup -->
<i>external</i> text
```

More.dtd:

```
<!-- a file with more DTD declarations -->
<!ENTITY ent1 "xx">
```

```
<!ENTITY ent2 "yy">
<!ELEMENT elem1 (%entity2;)>
```

The following lists the entities that would appear in the DOM document. Their values are also listed. Notice the parameter entities entity2 and entity4 do not appear in the list.

```
entity1=an internal entity
entity3=<i>external</i> text
ent1=xx
ent2=yy
ent5=null
```

If the input file were parsed with entity expansion, the resulting XML would be:

```
<?xml version="1.0" encoding="UTF-8"?>
<root a="an internal entity">
    an internal entity
    <!– a file with XML markup –>
<i>external</i> text

    xx
    yy
    <elem2 attr="entity5"/>
</root>
```

Note: The J2SE 1.4 DOM writing routines don't appear to write entity references properly. In particular, only text nodes that are descendants of the entity reference are written; all other node types are simply not printed.

ε530. Getting the Value of an Entity Reference in a DOM Document

The value of an entity reference is kept in the child nodes of the EntityReference node. This example demonstrates an entity reference with three children.

Note: By default, a parser expands entity references while constructing the DOM tree. See "ε516. Preventing Expansion of Entity References While Parsing an XML File" to prevent expansion.

```
// Obtain a document; the following method is implemented in
// "ε516. Preventing Expansion of Entity References While Parsing an XML File"
Document doc = parseXmlFileNoExpandER("infilename.xml", false);

// Get the entity reference (see input file)
Element root = doc.getDocumentElement();
EntityReference eref = (EntityReference)root.getFirstChild();

// The first child of the entity reference is comment
Comment comment = (Comment)eref.getFirstChild(); // comment

// The second child of the entity reference is an element
Element elem = (Element)eref.getFirstChild().getNextSibling(); // <i>

// The third child of the entity reference is a text
Text text = (Text)eref.getLastChild(); // text
```

This is the sample input for the example:

```
<?xml version="1.0" encoding="UTF-8"?>
<!DOCTYPE root [
    <!ENTITY entity "<!–comment–><i/>text">
]>
<root>&entity;</root>
```

Class   *Interface* —extends - - -implements ○ abstract ● final ˆ—has superclass ˏ—has subclass package—see other volume

Elements

ε531. Getting a DOM Element by Id

```
// Obtain an XML document; this method is implemented in
// "ε510. The Quintessential Program to Create a DOM Document from an XML File"
Document doc = parseXmlFile("infilename.xml", true);

// Retrieve the element using id
Element element = doc.getElementById("key1");

// Get the element's attribute
String attrValue = element.getAttribute("value"); // value1
```

This is the sample input for the example:

```
<?xml version="1.0" encoding="UTF-8"?>
<!DOCTYPE map [ <!ELEMENT map (entry*) >
                <!ELEMENT entry EMPTY >
                <!ATTLIST entry key ID #REQUIRED
                                value CDATA "default"> ]>
<map>
    <entry key="key1" value="value1"/>
    <entry key="key2" />
</map>
```

ε532. Visiting All the Elements in a DOM Document

```
// Obtain an XML document; this method is implemented in
// "ε510. The Quintessential Program to Create a DOM Document from an XML File"
Document doc = parseXmlFile("infilename.xml", false);

// Get a list of all elements in the document
NodeList list = doc.getElementsByTagName("*");
for (int i=0; i<list.getLength(); i++) {
    // Get element
    Element element = (Element)list.item(i);
}
```

ε533. Changing the Name of an DOM Element

There is no method to change the name of an element. The only way to change the name is to create another element with the new name, copy the attributes, copy the children, and finally replace the node.

```
// Obtain a document; this method is implemented in
// "ε510. The Quintessential Program to Create a DOM Document from an XML File"
Document doc = parseXmlFile("infilename.xml", false);

// Obtain the root element
Element element = doc.getDocumentElement();

// Create an element with the new name
Element element2 = doc.createElement("newname");

// Copy the attributes to the new element
NamedNodeMap attrs = element.getAttributes();
for (int i=0; i<attrs.getLength(); i++) {
    Attr attr2 = (Attr)doc.importNode(attrs.item(i), true);
    element2.getAttributes().setNamedItem(attr2);
}

// Move all the children
while (element.hasChildNodes()) {
```

Packages

393

```
            element2.appendChild(element.getFirstChild());
    }

    // Replace the old node with the new node
    element.getParentNode().replaceChild(element2, element);
```

Element Attributes

ε534. Getting and Setting an Attribute in a DOM Element

```
    // Obtain an XML document; this method is implemented in
    // "ε510. The Quintessential Program to Create a DOM Document from an XML File"
    Document doc = parseXmlFile("infilename.xml", false);

    // Obtain an element
    Element element = doc.getElementById("key1");

    // Determine the presence of an attribute
    boolean has = element.hasAttribute("value"); // true

    // Get an attribute value; returns null if not present
    String attrValue = element.getAttribute("value"); // value1

    // Change the value of an attribute
    element.setAttribute("value", "newValue1");

    // If an attribute is not specified in the XML but has a
    // default value, the attribute is automatically created
    element = doc.getElementById("key2");
    has = element.hasAttribute("value"); // true
    attrValue = element.getAttribute("value"); // value2

    // If the attribute value contains special characters,
    // they are automatically converted to entities when the
    // document in dumped
    element.setAttribute("value", "a<\"&>z");
```

This is the sample input for the example:

```
    <?xml version="1.0" encoding="UTF-8"?>
    <!DOCTYPE map [ <!ELEMENT map (entry*) >
                    <!ELEMENT entry EMPTY >
                    <!ATTLIST entry key ID #REQUIRED
                                    value CDATA "default"> ]>
    <map>
        <entry key="key1" value="value1"/>
        <entry key="key2" />
    </map>
```

The resulting XML from running the example is:

```
    <?xml version="1.0" encoding="UTF-8"?>
    <map>
        <entry key="key1" value="newValue1"/>
        <entry key="key2" value="a&lt;&quot;'&amp;&gt;z"/>
    </map>
```

Class *Interface* —extends - - -implements ○ abstract ● final ʌ—has superclass ⌄—has subclass package—see other volume

ε535. Adding and Removing an Attribute in a DOM Element

If any special characters appear in the value of an attribute (e.g., <>"), they are automatically converted to entities by the XML writers.

```
// Obtain an element; this method is implemented in
// "ε510. The Quintessential Program to Create a DOM Document from an XML File"
Document doc = parseXmlFile("infilename.xml", true);
Element element = doc.getElementById("key1");

// Add an attribute
element.setAttribute("newAttrName", "attrValue");

// Change the value of an attribute.
// Special characters are automatically converted to entities by the XML writer.
element.setAttribute("newAttrName", "<>&\"");

// Remove an attribute
element.removeAttribute("value");

// If the attribute has a default value, the attribute
// cannot be removed
boolean has = element.hasAttribute("value"); // true

// The effect of removing an attribute with a default value
// is to set the attribute to the default value
String attrValue = element.getAttribute("value"); // default
```

This is the sample input for the example:

```
<?xml version="1.0" encoding="UTF-8"?>
<!DOCTYPE map [ <!ELEMENT map (entry*) >
                <!ELEMENT entry EMPTY >
                <!ATTLIST entry key ID #REQUIRED
                                value CDATA "default"> ]>
<map>
    <entry key="key1" value="value1"/>
    <entry key="key2" />
</map>
```

The resulting XML from running the example is:

```
<?xml version="1.0" encoding="UTF-8"?>
<map>
    <entry key="key1" newAttrName="&lt;&gt;&amp;&quot;" value="default"/>
    <entry key="key2" value="default"/>
</map>
```

ε536. Listing All the Attributes of a DOM Element

```
// Get all the attributes of an element in a map
NamedNodeMap attrs = element.getAttributes();

// Get number of attributes in the element
int numAttrs = attrs.getLength();

// Process each attribute
for (int i=0; i<numAttrs; i++) {
    Attr attr = (Attr)attrs.item(i);

    // Get attribute name and value
    String attrName = attr.getNodeName();
    String attrValue = attr.getNodeValue();
}
```

Packages

ε537. Removing All the Attributes in a DOM Element

The tricky part of removing all the attributes in an XML element is to realize that attributes with a default value cannot be removed. Therefore, the following code will never terminate if the element has an attribute with a default value:

```
// Very bad code
NamedNodeMap attrs = element.getAttributes();
while (attrs.getLength() > 0) {
    attrs.removeNamedItem(attrs.item(0).getNodeName());
}
```

This example copies the names of all the attributes and then uses that list to remove the

```
// Remove all the attributes of an element
NamedNodeMap attrs = element.getAttributes();
String[] names = new String[attrs.getLength()];
for (int i=0; i<names.length; i++) {
    names[i] = attrs.item(i).getNodeName();
}
for (int i=0; i<names.length; i++) {
    attrs.removeNamedItem(names[i]);
}
```

ε538. Determining If an Attribute Was Supplied in a DOM Element

In the case of an attribute with a default value, it is possible to determine if the attribute was explicitly supplied in the original XML document or automatically created when it was parsed.

Note: If the attribute value is changed in the DOM document, the attributed is considered to have been supplied, even if the new value is the same as the default value.

```
// Get Attr node
Attr attr = (Attr)element.getAttributeNode("attrName");
boolean wasSpecified = attr != null && attr.getSpecified();
```

Adding and Removing Nodes

ε539. Adding a Node to a DOM Document

This example demonstrates how to insert a node into a DOM relative to another node. In particular, a text node is inserted around an element node.

```
// Create a new DOM document; this method is implemented in
// "ε511. Creating an Empty DOM Document"
Document doc = createDomDocument();

// Insert the root element node
Element element = doc.createElement("root");
doc.appendChild(element);

// Insert a comment in front of the element node
Comment comment = doc.createComment("a comment");
doc.insertBefore(comment, element);

// Add a text node to the element
element.appendChild(doc.createTextNode("D"));

// Add a text node to the beginning of the element
element.insertBefore(doc.createTextNode("A"), element.getFirstChild());
```

Class *Interface* —extends - - -implements ○ abstract ● final ^—has superclass ⌐—has subclass package—see other volume

```
// Add a text node before the last child of the element
element.insertBefore(doc.createTextNode("C"), element.getLastChild());

// Add another element after the first child of the root element
Element element2 = doc.createElement("item");
element.insertBefore(element2, element.getFirstChild().getNextSibling());

// Add a text node in front of the new item element
element2.getParentNode().insertBefore(doc.createTextNode("B"), element2);
```

This is the resulting XML:

```
<?xml version="1.0" encoding="UTF-8"?>
<!–a comment–><root>AB<item/>CD</root>
```

ε540. Adding a CDATA Section to a DOM Document

If ']]>' appears in the CDATA section's text, the default XML writers in J2SE 1.4 automatically break the CDATA section into two CDATA sections; ']]' will appear at the end of the first section while '>' will appear at the beginning of the second section.

```
// Obtain an XML document; this method is implemented in
// "ε510. The Quintessential Program to Create a DOM Document from an XML File"
Document doc = parseXmlFile("infilename.xml", false);

// Add a CDATA section to the root element
Element element = doc.getDocumentElement();
CDATASection cdata = doc.createCDATASection("data");
element.appendChild(cdata);

// If "]]>" appears in the text, two CDATA sections will be written out
cdata = doc.createCDATASection("more]]>data");
element.appendChild(cdata);
```

This is the sample input for the example:

```
<?xml version="1.0" encoding="UTF-8"?>
<map>
    <entry key="key1" value="value1" />
    <entry key="key2" />
</map>
```

The resulting XML from running the example is:

```
<?xml version="1.0" encoding="UTF-8"?>
<map>
    <entry key="key1" value="value1"/>
    <entry key="key2"/>
<![CDATA[data]]><![CDATA[more]]]]><![CDATA[>data]]></map>
```

ε541. Adding a Comment to a DOM Document

When creating a comment node, the string '–' must never appear in the comment text. The default XML writers in J2SE 1.4 will output the comment text with the '–' and therefore generate invalid XML.

```
// Obtain an XML document; this method is implemented in
// "ε510. The Quintessential Program to Create a DOM Document from an XML File"
Document doc = parseXmlFile("infilename.xml", false);

// Add a comment at the beginning of the document
Element element = doc.getDocumentElement();
Comment comment = doc.createComment("A Document Comment");
element.getParentNode().insertBefore(comment, element);
```

```
// Find all elements with the name "entry" and append a comment
NodeList list = doc.getElementsByTagName("entry");
for (int i=0; i<list.getLength(); i++) {
    element = (Element)list.item(i);
    comment = doc.createComment("index="+i);

    // Add the comment after this element
    element.getParentNode().insertBefore(comment, element.getNextSibling());
}

// "−" must never appear in the text used to create the comment
comment = doc.createComment("invalid − comment");
boolean validComment = comment.getNodeValue().indexOf("−") < 0;
```

This is the sample input for the example:

```
<?xml version="1.0" encoding="UTF-8"?>
<map>
    <entry key="key1" value="value1" />
    <entry key="key2" />
</map>
```

The resulting XML from running the example is:

```
<?xml version="1.0" encoding="UTF-8"?>
<!−A Document Comment−><map>
    <entry key="key1" value="value1"/><!−index=0−>
    <entry key="key2"/><!−index=1−>
</map>
```

ε542. Adding a Processing Instruction to a DOM Document

```
// Obtain an XML document; this method is implemented in
// "ε510. The Quintessential Program to Create a DOM Document from an XML File"
Document doc = parseXmlFile("infilename.xml", false);

// Add a PI at the beginning of the document
Element element = doc.getDocumentElement();
ProcessingInstruction pi = doc.createProcessingInstruction("target", "instruction");
element.getParentNode().insertBefore(pi, element);

// Find all elements with the name "entry" and add a child PI
NodeList list = doc.getElementsByTagName("entry");
for (int i=0; i<list.getLength(); i++) {
    element = (Element)list.item(i);
    pi = doc.createProcessingInstruction("target", "instruction="+i);

    // Add the comment to this element
    element.appendChild(pi);
}
```

This is the sample input for the example:

```
<?xml version="1.0" encoding="UTF-8"?>
<map>
    <entry key="key1" value="value1" />
    <entry key="key2" />
</map>
```

The resulting XML from running the example is:

```
<?xml version="1.0" encoding="UTF-8"?>
<?target instruction?>
<map>
    <entry key="key1" value="value1"><?target instruction=0?></entry>
    <entry key="key2"><?target instruction=1?></entry>
</map>
```

ε543. Adding a Text Node to a DOM Document

If any special characters appear in the text of a text node (e.g., <>"), they are automatically converted to entities by the XML writers.

```
// Obtain an XML document; this method is implemented in
// "ε510. The Quintessential Program to Create a DOM Document from an XML File"
Document doc = parseXmlFile("infilename.xml", false);

// Add a CDATA section to the root element
Element element = doc.getDocumentElement();
Text text = doc.createTextNode("data\n");
element.appendChild(text);

// Special characters are automatically converted to entities by the XML writers
text = doc.createTextNode("<>&\"");
element.appendChild(text);
```

This is the sample input for the example:

```
<?xml version="1.0" encoding="UTF-8"?>
<map>
    <entry key="key1" value="value1" />
    <entry key="key2" />
</map>
```

The resulting XML from running the example is:

```
<?xml version="1.0" encoding="UTF-8"?>
<map>
    <entry key="key1" value="value1"/>
    <entry key="key2"/>
data
&lt;&gt;&amp;"'</map>
```

ε544. Removing a Node from a DOM Document

This example demonstrates how to remove a single node and all nodes of a particular type.

```
// Obtain an XML document; this method is implemented in
// "ε510. The Quintessential Program to Create a DOM Document from an XML File"
Document doc = parseXmlFile("infilename.xml", false);

// Obtain a node
Element element = (Element)doc.getElementsByTagName("junk").item(0);

// Remove the node
element.getParentNode().removeChild(element);

// Remove all <junk> elements
removeAll(doc, Node.ELEMENT_NODE, "junk");

// Remove all comment nodes
removeAll(doc, Node.COMMENT_NODE, null);

// Normalize the DOM tree to combine all adjacent text nodes
doc.normalize();
```

```
    // This method walks the document and removes all nodes
    // of the specified type and specified name.
    // If name is null, then the node is removed if the type matches.
    public static void removeAll(Node node, short nodeType, String name) {
        if (node.getNodeType() == nodeType &&
                (name == null || node.getNodeName().equals(name))) {
            node.getParentNode().removeChild(node);
        } else {
            // Visit the children
            NodeList list = node.getChildNodes();
            for (int i=0; i<list.getLength(); i++) {
                removeAll(list.item(i), nodeType, name);
            }
        }
    }
```

This is the sample input for the example:

```
    <?xml version="1.0" encoding="UTF-8"?>
    <root>
        <!--comment1-->
        <elem>a</elem>
        <junk>b</junk>
        <elem>
            <!--comment2-->
            <junk>c<junk>d</junk></junk>
        </elem>
        <!--comment3-->
        <junk>e</junk>
    </root>
```

This is the resulting XML:

```
    <?xml version="1.0" encoding="UTF-8"?>
    <root>

        <elem>a</elem>

        <elem>

        </elem>

    </root>
```

Text Nodes

ε545. Editing Text in a CDATA, Comment, and Text Node of a DOM Document

This example demonstrates all the available methods to get, set and modify data in a CDATA, comment, or text node.

```
    // Obtain a CDATA, comment, and text node
    Document doc = createDomDocument();
    CDATASection cdataNode = doc.createCDATASection("");
    Comment commentNode = doc.createComment("");
    Text textNode = doc.createTextNode("");
```

Class *Interface* —extends - - -implements ○ abstract ● final ˆ—has superclass ˍ—has subclass package—see other volume

```
// All three types of nodes implement the CharacterData interface
CharacterData cdata = cdataNode;
cdata = commentNode;
cdata = textNode;

// Set the value of the node
cdata.setData("some data");

// Get the length of the text
int len = cdata.getLength(); // 9

// Get part of the text
int offset = 5;
len = 4;
String s = cdata.substringData(offset, len); // data

// Insert text
offset = 5;
cdata.insertData(offset, "more "); // some more data

// Append text
cdata.appendData(" please"); // some more data please

// Delete text
offset = 0;
len = 5;
cdata.deleteData(offset, len); // more data please

// Replace text
String replacement = "now";
offset = 10;
len = 6;
cdata.replaceData(offset, len, replacement);// more data please
```

ε546. Splitting a Text Node in a DOM Document

This example wraps a substring in an element. This requires breaking a text node in two places and then replacing the middle text node with an element node.

```
// Obtain a document; this method is implemented in
// "ε510. The Quintessential Program to Create a DOM Document from an XML File"
Document doc = parseXmlFile("infilename.xml", false);

// Obtain the root element
Element element = doc.getDocumentElement();

// Get the text node
Text text1 = (Text)element.getFirstChild();
String string = text1.getData();

// Split the node at the beginning of the word
String word = "some";
Text text2 = text1.splitText(string.indexOf(word));

// Split the new text node at the end of the word
Text text3 = text2.splitText(word.length());

// Create a new element and move the middle text node to it
Element newElement = doc.createElement("b");
newElement.appendChild(text2);

// Insert the new element where the middle node used to be
element.insertBefore(newElement, text3);
```

Packages

This is the sample input for the example:

```
<?xml version="1.0" encoding="UTF-8"?>
<root>
    Here is some text
</root>
```

This is the resulting XML:

```
<?xml version="1.0" encoding="UTF-8"?>
<root>
    Here is <b>some</b> text
</root>
```

ε547. Merging Text Nodes in a DOM Document

This example removes an element node and inserts its children nodes into the element node's parent. This can cause two text nodes to be adjacent. Normalizing the document merges adjacent text nodes into one and removes empty text nodes.

```
// Obtain a document; this method is implemented in
// "ε510. The Quintessential Program to Create a DOM Document from an XML File"
Document doc = parseXmlFile("infilename.xml", false);

// Obtain the root element to remove
Element element = (Element)doc.getElementsByTagName("b").item(0);

// Get the parent of the element
Node parent = element.getParentNode();

// Move all children of the element in front of the element
while (element.hasChildNodes()) {
    parent.insertBefore(element.getFirstChild(), element);
}
// Remove the element
parent.removeChild(element);

// Merge all text nodes under the parent
parent.normalize();
```

This is the sample input for the example:

```
<?xml version="1.0" encoding="UTF-8"?>
<root>
    Here is <b>some</b> text
</root>
```

This is the resulting XML:

```
<?xml version="1.0" encoding="UTF-8"?>
<root>
    Here is some text
</root>
```

org.xml.sax

This package provides the classes and interfaces for the Simple API for XML (SAX), a standard interface for event-based XML parsing.

Class *Interface* —extends - - -implements ○ abstract ● final ^—has superclass ⌐—has subclass package—see other volume

```
java.lang.Object
D      ├ HandlerBase - - - - - - - - - - - - - - - - - - - - - - - - - DTDHandler, DocumentHandler, EntityResolver,
                                                                         ErrorHandler
1.4    ├ InputSource
       └ java.lang.Throwable - - - - - - - - - - - - - - - - - - - - - - java.io.Serializable
            └ java.lang.Exception
1.4           └ SAXException
1.4              ├ SAXNotRecognizedException
1.4              ├ SAXNotSupportedException
1.4              └ SAXParseException

D      AttributeList
1.4    Attributes
1.4    ContentHandler
1.4    DTDHandler
D      DocumentHandler
1.4    EntityResolver
1.4    ErrorHandler
1.4    Locator
D      Parser
1.4    XMLFilter ─────────────────────────────── XMLReader
1.4    XMLReader
```

Packages

ε548. Intercepting All Accesses to External Entities During XML SAX Parsing

This capability is useful in situations where the public or system id in an XML file do not refer to actual resources and must be redirected. An EntityResolver object must be installed on the parser in order to intercept the accesses. If a mapping is made, the entity resolver must return an InputSource object to the resource.

```
try {
    // Create an XML parser
    DocumentBuilder builder = DocumentBuilderFactory.newInstance().newDocumentBuilder();

    // Install the entity resolver
    builder.setEntityResolver(new MyResolver());

    // Parse the XML file
```

```
            Document doc = builder.parse(new File("infilename.xml"));
        } catch (SAXException e) {
            // A parsing error occurred; the xml input is not valid
        } catch (ParserConfigurationException e) {
        } catch (IOException e) {
        }

        public class MyResolver implements EntityResolver {
            // This method is called whenever an external entity is accessed
            // for the first time.
            public InputSource resolveEntity (String publicId, String systemId) {
                try {
                    // Wrap the systemId in a URI object to make it convenient
                    // to extract the components of the systemId
                    URI uri = new URI(systemId);

                    // Check if external source is a file
                    if ("file".equals(uri.getScheme())) {
                        String filename = uri.getSchemeSpecificPart();
                        return new InputSource(new FileReader(filename));
                    }
                } catch (URISyntaxException e) {
                } catch (IOException e) {
                }

                // Returning null causes the caller to try accessing the systemid
                return null;
            }
        }
```

This is the sample input for the example:

```
<?xml version="1.0" encoding="UTF-8"?>
<!DOCTYPE root SYSTEM "System.dtd" [
    <!ENTITY entity1 SYSTEM "External.xml">
    <!ENTITY entity2 SYSTEM "http://hostname.com/my.dtd">
    <!ENTITY % entity3 SYSTEM "More.dtd">
    %entity3;
]>
<root>
    &entity1;
    &entity2;
</root>
```

The resulting system ids passed into MyResolve.resolveEntity() are:

```
file:d:/almanac/1.4/egs/org.xml.sax/More.dtd
file:d:/almanac/1.4/egs/org.xml.sax/Systemid.dtd
file:d:/almanac/1.4/egs/org.xml.sax/External.dtd
http://hostname.com/my.dtd
```

ε549. Getting the Attributes of an Element During XML SAX Parsing

```
// Create a handler for SAX events
DefaultHandler handler = new MyHandler();

// Parse an XML file using SAX;
// "ε517. The Quintessential Program to Parse an XML File Using SAX"
parseXmlFile("infilename.xml", handler, true);
```

```
// This class listens for startElement SAX events
static class MyHandler extends DefaultHandler {
    // This method is called when an element is encountered
    public void startElement(String namespaceURI, String localName,
                             String qName, Attributes atts) {
        // Get the number of attribute
        int length = atts.getLength();

        // Process each attribute
        for (int i=0; i<length; i++) {
            // Get names and values for each attribute
            String name = atts.getQName(i);
            String value = atts.getValue(i);

            // The following methods are valid only if the parser is namespace-aware

            // The uri of the attribute's namespace
            String nsUri = atts.getURI(i);

            // This is the name without the prefix
            String lName = atts.getLocalName(i);
        }
    }
}
```

ε550. Determining the Parsing Location of an XML SAX Parser

To get the current URI and location of a SAX parser during parsing, you need to obtain a Locator object. This object can be obtained by installing a ContentHandler and overriding the setDocumentLocator() method. The SAX parser will call this method and deliver the Locator object that you can use anytime it delivers an event (i.e. invokes a callback method in a handler). This method will be called before any other ContentHandler method.

Note: Not all SAX parser support a Locator. If it doesn't, the setDocumentLocator() method will not be called.

This example captures the Locator object and uses it whenever it gets a startElement event.

```
// Create a handler for SAX events
DefaultHandler handler = new MyHandler();

// Parse an XML file using SAX;
// "ε517. The Quintessential Program to Parse an XML File Using SAX"
parseXmlFile("infilename.xml", handler, false);

// This class listens for startElement SAX events
static class MyHandler extends DefaultHandler {
    Locator locator;
    public void setDocumentLocator(Locator locator) {
        this.locator = locator;
    }
    // This method is called when an element is encountered
    public void startElement(String namespaceURI, String localName,
                             String qName, Attributes atts) {
        if (locator != null) {
            int col = locator.getColumnNumber();
            int line = locator.getLineNumber();
            String publicId = locator.getPublicId();
            String systemId = locator.getSystemId();
        }
    }
}
```

Packages

org.xml.sax.ext

This package contains extension classes for the Simple API for XML (SAX), a standard interface for event-based XML parsing.

org.xml.sax.helpers

This package provides helper classes for the Simple API for XML (SAX), a standard interface for event-based XML parsing.

```
      java.lang.Object
 D      ├ AttributeListImpl - - - - - - - - - - - - - - - - - - - - - - - - - - - - - org.xml.sax.AttributeList
 1.4    ├ AttributesImpl - - - - - - - - - - - - - - - - - - - - - - - - - - - - - - org.xml.sax.Attributes
 1.4    ├ DefaultHandler - - - - - - - - - - - - - - - - - - - - - - - - - - - - - - org.xml.sax.ContentHandler,
                                                            org.xml.sax.DTDHandler,
                                                            org.xml.sax.EntityResolver,
                                                            org.xml.sax.ErrorHandler
 1.4    ├ LocatorImpl - - - - - - - - - - - - - - - - - - - - - - - - - - - - - - - org.xml.sax.Locator
 1.4    ├ NamespaceSupport
 1.4    ├ ParserAdapter - - - - - - - - - - - - - - - - - - - - - - - - - - - - - - org.xml.sax.DocumentHandler,
                                                            org.xml.sax.XMLReader
 D      ├ ParserFactory
 1.4    ├ XMLFilterImpl - - - - - - - - - - - - - - - - - - - - - - - - - - - - - - org.xml.sax.ContentHandler,
                                                            org.xml.sax.DTDHandler,
                                                            org.xml.sax.EntityResolver,
                                                            org.xml.sax.ErrorHandler,
                                                            org.xml.sax.XMLFilter^
 1.4    ├ XMLReaderAdapter - - - - - - - - - - - - - - - - - - - - - - - - - - - - org.xml.sax.ContentHandler, org.xml.sax.Parser
 1.4 ●  └ XMLReaderFactory
```

Class   *Interface*   —extends   - - -implements   ○ abstract   ● final   ^—has superclass   —has subclass   package —see other volume

Part 2
CLASSES

This part contains information about each class in every package. For easy lookup, the classes are arranged alphabetically by class name without regard to package. The following legend describes the layout of the class information.

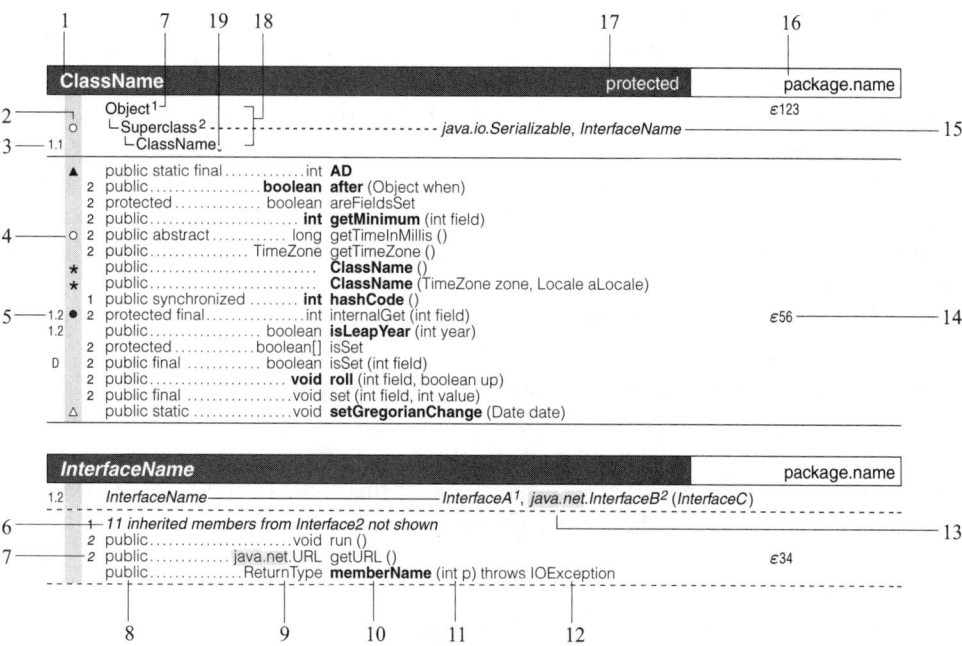

1. The class or interface name (interface names are italicized)
2. A symbolic representation of a class's modifier set:
   - ○ An abstract class
   - ● A final class
3. The version of Java in which this class or interface was introduced
   You need the specified version of Java or higher in order to use the class. If the field is blank, the class or interface was introduced in Java 1.0.
4. A symbolic representation of a member's modifier set, which is used to quickly locate members by their modifiers:

407

○　An abstract member

●　A final member

△　A static member

▲　A static final member

*　A constructor

5. The version of Java in which this member was introduced

You need the specified version of Java or higher in order to use the member. If the field is blank, the version is the same as that of the current class or interface. If the field contains a D, the member has been deprecated.

6. The number and source of inherited members that are not shown in the member list

7. The tree-reference

The number in this field corresponds to one of the classes or interfaces in the class tree. If this member has been inherited, the tree-reference refers to the class from which the member was inherited. If this member is an override, the tree-reference refers to the class that contains the overridden member. If this is a declared method and the method is required because of an interface, the tree-reference shows which interface.

8. The list of modifiers of a member

9. The return type of a member

A return type in bold type signifies that the member overrides a member from a superclass.

10. The member name

A member name in bold type signifies that the member has been declared in the current class or interface. A non-bold member name signifies that the member was inherited from a superclass. Inherited members from `java.lang.Object` and `java.lang.Throwable` are not shown (in order to save space).

11. The list of parameters of a member

12. The declared exceptions of a member

13. The shaded background behind a package name indicates that the details of this class is covered in another volume

14. A list of one or more example numbers

The example number identifies an example that uses this method, or an inherited version of it. The examples are located in the "Packages" part of this book.

15.

16. Package name

The name of the package that contains this class or interface

17. Class modifiers

Currently, only the modifier "protected" can appear in this space.

18. The class tree

If the current entity is a class, the class tree shows the superclasses of the current class. Also shown are the interfaces that each class implements, if any. If the current entity is an interface, the class tree shows all of the interfaces from which the current interface extends, if any.

A solid line means "extends" and a dotted line means "implements."

19. Has subclass

When on a class, the indicator signifies that the class has one or more subclasses. When on an interface, the indicator signifies that the interface is extended by one or more interfaces.

Note: For types appearing in a method's or constructor's signature, unless the type is from the same package or from the `java.lang` package, it is qualified with its package name.

Legend

A legend appears on all left-hand pages to remind you of the meanings of the symbols. Here are the symbols shown in the legend:

Class	Class names are not italicized
Interface	Interface names are italicized
○	An abstract member or class
●	A final member
⬠	A static member
▲	A static final member
*	A constructor
----	Implements
	Extends
x x	Inherited
x **x**	Declared
x x	Overridden
ε N	A list of examples that use this class or member
⌄	Has one or more subclasses

The x x's represent the pattern of light and bold type for the return type and member name. Spelled out, this pattern is:

return type	member name	Inherited
return type	**member name**	Declared
return type	**member name**	Overridden

_BindingIteratorImplBase	org.omg.CosNaming

```
        Object
1.2 ○    └org.omg.CORBA.portable.ObjectImpl¹ ----- org.omg.CORBA.Object ˎ
D
1.2 ○       └org.omg.CORBA.DynamicImplementation²
              └_BindingIteratorImplBase ------------ BindingIterator (BindingIteratorOperations,
                                                      org.omg.CORBA.Object, org.omg.CORBA.portable.IDLEntity
                                                      (java.io.Serializable))
```

	1	*25 inherited members from org.omg.CORBA.portable.ObjectImpl not shown*
✳		public........................... **_BindingIteratorImplBase** ()
	2	public................. **String[] _ids** ()
	2	public..................... **void invoke** (org.omg.CORBA.ServerRequest r)

_BindingIteratorStub	org.omg.CosNaming

```
        Object
1.2 ○    └org.omg.CORBA.portable.ObjectImpl¹ ------ org.omg.CORBA.Object ˎ
1.2       └_BindingIteratorStub ------------------ BindingIterator (BindingIteratorOperations²,
                                                    org.omg.CORBA.Object, org.omg.CORBA.portable.IDLEntity
                                                    (java.io.Serializable))
```

	1	*25 inherited members from org.omg.CORBA.portable.ObjectImpl not shown*
1.4 ✳		public........................... **_BindingIteratorStub** ()
	1	public................. **String[] _ids** ()
	2	public....................void **destroy** ()
	2	public................. boolean **next_n** (int how_many, BindingListHolder bl)
	2	public................. boolean **next_one** (BindingHolder b)

_DynAnyFactoryStub	org.omg.DynamicAny

```
        Object
1.2 ○    └org.omg.CORBA.portable.ObjectImpl¹ ------ org.omg.CORBA.Object ˎ
1.4       └_DynAnyFactoryStub ----------------- DynAnyFactory (DynAnyFactoryOperations²,
                                                 org.omg.CORBA.Object, org.omg.CORBA.portable.IDLEntity
                                                 (java.io.Serializable))
```

	1	*25 inherited members from org.omg.CORBA.portable.ObjectImpl not shown*
✳		public........................... **_DynAnyFactoryStub** ()
	1	public................. **String[] _ids** ()
▲		public static final .... Class **_opsClass**
	2	public..................*DynAny* **create_dyn_any** (org.omg.CORBA.Any value) throws org.omg.DynamicAny.DynAnyFactoryPackage.InconsistentTypeCode
	2	public..................*DynAny* **create_dyn_any_from_type_code** (org.omg.CORBA.TypeCode type) throws org.omg.DynamicAny.DynAnyFactoryPackage.InconsistentTypeCode

_DynAnyStub	org.omg.DynamicAny

```
        Object
1.2 ○    └org.omg.CORBA.portable.ObjectImpl¹ ------ org.omg.CORBA.Object ˎ
1.4       └_DynAnyStub ----------------------- DynAny ˎ (DynAnyOperations², org.omg.CORBA.Object,
                                               org.omg.CORBA.portable.IDLEntity (java.io.Serializable))
```

	1	*25 inherited members from org.omg.CORBA.portable.ObjectImpl not shown*
✳		public........................... **_DynAnyStub** ()
	1	public................. **String[] _ids** ()
▲		public static final .... Class **_opsClass**
	2	public.....................void **assign** (*DynAny* dyn_any) throws org.omg.DynamicAny.DynAnyPackage ↵ .TypeMismatch
	2	public.....................int **component_count** ()
	2	public..................*DynAny* **copy** ()
	2	public..................*DynAny* **current_component** () throws org.omg.DynamicAny.DynAnyPackage ↵ .TypeMismatch
	2	public.....................void **destroy** ()
	2	public................. boolean **equal** (*DynAny* dyn_any)

Class *Interface* —extends - - -implements ○ abstract ● final △ static ▲ static final ✳ constructor x x—inherited x **x**—declared **x x**—overridden
ε*n*—examples of usage ˎ—has subclass package—see other volume

2 public . . . . void **from_any** (org.omg.CORBA.Any value) throws org↵
.omg.DynamicAny.DynAnyPackage.TypeMismatch,
org.omg.DynamicAny.DynAnyPackage.InvalidValue

2 public . . . . org.omg.CORBA.Any **get_any** () throws org.omg.DynamicAny.DynAnyPackage.TypeMismatch,
org.omg.DynamicAny.DynAnyPackage.InvalidValue

2 public . . . . boolean **get_boolean** () throws org.omg.DynamicAny.DynAnyPackage.TypeMismatch,
org.omg.DynamicAny.DynAnyPackage.InvalidValue

2 public . . . . char **get_char** () throws org.omg.DynamicAny.DynAnyPackage.TypeMismatch,
org.omg.DynamicAny.DynAnyPackage.InvalidValue

2 public . . . . double **get_double** () throws org.omg.DynamicAny.DynAnyPackage.TypeMismatch,
org.omg.DynamicAny.DynAnyPackage.InvalidValue

2 public . . . . *DynAny* **get_dyn_any** () throws org.omg.DynamicAny.DynAnyPackage.TypeMismatch,
org.omg.DynamicAny.DynAnyPackage.InvalidValue

2 public . . . . float **get_float** () throws org.omg.DynamicAny.DynAnyPackage.TypeMismatch,
org.omg.DynamicAny.DynAnyPackage.InvalidValue

2 public . . . . int **get_long** () throws org.omg.DynamicAny.DynAnyPackage.TypeMismatch,
org.omg.DynamicAny.DynAnyPackage.InvalidValue

2 public . . . . long **get_longlong** () throws org.omg.DynamicAny.DynAnyPackage.TypeMismatch,
org.omg.DynamicAny.DynAnyPackage.InvalidValue

2 public . . . . byte **get_octet** () throws org.omg.DynamicAny.DynAnyPackage.TypeMismatch,
org.omg.DynamicAny.DynAnyPackage.InvalidValue

2 public *org.omg.CORBA.Object* **get_reference** () throws org.omg.DynamicAny.DynAnyPackage.TypeMismatch,
org.omg.DynamicAny.DynAnyPackage.InvalidValue

2 public . . . . short **get_short** () throws org.omg.DynamicAny.DynAnyPackage.TypeMismatch,
org.omg.DynamicAny.DynAnyPackage.InvalidValue

2 public . . . . String **get_string** () throws org.omg.DynamicAny.DynAnyPackage.TypeMismatch,
org.omg.DynamicAny.DynAnyPackage.InvalidValue

2 public . . . . **get_typecode** () throws org.omg.DynamicAny.DynAnyPackage.TypeMismatch,
. org.omg.CORBA.TypeCode   org.omg.DynamicAny.DynAnyPackage.InvalidValue

2 public . . . . int **get_ulong** () throws org.omg.DynamicAny.DynAnyPackage.TypeMismatch,
org.omg.DynamicAny.DynAnyPackage.InvalidValue

2 public . . . . long **get_ulonglong** () throws org.omg.DynamicAny.DynAnyPackage.TypeMismatch,
org.omg.DynamicAny.DynAnyPackage.InvalidValue

2 public . . . . short **get_ushort** () throws org.omg.DynamicAny.DynAnyPackage.TypeMismatch,
org.omg.DynamicAny.DynAnyPackage.InvalidValue

2 public . . . . *java.io.Serializable* **get_val** () throws org.omg.DynamicAny.DynAnyPackage.TypeMismatch,
org.omg.DynamicAny.DynAnyPackage.InvalidValue

2 public . . . . char **get_wchar** () throws org.omg.DynamicAny.DynAnyPackage.TypeMismatch,
org.omg.DynamicAny.DynAnyPackage.InvalidValue

2 public . . . . String **get_wstring** () throws org.omg.DynamicAny.DynAnyPackage.TypeMismatch,
org.omg.DynamicAny.DynAnyPackage.InvalidValue

2 public . . . . void **insert_any** (org.omg.CORBA.Any value) throws org↵
.omg.DynamicAny.DynAnyPackage.TypeMismatch,
org.omg.DynamicAny.DynAnyPackage.InvalidValue

2 public . . . . void **insert_boolean** (boolean value) throws org.omg.DynamicAny.DynAnyPackage↵
.TypeMismatch, org.omg.DynamicAny.DynAnyPackage.InvalidValue

2 public . . . . void **insert_char** (char value) throws org.omg.DynamicAny.DynAnyPackage↵
.TypeMismatch, org.omg.DynamicAny.DynAnyPackage.InvalidValue

2 public . . . . void **insert_double** (double value) throws org.omg.DynamicAny.DynAnyPackage↵
.TypeMismatch, org.omg.DynamicAny.DynAnyPackage.InvalidValue

2 public . . . . void **insert_dyn_any** (*DynAny* value) throws org.omg.DynamicAny.DynAnyPackage↵
.TypeMismatch, org.omg.DynamicAny.DynAnyPackage.InvalidValue

2 public . . . . void **insert_float** (float value) throws org.omg.DynamicAny.DynAnyPackage↵
.TypeMismatch, org.omg.DynamicAny.DynAnyPackage.InvalidValue

2 public . . . . void **insert_long** (int value) throws org.omg.DynamicAny.DynAnyPackage↵
.TypeMismatch, org.omg.DynamicAny.DynAnyPackage.InvalidValue

2 public . . . . void **insert_longlong** (long value) throws org.omg.DynamicAny.DynAnyPackage↵
.TypeMismatch, org.omg.DynamicAny.DynAnyPackage.InvalidValue

2 public . . . . void **insert_octet** (byte value) throws org.omg.DynamicAny.DynAnyPackage↵
.TypeMismatch, org.omg.DynamicAny.DynAnyPackage.InvalidValue

2 public . . . . void **insert_reference** (*org.omg.CORBA.Object* value) throws
org.omg.DynamicAny.DynAnyPackage.TypeMismatch,
org.omg.DynamicAny.DynAnyPackage.InvalidValue

2 public . . . . void **insert_short** (short value) throws org.omg.DynamicAny.DynAnyPackage↵
.TypeMismatch, org.omg.DynamicAny.DynAnyPackage.InvalidValue

2 public . . . . void **insert_string** (String value) throws org.omg.DynamicAny.DynAnyPackage↵
.TypeMismatch, org.omg.DynamicAny.DynAnyPackage.InvalidValue

2 public . . . . void **insert_typecode** (org.omg.CORBA.TypeCode value)
throws org.omg.DynamicAny.DynAnyPackage.TypeMismatch,
org.omg.DynamicAny.DynAnyPackage.InvalidValue

2 public . . . . void **insert_ulong** (int value) throws org.omg.DynamicAny.DynAnyPackage↵
.TypeMismatch, org.omg.DynamicAny.DynAnyPackage.InvalidValue

Classes

411

_DynAnyStub

2	public	void	**insert_ulonglong** (long value) throws org.omg.DynamicAny.DynAnyPackage↵
			.TypeMismatch, org.omg.DynamicAny.DynAnyPackage.InvalidValue
2	public	void	**insert_ushort** (short value) throws org.omg.DynamicAny.DynAnyPackage↵
			.TypeMismatch, org.omg.DynamicAny.DynAnyPackage.InvalidValue
2	public	void	**insert_val** (*java.io.Serializable* value) throws org↵
			.omg.DynamicAny.DynAnyPackage.TypeMismatch,
			org.omg.DynamicAny.DynAnyPackage.InvalidValue
2	public	void	**insert_wchar** (char value) throws org.omg.DynamicAny.DynAnyPackage↵
			.TypeMismatch, org.omg.DynamicAny.DynAnyPackage.InvalidValue
2	public	void	**insert_wstring** (String value) throws org.omg.DynamicAny.DynAnyPackage↵
			.TypeMismatch, org.omg.DynamicAny.DynAnyPackage.InvalidValue
2	public	boolean	**next** ()
2	public	void	**rewind** ()
2	public	boolean	**seek** (int index)
2	public	org.omg.CORBA.Any	**to_any** ()
2	public		**type** ()
	. org.omg.CORBA.TypeCode		

_DynArrayStub org.omg.DynamicAny

```
      Object
1.2 ○  └org.omg.CORBA.portable.ObjectImpl 1 ------ org.omg.CORBA.Object ˅
1.4       └_DynArrayStub --------------------- DynArray (DynArrayOperations 2 (DynAnyOperations 3),
                                              DynAny (DynAnyOperations 3, org.omg.CORBA.Object,
                                              org.omg.CORBA.portable.IDLEntity (java.io.Serializable)),
                                              org.omg.CORBA.portable.IDLEntity (java.io.Serializable))
```

	1	*25 inherited members from org.omg.CORBA.portable.ObjectImpl not shown*	
✳		public	**_DynArrayStub** ()
	1	public	**String[] _ids** ()
▲		public static final Class	**_opsClass**
	3	public	void **assign** (*DynAny* dyn_any) throws org.omg.DynamicAny.DynAnyPackage↵
			.TypeMismatch
	3	public	int **component_count** ()
	3	public *DynAny*	**copy** ()
	3	public *DynAny*	**current_component** () throws org.omg.DynamicAny.DynAnyPackage↵
			.TypeMismatch
	3	public	void **destroy** ()
	3	public	boolean **equal** (*DynAny* dyn_any)
	3	public	void **from_any** (org.omg.CORBA.Any value) throws org↵
			.omg.DynamicAny.DynAnyPackage.TypeMismatch,
			org.omg.DynamicAny.DynAnyPackage.InvalidValue
	3	public org.omg.CORBA.Any	**get_any** () throws org.omg.DynamicAny.DynAnyPackage.TypeMismatch,
			org.omg.DynamicAny.DynAnyPackage.InvalidValue
	3	public	boolean **get_boolean** () throws org.omg.DynamicAny.DynAnyPackage.TypeMismatch,
			org.omg.DynamicAny.DynAnyPackage.InvalidValue
	3	public	char **get_char** () throws org.omg.DynamicAny.DynAnyPackage.TypeMismatch,
			org.omg.DynamicAny.DynAnyPackage.InvalidValue
	3	public	double **get_double** () throws org.omg.DynamicAny.DynAnyPackage.TypeMismatch,
			org.omg.DynamicAny.DynAnyPackage.InvalidValue
	3	public *DynAny*	**get_dyn_any** () throws org.omg.DynamicAny.DynAnyPackage.TypeMismatch,
			org.omg.DynamicAny.DynAnyPackage.InvalidValue
	2	public org.omg.CORBA.Any[]	**get_elements** ()
	2	public *DynAny[]*	**get_elements_as_dyn_any** ()
	3	public	float **get_float** () throws org.omg.DynamicAny.DynAnyPackage.TypeMismatch,
			org.omg.DynamicAny.DynAnyPackage.InvalidValue
	3	public	int **get_long** () throws org.omg.DynamicAny.DynAnyPackage.TypeMismatch,
			org.omg.DynamicAny.DynAnyPackage.InvalidValue
	3	public	long **get_longlong** () throws org.omg.DynamicAny.DynAnyPackage.TypeMismatch,
			org.omg.DynamicAny.DynAnyPackage.InvalidValue
	3	public	byte **get_octet** () throws org.omg.DynamicAny.DynAnyPackage.TypeMismatch,
			org.omg.DynamicAny.DynAnyPackage.InvalidValue
	3	public *org.omg.CORBA.Object*	**get_reference** () throws org.omg.DynamicAny.DynAnyPackage.TypeMismatch,
			org.omg.DynamicAny.DynAnyPackage.InvalidValue
	3	public	short **get_short** () throws org.omg.DynamicAny.DynAnyPackage.TypeMismatch,
			org.omg.DynamicAny.DynAnyPackage.InvalidValue
	3	public	String **get_string** () throws org.omg.DynamicAny.DynAnyPackage.TypeMismatch,
			org.omg.DynamicAny.DynAnyPackage.InvalidValue

Class *Interface* —extends - - -implements ○ abstract ● final △ static ▲ static final ✳ constructor x x—inherited x **x**—declared **x x**—overridden
εn—examples of usage ˅—has subclass package—see other volume

3	public org.omg.CORBA.TypeCode	**get_typecode** () throws org.omg.DynamicAny.DynAnyPackage.TypeMismatch, org.omg.DynamicAny.DynAnyPackage.InvalidValue
3	public int	**get_ulong** () throws org.omg.DynamicAny.DynAnyPackage.TypeMismatch, org.omg.DynamicAny.DynAnyPackage.InvalidValue
3	public long	**get_ulonglong** () throws org.omg.DynamicAny.DynAnyPackage.TypeMismatch, org.omg.DynamicAny.DynAnyPackage.InvalidValue
3	public short	**get_ushort** () throws org.omg.DynamicAny.DynAnyPackage.TypeMismatch, org.omg.DynamicAny.DynAnyPackage.InvalidValue
3	public *java.io.Serializable*	**get_val** () throws org.omg.DynamicAny.DynAnyPackage.TypeMismatch, org.omg.DynamicAny.DynAnyPackage.InvalidValue
3	public char	**get_wchar** () throws org.omg.DynamicAny.DynAnyPackage.TypeMismatch, org.omg.DynamicAny.DynAnyPackage.InvalidValue
3	public String	**get_wstring** () throws org.omg.DynamicAny.DynAnyPackage.TypeMismatch, org.omg.DynamicAny.DynAnyPackage.InvalidValue
3	public void	**insert_any** (org.omg.CORBA.Any value) throws org.omg.DynamicAny.DynAnyPackage.TypeMismatch, org.omg.DynamicAny.DynAnyPackage.InvalidValue
3	public void	**insert_boolean** (boolean value) throws org.omg.DynamicAny.DynAnyPackage.TypeMismatch, org.omg.DynamicAny.DynAnyPackage.InvalidValue
3	public void	**insert_char** (char value) throws org.omg.DynamicAny.DynAnyPackage.TypeMismatch, org.omg.DynamicAny.DynAnyPackage.InvalidValue
3	public void	**insert_double** (double value) throws org.omg.DynamicAny.DynAnyPackage.TypeMismatch, org.omg.DynamicAny.DynAnyPackage.InvalidValue
3	public void	**insert_dyn_any** (*DynAny* value) throws org.omg.DynamicAny.DynAnyPackage.TypeMismatch, org.omg.DynamicAny.DynAnyPackage.InvalidValue
3	public void	**insert_float** (float value) throws org.omg.DynamicAny.DynAnyPackage.TypeMismatch, org.omg.DynamicAny.DynAnyPackage.InvalidValue
3	public void	**insert_long** (int value) throws org.omg.DynamicAny.DynAnyPackage.TypeMismatch, org.omg.DynamicAny.DynAnyPackage.InvalidValue
3	public void	**insert_longlong** (long value) throws org.omg.DynamicAny.DynAnyPackage.TypeMismatch, org.omg.DynamicAny.DynAnyPackage.InvalidValue
3	public void	**insert_octet** (byte value) throws org.omg.DynamicAny.DynAnyPackage.TypeMismatch, org.omg.DynamicAny.DynAnyPackage.InvalidValue
3	public void	**insert_reference** (*org.omg.CORBA.Object* value) throws org.omg.DynamicAny.DynAnyPackage.TypeMismatch, org.omg.DynamicAny.DynAnyPackage.InvalidValue
3	public void	**insert_short** (short value) throws org.omg.DynamicAny.DynAnyPackage.TypeMismatch, org.omg.DynamicAny.DynAnyPackage.InvalidValue
3	public void	**insert_string** (String value) throws org.omg.DynamicAny.DynAnyPackage.TypeMismatch, org.omg.DynamicAny.DynAnyPackage.InvalidValue
3	public void	**insert_typecode** (org.omg.CORBA.TypeCode value) throws org.omg.DynamicAny.DynAnyPackage.TypeMismatch, org.omg.DynamicAny.DynAnyPackage.InvalidValue
3	public void	**insert_ulong** (int value) throws org.omg.DynamicAny.DynAnyPackage.TypeMismatch, org.omg.DynamicAny.DynAnyPackage.InvalidValue
3	public void	**insert_ulonglong** (long value) throws org.omg.DynamicAny.DynAnyPackage.TypeMismatch, org.omg.DynamicAny.DynAnyPackage.InvalidValue
3	public void	**insert_ushort** (short value) throws org.omg.DynamicAny.DynAnyPackage.TypeMismatch, org.omg.DynamicAny.DynAnyPackage.InvalidValue
3	public void	**insert_val** (*java.io.Serializable* value) throws org.omg.DynamicAny.DynAnyPackage.TypeMismatch, org.omg.DynamicAny.DynAnyPackage.InvalidValue
3	public void	**insert_wchar** (char value) throws org.omg.DynamicAny.DynAnyPackage.TypeMismatch, org.omg.DynamicAny.DynAnyPackage.InvalidValue
3	public void	**insert_wstring** (String value) throws org.omg.DynamicAny.DynAnyPackage.TypeMismatch, org.omg.DynamicAny.DynAnyPackage.InvalidValue
3	public boolean	**next** ()
3	public void	**rewind** ()
3	public boolean	**seek** (int index)
2	public void	**set_elements** (org.omg.CORBA.Any[] value) throws org.omg.DynamicAny.DynAnyPackage.TypeMismatch, org.omg.DynamicAny.DynAnyPackage.InvalidValue
2	public void	**set_elements_as_dyn_any** (*DynAny[]* value) throws org.omg.DynamicAny.DynAnyPackage.TypeMismatch, org.omg.DynamicAny.DynAnyPackage.InvalidValue
3	public org.omg.CORBA.Any	**to_any** ()
3	public org.omg.CORBA.TypeCode	**type** ()

Classes

_DynEnumStub	org.omg.DynamicAny

```
        Object
1.2 ○   └─org.omg.CORBA.portable.ObjectImpl 1 ------ org.omg.CORBA.Object ⌄
1.4         └─_DynEnumStub ------------------- DynEnum (DynEnumOperations 2 (DynAnyOperations 3),
                                                 DynAny (DynAnyOperations 3, org.omg.CORBA.Object,
                                                 org.omg.CORBA.portable.IDLEntity (java.io.Serializable)),
                                                 org.omg.CORBA.portable.IDLEntity (java.io.Serializable))
```

	1	*25 inherited members from org.omg.CORBA.portable.ObjectImpl not shown*	
✱		public	**_DynEnumStub** ()
	1	public .... **String[]**	**_ids** ()
▲		public static final .... Class	**_opsClass**
	3	public ....void	**assign** (*DynAny* dyn_any) throws org.omg.DynamicAny.DynAnyPackage↵ .TypeMismatch
	3	public ....int	**component_count** ()
	3	public ....*DynAny*	**copy** ()
	3	public ....*DynAny*	**current_component** () throws org.omg.DynamicAny.DynAnyPackage↵ .TypeMismatch
	3	public ....void	**destroy** ()
	3	public .... boolean	**equal** (*DynAny* dyn_any)
	3	public ....void	**from_any** (org.omg.CORBA.Any value) throws org↵ .omg.DynamicAny.DynAnyPackage.TypeMismatch, org.omg.DynamicAny.DynAnyPackage.InvalidValue
	3	public ....org.omg.CORBA.Any	**get_any** () throws org.omg.DynamicAny.DynAnyPackage.TypeMismatch, org.omg.DynamicAny.DynAnyPackage.InvalidValue
	2	public ....String	**get_as_string** ()
	2	public ....int	**get_as_ulong** ()
	3	public .... boolean	**get_boolean** () throws org.omg.DynamicAny.DynAnyPackage.TypeMismatch, org.omg.DynamicAny.DynAnyPackage.InvalidValue
	3	public .... char	**get_char** () throws org.omg.DynamicAny.DynAnyPackage.TypeMismatch, org.omg.DynamicAny.DynAnyPackage.InvalidValue
	3	public ....double	**get_double** () throws org.omg.DynamicAny.DynAnyPackage.TypeMismatch, org.omg.DynamicAny.DynAnyPackage.InvalidValue
	3	public ....*DynAny*	**get_dyn_any** () throws org.omg.DynamicAny.DynAnyPackage.TypeMismatch, org.omg.DynamicAny.DynAnyPackage.InvalidValue
	3	public ....float	**get_float** () throws org.omg.DynamicAny.DynAnyPackage.TypeMismatch, org.omg.DynamicAny.DynAnyPackage.InvalidValue
	3	public ....int	**get_long** () throws org.omg.DynamicAny.DynAnyPackage.TypeMismatch, org.omg.DynamicAny.DynAnyPackage.InvalidValue
	3	public .... long	**get_longlong** () throws org.omg.DynamicAny.DynAnyPackage.TypeMismatch, org.omg.DynamicAny.DynAnyPackage.InvalidValue
	3	public .... byte	**get_octet** () throws org.omg.DynamicAny.DynAnyPackage.TypeMismatch, org.omg.DynamicAny.DynAnyPackage.InvalidValue
	3	public *org.omg.CORBA.Object*	**get_reference** () throws org.omg.DynamicAny.DynAnyPackage.TypeMismatch, org.omg.DynamicAny.DynAnyPackage.InvalidValue
	3	public ....short	**get_short** () throws org.omg.DynamicAny.DynAnyPackage.TypeMismatch, org.omg.DynamicAny.DynAnyPackage.InvalidValue
	3	public ....String	**get_string** () throws org.omg.DynamicAny.DynAnyPackage.TypeMismatch, org.omg.DynamicAny.DynAnyPackage.InvalidValue
	3	public . org.omg.CORBA.TypeCode	**get_typecode** () throws org.omg.DynamicAny.DynAnyPackage.TypeMismatch, org.omg.DynamicAny.DynAnyPackage.InvalidValue
	3	public ....int	**get_ulong** () throws org.omg.DynamicAny.DynAnyPackage.TypeMismatch, org.omg.DynamicAny.DynAnyPackage.InvalidValue
	3	public .... long	**get_ulonglong** () throws org.omg.DynamicAny.DynAnyPackage.TypeMismatch, org.omg.DynamicAny.DynAnyPackage.InvalidValue
	3	public ....short	**get_ushort** () throws org.omg.DynamicAny.DynAnyPackage.TypeMismatch, org.omg.DynamicAny.DynAnyPackage.InvalidValue
	3	public ....*java.io.Serializable*	**get_val** () throws org.omg.DynamicAny.DynAnyPackage.TypeMismatch, org.omg.DynamicAny.DynAnyPackage.InvalidValue
	3	public .... char	**get_wchar** () throws org.omg.DynamicAny.DynAnyPackage.TypeMismatch, org.omg.DynamicAny.DynAnyPackage.InvalidValue
	3	public ....String	**get_wstring** () throws org.omg.DynamicAny.DynAnyPackage.TypeMismatch, org.omg.DynamicAny.DynAnyPackage.InvalidValue
	3	public ....void	**insert_any** (org.omg.CORBA.Any value) throws org↵ .omg.DynamicAny.DynAnyPackage.TypeMismatch, org.omg.DynamicAny.DynAnyPackage.InvalidValue
	3	public ....void	**insert_boolean** (boolean value) throws org.omg.DynamicAny.DynAnyPackage↵ .TypeMismatch, org.omg.DynamicAny.DynAnyPackage.InvalidValue

---

Class   *Interface*   —extends   - - -implements   ○ abstract   ● final   △ static   ▲ static final   ✱ constructor   x x—inherited   x **x**—declared   **x x**—overridden
ε*n*—examples of usage   ⌄—has subclass   package—see other volume

3	public	void	**insert_char** (char value) throws org.omg.DynamicAny.DynAnyPackage ↵ .TypeMismatch, org.omg.DynamicAny.DynAnyPackage.InvalidValue
3	public	void	**insert_double** (double value) throws org.omg.DynamicAny.DynAnyPackage ↵ .TypeMismatch, org.omg.DynamicAny.DynAnyPackage.InvalidValue
3	public	void	**insert_dyn_any** (*DynAny* value) throws org.omg.DynamicAny.DynAnyPackage ↵ .TypeMismatch, org.omg.DynamicAny.DynAnyPackage.InvalidValue
3	public	void	**insert_float** (float value) throws org.omg.DynamicAny.DynAnyPackage ↵ .TypeMismatch, org.omg.DynamicAny.DynAnyPackage.InvalidValue
3	public	void	**insert_long** (int value) throws org.omg.DynamicAny.DynAnyPackage ↵ .TypeMismatch, org.omg.DynamicAny.DynAnyPackage.InvalidValue
3	public	void	**insert_longlong** (long value) throws org.omg.DynamicAny.DynAnyPackage ↵ .TypeMismatch, org.omg.DynamicAny.DynAnyPackage.InvalidValue
3	public	void	**insert_octet** (byte value) throws org.omg.DynamicAny.DynAnyPackage ↵ .TypeMismatch, org.omg.DynamicAny.DynAnyPackage.InvalidValue
3	public	void	**insert_reference** (*org.omg.CORBA.Object* value) throws org.omg.DynamicAny.DynAnyPackage.TypeMismatch, org.omg.DynamicAny.DynAnyPackage.InvalidValue
3	public	void	**insert_short** (short value) throws org.omg.DynamicAny.DynAnyPackage ↵ .TypeMismatch, org.omg.DynamicAny.DynAnyPackage.InvalidValue
3	public	void	**insert_string** (String value) throws org.omg.DynamicAny.DynAnyPackage ↵ .TypeMismatch, org.omg.DynamicAny.DynAnyPackage.InvalidValue
3	public	void	**insert_typecode** (org.omg.CORBA.TypeCode value) throws org.omg.DynamicAny.DynAnyPackage.TypeMismatch, org.omg.DynamicAny.DynAnyPackage.InvalidValue
3	public	void	**insert_ulong** (int value) throws org.omg.DynamicAny.DynAnyPackage ↵ .TypeMismatch, org.omg.DynamicAny.DynAnyPackage.InvalidValue
3	public	void	**insert_ulonglong** (long value) throws org.omg.DynamicAny.DynAnyPackage ↵ .TypeMismatch, org.omg.DynamicAny.DynAnyPackage.InvalidValue
3	public	void	**insert_ushort** (short value) throws org.omg.DynamicAny.DynAnyPackage ↵ .TypeMismatch, org.omg.DynamicAny.DynAnyPackage.InvalidValue
3	public	void	**insert_val** (*java.io.Serializable* value) throws org ↵ .omg.DynamicAny.DynAnyPackage.TypeMismatch, org.omg.DynamicAny.DynAnyPackage.InvalidValue
3	public	void	**insert_wchar** (char value) throws org.omg.DynamicAny.DynAnyPackage ↵ .TypeMismatch, org.omg.DynamicAny.DynAnyPackage.InvalidValue
3	public	void	**insert_wstring** (String value) throws org.omg.DynamicAny.DynAnyPackage ↵ .TypeMismatch, org.omg.DynamicAny.DynAnyPackage.InvalidValue
3	public	boolean	**next** ()
3	public	void	**rewind** ()
3	public	boolean	**seek** (int index)
2	public	void	**set_as_string** (String value) throws org.omg.DynamicAny.DynAnyPackage ↵ .InvalidValue
2	public	void	**set_as_ulong** (int value) throws org.omg.DynamicAny.DynAnyPackage.InvalidValue
3	public	org.omg.CORBA.Any	**to_any** ()
3	public	. org.omg.CORBA.TypeCode	**type** ()

_DynFixedStub

org.omg.DynamicAny

```
       Object
1.2 O  └─org.omg.CORBA.portable.ObjectImpl 1 ------ org.omg.CORBA.Object ┘
1.4       └─_DynFixedStub --------------------- DynFixed (DynFixedOperations 2 (DynAnyOperations 3),
                                                DynAny (DynAnyOperations 3, org.omg.CORBA.Object,
                                                org.omg.CORBA.portable.IDLEntity (java.io.Serializable)),
                                                org.omg.CORBA.portable.IDLEntity (java.io.Serializable))
```

Classes

1	*25 inherited members from org.omg.CORBA.portable.ObjectImpl not shown*		
∗	public		**_DynFixedStub** ()
1	public	String[]	**_ids** ()
▲	public static final	Class	**_opsClass**
3	public	void	**assign** (*DynAny* dyn_any) throws org.omg.DynamicAny.DynAnyPackage ↵ .TypeMismatch
3	public	int	**component_count** ()
3	public	*DynAny*	**copy** ()
3	public	*DynAny*	**current_component** () throws org.omg.DynamicAny.DynAnyPackage ↵ .TypeMismatch
3	public	void	**destroy** ()
3	public	boolean	**equal** (*DynAny* dyn_any)
3	public	void	**from_any** (org.omg.CORBA.Any value) throws org ↵ .omg.DynamicAny.DynAnyPackage.TypeMismatch, org.omg.DynamicAny.DynAnyPackage.InvalidValue

_DynFixedStub

3	public . . . . .org.omg.CORBA.Any	**get_any** () throws org.omg.DynamicAny.DynAnyPackage.TypeMismatch, org.omg.DynamicAny.DynAnyPackage.InvalidValue
3	public . . . . boolean	**get_boolean** () throws org.omg.DynamicAny.DynAnyPackage.TypeMismatch, org.omg.DynamicAny.DynAnyPackage.InvalidValue
3	public . . . . char	**get_char** () throws org.omg.DynamicAny.DynAnyPackage.TypeMismatch, org.omg.DynamicAny.DynAnyPackage.InvalidValue
3	public . . . . .double	**get_double** () throws org.omg.DynamicAny.DynAnyPackage.TypeMismatch, org.omg.DynamicAny.DynAnyPackage.InvalidValue
3	public . . . .*DynAny*	**get_dyn_any** () throws org.omg.DynamicAny.DynAnyPackage.TypeMismatch, org.omg.DynamicAny.DynAnyPackage.InvalidValue
3	public . . . . .float	**get_float** () throws org.omg.DynamicAny.DynAnyPackage.TypeMismatch, org.omg.DynamicAny.DynAnyPackage.InvalidValue
3	public . . . . .int	**get_long** () throws org.omg.DynamicAny.DynAnyPackage.TypeMismatch, org.omg.DynamicAny.DynAnyPackage.InvalidValue
3	public . . . . long	**get_longlong** () throws org.omg.DynamicAny.DynAnyPackage.TypeMismatch, org.omg.DynamicAny.DynAnyPackage.InvalidValue
3	public . . . . byte	**get_octet** () throws org.omg.DynamicAny.DynAnyPackage.TypeMismatch, org.omg.DynamicAny.DynAnyPackage.InvalidValue
3	public *org.omg.CORBA.Object*	**get_reference** () throws org.omg.DynamicAny.DynAnyPackage.TypeMismatch, org.omg.DynamicAny.DynAnyPackage.InvalidValue
3	public . . . . short	**get_short** () throws org.omg.DynamicAny.DynAnyPackage.TypeMismatch, org.omg.DynamicAny.DynAnyPackage.InvalidValue
3	public . . . . String	**get_string** () throws org.omg.DynamicAny.DynAnyPackage.TypeMismatch, org.omg.DynamicAny.DynAnyPackage.InvalidValue
3	public . . . . org.omg.CORBA.TypeCode	**get_typecode** () throws org.omg.DynamicAny.DynAnyPackage.TypeMismatch, org.omg.DynamicAny.DynAnyPackage.InvalidValue
3	public . . . . .int	**get_ulong** () throws org.omg.DynamicAny.DynAnyPackage.TypeMismatch, org.omg.DynamicAny.DynAnyPackage.InvalidValue
3	public . . . . long	**get_ulonglong** () throws org.omg.DynamicAny.DynAnyPackage.TypeMismatch, org.omg.DynamicAny.DynAnyPackage.InvalidValue
3	public . . . . .short	**get_ushort** () throws org.omg.DynamicAny.DynAnyPackage.TypeMismatch, org.omg.DynamicAny.DynAnyPackage.InvalidValue
3	public . . . . *java.io.Serializable*	**get_val** () throws org.omg.DynamicAny.DynAnyPackage.TypeMismatch, org.omg.DynamicAny.DynAnyPackage.InvalidValue
2	public . . . . String	**get_value** ()
3	public . . . . char	**get_wchar** () throws org.omg.DynamicAny.DynAnyPackage.TypeMismatch, org.omg.DynamicAny.DynAnyPackage.InvalidValue
3	public . . . . String	**get_wstring** () throws org.omg.DynamicAny.DynAnyPackage.TypeMismatch, org.omg.DynamicAny.DynAnyPackage.InvalidValue
3	public . . . . .void	**insert_any** (org.omg.CORBA.Any value) throws org↵ .omg.DynamicAny.DynAnyPackage.TypeMismatch, org.omg.DynamicAny.DynAnyPackage.InvalidValue
3	public . . . . .void	**insert_boolean** (boolean value) throws org.omg.DynamicAny.DynAnyPackage↵ .TypeMismatch, org.omg.DynamicAny.DynAnyPackage.InvalidValue
3	public . . . . .void	**insert_char** (char value) throws org.omg.DynamicAny.DynAnyPackage↵ .TypeMismatch, org.omg.DynamicAny.DynAnyPackage.InvalidValue
3	public . . . . .void	**insert_double** (double value) throws org.omg.DynamicAny.DynAnyPackage↵ .TypeMismatch, org.omg.DynamicAny.DynAnyPackage.InvalidValue
3	public . . . . .void	**insert_dyn_any** (*DynAny* value) throws org.omg.DynamicAny.DynAnyPackage↵ .TypeMismatch, org.omg.DynamicAny.DynAnyPackage.InvalidValue
3	public . . . . .void	**insert_float** (float value) throws org.omg.DynamicAny.DynAnyPackage↵ .TypeMismatch, org.omg.DynamicAny.DynAnyPackage.InvalidValue
3	public . . . . .void	**insert_long** (int value) throws org.omg.DynamicAny.DynAnyPackage↵ .TypeMismatch, org.omg.DynamicAny.DynAnyPackage.InvalidValue
3	public . . . . .void	**insert_longlong** (long value) throws org.omg.DynamicAny.DynAnyPackage↵ .TypeMismatch, org.omg.DynamicAny.DynAnyPackage.InvalidValue
3	public . . . . .void	**insert_octet** (byte value) throws org.omg.DynamicAny.DynAnyPackage↵ .TypeMismatch, org.omg.DynamicAny.DynAnyPackage.InvalidValue
3	public . . . . .void	**insert_reference** (*org.omg.CORBA.Object* value) throws org.omg.DynamicAny.DynAnyPackage.TypeMismatch, org.omg.DynamicAny.DynAnyPackage.InvalidValue
3	public . . . . .void	**insert_short** (short value) throws org.omg.DynamicAny.DynAnyPackage↵ .TypeMismatch, org.omg.DynamicAny.DynAnyPackage.InvalidValue
3	public . . . . .void	**insert_string** (String value) throws org.omg.DynamicAny.DynAnyPackage↵ .TypeMismatch, org.omg.DynamicAny.DynAnyPackage.InvalidValue
3	public . . . . .void	**insert_typecode** (org.omg.CORBA.TypeCode value) throws org.omg.DynamicAny.DynAnyPackage.TypeMismatch, org.omg.DynamicAny.DynAnyPackage.InvalidValue
3	public . . . . .void	**insert_ulong** (int value) throws org.omg.DynamicAny.DynAnyPackage↵ .TypeMismatch, org.omg.DynamicAny.DynAnyPackage.InvalidValue

Class *Interface* —extends - - -implements ○ abstract ● final △ static ▲ static final ✳ constructor x x—inherited x **x**—declared **x x**—overridden
εn—examples of usage ⌐—has subclass package—see other volume

3	public	void	**insert_ulonglong** (long value) throws org.omg.DynamicAny.DynAnyPackage↵
			.TypeMismatch, org.omg.DynamicAny.DynAnyPackage.InvalidValue
3	public	void	**insert_ushort** (short value) throws org.omg.DynamicAny.DynAnyPackage↵
			.TypeMismatch, org.omg.DynamicAny.DynAnyPackage.InvalidValue
3	public	void	**insert_val** (*java.io.Serializable* value) throws org↵
			.omg.DynamicAny.DynAnyPackage.TypeMismatch,
			org.omg.DynamicAny.DynAnyPackage.InvalidValue
3	public	void	**insert_wchar** (char value) throws org.omg.DynamicAny.DynAnyPackage↵
			.TypeMismatch, org.omg.DynamicAny.DynAnyPackage.InvalidValue
3	public	void	**insert_wstring** (String value) throws org.omg.DynamicAny.DynAnyPackage↵
			.TypeMismatch, org.omg.DynamicAny.DynAnyPackage.InvalidValue
3	public	boolean	**next** ()
3	public	void	**rewind** ()
3	public	boolean	**seek** (int index)
2	public	boolean	**set_value** (String val) throws org.omg.DynamicAny.DynAnyPackage.TypeMismatch,
			org.omg.DynamicAny.DynAnyPackage.InvalidValue
3	public	org.omg.CORBA.Any	**to_any** ()
3	public		**type** ()
	. org.omg.CORBA.TypeCode		

_DynSequenceStub   org.omg.DynamicAny

```
Object
```
1.2 ○   └org.omg.CORBA.portable.ObjectImpl[1] ------ *org.omg.CORBA.Object*
1.4   └_DynSequenceStub ----------------- *DynSequence (DynSequenceOperations[2] (DynAnyOperations[3]),*
                                        DynAny (DynAnyOperations[3], org.omg.CORBA.Object,
                                        org.omg.CORBA.portable.IDLEntity (java.io.Serializable)),
                                        org.omg.CORBA.portable.IDLEntity (java.io.Serializable))

1	*25 inherited members from org.omg.CORBA.portable.ObjectImpl not shown*		
✳	public		**_DynSequenceStub** ()
1	public	String[]	**_ids** ()
▲	public static final	Class	**_opsClass**
3	public	void	**assign** (*DynAny* dyn_any) throws org.omg.DynamicAny.DynAnyPackage↵
			.TypeMismatch
3	public	int	**component_count** ()
3	public	*DynAny*	**copy** ()
3	public	*DynAny*	**current_component** () throws org.omg.DynamicAny.DynAnyPackage↵
			.TypeMismatch
3	public	void	**destroy** ()
3	public	boolean	**equal** (*DynAny* dyn_any)
3	public	void	**from_any** (org.omg.CORBA.Any value) throws org↵
			.omg.DynamicAny.DynAnyPackage.TypeMismatch,
			org.omg.DynamicAny.DynAnyPackage.InvalidValue
3	public	org.omg.CORBA.Any	**get_any** () throws org.omg.DynamicAny.DynAnyPackage.TypeMismatch,
			org.omg.DynamicAny.DynAnyPackage.InvalidValue
3	public	boolean	**get_boolean** () throws org.omg.DynamicAny.DynAnyPackage.TypeMismatch,
			org.omg.DynamicAny.DynAnyPackage.InvalidValue
3	public	char	**get_char** () throws org.omg.DynamicAny.DynAnyPackage.TypeMismatch,
			org.omg.DynamicAny.DynAnyPackage.InvalidValue
3	public	double	**get_double** () throws org.omg.DynamicAny.DynAnyPackage.TypeMismatch,
			org.omg.DynamicAny.DynAnyPackage.InvalidValue
3	public	*DynAny*	**get_dyn_any** () throws org.omg.DynamicAny.DynAnyPackage.TypeMismatch,
			org.omg.DynamicAny.DynAnyPackage.InvalidValue
2	public	org.omg.CORBA.Any[]	**get_elements** ()
2	public	*DynAny[]*	**get_elements_as_dyn_any** ()
3	public	float	**get_float** () throws org.omg.DynamicAny.DynAnyPackage.TypeMismatch,
			org.omg.DynamicAny.DynAnyPackage.InvalidValue
2	public	int	**get_length** ()
3	public	int	**get_long** () throws org.omg.DynamicAny.DynAnyPackage.TypeMismatch,
			org.omg.DynamicAny.DynAnyPackage.InvalidValue
3	public	long	**get_longlong** () throws org.omg.DynamicAny.DynAnyPackage.TypeMismatch,
			org.omg.DynamicAny.DynAnyPackage.InvalidValue
3	public	byte	**get_octet** () throws org.omg.DynamicAny.DynAnyPackage.TypeMismatch,
			org.omg.DynamicAny.DynAnyPackage.InvalidValue
3	public	*org.omg.CORBA.Object*	**get_reference** () throws org.omg.DynamicAny.DynAnyPackage.TypeMismatch,
			org.omg.DynamicAny.DynAnyPackage.InvalidValue
3	public	short	**get_short** () throws org.omg.DynamicAny.DynAnyPackage.TypeMismatch,
			org.omg.DynamicAny.DynAnyPackage.InvalidValue
3	public	String	**get_string** () throws org.omg.DynamicAny.DynAnyPackage.TypeMismatch,
			org.omg.DynamicAny.DynAnyPackage.InvalidValue

Classes

417

_DynSequenceStub

3	public	org.omg.CORBA.TypeCode	**get_typecode** () throws org.omg.DynamicAny.DynAnyPackage.TypeMismatch, org.omg.DynamicAny.DynAnyPackage.InvalidValue
3	public	int	**get_ulong** () throws org.omg.DynamicAny.DynAnyPackage.TypeMismatch, org.omg.DynamicAny.DynAnyPackage.InvalidValue
3	public	long	**get_ulonglong** () throws org.omg.DynamicAny.DynAnyPackage.TypeMismatch, org.omg.DynamicAny.DynAnyPackage.InvalidValue
3	public	short	**get_ushort** () throws org.omg.DynamicAny.DynAnyPackage.TypeMismatch, org.omg.DynamicAny.DynAnyPackage.InvalidValue
3	public	*java.io.Serializable*	**get_val** () throws org.omg.DynamicAny.DynAnyPackage.TypeMismatch, org.omg.DynamicAny.DynAnyPackage.InvalidValue
3	public	char	**get_wchar** () throws org.omg.DynamicAny.DynAnyPackage.TypeMismatch, org.omg.DynamicAny.DynAnyPackage.InvalidValue
3	public	String	**get_wstring** () throws org.omg.DynamicAny.DynAnyPackage.TypeMismatch, org.omg.DynamicAny.DynAnyPackage.InvalidValue
3	public	void	**insert_any** (org.omg.CORBA.Any value) throws org.omg.DynamicAny.DynAnyPackage.TypeMismatch, org.omg.DynamicAny.DynAnyPackage.InvalidValue
3	public	void	**insert_boolean** (boolean value) throws org.omg.DynamicAny.DynAnyPackage.TypeMismatch, org.omg.DynamicAny.DynAnyPackage.InvalidValue
3	public	void	**insert_char** (char value) throws org.omg.DynamicAny.DynAnyPackage.TypeMismatch, org.omg.DynamicAny.DynAnyPackage.InvalidValue
3	public	void	**insert_double** (double value) throws org.omg.DynamicAny.DynAnyPackage.TypeMismatch, org.omg.DynamicAny.DynAnyPackage.InvalidValue
3	public	void	**insert_dyn_any** (*DynAny* value) throws org.omg.DynamicAny.DynAnyPackage.TypeMismatch, org.omg.DynamicAny.DynAnyPackage.InvalidValue
3	public	void	**insert_float** (float value) throws org.omg.DynamicAny.DynAnyPackage.TypeMismatch, org.omg.DynamicAny.DynAnyPackage.InvalidValue
3	public	void	**insert_long** (int value) throws org.omg.DynamicAny.DynAnyPackage.TypeMismatch, org.omg.DynamicAny.DynAnyPackage.InvalidValue
3	public	void	**insert_longlong** (long value) throws org.omg.DynamicAny.DynAnyPackage.TypeMismatch, org.omg.DynamicAny.DynAnyPackage.InvalidValue
3	public	void	**insert_octet** (byte value) throws org.omg.DynamicAny.DynAnyPackage.TypeMismatch, org.omg.DynamicAny.DynAnyPackage.InvalidValue
3	public	void	**insert_reference** (*org.omg.CORBA.Object* value) throws org.omg.DynamicAny.DynAnyPackage.TypeMismatch, org.omg.DynamicAny.DynAnyPackage.InvalidValue
3	public	void	**insert_short** (short value) throws org.omg.DynamicAny.DynAnyPackage.TypeMismatch, org.omg.DynamicAny.DynAnyPackage.InvalidValue
3	public	void	**insert_string** (String value) throws org.omg.DynamicAny.DynAnyPackage.TypeMismatch, org.omg.DynamicAny.DynAnyPackage.InvalidValue
3	public	void	**insert_typecode** (org.omg.CORBA.TypeCode value) throws org.omg.DynamicAny.DynAnyPackage.TypeMismatch, org.omg.DynamicAny.DynAnyPackage.InvalidValue
3	public	void	**insert_ulong** (int value) throws org.omg.DynamicAny.DynAnyPackage.TypeMismatch, org.omg.DynamicAny.DynAnyPackage.InvalidValue
3	public	void	**insert_ulonglong** (long value) throws org.omg.DynamicAny.DynAnyPackage.TypeMismatch, org.omg.DynamicAny.DynAnyPackage.InvalidValue
3	public	void	**insert_ushort** (short value) throws org.omg.DynamicAny.DynAnyPackage.TypeMismatch, org.omg.DynamicAny.DynAnyPackage.InvalidValue
3	public	void	**insert_val** (*java.io.Serializable* value) throws org.omg.DynamicAny.DynAnyPackage.TypeMismatch, org.omg.DynamicAny.DynAnyPackage.InvalidValue
3	public	void	**insert_wchar** (char value) throws org.omg.DynamicAny.DynAnyPackage.TypeMismatch, org.omg.DynamicAny.DynAnyPackage.InvalidValue
3	public	void	**insert_wstring** (String value) throws org.omg.DynamicAny.DynAnyPackage.TypeMismatch, org.omg.DynamicAny.DynAnyPackage.InvalidValue
3	public	boolean	**next** ()
3	public	void	**rewind** ()
3	public	boolean	**seek** (int index)
2	public	void	**set_elements** (org.omg.CORBA.Any[] value) throws org.omg.DynamicAny.DynAnyPackage.TypeMismatch, org.omg.DynamicAny.DynAnyPackage.InvalidValue
2	public	void	**set_elements_as_dyn_any** (*DynAny[]* value) throws org.omg.DynamicAny.DynAnyPackage.TypeMismatch, org.omg.DynamicAny.DynAnyPackage.InvalidValue
2	public	void	**set_length** (int len) throws org.omg.DynamicAny.DynAnyPackage.InvalidValue
3	public	org.omg.CORBA.Any	**to_any** ()
3	public	org.omg.CORBA.TypeCode	**type** ()

Class *Interface* —extends - - -implements ○ abstract ● final △ static ▲ static final ✻ constructor x x—inherited x **x**—declared **x x**—overridden
εn—examples of usage ⌐—has subclass package—see other volume

| **_DynStructStub** | org.omg.DynamicAny |

```
        Object
1.2 ○   └─org.omg.CORBA.portable.ObjectImpl 1 - - - - - - org.omg.CORBA.Object ↙
1.4         └─_DynStructStub - - - - - - - - - - - - - - - - - - - - DynStruct (DynStructOperations 2 (DynAnyOperations 3),
                                                     DynAny (DynAnyOperations 3, org.omg.CORBA.Object,
                                                     org.omg.CORBA.portable.IDLEntity (java.io.Serializable)),
                                                     org.omg.CORBA.portable.IDLEntity (java.io.Serializable))
```

	1	*25 inherited members from org.omg.CORBA.portable.ObjectImpl not shown*
✻		public.......................... **_DynStructStub** ()
	1	public................ **String[]** **_ids** ()
▲		public static final .... Class **_opsClass**
	3	public.......................void **assign** (*DynAny* dyn_any) throws org.omg.DynamicAny.DynAnyPackage ↩ .TypeMismatch
	3	public......................int **component_count** ()
	3	public...................*DynAny* **copy** ()
	3	public...................*DynAny* **current_component** () throws org.omg.DynamicAny.DynAnyPackage ↩ .TypeMismatch
	2	public.......................... .....org.omg.CORBA.TCKind **current_member_kind** () throws org.omg.DynamicAny.DynAnyPackage ↩ .TypeMismatch, org.omg.DynamicAny.DynAnyPackage.InvalidValue
	2	public.....................String **current_member_name** () throws org.omg.DynamicAny.DynAnyPackage ↩ .TypeMismatch, org.omg.DynamicAny.DynAnyPackage.InvalidValue
	3	public......................void **destroy** ()
	3	public................ boolean **equal** (*DynAny* dyn_any)
	3	public......................void **from_any** (org.omg.CORBA.Any value) throws org ↩ .omg.DynamicAny.DynAnyPackage.TypeMismatch, org.omg.DynamicAny.DynAnyPackage.InvalidValue
	3	public....org.omg.CORBA.Any **get_any** () throws org.omg.DynamicAny.DynAnyPackage.TypeMismatch, org.omg.DynamicAny.DynAnyPackage.InvalidValue
	3	public................. boolean **get_boolean** () throws org.omg.DynamicAny.DynAnyPackage.TypeMismatch, org.omg.DynamicAny.DynAnyPackage.InvalidValue
	3	public......................char **get_char** () throws org.omg.DynamicAny.DynAnyPackage.TypeMismatch, org.omg.DynamicAny.DynAnyPackage.InvalidValue
	3	public..................double **get_double** () throws org.omg.DynamicAny.DynAnyPackage.TypeMismatch, org.omg.DynamicAny.DynAnyPackage.InvalidValue
	3	public...................*DynAny* **get_dyn_any** () throws org.omg.DynamicAny.DynAnyPackage.TypeMismatch, org.omg.DynamicAny.DynAnyPackage.InvalidValue
	3	public......................float **get_float** () throws org.omg.DynamicAny.DynAnyPackage.TypeMismatch, org.omg.DynamicAny.DynAnyPackage.InvalidValue
	3	public........................int **get_long** () throws org.omg.DynamicAny.DynAnyPackage.TypeMismatch, org.omg.DynamicAny.DynAnyPackage.InvalidValue
	3	public......................long **get_longlong** () throws org.omg.DynamicAny.DynAnyPackage.TypeMismatch, org.omg.DynamicAny.DynAnyPackage.InvalidValue
	2	public.........NameValuePair[] **get_members** ()
	2	public...... NameDynAnyPair[] **get_members_as_dyn_any** ()
	3	public......................byte **get_octet** () throws org.omg.DynamicAny.DynAnyPackage.TypeMismatch, org.omg.DynamicAny.DynAnyPackage.InvalidValue
	3	public *org.omg.CORBA.Object* **get_reference** () throws org.omg.DynamicAny.DynAnyPackage.TypeMismatch, org.omg.DynamicAny.DynAnyPackage.InvalidValue
	3	public.....................short **get_short** () throws org.omg.DynamicAny.DynAnyPackage.TypeMismatch, org.omg.DynamicAny.DynAnyPackage.InvalidValue
	3	public.....................String **get_string** () throws org.omg.DynamicAny.DynAnyPackage.TypeMismatch, org.omg.DynamicAny.DynAnyPackage.InvalidValue
	3	public.......................... . org.omg.CORBA.TypeCode **get_typecode** () throws org.omg.DynamicAny.DynAnyPackage.TypeMismatch, org.omg.DynamicAny.DynAnyPackage.InvalidValue
	3	public........................int **get_ulong** () throws org.omg.DynamicAny.DynAnyPackage.TypeMismatch, org.omg.DynamicAny.DynAnyPackage.InvalidValue
	3	public...................... long **get_ulonglong** () throws org.omg.DynamicAny.DynAnyPackage.TypeMismatch, org.omg.DynamicAny.DynAnyPackage.InvalidValue
	3	public.....................short **get_ushort** () throws org.omg.DynamicAny.DynAnyPackage.TypeMismatch, org.omg.DynamicAny.DynAnyPackage.InvalidValue
	3	public.......*java.io.Serializable* **get_val** () throws org.omg.DynamicAny.DynAnyPackage.TypeMismatch, org.omg.DynamicAny.DynAnyPackage.InvalidValue
	3	public......................char **get_wchar** () throws org.omg.DynamicAny.DynAnyPackage.TypeMismatch, org.omg.DynamicAny.DynAnyPackage.InvalidValue
	3	public.....................String **get_wstring** () throws org.omg.DynamicAny.DynAnyPackage.TypeMismatch, org.omg.DynamicAny.DynAnyPackage.InvalidValue
	3	public......................void **insert_any** (org.omg.CORBA.Any value) throws org ↩ .omg.DynamicAny.DynAnyPackage.TypeMismatch, org.omg.DynamicAny.DynAnyPackage.InvalidValue

Classes

_DynStructStub

3	public	void	**insert_boolean** (boolean value) throws org.omg.DynamicAny.DynAnyPackage↩ .TypeMismatch, org.omg.DynamicAny.DynAnyPackage.InvalidValue
3	public	void	**insert_char** (char value) throws org.omg.DynamicAny.DynAnyPackage↩ .TypeMismatch, org.omg.DynamicAny.DynAnyPackage.InvalidValue
3	public	void	**insert_double** (double value) throws org.omg.DynamicAny.DynAnyPackage↩ .TypeMismatch, org.omg.DynamicAny.DynAnyPackage.InvalidValue
3	public	void	**insert_dyn_any** (*DynAny* value) throws org.omg.DynamicAny.DynAnyPackage↩ .TypeMismatch, org.omg.DynamicAny.DynAnyPackage.InvalidValue
3	public	void	**insert_float** (float value) throws org.omg.DynamicAny.DynAnyPackage↩ .TypeMismatch, org.omg.DynamicAny.DynAnyPackage.InvalidValue
3	public	void	**insert_long** (int value) throws org.omg.DynamicAny.DynAnyPackage↩ .TypeMismatch, org.omg.DynamicAny.DynAnyPackage.InvalidValue
3	public	void	**insert_longlong** (long value) throws org.omg.DynamicAny.DynAnyPackage↩ .TypeMismatch, org.omg.DynamicAny.DynAnyPackage.InvalidValue
3	public	void	**insert_octet** (byte value) throws org.omg.DynamicAny.DynAnyPackage↩ .TypeMismatch, org.omg.DynamicAny.DynAnyPackage.InvalidValue
3	public	void	**insert_reference** (*org.omg.CORBA.Object* value) throws org.omg.DynamicAny.DynAnyPackage.TypeMismatch, org.omg.DynamicAny.DynAnyPackage.InvalidValue
3	public	void	**insert_short** (short value) throws org.omg.DynamicAny.DynAnyPackage↩ .TypeMismatch, org.omg.DynamicAny.DynAnyPackage.InvalidValue
3	public	void	**insert_string** (String value) throws org.omg.DynamicAny.DynAnyPackage↩ .TypeMismatch, org.omg.DynamicAny.DynAnyPackage.InvalidValue
3	public	void	**insert_typecode** (org.omg.CORBA.TypeCode value) throws org.omg.DynamicAny.DynAnyPackage.TypeMismatch, org.omg.DynamicAny.DynAnyPackage.InvalidValue
3	public	void	**insert_ulong** (int value) throws org.omg.DynamicAny.DynAnyPackage↩ .TypeMismatch, org.omg.DynamicAny.DynAnyPackage.InvalidValue
3	public	void	**insert_ulonglong** (long value) throws org.omg.DynamicAny.DynAnyPackage↩ .TypeMismatch, org.omg.DynamicAny.DynAnyPackage.InvalidValue
3	public	void	**insert_ushort** (short value) throws org.omg.DynamicAny.DynAnyPackage↩ .TypeMismatch, org.omg.DynamicAny.DynAnyPackage.InvalidValue
3	public	void	**insert_val** (*java.io.Serializable* value) throws org↩ .omg.DynamicAny.DynAnyPackage.TypeMismatch, org.omg.DynamicAny.DynAnyPackage.InvalidValue
3	public	void	**insert_wchar** (char value) throws org.omg.DynamicAny.DynAnyPackage↩ .TypeMismatch, org.omg.DynamicAny.DynAnyPackage.InvalidValue
3	public	void	**insert_wstring** (String value) throws org.omg.DynamicAny.DynAnyPackage↩ .TypeMismatch, org.omg.DynamicAny.DynAnyPackage.InvalidValue
3	public	boolean	**next** ()
3	public	void	**rewind** ()
3	public	boolean	**seek** (int index)
2	public	void	**set_members** (NameValuePair[] value) throws org↩ .omg.DynamicAny.DynAnyPackage.TypeMismatch, org.omg.DynamicAny.DynAnyPackage.InvalidValue
2	public	void	**set_members_as_dyn_any** (NameDynAnyPair[] value) throws org.omg.DynamicAny.DynAnyPackage.TypeMismatch, org.omg.DynamicAny.DynAnyPackage.InvalidValue
3	public	org.omg.CORBA.Any	**to_any** ()
3	public	**type** () . org.omg.CORBA.TypeCode	

_DynUnionStub org.omg.DynamicAny

```
        Object
1.2 ○   └org.omg.CORBA.portable.ObjectImpl 1 ------ org.omg.CORBA.Object.
1.4        └_DynUnionStub --------------------- DynUnion (DynUnionOperations 2 (DynAnyOperations 3),
                                               DynAny (DynAnyOperations 3, org.omg.CORBA.Object,
                                               org.omg.CORBA.portable.IDLEntity (java.io.Serializable)),
                                               org.omg.CORBA.portable.IDLEntity (java.io.Serializable))
```

	1	*25 inherited members from org.omg.CORBA.portable.ObjectImpl not shown*		
✳		public		**_DynUnionStub** ()
	1	public	String[]	**_ids** ()
▲		public static final	Class	**_opsClass**
	3	public	void	**assign** (*DynAny* dyn_any) throws org.omg.DynamicAny.DynAnyPackage↩ .TypeMismatch
	3	public	int	**component_count** ()

Class *Interface* —extends - - -implements ○ abstract ● final △ static ▲ static final ✳ constructor x x—inherited x **x**—declared **x x**—overridden
εn—examples of usage ⌐—has subclass package—see other volume

3	public	*DynAny*	**copy** ()
3	public	*DynAny*	**current_component** () throws org.omg.DynamicAny.DynAnyPackage↵ .TypeMismatch
3	public	void	**destroy** ()
2	public		**discriminator_kind** ()
	.....org.omg.CORBA.TCKind		
3	public	boolean	**equal** (*DynAny* dyn_any)
3	public	void	**from_any** (org.omg.CORBA.Any value) throws org↵ .omg.DynamicAny.DynAnyPackage.TypeMismatch, org.omg.DynamicAny.DynAnyPackage.InvalidValue
3	public....org.omg.CORBA.Any		**get_any** () throws org.omg.DynamicAny.DynAnyPackage.TypeMismatch, org.omg.DynamicAny.DynAnyPackage.InvalidValue
3	public	boolean	**get_boolean** () throws org.omg.DynamicAny.DynAnyPackage.TypeMismatch, org.omg.DynamicAny.DynAnyPackage.InvalidValue
3	public	char	**get_char** () throws org.omg.DynamicAny.DynAnyPackage.TypeMismatch, org.omg.DynamicAny.DynAnyPackage.InvalidValue
2	public	*DynAny*	**get_discriminator** ()
3	public	double	**get_double** () throws org.omg.DynamicAny.DynAnyPackage.TypeMismatch, org.omg.DynamicAny.DynAnyPackage.InvalidValue
3	public	*DynAny*	**get_dyn_any** () throws org.omg.DynamicAny.DynAnyPackage.TypeMismatch, org.omg.DynamicAny.DynAnyPackage.InvalidValue
3	public	float	**get_float** () throws org.omg.DynamicAny.DynAnyPackage.TypeMismatch, org.omg.DynamicAny.DynAnyPackage.InvalidValue
3	public	int	**get_long** () throws org.omg.DynamicAny.DynAnyPackage.TypeMismatch, org.omg.DynamicAny.DynAnyPackage.InvalidValue
3	public	long	**get_longlong** () throws org.omg.DynamicAny.DynAnyPackage.TypeMismatch, org.omg.DynamicAny.DynAnyPackage.InvalidValue
3	public	byte	**get_octet** () throws org.omg.DynamicAny.DynAnyPackage.TypeMismatch, org.omg.DynamicAny.DynAnyPackage.InvalidValue
3	public *org.omg.CORBA.Object*		**get_reference** () throws org.omg.DynamicAny.DynAnyPackage.TypeMismatch, org.omg.DynamicAny.DynAnyPackage.InvalidValue
3	public	short	**get_short** () throws org.omg.DynamicAny.DynAnyPackage.TypeMismatch, org.omg.DynamicAny.DynAnyPackage.InvalidValue
3	public	String	**get_string** () throws org.omg.DynamicAny.DynAnyPackage.TypeMismatch, org.omg.DynamicAny.DynAnyPackage.InvalidValue
3	public		**get_typecode** () throws org.omg.DynamicAny.DynAnyPackage.TypeMismatch,
	. org.omg.CORBA.TypeCode		org.omg.DynamicAny.DynAnyPackage.InvalidValue
3	public	int	**get_ulong** () throws org.omg.DynamicAny.DynAnyPackage.TypeMismatch, org.omg.DynamicAny.DynAnyPackage.InvalidValue
3	public	long	**get_ulonglong** () throws org.omg.DynamicAny.DynAnyPackage.TypeMismatch, org.omg.DynamicAny.DynAnyPackage.InvalidValue
3	public	short	**get_ushort** () throws org.omg.DynamicAny.DynAnyPackage.TypeMismatch, org.omg.DynamicAny.DynAnyPackage.InvalidValue
3	public	*java.io.Serializable*	**get_val** () throws org.omg.DynamicAny.DynAnyPackage.TypeMismatch, org.omg.DynamicAny.DynAnyPackage.InvalidValue
3	public	char	**get_wchar** () throws org.omg.DynamicAny.DynAnyPackage.TypeMismatch, org.omg.DynamicAny.DynAnyPackage.InvalidValue
3	public	String	**get_wstring** () throws org.omg.DynamicAny.DynAnyPackage.TypeMismatch, org.omg.DynamicAny.DynAnyPackage.InvalidValue
2	public	boolean	**has_no_active_member** ()
3	public	void	**insert_any** (org.omg.CORBA.Any value) throws org↵ .omg.DynamicAny.DynAnyPackage.TypeMismatch, org.omg.DynamicAny.DynAnyPackage.InvalidValue
3	public	void	**insert_boolean** (boolean value) throws org.omg.DynamicAny.DynAnyPackage↵ .TypeMismatch, org.omg.DynamicAny.DynAnyPackage.InvalidValue
3	public	void	**insert_char** (char value) throws org.omg.DynamicAny.DynAnyPackage↵ .TypeMismatch, org.omg.DynamicAny.DynAnyPackage.InvalidValue
3	public	void	**insert_double** (double value) throws org.omg.DynamicAny.DynAnyPackage↵ .TypeMismatch, org.omg.DynamicAny.DynAnyPackage.InvalidValue
3	public	void	**insert_dyn_any** (*DynAny* value) throws org.omg.DynamicAny.DynAnyPackage↵ .TypeMismatch, org.omg.DynamicAny.DynAnyPackage.InvalidValue
3	public	void	**insert_float** (float value) throws org.omg.DynamicAny.DynAnyPackage↵ .TypeMismatch, org.omg.DynamicAny.DynAnyPackage.InvalidValue
3	public	void	**insert_long** (int value) throws org.omg.DynamicAny.DynAnyPackage↵ .TypeMismatch, org.omg.DynamicAny.DynAnyPackage.InvalidValue
3	public	void	**insert_longlong** (long value) throws org.omg.DynamicAny.DynAnyPackage↵ .TypeMismatch, org.omg.DynamicAny.DynAnyPackage.InvalidValue
3	public	void	**insert_octet** (byte value) throws org.omg.DynamicAny.DynAnyPackage↵ .TypeMismatch, org.omg.DynamicAny.DynAnyPackage.InvalidValue
3	public	void	**insert_reference** (*org.omg.CORBA.Object* value) throws org.omg.DynamicAny.DynAnyPackage.TypeMismatch, org.omg.DynamicAny.DynAnyPackage.InvalidValue

Classes

_DynUnionStub

3	public	void	**insert_short** (short value) throws org.omg.DynamicAny.DynAnyPackage↵ .TypeMismatch, org.omg.DynamicAny.DynAnyPackage.InvalidValue
3	public	void	**insert_string** (String value) throws org.omg.DynamicAny.DynAnyPackage↵ .TypeMismatch, org.omg.DynamicAny.DynAnyPackage.InvalidValue
3	public	void	**insert_typecode** (org.omg.CORBA.TypeCode value) throws org.omg.DynamicAny.DynAnyPackage.TypeMismatch, org.omg.DynamicAny.DynAnyPackage.InvalidValue
3	public	void	**insert_ulong** (int value) throws org.omg.DynamicAny.DynAnyPackage↵ .TypeMismatch, org.omg.DynamicAny.DynAnyPackage.InvalidValue
3	public	void	**insert_ulonglong** (long value) throws org.omg.DynamicAny.DynAnyPackage↵ .TypeMismatch, org.omg.DynamicAny.DynAnyPackage.InvalidValue
3	public	void	**insert_ushort** (short value) throws org.omg.DynamicAny.DynAnyPackage↵ .TypeMismatch, org.omg.DynamicAny.DynAnyPackage.InvalidValue
3	public	void	**insert_val** (*java.io.Serializable* value) throws org↵ .omg.DynamicAny.DynAnyPackage.TypeMismatch, org.omg.DynamicAny.DynAnyPackage.InvalidValue
3	public	void	**insert_wchar** (char value) throws org.omg.DynamicAny.DynAnyPackage↵ .TypeMismatch, org.omg.DynamicAny.DynAnyPackage.InvalidValue
3	public	void	**insert_wstring** (String value) throws org.omg.DynamicAny.DynAnyPackage↵ .TypeMismatch, org.omg.DynamicAny.DynAnyPackage.InvalidValue
2	public	*DynAny*	**member** () throws org.omg.DynamicAny.DynAnyPackage.InvalidValue
2	public	org.omg.CORBA.TCKind	**member_kind** () throws org.omg.DynamicAny.DynAnyPackage.InvalidValue
2	public	String	**member_name** () throws org.omg.DynamicAny.DynAnyPackage.InvalidValue
3	public	boolean	**next** ()
3	public	void	**rewind** ()
3	public	boolean	**seek** (int index)
2	public	void	**set_discriminator** (*DynAny* d) throws org.omg.DynamicAny.DynAnyPackage↵ .TypeMismatch
2	public	void	**set_to_default_member** () throws org.omg.DynamicAny.DynAnyPackage↵ .TypeMismatch
2	public	void	**set_to_no_active_member** () throws org.omg.DynamicAny.DynAnyPackage↵ .TypeMismatch
3	public	org.omg.CORBA.Any	**to_any** ()
3	public	org.omg.CORBA.TypeCode	**type** ()

_DynValueStub   org.omg.DynamicAny

```
Object
1.2 ○ └org.omg.CORBA.portable.ObjectImpl¹ ------ org.omg.CORBA.Object ˌ
1.4     └_DynValueStub -------------------- DynValue (DynValueOperations² (DynValueCommonOperations³
                                              (DynAnyOperations⁴)), DynValueCommon
                                              (DynValueCommonOperations³ (DynAnyOperations⁴),
                                              DynAny (DynAnyOperations⁴, org.omg.CORBA.Object,
                                              org.omg.CORBA.portable.IDLEntity (java.io.Serializable)),
                                              org.omg.CORBA.portable.IDLEntity (java.io.Serializable)),
                                              org.omg.CORBA.portable.IDLEntity (java.io.Serializable))
```

*	1		*25 inherited members from org.omg.CORBA.portable.ObjectImpl not shown*
*		public	**_DynValueStub** ()
	1	public ..... String[]	**_ids** ()
▲		public static final ..... Class	**_opsClass**
	4	public ..... void	**assign** (*DynAny* dyn_any) throws org.omg.DynamicAny.DynAnyPackage↵ .TypeMismatch
	4	public ..... int	**component_count** ()
	4	public ..... *DynAny*	**copy** ()
	4	public ..... *DynAny*	**current_component** () throws org.omg.DynamicAny.DynAnyPackage↵ .TypeMismatch
	2	public ..... org.omg.CORBA.TCKind	**current_member_kind** () throws org.omg.DynamicAny.DynAnyPackage↵ .TypeMismatch, org.omg.DynamicAny.DynAnyPackage.InvalidValue
	2	public ..... String	**current_member_name** () throws org.omg.DynamicAny.DynAnyPackage↵ .TypeMismatch, org.omg.DynamicAny.DynAnyPackage.InvalidValue
	4	public ..... void	**destroy** ()
	4	public ..... boolean	**equal** (*DynAny* dyn_any)
	4	public ..... void	**from_any** (org.omg.CORBA.Any value) throws org↵ .omg.DynamicAny.DynAnyPackage.TypeMismatch, org.omg.DynamicAny.DynAnyPackage.InvalidValue

---

Class *Interface* —extends - - -implements ○ abstract ● final △ static ▲ static final ✳ constructor x x—inherited x **x**—declared **x x**—overridden
εn—examples of usage ˌ—has subclass package—see other volume

4	public ....org.omg.CORBA.Any	**get_any** () throws org.omg.DynamicAny.DynAnyPackage.TypeMismatch, org.omg.DynamicAny.DynAnyPackage.InvalidValue
4	public .... boolean	**get_boolean** () throws org.omg.DynamicAny.DynAnyPackage.TypeMismatch, org.omg.DynamicAny.DynAnyPackage.InvalidValue
4	public .... char	**get_char** () throws org.omg.DynamicAny.DynAnyPackage.TypeMismatch, org.omg.DynamicAny.DynAnyPackage.InvalidValue
4	public ....double	**get_double** () throws org.omg.DynamicAny.DynAnyPackage.TypeMismatch, org.omg.DynamicAny.DynAnyPackage.InvalidValue
4	public ...._DynAny_	**get_dyn_any** () throws org.omg.DynamicAny.DynAnyPackage.TypeMismatch, org.omg.DynamicAny.DynAnyPackage.InvalidValue
4	public ....float	**get_float** () throws org.omg.DynamicAny.DynAnyPackage.TypeMismatch, org.omg.DynamicAny.DynAnyPackage.InvalidValue
4	public ....int	**get_long** () throws org.omg.DynamicAny.DynAnyPackage.TypeMismatch, org.omg.DynamicAny.DynAnyPackage.InvalidValue
4	public .... long	**get_longlong** () throws org.omg.DynamicAny.DynAnyPackage.TypeMismatch, org.omg.DynamicAny.DynAnyPackage.InvalidValue
2	public ....NameValuePair[]	**get_members** () throws org.omg.DynamicAny.DynAnyPackage.InvalidValue
2	public ...... NameDynAnyPair[]	**get_members_as_dyn_any** () throws org.omg.DynamicAny.DynAnyPackage↵.InvalidValue
4	public .... byte	**get_octet** () throws org.omg.DynamicAny.DynAnyPackage.TypeMismatch, org.omg.DynamicAny.DynAnyPackage.InvalidValue
4	public _org.omg.CORBA.Object_	**get_reference** () throws org.omg.DynamicAny.DynAnyPackage.TypeMismatch, org.omg.DynamicAny.DynAnyPackage.InvalidValue
4	public ....short	**get_short** () throws org.omg.DynamicAny.DynAnyPackage.TypeMismatch, org.omg.DynamicAny.DynAnyPackage.InvalidValue
4	public .... String	**get_string** () throws org.omg.DynamicAny.DynAnyPackage.TypeMismatch, org.omg.DynamicAny.DynAnyPackage.InvalidValue
4	public .... org.omg.CORBA.TypeCode	**get_typecode** () throws org.omg.DynamicAny.DynAnyPackage.TypeMismatch, org.omg.DynamicAny.DynAnyPackage.InvalidValue
4	public ....int	**get_ulong** () throws org.omg.DynamicAny.DynAnyPackage.TypeMismatch, org.omg.DynamicAny.DynAnyPackage.InvalidValue
4	public .... long	**get_ulonglong** () throws org.omg.DynamicAny.DynAnyPackage.TypeMismatch, org.omg.DynamicAny.DynAnyPackage.InvalidValue
4	public ....short	**get_ushort** () throws org.omg.DynamicAny.DynAnyPackage.TypeMismatch, org.omg.DynamicAny.DynAnyPackage.InvalidValue
4	public ...._java.io.Serializable_	**get_val** () throws org.omg.DynamicAny.DynAnyPackage.TypeMismatch, org.omg.DynamicAny.DynAnyPackage.InvalidValue
4	public .... char	**get_wchar** () throws org.omg.DynamicAny.DynAnyPackage.TypeMismatch, org.omg.DynamicAny.DynAnyPackage.InvalidValue
4	public .... String	**get_wstring** () throws org.omg.DynamicAny.DynAnyPackage.TypeMismatch, org.omg.DynamicAny.DynAnyPackage.InvalidValue
4	public ....void	**insert_any** (org.omg.CORBA.Any value) throws org↵.omg.DynamicAny.DynAnyPackage.TypeMismatch, org.omg.DynamicAny.DynAnyPackage.InvalidValue
4	public ....void	**insert_boolean** (boolean value) throws org.omg.DynamicAny.DynAnyPackage↵.TypeMismatch, org.omg.DynamicAny.DynAnyPackage.InvalidValue
4	public ....void	**insert_char** (char value) throws org.omg.DynamicAny.DynAnyPackage↵.TypeMismatch, org.omg.DynamicAny.DynAnyPackage.InvalidValue
4	public ....void	**insert_double** (double value) throws org.omg.DynamicAny.DynAnyPackage↵.TypeMismatch, org.omg.DynamicAny.DynAnyPackage.InvalidValue
4	public ....void	**insert_dyn_any** (_DynAny_ value) throws org.omg.DynamicAny.DynAnyPackage↵.TypeMismatch, org.omg.DynamicAny.DynAnyPackage.InvalidValue
4	public ....void	**insert_float** (float value) throws org.omg.DynamicAny.DynAnyPackage↵.TypeMismatch, org.omg.DynamicAny.DynAnyPackage.InvalidValue
4	public ....void	**insert_long** (int value) throws org.omg.DynamicAny.DynAnyPackage↵.TypeMismatch, org.omg.DynamicAny.DynAnyPackage.InvalidValue
4	public ....void	**insert_longlong** (long value) throws org.omg.DynamicAny.DynAnyPackage↵.TypeMismatch, org.omg.DynamicAny.DynAnyPackage.InvalidValue
4	public ....void	**insert_octet** (byte value) throws org.omg.DynamicAny.DynAnyPackage↵.TypeMismatch, org.omg.DynamicAny.DynAnyPackage.InvalidValue
4	public ....void	**insert_reference** (_org.omg.CORBA.Object_ value) throws org.omg.DynamicAny.DynAnyPackage.TypeMismatch, org.omg.DynamicAny.DynAnyPackage.InvalidValue
4	public ....void	**insert_short** (short value) throws org.omg.DynamicAny.DynAnyPackage↵.TypeMismatch, org.omg.DynamicAny.DynAnyPackage.InvalidValue
4	public ....void	**insert_string** (String value) throws org.omg.DynamicAny.DynAnyPackage↵.TypeMismatch, org.omg.DynamicAny.DynAnyPackage.InvalidValue
4	public ....void	**insert_typecode** (org.omg.CORBA.TypeCode value) throws org.omg.DynamicAny.DynAnyPackage.TypeMismatch, org.omg.DynamicAny.DynAnyPackage.InvalidValue
4	public ....void	**insert_ulong** (int value) throws org.omg.DynamicAny.DynAnyPackage↵.TypeMismatch, org.omg.DynamicAny.DynAnyPackage.InvalidValue

Classes

_DynValueStub

4	public......................void	**insert_ulonglong** (long value) throws org.omg.DynamicAny.DynAnyPackage ↵ .TypeMismatch, org.omg.DynamicAny.DynAnyPackage.InvalidValue
4	public......................void	**insert_ushort** (short value) throws org.omg.DynamicAny.DynAnyPackage ↵ .TypeMismatch, org.omg.DynamicAny.DynAnyPackage.InvalidValue
4	public......................void	**insert_val** (*java.io.Serializable* value) throws org ↵ .omg.DynamicAny.DynAnyPackage.TypeMismatch, org.omg.DynamicAny.DynAnyPackage.InvalidValue
4	public......................void	**insert_wchar** (char value) throws org.omg.DynamicAny.DynAnyPackage ↵ .TypeMismatch, org.omg.DynamicAny.DynAnyPackage.InvalidValue
4	public......................void	**insert_wstring** (String value) throws org.omg.DynamicAny.DynAnyPackage ↵ .TypeMismatch, org.omg.DynamicAny.DynAnyPackage.InvalidValue
3	public............... boolean	**is_null** ()
4	public............... boolean	**next** ()
4	public......................void	**rewind** ()
4	public............... boolean	**seek** (int index)
2	public......................void	**set_members** (NameValuePair[] value) throws org ↵ .omg.DynamicAny.DynAnyPackage.TypeMismatch, org.omg.DynamicAny.DynAnyPackage.InvalidValue
2	public......................void	**set_members_as_dyn_any** (NameDynAnyPair[] value) throws org.omg.DynamicAny.DynAnyPackage.TypeMismatch, org.omg.DynamicAny.DynAnyPackage.InvalidValue
3	public......................void	**set_to_null** ()
3	public......................void	**set_to_value** ()
4	public....org.omg.CORBA.Any	**to_any** ()
4	public.......................... . org.omg.CORBA.TypeCode	**type** ()

_IDLTypeStub | org.omg.CORBA

```
        Object
1.2 ○   └─org.omg.CORBA.portable.ObjectImpl¹ ------ Object ˌ
1.3         └─_IDLTypeStub ----------------------- IDLType (IDLTypeOperations² (IRObjectOperations³),
                                                   IRObject (IRObjectOperations³, Object,
                                                   org.omg.CORBA.portable.IDLEntity (java.io.Serializable)),
                                                   org.omg.CORBA.portable.IDLEntity (java.io.Serializable))
```

1	*25 inherited members from org.omg.CORBA.portable.ObjectImpl not shown*	
✳	public..........................	**_IDLTypeStub** ()
✳	public..........................	**_IDLTypeStub** (org.omg.CORBA.portable.Delegate delegate)
1	public................. **String[]**	**_ids** ()
3	public............DefinitionKind	**def_kind** ()
3	public......................void	**destroy** ()
2	public...............TypeCode	**type** ()

_NamingContextExtStub | org.omg.CosNaming

```
        Object
1.2 ○   └─org.omg.CORBA.portable.ObjectImpl¹ ------ org.omg.CORBA.Object ˌ
1.4         └─_NamingContextExtStub --------------- NamingContextExt (NamingContextExtOperations²
                                                    (NamingContextOperations³), NamingContext
                                                    (NamingContextOperations³, org.omg.CORBA.Object,
                                                    org.omg.CORBA.portable.IDLEntity (java.io.Serializable)),
                                                    org.omg.CORBA.portable.IDLEntity (java.io.Serializable))
```

1	*25 inherited members from org.omg.CORBA.portable.ObjectImpl not shown*	
1	public................. **String[]**	**_ids** ()
✳	public..........................	**_NamingContextExtStub** ()
3	public......................void	**bind** (NameComponent[] n, *org.omg.CORBA.Object* obj) throws org.omg.CosNaming.NamingContextPackage.NotFound, org.omg.CosNaming.NamingContextPackage.CannotProceed, org.omg.CosNaming.NamingContextPackage.InvalidName, org.omg.CosNaming.NamingContextPackage.AlreadyBound
3	public......................void	**bind_context** (NameComponent[] n, *NamingContext* nc) throws org.omg.CosNaming.NamingContextPackage.NotFound, org.omg.CosNaming.NamingContextPackage.CannotProceed, org.omg.CosNaming.NamingContextPackage.InvalidName, org.omg.CosNaming.NamingContextPackage.AlreadyBound

---

Class *Interface* ──extends - - -implements ○ abstract ● final △ static ▲ static final ✳ constructor x x──inherited x **x**──declared **x x**──overridden
εn──examples of usage ˌ──has subclass package──see other volume

3	public	*NamingContext*	**bind_new_context** (NameComponent[] n) throws

          org.omg.CosNaming.NamingContextPackage.NotFound,
          org.omg.CosNaming.NamingContextPackage.AlreadyBound,
          org.omg.CosNaming.NamingContextPackage.CannotProceed,
          org.omg.CosNaming.NamingContextPackage.InvalidName

3 public . . . . void **destroy** () throws org.omg.CosNaming.NamingContextPackage.NotEmpty

3 public . . . . void **list** (int how_many, BindingListHolder bl, BindingIteratorHolder bi)

3 public . . . . *NamingContext* **new_context** ()

3 public . . . . void **rebind** (NameComponent[] n, *org.omg.CORBA.Object* obj)
          throws org.omg.CosNaming.NamingContextPackage.NotFound,
          org.omg.CosNaming.NamingContextPackage.CannotProceed,
          org.omg.CosNaming.NamingContextPackage.InvalidName

3 public . . . . void **rebind_context** (NameComponent[] n, *NamingContext* nc)
          throws org.omg.CosNaming.NamingContextPackage.NotFound,
          org.omg.CosNaming.NamingContextPackage.CannotProceed,
          org.omg.CosNaming.NamingContextPackage.InvalidName

3 public *org.omg.CORBA.Object* **resolve** (NameComponent[] n) throws org.omg↵
          .CosNaming.NamingContextPackage.NotFound, org↵
          .omg.CosNaming.NamingContextPackage.CannotProceed,
          org.omg.CosNaming.NamingContextPackage.InvalidName

2 public *org.omg.CORBA.Object* **resolve_str** (String sn) throws org.omg.CosNaming.NamingContextPackage↵
          .NotFound, org.omg.CosNaming.NamingContextPackage.CannotProceed,
          org.omg.CosNaming.NamingContextPackage.InvalidName

2 public . . . . . . NameComponent[] **to_name** (String sn) throws org.omg.CosNaming.NamingContextPackage↵
          .InvalidName

2 public . . . . String **to_string** (NameComponent[] n) throws org.omg.CosNaming↵
          .NamingContextPackage.InvalidName

2 public . . . . String **to_url** (String addr, String sn) throws org.omg.CosNaming↵
          .NamingContextExtPackage.InvalidAddress, org.omg.CosNaming↵
          .NamingContextPackage.InvalidName

3 public . . . . void **unbind** (NameComponent[] n) throws org.omg↵
          .CosNaming.NamingContextPackage.NotFound, org↵
          .omg.CosNaming.NamingContextPackage.CannotProceed,
          org.omg.CosNaming.NamingContextPackage.InvalidName

_NamingContextImplBase　　　　　　　　　　　　　　　　org.omg.CosNaming

Object
1.2 O   └org.omg.CORBA.portable.ObjectImpl [1] - - - - - - *org.omg.CORBA.Object*
D   └org.omg.CORBA.DynamicImplementation [2]
1.2 O   └_NamingContextImplBase - - - - - - - - - - - *NamingContext* (NamingContextOperations,
                           org.omg.CORBA.Object, org.omg.CORBA.portable.IDLEntity
                           (*java.io.Serializable*))

---

1 *25 inherited members from org.omg.CORBA.portable.ObjectImpl not shown*
2 public . . . . **String[] _ids** ()
* public . . . . **_NamingContextImplBase** ()
2 public . . . . void **invoke** (org.omg.CORBA.ServerRequest r)

Classes

_NamingContextStub　　　　　　　　　　　　　　　　　　org.omg.CosNaming

Object
1.2 O   └org.omg.CORBA.portable.ObjectImpl [1] - - - - - - *org.omg.CORBA.Object*
1.2   └_NamingContextStub - - - - - - - - - - - - - - - - - *NamingContext* (NamingContextOperations [2],
                           org.omg.CORBA.Object, org.omg.CORBA.portable.IDLEntity
                           (*java.io.Serializable*))

---

1 *25 inherited members from org.omg.CORBA.portable.ObjectImpl not shown*
1 public . . . . **String[] _ids** ()
1.4 * public . . . . **_NamingContextStub** ()
2 public . . . . void **bind** (NameComponent[] n, *org.omg.CORBA.Object* obj)
          throws org.omg.CosNaming.NamingContextPackage.NotFound,
          org.omg.CosNaming.NamingContextPackage.CannotProceed,
          org.omg.CosNaming.NamingContextPackage.InvalidName,
          org.omg.CosNaming.NamingContextPackage.AlreadyBound

_NamingContextStub

2	public	void	**bind_context** (NameComponent[] n, *NamingContext* nc)

2 public....................void **bind_context** (NameComponent[] n, *NamingContext* nc)
throws org.omg.CosNaming.NamingContextPackage.NotFound,
org.omg.CosNaming.NamingContextPackage.CannotProceed,
org.omg.CosNaming.NamingContextPackage.InvalidName,
org.omg.CosNaming.NamingContextPackage.AlreadyBound

2 public.......... *NamingContext* **bind_new_context** (NameComponent[] n) throws
org.omg.CosNaming.NamingContextPackage.NotFound,
org.omg.CosNaming.NamingContextPackage.AlreadyBound,
org.omg.CosNaming.NamingContextPackage.CannotProceed,
org.omg.CosNaming.NamingContextPackage.InvalidName

2 public....................void **destroy** () throws org.omg.CosNaming.NamingContextPackage.NotEmpty

2 public....................void **list** (int how_many, BindingListHolder bl, BindingIteratorHolder bi)

2 public.......... *NamingContext* **new_context** ()

2 public....................void **rebind** (NameComponent[] n, *org.omg.CORBA.Object* obj)
throws org.omg.CosNaming.NamingContextPackage.NotFound,
org.omg.CosNaming.NamingContextPackage.CannotProceed,
org.omg.CosNaming.NamingContextPackage.InvalidName

2 public....................void **rebind_context** (NameComponent[] n, *NamingContext* nc)
throws org.omg.CosNaming.NamingContextPackage.NotFound,
org.omg.CosNaming.NamingContextPackage.CannotProceed,
org.omg.CosNaming.NamingContextPackage.InvalidName

2 public *org.omg.CORBA.Object* **resolve** (NameComponent[] n) throws org.omg↵
.CosNaming.NamingContextPackage.NotFound, org↵
.omg.CosNaming.NamingContextPackage.CannotProceed,
org.omg.CosNaming.NamingContextPackage.InvalidName

2 public....................void **unbind** (NameComponent[] n) throws org.omg↵
.CosNaming.NamingContextPackage.NotFound, org↵
.omg.CosNaming.NamingContextPackage.CannotProceed,
org.omg.CosNaming.NamingContextPackage.InvalidName

_PolicyStub — org.omg.CORBA

Object
1.2 O └org.omg.CORBA.portable.ObjectImpl[1] ------ *Object*ˇ
1.3   └_PolicyStub ----------------------- *Policy*ˇ (*PolicyOperations*[2], *Object*,
                                                org.omg.CORBA.portable.IDLEntity (*java.io.Serializable*))

1 *25 inherited members from org.omg.CORBA.portable.ObjectImpl not shown*
1 public.................. **String[]** **_ids** ()
∗ public.......................... **_PolicyStub** ()
∗ public.......................... **_PolicyStub** (org.omg.CORBA.portable.Delegate delegate)
2 public....................*Policy* **copy** ()
2 public....................void **destroy** ()
2 public....................int **policy_type** ()

_Remote_Stub — org.omg.stub.java.rmi

Object
1.2 O └org.omg.CORBA.portable.ObjectImpl[1] ------ *org.omg.CORBA.Object*ˇ
1.3 O   └org.omg.CORBA_2_3.portable.ObjectImpl[2]
1.3 O   └javax.rmi.CORBA.Stub[3] ------------- *java.io.Serializable*ˇ
1.3 ●   └_Remote_Stub ------------------- *java.rmi.Remote*ˇ

1 *22 inherited members from org.omg.CORBA.portable.ObjectImpl not shown*
3 *4 inherited members from javax.rmi.CORBA.Stub not shown*
2 public....................String _get_codebase ()
1 public.................. **String[]** **_ids** ()
∗ public.......................... **_Remote_Stub** ()

Class *Interface* —extends - - -implements O abstract ● final △ static ▲ static final ∗ constructor × x—inherited × **x**—declared **x x**—overridden
εn—examples of usage ˇ—has subclass package—see other volume

426

_ServantActivatorStub | org.omg.PortableServer

```
      Object
1.2 O └org.omg.CORBA.portable.ObjectImpl¹ ------ org.omg.CORBA.Object
1.4        └_ServantActivatorStub --------------- ServantActivator (ServantActivatorOperations²
                                    (ServantManagerOperations), ServantManager
                                    (ServantManagerOperations, org.omg.CORBA.Object,
                                    org.omg.CORBA.portable.IDLEntity (java.io.Serializable)),
                                    org.omg.CORBA.portable.IDLEntity (java.io.Serializable))
```

	1	*25 inherited members from org.omg.CORBA.portable.ObjectImpl not shown*	
	1	public .... **String[] _ids** ()	
▲		public static final .... Class **_opsClass**	
✳		public .... **_ServantActivatorStub** ()	
	2	public .... void **etherealize** (byte[] oid, *POA* adapter, Servant serv, boolean cleanup_in_progress, boolean remaining_activations)	
	2	public .... Servant **incarnate** (byte[] oid, *POA* adapter) throws ForwardRequest	

_ServantLocatorStub | org.omg.PortableServer

```
      Object
1.2 O └org.omg.CORBA.portable.ObjectImpl¹ ------ org.omg.CORBA.Object
1.4        └_ServantLocatorStub --------------- ServantLocator (ServantLocatorOperations²
                                    (ServantManagerOperations), ServantManager
                                    (ServantManagerOperations, org.omg.CORBA.Object,
                                    org.omg.CORBA.portable.IDLEntity (java.io.Serializable)),
                                    org.omg.CORBA.portable.IDLEntity (java.io.Serializable))
```

	1	*25 inherited members from org.omg.CORBA.portable.ObjectImpl not shown*
	1	public .... **String[] _ids** ()
▲		public static final .... Class **_opsClass**
✳		public .... **_ServantLocatorStub** ()
	2	public .... void **postinvoke** (byte[] oid, *POA* adapter, String operation, Object the_cookie, Servant the_servant)
	2	public .... Servant **preinvoke** (byte[] oid, *POA* adapter, String operation, org.omg.PortableServer↵ .ServantLocatorPackage.CookieHolder the_cookie) throws ForwardRequest

AbstractCollection | java.util

```
      Object¹
1.2 O └AbstractCollection --------------------- Collection ²
```

✳		protected .... **AbstractCollection** ()	
	2	public .... boolean **add** (Object o)	ε342,349,352,354,358
	2	public .... boolean **addAll** (*Collection* c)	ε351,353
	2	public .... void **clear** ()	ε351,353
	2	public .... boolean **contains** (Object o)	ε352
	2	public .... boolean **containsAll** (*Collection* c)	
	2	public .... boolean **isEmpty** ()	ε102
O	2	public abstract .... *Iterator* **iterator** ()	ε345,352,354,355,356
	2	public .... boolean **remove** (Object o)	ε349,352
	2	public .... boolean **removeAll** (*Collection* c)	ε351,353
	2	public .... boolean **retainAll** (*Collection* c)	ε351,353
O	2	public abstract .... int **size** ()	ε340,349,351,352,358
	2	public .... Object[] **toArray** ()	ε340
	2	public .... Object[] **toArray** (Object[] a)	ε340,352,358,194,508
	1	public .... **String toString** ()	

AbstractInterruptibleChannel | java.nio.channels.spi

```
      Object                                                          ε178,183
1.4 O └AbstractInterruptibleChannel ------------- java.nio.channels.Channel ¹, java.nio.channels↵
                                    .InterruptibleChannel (java.nio.channels.Channel ¹)
```

✳		protected .... **AbstractInterruptibleChannel** ()	
●		protected final .... void **begin** ()	
●	1	public final .... void **close** () throws java.io.IOException	ε167,170,171,172,174
●		protected final .... void **end** (boolean completed) throws java.nio.channels.AsynchronousCloseException	
O		protected abstract .... void **implCloseChannel** () throws java.io.IOException	

A

Classes

AbstractInterruptibleChannel

● *1* public final .... boolean **isOpen** ()

AbstractList | java.util

Object[1]
1.2 ○ └ AbstractCollection[2] - *Collection*
1.2 ○ └ AbstractList - *List*[3] (*Collection*)

✳		protected	**AbstractList** ()	
	2	public ....**boolean**	**add** (Object o)	ε342,349,352,354,358
	3	public ....void	**add** (int index, Object element)	ε349,362
	2	public .... boolean	**addAll** (*Collection* c)	ε351,353
	3	public .... boolean	**addAll** (int index, *Collection* c)	
	2	public .... **void clear** ()		ε351,353
	2	public .... boolean contains (Object o)		ε352
	2	public .... boolean containsAll (*Collection* c)		
	1	public ....**boolean equals** (Object o)		
○	3	public abstract .... Object **get** (int index)		ε349,234
	1	public ....**int hashCode** ()		
	3	public ....int **indexOf** (Object o)		
	2	public .... boolean isEmpty ()		ε102
	2	public .... ***Iterator* iterator** ()		ε345,352,354,355,356
	3	public ....int **lastIndexOf** (Object o)		
	3	public ......*ListIterator* **listIterator** ()		
	3	public ......*ListIterator* **listIterator** (int index)		
		protected transient ....int **modCount**		
	3	public .... Object **remove** (int index)		ε349
	2	public .... boolean remove (Object o)		ε349,352
	2	public .... boolean removeAll (*Collection* c)		ε351,353
		protected ....void **removeRange** (int fromIndex, int toIndex)		
	2	public .... boolean retainAll (*Collection* c)		ε351,353
	3	public .... Object **set** (int index, Object element)		ε348
○	2	public abstract ....int size ()		ε340,349,351,352,358
	3	public .... *List* **subList** (int fromIndex, int toIndex)		ε351
	2	public .... Object[] toArray ()		ε340
	2	public .... Object[] toArray (Object[] a)		ε340,352,358,194,508
	2	public .... String toString ()		

AbstractMap | java.util

Object[1]
1.2 ○ └ AbstractMap - *Map*[2]

✳		protected	**AbstractMap** ()	
	2	public ....void **clear** ()		
	1	protected ....**Object clone** () throws CloneNotSupportedException		
	2	public .... boolean **containsKey** (Object key)		ε344
	2	public .... boolean **containsValue** (Object value)		
○	2	public abstract .... *Set* **entrySet** ()		ε345
	1	public ....**boolean equals** (Object o)		
	2	public .... Object **get** (Object key)		ε337,344,346,356,357
	1	public ....**int hashCode** ()		
	2	public .... boolean **isEmpty** ()		
	2	public .... *Set* **keySet** ()		ε194,340,345,355,356
	2	public .... Object **put** (Object key, Object value)		ε337,344,346,355,356
	2	public ....void **putAll** (*Map* t)		
	2	public .... Object **remove** (Object key)		ε355
	2	public ....int **size** ()		ε355
	1	public ....**String toString** ()		
	2	public .... *Collection* **values** ()		ε340,345,355

Class *Interface* —extends - - -implements ○ abstract ● final △ static ▲ static final ✳ constructor x x—inherited x **x**—declared **x x**—overridden
ε*n*—examples of usage ⌐has subclass package—see other volume

AbstractMethodError — java.lang

```
Object
└ Throwable ---------------------------- java.io.Serializable
  └ Error
    └ LinkageError
      └ IncompatibleClassChangeError
        └ AbstractMethodError
```

∗	public	**AbstractMethodError** ()	
∗	public	**AbstractMethodError** (String s)	

AbstractPreferences — java.util.prefs

```
       Object
1.4 ○  └ Preferences¹
1.4 ○    └ AbstractPreferences
```

		type	member	page
	1	public	**String** **absolutePath** ()	ε411
∗		protected	**AbstractPreferences** (AbstractPreferences parent, String name)	
	1	public	**void** **addNodeChangeListener** (*NodeChangeListener* ncl)	ε422
	1	public	**void** **addPreferenceChangeListener** (*PreferenceChangeListener* pcl)	ε421
●		protected final .... AbstractPreferences[]	**cachedChildren** ()	
	1	public	**String[]** **childrenNames** () throws BackingStoreException	ε416,417
○		protected abstract ..... String[]	**childrenNamesSpi** () throws BackingStoreException	
○		protected abstract .... AbstractPreferences	**childSpi** (String name)	
	1	public	**void** **clear** () throws BackingStoreException	ε408
	1	public	**void** **exportNode** (java.io.OutputStream os) throws java.io.IOException, BackingStoreException	ε419
	1	public	**void** **exportSubtree** (java.io.OutputStream os) throws java.io.IOException, BackingStoreException	ε420
	1	public	**void** **flush** () throws BackingStoreException	
○		protected abstract	**void** **flushSpi** () throws BackingStoreException	
	1	public	**String** **get** (String key, String def)	ε405,406,407,409
	1	public	**boolean** **getBoolean** (String key, boolean def)	ε409
	1	public	**byte[]** **getByteArray** (String key, byte[] def)	ε409
		protected .AbstractPreferences	**getChild** (String nodeName) throws BackingStoreException	
	1	public	**double** **getDouble** (String key, double def)	ε409
	1	public	**float** **getFloat** (String key, float def)	ε409
	1	public	**int** **getInt** (String key, int def)	ε409
	1	public	**long** **getLong** (String key, long def)	ε409
○		protected abstract .... String	**getSpi** (String key)	
△	1	public static	**void** importPreferences (java.io.InputStream is) throws java.io.IOException, InvalidPreferencesFormatException	ε418
		protected .... boolean	**isRemoved** ()	
	1	public	**boolean** **isUserNode** ()	
	1	public	**String[]** **keys** () throws BackingStoreException	ε407
○		protected abstract ..... String[]	**keysSpi** () throws BackingStoreException	
●		protected final .... Object	**lock**	
	1	public	**String** **name** ()	ε411
		protected .... boolean	**newNode**	
	1	public	**Preferences** **node** (String path)	ε415,413,414,416,417
	1	public	**boolean** **nodeExists** (String path) throws BackingStoreException	ε414,415
	1	public	**Preferences** **parent** ()	ε411,416,420
	1	public	**void** **put** (String key, String value)	ε405,409,419,420,421
	1	public	**void** **putBoolean** (String key, boolean value)	ε409,419,420
	1	public	**void** **putByteArray** (String key, byte[] value)	ε409,419,420
	1	public	**void** **putDouble** (String key, double value)	ε409,419,420
	1	public	**void** **putFloat** (String key, float value)	ε409,419,420
	1	public	**void** **putInt** (String key, int value)	ε409,419,420
	1	public	**void** **putLong** (String key, long value)	ε409,419,420
○		protected abstract .... void	**putSpi** (String key, String value)	
	1	public	**void** **remove** (String key)	ε408,421
	1	public	**void** **removeNode** () throws BackingStoreException	ε414,415,422
	1	public	**void** **removeNodeChangeListener** (*NodeChangeListener* ncl)	
○		protected abstract .... void	**removeNodeSpi** () throws BackingStoreException	
	1	public	**void** **removePreferenceChangeListener** (*PreferenceChangeListener* pcl)	
○		protected abstract .... void	**removeSpi** (String key)	
	1	public	**void** **sync** () throws BackingStoreException	

AbstractPreferences

○		protected abstract ....void	**syncSpi** () throws BackingStoreException		
△	1	public static .... Preferences	systemNodeForPackage (Class c)		ε413
△	1	public static .... Preferences	systemRoot ()		ε411,413
	1	public.................. **String**	**toString** ()		
△	1	public static .... Preferences	userNodeForPackage (Class c)		ε405,408,409,413,416
△	1	public static .... Preferences	userRoot ()		ε411,413,414,415,417

AbstractSelectableChannel	java.nio.channels.spi

Object   ε178,183

1.4 ○ └AbstractInterruptibleChannel[1] - - - - - - - - - - - - *java.nio.channels.Channel* ◡, *java.nio.channels.InterruptibleChannel*
                                                   (*java.nio.channels.Channel*)

1.4 ○   └java.nio.channels.SelectableChannel[2]
1.4 ○   └AbstractSelectableChannel ◡

✳		protected	**AbstractSelectableChannel** (SelectorProvider provider)	
●	1	protected final............void	begin ()	
●	2	public final ....**Object**	**blockingLock** ()	
●	1	public final ....void	close () throws java.io.IOException	ε167,170,171,172,174
●	2	public final ....**java.nio.channels** ◡ **.SelectableChannel**	**configureBlocking** (boolean block) throws java.io.IOException ε173,177,179	
●	1	protected final.............void	end (boolean completed) throws java.nio.channels.AsynchronousCloseException	
●	1	protected final............ **void**	**implCloseChannel** () throws java.io.IOException	
○		protected abstract ....void	**implCloseSelectableChannel** () throws java.io.IOException	
○		protected abstract ....void	**implConfigureBlocking** (boolean block) throws java.io.IOException	
●	2	public final ....**boolean**	**isBlocking** ()	
●	1	public final .... boolean	isOpen ()	
●	2	public final ....**boolean**	**isRegistered** ()	
●	2	public final .... **java.nio** ◡ **.channels.SelectionKey**	**keyFor** (java.nio.channels.Selector sel)	
●	2	public final . **SelectorProvider**	**provider** ()	
●	2	public final .... java ◡ .nio.channels.SelectionKey	register (java.nio.channels.Selector sel, int ops) throws java.nio.channels.ClosedChannelException	ε176,179
●	2	public final .... **java.nio** ◡ **.channels.SelectionKey**	**register** (java.nio.channels.Selector sel, int ops, Object att) throws java.nio.channels.ClosedChannelException	
○	2	public abstract ....int	validOps ()	ε176

AbstractSelectionKey	java.nio.channels.spi

Object

1.4 ○ └java.nio.channels.SelectionKey[1]
1.4 ○   └AbstractSelectionKey

✳		protected	**AbstractSelectionKey** ()	
●	1	public final ....Object	attach (Object ob)	
●	1	public final ....Object	attachment ()	
●	1	public final .... **void**	**cancel** ()	ε176
○	1	public abstract .... java.nio.channels ◡ .SelectableChannel	channel ()	ε176,179
○	1	public abstract ....int	interestOps ()	
○	1	public abstract .... java ◡ .nio.channels.SelectionKey	interestOps (int ops)	
●	1	public final .... boolean	isAcceptable ()	ε179
●	1	public final .... boolean	isConnectable ()	ε176
●	1	public final .... boolean	isReadable ()	ε176
●	1	public final ....**boolean**	**isValid** ()	ε176
●	1	public final .... boolean	isWritable ()	ε176
○	1	public abstract ....int	readyOps ()	
○	1	public abstract .... java.nio.channels.Selector	selector ()	

Class   *Interface* ——extends - - -implements ○ abstract ● final △ static ▲ static final ✳ constructor x x—inherited x **x**—declared **x x**—overridden
ε*n*—examples of usage ◡—has subclass package—see other volume

		AbstractSelector		java.nio.channels.spi

Object
- 1.4 ○ └java.nio.channels.Selector [1]
- 1.4 ○   └AbstractSelector

✳		protected......................	**AbstractSelector** (SelectorProvider provider)	
●		protected final..............void	**begin** ()	
●		protected final......*java.util.Set*	**cancelledKeys** ()	
●	1	public final .... **void**	**close** () throws java.io.IOException	
●		protected final.............void	**deregister** (AbstractSelectionKey key)	
●		protected final............void	**end** ()	
○		protected abstract ....void	**implCloseSelector** () throws java.io.IOException	
●	1	public final ....**boolean**	**isOpen** ()	
○	1	public abstract.....*java.util.Set*	keys ()	
△	1	public static	open () throws java.io.IOException	ε176,179
		... java.nio.channels.Selector		
●	1	public final . **SelectorProvider**	**provider** ()	
○		protected abstract ...... java↩	**register** (AbstractSelectableChannel ch, int ops, Object att)	
		.nio.channels.SelectionKey		
○	1	public abstract..............int	select () throws java.io.IOException	ε176,179
○	1	public abstract..............int	select (long timeout) throws java.io.IOException	
○	1	public abstract.....*java.util.Set*	selectedKeys ()	ε176,179
○	1	public abstract..............int	selectNow () throws java.io.IOException	
○	1	public abstract.................	wakeup ()	
		... java.nio.channels.Selector		

		AbstractSequentialList		java.util

Object
- 1.2 ○ └AbstractCollection [1] - *Collection*
- 1.2 ○   └AbstractList [2] - *List* (*Collection*)
- 1.2 ○   └AbstractSequentialList

✳		protected......................	**AbstractSequentialList** ()	
	2	public.................. boolean	add (Object o)	ε342,349,352,354,358
	2	public...................... **void**	**add** (int index, Object element)	ε349,362
	1	public.................. boolean	addAll (*Collection* c)	ε351,353
	2	public................**boolean**	**addAll** (int index, *Collection* c)	
	2	public.....................void	clear ()	ε351,353
	1	public.................. boolean	contains (Object o)	ε352
	1	public.................. boolean	containsAll (*Collection* c)	
	2	public.................. boolean	equals (Object o)	
	2	public.............**Object get** (int index)		ε349,234
	2	public......................int	hashCode ()	
	2	public......................int	indexOf (Object o)	
	1	public.................. boolean	isEmpty ()	ε102
	2	public.............*Iterator* **iterator** ()		ε345,352,354,355,356
	2	public......................int	lastIndexOf (Object o)	
	2	public...............*ListIterator* listIterator ()		
○	2	public abstract .... **ListIterator** **listIterator** (int index)		
	2	protected transient...........int	modCount	
	2	public................**Object remove** (int index)		ε349
	1	public.................. boolean	remove (Object o)	ε349,352
	1	public.................. boolean	removeAll (*Collection* c)	ε351,353
	2	protected...................void	removeRange (int fromIndex, int toIndex)	
	1	public.................. boolean	retainAll (*Collection* c)	ε351,353
	2	public................**Object set** (int index, Object element)		ε348
○	1	public abstract..............int	size ()	ε340,349,351,352,358
	2	public..................... *List*	subList (int fromIndex, int toIndex)	ε351
	1	public.................. Object[]	toArray ()	ε340
	1	public.................. Object[]	toArray (Object[] a)	ε340,352,358,194,508
	1	public.................... String	toString ()	

		AbstractSet		java.util

Object [1]
- 1.2 ○ └AbstractCollection [2] - *Collection*
- 1.2 ○   └AbstractSet - *Set* (*Collection*)

AbstractSet

✱	protected		**AbstractSet** ()	
2	public	boolean	add (Object o)	ε342,349,352,354,358
2	public	boolean	addAll (*Collection* c)	ε351,353
2	public	void	clear ()	ε351,353
2	public	boolean	contains (Object o)	ε352
2	public	boolean	containsAll (*Collection* c)	
1	public	**boolean**	**equals** (Object o)	
1	public	**int**	**hashCode** ()	
2	public	boolean	isEmpty ()	ε102
○ 2	public abstract	*Iterator*	iterator ()	ε345,352,354,355,356
2	public	boolean	remove (Object o)	ε349,352
2	public	**boolean**	**removeAll** (*Collection* c)	ε351,353
2	public	boolean	retainAll (*Collection* c)	ε351,353
○ 2	public abstract	int	size ()	ε340,349,351,352,358
2	public	Object[]	toArray ()	ε340
2	public	Object[]	toArray (Object[] a)	ε340,352,358,194,508
2	public	String	toString ()	

AccessControlContext   java.security

Object[1]
└ AccessControlContext
1.2 ●

✱	public	**AccessControlContext** (ProtectionDomain[] context)
1.3 ✱	public	**AccessControlContext** (AccessControlContext acc, *DomainCombiner* combiner)
	public . . . . void	**checkPermission** (Permission perm) throws AccessControlException
1	public	**boolean**	**equals** (Object obj)
1.3	public	*DomainCombiner*	**getDomainCombiner** ()
1	public	**int**	**hashCode** ()

AccessControlException   java.security

Object   ε216
└ Throwable - *java.io.Serializable*
  └ Exception
    └ RuntimeException
      └ SecurityException
1.2   └ AccessControlException

✱	public	**AccessControlException** (String s)
✱	public	**AccessControlException** (String s, Permission p)
	public . . . . Permission	**getPermission** ()

AccessController   java.security

Object
└ AccessController
1.2 ●

△	public static . . . . void	**checkPermission** (Permission perm) throws AccessControlException
			ε213
△	public static native . . . . . . Object	**doPrivileged** (*PrivilegedAction* action)
△	public static native . . . . . . Object	**doPrivileged** (*PrivilegedExceptionAction* action) throws PrivilegedActionException
△	public static native . . . . . . Object	**doPrivileged** (*PrivilegedAction* action, AccessControlContext context)
△	public static native . . . . . . Object	**doPrivileged** (*PrivilegedExceptionAction* action, AccessControlContext context)
			throws PrivilegedActionException
△	public static	**getContext** ()
	. . . . AccessControlContext	

Class *Interface* —extends - - -implements ○ abstract ● final △ static ▲ static final ✱ constructor x x—inherited x **x**—declared **x x**—overridden
ε*n*—examples of usage ⌐—has subclass package—see other volume

AccessException

```
     Object
      └Throwable  - - - - - - - - - - - - - - - - - - - - - - - - - java.io.Serializable
        └Exception
          └java.io.IOException
1.1         └RemoteException¹
1.1           └AccessException
```

*	public.........................		**AccessException** (String s)
*	public.........................		**AccessException** (String s, Exception ex)
	1 public................Throwable		detail
1.4	1 public................Throwable		getCause ()
	1 public.....................String		getMessage ()

AccessibleObject

```
     Object
1.2   └AccessibleObject
```

*	protected......................		**AccessibleObject** ()
	public.................boolean		**isAccessible** ()
	public.........................void		**setAccessible** (boolean flag) throws SecurityException ε110
△	public static ....void		**setAccessible** (AccessibleObject[] array, boolean flag) throws SecurityException

AccountExpiredException

```
     Object
      └Throwable  - - - - - - - - - - - - - - - - - - - - - - - - - java.io.Serializable
        └Exception
1.2       └java.security.GeneralSecurityException
1.4         └LoginException
1.4           └AccountExpiredException
```

*	public.........................		**AccountExpiredException** ()
*	public.........................		**AccountExpiredException** (String msg)

Acl

```
1.1   Acl——————————————————————— Owner ¹
```

public.................boolean	**addEntry** (*java.security.Principal* caller, *AclEntry* entry) throws NotOwnerException
1 public.................boolean	addOwner (*java.security.Principal* caller, *java.security.Principal* owner)
	throws NotOwnerException
public.................boolean	**checkPermission** (*java.security.Principal* principal, *Permission* permission)
1 public.................boolean	deleteOwner (*java.security.Principal* caller, *java.security.Principal* owner)
	throws NotOwnerException, LastOwnerException
public.... *java.util.Enumeration*	**entries** ()
public.....................String	**getName** ()
public.... *java.util.Enumeration*	**getPermissions** (*java.security.Principal* user)
1 public.................boolean	isOwner (*java.security.Principal* user)
public.................boolean	**removeEntry** (*java.security.Principal* caller, *AclEntry* entry)
	throws NotOwnerException
public.....................void	**setName** (*java.security.Principal* caller, String name) throws NotOwnerException
public.....................String	**toString** ()

AclEntry

```
1.1   AclEntry—————————————————————— Cloneable
```

public.................boolean	**addPermission** (*Permission* permission)
public.................boolean	**checkPermission** (*Permission* permission)
public...................Object	**clone** ()
public... *java.security.Principal*	**getPrincipal** ()
public.................boolean	**isNegative** ()
public.... *java.util.Enumeration*	**permissions** ()
public.................boolean	**removePermission** (*Permission* permission)
public.....................void	**setNegativePermissions** ()
public.................boolean	**setPrincipal** (*java.security.Principal* user)

| | public | String | **toString** () |

- -

A

AclNotFoundException | java.security.acl

```
Object
└ Throwable  - - - - - - - - - - - - - - - - - - - - - - - - - - -  java.io.Serializable
    └ Exception
1.1     └ AclNotFoundException
```

| ✳ | public | **AclNotFoundException** () |

Activatable | java.rmi.activation

ε188

```
    Object
1.1 ○ └ java.rmi.server.RemoteObject¹  - - - - - - - - - - - -  java.rmi.Remote, java.io.Serializable
1.1 ○     └ java.rmi.server.RemoteServer²
1.2 ○         └ Activatable
```

✳	protected		**Activatable** (ActivationID id, int port) throws java.rmi.RemoteException
✳	protected		**Activatable** (String location, java.rmi.MarshalledObject data, boolean restart, int port) throws ActivationException, java.rmi.RemoteException
✳	protected		**Activatable** (ActivationID id, int port, *java.rmi.server.RMIClientSocketFactory* csf, *java.rmi.server.RMIServerSocketFactory* ssf) throws java.rmi.RemoteException
✳	protected		**Activatable** (String location, java.rmi.MarshalledObject data, boolean restart, int port, *java.rmi.server.RMIClientSocketFactory* csf, *java.rmi.server.RMIServerSocketFactory* ssf) throws ActivationException, java.rmi.RemoteException
	1	public	boolean	equals (Object obj)
△		public static .. *java.rmi.Remote*	**exportObject** (*java.rmi.Remote* obj, ActivationID id, int port) throws java.rmi.RemoteException
△		public static .. *java.rmi.Remote*	**exportObject** (*java.rmi.Remote* obj, ActivationID id, int port, *java.rmi.server.RMIClientSocketFactory* csf, *java.rmi.server.RMIServerSocketFactory* ssf) throws java.rmi.RemoteException
△		public static .... ActivationID	**exportObject** (*java.rmi.Remote* obj, String location, java.rmi.MarshalledObject data, boolean restart, int port) throws ActivationException, java.rmi.RemoteException
△		public static .... ActivationID	**exportObject** (*java.rmi.Remote* obj, String location, java.rmi.MarshalledObject data, boolean restart, int port, *java.rmi.server.RMIClientSocketFactory* csf, *java.rmi.server.RMIServerSocketFactory* ssf) throws ActivationException, java.rmi.RemoteException
△	2	public static .... String	getClientHost () throws java.rmi.server.ServerNotActiveException
		protected .... ActivationID	**getID** ()
△	2	public static java.io.PrintStream	getLog ()
	1	public	getRef () ... *java.rmi.server.RemoteRef*
	1	public	int	hashCode ()
△		public static .... boolean	**inactive** (ActivationID id) throws UnknownObjectException, ActivationException, java.rmi.RemoteException
	1	protected transient	ref ... *java.rmi.server.RemoteRef*
△		public static .. *java.rmi.Remote*	**register** (ActivationDesc desc) throws UnknownGroupException, ActivationException, java.rmi.RemoteException
△	2	public static .... void	setLog (java.io.OutputStream out)
	1	public	String	toString ()
△	1	public static .. *java.rmi.Remote*	toStub (*java.rmi.Remote* obj) throws java.rmi.NoSuchObjectException
△		public static .... boolean	**unexportObject** (*java.rmi.Remote* obj, boolean force) throws java.rmi.NoSuchObjectException
△		public static .... void	**unregister** (ActivationID id) throws UnknownObjectException, ActivationException, java.rmi.RemoteException

---

Class *Interface* —extends - - -implements ○ abstract ● final △ static ▲ static final ✳ constructor x x—inherited x **x**—declared **x x**—overridden
ε*n*—examples of usage ⌄—has subclass package—see other volume

ActivateFailedException | java.rmi.activation

```
        Object
        └Throwable  - - - - - - - - - - - - - - - - - - - - - - - - -  java.io.Serializable
          └Exception
            └java.io.IOException
1.1           └java.rmi.RemoteException 1
1.2             └ActivateFailedException
```

*	public		**ActivateFailedException** (String s)
*	public		**ActivateFailedException** (String s, Exception ex)
	1 public	Throwable	detail
1.4	1 public	Throwable	getCause ()
	1 public	String	getMessage ()

ActivationDesc | java.rmi.activation

```
         Object 1
1.2 ●    └ActivationDesc - - - - - - - - - - - - - - - - - - - - - - -  java.io.Serializable
```

*	public		**ActivationDesc** (String className, String location, java.rmi.MarshalledObject data) throws ActivationException
*	public		**ActivationDesc** (String className, String location, java.rmi.MarshalledObject data, boolean restart) throws ActivationException
*	public		**ActivationDesc** (ActivationGroupID groupID, String className, String location, java.rmi.MarshalledObject data)
*	public		**ActivationDesc** (ActivationGroupID groupID, String className, String location, java.rmi.MarshalledObject data, boolean restart)
	1 public	**boolean**	**equals** (Object obj)
	public	String	**getClassName** ()
	public		**getData** ()
		... java.rmi.MarshalledObject	
	public	ActivationGroupID	**getGroupID** ()
	public	String	**getLocation** ()
	public	boolean	**getRestartMode** ()
	1 public	**int**	**hashCode** ()

ActivationException | java.rmi.activation

```
        Object
        └Throwable 1  - - - - - - - - - - - - - - - - - - - - - - - -  java.io.Serializable
          └Exception
1.2         └ActivationException
```

*	public		**ActivationException** ()
*	public		**ActivationException** (String s)
*	public		**ActivationException** (String s, Throwable ex)
	public	Throwable	**detail**
1.4	1 public	**Throwable**	**getCause** ()
	1 public	**String**	**getMessage** ()

ActivationGroup | java.rmi.activation

```
                                                              ε188
         Object
1.1 ○    └java.rmi.server.RemoteObject 1  - - - - - - - - - - -  java.rmi.Remote , java.io.Serializable
1.1 ○      └java.rmi.server.RemoteServer 2
1.1          └java.rmi.server.UnicastRemoteObject 3
1.2 ○          └ActivationGroup - - - - - - - - - - - - - - - - -  ActivationInstantiator (java.rmi.Remote)
```

*	protected		**ActivationGroup** (ActivationGroupID groupID) throws java.rmi.RemoteException
○	public abstract	void	**activeObject** (ActivationID id, *java.rmi.Remote* obj) throws ActivationException, UnknownObjectException, java.rmi.RemoteException
	protected	void	**activeObject** (ActivationID id, java.rmi.MarshalledObject mobj) throws ActivationException, UnknownObjectException, java.rmi.RemoteException
	3 public	Object	clone () throws CloneNotSupportedException
△	public static synchronized		**createGroup** (ActivationGroupID id, ActivationGroupDesc desc, long incarnation) throws ActivationException
		ActivationGroup	
△	public static synchronized		**currentGroupID** ()
		ActivationGroupID	

A

Classes

ActivationGroup

	1	public.................. boolean	equals (Object obj)
△	3	public static	exportObject (*java.rmi.Remote* obj) throws java.rmi.RemoteException
		..java.rmi.server.RemoteStub	
△	3	public static .. *java.rmi.Remote*	exportObject (*java.rmi.Remote* obj, int port) throws java.rmi.RemoteException
△	3	public static .. *java.rmi.Remote*	exportObject (*java.rmi.Remote* obj, int port, *java.rmi.server.RMIClientSocketFactory*
			csf, *java.rmi.server.RMIServerSocketFactory* ssf)
			throws java.rmi.RemoteException
△	2	public static ....String	getClientHost () throws java.rmi.server.ServerNotActiveException
△	2	public static java.io.PrintStream	getLog ()
	1	public............................	getRef ()
		... *java.rmi.server.RemoteRef*	
△		public static synchronized	**getSystem** () throws ActivationException
		.... *ActivationSystem*	
	1	public.........................int	hashCode ()
		protected ....void	**inactiveGroup** () throws UnknownGroupException, java.rmi.RemoteException
		public................. boolean	**inactiveObject** (ActivationID id) throws ActivationException,
			UnknownObjectException, java.rmi.RemoteException
	1	protected transient.............	ref
		... *java.rmi.server.RemoteRef*	
△	2	public static ....void	setLog (java.io.OutputStream out)
△		public static synchronized void	**setSystem** (*ActivationSystem* system) throws ActivationException
	1	public....................String	toString ()
△	1	public static .. *java.rmi.Remote*	toStub (*java.rmi.Remote* obj) throws java.rmi.NoSuchObjectException
△	3	public static .... boolean	unexportObject (*java.rmi.Remote* obj, boolean force)
			throws java.rmi.NoSuchObjectException

ActivationGroup_Stub | java.rmi.activation

ε188

Object
1.1 ○ └java.rmi.server.RemoteObject[1] - - - - - - - - - - - *java.rmi.Remote*˸, *java.io.Serializable*˸
1.1 ○   └java.rmi.server.RemoteStub
1.2 ●   └ActivationGroup_Stub - - - - - - - - - - - - - - - *ActivationInstantiator* [2] (*java.rmi.Remote*)

✳		public........................	**ActivationGroup_Stub** (*java.rmi.server.RemoteRef*)
	1	public................. boolean	equals (Object obj)
	1	public........................	getRef ()
		... *java.rmi.server.RemoteRef*	
	1	public......................int	hashCode ()
	2	public........................	**newInstance** (ActivationID, ActivationDesc) throws java.rmi.RemoteException,
		... java.rmi.MarshalledObject	ActivationException
	1	protected transient............	ref
		... *java.rmi.server.RemoteRef*	
	1	public....................String	toString ()
△	1	public static .. *java.rmi.Remote*	toStub (*java.rmi.Remote* obj) throws java.rmi.NoSuchObjectException

---

ActivationGroupDesc | java.rmi.activation

Object[1]
1.2 ● └ActivationGroupDesc - - - - - - - - - - - - - - - - - - - *java.io.Serializable*˸

✳		public........................	**ActivationGroupDesc** (java.util.Properties overrides,
			ActivationGroupDesc.CommandEnvironment cmd)
✳		public........................	**ActivationGroupDesc** (String className, String location,
			java.rmi.MarshalledObject data, java.util.Properties overrides,
			ActivationGroupDesc.CommandEnvironment cmd)
	1	public................**boolean**	**equals** (Object obj)
		public....................String	**getClassName** ()
		public . ActivationGroupDesc ↵	**getCommandEnvironment** ()
		.CommandEnvironment	
		public........................	**getData** ()
		... java.rmi.MarshalledObject	
		public....................String	**getLocation** ()
		public.......java.util.Properties	**getPropertyOverrides** ()
	1	public...................... **int**	**hashCode** ()

Class   *Interface*   —extends   - - -implements   ○ abstract   ● final   △ static   ▲ static final   ✳ constructor   x x—inherited   x **x**—declared   **x x**—overridden
ε*n*—examples of usage   ˸—has subclass   package—see other volume

ActivationGroupDesc.CommandEnvironment · java.rmi.activation

Object[1]
1.2 └─ActivationGroupDesc.CommandEnvironment - *java.io.Serializable*

*	public..........................		**ActivationGroupDesc.CommandEnvironment** (String cmdpath, String[] argv)
1	public.................	**boolean**	**equals** (Object obj)
	public...................	String[]	**getCommandOptions** ()
	public...................	String	**getCommandPath** ()
1	public.......................	**int**	**hashCode** ()

ActivationGroupID · java.rmi.activation

Object[1]
1.2 └─ActivationGroupID - *java.io.Serializable*

*	public..........................		**ActivationGroupID** (*ActivationSystem* system)
1	public.................	**boolean**	**equals** (Object obj)
	public........	*ActivationSystem*	**getSystem** ()
1	public.......................	**int**	**hashCode** ()

ActivationID · java.rmi.activation

Object[1]
1.2 └─ActivationID - *java.io.Serializable*

	public.........	*java.rmi.Remote*	**activate** (boolean force) throws ActivationException, UnknownObjectException, java.rmi.RemoteException
*	public..........................		**ActivationID** (*Activator* activator)
1	public.................	**boolean**	**equals** (Object obj)
1	public.......................	**int**	**hashCode** ()

ActivationInstantiator · java.rmi.activation

1.2 *ActivationInstantiator* ──────────── *java.rmi.Remote*

	public......................		**newInstance** (ActivationID id, ActivationDesc desc)
	... java.rmi.MarshalledObject		throws ActivationException, java.rmi.RemoteException

---

ActivationMonitor · java.rmi.activation

1.2 *ActivationMonitor* ──────────── *java.rmi.Remote*

	public......................	void	**activeObject** (ActivationID id, java.rmi.MarshalledObject obj) throws UnknownObjectException, java.rmi.RemoteException
	public......................	void	**inactiveGroup** (ActivationGroupID id, long incarnation) throws UnknownGroupException, java.rmi.RemoteException
	public......................	void	**inactiveObject** (ActivationID id) throws UnknownObjectException, java.rmi.RemoteException

---

ActivationSystem · java.rmi.activation

1.2 *ActivationSystem* ──────────── *java.rmi.Remote*

	public........	*ActivationMonitor*	**activeGroup** (ActivationGroupID id, *ActivationInstantiator* group, long incarnation) throws UnknownGroupException, ActivationException, java.rmi.RemoteException
	public...........	ActivationDesc	**getActivationDesc** (ActivationID id) throws ActivationException, UnknownObjectException, java.rmi.RemoteException
	public....	ActivationGroupDesc	**getActivationGroupDesc** (ActivationGroupID id) throws ActivationException, UnknownGroupException, java.rmi.RemoteException
	public.......	ActivationGroupID	**registerGroup** (ActivationGroupDesc desc) throws ActivationException, java.rmi.RemoteException
	public..............	ActivationID	**registerObject** (ActivationDesc desc) throws ActivationException, UnknownGroupException, java.rmi.RemoteException
	public...........	ActivationDesc	**setActivationDesc** (ActivationID id, ActivationDesc desc) throws ActivationException, UnknownObjectException, UnknownGroupException, java.rmi.RemoteException
	public....	ActivationGroupDesc	**setActivationGroupDesc** (ActivationGroupID id, ActivationGroupDesc desc) throws ActivationException, UnknownGroupException, java.rmi.RemoteException

ActivationSystem

public	void	**shutdown** () throws java.rmi.RemoteException	
▲	public static final	int	**SYSTEM_PORT** = 1098
public	void	**unregisterGroup** (ActivationGroupID id) throws ActivationException, UnknownGroupException, java.rmi.RemoteException	
public	void	**unregisterObject** (ActivationID id) throws ActivationException, UnknownObjectException, java.rmi.RemoteException	

Activator   java.rmi.activation

1.2   *Activator*————————————————*java.rmi.Remote*˅

public .... **activate** (ActivationID id, boolean force) throws ActivationException,
... java.rmi.MarshalledObject   UnknownObjectException, java.rmi.RemoteException

---

AdapterActivator   org.omg.PortableServer

1.4   *AdapterActivator*————————————*AdapterActivatorOperations*˅[1], *org.omg.CORBA.Object*˅[2],
                                             org.omg.CORBA.portable.IDLEntity˅ (*java.io.Serializable*)

   [2] *13 inherited members from org.omg.CORBA.Object not shown*
   [1] public .... boolean unknown_adapter (*POA* parent, String name)

AdapterActivatorOperations   org.omg.PortableServer

1.4   *AdapterActivatorOperations*˅

public .... boolean **unknown_adapter** (*POA* parent, String name)

AdapterAlreadyExists   org.omg.PortableServer.POAPackage

Object
└Throwable - *java.io.Serializable*˅
   └Exception
1.2 ○   └org.omg.CORBA.UserException - - - - - - *org.omg.CORBA.portable.IDLEntity*˅ (*java.io.Serializable*)
1.4 ●   └AdapterAlreadyExists

✽	public	**AdapterAlreadyExists** ()
✽	public	**AdapterAlreadyExists** (String $reason)

AdapterAlreadyExistsHelper   org.omg.PortableServer.POAPackage

Object
1.4 ○   └AdapterAlreadyExistsHelper

✽	public	**AdapterAlreadyExistsHelper** ()
△	public static .... AdapterAlreadyExists	**extract** (org.omg.CORBA.Any a)
△	public static .... String	**id** ()
△	public static .... void	**insert** (org.omg.CORBA.Any a, AdapterAlreadyExists that)
△	public static .... void .... AdapterAlreadyExists	**read** (org.omg.CORBA.portable.InputStream istream)
△	public static synchronized .... . org.omg.CORBA.TypeCode	**type** ()
△	public static .... void	**write** (org.omg.CORBA.portable.OutputStream ostream, AdapterAlreadyExists value)

AdapterInactive   org.omg.PortableServer.POAManagerPackage

Object
└Throwable - *java.io.Serializable*˅
   └Exception
1.2 ○   └org.omg.CORBA.UserException - - - - - - *org.omg.CORBA.portable.IDLEntity*˅ (*java.io.Serializable*)
1.4 ●   └AdapterInactive

Class   *Interface*   —extends   - - -implements   ○ abstract   ● final   △ static   ▲ static final   ✽ constructor   x x—inherited   x **x**—declared   **x x**—overridden
εn—examples of usage   ˅—has subclass   package—see other volume

*	public.........................	**AdapterInactive** ()
*	public.........................	**AdapterInactive** (String $reason)

AdapterInactive Helper — org.omg.PortableServer.POAManagerPackage

AdapterInactiveHelper   org.omg.PortableServer.POAManagerPackage

Object
1.4 O   └AdapterInactiveHelper

*	public.........................	**AdapterInactiveHelper** ()
△	public static ...AdapterInactive	**extract** (org.omg.CORBA.Any a)
△	public static ....String	**id** ()
△	public static ....void	**insert** (org.omg.CORBA.Any a, AdapterInactive that)
△	public static ...AdapterInactive	**read** (org.omg.CORBA.portable.InputStream istream)
△	public static synchronized .... . org.omg.CORBA.TypeCode	**type** ()
△	. public static ....void	**write** (org.omg.CORBA.portable.OutputStream ostream, AdapterInactive value)

AdapterNonExistent   org.omg.PortableServer.POAPackage

Object
  └Throwable - *java.io.Serializable*
    └Exception
1.2 O   └org.omg.CORBA.UserException - - - - - - *org.omg.CORBA.portable.IDLEntity* (*java.io.Serializable*)
1.4 ●   └AdapterNonExistent

*	public.........................	**AdapterNonExistent** ()
*	public.........................	**AdapterNonExistent** (String $reason)

AdapterNonExistentHelper   org.omg.PortableServer.POAPackage

Object
1.4 O   └AdapterNonExistentHelper

*	public.........................	**AdapterNonExistentHelper** ()
△	public static .... AdapterNonExistent	**extract** (org.omg.CORBA.Any a)
△	public static ....String	**id** ()
△	public static ....void	**insert** (org.omg.CORBA.Any a, AdapterNonExistent that)
△	public static .... AdapterNonExistent	**read** (org.omg.CORBA.portable.InputStream istream)
△	public static synchronized .... . org.omg.CORBA.TypeCode	**type** ()
△	public static ....void	**write** (org.omg.CORBA.portable.OutputStream ostream, AdapterNonExistent value)

AddressHelper   org.omg.CosNaming.NamingContextExtPackage

Object
1.4 O   └AddressHelper

*	public.........................	**AddressHelper** ()
△	public static ....String	**extract** (org.omg.CORBA.Any a)
△	public static ....String	**id** ()
△	public static ....void	**insert** (org.omg.CORBA.Any a, String that)
△	public static ....String	**read** (org.omg.CORBA.portable.InputStream istream)
△	public static synchronized .... . org.omg.CORBA.TypeCode	**type** ()
△	public static ....void	**write** (org.omg.CORBA.portable.OutputStream ostream, String value)

Adler32   java.util.zip

Object
1.1   └Adler32 - *Checksum* [1]

*	public.........................	**Adler32** ()	ε456,457
1	public.................... long	**getValue** ()	ε456,457
1	public....................void	**reset** ()	ε456
	public....................void	**update** (byte[] b)	
1	public....................void	**update** (int b)	

Classes

1	public.....................void	**update** (byte[] b, int off, int len)	*ε*456

AlgorithmParameterGenerator   java.security

Object
1.2 └AlgorithmParameterGenerator

✳	protected	**AlgorithmParameterGenerator** (AlgorithmParameterGeneratorSpi paramGenSpi, Provider provider, String algorithm)
●	public final .... AlgorithmParameters	**generateParameters** () *ε*470
●	public final ....String	**getAlgorithm** ()
△	public static ....Algorithm-ParameterGenerator	**getInstance** (String algorithm) throws NoSuchAlgorithmException *ε*470
1.4 △	public static .... Algorithm-ParameterGenerator	**getInstance** (String algorithm, Provider provider) throws NoSuchAlgorithmException
△	public static .... Algorithm-ParameterGenerator	**getInstance** (String algorithm, String provider) throws NoSuchAlgorithmException, NoSuchProviderException
●	public final .... Provider	**getProvider** ()
●	public final ....void	**init** (int size) *ε*470
●	public final ....void	**init** (*java.security.spec.AlgorithmParameterSpec* genParamSpec) throws InvalidAlgorithmParameterException
●	public final ....void	**init** (int size, SecureRandom random)
●	public final ....void	**init** (*java.security.spec.AlgorithmParameterSpec* genParamSpec, SecureRandom random) throws InvalidAlgorithmParameterException

---

AlgorithmParameterGeneratorSpi   java.security

Object
1.2 ○ └AlgorithmParameterGeneratorSpi

✳	public..........................	**AlgorithmParameterGeneratorSpi** ()
○	protected abstract .... AlgorithmParameters	**engineGenerateParameters** ()
○	protected abstract ....void	**engineInit** (int size, SecureRandom random)
○	protected abstract ....void	**engineInit** (*java.security.spec.AlgorithmParameterSpec* genParamSpec, SecureRandom random) throws InvalidAlgorithmParameterException

---

AlgorithmParameters   java.security

Object [1]
1.2 └AlgorithmParameters

✳	protected	**AlgorithmParameters** (AlgorithmParametersSpi paramSpi, Provider provider, String algorithm)
●	public final ....String	**getAlgorithm** ()
●	public final ....byte[]	**getEncoded** () throws java.io.IOException
●	public final ....byte[]	**getEncoded** (String format) throws java.io.IOException
△	public static .... AlgorithmParameters	**getInstance** (String algorithm) throws NoSuchAlgorithmException
△	public static .... AlgorithmParameters	**getInstance** (String algorithm, String provider) throws NoSuchAlgorithmException, NoSuchProviderException
1.4 △	public static .... AlgorithmParameters	**getInstance** (String algorithm, Provider provider) throws NoSuchAlgorithmException
●	public final .... *java.security.spec↩ .AlgorithmParameterSpec*	**getParameterSpec** (Class paramSpec) throws java.security.spec↩ .InvalidParameterSpecException *ε*470
●	public final .... Provider	**getProvider** ()
●	public final ....void	**init** (byte[] params) throws java.io.IOException
●	public final ....void	**init** (*java.security.spec.AlgorithmParameterSpec* paramSpec) throws java.security.spec.InvalidParameterSpecException
●	public final ....void	**init** (byte[] params, String format) throws java.io.IOException
● 1	public final .... **String**	**toString** ()

Class *Interface* —extends - - -implements ○ abstract ● final △ static ▲ static final ✳ constructor x x—inherited x **x**—declared **x x**—overridden
εn—examples of usage ˌ—has subclass package—see other volume

AlgorithmParameterSpec		java.security.spec

1.2 *AlgorithmParameterSpec* ε463,464

AlgorithmParametersSpi		java.security

Object
1.2 ○ └AlgorithmParametersSpi

✳	public...........................	**AlgorithmParametersSpi** ()
○	protected abstract .... byte[]	**engineGetEncoded** () throws java.io.IOException
○	protected abstract .... byte[]	**engineGetEncoded** (String format) throws java.io.IOException
○	protected abstract	**engineGetParameterSpec** (Class paramSpec) throws
	.... java.security.spec ↵	java.security.spec.InvalidParameterSpecException
	.AlgorithmParameterSpec	
○	protected abstract ....void	**engineInit** (byte[] params) throws java.io.IOException
○	protected abstract ....void	**engineInit** (*java.security.spec.AlgorithmParameterSpec* paramSpec)
		throws java.security.spec.InvalidParameterSpecException
○	protected abstract ....void	**engineInit** (byte[] params, String format) throws java.io.IOException
○	protected abstract ....String	**engineToString** ()

AllPermission		java.security

Object   ε217,218
1.2 ○ └Permission [1] -------------------------- *Guard, java.io.Serializable*⌣
1.2 ●   └AllPermission

✳	public...........................	**AllPermission** ()
✳	public...........................	**AllPermission** (String name, String actions)
1	public...................void	checkGuard (Object object) throws SecurityException
1	public.................**boolean**	**equals** (Object obj) ε215
1	public.................**String**	**getActions** () ε215
● 1	public final ....String	getName ()
1	public..................... **int**	**hashCode** () ε215
1	public.................**boolean**	**implies** (Permission p) ε214,215
1	public.. **PermissionCollection**	**newPermissionCollection** ()
1	public...................String	toString ()

AlreadyBound		org.omg.CosNaming.NamingContextPackage

Object
└Throwable -------------------------- *java.io.Serializable*⌣
  └Exception
1.2 ○   └org.omg.CORBA.UserException ------- *org.omg.CORBA.portable.IDLEntity*⌣ (*java.io.Serializable*)
1.2 ●   └AlreadyBound

✳	public...........................	**AlreadyBound** ()
1.4 ✳	public...........................	**AlreadyBound** (String $reason)

AlreadyBoundException		java.rmi

Object
└Throwable -------------------------- *java.io.Serializable*⌣
  └Exception
1.1   └AlreadyBoundException

✳	public...........................	**AlreadyBoundException** ()
✳	public...........................	**AlreadyBoundException** (String s)

AlreadyBoundHelper		org.omg.CosNaming.NamingContextPackage

Object
1.2 ○ └AlreadyBoundHelper

1.4 ✳	public...........................	**AlreadyBoundHelper** ()
△	public static .... AlreadyBound	**extract** (org.omg.CORBA.Any a)
△	public static ....String	**id** ()
△	public static ....void	**insert** (org.omg.CORBA.Any a, AlreadyBound that)

AlreadyBoundHelper

△	public static .... AlreadyBound	**read** (org.omg.CORBA.portable.InputStream istream)
△	public static synchronized .... . org.omg.CORBA.TypeCode	**type** ()
△	public static ....void	**write** (org.omg.CORBA.portable.OutputStream ostream, AlreadyBound value)

AlreadyBoundHolder	org.omg.CosNaming.NamingContextPackage

Object
  └AlreadyBoundHolder - *org.omg.CORBA.portable.Streamable* [1]

1.2 ●

1	public.......................void	**_read** (org.omg.CORBA.portable.InputStream i)
1	public............................ . org.omg.CORBA.TypeCode	**_type** ()
1	public.......................void	**_write** (org.omg.CORBA.portable.OutputStream o)
✳	public...........................	**AlreadyBoundHolder** ()
✳	public...........................	**AlreadyBoundHolder** (AlreadyBound initialValue)
	public........... AlreadyBound	**value**

AlreadyConnectedException	java.nio.channels

Object
  └Throwable - *java.io.Serializable*
    └Exception
      └RuntimeException
        └IllegalStateException
          └AlreadyConnectedException

1.1
1.4

✳	public...........................	**AlreadyConnectedException** ()

Annotation	java.text

Object [1]
  └Annotation

1.2

✳	public............................	**Annotation** (Object value)
	public....................Object	**getValue** ()
1	public................... String	**toString** ()

Any	org.omg.CORBA

Object
  └Any - *org.omg.CORBA.portable.IDLEntity* (*java.io.Serializable*)

1.2 ○

✳	public...........................	**Any** ()
○	public abstract ....org.omg.CORBA↵ .portable.InputStream	**create_input_stream** ()
○	public abstract ....org.omg.CORBA↵ .portable.OutputStream	**create_output_stream** ()
○	public abstract .... boolean	**equal** (Any a)
○	public abstract .... Any	**extract_any** () throws BAD_OPERATION
○	public abstract .... boolean	**extract_boolean** () throws BAD_OPERATION
○	public abstract .... char	**extract_char** () throws BAD_OPERATION
○	public abstract ....double	**extract_double** () throws BAD_OPERATION
	public... java.math.BigDecimal	**extract_fixed** ()
○	public abstract ....float	**extract_float** () throws BAD_OPERATION
○	public abstract .... int	**extract_long** () throws BAD_OPERATION
○	public abstract .... long	**extract_longlong** () throws BAD_OPERATION
○	public abstract .... *Object*	**extract_Object** () throws BAD_OPERATION
○	public abstract .... byte	**extract_octet** () throws BAD_OPERATION
D	public.................Principal	**extract_Principal** () throws BAD_OPERATION
○	public abstract ....short	**extract_short** () throws BAD_OPERATION
1.4	public...... *org.omg.CORBA*↵ *.portable.Streamable*	**extract_Streamable** () throws BAD_INV_ORDER
○	public abstract ....String	**extract_string** () throws BAD_OPERATION

Class *Interface* —extends - - -implements ○ abstract ● final △ static ▲ static final ✳ constructor x x—inherited x **x**—declared **x x**—overridden
εn—examples of usage ‿—has subclass package—see other volume

A

○	public abstract ...... TypeCode	**extract_TypeCode** () throws BAD_OPERATION	
○	public abstract ....int	**extract_ulong** () throws BAD_OPERATION	
○	public abstract .... long	**extract_ulonglong** () throws BAD_OPERATION	
○	public abstract ....short	**extract_ushort** () throws BAD_OPERATION	
○	public abstract .... *java.io.Serializable*	**extract_Value** () throws BAD_OPERATION	
○	public abstract .... char	**extract_wchar** () throws BAD_OPERATION	
○	public abstract ....String	**extract_wstring** () throws BAD_OPERATION	
○	public abstract ....void	**insert_any** (Any a)	
○	public abstract ....void	**insert_boolean** (boolean b)	
○	public abstract ....void	**insert_char** (char c) throws DATA_CONVERSION	
○	public abstract ....void	**insert_double** (double d)	
	public.................void	**insert_fixed** (java.math.BigDecimal value)	
	public.................void	**insert_fixed** (java.math.BigDecimal value, TypeCode type) throws BAD_INV_ORDER	
○	public abstract ....void	**insert_float** (float f)	
○	public abstract ....void	**insert_long** (int l)	
○	public abstract ....void	**insert_longlong** (long l)	
○	public abstract ....void	**insert_Object** (*Object* o)	
○	public abstract ....void	**insert_Object** (*Object* o, TypeCode t) throws BAD_PARAM	
○	public abstract ....void	**insert_octet** (byte b)	
D	public.................void	**insert_Principal** (Principal p)	
○	public abstract ....void	**insert_short** (short s)	
	public.................void	**insert_Streamable** (*org.omg.CORBA.portable.Streamable* s)	
○	public abstract ....void	**insert_string** (String s) throws DATA_CONVERSION, MARSHAL	
○	public abstract ....void	**insert_TypeCode** (TypeCode t)	
○	public abstract ....void	**insert_ulong** (int l)	
○	public abstract ....void	**insert_ulonglong** (long l)	
○	public abstract ....void	**insert_ushort** (short s)	
○	public abstract ....void	**insert_Value** (*java.io.Serializable* v)	
○	public abstract ....void	**insert_Value** (*java.io.Serializable* v, TypeCode t) throws MARSHAL	
○	public abstract ....void	**insert_wchar** (char c)	
○	public abstract ....void	**insert_wstring** (String s) throws MARSHAL	
○	public abstract ....void	**read_value** (org.omg.CORBA.portable.InputStream is, TypeCode t) throws MARSHAL	
○	public abstract ...... TypeCode	**type** ()	
○	public abstract ....void	**type** (TypeCode t)	
○	public abstract ....void	**write_value** (org.omg.CORBA.portable.OutputStream os)	

AnyHolder   org.omg.CORBA

Object
1.2 ● └AnyHolder -------------------------- *org.omg.CORBA.portable.Streamable* [1]

	1 public.................void	**_read** (org.omg.CORBA.portable.InputStream input)	
	1 public.............TypeCode	**_type** ()	
	1 public.................void	**_write** (org.omg.CORBA.portable.OutputStream output)	
∗	public.................	**AnyHolder** ()	
∗	public.................	**AnyHolder** (Any initial)	
	public................. Any	**value**	

AnySeqHelper❶   org.omg.CORBA

Object
1.3 ○ └AnySeqHelper

∗	public.................	**AnySeqHelper** ()	
△	public static .... Any[]	**extract** (Any a)	
△	public static ....String	**id** ()	
△	public static ....void	**insert** (Any a, Any[] that)	
△	public static .... Any[]	**read** (org.omg.CORBA.portable.InputStream istream)	
△	public static synchronized .... TypeCode	**type** ()	
△	public static ....void	**write** (org.omg.CORBA.portable.OutputStream ostream, Any[] value)	

AnySeqHelper❷   org.omg.DynamicAny

Object
1.4 ○ └AnySeqHelper

Classes

AnySeqHelper ❷

✳	public........................	**AnySeqHelper** ()
△	public static .... org.omg.CORBA.Any[]	**extract** (org.omg.CORBA.Any a)
△	public static ....String	**id** ()
△	public static ....void	**insert** (org.omg.CORBA.Any a, org.omg.CORBA.Any[] that)
△	public static .... org.omg.CORBA.Any[]	**read** (org.omg.CORBA.portable.InputStream istream)
△	public static synchronized .... . org.omg.CORBA.TypeCode	**type** ()
△	public static ....void	**write** (org.omg.CORBA.portable.OutputStream ostream, org.omg.CORBA.Any[] value)

AnySeqHolder   org.omg.CORBA

Object
1.3 ● └AnySeqHolder ------------------------- *org.omg.CORBA.portable.Streamable* ⌐ [1]

1	public.................extends....void	**_read** (org.omg.CORBA.portable.InputStream i)
1	public.............TypeCode	**_type** ()
1	public.................extends....void	**_write** (org.omg.CORBA.portable.OutputStream o)
✳	public........................	**AnySeqHolder** ()
✳	public........................	**AnySeqHolder** (Any[] initialValue)
	public...................Any[]	**value**

AppConfigurationEntry   javax.security.auth.login

Object
1.4 └AppConfigurationEntry

✳	public.........................	**AppConfigurationEntry** (String loginModuleName, AppConfigurationEntry ↵ .LoginModuleControlFlag controlFlag, *java.util.Map* options)	
	public......................... .... AppConfigurationEntry ↵ .LoginModuleControlFlag	**getControlFlag** ()	ε507
	public.....................String	**getLoginModuleName** ()	ε507
	public.............*java.util.Map*	**getOptions** ()	

AppConfigurationEntry.LoginModuleControlFlag   javax.security.auth.login

Object [1]
1.4 └AppConfigurationEntry ↵ .LoginModuleControlFlag

▲	public static final .... AppConfigurationEntry ↵ .LoginModuleControlFlag	**OPTIONAL**	ε507
▲	public static final .... AppConfigurationEntry ↵ .LoginModuleControlFlag	**REQUIRED**	ε507
▲	public static final .... AppConfigurationEntry ↵ .LoginModuleControlFlag	**REQUISITE**	ε507
▲	public static final .... AppConfigurationEntry ↵ .LoginModuleControlFlag	**SUFFICIENT**	ε507
1	public...................**String**	**toString** ()	

AppletInitializer   java.beans

1.2 *AppletInitializer*

	public......................void	**activate** (java.applet.Applet newApplet)
	public......................void	**initialize** (java.applet.Applet newAppletBean, *java.beans.beancontext* ↵ .BeanContext bCtxt)

Class *Interface* —extends - - -implements ○ abstract ● final △ static ▲ static final ✳ constructor x x—inherited x **x**—declared **x x**—overridden
ε*n*—examples of usage ⌐—has subclass package—see other volume

444

ApplicationException		org.omg.CORBA.portable

```
Object
 └Throwable --------------------------- java.io.Serializable ˌ
   └Exception
     └ApplicationException
```
1.2

*	public...........................	**ApplicationException** (String id, InputStream ins)
	public...................String	**getId** ()
	public............. InputStream	**getInputStream** ()

ARG_IN		org.omg.CORBA

1.2　　*ARG_IN*

▲　　public static final.............int **value** = 1

ARG_INOUT		org.omg.CORBA

1.2　　*ARG_INOUT*

▲　　public static final.............int **value** = 3

ARG_OUT		org.omg.CORBA

1.2　　*ARG_OUT*

▲　　public static final.............int **value** = 2

ArithmeticException		java.lang

```
Object
 └Throwable --------------------------- java.io.Serializable ˌ
   └Exception
     └RuntimeException
       └ArithmeticException
```

*	public...........................	**ArithmeticException** ()
*	public...........................	**ArithmeticException** (String s)

Array❶		java.lang.reflect

```
        Object
1.1 ●    └Array
```

△	public static native......Object	**get** (Object array, int index) throws IllegalArgumentException, ArrayIndexOutOfBoundsException	ε125
△	public static native.... boolean	**getBoolean** (Object array, int index) throws IllegalArgumentException, ArrayIndexOutOfBoundsException	
△	public static native........ byte	**getByte** (Object array, int index) throws IllegalArgumentException, ArrayIndexOutOfBoundsException	
△	public static native........ char	**getChar** (Object array, int index) throws IllegalArgumentException, ArrayIndexOutOfBoundsException	
△	public static native......double	**getDouble** (Object array, int index) throws IllegalArgumentException, ArrayIndexOutOfBoundsException	
△	public static native........float	**getFloat** (Object array, int index) throws IllegalArgumentException, ArrayIndexOutOfBoundsException	
△	public static native...........int	**getInt** (Object array, int index) throws IllegalArgumentException, ArrayIndexOutOfBoundsException	
△	public static native...........int	**getLength** (Object array) throws IllegalArgumentException	ε121,124
△	public static native........ long	**getLong** (Object array, int index) throws IllegalArgumentException, ArrayIndexOutOfBoundsException	
△	public static native........short	**getShort** (Object array, int index) throws IllegalArgumentException, ArrayIndexOutOfBoundsException	
△	public static ....Object	**newInstance** (Class componentType, int[] dimensions) throws IllegalArgumentException, NegativeArraySizeException	ε123
△	public static ....Object	**newInstance** (Class componentType, int length) throws NegativeArraySizeException	ε123,124

A

Classes

445

Array ❶

△	public static native.........void	**set** (Object array, int index, Object value) throws IllegalArgumentException, ArrayIndexOutOfBoundsException	ε125
△	public static native.........void	**setBoolean** (Object array, int index, boolean z) throws IllegalArgumentException, ArrayIndexOutOfBoundsException	
△	public static native.........void	**setByte** (Object array, int index, byte b) throws IllegalArgumentException, ArrayIndexOutOfBoundsException	
△	public static native.........void	**setChar** (Object array, int index, char c) throws IllegalArgumentException, ArrayIndexOutOfBoundsException	
△	public static native.........void	**setDouble** (Object array, int index, double d) throws IllegalArgumentException, ArrayIndexOutOfBoundsException	
△	public static native.........void	**setFloat** (Object array, int index, float f) throws IllegalArgumentException, ArrayIndexOutOfBoundsException	
△	public static native.........void	**setInt** (Object array, int index, int i) throws IllegalArgumentException, ArrayIndexOutOfBoundsException	
△	public static native.........void	**setLong** (Object array, int index, long l) throws IllegalArgumentException, ArrayIndexOutOfBoundsException	
△	public static native.........void	**setShort** (Object array, int index, short s) throws IllegalArgumentException, ArrayIndexOutOfBoundsException	

Array ❷ — java.sql

1.2 | *Array*

public...................Object	**getArray** () throws SQLException
public...................Object	**getArray** (*java.util.Map* map) throws SQLException
public...................Object	**getArray** (long index, int count) throws SQLException
public...................Object	**getArray** (long index, int count, *java.util.Map* map) throws SQLException
public.......................int	**getBaseType** () throws SQLException
public...................String	**getBaseTypeName** () throws SQLException
public...................*ResultSet*	**getResultSet** () throws SQLException
public...................*ResultSet*	**getResultSet** (*java.util.Map* map) throws SQLException
public...................*ResultSet*	**getResultSet** (long index, int count) throws SQLException
public...................*ResultSet*	**getResultSet** (long index, int count, *java.util.Map* map) throws SQLException

ArrayIndexOutOfBoundsException — java.lang

```
Object
└Throwable - - - - - - - - - - - - - - - - - - - - - - - - - - - java.io.Serializable⌐
  └Exception
    └RuntimeException
      └IndexOutOfBoundsException
        └ArrayIndexOutOfBoundsException
```

✳	public...........................	**ArrayIndexOutOfBoundsException** ()
✳	public...........................	**ArrayIndexOutOfBoundsException** (int index)
✳	public...........................	**ArrayIndexOutOfBoundsException** (String s)

ArrayList — java.util

```
        Object¹
1.2 ○   └AbstractCollection² - - - - - - - - - - - - - - - - - - - - - Collection⌐
1.2 ○     └AbstractList³ - - - - - - - - - - - - - - - - - - - - - - List (Collection)
1.2         └ArrayList - - - - - - - - - - - - - - - - - - - - - - RandomAccess, Cloneable⌐, java.io.Serializable⌐
```

3	public.................**boolean add** (Object o)			ε342,349,352,354,358
3	public........................ **void add** (int index, Object element)			ε349,362
2	public.................**boolean addAll** (*Collection* c)			ε351,353
3	public.................**boolean addAll** (int index, *Collection* c)			
✳	public........................ **ArrayList** ()			ε339,349,351
✳	public........................ **ArrayList** (int initialCapacity)			
✳	public........................ **ArrayList** (*Collection* c)			ε347,348
3	public.................... **void clear** ()			ε351,353
1	public....................**Object clone** ()			
2	public.................**boolean contains** (Object elem)			ε352
2	public................. boolean containsAll (*Collection* c)			
	public....................void **ensureCapacity** (int minCapacity)			
3	public................. boolean equals (Object o)			

Class *Interface* —extends - - -implements ○ abstract ● final △ static ▲ static final ✳ constructor x x—inherited x **x**—declared **x x**—overridden
ε*n*—examples of usage ⌐—has subclass package—see other volume

3	public	**Object**	**get** (int index)	ε349,234
3	public	int	hashCode ()	
3	public	int	**indexOf** (Object elem)	
2	public	**boolean**	**isEmpty** ()	ε102
3	public	*Iterator*	iterator ()	ε345,352,354,355,356
3	public	int	**lastIndexOf** (Object elem)	
3	public	*ListIterator*	listIterator ()	
3	public	*ListIterator*	listIterator (int index)	
3	protected transient	int	modCount	
3	public	**Object**	**remove** (int index)	ε349
2	public	boolean	remove (Object o)	ε349,352
2	public	boolean	removeAll (*Collection* c)	ε351,353
3	protected	**void**	**removeRange** (int fromIndex, int toIndex)	
2	public	boolean	retainAll (*Collection* c)	ε351,353
3	public	**Object**	**set** (int index, Object element)	ε348
2	public	int	**size** ()	ε340,349,351,352,358
3	public	*List*	subList (int fromIndex, int toIndex)	ε351
2	public	**Object[]**	**toArray** ()	ε340
2	public	**Object[]**	**toArray** (Object[] a)	ε340,352,358,194,508
2	public	String	toString ()	
	public	void	**trimToSize** ()	

Arrays

java.util

```
Object
 └Arrays
```
1.2

△	public static	*List*	**asList** (Object[] a)	ε339,341,347,348,350
△	public static	int	**binarySearch** (byte[] a, byte key)	
△	public static	int	**binarySearch** (char[] a, char key)	
△	public static	int	**binarySearch** (double[] a, double key)	
△	public static	int	**binarySearch** (float[] a, float key)	
△	public static	int	**binarySearch** (int[] a, int key)	
△	public static	int	**binarySearch** (Object[] a, Object key)	ε360
△	public static	int	**binarySearch** (long[] a, long key)	
△	public static	int	**binarySearch** (short[] a, short key)	
△	public static	int	**binarySearch** (Object[] a, Object key, *Comparator* c)	
△	public static	boolean	**equals** (boolean[] a, boolean[] a2)	ε338
△	public static	boolean	**equals** (byte[] a, byte[] a2)	ε338
△	public static	boolean	**equals** (char[] a, char[] a2)	ε338
△	public static	boolean	**equals** (double[] a, double[] a2)	ε338
△	public static	boolean	**equals** (float[] a, float[] a2)	ε338
△	public static	boolean	**equals** (int[] a, int[] a2)	ε338
△	public static	boolean	**equals** (Object[] a, Object[] a2)	ε338
△	public static	boolean	**equals** (long[] a, long[] a2)	ε338
△	public static	boolean	**equals** (short[] a, short[] a2)	ε338
△	public static	void	**fill** (boolean[] a, boolean val)	
△	public static	void	**fill** (byte[] a, byte val)	
△	public static	void	**fill** (char[] a, char val)	
△	public static	void	**fill** (double[] a, double val)	
△	public static	void	**fill** (float[] a, float val)	
△	public static	void	**fill** (int[] a, int val)	
△	public static	void	**fill** (Object[] a, Object val)	
△	public static	void	**fill** (long[] a, long val)	
△	public static	void	**fill** (short[] a, short val)	
△	public static	void	**fill** (boolean[] a, int fromIndex, int toIndex, boolean val)	
△	public static	void	**fill** (byte[] a, int fromIndex, int toIndex, byte val)	
△	public static	void	**fill** (char[] a, int fromIndex, int toIndex, char val)	
△	public static	void	**fill** (double[] a, int fromIndex, int toIndex, double val)	
△	public static	void	**fill** (float[] a, int fromIndex, int toIndex, float val)	
△	public static	void	**fill** (int[] a, int fromIndex, int toIndex, int val)	
△	public static	void	**fill** (Object[] a, int fromIndex, int toIndex, Object val)	
△	public static	void	**fill** (long[] a, int fromIndex, int toIndex, long val)	
△	public static	void	**fill** (short[] a, int fromIndex, int toIndex, short val)	
△	public static	void	**sort** (byte[] a)	
△	public static	void	**sort** (char[] a)	
△	public static	void	**sort** (double[] a)	
△	public static	void	**sort** (float[] a)	
△	public static	void	**sort** (int[] a)	ε359
△	public static	void	**sort** (Object[] a)	ε359
△	public static	void	**sort** (long[] a)	
△	public static	void	**sort** (short[] a)	
△	public static	void	**sort** (Object[] a, *Comparator* c)	ε359

Classes

447

Arrays

△	public static	...............void	**sort** (byte[] a, int fromIndex, int toIndex)
△	public static	...............void	**sort** (char[] a, int fromIndex, int toIndex)
△	public static	...............void	**sort** (double[] a, int fromIndex, int toIndex)
△	public static	...............void	**sort** (float[] a, int fromIndex, int toIndex)
△	public static	...............void	**sort** (int[] a, int fromIndex, int toIndex)
△	public static	..............void	**sort** (Object[] a, int fromIndex, int toIndex)
△	public static	...............void	**sort** (long[] a, int fromIndex, int toIndex)
△	public static	...............void	**sort** (short[] a, int fromIndex, int toIndex)
△	public static	...............void	**sort** (Object[] a, int fromIndex, int toIndex, *Comparator* c)

ArrayStoreException   java.lang

```
Object
└ Throwable ------------------------------ java.io.Serializable
  └ Exception
    └ RuntimeException
      └ ArrayStoreException
```

✳	public..........................	**ArrayStoreException** ()
✳	public..........................	**ArrayStoreException** (String s)

AssertionError   java.lang

```
Object
└ Throwable 1 ------------------------------ java.io.Serializable
  └ Error
    └ AssertionError
```
1.4

✳	public..........................		**AssertionError** ()
✳	public..........................		**AssertionError** (boolean detailMessage)
✳	public..........................		**AssertionError** (char detailMessage)
✳	public..........................		**AssertionError** (double detailMessage)
✳	public..........................		**AssertionError** (float detailMessage)
✳	public..........................		**AssertionError** (int detailMessage)
✳	public..........................		**AssertionError** (Object detailMessage)
✳	public..........................		**AssertionError** (long detailMessage)
1	public...................	String	getMessage ()	ε105

AsynchronousCloseException   java.nio.channels

```
Object
└ Throwable ------------------------------ java.io.Serializable
  └ Exception
    └ java.io.IOException
      └ ClosedChannelException
        └ AsynchronousCloseException
```
1.4
1.4

✳	public..........................	**AsynchronousCloseException** ()

Attr   org.w3c.dom

1.4	*Attr* ———————————————— *Node* 1		ε533,524,526,529,530

	1 35 inherited members from Node not shown			
	public...................	String	**getName** ()	
1	public...................	String	getNodeName ()	ε536,528,529,537,544
1	public...................	String	getNodeValue () throws DOMException	ε536,541
	public................	*Element*	**getOwnerElement** ()	
	public...................	boolean	**getSpecified** ()	ε538
	public...................	String	**getValue** ()	
	public...................	void	**setValue** (String value) throws DOMException	

Class *Interface* —extends - - -implements ○ abstract ● final △ static ▲ static final ✳ constructor x x—inherited x **x**—declared **x x**—overridden
εn—examples of usage ˅—has subclass package—see other volume

Attribute ❶				javax.naming.directory

1.3		*Attribute*────────────────────── *Cloneable*, *java.io.Serializable*	ε482
	public................. boolean	**add** (Object attrVal)	ε484,485
	public........................void	**add** (int ix, Object attrVal)	
	public........................void	**clear** ()	
	public....................Object	**clone** ()	
	public.................. boolean	**contains** (Object attrVal)	
	public....................Object	**get** () throws javax.naming.NamingException	
	public....................Object	**get** (int ix) throws javax.naming.NamingException	
	public.........*javax.naming* ↵	**getAll** () throws javax.naming.NamingException	
	.NamingEnumeration		
	public...............*DirContext*	**getAttributeDefinition** () throws javax.naming.NamingException	
			ε491
	public...............*DirContext*	**getAttributeSyntaxDefinition** () throws javax.naming.NamingException	
	public....................String	**getID** ()	
	public.................. boolean	**isOrdered** ()	
	public....................Object	**remove** (int ix)	
	public.................. boolean	**remove** (Object attrval)	
▲	public static final .... long	**serialVersionUID** = 8707690322213556804	
	public....................Object	**set** (int ix, Object attrVal)	
	public........................int	**size** ()	

AttributedCharacterIterator		java.text

1.2		*AttributedCharacterIterator*──────── *CharacterIterator*, [1] (*Cloneable*)	
1	public....................Object	clone ()	
1	public.................... char	current ()	ε307
1	public.................... char	first ()	ε307
	public.............*java.util.Set*	**getAllAttributeKeys** ()	
	public....................Object	**getAttribute** (AttributedCharacterIterator.Attribute attribute)	
	public...........*java.util.Map*	**getAttributes** ()	
1	public........................int	getBeginIndex ()	
1	public........................int	getEndIndex ()	
1	public........................int	getIndex ()	ε307
	public........................int	**getRunLimit** ()	
	public........................int	**getRunLimit** (AttributedCharacterIterator.Attribute attribute)	
	public........................int	**getRunLimit** (*java.util.Set* attributes)	
	public........................int	**getRunStart** ()	
	public........................int	**getRunStart** (AttributedCharacterIterator.Attribute attribute)	
	public........................int	**getRunStart** (*java.util.Set* attributes)	
1	public.................... char	last ()	ε307
1	public.................... char	next ()	ε307
1	public.................... char	previous ()	ε307
1	public.................... char	setIndex (int position)	ε307

AttributedCharacterIterator.Attribute		java.text

		Object [1]	
1.2		└AttributedCharacterIterator.Attribute, ------- *java.io.Serializable*,	
*	protected......................	**AttributedCharacterIterator.Attribute** (String name)	ε308
● 1	public final ....**boolean**	**equals** (Object obj)	
	protected.................String	**getName** ()	
● 1	public final .... **int**	**hashCode** ()	
▲	public static final	**INPUT_METHOD_SEGMENT**	
	AttributedCharacterIterator ↵		
	.Attribute		
▲	public static final	**LANGUAGE**	
	AttributedCharacterIterator ↵		
	.Attribute		
▲	public static final	**READING**	
	AttributedCharacterIterator ↵		
	.Attribute		
	protected ....Object	**readResolve** () throws java.io.InvalidObjectException	
1	public.................. **String**	**toString** ()	

AttributedString

			java.text

1.2
```
Object
 └AttributedString
```

	public	void	**addAttribute** (AttributedCharacterIterator.Attribute attribute, Object value)
	public	void	**addAttribute** (AttributedCharacterIterator.Attribute attribute, Object value, int beginIndex, int endIndex) ε308
	public	void	**addAttributes** (*java.util.Map* attributes, int beginIndex, int endIndex)
*	public		**AttributedString** (String text) ε308
*	public		**AttributedString** (*AttributedCharacterIterator* text)
*	public		**AttributedString** (String text, *java.util.Map* attributes)
*	public		**AttributedString** (*AttributedCharacterIterator* text, int beginIndex, int endIndex)
*	public		**AttributedString** (*AttributedCharacterIterator* text, int beginIndex, int endIndex, AttributedCharacterIterator.Attribute[] attributes)
	public .. *AttributedCharacterIterator*		**getIterator** ()
	public .. *AttributedCharacterIterator*		**getIterator** (AttributedCharacterIterator.Attribute[] attributes)
	public .. *AttributedCharacterIterator*		**getIterator** (AttributedCharacterIterator.Attribute[] attributes, int beginIndex, int endIndex)

AttributeInUseException

			javax.naming.directory

```
Object
 └Throwable ----------------------------- java.io.Serializable ⌐
   └Exception
```
1.3   └javax.naming.NamingException [1]
1.3   └AttributeInUseException

[1]	*20 inherited members from javax.naming.NamingException not shown*		
*	public		**AttributeInUseException** ()
*	public		**AttributeInUseException** (String explanation)

AttributeList ❷

			org.xml.sax

D   *AttributeList*

D	public	int	**getLength** ()
D	public	String	**getName** (int i)
D	public	String	**getType** (int i)
D	public	String	**getType** (String name)
D	public	String	**getValue** (int i)
D	public	String	**getValue** (String name)

AttributeListImpl

			org.xml.sax.helpers

```
     Object
D     └AttributeListImpl ----------------------- org.xml.sax.AttributeList [1]
```

D		public	void	**addAttribute** (String name, String type, String value)
D	*	public		**AttributeListImpl** ()
D	*	public		**AttributeListImpl** (*org.xml.sax.AttributeList* atts)
D		public	void	**clear** ()
D	1	public	int	**getLength** ()
D	1	public	String	**getName** (int i)
D	1	public	String	**getType** (int i)
D	1	public	String	**getType** (String name)
D	1	public	String	**getValue** (int i)
D	1	public	String	**getValue** (String name)
D		public	void	**removeAttribute** (String name)
D		public	void	**setAttributeList** (*org.xml.sax.AttributeList* atts)

Class *Interface* —extends - - -implements ○ abstract ● final △ static ▲ static final ✳ constructor x x—inherited x **x**—declared **x x**—overridden
ε*n*—examples of usage ⌐—has subclass package—see other volume

AttributeModificationException — javax.naming.directory

Object
└Throwable ---------------------------- *java.io.Serializable*
  └Exception
1.3 └javax.naming.NamingException[1]
1.3 └AttributeModificationException

1	*19 inherited members from javax.naming.NamingException not shown*		
*	public		**AttributeModificationException** ()
*	public		**AttributeModificationException** (String explanation)
	public	ModificationItem[]	**getUnexecutedModifications** ()
	public	void	**setUnexecutedModifications** (ModificationItem[] e)
1	public	**String**	**toString** ()

Attributes ❶ — java.util.jar

Object[1]
1.2 └Attributes ---------------------------- *java.util.Map*[2], *Cloneable*

*	public		**Attributes** ()	
*	public		**Attributes** (int size)	
*	public		**Attributes** (Attributes attr)	
2	public	void	**clear** ()	
1	public	**Object**	**clone** ()	
2	public	boolean	**containsKey** (Object name)	ε344
2	public	boolean	**containsValue** (Object value)	
2	public	*java.util.Set*	**entrySet** ()	ε345
1	public	**boolean**	**equals** (Object o)	
2	public	Object	**get** (Object name)	ε337,344,346,356,357
	public	String	**getValue** (String name)	
	public	String	**getValue** (Attributes.Name name)	ε380,381
1	public	**int**	**hashCode** ()	
2	public	boolean	**isEmpty** ()	
2	public	*java.util.Set*	**keySet** ()	ε380,381,194,340,345
	protected	*java.util.Map*	**map**	
2	public	Object	**put** (Object name, Object value)	ε337,344,346,355,356
2	public	void	**putAll** (*java.util.Map* attr)	
	public	String	**putValue** (String name, String value)	
2	public	Object	**remove** (Object name)	ε355
2	public	int	**size** ()	ε355
2	public	*java.util.Collection*	**values** ()	ε340,345,355

Attributes ❷ — javax.naming.directory

1.3 *Attributes* ———————————— *Cloneable*, *java.io.Serializable*

public	Object	**clone** ()	
public	*Attribute*	**get** (String attrID)	ε491
public	*javax.naming.NamingEnumeration*	**getAll** ()	ε482
public	*javax.naming.NamingEnumeration*	**getIDs** ()	
public	boolean	**isCaseIgnored** ()	
public	*Attribute*	**put** (*Attribute* attr)	ε484,485,486,489
public	*Attribute*	**put** (String attrID, Object val)	
public	*Attribute*	**remove** (String attrID)	
public	int	**size** ()	

Attributes ❸ — org.xml.sax

1.4 *Attributes* ε550

public	int	**getIndex** (String qName)	
public	int	**getIndex** (String uri, String localPart)	
public	int	**getLength** ()	ε549
public	String	**getLocalName** (int index)	ε549
public	String	**getQName** (int index)	ε549
public	String	**getType** (int index)	
public	String	**getType** (String qName)	
public	String	**getType** (String uri, String localName)	

Attributes ❸

public	String	**getURI** (int index)	ε549
public	String	**getValue** (int index)	ε549
public	String	**getValue** (String qName)	
public	String	**getValue** (String uri, String localName)	

Attributes.Name   java.util.jar

Object [1]   ε380,381
1.2   └ Attributes.Name

▲	public static final		**CLASS_PATH**	
		Attributes.Name		
▲	public static final		**CONTENT_TYPE**	
		Attributes.Name		
1	public	boolean	**equals** (Object o)	
1.3 ▲	public static final		**EXTENSION_INSTALLATION**	
		Attributes.Name		
1.3 ▲	public static final		**EXTENSION_LIST**	
		Attributes.Name		
1.3 ▲	public static final		**EXTENSION_NAME**	
		Attributes.Name		
1	public	int	**hashCode** ()	
▲	public static final		**IMPLEMENTATION_TITLE**	
		Attributes.Name		
1.3 ▲	public static final		**IMPLEMENTATION_URL**	
		Attributes.Name		
▲	public static final		**IMPLEMENTATION_VENDOR**	
		Attributes.Name		
1.3 ▲	public static final		**IMPLEMENTATION_VENDOR_ID**	
		Attributes.Name		
▲	public static final		**IMPLEMENTATION_VERSION**	
		Attributes.Name		
▲	public static final		**MAIN_CLASS**	
		Attributes.Name		
▲	public static final		**MANIFEST_VERSION**	
		Attributes.Name		
✻	public		**Attributes.Name** (String name)	
▲	public static final		**SEALED**	
		Attributes.Name		
▲	public static final		**SIGNATURE_VERSION**	
		Attributes.Name		
▲	public static final		**SPECIFICATION_TITLE**	
		Attributes.Name		
▲	public static final		**SPECIFICATION_VENDOR**	
		Attributes.Name		
▲	public static final		**SPECIFICATION_VERSION**	
		Attributes.Name		
1	public	String	**toString** ()	

AttributesImpl   org.xml.sax.helpers

Object
1.4   └ AttributesImpl - *org.xml.sax.Attributes* [1]

	public	void	**addAttribute** (String uri, String localName, String qName, String type, String value)	
✻	public		**AttributesImpl** ()	
✻	public		**AttributesImpl** (*org.xml.sax.Attributes* atts)	
	public	void	**clear** ()	
1	public	int	**getIndex** (String qName)	
1	public	int	**getIndex** (String uri, String localName)	
1	public	int	**getLength** ()	ε549
1	public	String	**getLocalName** (int index)	ε549
1	public	String	**getQName** (int index)	ε549
1	public	String	**getType** (int index)	
1	public	String	**getType** (String qName)	
1	public	String	**getType** (String uri, String localName)	
1	public	String	**getURI** (int index)	ε549
1	public	String	**getValue** (int index)	ε549
1	public	String	**getValue** (String qName)	

Class *Interface* —extends - - -implements ○ abstract ● final △ static ▲ static final ✻ constructor x x—inherited x **x**—declared **x x**—overridden
ε*n*—examples of usage ˷—has subclass package—see other volume

1	public	String	**getValue** (String uri, String localName)
	public	void	**removeAttribute** (int index)
	public	void	**setAttribute** (int index, String uri, String localName, String qName, String type, String value)
	public	void	**setAttributes** (*org.xml.sax.Attributes* atts)
	public	void	**setLocalName** (int index, String localName)
	public	void	**setQName** (int index, String qName)
	public	void	**setType** (int index, String type)
	public	void	**setURI** (int index, String uri)
	public	void	**setValue** (int index, String value)

AuthenticationException — javax.naming

```
Object
└Throwable --------------------------- java.io.Serializable
    └Exception
        └NamingException 1
            └NamingSecurityException
                └AuthenticationException
```

1.3
1.3 O
1.3

1	*20 inherited members from NamingException not shown*		
*	public		**AuthenticationException** ()
*	public		**AuthenticationException** (String explanation)

AuthenticationNotSupportedException — javax.naming

```
Object
└Throwable --------------------------- java.io.Serializable
    └Exception
        └NamingException 1
            └NamingSecurityException
                └AuthenticationNotSupportedException
```

1.3
1.3 O
1.3

1	*20 inherited members from NamingException not shown*		
*	public		**AuthenticationNotSupportedException** ()
*	public		**AuthenticationNotSupportedException** (String explanation)

Authenticator — java.net

```
Object
└Authenticator
```

1.2 O

*	public		**Authenticator** ()	
	protected	PasswordAuthentication	**getPasswordAuthentication** ()	ε139
1.4 ●	protected final	String	**getRequestingHost** ()	
●	protected final	int	**getRequestingPort** ()	
●	protected final	String	**getRequestingPrompt** ()	
●	protected final	String	**getRequestingProtocol** ()	
●	protected final	String	**getRequestingScheme** ()	
●	protected final	InetAddress	**getRequestingSite** ()	
△	public static	PasswordAuthentication	**requestPasswordAuthentication** (InetAddress addr, int port, String protocol, String prompt, String scheme)	
1.4 △	public static	PasswordAuthentication	**requestPasswordAuthentication** (String host, InetAddress addr, int port, String protocol, String prompt, String scheme)	
△	public static synchronized void		**setDefault** (Authenticator a)	ε139

AuthPermission — javax.security.auth

ε217,218

```
Object
└java.security.Permission 1 ---------------- java.security.Guard, java.io.Serializable
    └java.security.BasicPermission 2
        └AuthPermission
```

1.2 O
1.2 O
1.4 ●

*	public		**AuthPermission** (String name)	
*	public		**AuthPermission** (String name, String actions)	
1	public	void	checkGuard (Object object) throws SecurityException	
2	public	boolean	equals (Object obj)	ε215
2	public	String	getActions ()	ε215

AuthPermission

●	1	public final .... String	getName ()	
	2	public........................int	hashCode ()	ε215
	2	public.................. boolean	implies (java.security.Permission p)	ε214,215
	2	public..........java.security ↵ .PermissionCollection	newPermissionCollection ()	
	1	public.................... String	toString ()	

BackingStoreException	java.util.prefs

Object
└Throwable - *java.io.Serializable*˅   ε407,408,414,415,416
  └Exception
    └BackingStoreException

1.4

✳	public.......................... **BackingStoreException** (String s)
✳	public.......................... **BackingStoreException** (Throwable cause)

BAD_CONTEXT	org.omg.CORBA

Object
└Throwable - *java.io.Serializable*˅
  └Exception
    └RuntimeException
1.2 ○   └SystemException[1]
1.2 ●   └BAD_CONTEXT

	1	*3 inherited members from SystemException not shown*
✳		public.......................... **BAD_CONTEXT** ()
✳		public.......................... **BAD_CONTEXT** (String s)
✳		public.......................... **BAD_CONTEXT** (int minor, CompletionStatus completed)
✳		public.......................... **BAD_CONTEXT** (String s, int minor, CompletionStatus completed)

BAD_INV_ORDER	org.omg.CORBA

Object
└Throwable - *java.io.Serializable*˅
  └Exception
    └RuntimeException
1.2 ○   └SystemException[1]
1.2 ●   └BAD_INV_ORDER

	1	*3 inherited members from SystemException not shown*
✳		public.......................... **BAD_INV_ORDER** ()
✳		public.......................... **BAD_INV_ORDER** (String s)
✳		public.......................... **BAD_INV_ORDER** (int minor, CompletionStatus completed)
✳		public.......................... **BAD_INV_ORDER** (String s, int minor, CompletionStatus completed)

BAD_OPERATION	org.omg.CORBA

Object
└Throwable - *java.io.Serializable*˅
  └Exception
    └RuntimeException
1.2 ○   └SystemException[1]
1.2 ●   └BAD_OPERATION

	1	*3 inherited members from SystemException not shown*
✳		public.......................... **BAD_OPERATION** ()
✳		public.......................... **BAD_OPERATION** (String s)
✳		public.......................... **BAD_OPERATION** (int minor, CompletionStatus completed)
✳		public.......................... **BAD_OPERATION** (String s, int minor, CompletionStatus completed)

Class *Interface* —extends - - -implements ○ abstract ● final △ static ▲ static final ✳ constructor x x—inherited x **x**—declared **x x**—overridden
ε*n*—examples of usage ˅—has subclass package—see other volume

BAD_PARAM · org.omg.CORBA

```
Object
 └Throwable ---------------------------- java.io.Serializable
    └Exception
       └RuntimeException
          └SystemException[1]
             └BAD_PARAM
```
1.2 ○
1.2 ●

	[1]	*3 inherited members from SystemException not shown*
*	public..........................	**BAD_PARAM** ()
*	public..........................	**BAD_PARAM** (String s)
*	public..........................	**BAD_PARAM** (int minor, CompletionStatus completed)
*	public..........................	**BAD_PARAM** (String s, int minor, CompletionStatus completed)

BAD_POLICY · org.omg.CORBA

1.2 *BAD_POLICY*

▲ public static final..........short **value** = 0

BAD_POLICY_TYPE · org.omg.CORBA

1.2 *BAD_POLICY_TYPE*

▲ public static final..........short **value** = 2

BAD_POLICY_VALUE · org.omg.CORBA

1.2 *BAD_POLICY_VALUE*

▲ public static final..........short **value** = 3

BAD_TYPECODE · org.omg.CORBA

```
Object
 └Throwable ---------------------------- java.io.Serializable
    └Exception
       └RuntimeException
          └SystemException[1]
             └BAD_TYPECODE
```
1.2 ○
1.2 ●

	[1]	*3 inherited members from SystemException not shown*
*	public..........................	**BAD_TYPECODE** ()
*	public..........................	**BAD_TYPECODE** (String s)
*	public..........................	**BAD_TYPECODE** (int minor, CompletionStatus completed)
*	public..........................	**BAD_TYPECODE** (String s, int minor, CompletionStatus completed)

BadKind · org.omg.CORBA.TypeCodePackage

```
Object
 └Throwable ---------------------------- java.io.Serializable
    └Exception
       └org.omg.CORBA.UserException ------- org.omg.CORBA.portable.IDLEntity (java.io.Serializable)
          └BadKind
```
1.2 ○
1.2 ●

*	public..........................	**BadKind** ()
*	public..........................	**BadKind** (String reason)

Classes

BadPaddingException · javax.crypto

ε462,464,466

```
Object
 └Throwable ---------------------------- java.io.Serializable
    └Exception
       └java.security.GeneralSecurityException
          └BadPaddingException
```
1.2
1.4

BadPaddingException

*	public		**BadPaddingException** ()	
*	public		**BadPaddingException** (String msg)	

B

BasicAttribute | javax.naming.directory

Object[1]
1.3 └BasicAttribute ------------------------ *Attribute*[2] (*Cloneable, java.io.Serializable*)

	2	public .... boolean	**add** (Object attrVal)	ε484,485
	2	public .... void	**add** (int ix, Object attrVal)	
		protected .... String	**attrID**	
*		public	**BasicAttribute** (String id)	ε483,484,485,486,489
*		public	**BasicAttribute** (String id, boolean ordered)	
*		public	**BasicAttribute** (String id, Object value)	ε483,486,489
*		public	**BasicAttribute** (String id, Object value, boolean ordered)	
	2	public .... void	**clear** ()	
	1	public .... **Object**	**clone** ()	
	2	public .... boolean	**contains** (Object attrVal)	
	1	public .... **boolean**	**equals** (Object obj)	
	2	public .... Object	**get** () throws javax.naming.NamingException	
	2	public .... Object	**get** (int ix) throws javax.naming.NamingException	
	2	public .... *javax.naming*↵	**getAll** () throws javax.naming.NamingException	
		.NamingEnumeration		
	2	public .... *DirContext*	**getAttributeDefinition** () throws javax.naming.NamingException	
				ε491
	2	public .... *DirContext*	**getAttributeSyntaxDefinition** () throws javax.naming.NamingException	
	2	public .... String	**getID** ()	
	1	public .... **int**	**hashCode** ()	
	2	public .... boolean	**isOrdered** ()	
		protected .... boolean	**ordered**	
	2	public .... Object	**remove** (int ix)	
	2	public .... boolean	**remove** (Object attrval)	
	2	public .... Object	**set** (int ix, Object attrVal)	
	2	public .... int	**size** ()	
	1	public .... **String**	**toString** ()	
		protected transient	**values**	
		.... java.util.Vector		

BasicAttributes | javax.naming.directory

Object[1]
1.3 └BasicAttributes ------------------------ *Attributes*[2] (*Cloneable, java.io.Serializable*)

*		public	**BasicAttributes** ()	
*		public	**BasicAttributes** (boolean ignoreCase)	ε484,485,486,489
*		public	**BasicAttributes** (String attrID, Object val)	
*		public	**BasicAttributes** (String attrID, Object val, boolean ignoreCase)	
	1	public .... **Object**	**clone** ()	
	1	public .... **boolean**	**equals** (Object obj)	
	2	public .... *Attribute*	**get** (String attrID)	ε491
	2	public .... *javax.naming*↵	**getAll** ()	ε482
		.NamingEnumeration		
	2	public .... *javax.naming*↵	**getIDs** ()	
		.NamingEnumeration		
	1	public .... **int**	**hashCode** ()	
	2	public .... boolean	**isCaseIgnored** ()	
	2	public .... *Attribute*	**put** (*Attribute* attr)	ε484,485,486,489
	2	public .... *Attribute*	**put** (String attrID, Object val)	
	2	public .... *Attribute*	**remove** (String attrID)	
	2	public .... int	**size** ()	
	1	public .... **String**	**toString** ()	

Class *Interface* —extends - - -implements ○ abstract ● final △ static ▲ static final ✳ constructor x x—inherited x **x**—declared **x x**—overridden
ε*n*—examples of usage ↵—has subclass package—see other volume

BasicPermission | java.security

		Object	ε217,218
1.2 ○		└ Permission [1] - *Guard, java.io.Serializable*	
1.2 ○		└ BasicPermission	

*	public		**BasicPermission** (String name)	
*	public		**BasicPermission** (String name, String actions)	
	1	public	void checkGuard (Object object) throws SecurityException	
	1	public	**boolean equals** (Object obj)	ε215
	1	public	**String getActions** ()	ε215
●	1	public final	String getName ()	
	1	public	**int hashCode** ()	ε215
	1	public	**boolean implies** (Permission p)	ε214,215
	1	public	**PermissionCollection newPermissionCollection** ()	
	1	public	String toString ()	

BatchUpdateException | java.sql

		Object	
		└ Throwable - *java.io.Serializable*	
		└ Exception	
1.1		└ SQLException [1]	
1.2		└ BatchUpdateException	

*	public		**BatchUpdateException** ()	
*	public		**BatchUpdateException** (int[] updateCounts)	
*	public		**BatchUpdateException** (String reason, int[] updateCounts)	
*	public		**BatchUpdateException** (String reason, String SQLState, int[] updateCounts)	
*	public		**BatchUpdateException** (String reason, String SQLState, int vendorCode, int[] updateCounts)	
	1	public	int getErrorCode ()	
	1	public	SQLException getNextException ()	
	1	public	String getSQLState ()	
		public	int[] **getUpdateCounts** ()	ε265
	1	public synchronized	void setNextException (SQLException ex)	

BeanContext | java.beans.beancontext

1.2		*BeanContext* ———————— *BeanContextChild* [1], *java.util.Collection* [2], *java.beans.DesignMode* [3], *java.beans.Visibility* [4]	

	2	public	boolean add (Object o)	ε342,349,352,354,358
	2	public	boolean addAll (*java.util.Collection* c)	ε351,353
		public	void **addBeanContextMembershipListener** (*BeanContextMembershipListener* bcml)	
	1	public	void addPropertyChangeListener (String name, *java.beans.PropertyChangeListener* pcl)	
	1	public	void addVetoableChangeListener (String name, *java.beans.VetoableChangeListener* vcl)	
	4	public	boolean avoidingGui ()	
	2	public	void clear ()	ε351,353
	2	public	boolean contains (Object o)	ε352
	2	public	boolean containsAll (*java.util.Collection* c)	
	4	public	void dontUseGui ()	
	2	public	boolean equals (Object o)	
	1	public	*BeanContext* getBeanContext ()	
		public	java.net.URL **getResource** (String name, *BeanContextChild* bcc) throws IllegalArgumentException	
		public	java.io.InputStream **getResourceAsStream** (String name, *BeanContextChild* bcc) throws IllegalArgumentException	
▲		public static final	Object **globalHierarchyLock**	
	2	public	int hashCode ()	
		public	Object **instantiateChild** (String beanName) throws java.io.IOException, ClassNotFoundException	
	3	public	boolean isDesignTime ()	
	2	public	boolean isEmpty ()	ε102
	2	public	*java.util.Iterator* iterator ()	ε345,352,354,355,356
	4	public	boolean needsGui ()	
	4	public	void okToUseGui ()	
	2	public	boolean remove (Object o)	ε349,352
	2	public	boolean removeAll (*java.util.Collection* c)	ε351,353
		public	void **removeBeanContextMembershipListener** (*BeanContextMembershipListener* bcml)	

B

Classes

BeanContext

1	public	void	removePropertyChangeListener (String name, *java.beans.PropertyChangeListener* pcl)	
1	public	void	removeVetoableChangeListener (String name, *java.beans.VetoableChangeListener* vcl)	
2	public	boolean	retainAll (*java.util.Collection* c)	ε351,353
1	public	void	setBeanContext (*BeanContext* bc) throws java.beans.PropertyVetoException	
3	public	void	setDesignTime (boolean designTime)	
2	public	int	size ()	ε340,349,351,352,358
2	public	Object[]	toArray ()	ε340
2	public	Object[]	toArray (Object[] a)	ε340,352,358,194,508

BeanContextChild   java.beans.beancontext

1.2 | *BeanContextChild* ⌄

public	void	**addPropertyChangeListener** (String name, *java.beans.PropertyChangeListener* pcl)	
public	void	**addVetoableChangeListener** (String name, *java.beans.VetoableChangeListener* vcl)	
public	*BeanContext*	**getBeanContext** ()	
public	void	**removePropertyChangeListener** (String name, *java.beans↩.PropertyChangeListener* pcl)	
public	void	**removeVetoableChangeListener** (String name, *java.beans↩.VetoableChangeListener* vcl)	
public	void	**setBeanContext** (*BeanContext* bc) throws java.beans.PropertyVetoException	

BeanContextChildComponentProxy   java.beans.beancontext

1.2 | *BeanContextChildComponentProxy*

public	java.awt.Component	**getComponent** ()

BeanContextChildSupport   java.beans.beancontext

Object
└ BeanContextChildSupport ⌄ - - - - - - - - - - - - - - - - *BeanContextChild* ⌄ [1], *BeanContextServicesListener* ⌄ [2]
1.2   (*BeanContextServiceRevokedListener* [3]
                                                        (*java.util.EventListener*)), *java.io.Serializable* ⌄

1	public	void	**addPropertyChangeListener** (String name, *java.beans.PropertyChangeListener* pcl)
1	public	void	**addVetoableChangeListener** (String name, *java.beans.VetoableChangeListener* vcl)
	protected transient *BeanContext*		**beanContext**
	public *BeanContextChild*		**beanContextChildPeer**
✳	public		**BeanContextChildSupport** ()
✳	public		**BeanContextChildSupport** (*BeanContextChild* bcc)
	public	void	**firePropertyChange** (String name, Object oldValue, Object newValue)
	public	void	**fireVetoableChange** (String name, Object oldValue, Object newValue) throws java.beans.PropertyVetoException
1	public synchronized *BeanContext*		**getBeanContext** ()
	public *BeanContextChild*		**getBeanContextChildPeer** ()
	protected	void	**initializeBeanContextResources** ()
	public	boolean	**isDelegated** ()
	protected java.beans↩.PropertyChangeSupport		**pcSupport**
	protected transient	boolean	**rejectedSetBCOnce**
	protected	void	**releaseBeanContextResources** ()
1	public	void	**removePropertyChangeListener** (String name, *java.beans↩.PropertyChangeListener* pcl)
1	public	void	**removeVetoableChangeListener** (String name, *java.beans↩.VetoableChangeListener* vcl)
2	public	void	**serviceAvailable** (BeanContextServiceAvailableEvent bcsae)
3	public	void	**serviceRevoked** (BeanContextServiceRevokedEvent bcsre)
1	public synchronized	void	**setBeanContext** (*BeanContext* bc) throws java.beans.PropertyVetoException
	public	boolean	**validatePendingSetBeanContext** (*BeanContext* newValue)

Class   *Interface*   —extends   - - -implements   ○ abstract   ● final   △ static   ▲ static final   ✳ constructor   x x—inherited   x **x**—declared   **x x**—overridden
ε*n*—examples of usage   ⌄—has subclass   package—see other volume

protected........ java.beans↩ **vcSupport**
.VetoableChangeSupport

BeanContextContainerProxy	java.beans.beancontext

| 1.2 | *BeanContextContainerProxy* |

public...... java.awt.Container **getContainer** ()

BeanContextEvent	java.beans.beancontext

Object   ε333
1.1   └java.util.EventObject[1] - - - - - - - - - - - - - - - - - *java.io.Serializable*
1.2 ○   └BeanContextEvent

∗	protected......................	**BeanContextEvent** (*BeanContext* bc)
	public............. *BeanContext*	**getBeanContext** ()
	public synchronized	**getPropagatedFrom** ()
	.... *BeanContext*	
1	public.................... Object	getSource ()
	public synchronized .. boolean	**isPropagated** ()
	protected......... *BeanContext*	**propagatedFrom**
	public synchronized ....void	**setPropagatedFrom** (*BeanContext* bc)
1	protected transient...... Object	source
1	public.................... String	toString ()

BeanContextMembershipEvent	java.beans.beancontext

Object   ε333
1.1   └java.util.EventObject[1] - - - - - - - - - - - - - - - - - *java.io.Serializable*
1.2 ○   └BeanContextEvent[2]
1.2   └BeanContextMembershipEvent

∗	public...........................	**BeanContextMembershipEvent** (*BeanContext* bc, *java.util.Collection* changes)
∗	public...........................	**BeanContextMembershipEvent** (*BeanContext* bc, Object[] changes)
	protected ... *java.util.Collection*	**children**
	public................. boolean	**contains** (Object child)
2	public............. *BeanContext*	getBeanContext ()
2	public synchronized	getPropagatedFrom ()
	.... *BeanContext*	
1	public.................... Object	getSource ()
2	public synchronized .. boolean	isPropagated ()
	public.......... *java.util.Iterator*	**iterator** ()
2	protected......... *BeanContext*	propagatedFrom
2	public synchronized ....void	setPropagatedFrom (*BeanContext* bc)
	public........................int	**size** ()
1	protected transient...... Object	source
	public.................. Object[]	**toArray** ()
1	public.................... String	toString ()

BeanContextMembershipListener	java.beans.beancontext

| 1.2 | *BeanContextMembershipListener*————————*java.util.EventListener*   ε2,3,333,493,494 |

public....................... void **childrenAdded** (BeanContextMembershipEvent bcme)
public....................... void **childrenRemoved** (BeanContextMembershipEvent bcme)

BeanContextProxy	java.beans.beancontext

| 1.2 | *BeanContextProxy* |

public....... *BeanContextChild* **getBeanContextProxy** ()

BeanContextServiceAvailableEvent

BeanContextServiceAvailableEvent				java.beans.beancontext

Object   ε333
1.1   └java.util.EventObject[1] - - - - - - - - - - - - - - - - - - - *java.io.Serializable*⌄
1.2 ○   └BeanContextEvent[2]
1.2   └BeanContextServiceAvailableEvent

✳	public........................	**BeanContextServiceAvailableEvent** (*BeanContextServices* bcs, Class sc)
2	public............. *BeanContext*	getBeanContext ()
	public......... *java.util.Iterator*	**getCurrentServiceSelectors** ()
2	public synchronized .... *BeanContext*	getPropagatedFrom ()
	public....................Class	**getServiceClass** ()
1	public...................Object	getSource ()
	public... *BeanContextServices*	**getSourceAsBeanContextServices** ()
2	public synchronized .. boolean	isPropagated ()
2	protected......... *BeanContext*	propagatedFrom
	protected................Class	**serviceClass**
2	public synchronized ....void	setPropagatedFrom (*BeanContext* bc)
1	protected transient......Object	source
1	public...................String	toString ()

BeanContextServiceProvider				java.beans.beancontext

1.2   *BeanContextServiceProvider*
- -
public.......... *java.util.Iterator* **getCurrentServiceSelectors** (*BeanContextServices* bcs, Class serviceClass)
public...................Object **getService** (*BeanContextServices* bcs, Object requestor, Class serviceClass,
                    Object serviceSelector)
public.......................void **releaseService** (*BeanContextServices* bcs, Object requestor, Object service)
- -

BeanContextServiceProviderBeanInfo				java.beans.beancontext

1.2   *BeanContextServiceProviderBeanInfo*————*java.beans.BeanInfo*⌄[1]
- -
1 public... *java.beans.BeanInfo[]* getAdditionalBeanInfo ()
1 public.......................... getBeanDescriptor ()
   .. java.beans.BeanDescriptor
1 public.........................int getDefaultEventIndex ()
1 public.........................int getDefaultPropertyIndex ()
1 public...................java↩ getEventSetDescriptors ()
   .beans.EventSetDescriptor[]
1 public......... java.awt.Image getIcon (int iconKind)
1 public...................java↩ getMethodDescriptors ()
   .beans.MethodDescriptor[]
1 public...................java↩ getPropertyDescriptors ()   ε5,9
   .beans.PropertyDescriptor[]
   public... *java.beans.BeanInfo[]* **getServicesBeanInfo** ()
- -

BeanContextServiceRevokedEvent				java.beans.beancontext

Object   ε333
1.1   └java.util.EventObject[1] - - - - - - - - - - - - - - - - - - - *java.io.Serializable*⌄
1.2 ○   └BeanContextEvent[2]
1.2   └BeanContextServiceRevokedEvent

✳	public........................	**BeanContextServiceRevokedEvent** (*BeanContextServices* bcs, Class sc,
		boolean invalidate)
2	public............. *BeanContext*	getBeanContext ()
2	public synchronized .... *BeanContext*	getPropagatedFrom ()
	public....................Class	**getServiceClass** ()
1	public...................Object	getSource ()
	public... *BeanContextServices*	**getSourceAsBeanContextServices** ()
	public................. boolean	**isCurrentServiceInvalidNow** ()
2	public synchronized .. boolean	isPropagated ()
	public................. boolean	**isServiceClass** (Class service)
2	protected......... *BeanContext*	propagatedFrom

Class *Interface* —extends - - -implements ○ abstract ● final △ static ▲ static final ✳ constructor x x—inherited x **x**—declared **x x**—overridden
ε*n*—examples of usage ⌄—has subclass package—see other volume

460

	protected	.... Class	**serviceClass**
2	public synchronized	.... void	setPropagatedFrom (*BeanContext* bc)
1	protected transient	...... Object	source
1	public	.... String	toString ()

BeanContextServiceRevokedListener — java.beans.beancontext

1.2	*BeanContextServiceRevokedListener* ———— *java.util.EventListener*	ε2,3,333,493,494

	public	.... void	**serviceRevoked** (BeanContextServiceRevokedEvent bcsre)

BeanContextServices — java.beans.beancontext

1.2	*BeanContextServices* ———————————— *BeanContext* [1] (*BeanContextChild* [2], *java.util.Collection* [3], *java.beans* ↵ *.DesignMode* [4], *java.beans.Visibility* [5]), *BeanContextServicesListener* [6] (*BeanContextServiceRevokedListener* [7] (*java.util.EventListener*))	ε2,3,333,493,494

3	public	.... boolean	add (Object o)	ε342,349,352,354,358
3	public	.... boolean	addAll (*java.util.Collection* c)	ε351,353
1	public	.... void	addBeanContextMembershipListener (*BeanContextMembershipListener* bcml)	
	public	.... void	**addBeanContextServicesListener** (*BeanContextServicesListener* bcsl)	
2	public	.... void	addPropertyChangeListener (String name, *java.beans.PropertyChangeListener* pcl)	
	public	.... boolean	**addService** (Class serviceClass, *BeanContextServiceProvider* serviceProvider)	
2	public	.... void	addVetoableChangeListener (String name, *java.beans.VetoableChangeListener* vcl)	
5	public	.... boolean	avoidingGui ()	
3	public	.... void	clear ()	ε351,353
3	public	.... boolean	contains (Object o)	ε352
3	public	.... boolean	containsAll (*java.util.Collection* c)	
5	public	.... void	dontUseGui ()	
3	public	.... boolean	equals (Object o)	
2	public	...... *BeanContext*	getBeanContext ()	
	public	.... *java.util.Iterator*	**getCurrentServiceClasses** ()	
	public	.... *java.util.Iterator*	**getCurrentServiceSelectors** (Class serviceClass)	
1	public	.... java.net.URL	getResource (String name, *BeanContextChild* bcc) throws IllegalArgumentException	
1	public	...... java.io.InputStream	getResourceAsStream (String name, *BeanContextChild* bcc) throws IllegalArgumentException	
	public	.... Object	**getService** (*BeanContextChild* child, Object requestor, Class serviceClass, Object serviceSelector, *BeanContextServiceRevokedListener* bcsrl) throws java.util.TooManyListenersException	
3	public	.... int	hashCode ()	
	public	.... boolean	**hasService** (Class serviceClass)	
1	public	.... Object	instantiateChild (String beanName) throws java.io.IOException, ClassNotFoundException	
4	public	.... boolean	isDesignTime ()	
3	public	.... boolean	isEmpty ()	ε102
3	public	.... *java.util.Iterator*	iterator ()	ε345,352,354,355,356
5	public	.... boolean	needsGui ()	
5	public	.... void	okToUseGui ()	
	public	.... void	**releaseService** (*BeanContextChild* child, Object requestor, Object service)	
3	public	.... boolean	remove (Object o)	ε349,352
3	public	.... boolean	removeAll (*java.util.Collection* c)	ε351,353
1	public	.... void	removeBeanContextMembershipListener (*BeanContextMembershipListener* bcml)	
	public	.... void	**removeBeanContextServicesListener** (*BeanContextServicesListener* bcsl)	
2	public	.... void	removePropertyChangeListener (String name, *java.beans.PropertyChangeListener* pcl)	
2	public	.... void	removeVetoableChangeListener (String name, *java.beans.VetoableChangeListener* vcl)	
3	public	.... boolean	retainAll (*java.util.Collection* c)	ε351,353
	public	.... void	**revokeService** (Class serviceClass, *BeanContextServiceProvider* serviceProvider, boolean revokeCurrentServicesNow)	
6	public	.... void	serviceAvailable (BeanContextServiceAvailableEvent bcsae)	
7	public	.... void	serviceRevoked (BeanContextServiceRevokedEvent bcsre)	
2	public	.... void	setBeanContext (*BeanContext* bc) throws java.beans.PropertyVetoException	
4	public	.... void	setDesignTime (boolean designTime)	
3	public	.... int	size ()	ε340,349,351,352,358
3	public	.... Object[]	toArray ()	ε340
3	public	.... Object[]	toArray (Object[] a)	ε340,352,358,194,508

BeanContextServicesListener	java.beans.beancontext

1.2	*BeanContextServicesListener* ⌄ ──────── *BeanContextServiceRevokedListener* ⌄[1] (*java.util.EventListener*)	ε2,3,333,493,494

	public.....................void **serviceAvailable** (BeanContextServiceAvailableEvent bcsae)
1	public.....................void serviceRevoked (BeanContextServiceRevokedEvent bcsre)

BeanContextServicesSupport	java.beans.beancontext

	Object
1.2	└─BeanContextChildSupport[1] ············· *BeanContextChild* ⌄, *BeanContextServicesListener* ⌄ (*BeanContextServiceRevokedListener* (*java.util.EventListener*)), *java.io.Serializable* ⌄
1.2	└─BeanContextSupport[2] ············· *BeanContextChild, java.util.Collection,* *java.beans.DesignMode, java.beans.Visibility*), *java.beans.PropertyChangeListener* (*java.util.EventListener*), *java.beans.VetoableChangeListener* (*java.util.EventListener*)
1.2	└─BeanContextServicesSupport ·········· *BeanContextServices*[3] (*BeanContext* (*BeanContextChild,* *java.util.Collection, java.beans.DesignMode,* *java.beans.Visibility*), *BeanContextServicesListener* (*BeanContextServiceRevokedListener* (*java.util.EventListener*)))

	2	*56 inherited members from BeanContextSupport not shown*
	3	public.....................void **addBeanContextServicesListener** (*BeanContextServicesListener* bcsl)
	1	public.....................void addPropertyChangeListener (String name, *java.beans.PropertyChangeListener* pcl)
	3	public................. boolean **addService** (Class serviceClass, *BeanContextServiceProvider* bcsp)
		protected .... boolean **addService** (Class serviceClass, *BeanContextServiceProvider* bcsp, boolean fireEvent)
	1	public.....................void addVetoableChangeListener (String name, *java.beans.VetoableChangeListener* vcl)
		protected transient............. .... java.util.ArrayList **bcsListeners**
	2	protected synchronized .. **void bcsPreDeserializationHook** (java.io.ObjectInputStream ois) throws java.io.IOException, ClassNotFoundException
	2	protected synchronized .. **void bcsPreSerializationHook** (java.io.ObjectOutputStream oos) throws java.io.IOException
	1	protected transient............. .... BeanContext beanContext
	1	public....... *BeanContextChild* beanContextChildPeer
∗		public.......................... **BeanContextServicesSupport** ()
∗		public.......................... **BeanContextServicesSupport** (*BeanContextServices* peer)
∗		public.......................... **BeanContextServicesSupport** (*BeanContextServices* peer, java.util.Locale lcle)
∗		public.......................... **BeanContextServicesSupport** (*BeanContextServices* peer, java.util.Locale lcle, boolean dtime)
∗		public.......................... **BeanContextServicesSupport** (*BeanContextServices* peer, java.util.Locale lcle, boolean dTime, boolean visible)
	2	protected .... **void childJustRemovedHook** (Object child, BeanContextSupport.BCSChild bcsc)
	2	protected .... **createBCSChild** (Object targetChild, Object peer) .....**BeanContextSupport**↵ .BCSChild
		protected .... BeanContextServicesSupport↵ .BCSSServiceProvider **createBCSSServiceProvider** (Class sc, *BeanContextServiceProvider* bcsp)
	1	public.......................void firePropertyChange (String name, Object oldValue, Object newValue)
●		protected final..............void **fireServiceAdded** (BeanContextServiceAvailableEvent bcssae)
●		protected final..............void **fireServiceAdded** (Class serviceClass)
●		protected final..............void **fireServiceRevoked** (BeanContextServiceRevokedEvent bcsre)
●		protected final..............void **fireServiceRevoked** (Class serviceClass, boolean revokeNow)
	1	public.......................void fireVetoableChange (String name, Object oldValue, Object newValue) throws java.beans.PropertyVetoException
	1	public synchronized .... BeanContext getBeanContext ()
	1	public....... *BeanContextChild* getBeanContextChildPeer ()
		public... *BeanContextServices* **getBeanContextServicesPeer** ()
▲		protected static final .....*Bean*- **getChildBeanContextServicesListener** (Object child) *ContextServicesListener*
	3	public......... *java.util.Iterator* **getCurrentServiceClasses** ()
	3	public......... *java.util.Iterator* **getCurrentServiceSelectors** (Class serviceClass)

Class *Interface* ──extends - - -implements ○ abstract ● final △ static ▲ static final ∗ constructor x x─inherited x **x**─declared **x x**─overridden
ε*n*─examples of usage ⌄─has subclass package─see other volume

3	public	Object	**getService** (*BeanContextChild* child, Object requestor, Class serviceClass, Object serviceSelector, *BeanContextServiceRevokedListener* bcsrl) throws java.util.TooManyListenersException
3	public synchronized ..	boolean	**hasService** (Class serviceClass)
2	public	**void**	**initialize** ()
1	protected synchronized ..	**void**	**initializeBeanContextResources** ()
1	public	boolean	isDelegated ()
1	protected	java.beans ↵ .PropertyChangeSupport	pcSupport
	protected transient		**proxy**
		BeanContextServicesSupport ↵ .BCSSProxyServiceProvider	
1	protected transient....	boolean	rejectedSetBCOnce
1	protected synchronized ..	**void**	**releaseBeanContextResources** ()
3	public	void	**releaseService** (*BeanContextChild* child, Object requestor, Object service)
3	public	void	**removeBeanContextServicesListener** (*BeanContextServicesListener* bcsl)
1	public	void	removePropertyChangeListener (String name, *java.beans.PropertyChangeListener* pcl)
1	public	void	removeVetoableChangeListener (String name, *java.beans.VetoableChangeListener* vcl)
3	public	void	**revokeService** (Class serviceClass, *BeanContextServiceProvider* bcsp, boolean revokeCurrentServicesNow)
	protected transient	int	**serializable**
1	public	**void**	**serviceAvailable** (BeanContextServiceAvailableEvent bcssae)
1	public	**void**	**serviceRevoked** (BeanContextServiceRevokedEvent bcssre)
	protected transient	java.util.HashMap	**services**
1	public synchronized	void	setBeanContext (*BeanContext* bc) throws java.beans.PropertyVetoException
1	public	boolean	validatePendingSetBeanContext (*BeanContext* newValue)
1	protected	java.beans ↵ .VetoableChangeSupport	vcSupport

BeanContextServicesSupport.BCSSChild	protected	java.beans.beancontext

	Object
1.2	└ BeanContextSupport.BCSChild - - - - - - - - - - - *java.io.Serializable*⌄
1.2	└ BeanContextServicesSupport.BCSSChild

BeanContextServicesSupport.BCSSProxyServiceProvider	protected	java.beans.beancontext

	Object
1.2	└ BeanContextServicesSupport ↵ - - - - - - - - - - - *BeanContextServiceProvider* [1], *BeanContextServiceRevokedListener*⌄ [2]
	.BCSSProxyServiceProvider (*java.util.EventListener*)

1	public	*java.util.Iterator*	**getCurrentServiceSelectors** (*BeanContextServices* bcs, Class serviceClass)
1	public	Object	**getService** (*BeanContextServices* bcs, Object requestor, Class serviceClass, Object serviceSelector)
1	public	void	**releaseService** (*BeanContextServices* bcs, Object requestor, Object service)
2	public	void	**serviceRevoked** (BeanContextServiceRevokedEvent bcsre)

BeanContextServicesSupport.BCSSServiceProvider	protected	java.beans.beancontext

	Object
1.2	└ BeanContextServicesSupport ↵ - - - - - - - - - - - *java.io.Serializable*⌄
	.BCSSServiceProvider

protected		**getServiceProvider** ()
BeanContextServiceProvider		
protected		**serviceProvider**
BeanContextServiceProvider		

B

			BeanContextSupport	java.beans.beancontext

Object
1.2 └─BeanContextChildSupport [1] - - - - - - - - - - - - - *BeanContextChild*, *BeanContextServicesListener*,
                          (*BeanContextServiceRevokedListener* (*java.util.EventListener*)),
                          java.io.Serializable
1.2   └─BeanContextSupport - - - - - - - - - - - - - - - - - *BeanContext* [2] (*BeanContextChild*, *java.util.Collection* [3],
                          java.beans.DesignMode [4], *java.beans.Visibility* [5],
                          java.beans.PropertyChangeListener [6] (*java.util.EventListener*),
                          java.beans.VetoableChangeListener [7] (*java.util.EventListener*))

3	public	boolean	**add** (Object targetChild)	ε342,349,352,354,358
3	public	boolean	**addAll** (*java.util.Collection* c)	ε351,353
2	public	void	**addBeanContextMembershipListener** (*BeanContextMembershipListener* bcml)	
1	public	void	addPropertyChangeListener (String name, *java.beans.PropertyChangeListener* pcl)	
1	public	void	addVetoableChangeListener (String name, *java.beans.VetoableChangeListener* vcl)	
5	public	boolean	**avoidingGui** ()	
	protected transient		**bcmListeners**	
		java.util.ArrayList		
	protected	*java.util.Iterator*	**bcsChildren** ()	
	protected	void	**bcsPreDeserializationHook** (java.io.ObjectInputStream ois)	
			throws java.io.IOException, ClassNotFoundException	
	protected	void	**bcsPreSerializationHook** (java.io.ObjectOutputStream oos)	
			throws java.io.IOException	
1	protected transient		beanContext	
		BeanContext		
1	public	*BeanContextChild*	beanContextChildPeer	
*	public		**BeanContextSupport** ()	
*	public		**BeanContextSupport** (*BeanContext* peer)	
*	public		**BeanContextSupport** (*BeanContext* peer, java.util.Locale lcle)	
*	public		**BeanContextSupport** (*BeanContext* peer, java.util.Locale lcle, boolean dtime)	
*	public		**BeanContextSupport** (*BeanContext* peer, java.util.Locale lcle, boolean dTime, boolean visible)	
	protected	void	**childDeserializedHook** (Object child, BeanContextSupport.BCSChild bcsc)	
	protected	void	**childJustAddedHook** (Object child, BeanContextSupport.BCSChild bcsc)	
	protected	void	**childJustRemovedHook** (Object child, BeanContextSupport.BCSChild bcsc)	
	protected transient		**children**	
		java.util.HashMap		
▲	protected static final	boolean	**classEquals** (Class first, Class second)	
3	public	void	**clear** ()	ε351,353
3	public	boolean	**contains** (Object o)	ε352
3	public	boolean	**containsAll** (*java.util.Collection* c)	
	public	boolean	**containsKey** (Object o)	
●	protected final	Object[]	**copyChildren** ()	
	protected		**createBCSChild** (Object targetChild, Object peer)	
		BeanContextSupport↩		
		.BCSChild		
●	protected final	void	**deserialize** (java.io.ObjectInputStream ois, *java.util.Collection* coll)	
			throws java.io.IOException, ClassNotFoundException	
	protected	boolean	**designTime**	
5	public synchronized	void	**dontUseGui** ()	
●	protected final	void	**fireChildrenAdded** (BeanContextMembershipEvent bcme)	
●	protected final	void	**fireChildrenRemoved** (BeanContextMembershipEvent bcme)	
1	public	void	firePropertyChange (String name, Object oldValue, Object newValue)	
1	public	void	fireVetoableChange (String name, Object oldValue, Object newValue)	
			throws java.beans.PropertyVetoException	
1	public synchronized		getBeanContext ()	
		BeanContext		
1	public	*BeanContextChild*	getBeanContextChildPeer ()	
	public	*BeanContext*	**getBeanContextPeer** ()	
▲	protected static final		**getChildBeanContextChild** (Object child)	
		BeanContextChild		
▲	protected static final	*Bean-*	**getChildBeanContextMembershipListener** (Object child)	
	ContextMembershipListener			
▲	protected static final		**getChildPropertyChangeListener** (Object child)	
		java.beans↩		
		.PropertyChangeListener		
▲	protected static final		**getChildSerializable** (Object child)	
		java.io.Serializable		

Class   *Interface*   —extends   - - -implements   ○ abstract   ● final   △ static   ▲ static final   ✱ constructor   x x—inherited   x **x**—declared   **x x**—overridden
ε*n*—examples of usage   ↵—has subclass   package—see other volume

▲	protected static final .... *java.beans*↩ *.VetoableChangeListener*	**getChildVetoableChangeListener** (Object child)	
▲	protected static final .... *java.beans.Visibility*	**getChildVisibility** (Object child)	
	public synchronized ....java.util.Locale	**getLocale** ()	
2	public............. java.net.URL	**getResource** (String name, *BeanContextChild* bcc)	
2	public...... java.io.InputStream	**getResourceAsStream** (String name, *BeanContextChild* bcc)	
	protected synchronized ...void	**initialize** ()	
1	protected....................void	initializeBeanContextResources ()	
2	public................... Object	**instantiateChild** (String beanName) throws java.io.IOException, ClassNotFoundException	
1	public............... boolean	isDelegated ()	
4	public synchronized .. boolean	**isDesignTime** ()	
3	public................. boolean	**isEmpty** ()	ε102
	public................. boolean	**isSerializing** ()	
3	public.......... *java.util.Iterator*	**iterator** ()	ε345,352,354,355,356
	protected.......java.util.Locale	**locale**	
5	public synchronized .. boolean	**needsGui** ()	
5	public synchronized ......void	**okToUseGui** ()	
	protected .... boolean	**okToUseGui**	
1	protected........ java.beans↩ .PropertyChangeSupport	pcSupport	
6	public...................void	**propertyChange** (java.beans.PropertyChangeEvent pce)	ε11,404
●	public final ....void	**readChildren** (java.io.ObjectInputStream ois) throws java.io.IOException, ClassNotFoundException	
1	protected transient.... boolean	rejectedSetBCOnce	
1	protected..............void	releaseBeanContextResources ()	
3	public................. boolean	**remove** (Object targetChild)	ε349,352
	protected............. boolean	**remove** (Object targetChild, boolean callChildSetBC)	
3	public................. boolean	**removeAll** (*java.util.Collection* c)	ε351,353
2	public...................void	**removeBeanContextMembershipListener** (*BeanContextMembershipListener* bcml)	
1	public...................void	removePropertyChangeListener (String name, *java.beans.PropertyChangeListener* pcl)	
1	public...................void	removeVetoableChangeListener (String name, *java.beans.VetoableChangeListener* vcl)	
3	public................. boolean	**retainAll** (*java.util.Collection* c)	ε351,353
●	protected final..............void	**serialize** (java.io.ObjectOutputStream oos, *java.util.Collection* coll) throws java.io.IOException	
1	public...................void	serviceAvailable (BeanContextServiceAvailableEvent bcsae)	
1	public...................void	serviceRevoked (BeanContextServiceRevokedEvent bcsre)	
1	public synchronized ....void	setBeanContext (*BeanContext* bc) throws java.beans.PropertyVetoException	
4	public synchronized ....void	**setDesignTime** (boolean dTime)	
	public synchronized ....void	setLocale (java.util.Locale newLocale) throws java.beans.PropertyVetoException	
3	public........................int	**size** ()	ε340,349,351,352,358
3	public........................ Object[]	**toArray** ()	ε340
3	public........................ Object[]	**toArray** (Object[] arry)	ε340,352,358,194,508
	protected .... boolean	**validatePendingAdd** (Object targetChild)	
	protected .... boolean	**validatePendingRemove** (Object targetChild)	
1	public................. boolean	validatePendingSetBeanContext (*BeanContext* newValue)	
1	protected........ java.beans↩ .VetoableChangeSupport	vcSupport	
7	public...................void	**vetoableChange** (java.beans.PropertyChangeEvent pce) throws java.beans.PropertyVetoException	ε12
●	public final ....void	**writeChildren** (java.io.ObjectOutputStream oos) throws java.io.IOException	

Classes

BeanContextSupport.BCSChild   protected   java.beans.beancontext

Object
1.2 └BeanContextSupport.BCSChild˷ ----------- *java.io.Serializable*˷

BeanContextSupport.BCSIterator   protected   java.beans.beancontext

Object
1.2 ● └BeanContextSupport.BCSIterator --------- *java.util.Iterator* ˷ [1]

1	public.................. boolean	**hasNext** ()	ε345,352,354,355,356
1	public................... Object	**next** ()	ε345,352,354,355,356

| | 1 | public | void | **remove** () | ε176,179 |

B **BeanDescriptor** java.beans

Object
1.1 └FeatureDescriptor [1]
1.1   └BeanDescriptor

	1	public	*java.util.Enumeration*	attributeNames ()
*		public		**BeanDescriptor** (Class beanClass)
*		public		**BeanDescriptor** (Class beanClass, Class customizerClass)
		public	Class	**getBeanClass** ()
		public	Class	**getCustomizerClass** ()
	1	public	String	getDisplayName ()
	1	public	String	getName () ε5,9
	1	public	String	getShortDescription ()
	1	public	Object	getValue (String attributeName)
	1	public	boolean	isExpert ()
	1	public	boolean	isHidden ()
1.2	1	public	boolean	isPreferred ()
	1	public	void	setDisplayName (String displayName)
	1	public	void	setExpert (boolean expert)
	1	public	void	setHidden (boolean hidden)
	1	public	void	setName (String name)
1.2	1	public	void	setPreferred (boolean preferred)
	1	public	void	setShortDescription (String text)
	1	public	void	setValue (String attributeName, Object value) ε9

BeanInfo java.beans

1.1 *BeanInfo*

public	*BeanInfo[]*	**getAdditionalBeanInfo** ()
public	BeanDescriptor	**getBeanDescriptor** ()
public	int	**getDefaultEventIndex** ()
public	int	**getDefaultPropertyIndex** ()
public	EventSetDescriptor[]	**getEventSetDescriptors** ()
public	java.awt.Image	**getIcon** (int iconKind)
public	MethodDescriptor[]	**getMethodDescriptors** ()
public	PropertyDescriptor[]	**getPropertyDescriptors** () ε5,9
▲	public static final	int	**ICON_COLOR_16x16** = 1
▲	public static final	int	**ICON_COLOR_32x32** = 2
▲	public static final	int	**ICON_MONO_16x16** = 3
▲	public static final	int	**ICON_MONO_32x32** = 4

Beans java.beans

Object
1.1 └Beans

*	public		**Beans** ()
△	public static	Object	**getInstanceOf** (Object bean, Class targetType)
△	public static	Object	**instantiate** (ClassLoader cls, String beanName) throws java.io.IOException,
			ClassNotFoundException ε4
1.2 △	public static	Object	**instantiate** (ClassLoader cls, String beanName, *java.beans.beancontext*↵
			.BeanContext beanContext) throws java.io.IOException, ClassNotFoundException
1.2 △	public static	Object	**instantiate** (ClassLoader cls, String beanName, *java.beans*↵
			.beancontext.BeanContext beanContext, *AppletInitializer* initializer)
			throws java.io.IOException, ClassNotFoundException
△	public static	boolean	**isDesignTime** ()
△	public static	boolean	**isGuiAvailable** ()
△	public static	boolean	**isInstanceOf** (Object bean, Class targetType)
△	public static	void	**setDesignTime** (boolean isDesignTime) throws SecurityException
△	public static	void	**setGuiAvailable** (boolean isGuiAvailable) throws SecurityException

---

Class   *Interface*   —extends   - - -implements   ○ abstract   ● final   △ static   ▲ static final   ＊ constructor   x x—inherited   x **x**—declared   **x x**—overridden
εn—examples of usage   ˅—has subclass   package—see other volume

Bidi   java.text

```
           Object 1
1.4  ●      └Bidi
```

	public	boolean	**baseIsLeftToRight** ()
*	public		**Bidi** (*AttributedCharacterIterator* paragraph)
*	public		**Bidi** (String paragraph, int flags)
*	public		**Bidi** (char[] text, int textStart, byte[] embeddings, int embStart, int paragraphLength, int flags)
	public	Bidi	**createLineBidi** (int lineStart, int lineLimit)
▲	public static final	int	**DIRECTION_DEFAULT_LEFT_TO_RIGHT** = -2
▲	public static final	int	**DIRECTION_DEFAULT_RIGHT_TO_LEFT** = -1
▲	public static final	int	**DIRECTION_LEFT_TO_RIGHT** = 0
▲	public static final	int	**DIRECTION_RIGHT_TO_LEFT** = 1
	public	int	**getBaseLevel** ()
	public	int	**getLength** ()
	public	int	**getLevelAt** (int offset)
	public	int	**getRunCount** ()
	public	int	**getRunLevel** (int run)
	public	int	**getRunLimit** (int run)
	public	int	**getRunStart** (int run)
	public	boolean	**isLeftToRight** ()
	public	boolean	**isMixed** ()
	public	boolean	**isRightToLeft** ()
△	public static	void	**reorderVisually** (byte[] levels, int levelStart, Object[] objects, int objectStart, int count)
△	public static	boolean	**requiresBidi** (char[] text, int start, int limit)
1	public	String	**toString** ()

BigDecimal   java.math

ε252,299,304,200,201

```
           Object 1
    O       └Number 2 - - - - - - - - - - - - - - - - - - - - - - - - - - - - java.io.Serializable
1.1          └BigDecimal - - - - - - - - - - - - - - - - - - - - - - - - - Comparable 3
```

	public	BigDecimal	**abs** ()	
	public	BigDecimal	**add** (BigDecimal val)	ε127
*	public		**BigDecimal** (double val)	ε259,298
*	public		**BigDecimal** (String val)	ε127
*	public		**BigDecimal** (BigInteger val)	
*	public		**BigDecimal** (BigInteger unscaledVal, int scale)	
2	public	byte	byteValue ()	ε58
1.2 3	public	int	**compareTo** (Object o)	ε53
	public	int	**compareTo** (BigDecimal val)	
	public	BigDecimal	**divide** (BigDecimal val, int roundingMode)	ε127
	public	BigDecimal	**divide** (BigDecimal val, int scale, int roundingMode)	
2	public	double	**doubleValue** ()	ε58
1	public	boolean	**equals** (Object x)	
2	public	float	**floatValue** ()	ε58
1	public	int	**hashCode** ()	
2	public	int	**intValue** ()	ε58,6,346
2	public	long	**longValue** ()	ε58
	public	BigDecimal	**max** (BigDecimal val)	
	public	BigDecimal	**min** (BigDecimal val)	
	public	BigDecimal	**movePointLeft** (int n)	
	public	BigDecimal	**movePointRight** (int n)	
	public	BigDecimal	**multiply** (BigDecimal val)	ε127
	public	BigDecimal	**negate** ()	ε127
▲	public static final	int	**ROUND_CEILING** = 2	
▲	public static final	int	**ROUND_DOWN** = 1	ε128
▲	public static final	int	**ROUND_FLOOR** = 3	
▲	public static final	int	**ROUND_HALF_DOWN** = 5	
▲	public static final	int	**ROUND_HALF_EVEN** = 6	
▲	public static final	int	**ROUND_HALF_UP** = 4	
▲	public static final	int	**ROUND_UNNECESSARY** = 7	
▲	public static final	int	**ROUND_UP** = 0	ε127
	public	int	**scale** ()	
	public	BigDecimal	**setScale** (int scale)	
	public	BigDecimal	**setScale** (int scale, int roundingMode)	ε128
2	public	short	shortValue ()	ε58
	public	int	**signum** ()	
	public	BigDecimal	**subtract** (BigDecimal val)	ε127

BigDecimal

	public	BigInteger	**toBigInteger** ()	
1	public	**String**	**toString** ()	ε128
1.2	public	BigInteger	**unscaledValue** ()	
△	public static	BigDecimal	**valueOf** (long val)	ε127
△	public static	BigDecimal	**valueOf** (long unscaledVal, int scale)	

B

BigInteger   java.math

Object[1]   ε200,201,252,299,304
○ └Number[2] - *java.io.Serializable*
1.1   └BigInteger - *Comparable*[3]

		public	BigInteger	**abs** ()	
		public	BigInteger	**add** (BigInteger val)	ε126
		public	BigInteger	**and** (BigInteger val)	ε129
		public	BigInteger	**andNot** (BigInteger val)	ε129
	✳	public		**BigInteger** (byte[] val)	ε129,131,471
	✳	public		**BigInteger** (String val)	ε126,130,131,471
	✳	public		**BigInteger** (int numBits, java.util.Random rnd)	
	✳	public		**BigInteger** (int signum, byte[] magnitude)	
	✳	public		**BigInteger** (String val, int radix)	ε130,131
	✳	public		**BigInteger** (int bitLength, int certainty, java.util.Random rnd)	
		public	int	**bitCount** ()	
		public	int	**bitLength** ()	
	2	public	byte	byteValue ()	ε58
		public	BigInteger	**clearBit** (int n)	ε129
1.2	3	public	int	**compareTo** (Object o)	ε53
		public	int	**compareTo** (BigInteger val)	
		public	BigInteger	**divide** (BigInteger val)	ε126
		public	BigInteger[]	**divideAndRemainder** (BigInteger val)	
	2	public	double	**doubleValue** ()	ε58
	1	public	**boolean**	**equals** (Object x)	
		public	BigInteger	**flipBit** (int n)	ε129
	2	public	float	**floatValue** ()	ε58
		public	BigInteger	**gcd** (BigInteger val)	
		public	int	**getLowestSetBit** ()	
	1	public	int	**hashCode** ()	
	2	public	int	**intValue** ()	ε58,6,346
		public	boolean	**isProbablePrime** (int certainty)	
	2	public	long	**longValue** ()	ε58
		public	BigInteger	**max** (BigInteger val)	
		public	BigInteger	**min** (BigInteger val)	
		public	BigInteger	**mod** (BigInteger m)	
		public	BigInteger	**modInverse** (BigInteger m)	
		public	BigInteger	**modPow** (BigInteger exponent, BigInteger m)	
		public	BigInteger	**multiply** (BigInteger val)	ε126
		public	BigInteger	**negate** ()	ε126
		public	BigInteger	**not** ()	ε129
1.2 ▲		public static final	BigInteger	**ONE**	
		public	BigInteger	**or** (BigInteger val)	ε129
		public	BigInteger	**pow** (int exponent)	ε126
1.4 △		public static	BigInteger	**probablePrime** (int bitLength, java.util.Random rnd)	
		public	BigInteger	**remainder** (BigInteger val)	
		public	BigInteger	**setBit** (int n)	ε129
		public	BigInteger	**shiftLeft** (int n)	ε129
		public	BigInteger	**shiftRight** (int n)	ε129
	2	public	short	shortValue ()	ε58
		public	int	**signum** ()	
		public	BigInteger	**subtract** (BigInteger val)	ε126
		public	boolean	**testBit** (int n)	ε129
		public	byte[]	**toByteArray** ()	ε129,131
	1	public	**String**	**toString** ()	ε130,131
		public	String	**toString** (int radix)	ε130,131
	△	public static	BigInteger	**valueOf** (long val)	ε126
		public	BigInteger	**xor** (BigInteger val)	ε129
1.2 ▲		public static final	BigInteger	**ZERO**	

Class   *Interface*   —extends   - - -implements   ○ abstract   ● final   △ static   ▲ static final   ✳ constructor   x x—inherited   x **x**—declared   **x x**—overridden
ε*n*—examples of usage   ⌐—has subclass   package—see other volume

		BinaryRefAddr		javax.naming

Object
1.3 ○ └RefAddr[1] - *java.io.Serializable*⌐
1.3   └BinaryRefAddr

B

1	protected	String	addrType	
✳	public		**BinaryRefAddr** (String addrType, byte[] src)	
✳	public		**BinaryRefAddr** (String addrType, byte[] src, int offset, int count)	
1	public	**boolean**	**equals** (Object obj)	
1	public	**Object**	**getContent** ()	
1	public	String	getType ()	
1	public	**int**	**hashCode** ()	
1	public	**String**	**toString** ()	

		BindException		java.net

Object
└Throwable - *java.io.Serializable*⌐
 └Exception
  └java.io.IOException
   └SocketException
1.1   └BindException

✳	public	**BindException** ()	
✳	public	**BindException** (String msg)	

		Binding❶		javax.naming

Object   ε474,486,487,488,489
1.3 └NameClassPair[1] - *java.io.Serializable*⌐
1.3   └Binding⌐

✳	public		**Binding** (String name, Object obj)	
✳	public		**Binding** (String name, String className, Object obj)	
✳	public		**Binding** (String name, Object obj, boolean isRelative)	
✳	public		**Binding** (String name, String className, Object obj, boolean isRelative)	
1	public	**String**	**getClassName** ()	
1	public	String	getName ()	
	public	Object	**getObject** ()	
1	public	boolean	isRelative ()	
1	public	void	setClassName (String name)	
1	public	void	setName (String name)	
	public	void	**setObject** (Object obj)	
1	public	void	setRelative (boolean r)	
1	public	**String**	**toString** ()	

		Binding❷		org.omg.CosNaming

Object
1.2 ● └Binding - *org.omg.CORBA.portable.IDLEntity*⌐ (*java.io.Serializable*)

✳	public		**Binding** ()	
✳	public		**Binding** (NameComponent[] _binding_name, BindingType _binding_type)	
	public	NameComponent[]	**binding_name**	
	public	BindingType	**binding_type**	

		BindingHelper		org.omg.CosNaming

Object
1.2 ○ └BindingHelper

1.4 ✳	public		**BindingHelper** ()	
△	public static	Binding	**extract** (org.omg.CORBA.Any a)	
△	public static	String	**id** ()	
△	public static	void	**insert** (org.omg.CORBA.Any a, Binding that)	
△	public static	Binding	**read** (org.omg.CORBA.portable.InputStream istream)	
△	public static synchronized		**type** ()	
	. org.omg.CORBA.TypeCode			

Classes

BindingHelper

△	public static ....void	**write** (org.omg.CORBA.portable.OutputStream ostream, Binding value)

BindingHolder   org.omg.CosNaming

	Object	
1.2 ●	└BindingHolder ------------------------ *org.omg.CORBA.portable.Streamable* ˌ[1]	

1	public.......................void	**_read** (org.omg.CORBA.portable.InputStream i)
1	public...........................	**_type** ()
	. org.omg.CORBA.TypeCode	
1	public.......................void	**_write** (org.omg.CORBA.portable.OutputStream o)
✳	public...........................	**BindingHolder** ()
✳	public...........................	**BindingHolder** (Binding initialValue)
	public.................Binding	**value**

BindingIterator   org.omg.CosNaming

1.2	*BindingIterator*——————————————— *BindingIteratorOperations* ˌ[1], *org.omg.CORBA.Object* ˌ[2],	
	org.omg.CORBA.portable.IDLEntity ˌ (*java.io.Serializable*)	

2	*13 inherited members from org.omg.CORBA.Object not shown*
1	*3 inherited members from BindingIteratorOperations not shown*

BindingIteratorHelper   org.omg.CosNaming

	Object	
1.2 ○	└BindingIteratorHelper	

1.4 ✳	public...........................	**BindingIteratorHelper** ()
△	public static .... *BindingIterator*	**extract** (org.omg.CORBA.Any a)
△	public static ....String	**id** ()
△	public static ....void	**insert** (org.omg.CORBA.Any a, *BindingIterator* that)
△	public static .... *BindingIterator*	**narrow** (*org.omg.CORBA.Object* obj)
△	public static .... *BindingIterator*	**read** (org.omg.CORBA.portable.InputStream istream)
△	public static synchronized	**type** ()
	. org.omg.CORBA.TypeCode	
△	public static ....void	**write** (org.omg.CORBA.portable.OutputStream ostream, *BindingIterator* value)

BindingIteratorHolder   org.omg.CosNaming

	Object	
1.2 ●	└BindingIteratorHolder ------------------ *org.omg.CORBA.portable.Streamable* ˌ[1]	

1	public.......................void	**_read** (org.omg.CORBA.portable.InputStream i)
1	public...........................	**_type** ()
	. org.omg.CORBA.TypeCode	
1	public.......................void	**_write** (org.omg.CORBA.portable.OutputStream o)
✳	public...........................	**BindingIteratorHolder** ()
✳	public...........................	**BindingIteratorHolder** (*BindingIterator* initialValue)
	public.......... *BindingIterator*	**value**

BindingIteratorOperations   org.omg.CosNaming

1.3	*BindingIteratorOperations* ˌ

	public.......................void	**destroy** ()
	public.................boolean	**next_n** (int how_many, BindingListHolder bl)
	public.................boolean	**next_one** (BindingHolder b)

Class   *Interface*   —extends   - - -implements   ○ abstract   ● final   △ static   ▲ static final   ✳ constructor   ˌx x—inherited   x **x**—declared   **x x**—overridden
ε*n*—examples of usage   ˌ—has subclass   package—see other volume

	BindingIteratorPOA	org.omg.CosNaming

Object
- 1.4 O └─org.omg.PortableServer.Servant [1]
- 1.4 O └─BindingIteratorPOA - - - - - - - - - - - - - - - - - - - *BindingIteratorOperations*, *org.omg.CORBA.portable↵ .InvokeHandler* [2]

1	*11 inherited members from org.omg.PortableServer.Servant not shown*		
1	public	**String[]**	**_all_interfaces** (*org.omg.PortableServer.POA* poa, byte[] objectId)
2	public	org.omg.CORBA↵ .portable.OutputStream	**_invoke** (String $method, org.omg.CORBA.portable.InputStream in, *org.omg.CORBA.portable.ResponseHandler* $rh)
	public	*BindingIterator*	**_this** ()
	public	*BindingIterator*	**_this** (org.omg.CORBA.ORB orb)
∗	public		**BindingIteratorPOA** ()

	BindingListHelper	org.omg.CosNaming

Object
- 1.2 O └─BindingListHelper

1.4 ∗	public		**BindingListHelper** ()
△	public static	Binding[]	**extract** (org.omg.CORBA.Any a)
△	public static	String	**id** ()
△	public static	void	**insert** (org.omg.CORBA.Any a, Binding[] that)
△	public static	Binding[]	**read** (org.omg.CORBA.portable.InputStream istream)
△	public static synchronized	org.omg.CORBA.TypeCode	**type** ()
△	public static	void	**write** (org.omg.CORBA.portable.OutputStream ostream, Binding[] value)

	BindingListHolder	org.omg.CosNaming

Object
- 1.2 ● └─BindingListHolder - *org.omg.CORBA.portable.Streamable* [1]

1	public	void	**_read** (org.omg.CORBA.portable.InputStream i)
1	public	org.omg.CORBA.TypeCode	**_type** ()
1	public	void	**_write** (org.omg.CORBA.portable.OutputStream o)
∗	public		**BindingListHolder** ()
∗	public		**BindingListHolder** (Binding[] initialValue)
	public	Binding[]	**value**

	BindingType	org.omg.CosNaming

Object
- 1.2 └─BindingType - *org.omg.CORBA.portable.IDLEntity* (*java.io.Serializable*)

▲	public static final	int	**_ncontext** = 1
▲	public static final	int	**_nobject** = 0
1.4 ∗	protected		**BindingType** (int value)
△	public static	BindingType	**from_int** (int value)
▲	public static final	BindingType	**ncontext**
▲	public static final	BindingType	**nobject**
	public	int	**value** ()

	BindingTypeHelper	org.omg.CosNaming

Object
- 1.2 O └─BindingTypeHelper

1.4 ∗	public		**BindingTypeHelper** ()
△	public static	BindingType	**extract** (org.omg.CORBA.Any a)
△	public static	String	**id** ()
△	public static	void	**insert** (org.omg.CORBA.Any a, BindingType that)
△	public static	BindingType	**read** (org.omg.CORBA.portable.InputStream istream)
△	public static synchronized	org.omg.CORBA.TypeCode	**type** ()
△	public static	void	**write** (org.omg.CORBA.portable.OutputStream ostream, BindingType value)

BindingTypeHolder

BindingTypeHolder				org.omg.CosNaming

Object
└ BindingTypeHolder - *org.omg.CORBA.portable.Streamable* [1]

1.2 ●

1	public......................void	**_read** (org.omg.CORBA.portable.InputStream i)	
1	public.............................	**_type** ()	
	. org.omg.CORBA.TypeCode		
1	public......................void	**_write** (org.omg.CORBA.portable.OutputStream o)	
*	public............................	**BindingTypeHolder** ()	
*	public............................	**BindingTypeHolder** (BindingType initialValue)	
	public............. BindingType	**value**	

BitSet				java.util

Object [1]
└ BitSet - *Cloneable* , *java.io.Serializable*

	public......................void	**and** (BitSet set)	ε363
1.2	public......................void	**andNot** (BitSet set)	ε363
*	public............................	**BitSet** ()	ε363,364,215
*	public............................	**BitSet** (int nbits)	
1.4	public........................int	**cardinality** ()	
1.4	public......................void	**clear** ()	
	public......................void	**clear** (int bitIndex)	ε363
1.4	public......................void	**clear** (int fromIndex, int toIndex)	
1	public..................**Object**	**clone** ()	ε215
1	public.................**boolean**	**equals** (Object obj)	ε215
1.4	public......................void	**flip** (int bitIndex)	
1.4	public......................void	**flip** (int fromIndex, int toIndex)	ε363
	public.................. boolean	**get** (int bitIndex)	ε363,364
1.4	public...................BitSet	**get** (int fromIndex, int toIndex)	
1	public....................... **int**	**hashCode** ()	ε215
1.4	public................. boolean	**intersects** (BitSet set)	
1.4	public................. boolean	**isEmpty** ()	
1.2	public........................int	**length** ()	ε363,364
1.4	public........................int	**nextClearBit** (int fromIndex)	
1.4	public........................int	**nextSetBit** (int fromIndex)	
	public......................void	**or** (BitSet set)	ε363,215
	public......................void	**set** (int bitIndex)	ε363,364
1.4	public......................void	**set** (int bitIndex, boolean value)	
1.4	public......................void	**set** (int fromIndex, int toIndex)	ε363,215
1.4	public......................void	**set** (int fromIndex, int toIndex, boolean value)	
	public........................int	**size** ()	
1	public.................. **String**	**toString** ()	
	public......................void	**xor** (BitSet set)	ε363

Blob				java.sql

1.2   *Blob*   ε252

	public...... java.io.InputStream	**getBinaryStream** () throws SQLException	ε256
	public....................byte[]	**getBytes** (long pos, int length) throws SQLException	ε256
	public.......................long	**length** () throws SQLException	ε256
	public.......................long	**position** (byte[] pattern, long start) throws SQLException	
	public.......................long	**position** (*Blob* pattern, long start) throws SQLException	
1.4	public.... java.io.OutputStream	**setBinaryStream** (long pos) throws SQLException	
1.4	public........................int	**setBytes** (long pos, byte[] bytes) throws SQLException	
1.4	public........................int	**setBytes** (long pos, byte[] bytes, int offset, int len) throws SQLException	
1.4	public......................void	**truncate** (long len) throws SQLException	

Boolean				java.lang

Object [1]
└ Boolean - *java.io.Serializable*

●

*	public...........................	**Boolean** (boolean value)	ε58,387
*	public...........................	**Boolean** (String s)	

Class   *Interface*   —extends   - - -implements   ○ abstract   ● final   △ static   ▲ static final   * constructor   x x—inherited   x **x**—declared   **x x**—overridden
ε*n*—examples of usage   —has subclass   package—see other volume

	public	boolean	**booleanValue** ()		ε58
1	public	**boolean**	**equals** (Object obj)		
▲	public static final	Boolean	**FALSE** = new Boolean(false)		
△	public static	boolean	**getBoolean** (String name)		
1	public	**int**	**hashCode** ()		
1	public	**String**	**toString** ()		
1.4 △	public static	String	**toString** (boolean b)		
▲	public static final	Boolean	**TRUE** = new Boolean(true)		ε9
1.1 ▲	public static final	Class	**TYPE**		
1.4 △	public static	Boolean	**valueOf** (boolean b)		
△	public static	Boolean	**valueOf** (String s)		

BooleanHolder   org.omg.CORBA

Object
  └BooleanHolder -------------------------- *org.omg.CORBA.portable.Streamable* ˬ *[1]*   1.2 ●

1	public	void	**_read** (org.omg.CORBA.portable.InputStream input)
1	public	TypeCode	**_type** ()
1	public	void	**_write** (org.omg.CORBA.portable.OutputStream output)
✳	public		**BooleanHolder** ()
✳	public		**BooleanHolder** (boolean initial)
	public	boolean	**value**

BooleanSeqHelper   org.omg.CORBA

Object
  └BooleanSeqHelper   1.3 ○

✳	public		**BooleanSeqHelper** ()
△	public static	boolean[]	**extract** (Any a)
△	public static	String	**id** ()
△	public static	void	**insert** (Any a, boolean[] that)
△	public static	boolean[]	**read** (org.omg.CORBA.portable.InputStream istream)
△	public static synchronized	TypeCode	**type** ()
△	public static	void	**write** (org.omg.CORBA.portable.OutputStream ostream, boolean[] value)

BooleanSeqHolder   org.omg.CORBA

Object
  └BooleanSeqHolder --------------------- *org.omg.CORBA.portable.Streamable* ˬ *[1]*   1.3 ●

1	public	void	**_read** (org.omg.CORBA.portable.InputStream i)
1	public	TypeCode	**_type** ()
1	public	void	**_write** (org.omg.CORBA.portable.OutputStream o)
✳	public		**BooleanSeqHolder** ()
✳	public		**BooleanSeqHolder** (boolean[] initialValue)
	public	boolean[]	**value**

Bounds❶   org.omg.CORBA

Object
  └Throwable -------------------------------- *java.io.Serializable* ˬ
    └Exception
      └UserException --------------------- *org.omg.CORBA.portable.IDLEntity* ˬ (*java.io.Serializable*)   1.2 ○
        └Bounds   1.2 ●

✳	public		**Bounds** ()
✳	public		**Bounds** (String reason)

Bounds❷ | org.omg.CORBA.TypeCodePackage

```
Object
 └ Throwable ------------------------------ java.io.Serializable ﹀
    └ Exception
1.2 ○     └ org.omg.CORBA.UserException ------ org.omg.CORBA.portable.IDLEntity ﹀ (java.io.Serializable)
1.2 ●        └ Bounds
```

✳	public.........................	**Bounds** ()	
✳	public.........................	**Bounds** (String reason)	

BoxedValueHelper | org.omg.CORBA.portable

```
1.3    BoxedValueHelper
```

public.....................String	**get_id** ()	
public.......*java.io.Serializable*	**read_value** (InputStream is)	
public.....................void	**write_value** (OutputStream os, *java.io.Serializable* value)	

BreakIterator | java.text

```
     Object¹
1.1 ○ └ BreakIterator ------------------------- Cloneable ﹀
```

✳		protected.....................	**BreakIterator** ()	
	1	public....................**Object**	**clone** ()	
○		public abstract...............int	**current** ()	
▲		public static final.............int	**DONE** = -1	ε327,328,329,330
○		public abstract...............int	**first** ()	ε327,328,329,330
○		public abstract...............int	**following** (int offset)	
△		public static synchronized	**getAvailableLocales** ()	
		...............java.util.Locale[]		
△		public static ......BreakIterator	**getCharacterInstance** ()	
△		public static ......BreakIterator	**getCharacterInstance** (java.util.Locale where)	ε327
△		public static ......BreakIterator	**getLineInstance** ()	
△		public static ......BreakIterator	**getLineInstance** (java.util.Locale where)	ε330
△		public static ......BreakIterator	**getSentenceInstance** ()	
△		public static ......BreakIterator	**getSentenceInstance** (java.util.Locale where)	ε329
○		public abstract..................	**getText** ()	
		..............*CharacterIterator*		
△		public static ......BreakIterator	**getWordInstance** ()	
△		public static ......BreakIterator	**getWordInstance** (java.util.Locale where)	ε328
1.2		public................. boolean	**isBoundary** (int offset)	
○		public abstract...............int	**last** ()	
○		public abstract...............int	**next** ()	ε327,328,329,330
○		public abstract...............int	**next** (int n)	
1.2		public...................int	**preceding** (int offset)	
○		public abstract...............int	**previous** ()	
		public.....................void	**setText** (String newText)	ε327,328,329,330
○		public abstract..............void	**setText** (*CharacterIterator* newText)	

Buffer | java.nio

```
     Object                                              ε163,166,171,425
1.4 ○ └ Buffer ﹀
```

●	public final ....int	**capacity** ()	ε159,160,161
●	public final ....Buffer	**clear** ()	ε161,170,174
●	public final ....Buffer	**flip** ()	ε162,164,170,174,175
●	public final .... boolean	**hasRemaining** ()	ε170,184
○	public abstract .... boolean	**isReadOnly** ()	
●	public final ....int	**limit** ()	
●	public final ....Buffer	**limit** (int newLimit)	ε159,160
●	public final ....Buffer	**mark** ()	
●	public final ....int	**position** ()	ε159,160
●	public final ....Buffer	**position** (int newPosition)	ε159,160
●	public final ....int	**remaining** ()	ε159,160,161,184
●	public final ....Buffer	**reset** ()	

Class *Interface* —extends - - -implements ○ abstract ● final △ static ▲ static final ✳ constructor x x—inherited x **x**—declared **x x**—overridden
ε*n*—examples of usage ﹀—has subclass package—see other volume

● public final .... Buffer **rewind** () ε159,160,169

BufferedInputStream	java.io

Object ε252,382,418
○ └InputStream
   └FilterInputStream [1]
     └BufferedInputStream

1	public synchronized .... **int available** () throws IOException	
	protected .... byte[] **buf**	
*	public........................... **BufferedInputStream** (InputStream in)	ε8,418
*	public........................... **BufferedInputStream** (InputStream in, int size)	
1	public..................... **void close** () throws IOException	ε14,36,45,452,455
	protected .... int **count**	
1	protected .... InputStream **in**	
1	public synchronized ...... **void mark** (int readlimit)	
	protected .... int **marklimit**	
	protected .... int **markpos**	
1	public.................. **boolean markSupported** ()	
	protected .... int **pos**	
1	public synchronized .... **int read** () throws IOException	ε90,184,256
1	public....................... int read (byte[] b) throws IOException	ε452,455,457,170,451
1	public synchronized .... **int read** (byte[] b, int off, int len) throws IOException	ε36
1	public synchronized ...... **void reset** () throws IOException	
1	public synchronized ...... **long skip** (long n) throws IOException	

BufferedOutputStream	java.io

Object ε183
○ └OutputStream
   └FilterOutputStream [1]
     └BufferedOutputStream

	protected .... byte[] **buf**	
*	public........................... **BufferedOutputStream** (OutputStream out)	ε7,9,10
*	public........................... **BufferedOutputStream** (OutputStream out, int size)	
1	public....................... void close () throws IOException	ε451,453,91,211,224
	protected .... int **count**	
1	public synchronized ...... **void flush** () throws IOException	ε27,54
1	protected .... OutputStream **out**	
1	public....................... void write (byte[] b) throws IOException	ε27,91,224
1	public synchronized ...... **void write** (int b) throws IOException	ε184
1	public synchronized ...... **void write** (byte[] b, int off, int len) throws IOException	ε451,453,54,449,450

BufferedReader	java.io

Object
1.1 ○ └Reader [1]
1.1   └BufferedReader

*	public........................... **BufferedReader** (Reader in)	ε34,35,40,42,135
*	public........................... **BufferedReader** (Reader in, int sz)	
1	public..................... **void close** () throws IOException	ε35,135,136,139,149
1	protected .... Object **lock**	
1	public..................... **void mark** (int readAheadLimit) throws IOException	
1	public.................. **boolean markSupported** ()	ε442
1	public..................... **int read** () throws IOException	
1	public....................... int read (char[] cbuf) throws IOException	ε434
1	public..................... **int read** (char[] cbuf, int off, int len) throws IOException	
	public.................... String **readLine** () throws IOException	ε34,35,40,42,135
1	public.................. **boolean ready** () throws IOException	ε442
1	public..................... **void reset** () throws IOException	
1	public..................... **long skip** (long n) throws IOException	

B

BufferedWriter				java.io

Object
1.1 ○ └Writer [1]
1.1   └BufferedWriter

*		public............................	**BufferedWriter** (Writer out)	ε23,37,38,41,43
*		public............................	**BufferedWriter** (Writer out, int sz)	
	1	public.....................**void**	**close** () throws IOException	ε23,37,38,41,43
	1	public.....................**void**	**flush** () throws IOException	ε150,135,224
	1	protected ....Object	lock	
		public............................void	**newLine** () throws IOException	
	1	public.....................void	write (char[] cbuf) throws IOException	
	1	public.....................**void**	**write** (int c) throws IOException	
	1	public.....................void	write (String str) throws IOException	ε23,37,38,150,41
	1	public.....................**void**	**write** (char[] cbuf, int off, int len) throws IOException	
	1	public.....................**void**	**write** (String s, int off, int len) throws IOException	

BufferOverflowException				java.nio

Object
└Throwable - *java.io.Serializable*
  └Exception
    └RuntimeException
1.4   └BufferOverflowException

*	public...........................	**BufferOverflowException** ()	

BufferUnderflowException				java.nio

Object
└Throwable - *java.io.Serializable*
  └Exception
    └RuntimeException
1.4   └BufferUnderflowException

*	public...........................	**BufferUnderflowException** ()	

Byte				java.lang

Object [1]   ε200,201,252,299,304
○ └Number [2] - *java.io.Serializable*
1.1 ●   └Byte - *Comparable* [3]

*		public...........................	**Byte** (byte value)	ε58
*		public...........................	**Byte** (String s) throws NumberFormatException	
	2	public.....................**byte**	**byteValue** ()	ε58
1.2		public.....................int	**compareTo** (Byte anotherByte)	
1.2	3	public.....................int	**compareTo** (Object o)	ε53
△		public static .... Byte	**decode** (String nm) throws NumberFormatException	
	2	public.................**double**	**doubleValue** ()	ε58
	1	public.................**boolean**	**equals** (Object obj)	
	2	public.....................**float**	**floatValue** ()	ε58
	1	public.....................**int**	**hashCode** ()	
	2	public.....................**int**	**intValue** ()	ε58,6,346
	2	public.....................**long**	**longValue** ()	ε58
▲		public static final .... byte	**MAX_VALUE** = 127	
▲		public static final .... byte	**MIN_VALUE** = -128	
△		public static .... byte	**parseByte** (String s) throws NumberFormatException	ε82
△		public static .... byte	**parseByte** (String s, int radix) throws NumberFormatException	
	2	public.....................**short**	**shortValue** ()	ε58
	1	public.................**String**	**toString** ()	
△		public static ....String	**toString** (byte b)	
▲		public static final .... Class	**TYPE**	
△		public static .... Byte	**valueOf** (String s) throws NumberFormatException	
△		public static .... Byte	**valueOf** (String s, int radix) throws NumberFormatException	

Class *Interface* —extends - - -implements ○ abstract ● final △ static ▲ static final * constructor x x—inherited x **x**—declared **x x**—overridden
ε*n*—examples of usage ⌄—has subclass package—see other volume

ByteArrayInputStream				java.io

		Object		ε252,382,418
○		└InputStream[1]		
		└ByteArrayInputStream		

	1	public synchronized .... **int**	**available** ()	
		protected .... byte[]	**buf**	
✳		public	**ByteArrayInputStream** (byte[] buf)	ε45,382,506
✳		public	**ByteArrayInputStream** (byte[] buf, int offset, int length)	
	1	public .... **void**	**close** () throws IOException	ε14,36,45,452,455
		protected .... int	**count**	
1.1		protected .... int	**mark**	
	1	public .... **void**	**mark** (int readAheadLimit)	
	1	public .... **boolean**	**markSupported** ()	
		protected .... int	**pos**	
	1	public synchronized .... **int**	**read** ()	ε90,184,256
	1	public .... int	read (byte[] b) throws IOException	ε452,455,457,170,451
	1	public synchronized .... **int**	**read** (byte[] b, int off, int len)	ε36
	1	public synchronized ...... **void**	**reset** ()	
	1	public synchronized ...... **long**	**skip** (long n)	

ByteArrayOutputStream				java.io

		Object[1]		ε183
○		└OutputStream[2]		
		└ByteArrayOutputStream		

		protected .... byte[]	**buf**	
✳		public	**ByteArrayOutputStream** ()	ε44,450
✳		public	**ByteArrayOutputStream** (int size)	ε449,450
	2	public .... **void**	**close** () throws IOException	ε449,450,451,453,91
		protected .... int	**count**	
	2	public .... void	flush () throws IOException	ε27,54
		public synchronized ...... void	**reset** ()	
		public .... int	**size** ()	
		public synchronized .... byte[]	**toByteArray** ()	ε44,449,450
	1	public .... **String**	**toString** ()	
D		public .... String	**toString** (int hibyte)	
1.1		public .... String	**toString** (String enc) throws UnsupportedEncodingException	
	2	public .... void	write (byte[] b) throws IOException	ε27,91,224
	2	public synchronized ...... **void**	**write** (int b)	ε184
	2	public synchronized ...... **void**	**write** (byte[] b, int off, int len)	ε449,450,451,453,54
		public synchronized ...... void	**writeTo** (OutputStream out) throws IOException	

ByteBuffer				java.nio

		Object[1]		ε166,171,425,163
1.4 ○		└Buffer[2]		
1.4 ○		└ByteBuffer - *Comparable*[3]		

△		public static .... ByteBuffer	**allocate** (int capacity)	ε158,159,160,162,163
△		public static .... ByteBuffer	**allocateDirect** (int capacity)	ε158,168,169,170,174
●		public final .... byte[]	**array** ()	
●		public final .... int	**arrayOffset** ()	
○		public abstract ..... CharBuffer	**asCharBuffer** ()	ε163,164
○		public abstract ... DoubleBuffer	**asDoubleBuffer** ()	ε163
○		public abstract ..... FloatBuffer	**asFloatBuffer** ()	ε163
○		public abstract .... IntBuffer	**asIntBuffer** ()	ε163
○		public abstract ..... LongBuffer	**asLongBuffer** ()	ε163
○		public abstract ..... ByteBuffer	**asReadOnlyBuffer** ()	
○		public abstract ..... ShortBuffer	**asShortBuffer** ()	ε163
●	2	public final .... int	**capacity** ()	ε159,160,161
●	2	public final .... Buffer	clear ()	ε161,170,174
○		public abstract ...... ByteBuffer	**compact** ()	ε170
	3	public .... int	**compareTo** (Object ob)	ε53
○		public abstract ...... ByteBuffer	**duplicate** ()	
	1	public .... **boolean**	**equals** (Object ob)	
●	2	public final .... Buffer	flip ()	ε162,170,174,175,186
○		public abstract .... byte	**get** ()	ε159,169,184
		public .... ByteBuffer	**get** (byte[] dst)	

ByteBuffer

O		public abstract	byte	**get** (int index)	ε159,165,184
		public	ByteBuffer	**get** (byte[] dst, int offset, int length)	ε161,184
O		public abstract	char	**getChar** ()	ε162
O		public abstract	char	**getChar** (int index)	
O		public abstract	double	**getDouble** ()	ε162
O		public abstract	double	**getDouble** (int index)	
O		public abstract	float	**getFloat** ()	ε162
O		public abstract	float	**getFloat** (int index)	
O		public abstract	int	**getInt** ()	ε162
O		public abstract	int	**getInt** (int index)	
O		public abstract	long	**getLong** ()	ε162
O		public abstract	long	**getLong** (int index)	
O		public abstract	short	**getShort** ()	ε162
O		public abstract	short	**getShort** (int index)	
●		public final	boolean	**hasArray** ()	
	1	public	int	**hashCode** ()	
●	2	public final	boolean	hasRemaining ()	ε170,184
O		public abstract	boolean	**isDirect** ()	ε168
O	2	public abstract	boolean	isReadOnly ()	
●	2	public final	int	limit ()	
●	2	public final	Buffer	limit (int newLimit)	ε159,160
●	2	public final	Buffer	mark ()	
●		public final	ByteOrder	**order** ()	ε165
●		public final	ByteBuffer	**order** (ByteOrder bo)	ε165
●	2	public final	int	position ()	ε159,160
●	2	public final	Buffer	position (int newPosition)	ε159,160
O		public abstract	ByteBuffer	**put** (byte b)	ε160,170,175,184
●		public final	ByteBuffer	**put** (byte[] src)	
		public	ByteBuffer	**put** (ByteBuffer src)	
O		public abstract	ByteBuffer	**put** (int index, byte b)	ε167
		public	ByteBuffer	**put** (byte[] src, int offset, int length)	ε184
O		public abstract	ByteBuffer	**putChar** (char value)	ε162
O		public abstract	ByteBuffer	**putChar** (int index, char value)	
O		public abstract	ByteBuffer	**putDouble** (double value)	ε162
O		public abstract	ByteBuffer	**putDouble** (int index, double value)	
O		public abstract	ByteBuffer	**putFloat** (float value)	ε162
O		public abstract	ByteBuffer	**putFloat** (int index, float value)	
O		public abstract	ByteBuffer	**putInt** (int value)	ε162
O		public abstract	ByteBuffer	**putInt** (int index, int value)	
O		public abstract	ByteBuffer	**putLong** (long value)	ε162
O		public abstract	ByteBuffer	**putLong** (int index, long value)	
O		public abstract	ByteBuffer	**putShort** (short value)	ε162
O		public abstract	ByteBuffer	**putShort** (int index, short value)	ε165
●	2	public final	int	remaining ()	ε159,160,161,184
●	2	public final	Buffer	reset ()	
●	2	public final	Buffer	rewind ()	ε159,160,169
O		public abstract	ByteBuffer	**slice** ()	
	1	public	String	**toString** ()	
△		public static	ByteBuffer	**wrap** (byte[] array)	ε158,161,168
△		public static	ByteBuffer	**wrap** (byte[] array, int offset, int length)	

ByteChannel	java.nio.channels

1.4	*ByteChannel*————————*ReadableByteChannel* [1] (*Channel* [2]), *WritableByteChannel* [3] (*Channel* [2])

	2	public	void	close () throws java.io.IOException	ε167,170,171,172,174
	2	public	boolean	isOpen ()	
	1	public	int	read (java.nio.ByteBuffer dst) throws java.io.IOException	ε180,169,174
	3	public	int	write (java.nio.ByteBuffer src) throws java.io.IOException	ε180,170,171,175

ByteHolder	org.omg.CORBA

	Object
1.2 ●	└ByteHolder - *org.omg.CORBA.portable.Streamable* [1]

	1	public	void	**_read** (org.omg.CORBA.portable.InputStream input)
	1	public	TypeCode	**_type** ()
	1	public	void	**_write** (org.omg.CORBA.portable.OutputStream output)

Class *Interface* —extends - - -implements O abstract ● final △ static ▲ static final ✳ constructor x x—inherited x **x**—declared **x x**—overridden
ε*n*—examples of usage ⌐—has subclass package—see other volume

478

✳	public.........................	**ByteHolder** ()	
✳	public.........................	**ByteHolder** (byte initial)	
	public.................... byte	**value**	

ByteOrder
java.nio

Object[1]
1.4 ● └ByteOrder

▲	public static final .... ByteOrder **BIG_ENDIAN**	ε165
▲	public static final .... ByteOrder **LITTLE_ENDIAN**	ε165
△	public static .... ByteOrder **nativeOrder** ()	
1	public................... **String** **toString** ()	

Calendar
java.util

Object[1]
1.1 ○ └Calendar ---------------------------- *java.io.Serializable*, *Cloneable*

○	public abstract ....void	**add** (int field, int amount)	ε377
	public.................. boolean	**after** (Object when)	ε376
▲	public static final...........int	**AM** = 0	ε370,372
▲	public static final...........int	**AM_PM** = 9	ε369,370,372
▲	public static final...........int	**APRIL** = 3	
	protected .... boolean	**areFieldsSet**	
▲	public static final...........int	**AUGUST** = 7	
	public.................. boolean	**before** (Object when)	ε376,377
✳	protected.....................	**Calendar** ()	
✳	protected.....................	**Calendar** (TimeZone zone, Locale aLocale)	
●	public final ....void	**clear** ()	
●	public final ....void	**clear** (int field)	
1	public................**Object**	**clone** ()	
	protected ....void	**complete** ()	
○	protected abstract ....void	**computeFields** ()	
○	protected abstract ....void	**computeTime** ()	
▲	public static final...........int	**DATE** = 5	
▲	public static final...........int	**DAY_OF_MONTH** = 5	ε373,375
▲	public static final...........int	**DAY_OF_WEEK** = 7	ε373,379
▲	public static final...........int	**DAY_OF_WEEK_IN_MONTH** = 8	
▲	public static final...........int	**DAY_OF_YEAR** = 6	
▲	public static final...........int	**DECEMBER** = 11	ε374,376,379
▲	public static final...........int	**DST_OFFSET** = 16	
1	public................**boolean**	**equals** (Object obj)	
▲	public static final...........int	**ERA** = 0	ε373
▲	public static final...........int	**FEBRUARY** = 1	ε375
▲	public static final...........int	**FIELD_COUNT** = 17	
	protected ....int[]	**fields**	
▲	public static final...........int	**FRIDAY** = 6	
	public......................int	**get** (int field)	ε369,370,372,373,377
1.2	public......................int	**getActualMaximum** (int field)	ε375
1.2	public......................int	**getActualMinimum** (int field)	
△	public static synchronized	**getAvailableLocales** ()	
	.... Locale[]		
	public......................int	**getFirstDayOfWeek** ()	
○	public abstract ....int	**getGreatestMinimum** (int field)	
△	public static .... Calendar	**getInstance** ()	ε377
△	public static .... Calendar	**getInstance** (Locale aLocale)	
△	public static .... Calendar	**getInstance** (TimeZone zone)	
△	public static .... Calendar	**getInstance** (TimeZone zone, Locale aLocale)	
○	public abstract ....int	**getLeastMaximum** (int field)	
○	public abstract ....int	**getMaximum** (int field)	
	public......................int	**getMinimalDaysInFirstWeek** ()	
○	public abstract ....int	**getMinimum** (int field)	
●	public final .... Date	**getTime** ()	ε374
	public.................... long	**getTimeInMillis** ()	ε372,376
	public.............. TimeZone	**getTimeZone** ()	
1	public................... **int**	**hashCode** ()	
▲	public static final...........int	**HOUR** = 10	ε369,370,372
▲	public static final...........int	**HOUR_OF_DAY** = 11	ε369,370,372
●	protected final...............int	**internalGet** (int field)	
	public.................. boolean	**isLenient** ()	
	protected ....boolean[]	**isSet**	

Calendar

●	public final	.... boolean	**isSet** (int field)	
	protected	.... boolean	**isTimeSet**	
▲	public static final	........int	**JANUARY** = 0	ε376,377,379
▲	public static final	............int	**JULY** = 6	
▲	public static final	............int	**JUNE** = 5	
▲	public static final	............int	**MARCH** = 2	
▲	public static final	............int	**MAY** = 4	
▲	public static final	............int	**MILLISECOND** = 14	ε369
▲	public static final	............int	**MINUTE** = 12	ε369,370,372
▲	public static final	............int	**MONDAY** = 2	
▲	public static final	............int	**MONTH** = 2	ε373
▲	public static final	............int	**NOVEMBER** = 10	
▲	public static final	............int	**OCTOBER** = 9	
▲	public static final	............int	**PM** = 1	
○	public abstract	............void	**roll** (int field, boolean up)	
1.2	public	............void	**roll** (int field, int amount)	
▲	public static final	............int	**SATURDAY** = 7	
▲	public static final	............int	**SECOND** = 13	ε369,370,372
▲	public static final	............int	**SEPTEMBER** = 8	
	public	............void	**set** (int field, int value)	ε372
●	public final	............void	**set** (int year, int month, int date)	
●	public final	............void	**set** (int year, int month, int date, int hour, int minute)	
●	public final	............void	**set** (int year, int month, int date, int hour, int minute, int second)	
	public	............void	**setFirstDayOfWeek** (int value)	
	public	............void	**setLenient** (boolean lenient)	
	public	............void	**setMinimalDaysInFirstWeek** (int value)	
●	public final	............void	**setTime** (Date date)	
	public	............void	**setTimeInMillis** (long millis)	ε372
	public	............void	**setTimeZone** (TimeZone value)	ε370
▲	public static final	............int	**SUNDAY** = 1	
▲	public static final	............int	**THURSDAY** = 5	
	protected	.... long	**time**	
1	public	.... **String**	**toString** ()	
▲	public static final	............int	**TUESDAY** = 3	
▲	public static final	............int	**UNDECIMBER** = 12	
▲	public static final	............int	**WEDNESDAY** = 4	
▲	public static final	............int	**WEEK_OF_MONTH** = 4	
▲	public static final	............int	**WEEK_OF_YEAR** = 3	
▲	public static final	............int	**YEAR** = 1	ε373,377
▲	public static final	............int	**ZONE_OFFSET** = 15	

CallableStatement   java.sql

1.1	*CallableStatement*——————————————*PreparedStatement* ˅ [1] (*Statement* [2])	ε267
	[1] 35 inherited members from PreparedStatement not shown	
	[2] 44 inherited members from Statement not shown	
1	public .... boolean **execute** () throws SQLException	ε281,282,298,303
1.2	public .... *Array* **getArray** (int i) throws SQLException	
1.4	public .... *Array* **getArray** (String parameterName) throws SQLException	
1.2	public ... java.math.BigDecimal **getBigDecimal** (int parameterIndex) throws SQLException	
1.4	public ... java.math.BigDecimal **getBigDecimal** (String parameterName) throws SQLException	
D	public ... java.math.BigDecimal **getBigDecimal** (int parameterIndex, int scale) throws SQLException	
1.2	public .... *Blob* **getBlob** (int i) throws SQLException	
1.4	public .... *Blob* **getBlob** (String parameterName) throws SQLException	
	public .... boolean **getBoolean** (int parameterIndex) throws SQLException	
1.4	public .... boolean **getBoolean** (String parameterName) throws SQLException	
	public .... byte **getByte** (int parameterIndex) throws SQLException	
1.4	public .... byte **getByte** (String parameterName) throws SQLException	
	public .... byte[] **getBytes** (int parameterIndex) throws SQLException	
1.4	public .... byte[] **getBytes** (String parameterName) throws SQLException	
1.2	public .... *Clob* **getClob** (int i) throws SQLException	
1.4	public .... *Clob* **getClob** (String parameterName) throws SQLException	
	public .... Date **getDate** (int parameterIndex) throws SQLException	
1.4	public .... Date **getDate** (String parameterName) throws SQLException	
1.2	public .... Date **getDate** (int parameterIndex, java.util.Calendar cal) throws SQLException	
1.4	public .... Date **getDate** (String parameterName, java.util.Calendar cal) throws SQLException	
	public ....double **getDouble** (int parameterIndex) throws SQLException	
1.4	public ....double **getDouble** (String parameterName) throws SQLException	
	public .... float **getFloat** (int parameterIndex) throws SQLException	

Class *Interface* —extends - - -implements ○ abstract ● final △ static ▲ static final ✳ constructor x x—inherited x **x**—declared **x x**—overridden
ε*n*—examples of usage ˅—has subclass package—see other volume

1.4	public	float	**getFloat** (String parameterName) throws SQLException	
	public	int	**getInt** (int parameterIndex) throws SQLException	
1.4	public	int	**getInt** (String parameterName) throws SQLException	
	public	long	**getLong** (int parameterIndex) throws SQLException	
1.4	public	long	**getLong** (String parameterName) throws SQLException	
	public	Object	**getObject** (int parameterIndex) throws SQLException	
1.4	public	Object	**getObject** (String parameterName) throws SQLException	
1.2	public	Object	**getObject** (int i, *java.util.Map* map) throws SQLException	
1.4	public	Object	**getObject** (String parameterName, *java.util.Map* map) throws SQLException	
1.2	public	*Ref*	**getRef** (int i) throws SQLException	
1.4	public	*Ref*	**getRef** (String parameterName) throws SQLException	
	public	short	**getShort** (int parameterIndex) throws SQLException	
1.4	public	short	**getShort** (String parameterName) throws SQLException	
	public	String	**getString** (int parameterIndex) throws SQLException	ε281,282
1.4	public	String	**getString** (String parameterName) throws SQLException	
	public	Time	**getTime** (int parameterIndex) throws SQLException	
1.4	public	Time	**getTime** (String parameterName) throws SQLException	
1.2	public	Time	**getTime** (int parameterIndex, java.util.Calendar cal) throws SQLException	
1.4	public	Time	**getTime** (String parameterName, java.util.Calendar cal) throws SQLException	
	public	Timestamp	**getTimestamp** (int parameterIndex) throws SQLException	
1.4	public	Timestamp	**getTimestamp** (String parameterName) throws SQLException	
1.2	public	Timestamp	**getTimestamp** (int parameterIndex, java.util.Calendar cal) throws SQLException	
1.4	public	Timestamp	**getTimestamp** (String parameterName, java.util.Calendar cal) throws SQLException	
1.4	public	java.net.URL	**getURL** (int parameterIndex) throws SQLException	
1.4	public	java.net.URL	**getURL** (String parameterName) throws SQLException	
	public	void	**registerOutParameter** (int parameterIndex, int sqlType) throws SQLException ε281,282	
1.4	public	void	**registerOutParameter** (String parameterName, int sqlType) throws SQLException	
1.2	public	void	**registerOutParameter** (int paramIndex, int sqlType, String typeName) throws SQLException	
	public	void	**registerOutParameter** (int parameterIndex, int sqlType, int scale) throws SQLException	
1.4	public	void	**registerOutParameter** (String parameterName, int sqlType, String typeName) throws SQLException	
1.4	public	void	**registerOutParameter** (String parameterName, int sqlType, int scale) throws SQLException	
1.4	public	void	**setAsciiStream** (String parameterName, java.io.InputStream x, int length) throws SQLException	
1.4	public	void	**setBigDecimal** (String parameterName, java.math.BigDecimal x) throws SQLException	
1.4	public	void	**setBinaryStream** (String parameterName, java.io.InputStream x, int length) throws SQLException	
1.4	public	void	**setBoolean** (String parameterName, boolean x) throws SQLException	
1.4	public	void	**setByte** (String parameterName, byte x) throws SQLException	
1.4	public	void	**setBytes** (String parameterName, byte[] x) throws SQLException	
1.4	public	void	**setCharacterStream** (String parameterName, java.io.Reader reader, int length) throws SQLException	
1.4	public	void	**setDate** (String parameterName, Date x) throws SQLException	
1.4	public	void	**setDate** (String parameterName, Date x, java.util.Calendar cal) throws SQLException	
1.4	public	void	**setDouble** (String parameterName, double x) throws SQLException	
1.4	public	void	**setFloat** (String parameterName, float x) throws SQLException	
1.4	public	void	**setInt** (String parameterName, int x) throws SQLException	
1.4	public	void	**setLong** (String parameterName, long x) throws SQLException	
1.4	public	void	**setNull** (String parameterName, int sqlType) throws SQLException	
1.4	public	void	**setNull** (String parameterName, int sqlType, String typeName) throws SQLException	
1.4	public	void	**setObject** (String parameterName, Object x) throws SQLException	
1.4	public	void	**setObject** (String parameterName, Object x, int targetSqlType) throws SQLException	
1.4	public	void	**setObject** (String parameterName, Object x, int targetSqlType, int scale) throws SQLException	
1.4	public	void	**setShort** (String parameterName, short x) throws SQLException	
1	public	void	setString (int parameterIndex, String x) throws SQLException ε281,282,259,262,265	
1.4	public	void	**setString** (String parameterName, String x) throws SQLException	
1.4	public	void	**setTime** (String parameterName, Time x) throws SQLException	
1.4	public	void	**setTime** (String parameterName, Time x, java.util.Calendar cal) throws SQLException	
1.4	public	void	**setTimestamp** (String parameterName, Timestamp x) throws SQLException	
1.4	public	void	**setTimestamp** (String parameterName, Timestamp x, java.util.Calendar cal) throws SQLException	
1.4	public	void	**setURL** (String parameterName, java.net.URL val) throws SQLException	
	public	boolean	**wasNull** () throws SQLException	

Callback

Callback — javax.security.auth.callback

1.4	*Callback* · ε509

CallbackHandler — javax.security.auth.callback

1.4	*CallbackHandler*
	public .... void **handle** (*Callback[]* callbacks) throws java.io.IOException, UnsupportedCallbackException · ε509

CancelledKeyException — java.nio.channels

```
Object
└Throwable ------------------------------ java.io.Serializable
  └Exception
    └RuntimeException
```
1.1	└IllegalStateException
1.4	└CancelledKeyException

✳	public .... **CancelledKeyException** ()

CannotProceed — org.omg.CosNaming.NamingContextPackage

```
Object
└Throwable ------------------------------ java.io.Serializable
  └Exception
```
1.2 ○	└org.omg.CORBA.UserException ------ *org.omg.CORBA.portable.IDLEntity* (*java.io.Serializable*)
1.2 ●	└CannotProceed

✳	public .... **CannotProceed** ()
✳	public .... **CannotProceed** (*org.omg.CosNaming.NamingContext* _cxt, org.omg.CosNaming.NameComponent[] _rest_of_name)
1.4 ✳	public .... **CannotProceed** (String $reason, *org.omg.CosNaming.NamingContext* _cxt, org.omg.CosNaming.NameComponent[] _rest_of_name)
	public .... *org.omg*↵ **cxt** *.CosNaming.NamingContext*
	public . org.omg.CosNaming↵ **rest_of_name** .NameComponent[]

CannotProceedException — javax.naming

```
Object
└Throwable ------------------------------ java.io.Serializable
  └Exception
```
1.3	└NamingException [1]
1.3	└CannotProceedException

[1]	*20 inherited members from NamingException not shown*
	protected .... *Name* **altName**
	protected .... *Context* **altNameCtx**
✳	public .... **CannotProceedException** ()
✳	public .... **CannotProceedException** (String explanation)
	protected ... java.util.Hashtable **environment**
	public .... *Name* **getAltName** ()
	public .... *Context* **getAltNameCtx** ()
	public .... java.util.Hashtable **getEnvironment** ()
	public .... *Name* **getRemainingNewName** ()
	protected .... *Name* **remainingNewName**
	public .... void **setAltName** (*Name* altName)
	public .... void **setAltNameCtx** (*Context* altNameCtx)
	public .... void **setEnvironment** (java.util.Hashtable environment)
	public .... void **setRemainingNewName** (*Name* newName)

Class *Interface* —extends - - -implements ○ abstract ● final △ static ▲ static final ✳ constructor x x—inherited x **x**—declared **x x**—overridden
ε*n*—examples of usage ⌄—has subclass package—see other volume

			CannotProceedHelper	org.omg.CosNaming.NamingContextPackage

		Object	
1.2	O	└CannotProceedHelper	

1.4	✳	public............................	**CannotProceedHelper** ()
	△	public static ... CannotProceed	**extract** (org.omg.CORBA.Any a)
	△	public static ....String	**id** ()
	△	public static ....void	**insert** (org.omg.CORBA.Any a, CannotProceed that)
	△	public static ... CannotProceed	**read** (org.omg.CORBA.portable.InputStream istream)
	△	public static synchronized ..... . org.omg.CORBA.TypeCode	**type** ()
	△	public static ....void	**write** (org.omg.CORBA.portable.OutputStream ostream, CannotProceed value)

C

			CannotProceedHolder	org.omg.CosNaming.NamingContextPackage

		Object		
1.2	●	└CannotProceedHolder ------------------ *org.omg.CORBA.portable.Streamable* [1]	

	1	public........................void	**_read** (org.omg.CORBA.portable.InputStream i)
	1	public............................ . org.omg.CORBA.TypeCode	**_type** ()
	1	public........................void	**_write** (org.omg.CORBA.portable.OutputStream o)
	✳	public............................	**CannotProceedHolder** ()
	✳	public............................	**CannotProceedHolder** (CannotProceed initialValue)
		public..........CannotProceed	**value**

			CDATASection	org.w3c.dom

1.4		CDATASection————————— *Text* [1] (*CharacterData* [2] (*Node* [3]))	ε540,545,524,526,529

	3	*37 inherited members from Node not shown*	
	2	public........................void	appendData (String arg) throws DOMException	ε545
	2	public........................void	deleteData (int offset, int count) throws DOMException	ε545
	2	public......................String	getData () throws DOMException	ε546
	2	public..........................int	getLength ()	ε545
	2	public........................void	insertData (int offset, String arg) throws DOMException	ε545
	2	public........................void	replaceData (int offset, int count, String arg) throws DOMException	ε545
	2	public........................void	setData (String data) throws DOMException	ε545
	1	public........................*Text*	splitText (int offset) throws DOMException	ε546
	2	public......................String	substringData (int offset, int count) throws DOMException	ε545

			Certificate❶	java.security.cert

		Object [1]		ε225,227,229,209,211
1.2	O	└Certificate ------------------------- *java.io.Serializable*	

	✳	protected.......................	**Certificate** (String type)	
	1	public..................**boolean**	**equals** (Object other)	
	O	public abstract ....byte[]	**getEncoded** () throws CertificateEncodingException	ε224
	O	public abstract .... *java.security.PublicKey*	**getPublicKey** ()	ε210
	●	public final ....String	**getType** ()	
	1	public........................ **int**	**hashCode** ()	
	O 1	public abstract ....**String**	**toString** ()	
	O	public abstract ....void	**verify** (*java.security.PublicKey* key) throws CertificateException, java.security.NoSuchAlgorithmException, java.security.InvalidKeyException, java.security.NoSuchProviderException, java.security.SignatureException	
	O	public abstract ....void	**verify** (*java.security.PublicKey* key, String sigProvider) throws CertificateException, java.security.NoSuchAlgorithmException, java.security.InvalidKeyException, java.security.NoSuchProviderException, java.security.SignatureException	
1.3		protected ....Object	**writeReplace** () throws java.io.ObjectStreamException	

Classes

			Certificate❷	java.security

D		*Certificate*	

D		public........................void	**decode** (java.io.InputStream stream) throws KeyException, java.io.IOException
D		public........................void	**encode** (java.io.OutputStream stream) throws KeyException, java.io.IOException

Certificate ❷

D	public	String	**getFormat** ()
D	public	*Principal*	**getGuarantor** ()
D	public	*Principal*	**getPrincipal** ()
D	public	*PublicKey*	**getPublicKey** ()
D	public	String	**toString** (boolean detailed)

C

Certificate ❸   javax.security.cert

Object[1]
1.4 ○ └─Certificate⌄

✳	public		**Certificate** ()	
1	public	**boolean**	**equals** (Object other)	
○	public abstract	byte[]	**getEncoded** () throws CertificateEncodingException	ε506
○	public abstract		**getPublicKey** ()	
	...... *java.security.PublicKey*			
1	public	**int**	**hashCode** ()	
○ 1	public abstract	**String**	**toString** ()	
○	public abstract	void	**verify** (*java.security.PublicKey* key) throws CertificateException,	
			java.security.NoSuchAlgorithmException, java.security.InvalidKeyException,	
			java.security.NoSuchProviderException, java.security.SignatureException	
○	public abstract	void	**verify** (*java.security.PublicKey* key, String sigProvider) throws CertificateException,	
			java.security.NoSuchAlgorithmException, java.security.InvalidKeyException,	
			java.security.NoSuchProviderException, java.security.SignatureException	

Certificate.CertificateRep   protected   java.security.cert

Object
1.3 └─Certificate.CertificateRep ---------------- *java.io.Serializable*⌄

✳	protected		**Certificate.CertificateRep** (String type, byte[] data)
	protected	Object	**readResolve** () throws java.io.ObjectStreamException

---

CertificateEncodingException ❶   java.security.cert

Object   ε224,229,501,506
└─Throwable -------------------------- *java.io.Serializable*⌄
　└─Exception
1.2 　　└─java.security.GeneralSecurityException
1.2 　　　└─CertificateException
1.2 　　　　└─CertificateEncodingException

✳	public		**CertificateEncodingException** ()
✳	public		**CertificateEncodingException** (String message)

CertificateEncodingException ❷   javax.security.cert

Object   ε506
└─Throwable -------------------------- *java.io.Serializable*⌄
　└─Exception
1.4 　　└─CertificateException
1.4 　　　└─CertificateEncodingException

✳	public		**CertificateEncodingException** ()
✳	public		**CertificateEncodingException** (String message)

CertificateException ❶   java.security.cert

Object   ε225,229,230,231,208
└─Throwable -------------------------- *java.io.Serializable*⌄
　└─Exception
1.2 　　└─java.security.GeneralSecurityException
1.2 　　　└─CertificateException⌄

Class　*Interface*　—extends　- - -implements　○ abstract　● final　△ static　▲ static final　✳ constructor　x x—inherited　x **x**—declared　**x x**—overridden
ε*n*—examples of usage　⌄—has subclass　package—see other volume

✳	public........................	**CertificateException** ()
✳	public........................	**CertificateException** (String msg)

CertificateException ❷ | javax.security.cert

ε506

Object
└Throwable - *java.io.Serializable*⌄
  └Exception
1.4   └CertificateException⌄

✳	public........................	**CertificateException** ()
✳	public........................	**CertificateException** (String msg)

CertificateExpiredException ❶ | java.security.cert

Object
└Throwable - *java.io.Serializable*⌄
  └Exception
1.2   └java.security.GeneralSecurityException
1.2   └CertificateException
1.2   └CertificateExpiredException

✳	public........................	**CertificateExpiredException** ()
✳	public........................	**CertificateExpiredException** (String message)

CertificateExpiredException ❷ | javax.security.cert

Object
└Throwable - *java.io.Serializable*⌄
  └Exception
1.4   └CertificateException
1.4   └CertificateExpiredException

✳	public........................	**CertificateExpiredException** ()
✳	public........................	**CertificateExpiredException** (String message)

CertificateFactory | java.security.cert

ε226

Object
1.2 └CertificateFactory

✳	protected	**CertificateFactory** (CertificateFactorySpi certFacSpi, java.security.Provider provider, String type)
●	public final ....Certificate	**generateCertificate** (java.io.InputStream inStream) throws CertificateException ε225,506
●	public final . *java.util.Collection*	**generateCertificates** (java.io.InputStream inStream) throws CertificateException
1.4 ●	public final ....CertPath	**generateCertPath** (java.io.InputStream inStream) throws CertificateException
1.4 ●	public final ....CertPath	**generateCertPath** (*java.util.List* certificates) throws CertificateException ε229
1.4 ●	public final ....CertPath	**generateCertPath** (java.io.InputStream inStream, String encoding) throws CertificateException
●	public final .... CRL	**generateCRL** (java.io.InputStream inStream) throws CRLException
●	public final . *java.util.Collection*	**generateCRLs** (java.io.InputStream inStream) throws CRLException
1.4 ●	public final .... *java.util.Iterator*	**getCertPathEncodings** ()
▲	public static final............... CertificateFactory	**getInstance** (String type) throws CertificateException ε225,229,506
1.4 ▲	public static final............... CertificateFactory	**getInstance** (String type, java.security.Provider provider) throws CertificateException
▲	public static final............... CertificateFactory	**getInstance** (String type, String provider) throws CertificateException, java.security.NoSuchProviderException
●	public final .... java.security.Provider	**getProvider** ()
●	public final ....String	**getType** ()

CertificateFactorySpi

java.security.cert

Object
└CertificateFactorySpi

1.2 ○

✱	public	**CertificateFactorySpi** ()
○	public abstract ...... Certificate	**engineGenerateCertificate** (java.io.InputStream inStream)
		throws CertificateException
○	public abstract	**engineGenerateCertificates** (java.io.InputStream inStream)
	.... *java.util.Collection*	throws CertificateException
1.4	public .... CertPath	**engineGenerateCertPath** (java.io.InputStream inStream)
		throws CertificateException
1.4	public .... CertPath	**engineGenerateCertPath** (*java.util.List* certificates) throws CertificateException
1.4	public .... CertPath	**engineGenerateCertPath** (java.io.InputStream inStream, String encoding)
		throws CertificateException
○	public abstract .... CRL	**engineGenerateCRL** (java.io.InputStream inStream) throws CRLException
○	public abstract	**engineGenerateCRLs** (java.io.InputStream inStream) throws CRLException
	.... *java.util.Collection*	
1.4	public .... *java.util.Iterator*	**engineGetCertPathEncodings** ()

CertificateNotYetValidException❶

java.security.cert

Object
└Throwable - *java.io.Serializable*⌐
  └Exception
1.2   └java.security.GeneralSecurityException
1.2   └CertificateException
1.2   └CertificateNotYetValidException

✱	public	**CertificateNotYetValidException** ()
✱	public	**CertificateNotYetValidException** (String message)

CertificateNotYetValidException❷

javax.security.cert

Object
└Throwable - *java.io.Serializable*⌐
  └Exception
1.4   └CertificateException
1.4   └CertificateNotYetValidException

✱	public	**CertificateNotYetValidException** ()
✱	public	**CertificateNotYetValidException** (String message)

CertificateParsingException❶

java.security.cert

Object
└Throwable - *java.io.Serializable*⌐
  └Exception
1.2   └java.security.GeneralSecurityException
1.2   └CertificateException
1.2   └CertificateParsingException

✱	public	**CertificateParsingException** ()
✱	public	**CertificateParsingException** (String message)

CertificateParsingException❷

javax.security.cert

Object
└Throwable - *java.io.Serializable*⌐
  └Exception
1.4   └CertificateException
1.4   └CertificateParsingException

✱	public	**CertificateParsingException** ()
✱	public	**CertificateParsingException** (String message)

Class   *Interface*   —extends   - - -implements   ○ abstract   ● final   △ static   ▲ static final   ✱ constructor   x x—inherited   x **x**—declared   **x x**—overridden
εn—examples of usage   ⌐—has subclass   package—see other volume

CertPath — java.security.cert

		Object[1]				ε229
1.4	O	└CertPath ------------------------------- *java.io.Serializable*				

*		protected	**CertPath** (String type)	
	1	public.................**boolean**	**equals** (Object other)	
O		public abstract .... *java.util.List*	**getCertificates** ()	
O		public abstract ....byte[]	**getEncoded** () throws CertificateEncodingException	
O		public abstract ....byte[]	**getEncoded** (String encoding) throws CertificateEncodingException	
O		public abstract *java.util.Iterator*	**getEncodings** ()	
		public.....................String	**getType** ()	
	1	public.....................**int**	**hashCode** ()	
	1	public.................**String**	**toString** ()	
		protected ....Object	**writeReplace** () throws java.io.ObjectStreamException	

CertPath.CertPathRep — protected — java.security.cert

	Object	
1.4	└CertPath.CertPathRep ------------------ *java.io.Serializable*	

*	protected.....................	**CertPath.CertPathRep** (String type, byte[] data)
	protected ....Object	**readResolve** () throws java.io.ObjectStreamException

CertPathBuilder — java.security.cert

	Object
1.4	└CertPathBuilder

●	public final	**build** (*CertPathParameters* params) throws CertPathBuilderException,
	.... *CertPathBuilderResult*	java.security.InvalidAlgorithmParameterException
*	protected	**CertPathBuilder** (CertPathBuilderSpi builderSpi, java.security.Provider provider,
		String algorithm)
●	public final ....String	**getAlgorithm** ()
▲	public static final ....String	**getDefaultType** ()
△	public static ...CertPathBuilder	**getInstance** (String algorithm) throws java.security.NoSuchAlgorithmException
△	public static ...CertPathBuilder	**getInstance** (String algorithm, java.security.Provider provider)
		throws java.security.NoSuchAlgorithmException
△	public static ...CertPathBuilder	**getInstance** (String algorithm, String provider) throws java.security↵
		.NoSuchAlgorithmException, java.security.NoSuchProviderException
●	public final	**getProvider** ()
	.... java.security.Provider	

CertPathBuilderException — java.security.cert

	Object
	└Throwable[1] ------------------------- *java.io.Serializable*
	└Exception
1.2	└java.security.GeneralSecurityException
1.4	└CertPathBuilderException

*		public.........................	**CertPathBuilderException** ()
*		public.........................	**CertPathBuilderException** (String msg)
*		public.........................	**CertPathBuilderException** (Throwable cause)
*		public.........................	**CertPathBuilderException** (String msg, Throwable cause)
	1	public.............**Throwable**	**getCause** ()
	1	public.................**String**	**getMessage** ()
	1	public...................**void**	**printStackTrace** ()
	1	public...................**void**	**printStackTrace** (java.io.PrintStream ps)
	1	public...................**void**	**printStackTrace** (java.io.PrintWriter pw)
	1	public.................**String**	**toString** ()

CertPathBuilderResult — java.security.cert

1.4	*CertPathBuilderResult*————————————*Cloneable*

public...................Object	**clone** ()
public.................CertPath	**getCertPath** ()

CertPathBuilderSpi

CertPathBuilderSpi	java.security.cert

Object
└CertPathBuilderSpi

1.4 O

*	public.........................	**CertPathBuilderSpi** ()
O	public abstract	**engineBuild** (*CertPathParameters* params) throws CertPathBuilderException,
	.... *CertPathBuilderResult*	java.security.InvalidAlgorithmParameterException

CertPathParameters	java.security.cert

1.4   *CertPathParameters*————————————*Cloneable* ⌄

- -

public.....................Object **clone** ()

- -

CertPathValidator	java.security.cert

Object   ε228
1.4   └CertPathValidator

*	protected	**CertPathValidator** (CertPathValidatorSpi validatorSpi,
		java.security.Provider provider, String algorithm)
●	public final ....String	**getAlgorithm** ()
▲	public static final.........String	**getDefaultType** () ε231
△	public static . CertPathValidator	**getInstance** (String algorithm) throws java.security.NoSuchAlgorithmException
		ε231
△	public static . CertPathValidator	**getInstance** (String algorithm, String provider) throws java.security ↵
		.NoSuchAlgorithmException, java.security.NoSuchProviderException
△	public static . CertPathValidator	**getInstance** (String algorithm, java.security.Provider provider)
		throws java.security.NoSuchAlgorithmException
●	public final	**getProvider** ()
	.... java.security.Provider	
●	public final	**validate** (CertPath certPath, *CertPathParameters* params) throws
	...... *CertPathValidatorResult*	CertPathValidatorException, java.security.InvalidAlgorithmParameterException
		ε231

CertPathValidatorException	java.security.cert

Object   ε231
└Throwable [1] - *java.io.Serializable* ⌄
  └Exception
1.2   └java.security.GeneralSecurityException
1.4   └CertPathValidatorException

*	public.........................	**CertPathValidatorException** ()
*	public.........................	**CertPathValidatorException** (String msg)
*	public.........................	**CertPathValidatorException** (Throwable cause)
*	public.........................	**CertPathValidatorException** (String msg, Throwable cause)
*	public.........................	**CertPathValidatorException** (String msg, Throwable cause, CertPath certPath,
		int index)
1	public..............**Throwable**	**getCause** ()
	public...............CertPath	**getCertPath** ()
	public.....................int	**getIndex** ()
1	public...................**String**	**getMessage** ()
1	public.................. **void**	**printStackTrace** ()
1	public.................. **void**	**printStackTrace** (java.io.PrintStream ps)
1	public.................. **void**	**printStackTrace** (java.io.PrintWriter pw)
1	public...................**String**	**toString** ()

CertPathValidatorResult	java.security.cert

1.4   *CertPathValidatorResult*————————————*Cloneable* ⌄   ε231

- -

public.................Object **clone** ()

- -

Class   *Interface*   —extends   - - -implements   O abstract   ● final   △ static   ▲ static final   * constructor   x x—inherited   x **x**—declared   **x x**—overridden
ε*n*—examples of usage   ⌄—has subclass   package—see other volume

	CertPathValidatorSpi	java.security.cert

Object
└CertPathValidatorSpi

1.4 ○

✳	public.........................	**CertPathValidatorSpi** ()
○	public abstract	**engineValidate** (CertPath certPath, *CertPathParameters* params) throws
	...... *CertPathValidatorResult*	CertPathValidatorException, java.security.InvalidAlgorithmParameterException

	CertSelector	java.security.cert

1.4 | *CertSelector*————————————————*Cloneable* ˅

	public.................... Object	**clone** ()
	public................. boolean	**match** (Certificate cert)

	CertStore	java.security.cert

Object
└CertStore

1.4

✳	protected	**CertStore** (CertStoreSpi storeSpi, java.security.Provider provider, String type, *CertStoreParameters* params)
●	public final . *java.util.Collection*	**getCertificates** (*CertSelector* selector) throws CertStoreException
●	public final .... *CertStoreParameters*	**getCertStoreParameters** ()
●	public final . *java.util.Collection*	**getCRLs** (*CRLSelector* selector) throws CertStoreException
▲	public static final .... String	**getDefaultType** ()
△	public static .... CertStore	**getInstance** (String type, *CertStoreParameters* params) throws java.security ↵ .InvalidAlgorithmParameterException, java.security.NoSuchAlgorithmException
△	public static .... CertStore	**getInstance** (String type, *CertStoreParameters* params, java.security.Provider provider) throws java.security.NoSuchAlgorithmException, java.security.InvalidAlgorithmParameterException
△	public static .... CertStore	**getInstance** (String type, *CertStoreParameters* params, String provider) throws java.security.InvalidAlgorithmParameterException, java.security ↵ .NoSuchAlgorithmException, java.security.NoSuchProviderException
●	public final .... java.security.Provider	**getProvider** ()
●	public final .... String	**getType** ()

	CertStoreException	java.security.cert

Object
└Throwable [1] - *java.io.Serializable* ˅
  └Exception
    └java.security.GeneralSecurityException
      └CertStoreException

1.2
1.4

✳	public..........................	**CertStoreException** ()
✳	public..........................	**CertStoreException** (String msg)
✳	public..........................	**CertStoreException** (Throwable cause)
✳	public..........................	**CertStoreException** (String msg, Throwable cause)
1	public............... **Throwable**	**getCause** ()
1	public.................. **String**	**getMessage** ()
1	public..................... **void**	**printStackTrace** ()
1	public..................... **void**	**printStackTrace** (java.io.PrintStream ps)
1	public..................... **void**	**printStackTrace** (java.io.PrintWriter pw)
1	public.................. **String**	**toString** ()

	CertStoreParameters	java.security.cert

1.4 | *CertStoreParameters*————————————— *Cloneable* ˅

	public.................... Object	**clone** ()

CertStoreSpi

CertStoreSpi — java.security.cert

Object
└ CertStoreSpi — 1.4 ○

∗	public........................	**CertStoreSpi** (*CertStoreParameters* params) throws java.security.InvalidAlgorithmParameterException
○	public abstract................. *java.util.Collection*	**engineGetCertificates** (*CertSelector* selector) throws CertStoreException
○	public abstract................. *java.util.Collection*	**engineGetCRLs** (*CRLSelector* selector) throws CertStoreException

Channel — java.nio.channels

1.4   *Channel*

public......................void	**close** () throws java.io.IOException	ε167,170,171,172,174
public......................boolean	**isOpen** ()	

ChannelBinding — org.ietf.jgss

Object[1]
└ ChannelBinding — 1.4

∗	public........................	**ChannelBinding** (byte[] appData)	
∗	public........................	**ChannelBinding** (java.net.InetAddress initAddr, java.net.InetAddress acceptAddr, byte[] appData)	
1	public................**boolean**	**equals** (Object obj)	
	public.... java.net.InetAddress	**getAcceptorAddress** ()	
	public....................byte[]	**getApplicationData** ()	
	public.... java.net.InetAddress	**getInitiatorAddress** ()	
1	public.......................**int**	**hashCode** ()	

Channels — java.nio.channels

Object
└ Channels — 1.4 ●

△	public static .... *ReadableByteChannel*	**newChannel** (java.io.InputStream in)
△	public static .... *WritableByteChannel*	**newChannel** (java.io.OutputStream out)
△	public static .... java.io.InputStream	**newInputStream** (*ReadableByteChannel* ch) ε183
△	public static .... java.io.OutputStream	**newOutputStream** (*WritableByteChannel* ch) ε183
△	public static .... java.io.Reader	**newReader** (*ReadableByteChannel* ch, String csName)
△	public static .... java.io.Reader	**newReader** (*ReadableByteChannel* ch, java.nio.charset.CharsetDecoder dec, int minBufferCap)
△	public static ...... java.io.Writer	**newWriter** (*WritableByteChannel* ch, String csName)
△	public static ...... java.io.Writer	**newWriter** (*WritableByteChannel* ch, java.nio.charset.CharsetEncoder enc, int minBufferCap)

Character — java.lang

Object[1]
└ Character - *java.io.Serializable*, *Comparable*[2] ●

∗		public........................	**Character** (char value) ε58
		public......................char	**charValue** () ε58
1.1 ▲		public static final .... byte	**COMBINING_SPACING_MARK** = 8
1.2		public......................int	**compareTo** (Character anotherCharacter)
1.2	2	public......................int	**compareTo** (Object o) ε53
1.1 ▲		public static final .... byte	**CONNECTOR_PUNCTUATION** = 23
1.1 ▲		public static final .... byte	**CONTROL** = 15
1.1 ▲		public static final .... byte	**CURRENCY_SYMBOL** = 26

Class   *Interface*   —extends   - - -implements   ○ abstract   ● final   △ static   ▲ static final   ∗ constructor   x x—inherited   x **x**—declared   x **x**—overridden
ε*n*—examples of usage   ⌄—has subclass   package—see other volume

C

1.1	▲	public static final	.... byte	**DASH_PUNCTUATION** = 20	
1.1	▲	public static final	.... byte	**DECIMAL_DIGIT_NUMBER** = 9	
	△	public static	.... int	**digit** (char ch, int radix)	
1.4	▲	public static final	.... byte	**DIRECTIONALITY_ARABIC_NUMBER** = 6	
1.4	▲	public static final	.... byte	**DIRECTIONALITY_BOUNDARY_NEUTRAL** = 9	
1.4	▲	public static final	.... byte	**DIRECTIONALITY_COMMON_NUMBER_SEPARATOR** = 7	
1.4	▲	public static final	.... byte	**DIRECTIONALITY_EUROPEAN_NUMBER** = 3	
1.4	▲	public static final	.... byte	**DIRECTIONALITY_EUROPEAN_NUMBER_SEPARATOR** = 4	
1.4	▲	public static final	.... byte	**DIRECTIONALITY_EUROPEAN_NUMBER_TERMINATOR** = 5	
1.4	▲	public static final	.... byte	**DIRECTIONALITY_LEFT_TO_RIGHT** = 0	
1.4	▲	public static final	.... byte	**DIRECTIONALITY_LEFT_TO_RIGHT_EMBEDDING** = 14	
1.4	▲	public static final	.... byte	**DIRECTIONALITY_LEFT_TO_RIGHT_OVERRIDE** = 15	
1.4	▲	public static final	.... byte	**DIRECTIONALITY_NONSPACING_MARK** = 8	
1.4	▲	public static final	.... byte	**DIRECTIONALITY_OTHER_NEUTRALS** = 13	
1.4	▲	public static final	.... byte	**DIRECTIONALITY_PARAGRAPH_SEPARATOR** = 10	
1.4	▲	public static final	.... byte	**DIRECTIONALITY_POP_DIRECTIONAL_FORMAT** = 18	
1.4	▲	public static final	.... byte	**DIRECTIONALITY_RIGHT_TO_LEFT** = 1	
1.4	▲	public static final	.... byte	**DIRECTIONALITY_RIGHT_TO_LEFT_ARABIC** = 2	
1.4	▲	public static final	.... byte	**DIRECTIONALITY_RIGHT_TO_LEFT_EMBEDDING** = 16	
1.4	▲	public static final	.... byte	**DIRECTIONALITY_RIGHT_TO_LEFT_OVERRIDE** = 17	
1.4	▲	public static final	.... byte	**DIRECTIONALITY_SEGMENT_SEPARATOR** = 11	
1.4	▲	public static final	.... byte	**DIRECTIONALITY_UNDEFINED** = -1	
1.4	▲	public static final	.... byte	**DIRECTIONALITY_WHITESPACE** = 12	
1.1	▲	public static final	.... byte	**ENCLOSING_MARK** = 7	
1.1	▲	public static final	.... byte	**END_PUNCTUATION** = 22	
	1	public	.... boolean	**equals** (Object obj)	
1.4	▲	public static final	.... byte	**FINAL_QUOTE_PUNCTUATION** = 30	
	△	public static	.... char	**forDigit** (int digit, int radix)	
1.1	▲	public static final	.... byte	**FORMAT** = 16	
1.4	△	public static	.... byte	**getDirectionality** (char c)	
1.1	△	public static	.... int	**getNumericValue** (char ch)	
1.1	△	public static	.... int	**getType** (char ch)	
	1	public	.... int	**hashCode** ()	
1.4	▲	public static final	.... byte	**INITIAL_QUOTE_PUNCTUATION** = 29	
	△	public static	.... boolean	**isDefined** (char ch)	
	△	public static	.... boolean	**isDigit** (char ch)	ε305
1.1	△	public static	.... boolean	**isIdentifierIgnorable** (char ch)	
1.1	△	public static	.... boolean	**isISOControl** (char ch)	
1.1	△	public static	.... boolean	**isJavaIdentifierPart** (char ch)	ε81
1.1	△	public static	.... boolean	**isJavaIdentifierStart** (char ch)	ε81
D	△	public static	.... boolean	**isJavaLetter** (char ch)	
D	△	public static	.... boolean	**isJavaLetterOrDigit** (char ch)	
	△	public static	.... boolean	**isLetter** (char ch)	ε305
	△	public static	.... boolean	**isLetterOrDigit** (char ch)	
	△	public static	.... boolean	**isLowerCase** (char ch)	ε305
1.4	△	public static	.... boolean	**isMirrored** (char c)	
D	△	public static	.... boolean	**isSpace** (char ch)	
1.1	△	public static	.... boolean	**isSpaceChar** (char ch)	
	△	public static	.... boolean	**isTitleCase** (char ch)	
1.1	△	public static	.... boolean	**isUnicodeIdentifierPart** (char ch)	
1.1	△	public static	.... boolean	**isUnicodeIdentifierStart** (char ch)	
	△	public static	.... boolean	**isUpperCase** (char ch)	ε305
1.1	△	public static	.... boolean	**isWhitespace** (char ch)	
1.1	▲	public static final	.... byte	**LETTER_NUMBER** = 10	
1.1	▲	public static final	.... byte	**LINE_SEPARATOR** = 13	
1.1	▲	public static final	.... byte	**LOWERCASE_LETTER** = 2	
1.1	▲	public static final	.... byte	**MATH_SYMBOL** = 25	
	▲	public static final	.... int	**MAX_RADIX** = 36	
	▲	public static final	.... char	**MAX_VALUE** = '?'	
	▲	public static final	.... int	**MIN_RADIX** = 2	
	▲	public static final	.... char	**MIN_VALUE**	
1.1	▲	public static final	.... byte	**MODIFIER_LETTER** = 4	
1.1	▲	public static final	.... byte	**MODIFIER_SYMBOL** = 27	
1.1	▲	public static final	.... byte	**NON_SPACING_MARK** = 6	
1.1	▲	public static final	.... byte	**OTHER_LETTER** = 5	
1.1	▲	public static final	.... byte	**OTHER_NUMBER** = 11	
1.1	▲	public static final	.... byte	**OTHER_PUNCTUATION** = 24	
1.1	▲	public static final	.... byte	**OTHER_SYMBOL** = 28	
1.1	▲	public static final	.... byte	**PARAGRAPH_SEPARATOR** = 14	
1.1	▲	public static final	.... byte	**PRIVATE_USE** = 18	
1.1	▲	public static final	.... byte	**SPACE_SEPARATOR** = 12	
1.1	▲	public static final	.... byte	**START_PUNCTUATION** = 21	
1.1	▲	public static final	.... byte	**SURROGATE** = 19	
1.1	▲	public static final	.... byte	**TITLECASE_LETTER** = 3	

Classes

Character

	△	public static .... char	**toLowerCase** (char ch)	
	1	public................... **String**	**toString** ()	
1.4	△	public static ....String	**toString** (char c)	
	△	public static .... char	**toTitleCase** (char ch)	
	△	public static .... char	**toUpperCase** (char ch)	
1.1	▲	public static final .... Class	**TYPE**	
1.1	▲	public static final .... byte	**UNASSIGNED** = 0	
1.1	▲	public static final .... byte	**UPPERCASE_LETTER** = 1	

Character.Subset   java.lang

Object[1]
1.2 └Character.Subset

●	1	public final .... **boolean**	**equals** (Object obj)
●	1	public final .... **int**	**hashCode** ()
*		protected	**Character.Subset** (String name)
●	1	public final .... **String**	**toString** ()

Character.UnicodeBlock   java.lang

Object
1.2 └Character.Subset[1]
1.2 ● └Character.UnicodeBlock

	▲	public static final .... Character.UnicodeBlock	**ALPHABETIC_PRESENTATION_FORMS**
	▲	public static final .... Character.UnicodeBlock	**ARABIC**
	▲	public static final .... Character.UnicodeBlock	**ARABIC_PRESENTATION_FORMS_A**
	▲	public static final .... Character.UnicodeBlock	**ARABIC_PRESENTATION_FORMS_B**
	▲	public static final .... Character.UnicodeBlock	**ARMENIAN**
	▲	public static final .... Character.UnicodeBlock	**ARROWS**
	▲	public static final .... Character.UnicodeBlock	**BASIC_LATIN**
	▲	public static final .... Character.UnicodeBlock	**BENGALI**
	▲	public static final .... Character.UnicodeBlock	**BLOCK_ELEMENTS**
	▲	public static final .... Character.UnicodeBlock	**BOPOMOFO**
1.4	▲	public static final .... Character.UnicodeBlock	**BOPOMOFO_EXTENDED**
	▲	public static final .... Character.UnicodeBlock	**BOX_DRAWING**
1.4	▲	public static final .... Character.UnicodeBlock	**BRAILLE_PATTERNS**
1.4	▲	public static final .... Character.UnicodeBlock	**CHEROKEE**
	▲	public static final .... Character.UnicodeBlock	**CJK_COMPATIBILITY**
	▲	public static final .... Character.UnicodeBlock	**CJK_COMPATIBILITY_FORMS**
	▲	public static final .... Character.UnicodeBlock	**CJK_COMPATIBILITY_IDEOGRAPHS**
1.4	▲	public static final .... Character.UnicodeBlock	**CJK_RADICALS_SUPPLEMENT**
	▲	public static final .... Character.UnicodeBlock	**CJK_SYMBOLS_AND_PUNCTUATION**
	▲	public static final .... Character.UnicodeBlock	**CJK_UNIFIED_IDEOGRAPHS**
1.4	▲	public static final .... Character.UnicodeBlock	**CJK_UNIFIED_IDEOGRAPHS_EXTENSION_A**

Class *Interface* —extends - - -implements ○ abstract ● final △ static ▲ static final * constructor x x—inherited x **x**—declared **x x**—overridden
εn—examples of usage ˌ—has subclass package—see other volume

▲ public static final .... **COMBINING_DIACRITICAL_MARKS**
..... Character.UnicodeBlock
▲ public static final .... **COMBINING_HALF_MARKS**
..... Character.UnicodeBlock
▲ public static final .... **COMBINING_MARKS_FOR_SYMBOLS**
..... Character.UnicodeBlock
▲ public static final .... **CONTROL_PICTURES**
..... Character.UnicodeBlock
▲ public static final .... **CURRENCY_SYMBOLS**
..... Character.UnicodeBlock
▲ public static final .... **CYRILLIC**
..... Character.UnicodeBlock
▲ public static final .... **DEVANAGARI**
..... Character.UnicodeBlock
▲ public static final .... **DINGBATS**
..... Character.UnicodeBlock
▲ public static final .... **ENCLOSED_ALPHANUMERICS**
..... Character.UnicodeBlock
▲ public static final .... **ENCLOSED_CJK_LETTERS_AND_MONTHS**
..... Character.UnicodeBlock
● 1 public final .... boolean equals (Object obj)
1.4 ▲ public static final .... **ETHIOPIC**
..... Character.UnicodeBlock
▲ public static final .... **GENERAL_PUNCTUATION**
..... Character.UnicodeBlock
▲ public static final .... **GEOMETRIC_SHAPES**
..... Character.UnicodeBlock
▲ public static final .... **GEORGIAN**
..... Character.UnicodeBlock
▲ public static final .... **GREEK**
..... Character.UnicodeBlock
▲ public static final .... **GREEK_EXTENDED**
..... Character.UnicodeBlock
▲ public static final .... **GUJARATI**
..... Character.UnicodeBlock
▲ public static final .... **GURMUKHI**
..... Character.UnicodeBlock
▲ public static final .... **HALFWIDTH_AND_FULLWIDTH_FORMS**
..... Character.UnicodeBlock
▲ public static final .... **HANGUL_COMPATIBILITY_JAMO**
..... Character.UnicodeBlock
▲ public static final .... **HANGUL_JAMO**
..... Character.UnicodeBlock
▲ public static final .... **HANGUL_SYLLABLES**
..... Character.UnicodeBlock
● 1 public final ....int hashCode ()
▲ public static final .... **HEBREW**
..... Character.UnicodeBlock
▲ public static final .... **HIRAGANA**
..... Character.UnicodeBlock
1.4 ▲ public static final .... **IDEOGRAPHIC_DESCRIPTION_CHARACTERS**
..... Character.UnicodeBlock
▲ public static final .... **IPA_EXTENSIONS**
..... Character.UnicodeBlock
▲ public static final .... **KANBUN**
..... Character.UnicodeBlock
1.4 ▲ public static final .... **KANGXI_RADICALS**
..... Character.UnicodeBlock
▲ public static final .... **KANNADA**
..... Character.UnicodeBlock
▲ public static final .... **KATAKANA**
..... Character.UnicodeBlock
1.4 ▲ public static final .... **KHMER**
..... Character.UnicodeBlock
▲ public static final .... **LAO**
..... Character.UnicodeBlock
▲ public static final .... **LATIN_1_SUPPLEMENT**
..... Character.UnicodeBlock
▲ public static final .... **LATIN_EXTENDED_A**
..... Character.UnicodeBlock
▲ public static final .... **LATIN_EXTENDED_ADDITIONAL**
..... Character.UnicodeBlock

C

Classes

▲		public static final . . . . Character.UnicodeBlock	**LATIN_EXTENDED_B**	
▲		public static final . . . . Character.UnicodeBlock	**LETTERLIKE_SYMBOLS**	
▲		public static final . . . . Character.UnicodeBlock	**MALAYALAM**	
▲		public static final . . . . Character.UnicodeBlock	**MATHEMATICAL_OPERATORS**	
▲		public static final . . . . Character.UnicodeBlock	**MISCELLANEOUS_SYMBOLS**	
▲		public static final . . . . Character.UnicodeBlock	**MISCELLANEOUS_TECHNICAL**	
1.4 ▲		public static final . . . . Character.UnicodeBlock	**MONGOLIAN**	
1.4 ▲		public static final . . . . Character.UnicodeBlock	**MYANMAR**	
▲		public static final . . . . Character.UnicodeBlock	**NUMBER_FORMS**	
△		public static . . . . Character.UnicodeBlock	**of** (char c)	ε80
1.4 ▲		public static final . . . . Character.UnicodeBlock	**OGHAM**	
▲		public static final . . . . Character.UnicodeBlock	**OPTICAL_CHARACTER_RECOGNITION**	
▲		public static final . . . . Character.UnicodeBlock	**ORIYA**	
▲		public static final . . . . Character.UnicodeBlock	**PRIVATE_USE_AREA**	
1.4 ▲		public static final . . . . Character.UnicodeBlock	**RUNIC**	
1.4 ▲		public static final . . . . Character.UnicodeBlock	**SINHALA**	
▲		public static final . . . . Character.UnicodeBlock	**SMALL_FORM_VARIANTS**	
▲		public static final . . . . Character.UnicodeBlock	**SPACING_MODIFIER_LETTERS**	
▲		public static final . . . . Character.UnicodeBlock	**SPECIALS**	
▲		public static final . . . . Character.UnicodeBlock	**SUPERSCRIPTS_AND_SUBSCRIPTS**	
▲		public static final . . . . Character.UnicodeBlock	**SURROGATES_AREA**	
1.4 ▲		public static final . . . . Character.UnicodeBlock	**SYRIAC**	
▲		public static final . . . . Character.UnicodeBlock	**TAMIL**	
▲		public static final . . . . Character.UnicodeBlock	**TELUGU**	
1.4 ▲		public static final . . . . Character.UnicodeBlock	**THAANA**	
▲		public static final . . . . Character.UnicodeBlock	**THAI**	
▲		public static final . . . . Character.UnicodeBlock	**TIBETAN**	
●	1	public final . . . . String	toString ()	
1.4 ▲		public static final . . . . Character.UnicodeBlock	**UNIFIED_CANADIAN_ABORIGINAL_SYLLABICS**	
1.4 ▲		public static final . . . . Character.UnicodeBlock	**YI_RADICALS**	
1.4 ▲		public static final . . . . Character.UnicodeBlock	**YI_SYLLABLES**	

CharacterCodingException	java.nio.charset

Object
 └Throwable ------------------------ *java.io.Serializable*⌄
  └Exception
   └java.io.IOException
1.4   └CharacterCodingException⌄

ε186

| ✳ | public......................... | **CharacterCodingException** () |

CharacterData	org.w3c.dom

1.4 *CharacterData*⌄─────────────── *Node*⌄[1]   ε524,526,529,530,532

 1 *37 inherited members from Node not shown*
  public.....................void **appendData** (String arg) throws DOMException ε545
  public.....................void **deleteData** (int offset, int count) throws DOMException ε545
  public.....................String **getData** () throws DOMException ε546
  public.....................int **getLength** () ε545
  public.....................void **insertData** (int offset, String arg) throws DOMException ε545
  public.....................void **replaceData** (int offset, int count, String arg) throws DOMException ε545
  public.....................void **setData** (String data) throws DOMException ε545
  public.....................String **substringData** (int offset, int count) throws DOMException ε545

CharacterIterator	java.text

1.1 *CharacterIterator*⌄────────────── *Cloneable*⌄

  public.....................Object **clone** ()
  public.....................char **current** () ε307
▲ public static final..........char **DONE** = '?' ε307
  public.....................char **first** () ε307
  public.....................int **getBeginIndex** ()
  public.....................int **getEndIndex** ()
  public.....................int **getIndex** () ε307
  public.....................char **last** () ε307
  public.....................char **next** () ε307
  public.....................char **previous** () ε307
  public.....................char **setIndex** (int position) ε307

CharArrayReader	java.io

Object
1.1 ○ └Reader[1]
1.1 └CharArrayReader

  protected.................char[] **buf**
✳ public......................... **CharArrayReader** (char[] buf)
✳ public......................... **CharArrayReader** (char[] buf, int offset, int length)
1 public..................... **void close** () ε35,47,135,136,139
  protected.....................int **count**
1 protected.................Object **lock**
1 public..................... **void mark** (int readAheadLimit) throws IOException
  protected.....................int **markedPos**
1 public.................**boolean markSupported** () ε442
  protected.....................int **pos**
1 public..................... **int read** () throws IOException
1 public.....................int read (char[] cbuf) throws IOException ε434
1 public..................... **int read** (char[] b, int off, int len) throws IOException
1 public.................**boolean ready** () throws IOException ε442
1 public..................... **void reset** () throws IOException
1 public..................... **long skip** (long n) throws IOException

CharArrayWriter	java.io

Object[1]
1.1 ○ └Writer[2]
1.1 └CharArrayWriter

CharArrayWriter

		protected .... char[]	**buf**	
*		public	**CharArrayWriter** ()	
*		public	**CharArrayWriter** (int initialSize)	
	2	public .... **void**	**close** ()	ε23,37,38,41,43
		protected .... int	**count**	
	2	public .... **void**	**flush** ()	ε135,150,224
	2	protected .... Object	lock	
		public .... void	**reset** ()	
		public .... int	**size** ()	
		public .... char[]	**toCharArray** ()	
	1	public .... **String**	**toString** ()	
	2	public .... void	write (char[] cbuf) throws IOException	
	2	public .... **void**	**write** (int c)	
	2	public .... void	write (String str) throws IOException	ε23,37,38,41,43
	2	public .... **void**	**write** (char[] c, int off, int len)	
	2	public .... **void**	**write** (String str, int off, int len)	
		public .... void	**writeTo** (Writer out) throws IOException	

CharBuffer   java.nio

		Object[1]		ε163,425,166,171
1.4 O		└Buffer[2]		
1.4 O		└CharBuffer - Comparable[3], CharSequence[4]		
△		public static .... CharBuffer	**allocate** (int capacity)	ε186
●		public final .... char[]	**array** ()	
●		public final .... int	**arrayOffset** ()	
O		public abstract ..... CharBuffer	**asReadOnlyBuffer** ()	
●	2	public final .... int	capacity ()	ε159,160,161
●	4	public final .... char	**charAt** (int index)	ε81,442
●	2	public final .... Buffer	clear ()	ε161,170,174
O		public abstract ..... CharBuffer	**compact** ()	
	3	public .... int	**compareTo** (Object ob)	ε53
O		public abstract ..... CharBuffer	**duplicate** ()	
	1	public .... **boolean**	**equals** (Object ob)	
●	2	public final .... Buffer	flip ()	ε164,186,162,170,174
O		public abstract .... char	**get** ()	
		public .... CharBuffer	**get** (char[] dst)	
O		public abstract .... char	**get** (int index)	
		public .... CharBuffer	**get** (char[] dst, int offset, int length)	
●		public final .... boolean	**hasArray** ()	
	1	public .... **int**	**hashCode** ()	
●	2	public final .... boolean	hasRemaining ()	ε170,184
O		public abstract .... boolean	**isDirect** ()	
O	2	public abstract .... boolean	isReadOnly ()	
●	4	public final ....int	**length** ()	ε76,81,109,131,194
●	2	public final ....int	limit ()	
●	2	public final .... Buffer	limit (int newLimit)	ε159,160
●	2	public final .... Buffer	mark ()	
O		public abstract ...... ByteOrder	**order** ()	
●	2	public final ....int	position ()	ε159,160
●	2	public final .... Buffer	position (int newPosition)	ε159,160
O		public abstract ..... CharBuffer	**put** (char c)	
●		public final .... CharBuffer	**put** (char[] src)	
●		public final .... CharBuffer	**put** (String src)	ε164
		public .... CharBuffer	**put** (CharBuffer src)	
O		public abstract ..... CharBuffer	**put** (int index, char c)	
		public .... CharBuffer	**put** (char[] src, int offset, int length)	
		public .... CharBuffer	**put** (String src, int start, int end)	
●	2	public final ....int	remaining ()	ε159,160,161,184
●	2	public final .... Buffer	reset ()	
●	2	public final .... Buffer	rewind ()	ε159,160,169
O		public abstract ..... CharBuffer	**slice** ()	
O	4	public abstract . CharSequence	**subSequence** (int start, int end)	ε164,437
	1	public .... **String**	**toString** ()	ε164,186,70,76,131
△		public static .... CharBuffer	**wrap** (char[] array)	
△		public static .... CharBuffer	**wrap** (CharSequence csq)	ε186
△		public static .... CharBuffer	**wrap** (char[] array, int offset, int length)	
△		public static .... CharBuffer	**wrap** (CharSequence csq, int start, int end)	

Class   *Interface*   —extends   - - -implements   O abstract   ● final   △ static   ▲ static final   * constructor   x x—inherited   x **x**—declared   **x x**—overridden
ε*n*—examples of usage   ⌐—has subclass   package—see other volume

CharConversionException — java.io

```
Object
└Throwable ------------------------------ Serializable ⌄
  └Exception
    └IOException
      └CharConversionException
```
1.1

*	public........................	**CharConversionException** ()
*	public........................	**CharConversionException** (String s)

CharHolder — org.omg.CORBA

```
Object
└CharHolder ------------------------ org.omg.CORBA.portable.Streamable ⌄ 1
```
1.2 ●

1	public.....................void	**_read** (org.omg.CORBA.portable.InputStream input)
1	public.................TypeCode	**_type** ()
1	public.....................void	**_write** (org.omg.CORBA.portable.OutputStream output)
*	public........................	**CharHolder** ()
*	public........................	**CharHolder** (char initial)
	public...................char	**value**

CharSeqHelper — org.omg.CORBA

```
Object
└CharSeqHelper
```
1.3 ○

*	public........................	**CharSeqHelper** ()
△	public static ....char[]	**extract** (Any a)
△	public static ....String	**id** ()
△	public static ....void	**insert** (Any a, char[] that)
△	public static ....char[]	**read** (org.omg.CORBA.portable.InputStream istream)
△	public static synchronized	**type** ()
	....................TypeCode	
△	public static ....void	**write** (org.omg.CORBA.portable.OutputStream ostream, char[] value)

CharSeqHolder — org.omg.CORBA

```
Object
└CharSeqHolder ----------------------- org.omg.CORBA.portable.Streamable ⌄ 1
```
1.3 ●

1	public.....................void	**_read** (org.omg.CORBA.portable.InputStream i)
1	public.................TypeCode	**_type** ()
1	public.....................void	**_write** (org.omg.CORBA.portable.OutputStream o)
*	public........................	**CharSeqHolder** ()
*	public........................	**CharSeqHolder** (char[] initialValue)
	public...................char[]	**value**

CharSequence — java.lang

1.4 *CharSequence* ε164,423,424,426,427

public.................. char	**charAt** (int index)	ε81,442
public....................int	**length** ()	ε76,81,109,131,194
public..........*CharSequence*	**subSequence** (int start, int end)	ε437
public...................String	**toString** ()	ε70,76,164,186,131

Charset — java.nio.charset

```
Object 1
└Charset ---------------------------- Comparable 2
```
1.4 ○

●	public final ....*java.util.Set*	**aliases** ()	
△	public static	**availableCharsets** ()	ε185
	...........*java.util.SortedMap*		
	public.................. boolean	**canEncode** ()	
*	protected	**Charset** (String canonicalName, String[] aliases)	
● 2	public final ....int	**compareTo** (Object ob)	ε53

C

Classes

497

Charset

○	public abstract .... boolean	**contains** (Charset cs)	
●	public final java.nio.CharBuffer	**decode** (java.nio.ByteBuffer bb)	
	public.....................String	**displayName** ()	
	public.....................String	**displayName** (java.util.Locale locale)	
●	public final java.nio.ByteBuffer	**encode** (String str)	
●	public final java.nio.ByteBuffer	**encode** (java.nio.CharBuffer cb)	
● 1	public final ....**boolean**	**equals** (Object ob)	
△	public static ....Charset	**forName** (String charsetName)	ε185,186,224,425
● 1	public final ....**int**	**hashCode** ()	
●	public final .... boolean	**isRegistered** ()	
△	public static .... boolean	**isSupported** (String charsetName)	
●	public final ....String	**name** ()	
○	public abstract.................. CharsetDecoder	**newDecoder** ()	ε186,425
○	public abstract............... CharsetEncoder	**newEncoder** ()	ε186
● 1	public final .... **String**	**toString** ()	

CharsetDecoder java.nio.charset

Object
└CharsetDecoder

1.4 ○

●	public final ....float	**averageCharsPerByte** ()
●	public final ....Charset	**charset** ()
✱	protected......................	**CharsetDecoder** (Charset cs, float averageCharsPerByte, float maxCharsPerByte)
●	public final java.nio.CharBuffer	**decode** (java.nio.ByteBuffer in) throws CharacterCodingException
		ε186,425
●	public final .... CoderResult	**decode** (java.nio.ByteBuffer in, java.nio.CharBuffer out, boolean endOfInput)
		ε186
○	protected abstract .... CoderResult	**decodeLoop** (java.nio.ByteBuffer in, java.nio.CharBuffer out)
	public...................Charset	**detectedCharset** ()
●	public final .... CoderResult	**flush** (java.nio.CharBuffer out)
	protected .... CoderResult	**implFlush** (java.nio.CharBuffer out)
	protected ....void	**implOnMalformedInput** (CodingErrorAction newAction)
	protected ....void	**implOnUnmappableCharacter** (CodingErrorAction newAction)
	protected ....void	**implReplaceWith** (String newReplacement)
	protected ....void	**implReset** ()
	public................. boolean	**isAutoDetecting** ()
	public................. boolean	**isCharsetDetected** ()
	public.......CodingErrorAction	**malformedInputAction** ()
●	public final ....float	**maxCharsPerByte** ()
●	public final ... CharsetDecoder	**onMalformedInput** (CodingErrorAction newAction)
●	public final ... CharsetDecoder	**onUnmappableCharacter** (CodingErrorAction newAction)
●	public final ....String	**replacement** ()
●	public final ... CharsetDecoder	**replaceWith** (String newReplacement)
●	public final ... CharsetDecoder	**reset** ()
	public.......CodingErrorAction	**unmappableCharacterAction** ()

CharsetEncoder java.nio.charset

Object
└CharsetEncoder

1.4 ○

●	public final ....float	**averageBytesPerChar** ()
	public................. boolean	**canEncode** (char c)
	public................. boolean	**canEncode** (*CharSequence* cs)
●	public final ....Charset	**charset** ()
✱	protected......................	**CharsetEncoder** (Charset cs, float averageBytesPerChar, float maxBytesPerChar)
✱	protected......................	**CharsetEncoder** (Charset cs, float averageBytesPerChar, float maxBytesPerChar, byte[] replacement)
●	public final java.nio.ByteBuffer	**encode** (java.nio.CharBuffer in) throws CharacterCodingException
		ε186
●	public final .... CoderResult	**encode** (java.nio.CharBuffer in, java.nio.ByteBuffer out, boolean endOfInput)
		ε186
○	protected abstract .... CoderResult	**encodeLoop** (java.nio.CharBuffer in, java.nio.ByteBuffer out)
●	public final .... CoderResult	**flush** (java.nio.ByteBuffer out)

Class   *Interface*   —extends   - - -implements   ○ abstract   ● final   △ static   ▲ static final   ✱ constructor   x x—inherited   x **x**—declared   **x x**—overridden
ε*n*—examples of usage   ˌ—has subclass   package—see other volume

protected	CoderResult	**implFlush** (java.nio.ByteBuffer out)	
protected	void	**implOnMalformedInput** (CodingErrorAction newAction)	
protected	void	**implOnUnmappableCharacter** (CodingErrorAction newAction)	
protected	void	**implReplaceWith** (byte[] newReplacement)	
protected	void	**implReset** ()	
public	boolean	**isLegalReplacement** (byte[] repl)	
public	CodingErrorAction	**malformedInputAction** ()	
● public final	float	**maxBytesPerChar** ()	
● public final	... CharsetEncoder	**onMalformedInput** (CodingErrorAction newAction)	
● public final	... CharsetEncoder	**onUnmappableCharacter** (CodingErrorAction newAction)	
● public final	byte[]	**replacement** ()	
● public final	... CharsetEncoder	**replaceWith** (byte[] newReplacement)	
● public final	... CharsetEncoder	**reset** ()	
public	CodingErrorAction	**unmappableCharacterAction** ()	

CharsetProvider — java.nio.charset.spi

Object
1.4 ○ └CharsetProvider

○	public abstract	**charsetForName** (String charsetName)	
	..... java.nio.charset.Charset		
*	protected	**CharsetProvider** ()	
○	public abstract *java.util.Iterator*	**charsets** ()	

CheckedInputStream — java.util.zip

Object   ε252,382,418
○ └java.io.InputStream
  └java.io.FilterInputStream [1]
1.1   └CheckedInputStream

1	public	int available () throws java.io.IOException	
*	public	**CheckedInputStream** (java.io.InputStream in, *Checksum* cksum)	
			ε457
1	public	void close () throws java.io.IOException	ε14,36,45,452,455
	public	*Checksum* **getChecksum** ()	ε457
1	protected .. java.io.InputStream	in	
1	public synchronized	void mark (int readlimit)	
1	public	boolean markSupported ()	
1	public	**int read** () throws java.io.IOException	ε90,184,256
1	public	int read (byte[] b) throws java.io.IOException	ε457,452,455,170,451
1	public	**int read** (byte[] buf, int off, int len) throws java.io.IOException	ε36
1	public synchronized	void reset () throws java.io.IOException	
1	public	**long skip** (long n) throws java.io.IOException	

CheckedOutputStream — java.util.zip

Object   ε183
○ └java.io.OutputStream
  └java.io.FilterOutputStream [1]
1.1   └CheckedOutputStream

*	public	**CheckedOutputStream** (java.io.OutputStream out, *Checksum* cksum)	
1	public	void close () throws java.io.IOException	ε451,453,91,211,224
1	public	void flush () throws java.io.IOException	ε27,54
	public	*Checksum* **getChecksum** ()	
1	protected java.io.OutputStream	out	
1	public	void write (byte[] b) throws java.io.IOException	ε27,91,224
1	public	**void write** (int b) throws java.io.IOException	ε184
1	public	**void write** (byte[] b, int off, int len) throws java.io.IOException	ε451,453,54,449,450

Checksum — java.util.zip

1.1 *Checksum*

public	long	**getValue** ()	ε456,457
public	void	**reset** ()	ε456
public	void	**update** (int b)	

public	void	**update** (byte[] b, int off, int len)	ε456

ChoiceCallback   javax.security.auth.callback

Object
1.4 └ChoiceCallback ----------------------- *Callback*, *java.io.Serializable*⌄

	public	boolean **allowMultipleSelections** ()
*	public	**ChoiceCallback** (String prompt, String[] choices, int defaultChoice, boolean multipleSelectionsAllowed)
	public	String[] **getChoices** ()
	public	int **getDefaultChoice** ()
	public	String **getPrompt** ()
	public	int[] **getSelectedIndexes** ()
	public	void **setSelectedIndex** (int selection)
	public	void **setSelectedIndexes** (int[] selections)

ChoiceFormat   java.text

Object
1.1 ○ └Format[1] ---------------------------- *java.io.Serializable*⌄, *Cloneable*⌄
1.1 ○   └NumberFormat[2]
1.1   └ChoiceFormat

2	*32 inherited members from NumberFormat not shown*		
	public	void **applyPattern** (String newPattern)	
*	public	**ChoiceFormat** (String newPattern)	
*	public	**ChoiceFormat** (double[] limits, String[] formats)	
2	public	**Object** **clone** ()	
2	public	**boolean** **equals** (Object obj)	
● 1	public final	String format (Object obj)	ε316,320
2	public	**StringBuffer** **format** (double number, StringBuffer toAppendTo, FieldPosition status)	
2	public	**StringBuffer** **format** (long number, StringBuffer toAppendTo, FieldPosition status)	
1.4 1	public	formatToCharacterIterator (Object obj)	
		.. *AttributedCharacterIterator*	
	public	Object[] **getFormats** ()	
	public	double[] **getLimits** ()	
2	public	int **hashCode** ()	
▲	public static final	double **nextDouble** (double d)	ε309
△	public static	double **nextDouble** (double d, boolean positive)	
2	public	**Number** **parse** (String text, ParsePosition status)	
1	public	Object parseObject (String source) throws ParseException	
▲	public static final	double **previousDouble** (double d)	ε309
	public	void **setChoices** (double[] limits, String[] formats)	
	public	String **toPattern** ()	

Cipher   javax.crypto

Object   ε461
1.4 └Cipher⌄

*	protected	**Cipher** (CipherSpi cipherSpi, java.security.Provider provider, String transformation)	
▲	public static final	int **DECRYPT_MODE** = 2	ε462,463,464,466
●	public final	byte[] **doFinal** () throws IllegalStateException, IllegalBlockSizeException, BadPaddingException	
●	public final	byte[] **doFinal** (byte[] input) throws IllegalStateException, IllegalBlockSizeException, BadPaddingException	ε462,464
●	public final	int **doFinal** (byte[] output, int outputOffset) throws IllegalStateException, IllegalBlockSizeException, ShortBufferException, BadPaddingException	
●	public final	byte[] **doFinal** (byte[] input, int inputOffset, int inputLen) throws IllegalStateException, IllegalBlockSizeException, BadPaddingException	
●	public final	int **doFinal** (byte[] input, int inputOffset, int inputLen, byte[] output) throws IllegalStateException, ShortBufferException, IllegalBlockSizeException, BadPaddingException	
●	public final	int **doFinal** (byte[] input, int inputOffset, int inputLen, byte[] output, int outputOffset) throws IllegalStateException, ShortBufferException, IllegalBlockSizeException, BadPaddingException	

Class *Interface* —extends - - -implements ○ abstract ● final △ static ▲ static final ✳ constructor x x—inherited x **x**—declared **x x**—overridden
ε*n*—examples of usage ⌄—has subclass package—see other volume

▲	public static final . . . . int	**ENCRYPT_MODE** = 1		ε462,463,464,466
●	public final . . . . String	**getAlgorithm** ()		
●	public final . . . . int	**getBlockSize** ()		
●	public final . . . . ExemptionMechanism	**getExemptionMechanism** ()		
▲	public static final . . . . Cipher	**getInstance** (String transformation) throws java.security↵.NoSuchAlgorithmException, NoSuchPaddingException		ε462,463,464,466
▲	public static final . . . . Cipher	**getInstance** (String transformation, String provider) throws java.security.NoSuchAlgorithmException, java.security.NoSuchProviderException, NoSuchPaddingException		
▲	public static final . . . . Cipher	**getInstance** (String transformation, java.security.Provider provider) throws java.security.NoSuchAlgorithmException, NoSuchPaddingException		
●	public final . . . . byte[]	**getIV** ()		
●	public final . . . . int	**getOutputSize** (int inputLen) throws IllegalStateException		
●	public final . . . . . java.security↵.AlgorithmParameters	**getParameters** ()		
●	public final . . . . java.security.Provider	**getProvider** ()		
●	public final . . . . void	**init** (int opmode, java.security.cert.Certificate certificate) throws java.security.InvalidKeyException		
●	public final . . . . void	**init** (int opmode, *java.security.Key* key) throws java.security.InvalidKeyException		ε462,466
●	public final . . . . void	**init** (int opmode, *java.security.Key* key, java.security.SecureRandom random) throws java.security.InvalidKeyException		
●	public final . . . . void	**init** (int opmode, *java.security.Key* key, *java.security.spec.AlgorithmParameterSpec* params) throws java.security.InvalidKeyException, java.security.InvalidAlgorithmParameterException		ε463,464
●	public final . . . . void	**init** (int opmode, *java.security.Key* key, java.security.AlgorithmParameters params) throws java.security.InvalidKeyException, java.security.InvalidAlgorithmParameterException		
●	public final . . . . void	**init** (int opmode, java.security.cert.Certificate certificate, java.security.SecureRandom random) throws java.security.InvalidKeyException		
●	public final . . . . void	**init** (int opmode, *java.security.Key* key, *java.security.spec.AlgorithmParameterSpec* params, java.security.SecureRandom random) throws java.security↵.InvalidKeyException, java.security.InvalidAlgorithmParameterException		
●	public final . . . . void	**init** (int opmode, *java.security.Key* key, java.security.AlgorithmParameters params, java.security.SecureRandom random) throws java.security.InvalidKeyException, java.security.InvalidAlgorithmParameterException		
▲	public static final . . . . int	**PRIVATE_KEY** = 2		
▲	public static final . . . . int	**PUBLIC_KEY** = 1		
▲	public static final . . . . int	**SECRET_KEY** = 3		
	public final . . *java.security.Key*	**unwrap** (byte[] wrappedKey, String wrappedKeyAlgorithm, int wrappedKeyType) throws IllegalStateException, java.security.InvalidKeyException, java.security.NoSuchAlgorithmException		
▲	public static final . . . . int	**UNWRAP_MODE** = 4		
●	public final . . . . byte[]	**update** (byte[] input) throws IllegalStateException		
●	public final . . . . byte[]	**update** (byte[] input, int inputOffset, int inputLen) throws IllegalStateException		
●	public final . . . . int	**update** (byte[] input, int inputOffset, int inputLen, byte[] output) throws IllegalStateException, ShortBufferException		
●	public final . . . . int	**update** (byte[] input, int inputOffset, int inputLen, byte[] output, int outputOffset) throws IllegalStateException, ShortBufferException		
●	public final . . . . byte[]	**wrap** (*java.security.Key* key) throws IllegalStateException, IllegalBlockSizeException, java.security.InvalidKeyException		
▲	public static final . . . . int	**WRAP_MODE** = 3		

CipherInputStream javax.crypto

ε252,382,418

```
      Object
  ○   └java.io.InputStream
        └java.io.FilterInputStream 1
1.4       └CipherInputStream
```

1	public . . . . **int**	**available** () throws java.io.IOException		
*	protected	**CipherInputStream** (java.io.InputStream is)		
*	public	**CipherInputStream** (java.io.InputStream is, Cipher c)		ε463
1	public . . . . **void**	**close** () throws java.io.IOException		ε14,36,45,452,455
1	protected . . java.io.InputStream	in		
1	public synchronized . . . . void	mark (int readlimit)		
1	public . . . . **boolean**	**markSupported** ()		
1	public . . . . **int**	**read** () throws java.io.IOException		ε90,184,256
1	public . . . . **int**	**read** (byte[] b) throws java.io.IOException		ε452,455,457,170,451
1	public . . . . **int**	**read** (byte[] b, int off, int len) throws java.io.IOException		ε36

CipherInputStream

	1	public synchronized .... void	**reset** () throws java.io.IOException
	1	public..................... **long**	**skip** (long n) throws java.io.IOException

---

CipherOutputStream   javax.crypto

Object	ε183
└java.io.OutputStream	
└java.io.FilterOutputStream [1]	
1.4 └CipherOutputStream	

*		protected	**CipherOutputStream** (java.io.OutputStream os)	
*		public..........................	**CipherOutputStream** (java.io.OutputStream os, Cipher c)	ε463
	1	public................... **void**	**close** () throws java.io.IOException	ε451,453,91,211,224
	1	public................... **void**	**flush** () throws java.io.IOException	ε27,54
	1	protected java.io.OutputStream	out	
	1	public................... **void**	**write** (byte[] b) throws java.io.IOException	ε27,91,224
	1	public................... **void**	**write** (int b) throws java.io.IOException	ε184
	1	public................... **void**	**write** (byte[] b, int off, int len) throws java.io.IOException	ε451,453,54,449,450

CipherSpi   javax.crypto

Object
1.4 O └CipherSpi

*	public..........................	**CipherSpi** ()
O	protected abstract .... byte[]	**engineDoFinal** (byte[] input, int inputOffset, int inputLen)
		throws IllegalBlockSizeException, BadPaddingException
O	protected abstract .... int	**engineDoFinal** (byte[] input, int inputOffset, int inputLen, byte[] output,
		int outputOffset) throws ShortBufferException, IllegalBlockSizeException,
		BadPaddingException
O	protected abstract .... int	**engineGetBlockSize** ()
O	protected abstract .... byte[]	**engineGetIV** ()
	protected .... int	**engineGetKeySize** (*java.security.Key* key) throws java.security.InvalidKeyException
O	protected abstract .... int	**engineGetOutputSize** (int inputLen)
O	protected abstract	**engineGetParameters** ()
	.... java.security ↵	
	.AlgorithmParameters	
O	protected abstract .... void	**engineInit** (int opmode, *java.security.Key* key, java.security.SecureRandom random)
		throws java.security.InvalidKeyException
O	protected abstract .... void	**engineInit** (int opmode, *java.security.Key* key, *java↵*
		.security.spec.AlgorithmParameterSpec params,
		java.security.SecureRandom random) throws java.security.InvalidKeyException,
		java.security.InvalidAlgorithmParameterException
O	protected abstract .... void	**engineInit** (int opmode, *java.security.Key* key, java.security.AlgorithmParameters
		params, java.security.SecureRandom random) throws java.security ↵
		.InvalidKeyException, java.security.InvalidAlgorithmParameterException
O	protected abstract .... void	**engineSetMode** (String mode) throws java.security.NoSuchAlgorithmException
O	protected abstract .... void	**engineSetPadding** (String padding) throws NoSuchPaddingException
	protected .... *java.security.Key*	**engineUnwrap** (byte[] wrappedKey, String wrappedKeyAlgorithm,
		int wrappedKeyType) throws java.security.InvalidKeyException,
		java.security.NoSuchAlgorithmException
O	protected abstract .... byte[]	**engineUpdate** (byte[] input, int inputOffset, int inputLen)
O	protected abstract .... int	**engineUpdate** (byte[] input, int inputOffset, int inputLen, byte[] output,
		int outputOffset) throws ShortBufferException
	protected .... byte[]	**engineWrap** (*java.security.Key* key) throws IllegalBlockSizeException,
		java.security.InvalidKeyException

Class   java.lang

Object [1]	ε68
● └Class - *java.io.Serializable* ↵	

1.4	public................. boolean	**desiredAssertionStatus** ()
△	public static .... Class	**forName** (String className) throws ClassNotFoundException ε233,59,235,236,237
1.2 △	public static .... Class	**forName** (String name, boolean initialize, ClassLoader loader)
		throws ClassNotFoundException
1.1	public................. Class[]	**getClasses** ()

Class *Interface* —extends - - -implements O abstract ● final △ static ▲ static final * constructor x x—inherited x **x**—declared **x x**—overridden
ε*n*—examples of usage ↵—has subclass package—see other volume

---

ClassCastException

```
Object
└Throwable -------------------------- java.io.Serializable┘
  └Exception
    └RuntimeException
      └ClassCastException
```

	public...........................	**ClassCastException** ()
*		
*	public...........................	**ClassCastException** (String s)

ClassCircularityError

```
Object
└Throwable -------------------------- java.io.Serializable┘
  └Error
    └LinkageError
      └ClassCircularityError
```

	public...........................	**ClassCircularityError** ()
*		
*	public...........................	**ClassCircularityError** (String s)

			ClassDesc	javax.rmi.CORBA

Object
└ClassDesc `- - - - - - - - - - - - - - - - - - - - - - - - - - -` *java.io.Serializable*

1.3

* ∗ public......................... **ClassDesc** ()

ClassFormatError	java.lang

Object
└Throwable `- - - - - - - - - - - - - - - - - - - - - - - - -` *java.io.Serializable*
  └Error
    └LinkageError
      └ClassFormatError

* ∗ public.......................... **ClassFormatError** ()
* ∗ public.......................... **ClassFormatError** (String s)

ClassLoader	java.lang

Object
○ └ClassLoader

	∗	protected	**ClassLoader** ()	
1.2	∗	protected	**ClassLoader** (ClassLoader parent)	
1.4		public synchronized ....void	**clearAssertionStatus** ()	
D	●	protected final .... Class	**defineClass** (byte[] b, int off, int len) throws ClassFormatError	
1.1	●	protected final .... Class	**defineClass** (String name, byte[] b, int off, int len) throws ClassFormatError	
1.2	●	protected final .... Class	**defineClass** (String name, byte[] b, int off, int len,	
			java.security.ProtectionDomain protectionDomain) throws ClassFormatError	
1.2		protected .... Package	**definePackage** (String name, String specTitle, String specVersion,	
			String specVendor, String implTitle, String implVersion, String implVendor,	
			java.net.URL sealBase) throws IllegalArgumentException	
1.2		protected .... Class	**findClass** (String name) throws ClassNotFoundException	
1.2		protected .... String	**findLibrary** (String libname)	
1.1	●	protected final native .... Class	**findLoadedClass** (String name)	
1.2		protected .... java.net.URL	**findResource** (String name)	
1.2		protected *java.util.Enumeration*	**findResources** (String name) throws java.io.IOException	
	●	protected final .... Class	**findSystemClass** (String name) throws ClassNotFoundException	
1.2		protected .... Package	**getPackage** (String name)	
1.2		protected ....Package[]	**getPackages** ()	
1.2	●	public final .... ClassLoader	**getParent** ()	
1.1		public............. java.net.URL	**getResource** (String name)	
1.1		public...... java.io.InputStream	**getResourceAsStream** (String name)	
1.2	●	public final	**getResources** (String name) throws java.io.IOException	
		.... *java.util.Enumeration*		
1.2	△	public static ...... ClassLoader	**getSystemClassLoader** ()	ε4
1.1	△	public static ...... java.net.URL	**getSystemResource** (String name)	
1.1	△	public static	**getSystemResourceAsStream** (String name)	
		.... java.io.InputStream		
1.2	△	public static	**getSystemResources** (String name) throws java.io.IOException	
		.... *java.util.Enumeration*		
1.1		public............. Class	**loadClass** (String name) throws ClassNotFoundException	ε68,69
		protected synchronized . Class	**loadClass** (String name, boolean resolve) throws ClassNotFoundException	
	●	protected final.............void	**resolveClass** (Class c)	
1.4		public synchronized ......void	**setClassAssertionStatus** (String className, boolean enabled)	
1.4		public synchronized ......void	**setDefaultAssertionStatus** (boolean enabled)	
1.4		public synchronized ......void	**setPackageAssertionStatus** (String packageName, boolean enabled)	
1.1	●	protected final.............void	**setSigners** (Class c, Object[] signers)	

ClassNotFoundException	java.lang

Object   ε59,68,69,4,45
└Throwable[1] `- - - - - - - - - - - - - - - - - - - - - - - - -` *java.io.Serializable*
  └Exception
    └ClassNotFoundException

Class *Interface* —extends `- - -`implements ○ abstract ● final △ static ▲ static final ∗ constructor x x—inherited x **x**—declared x **x**—overridden
ε*n*—examples of usage ͺ—has subclass package—see other volume

*		public	....	**ClassNotFoundException** ()
*		public	....	**ClassNotFoundException** (String s)
1.2	*	public	....	**ClassNotFoundException** (String s, Throwable ex)
1.4	1	public	.... **Throwable**	**getCause** ()
1.2		public	.... Throwable	**getException** ()
	1	public	.... String	getMessage () ε105

C

ClientRequestInfo	org.omg.PortableInterceptor

1.4	*ClientRequestInfo*——————————*ClientRequestInfoOperations*₎[1] (*RequestInfoOperations*[2]), *RequestInfo*₎ (*RequestInfoOperations*[2], *org.omg.CORBA.Object*[3], org.omg.CORBA.portable.IDLEntity (java.io.Serializable)), org.omg.CORBA.portable.IDLEntity₎ (java.io.Serializable)

- [1] 9 inherited members from ClientRequestInfoOperations not shown
- [3] 13 inherited members from org.omg.CORBA.Object not shown
- [2] 14 inherited members from RequestInfoOperations not shown

---

ClientRequestInfoOperations	org.omg.PortableInterceptor

1.4	*ClientRequestInfoOperations*₎——————————*RequestInfoOperations*₎[1]

[1] 14 inherited members from RequestInfoOperations not shown

public	.......................void	**add_request_service_context** (org.omg.IOP.ServiceContext service_context, boolean replace)
public	....	**effective_profile** ()
.. org.omg.IOP.TaggedProfile		
public *org.omg.CORBA.Object*		**effective_target** ()
public	.... org.omg ↵ .IOP.TaggedComponent	**get_effective_component** (int id)
public	.... org.omg ↵ .IOP.TaggedComponent[]	**get_effective_components** (int id)
public. *org.omg.CORBA.Policy*		**get_request_policy** (int type)
public	....org.omg.CORBA.Any	**received_exception** ()
public	.......................String	**received_exception_id** ()
public *org.omg.CORBA.Object*		**target** ()

ClientRequestInterceptor	org.omg.PortableInterceptor

1.4	*ClientRequestInterceptor*——————————*ClientRequestInterceptorOperations*₎[1] (*InterceptorOperations*[2]), *Interceptor*₎ (*InterceptorOperations*[2], *org.omg.CORBA.Object*[3], org.omg.CORBA.portable.IDLEntity (java.io.Serializable)), org.omg.CORBA.portable.IDLEntity₎ (java.io.Serializable)

- [2] 2 inherited members from InterceptorOperations not shown
- [3] 13 inherited members from org.omg.CORBA.Object not shown
- [1] 5 inherited members from ClientRequestInterceptorOperations not shown

---

ClientRequestInterceptorOperations	org.omg.PortableInterceptor

Classes

1.4	*ClientRequestInterceptorOperations*₎——————— *InterceptorOperations*₎[1]

[1] 2 inherited members from InterceptorOperations not shown

public	.......................void	**receive_exception** (*ClientRequestInfo* ri) throws ForwardRequest
public	.......................void	**receive_other** (*ClientRequestInfo* ri) throws ForwardRequest
public	.......................void	**receive_reply** (*ClientRequestInfo* ri)
public	.......................void	**send_poll** (*ClientRequestInfo* ri)
public	.......................void	**send_request** (*ClientRequestInfo* ri) throws ForwardRequest

---

Clob	java.sql

1.2	*Clob*

public	...... java.io.InputStream	**getAsciiStream** () throws SQLException
public	.... java.io.Reader	**getCharacterStream** () throws SQLException
public	.... String	**getSubString** (long pos, int length) throws SQLException
public	.... long	**length** () throws SQLException
public	.... long	**position** (String searchstr, long start) throws SQLException

	public..................... long	**position** (*Clob* searchstr, long start) throws SQLException
1.4	public.... java.io.OutputStream	**setAsciiStream** (long pos) throws SQLException
1.4	public............ java.io.Writer	**setCharacterStream** (long pos) throws SQLException
1.4	public.........................int	**setString** (long pos, String str) throws SQLException
1.4	public.........................int	**setString** (long pos, String str, int offset, int len) throws SQLException
1.4	public.......................void	**truncate** (long len) throws SQLException

C

Cloneable   java.lang

Cloneable ⌄   *ε56*

CloneNotSupportedException   java.lang

```
Object
└Throwable ------------------------- java.io.Serializable ⌄
  └Exception
    └CloneNotSupportedException ⌄
```

✳	public..........................	**CloneNotSupportedException** ()
✳	public..........................	**CloneNotSupportedException** (String s)

ClosedByInterruptException   java.nio.channels

```
Object
└Throwable ------------------------- java.io.Serializable ⌄
  └Exception
    └java.io.IOException
```
1.4	└ClosedChannelException
1.4	└AsynchronousCloseException
1.4	└ClosedByInterruptException

✳	public..........................	**ClosedByInterruptException** ()

ClosedChannelException   java.nio.channels

```
Object
└Throwable ------------------------- java.io.Serializable ⌄
  └Exception
    └java.io.IOException
```
| 1.4 | └ClosedChannelException ⌄ |

✳	public..........................	**ClosedChannelException** ()

ClosedSelectorException   java.nio.channels

```
Object
└Throwable ------------------------- java.io.Serializable ⌄
  └Exception
    └RuntimeException
```
| 1.1 | └IllegalStateException |
| 1.4 | └ClosedSelectorException |

✳	public..........................	**ClosedSelectorException** ()

Codec   org.omg.IOP

| 1.4 | *Codec*————————————— *CodecOperations* ⌄ [1], *org.omg.CORBA.Object* ⌄ [2], |
| | *org.omg.CORBA.portable.IDLEntity* ⌄ (*java.io.Serializable*) |

1 4 inherited members from CodecOperations not shown
2 13 inherited members from org.omg.CORBA.Object not shown

Class *Interface* —extends - - -implements ○ abstract ● final △ static ▲ static final ✳ constructor x x—inherited x **x**—declared **x x**—overridden
εn—examples of usage ⌄—has subclass package—see other volume

	CodecFactory	org.omg.IOP

1.4	*CodecFactory*——————————————— *CodecFactoryOperations*, [1], *org.omg.CORBA.Object*, [2], *org.omg.CORBA.portable.IDLEntity*, (*java.io.Serializable*)	

---

   [2] *13 inherited members from org.omg.CORBA.Object not shown*
   [1] public.................... *Codec* create_codec (Encoding enc) throws org.omg.IOP.CodecFactoryPackage ↵
      .UnknownEncoding

C

	CodecFactoryHelper	org.omg.IOP

Object
1.4 ○ └─CodecFactoryHelper

---

*   public........................... **CodecFactoryHelper** ()
△   public static .... *CodecFactory* **extract** (org.omg.CORBA.Any a)
△   public static ....String **id** ()
△   public static ....void **insert** (org.omg.CORBA.Any a, *CodecFactory* that)
△   public static .... *CodecFactory* **narrow** (*org.omg.CORBA.Object* obj)
△   public static .... *CodecFactory* **read** (org.omg.CORBA.portable.InputStream istream)
  public static synchronized .... **type** ()
  . org.omg.CORBA.TypeCode
△   public static ....void **write** (org.omg.CORBA.portable.OutputStream ostream, *CodecFactory* value)

	CodecFactoryOperations	org.omg.IOP

1.4	*CodecFactoryOperations*,	

public.................... *Codec* **create_codec** (Encoding enc) throws org.omg.IOP.CodecFactoryPackage ↵
    .UnknownEncoding

	CodecOperations	org.omg.IOP

1.4	*CodecOperations*,	

public....org.omg.CORBA.Any **decode** (byte[] data) throws org.omg.IOP.CodecPackage.FormatMismatch
public....org.omg.CORBA.Any **decode_value** (byte[] data, org.omg.CORBA.TypeCode tc) throws org.omg.IOP ↵
    .CodecPackage.FormatMismatch, org.omg.IOP.CodecPackage.TypeMismatch
public.................... byte[] **encode** (org.omg.CORBA.Any data) throws org.omg.IOP.CodecPackage ↵
    .InvalidTypeForEncoding
public.................... byte[] **encode_value** (org.omg.CORBA.Any data) throws
    org.omg.IOP.CodecPackage.InvalidTypeForEncoding

	CoderMalfunctionError	java.nio.charset

Object
└─Throwable ------------------------- *java.io.Serializable*,
  └─Error
1.4   └─CoderMalfunctionError

---

*   public........................... **CoderMalfunctionError** (Exception cause)

Classes

	CoderResult	java.nio.charset

Object[1]
1.4 └─CoderResult

---

public.................. boolean **isError** ()
public.................. boolean **isMalformed** ()
public.................. boolean **isOverflow** ()
public.................. boolean **isUnderflow** ()
public.................. boolean **isUnmappable** ()
public.........................int **length** ()
△   public static ...... CoderResult **malformedForLength** (int length)
▲   public static final . CoderResult **OVERFLOW**
public.......................void **throwException** () throws CharacterCodingException
[1] public.................... **String toString** ()
▲   public static final . CoderResult **UNDERFLOW**
△   public static ...... CoderResult **unmappableForLength** (int length)

CodeSets

		org.omg.IOP

1.4   *CodeSets*

▲   public static final .... int **value** = 1

CodeSource

		java.security

Object [1]
1.2   └CodeSource - *java.io.Serializable*⌄

*   public......................... **CodeSource** (java.net.URL url, java.security.cert.Certificate[] certs)
                                                  *ε*218
   1   public................... **boolean equals** (Object obj)
●   public final .... java↵ **getCertificates** ()
           .security.cert.Certificate[]
●   public final .... java.net.URL **getLocation** ()   *ε*67
   1   public...................... **int hashCode** ()
     public................... boolean **implies** (CodeSource codesource)
   1   public................... **String toString** ()

CodingErrorAction

		java.nio.charset

Object [1]
1.4   └CodingErrorAction

▲   public static final .... **IGNORE**
             ....CodingErrorAction
▲   public static final .... **REPLACE**
             ....CodingErrorAction
▲   public static final .... **REPORT**
             ....CodingErrorAction
   1   public................... **String toString** ()

CollationElementIterator

		java.text

Object
1.1 ●   └CollationElementIterator

1.2   public........................int **getMaxExpansion** (int order)
1.2   public........................int **getOffset** ()
     public........................int **next** ()
▲   public static final.............int **NULLORDER** = -1
1.2   public........................int **previous** ()
▲   public static final.............int **primaryOrder** (int order)
     public........................void **reset** ()
▲   public static final.........short **secondaryOrder** (int order)
1.2   public........................void **setOffset** (int newOffset)
1.2   public........................void **setText** (String source)
1.2   public........................void **setText** (*CharacterIterator* source)
▲   public static final.........short **tertiaryOrder** (int order)

CollationKey

		java.text

Object [1]
1.1 ●   └CollationKey - *Comparable* [2]

1.2   2 public........................int **compareTo** (Object o)   *ε*53
     public........................int **compareTo** (CollationKey target)
   1   public................... **boolean equals** (Object target)
     public....................String **getSourceString** ()
   1   public...................... **int hashCode** ()
     public....................byte[] **toByteArray** ()

Class   *Interface*   —extends   - - -implements   ○ abstract   ● final   △ static   ▲ static final   * constructor   x x—inherited   x **x**—declared   **x x**—overridden
εn—examples of usage   ⌄—has subclass   package—see other volume

Collator

```
        Object 1
1.1  O   └ Collator ------------------------------ java.util.Comparator 2, Cloneable
```

▲		public static final .... int		**CANONICAL_DECOMPOSITION** = 1	
	1	public .... **Object**		**clone** ()	
*		protected		**Collator** ()	
1.2	2	public .... int		**compare** (Object o1, Object o2)	
O		public abstract .... int		**compare** (String source, String target)	ε306
	1	public .... **boolean**		**equals** (Object that)	
		public .... boolean		**equals** (String source, String target)	
▲		public static final .... int		**FULL_DECOMPOSITION** = 2	
△		public static synchronized .... java.util.Locale[]		**getAvailableLocales** ()	
O		public abstract ... CollationKey		**getCollationKey** (String source)	
		public synchronized .... int		**getDecomposition** ()	
△		public static synchronized .... Collator		**getInstance** ()	
△		public static synchronized .... Collator		**getInstance** (java.util.Locale desiredLocale)	ε306
		public synchronized .... int		**getStrength** ()	
O	1	public abstract .... **int**		**hashCode** ()	
▲		public static final .... int		**IDENTICAL** = 3	
▲		public static final .... int		**NO_DECOMPOSITION** = 0	
▲		public static final .... int		**PRIMARY** = 0	
▲		public static final .... int		**SECONDARY** = 1	
		public synchronized .... void		**setDecomposition** (int decompositionMode)	
		public synchronized .... void		**setStrength** (int newStrength)	
▲		public static final .... int		**TERTIARY** = 2	

Collection

ε339,341,347,348,350

```
1.2     Collection
```

		ε342,349,352,354,358
public .... boolean	**add** (Object o)	ε342,349,352,354,358
public .... boolean	**addAll** (Collection c)	ε351,353
public .... void	**clear** ()	ε351,353
public .... boolean	**contains** (Object o)	ε352
public .... boolean	**containsAll** (Collection c)	
public .... boolean	**equals** (Object o)	
public .... int	**hashCode** ()	
public .... boolean	**isEmpty** ()	ε102
public .... Iterator	**iterator** ()	ε345,355
public .... boolean	**remove** (Object o)	ε349,352
public .... boolean	**removeAll** (Collection c)	ε351,353
public .... boolean	**retainAll** (Collection c)	ε351,353
public .... int	**size** ()	ε340,349,351,352,358
public .... Object[]	**toArray** ()	ε340
public .... Object[]	**toArray** (Object[] a)	ε340

CollectionCertStoreParameters

```
        Object 1
1.4  └ CollectionCertStoreParameters ----------- CertStoreParameters (Cloneable)
```

	1	public .... **Object**	**clone** ()
*		public	**CollectionCertStoreParameters** ()
*		public	**CollectionCertStoreParameters** (java.util.Collection collection)
		public .... java.util.Collection	**getCollection** ()
	1	public .... **String**	**toString** ()

Collections

```
        Object
1.2     └ Collections
```

△	public static .... int	**binarySearch** (List list, Object key)	ε361,362
△	public static .... int	**binarySearch** (List list, Object key, Comparator c)	
△	public static .... void	**copy** (List dest, List src)	
▲	public static final .... List	**EMPTY_LIST**	

C

Classes

Collections

COMM_FAILURE
org.omg.CORBA

```
Object
└Throwable --------------------------- java.io.Serializable⌄
  └Exception
    └RuntimeException
      └SystemException 1
1.2 O
        └COMM_FAILURE
1.2 ●
```

1   *3 inherited members from SystemException not shown*

✳	public		**COMM_FAILURE** ()
✳	public		**COMM_FAILURE** (String s)
✳	public		**COMM_FAILURE** (int minor, CompletionStatus completed)
✳	public		**COMM_FAILURE** (String s, int minor, CompletionStatus completed)

Comment
org.w3c.dom

1.4	*Comment*————————————*CharacterData*⌄ 1 (*Node* 2)			ε530,539,545,524,526

2   *36 inherited members from Node not shown*

1	public	void	appendData (String arg) throws DOMException	ε545
1	public	void	deleteData (int offset, int count) throws DOMException	ε545
1	public	String	getData () throws DOMException	ε546
1	public	int	getLength ()	ε545
2	public	String	getNodeValue () throws DOMException	ε541,536
1	public	void	insertData (int offset, String arg) throws DOMException	ε545
1	public	void	replaceData (int offset, int count, String arg) throws DOMException	ε545
1	public	void	setData (String data) throws DOMException	ε545
1	public	String	substringData (int offset, int count) throws DOMException	ε545

Class *Interface* —extends - - -implements O abstract ● final △ static ▲ static final ✳ constructor x x—inherited x **x**—declared **x x**—overridden
ε*n*—examples of usage ⌄—has subclass package—see other volume

	CommunicationException	javax.naming

```
        Object
        └Throwable ---------------------------- java.io.Serializable
           └Exception
1.3          └NamingException 1
1.3             └CommunicationException
```

	1	20 inherited members from NamingException not shown	
*	public..........................	**CommunicationException** ()	
*	public..........................	**CommunicationException** (String explanation)	

C

	Comparable	java.lang

1.2	*Comparable*	
	public..........................int **compareTo** (Object o)	ε53

	Comparator	java.util

1.2	*Comparator*	
	public..........................int **compare** (Object o1, Object o2)	
	public..................boolean **equals** (Object obj)	

	Compiler	java.lang

```
        Object
●       └Compiler
```

△	public static native......Object **command** (Object any)
△	public static native....boolean **compileClass** (Class clazz)
△	public static native....boolean **compileClasses** (String string)
△	public static native.........void **disable** ()
△	public static native.........void **enable** ()

	CompletionStatus	org.omg.CORBA

```
        Object
1.2 ●   └CompletionStatus --------------------- org.omg.CORBA.portable.IDLEntity (java.io.Serializable)
```

▲	public static final..............int **_COMPLETED_MAYBE** = 2
▲	public static final..............int **_COMPLETED_NO** = 1
▲	public static final..............int **_COMPLETED_YES** = 0
▲	public static final............... CompletionStatus **COMPLETED_MAYBE**
▲	public static final............... CompletionStatus **COMPLETED_NO**
▲	public static final............... CompletionStatus **COMPLETED_YES**
△	public static .CompletionStatus **from_int** (int i)
	public..........................int **value** ()

Classes

	CompletionStatusHelper	org.omg.CORBA

```
        Object
1.3 ○   └CompletionStatusHelper
```

*	public.......................... **CompletionStatusHelper** ()
△	public static .CompletionStatus **extract** (Any a)
△	public static ....String **id** ()
△	public static ....void **insert** (Any a, CompletionStatus that)
△	public static .CompletionStatus **read** (org.omg.CORBA.portable.InputStream istream)
△	public static synchronized .... TypeCode **type** ()
△	public static ....void **write** (org.omg.CORBA.portable.OutputStream ostream, CompletionStatus value)

ComponentIdHelper

			org.omg.IOP

Object
1.4 ○ └ComponentIdHelper

∗	public..........................		**ComponentIdHelper** ()
△	public static ....int		**extract** (org.omg.CORBA.Any a)
△	public static ....String		**id** ()
△	public static ....void		**insert** (org.omg.CORBA.Any a, int that)
△	public static ....int		**read** (org.omg.CORBA.portable.InputStream istream)
△	public static synchronized .... . org.omg.CORBA.TypeCode		**type** ()
△	public static ....void		**write** (org.omg.CORBA.portable.OutputStream ostream, int value)

CompositeName

			javax.naming

Object[1]
1.3 └CompositeName --------------------- Name[2] (Cloneable, java.io.Serializable)

2	public.....................Name	**add** (String comp) throws InvalidNameException		ε480
2	public.....................Name	**add** (int posn, String comp) throws InvalidNameException		ε479,480
2	public.....................Name	**addAll** (Name suffix) throws InvalidNameException		
2	public.....................Name	**addAll** (int posn, Name n) throws InvalidNameException		
1	public....................**Object**	**clone** ()		
2	public......................int	**compareTo** (Object obj)		
∗	public..........................	**CompositeName** ()		
∗	public..........................	**CompositeName** (String n) throws InvalidNameException		ε479
∗	protected......................	**CompositeName** (java.util.Enumeration comps)		
2	public.............. boolean	**endsWith** (Name n)		
1	public..............**boolean**	**equals** (Object obj)		
2	public.................String	**get** (int posn)		ε479
2	public.... java.util.Enumeration	**getAll** ()		
2	public.....................Name	**getPrefix** (int posn)		
2	public.....................Name	**getSuffix** (int posn)		
1	public.............. **int**	**hashCode** ()		
2	public.............. boolean	**isEmpty** ()		
2	public..................Object	**remove** (int posn) throws InvalidNameException		ε479,480
2	public......................int	**size** ()		ε479
2	public.............. boolean	**startsWith** (Name n)		
1	public.............. **String**	**toString** ()		

CompoundName

			javax.naming

Object[1]
1.3 └CompoundName --------------------- Name[2] (Cloneable, java.io.Serializable)

2	public.....................Name	**add** (String comp) throws InvalidNameException		ε480
2	public.....................Name	**add** (int posn, String comp) throws InvalidNameException		ε479,480
2	public.....................Name	**addAll** (Name suffix) throws InvalidNameException		
2	public.....................Name	**addAll** (int posn, Name n) throws InvalidNameException		
1	public....................**Object**	**clone** ()		
2	public......................int	**compareTo** (Object obj)		
∗	public..........................	**CompoundName** (String n, java.util.Properties syntax) throws InvalidNameException		
∗	protected......................	**CompoundName** (java.util.Enumeration comps, java.util.Properties syntax)		
2	public.............. boolean	**endsWith** (Name n)		
1	public..............**boolean**	**equals** (Object obj)		
2	public.................String	**get** (int posn)		ε479
2	public.... java.util.Enumeration	**getAll** ()		
2	public.....................Name	**getPrefix** (int posn)		
2	public.....................Name	**getSuffix** (int posn)		
1	public.............. **int**	**hashCode** ()		
	protected transient............ ..... javax.naming.NameImpl	**impl**		
2	public.............. boolean	**isEmpty** ()		
	protected transient............ ....java.util.Properties	**mySyntax**		
2	public..................Object	**remove** (int posn) throws InvalidNameException		ε479,480

Class *Interface* —extends - - -implements ○ abstract ● final △ static ▲ static final ∗ constructor x x—inherited x **x**—declared **x x**—overridden
ε*n*—examples of usage └—has subclass package—see other volume

512

2	public........................int	**size** ()	
2	public.................boolean	**startsWith** (*Name* n)	
1	public...................**String**	**toString** ()	

ε479

ConcurrentModificationException java.util

C

```
Object
└Throwable -------------------------- java.io.Serializable⌄
  └Exception
    └RuntimeException
      └ConcurrentModificationException
```
1.2

*	public.........................	**ConcurrentModificationException** ()
*	public.........................	**ConcurrentModificationException** (String message)

Configuration javax.security.auth.login

```
Object
└Configuration
```
1.4 ○

*	protected......................	**Configuration** ()	
○	public abstract	**getAppConfigurationEntry** (String applicationName)	*ε507*
	.... AppConfigurationEntry[]		
△	public static synchronized	**getConfiguration** ()	*ε507*
	.... Configuration		
○	public abstract ....void	**refresh** ()	
△	public static ....void	**setConfiguration** (Configuration configuration)	

ConfigurationException javax.naming

```
Object
└Throwable -------------------------- java.io.Serializable⌄
  └Exception
    └NamingException[1]
      └ConfigurationException
```
1.3
1.3

1	*20 inherited members from NamingException not shown*	
*	public.........................	**ConfigurationException** ()
*	public.........................	**ConfigurationException** (String explanation)

ConfirmationCallback javax.security.auth.callback

```
Object
└ConfirmationCallback ------------------- Callback, java.io.Serializable⌄
```
1.4

▲	public static final ....int	**CANCEL** = 2
*	public.........................	**ConfirmationCallback** (int messageType, String[] options, int defaultOption)
*	public.........................	**ConfirmationCallback** (int messageType, int optionType, int defaultOption)
*	public.........................	**ConfirmationCallback** (String prompt, int messageType, int optionType, int defaultOption)
*	public.........................	**ConfirmationCallback** (String prompt, int messageType, String[] options, int defaultOption)
▲	public static final ....int	**ERROR** = 2
	public......................int	**getDefaultOption** ()
	public......................int	**getMessageType** ()
	public...................String[]	**getOptions** ()
	public......................int	**getOptionType** ()
	public...................String	**getPrompt** ()
	public......................int	**getSelectedIndex** ()
▲	public static final ....int	**INFORMATION** = 0
▲	public static final ....int	**NO** = 1
▲	public static final ....int	**OK** = 3
▲	public static final ....int	**OK_CANCEL_OPTION** = 2
	public.....................void	**setSelectedIndex** (int selection)
▲	public static final ....int	**UNSPECIFIED_OPTION** = -1
▲	public static final ....int	**WARNING** = 1
▲	public static final ....int	**YES** = 0
▲	public static final ....int	**YES_NO_CANCEL_OPTION** = 1
▲	public static final ....int	**YES_NO_OPTION** = 0

Classes

C

ConnectException ❶ `java.net`

```
Object
└Throwable ------------------------- java.io.Serializable ˷
  └Exception
    └java.io.IOException
      └SocketException
1.1     └ConnectException
```

✳	public..........................		**ConnectException** ()
✳	public..........................		**ConnectException** (String msg)

ConnectException ❷ `java.rmi`

```
Object
└Throwable ------------------------- java.io.Serializable ˷
  └Exception
    └java.io.IOException
1.1   └RemoteException¹
1.1     └ConnectException
```

✳		public..........................		**ConnectException** (String s)
✳		public..........................		**ConnectException** (String s, Exception ex)
	1	public...............Throwable	detail	
1.4	1	public...............Throwable	getCause ()	
	1	public....................String	getMessage ()	

ConnectIOException `java.rmi`

```
Object
└Throwable ------------------------- java.io.Serializable ˷
  └Exception
    └java.io.IOException
1.1   └RemoteException¹
1.1     └ConnectIOException
```

✳		public..........................		**ConnectIOException** (String s)
✳		public..........................		**ConnectIOException** (String s, Exception ex)
	1	public...............Throwable	detail	
1.4	1	public...............Throwable	getCause ()	
	1	public....................String	getMessage ()	

Connection `java.sql`

1.1	*Connection*		ε235,236,237

	public.......................void	**clearWarnings** () throws SQLException	
	public.......................void	**close** () throws SQLException	ε260
	public.......................void	**commit** () throws SQLException	ε240,265
	public...............*Statement*	**createStatement** () throws SQLException	ε242,244,245,246,248
1.2	public...............*Statement*	**createStatement** (int resultSetType, int resultSetConcurrency) throws SQLException	
			ε267,269,270,271,273
1.4	public...............*Statement*	**createStatement** (int resultSetType, int resultSetConcurrency, int resultSetHoldability) throws SQLException	
	public.................boolean	**getAutoCommit** () throws SQLException	
	public......................String	**getCatalog** () throws SQLException	
1.4	public............................int	**getHoldability** () throws SQLException	
	public......*DatabaseMetaData*	**getMetaData** () throws SQLException	ε239,241,243,247,264
	public............................int	**getTransactionIsolation** () throws SQLException	
1.2	public.............*java.util.Map*	**getTypeMap** () throws SQLException	
	public..............SQLWarning	**getWarnings** () throws SQLException	ε242
	public.................boolean	**isClosed** () throws SQLException	
	public.................boolean	**isReadOnly** () throws SQLException	
	public......................String	**nativeSQL** (String sql) throws SQLException	
	public.......*CallableStatement*	**prepareCall** (String sql) throws SQLException	ε281,282
1.2	public.......*CallableStatement*	**prepareCall** (String sql, int resultSetType, int resultSetConcurrency) throws SQLException	

Class *Interface* —extends - - -implements ○ abstract ● final △ static ▲ static final ✳ constructor x x—inherited x **x**—declared **x x**—overridden
ε*n*—examples of usage ˷—has subclass package—see other volume

1.4	public....... *CallableStatement*	**prepareCall** (String sql, int resultSetType, int resultSetConcurrency, int resultSetHoldability) throws SQLException	
	public...... *PreparedStatement*	**prepareStatement** (String sql) throws SQLException	ε259,260,262,265,298
1.4	public...... *PreparedStatement*	**prepareStatement** (String sql, int autoGeneratedKeys) throws SQLException	
1.4	public...... *PreparedStatement*	**prepareStatement** (String sql, int[] columnIndexes) throws SQLException	
1.4	public...... *PreparedStatement*	**prepareStatement** (String sql, String[] columnNames) throws SQLException	
1.2	public...... *PreparedStatement*	**prepareStatement** (String sql, int resultSetType, int resultSetConcurrency) throws SQLException	
1.4	public...... *PreparedStatement*	**prepareStatement** (String sql, int resultSetType, int resultSetConcurrency, int resultSetHoldability) throws SQLException	
1.4	public....................void	**releaseSavepoint** (*Savepoint* savepoint) throws SQLException	
	public....................void	**rollback** () throws SQLException	ε240,265
1.4	public....................void	**rollback** (*Savepoint* savepoint) throws SQLException	
	public....................void	**setAutoCommit** (boolean autoCommit) throws SQLException	ε240,265
	public....................void	**setCatalog** (String catalog) throws SQLException	
1.4	public....................void	**setHoldability** (int holdability) throws SQLException	
	public....................void	**setReadOnly** (boolean readOnly) throws SQLException	
1.4	public................*Savepoint*	**setSavepoint** () throws SQLException	
1.4	public................*Savepoint*	**setSavepoint** (String name) throws SQLException	
	public....................void	**setTransactionIsolation** (int level) throws SQLException	
1.2	public....................void	**setTypeMap** (*java.util.Map* map) throws SQLException	
▲	public static final...........int	**TRANSACTION_NONE** = 0	
▲	public static final...........int	**TRANSACTION_READ_COMMITTED** = 2	
▲	public static final...........int	**TRANSACTION_READ_UNCOMMITTED** = 1	
▲	public static final...........int	**TRANSACTION_REPEATABLE_READ** = 4	
▲	public static final...........int	**TRANSACTION_SERIALIZABLE** = 8	

C

ConnectionEvent — javax.sql

Object
  └java.util.EventObject[1] - - - - - - - - - - - - - - - - - - *java.io.Serializable* ˌ
    └ConnectionEvent

(1.1, 1.4) ε333

*	public...........................	**ConnectionEvent** (*PooledConnection* con)	
*	public...........................	**ConnectionEvent** (*PooledConnection* con, java.sql.SQLException ex)	
1	public.....................Object	getSource ()	
	public.. java.sql.SQLException	**getSQLException** ()	
1	protected transient......Object	source	
1	public.....................String	toString ()	

ConnectionEventListener — javax.sql

ConnectionEventListener————————*java.util.EventListener* ˌ

(1.4) ε2,3,333,493,494

public........................void	**connectionClosed** (ConnectionEvent event)	
public........................void	**connectionErrorOccurred** (ConnectionEvent event)	

ConnectionPendingException — java.nio.channels

Object
  └Throwable - *java.io.Serializable* ˌ
    └Exception
      └RuntimeException
        └IllegalStateException
          └ConnectionPendingException

(1.1, 1.4)

*	public...........................	**ConnectionPendingException** ()

ConnectionPoolDataSource — javax.sql

ConnectionPoolDataSource

(1.4)

public...........................int	**getLoginTimeout** () throws java.sql.SQLException	
public........java.io.PrintWriter	**getLogWriter** () throws java.sql.SQLException	
public....... *PooledConnection*	**getPooledConnection** () throws java.sql.SQLException	
public....... *PooledConnection*	**getPooledConnection** (String user, String password) throws java.sql.SQLException	
public........................void	**setLoginTimeout** (int seconds) throws java.sql.SQLException	
public........................void	**setLogWriter** (java.io.PrintWriter out) throws java.sql.SQLException	

Classes

ConsoleHandler
java.util.logging

```
        Object
1.4  O   └Handler¹
1.4      └StreamHandler²
1.4          └ConsoleHandler
```

2	public	**void**	**close** ()	
*	public		**ConsoleHandler** ()	ε392,394
2	public synchronized	void	flush ()	
1	public	String	getEncoding ()	
1	public	ErrorManager	getErrorManager ()	
1	public	*Filter*	getFilter ()	
1	public	Formatter	getFormatter ()	
1	public synchronized	Level	getLevel ()	
2	public	boolean	isLoggable (LogRecord record)	
2	public	**void**	**publish** (LogRecord record)	ε393
1	protected	void	reportError (String msg, Exception ex, int code)	
2	public	void	setEncoding (String encoding) throws SecurityException, java.io.UnsupportedEncodingException	
1	public	void	setErrorManager (ErrorManager em)	
1	public	void	setFilter (*Filter* newFilter) throws SecurityException	ε394
1	public	void	setFormatter (Formatter newFormatter) throws SecurityException	ε399,400
1	public synchronized	void	setLevel (Level newLevel) throws SecurityException	
2	protected synchronized	void	setOutputStream (java.io.OutputStream out) throws SecurityException	

Constructor
java.lang.reflect

```
        Object¹
1.2     └AccessibleObject²
1.1 ●     └Constructor ----------------------- Member³
```

	1	public	**boolean**	**equals** (Object obj)	
	3	public	Class	**getDeclaringClass** ()	
		public	Class[]	**getExceptionTypes** ()	
	3	public	int	**getModifiers** ()	ε113
	3	public	String	**getName** ()	ε109,291
		public	Class[]	**getParameterTypes** ()	ε116
	1	public	**int**	**hashCode** ()	
1.2	2	public	boolean	isAccessible ()	
		public	Object	**newInstance** (Object[] initargs) throws InstantiationException, IllegalAccessException, IllegalArgumentException, InvocationTargetException	ε117
1.2	2	public	void	setAccessible (boolean flag) throws SecurityException	ε110
1.2 △	2	public static	void	setAccessible (AccessibleObject[] array, boolean flag) throws SecurityException	
	1	public	**String**	**toString** ()	

ContentHandler ❶
java.net

```
     Object
 O   └ContentHandler
```

*	public		**ContentHandler** ()	
O	public abstract	Object	**getContent** (URLConnection urlc) throws java.io.IOException	
1.3	public	Object	**getContent** (URLConnection urlc, Class[] classes) throws java.io.IOException	

ContentHandler ❷
org.xml.sax

```
1.4  ContentHandler
```

public	void	**characters** (char[] ch, int start, int length) throws SAXException	
public	void	**endDocument** () throws SAXException	
public	void	**endElement** (String namespaceURI, String localName, String qName) throws SAXException	
public	void	**endPrefixMapping** (String prefix) throws SAXException	
public	void	**ignorableWhitespace** (char[] ch, int start, int length) throws SAXException	

public	.... void	**processingInstruction** (String target, String data) throws SAXException	
public	.... void	**setDocumentLocator** (*Locator* locator)	ε550
public	.... void	**skippedEntity** (String name) throws SAXException	
public	.... void	**startDocument** () throws SAXException	
public	.... void	**startElement** (String namespaceURI, String localName, String qName,	
		Attributes atts) throws SAXException	ε549,550
public	.... void	**startPrefixMapping** (String prefix, String uri) throws SAXException	

ContentHandlerFactory   java.net

ContentHandlerFactory

public	.... ContentHandler	**createContentHandler** (String mimetype)

Context ❶   javax.naming

			ε484
1.3	*Context*		
	public	.... Object	**addToEnvironment** (String propName, Object propVal) throws NamingException
▲	public static final	.... String	**APPLET** = "java.naming.applet"
▲	public static final	.... String	**AUTHORITATIVE** = "java.naming.authoritative"
▲	public static final	.... String	**BATCHSIZE** = "java.naming.batchsize"
	public	.... void	**bind** (String name, Object obj) throws NamingException ε475
	public	.... void	**bind** (*Name* name, Object obj) throws NamingException
	public	.... void	**close** () throws NamingException
	public	.... String	**composeName** (String name, String prefix) throws NamingException
	public	.... *Name*	**composeName** (*Name* name, *Name* prefix) throws NamingException
	public	.... *Context*	**createSubcontext** (String name) throws NamingException ε476
	public	.... *Context*	**createSubcontext** (*Name* name) throws NamingException
	public	.... void	**destroySubcontext** (String name) throws NamingException ε476
	public	.... void	**destroySubcontext** (*Name* name) throws NamingException
▲	public static final	.... String	**DNS_URL** = "java.naming.dns.url"
	public	.... java.util.Hashtable	**getEnvironment** () throws NamingException
	public	.... String	**getNameInNamespace** () throws NamingException ε477
	public	.... *NameParser*	**getNameParser** (String name) throws NamingException ε480
	public	.... *NameParser*	**getNameParser** (*Name* name) throws NamingException
▲	public static final	.... String	**INITIAL_CONTEXT_FACTORY** = "java.naming.factory.initial" ε472,481,492
▲	public static final	.... String	**LANGUAGE** = "java.naming.language"
	public	..... *NamingEnumeration*	**list** (String name) throws NamingException ε474
	public	..... *NamingEnumeration*	**list** (*Name* name) throws NamingException
	public	..... *NamingEnumeration*	**listBindings** (String name) throws NamingException
	public	..... *NamingEnumeration*	**listBindings** (*Name* name) throws NamingException
	public	.... Object	**lookup** (String name) throws NamingException ε473,477
	public	.... Object	**lookup** (*Name* name) throws NamingException
	public	.... Object	**lookupLink** (String name) throws NamingException
	public	.... Object	**lookupLink** (*Name* name) throws NamingException
▲	public static final	.... String	**OBJECT_FACTORIES** = "java.naming.factory.object"
▲	public static final	.... String	**PROVIDER_URL** = "java.naming.provider.url" ε472,481,492
	public	.... void	**rebind** (String name, Object obj) throws NamingException ε475
	public	.... void	**rebind** (*Name* name, Object obj) throws NamingException
▲	public static final	.... String	**REFERRAL** = "java.naming.referral"
	public	.... Object	**removeFromEnvironment** (String propName) throws NamingException
	public	.... void	**rename** (String oldName, String newName) throws NamingException
			ε475
	public	.... void	**rename** (*Name* oldName, *Name* newName) throws NamingException
▲	public static final	.... String	**SECURITY_AUTHENTICATION** = "java.naming.security.authentication"
			ε492
▲	public static final	.... String	**SECURITY_CREDENTIALS** = "java.naming.security.credentials"
			ε492
▲	public static final	.... String	**SECURITY_PRINCIPAL** = "java.naming.security.principal" ε492
▲	public static final	.... String	**SECURITY_PROTOCOL** = "java.naming.security.protocol"
▲	public static final	.... String	**STATE_FACTORIES** = "java.naming.factory.state"
	public	.... void	**unbind** (String name) throws NamingException ε475
	public	.... void	**unbind** (*Name* name) throws NamingException
▲	public static final	.... String	**URL_PKG_PREFIXES** = "java.naming.factory.url.pkgs"

Context ❷   org.omg.CORBA

Object
1.2 ○   └─Context

Context ❷

✳	public		**Context** ()
○	public abstract	String	**context_name** ()
○	public abstract	Context	**create_child** (String child_ctx_name)
○	public abstract	void	**delete_values** (String propname)
○	public abstract	NVList	**get_values** (String start_scope, int op_flags, String pattern)
○	public abstract	Context	**parent** ()
○	public abstract	void	**set_one_value** (String propname, Any propvalue)
○	public abstract	void	**set_values** (NVList values)

ContextList org.omg.CORBA

Object
  └ContextList

1.2 ○

○	public abstract	void	**add** (String ctx)
✳	public		**ContextList** ()
○	public abstract	int	**count** ()
○	public abstract	String	**item** (int index) throws Bounds
○	public abstract	void	**remove** (int index) throws Bounds

ContextNotEmptyException javax.naming

Object
  └Throwable - *java.io.Serializable*
    └Exception
1.3   └NamingException [1]
1.3   └ContextNotEmptyException

	[1]	*20 inherited members from NamingException not shown*
✳	public	**ContextNotEmptyException** ()
✳	public	**ContextNotEmptyException** (String explanation)

Control ❶ javax.naming.ldap

1.3   *Control* ———————————————— *java.io.Serializable*   ε495

▲	public static final	boolean	**CRITICAL** = true	ε496
	public	byte[]	**getEncodedValue** ()	
	public	String	**getID** ()	
	public	boolean	**isCritical** ()	
▲	public static final	boolean	**NONCRITICAL** = false	

ControlFactory javax.naming.ldap

Object
1.3 ○   └ControlFactory

✳	protected		**ControlFactory** ()
○	public abstract	*Control*	**getControlInstance** (*Control* ctl) throws javax.naming.NamingException
△	public static	*Control*	**getControlInstance** (*Control* ctl, *javax.naming.Context* ctx, java.util.Hashtable env) throws javax.naming.NamingException

---

CookieHolder org.omg.PortableServer.ServantLocatorPackage

Object
1.4 ●   └CookieHolder - *org.omg.CORBA.portable.Streamable* [1]

	[1] public	void	**_read** (org.omg.CORBA.portable.InputStream is)
	[1] public		**_type** ()
		org.omg.CORBA.TypeCode	
	[1] public	void	**_write** (org.omg.CORBA.portable.OutputStream os)
✳	public		**CookieHolder** ()
✳	public		**CookieHolder** (Object initial)
	public	Object	**value**

Class *Interface* —extends - - -implements ○ abstract ● final △ static ▲ static final ✳ constructor x x—inherited x **x**—declared **x x**—overridden
ε*n*—examples of usage ˽—has subclass package—see other volume

CRC32 | java.util.zip

		Object		
1.1		└CRC32 ----------------------------- *Checksum* [1]		
*		public...........................	**CRC32** ()	ε456
	1	public..................... long	**getValue** ()	ε456,457
	1	public.....................void	**reset** ()	ε456
		public.....................void	**update** (byte[] b)	
	1	public.....................void	**update** (int b)	
	1	public.....................void	**update** (byte[] b, int off, int len)	ε456

CredentialExpiredException | javax.security.auth.login

		Object	
		└Throwable --------------------------- *java.io.Serializable*	
		└Exception	
1.2		└java.security.GeneralSecurityException	
1.4		└LoginException	
1.4		└CredentialExpiredException	
*		public...........................	**CredentialExpiredException** ()
*		public...........................	**CredentialExpiredException** (String msg)

CRL | java.security.cert

		Object [1]		
1.2	O	└CRL		
*		protected......................	**CRL** (String type)	
●		public final ....String	**getType** ()	
O		public abstract .... boolean	**isRevoked** (Certificate cert)	
O	1	public abstract .... String	**toString** ()	

CRLException | java.security.cert

		Object	
		└Throwable -------------------------- *java.io.Serializable*	
		└Exception	
1.2		└java.security.GeneralSecurityException	
1.2		└CRLException	
*		public...........................	**CRLException** ()
*		public...........................	**CRLException** (String message)

CRLSelector | java.security.cert

1.4		*CRLSelector* ─────────────── *Cloneable*	
		public.................Object	**clone** ()
		public................. boolean	**match** (CRL crl)

CTX_RESTRICT_SCOPE | org.omg.CORBA

1.2		*CTX_RESTRICT_SCOPE*	
▲		public static final.............int	**value** = 15

Currency | java.util

		Object [1]		
1.4	●	└Currency ----------------------------- *java.io.Serializable*		
		public....................String	**getCurrencyCode** ()	
		public.......................int	**getDefaultFractionDigits** ()	
	△	public static .... Currency	**getInstance** (String currencyCode)	
	△	public static .... Currency	**getInstance** (Locale locale)	
		public....................String	**getSymbol** ()	

Currency

public	String	**getSymbol** (Locale locale)	
1 public	**String**	**toString** ()	

Current ❶   org.omg.CORBA

1.2   *Current* ──────────────── *CurrentOperations*, *Object* [1], *org.omg.CORBA.portable.IDLEntity*
                   (*java.io.Serializable*)

- -

   1   *13 inherited members from Object not shown*

Current ❷   org.omg.PortableInterceptor

1.4   *Current* ──────────────── *CurrentOperations* [1] (*org.omg.CORBA.CurrentOperations*),
                   org.omg.CORBA.Current (*org.omg.CORBA.CurrentOperations*,
                   org.omg.CORBA.Object [2], *org.omg.CORBA.portable.IDLEntity*
                   (*java.io.Serializable*)), *org.omg.CORBA.portable.IDLEntity*
                   (*java.io.Serializable*)

- -

   2   *13 inherited members from org.omg.CORBA.Object not shown*
   1   *2 inherited members from CurrentOperations not shown*

Current ❸   org.omg.PortableServer

1.4   *Current* ──────────────── *CurrentOperations* [1] (*org.omg.CORBA.CurrentOperations*),
                   org.omg.CORBA.Current (*org.omg.CORBA.CurrentOperations*,
                   org.omg.CORBA.Object [2], *org.omg.CORBA.portable.IDLEntity*
                   (*java.io.Serializable*)), *org.omg.CORBA.portable.IDLEntity*
                   (*java.io.Serializable*)

- -

   2   *13 inherited members from org.omg.CORBA.Object not shown*
   1   *2 inherited members from CurrentOperations not shown*

CurrentHelper ❶   org.omg.CORBA

   Object
1.3 ○   └CurrentHelper

✳	public		**CurrentHelper** ()
△	public static	*Current*	**extract** (Any a)
△	public static	String	**id** ()
△	public static	void	**insert** (Any a, *Current* that)
△	public static	*Current*	**narrow** (*Object* obj)
△	public static	*Current*	**read** (org.omg.CORBA.portable.InputStream istream)
△	public static synchronized	TypeCode	**type** ()
△	public static	void	**write** (org.omg.CORBA.portable.OutputStream ostream, *Current* value)

CurrentHelper ❷   org.omg.PortableInterceptor

   Object
1.4 ○   └CurrentHelper

✳	public		**CurrentHelper** ()
△	public static	*Current*	**extract** (org.omg.CORBA.Any a)
△	public static	String	**id** ()
△	public static	void	**insert** (org.omg.CORBA.Any a, *Current* that)
△	public static	*Current*	**narrow** (*org.omg.CORBA.Object* obj)
△	public static	*Current*	**read** (org.omg.CORBA.portable.InputStream istream)
	public static synchronized	org.omg.CORBA.TypeCode	**type** ()
△	public static	void	**write** (org.omg.CORBA.portable.OutputStream ostream, *Current* value)

Class   *Interface*   ──extends   - - -implements   ○ abstract   ● final   △ static   ▲ static final   ✳ constructor   x x──inherited   x **x**──declared   **x x**──overridden
εn──examples of usage   ⌐has subclass   package──see other volume

CurrentHelper ❸ | org.omg.PortableServer

```
        Object
1.4 ○   └CurrentHelper
```

✳	public......................... **CurrentHelper** ()
△	public static .... *Current* **extract** (org.omg.CORBA.Any a)
△	public static ....String **id** ()
△	public static ....void **insert** (org.omg.CORBA.Any a, *Current* that)
△	public static .... *Current* **narrow** (*org.omg.CORBA.Object* obj)
△	public static .... *Current* **read** (org.omg.CORBA.portable.InputStream istream)
△	public static synchronized .... **type** ()
	. org.omg.CORBA.TypeCode
△	public static ....void **write** (org.omg.CORBA.portable.OutputStream ostream, *Current* value)

CurrentHolder | org.omg.CORBA

```
        Object
1.3 ●   └CurrentHolder ------------------------- org.omg.CORBA.portable.Streamable ⌐1
```

1	public.......................void **_read** (org.omg.CORBA.portable.InputStream i)
1	public...............TypeCode **_type** ()
1	public.......................void **_write** (org.omg.CORBA.portable.OutputStream o)
✳	public......................... **CurrentHolder** ()
✳	public......................... **CurrentHolder** (*Current* initialValue)
	public.................. *Current* **value**

CurrentOperations ❶ | org.omg.CORBA

```
1.3     CurrentOperations ⌐
```

CurrentOperations ❷ | org.omg.PortableInterceptor

```
1.4     CurrentOperations ⌐—————————————— org.omg.CORBA.CurrentOperations ⌐
```

	public....org.omg.CORBA.Any **get_slot** (int id) throws InvalidSlot
	public.......................void **set_slot** (int id, org.omg.CORBA.Any data) throws InvalidSlot

CurrentOperations ❸ | org.omg.PortableServer

```
1.4     CurrentOperations ⌐—————————————— org.omg.CORBA.CurrentOperations ⌐
```

	public.....................byte[] **get_object_id** () throws org.omg.PortableServer.CurrentPackage.NoContext
	public..................... *POA* **get_POA** () throws org.omg.PortableServer.CurrentPackage.NoContext

Customizer | java.beans

```
1.1     Customizer
```

	public.......................void **addPropertyChangeListener** (*PropertyChangeListener* listener)
	public.......................void **removePropertyChangeListener** (*PropertyChangeListener* listener)
	public.......................void **setObject** (Object bean)

CustomMarshal | org.omg.CORBA

```
1.3     CustomMarshal ⌐
```

	public.......................void **marshal** (*DataOutputStream* os)
	public.......................void **unmarshal** (*DataInputStream* is)

CustomValue | org.omg.CORBA.portable

```
1.3     CustomValue——————————————— ValueBase ⌐1 (IDLEntity (java.io.Serializable)),
                                        org.omg.CORBA.CustomMarshal ⌐2
```

2	2 inherited members from org.omg.CORBA.CustomMarshal not shown
1	public.................... String[] **_truncatable_ids** ()

C

Classes

521

DATA_CONVERSION	org.omg.CORBA

```
Object
 └Throwable ------------------------------ java.io.Serializable ˬ
   └Exception
     └RuntimeException
1.2 ○         └SystemException 1
1.2 ●           └DATA_CONVERSION
```

D

	1	*3 inherited members from SystemException not shown*
✳	public.........................	**DATA_CONVERSION** ()
✳	public.........................	**DATA_CONVERSION** (String s)
✳	public.........................	**DATA_CONVERSION** (int minor, CompletionStatus completed)
✳	public.........................	**DATA_CONVERSION** (String s, int minor, CompletionStatus completed)

DatabaseMetaData	java.sql

1.1	*DatabaseMetaData*	
	public.................. boolean	**allProceduresAreCallable** () throws SQLException
	public.................. boolean	**allTablesAreSelectable** () throws SQLException
1.4 ▲	public static final......... short	**attributeNoNulls** = 0
1.4 ▲	public static final......... short	**attributeNullable** = 1
1.4 ▲	public static final......... short	**attributeNullableUnknown** = 2
▲	public static final.......... int	**bestRowNotPseudo** = 1
▲	public static final.......... int	**bestRowPseudo** = 2
▲	public static final.......... int	**bestRowSession** = 2
▲	public static final.......... int	**bestRowTemporary** = 0
▲	public static final.......... int	**bestRowTransaction** = 1
▲	public static final.......... int	**bestRowUnknown** = 0
▲	public static final.......... int	**columnNoNulls** = 0
▲	public static final.......... int	**columnNullable** = 1
▲	public static final.......... int	**columnNullableUnknown** = 2
	public.................. boolean	**dataDefinitionCausesTransactionCommit** () throws SQLException
	public.................. boolean	**dataDefinitionIgnoredInTransactions** () throws SQLException
1.2	public.................. boolean	**deletesAreDetected** (int type) throws SQLException
	public.................. boolean	**doesMaxRowSizeIncludeBlobs** () throws SQLException
1.4	public.................. ResultSet	**getAttributes** (String catalog, String schemaPattern, String typeNamePattern, String attributeNamePattern) throws SQLException
	public.................. ResultSet	**getBestRowIdentifier** (String catalog, String schema, String table, int scope, boolean nullable) throws SQLException
	public.................. ResultSet	**getCatalogs** () throws SQLException
	public.................. String	**getCatalogSeparator** () throws SQLException
	public.................. String	**getCatalogTerm** () throws SQLException
	public.................. ResultSet	**getColumnPrivileges** (String catalog, String schema, String table, String columnNamePattern) throws SQLException
	public.................. ResultSet	**getColumns** (String catalog, String schemaPattern, String tableNamePattern, String columnNamePattern) throws SQLException
1.2	public.................. Connection	**getConnection** () throws SQLException
	public.................. ResultSet	**getCrossReference** (String primaryCatalog, String primarySchema, String primaryTable, String foreignCatalog, String foreignSchema, String foreignTable) throws SQLException
1.4	public.................. int	**getDatabaseMajorVersion** () throws SQLException
1.4	public.................. int	**getDatabaseMinorVersion** () throws SQLException
	public.................. String	**getDatabaseProductName** () throws SQLException
	public.................. String	**getDatabaseProductVersion** () throws SQLException
	public.................. int	**getDefaultTransactionIsolation** () throws SQLException
	public.................. int	**getDriverMajorVersion** ()
	public.................. int	**getDriverMinorVersion** ()
	public.................. String	**getDriverName** () throws SQLException ε241,243
	public.................. String	**getDriverVersion** () throws SQLException
	public.................. ResultSet	**getExportedKeys** (String catalog, String schema, String table) throws SQLException
	public.................. String	**getExtraNameCharacters** () throws SQLException
	public.................. String	**getIdentifierQuoteString** () throws SQLException
	public.................. ResultSet	**getImportedKeys** (String catalog, String schema, String table) throws SQLException
	public.................. ResultSet	**getIndexInfo** (String catalog, String schema, String table, boolean unique, boolean approximate) throws SQLException
1.4	public.................. int	**getJDBCMajorVersion** () throws SQLException
1.4	public.................. int	**getJDBCMinorVersion** () throws SQLException

Class *Interface* —extends - - -implements ○ abstract ● final △ static ▲ static final ✳ constructor x x—inherited x **x**—declared **x x**—overridden
ε*n*—examples of usage ˬ—has subclass package—see other volume

public	int	**getMaxBinaryLiteralLength** () throws SQLException	
public	int	**getMaxCatalogNameLength** () throws SQLException	
public	int	**getMaxCharLiteralLength** () throws SQLException	
public	int	**getMaxColumnNameLength** () throws SQLException	
public	int	**getMaxColumnsInGroupBy** () throws SQLException	
public	int	**getMaxColumnsInIndex** () throws SQLException	
public	int	**getMaxColumnsInOrderBy** () throws SQLException	
public	int	**getMaxColumnsInSelect** () throws SQLException	
public	int	**getMaxColumnsInTable** () throws SQLException	
public	int	**getMaxConnections** () throws SQLException	
public	int	**getMaxCursorNameLength** () throws SQLException	
public	int	**getMaxIndexLength** () throws SQLException	
public	int	**getMaxProcedureNameLength** () throws SQLException	
public	int	**getMaxRowSize** () throws SQLException	
public	int	**getMaxSchemaNameLength** () throws SQLException	
public	int	**getMaxStatementLength** () throws SQLException	
public	int	**getMaxStatements** () throws SQLException	
public	int	**getMaxTableNameLength** () throws SQLException	ε289
public	int	**getMaxTablesInSelect** () throws SQLException	
public	int	**getMaxUserNameLength** () throws SQLException	
public	String	**getNumericFunctions** () throws SQLException	ε286
public	ResultSet	**getPrimaryKeys** (String catalog, String schema, String table) throws SQLException	
public	ResultSet	**getProcedureColumns** (String catalog, String schemaPattern, String procedureNamePattern, String columnNamePattern) throws SQLException	
public	ResultSet	**getProcedures** (String catalog, String schemaPattern, String procedureNamePattern) throws SQLException	ε280
public	String	**getProcedureTerm** () throws SQLException	
1.4 public	int	**getResultSetHoldability** () throws SQLException	
public	ResultSet	**getSchemas** () throws SQLException	
public	String	**getSchemaTerm** () throws SQLException	
public	String	**getSearchStringEscape** () throws SQLException	
public	String	**getSQLKeywords** () throws SQLException	ε284
1.4 public	int	**getSQLStateType** () throws SQLException	
public	String	**getStringFunctions** () throws SQLException	ε285
1.4 public	ResultSet	**getSuperTables** (String catalog, String schemaPattern, String tableNamePattern) throws SQLException	
1.4 public	ResultSet	**getSuperTypes** (String catalog, String schemaPattern, String typeNamePattern) throws SQLException	
public	String	**getSystemFunctions** () throws SQLException	ε287
public	ResultSet	**getTablePrivileges** (String catalog, String schemaPattern, String tableNamePattern) throws SQLException	
public	ResultSet	**getTables** (String catalog, String schemaPattern, String tableNamePattern, String[] types) throws SQLException	ε247
public	ResultSet	**getTableTypes** () throws SQLException	
public	String	**getTimeDateFunctions** () throws SQLException	ε288
public	ResultSet	**getTypeInfo** () throws SQLException	ε290
1.2 public	ResultSet	**getUDTs** (String catalog, String schemaPattern, String typeNamePattern, int[] types) throws SQLException	
public	String	**getURL** () throws SQLException	
public	String	**getUserName** () throws SQLException	
public	ResultSet	**getVersionColumns** (String catalog, String schema, String table) throws SQLException	
▲ public static final	int	**importedKeyCascade** = 0	
▲ public static final	int	**importedKeyInitiallyDeferred** = 5	
▲ public static final	int	**importedKeyInitiallyImmediate** = 6	
▲ public static final	int	**importedKeyNoAction** = 3	
▲ public static final	int	**importedKeyNotDeferrable** = 7	
▲ public static final	int	**importedKeyRestrict** = 1	
▲ public static final	int	**importedKeySetDefault** = 4	
▲ public static final	int	**importedKeySetNull** = 2	
1.2 public	boolean	**insertsAreDetected** (int type) throws SQLException	
public	boolean	**isCatalogAtStart** () throws SQLException	
public	boolean	**isReadOnly** () throws SQLException	
1.4 public	boolean	**locatorsUpdateCopy** () throws SQLException	
public	boolean	**nullPlusNonNullIsNull** () throws SQLException	
public	boolean	**nullsAreSortedAtEnd** () throws SQLException	
public	boolean	**nullsAreSortedAtStart** () throws SQLException	
public	boolean	**nullsAreSortedHigh** () throws SQLException	
public	boolean	**nullsAreSortedLow** () throws SQLException	
1.2 public	boolean	**othersDeletesAreVisible** (int type) throws SQLException	
1.2 public	boolean	**othersInsertsAreVisible** (int type) throws SQLException	
1.2 public	boolean	**othersUpdatesAreVisible** (int type) throws SQLException	
1.2 public	boolean	**ownDeletesAreVisible** (int type) throws SQLException	
1.2 public	boolean	**ownInsertsAreVisible** (int type) throws SQLException	

DatabaseMetaData

1.2	public	boolean	**ownUpdatesAreVisible** (int type) throws SQLException
▲	public static final	int	**procedureColumnIn** = 1
▲	public static final	int	**procedureColumnInOut** = 2
▲	public static final	int	**procedureColumnOut** = 4
▲	public static final	int	**procedureColumnResult** = 3
▲	public static final	int	**procedureColumnReturn** = 5
▲	public static final	int	**procedureColumnUnknown** = 0
▲	public static final	int	**procedureNoNulls** = 0
▲	public static final	int	**procedureNoResult** = 1
▲	public static final	int	**procedureNullable** = 1
▲	public static final	int	**procedureNullableUnknown** = 2
▲	public static final	int	**procedureResultUnknown** = 0
▲	public static final	int	**procedureReturnsResult** = 2
1.4 ▲	public static final	int	**sqlStateSQL99** = 2
1.4 ▲	public static final	int	**sqlStateXOpen** = 1
	public	boolean	**storesLowerCaseIdentifiers** () throws SQLException
	public	boolean	**storesLowerCaseQuotedIdentifiers** () throws SQLException
	public	boolean	**storesMixedCaseIdentifiers** () throws SQLException
	public	boolean	**storesMixedCaseQuotedIdentifiers** () throws SQLException
	public	boolean	**storesUpperCaseIdentifiers** () throws SQLException
	public	boolean	**storesUpperCaseQuotedIdentifiers** () throws SQLException
	public	boolean	**supportsAlterTableWithAddColumn** () throws SQLException
	public	boolean	**supportsAlterTableWithDropColumn** () throws SQLException
	public	boolean	**supportsANSI92EntryLevelSQL** () throws SQLException
	public	boolean	**supportsANSI92FullSQL** () throws SQLException
	public	boolean	**supportsANSI92IntermediateSQL** () throws SQLException
1.2	public	boolean	**supportsBatchUpdates** () throws SQLException　　　ε264
	public	boolean	**supportsCatalogsInDataManipulation** () throws SQLException
	public	boolean	**supportsCatalogsInIndexDefinitions** () throws SQLException
	public	boolean	**supportsCatalogsInPrivilegeDefinitions** () throws SQLException
	public	boolean	**supportsCatalogsInProcedureCalls** () throws SQLException
	public	boolean	**supportsCatalogsInTableDefinitions** () throws SQLException
	public	boolean	**supportsColumnAliasing** () throws SQLException
	public	boolean	**supportsConvert** () throws SQLException
	public	boolean	**supportsConvert** (int fromType, int toType) throws SQLException
	public	boolean	**supportsCoreSQLGrammar** () throws SQLException
	public	boolean	**supportsCorrelatedSubqueries** () throws SQLException
	public	boolean	**supportsDataDefinitionAndDataManipulationTransactions** () throws SQLException
	public	boolean	**supportsDataManipulationTransactionsOnly** () throws SQLException
	public	boolean	**supportsDifferentTableCorrelationNames** () throws SQLException
	public	boolean	**supportsExpressionsInOrderBy** () throws SQLException
	public	boolean	**supportsExtendedSQLGrammar** () throws SQLException
	public	boolean	**supportsFullOuterJoins** () throws SQLException
1.4	public	boolean	**supportsGetGeneratedKeys** () throws SQLException
	public	boolean	**supportsGroupBy** () throws SQLException
	public	boolean	**supportsGroupByBeyondSelect** () throws SQLException
	public	boolean	**supportsGroupByUnrelated** () throws SQLException
	public	boolean	**supportsIntegrityEnhancementFacility** () throws SQLException
	public	boolean	**supportsLikeEscapeClause** () throws SQLException
	public	boolean	**supportsLimitedOuterJoins** () throws SQLException
	public	boolean	**supportsMinimumSQLGrammar** () throws SQLException
	public	boolean	**supportsMixedCaseIdentifiers** () throws SQLException
	public	boolean	**supportsMixedCaseQuotedIdentifiers** () throws SQLException
1.4	public	boolean	**supportsMultipleOpenResults** () throws SQLException
	public	boolean	**supportsMultipleResultSets** () throws SQLException
	public	boolean	**supportsMultipleTransactions** () throws SQLException
1.4	public	boolean	**supportsNamedParameters** () throws SQLException
	public	boolean	**supportsNonNullableColumns** () throws SQLException
	public	boolean	**supportsOpenCursorsAcrossCommit** () throws SQLException
	public	boolean	**supportsOpenCursorsAcrossRollback** () throws SQLException
	public	boolean	**supportsOpenStatementsAcrossCommit** () throws SQLException
	public	boolean	**supportsOpenStatementsAcrossRollback** () throws SQLException
	public	boolean	**supportsOrderByUnrelated** () throws SQLException
	public	boolean	**supportsOuterJoins** () throws SQLException
	public	boolean	**supportsPositionedDelete** () throws SQLException
	public	boolean	**supportsPositionedUpdate** () throws SQLException
1.2	public	boolean	**supportsResultSetConcurrency** (int type, int concurrency) throws SQLException　　ε272
1.4	public	boolean	**supportsResultSetHoldability** (int holdability) throws SQLException
1.2	public	boolean	**supportsResultSetType** (int type) throws SQLException　　　ε266

D

Class *Interface* —extends - - -implements ○ abstract ● final △ static ▲ static final ✳ constructor x x—inherited x **x**—declared **x x**—overridden
ε*n*—examples of usage ⌐—has subclass package—see other volume

1.4	public	boolean	**supportsSavepoints** () throws SQLException	
	public	boolean	**supportsSchemasInDataManipulation** () throws SQLException	
	public	boolean	**supportsSchemasInIndexDefinitions** () throws SQLException	
	public	boolean	**supportsSchemasInPrivilegeDefinitions** () throws SQLException	
	public	boolean	**supportsSchemasInProcedureCalls** () throws SQLException	
	public	boolean	**supportsSchemasInTableDefinitions** () throws SQLException	
	public	boolean	**supportsSelectForUpdate** () throws SQLException	
1.4	public	boolean	**supportsStatementPooling** () throws SQLException	
	public	boolean	**supportsStoredProcedures** () throws SQLException	
	public	boolean	**supportsSubqueriesInComparisons** () throws SQLException	
	public	boolean	**supportsSubqueriesInExists** () throws SQLException	
	public	boolean	**supportsSubqueriesInIns** () throws SQLException	
	public	boolean	**supportsSubqueriesInQuantifieds** () throws SQLException	
	public	boolean	**supportsTableCorrelationNames** () throws SQLException	
	public	boolean	**supportsTransactionIsolationLevel** (int level) throws SQLException	
	public	boolean	**supportsTransactions** () throws SQLException	ε239
	public	boolean	**supportsUnion** () throws SQLException	
	public	boolean	**supportsUnionAll** () throws SQLException	
▲	public static final	short	**tableIndexClustered** = 1	
▲	public static final	short	**tableIndexHashed** = 2	
▲	public static final	short	**tableIndexOther** = 3	
▲	public static final	short	**tableIndexStatistic** = 0	
▲	public static final	int	**typeNoNulls** = 0	
▲	public static final	int	**typeNullable** = 1	
▲	public static final	int	**typeNullableUnknown** = 2	
▲	public static final	int	**typePredBasic** = 2	
▲	public static final	int	**typePredChar** = 1	
▲	public static final	int	**typePredNone** = 0	
▲	public static final	int	**typeSearchable** = 3	
1.2	public	boolean	**updatesAreDetected** (int type) throws SQLException	
	public	boolean	**usesLocalFilePerTable** () throws SQLException	
	public	boolean	**usesLocalFiles** () throws SQLException	
▲	public static final	int	**versionColumnNotPseudo** = 1	
▲	public static final	int	**versionColumnPseudo** = 2	
▲	public static final	int	**versionColumnUnknown** = 0	

DataFormatException | java.util.zip

```
Object                                                                    ε450
 └Throwable ---------------------------- java.io.Serializable
    └Exception
1.1      └DataFormatException
```

| ✳ | public | **DataFormatException** () |
| ✳ | public | **DataFormatException** (String s) |

DatagramChannel | java.nio.channels

```
       Object                                                             ε178,183
1.4 ○  └java.nio.channels.spi ↵ -------------------- Channel, InterruptibleChannel (Channel)
          .AbstractInterruptibleChannel 1
1.4 ○     └SelectableChannel 2
1.4 ○        └java.nio.channels.spi ↵
                .AbstractSelectableChannel 3
1.4 ○           └DatagramChannel ---------------- ByteChannel (ReadableByteChannel 4 (Channel),
                                                  WritableByteChannel 5 (Channel)), ScatteringByteChannel 6
                                                  (ReadableByteChannel 4 (Channel)), GatheringByteChannel 7
                                                  (WritableByteChannel 5 (Channel))
```

● 1	protected final	void	begin ()	
● 3	public final	Object	blockingLock ()	
● 1	public final	void	close () throws java.io.IOException	ε167,170,171,172,174
● 3	public final	SelectableChannel	configureBlocking (boolean block) throws java.io.IOException	ε173,177,179
○	public abstract .... DatagramChannel		**connect** (java.net.SocketAddress remote) throws java.io.IOException	
✳	protected		**DatagramChannel** (java.nio.channels.spi.SelectorProvider provider)	
○	public abstract .... DatagramChannel		**disconnect** () throws java.io.IOException	
● 1	protected final	void	end (boolean completed) throws AsynchronousCloseException	
● 3	protected final	void	implCloseChannel () throws java.io.IOException	
○ 3	protected abstract	void	implCloseSelectableChannel () throws java.io.IOException	

DatagramChannel

○	3	protected abstract ....void	implConfigureBlocking (boolean block) throws java.io.IOException	
●	3	public final .... boolean	isBlocking ()	
○		public abstract .... boolean	**isConnected** ()	
●	1	public final .... boolean	isOpen ()	
●	3	public final .... boolean	isRegistered ()	
●	3	public final ......SelectionKey	keyFor (Selector sel)	
△		public static DatagramChannel	**open** () throws java.io.IOException	
●	3	public final java.nio.channels↩ .spi.SelectorProvider	provider ()	
○	4	public abstract ....int	**read** (java.nio.ByteBuffer dst) throws java.io.IOException	ε180,169,174
●	6	public final .... long	**read** (java.nio.ByteBuffer[] dsts) throws java.io.IOException	
○	6	public abstract .... long	**read** (java.nio.ByteBuffer[] dsts, int offset, int length) throws java.io.IOException	
○		public abstract .... java.net.SocketAddress	**receive** (java.nio.ByteBuffer dst) throws java.io.IOException	
●	2	public final ....SelectionKey	register (Selector sel, int ops) throws ClosedChannelException ε176,179	
●	3	public final ....SelectionKey	register (Selector sel, int ops, Object att) throws ClosedChannelException	
○		public abstract ....int	**send** (java.nio.ByteBuffer src, java.net.SocketAddress target) throws java.io.IOException	
○		public abstract .... java.net.DatagramSocket	**socket** ()	
●	2	public final .... **int**	**validOps** ()	ε176
○	5	public abstract ....int	**write** (java.nio.ByteBuffer src) throws java.io.IOException	ε180,170,171,175
●	7	public final .... long	**write** (java.nio.ByteBuffer[] srcs) throws java.io.IOException	
○	7	public abstract .... long	**write** (java.nio.ByteBuffer[] srcs, int offset, int length) throws java.io.IOException	

DatagramPacket   java.net

Object
└DatagramPacket

●

*		public...........................	**DatagramPacket** (byte[] buf, int length)	ε151,152,154
1.4 *		public...........................	**DatagramPacket** (byte[] buf, int length, SocketAddress address) throws SocketException	
1.2 *		public...........................	**DatagramPacket** (byte[] buf, int offset, int length)	
*		public...........................	**DatagramPacket** (byte[] buf, int length, InetAddress address, int port)	ε151,152
1.4 *		public...........................	**DatagramPacket** (byte[] buf, int offset, int length, SocketAddress address) throws SocketException	
1.2 *		public...........................	**DatagramPacket** (byte[] buf, int offset, int length, InetAddress address, int port)	
		public synchronized ....InetAddress	**getAddress** ()	
		public synchronized ..... byte[]	**getData** ()	
		public synchronized ....int	**getLength** ()	ε152,154
1.2		public synchronized ....int	**getOffset** ()	
		public synchronized ....int	**getPort** ()	
1.4		public synchronized ....SocketAddress	**getSocketAddress** ()	
1.1		public synchronized ....void	**setAddress** (InetAddress iaddr)	
1.1		public synchronized ....void	**setData** (byte[] buf)	
1.2		public synchronized ....void	**setData** (byte[] buf, int offset, int length)	
1.1		public synchronized ....void	**setLength** (int length)	
1.1		public synchronized ....void	**setPort** (int iport)	
1.4		public synchronized ....void	**setSocketAddress** (SocketAddress address)	

DatagramSocket   java.net

Object
└DatagramSocket

1.4		public synchronized ....void	**bind** (SocketAddress addr) throws SocketException	
		public.......................void	**close** ()	
1.4		public.......................void	**connect** (SocketAddress addr) throws SocketException	
1.2		public.......................void	**connect** (InetAddress address, int port)	
*		public...........................	**DatagramSocket** () throws SocketException	ε151,152
*		public...........................	**DatagramSocket** (int port) throws SocketException	
1.4 *		protected......................	**DatagramSocket** (DatagramSocketImpl impl)	
1.4 *		public...........................	**DatagramSocket** (SocketAddress bindaddr) throws SocketException	
1.1 *		public...........................	**DatagramSocket** (int port, InetAddress laddr) throws SocketException	

Class   *Interface*   —extends   - - -implements   ○ abstract   ● final   △ static   ▲ static final   ✳ constructor   x x—inherited   x **x**—declared   **x x**—overridden
ε*n*—examples of usage   ˌ—has subclass   package—see other volume

1.2	public	void	**disconnect** ()
1.4	public synchronized ..	boolean	**getBroadcast** () throws SocketException
1.4	public	java.nio↵	**getChannel** ()
	.channels.DatagramChannel		
1.2	public	InetAddress	**getInetAddress** ()
1.1	public	InetAddress	**getLocalAddress** ()
	public	int	**getLocalPort** ()
1.4	public	SocketAddress	**getLocalSocketAddress** ()
1.2	public	int	**getPort** ()
1.2	public synchronized	int	**getReceiveBufferSize** () throws SocketException
1.4	public	SocketAddress	**getRemoteSocketAddress** ()
1.4	public synchronized ..	boolean	**getReuseAddress** () throws SocketException
1.2	public synchronized	int	**getSendBufferSize** () throws SocketException
1.1	public synchronized	int	**getSoTimeout** () throws SocketException
1.4	public synchronized	int	**getTrafficClass** () throws SocketException
1.4	public	boolean	**isBound** ()
1.4	public	boolean	**isClosed** ()
1.4	public	boolean	**isConnected** ()
	public synchronized	void	**receive** (DatagramPacket p) throws java.io.IOException ε152
	public	void	**send** (DatagramPacket p) throws java.io.IOException ε151
1.4	public synchronized	void	**setBroadcast** (boolean on) throws SocketException
1.3 △	public static synchronized	void	**setDatagramSocketImplFactory** (*DatagramSocketImplFactory* fac)
			throws java.io.IOException
1.2	public synchronized	void	**setReceiveBufferSize** (int size) throws SocketException
1.4	public synchronized	void	**setReuseAddress** (boolean on) throws SocketException
1.2	public synchronized	void	**setSendBufferSize** (int size) throws SocketException
1.1	public synchronized	void	**setSoTimeout** (int timeout) throws SocketException
1.4	public synchronized	void	**setTrafficClass** (int tc) throws SocketException

DatagramSocketImpl   java.net

Object
  └ DatagramSocketImpl - *SocketOptions*   (1.1 ○)

○	protected abstract	void	**bind** (int lport, InetAddress laddr) throws SocketException
○	protected abstract	void	**close** ()
1.4	protected	void	**connect** (InetAddress address, int port) throws SocketException
○	protected abstract	void	**create** () throws SocketException
*	public		**DatagramSocketImpl** ()
1.4	protected	void	**disconnect** ()
	protected java.io.FileDescriptor		**fd**
	protected java.io.FileDescriptor		**getFileDescriptor** ()
	protected	int	**getLocalPort** ()
1.2 ○	protected abstract	int	**getTimeToLive** () throws java.io.IOException
D ○	protected abstract	byte	**getTTL** () throws java.io.IOException
○	protected abstract	void	**join** (InetAddress inetaddr) throws java.io.IOException
1.4 ○	protected abstract	void	**joinGroup** (SocketAddress mcastaddr, NetworkInterface netIf)
			throws java.io.IOException
○	protected abstract	void	**leave** (InetAddress inetaddr) throws java.io.IOException
1.4 ○	protected abstract	void	**leaveGroup** (SocketAddress mcastaddr, NetworkInterface netIf)
			throws java.io.IOException
	protected	int	**localPort**
○	protected abstract	int	**peek** (InetAddress i) throws java.io.IOException
1.4 ○	protected abstract	int	**peekData** (DatagramPacket p) throws java.io.IOException
○	protected abstract	void	**receive** (DatagramPacket p) throws java.io.IOException
○	protected abstract	void	**send** (DatagramPacket p) throws java.io.IOException
1.2 ○	protected abstract	void	**setTimeToLive** (int ttl) throws java.io.IOException
D ○	protected abstract	void	**setTTL** (byte ttl) throws java.io.IOException

DatagramSocketImplFactory   java.net

1.3   *DatagramSocketImplFactory*
- -
    public .... DatagramSocketImpl **createDatagramSocketImpl** ()
- -

DataInput   java.io

  DataInput
- -
    public .... boolean **readBoolean** () throws IOException
    public .... byte **readByte** () throws IOException

D

Classes

DataInput

public	char	**readChar** () throws IOException
public	double	**readDouble** () throws IOException
public	float	**readFloat** () throws IOException
public	void	**readFully** (byte[] b) throws IOException
public	void	**readFully** (byte[] b, int off, int len) throws IOException
public	int	**readInt** () throws IOException
public	String	**readLine** () throws IOException
public	long	**readLong** () throws IOException
public	short	**readShort** () throws IOException
public	int	**readUnsignedByte** () throws IOException
public	int	**readUnsignedShort** () throws IOException
public	String	**readUTF** () throws IOException
public	int	**skipBytes** (int n) throws IOException

ε39

DataInputStream❶   java.io

```
Object                                                    ε252,382,418
O └InputStream
    └FilterInputStream¹
      └DataInputStream ------------------ DataInput ²
```

	1	public	int	available () throws IOException
	1	public	void	close () throws IOException
*		public		**DataInputStream** (InputStream in)
	1	protected	InputStream	in
	1	public synchronized	void	mark (int readlimit)
	1	public	boolean	markSupported ()
	1	public	int	read () throws IOException
●	1	public final	**int read** (byte[] b) throws IOException
●	1	public final	**int read** (byte[] b, int off, int len) throws IOException
●	2	public final	boolean	**readBoolean** () throws IOException
●	2	public final	byte	**readByte** () throws IOException
●	2	public final	char	**readChar** () throws IOException
●	2	public final	double	**readDouble** () throws IOException
●	2	public final	float	**readFloat** () throws IOException
●	2	public final	void	**readFully** (byte[] b) throws IOException
●	2	public final	void	**readFully** (byte[] b, int off, int len) throws IOException
●	2	public final	int	**readInt** () throws IOException
●	2	public final	String	**readLine** () throws IOException
●	2	public final	long	**readLong** () throws IOException
●	2	public final	short	**readShort** () throws IOException
●	2	public final	int	**readUnsignedByte** () throws IOException
●	2	public final	int	**readUnsignedShort** () throws IOException
●	2	public final	String	**readUTF** () throws IOException
▲		public static final	String	**readUTF** (DataInput in) throws IOException
	1	public synchronized	void	reset () throws IOException
	1	public	long	skip (long n) throws IOException
●	2	public final	int	**skipBytes** (int n) throws IOException

ε14,36,45,452,455

ε90,184,256
ε452,455,457,170,451
ε36

ε39

DataInputStream❷   org.omg.CORBA

```
1.3   DataInputStream——————————— org.omg.CORBA.portable.ValueBase ¹
                                   (org.omg.CORBA.portable.IDLEntity (java.io.Serializable))
```

	1	public	String[] **_truncatable_ids** ()
		public	Object **read_Abstract** ()
		public	Any **read_any** ()
		public	void **read_any_array** (AnySeqHolder seq, int offset, int length)
		public	boolean **read_boolean** ()
		public	void **read_boolean_array** (BooleanSeqHolder seq, int offset, int length)
		public	char **read_char** ()
		public	void **read_char_array** (CharSeqHolder seq, int offset, int length)
		public	double **read_double** ()
		public	void **read_double_array** (DoubleSeqHolder seq, int offset, int length)
		public	float **read_float** ()
		public	void **read_float_array** (FloatSeqHolder seq, int offset, int length)
		public	int **read_long** ()
		public	void **read_long_array** (LongSeqHolder seq, int offset, int length)
		public	long **read_longlong** ()

Class   *Interface*   —extends   - - -implements   O abstract   ● final   △ static   ▲ static final   ✳ constructor   x x—inherited   x **x**—declared   **x x**—overridden
εn—examples of usage   ⌐—has subclass   package—see other volume

```
public.......................void  read_longlong_array (LongLongSeqHolder seq, int offset, int length)
public...................Object  read_Object ()
public....................byte  read_octet ()
public.......................void  read_octet_array (OctetSeqHolder seq, int offset, int length)
public...................short  read_short ()
public.......................void  read_short_array (ShortSeqHolder seq, int offset, int length)
public..................String  read_string ()
public...............TypeCode  read_TypeCode ()
public........................int  read_ulong ()
public.......................void  read_ulong_array (ULongSeqHolder seq, int offset, int length)
public.....................long  read_ulonglong ()
public.......................void  read_ulonglong_array (ULongLongSeqHolder seq, int offset, int length)
public...................short  read_ushort ()
public.......................void  read_ushort_array (UShortSeqHolder seq, int offset, int length)
public.......java.io.Serializable  read_Value ()
public....................char  read_wchar ()
public.......................void  read_wchar_array (WCharSeqHolder seq, int offset, int length)
public..................String  read_wstring ()
```

DataOutput | java.io

DataOutput

```
public.......................void  write (byte[] b) throws IOException
public.......................void  write (int b) throws IOException
public.......................void  write (byte[] b, int off, int len) throws IOException
public.......................void  writeBoolean (boolean v) throws IOException
public.......................void  writeByte (int v) throws IOException
public.......................void  writeBytes (String s) throws IOException
public.......................void  writeChar (int v) throws IOException
public.......................void  writeChars (String s) throws IOException                ε39
public.......................void  writeDouble (double v) throws IOException
public.......................void  writeFloat (float v) throws IOException
public.......................void  writeInt (int v) throws IOException
public.......................void  writeLong (long v) throws IOException
public.......................void  writeShort (int v) throws IOException
public.......................void  writeUTF (String str) throws IOException
```

DataOutputStream ❶ | java.io

```
Object                                                            ε183
o  └OutputStream
     └FilterOutputStream 1
        └DataOutputStream ------------------ DataOutput 2
```

```
   1  public.......................void  close () throws IOException              ε451,453,91,211,224
*     public...........................  DataOutputStream (OutputStream out)
   1  public...............void  flush () throws IOException                      ε27,54
   1  protected........OutputStream  out
●     public final ....................int  size ()
   1  public.......................void  write (byte[] b) throws IOException       ε27,91,224
   1  public synchronized ......void  write (int b) throws IOException            ε184
   1  public synchronized ......void  write (byte[] b, int off, int len) throws IOException  ε451,453,54,449,450
● 2  public final ...............void  writeBoolean (boolean v) throws IOException
● 2  public final ...............void  writeByte (int v) throws IOException
● 2  public final ...............void  writeBytes (String s) throws IOException
● 2  public final ...............void  writeChar (int v) throws IOException
● 2  public final ...............void  writeChars (String s) throws IOException   ε39
● 2  public final ...............void  writeDouble (double v) throws IOException
● 2  public final ...............void  writeFloat (float v) throws IOException
● 2  public final ...............void  writeInt (int v) throws IOException
● 2  public final ...............void  writeLong (long v) throws IOException
● 2  public final ...............void  writeShort (int v) throws IOException
● 2  public final ...............void  writeUTF (String str) throws IOException
      protected.......................int  written
```

DataOutputStream❷				org.omg.CORBA

1.3   *DataOutputStream*————————— *org.omg.CORBA.portable.ValueBase* [1]
                                                        (org.omg.CORBA.portable.IDLEntity (java.io.Serializable))

1 public	String[]	**_truncatable_ids** ()
public	void	**write_Abstract** (Object value)
public	void	**write_any** (Any value)
public	void	**write_any_array** (Any[] seq, int offset, int length)
public	void	**write_boolean** (boolean value)
public	void	**write_boolean_array** (boolean[] seq, int offset, int length)
public	void	**write_char** (char value)
public	void	**write_char_array** (char[] seq, int offset, int length)
public	void	**write_double** (double value)
public	void	**write_double_array** (double[] seq, int offset, int length)
public	void	**write_float** (float value)
public	void	**write_float_array** (float[] seq, int offset, int length)
public	void	**write_long** (int value)
public	void	**write_long_array** (int[] seq, int offset, int length)
public	void	**write_longlong** (long value)
public	void	**write_longlong_array** (long[] seq, int offset, int length)
public	void	**write_Object** (*Object* value)
public	void	**write_octet** (byte value)
public	void	**write_octet_array** (byte[] seq, int offset, int length)
public	void	**write_short** (short value)
public	void	**write_short_array** (short[] seq, int offset, int length)
public	void	**write_string** (String value)
public	void	**write_TypeCode** (TypeCode value)
public	void	**write_ulong** (int value)
public	void	**write_ulong_array** (int[] seq, int offset, int length)
public	void	**write_ulonglong** (long value)
public	void	**write_ulonglong_array** (long[] seq, int offset, int length)
public	void	**write_ushort** (short value)
public	void	**write_ushort_array** (short[] seq, int offset, int length)
public	void	**write_Value** (*java.io.Serializable* value)
public	void	**write_wchar** (char value)
public	void	**write_wchar_array** (char[] seq, int offset, int length)
public	void	**write_wstring** (String value)

DataSource				javax.sql

1.4   *DataSource*

public	*java.sql.Connection*	**getConnection** () throws java.sql.SQLException
public	*java.sql.Connection*	**getConnection** (String username, String password) throws java.sql.SQLException
public	int	**getLoginTimeout** () throws java.sql.SQLException
public	java.io.PrintWriter	**getLogWriter** () throws java.sql.SQLException
public	void	**setLoginTimeout** (int seconds) throws java.sql.SQLException
public	void	**setLogWriter** (java.io.PrintWriter out) throws java.sql.SQLException

DataTruncation				java.sql

Object
└Throwable - *java.io.Serializable*
   └Exception
1.1   └SQLException [1]
1.1   └SQLWarning [2]
1.1   └DataTruncation

✳	public		**DataTruncation** (int index, boolean parameter, boolean read, int dataSize, int transferSize)	
	public	int	**getDataSize** ()	
1	public	int	getErrorCode ()	
	public	int	**getIndex** ()	
1	public	SQLException	getNextException ()	
2	public	SQLWarning	getNextWarning ()	ε242
	public	boolean	**getParameter** ()	
	public	boolean	**getRead** ()	
1	public	String	getSQLState ()	

Class   *Interface*   —extends   - - -implements   ○ abstract   ● final   △ static   ▲ static final   ✳ constructor   x x—inherited   x **x**—declared   **x x**—overridden
ε*n*—examples of usage   ⌐has subclass   package—see other volume

		public	int	**getTransferSize** ()	
	1	public synchronized	void	setNextException (SQLException ex)	
	2	public	void	setNextWarning (SQLWarning w)	

Date ❶   java.sql

Object   ε252,374,317,321
└java.util.Date [1] ----------------------- *java.io.Serializable* ˎ, *Cloneable* ˎ, *Comparable*
     └Date

	1	public	boolean	after (java.util.Date when)	
	1	public	boolean	before (java.util.Date when)	
	1	public	Object	clone ()	
1.2	1	public	int	compareTo (Object o)	ε53
1.2	1	public	int	compareTo (java.util.Date anotherDate)	
	✳	public		**Date** (long date)	ε259
D	✳	public		**Date** (int year, int month, int day)	
	1	public	boolean	equals (Object obj)	
D	1	public	**int**	**getHours** ()	
D	1	public	**int**	**getMinutes** ()	
D	1	public	**int**	**getSeconds** ()	
	1	public	long	getTime ()	
	1	public	int	hashCode ()	
D	1	public	**void**	**setHours** (int i)	
D	1	public	**void**	**setMinutes** (int i)	
D	1	public	**void**	**setSeconds** (int i)	
	1	public	**void**	**setTime** (long date)	
	1	public	**String**	**toString** ()	
△		public static	Date	**valueOf** (String s)	

Date ❷   java.util

Object [1]   ε374,317,321
└Date ˎ ----------------------------- *java.io.Serializable* ˎ, *Cloneable* ˎ, *Comparable* [2]

		public	boolean	**after** (Date when)	
		public	boolean	**before** (Date when)	
	1	public	**Object**	**clone** ()	
1.2	2	public	int	**compareTo** (Object o)	ε53
1.2		public	int	**compareTo** (Date anotherDate)	
	✳	public		**Date** ()	ε371,400,275,276,316
D	✳	public		**Date** (String s)	
	✳	public		**Date** (long date)	ε367,325
D	✳	public		**Date** (int year, int month, int date)	
D	✳	public		**Date** (int year, int month, int date, int hrs, int min)	
D	✳	public		**Date** (int year, int month, int date, int hrs, int min, int sec)	
	1	public	**boolean**	**equals** (Object obj)	
D		public	int	**getDate** ()	
D		public	int	**getDay** ()	
D		public	int	**getHours** ()	
D		public	int	**getMinutes** ()	
D		public	int	**getMonth** ()	
D		public	int	**getSeconds** ()	
		public	long	**getTime** ()	
D		public	int	**getTimezoneOffset** ()	
D		public	int	**getYear** ()	
	1	public	**int**	**hashCode** ()	
D	△	public static	long	**parse** (String s)	
D		public	void	**setDate** (int date)	
D		public	void	**setHours** (int hours)	
D		public	void	**setMinutes** (int minutes)	
D		public	void	**setMonth** (int month)	
D		public	void	**setSeconds** (int seconds)	
		public	void	**setTime** (long time)	
D		public	void	**setYear** (int year)	
D		public	String	**toGMTString** ()	
D		public	String	**toLocaleString** ()	
	1	public	**String**	**toString** ()	
D	△	public static	long	**UTC** (int year, int month, int date, int hrs, int min, int sec)	

DateFormat

DateFormat	java.text

Object[1]
1.1 ○ └Format[2] - *java.io.Serializable* ⌐, *Cloneable* ⌐
1.1 ○   └DateFormat ⌐

▲		public static final ....int	**AM_PM_FIELD** = 14	
		protected .... java.util.Calendar	**calendar**	
	2	public....................**Object**	**clone** ()	
▲		public static final ....int	**DATE_FIELD** = 3	
✳		protected	**DateFormat** ()	
▲		public static final ....int	**DAY_OF_WEEK_FIELD** = 9	
▲		public static final ....int	**DAY_OF_WEEK_IN_MONTH_FIELD** = 11	
▲		public static final ....int	**DAY_OF_YEAR_FIELD** = 10	
▲		public static final ....int	**DEFAULT** = 2	ε318,322
	1	public..................**boolean**	**equals** (Object obj)	
▲		public static final ....int	**ERA_FIELD** = 0	
●	2	public final ....String	format (Object obj)	ε316,320
●		public final ....String	**format** (java.util.Date date)	ε318,319,322,323
●	2	public final ......**StringBuffer**	**format** (Object obj, StringBuffer toAppendTo, FieldPosition fieldPosition)	
○		public abstract .... StringBuffer	**format** (java.util.Date date, StringBuffer toAppendTo, FieldPosition fieldPosition)	
1.4	2	public..........................	formatToCharacterIterator (Object obj)	
		.. *AttributedCharacterIterator*		
▲		public static final ....int	**FULL** = 0	ε318,322
△		public static .. java.util.Locale[]	**getAvailableLocales** ()	
		public........ java.util.Calendar	**getCalendar** ()	
▲		public static final .. DateFormat	**getDateInstance** ()	
▲		public static final .. DateFormat	**getDateInstance** (int style)	ε322
▲		public static final .. DateFormat	**getDateInstance** (int style, java.util.Locale aLocale)	ε323
▲		public static final .. DateFormat	**getDateTimeInstance** ()	
▲		public static final .. DateFormat	**getDateTimeInstance** (int dateStyle, int timeStyle)	
▲		public static final .. DateFormat	**getDateTimeInstance** (int dateStyle, int timeStyle, java.util.Locale aLocale)	
▲		public static final .. DateFormat	**getInstance** ()	
		public..........NumberFormat	**getNumberFormat** ()	
▲		public static final .. DateFormat	**getTimeInstance** ()	
▲		public static final .. DateFormat	**getTimeInstance** (int style)	
▲		public static final .. DateFormat	**getTimeInstance** (int style, java.util.Locale aLocale)	ε318,319
		public....... java.util.TimeZone	**getTimeZone** ()	
	1	public........................**int**	**hashCode** ()	
▲		public static final ....int	**HOUR0_FIELD** = 16	
▲		public static final ....int	**HOUR1_FIELD** = 15	
▲		public static final ....int	**HOUR_OF_DAY0_FIELD** = 5	
▲		public static final ....int	**HOUR_OF_DAY1_FIELD** = 4	
		public.................. boolean	**isLenient** ()	
▲		public static final ....int	**LONG** = 1	ε318,322
▲		public static final ....int	**MEDIUM** = 2	ε318,319,322,323
▲		public static final ....int	**MILLISECOND_FIELD** = 8	
▲		public static final ....int	**MINUTE_FIELD** = 6	
▲		public static final ....int	**MONTH_FIELD** = 2	
		protected ....NumberFormat	**numberFormat**	
		public............. java.util.Date	**parse** (String source) throws ParseException	ε317,318,319,321,322
○		public abstract ... java.util.Date	**parse** (String source, ParsePosition pos)	
	2	public....................Object	parseObject (String source) throws ParseException	
	2	public....................**Object**	**parseObject** (String source, ParsePosition pos)	
▲		public static final ....int	**SECOND_FIELD** = 7	
		public.....................void	**setCalendar** (java.util.Calendar newCalendar)	
		public.....................void	**setLenient** (boolean lenient)	
		public.....................void	**setNumberFormat** (NumberFormat newNumberFormat)	
		public.....................void	**setTimeZone** (java.util.TimeZone zone)	
▲		public static final ....int	**SHORT** = 3	ε318,322
▲		public static final ....int	**TIMEZONE_FIELD** = 17	
▲		public static final ....int	**WEEK_OF_MONTH_FIELD** = 13	
▲		public static final ....int	**WEEK_OF_YEAR_FIELD** = 12	
▲		public static final ....int	**YEAR_FIELD** = 1	

Class *Interface* —extends - - -implements ○ abstract ● final △ static ▲ static final ✳ constructor x x—inherited x **x**—declared **x x**—overridden
ε*n*—examples of usage ⌐—has subclass package—see other volume

532

Object
1.2 └AttributedCharacterIterator.Attribute [1] - - - - - - *java.io.Serializable*ˬ
1.4   └Format.Field
1.4   └DateFormat.Field

D

▲	public static final		**AM_PM**
	.... DateFormat.Field		
▲	public static final		**DAY_OF_MONTH**
	.... DateFormat.Field		
▲	public static final		**DAY_OF_WEEK**
	.... DateFormat.Field		
▲	public static final		**DAY_OF_WEEK_IN_MONTH**
	.... DateFormat.Field		
▲	public static final		**DAY_OF_YEAR**
	.... DateFormat.Field		
● 1	public final .... boolean		equals (Object obj)
▲	public static final		**ERA**
	.... DateFormat.Field		
✳	protected		**DateFormat.Field** (String name, int calendarField)
	public.......................int		**getCalendarField** ()
1	protected ....String		getName ()
● 1	public final ....int		hashCode ()
▲	public static final		**HOUR0**
	.... DateFormat.Field		
▲	public static final		**HOUR1**
	.... DateFormat.Field		
▲	public static final		**HOUR_OF_DAY0**
	.... DateFormat.Field		
▲	public static final		**HOUR_OF_DAY1**
	.... DateFormat.Field		
▲	public static final		**MILLISECOND**
	.... DateFormat.Field		
▲	public static final		**MINUTE**
	.... DateFormat.Field		
▲	public static final		**MONTH**
	.... DateFormat.Field		
△	public static . DateFormat.Field		**ofCalendarField** (int calendarField)
1	protected ....**Object**		**readResolve** () throws java.io.InvalidObjectException
▲	public static final		**SECOND**
	.... DateFormat.Field		
▲	public static final		**TIME_ZONE**
	.... DateFormat.Field		
1	public....................String		toString ()
▲	public static final		**WEEK_OF_MONTH**
	.... DateFormat.Field		
▲	public static final		**WEEK_OF_YEAR**
	.... DateFormat.Field		
▲	public static final		**YEAR**
	.... DateFormat.Field		

Object [1]
1.1 └DateFormatSymbols - *java.io.Serializable*ˬ, *Cloneable*ˬ

1	public..................**Object**	**clone** ()
✳	public.....................	**DateFormatSymbols** ()
✳	public.....................	**DateFormatSymbols** (java.util.Locale locale)
1	public..................**boolean**	**equals** (Object obj)
	public.................. String[]	**getAmPmStrings** ()
	public.................. String[]	**getEras** ()
	public..................String	**getLocalPatternChars** ()
	public.................. String[]	**getMonths** ()
	public.................. String[]	**getShortMonths** ()
	public.................. String[]	**getShortWeekdays** ()
	public.................. String[]	**getWeekdays** ()
	public.................. String[][]	**getZoneStrings** ()
1	public...................... **int**	**hashCode** ()
	public......................void	**setAmPmStrings** (String[] newAmpms)
	public......................void	**setEras** (String[] newEras)

DateFormatSymbols

```
public.....................void  setLocalPatternChars (String newLocalPatternChars)
public.....................void  setMonths (String[] newMonths)
public.....................void  setShortMonths (String[] newShortMonths)
public.....................void  setShortWeekdays (String[] newShortWeekdays)
public.....................void  setWeekdays (String[] newWeekdays)
public.....................void  setZoneStrings (String[][] newZoneStrings)
```

DecimalFormat	java.text

```
        Object
1.1 ○   └Format 1 ---------------------------- java.io.Serializable ॖ , Cloneable ॖ
1.1 ○     └NumberFormat 2
1.1         └DecimalFormat

     2  26 inherited members from NumberFormat not shown
        public.....................void  applyLocalizedPattern (String pattern)
        public.....................void  applyPattern (String pattern)
     2  public.................Object  clone ()
 *      public......................  DecimalFormat ()
 *      public......................  DecimalFormat (String pattern)                      ε311,313
 *      public......................  DecimalFormat (String pattern, DecimalFormatSymbols symbols)
     2  public.............boolean  equals (Object obj)
 ● 1  public final .............String  format (Object obj)                                ε316,320
     2  public...........StringBuffer  format (double number, StringBuffer result, FieldPosition fieldPosition)
     2  public...........StringBuffer  format (long number, StringBuffer result, FieldPosition fieldPosition)
1.4 1  public......................  formatToCharacterIterator (Object obj)
        AttributedCharacterIterator
1.4 2  public......java.util.Currency  getCurrency ()
        public. DecimalFormatSymbols  getDecimalFormatSymbols ()
        public.....................int  getGroupingSize ()
        public.....................int  getMultiplier ()
        public.................String  getNegativePrefix ()
        public.................String  getNegativeSuffix ()
        public.................String  getPositivePrefix ()
        public.................String  getPositiveSuffix ()
     2  public.....................int  hashCode ()
        public................boolean  isDecimalSeparatorAlwaysShown ()
     2  public.............Number  parse (String text, ParsePosition pos)
     1  public.................Object  parseObject (String source) throws ParseException
1.4 2  public...................void  setCurrency (java.util.Currency currency)
        public.....................void  setDecimalFormatSymbols (DecimalFormatSymbols newSymbols)
        public.....................void  setDecimalSeparatorAlwaysShown (boolean newValue)
        public.....................void  setGroupingSize (int newValue)
     2  public...................void  setMaximumFractionDigits (int newValue)
     2  public...................void  setMaximumIntegerDigits (int newValue)
     2  public...................void  setMinimumFractionDigits (int newValue)
     2  public...................void  setMinimumIntegerDigits (int newValue)
        public.....................void  setMultiplier (int newValue)
        public.....................void  setNegativePrefix (String newValue)
        public.....................void  setNegativeSuffix (String newValue)
        public.....................void  setPositivePrefix (String newValue)
        public.....................void  setPositiveSuffix (String newValue)
        public.................String  toLocalizedPattern ()
        public.................String  toPattern ()
```

DecimalFormatSymbols	java.text

```
        Object 1
1.1 ●   └DecimalFormatSymbols ----------------- Cloneable ॖ , java.io.Serializable ॖ

     1  public................Object  clone ()
 *      public......................  DecimalFormatSymbols ()
 *      public......................  DecimalFormatSymbols (java.util.Locale locale)
     1  public.............boolean  equals (Object obj)
1.4    public.......java.util.Currency  getCurrency ()
1.2    public.................String  getCurrencySymbol ()
        public....................char  getDecimalSeparator ()
        public....................char  getDigit ()
        public....................char  getGroupingSeparator ()
```

Class *Interface* —extends - - -implements ○ abstract ● final △ static ▲ static final ✳ constructor x x—inherited x **x**—declared **x x**—overridden
ε*n*—examples of usage ॖ—has subclass package—see other volume

	public	String	**getInfinity** ()
1.2	public	String	**getInternationalCurrencySymbol** ()
	public	char	**getMinusSign** ()
1.2	public	char	**getMonetaryDecimalSeparator** ()
	public	String	**getNaN** ()
	public	char	**getPatternSeparator** ()
	public	char	**getPercent** ()
	public	char	**getPerMill** ()
	public	char	**getZeroDigit** ()
1	public	int	**hashCode** ()
1.4	public	void	**setCurrency** (java.util.Currency currency)
1.2	public	void	**setCurrencySymbol** (String currency)
	public	void	**setDecimalSeparator** (char decimalSeparator)
	public	void	**setDigit** (char digit)
	public	void	**setGroupingSeparator** (char groupingSeparator)
	public	void	**setInfinity** (String infinity)
1.2	public	void	**setInternationalCurrencySymbol** (String currencyCode)
	public	void	**setMinusSign** (char minusSign)
1.2	public	void	**setMonetaryDecimalSeparator** (char sep)
	public	void	**setNaN** (String NaN)
	public	void	**setPatternSeparator** (char patternSeparator)
	public	void	**setPercent** (char percent)
	public	void	**setPerMill** (char perMill)
	public	void	**setZeroDigit** (char zeroDigit)

D

DeclHandler   org.xml.sax.ext

1.4	*DeclHandler*

	public	void	**attributeDecl** (String eName, String aName, String type, String valueDefault, String value) throws org.xml.sax.SAXException
	public	void	**elementDecl** (String name, String model) throws org.xml.sax.SAXException
	public	void	**externalEntityDecl** (String name, String publicId, String systemId) throws org.xml.sax.SAXException
	public	void	**internalEntityDecl** (String name, String value) throws org.xml.sax.SAXException

---

DefaultHandler   org.xml.sax.helpers

	Object	ε517,523
1.4	└ DefaultHandler - *org.xml.sax.EntityResolver* [1], *org.xml.sax.DTDHandler* [2], *org.xml.sax.ContentHandler* [3], *org.xml.sax.ErrorHandler* [4]

3	public	void	**characters** (char[] ch, int start, int length) throws org.xml.sax.SAXException
*	public		**DefaultHandler** ()
3	public	void	**endDocument** () throws org.xml.sax.SAXException
3	public	void	**endElement** (String uri, String localName, String qName) throws org.xml.sax.SAXException
3	public	void	**endPrefixMapping** (String prefix) throws org.xml.sax.SAXException
4	public	void	**error** (org.xml.sax.SAXParseException e) throws org.xml.sax.SAXException
			ε513
4	public	void	**fatalError** (org.xml.sax.SAXParseException e) throws org.xml.sax.SAXException
			ε513
3	public	void	**ignorableWhitespace** (char[] ch, int start, int length) throws org.xml.sax.SAXException
2	public	void	**notationDecl** (String name, String publicId, String systemId) throws org.xml.sax.SAXException
3	public	void	**processingInstruction** (String target, String data) throws org.xml.sax.SAXException
1	public org.xml.sax.InputSource		**resolveEntity** (String publicId, String systemId) throws org.xml.sax.SAXException
			ε548
3	public	void	**setDocumentLocator** (*org.xml.sax.Locator* locator) ε550
3	public	void	**skippedEntity** (String name) throws org.xml.sax.SAXException
3	public	void	**startDocument** () throws org.xml.sax.SAXException
3	public	void	**startElement** (String uri, String localName, String qName, *org.xml.sax.Attributes* attributes) throws org.xml.sax.SAXException ε549,550
3	public	void	**startPrefixMapping** (String prefix, String uri) throws org.xml.sax.SAXException
2	public	void	**unparsedEntityDecl** (String name, String publicId, String systemId, String notationName) throws org.xml.sax.SAXException
4	public	void	**warning** (org.xml.sax.SAXParseException e) throws org.xml.sax.SAXException
			ε513

Classes

DefaultPersistenceDelegate

DefaultPersistenceDelegate	java.beans

```
              Object
1.4 ○         └PersistenceDelegate 1
1.4               └DefaultPersistenceDelegate
```

✳	public.........................	**DefaultPersistenceDelegate** ()
✳	public.........................	**DefaultPersistenceDelegate** (String[] constructorPropertyNames)
		ε10
1	protected................. **void**	**initialize** (Class type, Object oldInstance, Object newInstance, Encoder out)
1	protected.......... **Expression**	**instantiate** (Object oldInstance, Encoder out)
1	protected.............. **boolean**	**mutatesTo** (Object oldInstance, Object newInstance)
1	public......................void	writeObject (Object oldInstance, Encoder out)

D

DefinitionKind	org.omg.CORBA

```
              Object
1.2           └DefinitionKind ------------------------- org.omg.CORBA.portable.IDLEntity ⌐ (java.io.Serializable)
```

1.4 ▲	public static final ....int	**_dk_AbstractInterface** = 24
▲	public static final ....int	**_dk_Alias** = 9
▲	public static final ....int	**_dk_all** = 1
▲	public static final ....int	**_dk_Array** = 16
▲	public static final ....int	**_dk_Attribute** = 2
▲	public static final ....int	**_dk_Constant** = 3
▲	public static final ....int	**_dk_Enum** = 12
▲	public static final ....int	**_dk_Exception** = 4
▲	public static final ....int	**_dk_Fixed** = 19
▲	public static final ....int	**_dk_Interface** = 5
▲	public static final ....int	**_dk_Module** = 6
▲	public static final ....int	**_dk_Native** = 23
▲	public static final ....int	**_dk_none** = 0
▲	public static final ....int	**_dk_Operation** = 7
▲	public static final ....int	**_dk_Primitive** = 13
▲	public static final ....int	**_dk_Repository** = 17
▲	public static final ....int	**_dk_Sequence** = 15
▲	public static final ....int	**_dk_String** = 14
▲	public static final ....int	**_dk_Struct** = 10
▲	public static final ....int	**_dk_Typedef** = 8
▲	public static final ....int	**_dk_Union** = 11
▲	public static final ....int	**_dk_Value** = 20
▲	public static final ....int	**_dk_ValueBox** = 21
▲	public static final ....int	**_dk_ValueMember** = 22
▲	public static final ....int	**_dk_Wstring** = 18
✳	protected.....................	**DefinitionKind** (int _value)
1.4 ▲	public static final DefinitionKind	**dk_AbstractInterface**
▲	public static final DefinitionKind	**dk_Alias**
▲	public static final DefinitionKind	**dk_all**
▲	public static final DefinitionKind	**dk_Array**
▲	public static final DefinitionKind	**dk_Attribute**
▲	public static final DefinitionKind	**dk_Constant**
▲	public static final DefinitionKind	**dk_Enum**
▲	public static final DefinitionKind	**dk_Exception**
▲	public static final DefinitionKind	**dk_Fixed**
▲	public static final DefinitionKind	**dk_Interface**
▲	public static final DefinitionKind	**dk_Module**
▲	public static final DefinitionKind	**dk_Native**
▲	public static final DefinitionKind	**dk_none**
▲	public static final DefinitionKind	**dk_Operation**
▲	public static final DefinitionKind	**dk_Primitive**
▲	public static final DefinitionKind	**dk_Repository**
▲	public static final DefinitionKind	**dk_Sequence**
▲	public static final DefinitionKind	**dk_String**
▲	public static final DefinitionKind	**dk_Struct**
▲	public static final DefinitionKind	**dk_Typedef**
▲	public static final DefinitionKind	**dk_Union**
▲	public static final DefinitionKind	**dk_Value**
▲	public static final DefinitionKind	**dk_ValueBox**
▲	public static final DefinitionKind	**dk_ValueMember**
▲	public static final DefinitionKind	**dk_Wstring**

Class *Interface* —extends - - -implements ○ abstract ● final △ static ▲ static final ✳ constructor x x—inherited x **x**—declared **x x**—overridden
ε*n*—examples of usage ⌐—has subclass package—see other volume

△	public static ..... DefinitionKind	**from_int** (int i)
	public........................int	**value** ()

DefinitionKindHelper　　　　　　　　　　　　　　　org.omg.CORBA

```
      Object
1.3 ○  └DefinitionKindHelper
```

✳	public...........................	**DefinitionKindHelper** ()
△	public static ..... DefinitionKind	**extract** (Any a)
△	public static ....String	**id** ()
△	public static ....void	**insert** (Any a, DefinitionKind that)
△	public static ..... DefinitionKind	**read** (org.omg.CORBA.portable.InputStream istream)
△	public static synchronized .... TypeCode	**type** ()
△	public static ....void	**write** (org.omg.CORBA.portable.OutputStream ostream, DefinitionKind value)

Deflater　　　　　　　　　　　　　　　　　　　　　　java.util.zip

```
      Object 1
1.1    └Deflater
```

▲	public static final ....int	**BEST_COMPRESSION** = 9	ε449
▲	public static final ....int	**BEST_SPEED** = 1	
▲	public static final ....int	**DEFAULT_COMPRESSION** = -1	
▲	public static final ....int	**DEFAULT_STRATEGY** = 0	
	public........................int	**deflate** (byte[] b)	ε449
	public synchronized ....int	**deflate** (byte[] b, int off, int len)	
▲	public static final ....int	**DEFLATED** = 8	
✳	public...........................	**Deflater** ()	ε449
✳	public...........................	**Deflater** (int level)	
✳	public...........................	**Deflater** (int level, boolean nowrap)	
	public synchronized ....void	**end** ()	
▲	public static final ....int	**FILTERED** = 1	
1	protected .... void	**finalize** ()	
	public synchronized ......void	**finish** ()	ε449
	public synchronized .. boolean	**finished** ()	ε449,450
	public synchronized ....int	**getAdler** ()	
	public synchronized ....int	**getTotalIn** ()	
	public synchronized ....int	**getTotalOut** ()	
▲	public static final ....int	**HUFFMAN_ONLY** = 2	
	public................. boolean	**needsInput** ()	
▲	public static final ....int	**NO_COMPRESSION** = 0	
	public synchronized ......void	**reset** ()	
	public........................void	**setDictionary** (byte[] b)	
	public synchronized ......void	**setDictionary** (byte[] b, int off, int len)	
	public........................void	**setInput** (byte[] b)	ε449,450
	public synchronized ......void	**setInput** (byte[] b, int off, int len)	
	public synchronized ......void	**setLevel** (int level)	ε449
	public synchronized ......void	**setStrategy** (int strategy)	

DeflaterOutputStream　　　　　　　　　　　　　　　　java.util.zip

```
      Object                                                    ε183
 ○    └java.io.OutputStream
        └java.io.FilterOutputStream 1
1.1        └DeflaterOutputStream ⌄
```

	protected ....byte[]	**buf**	
1	public..................... **void**	**close** () throws java.io.IOException	ε451,453,91,211,224
	protected ....Deflater	**def**	
	protected ....void	**deflate** () throws java.io.IOException	
✳	public...........................	**DeflaterOutputStream** (java.io.OutputStream out)	
✳	public...........................	**DeflaterOutputStream** (java.io.OutputStream out, Deflater def)	
✳	public...........................	**DeflaterOutputStream** (java.io.OutputStream out, Deflater def, int size)	
	public........................void	**finish** () throws java.io.IOException	ε451
1	public........................void	flush () throws java.io.IOException	ε27,54
1	protected java.io.OutputStream	out	
1	public........................void	write (byte[] b) throws java.io.IOException	ε27,91,224
1	public..................... **void**	write (int b) throws java.io.IOException	ε184

DeflaterOutputStream

▨	1	public.....................	**void** **write** (byte[] b, int off, int len) throws java.io.IOException		ε451,453,54,449,450

Delegate❶   org.omg.CORBA.portable

Object
1.2 ○ └Delegate˅

○	public abstract ....org.omg.CORBA.Request	**create_request** (*org.omg.CORBA.Object* obj, org.omg.CORBA.Context ctx, String operation, org.omg.CORBA.NVList arg_list, org.omg.CORBA.NamedValue result)
○	public abstract ....org.omg.CORBA.Request	**create_request** (*org.omg.CORBA.Object* obj, org.omg.CORBA.Context ctx, String operation, org.omg.CORBA.NVList arg_list, org.omg.CORBA.NamedValue result, org.omg.CORBA.ExceptionList exclist, org.omg.CORBA.ContextList ctxlist)
✳	public..........................	**Delegate** ()
○	public abstract .... *org.omg.CORBA.Object*	**duplicate** (*org.omg.CORBA.Object* obj)
	public .... boolean	**equals** (*org.omg.CORBA.Object* self, Object obj)
	public............... *org.omg↩* .*CORBA.DomainManager[]*	**get_domain_managers** (*org.omg.CORBA.Object* self)
○	public abstract .... *org.omg.CORBA.Object*	**get_interface_def** (*org.omg.CORBA.Object* self)
	public. *org.omg.CORBA.Policy*	**get_policy** (*org.omg.CORBA.Object* self, int policy_type)
○	public abstract ....int	**hash** (*org.omg.CORBA.Object* obj, int max)
	public.......................int	**hashCode** (*org.omg.CORBA.Object* self)
	public............. InputStream	**invoke** (*org.omg.CORBA.Object* self, OutputStream output) throws ApplicationException, RemarshalException
○	public abstract .... boolean	**is_a** (*org.omg.CORBA.Object* obj, String repository_id)
○	public abstract .... boolean	**is_equivalent** (*org.omg.CORBA.Object* obj, *org.omg.CORBA.Object* other)
	public.................. boolean	**is_local** (*org.omg.CORBA.Object* self)
○	public abstract .... boolean	**non_existent** (*org.omg.CORBA.Object* obj)
	public...org.omg.CORBA.ORB	**orb** (*org.omg.CORBA.Object* obj)
○	public abstract ....void	**release** (*org.omg.CORBA.Object* obj)
	public......................void	**releaseReply** (*org.omg.CORBA.Object* self, InputStream input)
○	public abstract ....org.omg.CORBA.Request	**request** (*org.omg.CORBA.Object* obj, String operation)
	public........... OutputStream	**request** (*org.omg.CORBA.Object* self, String operation, boolean responseExpected)
	public......................void	**servant_postinvoke** (*org.omg.CORBA.Object* self, ServantObject servant)
	public............. ServantObject	**servant_preinvoke** (*org.omg.CORBA.Object* self, String operation, Class expectedType)
	public *org.omg.CORBA.Object*	**set_policy_override** (*org.omg.CORBA.Object* self, *org.omg.CORBA.Policy[]* policies, org.omg.CORBA.SetOverrideType set_add)
	public.................... String	**toString** (*org.omg.CORBA.Object* self)

Delegate❷   org.omg.CORBA_2_3.portable

Object
1.2 ○ └org.omg.CORBA.portable.Delegate [1]
1.3 ○   └Delegate

	1	*23 inherited members from org.omg.CORBA.portable.Delegate not shown*
✳	public........................	**Delegate** ()
	public.................... String	**get_codebase** (*org.omg.CORBA.Object* self)

Delegate❸   org.omg.PortableServer.portable

1.4 *Delegate*
- -

public........................*org↩* .*omg.PortableServer.POA*	**default_POA** (org.omg.PortableServer.Servant Self)
public *org.omg.CORBA.Object*	**get_interface_def** (org.omg.PortableServer.Servant self)
public.................. boolean	**is_a** (org.omg.PortableServer.Servant Self, String Repository_Id)
public.................. boolean	**non_existent** (org.omg.PortableServer.Servant Self)
public.......................byte[]	**object_id** (org.omg.PortableServer.Servant Self)
public...org.omg.CORBA.ORB	**orb** (org.omg.PortableServer.Servant Self)
public.....................*org↩* .*omg.PortableServer.POA*	**poa** (org.omg.PortableServer.Servant Self)
public *org.omg.CORBA.Object*	**this_object** (org.omg.PortableServer.Servant Self)

- -

Class *Interface* —extends - - -implements ○ abstract ● final △ static ▲ static final ✳ constructor x x—inherited x **x**—declared **x x**—overridden
ε*n*—examples of usage ˅—has subclass package—see other volume

DelegationPermission — javax.security.auth.kerberos

```
Object
 └java.security.Permission¹ - - - - - - - - - - - - - - - java.security.Guard, java.io.Serializable
    └java.security.BasicPermission²
       └DelegationPermission
```
ε217,218

1.2 O			
1.2 O			
1.4 ●			

	1	public	void	checkGuard (Object object) throws SecurityException
*		public		**DelegationPermission** (String principals)
*		public		**DelegationPermission** (String principals, String actions)
	2	public	boolean	**equals** (Object obj)
	2	public	String	getActions ()
●	1	public final	String	getName ()
	2	public	int	**hashCode** ()
	2	public	boolean	**implies** (java.security.Permission p)
	2	public	java.security ↵ .PermissionCollection	**newPermissionCollection** ()
	1	public	String	toString ()

ε215, ε215, ε215, ε214,215

DESedeKeySpec — javax.crypto.spec

```
Object
 └DESedeKeySpec - - - - - - - - - - - - - - - - java.security.spec.KeySpec
```
1.4

▲	public static final	int	**DES_EDE_KEY_LEN** = 24
*	public		**DESedeKeySpec** (byte[] key) throws java.security.InvalidKeyException
*	public		**DESedeKeySpec** (byte[] key, int offset) throws java.security.InvalidKeyException
	public	byte[]	**getKey** ()
△	public static	boolean	**isParityAdjusted** (byte[] key, int offset) throws java.security.InvalidKeyException

DesignMode — java.beans

DesignMode
1.2

	public	boolean	**isDesignTime** ()
▲	public static final	String	**PROPERTYNAME** = "designTime"
	public	void	**setDesignTime** (boolean designTime)

DESKeySpec — javax.crypto.spec

```
Object
 └DESKeySpec - - - - - - - - - - - - - - - - java.security.spec.KeySpec
```
1.4

▲	public static final	int	**DES_KEY_LEN** = 8
*	public		**DESKeySpec** (byte[] key) throws java.security.InvalidKeyException
*	public		**DESKeySpec** (byte[] key, int offset) throws java.security.InvalidKeyException
	public	byte[]	**getKey** ()
△	public static	boolean	**isParityAdjusted** (byte[] key, int offset) throws java.security.InvalidKeyException
△	public static	boolean	**isWeak** (byte[] key, int offset) throws java.security.InvalidKeyException

ε465

Destroyable — javax.security.auth

Destroyable
1.4

	public	void	**destroy** () throws DestroyFailedException
	public	boolean	**isDestroyed** ()

DestroyFailedException — javax.security.auth

```
Object
 └Throwable - - - - - - - - - - - - - - - - java.io.Serializable
    └Exception
       └DestroyFailedException
```
1.4

*	public		**DestroyFailedException** ()
*	public		**DestroyFailedException** (String msg)

DGC | java.rmi.dgc

1.1	*DGC*────────────────────────────*java.rmi.Remote*	

public.........................void **clean** (java.rmi.server.ObjID[] ids, long sequenceNum, VMID vmid, boolean strong)
　　　　　　　　　　　　　　　　　　throws java.rmi.RemoteException
public....................Lease **dirty** (java.rmi.server.ObjID[] ids, long sequenceNum, Lease lease)
　　　　　　　　　　　　　　　　　　throws java.rmi.RemoteException

DHGenParameterSpec | javax.crypto.spec

Object
　└DHGenParameterSpec - - - - - - - - - - - - - - - - - *java.security.spec.AlgorithmParameterSpec*
1.4

*	public........................ **DHGenParameterSpec** (int primeSize, int exponentSize)	
	public........................int **getExponentSize** ()	
	public........................int **getPrimeSize** ()	

DHKey | javax.crypto.interfaces

1.4	*DHKey*	

public...........javax.crypto↩ **getParams** ()
　　　　　.spec.DHParameterSpec

DHParameterSpec | javax.crypto.spec

Object
　└DHParameterSpec - *java.security.spec.AlgorithmParameterSpec*
1.4

*	public........................ **DHParameterSpec** (java.math.BigInteger p, java.math.BigInteger g)	
*	public........................ **DHParameterSpec** (java.math.BigInteger p, java.math.BigInteger g, int l)	
		ε471
	public.... java.math.BigInteger **getG** ()	ε470
	public........................int **getL** ()	ε470
	public.... java.math.BigInteger **getP** ()	ε470

DHPrivateKey | javax.crypto.interfaces

1.4	*DHPrivateKey*────────────────────────*DHKey* ‿[1], *java.security.PrivateKey* ‿	ε198,201,210,459,462
	(*java.security.Key* [2] (*java.io.Serializable*))	

2	public.....................String	getAlgorithm ()	ε203,204,205,464,469
2	public.....................byte[]	getEncoded ()	ε199,460,471,471
2	public.....................String	getFormat ()	ε199
1	public...........javax.crypto↩	getParams ()	
	.spec.DHParameterSpec		
	public.... java.math.BigInteger	**getX** ()	

DHPrivateKeySpec | javax.crypto.spec

Object
　└DHPrivateKeySpec - *java.security.spec.KeySpec*
1.4

*	public........................ **DHPrivateKeySpec** (java.math.BigInteger x, java.math.BigInteger p,	
	java.math.BigInteger g)	
	public.... java.math.BigInteger **getG** ()	
	public.... java.math.BigInteger **getP** ()	
	public.... java.math.BigInteger **getX** ()	

Class *Interface* ──extends - - -implements ○ abstract ● final △ static ▲ static final ✳ constructor x x—inherited x **x**—declared **x x**—overridden
ε*n*—examples of usage ‿—has subclass package—see other volume

DHPublicKey | javax.crypto.interfaces

1.4		*DHPublicKey*——————————————————*DHKey* ⌄ [1], *java.security.PublicKey* ⌄	ε198,201,210,459,462
		(*java.security.Key* [2] (*java.io.Serializable*))	
	2	public.....................String getAlgorithm ()	ε203,204,205,464,469
	2	public.....................byte[] getEncoded ()	ε199,460,471,471
	2	public.....................String getFormat ()	ε199
	1	public..........javax.crypto ↩ getParams ()	
		.spec.DHParameterSpec	
		public....java.math.BigInteger **getY** ()	

DHPublicKeySpec | javax.crypto.spec

		Object	
1.4		└DHPublicKeySpec - *java.security.spec.KeySpec*	
*		public...........................**DHPublicKeySpec** (java.math.BigInteger y, java.math.BigInteger p,	
		java.math.BigInteger g)	
		public....java.math.BigInteger **getG** ()	
		public....java.math.BigInteger **getP** ()	
		public....java.math.BigInteger **getY** ()	

Dictionary | java.util

		Object	
○		└Dictionary ⌄	
*		public........................... **Dictionary** ()	
○		public abstract ... *Enumeration* **elements** ()	
○		public abstract ....Object **get** (Object key)	ε88
○		public abstract .... boolean **isEmpty** ()	
○		public abstract ... *Enumeration* **keys** ()	
○		public abstract ....Object **put** (Object key, Object value)	ε472,481,484,485,486
○		public abstract ....Object **remove** (Object key)	
○		public abstract ....int **size** ()	

DigestException | java.security

		Object	
		└Throwable - *java.io.Serializable* ⌄	
		└Exception	
1.2		└GeneralSecurityException	
1.1		└DigestException	
*		public........................... **DigestException** ()	
*		public........................... **DigestException** (String msg)	

DigestInputStream | java.security

		Object[1]	ε252,382,418
○		└java.io.InputStream	
		└java.io.FilterInputStream[2]	
1.1		└DigestInputStream	
	2	public.......................int available () throws java.io.IOException	
	2	public.......................void close () throws java.io.IOException	ε14,36,45,452,455
		protected ...... MessageDigest **digest**	
*		public........................... **DigestInputStream** (java.io.InputStream stream, MessageDigest digest)	
		public.........MessageDigest **getMessageDigest** ()	
	2	protected .. java.io.InputStream in	
	2	public synchronized ....void mark (int readlimit)	
	2	public.................... boolean markSupported ()	
		public.......................void **on** (boolean on)	
	2	public........................ **int read** () throws java.io.IOException	ε90,184,256
	2	public.......................int read (byte[] b) throws java.io.IOException	ε452,455,457,170,451
	2	public........................ **int read** (byte[] b, int off, int len) throws java.io.IOException	ε36
	2	public synchronized ....void reset () throws java.io.IOException	
		public.......................void **setMessageDigest** (MessageDigest digest)	
	2	public.................... long skip (long n) throws java.io.IOException	

DigestInputStream

1	public.................... **String toString** ()	

DigestOutputStream   java.security

```
      Object 1                                                    ε183
  o   └java.io.OutputStream
          └java.io.FilterOutputStream 2
1.1          └DigestOutputStream
```

2	public.....................void	close () throws java.io.IOException	ε451,453,91,211,224
	protected ...... MessageDigest	**digest**	
*	public..........................	**DigestOutputStream** (java.io.OutputStream stream, MessageDigest digest)	
2	public.....................void	flush () throws java.io.IOException	ε27,54
	public......... MessageDigest	**getMessageDigest** ()	
	public.....................void	**on** (boolean on)	
2	protected java.io.OutputStream	out	
	public.....................void	**setMessageDigest** (MessageDigest digest)	
1	public................. **String toString** ()		
2	public.....................void	write (byte[] b) throws java.io.IOException	ε27,91,224
2	public.................... **void write** (int b) throws java.io.IOException		ε184
2	public.................... **void write** (byte[] b, int off, int len) throws java.io.IOException		ε451,453,54,449,450

DirContext   javax.naming.directory

1.3	*DirContext* ─────────────────── *javax.naming.Context* [1]	ε481,492,484,495

```
    1  44 inherited members from javax.naming.Context not shown
```

▲	public static final ....int	**ADD_ATTRIBUTE** = 1	ε483
	public.....................void	**bind** (String name, Object obj, *Attributes* attrs) throws	
		javax.naming.NamingException	ε485
	public.....................void	**bind** (*javax.naming.Name* name, Object obj, *Attributes* attrs)	
		throws javax.naming.NamingException	
	public...............*DirContext*	**createSubcontext** (String name, *Attributes* attrs) throws	
		javax.naming.NamingException	ε484
	public...............*DirContext*	**createSubcontext** (*javax.naming.Name* name, *Attributes* attrs)	
		throws javax.naming.NamingException	
	public.................*Attributes*	**getAttributes** (String name) throws javax.naming.NamingException	
			ε491
	public.................*Attributes*	**getAttributes** (*javax.naming.Name* name) throws javax.naming.NamingException	
	public.................*Attributes*	**getAttributes** (String name, String[] attrIds) throws javax.naming.NamingException	
			ε482,491
	public.................*Attributes*	**getAttributes** (*javax.naming.Name* name, String[] attrIds)	
		throws javax.naming.NamingException	
	public...............*DirContext*	**getSchema** (String name) throws javax.naming.NamingException	
	public...............*DirContext*	**getSchema** (*javax.naming.Name* name) throws javax.naming.NamingException	
	public...............*DirContext*	**getSchemaClassDefinition** (String name) throws javax.naming.NamingException	
			ε490
	public...............*DirContext*	**getSchemaClassDefinition** (*javax.naming.Name* name)	
		throws javax.naming.NamingException	
	public.....................void	**modifyAttributes** (String name, ModificationItem[] mods)	
		throws javax.naming.NamingException	ε483
	public.....................void	**modifyAttributes** (*javax.naming.Name* name, ModificationItem[] mods)	
		throws javax.naming.NamingException	
	public.....................void	**modifyAttributes** (String name, int mod_op, *Attributes* attrs)	
		throws javax.naming.NamingException	
	public.....................void	**modifyAttributes** (*javax.naming.Name* name, int mod_op, *Attributes* attrs)	
		throws javax.naming.NamingException	
	public.....................void	**rebind** (String name, Object obj, *Attributes* attrs) throws	
		javax.naming.NamingException	
	public.....................void	**rebind** (*javax.naming.Name* name, Object obj, *Attributes* attrs)	
		throws javax.naming.NamingException	
▲	public static final ....int	**REMOVE_ATTRIBUTE** = 3	ε483
▲	public static final ....int	**REPLACE_ATTRIBUTE** = 2	ε483
	public.........*javax.naming*↵	**search** (String name, *Attributes* matchingAttributes)	
	.NamingEnumeration	throws javax.naming.NamingException	ε489,490
	public.........*javax.naming*↵	**search** (*javax.naming.Name* name, *Attributes* matchingAttributes)	
	.NamingEnumeration	throws javax.naming.NamingException	

Class   *Interface*   —extends   - - -implements   O abstract   ● final   △ static   ▲ static final   ✳ constructor   x x—inherited   x **x**—declared   **x x**—overridden
ε*n*—examples of usage   ⌐has subclass   package—see other volume

```
      public..........javax.naming↩ search (String name, String filter, SearchControls cons)
              .NamingEnumeration   throws javax.naming.NamingException              ε487,488
      public..........javax.naming↩ search (String name, Attributes matchingAttributes, String[] attributesToReturn)
              .NamingEnumeration   throws javax.naming.NamingException              ε486
      public..........javax.naming↩ search (javax.naming.Name name, Attributes matchingAttributes,
              .NamingEnumeration   String[] attributesToReturn) throws javax.naming.NamingException
      public..........javax.naming↩ search (javax.naming.Name name, String filter, SearchControls cons)
              .NamingEnumeration   throws javax.naming.NamingException
      public..........javax.naming↩ search (String name, String filterExpr, Object[] filterArgs, SearchControls cons)
              .NamingEnumeration   throws javax.naming.NamingException
      public..........javax.naming↩ search (javax.naming.Name name, String filterExpr, Object[] filterArgs,
              .NamingEnumeration   SearchControls cons) throws javax.naming.NamingException
```

DirectoryManager   javax.naming.spi

```
        Object
1.3     └NamingManager 1
1.3        └DirectoryManager
```

```
△ 1   public static ...................  getContinuationContext (javax.naming.CannotProceedException cpe)
      ........ javax.naming.Context        throws javax.naming.NamingException
△     public static ...........javax↩ getContinuationDirContext (javax.naming.CannotProceedException cpe)
      .naming.directory.DirContext       throws javax.naming.NamingException
△ 1   public static ...................  getInitialContext (java.util.Hashtable env) throws javax.naming.NamingException
      ........ javax.naming.Context
△ 1   public static ............Object getObjectInstance (Object refInfo, javax.naming.Name name, javax.naming.Context
                                        nameCtx, java.util.Hashtable environment) throws Exception
△     public static ............Object getObjectInstance (Object refInfo, javax.naming.Name name,
                                        javax.naming.Context nameCtx, java.util.Hashtable environment,
                                        javax.naming.directory.Attributes attrs) throws Exception
△ 1   public static ............Object getStateToBind (Object obj, javax.naming.Name name, javax.naming.Context
                                        nameCtx, java.util.Hashtable environment) throws javax.naming.NamingException
△     public static ...................  getStateToBind (Object obj, javax.naming.Name name,
      ........DirStateFactory.Result     javax.naming.Context nameCtx, java.util.Hashtable environment,
                                        javax.naming.directory.Attributes attrs) throws javax.naming.NamingException
△ 1   public static ...................  getURLContext (String scheme, java.util.Hashtable environment)
      ........ javax.naming.Context       throws javax.naming.NamingException
△ 1   public static ........... boolean hasInitialContextFactoryBuilder ()
△ 1   public static synchronized void setInitialContextFactoryBuilder (InitialContextFactoryBuilder builder)
                                        throws javax.naming.NamingException
△ 1   public static synchronized void setObjectFactoryBuilder (ObjectFactoryBuilder builder)
                                        throws javax.naming.NamingException
```

DirObjectFactory   javax.naming.spi

```
1.3     DirObjectFactory——————————————ObjectFactory 1
```

```
  1   public...................Object getObjectInstance (Object obj, javax.naming.Name name, javax.naming.Context
                                      nameCtx, java.util.Hashtable environment) throws Exception
      public...................Object getObjectInstance (Object obj, javax.naming.Name name,
                                      javax.naming.Context nameCtx, java.util.Hashtable environment,
                                      javax.naming.directory.Attributes attrs) throws Exception
```

DirStateFactory   javax.naming.spi

```
1.3     DirStateFactory————————————————StateFactory 1
```

```
  1   public...................Object getStateToBind (Object obj, javax.naming.Name name, javax.naming.Context
                                      nameCtx, java.util.Hashtable environment) throws javax.naming.NamingException
      public...DirStateFactory.Result getStateToBind (Object obj, javax.naming.Name name,
                                      javax.naming.Context nameCtx, java.util.Hashtable environment,
                                      javax.naming.directory.Attributes inAttrs) throws javax.naming.NamingException
```

DirStateFactory.Result   javax.naming.spi

```
        Object
1.3     └DirStateFactory.Result
```

DirStateFactory.Result

	public	*javax*↩	**getAttributes** ()
		.naming.directory.Attributes	
	public	Object	**getObject** ()
*	public		**DirStateFactory.Result** (Object obj, *javax.naming.directory.Attributes* outAttrs)

D

Document ❷   `org.w3c.dom`

1.4	*Document* ————————————————— *Node* ₁	ε524,510,511,513,514

	1	*34 inherited members from Node not shown*	
	1	public .... *Node*	appendChild (*Node* newChild) throws DOMException	ε539,526,533,540,542
		public .... *Attr*	**createAttribute** (String name) throws DOMException	
		public .... *Attr*	**createAttributeNS** (String namespaceURI, String qualifiedName)	
			throws DOMException	
		public .... *CDATASection*	**createCDATASection** (String data) throws DOMException	ε540,545
		public .... *Comment*	**createComment** (String data)	ε539,541,545
		public ..... *DocumentFragment*	**createDocumentFragment** ()	ε512
		public .... *Element*	**createElement** (String tagName) throws DOMException	ε533,539,546
		public .... *Element*	**createElementNS** (String namespaceURI, String qualifiedName)	
			throws DOMException	
		public .... *EntityReference*	**createEntityReference** (String name) throws DOMException	
		public ... *ProcessingInstruction*	**createProcessingInstruction** (String target, String data) throws DOMException	
				ε542
		public .... *Text*	**createTextNode** (String data)	ε539,543,545
		public .... *DocumentType*	**getDoctype** ()	ε528,529
		public .... *Element*	**getDocumentElement** ()	ε526,530,533,540,541
		public .... *Element*	**getElementById** (String elementId)	ε531,534,535
		public .... *NodeList*	**getElementsByTagName** (String tagname)	ε525,526,532,541,542
		public .... *NodeList*	**getElementsByTagNameNS** (String namespaceURI, String localName)	
		public .... *DOMImplementation*	**getImplementation** ()	
		public .... *Node*	**importNode** (*Node* importedNode, boolean deep) throws DOMException	
				ε526,533,512
	1	public .... *Node*	insertBefore (*Node* newChild, *Node* refChild) throws DOMException	
				ε539,525,541,542,546
	1	public ....void	normalize ()	ε544,547

DocumentBuilder   `javax.xml.parsers`

1.4	○	Object ∟DocumentBuilder

*		protected	**DocumentBuilder** ()	
○		public abstract ...... *org.w3c*↩	**getDOMImplementation** ()	
		.dom.DOMImplementation		
○		public abstract .... boolean	**isNamespaceAware** ()	
○		public abstract .... boolean	**isValidating** ()	
○		public abstract	**newDocument** ()	ε511,522
		..... *org.w3c.dom.Document*		
		public *org.w3c.dom.Document*	**parse** (java.io.File f) throws org.xml.sax.SAXException, java.io.IOException	
				ε513,510,514,515,516
		public *org.w3c.dom.Document*	**parse** (java.io.InputStream is) throws org.xml.sax.SAXException, java.io.IOException	
		public *org.w3c.dom.Document*	**parse** (String uri) throws org.xml.sax.SAXException, java.io.IOException	
○		public abstract	**parse** (org.xml.sax.InputSource is) throws org.xml.sax.SAXException,	
		..... *org.w3c.dom.Document*	java.io.IOException	ε512
		public *org.w3c.dom.Document*	**parse** (java.io.InputStream is, String systemId) throws org.xml.sax.SAXException,	
			java.io.IOException	
○		public abstract ....void	**setEntityResolver** (*org.xml.sax.EntityResolver* er)	ε548
○		public abstract ....void	**setErrorHandler** (*org.xml.sax.ErrorHandler* eh)	ε513

DocumentBuilderFactory   `javax.xml.parsers`

1.4	○	Object ∟DocumentBuilderFactory

*	protected	**DocumentBuilderFactory** ()	
○	public abstract .... Object	**getAttribute** (String name) throws IllegalArgumentException	
	public .... boolean	**isCoalescing** ()	
	public .... boolean	**isExpandEntityReferences** ()	

Class   *Interface*   —extends   - - -implements   ○ abstract   ● final   △ static   ▲ static final   ✳ constructor   x x—inherited   x **x**—declared   **x x**—overridden
ε*n*—examples of usage   ⌄—has subclass   package —see other volume

	public .... boolean	**isIgnoringComments** ()	
	public .... boolean	**isIgnoringElementContentWhitespace** ()	
	public .... boolean	**isNamespaceAware** ()	
	public .... boolean	**isValidating** ()	
○	public abstract .... DocumentBuilder	**newDocumentBuilder** () throws ParserConfigurationException	ε510,511,512,513,514
△	public static .... DocumentBuilderFactory	**newInstance** () throws FactoryConfigurationError	ε510,511,512,513,514
○	public abstract .... void	**setAttribute** (String name, Object value) throws IllegalArgumentException
	public .... void	**setCoalescing** (boolean coalescing)	ε514
	public .... void	**setExpandEntityReferences** (boolean expandEntityRef)	ε516
	public .... void	**setIgnoringComments** (boolean ignoreComments)	ε515
	public .... void	**setIgnoringElementContentWhitespace** (boolean whitespace)
	public .... void	**setNamespaceAware** (boolean awareness)
	public .... void	**setValidating** (boolean validating)	ε510,516

DocumentFragment org.w3c.dom

1.4	*DocumentFragment* ——————————— *Node* ˎ[1]	ε524,526,529,530,532

> 1 *36 inherited members from Node not shown*
> 1 public .... *Node* appendChild (*Node* newChild) throws DOMException ε512,526,533,539,540

DocumentHandler org.xml.sax

D	*DocumentHandler*	
D	public .... void	**characters** (char[] ch, int start, int length) throws SAXException
D	public .... void	**endDocument** () throws SAXException
D	public .... void	**endElement** (String name) throws SAXException
D	public .... void	**ignorableWhitespace** (char[] ch, int start, int length) throws SAXException
D	public .... void	**processingInstruction** (String target, String data) throws SAXException
D	public .... void	**setDocumentLocator** (*Locator* locator)
D	public .... void	**startDocument** () throws SAXException
D	public .... void	**startElement** (String name, *AttributeList* atts) throws SAXException

---

DocumentType org.w3c.dom

1.4	*DocumentType* ——————————— *Node* ˎ[1]	ε524,526,529,530,532

> 1 *37 inherited members from Node not shown*
> public .... *NamedNodeMap* **getEntities** () — ε529
> public .... String **getInternalSubset** ()
> public .... String **getName** ()
> public .... *NamedNodeMap* **getNotations** () — ε528
> public .... String **getPublicId** ()
> public .... String **getSystemId** ()

DomainCombiner java.security

1.3	*DomainCombiner*

> public ...... ProtectionDomain[] **combine** (ProtectionDomain[] currentDomains, ProtectionDomain[] assignedDomains)

DomainManager org.omg.CORBA

1.2	*DomainManager* ——————————— *DomainManagerOperations* ˎ[1], *Object* ˎ[2], org.omg.CORBA.portable.IDLEntity ˎ (*java.io.Serializable*)

> 2 *13 inherited members from Object not shown*
> 1.3 1 public .... *Policy* get_domain_policy (int policy_type)

DomainManagerOperations org.omg.CORBA

1.3	*DomainManagerOperations* ˎ

> public .... *Policy* **get_domain_policy** (int policy_type)

DOMException

	DOMException		org.w3c.dom

```
Object
└Throwable ------------------------- java.io.Serializable.
  └Exception
    └RuntimeException
      └DOMException
```
1.4

	public	short	**code**
＊	public		**DOMException** (short code, String message)
▲	public static final	short	**DOMSTRING_SIZE_ERR** = 2
▲	public static final	short	**HIERARCHY_REQUEST_ERR** = 3
▲	public static final	short	**INDEX_SIZE_ERR** = 1
▲	public static final	short	**INUSE_ATTRIBUTE_ERR** = 10
▲	public static final	short	**INVALID_ACCESS_ERR** = 15
▲	public static final	short	**INVALID_CHARACTER_ERR** = 5
▲	public static final	short	**INVALID_MODIFICATION_ERR** = 13
▲	public static final	short	**INVALID_STATE_ERR** = 11
▲	public static final	short	**NAMESPACE_ERR** = 14
▲	public static final	short	**NO_DATA_ALLOWED_ERR** = 6
▲	public static final	short	**NO_MODIFICATION_ALLOWED_ERR** = 7
▲	public static final	short	**NOT_FOUND_ERR** = 8
▲	public static final	short	**NOT_SUPPORTED_ERR** = 9
▲	public static final	short	**SYNTAX_ERR** = 12
▲	public static final	short	**WRONG_DOCUMENT_ERR** = 4

	DOMImplementation		org.w3c.dom

1.4   *DOMImplementation*

public	*Document*	**createDocument** (String namespaceURI, String qualifiedName, *DocumentType* doctype) throws DOMException
public	*DocumentType*	**createDocumentType** (String qualifiedName, String publicId, String systemId) throws DOMException
public	boolean	**hasFeature** (String feature, String version)

	DOMLocator		javax.xml.transform.dom

1.4   *DOMLocator* ──────────────── *javax.xml.transform.SourceLocator*.[1]

1	public	int	getColumnNumber ()	ε521
1	public	int	getLineNumber ()	ε521
	public	*org.w3c.dom.Node*	**getOriginatingNode** ()	
1	public	String	getPublicId ()	ε521
1	public	String	getSystemId ()	ε521

	DOMResult		javax.xml.transform.dom

```
Object
└DOMResult ------------------------- javax.xml.transform.Result [1]
```
1.4

＊	public		**DOMResult** ()	
＊	public		**DOMResult** (*org.w3c.dom.Node* node)	ε522
＊	public		**DOMResult** (*org.w3c.dom.Node* node, String systemID)	
▲	public static final	String	**FEATURE** = "http://javax.xml.transform.dom.DOMResult/feature"	
	public	*org.w3c.dom.Node*	**getNode** ()	
1	public	String	**getSystemId** ()	
	public	void	**setNode** (*org.w3c.dom.Node* node)	
1	public	void	**setSystemId** (String systemId)	

	DOMSource		javax.xml.transform.dom

```
Object
└DOMSource ------------------------- javax.xml.transform.Source [1]
```
1.4

＊	public	**DOMSource** ()	
＊	public	**DOMSource** (*org.w3c.dom.Node* n)	ε518,519,520,523

*		public	....	**DOMSource** (*org.w3c.dom.Node* node, String systemID)	
▲		public static final	.... String	**FEATURE** = "http://javax.xml.transform.dom.DOMSource/feature"	
		public	...... *org.w3c.dom.Node*	**getNode** ()	
	1	public	.... String	**getSystemId** ()	
		public	.... void	**setNode** (*org.w3c.dom.Node* node)	
	1	public	.... void	**setSystemId** (String baseID)	ε523

Double | java.lang

Object[1]   ε200,201,252,299,304
○   └Number[2] ------------------------------ *java.io.Serializable*
●   └Double ---------------------------- *Comparable*[3]

1.1	2	public	.... **byte**	**byteValue** ()	ε58
1.4 △		public static	.... int	**compare** (double d1, double d2)	
1.2		public	.... int	**compareTo** (Double anotherDouble)	
1.2	3	public	.... int	**compareTo** (Object o)	ε53
*		public	....	**Double** (double value)	ε58,324
*		public	....	**Double** (String s) throws NumberFormatException	
△		public static native	.... long	**doubleToLongBits** (double value)	
1.3 △		public static native	.... long	**doubleToRawLongBits** (double value)	
	2	public	.... **double**	**doubleValue** ()	ε58
	1	public	................**boolean**	**equals** (Object obj)	
	2	public	.... **float**	**floatValue** ()	ε58
	1	public	.... **int**	**hashCode** ()	
	2	public	.... **int**	**intValue** ()	ε58,6,346
		public	.... boolean	**isInfinite** ()	
△		public static	.... boolean	**isInfinite** (double v)	
		public	.... boolean	**isNaN** ()	
△		public static	.... boolean	**isNaN** (double v)	
△		public static native	...... double	**longBitsToDouble** (long bits)	
	2	public	.... **long**	**longValue** ()	ε58
▲		public static final	.... double	**MAX_VALUE** = 1.7976931348623157E308	
▲		public static final	.... double	**MIN_VALUE** = 4.9E-324	
▲		public static final	.... double	**NaN** = NaN	
▲		public static final	.... double	**NEGATIVE_INFINITY** = -Infinity	
1.2 △		public static	.... double	**parseDouble** (String s) throws NumberFormatException	ε82
▲		public static final	.... double	**POSITIVE_INFINITY** = Infinity	
1.1	2	public	.... **short**	**shortValue** ()	ε58
	1	public	.... **String**	**toString** ()	
△		public static	.... String	**toString** (double d)	
1.1 ▲		public static final	.... Class	**TYPE**	
△		public static	.... Double	**valueOf** (String s) throws NumberFormatException	

DoubleBuffer | java.nio

Object[1]   ε163,166,171,425
1.4 ○   └Buffer[2]
1.4 ○   └DoubleBuffer ----------------------- *Comparable*[3]

△		public static	...... DoubleBuffer	**allocate** (int capacity)	
●		public final	.... double[]	**array** ()	
●		public final	.... int	**arrayOffset** ()	
○		public abstract	...DoubleBuffer	**asReadOnlyBuffer** ()	
●	2	public final	.................int	capacity ()	ε159,160,161
●	2	public final	.... Buffer	clear ()	ε161,170,174
○		public abstract	...DoubleBuffer	**compact** ()	
	3	public	.....................int	**compareTo** (Object ob)	ε53
○		public abstract	...DoubleBuffer	**duplicate** ()	
	1	public	.... **boolean**	**equals** (Object ob)	
●	2	public final	.... Buffer	flip ()	ε162,164,170,174,175
○		public abstract	..........double	**get** ()	
		public	.... DoubleBuffer	**get** (double[] dst)	
○		public abstract	.........double	**get** (int index)	
		public	.... DoubleBuffer	**get** (double[] dst, int offset, int length)	
●		public final	.... boolean	**hasArray** ()	
	1	public	.... **int**	**hashCode** ()	
●	2	public final	.... boolean	hasRemaining ()	ε170,184
○		public abstract	.... boolean	**isDirect** ()	
○	2	public abstract	.... boolean	isReadOnly ()	
●	2	public final	....................int	limit ()	

public .... boolean **jdbcCompliant** ()   ε234

DriverManager   java.sql

Object
1.1   └DriverManager

△	public static synchronized void **deregisterDriver** (*Driver* driver) throws SQLException	
△	public static synchronized .... *Connection* **getConnection** (String url) throws SQLException	
△	public static synchronized .... *Connection* **getConnection** (String url, java.util.Properties info) throws SQLException	
△	public static synchronized .... *Connection* **getConnection** (String url, String user, String password) throws SQLException	ε235,236,237,243
△	public static synchronized .... *Driver* **getDriver** (String url) throws SQLException	ε238,243
△	public static synchronized .... *java.util.Enumeration* **getDrivers** ()	ε234
△	public static .... int **getLoginTimeout** ()	
D △	public static java.io.PrintStream **getLogStream** ()	
1.2 △	public static . java.io.PrintWriter **getLogWriter** ()	
△	public static ....void **println** (String message)	
△	public static synchronized void **registerDriver** (*Driver* driver) throws SQLException	
△	public static ....void **setLoginTimeout** (int seconds)	
D △	public static synchronized void **setLogStream** (java.io.PrintStream out)	
1.2 △	public static ....void **setLogWriter** (java.io.PrintWriter out)	

DriverPropertyInfo   java.sql

Object
1.1   └DriverPropertyInfo

	public .... String[] **choices**	ε238
	public .... String **description**	ε238
*	public .... **DriverPropertyInfo** (String name, String value)	
	public .... String **name**	ε238
	public .... boolean **required**	ε238
	public .... String **value**	ε238

DSAKey   java.security.interfaces

1.1   *DSAKey*

public .... *DSAParams* **getParams** ()   ε200

DSAKeyPairGenerator   java.security.interfaces

1.1   *DSAKeyPairGenerator*

public ....void **initialize** (*DSAParams* params, java.security.SecureRandom random)
         throws java.security.InvalidParameterException
public ....void **initialize** (int modlen, boolean genParams, java.security.SecureRandom random)
         throws java.security.InvalidParameterException

DSAParameterSpec   java.security.spec

Object
1.2   └DSAParameterSpec -------------------- *AlgorithmParameterSpec, java.security.interfaces.DSAParams* [1]

*	public .... **DSAParameterSpec** (java.math.BigInteger p, java.math.BigInteger q, java.math.BigInteger g)	
[1]	public .... java.math.BigInteger **getG** ()	ε200
[1]	public .... java.math.BigInteger **getP** ()	ε200
[1]	public .... java.math.BigInteger **getQ** ()	ε200

D

Classes

DSAParams | java.security.interfaces

1.1	*DSAParams*	
	public.... java.math.BigInteger **getG** ()	ε200
	public.... java.math.BigInteger **getP** ()	ε200
	public.... java.math.BigInteger **getQ** ()	ε200

D

DSAPrivateKey | java.security.interfaces

1.1	*DSAPrivateKey*————————————— *DSAKey* ⌄ [1], *java.security.PrivateKey* ⌄ [2]	ε198,201,210,459,462
	(*java.security.Key* [3] (*java.io.Serializable*))	
3	public......................String getAlgorithm ()	ε203,204,205,464,469
3	public......................byte[] getEncoded ()	ε199,460,471,471
3	public......................String getFormat ()	ε199
1	public.............*DSAParams* getParams ()	ε200
	public.... java.math.BigInteger **getX** ()	ε200
1.2 ▲ 2	public static final.......... **long getX** **serialVersionUID** = 7776497482533790279	

DSAPrivateKeySpec | java.security.spec

	Object	
1.2	└DSAPrivateKeySpec - *KeySpec*	
✱	public........................... **DSAPrivateKeySpec** (java.math.BigInteger x, java.math.BigInteger p,	
	java.math.BigInteger q, java.math.BigInteger g)	ε201
	public.... java.math.BigInteger **getG** ()	
	public.... java.math.BigInteger **getP** ()	
	public.... java.math.BigInteger **getQ** ()	
	public.... java.math.BigInteger **getX** ()	

DSAPublicKey | java.security.interfaces

1.1	*DSAPublicKey*————————————— *DSAKey* ⌄ [1], *java.security.PublicKey* ⌄ [2]	ε198,201,210,459,462
	(*java.security.Key* [3] (*java.io.Serializable*))	
3	public......................String getAlgorithm ()	ε203,204,205,464,469
3	public......................byte[] getEncoded ()	ε199,460,471,471
3	public......................String getFormat ()	ε199
1	public.............*DSAParams* getParams ()	ε200
	public.... java.math.BigInteger **getY** ()	ε200
1.2 ▲ 2	public static final.......... **long serialVersionUID** = 1234526332779022332	

DSAPublicKeySpec | java.security.spec

	Object	
1.2	└DSAPublicKeySpec - *KeySpec*	
✱	public........................... **DSAPublicKeySpec** (java.math.BigInteger y, java.math.BigInteger p,	
	java.math.BigInteger q, java.math.BigInteger g)	ε201
	public.... java.math.BigInteger **getG** ()	
	public.... java.math.BigInteger **getP** ()	
	public.... java.math.BigInteger **getQ** ()	
	public.... java.math.BigInteger **getY** ()	

DTDHandler | org.xml.sax

1.4	*DTDHandler* ⌄	
	public........................void **notationDecl** (String name, String publicId, String systemId) throws SAXException	
	public........................void **unparsedEntityDecl** (String name, String publicId, String systemId,	
	String notationName) throws SAXException	

Class *Interface* —extends - - -implements ○ abstract ● final △ static ▲ static final ✱ constructor x x—inherited x **x**—declared **x x**—overridden
ε*n*—examples of usage ⌄—has subclass package—see other volume

DuplicateName   org.omg.PortableInterceptor.ORBInitInfoPackage

```
Object
└Throwable --------------------------- java.io.Serializable ◝
  └Exception
```
1.2 ○   └org.omg.CORBA.UserException ------- org.omg.CORBA.portable.IDLEntity ◝ (java.io.Serializable)
1.4 ●   └DuplicateName

✳	public........................	**DuplicateName** ()
✳	public........................	**DuplicateName** (String _name)
✳	public........................	**DuplicateName** (String $reason, String _name)
	public...................String	**name**

DuplicateNameHelper   org.omg.PortableInterceptor.ORBInitInfoPackage

```
Object
```
1.4 ○   └DuplicateNameHelper

✳	public........................	**DuplicateNameHelper** ()
△	public static ... DuplicateName	**extract** (org.omg.CORBA.Any a)
△	public static ....String	**id** ()
△	public static ....void	**insert** (org.omg.CORBA.Any a, DuplicateName that)
△	public static ... DuplicateName	**read** (org.omg.CORBA.portable.InputStream istream)
△	public static synchronized .... . org.omg.CORBA.TypeCode	**type** ()
△	public static ....void	**write** (org.omg.CORBA.portable.OutputStream ostream, DuplicateName value)

DynamicImplementation ❶   org.omg.CORBA

```
Object
```
1.2 ○   └org.omg.CORBA.portable.ObjectImpl¹ ------ Object ◝
D   └DynamicImplementation ◝

D	1	*25 inherited members from org.omg.CORBA.portable.ObjectImpl not shown*	
D	1	public................. **String[]**	**_ids** ()
D	✳	public........................	**DynamicImplementation** ()
D		public......................void	**invoke** (ServerRequest request)

DynamicImplementation ❷   org.omg.PortableServer

```
Object
```
1.4 ○   └Servant¹
1.4 ○   └DynamicImplementation

	1	*12 inherited members from Servant not shown*	
✳		public........................	**DynamicImplementation** ()
○		public abstract ....void	**invoke** (org.omg.CORBA.ServerRequest request)

DynAny ❶   org.omg.CORBA

1.2   *DynAny* ◝ ———————————————— *Object* ◝¹

1	*13 inherited members from Object not shown*
public......................void	**assign** (*DynAny* dyn_any) throws org.omg.CORBA.DynAnyPackage.Invalid
public.....................*DynAny*	**copy** ()
public.....................*DynAny*	**current_component** ()
public......................void	**destroy** ()
public......................void	**from_any** (Any value) throws org.omg.CORBA.DynAnyPackage.Invalid
public........................ Any	**get_any** () throws org.omg.CORBA.DynAnyPackage.TypeMismatch
public................... boolean	**get_boolean** () throws org.omg.CORBA.DynAnyPackage.TypeMismatch
public...................... char	**get_char** () throws org.omg.CORBA.DynAnyPackage.TypeMismatch
public....................double	**get_double** () throws org.omg.CORBA.DynAnyPackage.TypeMismatch
public......................float	**get_float** () throws org.omg.CORBA.DynAnyPackage.TypeMismatch
public........................int	**get_long** () throws org.omg.CORBA.DynAnyPackage.TypeMismatch
public...................... long	**get_longlong** () throws org.omg.CORBA.DynAnyPackage.TypeMismatch
public...................... byte	**get_octet** () throws org.omg.CORBA.DynAnyPackage.TypeMismatch
public.....................*Object*	**get_reference** () throws org.omg.CORBA.DynAnyPackage.TypeMismatch
public...................... short	**get_short** () throws org.omg.CORBA.DynAnyPackage.TypeMismatch
public....................String	**get_string** () throws org.omg.CORBA.DynAnyPackage.TypeMismatch

DynAny ❶

public	TypeCode	**get_typecode**	() throws org.omg.CORBA.DynAnyPackage.TypeMismatch
public	int	**get_ulong**	() throws org.omg.CORBA.DynAnyPackage.TypeMismatch
public	long	**get_ulonglong**	() throws org.omg.CORBA.DynAnyPackage.TypeMismatch
public	short	**get_ushort**	() throws org.omg.CORBA.DynAnyPackage.TypeMismatch
public	*java.io.Serializable*	**get_val**	() throws org.omg.CORBA.DynAnyPackage.TypeMismatch
public	char	**get_wchar**	() throws org.omg.CORBA.DynAnyPackage.TypeMismatch
public	String	**get_wstring**	() throws org.omg.CORBA.DynAnyPackage.TypeMismatch
public	void	**insert_any**	(Any value) throws org.omg.CORBA.DynAnyPackage.InvalidValue
public	void	**insert_boolean**	(boolean value) throws org.omg.CORBA.DynAnyPackage↵.InvalidValue
public	void	**insert_char**	(char value) throws org.omg.CORBA.DynAnyPackage.InvalidValue
public	void	**insert_double**	(double value) throws org.omg.CORBA.DynAnyPackage↵.InvalidValue
public	void	**insert_float**	(float value) throws org.omg.CORBA.DynAnyPackage.InvalidValue
public	void	**insert_long**	(int value) throws org.omg.CORBA.DynAnyPackage.InvalidValue
public	void	**insert_longlong**	(long value) throws org.omg.CORBA.DynAnyPackage.InvalidValue
public	void	**insert_octet**	(byte value) throws org.omg.CORBA.DynAnyPackage.InvalidValue
public	void	**insert_reference**	(*Object* value) throws org.omg.CORBA.DynAnyPackage↵.InvalidValue
public	void	**insert_short**	(short value) throws org.omg.CORBA.DynAnyPackage.InvalidValue
public	void	**insert_string**	(String value) throws org.omg.CORBA.DynAnyPackage.InvalidValue
public	void	**insert_typecode**	(TypeCode value) throws org.omg.CORBA.DynAnyPackage↵.InvalidValue
public	void	**insert_ulong**	(int value) throws org.omg.CORBA.DynAnyPackage.InvalidValue
public	void	**insert_ulonglong**	(long value) throws org.omg.CORBA.DynAnyPackage↵.InvalidValue
public	void	**insert_ushort**	(short value) throws org.omg.CORBA.DynAnyPackage.InvalidValue
public	void	**insert_val**	(*java.io.Serializable* value) throws org.omg.CORBA.DynAnyPackage↵.InvalidValue
public	void	**insert_wchar**	(char value) throws org.omg.CORBA.DynAnyPackage.InvalidValue
public	void	**insert_wstring**	(String value) throws org.omg.CORBA.DynAnyPackage.InvalidValue
public	boolean	**next**	()
public	void	**rewind**	()
public	boolean	**seek**	(int index)
public	Any	**to_any**	() throws org.omg.CORBA.DynAnyPackage.Invalid
public	TypeCode	**type**	()

DynAny ❷　　　　　　　　　　　　　　　　　　　org.omg.DynamicAny

1.4　*DynAny* ⌐————————————— *DynAnyOperations* ⌐[1], org.omg.CORBA.Object ⌐[2],
　　　　　　　　　　　　　　　　org.omg.CORBA.portable.IDLEntity ⌐ (java.io.Serializable)

　2 *13 inherited members from org.omg.CORBA.Object not shown*
　1 *50 inherited members from DynAnyOperations not shown*

DynAnyFactory　　　　　　　　　　　　　　　　　org.omg.DynamicAny

1.4　*DynAnyFactory*————————————— *DynAnyFactoryOperations* ⌐[1], org.omg.CORBA.Object ⌐[2],
　　　　　　　　　　　　　　　　org.omg.CORBA.portable.IDLEntity ⌐ (java.io.Serializable)

　2 *13 inherited members from org.omg.CORBA.Object not shown*
　1 *2 inherited members from DynAnyFactoryOperations not shown*

DynAnyFactoryHelper　　　　　　　　　　　　　　org.omg.DynamicAny

Object
└DynAnyFactoryHelper

1.4 ○

✳	public		**DynAnyFactoryHelper**	()
△	public static	*DynAnyFactory*	**extract**	(org.omg.CORBA.Any a)
△	public static	String	**id**	()
△	public static	void	**insert**	(org.omg.CORBA.Any a, *DynAnyFactory* that)
△	public static	*DynAnyFactory*	**narrow**	(*org.omg.CORBA.Object* obj)
△	public static	*DynAnyFactory*	**read**	(org.omg.CORBA.portable.InputStream istream)
△	public static synchronized org.omg.CORBA.TypeCode		**type**	()
△	public static	void	**write**	(org.omg.CORBA.portable.OutputStream ostream, *DynAnyFactory* value)

Class　*Interface*　—extends　- - -implements　○ abstract　● final　△ static　▲ static final　✳ constructor　x x—inherited　x **x**—declared　**x x**—overridden
εn—examples of usage　⌐—has subclass　package—see other volume

DynAnyFactoryOperations		org.omg.DynamicAny

1.4   *DynAnyFactoryOperations*

    public...................*DynAny* **create_dyn_any** (org.omg.CORBA.Any value) throws
            org.omg.DynamicAny.DynAnyFactoryPackage.InconsistentTypeCode
    public...................*DynAny* **create_dyn_any_from_type_code** (org.omg.CORBA.TypeCode type)
            throws org.omg.DynamicAny.DynAnyFactoryPackage.InconsistentTypeCode

D

DynAnyHelper		org.omg.DynamicAny

    Object
1.4 O   └DynAnyHelper

*   public......................... **DynAnyHelper** ()
△   public static ....*DynAny* **extract** (org.omg.CORBA.Any a)
△   public static ....String **id** ()
△   public static ....void **insert** (org.omg.CORBA.Any a, *DynAny* that)
△   public static ....*DynAny* **narrow** (*org.omg.CORBA.Object* obj)
△   public static ....*DynAny* **read** (org.omg.CORBA.portable.InputStream istream)
△   public static synchronized .... **type** ()
   . org.omg.CORBA.TypeCode
△   public static ....void **write** (org.omg.CORBA.portable.OutputStream ostream, *DynAny* value)

DynAnyOperations		org.omg.DynamicAny

1.4   *DynAnyOperations*

    public......................void **assign** (*DynAny* dyn_any) throws org.omg.DynamicAny.DynAnyPackage↵
            .TypeMismatch
    public......................int **component_count** ()
    public...................*DynAny* **copy** ()
    public...................*DynAny* **current_component** () throws org.omg.DynamicAny.DynAnyPackage↵
            .TypeMismatch
    public......................void **destroy** ()
    public...................boolean **equal** (*DynAny* dyn_any)
    public......................void **from_any** (org.omg.CORBA.Any value) throws org↵
            .omg.DynamicAny.DynAnyPackage.TypeMismatch,
            org.omg.DynamicAny.DynAnyPackage.InvalidValue
    public....org.omg.CORBA.Any **get_any** () throws org.omg.DynamicAny.DynAnyPackage.TypeMismatch,
            org.omg.DynamicAny.DynAnyPackage.InvalidValue
    public...................boolean **get_boolean** () throws org.omg.DynamicAny.DynAnyPackage.TypeMismatch,
            org.omg.DynamicAny.DynAnyPackage.InvalidValue
    public......................char **get_char** () throws org.omg.DynamicAny.DynAnyPackage.TypeMismatch,
            org.omg.DynamicAny.DynAnyPackage.InvalidValue
    public...................double **get_double** () throws org.omg.DynamicAny.DynAnyPackage.TypeMismatch,
            org.omg.DynamicAny.DynAnyPackage.InvalidValue
    public...................*DynAny* **get_dyn_any** () throws org.omg.DynamicAny.DynAnyPackage.TypeMismatch,
            org.omg.DynamicAny.DynAnyPackage.InvalidValue
    public......................float **get_float** () throws org.omg.DynamicAny.DynAnyPackage.TypeMismatch,
            org.omg.DynamicAny.DynAnyPackage.InvalidValue
    public......................int **get_long** () throws org.omg.DynamicAny.DynAnyPackage.TypeMismatch,
            org.omg.DynamicAny.DynAnyPackage.InvalidValue
    public......................long **get_longlong** () throws org.omg.DynamicAny.DynAnyPackage.TypeMismatch,
            org.omg.DynamicAny.DynAnyPackage.InvalidValue
    public......................byte **get_octet** () throws org.omg.DynamicAny.DynAnyPackage.TypeMismatch,
            org.omg.DynamicAny.DynAnyPackage.InvalidValue
    public *org.omg.CORBA.Object* **get_reference** () throws org.omg.DynamicAny.DynAnyPackage.TypeMismatch,
            org.omg.DynamicAny.DynAnyPackage.InvalidValue
    public...................short **get_short** () throws org.omg.DynamicAny.DynAnyPackage.TypeMismatch,
            org.omg.DynamicAny.DynAnyPackage.InvalidValue
    public...................String **get_string** () throws org.omg.DynamicAny.DynAnyPackage.TypeMismatch,
            org.omg.DynamicAny.DynAnyPackage.InvalidValue
    public......................... **get_typecode** () throws org.omg.DynamicAny.DynAnyPackage.TypeMismatch,
    . org.omg.CORBA.TypeCode org.omg.DynamicAny.DynAnyPackage.InvalidValue
    public......................int **get_ulong** () throws org.omg.DynamicAny.DynAnyPackage.TypeMismatch,
            org.omg.DynamicAny.DynAnyPackage.InvalidValue
    public......................long **get_ulonglong** () throws org.omg.DynamicAny.DynAnyPackage.TypeMismatch,
            org.omg.DynamicAny.DynAnyPackage.InvalidValue
    public...................short **get_ushort** () throws org.omg.DynamicAny.DynAnyPackage.TypeMismatch,
            org.omg.DynamicAny.DynAnyPackage.InvalidValue

Classes

DynAnyOperations

public.......*java.io.Serializable* **get_val** () throws org.omg.DynamicAny.DynAnyPackage.TypeMismatch, org.omg.DynamicAny.DynAnyPackage.InvalidValue

public...................... char **get_wchar** () throws org.omg.DynamicAny.DynAnyPackage.TypeMismatch, org.omg.DynamicAny.DynAnyPackage.InvalidValue

public...................... String **get_wstring** () throws org.omg.DynamicAny.DynAnyPackage.TypeMismatch, org.omg.DynamicAny.DynAnyPackage.InvalidValue

public...................... void **insert_any** (org.omg.CORBA.Any value) throws org↵ .omg.DynamicAny.DynAnyPackage.TypeMismatch, org.omg.DynamicAny.DynAnyPackage.InvalidValue

public...................... void **insert_boolean** (boolean value) throws org.omg.DynamicAny.DynAnyPackage↵ .TypeMismatch, org.omg.DynamicAny.DynAnyPackage.InvalidValue

public...................... void **insert_char** (char value) throws org.omg.DynamicAny.DynAnyPackage↵ .TypeMismatch, org.omg.DynamicAny.DynAnyPackage.InvalidValue

public...................... void **insert_double** (double value) throws org.omg.DynamicAny.DynAnyPackage↵ .TypeMismatch, org.omg.DynamicAny.DynAnyPackage.InvalidValue

public...................... void **insert_dyn_any** (*DynAny* value) throws org.omg.DynamicAny.DynAnyPackage↵ .TypeMismatch, org.omg.DynamicAny.DynAnyPackage.InvalidValue

public...................... void **insert_float** (float value) throws org.omg.DynamicAny.DynAnyPackage↵ .TypeMismatch, org.omg.DynamicAny.DynAnyPackage.InvalidValue

public...................... void **insert_long** (int value) throws org.omg.DynamicAny.DynAnyPackage↵ .TypeMismatch, org.omg.DynamicAny.DynAnyPackage.InvalidValue

public...................... void **insert_longlong** (long value) throws org.omg.DynamicAny.DynAnyPackage↵ .TypeMismatch, org.omg.DynamicAny.DynAnyPackage.InvalidValue

public...................... void **insert_octet** (byte value) throws org.omg.DynamicAny.DynAnyPackage↵ .TypeMismatch, org.omg.DynamicAny.DynAnyPackage.InvalidValue

public...................... void **insert_reference** (*org.omg.CORBA.Object* value) throws org.omg.DynamicAny.DynAnyPackage.TypeMismatch, org.omg.DynamicAny.DynAnyPackage.InvalidValue

public...................... void **insert_short** (short value) throws org.omg.DynamicAny.DynAnyPackage↵ .TypeMismatch, org.omg.DynamicAny.DynAnyPackage.InvalidValue

public...................... void **insert_string** (String value) throws org.omg.DynamicAny.DynAnyPackage↵ .TypeMismatch, org.omg.DynamicAny.DynAnyPackage.InvalidValue

public...................... void **insert_typecode** (org.omg.CORBA.TypeCode value) throws org.omg.DynamicAny.DynAnyPackage.TypeMismatch, org.omg.DynamicAny.DynAnyPackage.InvalidValue

public...................... void **insert_ulong** (int value) throws org.omg.DynamicAny.DynAnyPackage↵ .TypeMismatch, org.omg.DynamicAny.DynAnyPackage.InvalidValue

public...................... void **insert_ulonglong** (long value) throws org.omg.DynamicAny.DynAnyPackage↵ .TypeMismatch, org.omg.DynamicAny.DynAnyPackage.InvalidValue

public...................... void **insert_ushort** (short value) throws org.omg.DynamicAny.DynAnyPackage↵ .TypeMismatch, org.omg.DynamicAny.DynAnyPackage.InvalidValue

public...................... void **insert_val** (*java.io.Serializable* value) throws org↵ .omg.DynamicAny.DynAnyPackage.TypeMismatch, org.omg.DynamicAny.DynAnyPackage.InvalidValue

public...................... void **insert_wchar** (char value) throws org.omg.DynamicAny.DynAnyPackage↵ .TypeMismatch, org.omg.DynamicAny.DynAnyPackage.InvalidValue

public...................... void **insert_wstring** (String value) throws org.omg.DynamicAny.DynAnyPackage↵ .TypeMismatch, org.omg.DynamicAny.DynAnyPackage.InvalidValue

public................. boolean **next** ()

public...................... void **rewind** ()

public................. boolean **seek** (int index)

public....org.omg.CORBA.Any **to_any** ()

public.......................... **type** ()
. org.omg.CORBA.TypeCode

- -

DynAnySeqHelper   org.omg.DynamicAny

Object
└DynAnySeqHelper

1.4 ○

* public.......................... **DynAnySeqHelper** ()
△ public static .... *DynAny[]* **extract** (org.omg.CORBA.Any a)
△ public static .... String **id** ()
△ public static ....void **insert** (org.omg.CORBA.Any a, *DynAny[]* that)
△ public static .... *DynAny[]* **read** (org.omg.CORBA.portable.InputStream istream)
△ public static synchronized .... **type** ()
. org.omg.CORBA.TypeCode
△ public static ....void **write** (org.omg.CORBA.portable.OutputStream ostream, *DynAny[]* value)

Class *Interface* —extends - - -implements ○ abstract ● final △ static ▲ static final ✳ constructor x x—inherited x **x**—declared **x x**—overridden
εn—examples of usage ⌐—has subclass package—see other volume

554

DynArray ❶ — org.omg.CORBA

1.2	*DynArray*————————————*Object* ,[1], *DynAny* ,[2] (*Object* [1])

```
    2  46 inherited members from DynAny not shown
    1  13 inherited members from Object not shown
       public.................... Any[] get_elements ()
       public.....................void set_elements (Any[] value) throws org.omg.CORBA.DynAnyPackage.InvalidSeq
```

D

DynArray ❷ — org.omg.DynamicAny

1.4	*DynArray*————————————*DynArrayOperations* ,[1] (*DynAnyOperations* [2]), *DynAny* , (*DynAnyOperations* [2], *org.omg.CORBA.Object* [3], *org.omg.CORBA.portable.IDLEntity* (*java.io.Serializable*)), *org.omg.CORBA.portable.IDLEntity* , (*java.io.Serializable*)

```
    1   4 inherited members from DynArrayOperations not shown
    3  13 inherited members from org.omg.CORBA.Object not shown
    2  50 inherited members from DynAnyOperations not shown
```

DynArrayHelper — org.omg.DynamicAny

```
       Object
1.4 ○  └DynArrayHelper
```

✳	public.........................	**DynArrayHelper** ()
△	public static ....*DynArray*	**extract** (org.omg.CORBA.Any a)
△	public static ....String	**id** ()
△	public static ....void	**insert** (org.omg.CORBA.Any a, *DynArray* that)
△	public static ....*DynArray*	**narrow** (*org.omg.CORBA.Object* obj)
△	public static ....*DynArray*	**read** (org.omg.CORBA.portable.InputStream istream)
	public static synchronized .... . org.omg.CORBA.TypeCode	**type** ()
△	public static ....void	**write** (org.omg.CORBA.portable.OutputStream ostream, *DynArray* value)

DynArrayOperations — org.omg.DynamicAny

1.4	*DynArrayOperations* ————————*DynAnyOperations* ,[1]

```
    1  50 inherited members from DynAnyOperations not shown
       public.. org.omg.CORBA.Any[] get_elements ()
       public.................DynAny[] get_elements_as_dyn_any ()
       public.....................void set_elements (org.omg.CORBA.Any[] value) throws
                           org.omg.DynamicAny.DynAnyPackage.TypeMismatch,
                           org.omg.DynamicAny.DynAnyPackage.InvalidValue
       public.....................void set_elements_as_dyn_any (DynAny[] value) throws
                           org.omg.DynamicAny.DynAnyPackage.TypeMismatch,
                           org.omg.DynamicAny.DynAnyPackage.InvalidValue
```

DynEnum ❶ — org.omg.CORBA

1.2	*DynEnum*————————————*Object* ,[1], *DynAny* ,[2] (*Object* [1])

```
    2  46 inherited members from DynAny not shown
    1  13 inherited members from Object not shown
       public....................String value_as_string ()
       public.....................void value_as_string (String arg)
       public......................int value_as_ulong ()
       public.....................void value_as_ulong (int arg)
```

DynEnum ❷ — org.omg.DynamicAny

1.4	*DynEnum*————————————*DynEnumOperations* ,[1] (*DynAnyOperations* [2]), *DynAny* , (*DynAnyOperations* [2], *org.omg.CORBA.Object* [3], *org.omg.CORBA.portable.IDLEntity* (*java.io.Serializable*)), *org.omg.CORBA.portable.IDLEntity* , (*java.io.Serializable*)

```
    3  13 inherited members from org.omg.CORBA.Object not shown
    1   4 inherited members from DynEnumOperations not shown
```

Classes

░ *2 50 inherited members from DynAnyOperations not shown*

DynEnumHelper	org.omg.DynamicAny

Object
1.4 ○ └DynEnumHelper

✳	public......................... **DynEnumHelper** ()
△	public static .... *DynEnum* **extract** (org.omg.CORBA.Any a)
△	public static ....String **id** ()
△	public static ....void **insert** (org.omg.CORBA.Any a, *DynEnum* that)
△	public static .... *DynEnum* **narrow** (*org.omg.CORBA.Object* obj)
△	public static .... *DynEnum* **read** (org.omg.CORBA.portable.InputStream istream)
△	public static synchronized .... **type** () . org.omg.CORBA.TypeCode
△	public static ....void **write** (org.omg.CORBA.portable.OutputStream ostream, *DynEnum* value)

DynEnumOperations	org.omg.DynamicAny

1.4   *DynEnumOperations*⌣────────────────*DynAnyOperations*⌣[1]

1 50 inherited members from DynAnyOperations not shown
public.....................String **get_as_string** ()
public.......................int **get_as_ulong** ()
public.....................void **set_as_string** (String value) throws org.omg.DynamicAny.DynAnyPackage↵
.InvalidValue
public.....................void **set_as_ulong** (int value) throws org.omg.DynamicAny.DynAnyPackage.InvalidValue

---

DynFixed ❶	org.omg.CORBA

1.2   *DynFixed*────────────────── *Object*⌣[1], *DynAny*⌣[2] (*Object*[1])

2 46 inherited members from DynAny not shown
1 13 inherited members from Object not shown
public.....................byte[] **get_value** ()
public.....................void **set_value** (byte[] val) throws org.omg.CORBA.DynAnyPackage.InvalidValue

---

DynFixed ❷	org.omg.DynamicAny

1.4   *DynFixed*──────────────── *DynFixedOperations*⌣[1] (*DynAnyOperations*[2]), *DynAny*⌣
(*DynAnyOperations*[2], *org.omg.CORBA.Object*[3],
org.omg.CORBA.portable.IDLEntity (*java.io.Serializable*)),
org.omg.CORBA.portable.IDLEntity⌣ (*java.io.Serializable*)

1 2 inherited members from DynFixedOperations not shown
3 13 inherited members from org.omg.CORBA.Object not shown
2 50 inherited members from DynAnyOperations not shown

DynFixedHelper	org.omg.DynamicAny

Object
1.4 ○ └DynFixedHelper

✳	public......................... **DynFixedHelper** ()
△	public static .... *DynFixed* **extract** (org.omg.CORBA.Any a)
△	public static ....String **id** ()
△	public static ....void **insert** (org.omg.CORBA.Any a, *DynFixed* that)
△	public static .... *DynFixed* **narrow** (*org.omg.CORBA.Object* obj)
△	public static .... *DynFixed* **read** (org.omg.CORBA.portable.InputStream istream)
△	public static synchronized .... **type** () . org.omg.CORBA.TypeCode
△	public static ....void **write** (org.omg.CORBA.portable.OutputStream ostream, *DynFixed* value)

Class *Interface* —extends - - -implements ○ abstract ● final △ static ▲ static final ✳ constructor x x—inherited x **x**—declared **x x**—overridden
εn—examples of usage ⌣—has subclass package—see other volume

556

DynFixedOperations
org.omg.DynamicAny

1.4   *DynFixedOperations* ───────────── *DynAnyOperations* [1]

---

   1   *50 inherited members from DynAnyOperations not shown*
     public.....................String **get_value** ()
     public.................boolean **set_value** (String val) throws org.omg.DynamicAny.DynAnyPackage.TypeMismatch,
                                org.omg.DynamicAny.DynAnyPackage.InvalidValue

---

DynSequence❶
org.omg.CORBA

1.2   *DynSequence* ───────────────── *Object* [1], *DynAny* [2] (*Object* [1])

---

   2   *46 inherited members from DynAny not shown*
   1   *13 inherited members from Object not shown*
     public..................... Any[] **get_elements** ()
     public.........................int **length** ()
     public.........................void **length** (int arg)
     public.........................void **set_elements** (Any[] value) throws org.omg.CORBA.DynAnyPackage.InvalidSeq

---

DynSequence❷
org.omg.DynamicAny

1.4   *DynSequence* ───────────────── *DynSequenceOperations* [1] (*DynAnyOperations* [2]), *DynAny*
                             (*DynAnyOperations* [2], *org.omg.CORBA.Object* [3],
                             org.omg.CORBA.portable.IDLEntity (*java.io.Serializable*)),
                             org.omg.CORBA.portable.IDLEntity (*java.io.Serializable*))

---

   3   *13 inherited members from org.omg.CORBA.Object not shown*
   1   *6 inherited members from DynSequenceOperations not shown*
   2   *50 inherited members from DynAnyOperations not shown*

DynSequenceHelper
org.omg.DynamicAny

     Object
1.4 ○   └DynSequenceHelper

✳   public......................... **DynSequenceHelper** ()
△   public static ..... *DynSequence* **extract** (org.omg.CORBA.Any a)
△   public static ....String **id** ()
△   public static ....void **insert** (org.omg.CORBA.Any a, *DynSequence* that)
△   public static ..... *DynSequence* **narrow** (*org.omg.CORBA.Object* obj)
△   public static ..... *DynSequence* **read** (org.omg.CORBA.portable.InputStream istream)
△   public static synchronized .... **type** ()
     . org.omg.CORBA.TypeCode
△   public static ....void **write** (org.omg.CORBA.portable.OutputStream ostream, *DynSequence* value)

DynSequenceOperations
org.omg.DynamicAny

1.4   *DynSequenceOperations* ───────────── *DynAnyOperations* [1]

---

   1   *50 inherited members from DynAnyOperations not shown*
     public.. org.omg.CORBA.Any[] **get_elements** ()
     public................. *DynAny[]* **get_elements_as_dyn_any** ()
     public.........................int **get_length** ()
     public.........................void **set_elements** (org.omg.CORBA.Any[] value) throws
                               org.omg.DynamicAny.DynAnyPackage.TypeMismatch,
                               org.omg.DynamicAny.DynAnyPackage.InvalidValue
     public.........................void **set_elements_as_dyn_any** (*DynAny[]* value) throws
                               org.omg.DynamicAny.DynAnyPackage.TypeMismatch,
                               org.omg.DynamicAny.DynAnyPackage.InvalidValue
     public.........................void **set_length** (int len) throws org.omg.DynamicAny.DynAnyPackage.InvalidValue

---

DynStruct❶
org.omg.CORBA

1.2   *DynStruct* ───────────────── *Object* [1], *DynAny* [2] (*Object* [1])

---

   2   *46 inherited members from DynAny not shown*
   1   *13 inherited members from Object not shown*
     public................. TCKind **current_member_kind** ()
     public..................... String **current_member_name** ()

D

Classes

DynStruct ❶

```
public.........NameValuePair[] get_members ()
public.....................void set_members (NameValuePair[] value) throws org.omg.CORBA.DynAnyPackage↵
                                   .InvalidSeq
```

DynStruct ❷   org.omg.DynamicAny

```
1.4      DynStruct——————————————————DynStructOperations ¹ (DynAnyOperations²), DynAny
                                              (DynAnyOperations², org.omg.CORBA.Object ³,
                                              org.omg.CORBA.portable.IDLEntity (java.io.Serializable)),
                                              org.omg.CORBA.portable.IDLEntity (java.io.Serializable)
```

```
    1  6 inherited members from DynStructOperations not shown
    3  13 inherited members from org.omg.CORBA.Object not shown
    2  50 inherited members from DynAnyOperations not shown
```

DynStructHelper   org.omg.DynamicAny

```
        Object
1.4 ○   └DynStructHelper
```

```
∗   public.......................... DynStructHelper ()
△   public static ......... DynStruct extract (org.omg.CORBA.Any a)
△   public static ............. String id ()
△   public static ...............void insert (org.omg.CORBA.Any a, DynStruct that)
△   public static ......... DynStruct narrow (org.omg.CORBA.Object obj)
△   public static ......... DynStruct read (org.omg.CORBA.portable.InputStream istream)
△   public static synchronized .... type ()
      . org.omg.CORBA.TypeCode
△   public static ...............void write (org.omg.CORBA.portable.OutputStream ostream, DynStruct value)
```

DynStructOperations   org.omg.DynamicAny

```
1.4      DynStructOperations ——————————————DynAnyOperations ¹
```

```
    1  50 inherited members from DynAnyOperations not shown
        public.......................... current_member_kind () throws org.omg.DynamicAny.DynAnyPackage↵
          .....org.omg.CORBA.TCKind    .TypeMismatch, org.omg.DynamicAny.DynAnyPackage.InvalidValue
        public....................String current_member_name () throws org.omg.DynamicAny.DynAnyPackage↵
                                         .TypeMismatch, org.omg.DynamicAny.DynAnyPackage.InvalidValue
        public.........NameValuePair[] get_members ()
        public...... NameDynAnyPair[] get_members_as_dyn_any ()
        public.....................void set_members (NameValuePair[] value) throws org↵
                                         .omg.DynamicAny.DynAnyPackage.TypeMismatch,
                                         org.omg.DynamicAny.DynAnyPackage.InvalidValue
        public.....................void set_members_as_dyn_any (NameDynAnyPair[] value)
                                         throws org.omg.DynamicAny.DynAnyPackage.TypeMismatch,
                                         org.omg.DynamicAny.DynAnyPackage.InvalidValue
```

DynUnion ❶   org.omg.CORBA

```
1.2      DynUnion——————————————————————Object ¹, DynAny ² (Object ¹)
```

```
    2  46 inherited members from DynAny not shown
    1  13 inherited members from Object not shown
        public...................DynAny discriminator ()
        public.................TCKind discriminator_kind ()
        public...................DynAny member ()
        public.................TCKind member_kind ()
        public...................String member_name ()
        public.....................void member_name (String arg)
        public................ boolean set_as_default ()
        public.....................void set_as_default (boolean arg)
```

DynUnion❷ | org.omg.DynamicAny

| 1.4 | *DynUnion*────────── *DynUnionOperations* [1] (*DynAnyOperations* [2]), *DynAny* (*DynAnyOperations* [2], *org.omg.CORBA.Object* [3], *org.omg.CORBA.portable.IDLEntity* (*java.io.Serializable*)), *org.omg.CORBA.portable.IDLEntity* (*java.io.Serializable*) |

> [3] *13 inherited members from org.omg.CORBA.Object not shown*
> [1] *9 inherited members from DynUnionOperations not shown*
> [2] *50 inherited members from DynAnyOperations not shown*

DynUnionHelper | org.omg.DynamicAny

Object
1.4 ○ └DynUnionHelper

∗	public........................		**DynUnionHelper** ()
△	public static	*DynUnion*	**extract** (org.omg.CORBA.Any a)
△	public static ....String		**id** ()
△	public static ....void		**insert** (org.omg.CORBA.Any a, *DynUnion* that)
△	public static	*DynUnion*	**narrow** (*org.omg.CORBA.Object* obj)
△	public static	*DynUnion*	**read** (org.omg.CORBA.portable.InputStream istream)
△	public static synchronized .... org.omg.CORBA.TypeCode		**type** ()
△	public static ....void		**write** (org.omg.CORBA.portable.OutputStream ostream, *DynUnion* value)

DynUnionOperations | org.omg.DynamicAny

| 1.4 | *DynUnionOperations* ──────────── *DynAnyOperations* [1] |

> [1] *50 inherited members from DynAnyOperations not shown*

public.......................... .....org.omg.CORBA.TCKind	**discriminator_kind** ()
public...................*DynAny*	**get_discriminator** ()
public.................. boolean	**has_no_active_member** ()
public...................*DynAny*	**member** () throws org.omg.DynamicAny.DynAnyPackage.InvalidValue
public.......................... .....org.omg.CORBA.TCKind	**member_kind** () throws org.omg.DynamicAny.DynAnyPackage.InvalidValue
public...................String	**member_name** () throws org.omg.DynamicAny.DynAnyPackage.InvalidValue
public.......................void	**set_discriminator** (*DynAny* d) throws org.omg.DynamicAny.DynAnyPackage↵ .TypeMismatch
public.......................void	**set_to_default_member** () throws org.omg.DynamicAny.DynAnyPackage↵ .TypeMismatch
public.......................void	**set_to_no_active_member** () throws org.omg.DynamicAny.DynAnyPackage↵ .TypeMismatch

DynValue❶ | org.omg.CORBA

| 1.2 | *DynValue*──────────── *Object* [1], *DynAny* [2] (*Object* [1]) |

> [2] *46 inherited members from DynAny not shown*
> [1] *13 inherited members from Object not shown*

public...................TCKind	**current_member_kind** ()
public...................String	**current_member_name** ()
public.........NameValuePair[]	**get_members** ()
public.......................void	**set_members** (NameValuePair[] value) throws org.omg.CORBA.DynAnyPackage↵ .InvalidSeq

DynValue❷ | org.omg.DynamicAny

| 1.4 | *DynValue*──────────── *DynValueOperations* [1] (*DynValueCommonOperations* [2] (*DynAnyOperations* [3])), *DynValueCommon* (*DynValueCommonOperations* [2] (*DynAnyOperations* [3]), *DynAny* (*DynAnyOperations* [3], *org.omg.CORBA.Object* [4], *org.omg.CORBA.portable.IDLEntity* (*java.io.Serializable*)), *org.omg.CORBA.portable.IDLEntity* (*java.io.Serializable*)), *org.omg.CORBA.portable.IDLEntity* (*java.io.Serializable*) |

> [4] *13 inherited members from org.omg.CORBA.Object not shown*
> [1] *6 inherited members from DynValueOperations not shown*

D

Classes

> 3 50 inherited members from DynAnyOperations not shown
> 2 3 inherited members from DynValueCommonOperations not shown

---

DynValueBox   org.omg.DynamicAny

1.4   *DynValueBox*────────────────── *DynValueBoxOperations* [1] (*DynValueCommonOperations* [2]
                                         (*DynAnyOperations* [3])), *DynValueCommon*
                                         (*DynValueCommonOperations* [2] (*DynAnyOperations* [3]),
                                         DynAny (*DynAnyOperations* [3], *org.omg.CORBA.Object* [4],
                                         org.omg.CORBA.portable.IDLEntity (*java.io.Serializable*)),
                                         org.omg.CORBA.portable.IDLEntity (*java.io.Serializable*)),
                                         org.omg.CORBA.portable.IDLEntity (*java.io.Serializable*)

> 1 4 inherited members from DynValueBoxOperations not shown
> 4 13 inherited members from org.omg.CORBA.Object not shown
> 3 50 inherited members from DynAnyOperations not shown
> 2 3 inherited members from DynValueCommonOperations not shown

---

DynValueBoxOperations   org.omg.DynamicAny

1.4   *DynValueBoxOperations*──────────── *DynValueCommonOperations* [1] (*DynAnyOperations* [2])

> 2 50 inherited members from DynAnyOperations not shown
> 1 3 inherited members from DynValueCommonOperations not shown

public....org.omg.CORBA.Any **get_boxed_value** () throws org.omg.DynamicAny.DynAnyPackage.InvalidValue
public..................*DynAny* **get_boxed_value_as_dyn_any** () throws org.omg.DynamicAny.DynAnyPackage ↵
                         .InvalidValue
public......................void **set_boxed_value** (org.omg.CORBA.Any boxed) throws
                         org.omg.DynamicAny.DynAnyPackage.TypeMismatch
public......................void **set_boxed_value_as_dyn_any** (*DynAny* boxed) throws
                         org.omg.DynamicAny.DynAnyPackage.TypeMismatch

---

DynValueCommon   org.omg.DynamicAny

1.4   *DynValueCommon*────────────────── *DynValueCommonOperations* [1] (*DynAnyOperations* [2]),
                                         DynAny (*DynAnyOperations* [2], *org.omg.CORBA.Object* [3],
                                         org.omg.CORBA.portable.IDLEntity (*java.io.Serializable*)),
                                         org.omg.CORBA.portable.IDLEntity (*java.io.Serializable*)

> 3 13 inherited members from org.omg.CORBA.Object not shown
> 2 50 inherited members from DynAnyOperations not shown
> 1 3 inherited members from DynValueCommonOperations not shown

---

DynValueCommonOperations   org.omg.DynamicAny

1.4   *DynValueCommonOperations*──────────── *DynAnyOperations* [1]

> 1 50 inherited members from DynAnyOperations not shown

public................. boolean **is_null** ()
public......................void **set_to_null** ()
public......................void **set_to_value** ()

DynValueHelper   org.omg.DynamicAny

         Object
1.4 ○   └DynValueHelper

✳   public........................... **DynValueHelper** ()
△   public static ....*DynValue* **extract** (org.omg.CORBA.Any a)
△   public static ....String **id** ()
△   public static ....void **insert** (org.omg.CORBA.Any a, *DynValue* that)
△   public static ....*DynValue* **narrow** (*org.omg.CORBA.Object* obj)
△   public static ....*DynValue* **read** (org.omg.CORBA.portable.InputStream istream)
△   public static synchronized .... **type** ()
     . org.omg.CORBA.TypeCode
△   public static ....void **write** (org.omg.CORBA.portable.OutputStream ostream, *DynValue* value)

Class *Interface* —extends - - -implements ○ abstract ● final △ static ▲ static final ✳ constructor x x—inherited x **x**—declared **x x**—overridden
εn—examples of usage ˍ—has subclass package—see other volume

DynValueOperations | org.omg.DynamicAny

1.4   *DynValueOperations* ──────────────── *DynValueCommonOperations* [1] (*DynAnyOperations* [2])

  2 *50 inherited members from DynAnyOperations not shown*
  1 *3 inherited members from DynValueCommonOperations not shown*
    public.......................... **current_member_kind** () throws org.omg.DynamicAny.DynAnyPackage ↵
    .....org.omg.CORBA.TCKind .TypeMismatch, org.omg.DynamicAny.DynAnyPackage.InvalidValue
    public.....................String **current_member_name** () throws org.omg.DynamicAny.DynAnyPackage ↵
    .TypeMismatch, org.omg.DynamicAny.DynAnyPackage.InvalidValue
    public.........NameValuePair[] **get_members** () throws org.omg.DynamicAny.DynAnyPackage.InvalidValue
    public......NameDynAnyPair[] **get_members_as_dyn_any** () throws org.omg.DynamicAny.DynAnyPackage ↵
    .InvalidValue
    public......................void **set_members** (NameValuePair[] value) throws org ↵
    .omg.DynamicAny.DynAnyPackage.TypeMismatch,
    org.omg.DynamicAny.DynAnyPackage.InvalidValue
    public......................void **set_members_as_dyn_any** (NameDynAnyPair[] value)
    throws org.omg.DynamicAny.DynAnyPackage.TypeMismatch,
    org.omg.DynamicAny.DynAnyPackage.InvalidValue

Element ❸ | org.w3c.dom

1.4   *Element* ──────────────── *Node* [1]   ε532,524,526,529,530

  1 *28 inherited members from Node not shown*
  1 public.................... *Node* appendChild (*Node* newChild) throws DOMException ε526,533,539,540,542
  1 public.................... *Node* cloneNode (boolean deep) ε525
    public....................String **getAttribute** (String name) ε531,534,535
    public..................... *Attr* **getAttributeNode** (String name) ε538
    public..................... *Attr* **getAttributeNodeNS** (String namespaceURI, String localName)
    public....................String **getAttributeNS** (String namespaceURI, String localName)
  1 public........ *NamedNodeMap* getAttributes () ε533,536,537
    public................. *NodeList* **getElementsByTagName** (String name)
    public................. *NodeList* **getElementsByTagNameNS** (String namespaceURI, String localName)
  1 public.................... *Node* getFirstChild () ε527,530,533,539,546
  1 public.................... *Node* getLastChild () ε527,539,530
  1 public.................... *Node* getNextSibling () ε525,541,527,530,539
  1 public.................... *Node* getParentNode () ε525,527,533,539,541
    public....................String **getTagName** ()
    public................. boolean **hasAttribute** (String name) ε534,535
    public................. boolean **hasAttributeNS** (String namespaceURI, String localName)
  1 public................. boolean hasChildNodes () ε533,547,512
  1 public.................... *Node* insertBefore (*Node* newChild, *Node* refChild) throws DOMException
    ε539,546,525,541,542
    public......................void **removeAttribute** (String name) throws DOMException ε535
    public..................... *Attr* **removeAttributeNode** (*Attr* oldAttr) throws DOMException
    public......................void **removeAttributeNS** (String namespaceURI, String localName)
    throws DOMException
    public......................void **setAttribute** (String name, String value) throws DOMException ε534,535
    public..................... *Attr* **setAttributeNode** (*Attr* newAttr) throws DOMException
    public..................... *Attr* **setAttributeNodeNS** (*Attr* newAttr) throws DOMException
    public......................void **setAttributeNS** (String namespaceURI, String qualifiedName, String value)
    throws DOMException

EmptyStackException | java.util

    Object
    └Throwable ------------------------- *java.io.Serializable*
     └Exception
      └RuntimeException
       └EmptyStackException

  * public.......................... **EmptyStackException** ()

EncodedKeySpec | java.security.spec

    Object ε199
1.2 ○ └EncodedKeySpec -------------------- *KeySpec*

  * public.......................... **EncodedKeySpec** (byte[] encodedKey)
    public....................byte[] **getEncoded** ()

EncodedKeySpec

O	public abstract . . . . String **getFormat** ()

Encoder
java.beans

Object
1.4 └Encoder‿

∗	public. . . . . **Encoder** ()
	public. . . . . Object **get** (Object oldInstance)
	public. . . . . . . *ExceptionListener* **getExceptionListener** ()
	public. . . . PersistenceDelegate **getPersistenceDelegate** (Class type)
	public. . . . . Object **remove** (Object oldInstance)
	public. . . . . void **setExceptionListener** (*ExceptionListener* exceptionListener)
	public. . . . . void **setPersistenceDelegate** (Class type, PersistenceDelegate persistenceDelegate)
	ε10
	public. . . . . void **writeExpression** (Expression oldExp)
	protected . . . . void **writeObject** (Object o) ε7,9,10
	public. . . . . void **writeStatement** (Statement oldStm)

Encoding
org.omg.IOP

Object
1.4 ● └Encoding - *org.omg.CORBA.portable.IDLEntity*‿ (*java.io.Serializable*)

∗	public. . . . . **Encoding** ()
∗	public. . . . . **Encoding** (short _format, byte _major_version, byte _minor_version)
	public. . . . . short **format**
	public. . . . . byte **major_version**
	public. . . . . byte **minor_version**

ENCODING_CDR_ENCAPS
org.omg.IOP

ENCODING_CDR_ENCAPS
1.4

▲	public static final . . . . short **value** = 0

EncryptedPrivateKeyInfo
javax.crypto

Object
1.4 └EncryptedPrivateKeyInfo

∗	public. . . . . **EncryptedPrivateKeyInfo** (byte[] encoded) throws java.io.IOException
∗	public. . . . . **EncryptedPrivateKeyInfo** (String algName, byte[] encryptedData)
	throws java.security.NoSuchAlgorithmException
∗	public. . . . . **EncryptedPrivateKeyInfo** (java.security.AlgorithmParameters algParams,
	byte[] encryptedData) throws java.security.NoSuchAlgorithmException
	public. . . . . String **getAlgName** ()
	public. . . . . java.security↵ **getAlgParameters** ()
	.AlgorithmParameters
	public. . . . . byte[] **getEncoded** () throws java.io.IOException
	public. . . . . byte[] **getEncryptedData** ()
	public. . . . java.security.spec↵ **getKeySpec** (Cipher c) throws java.security.spec.InvalidKeySpecException
	.PKCS8EncodedKeySpec

Entity ❷
org.w3c.dom

1.4 *Entity*————————————————*Node*‿ [1]   ε524,526,529,530,532

1	*36 inherited members from Node not shown*
1	public. . . . . String getNodeName () ε529,528,536,537,544
	public. . . . . String **getNotationName** ()
	public. . . . . String **getPublicId** () ε529
	public. . . . . String **getSystemId** () ε529

Class *Interface* —extends - - -implements O abstract ● final △ static ▲ static final ∗ constructor x x—inherited x **x**—declared **x x**—overridden
ε*n*—examples of usage ‿—has subclass package—see other volume

EntityReference | org.w3c.dom

1.4	*EntityReference*————————————*Node*, [1]	ε529,524,526,530,532

1	*35 inherited members from Node not shown*	
1	public .... *Node* getFirstChild ()	ε530,527,533,539,546
1	public .... *Node* getLastChild ()	ε530,527,539

EntityResolver | org.xml.sax

1.4	*EntityResolver*

public .... InputSource **resolveEntity** (String publicId, String systemId) throws SAXException, java.io.IOException	ε548

Enumeration | java.util

Enumeration,

public .... boolean **hasMoreElements** ()	ε454,88,208,217,218
public .... Object **nextElement** ()	ε454,88,208,217,218

Environment | org.omg.CORBA

Object
  └Environment
1.2 ○

○	public abstract .... void **clear** ()
✳	public .... **Environment** ()
○	public abstract ...... Exception **exception** ()
○	public abstract .... void **exception** (Exception except)

EOFException | java.io

Object
  └Throwable ---------------------------- *Serializable*,
    └Exception
      └IOException
        └EOFException

✳	public .... **EOFException** ()
✳	public .... **EOFException** (String s)

Error | java.lang

Object
  └Throwable ---------------------------- *java.io.Serializable*,
    └Error,

✳	public .... **Error** ()
✳	public .... **Error** (String message)
1.4 ✳	public .... **Error** (Throwable cause)
1.4 ✳	public .... **Error** (String message, Throwable cause)

ErrorHandler | org.xml.sax

1.4	*ErrorHandler*

public .... void **error** (SAXParseException exception) throws SAXException	ε513
public .... void **fatalError** (SAXParseException exception) throws SAXException	ε513
public .... void **warning** (SAXParseException exception) throws SAXException	ε513

E

Classes

ErrorListener | javax.xml.transform

1.4   *ErrorListener*

    public......................void **error** (TransformerException exception) throws TransformerException
                                                ε513

    public......................void **fatalError** (TransformerException exception) throws TransformerException
                                                  ε513

    public......................void **warning** (TransformerException exception) throws TransformerException
                                                  ε513

ErrorManager | java.util.logging

     Object
1.4   └ErrorManager

▲   public static final.............int **CLOSE_FAILURE** = 3
    public synchronized.......void **error** (String msg, Exception ex, int code)
✳   public................................ **ErrorManager** ()
▲   public static final.............int **FLUSH_FAILURE** = 2
▲   public static final.............int **FORMAT_FAILURE** = 5
▲   public static final.............int **GENERIC_FAILURE** = 0
▲   public static final.............int **OPEN_FAILURE** = 4
▲   public static final.............int **WRITE_FAILURE** = 1

EventContext | javax.naming.event

1.3   *EventContext* ─────────────────── *javax.naming.Context* ⌐[1] ε481,484,492,495

    1 *44 inherited members from javax.naming.Context not shown*
    public......................void **addNamingListener** (String target, int scope, *NamingListener* l)
                     throws javax.naming.NamingException ε493
    public......................void **addNamingListener** (*javax.naming.Name* target, int scope, *NamingListener* l)
                     throws javax.naming.NamingException
▲   public static final.............int **OBJECT_SCOPE** = 0
▲   public static final.............int **ONELEVEL_SCOPE** = 1 ε493
    public......................void **removeNamingListener** (*NamingListener* l) throws javax.naming.NamingException
▲   public static final.............int **SUBTREE_SCOPE** = 2
    public.................boolean **targetMustExist** () throws javax.naming.NamingException

EventDirContext | javax.naming.event

1.3   *EventDirContext*──────────────── *EventContext* ⌐[1] (*javax.naming.Context* [2]), ε481,484,492,495
                                  javax.naming.directory.DirContext ⌐[3]
                                  (*javax.naming.Context* [2])

    2 *44 inherited members from javax.naming.Context not shown*
    3 *29 inherited members from javax.naming.directory.DirContext not shown*
    1 public......................void addNamingListener (String target, int scope, *NamingListener* l)
                     throws javax.naming.NamingException ε493
    1 public......................void addNamingListener (*javax.naming.Name* target, int scope, *NamingListener* l)
                     throws javax.naming.NamingException
    public......................void **addNamingListener** (String target, String filter, javax.naming.directory↵
                 .SearchControls ctls, *NamingListener* l) throws javax.naming.NamingException
                                                        ε494
    public......................void **addNamingListener** (*javax.naming.Name* target, String filter,
                 javax.naming.directory.SearchControls ctls, *NamingListener* l)
                 throws javax.naming.NamingException
    public......................void **addNamingListener** (String target, String filter, Object[] filterArgs,
                 javax.naming.directory.SearchControls ctls, *NamingListener* l)
                 throws javax.naming.NamingException
    public......................void **addNamingListener** (*javax.naming.Name* target, String filter, Object[] filterArgs,
                 javax.naming.directory.SearchControls ctls, *NamingListener* l)
                 throws javax.naming.NamingException
    1 public......................void removeNamingListener (*NamingListener* l) throws javax.naming.NamingException
    1 public.................boolean targetMustExist () throws javax.naming.NamingException

Class *Interface* —extends - - -implements ○ abstract ● final △ static ▲ static final ✳ constructor x x—inherited x **x**—declared **x x**—overridden
εn—examples of usage ⌐—has subclass package—see other volume

564

			EventHandler	java.beans
			Object	
1.4			└EventHandler - *java.lang.reflect.InvocationHandler* [1]	
△	public static .... Object	**create** (Class listenerInterface, Object target, String action)		
△	public static .... Object	**create** (Class listenerInterface, Object target, String action, String eventPropertyName)		
△	public static .... Object	**create** (Class listenerInterface, Object target, String action, String eventPropertyName, String listenerMethodName)		
*	public..........................	**EventHandler** (Object target, String action, String eventPropertyName, String listenerMethodName)		
	public.................... String	**getAction** ()		
	public.................... String	**getEventPropertyName** ()		
	public.................... String	**getListenerMethodName** ()		
	public.................... Object	**getTarget** ()		
[1]	public.................... Object	**invoke** (Object proxy, java.lang.reflect.Method method, Object[] arguments)		
				ε111

EventListener		java.util
1.1	*EventListener*	ε333

EventListenerProxy			java.util
	Object		
1.4 ○	└EventListenerProxy - *EventListener*		
*	public..........................	**EventListenerProxy** (*EventListener* listener)	
	public............ *EventListener*	**getListener** ()	

EventObject			java.util
	Object [1]		ε333
1.1	└EventObject - *java.io.Serializable*		
*	public..........................	**EventObject** (Object source)	
	public.................... Object	**getSource** ()	
	protected transient...... Object	**source**	
[1]	public.................... String	**toString** ()	

EventSetDescriptor			java.beans
	Object		
1.1	└FeatureDescriptor [1]		
1.1	└EventSetDescriptor		
[1]	public.... *java.util.Enumeration*	attributeNames ()	
*	public..........................	**EventSetDescriptor** (Class sourceClass, String eventSetName, Class listenerType, String listenerMethodName) throws IntrospectionException	
*	public..........................	**EventSetDescriptor** (String eventSetName, Class listenerType, MethodDescriptor[] listenerMethodDescriptors, java.lang.reflect.Method addListenerMethod, java.lang.reflect.Method removeListenerMethod) throws IntrospectionException	
*	public..........................	**EventSetDescriptor** (String eventSetName, Class java.lang↵ .reflect.Method[] listenerMethods, java.lang.reflect.Method addListenerMethod, java.lang.reflect.Method removeListenerMethod) throws IntrospectionException	
*	public..........................	**EventSetDescriptor** (Class sourceClass, String eventSetName, Class listenerType, String[] listenerMethodNames, String addListenerMethodName, String removeListenerMethodName) throws IntrospectionException	
1.4 *	public..........................	**EventSetDescriptor** (String eventSetName, Class listenerType, java.lang.reflect.Method[] listenerMethods, java.lang.reflect.Method addListenerMethod, java.lang.reflect.Method removeListenerMethod, java.lang.reflect.Method getListenerMethod) throws IntrospectionException	
1.4 *	public..........................	**EventSetDescriptor** (Class sourceClass, String eventSetName, Class listenerType, String[] listenerMethodNames, String addListenerMethodName, String removeListenerMethodName, String getListenerMethodName) throws IntrospectionException	
	public. java.lang.reflect.Method	**getAddListenerMethod** ()	

E

Classes

EventSetDescriptor

	1	public......................String	getDisplayName ()	
1.4		public.java.lang.reflect.Method	**getGetListenerMethod** ()	
		public......MethodDescriptor[]	**getListenerMethodDescriptors** ()	
		public.............................. ....java.lang.reflect.Method[]	**getListenerMethods** ()	
		public....................Class	**getListenerType** ()	
	1	public......................String	getName ()	ε5,9
		public.java.lang.reflect.Method	**getRemoveListenerMethod** ()	
	1	public......................String	getShortDescription ()	
	1	public....................Object	getValue (String attributeName)	
	1	public...........boolean	isExpert ()	
	1	public...........boolean	isHidden ()	
		public...........boolean	**isInDefaultEventSet** ()	
1.2	1	public...........boolean	isPreferred ()	
		public...........boolean	**isUnicast** ()	
	1	public..................void	setDisplayName (String displayName)	
	1	public..................void	setExpert (boolean expert)	
	1	public..................void	setHidden (boolean hidden)	
		public..................void	**setInDefaultEventSet** (boolean inDefaultEventSet)	
	1	public..................void	setName (String name)	
1.2	1	public..................void	setPreferred (boolean preferred)	
	1	public..................void	setShortDescription (String text)	
		public..................void	**setUnicast** (boolean unicast)	
	1	public..................void	setValue (String attributeName, Object value)	ε9

Exception   java.lang

Object   ε54,69,96,111,6
└Throwable - *java.io.Serializable*⌄
  └Exception⌄

*	public........................	**Exception** ()	
*	public........................	**Exception** (String message)	
1.4 *	public........................	**Exception** (Throwable cause)	
1.4 *	public........................	**Exception** (String message, Throwable cause)	

ExceptionInInitializerError   java.lang

Object
└Throwable[1] - *java.io.Serializable*⌄
  └Error
    └LinkageError
1.1   └ExceptionInInitializerError

*	public........................	**ExceptionInInitializerError** ()	
*	public........................	**ExceptionInInitializerError** (String s)	
*	public........................	**ExceptionInInitializerError** (Throwable thrown)	
1.4	1	public..........**Throwable**	**getCause** ()	
	public...............Throwable	**getException** ()	

ExceptionList   org.omg.CORBA

Object
1.2 ○ └ExceptionList

○	public abstract ....void	**add** (TypeCode exc)	
○	public abstract ....int	**count** ()	
*	public........................	**ExceptionList** ()	
○	public abstract ......TypeCode	**item** (int index) throws Bounds	
○	public abstract ....void	**remove** (int index) throws Bounds	

ExceptionListener   java.beans

1.4   *ExceptionListener*

	public......................void	**exceptionThrown** (Exception e)	

Class   *Interface*   —extends   - - -implements   ○ abstract   ● final   △ static   ▲ static final   * constructor   x x—inherited   x **x**—declared   **x x**—overridden
ε*n*—examples of usage   ⌄—has subclass   package—see other volume

	ExemptionMechanism	javax.crypto

Object [1]
  └ExemptionMechanism

1.4

✳	protected	**ExemptionMechanism** (ExemptionMechanismSpi exmechSpi, java.security.Provider provider, String mechanism)
1	protected . . . . **void finalize** ()	
●	public final . . . . byte[] **genExemptionBlob** () throws IllegalStateException, ExemptionMechanismException	
●	public final . . . . int **genExemptionBlob** (byte[] output) throws IllegalStateException, ShortBufferException, ExemptionMechanismException	
●	public final . . . . int **genExemptionBlob** (byte[] output, int outputOffset) throws IllegalStateException, ShortBufferException, ExemptionMechanismException	
▲	public static final . . . . ExemptionMechanism **getInstance** (String mechanism) throws java.security.NoSuchAlgorithmException	
▲	public static final . . . . ExemptionMechanism **getInstance** (String mechanism, java.security.Provider provider) throws java.security.NoSuchAlgorithmException	
▲	public static final . . . . ExemptionMechanism **getInstance** (String mechanism, String provider) throws java.security↵.NoSuchAlgorithmException, java.security.NoSuchProviderException	
●	public final . . . . String **getName** ()	
●	public final . . . . int **getOutputSize** (int inputLen) throws IllegalStateException	
●	public final . . . . java.security.Provider **getProvider** ()	
●	public final . . . . void **init** (*java.security.Key* key) throws java.security.InvalidKeyException, ExemptionMechanismException	
●	public final . . . . void **init** (*java.security.Key* key, java.security.AlgorithmParameters params) throws java.security.InvalidKeyException, java.security↵.InvalidAlgorithmParameterException, ExemptionMechanismException	
●	public final . . . . void **init** (*java.security.Key* key, *java.security.spec.AlgorithmParameterSpec* params) throws java.security.InvalidKeyException, java.security↵.InvalidAlgorithmParameterException, ExemptionMechanismException	
●	public final . . . . boolean **isCryptoAllowed** (*java.security.Key* key) throws ExemptionMechanismException	

E

	ExemptionMechanismException	javax.crypto

Object
 └Throwable - *java.io.Serializable*
   └Exception
    └java.security.GeneralSecurityException

1.2

     └ExemptionMechanismException

1.4

✳	public . . . . **ExemptionMechanismException** ()
✳	public . . . . **ExemptionMechanismException** (String msg)

	ExemptionMechanismSpi	javax.crypto

Object
 └ExemptionMechanismSpi

1.4 ○

○	protected abstract . . . . byte[] **engineGenExemptionBlob** () throws ExemptionMechanismException
○	protected abstract . . . . int **engineGenExemptionBlob** (byte[] output, int outputOffset) throws ShortBufferException, ExemptionMechanismException
○	protected abstract . . . . int **engineGetOutputSize** (int inputLen)
○	protected abstract . . . . void **engineInit** (*java.security.Key* key) throws java.security.InvalidKeyException, ExemptionMechanismException
○	protected abstract . . . . void **engineInit** (*java.security.Key* key, *java.security.spec.AlgorithmParameterSpec* params) throws java.security.InvalidKeyException, java.security↵.InvalidAlgorithmParameterException, ExemptionMechanismException
○	protected abstract . . . . void **engineInit** (*java.security.Key* key, java.security.AlgorithmParameters params) throws java.security.InvalidKeyException, java.security↵.InvalidAlgorithmParameterException, ExemptionMechanismException
✳	public . . . . **ExemptionMechanismSpi** ()

Classes

ExportException			java.rmi.server

```
Object
└Throwable ---------------------------- java.io.Serializable↲
  └Exception
    └java.io.IOException
1.1    └java.rmi.RemoteException¹
1.1      └ExportException↲
```

	1	public................Throwable	detail	
✳		public........................	**ExportException** (String s)	
✳		public........................	**ExportException** (String s, Exception ex)	
1.4	1	public................Throwable	getCause ()	
	1	public....................String	getMessage ()	

Expression			java.beans

```
Object
1.4  └Statement¹
1.4    └Expression
```

	1	public......................void	execute () throws Exception	ε6
✳		public.........................	**Expression** (Object target, String methodName, Object[] arguments)	
				ε6
✳		public.........................	**Expression** (Object value, Object target, String methodName, Object[] arguments)	
	1	public.................Object[]	getArguments ()	
	1	public....................String	getMethodName ()	
	1	public..................Object	getTarget ()	
		public..................Object	**getValue** () throws Exception	ε6
		public......................void	**setValue** (Object value)	
	1	public..................**String**	**toString** ()	

ExtendedRequest			javax.naming.ldap

1.3	*ExtendedRequest*————————*java.io.Serializable*↲	ε498

public..... *ExtendedResponse*	**createExtendedResponse** (String id, byte[] berValue, int offset, int length)	
	throws javax.naming.NamingException	
public....................byte[]	**getEncodedValue** ()	
public....................String	**getID** ()	

ExtendedResponse			javax.naming.ldap

1.3	*ExtendedResponse*↲————————————*java.io.Serializable*↲

public....................byte[]	**getEncodedValue** ()
public....................String	**getID** ()

Externalizable			java.io

1.1	*Externalizable*↲————————————*Serializable*↲

public......................void	**readExternal** (*ObjectInput* in) throws IOException, ClassNotFoundException
public......................void	**writeExternal** (*ObjectOutput* out) throws IOException

FactoryConfigurationError			javax.xml.parsers

```
Object
└Throwable¹ ---------------------------- java.io.Serializable↲
  └Error
1.4    └FactoryConfigurationError
```

✳		public........................	**FactoryConfigurationError** ()
✳		public........................	**FactoryConfigurationError** (Exception e)
✳		public........................	**FactoryConfigurationError** (String msg)
✳		public........................	**FactoryConfigurationError** (Exception e, String msg)

Class *Interface* —extends - - -implements ○ abstract ● final △ static ▲ static final ✳ constructor x x—inherited x **x**—declared **x x**—overridden
ε*n*—examples of usage ↲—has subclass package—see other volume

	public............... Exception	**getException** ()	
1	public.................... **String**	**getMessage** ()	

FailedLoginException
javax.security.auth.login

```
Object
 └Throwable -------------------------- java.io.Serializable⌄
   └Exception
1.2     └java.security.GeneralSecurityException
1.4       └LoginException
1.4         └FailedLoginException
```

*	public.........................	**FailedLoginException** ()	
*	public.........................	**FailedLoginException** (String msg)	

FeatureDescriptor
java.beans

```
Object
1.1 └FeatureDescriptor⌄
```

	public.... *java.util.Enumeration*	**attributeNames** ()	
*	public.........................	**FeatureDescriptor** ()	
	public....................String	**getDisplayName** ()	
	public....................String	**getName** ()	ε5,9
	public....................String	**getShortDescription** ()	
	public....................Object	**getValue** (String attributeName)	
	public............... boolean	**isExpert** ()	
	public............... boolean	**isHidden** ()	
1.2	public............... boolean	**isPreferred** ()	
	public......................void	**setDisplayName** (String displayName)	
	public......................void	**setExpert** (boolean expert)	
	public......................void	**setHidden** (boolean hidden)	
	public......................void	**setName** (String name)	
1.2	public......................void	**setPreferred** (boolean preferred)	
	public......................void	**setShortDescription** (String text)	
	public......................void	**setValue** (String attributeName, Object value)	ε9

Field
java.lang.reflect

```
Object¹
1.2 └AccessibleObject²
1.1● └Field ----------------------------- Member³
```

	1	public.................**boolean**	**equals** (Object obj)	
		public....................Object	**get** (Object obj) throws IllegalArgumentException, IllegalAccessException	ε291
		public............... boolean	**getBoolean** (Object obj) throws IllegalArgumentException, IllegalAccessException	
		public..................... byte	**getByte** (Object obj) throws IllegalArgumentException, IllegalAccessException	
		public..................... char	**getChar** (Object obj) throws IllegalArgumentException, IllegalAccessException	
	3	public.....................Class	**getDeclaringClass** ()	
		public....................double	**getDouble** (Object obj) throws IllegalArgumentException, IllegalAccessException	
		public.....................float	**getFloat** (Object obj) throws IllegalArgumentException, IllegalAccessException	
		public.........................int	**getInt** (Object obj) throws IllegalArgumentException, IllegalAccessException	ε115
		public..................... long	**getLong** (Object obj) throws IllegalArgumentException, IllegalAccessException	
	3	public.........................int	**getModifiers** ()	ε113
	3	public....................String	**getName** ()	ε109,291
		public....................short	**getShort** (Object obj) throws IllegalArgumentException, IllegalAccessException	
		public.....................Class	**getType** ()	ε114
	1	public................. **int**	**hashCode** ()	
1.2	2	public............... boolean	isAccessible ()	
		public......................void	**set** (Object obj, Object value) throws IllegalArgumentException, IllegalAccessException	
1.2	2	public......................void	setAccessible (boolean flag) throws SecurityException	ε110
1.2 △	2	public static ....void	setAccessible (AccessibleObject[] array, boolean flag) throws SecurityException	
		public......................void	**setBoolean** (Object obj, boolean z) throws IllegalArgumentException, IllegalAccessException	
		public......................void	**setByte** (Object obj, byte b) throws IllegalArgumentException, IllegalAccessException	
		public......................void	**setChar** (Object obj, char c) throws IllegalArgumentException, IllegalAccessException	

Field

	public	.................void	**setDouble** (Object obj, double d) throws IllegalArgumentException, IllegalAccessException
	public	.................void	**setFloat** (Object obj, float f) throws IllegalArgumentException, IllegalAccessException
	public	.................void	**setInt** (Object obj, int i) throws IllegalArgumentException, IllegalAccessException
			ε115
	public	.................void	**setLong** (Object obj, long l) throws IllegalArgumentException, IllegalAccessException
	public	.................void	**setShort** (Object obj, short s) throws IllegalArgumentException, IllegalAccessException
1	public	.................String	**toString** ()

FieldNameHelper❶   org.omg.CORBA

1.3 O
```
Object
 └FieldNameHelper
```

△	public static	.............String	**extract** (Any a)
✳	public	....	**FieldNameHelper** ()
△	public static	.............String	**id** ()
△	public static	............void	**insert** (Any a, String that)
△	public static	.............String	**read** (org.omg.CORBA.portable.InputStream istream)
△	public static synchronized ....TypeCode		**type** ()
△	public static	............void	**write** (org.omg.CORBA.portable.OutputStream ostream, String value)

FieldNameHelper❷   org.omg.DynamicAny

1.4 O
```
Object
 └FieldNameHelper
```

△	public static	.............String	**extract** (org.omg.CORBA.Any a)
✳	public	....	**FieldNameHelper** ()
△	public static	.............String	**id** ()
△	public static	............void	**insert** (org.omg.CORBA.Any a, String that)
△	public static	.............String	**read** (org.omg.CORBA.portable.InputStream istream)
△	public static synchronized .... . org.omg.CORBA.TypeCode		**type** ()
△	public static	............void	**write** (org.omg.CORBA.portable.OutputStream ostream, String value)

FieldPosition   java.text

1.1
```
Object¹
 └FieldPosition
```

	1	public	............boolean	**equals** (Object obj)
✳		public	....	**FieldPosition** (int field)
1.4	✳	public	....	**FieldPosition** (Format.Field attribute)
1.4	✳	public	....	**FieldPosition** (Format.Field attribute, int fieldID)
		public	............int	**getBeginIndex** ()
		public	............int	**getEndIndex** ()
		public	............int	**getField** ()
1.4		public	............Format.Field	**getFieldAttribute** ()
	1	public	............int	**hashCode** ()
1.2		public	............void	**setBeginIndex** (int bi)
1.2		public	............void	**setEndIndex** (int ei)
	1	public	............String	**toString** ()

File   java.io

1.1
```
Object¹                                                    ε211,224,225
 └File - - - - - - - - - - - - - - - - - - - - - - - - - - - Serializable‿, Comparable²
```

	public	............boolean	**canRead** ()
	public	............boolean	**canWrite** ()
1.2	public	............int	**compareTo** (File pathname)

Class *Interface* —extends - - -implements ○ abstract ● final △ static ▲ static final ✳ constructor x x—inherited x **x**—declared **x x**—overridden
ε*n*—examples of usage ‿—has subclass package—see other volume

1.2	*2*	public...................................int	**compareTo** (Object o)	ε53
1.2		public................... boolean	**createNewFile** () throws IOException	ε20
1.2 △		public static .... File	**createTempFile** (String prefix, String suffix) throws IOException	ε23
1.2 △		public static .... File	**createTempFile** (String prefix, String suffix, File directory) throws IOException	
		public................. boolean	**delete** ()	ε22,30
1.2		public....................void	**deleteOnExit** ()	ε23
	1	public.................. **boolean equals** (Object obj)		ε57,16
		public................. boolean	**exists** ()	ε19
*		public...................	**File** (String pathname)	ε16,14,15,17,18
1.4 *		public...................	**File** (java.net.URI uri)	
*		public...................	**File** (File parent, String child)	ε25,33
*		public...................	**File** (String parent, String child)	
1.2		public................ File	**getAbsoluteFile** ()	ε15
		public...............String	**getAbsolutePath** ()	
1.2		public................ File	**getCanonicalFile** () throws IOException	ε16
1.1		public...............String	**getCanonicalPath** () throws IOException	
		public...............String	**getName** ()	ε25,36
		public...............String	**getParent** ()	ε17
1.2		public................ File	**getParentFile** ()	ε17
		public...............String	**getPath** ()	
	1	public.................... **int hashCode** ()		ε57
		public................ boolean	**isAbsolute** ()	
		public................ boolean	**isDirectory** ()	ε18,31,33
		public................ boolean	**isFile** ()	
1.2		public................ boolean	**isHidden** ()	ε26
		public.................. long	**lastModified** ()	ε21,36,39,259,434
		public.................. long	**length** ()	ε31,33
		public...............String[]	**list** ()	ε31
		public...............String[]	**list** (*FilenameFilter* filter)	
1.2		public.................File[]	**listFiles** ()	ε31
1.2		public.................File[]	**listFiles** (*FileFilter* filter)	ε31
1.2		public.................File[]	**listFiles** (*FilenameFilter* filter)	
1.2 △		public static ....File[]	**listRoots** ()	ε32
		public................ boolean	**mkdir** ()	ε29
		public................ boolean	**mkdirs** ()	ε29
▲		public static final........String	**pathSeparator** = ";"	
▲		public static final......... char	**pathSeparatorChar** = ';'	
		public................ boolean	**renameTo** (File dest)	ε24,25
▲		public static final........String	**separator** = "\"	ε13,69
▲		public static final......... char	**separatorChar** = '\'	ε208,209,230,231
1.2		public................ boolean	**setLastModified** (long time)	ε26
1.2		public................ boolean	**setReadOnly** ()	
	1	public.................. **String toString** ()		
1.4		public.............java.net.URI	**toURI** ()	ε523
1.2		public.............java.net.URL	**toURL** () throws java.net.MalformedURLException	ε14,68,69,218

FileChannel   java.nio.channels

Object   ε183,178

1.4 ○ └─java.nio.channels.spi.↩ - - - - - - - - - - - - - - - - - - - *Channel* ., *InterruptibleChannel* (*Channel*)
       .AbstractInterruptibleChannel[1]

1.4 ○   └─FileChannel - *ByteChannel* (*ReadableByteChannel*[2] (*Channel*),
                                              WritableByteChannel[3] (*Channel*)), *GatheringByteChannel*[4]
                                              (*WritableByteChannel*[3] (*Channel*)), *ScatteringByteChannel*[5]
                                              (*ReadableByteChannel*[2] (*Channel*))

●	*1*	protected final..............void	begin ()	
●	*1*	public final ....void	close () throws java.io.IOException	ε167,171,172,181,182
●	*1*	protected final..............void	end (boolean completed) throws AsynchronousCloseException	
*		protected......................	**FileChannel** ()	
○		public abstract ....void	**force** (boolean metaData) throws java.io.IOException	
○	*1*	protected abstract ....void	implCloseChannel () throws java.io.IOException	
●	*1*	public final .... boolean	isOpen ()	
●		public final .... FileLock	**lock** () throws java.io.IOException	ε181
○		public abstract .... FileLock	**lock** (long position, long size, boolean shared) throws java.io.IOException	
				ε182
○		public abstract	**map** (FileChannel.MapMode mode, long position, long size)	
		.. java.nio.MappedByteBuffer	throws java.io.IOException	ε166,167,425
○		public abstract .... long	**position** () throws java.io.IOException	
○		public abstract .... FileChannel	**position** (long newPosition) throws java.io.IOException	
○	*2*	public abstract ....int	**read** (java.nio.ByteBuffer dst) throws java.io.IOException	ε180,169,174
●	*5*	public final .... long	**read** (java.nio.ByteBuffer[] dsts) throws java.io.IOException	

F

Classes

FileChannel

○		public abstract .... int	**read** (java.nio.ByteBuffer dst, long position) throws java.io.IOException	
○	5	public abstract .... long	**read** (java.nio.ByteBuffer[] dsts, int offset, int length) throws java.io.IOException	
○		public abstract .... long	**size** () throws java.io.IOException	ε166,167,172,425
○		public abstract .... long	**transferFrom** (*ReadableByteChannel* src, long position, long count)	
			throws java.io.IOException	ε172
○		public abstract .... long	**transferTo** (long position, long count, *WritableByteChannel* target)	
			throws java.io.IOException	
○		public abstract .... FileChannel	**truncate** (long size) throws java.io.IOException	
●		public final .... FileLock	**tryLock** () throws java.io.IOException	ε181
○		public abstract .... FileLock	**tryLock** (long position, long size, boolean shared) throws java.io.IOException	
				ε182
○	3	public abstract .... int	**write** (java.nio.ByteBuffer src) throws java.io.IOException	ε171,180,170,175
●	4	public final .... long	**write** (java.nio.ByteBuffer[] srcs) throws java.io.IOException	
○		public abstract .... int	**write** (java.nio.ByteBuffer src, long position) throws java.io.IOException	
○	4	public abstract .... long	**write** (java.nio.ByteBuffer[] srcs, int offset, int length) throws java.io.IOException	

FileChannel.MapMode java.nio.channels

Object[1]
1.4 └FileChannel.MapMode

▲		public static final	**PRIVATE**	
		.... FileChannel.MapMode		
▲		public static final	**READ_ONLY**	ε166,425
		.... FileChannel.MapMode		
▲		public static final	**READ_WRITE**	ε166,167
		.... FileChannel.MapMode		
	1	public................... String	**toString** ()	

FileDescriptor java.io

Object
● └FileDescriptor

▲	public static final FileDescriptor	**err**	
✱	public........................	**FileDescriptor** ()	
▲	public static final FileDescriptor	**in**	
▲	public static final FileDescriptor	**out**	
1.1	public native ....void	**sync** () throws SyncFailedException	ε27
	public................. boolean	**valid** ()	

FileFilter ❶ java.io

1.2 *FileFilter*

	public................. boolean	**accept** (File pathname)	ε31

FileHandler java.util.logging

Object ε400
1.4 ○ └Handler[1]
1.4 └StreamHandler[2]
1.4 └FileHandler

	2	public synchronized ...... **void**	**close** () throws SecurityException	
✱		public...........................	**FileHandler** () throws java.io.IOException, SecurityException	
✱		public........................	**FileHandler** (String pattern) throws java.io.IOException, SecurityException	
				ε391,393,399,400
✱		public........................	**FileHandler** (String pattern, boolean append) throws java.io.IOException,	
			SecurityException	ε391
✱		public........................	**FileHandler** (String pattern, int limit, int count) throws java.io.IOException,	
			SecurityException	ε401,402
✱		public........................	**FileHandler** (String pattern, int limit, int count, boolean append)	
			throws java.io.IOException, SecurityException	
	2	public synchronized ....void	**flush** ()	
	1	public................... String	**getEncoding** ()	

Class *Interface* —extends - - -implements ○ abstract ● final △ static ▲ static final ✱ constructor x x—inherited x **x**—declared **x x**—overridden
ε*n*—examples of usage ˌ—has subclass package—see other volume

1	public	ErrorManager	getErrorManager ()	
1	public	*Filter*	getFilter ()	
1	public	Formatter	getFormatter ()	
1	public synchronized	Level	getLevel ()	
2	public	boolean	isLoggable (LogRecord record)	
2	public synchronized	**void**	**publish** (LogRecord record)	ε393
1	protected	void	reportError (String msg, Exception ex, int code)	
2	public	void	setEncoding (String encoding) throws SecurityException, java.io.UnsupportedEncodingException	
1	public	void	setErrorManager (ErrorManager em)	
1	public	void	setFilter (*Filter* newFilter) throws SecurityException	ε394
1	public	void	setFormatter (Formatter newFormatter) throws SecurityException	ε399,400
1	public synchronized	void	setLevel (Level newLevel) throws SecurityException	
2	protected synchronized	void	setOutputStream (java.io.OutputStream out) throws SecurityException	

FileInputStream — java.io

Object[1]
○ └ InputStream[2]
    └ FileInputStream

ε252,382,418

2	public native	**int**	**available** () throws IOException	
2	public	**void**	**close** () throws IOException	ε208,211,451,453,501
*	public		**FileInputStream** (File file) throws FileNotFoundException	ε36,45,208,211,225
*	public		**FileInputStream** (FileDescriptor fdObj)	
*	public		**FileInputStream** (String name) throws FileNotFoundException	ε40,42,8,169,172
1	protected	**void**	**finalize** () throws IOException	
1.4	public	java↩ .nio.channels.FileChannel	**getChannel** ()	ε169,172,425
●	public final	FileDescriptor	**getFD** () throws IOException	
2	public synchronized	void	mark (int readlimit)	
2	public	boolean	markSupported ()	
2	public native	**int**	**read** () throws IOException	ε90,184,256
2	public	**int**	**read** (byte[] b) throws IOException	ε451,453,452,455,457
2	public	**int**	**read** (byte[] b, int off, int len) throws IOException	ε36
2	public synchronized	void	reset () throws IOException	
2	public native	**long**	**skip** (long n) throws IOException	

FileLock — java.nio.channels

1.4 ○
Object[1]
└ FileLock

●	public final	FileChannel	**channel** ()	
*	protected		**FileLock** (FileChannel channel, long position, long size, boolean shared)	
●	public final	boolean	**isShared** ()	ε182
○	public abstract	boolean	**isValid** ()	
●	public final	boolean	**overlaps** (long position, long size)	
●	public final	long	**position** ()	
○	public abstract	void	**release** () throws java.io.IOException	ε181,182
●	public final	long	**size** ()	
● 1	public final	**String**	**toString** ()	

FileLockInterruptionException — java.nio.channels

Object
└ Throwable - *java.io.Serializable*⌄
  └ Exception
    └ java.io.IOException
1.4   └ FileLockInterruptionException

*	public		**FileLockInterruptionException** ()

FilenameFilter — java.io

FilenameFilter

	public	boolean	**accept** (File dir, String name)	ε31

F

Classes

FileNameMap

			java.net
1.1	*FileNameMap*		
	public.....................String	**getContentTypeFor** (String fileName)	

FileNotFoundException

			java.io
	Object		ε7,8,9,10,54

Object
└Throwable [1] - *Serializable*
  └Exception
    └IOException
      └FileNotFoundException

*	public..........................	**FileNotFoundException** ()	
*	public..........................	**FileNotFoundException** (String s)	
1	public.......................void	printStackTrace ()	

FileOutputStream

			java.io
	Object [1]		ε183

O └OutputStream [2]
    └FileOutputStream

2	public.....................**void**	**close** () throws IOException	ε211,224,501,451,453
*	public..........................	**FileOutputStream** (File file) throws FileNotFoundException	ε211,224
*	public..........................	**FileOutputStream** (FileDescriptor fdObj)	
*	public..........................	**FileOutputStream** (String name) throws FileNotFoundException	ε27,41,43,44,7
1.4 *	public..........................	**FileOutputStream** (File file, boolean append) throws FileNotFoundException	
			ε171
1.1 *	public..........................	**FileOutputStream** (String name, boolean append) throws FileNotFoundException	
1	protected ....**void**	**finalize** () throws IOException	
2	public.....................void	flush () throws IOException	ε27,54
1.4	public......................java↩	**getChannel** ()	ε170,171,172
	.nio.channels.FileChannel		
●	public final ......FileDescriptor	**getFD** () throws IOException	ε27
2	public.....................**void**	**write** (byte[] b) throws IOException	ε27,224,91
2	public native ....**void**	**write** (int b) throws IOException	ε184
2	public.....................**void**	**write** (byte[] b, int off, int len) throws IOException	ε451,453,54,449,450

FilePermission

			java.io
	Object		ε217,218

1.2 O └java.security.Permission [1] - - - - - - - - - - - - - - - - *java.security.Guard*, *Serializable*
1.2 ●   └FilePermission

1	public.......................void	checkGuard (Object object) throws SecurityException	
1	public.................**boolean**	**equals** (Object obj)	ε215
*	public..........................	**FilePermission** (String path, String actions)	ε213,214
1	public..................**String**	**getActions** ()	ε215
●	public final ....String	getName ()	
1	public......................**int**	**hashCode** ()	ε215
1	public.................**boolean**	**implies** (java.security.Permission p)	ε214,215
1	public..........**java.security**↩	**newPermissionCollection** ()	
	.**PermissionCollection**		
1	public.....................String	toString ()	

FileReader

			java.io
	Object		

1.1 O └Reader [1]
1.1   └InputStreamReader [2]
1.1   └FileReader

2	public.......................void	close () throws IOException	ε47,35,135,136,139
*	public..........................	**FileReader** (File file) throws FileNotFoundException	ε434

Class *Interface* —extends - - -implements ○ abstract ● final △ static ▲ static final ✳ constructor x x—inherited x **x**—declared **x x**—overridden
ε*n*—examples of usage ⌐—has subclass package—see other volume

*	public..........................		**FileReader** (FileDescriptor fd)	
*	public..........................		**FileReader** (String fileName) throws FileNotFoundException	ε35,47,441,442,548
2	public....................	String	getEncoding ()	
1	protected	Object	lock	
1	public.....................	void	mark (int readAheadLimit) throws IOException	
1	public.....................	boolean	markSupported ()	ε442
2	public.....................	int	read () throws IOException	
1	public.....................	int	read (char[] cbuf) throws IOException	ε434
2	public.....................	int	read (char[] cbuf, int offset, int length) throws IOException	
2	public.....................	boolean	ready () throws IOException	ε442
1	public.....................	void	reset () throws IOException	
1	public.....................	long	skip (long n) throws IOException	

FileWriter — java.io

```
Object
└─Writer 1
   └─OutputStreamWriter 2
      └─FileWriter
```
(1.1)

2	public.....................	void	close () throws IOException	ε23,37,38,41,43
*	public..........................		**FileWriter** (File file) throws IOException	ε23
*	public..........................		**FileWriter** (FileDescriptor fd)	
*	public..........................		**FileWriter** (String fileName) throws IOException	ε37
1.4 *	public..........................		**FileWriter** (File file, boolean append) throws IOException	
*	public..........................		**FileWriter** (String fileName, boolean append) throws IOException	ε38
2	public.....................	void	flush () throws IOException	ε135,150,224
2	public....................	String	getEncoding ()	
1	protected	Object	lock	
1	public.....................	void	write (char[] cbuf) throws IOException	
2	public.....................	void	write (int c) throws IOException	
1	public.....................	void	write (String str) throws IOException	ε23,37,38,41,43
2	public.....................	void	write (char[] cbuf, int off, int len) throws IOException	
2	public.....................	void	write (String str, int off, int len) throws IOException	

Filter — java.util.logging

Filter (1.4)

	public.................	boolean	**isLoggable** (LogRecord record)	ε394

FilterInputStream — java.io

ε252,382,418

```
Object
└─InputStream 1
   └─FilterInputStream
```

1	public.....................	**int**	**available** () throws IOException	
1	public.....................	**void**	**close** () throws IOException	ε14,36,45,452,455
*	protected......................		**FilterInputStream** (InputStream in)	
	protected	InputStream	**in**	
1	public synchronized	**void**	**mark** (int readlimit)	
1	public.................	**boolean**	**markSupported** ()	
1	public.....................	**int**	**read** () throws IOException	ε90,184,256
1	public.....................	**int**	**read** (byte[] b) throws IOException	ε452,455,457,170,451
1	public.....................	**int**	**read** (byte[] b, int off, int len) throws IOException	ε36
1	public synchronized	**void**	**reset** () throws IOException	
1	public.....................	**long**	**skip** (long n) throws IOException	

Classes

FilterOutputStream — java.io

ε183

```
Object
└─OutputStream 1
   └─FilterOutputStream
```

1	public.....................	**void**	**close** () throws IOException	ε451,453,91,211,224
*	public..........................		**FilterOutputStream** (OutputStream out)	
1	public.....................	**void**	**flush** () throws IOException	ε27,54
	protected	OutputStream	**out**	

FilterOutputStream

	1	public	**void**	**write** (byte[] b) throws IOException	ε27,91,224
	1	public	**void**	**write** (int b) throws IOException	ε184
	1	public	**void**	**write** (byte[] b, int off, int len) throws IOException	ε451,453,54,449,450

FilterReader   java.io

```
          Object
1.1 ○     └Reader 1
1.1 ○        └FilterReader
```

	1	public	**void**	**close** () throws IOException	ε35,47,135,136,139
✳		protected		**FilterReader** (Reader in)	
		protected	Reader	**in**	
	1	protected	Object	lock	
	1	public	**void**	**mark** (int readAheadLimit) throws IOException	
	1	public	**boolean**	**markSupported** ()	ε442
	1	public	**int**	**read** () throws IOException	
	1	public	int	read (char[] cbuf) throws IOException	ε434
	1	public	**int**	**read** (char[] cbuf, int off, int len) throws IOException	
	1	public	**boolean**	**ready** () throws IOException	ε442
	1	public	**void**	**reset** () throws IOException	
	1	public	**long**	**skip** (long n) throws IOException	

FilterWriter   java.io

```
          Object
1.1 ○     └Writer 1
1.1 ○        └FilterWriter
```

	1	public	**void**	**close** () throws IOException	ε23,37,38,41,43
✳		protected		**FilterWriter** (Writer out)	
	1	public	**void**	**flush** () throws IOException	ε135,150,224
	1	protected	Object	lock	
		protected	Writer	**out**	
	1	public	void	write (char[] cbuf) throws IOException	
	1	public	**void**	**write** (int c) throws IOException	
	1	public	void	write (String str) throws IOException	ε23,37,38,41,43
	1	public	**void**	**write** (char[] cbuf, int off, int len) throws IOException	
	1	public	**void**	**write** (String str, int off, int len) throws IOException	

FixedHolder   org.omg.CORBA

```
          Object
1.2 ●     └FixedHolder - - - - - - - - - - - - - - - - - - - - - - - - - - - org.omg.CORBA.portable.Streamable 1
```

	1	public	void	**_read** (org.omg.CORBA.portable.InputStream input)	
	1	public	TypeCode	**_type** ()	
	1	public	void	**_write** (org.omg.CORBA.portable.OutputStream output)	
✳		public		**FixedHolder** ()	
✳		public		**FixedHolder** (java.math.BigDecimal initial)	
		public	java.math.BigDecimal	**value**	

Float   java.lang

```
          Object 1                                                            ε200,201,252,299,304
    ○     └Number 2 - - - - - - - - - - - - - - - - - - - - - - - - - - - - java.io.Serializable
    ●        └Float - - - - - - - - - - - - - - - - - - - - - - - - - - - Comparable 3
```

1.1	2	public	**byte**	**byteValue** ()	ε58
1.4 △		public static	int	**compare** (float f1, float f2)	
1.2		public	int	**compareTo** (Float anotherFloat)	
1.2	3	public	int	**compareTo** (Object o)	ε53
	2	public	**double**	**doubleValue** ()	ε58
	1	public	**boolean**	**equals** (Object obj)	
✳		public		**Float** (double value)	
✳		public		**Float** (float value)	ε58

---

*		public		**Float** (String s) throws NumberFormatException	
△		public static native	int	**floatToIntBits** (float value)	
1.3 △		public static native	int	**floatToRawIntBits** (float value)	
	2	public	**float**	**floatValue** ()	ε58
	1	public	**int**	**hashCode** ()	
△		public static native	float	**intBitsToFloat** (int bits)	
	2	public	**int**	**intValue** ()	ε58,6,346
		public	boolean	**isInfinite** ()	
△		public static	boolean	**isInfinite** (float v)	
		public	boolean	**isNaN** ()	
△		public static	boolean	**isNaN** (float v)	
	2	public	**long**	**longValue** ()	ε58
▲		public static final	float	**MAX_VALUE** = 3.4028235E38	
▲		public static final	float	**MIN_VALUE** = 1.4E-45	
▲		public static final	float	**NaN** = NaN	
▲		public static final	float	**NEGATIVE_INFINITY** = -Infinity	
1.2 △		public static	float	**parseFloat** (String s) throws NumberFormatException	ε82
▲		public static final	float	**POSITIVE_INFINITY** = Infinity	
1.1	2	public	**short**	**shortValue** ()	ε58
	1	public	**String**	**toString** ()	
△		public static	String	**toString** (float f)	
1.1 ▲		public static final	Class	**TYPE**	
△		public static	Float	**valueOf** (String s) throws NumberFormatException	

FloatBuffer					java.nio

		Object[1]			ε163,166,171,425
1.4 ○		└Buffer[2]			
1.4 ○		└FloatBuffer ------------------------- *Comparable*[3]			

△		public static	FloatBuffer	**allocate** (int capacity)	
●		public final	float[]	**array** ()	
●		public final	int	**arrayOffset** ()	
○		public abstract	FloatBuffer	**asReadOnlyBuffer** ()	
●	2	public final	int	capacity ()	ε159,160,161
●	2	public final	Buffer	clear ()	ε161,170,174
○		public abstract	FloatBuffer	**compact** ()	
	3	public	int	**compareTo** (Object ob)	ε53
○		public abstract	FloatBuffer	**duplicate** ()	
	1	public	**boolean**	**equals** (Object ob)	
●	2	public final	Buffer	flip ()	ε162,164,170,174,175
○		public abstract	float	**get** ()	
		public	FloatBuffer	**get** (float[] dst)	
○		public abstract	float	**get** (int index)	
		public	FloatBuffer	**get** (float[] dst, int offset, int length)	
●		public final	boolean	**hasArray** ()	
	1	public	**int**	**hashCode** ()	
●	2	public final	boolean	hasRemaining ()	ε170,184
○		public abstract	boolean	**isDirect** ()	
○	2	public abstract	boolean	**isReadOnly** ()	
●	2	public final	int	limit ()	
●	2	public final	Buffer	limit (int newLimit)	ε159,160
●	2	public final	Buffer	mark ()	
○		public abstract	ByteOrder	**order** ()	
●	2	public final	int	position ()	ε159,160
●	2	public final	Buffer	position (int newPosition)	ε159,160
○		public abstract	FloatBuffer	**put** (float f)	
●		public final	FloatBuffer	**put** (float[] src)	
		public	FloatBuffer	**put** (FloatBuffer src)	
○		public abstract	FloatBuffer	**put** (int index, float f)	
		public	FloatBuffer	**put** (float[] src, int offset, int length)	
●	2	public final	int	remaining ()	ε159,160,161,184
●	2	public final	Buffer	reset ()	
●	2	public final	Buffer	rewind ()	ε159,160,169
○		public abstract	FloatBuffer	**slice** ()	
	1	public	**String**	**toString** ()	
△		public static	FloatBuffer	**wrap** (float[] array)	
△		public static	FloatBuffer	**wrap** (float[] array, int offset, int length)	

FloatHolder

			org.omg.CORBA

Object
1.2 ● └FloatHolder ------------------------- *org.omg.CORBA.portable.Streamable*˛ [1]

1	public......................void	**_read** (org.omg.CORBA.portable.InputStream input)	
1	public...............TypeCode	**_type** ()	
1	public......................void	**_write** (org.omg.CORBA.portable.OutputStream output)	
✳	public...........................	**FloatHolder** ()	
✳	public...........................	**FloatHolder** (float initial)	
	public.....................float	**value**	

FloatSeqHelper

			org.omg.CORBA

Object
1.3 ○ └FloatSeqHelper

△	public static ....float[]	**extract** (Any a)	
✳	public...........................	**FloatSeqHelper** ()	
△	public static ....String	**id** ()	
△	public static ....void	**insert** (Any a, float[] that)	
△	public static ....float[]	**read** (org.omg.CORBA.portable.InputStream istream)	
△	public static synchronized ....TypeCode	**type** ()	
△	public static ....void	**write** (org.omg.CORBA.portable.OutputStream ostream, float[] value)	

FloatSeqHolder

			org.omg.CORBA

Object
1.3 ● └FloatSeqHolder ----------------------- *org.omg.CORBA.portable.Streamable*˛ [1]

1	public......................void	**_read** (org.omg.CORBA.portable.InputStream i)	
1	public...............TypeCode	**_type** ()	
1	public......................void	**_write** (org.omg.CORBA.portable.OutputStream o)	
✳	public...........................	**FloatSeqHolder** ()	
✳	public...........................	**FloatSeqHolder** (float[] initialValue)	
	public...................float[]	**value**	

Format

			java.text

Object [1]
1.1 ○ └Format˛ ----------------------------- *java.io.Serializable*˛, *Cloneable*˛

	1	public....................**Object clone** ()	
✳		public........................... **Format** ()	
●		public final ....String **format** (Object obj)	ε316,320
○		public abstract .... StringBuffer **format** (Object obj, StringBuffer toAppendTo, FieldPosition pos)	
1.4		public........................... **formatToCharacterIterator** (Object obj) .. *AttributedCharacterIterator*	
		public...................Object **parseObject** (String source) throws ParseException	
○		public abstract ....Object **parseObject** (String source, ParsePosition pos)	

Format.Field

			java.text

Object
1.2 └AttributedCharacterIterator.Attribute [1] ------- *java.io.Serializable*˛
1.4 └Format.Field˛

●	1	public final .... boolean **equals** (Object obj)	
✳		protected...................... **Format.Field** (String name)	
	1	protected.................String **getName** ()	
●	1	public final ....int **hashCode** ()	
	1	protected...............Object **readResolve** () throws java.io.InvalidObjectException	
	1	public....................String **toString** ()	

Class *Interface* —extends - - -implements ○ abstract ● final △ static ▲ static final ✳ constructor x x—inherited x **x**—declared **x x**—overridden
ε*n*—examples of usage ˛—has subclass package—see other volume

FormatMismatch	org.omg.IOP.CodecPackage

```
     Object
      └Throwable --------------------------- java.io.Serializable.
        └Exception
1.2 ○      └org.omg.CORBA.UserException ------ org.omg.CORBA.portable.IDLEntity. (java.io.Serializable)
1.4 ●        └FormatMismatch
```

∗	public.........................	**FormatMismatch** ()
∗	public.........................	**FormatMismatch** (String $reason)

FormatMismatchHelper	org.omg.IOP.CodecPackage

```
     Object
1.4 ○ └FormatMismatchHelper
```

△	public static .. FormatMismatch	**extract** (org.omg.CORBA.Any a)
∗	public.........................	**FormatMismatchHelper** ()
△	public static .... String	**id** ()
△	public static ....void	**insert** (org.omg.CORBA.Any a, FormatMismatch that)
△	public static .. FormatMismatch	**read** (org.omg.CORBA.portable.InputStream istream)
△	public static synchronized	**type** ()
	. org.omg.CORBA.TypeCode	
△	public static ....void	**write** (org.omg.CORBA.portable.OutputStream ostream, FormatMismatch value)

Formatter	java.util.logging

```
     Object
1.4 ○ └Formatter.
```

○	public abstract .... String	**format** (LogRecord record)	ε400
	public synchronized ..... String	**formatMessage** (LogRecord record)	
∗	protected	**Formatter** ()	
	public.................... String	**getHead** (Handler h)	ε400
	public.................... String	**getTail** (Handler h)	ε400

ForwardRequest❶	org.omg.PortableInterceptor

```
     Object
      └Throwable --------------------------- java.io.Serializable.
        └Exception
1.2 ○      └org.omg.CORBA.UserException ------ org.omg.CORBA.portable.IDLEntity. (java.io.Serializable)
1.4 ●        └ForwardRequest
```

	public org.omg.CORBA.Object	**forward**
∗	public.........................	**ForwardRequest** ()
∗	public.........................	**ForwardRequest** (org.omg.CORBA.Object _forward)
∗	public.........................	**ForwardRequest** (String $reason, org.omg.CORBA.Object _forward)

ForwardRequest❷	org.omg.PortableServer

```
     Object
      └Throwable --------------------------- java.io.Serializable.
        └Exception
1.2 ○      └org.omg.CORBA.UserException ------ org.omg.CORBA.portable.IDLEntity. (java.io.Serializable)
1.4 ●        └ForwardRequest
```

	public org.omg.CORBA.Object	**forward_reference**
∗	public.........................	**ForwardRequest** ()
∗	public.........................	**ForwardRequest** (org.omg.CORBA.Object _forward_reference)
∗	public.........................	**ForwardRequest** (String $reason, org.omg.CORBA.Object _forward_reference)

ForwardRequestHelper❶	org.omg.PortableInterceptor

```
     Object
1.4 ○ └ForwardRequestHelper
```

F

Classes

ForwardRequestHelper ❶

△	public static .. ForwardRequest	**extract** (org.omg.CORBA.Any a)	
✳	public..........................	**ForwardRequestHelper** ()	
△	public static ....String	**id** ()	
△	public static ....void	**insert** (org.omg.CORBA.Any a, ForwardRequest that)	
△	public static .. ForwardRequest	**read** (org.omg.CORBA.portable.InputStream istream)	
△	public static synchronized .... . org.omg.CORBA.TypeCode	**type** ()	
△	public static ....void	**write** (org.omg.CORBA.portable.OutputStream ostream, ForwardRequest value)	

F

ForwardRequestHelper ❷   org.omg.PortableServer

Object
1.4 ○ └ForwardRequestHelper

△	public static .. ForwardRequest	**extract** (org.omg.CORBA.Any a)
✳	public..........................	**ForwardRequestHelper** ()
△	public static ....String	**id** ()
△	public static ....void	**insert** (org.omg.CORBA.Any a, ForwardRequest that)
△	public static .. ForwardRequest	**read** (org.omg.CORBA.portable.InputStream istream)
△	public static synchronized .... . org.omg.CORBA.TypeCode	**type** ()
△	public static ....void	**write** (org.omg.CORBA.portable.OutputStream ostream, ForwardRequest value)

FREE_MEM   org.omg.CORBA

Object
 └Throwable - *java.io.Serializable*ˎ
  └Exception
   └RuntimeException
1.2 ○   └SystemException[1]
1.2 ●   └FREE_MEM

	1	*3 inherited members from SystemException not shown*	
✳	public..........................	**FREE_MEM** ()	
✳	public..........................	**FREE_MEM** (String s)	
✳	public..........................	**FREE_MEM** (int minor, CompletionStatus completed)	
✳	public..........................	**FREE_MEM** (String s, int minor, CompletionStatus completed)	

GatheringByteChannel   java.nio.channels

1.4   *GatheringByteChannel*────────── *WritableByteChannel* ˎ[1] (*Channel* [2])

	2	public.......................void	close () throws java.io.IOException	ε167,170,171,172,174
	2	public................ boolean	isOpen ()	
	1	public........................int	write (java.nio.ByteBuffer src) throws java.io.IOException	ε180,170,171,175
		public...................... long	**write** (java.nio.ByteBuffer[] srcs) throws java.io.IOException	
		public...................... long	**write** (java.nio.ByteBuffer[] srcs, int offset, int length) throws java.io.IOException	

GeneralSecurityException   java.security

Object
 └Throwable - *java.io.Serializable*ˎ
  └Exception
1.2 └GeneralSecurityExceptionˎ

✳	public..........................	**GeneralSecurityException** ()
✳	public..........................	**GeneralSecurityException** (String msg)

GregorianCalendar   java.util

Object
1.1 ○ └Calendar[1] - *java.io.Serializable*ˎ, *Cloneable*ˎ
1.1   └GregorianCalendar

Class   *Interface*   —extends   - - -implements   ○ abstract   ● final   △ static   ▲ static final   ✳ constructor   x x—inherited   x **x**—declared   **x x**—overridden
εn—examples of usage   ˎ—has subclass   package—see other volume

	1	*77 inherited members from Calendar not shown*		
▲	1	public static final............int	**AD** = 1	
	1	public................... **void**	**add** (int field, int amount)	ε377
▲	1	public static final............int	**BC** = 0	
	1	protected................. **void**	**computeFields** ()	
	1	protected................. **void**	**computeTime** ()	
	1	public................**boolean**	**equals** (Object obj)	
1.2	1	public........................ **int**	**getActualMaximum** (int field)	ε375
1.2	1	public........................ **int**	**getActualMinimum** (int field)	
	1	public........................ **int**	**getGreatestMinimum** (int field)	
●		public final .... Date	**getGregorianChange** ()	
	1	public........................ **int**	**getLeastMaximum** (int field)	
	1	public........................ **int**	**getMaximum** (int field)	
	1	public........................ **int**	**getMinimum** (int field)	
*		public	**GregorianCalendar** ()	ε369,370,372,373,378
*		public	**GregorianCalendar** (Locale aLocale)	
*		public	**GregorianCalendar** (TimeZone zone)	ε370,372
*		public	**GregorianCalendar** (TimeZone zone, Locale aLocale)	
*		public	**GregorianCalendar** (int year, int month, int date)	ε374,375,376,377,379
*		public	**GregorianCalendar** (int year, int month, int date, int hour, int minute)	
*		public	**GregorianCalendar** (int year, int month, int date, int hour, int minute, int second)	
	1	public........................ **int**	**hashCode** ()	
		public................ boolean	**isLeapYear** (int year)	ε378
	1	public................... **void**	**roll** (int field, boolean up)	
1.2	1	public................... **void**	**roll** (int field, int amount)	
		public......................void	**setGregorianChange** (Date date)	

G

Group	java.security.acl

1.1		*Group────────────────java.security.Principal 1*	
		public................. boolean	**addMember** (*java.security.Principal* user)
	1	public................. boolean	equals (Object another)
	1	public................... String	getName ()	ε227,508
	1	public......................int	hashCode ()
		public................. boolean	**isMember** (*java.security.Principal* member)
		public.... *java.util.Enumeration*	**members** ()
		public................. boolean	**removeMember** (*java.security.Principal* user)
	1	public................... String	toString ()

GSSContext	org.ietf.jgss

1.4		*GSSContext*	
		public......................void	**acceptSecContext** (java.io.InputStream inStream, java.io.OutputStream outStream) throws GSSException
		public......................byte[]	**acceptSecContext** (byte[] inToken, int offset, int len) throws GSSException
▲		public static final............int	**DEFAULT_LIFETIME** = 0
		public......................void	**dispose** () throws GSSException
		public......................byte[]	**export** () throws GSSException
		public................. boolean	**getAnonymityState** ()
		public................. boolean	**getConfState** ()
		public................. boolean	**getCredDelegState** ()
		public........... *GSSCredential*	**getDelegCred** () throws GSSException
		public................. boolean	**getIntegState** ()
		public......................int	**getLifetime** ()
		public.........................Oid	**getMech** () throws GSSException
		public......................void	**getMIC** (java.io.InputStream inStream, java.io.OutputStream outStream, MessageProp msgProp) throws GSSException
		public......................byte[]	**getMIC** (byte[] inMsg, int offset, int len, MessageProp msgProp) throws GSSException
		public................. boolean	**getMutualAuthState** ()
		public................. boolean	**getReplayDetState** ()
		public................. boolean	**getSequenceDetState** ()
		public..........*GSSName*	**getSrcName** () throws GSSException
		public..........*GSSName*	**getTargName** () throws GSSException
		public......................int	**getWrapSizeLimit** (int qop, boolean confReq, int maxTokenSize) throws GSSException
▲		public static final............int	**INDEFINITE_LIFETIME** = 2147483647
		public......................int	**initSecContext** (java.io.InputStream inStream, java.io.OutputStream outStream) throws GSSException
		public......................byte[]	**initSecContext** (byte[] inputBuf, int offset, int len) throws GSSException

Classes

GSSContext

public	boolean	**isEstablished** ()	
public	boolean	**isInitiator** () throws GSSException	
public	boolean	**isProtReady** ()	
public	boolean	**isTransferable** () throws GSSException	
public	void	**requestAnonymity** (boolean state) throws GSSException	
public	void	**requestConf** (boolean state) throws GSSException	
public	void	**requestCredDeleg** (boolean state) throws GSSException	
public	void	**requestInteg** (boolean state) throws GSSException	
public	void	**requestLifetime** (int lifetime) throws GSSException	
public	void	**requestMutualAuth** (boolean state) throws GSSException	
public	void	**requestReplayDet** (boolean state) throws GSSException	
public	void	**requestSequenceDet** (boolean state) throws GSSException	
public	void	**setChannelBinding** (ChannelBinding cb) throws GSSException	
public	void	**unwrap** (java.io.InputStream inStream, java.io.OutputStream outStream, MessageProp msgProp) throws GSSException	
public	byte[]	**unwrap** (byte[] inBuf, int offset, int len, MessageProp msgProp) throws GSSException	
public	void	**verifyMIC** (java.io.InputStream tokStream, java.io.InputStream msgStream, MessageProp msgProp) throws GSSException	
public	void	**verifyMIC** (byte[] inToken, int tokOffset, int tokLen, byte[] inMsg, int msgOffset, int msgLen, MessageProp msgProp) throws GSSException	
public	void	**wrap** (java.io.InputStream inStream, java.io.OutputStream outStream, MessageProp msgProp) throws GSSException	
public	byte[]	**wrap** (byte[] inBuf, int offset, int len, MessageProp msgProp) throws GSSException	

GSSCredential — org.ietf.jgss

1.4   *GSSCredential* ———————————— *Cloneable*

▲	public static final	int	**ACCEPT_ONLY** = 2	
	public	void	**add** (*GSSName* name, int initLifetime, int acceptLifetime, Oid mech, int usage) throws GSSException	
▲	public static final	int	**DEFAULT_LIFETIME** = 0	
	public	void	**dispose** () throws GSSException	
	public	boolean	**equals** (Object another)	
	public	Oid[]	**getMechs** () throws GSSException	
	public	*GSSName*	**getName** () throws GSSException	
	public	*GSSName*	**getName** (Oid mech) throws GSSException	
	public	int	**getRemainingAcceptLifetime** (Oid mech) throws GSSException	
	public	int	**getRemainingInitLifetime** (Oid mech) throws GSSException	
	public	int	**getRemainingLifetime** () throws GSSException	
	public	int	**getUsage** () throws GSSException	
	public	int	**getUsage** (Oid mech) throws GSSException	
	public	int	**hashCode** ()	
▲	public static final	int	**INDEFINITE_LIFETIME** = 2147483647	
▲	public static final	int	**INITIATE_AND_ACCEPT** = 0	
▲	public static final	int	**INITIATE_ONLY** = 1	

GSSException — org.ietf.jgss

Object
└Throwable[1] - *java.io.Serializable*
  └Exception
1.4   └GSSException

▲	public static final	int	**BAD_BINDINGS** = 1
▲	public static final	int	**BAD_MECH** = 2
▲	public static final	int	**BAD_MIC** = 6
▲	public static final	int	**BAD_NAME** = 3
▲	public static final	int	**BAD_NAMETYPE** = 4
▲	public static final	int	**BAD_QOP** = 14
▲	public static final	int	**BAD_STATUS** = 5
▲	public static final	int	**CONTEXT_EXPIRED** = 7
▲	public static final	int	**CREDENTIALS_EXPIRED** = 8
▲	public static final	int	**DEFECTIVE_CREDENTIAL** = 9
▲	public static final	int	**DEFECTIVE_TOKEN** = 10
▲	public static final	int	**DUPLICATE_ELEMENT** = 17
▲	public static final	int	**DUPLICATE_TOKEN** = 19
▲	public static final	int	**FAILURE** = 11

Class   *Interface*   —extends   - - -implements   ○ abstract   ● final   △ static   ▲ static final   ✱ constructor   x x—inherited   x **x**—declared   **x x**—overridden
εn—examples of usage   ⌄—has subclass   package—see other volume

▲	public static final	....	int	**GAP_TOKEN**	= 22
	public	....	int	**getMajor** ()	
	public	....	String	**getMajorString** ()	
1	public	....	**String**	**getMessage** ()	
	public	....	int	**getMinor** ()	
	public	....	String	**getMinorString** ()	
∗	public	....		**GSSException** (int majorCode)	
∗	public	....		**GSSException** (int majorCode, int minorCode, String minorString)	
▲	public static final	....	int	**NAME_NOT_MN**	= 18
▲	public static final	....	int	**NO_CONTEXT**	= 12
▲	public static final	....	int	**NO_CRED**	= 13
▲	public static final	....	int	**OLD_TOKEN**	= 20
	public	....	void	**setMinor** (int minorCode, String message)	
1	public	....	**String**	**toString** ()	
▲	public static final	....	int	**UNAUTHORIZED**	= 15
▲	public static final	....	int	**UNAVAILABLE**	= 16
▲	public static final	....	int	**UNSEQ_TOKEN**	= 21

G

GSSManager   org.ietf.jgss

Object
1.4 ○   └GSSManager

○	public abstract	....	void	**addProviderAtEnd** (java.security.Provider p, Oid mech) throws GSSException
○	public abstract	....	void	**addProviderAtFront** (java.security.Provider p, Oid mech) throws GSSException
○	public abstract	....	*GSSContext*	**createContext** (byte[] interProcessToken) throws GSSException
○	public abstract	....	*GSSContext*	**createContext** (*GSSCredential* myCred) throws GSSException
○	public abstract	....	*GSSContext*	**createContext** (*GSSName* peer, Oid mech, *GSSCredential* myCred, int lifetime) throws GSSException
○	public abstract	.	*GSSCredential*	**createCredential** (int usage) throws GSSException
○	public abstract	.	*GSSCredential*	**createCredential** (*GSSName* name, int lifetime, Oid[] mechs, int usage) throws GSSException
○	public abstract	.	*GSSCredential*	**createCredential** (*GSSName* name, int lifetime, Oid mech, int usage) throws GSSException
○	public abstract	......	*GSSName*	**createName** (byte[] name, Oid nameType) throws GSSException
○	public abstract	......	*GSSName*	**createName** (String nameStr, Oid nameType) throws GSSException
○	public abstract	......	*GSSName*	**createName** (byte[] name, Oid nameType, Oid mech) throws GSSException
○	public abstract	......	*GSSName*	**createName** (String nameStr, Oid nameType, Oid mech) throws GSSException
△	public static	.....	GSSManager	**getInstance** ()
○	public abstract	....	Oid[]	**getMechs** ()
○	public abstract	....	Oid[]	**getMechsForName** (Oid nameType)
○	public abstract	....	Oid[]	**getNamesForMech** (Oid mech) throws GSSException
∗	public	....		**GSSManager** ()

GSSName   org.ietf.jgss

1.4   *GSSName*

	public	....	*GSSName*	**canonicalize** (Oid mech) throws GSSException
	public	....	boolean	**equals** (Object another)
	public	....	boolean	**equals** (*GSSName* another) throws GSSException
	public	....	byte[]	**export** () throws GSSException
	public	....	Oid	**getStringNameType** () throws GSSException
	public	....	int	**hashCode** ()
	public	....	boolean	**isAnonymous** ()
	public	....	boolean	**isMN** ()
▲	public static final	....	Oid	**NT_ANONYMOUS**
▲	public static final	....	Oid	**NT_EXPORT_NAME**
▲	public static final	....	Oid	**NT_HOSTBASED_SERVICE**
▲	public static final	....	Oid	**NT_MACHINE_UID_NAME**
▲	public static final	....	Oid	**NT_STRING_UID_NAME**
▲	public static final	....	Oid	**NT_USER_NAME**
	public	....	String	**toString** ()

Guard   java.security

1.2   *Guard*   ε216

	public	....	void	**checkGuard** (Object object) throws SecurityException

Classes

GuardedObject

		java.security

1.2	Object └ GuardedObject ----------------------- *java.io.Serializable* ↲	

	public .... Object **getObject** () throws SecurityException		ε216
*	public .... **GuardedObject** (Object object, *Guard* guard)		ε216

GZIPInputStream

		java.util.zip

	Object	ε252,382,418
○	└ java.io.InputStream	
	└ java.io.FilterInputStream [1]	
1.1	└ InflaterInputStream [2]	
1.1	└ GZIPInputStream	

2	public .... int available () throws java.io.IOException	
2	protected .... byte[] buf	
2	public .... **void close** () throws java.io.IOException	ε452,14,36,45,455
	protected .... CRC32 **crc**	
	protected .... boolean **eos**	
2	protected .... void fill () throws java.io.IOException	
▲	public static final .... int **GZIP_MAGIC** = 35615	
*	public .... **GZIPInputStream** (java.io.InputStream in) throws java.io.IOException	ε452
*	public .... **GZIPInputStream** (java.io.InputStream in, int size) throws java.io.IOException	
1	protected .. java.io.InputStream in	
2	protected .... Inflater inf	
2	protected .... int len	
1	public synchronized .... void mark (int readlimit)	
1	public .... boolean markSupported ()	
2	public .... int read () throws java.io.IOException	ε90,184,256
1	public .... int read (byte[] b) throws java.io.IOException	ε452,455,457,170,451
2	**int read** (byte[] buf, int off, int len) throws java.io.IOException	ε36
1	public synchronized ...... void reset () throws java.io.IOException	
2	public .... long skip (long n) throws java.io.IOException	

GZIPOutputStream

		java.util.zip

	Object	ε183
○	└ java.io.OutputStream	
	└ java.io.FilterOutputStream [1]	
1.1	└ DeflaterOutputStream [2]	
1.1	└ GZIPOutputStream	

2	protected .... byte[] buf	
2	public .... void close () throws java.io.IOException	ε451,453,91,211,224
	protected .... CRC32 **crc**	
2	protected .... Deflater def	
2	protected .... void deflate () throws java.io.IOException	
2	public .... **void finish** () throws java.io.IOException	ε451
1	public .... void flush () throws java.io.IOException	ε27,54
*	public .... **GZIPOutputStream** (java.io.OutputStream out) throws java.io.IOException	ε451
*	public .... **GZIPOutputStream** (java.io.OutputStream out, int size) throws java.io.IOException	
1	protected java.io.OutputStream out	
1	public .... void write (byte[] b) throws java.io.IOException	ε27,91,224
2	public .... void write (int b) throws java.io.IOException	ε184
2	public synchronized ...... **void write** (byte[] buf, int off, int len) throws java.io.IOException	ε451,453,54,449,450

Handler

		java.util.logging

	Object	ε400
1.4 ○	└ Handler ↲	

○	public abstract .... void **close** () throws SecurityException	
○	public abstract .... void **flush** ()	

Class   *Interface*   —extends   - - -implements   ○ abstract   ● final   △ static   ▲ static final   * constructor   x x—inherited   x **x**—declared   **x x**—overridden
εn—examples of usage   ↲—has subclass   package—see other volume

	public .... String	**getEncoding** ()	
	public .... ErrorManager	**getErrorManager** ()	
	public .... *Filter*	**getFilter** ()	
	public .... Formatter	**getFormatter** ()	
	public synchronized ..... Level	**getLevel** ()	
✳	protected	**Handler** ()	
	public .... boolean	**isLoggable** (LogRecord record)	
○	public abstract .... void	**publish** (LogRecord record)	ε393
	protected .... void	**reportError** (String msg, Exception ex, int code)	
	public .... void	**setEncoding** (String encoding) throws SecurityException, java.io.UnsupportedEncodingException	
	public .... void	**setErrorManager** (ErrorManager em)	
	public .... void	**setFilter** (*Filter* newFilter) throws SecurityException	ε394
	public .... void	**setFormatter** (Formatter newFormatter) throws SecurityException	ε399,400
	public synchronized .... void	**setLevel** (Level newLevel) throws SecurityException	

HandlerBase — org.xml.sax

```
        Object
D       └HandlerBase -------------------------- EntityResolver 1, DTDHandler 2, DocumentHandler 3,
                                                 ErrorHandler 4
```

D	3	public .... void	**characters** (char[] ch, int start, int length) throws SAXException	
D	3	public .... void	**endDocument** () throws SAXException	
D	3	public .... void	**endElement** (String name) throws SAXException	
D	4	public .... void	**error** (SAXParseException e) throws SAXException	ε513
D	4	public .... void	**fatalError** (SAXParseException e) throws SAXException	ε513
D ✳		public	**HandlerBase** ()	
D	3	public .... void	**ignorableWhitespace** (char[] ch, int start, int length) throws SAXException	
D	2	public .... void	**notationDecl** (String name, String publicId, String systemId)	
D	3	public .... void	**processingInstruction** (String target, String data) throws SAXException	
D	1	public .... InputSource	**resolveEntity** (String publicId, String systemId) throws SAXException	ε548
D	3	public .... void	**setDocumentLocator** (*Locator* locator)	
D	3	public .... void	**startDocument** () throws SAXException	
D	3	public .... void	**startElement** (String name, *AttributeList* attributes) throws SAXException	
D	2	public .... void	**unparsedEntityDecl** (String name, String publicId, String systemId, String notationName)	
D	4	public .... void	**warning** (SAXParseException e) throws SAXException	ε513

HandshakeCompletedEvent — javax.net.ssl

ε333

```
        Object
1.1     └java.util.EventObject 1 ------------------- java.io.Serializable
1.4       └HandshakeCompletedEvent
```

	public .... String	**getCipherSuite** ()	
	public .... java↵ .security.cert.Certificate[]	**getLocalCertificates** ()	
	public .... javax.security↵ .cert.X509Certificate[]	**getPeerCertificateChain** () throws SSLPeerUnverifiedException	
	public .... java↵ .security.cert.Certificate[]	**getPeerCertificates** () throws SSLPeerUnverifiedException	
	public .... *SSLSession*	**getSession** ()	
	public .... SSLSocket	**getSocket** ()	
	public .... Object	getSource ()	
✳	public	**HandshakeCompletedEvent** (SSLSocket sock, *SSLSession* s)	
1	protected transient ...... Object	source	
1	public .... String	toString ()	

HandshakeCompletedListener — javax.net.ssl

```
1.4   HandshakeCompletedListener——————————java.util.EventListener     ε2,3,333,493,494
```

	public .... void	**handshakeCompleted** (HandshakeCompletedEvent event)

HasControls

HasControls	javax.naming.ldap

1.3	*HasControls* ˅	
	public .... *Control[]* **getControls** () throws javax.naming.NamingException	ε497

HashMap

HashMap	java.util

Object
1.2 ○	└ AbstractMap[1] ----------------------- *Map* ˅	
1.2	└ HashMap ˅ ----------------------- *Cloneable* ˅, *java.io.Serializable* ˅	

	1	public .... **void clear** ()		
	1	public .... **Object clone** ()		
	1	public .... **boolean containsKey** (Object key)		ε344
	1	public .... **boolean containsValue** (Object value)		
	1	public .... ***Set* entrySet** ()		ε345
	1	public .... boolean equals (Object o)		
	1	public .... **Object get** (Object key)		ε337,344,346,356,357
	1	public .... int hashCode ()		
*		public .... **HashMap** ()		ε346,347,348,355,291
*		public .... **HashMap** (int initialCapacity)		
*		public .... **HashMap** (*Map* m)		
*		public .... **HashMap** (int initialCapacity, float loadFactor)		
	1	public .... **boolean isEmpty** ()		
	1	public .... ***Set* keySet** ()		ε194,340,345,355,356
	1	public .... **Object put** (Object key, Object value)		ε337,344,346,355,356
	1	public .... **void putAll** (*Map* t)		
	1	public .... **Object remove** (Object key)		ε355
	1	public .... **int size** ()		ε355
	1	public .... String toString ()		
	1	public .... ***Collection* values** ()		ε340,345,355

HashSet

HashSet	java.util

Object[1]
1.2 ○	└ AbstractCollection[2] --------------------- *Collection* ˅	
1.2 ○	└ AbstractSet[3] ---------------------- *Set* ˅ (*Collection*)	
1.2	└ HashSet ˅ ----------------------- *Cloneable* ˅, *java.io.Serializable* ˅	

	2	public .... **boolean add** (Object o)	ε342,349,352,354,358
	2	public .... boolean addAll (*Collection* c)	ε351,353
	2	public .... **void clear** ()	ε351,353
	1	public .... **Object clone** ()	
	2	public .... **boolean contains** (Object o)	ε352
	2	public .... boolean containsAll (*Collection* c)	
	3	public .... boolean equals (Object o)	
	3	public .... int hashCode ()	
*		public .... **HashSet** ()	ε352,353,194
*		public .... **HashSet** (int initialCapacity)	
*		public .... **HashSet** (*Collection* c)	ε341,347,348
*		public .... **HashSet** (int initialCapacity, float loadFactor)	
	2	public .... **boolean isEmpty** ()	ε102
	2	public .... ***Iterator* iterator** ()	ε345,352,354,355,356
	2	public .... **boolean remove** (Object o)	ε349,352
	3	public .... boolean removeAll (*Collection* c)	ε351,353
	2	public .... boolean retainAll (*Collection* c)	ε351,353
	2	public .... **int size** ()	ε340,349,351,352,358
	2	public .... Object[] toArray ()	ε340
	2	public .... Object[] toArray (Object[] a)	ε340,352,358,194,508
	2	public .... String toString ()	

Hashtable

Hashtable	java.util

Object[1]
○	└ Dictionary[2]	
	└ Hashtable ˅ ----------------------- *Map* ˅[3], *Cloneable* ˅, *java.io.Serializable* ˅	

	3	public synchronized ....void	**clear** ()		
	1	public synchronized ....**Object**	**clone** ()		
		public synchronized .. boolean	**contains** (Object value)		
	3	public synchronized .. boolean	**containsKey** (Object key)		ε344
1.2	3	public................. boolean	**containsValue** (Object value)		
	2	public synchronized	**elements** ()		
		.... *Enumeration*			
1.2	3	public.......................*Set*	**entrySet** ()		ε345
	1	public synchronized .. **boolean**	**equals** (Object o)		
	2	public synchronized ....**Object**	**get** (Object key)		ε88
	1	public synchronized .... **int**	**hashCode** ()		
*		public........................	**Hashtable** ()		ε472,481,492
*		public........................	**Hashtable** (int initialCapacity)		
1.2 *		public........................	**Hashtable** (*Map* t)		
*		public........................	**Hashtable** (int initialCapacity, float loadFactor)		
	2	public synchronized .. **boolean**	**isEmpty** ()		
	2	public synchronized	**keys** ()		
		.... *Enumeration*			
1.2	3	public.......................*Set*	**keySet** ()		ε194,340,345,355,356
	2	public synchronized ....**Object**	**put** (Object key, Object value)		ε472,481,484,485,486
1.2	3	public synchronized ......void	**putAll** (*Map* t)		
		protected..................void	**rehash** ()		
	2	public synchronized ....**Object**	**remove** (Object key)		
	2	public synchronized .... **int**	**size** ()		
	1	public synchronized .... **String**	**toString** ()		
1.2	3	public................ *Collection*	**values** ()		ε340,345,355

HostnameVerifier	javax.net.ssl

1.4	*HostnameVerifier*

public................. boolean **verify** (String hostname, *SSLSession* session)

HttpsURLConnection	javax.net.ssl

	Object
○	└java.net.URLConnection [1]
1.1 ○	└java.net.HttpURLConnection [2]
1.4 ○	└HttpsURLConnection

	1	*50 inherited members from java.net.URLConnection not shown*		
	2	*53 inherited members from java.net.HttpURLConnection not shown*		
○		public abstract ....String	**getCipherSuite** ()	
△		public static . *HostnameVerifier*	**getDefaultHostnameVerifier** ()	
△		public static SSLSocketFactory	**getDefaultSSLSocketFactory** ()	ε501
		public........ *HostnameVerifier*	**getHostnameVerifier** ()	
○		public abstract .... java↩	**getLocalCertificates** ()	
		.security.cert.Certificate[]		
○		public abstract .... java↩	**getServerCertificates** () throws SSLPeerUnverifiedException	
		.security.cert.Certificate[]		
		public....... SSLSocketFactory	**getSSLSocketFactory** ()	
		protected .... *HostnameVerifier*	**hostnameVerifier**	
*		protected......................	**HttpsURLConnection** (java.net.URL url) throws java.io.IOException	
△		public static ....void	**setDefaultHostnameVerifier** (*HostnameVerifier* v)	
△		public static ....void	**setDefaultSSLSocketFactory** (SSLSocketFactory sf)	ε502
		public......................void	**setHostnameVerifier** (*HostnameVerifier* v)	
		public......................void	**setSSLSocketFactory** (SSLSocketFactory sf)	

HttpURLConnection	java.net

	Object
○	└URLConnection [1]
1.1 ○	└HttpURLConnection.

	1	*50 inherited members from URLConnection not shown*	
○		public abstract ....void	**disconnect** ()
1.2		public...... java.io.InputStream	**getErrorStream** ()
△		public static .... boolean	**getFollowRedirects** ()
	1	public.................... **long**	**getHeaderFieldDate** (String name, long Default)
1.3		public................. boolean	**getInstanceFollowRedirects** ()

H

Classes

HttpURLConnection

1.2	1	public............................	**getPermission** () throws java.io.IOException	
		... **java.security.Permission**		
		public.....................String	**getRequestMethod** ()	
		public..........................int	**getResponseCode** () throws java.io.IOException	
		public.....................String	**getResponseMessage** () throws java.io.IOException	
	▲	public static final.............int	**HTTP_ACCEPTED** = 202	
	▲	public static final.............int	**HTTP_BAD_GATEWAY** = 502	
	▲	public static final.............int	**HTTP_BAD_METHOD** = 405	
	▲	public static final.............int	**HTTP_BAD_REQUEST** = 400	
	▲	public static final.............int	**HTTP_CLIENT_TIMEOUT** = 408	
	▲	public static final.............int	**HTTP_CONFLICT** = 409	
	▲	public static final.............int	**HTTP_CREATED** = 201	
	▲	public static final.............int	**HTTP_ENTITY_TOO_LARGE** = 413	
	▲	public static final.............int	**HTTP_FORBIDDEN** = 403	
	▲	public static final.............int	**HTTP_GATEWAY_TIMEOUT** = 504	
	▲	public static final.............int	**HTTP_GONE** = 410	
	▲	public static final.............int	**HTTP_INTERNAL_ERROR** = 500	
	▲	public static final.............int	**HTTP_LENGTH_REQUIRED** = 411	
	▲	public static final.............int	**HTTP_MOVED_PERM** = 301	
	▲	public static final.............int	**HTTP_MOVED_TEMP** = 302	
	▲	public static final.............int	**HTTP_MULT_CHOICE** = 300	
	▲	public static final.............int	**HTTP_NO_CONTENT** = 204	
	▲	public static final.............int	**HTTP_NOT_ACCEPTABLE** = 406	
	▲	public static final.............int	**HTTP_NOT_AUTHORITATIVE** = 203	
	▲	public static final.............int	**HTTP_NOT_FOUND** = 404	
1.3	▲	public static final.............int	**HTTP_NOT_IMPLEMENTED** = 501	
	▲	public static final.............int	**HTTP_NOT_MODIFIED** = 304	
	▲	public static final.............int	**HTTP_OK** = 200	
	▲	public static final.............int	**HTTP_PARTIAL** = 206	
	▲	public static final.............int	**HTTP_PAYMENT_REQUIRED** = 402	
	▲	public static final.............int	**HTTP_PRECON_FAILED** = 412	
	▲	public static final.............int	**HTTP_PROXY_AUTH** = 407	
	▲	public static final.............int	**HTTP_REQ_TOO_LONG** = 414	
	▲	public static final.............int	**HTTP_RESET** = 205	
	▲	public static final.............int	**HTTP_SEE_OTHER** = 303	
D	▲	public static final.............int	**HTTP_SERVER_ERROR** = 500	
	▲	public static final.............int	**HTTP_UNAUTHORIZED** = 401	
	▲	public static final.............int	**HTTP_UNAVAILABLE** = 503	
	▲	public static final.............int	**HTTP_UNSUPPORTED_TYPE** = 415	
	▲	public static final.............int	**HTTP_USE_PROXY** = 305	
	▲	public static final.............int	**HTTP_VERSION** = 505	
	✳	protected.........................	**HttpURLConnection** (URL u)	
1.3		protected..............boolean	**instanceFollowRedirects**	
		protected.................String	**method**	
		protected.....................int	**responseCode**	
		protected.................String	**responseMessage**	
	△	public static ....void	**setFollowRedirects** (boolean set)	ε143
1.3		public.......................void	**setInstanceFollowRedirects** (boolean followRedirects)	ε143
		public.......................void	**setRequestMethod** (String method) throws ProtocolException	
	○	public abstract .... boolean	**usingProxy** ()	

ID_ASSIGNMENT_POLICY_ID	org.omg.PortableServer

1.4	*ID_ASSIGNMENT_POLICY_ID*
▲	public static final.............int **value** = 19

ID_UNIQUENESS_POLICY_ID	org.omg.PortableServer

1.4	*ID_UNIQUENESS_POLICY_ID*
▲	public static final.............int **value** = 18

Class   *Interface*   —extends   - - -implements   ○ abstract   ● final   △ static   ▲ static final   ✳ constructor   x x—inherited   x **x**—declared   **x x**—overridden
εn—examples of usage   ˌ—has subclass   package—see other volume

IdAssignmentPolicy — org.omg.PortableServer

1.4   *IdAssignmentPolicy*────────── *IdAssignmentPolicyOperations* [1] (*org.omg.CORBA* ↩
              .PolicyOperations [2]), *org.omg.CORBA.Policy*
              (*org.omg.CORBA.PolicyOperations* [2], *org.omg.CORBA.Object* [3],
              org.omg.CORBA.portable.IDLEntity (*java.io.Serializable*)),
              org.omg.CORBA.portable.IDLEntity (*java.io.Serializable*)

   3   *13 inherited members from org.omg.CORBA.Object not shown*
   2   *3 inherited members from org.omg.CORBA.PolicyOperations not shown*
   1   public.......................... **value** ()
      .... IdAssignmentPolicyValue

IdAssignmentPolicyOperations — org.omg.PortableServer

1.4   *IdAssignmentPolicyOperations* ──────── *org.omg.CORBA.PolicyOperations* [1]

   1   *3 inherited members from org.omg.CORBA.PolicyOperations not shown*
     public.......................... **value** ()
     .... IdAssignmentPolicyValue

IdAssignmentPolicyValue — org.omg.PortableServer

     Object
1.4   └IdAssignmentPolicyValue --------------- *org.omg.CORBA.portable.IDLEntity* (*java.io.Serializable*)

▲   public static final ....int **_SYSTEM_ID** = 1
▲   public static final ....int **_USER_ID** = 0
△   public static .... **from_int** (int value)
     .... IdAssignmentPolicyValue
∗   protected...................... **IdAssignmentPolicyValue** (int value)
▲   public static final .... **SYSTEM_ID**
     .... IdAssignmentPolicyValue
▲   public static final .... **USER_ID**
     .... IdAssignmentPolicyValue
   public.......................int **value** ()

IdentifierHelper — org.omg.CORBA

     Object
1.3 ○   └IdentifierHelper

△   public static ....String **extract** (Any a)
△   public static ....String **id** ()
∗   public.......................... **IdentifierHelper** ()
△   public static ....void **insert** (Any a, String that)
△   public static ....String **read** (org.omg.CORBA.portable.InputStream istream)
△   public static synchronized .... **type** ()
     .... TypeCode
△   public static ....void **write** (org.omg.CORBA.portable.OutputStream ostream, String value)

Identity — java.security

     Object [1]
D ○   └Identity ---------------------------- *Principal* [2], *java.io.Serializable*

D   public.......................void **addCertificate** (*Certificate* certificate) throws KeyManagementException
D   public............. *Certificate[]* **certificates** ()
D ● 1 public final ....**boolean equals** (Object identity)
D   public.......................String **getInfo** ()
D ● 2 public final ....String **getName** ()   ε227,508
D   public............... *PublicKey* **getPublicKey** ()
D ●   public final ...... IdentityScope **getScope** ()
D   1 public.......................**int hashCode** ()
D ∗   protected...................... **Identity** ()
D ∗   public.......................... **Identity** (String name)
D ∗   public.......................... **Identity** (String name, IdentityScope scope) throws KeyManagementException
D   protected.............. boolean **identityEquals** (Identity identity)
D   public.......................void **removeCertificate** (*Certificate* certificate) throws KeyManagementException
D   public.......................void **setInfo** (String info)

I

Classes

Identity

D		public	void	**setPublicKey** (*PublicKey* key) throws KeyManagementException	
D	1	public	**String**	**toString** ()	
D		public	String	**toString** (boolean detailed)	

IdentityHashMap   java.util

Object
- 1.2 ○ └AbstractMap [1] ------------------------ *Map*
- 1.4   └IdentityHashMap -------------------- *java.io.Serializable*, Cloneable

	1	public	**void**	**clear** ()	
	1	public	**Object**	**clone** ()	
	1	public	**boolean**	**containsKey** (Object key)	ε344
	1	public	**boolean**	**containsValue** (Object value)	
	1	public	*Set*	**entrySet** ()	ε345
	1	public	**boolean**	**equals** (Object o)	
	1	public	**Object**	**get** (Object key)	ε337,344,346,356,357
	1	public	**int**	**hashCode** ()	
*		public		**IdentityHashMap** ()	ε337
*		public		**IdentityHashMap** (int expectedMaxSize)	
*		public		**IdentityHashMap** (*Map* m)	
	1	public	**boolean**	**isEmpty** ()	
	1	public	*Set*	**keySet** ()	ε194,340,345,355,356
	1	public	**Object**	**put** (Object key, Object value)	ε337,344,346,355,356
	1	public	**void**	**putAll** (*Map* t)	
	1	public	**Object**	**remove** (Object key)	ε355
	1	public	**int**	**size** ()	ε355
	1	public	String	toString ()	
	1	public	*Collection*	**values** ()	ε340,345,355

IdentityScope   java.security

Object
- D ○ └Identity [1] ----------------------------- *Principal*, java.io.Serializable
- D ○   └IdentityScope

D	1	public	void	addCertificate (*Certificate* certificate) throws KeyManagementException	
D	○	public abstract	void	**addIdentity** (Identity identity) throws KeyManagementException	
D	1	public	*Certificate[]*	certificates ()	
D	● 1	public final	boolean	equals (Object identity)	
D	○	public abstract	Identity	**getIdentity** (String name)	
D	1	public	Identity	**getIdentity** (*Principal* principal)	
D	○	public abstract	Identity	**getIdentity** (*PublicKey* key)	
D	1	public	String	getInfo ()	
D	● 1	public final	String	getName ()	ε227,508
D	1	public	*PublicKey*	getPublicKey ()	
D	● 1	public final	IdentityScope	getScope ()	
D	△	public static	IdentityScope	**getSystemScope** ()	
D	1	public	int	hashCode ()	
D	○	public abstract		**identities** ()	
			java.util.Enumeration		
D	1	protected	boolean	identityEquals (Identity identity)	
D	*	protected		**IdentityScope** ()	
D	*	public		**IdentityScope** (String name)	
D	*	public		**IdentityScope** (String name, IdentityScope scope)	
				throws KeyManagementException	
D	1	public	void	removeCertificate (*Certificate* certificate) throws KeyManagementException	
D	○	public abstract	void	**removeIdentity** (Identity identity) throws KeyManagementException	
D	1	public	void	setInfo (String info)	
D	1	public	void	setPublicKey (*PublicKey* key) throws KeyManagementException	
D	△	protected static	void	**setSystemScope** (IdentityScope scope)	
D	○	public abstract	int	**size** ()	
D	1	public	**String**	**toString** ()	
D	1	public	String	toString (boolean detailed)	

Class   *Interface*   —extends   - - -implements   ○ abstract   ● final   △ static   ▲ static final   * constructor   x x—inherited   x **x**—declared   **x x**—overridden
ε*n*—examples of usage   —has subclass   package—see other volume

590

IDLEntity | org.omg.CORBA.portable

1.2   *IDLEntity* ───────────────────── *java.io.Serializable*

- -

IDLType | org.omg.CORBA

1.2   *IDLType*──────────────── *IDLTypeOperations* [1] (*IRObjectOperations* [2]),
                              IRObject (*IRObjectOperations* [2], *Object* [3],
                              org.omg.CORBA.portable.IDLEntity (java.io.Serializable)),
                              org.omg.CORBA.portable.IDLEntity (java.io.Serializable)

- -

     2   2 inherited members from IRObjectOperations not shown
     3   13 inherited members from Object not shown
1.3   *1*   public.............. TypeCode type ()

- -

IDLTypeHelper | org.omg.CORBA

      Object
1.3 ○   └IDLTypeHelper

△   public static .... *IDLType* **extract** (Any a)
△   public static .... String **id** ()
✱   public......................... **IDLTypeHelper** ()
△   public static .... void **insert** (Any a, *IDLType* that)
△   public static .... *IDLType* **narrow** (*Object* obj)
△   public static .... *IDLType* **read** (org.omg.CORBA.portable.InputStream istream)
△   public static synchronized .... **type** ()
              .... TypeCode
△   public static .... void **write** (org.omg.CORBA.portable.OutputStream ostream, *IDLType* value)

IDLTypeOperations | org.omg.CORBA

1.3   *IDLTypeOperations* ──────────────── *IRObjectOperations* [1]

- -

     1   2 inherited members from IRObjectOperations not shown
     public.............. TypeCode **type** ()

- -

IdUniquenessPolicy | org.omg.PortableServer

1.4   *IdUniquenessPolicy*──────────── *IdUniquenessPolicyOperations* [1] (*org.omg.CORBA↵*
                             .PolicyOperations [2]), *org.omg.CORBA.Policy*
                             (org.omg.CORBA.PolicyOperations [2], *org.omg.CORBA.Object* [3],
                             org.omg.CORBA.portable.IDLEntity (java.io.Serializable)),
                             org.omg.CORBA.portable.IDLEntity (java.io.Serializable)

- -

     3   13 inherited members from org.omg.CORBA.Object not shown
     2   3 inherited members from org.omg.CORBA.PolicyOperations not shown
     1   public.......................... **value** ()
       .... IdUniquenessPolicyValue

IdUniquenessPolicyOperations | org.omg.PortableServer

1.4   *IdUniquenessPolicyOperations* ──────────── *org.omg.CORBA.PolicyOperations* [1]

- -

     1   3 inherited members from org.omg.CORBA.PolicyOperations not shown
     public.......................... **value** ()
       .... IdUniquenessPolicyValue

- -

IdUniquenessPolicyValue | org.omg.PortableServer

      Object
1.4   └IdUniquenessPolicyValue - - - - - - - - - - - - - - - *org.omg.CORBA.portable.IDLEntity (java.io.Serializable)*

▲   public static final ....int **_MULTIPLE_ID** = 1
▲   public static final ....int **_UNIQUE_ID** = 0
△   public static .... **from_int** (int value)
      .... IdUniquenessPolicyValue
✱   protected...................... **IdUniquenessPolicyValue** (int value)

IdUniquenessPolicyValue

▲	public static final	**MULTIPLE_ID**
	. . . . IdUniquenessPolicyValue	
▲	public static final	**UNIQUE_ID**
	. . . . IdUniquenessPolicyValue	
	public . . . . int	**value** ()

IllegalAccessError   java.lang

```
Object
└Throwable --------------------------- java.io.Serializable
  └Error
    └LinkageError
      └IncompatibleClassChangeError
        └IllegalAccessError
```

✳	public	**IllegalAccessError** ()
✳	public	**IllegalAccessError** (String s)

IllegalAccessException   java.lang

ε69,115,117,119,291

```
Object
└Throwable --------------------------- java.io.Serializable
  └Exception
    └IllegalAccessException
```

✳	public	**IllegalAccessException** ()
✳	public	**IllegalAccessException** (String s)

IllegalArgumentException   java.lang

ε133

```
Object
└Throwable --------------------------- java.io.Serializable
  └Exception
    └RuntimeException
      └IllegalArgumentException
```

✳	public	**IllegalArgumentException** ()
✳	public	**IllegalArgumentException** (String s)

IllegalBlockingModeException   java.nio.channels

```
Object
└Throwable --------------------------- java.io.Serializable
  └Exception
    └RuntimeException
      └IllegalStateException
        └IllegalBlockingModeException
```

1.1
1.4

✳	public	**IllegalBlockingModeException** ()

IllegalBlockSizeException   javax.crypto

ε462,464,466

```
Object
└Throwable --------------------------- java.io.Serializable
  └Exception
    └java.security.GeneralSecurityException
      └IllegalBlockSizeException
```

1.2
1.4

✳	public	**IllegalBlockSizeException** ()
✳	public	**IllegalBlockSizeException** (String msg)

Class   *Interface*   —extends   - - -implements   ○ abstract   ● final   △ static   ▲ static final   ✳ constructor   x x—inherited   x **x**—declared   **x x**—overridden
ε*n*—examples of usage   ⌄—has subclass   package—see other volume

IllegalCharsetNameException

java.nio.charset

```
Object
└Throwable ------------------------- java.io.Serializable ⌄
  └Exception
    └RuntimeException
      └IllegalArgumentException
1.4     └IllegalCharsetNameException
```

	public.....................String	**getCharsetName** ()
∗	public..........................	**IllegalCharsetNameException** (String charsetName)

IllegalMonitorStateException

java.lang

```
Object
└Throwable ------------------------- java.io.Serializable ⌄
  └Exception
    └RuntimeException
      └IllegalMonitorStateException
```

∗	public..........................	**IllegalMonitorStateException** ()
∗	public..........................	**IllegalMonitorStateException** (String s)

IllegalSelectorException

java.nio.channels

```
Object
└Throwable ------------------------- java.io.Serializable ⌄
  └Exception
    └RuntimeException
      └IllegalArgumentException
1.4     └IllegalSelectorException
```

∗	public..........................	**IllegalSelectorException** ()

IllegalStateException

java.lang

```
Object
└Throwable ------------------------- java.io.Serializable ⌄
  └Exception
    └RuntimeException
1.1     └IllegalStateException ⌄
```

∗	public..........................	**IllegalStateException** ()	ε388
∗	public..........................	**IllegalStateException** (String s)	

IllegalThreadStateException

java.lang

```
Object
└Throwable ------------------------- java.io.Serializable ⌄
  └Exception
    └RuntimeException
      └IllegalArgumentException
        └IllegalThreadStateException
```

∗	public..........................	**IllegalThreadStateException** ()
∗	public..........................	**IllegalThreadStateException** (String s)

IMP_LIMIT

org.omg.CORBA

```
Object
└Throwable ------------------------- java.io.Serializable ⌄
  └Exception
    └RuntimeException
1.2 ○   └SystemException [1]
1.2 ●     └IMP_LIMIT
```

	[1]	*3 inherited members from SystemException not shown*
∗	public..........................	**IMP_LIMIT** ()

IMP_LIMIT

✳	public	IMP_LIMIT	(String s)
✳	public	IMP_LIMIT	(int minor, CompletionStatus completed)
✳	public	IMP_LIMIT	(String s, int minor, CompletionStatus completed)

IMPLICIT_ACTIVATION_POLICY_ID	org.omg.PortableServer

1.4	*IMPLICIT_ACTIVATION_POLICY_ID*
▲	public static final............int **value** = 20

ImplicitActivationPolicy	org.omg.PortableServer

1.4 *ImplicitActivationPolicy*————————*ImplicitActivationPolicyOperations* ˅ [1]
(*org.omg.CORBA.PolicyOperations* [2]), *org.omg.CORBA.Policy* ˅
(*org.omg.CORBA.PolicyOperations* [2], *org.omg.CORBA.Object* [3],
org.omg.CORBA.portable.IDLEntity (*java.io.Serializable*)),
org.omg.CORBA.portable.IDLEntity ˅ (*java.io.Serializable*)

3 13 inherited members from org.omg.CORBA.Object not shown
2 3 inherited members from org.omg.CORBA.PolicyOperations not shown
1 public........................ value ()
.ImplicitActivationPolicyValue

ImplicitActivationPolicyOperations	org.omg.PortableServer

1.4 *ImplicitActivationPolicyOperations* ˅————— *org.omg.CORBA.PolicyOperations* ˅ [1]

1 3 inherited members from org.omg.CORBA.PolicyOperations not shown
public........................ **value** ()
.ImplicitActivationPolicyValue

ImplicitActivationPolicyValue	org.omg.PortableServer

Object
└ImplicitActivationPolicyValue ------------- *org.omg.CORBA.portable.IDLEntity* ˅ (*java.io.Serializable*)

1.4

▲	public static final............int	**_IMPLICIT_ACTIVATION** = 0	
▲	public static final............int	**_NO_IMPLICIT_ACTIVATION** = 1	
△	public static....................	**from_int** (int value)	
	.ImplicitActivationPolicyValue		
▲	public static final...............	**IMPLICIT_ACTIVATION**	
	.ImplicitActivationPolicyValue		
✳	protected........................	**ImplicitActivationPolicyValue** (int value)	
▲	public static final...............	**NO_IMPLICIT_ACTIVATION**	
	.ImplicitActivationPolicyValue		
	public........................int	**value** ()	

IncompatibleClassChangeError	java.lang

Object
└Throwable ---------------------------- *java.io.Serializable* ˅
  └Error
    └LinkageError
      └IncompatibleClassChangeError ˅

✳	public........................	**IncompatibleClassChangeError** ()
✳	public........................	**IncompatibleClassChangeError** (String s)

Class *Interface* —extends - - -implements ○ abstract ● final △ static ▲ static final ✳ constructor x x—inherited x **x**—declared **x x**—overridden
εn—examples of usage ˅—has subclass package—see other volume

InconsistentTypeCode❶ | org.omg.CORBA.ORBPackage

```
Object
└Throwable ---------------------------- java.io.Serializable
  └Exception
1.2 ○   └org.omg.CORBA.UserException ------- org.omg.CORBA.portable.IDLEntity (java.io.Serializable)
1.2 ●     └InconsistentTypeCode
```

✳	public..........................	**InconsistentTypeCode** ()
✳	public..........................	**InconsistentTypeCode** (String reason)

InconsistentTypeCode❷ | org.omg.DynamicAny.DynAnyFactoryPackage

```
Object
└Throwable ---------------------------- java.io.Serializable
  └Exception
1.2 ○   └org.omg.CORBA.UserException ------- org.omg.CORBA.portable.IDLEntity (java.io.Serializable)
1.4 ●     └InconsistentTypeCode
```

✳	public..........................	**InconsistentTypeCode** ()
✳	public..........................	**InconsistentTypeCode** (String $reason)

InconsistentTypeCodeHelper | org.omg.DynamicAny.DynAnyFactoryPackage

```
Object
1.4 ○ └InconsistentTypeCodeHelper
```

△	public static	**extract** (org.omg.CORBA.Any a)
	.... InconsistentTypeCode	
△	public static .... String	**id** ()
✳	public..........................	**InconsistentTypeCodeHelper** ()
△	public static ....void	**insert** (org.omg.CORBA.Any a, InconsistentTypeCode that)
△	public static	**read** (org.omg.CORBA.portable.InputStream istream)
	.... InconsistentTypeCode	
△	public static synchronized	**type** ()
	. org.omg.CORBA.TypeCode	
△	public static ....void	**write** (org.omg.CORBA.portable.OutputStream ostream,
		InconsistentTypeCode value)

IndexedPropertyDescriptor | java.beans

```
Object
1.1 └FeatureDescriptor 1
1.1   └PropertyDescriptor 2
1.1     └IndexedPropertyDescriptor
```

1	public.... java.util.Enumeration	attributeNames ()	
2	public.................**boolean**	**equals** (Object obj)	
1	public....................String	getDisplayName ()	
	public....................Class	**getIndexedPropertyType** ()	
	public.java.lang.reflect.Method	**getIndexedReadMethod** ()	
	public.java.lang.reflect.Method	**getIndexedWriteMethod** ()	
1	public....................String	getName ()	ε5,9
2	public....................Class	getPropertyEditorClass ()	
2	public....................Class	getPropertyType ()	
2	public.java.lang.reflect.Method	getReadMethod ()	
1	public....................String	getShortDescription ()	
1	public....................Object	getValue (String attributeName)	
2	public.java.lang.reflect.Method	getWriteMethod ()	
✳	public..........................	**IndexedPropertyDescriptor** (String propertyName, Class beanClass)	
		throws IntrospectionException	
✳	public..........................	**IndexedPropertyDescriptor** (String propertyName, java.lang.reflect.Method getter,	
		java.lang.reflect.Method setter, java.lang.reflect.Method indexedGetter,	
		java.lang.reflect.Method indexedSetter) throws IntrospectionException	
✳	public..........................	**IndexedPropertyDescriptor** (String propertyName, Class beanClass,	
		String getterName, String setterName, String indexedGetterName,	
		String indexedSetterName) throws IntrospectionException	
2	public................. boolean	isBound ()	
2	public................. boolean	isConstrained ()	
1	public................. boolean	isExpert ()	

IndexedPropertyDescriptor

	1	public	boolean	isHidden ()
1.2	1	public	boolean	isPreferred ()
	2	public	void	setBound (boolean bound)
	2	public	void	setConstrained (boolean constrained)
	1	public	void	setDisplayName (String displayName)
	1	public	void	setExpert (boolean expert)
	1	public	void	setHidden (boolean hidden)
1.2		public	void	**setIndexedReadMethod** (java.lang.reflect.Method getter)
				throws IntrospectionException
1.2		public	void	**setIndexedWriteMethod** (java.lang.reflect.Method setter)
				throws IntrospectionException
	1	public	void	setName (String name)
1.2	1	public	void	setPreferred (boolean preferred)
	2	public	void	setPropertyEditorClass (Class propertyEditorClass)
1.2	2	public	void	setReadMethod (java.lang.reflect.Method getter) throws IntrospectionException
	1	public	void	setShortDescription (String text)
	1	public	void	setValue (String attributeName, Object value) ε9
1.2	2	public	void	setWriteMethod (java.lang.reflect.Method setter) throws IntrospectionException

---

IndexOutOfBoundsException   java.lang

```
Object
└Throwable ---------------------------- java.io.Serializable⌐
  └Exception
    └RuntimeException
      └IndexOutOfBoundsException⌐
```

*	public	**IndexOutOfBoundsException** ()
*	public	**IndexOutOfBoundsException** (String s)

IndirectionException   org.omg.CORBA.portable

```
Object
└Throwable ---------------------------- java.io.Serializable⌐
  └Exception
    └RuntimeException
```
1.2 O `      └org.omg.CORBA.SystemException`[1]
1.3 `        └IndirectionException`

	1	*3 inherited members from org.omg.CORBA.SystemException not shown*	
*		public	**IndirectionException** (int offset)
		public	int **offset**

Inet4Address   java.net

```
Object                                                       ε139,151
└InetAddress¹ -------------------------- java.io.Serializable⌐
```
1.4 ● `  └Inet4Address`

	1	public	**boolean**	**equals** (Object obj)
	1	public	**byte[]**	**getAddress** () ε144,146
△	1	public static	InetAddress[]	getAllByName (String host) throws UnknownHostException
△	1	public static	InetAddress	getByAddress (byte[] addr) throws UnknownHostException ε145
△	1	public static	InetAddress	getByAddress (String host, byte[] addr) throws UnknownHostException
△	1	public static	InetAddress	getByName (String host) throws UnknownHostException ε144,145,147,153
	1	public	String	getCanonicalHostName () ε145
	1	public	**String**	**getHostAddress** ()
	1	public	String	getHostName () ε145,146,173,176
△	1	public static synchronized .... InetAddress	getLocalHost () throws UnknownHostException ε146,173,176
	1	public	int	**hashCode** ()
	1	public	**boolean**	**isAnyLocalAddress** ()
	1	public	**boolean**	**isLinkLocalAddress** ()
	1	public	**boolean**	**isLoopbackAddress** ()
	1	public	**boolean**	**isMCGlobal** ()
	1	public	**boolean**	**isMCLinkLocal** ()
	1	public	**boolean**	**isMCNodeLocal** ()

Class *Interface* —extends - - -implements O abstract ● final △ static ▲ static final ✳ constructor x x—inherited x **x**—declared **x x**—overridden
εn—examples of usage ⌐—has subclass package—see other volume

	1	public	**boolean**	**isMCOrgLocal** ()	
	1	public	**boolean**	**isMCSiteLocal** ()	
	1	public	**boolean**	**isMulticastAddress** ()	
	1	public	**boolean**	**isSiteLocalAddress** ()	
	1	public	String	toString ()	

Inet6Address   java.net

Object   ε139,151
└ InetAddress[1] - *java.io.Serializable*
1.4 ●   └ Inet6Address

	1	public	**boolean**	**equals** (Object obj)	
	1	public	**byte[]**	**getAddress** ()	ε144,146
△	1	public static	InetAddress[]	getAllByName (String host) throws UnknownHostException	
△	1	public static	InetAddress	getByAddress (byte[] addr) throws UnknownHostException	ε145
△	1	public static	InetAddress	getByAddress (String host, byte[] addr) throws UnknownHostException	
△	1	public static	InetAddress	getByName (String host) throws UnknownHostException	ε144,145,147,153
	1	public	String	getCanonicalHostName ()	ε145
	1	public	**String**	**getHostAddress** ()	
	1	public	String	getHostName ()	ε145,146,173,176
△	1	public static synchronized InetAddress		getLocalHost () throws UnknownHostException	ε146,173,176
	1	public	**int**	**hashCode** ()	
	1	public	**boolean**	**isAnyLocalAddress** ()	
		public	boolean	**isIPv4CompatibleAddress** ()	
	1	public	**boolean**	**isLinkLocalAddress** ()	
	1	public	**boolean**	**isLoopbackAddress** ()	
	1	public	**boolean**	**isMCGlobal** ()	
	1	public	**boolean**	**isMCLinkLocal** ()	
	1	public	**boolean**	**isMCNodeLocal** ()	
	1	public	**boolean**	**isMCOrgLocal** ()	
	1	public	**boolean**	**isMCSiteLocal** ()	
	1	public	**boolean**	**isMulticastAddress** ()	
	1	public	**boolean**	**isSiteLocalAddress** ()	
	1	public	String	toString ()	

InetAddress   java.net

Object[1]   ε139,151
└ InetAddress - *java.io.Serializable*

	1	public	**boolean**	**equals** (Object obj)	
		public	byte[]	**getAddress** ()	ε144,146
△		public static	InetAddress[]	**getAllByName** (String host) throws UnknownHostException	
1.4 △		public static	InetAddress	**getByAddress** (byte[] addr) throws UnknownHostException	ε145
1.4 △		public static	InetAddress	**getByAddress** (String host, byte[] addr) throws UnknownHostException	
△		public static	InetAddress	**getByName** (String host) throws UnknownHostException	ε144,145,147,153
1.4		public	String	**getCanonicalHostName** ()	ε145
		public	String	**getHostAddress** ()	
		public	String	**getHostName** ()	ε145,146,173,176
△		public static synchronized InetAddress		**getLocalHost** () throws UnknownHostException	ε146,173,176
	1	public	**int**	**hashCode** ()	
1.4		public	boolean	**isAnyLocalAddress** ()	
1.4		public	boolean	**isLinkLocalAddress** ()	
1.4		public	boolean	**isLoopbackAddress** ()	
1.4		public	boolean	**isMCGlobal** ()	
1.4		public	boolean	**isMCLinkLocal** ()	
1.4		public	boolean	**isMCNodeLocal** ()	
1.4		public	boolean	**isMCOrgLocal** ()	
1.4		public	boolean	**isMCSiteLocal** ()	
1.1		public	boolean	**isMulticastAddress** ()	
1.4		public	boolean	**isSiteLocalAddress** ()	
	1	public	**String**	**toString** ()	

I

Classes

InetSocketAddress

InetSocketAddress					java.net

		Object[1]	ε147
1.4	O	└SocketAddress ------------------------ *java.io.Serializable* ⌄	
1.4		└InetSocketAddress	

●	1	public final ....**boolean**	**equals** (Object obj)	
●		public final ....InetAddress	**getAddress** ()	
●		public final ....String	**getHostName** ()	
●		public final ....int	**getPort** ()	
●	1	public final .... **int**	**hashCode** ()	
✳		public..........................	**InetSocketAddress** (int port)	ε177,179
✳		public..........................	**InetSocketAddress** (String hostname, int port)	ε173
✳		public..........................	**InetSocketAddress** (InetAddress addr, int port)	ε147,179
●		public final .... boolean	**isUnresolved** ()	
	1	public....................**String**	**toString** ()	

Inflater					java.util.zip

	Object[1]	
1.1	└Inflater	

		public synchronized ....void	**end** ()	
	1	protected..................**void**	**finalize** ()	
		public synchronized .. boolean	**finished** ()	ε450
		public synchronized ....int	**getAdler** ()	
		public synchronized ....int	**getRemaining** ()	
		public synchronized ....int	**getTotalIn** ()	
		public synchronized ....int	**getTotalOut** ()	
		public..........................int	**inflate** (byte[] b) throws DataFormatException	ε450
		public synchronized ....int	**inflate** (byte[] b, int off, int len) throws DataFormatException	
✳		public..........................	**Inflater** ()	ε450
✳		public..........................	**Inflater** (boolean nowrap)	
		public synchronized .. boolean	**needsDictionary** ()	
		public synchronized .. boolean	**needsInput** ()	
		public synchronized ....void	**reset** ()	
		public........................void	**setDictionary** (byte[] b)	
		public synchronized ......void	**setDictionary** (byte[] b, int off, int len)	
		public........................void	**setInput** (byte[] b)	ε450
		public synchronized ....void	**setInput** (byte[] b, int off, int len)	

InflaterInputStream					java.util.zip

		Object	ε252,382,418
	O	└java.io.InputStream	
		└java.io.FilterInputStream[1]	
1.1		└InflaterInputStream ⌄	

	1	public...................... **int**	**available** () throws java.io.IOException	
		protected ....byte[]	**buf**	
	1	public......................,.... **void**	**close** () throws java.io.IOException	ε14,36,45,452,455
		protected ....void	**fill** () throws java.io.IOException	
	1	protected .. java.io.InputStream	in	
		protected ....Inflater	**inf**	
✳		public..........................	**InflaterInputStream** (java.io.InputStream in)	
✳		public..........................	**InflaterInputStream** (java.io.InputStream in, Inflater inf)	
✳		public..........................	**InflaterInputStream** (java.io.InputStream in, Inflater inf, int size)	
		protected ....int	**len**	
	1	public synchronized ....void	mark (int readlimit)	
	1	public................... boolean	markSupported ()	
	1	public.......................... **int**	**read** () throws java.io.IOException	ε90,184,256
	1	public..........................int	read (byte[] b) throws java.io.IOException	ε452,455,457,170,451
	1	public.......................... **int**	**read** (byte[] b, int off, int len) throws java.io.IOException	ε36
	1	public synchronized ....void	reset () throws java.io.IOException	
	1	public.................... **long**	**skip** (long n) throws java.io.IOException	

Class *Interface* —extends - - -implements O abstract ● final △ static ▲ static final ✳ constructor x x—inherited x **x**—declared **x x**—overridden
ε*n*—examples of usage ⌄—has subclass package—see other volume

InheritableThreadLocal				java.lang

Object
1.2 └ ThreadLocal [1]
1.2   └ InheritableThreadLocal

	protected	Object	**childValue** (Object parentValue)	
1	public	Object	get ()	ε100
*	public		**InheritableThreadLocal** ()	
1	protected	Object	initialValue ()	
1	public	void	set (Object value)	ε100

InitialContext		javax.naming

Object
1.3 └ InitialContext ------------------------ *Context* [1]

1	public	Object	**addToEnvironment** (String propName, Object propVal) throws NamingException	
1	public	void	**bind** (String name, Object obj) throws NamingException	ε504,475
1	public	void	**bind** (*Name* name, Object obj) throws NamingException	
1	public	void	**close** () throws NamingException	
1	public	String	**composeName** (String name, String prefix) throws NamingException	
1	public	*Name*	**composeName** (*Name* name, *Name* prefix) throws NamingException	
1	public	*Context*	**createSubcontext** (String name) throws NamingException	ε476
1	public	*Context*	**createSubcontext** (*Name* name) throws NamingException	
	protected	*Context*	**defaultInitCtx**	
1	public	void	**destroySubcontext** (String name) throws NamingException	ε476
1	public	void	**destroySubcontext** (*Name* name) throws NamingException	
	protected	*Context*	**getDefaultInitCtx** () throws NamingException	
1	public	java.util.Hashtable	**getEnvironment** () throws NamingException	
1	public	String	**getNameInNamespace** () throws NamingException	ε477
1	public	*NameParser*	**getNameParser** (String name) throws NamingException	ε480
1	public	*NameParser*	**getNameParser** (*Name* name) throws NamingException	
	protected	*Context*	**getURLOrDefaultInitCtx** (String name) throws NamingException	
	protected	*Context*	**getURLOrDefaultInitCtx** (*Name* name) throws NamingException	
	protected	boolean	**gotDefault**	
	protected	void	**init** (java.util.Hashtable environment) throws NamingException	
*	public		**InitialContext** () throws NamingException	ε478,504,505
*	protected		**InitialContext** (boolean lazy) throws NamingException	
*	public		**InitialContext** (java.util.Hashtable environment) throws NamingException	
				ε472,493,494
1	public	*NamingEnumeration*	**list** (String name) throws NamingException	ε496,474
1	public	*NamingEnumeration*	**list** (*Name* name) throws NamingException	
1	public	*NamingEnumeration*	**listBindings** (String name) throws NamingException	
1	public	*NamingEnumeration*	**listBindings** (*Name* name) throws NamingException	
1	public	Object	**lookup** (String name) throws NamingException	ε478,493,494,505,473
1	public	Object	**lookup** (*Name* name) throws NamingException	
1	public	Object	**lookupLink** (String name) throws NamingException	
1	public	Object	**lookupLink** (*Name* name) throws NamingException	
	protected	java.util.Hashtable	**myProps**	
1	public	void	**rebind** (String name, Object obj) throws NamingException	ε475
1	public	void	**rebind** (*Name* name, Object obj) throws NamingException	
1	public	Object	**removeFromEnvironment** (String propName) throws NamingException	
1	public	void	**rename** (String oldName, String newName) throws NamingException	
				ε475
1	public	void	**rename** (*Name* oldName, *Name* newName) throws NamingException	
1	public	void	**unbind** (String name) throws NamingException	ε475
1	public	void	**unbind** (*Name* name) throws NamingException	

InitialContextFactory		javax.naming.spi

InitialContextFactory
- -
public... *javax.naming.Context* **getInitialContext** (java.util.Hashtable environment)
        throws javax.naming.NamingException
- -

I

Classes

InitialContextFactoryBuilder	javax.naming.spi

1.3   *InitialContextFactoryBuilder*

     public.....*InitialContextFactory* **createInitialContextFactory** (java.util.Hashtable environment)
            throws javax.naming.NamingException

InitialDirContext	javax.naming.directory

    Object
1.3   └javax.naming.InitialContext [1] - - - - - - - - - - - - - - *javax.naming.Context* ⌐
1.3   └InitialDirContext⌐ - - - - - - - - - - - - - - - - - - - *DirContext* ⌐[2] (*javax.naming.Context*)

	1	*36 inherited members from javax.naming.InitialContext not shown*	
	2	public......................void **bind** (String name, Object obj, *Attributes* attrs) throws	
		javax.naming.NamingException	ε485
	2	public......................void **bind** (*javax.naming.Name* name, Object obj, *Attributes* attrs)	
		throws javax.naming.NamingException	
	2	public...............*DirContext* **createSubcontext** (String name, *Attributes* attrs) throws	
		javax.naming.NamingException	ε484
	2	public...............*DirContext* **createSubcontext** (*javax.naming.Name* name, *Attributes* attrs)	
		throws javax.naming.NamingException	
	2	public.................*Attributes* **getAttributes** (String name) throws javax.naming.NamingException	
			ε491
	2	public.................*Attributes* **getAttributes** (*javax.naming.Name* name) throws javax.naming.NamingException	
	2	public.................*Attributes* **getAttributes** (String name, String[] attrIds) throws javax.naming.NamingException	
			ε482,491
	2	public.................*Attributes* **getAttributes** (*javax.naming.Name* name, String[] attrIds)	
		throws javax.naming.NamingException	
	2	public.................*DirContext* **getSchema** (String name) throws javax.naming.NamingException	
	2	public.................*DirContext* **getSchema** (*javax.naming.Name* name) throws javax.naming.NamingException	
	2	public.................*DirContext* **getSchemaClassDefinition** (String name) throws javax.naming.NamingException	
			ε490
	2	public.................*DirContext* **getSchemaClassDefinition** (*javax.naming.Name* name)	
		throws javax.naming.NamingException	
✳		public.......................... **InitialDirContext** () throws javax.naming.NamingException	
✳		protected...................... **InitialDirContext** (boolean lazy) throws javax.naming.NamingException	
✳		public.......................... **InitialDirContext** (java.util.Hashtable environment)	
		throws javax.naming.NamingException	ε481,492
	2	public......................void **modifyAttributes** (String name, ModificationItem[] mods)	
		throws javax.naming.NamingException	ε483
	2	public......................void **modifyAttributes** (*javax.naming.Name* name, ModificationItem[] mods)	
		throws javax.naming.NamingException	
	2	public......................void **modifyAttributes** (String name, int mod_op, *Attributes* attrs)	
		throws javax.naming.NamingException	
	2	public......................void **modifyAttributes** (*javax.naming.Name* name, int mod_op, *Attributes* attrs)	
		throws javax.naming.NamingException	
	2	public......................void **rebind** (String name, Object obj, *Attributes* attrs) throws	
		javax.naming.NamingException	
	2	public......................void **rebind** (*javax.naming.Name* name, Object obj, *Attributes* attrs)	
		throws javax.naming.NamingException	
	2	public..........*javax.naming*↩ **search** (String name, *Attributes* matchingAttributes)	
		.*NamingEnumeration* throws javax.naming.NamingException	ε489,490
	2	public..........*javax.naming*↩ **search** (*javax.naming.Name* name, *Attributes* matchingAttributes)	
		.*NamingEnumeration* throws javax.naming.NamingException	
	2	public..........*javax.naming*↩ **search** (String name, String filter, SearchControls cons)	
		.*NamingEnumeration* throws javax.naming.NamingException	ε487,488,497
	2	public..........*javax.naming*↩ **search** (String name, *Attributes* matchingAttributes, String[] attributesToReturn)	
		.*NamingEnumeration* throws javax.naming.NamingException	ε486
	2	public..........*javax.naming*↩ **search** (*javax.naming.Name* name, *Attributes* matchingAttributes,	
		.*NamingEnumeration* String[] attributesToReturn) throws javax.naming.NamingException	
	2	public..........*javax.naming*↩ **search** (*javax.naming.Name* name, String filter, SearchControls cons)	
		.*NamingEnumeration* throws javax.naming.NamingException	
	2	public..........*javax.naming*↩ **search** (String name, String filterExpr, Object[] filterArgs, SearchControls cons)	
		.*NamingEnumeration* throws javax.naming.NamingException	
	2	public..........*javax.naming*↩ **search** (*javax.naming.Name* name, String filterExpr, Object[] filterArgs,	
		.*NamingEnumeration* SearchControls cons) throws javax.naming.NamingException	

Class *Interface* —extends - - -implements ○ abstract ● final △ static ▲ static final ✳ constructor x x—inherited x **x**—declared **x x**—overridden
εn—examples of usage ⌐—has subclass package—see other volume

INITIALIZE · org.omg.CORBA

```
Object
└ Throwable - - - - - - - - - - - - - - - - - - - - - - - - - - java.io.Serializable ⌄
   └ Exception
      └ RuntimeException
         └ SystemException[1]
1.2 ○
1.2 ●        └ INITIALIZE
```

	1	*3 inherited members from SystemException not shown*	
*		public.........................	**INITIALIZE** ()
*		public.........................	**INITIALIZE** (String s)
*		public.........................	**INITIALIZE** (int minor, CompletionStatus completed)
*		public.........................	**INITIALIZE** (String s, int minor, CompletionStatus completed)

InitialLdapContext · javax.naming.ldap

```
      Object
1.3   └ javax.naming.InitialContext[1] - - - - - - - - - - - - - - javax.naming.Context ⌄
1.3      └ javax.naming.directory.InitialDirContext[2] - - - javax.naming.directory.DirContext ⌄ (javax.naming.Context)
1.3         └ InitialLdapContext - - - - - - - - - - - - - - - - - LdapContext[3] (javax.naming.directory.DirContext
                                                              (javax.naming.Context))
```

	1	*36 inherited members from javax.naming.InitialContext not shown*		
	2	*26 inherited members from javax.naming.directory.InitialDirContext not shown*		
	3	public..... *ExtendedResponse* **extendedOperation** (*ExtendedRequest* request) throws		
		javax.naming.NamingException	ε498	
	3	public.................*Control[]* **getConnectControls** () throws javax.naming.NamingException		
	3	public.................*Control[]* **getRequestControls** () throws javax.naming.NamingException		
	3	public.................*Control[]* **getResponseControls** () throws javax.naming.NamingException		
			ε497	
*		public.........................	**InitialLdapContext** () throws javax.naming.NamingException	
*		public.........................	**InitialLdapContext** (java.util.Hashtable environment, *Control[]* connCtls)	
		throws javax.naming.NamingException	ε495,496,497,498	
	3	public............. *LdapContext* **newInstance** (*Control[]* reqCtls) throws javax.naming.NamingException		
	3	public......................void **reconnect** (*Control[]* connCtls) throws javax.naming.NamingException		
	3	public.............void **setRequestControls** (*Control[]* requestControls) throws		
		javax.naming.NamingException	ε496	

InputSource · org.xml.sax

```
      Object
1.4   └ InputSource
```

	public...... java.io.InputStream **getByteStream** ()	
	public.......... java.io.Reader **getCharacterStream** ()	
	public.....................String **getEncoding** ()	
	public.....................String **getPublicId** ()	
	public.....................String **getSystemId** ()	
*	public......................... **InputSource** ()	
*	public......................... **InputSource** (java.io.InputStream byteStream)	
*	public......................... **InputSource** (java.io.Reader characterStream)	ε548,512
*	public......................... **InputSource** (String systemId)	
	public......................void **setByteStream** (java.io.InputStream byteStream)	
	public......................void **setCharacterStream** (java.io.Reader characterStream)	
	public......................void **setEncoding** (String encoding)	
	public......................void **setPublicId** (String publicId)	
	public......................void **setSystemId** (String systemId)	

InputStream❶ · java.io

			ε252,382,418
	Object		
○	└ InputStream ⌄		

	public........................int **available** () throws IOException	
	public......................void **close** () throws IOException	ε14,36,45,90,183
*	public......................... **InputStream** ()	ε184
	public synchronized ....void **mark** (int readlimit)	
	public................. boolean **markSupported** ()	
○	public abstract...............int **read** () throws IOException	ε90,184,256

InputStream ❶

public .... int	**read** (byte[] b) throws IOException	ε170,463
public .... int	**read** (byte[] b, int off, int len) throws IOException	ε36
public synchronized .... void	**reset** () throws IOException	
public .... long	**skip** (long n) throws IOException	

InputStream ❷   org.omg.CORBA.portable

Object   ε252,382,418
   ○ └java.io.InputStream [1]
1.2 ○   └InputStream

1		8 inherited members from java.io.InputStream not shown	
✳	public	**InputStream** ()	
	public ... org.omg.CORBA.ORB	**orb** ()	
1	public .... int	**read** () throws java.io.IOException	ε90,184,256
○	public abstract	**read_any** ()	
	.........org.omg.CORBA.Any		
○	public abstract .... boolean	**read_boolean** ()	
○	public abstract ....void	**read_boolean_array** (boolean[] value, int offset, int length)	
○	public abstract .... char	**read_char** ()	
○	public abstract ....void	**read_char_array** (char[] value, int offset, int length)	
	public	**read_Context** ()	
	.... org.omg.CORBA.Context		
○	public abstract ....double	**read_double** ()	
○	public abstract ....void	**read_double_array** (double[] value, int offset, int length)	
	public... java.math.BigDecimal	**read_fixed** ()	
○	public abstract ....float	**read_float** ()	
○	public abstract ....void	**read_float_array** (float[] value, int offset, int length)	
○	public abstract ....int	**read_long** ()	
○	public abstract ....void	**read_long_array** (int[] value, int offset, int length)	
○	public abstract .... long	**read_longlong** ()	
○	public abstract ....void	**read_longlong_array** (long[] value, int offset, int length)	
○	public abstract	**read_Object** ()	
	..... org.omg.CORBA.Object		
	public org.omg.CORBA.Object	**read_Object** (Class clz)	
○	public abstract .... byte	**read_octet** ()	
○	public abstract ....void	**read_octet_array** (byte[] value, int offset, int length)	
D	public	**read_Principal** ()	
	... org.omg.CORBA.Principal		
○	public abstract ....short	**read_short** ()	
○	public abstract ....void	**read_short_array** (short[] value, int offset, int length)	
○	public abstract ....String	**read_string** ()	
○	public abstract	**read_TypeCode** ()	
	. org.omg.CORBA.TypeCode		
○	public abstract ....int	**read_ulong** ()	
○	public abstract ....void	**read_ulong_array** (int[] value, int offset, int length)	
○	public abstract .... long	**read_ulonglong** ()	
○	public abstract ....void	**read_ulonglong_array** (long[] value, int offset, int length)	
○	public abstract ....short	**read_ushort** ()	
○	public abstract ....void	**read_ushort_array** (short[] value, int offset, int length)	
○	public abstract .... char	**read_wchar** ()	
○	public abstract ....void	**read_wchar_array** (char[] value, int offset, int length)	
○	public abstract ....String	**read_wstring** ()	

InputStream ❸   org.omg.CORBA_2_3.portable

Object   ε252,382,418
   ○ └java.io.InputStream [1]
1.2 ○   └org.omg.CORBA.portable.InputStream [2]
1.3 ○   └InputStream

1		8 inherited members from java.io.InputStream not shown	
2		35 inherited members from org.omg.CORBA.portable.InputStream not shown	
✳	public	**InputStream** ()	
	public .... Object	**read_abstract_interface** ()	
	public .... Object	**read_abstract_interface** (Class clz)	
	public .... java.io.Serializable	**read_value** ()	
	public .... java.io.Serializable	**read_value** (java.io.Serializable value)	

Class   *Interface*   —extends   - - -implements   ○ abstract   ● final   △ static   ▲ static final   ✳ constructor   x x—inherited   x **x**—declared   **x x**—overridden
ε*n*—examples of usage   .—has subclass   package—see other volume

602

public.......*java.io.Serializable* **read_value** (Class clz)
public.......*java.io.Serializable* **read_value** (String rep_id)
public.......*java.io.Serializable* **read_value** (*org.omg.CORBA.portable.BoxedValueHelper* factory)

InputStreamReader — java.io

Object
1.1 O └Reader[1]
1.1   └InputStreamReader

	1	public..................... **void**	**close** () throws IOException	ε35,47,135,136,139
		public.....................String	**getEncoding** ()	
*		public...........................	**InputStreamReader** (InputStream in)	ε34,135,136,139,149
1.4 *		public...........................	**InputStreamReader** (InputStream in, java.nio.charset.CharsetDecoder dec)	
1.4 *		public...........................	**InputStreamReader** (InputStream in, java.nio.charset.Charset cs)	
*		public...........................	**InputStreamReader** (InputStream in, String charsetName)	
			throws UnsupportedEncodingException	ε40,42
	1	protected ....Object	lock	
	1	public.....................void	mark (int readAheadLimit) throws IOException	
	1	public................. boolean	markSupported ()	ε442
	1	public..................... **int read** () throws IOException		
	1	public.....................int	read (char[] cbuf) throws IOException	ε434
	1	public..................... **int read** (char[] cbuf, int offset, int length) throws IOException		
	1	public.................**boolean ready** () throws IOException		ε442
	1	public.....................void	reset () throws IOException	
	1	public................. long	skip (long n) throws IOException	

InstantiationError — java.lang

Object
└Throwable --------------------------- *java.io.Serializable*
  └Error
    └LinkageError
      └IncompatibleClassChangeError
        └InstantiationError

*		public.........................	**InstantiationError** ()
*		public.........................	**InstantiationError** (String s)

InstantiationException — java.lang

Object   ε69,117
└Throwable --------------------------- *java.io.Serializable*
  └Exception
    └InstantiationException

*	public.........................	**InstantiationException** ()
*	public.........................	**InstantiationException** (String s)

InsufficientResourcesException — javax.naming

Object
└Throwable --------------------------- *java.io.Serializable*
  └Exception
1.3   └NamingException[1]
1.3   └InsufficientResourcesException

	1	*20 inherited members from NamingException not shown*	
*		public.........................	**InsufficientResourcesException** ()
*		public.........................	**InsufficientResourcesException** (String explanation)

IntBuffer — java.nio

Object[1]   ε163,166,171,425
1.4 O └Buffer[2]
1.4 O   └IntBuffer --------------------------- *Comparable*[3]

IntBuffer

△		public static	IntBuffer	**allocate** (int capacity)	
●		public final	int[]	**array** ()	
●		public final	int	**arrayOffset** ()	
○		public abstract	IntBuffer	**asReadOnlyBuffer** ()	
●	2	public final	int	capacity ()	ε159,160,161
●	2	public final	Buffer	clear ()	ε161,170,174
○		public abstract	IntBuffer	**compact** ()	
	3	public	int	**compareTo** (Object ob)	ε53
○		public abstract	IntBuffer	**duplicate** ()	
	1	public	boolean	**equals** (Object ob)	
●	2	public final	Buffer	flip ()	ε162,164,170,174,175
○		public abstract	int	**get** ()	
○		public abstract	int	**get** (int index)	
		public	IntBuffer	**get** (int[] dst)	
		public	IntBuffer	**get** (int[] dst, int offset, int length)	
●		public final	boolean	**hasArray** ()	
	1	public	int	**hashCode** ()	
●	2	public final	boolean	hasRemaining ()	ε170,184
○		public abstract	boolean	**isDirect** ()	
○	2	public abstract	boolean	isReadOnly ()	
●	2	public final	int	limit ()	
●	2	public final	Buffer	limit (int newLimit)	ε159,160
●	2	public final	Buffer	mark ()	
○		public abstract	ByteOrder	**order** ()	
●	2	public final	int	position ()	ε159,160
●	2	public final	Buffer	position (int newPosition)	ε159,160
○		public abstract	IntBuffer	**put** (int i)	
●		public final	IntBuffer	**put** (int[] src)	
		public	IntBuffer	**put** (IntBuffer src)	
○		public abstract	IntBuffer	**put** (int index, int i)	
		public	IntBuffer	**put** (int[] src, int offset, int length)	
●	2	public final	int	remaining ()	ε159,160,161,184
●	2	public final	Buffer	reset ()	
●	2	public final	Buffer	rewind ()	ε159,160,169
○		public abstract	IntBuffer	**slice** ()	
	1	public	String	**toString** ()	
△		public static	IntBuffer	**wrap** (int[] array)	
△		public static	IntBuffer	**wrap** (int[] array, int offset, int length)	

Integer   java.lang

			Object[1]			ε200,201,252,299,304
○			└Number[2] - *java.io.Serializable*			
●			└Integer - *Comparable*[3]			

1.1		2	public	byte	**byteValue** ()	ε58
1.2			public	int	**compareTo** (Integer anotherInteger)	
1.2		3	public	int	**compareTo** (Object o)	ε53
1.1	△		public static	Integer	**decode** (String nm) throws NumberFormatException	
		2	public	double	**doubleValue** ()	ε58
		1	public	boolean	**equals** (Object obj)	
		2	public	float	**floatValue** ()	ε58
	△		public static	Integer	**getInteger** (String nm)	
	△		public static	Integer	**getInteger** (String nm, Integer val)	
	△		public static	Integer	**getInteger** (String nm, int val)	
		1	public	int	**hashCode** ()	
	✱		public		**Integer** (int value)	ε58,117,119,2,3
	✱		public		**Integer** (String s) throws NumberFormatException	
		2	public	int	**intValue** ()	ε58,6,346
		2	public	long	**longValue** ()	ε58
	▲		public static final	int	**MAX_VALUE** = 2147483647	ε36
	▲		public static final	int	**MIN_VALUE** = -2147483648	
	△		public static	int	**parseInt** (String s) throws NumberFormatException	ε82,83,215,471
	△		public static	int	**parseInt** (String s, int radix) throws NumberFormatException	ε82,83
1.1		2	public	short	**shortValue** ()	ε58
	△		public static	String	**toBinaryString** (int i)	
	△		public static	String	**toHexString** (int i)	
	△		public static	String	**toOctalString** (int i)	
		1	public	String	**toString** ()	
	△		public static	String	**toString** (int i)	ε83

Class   *Interface*   —extends   - - -implements   ○ abstract   ● final   △ static   ▲ static final   ✱ constructor   x x—inherited   x **x**—declared   **x x**—overridden
ε*n*—examples of usage   ˌ—has subclass   package—see other volume

△	public static	String	**toString** (int i, int radix)	ε83,131
1.1 ▲	public static final	Class	**TYPE**	
△	public static	Integer	**valueOf** (String s) throws NumberFormatException	
△	public static	Integer	**valueOf** (String s, int radix) throws NumberFormatException	

Interceptor	org.omg.PortableInterceptor

1.4   *Interceptor* ─────────────── *InterceptorOperations* [1], *org.omg.CORBA.Object* [2], *org.omg.CORBA.portable.IDLEntity* (*java.io.Serializable*)

- - - - -
  1 *2 inherited members from InterceptorOperations not shown*
  2 *13 inherited members from org.omg.CORBA.Object not shown*

InterceptorOperations	org.omg.PortableInterceptor

1.4   *InterceptorOperations*

public......................void **destroy** ()
public......................String **name** ()

INTERNAL	org.omg.CORBA

```
Object
 └Throwable ------------------------- java.io.Serializable
   └Exception
     └RuntimeException
```
1.2 ○   └SystemException [1]
1.2 ●   └INTERNAL

  1 *3 inherited members from SystemException not shown*
* public.......................... **INTERNAL** ()
* public.......................... **INTERNAL** (String s)
* public.......................... **INTERNAL** (int minor, CompletionStatus completed)
* public.......................... **INTERNAL** (String s, int minor, CompletionStatus completed)

InternalError	java.lang

```
Object
 └Throwable ------------------------- java.io.Serializable
   └Error
```
○   └VirtualMachineError
      └InternalError

* public.......................... **InternalError** ()
* public.......................... **InternalError** (String s)

InterruptedException	java.lang

ε94,95,102,107,108

```
Object
 └Throwable ------------------------- java.io.Serializable
   └Exception
     └InterruptedException
```

* public.......................... **InterruptedException** ()
* public.......................... **InterruptedException** (String s)

InterruptedIOException	java.io

```
Object
 └Throwable ------------------------- Serializable
   └Exception
     └IOException
       └InterruptedIOException
```

public......................int **bytesTransferred**
* public.......................... **InterruptedIOException** ()
* public.......................... **InterruptedIOException** (String s)

I

Classes

InterruptedNamingException

InterruptedNamingException | javax.naming

```
     Object
      └Throwable ------------------------------ java.io.Serializable╴
         └Exception
1.3         └NamingException¹
1.3            └InterruptedNamingException
```

	1	*20 inherited members from NamingException not shown*
✳		public......................... **InterruptedNamingException** ()
✳		public......................... **InterruptedNamingException** (String explanation)

InterruptibleChannel | java.nio.channels

```
1.4    InterruptibleChannel─────────────────Channel╴¹
```

	1	public..................... **void close** () throws java.io.IOException	ε167,170,171,172,174
	1	public................. boolean isOpen ()

INTF_REPOS | org.omg.CORBA

```
       Object
        └Throwable ------------------------------ java.io.Serializable╴
           └Exception
              └RuntimeException
1.2 ○            └SystemException¹
1.2 ●               └INTF_REPOS
```

	1	*3 inherited members from SystemException not shown*
✳		public......................... **INTF_REPOS** ()
✳		public......................... **INTF_REPOS** (String s)
✳		public......................... **INTF_REPOS** (int minor, CompletionStatus completed)
✳		public......................... **INTF_REPOS** (String s, int minor, CompletionStatus completed)

IntHolder | org.omg.CORBA

```
       Object
1.2 ●  └IntHolder ---------------------------- org.omg.CORBA.portable.Streamable╴¹
```

	1	public.....................void **_read** (org.omg.CORBA.portable.InputStream input)
	1	public...............TypeCode **_type** ()
	1	public.....................void **_write** (org.omg.CORBA.portable.OutputStream output)
✳		public......................... **IntHolder** ()
✳		public......................... **IntHolder** (int initial)
		public.........................int **value**

IntrospectionException | java.beans

```
       Object                                                         ε5,9
        └Throwable¹ ------------------------------ java.io.Serializable╴
           └Exception
1.1          └IntrospectionException
```

✳		public......................... **IntrospectionException** (String mess)
	1	public.........................void printStackTrace ()

Introspector | java.beans

```
       Object
1.1    └Introspector
```

△		public static ....String **decapitalize** (String name)
1.2 △		public static ....void **flushCaches** ()
1.2 △		public static ....void **flushFromCaches** (Class clz)
△		public static .... *BeanInfo* **getBeanInfo** (Class beanClass) throws IntrospectionException ε5,9

Class *Interface* —extends - - -implements ○ abstract ● final △ static ▲ static final ✳ constructor x x—inherited x **x**—declared **x x**—overridden
ε*n*—examples of usage ╴—has subclass package—see other volume

△	public static	*BeanInfo*	**getBeanInfo** (Class beanClass, Class stopClass) throws IntrospectionException
1.2 △	public static	*BeanInfo*	**getBeanInfo** (Class beanClass, int flags) throws IntrospectionException
△	public static synchronized		**getBeanInfoSearchPath** ()
	.... String[]		
1.2 ▲	public static final .... int		**IGNORE_ALL_BEANINFO** = 3
1.2 ▲	public static final .... int		**IGNORE_IMMEDIATE_BEANINFO** = 2
△	public static synchronized void		**setBeanInfoSearchPath** (String[] path)
1.2 ▲	public static final .... int		**USE_ALL_BEANINFO** = 1

INV_FLAG org.omg.CORBA

```
Object
 └Throwable --------------------------- java.io.Serializable
    └Exception
       └RuntimeException
          └SystemException 1
             └INV_FLAG
```
1.2 ○
1.2 ●

1 *3 inherited members from SystemException not shown*

∗	public.........................	**INV_FLAG** ()
∗	public.........................	**INV_FLAG** (String s)
∗	public.........................	**INV_FLAG** (int minor, CompletionStatus completed)
∗	public.........................	**INV_FLAG** (String s, int minor, CompletionStatus completed)

INV_IDENT org.omg.CORBA

```
Object
 └Throwable --------------------------- java.io.Serializable
    └Exception
       └RuntimeException
          └SystemException 1
             └INV_IDENT
```
1.2 ○
1.2 ●

1 *3 inherited members from SystemException not shown*

∗	public.........................	**INV_IDENT** ()
∗	public.........................	**INV_IDENT** (String s)
∗	public.........................	**INV_IDENT** (int minor, CompletionStatus completed)
∗	public.........................	**INV_IDENT** (String s, int minor, CompletionStatus completed)

INV_OBJREF org.omg.CORBA

```
Object
 └Throwable --------------------------- java.io.Serializable
    └Exception
       └RuntimeException
          └SystemException 1
             └INV_OBJREF
```
1.2 ○
1.2 ●

1 *3 inherited members from SystemException not shown*

∗	public.........................	**INV_OBJREF** ()
∗	public.........................	**INV_OBJREF** (String s)
∗	public.........................	**INV_OBJREF** (int minor, CompletionStatus completed)
∗	public.........................	**INV_OBJREF** (String s, int minor, CompletionStatus completed)

INV_POLICY org.omg.CORBA

```
Object
 └Throwable --------------------------- java.io.Serializable
    └Exception
       └RuntimeException
          └SystemException 1
             └INV_POLICY
```
1.2 ○
1.2 ●

1 *3 inherited members from SystemException not shown*

∗	public.........................	**INV_POLICY** ()
∗	public.........................	**INV_POLICY** (String s)
∗	public.........................	**INV_POLICY** (int minor, CompletionStatus completed)
∗	public.........................	**INV_POLICY** (String s, int minor, CompletionStatus completed)

Classes

Invalid

Invalid		org.omg.CORBA.DynAnyPackage

```
Object
└ Throwable ------------------------------ java.io.Serializable ↲
  └ Exception
1.2 ○   └ org.omg.CORBA.UserException ------- org.omg.CORBA.portable.IDLEntity ↲ (java.io.Serializable)
1.2 ●     └ Invalid
```

✱	public..........................	**Invalid** ()
✱	public..........................	**Invalid** (String reason)

INVALID_TRANSACTION		org.omg.CORBA

```
Object
└ Throwable ------------------------------ java.io.Serializable ↲
  └ Exception
    └ RuntimeException
1.2 ○       └ SystemException 1
1.2 ●         └ INVALID_TRANSACTION
```

	1	*3 inherited members from SystemException not shown*
✱	public..........................	**INVALID_TRANSACTION** ()
✱	public..........................	**INVALID_TRANSACTION** (String s)
✱	public..........................	**INVALID_TRANSACTION** (int minor, CompletionStatus completed)
✱	public..........................	**INVALID_TRANSACTION** (String s, int minor, CompletionStatus completed)

InvalidAddress		org.omg.CosNaming.NamingContextExtPackage

```
Object
└ Throwable ------------------------------ java.io.Serializable ↲
  └ Exception
1.2 ○   └ org.omg.CORBA.UserException ------- org.omg.CORBA.portable.IDLEntity ↲ (java.io.Serializable)
1.4 ●     └ InvalidAddress
```

✱	public..........................	**InvalidAddress** ()
✱	public..........................	**InvalidAddress** (String $reason)

InvalidAddressHelper		org.omg.CosNaming.NamingContextExtPackage

```
Object
1.4 ○ └ InvalidAddressHelper
```

△	public static ....InvalidAddress	**extract** (org.omg.CORBA.Any a)
△	public static ....String	**id** ()
△	public static ....void	**insert** (org.omg.CORBA.Any a, InvalidAddress that)
✱	public..........................	**InvalidAddressHelper** ()
△	public static ....InvalidAddress	**read** (org.omg.CORBA.portable.InputStream istream)
△	public static synchronized .... . org.omg.CORBA.TypeCode	**type** ()
△	public static ....void	**write** (org.omg.CORBA.portable.OutputStream ostream, InvalidAddress value)

InvalidAddressHolder		org.omg.CosNaming.NamingContextExtPackage

```
Object
1.4 ● └ InvalidAddressHolder ------------------ org.omg.CORBA.portable.Streamable ↲ 1
```

1	public.......................void	**_read** (org.omg.CORBA.portable.InputStream i)
1	public.......................... . org.omg.CORBA.TypeCode	**_type** ()
1	public.......................void	**_write** (org.omg.CORBA.portable.OutputStream o)
✱	public..........................	**InvalidAddressHolder** ()
✱	public..........................	**InvalidAddressHolder** (InvalidAddress initialValue)
	public..........InvalidAddress	**value**

Class *Interface* —extends - - -implements ○ abstract ● final △ static ▲ static final ✱ constructor x x—inherited x **x**—declared **x x**—overridden
εn—examples of usage ↲—has subclass package—see other volume

608

	InvalidAlgorithmParameterException	java.security

```
        Object
        └Throwable ------------------------- java.io.Serializable↲
          └Exception
1.2         └GeneralSecurityException
1.2           └InvalidAlgorithmParameterException
```

✳	public........................	**InvalidAlgorithmParameterException** ()
✳	public.........................	**InvalidAlgorithmParameterException** (String msg)

	InvalidAttributeIdentifierException	javax.naming.directory

```
        Object
        └Throwable ------------------------- java.io.Serializable↲
          └Exception
1.3         └javax.naming.NamingException 1
1.3           └InvalidAttributeIdentifierException
```

1	*20 inherited members from javax.naming.NamingException not shown*	
✳	public.........................	**InvalidAttributeIdentifierException** ()
✳	public.........................	**InvalidAttributeIdentifierException** (String explanation)

	InvalidAttributesException	javax.naming.directory

```
        Object
        └Throwable ------------------------- java.io.Serializable↲
          └Exception
1.3         └javax.naming.NamingException 1
1.3           └InvalidAttributesException
```

1	*20 inherited members from javax.naming.NamingException not shown*	
✳	public.........................	**InvalidAttributesException** ()
✳	public.........................	**InvalidAttributesException** (String explanation)

	InvalidAttributeValueException	javax.naming.directory

```
        Object
        └Throwable ------------------------- java.io.Serializable↲
          └Exception
1.3         └javax.naming.NamingException 1
1.3           └InvalidAttributeValueException
```

1	*20 inherited members from javax.naming.NamingException not shown*	
✳	public.........................	**InvalidAttributeValueException** ()
✳	public.........................	**InvalidAttributeValueException** (String explanation)

	InvalidClassException	java.io

```
         Object
         └Throwable 1 ------------------------- Serializable↲
           └Exception
             └IOException
1.1 ○          └ObjectStreamException
1.1              └InvalidClassException
```

	public....................String	**classname**
1	public..................**String**	**getMessage** ()
✳	public.....................	**InvalidClassException** (String reason)
✳	public.........................	**InvalidClassException** (String cname, String reason)

InvalidKeyException

InvalidKeyException — java.security

ε203,204,205,462,463

```
Object
└ Throwable - - - - - - - - - - - - - - - - - - - - - - - - - - - java.io.Serializable ˯
     └ Exception
1.2       └ GeneralSecurityException
1.1          └ KeyException
1.1             └ InvalidKeyException
```

*	public..........................	**InvalidKeyException** ()
*	public..........................	**InvalidKeyException** (String msg)

InvalidKeySpecException — java.security.spec

ε199,201,464,471

```
Object
└ Throwable - - - - - - - - - - - - - - - - - - - - - - - - - - - java.io.Serializable ˯
     └ Exception
1.2       └ java.security.GeneralSecurityException
1.2          └ InvalidKeySpecException
```

*	public..........................	**InvalidKeySpecException** ()
*	public..........................	**InvalidKeySpecException** (String msg)

InvalidMarkException — java.nio

```
Object
└ Throwable - - - - - - - - - - - - - - - - - - - - - - - - - - - java.io.Serializable ˯
     └ Exception
        └ RuntimeException
1.1        └ IllegalStateException
1.4           └ InvalidMarkException
```

*	public..........................	**InvalidMarkException** ()

InvalidName❶ — org.omg.CORBA.ORBPackage

```
Object
└ Throwable - - - - - - - - - - - - - - - - - - - - - - - - - - - java.io.Serializable ˯
     └ Exception
1.2 ○     └ org.omg.CORBA.UserException - - - - - - org.omg.CORBA.portable.IDLEntity ˯ (java.io.Serializable)
1.2 ●        └ InvalidName
```

*	public..........................	**InvalidName** ()
*	public..........................	**InvalidName** (String reason)

InvalidName❷ — org.omg.CosNaming.NamingContextPackage

```
Object
└ Throwable - - - - - - - - - - - - - - - - - - - - - - - - - - - java.io.Serializable ˯
     └ Exception
1.2 ○     └ org.omg.CORBA.UserException - - - - - - org.omg.CORBA.portable.IDLEntity ˯ (java.io.Serializable)
1.2 ●        └ InvalidName
```

*	public..........................	**InvalidName** ()
1.4 *	public..........................	**InvalidName** (String $reason)

InvalidName❸ — org.omg.PortableInterceptor.ORBInitInfoPackage

```
Object
└ Throwable - - - - - - - - - - - - - - - - - - - - - - - - - - - java.io.Serializable ˯
     └ Exception
1.2 ○     └ org.omg.CORBA.UserException - - - - - - org.omg.CORBA.portable.IDLEntity ˯ (java.io.Serializable)
1.4 ●        └ InvalidName
```

Class   *Interface*   —extends   - - -implements   ○ abstract   ● final   △ static   ▲ static final   ✳ constructor   x x—inherited   x **x**—declared   **x x**—overridden
εn—examples of usage   ˯—has subclass   package—see other volume

610

✳	public.........................	**InvalidName** ()
✳	public.........................	**InvalidName** (String $reason)

InvalidNameException · javax.naming

Object
└Throwable ------------------------- *java.io.Serializable*␘
  └Exception
1.3   └NamingException[1]
1.3   └InvalidNameException

[1]	*20 inherited members from NamingException not shown*	
✳	public.........................	**InvalidNameException** ()
✳	public.........................	**InvalidNameException** (String explanation)

InvalidNameHelper ❶ · org.omg.CosNaming.NamingContextPackage

Object
1.2 ○ └InvalidNameHelper

△	public static ...... InvalidName	**extract** (org.omg.CORBA.Any a)
△	public static ....String	**id** ()
△	public static ....void	**insert** (org.omg.CORBA.Any a, InvalidName that)
1.4 ✳	public.........................	**InvalidNameHelper** ()
△	public static ...... InvalidName	**read** (org.omg.CORBA.portable.InputStream istream)
△	public static synchronized .... . org.omg.CORBA.TypeCode	**type** ()
△	public static ....void	**write** (org.omg.CORBA.portable.OutputStream ostream, InvalidName value)

InvalidNameHelper ❷ · org.omg.PortableInterceptor.ORBInitInfoPackage

Object
1.4 ○ └InvalidNameHelper

△	public static ...... InvalidName	**extract** (org.omg.CORBA.Any a)
△	public static ....String	**id** ()
△	public static ....void	**insert** (org.omg.CORBA.Any a, InvalidName that)
✳	public.........................	**InvalidNameHelper** ()
△	public static ...... InvalidName	**read** (org.omg.CORBA.portable.InputStream istream)
△	public static synchronized .... . org.omg.CORBA.TypeCode	**type** ()
△	public static ....void	**write** (org.omg.CORBA.portable.OutputStream ostream, InvalidName value)

InvalidNameHolder · org.omg.CosNaming.NamingContextPackage

Object
1.2 ● └InvalidNameHolder -------------------- *org.omg.CORBA.portable.Streamable*␘[1]

[1]	public......................void	**_read** (org.omg.CORBA.portable.InputStream i)
[1]	public......................... . org.omg.CORBA.TypeCode	**_type** ()
[1]	public......................void	**_write** (org.omg.CORBA.portable.OutputStream o)
✳	public.........................	**InvalidNameHolder** ()
✳	public.........................	**InvalidNameHolder** (InvalidName initialValue)
	public............ InvalidName	**value**

InvalidObjectException · java.io

Object
└Throwable ------------------------- *Serializable*␘
  └Exception
    └IOException
1.1 ○   └ObjectStreamException
1.1   └InvalidObjectException

✳	public.........................	**InvalidObjectException** (String reason)

InvalidParameterException

Class *Interface* —extends - - -implements ○ abstract ● final △ static ▲ static final ✳ constructor x x—inherited x **x**—declared **x x**—overridden
ε*n*—examples of usage ˯—has subclass package—see other volume

612

InvalidSearchControlsException | javax.naming.directory

```
Object
└Throwable ------------------------- java.io.Serializable ⌐
  └Exception
1.3    └javax.naming.NamingException[1]
1.3      └InvalidSearchControlsException
```

	[1] *20 inherited members from javax.naming.NamingException not shown*	
*	public.........................	**InvalidSearchControlsException** ()
*	public.........................	**InvalidSearchControlsException** (String msg)

InvalidSearchFilterException | javax.naming.directory

```
Object
└Throwable ------------------------- java.io.Serializable ⌐
  └Exception
1.3    └javax.naming.NamingException[1]
1.3      └InvalidSearchFilterException
```

	[1] *20 inherited members from javax.naming.NamingException not shown*	
*	public.........................	**InvalidSearchFilterException** ()
*	public.........................	**InvalidSearchFilterException** (String msg)

InvalidSeq | org.omg.CORBA.DynAnyPackage

```
Object
└Throwable ------------------------- java.io.Serializable ⌐
  └Exception
1.2 ○  └org.omg.CORBA.UserException ------- org.omg.CORBA.portable.IDLEntity ⌐ (java.io.Serializable)
1.2 ●    └InvalidSeq
```

*	public.........................	**InvalidSeq** ()
*	public.........................	**InvalidSeq** (String reason)

InvalidSlot | org.omg.PortableInterceptor

```
Object
└Throwable ------------------------- java.io.Serializable ⌐
  └Exception
1.2 ○  └org.omg.CORBA.UserException ------- org.omg.CORBA.portable.IDLEntity ⌐ (java.io.Serializable)
1.4 ●    └InvalidSlot
```

*	public.........................	**InvalidSlot** ()
*	public.........................	**InvalidSlot** (String $reason)

InvalidSlotHelper | org.omg.PortableInterceptor

```
Object
1.4 ○ └InvalidSlotHelper
```

△	public static ....InvalidSlot	**extract** (org.omg.CORBA.Any a)
△	public static ....String	**id** ()
△	public static ....void	**insert** (org.omg.CORBA.Any a, InvalidSlot that)
*	public.........................	**InvalidSlotHelper** ()
△	public static ....InvalidSlot	**read** (org.omg.CORBA.portable.InputStream istream)
△	public static synchronized	**type** ()
	. org.omg.CORBA.TypeCode	
△	public static ....void	**write** (org.omg.CORBA.portable.OutputStream ostream, InvalidSlot value)

I

Classes

613

InvalidTransactionException

	InvalidTransactionException			javax.transaction

```
Object
 └ Throwable ---------------------------- java.io.Serializable ⌣
    └ Exception
       └ java.io.IOException
```
		└ java.rmi.RemoteException [1]
1.1		
1.3		└ InvalidTransactionException

	1	public.............Throwable	detail	
1.4	1	public.............Throwable	getCause ()	
	1	public.....................String	getMessage ()	
✳		public.........................	**InvalidTransactionException** ()	
✳		public.........................	**InvalidTransactionException** (String msg)	

	InvalidTypeForEncoding		org.omg.IOP.CodecPackage

```
Object
 └ Throwable ---------------------------- java.io.Serializable ⌣
    └ Exception
```
1.2 ○	└ org.omg.CORBA.UserException ------ org.omg.CORBA.portable.IDLEntity ⌣ (java.io.Serializable)
1.4 ●	└ InvalidTypeForEncoding

✳	public.........................	**InvalidTypeForEncoding** ()	
✳	public.........................	**InvalidTypeForEncoding** (String $reason)	

	InvalidTypeForEncodingHelper		org.omg.IOP.CodecPackage

```
       Object
1.4 ○   └ InvalidTypeForEncodingHelper
```

△	public static .... InvalidTypeForEncoding	**extract** (org.omg.CORBA.Any a)	
△	public static ....String	**id** ()	
△	public static ....void	**insert** (org.omg.CORBA.Any a, InvalidTypeForEncoding that)	
✳	public.........................	**InvalidTypeForEncodingHelper** ()	
△	public static .... InvalidTypeForEncoding	**read** (org.omg.CORBA.portable.InputStream istream)	
△	public static synchronized .... . org.omg.CORBA.TypeCode	**type** ()	
△	public static ....void	**write** (org.omg.CORBA.portable.OutputStream ostream, InvalidTypeForEncoding value)	

	InvalidValue❶		org.omg.CORBA.DynAnyPackage

```
Object
 └ Throwable ---------------------------- java.io.Serializable ⌣
    └ Exception
```
1.2 ○	└ org.omg.CORBA.UserException ------ org.omg.CORBA.portable.IDLEntity ⌣ (java.io.Serializable)
1.2 ●	└ InvalidValue

✳	public.........................	**InvalidValue** ()	
✳	public.........................	**InvalidValue** (String reason)	

	InvalidValue❷		org.omg.DynamicAny.DynAnyPackage

```
Object
 └ Throwable ---------------------------- java.io.Serializable ⌣
    └ Exception
```
1.2 ○	└ org.omg.CORBA.UserException ------ org.omg.CORBA.portable.IDLEntity ⌣ (java.io.Serializable)
1.4 ●	└ InvalidValue

✳	public.........................	**InvalidValue** ()	
✳	public.........................	**InvalidValue** (String $reason)	

Class *Interface* —extends - - -implements ○ abstract ● final △ static ▲ static final ✳ constructor x x—inherited x **x**—declared **x x**—overridden
εn—examples of usage ⌣—has subclass package—see other volume

InvalidValueHelper | org.omg.DynamicAny.DynAnyPackage

```
       Object
1.4 O  └InvalidValueHelper
```

△	public static .... InvalidValue	**extract** (org.omg.CORBA.Any a)
△	public static .... String	**id** ()
△	public static .... void	**insert** (org.omg.CORBA.Any a, InvalidValue that)
✳	public..........................	**InvalidValueHelper** ()
△	public static .... InvalidValue	**read** (org.omg.CORBA.portable.InputStream istream)
△	public static synchronized .... . org.omg.CORBA.TypeCode	**type** ()
△	public static .... void	**write** (org.omg.CORBA.portable.OutputStream ostream, InvalidValue value)

InvocationHandler | java.lang.reflect

```
1.3    InvocationHandler
```

public.................... Object **invoke** (Object proxy, Method method, Object[] args) throws Throwable
ε111

InvocationTargetException | java.lang.reflect

ε111,117,119

```
       Object
       └Throwable 1 -------------------------- java.io.Serializable
         └Exception
1.1        └InvocationTargetException
```

1.4	1	public.............. **Throwable**	**getCause** ()
		public...................Throwable	**getTargetException** ()
✳		protected	**InvocationTargetException** ()
✳		public..........................	**InvocationTargetException** (Throwable target)
✳		public..........................	**InvocationTargetException** (Throwable target, String s)

InvokeHandler | org.omg.CORBA.portable

```
1.2    InvokeHandler
```

public............OutputStream **_invoke** (String method, InputStream input, *ResponseHandler* handler)
throws org.omg.CORBA.SystemException

IOException | java.io

ε14,16,20,23,27

```
       Object
       └Throwable 1 -------------------------- Serializable
         └Exception
           └IOException
```

✳	public..........................	**IOException** ()	ε388
✳	public..........................	**IOException** (String s)	ε36
1	public.....................void	printStackTrace ()	

IOR | org.omg.IOP

```
       Object
1.4 ●  └IOR ----------------------------------- org.omg.CORBA.portable.IDLEntity , (java.io.Serializable)
```

✳	public..........................	**IOR** ()	
✳	public..........................	**IOR** (String _type_id, TaggedProfile[] _profiles)	
	public............ TaggedProfile[]	**profiles**	
	public....................String	**type_id**	

IORHelper | org.omg.IOP

```
       Object
1.4 O  └IORHelper
```

I

Classes

IORHelper

△	public static .... IOR	**extract** (org.omg.CORBA.Any a)	
△	public static .... String	**id** ()	
△	public static .... void	**insert** (org.omg.CORBA.Any a, IOR that)	
✳	public..........................	**IORHelper** ()	
△	public static .... IOR	**read** (org.omg.CORBA.portable.InputStream istream)	
△	public static synchronized .... . org.omg.CORBA.TypeCode	**type** ()	
△	public static .... void	**write** (org.omg.CORBA.portable.OutputStream ostream, IOR value)	

IORHolder · org.omg.IOP

Object
1.4 ● └IORHolder - *org.omg.CORBA.portable.Streamable* [1]

	1	public.......................void	**_read** (org.omg.CORBA.portable.InputStream i)
	1	public........................... . org.omg.CORBA.TypeCode	**_type** ()
	1	public.......................void	**_write** (org.omg.CORBA.portable.OutputStream o)
✳		public...........................	**IORHolder** ()
✳		public...........................	**IORHolder** (IOR initialValue)
		public...................... IOR	**value**

IORInfo · org.omg.PortableInterceptor

1.4 *IORInfo*————————————*IORInfoOperations* [1], *org.omg.CORBA.Object* [2],
org.omg.CORBA.portable.IDLEntity (java.io.Serializable)

2 13 inherited members from org.omg.CORBA.Object not shown
1 3 inherited members from IORInfoOperations not shown

IORInfoOperations · org.omg.PortableInterceptor

1.4 *IORInfoOperations*

public.......................void	**add_ior_component** (org.omg.IOP.TaggedComponent tagged_component)	
public.......................void	**add_ior_component_to_profile** (org.omg.IOP.TaggedComponent tagged_component, int profile_id)	
public. *org.omg.CORBA.Policy*	**get_effective_policy** (int type)	

IORInterceptor · org.omg.PortableInterceptor

1.4 *IORInterceptor*————————————*IORInterceptorOperations* [1] (*InterceptorOperations* [2]),
Interceptor (*InterceptorOperations* [2], *org.omg.CORBA.Object* [3],
org.omg.CORBA.portable.IDLEntity (java.io.Serializable)),
org.omg.CORBA.portable.IDLEntity (java.io.Serializable)

2 2 inherited members from InterceptorOperations not shown
3 13 inherited members from org.omg.CORBA.Object not shown
1 public.......................void establish_components (*IORInfo* info)

IORInterceptorOperations · org.omg.PortableInterceptor

1.4 *IORInterceptorOperations*————————————*InterceptorOperations* [1]

1 2 inherited members from InterceptorOperations not shown
public.......................void **establish_components** (*IORInfo* info)

IRObject · org.omg.CORBA

1.2 *IRObject*————————————*IRObjectOperations* [1], *Object* [2], org.omg.CORBA.portable↩
.IDLEntity (java.io.Serializable)

1 2 inherited members from IRObjectOperations not shown
2 13 inherited members from Object not shown

Class *Interface* —extends - - -implements ○ abstract ● final △ static ▲ static final ✳ constructor x x—inherited x **x**—declared **x x**—overridden
εn—examples of usage —has subclass package—see other volume

IRObjectOperations   org.omg.CORBA

1.3		*IRObjectOperations* ⌄	

```
public ............ DefinitionKind  def_kind ()
public ...................... void  destroy ()
```

IstringHelper   org.omg.CosNaming

```
            Object
1.2 O       └ IstringHelper
```

△	public static .... String	**extract** (org.omg.CORBA.Any a)
△	public static .... String	**id** ()
△	public static .... void	**insert** (org.omg.CORBA.Any a, String that)
1.4 ✳	public	**IstringHelper** ()
△	public static .... String	**read** (org.omg.CORBA.portable.InputStream istream)
△	public static synchronized .... . org.omg.CORBA.TypeCode	**type** ()
△	public static .... void	**write** (org.omg.CORBA.portable.OutputStream ostream, String value)

Iterator   java.util

1.2		*Iterator* ⌄	

```
public ................. boolean  hasNext ()                          ε345,352,354,355,356
public .................... Object  next ()                           ε345,352,354,355,356
public ...................... void  remove ()                         ε176,179
```

IvParameterSpec   javax.crypto.spec

```
            Object
1.4         └ IvParameterSpec - - - - - - - - - - - - - - - - - - - - - - - - java.security.spec.AlgorithmParameterSpec
```

	public .... byte[]	**getIV** ()
✳	public	**IvParameterSpec** (byte[] iv) ε463
✳	public	**IvParameterSpec** (byte[] iv, int offset, int len)

JarEntry   java.util.jar

```
            Object                                                                    ε138,455
1.1         └ java.util.zip.ZipEntry¹ - - - - - - - - - - - - - - - - - - - java.util.zip.ZipConstants, Cloneable ⌄
1.2             └ JarEntry
```

1	public .... Object	clone ()	
	public .... Attributes	**getAttributes** () throws java.io.IOException	
	public .... java ↩ .security.cert.Certificate[]	**getCertificates** ()	
1	public .... String	getComment ()	
1	public .... long	getCompressedSize ()	
1	public .... long	getCrc ()	
1	public .... byte[]	getExtra ()	
1	public .... int	getMethod ()	
1	public .... String	getName ()	ε454
1	public .... long	getSize ()	
1	public .... long	getTime ()	
1	public .... int	hashCode ()	
1	public .... boolean	isDirectory ()	
✳	public	**JarEntry** (String name)	
✳	public	**JarEntry** (JarEntry je)	
✳	public	**JarEntry** (java.util.zip.ZipEntry ze)	
1	public .... void	setComment (String comment)	
1	public .... void	setCompressedSize (long csize)	
1	public .... void	setCrc (long crc)	
1	public .... void	setExtra (byte[] extra)	
1	public .... void	setMethod (int method)	
1	public .... void	setSize (long size)	
1	public .... void	setTime (long time)	
1	public .... String	toString ()	

J

Classes

JarException

	JarException			java.util.jar

```
        Object
        └ Throwable - - - - - - - - - - - - - - - - - - - - - - - - - - java.io.Serializable ˅
          └ Exception
            └ java.io.IOException
1.1           └ java.util.zip.ZipException
1.2             └ JarException
```

✳	public.........................	**JarException** ()
✳	public.........................	**JarException** (String s)

	JarFile	java.util.jar

```
        Object                                              ε138
1.1     └ java.util.zip.ZipFile 1 - - - - - - - - - - - - - - - - - - - - java.util.zip.ZipConstants
1.2       └ JarFile
```

1	public.........................void	close () throws java.io.IOException	
1	public.. ***java.util.Enumeration***	**entries** ()	ε454
1	protected ....void	finalize () throws java.io.IOException	
1	public... **java.util.zip.ZipEntry**	**getEntry** (String name)	
1	public synchronized	**getInputStream** (java.util.zip.ZipEntry ze) throws java.io.IOException	
	.... **java.io.InputStream**		
	public...............JarEntry	**getJarEntry** (String name)	
	public...............Manifest	**getManifest** () throws java.io.IOException	ε380,381,383
1	public...................String	getName ()	
✳	public...................	**JarFile** (java.io.File file) throws java.io.IOException	
✳	public...................	**JarFile** (String name) throws java.io.IOException	ε380,381,383
✳	public...................	**JarFile** (java.io.File file, boolean verify) throws java.io.IOException	
✳	public...................	**JarFile** (String name, boolean verify) throws java.io.IOException	
1.3 ✳	public...................	**JarFile** (java.io.File file, boolean verify, int mode) throws java.io.IOException	
▲	public static final ....String	**MANIFEST_NAME** = "META-INF/MANIFEST.MF"	
1	public.........................int	size ()	

	JarInputStream	java.util.jar

```
        Object                                              ε252,382,418
   O    └ java.io.InputStream
   ,      └ java.io.FilterInputStream 1
1.1         └ java.util.zip.InflaterInputStream 2
1.1           └ java.util.zip.ZipInputStream 3 - - - - - - - - - java.util.zip.ZipConstants
1.2             └ JarInputStream
```

3	public.........................int	available () throws java.io.IOException	
2	protected ....byte[]	buf	
3	public.......................void	close () throws java.io.IOException	ε14,36,45,452,455
3	public.......................void	closeEntry () throws java.io.IOException	
3	protected	**createZipEntry** (String name)	
	.... **java.util.zip.ZipEntry**		
2	protected ....void	fill () throws java.io.IOException	
	public.................Manifest	**getManifest** ()	
3	public.. **java.util.zip.ZipEntry**	**getNextEntry** () throws java.io.IOException	ε455
	public.................JarEntry	**getNextJarEntry** () throws java.io.IOException	
1	protected .. java.io.InputStream	in	
2	protected ...java.util.zip.Inflater	inf	
✳	public.........................	**JarInputStream** (java.io.InputStream in) throws java.io.IOException	
✳	public.........................	**JarInputStream** (java.io.InputStream in, boolean verify) throws java.io.IOException	
2	protected ....int	len	
1	public synchronized ....void	mark (int readlimit)	
1	public.................boolean	markSupported ()	
2	public.........................int	read () throws java.io.IOException	ε90,184,256
1	public.........................int	read (byte[] b) throws java.io.IOException	ε452,455,457,170,451
3	public......................... **int**	**read** (byte[] b, int off, int len) throws java.io.IOException	ε36
1	public synchronized ....void	reset () throws java.io.IOException	
3	public.....................long	skip (long n) throws java.io.IOException	

Class   *Interface*   —extends   - - -implements   O abstract   ● final   △ static   ▲ static final   ✳ constructor   x x—inherited   x **x**—declared   **x x**—overridden
ε*n*—examples of usage   ˅—has subclass   package—see other volume

JarOutputStream | java.util.jar

	Object	ε183
O	└java.io.OutputStream	
	└java.io.FilterOutputStream[1]	
1.1	└java.util.zip.DeflaterOutputStream[2]	
1.1	└java.util.zip.ZipOutputStream[3] - - - - - - java.util.zip.ZipConstants	
1.2	└JarOutputStream	

	2	protected .... byte[]	buf	
	3	public.....................void	close () throws java.io.IOException	ε451,453,91,211,224
	3	public.....................void	closeEntry () throws java.io.IOException	ε453
	2	protected . java.util.zip.Deflater	def	
	2	protected ....void	deflate () throws java.io.IOException	
	3	public.....................void	finish () throws java.io.IOException	ε451
	1	public.....................void	flush () throws java.io.IOException	ε27,54
*		public..........................	**JarOutputStream** (java.io.OutputStream out) throws java.io.IOException	
*		public..........................	**JarOutputStream** (java.io.OutputStream out, Manifest man) throws java.io.IOException	
	1	protected java.io.OutputStream	out	
	3	public..................... **void**	**putNextEntry** (java.util.zip.ZipEntry ze) throws java.io.IOException	
				ε453
	3	public.....................void	setComment (String comment)	
	3	public.....................void	setLevel (int level)	
	3	public.....................void	setMethod (int method)	
	1	public.....................void	write (byte[] b) throws java.io.IOException	ε27,91,224
	2	public.....................void	write (int b) throws java.io.IOException	ε184
	3	public synchronized ....void	write (byte[] b, int off, int len) throws java.io.IOException	ε451,453,54,449,450

K

JarURLConnection | java.net

	Object
O	└URLConnection[1]
1.2 O	└JarURLConnection

	1	*52 inherited members from URLConnection not shown*	
		public.... java.util.jar.Attributes	**getAttributes** () throws java.io.IOException
		public...................java↵ .security.cert.Certificate[]	**getCertificates** () throws java.io.IOException
		public.....................String	**getEntryName** ()	ε138
		public......java.util.jar.JarEntry	**getJarEntry** () throws java.io.IOException	ε138
O		public abstract .... java.util.jar.JarFile	**getJarFile** () throws java.io.IOException	ε138
		public..................... URL	**getJarFileURL** ()
		public..... java.util.jar.Attributes	**getMainAttributes** () throws java.io.IOException
		public..... java.util.jar.Manifest	**getManifest** () throws java.io.IOException
		protected ......URLConnection	**jarFileURLConnection**
*		protected	**JarURLConnection** (URL url) throws MalformedURLException

KerberosKey | javax.security.auth.kerberos

	Object[1]
1.4	└KerberosKey - *javax.crypto.SecretKey* ˷ (*java.security.Key* [2] (*java.io.Serializable*)), *javax.security.auth.Destroyable* [3]

	3	public.......................void	**destroy** () throws javax.security.auth.DestroyFailedException	
●	2	public final ....String	**getAlgorithm** ()	ε203,204,205,464,469
●	2	public final ....byte[]	**getEncoded** ()	ε199,460,471,471
●	2	public final ....String	**getFormat** ()	ε199
●		public final ....int	**getKeyType** ()	
●		public final . KerberosPrincipal	**getPrincipal** ()	
●		public final ....int	**getVersionNumber** ()	
	3	public.................. boolean	**isDestroyed** ()	
*		public..........................	**KerberosKey** (KerberosPrincipal principal, char[] password, String algorithm)	
*		public..........................	**KerberosKey** (KerberosPrincipal principal, byte[] keyBytes, int keyType, int versionNum)	
	1	public.................. **String**	**toString** ()	

Classes

619

KerberosPrincipal

KerberosPrincipal	javax.security.auth.kerberos

Object [1]
1.4 ● └KerberosPrincipal - *java.security.Principal* ⌄ [2], *java.io.Serializable* ⌄

1	public	**boolean**	**equals** (Object other)	
2	public	String	**getName** ()	*ε*227,508
	public	int	**getNameType** ()	
	public	String	**getRealm** ()	
1	public	**int**	**hashCode** ()	
✳	public		**KerberosPrincipal** (String name)	
✳	public		**KerberosPrincipal** (String name, int nameType)	
▲	public static final	int	**KRB_NT_PRINCIPAL** = 1	
▲	public static final	int	**KRB_NT_SRV_HST** = 3	
▲	public static final	int	**KRB_NT_SRV_INST** = 2	
▲	public static final	int	**KRB_NT_SRV_XHST** = 4	
▲	public static final	int	**KRB_NT_UID** = 5	
▲	public static final	int	**KRB_NT_UNKNOWN** = 0	
1	public	**String**	**toString** ()	

K

KerberosTicket	javax.security.auth.kerberos

Object [1]
1.4 └KerberosTicket - *javax.security.auth.Destroyable* [2], *javax.security.auth.Refreshable* [3],
java.io.Serializable ⌄

2	public	void	**destroy** () throws javax.security.auth.DestroyFailedException
●	public final	java.util.Date	**getAuthTime** ()
●	public final	KerberosPrincipal	**getClient** ()
●	public final		**getClientAddresses** ()
		java.net.InetAddress[]	
●	public final	byte[]	**getEncoded** ()
●	public final	java.util.Date	**getEndTime** ()
●	public final	boolean[]	**getFlags** ()
●	public final	java.util.Date	**getRenewTill** ()
●	public final	KerberosPrincipal	**getServer** ()
●	public final		**getSessionKey** ()
		javax.crypto.SecretKey	
●	public final	int	**getSessionKeyType** ()
●	public final	java.util.Date	**getStartTime** ()
3	public	boolean	**isCurrent** ()
2	public	boolean	**isDestroyed** ()
●	public final	boolean	**isForwardable** ()
●	public final	boolean	**isForwarded** ()
●	public final	boolean	**isInitial** ()
●	public final	boolean	**isPostdated** ()
●	public final	boolean	**isProxiable** ()
●	public final	boolean	**isProxy** ()
●	public final	boolean	**isRenewable** ()
✳	public		**KerberosTicket** (byte[] asn1Encoding, KerberosPrincipal client, KerberosPrincipal server, byte[] sessionKey, int keyType, boolean[] flags, java.util.Date authTime, java.util.Date startTime, java.util.Date endTime, java.util.Date renewTill, java.net.InetAddress[] clientAddresses)
3	public	void	**refresh** () throws javax.security.auth.RefreshFailedException
1	public	**String**	**toString** ()

Key	java.security

1.1 *Key* ⌄ ─────────────────────── *java.io.Serializable* ⌄   *ε*210

public	String	**getAlgorithm** ()	*ε*203,204,205,464,469
public	byte[]	**getEncoded** ()	*ε*199,460,471,471
public	String	**getFormat** ()	*ε*199
1.2 ▲ public static final	long	**serialVersionUID** = 6603384152749567654	

Class *Interface* —extends - - -implements ○ abstract ● final △ static ▲ static final ✳ constructor x x—inherited x **x**—declared **x x**—overridden
εn—examples of usage ⌄—has subclass package—see other volume

KeyAgreement		javax.crypto

Object
1.4 └KeyAgreement

● public final .. *java.security.Key* **doPhase** (*java.security.Key* key, boolean lastPhase) throws
java.security.InvalidKeyException, IllegalStateException ε471
● public final .... byte[] **generateSecret** () throws IllegalStateException
● public final .... *SecretKey* **generateSecret** (String algorithm) throws IllegalStateException,
java.security.NoSuchAlgorithmException, java.security.InvalidKeyException ε471
● public final .... int **generateSecret** (byte[] sharedSecret, int offset) throws IllegalStateException,
ShortBufferException
● public final .... String **getAlgorithm** ()
▲ public static final.............. **getInstance** (String algorithm) throws java.security.NoSuchAlgorithmException
.... KeyAgreement ε471
▲ public static final.............. **getInstance** (String algorithm, java.security.Provider provider)
.... KeyAgreement throws java.security.NoSuchAlgorithmException
▲ public static final.............. **getInstance** (String algorithm, String provider) throws java.security↵
.... KeyAgreement .NoSuchAlgorithmException, java.security.NoSuchProviderException
● public final .... **getProvider** ()
.... java.security.Provider
● public final ....void **init** (*java.security.Key* key) throws java.security.InvalidKeyException
ε471
● public final ....void **init** (*java.security.Key* key, *java.security.spec.AlgorithmParameterSpec*
params) throws java.security.InvalidKeyException,
java.security.InvalidAlgorithmParameterException
● public final ....void **init** (*java.security.Key* key, java.security.SecureRandom random)
throws java.security.InvalidKeyException
● public final ....void **init** (*java.security.Key* key, *java.security.spec.AlgorithmParameterSpec* params,
java.security.SecureRandom random) throws java.security.InvalidKeyException,
java.security.InvalidAlgorithmParameterException
✳ protected .... **KeyAgreement** (KeyAgreementSpi keyAgreeSpi, java.security.Provider provider,
String algorithm)

KeyAgreementSpi		javax.crypto

Object
1.4 ○ └KeyAgreementSpi

○ protected abstract .... **engineDoPhase** (*java.security.Key* key, boolean lastPhase)
.... *java.security.Key* throws java.security.InvalidKeyException, IllegalStateException
○ protected abstract .... byte[] **engineGenerateSecret** () throws IllegalStateException
○ protected abstract .. *SecretKey* **engineGenerateSecret** (String algorithm) throws IllegalStateException,
java.security.NoSuchAlgorithmException, java.security.InvalidKeyException
○ protected abstract ....int **engineGenerateSecret** (byte[] sharedSecret, int offset)
throws IllegalStateException, ShortBufferException
○ protected abstract ....void **engineInit** (*java.security.Key* key, java.security.SecureRandom random)
throws java.security.InvalidKeyException
○ protected abstract ....void **engineInit** (*java.security.Key* key, *java.security.spec.AlgorithmParameterSpec*
params, java.security.SecureRandom random) throws java.security↵
.InvalidKeyException, java.security.InvalidAlgorithmParameterException
✳ public.......................... **KeyAgreementSpi** ()

KeyException		java.security

Object
└Throwable - *java.io.Serializable*
└Exception
1.2 └GeneralSecurityException
1.1 └KeyException

✳ public.......................... **KeyException** ()
✳ public.......................... **KeyException** (String msg)

KeyFactory		java.security

Object
1.2 └KeyFactory

KeyFactory

●	public final .... *PrivateKey*	**generatePrivate** (*java.security.spec.KeySpec* keySpec)	
		throws java.security.spec.InvalidKeySpecException	ε199,201
●	public final .... *PublicKey*	**generatePublic** (*java.security.spec.KeySpec* keySpec)	
		throws java.security.spec.InvalidKeySpecException	ε199,201,471
●	public final ....String	**getAlgorithm** ()	
△	public static ....KeyFactory	**getInstance** (String algorithm) throws NoSuchAlgorithmException	
			ε199,201,471
1.4 △	public static ....KeyFactory	**getInstance** (String algorithm, Provider provider) throws NoSuchAlgorithmException	
△	public static ....KeyFactory	**getInstance** (String algorithm, String provider) throws NoSuchAlgorithmException,	
		NoSuchProviderException	
●	public final	**getKeySpec** (*Key* key, Class keySpec) throws java.security.spec ↵	
	. *java.security.spec.KeySpec*	.InvalidKeySpecException	
●	public final .... Provider	**getProvider** ()	
✳	protected.......................	**KeyFactory** (KeyFactorySpi keyFacSpi, Provider provider, String algorithm)	
●	public final .... *Key*	**translateKey** (*Key* key) throws InvalidKeyException	

KeyFactorySpi   java.security

Object
  └KeyFactorySpi   (1.2 ○)

○	protected abstract . *PrivateKey*	**engineGeneratePrivate** (*java.security.spec.KeySpec* keySpec)
		throws java.security.spec.InvalidKeySpecException
○	protected abstract .. *PublicKey*	**engineGeneratePublic** (*java.security.spec.KeySpec* keySpec)
		throws java.security.spec.InvalidKeySpecException
○	protected abstract	**engineGetKeySpec** (*Key* key, Class keySpec) throws
	. *java.security.spec.KeySpec*	java.security.spec.InvalidKeySpecException
○	protected abstract .... *Key*	**engineTranslateKey** (*Key* key) throws InvalidKeyException
✳	public...........................	**KeyFactorySpi** ()

KeyGenerator   javax.crypto

Object   ε458
  └KeyGenerator   (1.4)

●	public final .... *SecretKey*	**generateKey** ()	ε459,460,462,463,466
●	public final ....String	**getAlgorithm** ()	
▲	public static final KeyGenerator	**getInstance** (String algorithm) throws java.security.NoSuchAlgorithmException	
			ε459,460,462,463,466
▲	public static final KeyGenerator	**getInstance** (String algorithm, java.security.Provider provider)	
		throws java.security.NoSuchAlgorithmException	
▲	public static final KeyGenerator	**getInstance** (String algorithm, String provider) throws java.security ↵	
		.NoSuchAlgorithmException, java.security.NoSuchProviderException	
●	public final	**getProvider** ()	
	.... java.security.Provider		
●	public final ....void	**init** (int keysize)	
●	public final ....void	**init** (java.security.SecureRandom random)	
●	public final ....void	**init** (*java.security.spec.AlgorithmParameterSpec* params)	
		throws java.security.InvalidAlgorithmParameterException	
●	public final ....void	**init** (int keysize, java.security.SecureRandom random)	
●	public final ....void	**init** (*java.security.spec.AlgorithmParameterSpec* params,	
		java.security.SecureRandom random) throws java.security ↵	
		.InvalidAlgorithmParameterException	
✳	protected......................	**KeyGenerator** (KeyGeneratorSpi keyGenSpi, java.security.Provider provider,	
		String algorithm)	

KeyGeneratorSpi   javax.crypto

Object
  └KeyGeneratorSpi   (1.4 ○)

○	protected abstract .. *SecretKey*	**engineGenerateKey** ()
○	protected abstract ....void	**engineInit** (java.security.SecureRandom random)
○	protected abstract ....void	**engineInit** (int keysize, java.security.SecureRandom random)
○	protected abstract ....void	**engineInit** (*java.security.spec.AlgorithmParameterSpec*
		params, java.security.SecureRandom random) throws
		java.security.InvalidAlgorithmParameterException

Class   *Interface* —extends - - -implements ○ abstract ● final △ static ▲ static final ✳ constructor x x—inherited x **x**—declared **x x**—overridden
ε*n*—examples of usage ˌ—has subclass package—see other volume

*	public..........................	**KeyGeneratorSpi** ()

KeyManagementException
java.security

```
Object
 └Throwable --------------------------- java.io.Serializable
   └Exception
1.2    └GeneralSecurityException
1.1      └KeyException
1.1        └KeyManagementException
```

*	public..........................	**KeyManagementException** ()
*	public..........................	**KeyManagementException** (String msg)

KeyManager
javax.net.ssl

1.4	*KeyManager*

KeyManagerFactory
javax.net.ssl

```
Object
1.4 └KeyManagerFactory
```

●	public final ....String	**getAlgorithm** ()
▲	public static final ....String	**getDefaultAlgorithm** ()
▲	public static final ....KeyManagerFactory	**getInstance** (String algorithm) throws java.security.NoSuchAlgorithmException
▲	public static final ....KeyManagerFactory	**getInstance** (String algorithm, java.security.Provider provider) throws java.security.NoSuchAlgorithmException
▲	public static final ....KeyManagerFactory	**getInstance** (String algorithm, String provider) throws java.security↵ .NoSuchAlgorithmException, java.security.NoSuchProviderException
●	public final ..... *KeyManager[]*	**getKeyManagers** ()
●	public final .... java.security.Provider	**getProvider** ()
●	public final ....void	**init** (*ManagerFactoryParameters* spec) throws java.security↵ .InvalidAlgorithmParameterException
●	public final ....void	**init** (java.security.KeyStore ks, char[] password) throws java.security.KeyStoreException, java.security.NoSuchAlgorithmException, java.security.UnrecoverableKeyException
*	protected	**KeyManagerFactory** (KeyManagerFactorySpi factorySpi, java.security.Provider provider, String algorithm)

KeyManagerFactorySpi
javax.net.ssl

```
      Object
1.4 ○ └KeyManagerFactorySpi
```

○	protected abstract .... *KeyManager[]*	**engineGetKeyManagers** ()
○	protected abstract ....void	**engineInit** (*ManagerFactoryParameters* spec) throws java.security.InvalidAlgorithmParameterException
○	protected abstract ....void	**engineInit** (java.security.KeyStore ks, char[] password) throws java.security.KeyStoreException, java.security.NoSuchAlgorithmException, java.security.UnrecoverableKeyException
*	public..........................	**KeyManagerFactorySpi** ()

KeyPair
java.security

```
      Object
1.1 ● └KeyPair ------------------------------- java.io.Serializable
```

	public.............. *PrivateKey*	**getPrivate** ()	ε198,199,200,205,471
	public.............. *PublicKey*	**getPublic** ()	ε198,199,200,205,471
*	public..........................	**KeyPair** (*PublicKey* publicKey, *PrivateKey* privateKey)	ε210

K

Classes

KeyPairGenerator

KeyPairGenerator — java.security

		Object		ε197
1.2 ○		└KeyPairGeneratorSpi[1]		
1.1 ○		└KeyPairGenerator		

1.2	1	public................ **KeyPair**	**generateKeyPair** ()	ε471
1.2 ●		public final ....KeyPair	**genKeyPair** ()	ε198,199,200,205
		public....................String	**getAlgorithm** ()	
△		public static .KeyPairGenerator	**getInstance** (String algorithm) throws NoSuchAlgorithmException	ε198,199,200,205,471
△		public static .KeyPairGenerator	**getInstance** (String algorithm, String provider) throws NoSuchAlgorithmException, NoSuchProviderException	
1.4 △		public static .KeyPairGenerator	**getInstance** (String algorithm, Provider provider) throws NoSuchAlgorithmException	
1.2 ●		public final .... Provider	**getProvider** ()	
		public......................void	**initialize** (int keysize)	ε198,199,200,205
1.2		public......................void	**initialize** (*java.security.spec.AlgorithmParameterSpec* params) throws InvalidAlgorithmParameterException	ε471
	1	public................ **void**	**initialize** (int keysize, SecureRandom random)	
1.2	1	public................ **void**	**initialize** (*java.security.spec.AlgorithmParameterSpec* params, SecureRandom random) throws InvalidAlgorithmParameterException	
✳		protected	**KeyPairGenerator** (String algorithm)	

KeyPairGeneratorSpi — java.security

	Object		ε197
1.2 ○	└KeyPairGeneratorSpi‿		

○	public abstract ....KeyPair	**generateKeyPair** ()	ε471
○	public abstract ....void	**initialize** (int keysize, SecureRandom random)	
	public......................void	**initialize** (*java.security.spec.AlgorithmParameterSpec* params, SecureRandom random) throws InvalidAlgorithmParameterException	
✳	public..........................	**KeyPairGeneratorSpi** ()	

KeySpec — java.security.spec

1.2	*KeySpec*	ε201,464

KeyStore — java.security

	Object	
1.2	└KeyStore	

●	public final .... *java.util.Enumeration*	**aliases** () throws KeyStoreException	ε208,227
●	public final .... boolean	**containsAlias** (String alias) throws KeyStoreException	
●	public final ....void	**deleteEntry** (String alias) throws KeyStoreException	
●	public final .... java.security.cert.Certificate	**getCertificate** (String alias) throws KeyStoreException	ε209,210,227
●	public final ....String	**getCertificateAlias** (java.security.cert.Certificate cert) throws KeyStoreException	
●	public final .... java↵ .security.cert.Certificate[]	**getCertificateChain** (String alias) throws KeyStoreException	
●	public final ...... java.util.Date	**getCreationDate** (String alias) throws KeyStoreException	
▲	public static final ....String	**getDefaultType** ()	ε208,209,211,230,231
△	public static .... KeyStore	**getInstance** (String type) throws KeyStoreException	ε208,209,211,230,231
△	public static .... KeyStore	**getInstance** (String type, String provider) throws KeyStoreException, NoSuchProviderException	
1.4 △	public static .... KeyStore	**getInstance** (String type, Provider provider) throws KeyStoreException	
●	public final .... *Key*	**getKey** (String alias, char[] password) throws KeyStoreException, NoSuchAlgorithmException, UnrecoverableKeyException	ε210
●	public final .... Provider	**getProvider** ()	
●	public final ....String	**getType** ()	
●	public final .... boolean	**isCertificateEntry** (String alias) throws KeyStoreException	ε208
●	public final .... boolean	**isKeyEntry** (String alias) throws KeyStoreException	ε208
✳	protected	**KeyStore** (KeyStoreSpi keyStoreSpi, Provider provider, String type)	

Class *Interface* —extends - - -implements ○ abstract ● final △ static ▲ static final ✳ constructor x x—inherited x **x**—declared **x x**—overridden
ε*n*—examples of usage ‿—has subclass package—see other volume

●	public final ....void	**load** (java.io.InputStream stream, char[] password) throws java.io.IOException,
		NoSuchAlgorithmException, java.security.cert.CertificateException
		ε208,209,211,230,231
●	public final ....void	**setCertificateEntry** (String alias, java.security.cert.Certificate cert)
		throws KeyStoreException ε211
●	public final ....void	**setKeyEntry** (String alias, byte[] key, java.security.cert.Certificate[] chain)
		throws KeyStoreException
●	public final ....void	**setKeyEntry** (String alias, *Key* key, char[] password,
		java.security.cert.Certificate[] chain) throws KeyStoreException
●	public final ....int	**size** () throws KeyStoreException
●	public final ....void	**store** (java.io.OutputStream stream, char[] password)
		throws KeyStoreException, java.io.IOException, NoSuchAlgorithmException,
		java.security.cert.CertificateException ε211

KeyStoreException		java.security

```
      Object
       └Throwable - - - - - - - - - - - - - - - - - - - - - - - - - - java.io.Serializable ˎ          ε208,209,210,211,227
        └Exception
1.2       └GeneralSecurityException
1.2         └KeyStoreException
```

✳	public..........................	**KeyStoreException** ()
✳	public..........................	**KeyStoreException** (String msg)

KeyStoreSpi		java.security

```
      Object
1.2 ○  └KeyStoreSpi
```

○	public abstract	**engineAliases** ()
	.........java.util.Enumeration	
○	public abstract .... boolean	**engineContainsAlias** (String alias)
○	public abstract ....void	**engineDeleteEntry** (String alias) throws KeyStoreException
○	public abstract	**engineGetCertificate** (String alias)
	. java.security.cert.Certificate	
○	public abstract ....String	**engineGetCertificateAlias** (java.security.cert.Certificate cert)
○	public abstract .... java ↵	**engineGetCertificateChain** (String alias)
	.security.cert.Certificate[]	
○	public abstract ... java.util.Date	**engineGetCreationDate** (String alias)
○	public abstract .... *Key*	**engineGetKey** (String alias, char[] password) throws NoSuchAlgorithmException,
		UnrecoverableKeyException
○	public abstract .... boolean	**engineIsCertificateEntry** (String alias)
○	public abstract .... boolean	**engineIsKeyEntry** (String alias)
○	public abstract ....void	**engineLoad** (java.io.InputStream stream, char[] password) throws java.io ↵
		.IOException, NoSuchAlgorithmException, java.security.cert.CertificateException
○	public abstract ....void	**engineSetCertificateEntry** (String alias, java.security.cert.Certificate cert)
		throws KeyStoreException
○	public abstract ....void	**engineSetKeyEntry** (String alias, byte[] key, java.security.cert.Certificate[] chain)
		throws KeyStoreException
○	public abstract ....void	**engineSetKeyEntry** (String alias, *Key* key, char[] password,
		java.security.cert.Certificate[] chain) throws KeyStoreException
○	public abstract ....int	**engineSize** ()
○	public abstract ....void	**engineStore** (java.io.OutputStream stream, char[] password) throws java.io ↵
		.IOException, NoSuchAlgorithmException, java.security.cert.CertificateException
✳	public..........................	**KeyStoreSpi** ()

LanguageCallback		javax.security.auth.callback

```
      Object
1.4    └LanguageCallback - - - - - - - - - - - - - - - - - - - - Callback, java.io.Serializable ˎ
```

	public..........java.util.Locale	**getLocale** ()
✳	public..........................	**LanguageCallback** ()
	public.....................void	**setLocale** (java.util.Locale locale) ε509

L

Classes

LastOwnerException

Class *Interface* —extends - - -implements ○ abstract ● final △ static ▲ static final * constructor x x—inherited x **x**—declared **x x**—overridden
ε*n*—examples of usage ⌐—has subclass package—see other volume

Lease
java.rmi.dgc

1.1 ●		Object └Lease - *java.io.Serializable*		

	public	long	**getValue** ()
	public	VMID	**getVMID** ()
*	public		**Lease** (VMID id, long duration)

Level
java.util.logging

		Object[1]		ε396
1.4		└Level - *java.io.Serializable*		

▲		public static final	Level	**ALL**	ε395,400
▲		public static final	Level	**CONFIG**	ε397
	1	public	**boolean**	**equals** (Object ox)	
▲		public static final	Level	**FINE**	
▲		public static final	Level	**FINER**	ε387
▲		public static final	Level	**FINEST**	ε386,389
		public	String	**getLocalizedName** ()	
		public	String	**getName** ()	
		public	String	**getResourceBundleName** ()	
	1	public	**int**	**hashCode** ()	
▲		public static final	Level	**INFO**	ε395,397
●		public final	int	**intValue** ()	ε397,398,400
*		protected		**Level** (String name, int value)	
*		protected		**Level** (String name, int value, String resourceBundleName)	
▲		public static final	Level	**OFF**	ε393,395
△		public static synchronized Level		**parse** (String name) throws IllegalArgumentException	
▲		public static final	Level	**SEVERE**	ε388,393,513
●	1	public final	**String**	**toString** ()	
▲		public static final	Level	**WARNING**	ε513

LexicalHandler
org.xml.sax.ext

1.4		*LexicalHandler*	

	public	void	**comment** (char[] ch, int start, int length) throws org.xml.sax.SAXException
	public	void	**endCDATA** () throws org.xml.sax.SAXException
	public	void	**endDTD** () throws org.xml.sax.SAXException
	public	void	**endEntity** (String name) throws org.xml.sax.SAXException
	public	void	**startCDATA** () throws org.xml.sax.SAXException
	public	void	**startDTD** (String name, String publicId, String systemId) throws org.xml.sax.SAXException
	public	void	**startEntity** (String name) throws org.xml.sax.SAXException

LIFESPAN_POLICY_ID
org.omg.PortableServer

1.4		*LIFESPAN_POLICY_ID*

▲	public static final	int	**value** = 17

LifespanPolicy
org.omg.PortableServer

1.4		*LifespanPolicy*————————————————*LifespanPolicyOperations*. [1] (*org.omg.CORBA.PolicyOperations* [2]), *org.omg.CORBA.Policy* (*org.omg.CORBA.PolicyOperations* [2], *org.omg.CORBA.Object* [3], *org.omg.CORBA.portable.IDLEntity* (*java.io.Serializable*)), *org.omg.CORBA.portable.IDLEntity*. (*java.io.Serializable*)

	3	*13 inherited members from org.omg.CORBA.Object not shown*
	2	*3 inherited members from org.omg.CORBA.PolicyOperations not shown*
	1	public ..... LifespanPolicyValue **value** ()

LifespanPolicyOperations	org.omg.PortableServer

1.4	*LifespanPolicyOperations* ────────────── *org.omg.CORBA.PolicyOperations* [1]

   1 *3 inherited members from org.omg.CORBA.PolicyOperations not shown*
      public ..... LifespanPolicyValue **value** ()

LifespanPolicyValue	org.omg.PortableServer

1.4	Object └LifespanPolicyValue -------------------- *org.omg.CORBA.portable.IDLEntity* (*java.io.Serializable*)

▲	public static final .... int	**_PERSISTENT** = 1
▲	public static final .... int	**_TRANSIENT** = 0
△	public static	**from_int** (int value)
	.... LifespanPolicyValue	
✳	protected	**LifespanPolicyValue** (int value)
	.... LifespanPolicyValue	
▲	public static final	**PERSISTENT**
	.... LifespanPolicyValue	
▲	public static final	**TRANSIENT**
	.... LifespanPolicyValue	
	public .... int	**value** ()

LimitExceededException	javax.naming

	Object └Throwable --------------------------- *java.io.Serializable* └Exception
1.3	└NamingException [1]
1.3	└LimitExceededException

   1 *20 inherited members from NamingException not shown*
✳	public	**LimitExceededException** ()
✳	public	**LimitExceededException** (String explanation)

LineNumberInputStream	java.io
	ε252,382,418

	O	Object └InputStream └FilterInputStream [1]
D		└LineNumberInputStream

D	1	public .... **int**	**available** () throws IOException	
D	1	public .... void	close () throws IOException	ε14,36,45,452,455
D	1	public .... int	**getLineNumber** ()	
D	1	protected .... InputStream	in	
D	✳	public	**LineNumberInputStream** (InputStream in)	
D	1	public .... **void**	**mark** (int readlimit)	
D	1	public .... boolean	markSupported ()	
D	1	public .... **int**	**read** () throws IOException	ε90,184,256
D	1	public .... int	read (byte[] b) throws IOException	ε452,455,457,170,451
D	1	public .... **int**	**read** (byte[] b, int off, int len) throws IOException	ε36
D	1	public .... **void**	**reset** () throws IOException	
D		public .... void	**setLineNumber** (int lineNumber)	
D	1	public .... **long**	**skip** (long n) throws IOException	

LineNumberReader	java.io

1.1	O	Object └Reader [1]
1.1		└BufferedReader [2]
1.1		└LineNumberReader

	2	public .... void	close () throws IOException	ε35,47,135,136,139
		public .... int	**getLineNumber** ()	
	✳	public	**LineNumberReader** (Reader in)	

Class *Interface* —extends - - -implements O abstract ● final △ static ▲ static final ✳ constructor x x—inherited x **x**—declared **x x**—overridden
ε*n*—examples of usage —has subclass package—see other volume

*	public		**LineNumberReader** (Reader in, int sz)	
1	protected	Object	lock	
2	public	**void**	**mark** (int readAheadLimit) throws IOException	
2	public	boolean	markSupported ()	ε442
2	public	**int**	**read** () throws IOException	
1	public	int	read (char[] cbuf) throws IOException	ε434
2	public	**int**	**read** (char[] cbuf, int off, int len) throws IOException	
2	public	**String**	**readLine** () throws IOException	ε34,35,40,42,135
2	public	boolean	ready () throws IOException	ε442
2	public	**void**	**reset** () throws IOException	
	public	void	**setLineNumber** (int lineNumber)	
2	public	**long**	**skip** (long n) throws IOException	

LinkageError — java.lang

```
Object
└Throwable - - - - - - - - - - - - - - - - - - - - - - - - - - - java.io.Serializable‿
  └Error
    └LinkageError‿
```

*	public	**LinkageError** ()	
*	public	**LinkageError** (String s)	

L

LinkedHashMap — java.util

```
     Object
1.2 ○ └AbstractMap¹ - - - - - - - - - - - - - - - - - - - - - - - Map‿
1.2       └HashMap² - - - - - - - - - - - - - - - - - - - - - - - Cloneable‿, java.io.Serializable‿
1.4         └LinkedHashMap
```

2	public	**void**	**clear** ()	
2	public	Object	clone ()	
2	public	boolean	containsKey (Object key)	ε344
2	public	**boolean**	**containsValue** (Object value)	
2	public	Set	entrySet ()	ε345
1	public	boolean	equals (Object o)	
2	public	**Object**	**get** (Object key)	ε337,344,346,356,357
1	public	int	hashCode ()	
2	public	boolean	isEmpty ()	
2	public	Set	keySet ()	ε194,340,345,355,356
*	public		**LinkedHashMap** ()	ε356
*	public		**LinkedHashMap** (int initialCapacity)	
*	public		**LinkedHashMap** (Map m)	
*	public		**LinkedHashMap** (int initialCapacity, float loadFactor)	
*	public		**LinkedHashMap** (int initialCapacity, float loadFactor, boolean accessOrder)	
				ε344
2	public	Object	put (Object key, Object value)	ε337,344,346,355,356
2	public	void	putAll (Map t)	
2	public	Object	remove (Object key)	ε355
	protected	boolean	**removeEldestEntry** (Map.Entry eldest)	ε344
2	public	int	size ()	ε355
1	public	String	toString ()	
2	public	Collection	values ()	ε340,345,355

LinkedHashSet — java.util

```
       Object
1.2 ○ └AbstractCollection¹ - - - - - - - - - - - - - - - - - - - - Collection‿
1.2 ○   └AbstractSet² - - - - - - - - - - - - - - - - - - - - - - Set‿ (Collection)
1.2       └HashSet³ - - - - - - - - - - - - - - - - - - - - - - - Cloneable‿, java.io.Serializable‿
1.4         └LinkedHashSet
```

3	public	boolean	add (Object o)	ε342,349,352,354,358
1	public	boolean	addAll (Collection c)	ε351,353
3	public	void	clear ()	ε351,353
3	public	Object	clone ()	
3	public	boolean	contains (Object o)	ε352
1	public	boolean	containsAll (Collection c)	
2	public	boolean	equals (Object o)	
2	public	int	hashCode ()	

Classes

LinkedHashSet

3	public	boolean	isEmpty ()		ε102
3	public	*Iterator*	iterator ()		ε345,352,354,355,356
✳	public		**LinkedHashSet** ()		ε354
✳	public		**LinkedHashSet** (int initialCapacity)		
✳	public		**LinkedHashSet** (*Collection* c)		
✳	public		**LinkedHashSet** (int initialCapacity, float loadFactor)		
3	public	boolean	remove (Object o)		ε349,352
2	public	boolean	removeAll (*Collection* c)		ε351,353
1	public	boolean	retainAll (*Collection* c)		ε351,353
3	public	int	size ()		ε340,349,351,352,358
1	public	Object[]	toArray ()		ε340
1	public	Object[]	toArray (Object[] a)		ε340,352,358,194,508
1	public	String	toString ()		

LinkedList   java.util

Object[1]
  └AbstractCollection[2] - *Collection*˅   (1.2 ○)
    └AbstractList[3] - *List* (*Collection*)   (1.2 ○)
      └AbstractSequentialList[4]   (1.2 ○)
        └LinkedList - *Cloneable*˅, *java.io.Serializable*˅   (1.2)

3	public	**boolean**	**add** (Object o)		ε342,349,352,354,358
4	public	**void**	**add** (int index, Object element)		ε349,362
2	public	**boolean**	**addAll** (*Collection* c)		ε351,353
4	public	**boolean**	**addAll** (int index, *Collection* c)		
	public	void	**addFirst** (Object o)		ε343
	public	void	**addLast** (Object o)		ε102
3	public	**void**	**clear** ()		ε351,353
1	public	**Object**	**clone** ()		
2	public	**boolean**	**contains** (Object o)		ε352
2	public	boolean	containsAll (*Collection* c)		
3	public	boolean	equals (Object o)		
4	public	**Object**	**get** (int index)		ε349,234
	public	Object	**getFirst** ()		ε343
	public	Object	**getLast** ()		
3	public	int	hashCode ()		
3	public	**int**	**indexOf** (Object o)		
2	public	boolean	isEmpty ()		ε102
4	public	*Iterator*	iterator ()		ε345,352,354,355,356
3	public	**int**	**lastIndexOf** (Object o)		
✳	public		**LinkedList** ()		ε342,343,349,102
✳	public		**LinkedList** (*Collection* c)		ε341,347
3	public	*ListIterator*	listIterator ()		
4	public	***ListIterator***	**listIterator** (int index)		
3	protected transient	int	modCount		
4	public	**Object**	**remove** (int index)		ε349
2	public	**boolean**	**remove** (Object o)		ε349,352
2	public	boolean	removeAll (*Collection* c)		ε351,353
	public	Object	**removeFirst** ()		ε342,102
	public	Object	**removeLast** ()		
3	protected	void	removeRange (int fromIndex, int toIndex)		
2	public	boolean	retainAll (*Collection* c)		ε351,353
4	public	**Object**	**set** (int index, Object element)		ε348
2	public	**int**	**size** ()		ε340,349,351,352,358
3	public	*List*	subList (int fromIndex, int toIndex)		ε351
2	public	**Object[]**	**toArray** ()		ε340
2	public	**Object[]**	**toArray** (Object[] a)		ε340,352,358,194,508
2	public	String	toString ()		

LinkException   javax.naming

Object
  └Throwable - *java.io.Serializable*˅
    └Exception
      └NamingException[1]   (1.3)
        └LinkException˅   (1.3)

Class   *Interface*   —extends   - - -implements   ○ abstract   ● final   △ static   ▲ static final   ✳ constructor   x x—inherited   x **x**—declared   **x x**—overridden
ε*n*—examples of usage   ˅—has subclass   package—see other volume

	1	*18 inherited members from NamingException not shown*	
		public .... String	**getLinkExplanation** ()
		public .... *Name*	**getLinkRemainingName** ()
		public .... *Name*	**getLinkResolvedName** ()
		public .... Object	**getLinkResolvedObj** ()
*		public	**LinkException** ()
*		public	**LinkException** (String explanation)
		protected .... String	**linkExplanation**
		protected .... *Name*	**linkRemainingName**
		protected .... *Name*	**linkResolvedName**
		protected .... Object	**linkResolvedObj**
		public ....void	**setLinkExplanation** (String msg)
		public ....void	**setLinkRemainingName** (*Name* name)
		public ....void	**setLinkResolvedName** (*Name* name)
		public ....void	**setLinkResolvedObj** (Object obj)
	1	public .... **String**	**toString** ()
	1	public .... **String**	**toString** (boolean detail)

LinkLoopException — javax.naming

```
Object
└Throwable ---------------------------- java.io.Serializable
  └Exception
1.3   └NamingException 1
1.3     └LinkException 2
1.3       └LinkLoopException
```

	1	*18 inherited members from NamingException not shown*	
	2	public .... String	getLinkExplanation ()
	2	public .... *Name*	getLinkRemainingName ()
	2	public .... *Name*	getLinkResolvedName ()
	2	public .... Object	getLinkResolvedObj ()
	2	protected .... String	linkExplanation
*		public	**LinkLoopException** ()
*		public	**LinkLoopException** (String explanation)
	2	protected .... *Name*	linkRemainingName
	2	protected .... *Name*	linkResolvedName
	2	protected .... Object	linkResolvedObj
	2	public ....void	setLinkExplanation (String msg)
	2	public ....void	setLinkRemainingName (*Name* name)
	2	public ....void	setLinkResolvedName (*Name* name)
	2	public ....void	setLinkResolvedObj (Object obj)
	2	public .... String	toString ()
	2	public .... String	toString (boolean detail)

LinkRef — javax.naming

```
Object
1.3 └Reference 1 ------------------------- Cloneable, java.io.Serializable
1.3   └LinkRef
```

	1	public ....void	add (RefAddr addr)
	1	public ....void	add (int posn, RefAddr addr)
	1	protected .... java.util.Vector	addrs
	1	protected .... String	classFactory
	1	protected .... String	classFactoryLocation
	1	protected .... String	className
	1	public ....void	clear ()
	1	public .... Object	clone ()
	1	public .... boolean	equals (Object obj)
	1	public .... RefAddr	get (int posn)
	1	public .... RefAddr	get (String addrType)
	1	public .... *java.util.Enumeration*	getAll ()
	1	public .... String	getClassName ()
	1	public .... String	getFactoryClassLocation ()
	1	public .... String	getFactoryClassName ()
		public .... String	**getLinkName** () throws NamingException
	1	public ....int	hashCode ()
*		public	**LinkRef** (String linkName)
*		public	**LinkRef** (*Name* linkName)
	1	public .... Object	remove (int posn)

LinkRef

List ❷   java.util

1.2		List————————————————————Collection ‿[1]	ε339,341,347,350,348

	1	public	boolean	**add** (Object o)	ε349,362,342,352,354
		public	void	**add** (int index, Object element)	ε349,362
	1	public	boolean	**addAll** (*Collection* c)	ε351,353
		public	boolean	**addAll** (int index, *Collection* c)	
	1	public	void	**clear** ()	ε351,353
	1	public	boolean	**contains** (Object o)	ε352
	1	public	boolean	**containsAll** (*Collection* c)	
	1	public	boolean	**equals** (Object o)	
		public	Object	**get** (int index)	ε349,234
	1	public	int	**hashCode** ()	
		public	int	**indexOf** (Object o)	
	1	public	boolean	**isEmpty** ()	ε102
	1	public	*Iterator*	**iterator** ()	ε345,352,354,355,356
		public	int	**lastIndexOf** (Object o)	
		public	*ListIterator*	**listIterator** ()	
		public	*ListIterator*	**listIterator** (int index)	
		public	Object	**remove** (int index)	ε349
	1	public	boolean	**remove** (Object o)	ε349,352
	1	public	boolean	**removeAll** (*Collection* c)	ε351,353
	1	public	boolean	**retainAll** (*Collection* c)	ε351,353
		public	Object	**set** (int index, Object element)	ε348
	1	public	int	**size** ()	ε340,349,351,234,352
		public	*List*	**subList** (int fromIndex, int toIndex)	ε351
	1	public	**Object[]**	**toArray** ()	ε340
	1	public	**Object[]**	**toArray** (Object[] a)	ε340,352,358,194,508

ListIterator   java.util

1.2		ListIterator————————————————Iterator ‿[1]	

		public	void	**add** (Object o)	
	1	public	boolean	**hasNext** ()	ε345,352,354,355,356
		public	boolean	**hasPrevious** ()	
	1	public	**Object**	**next** ()	ε345,352,354,355,356
		public	int	**nextIndex** ()	
		public	Object	**previous** ()	
		public	int	**previousIndex** ()	
	1	public	void	**remove** ()	ε176,179
		public	void	**set** (Object o)	

ListResourceBundle   java.util

		Object	
1.1	O	└ResourceBundle[1]	
1.1	O	└ListResourceBundle‿	

▲	1	public static final ResourceBundle		**getBundle** (String baseName)	ε310
▲	1	public static final ResourceBundle		**getBundle** (String baseName, Locale locale)	ε310
1.2 △	1	public static .. ResourceBundle	**getBundle**	(String baseName, Locale locale, ClassLoader loader)	
O		protected abstract .. Object[][]	**getContents**	()	
	1	public	**Enumeration**	**getKeys** ()	
1.2	1	public	Locale	**getLocale** ()	
●	1	public final	Object	**getObject** (String key)	
●	1	public final	String	**getString** (String key)	ε310
●	1	public final	String[]	**getStringArray** (String key)	
●	1	public final	**Object**	**handleGetObject** (String key)	
✳		public		**ListResourceBundle** ()	
	1	protected	ResourceBundle	**parent**	
	1	protected	void	**setParent** (ResourceBundle parent)	

LoaderHandler			java.rmi.server

D		*LoaderHandler*
D	public...................Object	**getSecurityContext** (ClassLoader loader)
D	public....................Class	**loadClass** (String name) throws java.net.MalformedURLException, ClassNotFoundException
D	public....................Class	**loadClass** (java.net.URL codebase, String name) throws java.net.MalformedURLException, ClassNotFoundException
D ▲	public static final.........String	**packagePrefix** = "sun.rmi.server"

Locale			java.util

Object[1]

1.1 ●	└─Locale ------------------------------------- *Cloneable* ˎ, *java.io.Serializable* ˎ	
▲	public static final........Locale **CANADA** = new Locale("en", "CA", "")	ε306,312,314,315,327
▲	public static final........Locale **CANADA_FRENCH** = new Locale("fr", "CA", "")	
▲	public static final........Locale **CHINA** = new Locale("zh", "CN", "")	
▲	public static final........Locale **CHINESE** = new Locale("zh", "", "")	ε509
1	public.................**Object clone** ()	
▲	public static final........Locale **ENGLISH** = new Locale("en", "", "")	
1	public.................**boolean equals** (Object obj)	
▲	public static final........Locale **FRANCE** = new Locale("fr", "FR", "")	
▲	public static final........Locale **FRENCH** = new Locale("fr", "", "")	ε336,310,319,323
▲	public static final........Locale **GERMAN** = new Locale("de", "", "")	ε312
▲	public static final........Locale **GERMANY** = new Locale("de", "DE", "")	ε314
1.2 △	public static ....Locale[] **getAvailableLocales** ()	ε335
	public....................String **getCountry** ()	ε335
△	public static ....Locale **getDefault** ()	ε336
●	public final ....String **getDisplayCountry** ()	
	public....................String **getDisplayCountry** (Locale inLocale)	
●	public final ....String **getDisplayLanguage** ()	
	public....................String **getDisplayLanguage** (Locale inLocale)	
●	public final ....String **getDisplayName** ()	ε335
	public....................String **getDisplayName** (Locale inLocale)	
●	public final ....String **getDisplayVariant** ()	
	public....................String **getDisplayVariant** (Locale inLocale)	
	public....................String **getISO3Country** () throws MissingResourceException	
	public....................String **getISO3Language** () throws MissingResourceException	
1.2 △	public static ....String[] **getISOCountries** ()	
1.2 △	public static ....String[] **getISOLanguages** ()	
	public....................String **getLanguage** ()	ε335
	public....................String **getVariant** ()	
1	public synchronized .... **int hashCode** ()	
▲	public static final........Locale **ITALIAN** = new Locale("it", "", "")	ε318
▲	public static final........Locale **ITALY** = new Locale("it", "IT", "")	
▲	public static final........Locale **JAPAN** = new Locale("ja", "JP", "")	
▲	public static final........Locale **JAPANESE** = new Locale("ja", "", "")	
▲	public static final........Locale **KOREA** = new Locale("ko", "KR", "")	
▲	public static final........Locale **KOREAN** = new Locale("ko", "", "")	
1.4 *	public.......................... **Locale** (String language)	
*	public.......................... **Locale** (String language, String country)	ε336
*	public.......................... **Locale** (String language, String country, String variant)	
▲	public static final........Locale **PRC** = new Locale("zh", "CN", "")	
△	public static synchronized void **setDefault** (Locale newLocale)	ε336
▲	public static final........Locale **SIMPLIFIED_CHINESE** = new Locale("zh", "CN", "")	
▲	public static final........Locale **TAIWAN** = new Locale("zh", "TW", "")	
● 1	public final ....**String toString** ()	
▲	public static final........Locale **TRADITIONAL_CHINESE** = new Locale("zh", "TW", "")	
▲	public static final........Locale **UK** = new Locale("en", "GB", "")	
▲	public static final........Locale **US** = new Locale("en", "US", "")	

L

Classes

LocalObject			org.omg.CORBA

Object

1.4	└─LocalObject -------------------------- *Object* ˎ [1]	
1	public................Request **_create_request** (Context ctx, String operation, NVList arg_list, NamedValue result)	
1	public................Request **_create_request** (Context ctx, String operation, NVList arg_list, NamedValue result, ExceptionList exceptions, ContextList contexts)	
1	public................*Object* **_duplicate** ()	

LocalObject

	1	public........ *DomainManager[]*	**_get_domain_managers** ()
		public.................... *Object*	**_get_interface** ()
	1	public.................... *Object*	**_get_interface_def** ()
	1	public.................... *Policy*	**_get_policy** (int policy_type)
	1	public................................int	**_hash** (int maximum)
		public......org.omg.CORBA↵	**_invoke** (org.omg.CORBA.portable.OutputStream output)
		.portable.InputStream	throws org.omg.CORBA.portable.ApplicationException,
			org.omg.CORBA.portable.RemarshalException
	1	public.................. boolean	**_is_a** (String repository_id)
	1	public.................. boolean	**_is_equivalent** (*Object* that)
		public.................. boolean	**_is_local** ()
	1	public.................. boolean	**_non_existent** ()
		public.................... ORB	**_orb** ()
	1	public....................void	**_release** ()
		public....................void	**_releaseReply** (org.omg.CORBA.portable.InputStream input)
	1	public.................. Request	**_request** (String operation)
		public......org.omg.CORBA↵	**_request** (String operation, boolean responseExpected)
		.portable.OutputStream	
		public........................void	**_servant_postinvoke** (org.omg.CORBA.portable.ServantObject servant)
		public......org.omg.CORBA↵	**_servant_preinvoke** (String operation, Class expectedType)
		.portable.ServantObject	
	1	public.................... *Object*	**_set_policy_override** (*Policy[]* policies, SetOverrideType set_add)
	✳	public....................	**LocalObject** ()
		public.................. boolean	**validate_connection** ()

LocateRegistry java.rmi.registry

Object
└LocateRegistry   1.1 ●

△	public static .... *Registry*	**createRegistry** (int port) throws java.rmi.RemoteException
1.2 △	public static .... *Registry*	**createRegistry** (int port, *java.rmi.server.RMIClientSocketFactory* csf,
		java.rmi.server.RMIServerSocketFactory ssf) throws java.rmi.RemoteException
△	public static .... *Registry*	**getRegistry** () throws java.rmi.RemoteException
△	public static .... *Registry*	**getRegistry** (int port) throws java.rmi.RemoteException
△	public static .... *Registry*	**getRegistry** (String host) throws java.rmi.RemoteException
△	public static .... *Registry*	**getRegistry** (String host, int port) throws java.rmi.RemoteException
1.2 △	public static .... *Registry*	**getRegistry** (String host, int port, *java.rmi.server.RMIClientSocketFactory* csf)
		throws java.rmi.RemoteException

LOCATION_FORWARD org.omg.PortableInterceptor

1.4   *LOCATION_FORWARD*

▲   public static final..........short **value** = 3

Locator org.xml.sax

1.4   *Locator*

public........................int	**getColumnNumber** ()	ε550
public........................int	**getLineNumber** ()	ε550
public........................String	**getPublicId** ()	ε550
public........................String	**getSystemId** ()	ε550

LocatorImpl org.xml.sax.helpers

Object
└LocatorImpl ---------------------------- *org.xml.sax.Locator* [1]   1.4

1	public........................int	**getColumnNumber** ()	ε550
1	public........................int	**getLineNumber** ()	ε550
1	public........................String	**getPublicId** ()	ε550
1	public........................String	**getSystemId** ()	ε550
✳	public........................	**LocatorImpl** ()	
✳	public........................	**LocatorImpl** (*org.xml.sax.Locator* locator)	
	public........................void	**setColumnNumber** (int columnNumber)	

Class   *Interface*   —extends   - - -implements   ○ abstract   ● final   △ static   ▲ static final   ✳ constructor   x x—inherited   x **x**—declared   **x x**—overridden
εn—examples of usage   ⌐has subclass   package—see other volume

```
public.....................void  setLineNumber (int lineNumber)
public.....................void  setPublicId (String publicId)
public.....................void  setSystemId (String systemId)
```

Logger		java.util.logging

```
            Object
1.4         └Logger
```

	public synchronized ....void	**addHandler** (Handler handler) throws SecurityException	ε391,392,393,394,399
	public.....................void	**config** (String msg)	ε385,399
	public.....................void	**entering** (String sourceClass, String sourceMethod)	
	public.....................void	**entering** (String sourceClass, String sourceMethod, Object[] params)	
			ε387,400
	public.....................void	**entering** (String sourceClass, String sourceMethod, Object param1)	
	public.....................void	**exiting** (String sourceClass, String sourceMethod)	ε387
	public.....................void	**exiting** (String sourceClass, String sourceMethod, Object result)	ε387
	public.....................void	**fine** (String msg)	ε385,399
	public.....................void	**finer** (String msg)	ε385,399
	public.....................void	**finest** (String msg)	ε385,386,389,399
△	public static synchronized	**getAnonymousLogger** ()	
	.....................Logger		
△	public static synchronized	**getAnonymousLogger** (String resourceBundleName)	
	.....................Logger		
	public.....................*Filter*	**getFilter** ()	
	public synchronized . Handler[]	**getHandlers** ()	
	public.....................Level	**getLevel** ()	ε396
△	public static synchronized	**getLogger** (String name)	ε385,386,387,388,389
	.....................Logger		
△	public static synchronized	**getLogger** (String name, String resourceBundleName)	
	.....................Logger		
	public.....................String	**getName** ()	
	public.....................Logger	**getParent** ()	ε396
	public.....................	**getResourceBundle** ()	
	.....java.util.ResourceBundle		
	public.....................String	**getResourceBundleName** ()	
	public synchronized .. boolean	**getUseParentHandlers** ()	
▲	public static final ....Logger	**global**	
	public.....................void	**info** (String msg)	ε385,399,400
	public.....................boolean	**isLoggable** (Level level)	ε389,386,387
	public.....................void	**log** (LogRecord record)	
	public.....................void	**log** (Level level, String msg)	ε513
	public.....................void	**log** (Level level, String msg, Throwable thrown)	ε388,513
	public.....................void	**log** (Level level, String msg, Object[] params)	
	public.....................void	**log** (Level level, String msg, Object param1)	
*	protected	**Logger** (String name, String resourceBundleName)	
	public.....................void	**logp** (Level level, String sourceClass, String sourceMethod, String msg)	
	public.....................void	**logp** (Level level, String sourceClass, String sourceMethod, String msg, Object param1)	
	public.....................void	**logp** (Level level, String sourceClass, String sourceMethod, String msg, Object[] params)	
	public.....................void	**logp** (Level level, String sourceClass, String sourceMethod, String msg, Throwable thrown)	
	public.....................void	**logrb** (Level level, String sourceClass, String sourceMethod, String bundleName, String msg)	
	public.....................void	**logrb** (Level level, String sourceClass, String sourceMethod, String bundleName, String msg, Object[] params)	
	public.....................void	**logrb** (Level level, String sourceClass, String sourceMethod, String bundleName, String msg, Throwable thrown)	
	public.....................void	**logrb** (Level level, String sourceClass, String sourceMethod, String bundleName, String msg, Object param1)	
	public synchronized ....void	**removeHandler** (Handler handler) throws SecurityException	
	public.....................void	**setFilter** (*Filter* newFilter) throws SecurityException	
	public.....................void	**setLevel** (Level newLevel) throws SecurityException	ε395,400
	public.....................void	**setParent** (Logger parent)	
	public synchronized ....void	**setUseParentHandlers** (boolean useParentHandlers)	ε390
	public.....................void	**severe** (String msg)	ε385,399,400
	public.....................void	**throwing** (String sourceClass, String sourceMethod, Throwable thrown)	
			ε388
	public.....................void	**warning** (String msg)	ε385,399

L

Classes

LoggingPermission

				java.util.logging

Object
└java.security.Permission[1] - - - - - - - - - - - - - - - *java.security.Guard, java.io.Serializable*

1.2 ○

    └java.security.BasicPermission[2]

1.2 ○

        └LoggingPermission

1.4 ●

1	public	void	checkGuard (Object object) throws SecurityException	
2	public	boolean	equals (Object obj)	ε215
2	public	String	getActions ()	ε215
● 1	public final	String	getName ()	
2	public	int	hashCode ()	ε215
2	public	boolean	implies (java.security.Permission p)	ε214,215
✳	public		**LoggingPermission** (String name, String actions) throws IllegalArgumentException	
2	public	java.security ↵ .PermissionCollection	newPermissionCollection ()	
1	public	String	toString ()	

LoginContext

	javax.security.auth.login

Object
└LoginContext

1.4

	public .. javax.security.auth.Subject		**getSubject** ()	ε508
	public	void	**login** () throws LoginException	ε508
✳	public		**LoginContext** (String name) throws LoginException	
✳	public		**LoginContext** (String name, *javax.security.auth.callback.CallbackHandler* callbackHandler) throws LoginException	ε508,509
✳	public		**LoginContext** (String name, javax.security.auth.Subject subject) throws LoginException	
✳	public		**LoginContext** (String name, javax.security.auth.Subject subject, *javax.security .auth.callback.CallbackHandler* callbackHandler) throws LoginException	
	public	void	**logout** () throws LoginException	

LoginException

	javax.security.auth.login

Object — ε508,509
└Throwable - *java.io.Serializable*
    └Exception

1.2

        └java.security.GeneralSecurityException

1.4

            └LoginException

✳	public	**LoginException** ()
✳	public	**LoginException** (String msg)

LoginModule

	javax.security.auth.spi

LoginModule

1.4

public	boolean	**abort** () throws javax.security.auth.login.LoginException
public	boolean	**commit** () throws javax.security.auth.login.LoginException
public	void	**initialize** (javax.security.auth.Subject subject, *javax.security.auth .callback.CallbackHandler* callbackHandler, *java.util.Map* sharedState, *java.util.Map* options)
public	boolean	**login** () throws javax.security.auth.login.LoginException
public	boolean	**logout** () throws javax.security.auth.login.LoginException

---

LogManager

	java.util.logging

Object
└LogManager

1.4

public synchronized ..	boolean	**addLogger** (Logger logger)	
public	void	**addPropertyChangeListener** (*java.beans.PropertyChangeListener* l) throws SecurityException	ε404

Class   *Interface*   —extends   - - -implements   ○ abstract   ● final   △ static   ▲ static final   ✳ constructor   x x—inherited   x **x**—declared   **x x**—overridden
ε*n*—examples of usage   ⌣—has subclass   package—see other volume

```
       public.......................void  checkAccess () throws SecurityException
       public synchronized ... Logger  getLogger (String name)
       public synchronized ..........  getLoggerNames ()
       ......... java.util.Enumeration
△      public static ...... LogManager  getLogManager ()                                    ε404
       public......................String  getProperty (String name)
*      protected......................  LogManager ()
       public.......................void  readConfiguration () throws java.io.IOException, SecurityException
                                                                                            ε404
       public.......................void  readConfiguration (java.io.InputStream ins) throws java.io.IOException,
                                              SecurityException
       public.......................void  removePropertyChangeListener (java.beans.PropertyChangeListener l)
                                              throws SecurityException
       public.......................void  reset () throws SecurityException
```

LogRecord | java.util.logging

```
       Object                                                                               ε393,394
1.4    └LogRecord ----------------------------- java.io.Serializable
```

```
       public.................... Level  getLevel ()                                        ε400
       public....................String  getLoggerName ()
       public....................String  getMessage ()
       public.................... long  getMillis ()                                        ε400
       public................... Object[]  getParameters ()
       public........................  getResourceBundle ()
       .....java.util.ResourceBundle
       public....................String  getResourceBundleName ()
       public.................... long  getSequenceNumber ()
       public....................String  getSourceClassName ()
       public....................String  getSourceMethodName ()
       public.......................int  getThreadID ()
       public...............Throwable  getThrown ()
*      public........................  LogRecord (Level level, String msg)
       public.......................void  setLevel (Level level)
       public.......................void  setLoggerName (String name)
       public.......................void  setMessage (String message)
       public.......................void  setMillis (long millis)
       public.......................void  setParameters (Object[] parameters)
       public.......................void  setResourceBundle (java.util.ResourceBundle bundle)
       public.......................void  setResourceBundleName (String name)
       public.......................void  setSequenceNumber (long seq)
       public.......................void  setSourceClassName (String sourceClassName)
       public.......................void  setSourceMethodName (String sourceMethodName)
       public.......................void  setThreadID (int threadID)
       public.......................void  setThrown (Throwable thrown)
```

LogStream | java.rmi.server

```
       Object 1                                                                             ε183
○      └java.io.OutputStream
          └java.io.FilterOutputStream 2
             └java.io.PrintStream 3
D               └LogStream
```

```
D ▲    public static final.............int  BRIEF  = 10
D   3  public................. boolean  checkError ()
D   3  public.......................void  close ()                                      ε451,453,91,211,224
D   3  public.......................void  flush ()                                      ε27,54
D △    public static synchronized ....  getDefaultStream ()
       ...........java.io.PrintStream
D      public synchronized ..........  getOutputStream ()
       ........ java.io.OutputStream
D △    public static ........ LogStream  log (String name)
D   2  protected java.io.OutputStream  out
D △    public static .................int  parseLevel (String s)
D   3  public.......................void  print (boolean b)
D   3  public.......................void  print (char c)
D   3  public.......................void  print (char[] s)
D   3  public.......................void  print (double d)
D   3  public.......................void  print (float f)
```

LogStream

D	3	public ....void	print (int i)	
D	3	public ....void	print (Object obj)	ε34
D	3	public ....void	print (String s)	ε34
D	3	public ....void	print (long l)	
D	3	public ....void	println ()	
D	3	public ....void	println (boolean x)	
D	3	public ....void	println (char x)	
D	3	public ....void	println (char[] x)	
D	3	public ....void	println (double x)	
D	3	public ....void	println (float x)	
D	3	public ....void	println (int x)	ε262
D	3	public ....void	println (Object x)	ε69
D	3	public ....void	println (String x)	ε54,69,262
D	3	public ....void	println (long x)	
D	△	public static synchronized void	**setDefaultStream** (java.io.PrintStream newDefault)	
D	3	protected ....void	setError ()	
D		public synchronized ....void	**setOutputStream** (java.io.OutputStream out)	
D	▲	public static final ....int	**SILENT** = 0	
D	1	public ....**String**	**toString** ()	
D	▲	public static final ....int	**VERBOSE** = 20	
D	2	public ....void	write (byte[] b) throws java.io.IOException	ε27,91,224
D	3	public ....**void**	**write** (int b)	ε184
D	3	public ....**void**	**write** (byte[] b, int off, int len)	ε451,453,54,449,450

Long   java.lang

		Object[1]	ε312,314,315,200,201
	O	└Number[2] - java.io.Serializable⌐	
	●	└Long - Comparable[3]	

1.1	2	public ....**byte**	**byteValue** ()	ε58
1.2		public ....int	**compareTo** (Long anotherLong)	
1.2	3	public ....int	**compareTo** (Object o)	ε53
1.2	△	public static ....Long	**decode** (String nm) throws NumberFormatException	
	2	public ....**double**	**doubleValue** ()	ε58
	1	public ....**boolean**	**equals** (Object obj)	
	2	public ....**float**	**floatValue** ()	ε58
	△	public static ....Long	**getLong** (String nm)	
	△	public static ....Long	**getLong** (String nm, Long val)	
	△	public static ....Long	**getLong** (String nm, long val)	
	1	public ....**int**	**hashCode** ()	
	2	public ....**int**	**intValue** ()	ε58,6,346
	*	public	**Long** (String s) throws NumberFormatException	
	*	public	**Long** (long value)	ε58
	2	public ....**long**	**longValue** ()	ε58
	▲	public static final .... long	**MAX_VALUE** = 9223372036854775807	ε182
	▲	public static final .... long	**MIN_VALUE** = -9223372036854775808	
	△	public static .... long	**parseLong** (String s) throws NumberFormatException	ε82
	△	public static .... long	**parseLong** (String s, int radix) throws NumberFormatException	
1.1	2	public ....**short**	**shortValue** ()	ε58
	△	public static .... String	**toBinaryString** (long i)	
	△	public static .... String	**toHexString** (long i)	
	△	public static .... String	**toOctalString** (long i)	
	1	public ....**String**	**toString** ()	
	△	public static .... String	**toString** (long i)	
	△	public static .... String	**toString** (long i, int radix)	
1.1	▲	public static final .... Class	**TYPE**	
	△	public static ....Long	**valueOf** (String s) throws NumberFormatException	
	△	public static ....Long	**valueOf** (String s, int radix) throws NumberFormatException	

LongBuffer   java.nio

		Object[1]	ε163,166,171,425
1.4	O	└Buffer[2]	
1.4	O	└LongBuffer - Comparable[3]	

	△	public static .... LongBuffer	**allocate** (int capacity)
	●	public final ....long[]	**array** ()

Class *Interface* —extends - - -implements O abstract ● final △ static ▲ static final ✳ constructor x x—inherited x **x**—declared **x x**—overridden
εn—examples of usage ⌐—has subclass package—see other volume

●		public final	.... int	**arrayOffset** ()	
○		public abstract ..... LongBuffer	**asReadOnlyBuffer** ()	
●	2	public final	.... int	capacity ()	ε159,160,161
●	2	public final	.... Buffer	clear ()	ε161,170,174
○		public abstract ..... LongBuffer	**compact** ()	
	3	public .... int	**compareTo** (Object ob)	ε53
○		public abstract ..... LongBuffer	**duplicate** ()	
	1	public .... **boolean**	**equals** (Object ob)	
●	2	public final	.... Buffer	flip ()	ε162,164,170,174,175
○		public abstract .... long	**get** ()	
○		public abstract .... long	**get** (int index)	
		public .... LongBuffer	**get** (long[] dst)	
		public .... LongBuffer	**get** (long[] dst, int offset, int length)	
●		public final	.... boolean	**hasArray** ()	
	1	public .... **int**	**hashCode** ()	
●	2	public final	.... boolean	hasRemaining ()	ε170,184
○		public abstract .... boolean	**isDirect** ()	
○	2	public abstract .... boolean	isReadOnly ()	
●	2	public final	.... int	limit ()	
●	2	public final	.... Buffer	limit (int newLimit)	ε159,160
●	2	public final	.... Buffer	mark ()	
○		public abstract ...... ByteOrder	**order** ()	
●	2	public final	.... int	position ()	ε159,160
●	2	public final	.... Buffer	position (int newPosition)	ε159,160
		public .... LongBuffer	**put** (LongBuffer src)	
○		public abstract ..... LongBuffer	**put** (long l)	
●		public final	.... LongBuffer	**put** (long[] src)	
○		public abstract ..... LongBuffer	**put** (int index, long l)	
		public .... LongBuffer	**put** (long[] src, int offset, int length)	
●	2	public final	.... int	remaining ()	ε159,160,161,184
●	2	public final	.... Buffer	reset ()	
●	2	public final	.... Buffer	rewind ()	ε159,160,169
○		public abstract ..... LongBuffer	**slice** ()	
	1	public .... **String**	**toString** ()	
△		public static .... LongBuffer	**wrap** (long[] array)	
△		public static .... LongBuffer	**wrap** (long[] array, int offset, int length)	

L

LongHolder   org.omg.CORBA

Object
1.2 ● └LongHolder - *org.omg.CORBA.portable.Streamable*↲[1]

	1	public .... void	**_read** (org.omg.CORBA.portable.InputStream input)
	1	public .... TypeCode	**_type** ()
	1	public .... void	**_write** (org.omg.CORBA.portable.OutputStream output)
*		public	**LongHolder** ()
*		public	**LongHolder** (long initial)
		public .... long	**value**

LongLongSeqHelper   org.omg.CORBA

Object
1.3 ○ └LongLongSeqHelper

△	public static .... long[]	**extract** (Any a)
△	public static .... String	**id** ()
△	public static .... void	**insert** (Any a, long[] that)
*	public	**LongLongSeqHelper** ()
△	public static .... long[]	**read** (org.omg.CORBA.portable.InputStream istream)
△	public static synchronized	**type** ()
	.... TypeCode	
△	public static .... void	**write** (org.omg.CORBA.portable.OutputStream ostream, long[] value)

LongLongSeqHolder   org.omg.CORBA

Object
1.3 ● └LongLongSeqHolder - *org.omg.CORBA.portable.Streamable*↲[1]

	1	public .... void	**_read** (org.omg.CORBA.portable.InputStream i)
	1	public .... TypeCode	**_type** ()
	1	public .... void	**_write** (org.omg.CORBA.portable.OutputStream o)

Classes

LongLongSeqHolder

✳	public.........................	**LongLongSeqHolder** ()
✳	public.........................	**LongLongSeqHolder** (long[] initialValue)
	public....................long[]	**value**

LongSeqHelper

org.omg.CORBA

Object
1.3 ○ └LongSeqHelper

△	public static .... int[]	**extract** (Any a)
△	public static ....String	**id** ()
△	public static ....void	**insert** (Any a, int[] that)
✳	public.........................	**LongSeqHelper** ()
△	public static .... int[]	**read** (org.omg.CORBA.portable.InputStream istream)
△	public static synchronized	**type** ()
	...................TypeCode	
△	public static ....void	**write** (org.omg.CORBA.portable.OutputStream ostream, int[] value)

LongSeqHolder

org.omg.CORBA

Object
1.3 ● └LongSeqHolder - *org.omg.CORBA.portable.Streamable*‿[1]

	1 public.......................void	**_read** (org.omg.CORBA.portable.InputStream i)
	1 public...............TypeCode	**_type** ()
	1 public.......................void	**_write** (org.omg.CORBA.portable.OutputStream o)
✳	public.........................	**LongSeqHolder** ()
✳	public.........................	**LongSeqHolder** (int[] initialValue)
	public.....................int[]	**value**

Mac

javax.crypto

Object[1]
1.4 └Mac - *Cloneable*‿

● 1	public final ....**Object**	**clone** () throws CloneNotSupportedException
●	public final ....byte[]	**doFinal** () throws IllegalStateException
●	public final ....byte[]	**doFinal** (byte[] input) throws IllegalStateException ε469
●	public final ....void	**doFinal** (byte[] output, int outOffset) throws ShortBufferException, IllegalStateException
●	public final ....String	**getAlgorithm** ()
▲	public static final.......... Mac	**getInstance** (String algorithm) throws java.security.NoSuchAlgorithmException ε469
▲	public static final.......... Mac	**getInstance** (String algorithm, java.security.Provider provider) throws java.security.NoSuchAlgorithmException
▲	public static final.......... Mac	**getInstance** (String algorithm, String provider) throws java.security ↵ .NoSuchAlgorithmException, java.security.NoSuchProviderException
●	public final ....int	**getMacLength** ()
●	public final	**getProvider** ()
	.... java.security.Provider	
●	public final ....void	**init** (*java.security.Key* key) throws java.security.InvalidKeyException ε469
●	public final ....void	**init** (*java.security.Key* key, *java.security.spec.AlgorithmParameterSpec* params) throws java.security.InvalidKeyException, java.security.InvalidAlgorithmParameterException
✳	protected......................	**Mac** (MacSpi macSpi, java.security.Provider provider, String algorithm)
●	public final ....void	**reset** ()
●	public final ....void	**update** (byte input) throws IllegalStateException
●	public final ....void	**update** (byte[] input) throws IllegalStateException
●	public final ....void	**update** (byte[] input, int offset, int len) throws IllegalStateException

---

MacSpi

javax.crypto

Object[1]
1.4 ○ └MacSpi

Class *Interface* —extends - - -implements ○ abstract ● final △ static ▲ static final ✳ constructor x x—inherited x **x**—declared **x x**—overridden
εn—examples of usage ‿—has subclass package—see other volume

1	public	**Object**	**clone** () throws CloneNotSupportedException
○	protected abstract	byte[]	**engineDoFinal** ()
○	protected abstract	int	**engineGetMacLength** ()
○	protected abstract	void	**engineInit** (*java.security.Key* key, *java.security.spec.AlgorithmParameterSpec* params) throws java.security.InvalidKeyException, java.security.InvalidAlgorithmParameterException
○	protected abstract	void	**engineReset** ()
○	protected abstract	void	**engineUpdate** (byte input)
○	protected abstract	void	**engineUpdate** (byte[] input, int offset, int len)
∗	public		**MacSpi** ()

MalformedInputException · java.nio.charset

```
Object
└ Throwable 1 - - - - - - - - - - - - - - - - - - - - - - - - - - java.io.Serializable
    └ Exception
        └ java.io.IOException
1.4         └ CharacterCodingException
1.4             └ MalformedInputException
```

	public	int	**getInputLength** ()
1	public	**String**	**getMessage** ()
∗	public		**MalformedInputException** (int inputLength)

MalformedLinkException · javax.naming

```
Object
└ Throwable - - - - - - - - - - - - - - - - - - - - - - - - - - java.io.Serializable
    └ Exception
1.3     └ NamingException 1
1.3         └ LinkException 2
1.3             └ MalformedLinkException
```

1	*18 inherited members from NamingException not shown*		
2	public	String	getLinkExplanation ()
2	public	*Name*	getLinkRemainingName ()
2	public	*Name*	getLinkResolvedName ()
2	public	Object	getLinkResolvedObj ()
2	protected	String	linkExplanation
2	protected	*Name*	linkRemainingName
2	protected	*Name*	linkResolvedName
2	protected	Object	linkResolvedObj
∗	public		**MalformedLinkException** ()
∗	public		**MalformedLinkException** (String explanation)
2	public	void	setLinkExplanation (String msg)
2	public	void	setLinkRemainingName (*Name* name)
2	public	void	setLinkResolvedName (*Name* name)
2	public	void	setLinkResolvedObj (Object obj)
2	public	String	toString ()
2	public	String	toString (boolean detail)

MalformedURLException · java.net

*ε*132,133,134,136,137

```
Object
└ Throwable - - - - - - - - - - - - - - - - - - - - - - - - - - java.io.Serializable
    └ Exception
        └ java.io.IOException
            └ MalformedURLException
```

∗	public		**MalformedURLException** ()
∗	public		**MalformedURLException** (String msg)

ManagerFactoryParameters · javax.net.ssl

1.4	*ManagerFactoryParameters*

Manifest

Manifest					java.util.jar

```
         Object 1
1.2      └ Manifest ---------------------------------- Cloneable ⌄
```

	public......................void	**clear** ()		
1	public...................**Object**	**clone** ()		
1	public..................**boolean**	**equals** (Object o)		
	public......................Attributes	**getAttributes** (String name)		
	public...........*java.util.Map*	**getEntries** ()		ε380
	public......................Attributes	**getMainAttributes** ()		ε381
1	public.......................**int**	**hashCode** ()		
✳	public............................	**Manifest** ()		
✳	public............................	**Manifest** (java.io.InputStream is) throws java.io.IOException		ε382
✳	public............................	**Manifest** (Manifest man)		
	public......................void	**read** (java.io.InputStream is) throws java.io.IOException		
	public......................void	**write** (java.io.OutputStream out) throws java.io.IOException		ε383

Map					java.util

```
1.2      Map ⌄                                          ε347,348
```

public......................void	**clear** ()		
public..................boolean	**containsKey** (Object key)		ε344
public..................boolean	**containsValue** (Object value)		
public......................*Set*	**entrySet** ()		ε345
public..................boolean	**equals** (Object o)		
public......................Object	**get** (Object key)		ε337,344,346,356,357
public......................int	**hashCode** ()		
public..................boolean	**isEmpty** ()		
public......................*Set*	**keySet** ()		ε340,345,355,356,357
public......................Object	**put** (Object key, Object value)		ε337,344,346,355,356
public......................void	**putAll** (*Map* t)		
public......................Object	**remove** (Object key)		ε355
public......................int	**size** ()		ε355
public............*Collection*	**values** ()		ε340,345,355

Map.Entry					java.util

```
1.2      Map.Entry                                       ε344
```

public..................boolean	**equals** (Object o)		
public......................Object	**getKey** ()		ε345
public......................Object	**getValue** ()		ε345
public......................int	**hashCode** ()		
public......................Object	**setValue** (Object value)		

MappedByteBuffer					java.nio

```
          Object                                          ε163,166,171,425
1.4  ○    └ Buffer 1
1.4  ○      └ ByteBuffer 2 --------------------------- Comparable
1.4  ○        └ MappedByteBuffer
```

	2	*56 inherited members from ByteBuffer not shown*			
●	1	public final ....int	capacity ()		ε159,160,161
●	1	public final ....Buffer	clear ()		ε161,170,174
●	1	public final ....Buffer	flip ()		ε162,164,170,174,175
●		public final MappedByteBuffer	**force** ()		ε167
●	1	public final ....boolean	hasRemaining ()		ε170,184
●		public final ....boolean	**isLoaded** ()		
○	1	public abstract ....boolean	isReadOnly ()		
●	1	public final ....int	limit ()		
●	1	public final ....Buffer	limit (int newLimit)		ε159,160
●		public final MappedByteBuffer	**load** ()		
●	1	public final ....Buffer	mark ()		
●	1	public final ....int	position ()		ε159,160
●	1	public final ....Buffer	position (int newPosition)		ε159,160

Class *Interface* —extends - - -implements ○ abstract ● final △ static ▲ static final ✳ constructor x x—inherited x **x**—declared **x x**—overridden
ε*n*—examples of usage ⌄—has subclass package—see other volume

○	2	public abstract . . . . . . ByteBuffer	**put** (int index, byte b)		ε167
●	1	public final . . . . int	**remaining** ()		ε159,160,161,184
●	1	public final . . . . Buffer	**reset** ()		
●	1	public final . . . . Buffer	**rewind** ()		ε159,160,169

MARSHAL org.omg.CORBA

```
Object
└Throwable ------------------------- java.io.Serializable⌄
   └Exception
      └RuntimeException
1.2 ○       └SystemException¹
1.2 ●          └MARSHAL
```

	1	*3 inherited members from SystemException not shown*	
✳		public.	**MARSHAL** ()
✳		public.	**MARSHAL** (String s)
✳		public.	**MARSHAL** (int minor, CompletionStatus completed)
✳		public.	**MARSHAL** (String s, int minor, CompletionStatus completed)

MarshalException java.rmi

```
Object
└Throwable ------------------------- java.io.Serializable⌄
   └Exception
      └java.io.IOException
1.1       └RemoteException¹
1.1          └MarshalException
```

	1	public. . . . . Throwable	**detail**
1.4	1	public. . . . . Throwable	**getCause** ()
	1	public. . . . . String	**getMessage** ()
✳		public.	**MarshalException** (String s)
✳		public.	**MarshalException** (String s, Exception ex)

MarshalledObject java.rmi

```
Object¹
1.2 ●  └MarshalledObject -------------------- java.io.Serializable⌄
```

	1	public. . . . . **boolean**	**equals** (Object obj)
		public. . . . . Object	**get** () throws java.io.IOException, ClassNotFoundException
	1	public. . . . . **int**	**hashCode** ()
✳		public.	**MarshalledObject** (Object obj) throws java.io.IOException

---

Matcher java.util.regex

```
Object
1.4 ●  └Matcher
```

public. . . . . Matcher	**appendReplacement** (StringBuffer sb, String replacement)	ε430
public. . . . . StringBuffer	**appendTail** (StringBuffer sb)	ε430
public. . . . . int	**end** ()	ε423
public. . . . . int	**end** (int group)	ε437
public. . . . . boolean	**find** ()	ε423,425,427,430,435
public. . . . . boolean	**find** (int start)	
public. . . . . String	**group** ()	ε423,425,427,430,447
public. . . . . String	**group** (int group)	ε436,437,438,439,445
public. . . . . int	**groupCount** ()	ε436,437,438
public. . . . . boolean	**lookingAt** ()	ε424
public. . . . . boolean	**matches** ()	ε424,433,434,444
public. . . . . Pattern	**pattern** ()	
public. . . . . String	**replaceAll** (String replacement)	ε426,428,429,440,446
public. . . . . String	**replaceFirst** (String replacement)	
public. . . . . Matcher	**reset** ()	
public. . . . . Matcher	**reset** (*CharSequence* input)	ε424,439,441,442
public. . . . . int	**start** ()	ε423
public. . . . . int	**start** (int group)	ε437

Math

						java.lang
	Object					
●	└Math					

△	public static strictfp	.....double	**abs** (double a)			
△	public static strictfp	........float	**abs** (float a)			
△	public static strictfp	..........int	**abs** (int a)		ε371	
△	public static strictfp	.... long	**abs** (long a)			
△	public static strictfp	.....double	**acos** (double a)			
△	public static strictfp	.....double	**asin** (double a)			
△	public static strictfp	.....double	**atan** (double a)			
△	public static strictfp	.....double	**atan2** (double y, double x)			
△	public static strictfp	.....double	**ceil** (double a)			
△	public static strictfp	.....double	**cos** (double a)			
▲	public static final	........double	**E** = 2.718281828459045			
△	public static strictfp	.....double	**exp** (double a)			
△	public static strictfp	.....double	**floor** (double a)			
△	public static strictfp	.....double	**IEEEremainder** (double f1, double f2)			
△	public static strictfp	.....double	**log** (double a)			
△	public static strictfp	.....double	**max** (double a, double b)			
△	public static strictfp	........float	**max** (float a, float b)			
△	public static strictfp	..........int	**max** (int a, int b)			
△	public static strictfp	.... long	**max** (long a, long b)			
△	public static strictfp	.....double	**min** (double a, double b)			
△	public static strictfp	........float	**min** (float a, float b)			
△	public static strictfp	..........int	**min** (int a, int b)		ε85,184,442	
△	public static strictfp	.... long	**min** (long a, long b)			
▲	public static final	........double	**PI** = 3.141592653589793			
△	public static strictfp	.....double	**pow** (double a, double b)			
△	public static strictfp	.....double	**random** ()			
△	public static strictfp	.....double	**rint** (double a)			
△	public static strictfp	.... long	**round** (double a)			
△	public static strictfp	..........int	**round** (float a)			
△	public static strictfp	.....double	**sin** (double a)			
△	public static strictfp	.....double	**sqrt** (double a)			
△	public static strictfp	.....double	**tan** (double a)			
1.2 △	public static strictfp	.....double	**toDegrees** (double angrad)			
1.2 △	public static strictfp	.....double	**toRadians** (double angdeg)			

Member

						java.lang.reflect
1.1	*Member*					
▲	public static final	.............int	**DECLARED** = 1			
	public	.....................Class	**getDeclaringClass** ()			
	public	..........................int	**getModifiers** ()		ε113	
	public	.....................String	**getName** ()		ε109,291	
▲	public static final	.............int	**PUBLIC** = 0			

MemoryHandler

						java.util.logging
	Object				ε400	
1.4 ○	└Handler [1]					
1.4 ●	└MemoryHandler					
1	public	......................void	**close** () throws SecurityException			
1	public	......................void	**flush** ()			
1	public	.....................String	getEncoding ()			
1	public	..........ErrorManager	getErrorManager ()			
1	public	......................Filter	getFilter ()			
1	public	..............Formatter	getFormatter ()			
1	public synchronized	..... Level	getLevel ()			
	public synchronized	..... Level	**getPushLevel** ()			
1	public	..................boolean	**isLoggable** (LogRecord record)			
✳	public	....	**MemoryHandler** ()			
✳	public	....	**MemoryHandler** (Handler target, int size, Level pushLevel)		ε393	
1	public synchronized	...... void	**publish** (LogRecord record)		ε393	
	public synchronized	.......void	**push** ()			

Class   *Interface*   —extends   - - -implements   ○ abstract   ● final   △ static   ▲ static final   ✳ constructor   x x—inherited   x **x**—declared   **x x**—overridden
εn—examples of usage   ˌ—has subclass   package—see other volume

1	protected	. . . . void	reportError (String msg, Exception ex, int code)
1	public	. . . . void	setEncoding (String encoding) throws SecurityException,
			java.io.UnsupportedEncodingException
1	public	. . . . void	setErrorManager (ErrorManager em)
1	public	. . . . void	setFilter (*Filter* newFilter) throws SecurityException *ε*394
1	public	. . . . void	setFormatter (Formatter newFormatter) throws SecurityException
			*ε*399,400
1	public synchronized	. . . . void	setLevel (Level newLevel) throws SecurityException
	public	. . . . void	**setPushLevel** (Level newLevel) throws SecurityException

---

MessageDigest		java.security

Object[1]   *ε*206
1.2 ○ └MessageDigestSpi[2]
1.1 ○   └MessageDigest

	2	public	. . . . **Object**	**clone** () throws CloneNotSupportedException
		public	. . . . byte[]	**digest** ()
		public	. . . . byte[]	**digest** (byte[] input) *ε*207
1.2		public	. . . . int	**digest** (byte[] buf, int offset, int len) throws DigestException
1.2 ○	2	protected abstract	. . . . byte[]	engineDigest ()
1.2	2	protected	. . . . int	engineDigest (byte[] buf, int offset, int len) throws DigestException
1.2	2	protected	. . . . int	engineGetDigestLength ()
1.2 ○	2	protected abstract	. . . . void	engineReset ()
1.2 ○	2	protected abstract	. . . . void	engineUpdate (byte input)
1.2 ○	2	protected abstract	. . . . void	engineUpdate (byte[] input, int offset, int len)
●		public final	. . . . String	**getAlgorithm** ()
1.2 ●		public final	. . . . int	**getDigestLength** ()
△		public static	. . . MessageDigest	**getInstance** (String algorithm) throws NoSuchAlgorithmException
				*ε*207
1.4 △		public static	. . . MessageDigest	**getInstance** (String algorithm, Provider provider) throws NoSuchAlgorithmException
△		public static	. . . MessageDigest	**getInstance** (String algorithm, String provider) throws NoSuchAlgorithmException,
				NoSuchProviderException
1.2 ●		public final	. . . . Provider	**getProvider** ()
△		public static	. . . . boolean	**isEqual** (byte[] digesta, byte[] digestb)
✳		protected	. . . .	**MessageDigest** (String algorithm)
		public	. . . . void	**reset** ()
	1	public	. . . . **String**	**toString** ()
		public	. . . . void	**update** (byte input)
		public	. . . . void	**update** (byte[] input) *ε*207
		public	. . . . void	**update** (byte[] input, int offset, int len)

MessageDigestSpi		java.security

Object[1]   *ε*206
1.2 ○ └MessageDigestSpi

	1	public	. . . . **Object**	**clone** () throws CloneNotSupportedException
○		protected abstract	. . . . byte[]	**engineDigest** ()
		protected	. . . . int	**engineDigest** (byte[] buf, int offset, int len) throws DigestException
		protected	. . . . int	**engineGetDigestLength** ()
○		protected abstract	. . . . void	**engineReset** ()
○		protected abstract	. . . . void	**engineUpdate** (byte input)
○		protected abstract	. . . . void	**engineUpdate** (byte[] input, int offset, int len)
✳		public	. . . .	**MessageDigestSpi** ()

MessageFormat		java.text

Object[1]
1.1 ○ └Format[2] - *java.io.Serializable*, *Cloneable*
1.1   └MessageFormat

		public	. . . . void	**applyPattern** (String pattern)
	2	public	. . . . **Object**	**clone** ()
	1	public	. . . . **boolean**	**equals** (Object obj)
●	2	public final	. . . . String	format (Object obj) *ε*316,320
△		public static	. . . . String	**format** (String pattern, Object[] arguments) *ε*324,325
●	2	public final	. . . . . . **StringBuffer**	**format** (Object arguments, StringBuffer result, FieldPosition pos)
●		public final	. . . . StringBuffer	**format** (Object[] arguments, StringBuffer result, FieldPosition pos)
1.4	2	public	. . . .	**formatToCharacterIterator** (Object arguments)
		AttributedCharacterIterator		

MessageFormat

	public	Format[]	**getFormats** ()
1.4	public	Format[]	**getFormatsByArgumentIndex** ()
	public	java.util.Locale	**getLocale** ()
1	public	**int**	**hashCode** ()
✳	public		**MessageFormat** (String pattern)
1.4 ✳	public		**MessageFormat** (String pattern, java.util.Locale locale)
	public	Object[]	**parse** (String source) throws ParseException
	public	Object[]	**parse** (String source, ParsePosition pos)
2	public	Object	parseObject (String source) throws ParseException
2	public	**Object**	parseObject (String source, ParsePosition pos)
	public	void	**setFormat** (int formatElementIndex, Format newFormat)
1.4	public	void	**setFormatByArgumentIndex** (int argumentIndex, Format newFormat)
	public	void	**setFormats** (Format[] newFormats)
1.4	public	void	**setFormatsByArgumentIndex** (Format[] newFormats)
	public	void	**setLocale** (java.util.Locale locale)
	public	String	**toPattern** ()

MessageFormat.Field   java.text

Object
| 1.2 | └AttributedCharacterIterator.Attribute [1] - - - - - - *java.io.Serializable* ⌣
| 1.4 | └Format.Field
| 1.4 | └MessageFormat.Field

▲	public static final		**ARGUMENT**
		MessageFormat.Field	
● 1	public final	boolean	equals (Object obj)
✳	protected		**MessageFormat.Field** (String name)
1	protected	String	getName ()
● 1	public final	int	hashCode ()
1	protected	**Object**	**readResolve** () throws java.io.InvalidObjectException
1	public	String	toString ()

MessageProp   org.ietf.jgss

Object
| 1.4 | └MessageProp

	public	int	**getMinorStatus** ()
	public	String	**getMinorString** ()
	public	boolean	**getPrivacy** ()
	public	int	**getQOP** ()
	public	boolean	**isDuplicateToken** ()
	public	boolean	**isGapToken** ()
	public	boolean	**isOldToken** ()
	public	boolean	**isUnseqToken** ()
✳	public		**MessageProp** (boolean privState)
✳	public		**MessageProp** (int qop, boolean privState)
	public	void	**setPrivacy** (boolean privState)
	public	void	**setQOP** (int qop)
	public	void	**setSupplementaryStates** (boolean duplicate, boolean old, boolean unseq, boolean gap, int minorStatus, String minorString)

Method   java.lang.reflect

Object [1]
| 1.2 | └AccessibleObject [2]
| 1.1 ● | └Method - *Member* [3]

1	public	**boolean**	equals (Object obj)	
3	public	Class	**getDeclaringClass** ()	
	public	Class[]	**getExceptionTypes** ()	
3	public	int	**getModifiers** ()	ε113
3	public	String	**getName** ()	ε109,291
	public	Class[]	**getParameterTypes** ()	ε118
	public	Class	**getReturnType** ()	ε118
1	public	**int**	**hashCode** ()	

Class *Interface* —extends - - -implements ○ abstract ● final △ static ▲ static final ✳ constructor x x—inherited x **x**—declared **x x**—overridden
εn—examples of usage ⌣—has subclass package—see other volume

M

		public .... Object **invoke** (Object obj, Object[] args) throws IllegalAccessException, IllegalArgumentException, InvocationTargetException	ε111,119
1.2	2	public .... boolean isAccessible ()	
1.2	2	public .... void setAccessible (boolean flag) throws SecurityException	ε110
1.2 △	2	public static .... void setAccessible (AccessibleObject[] array, boolean flag) throws SecurityException	
	1	public .... **String toString** ()	

MethodDescriptor
java.beans

Object
  └ FeatureDescriptor [1] (1.1)
    └ MethodDescriptor (1.1)

	1	public .... *java.util.Enumeration* attributeNames ()	
	1	public .... String getDisplayName ()	
		public . java.lang.reflect.Method **getMethod** ()	
	1	public .... String getName ()	ε5,9
		public ... ParameterDescriptor[] **getParameterDescriptors** ()	
	1	public .... String getShortDescription ()	
	1	public .... Object getValue (String attributeName)	
	1	public .... boolean isExpert ()	
	1	public .... boolean isHidden ()	
1.2	1	public .... boolean isPreferred ()	
*		public .... **MethodDescriptor** (java.lang.reflect.Method method)	
*		public .... **MethodDescriptor** (java.lang.reflect.Method method, ParameterDescriptor[] parameterDescriptors)	
	1	public .... void setDisplayName (String displayName)	
	1	public .... void setExpert (boolean expert)	
	1	public .... void setHidden (boolean hidden)	
	1	public .... void setName (String name)	
1.2	1	public .... void setPreferred (boolean preferred)	
	1	public .... void setShortDescription (String text)	
	1	public .... void setValue (String attributeName, Object value)	ε9

M

MissingResourceException
java.util

Object   ε310
  └ Throwable - *java.io.Serializable*
    └ Exception
      └ RuntimeException
        └ MissingResourceException (1.1)

	public .... String **getClassName** ()	
	public .... String **getKey** ()	
*	public .... **MissingResourceException** (String s, String className, String key)	

ModificationItem
javax.naming.directory

Object [1]
  └ ModificationItem - *java.io.Serializable* (1.3)

	public .... *Attribute* **getAttribute** ()	
	public .... int **getModificationOp** ()	
*	public .... **ModificationItem** (int mod_op, *Attribute* attr)	ε483
1	public .... **String toString** ()	

Modifier
java.lang.reflect

Object
  └ Modifier (1.1)

▲	public static final .... int **ABSTRACT** = 1024	
▲	public static final .... int **FINAL** = 16	
▲	public static final .... int **INTERFACE** = 512	
△	public static .... boolean **isAbstract** (int mod)	
△	public static .... boolean **isFinal** (int mod)	
△	public static .... boolean **isInterface** (int mod)	
△	public static .... boolean **isNative** (int mod)	
△	public static .... boolean **isPrivate** (int mod)	

Classes

Modifier

△	public static	boolean	**isProtected** (int mod)	
△	public static	boolean	**isPublic** (int mod)	*ε*112,113
△	public static	boolean	**isStatic** (int mod)	
1.2 △	public static	boolean	**isStrict** (int mod)	
△	public static	boolean	**isSynchronized** (int mod)	
△	public static	boolean	**isTransient** (int mod)	
△	public static	boolean	**isVolatile** (int mod)	
✳	public		**Modifier** ()	
▲	public static final	int	**NATIVE** = 256	
▲	public static final	int	**PRIVATE** = 2	
▲	public static final	int	**PROTECTED** = 4	
▲	public static final	int	**PUBLIC** = 1	
▲	public static final	int	**STATIC** = 8	
1.2 ▲	public static final	int	**STRICT** = 2048	
▲	public static final	int	**SYNCHRONIZED** = 32	
△	public static	String	**toString** (int mod)	
▲	public static final	int	**TRANSIENT** = 128	
▲	public static final	int	**VOLATILE** = 64	

MulticastSocket   java.net

Object
└DatagramSocket[1]
1.1   └MulticastSocket

	1	*29 inherited members from DatagramSocket not shown*	
1.4		public	InetAddress **getInterface** () throws SocketException
1.4		public	boolean **getLoopbackMode** () throws SocketException
1.4		public	NetworkInterface **getNetworkInterface** () throws SocketException
1.2		public	int **getTimeToLive** () throws java.io.IOException
D		public	byte **getTTL** () throws java.io.IOException
		public	void **joinGroup** (InetAddress mcastaddr) throws java.io.IOException *ε*153
1.4		public	void **joinGroup** (SocketAddress mcastaddr, NetworkInterface netIf) throws java.io.IOException
		public	void **leaveGroup** (InetAddress mcastaddr) throws java.io.IOException
1.4		public	void **leaveGroup** (SocketAddress mcastaddr, NetworkInterface netIf) throws java.io.IOException
✳		public	**MulticastSocket** () throws java.io.IOException
✳		public	**MulticastSocket** (int port) throws java.io.IOException *ε*153
1.4 ✳		public	**MulticastSocket** (SocketAddress bindaddr) throws java.io.IOException
	1	public synchronized	void receive (DatagramPacket p) throws java.io.IOException *ε*154,152
D		public	void **send** (DatagramPacket p, byte ttl) throws java.io.IOException
		public	void **setInterface** (InetAddress inf) throws SocketException
1.4		public	void **setLoopbackMode** (boolean disable) throws SocketException
1.4		public	void **setNetworkInterface** (NetworkInterface netIf) throws SocketException
1.2		public	void **setTimeToLive** (int ttl) throws java.io.IOException
D		public	void **setTTL** (byte ttl) throws java.io.IOException

---

MultipleComponentProfileHelper   org.omg.IOP

Object
1.4 ○   └MultipleComponentProfileHelper

△	public static	TaggedComponent[]	**extract** (org.omg.CORBA.Any a)
△	public static	String	**id** ()
△	public static	void	**insert** (org.omg.CORBA.Any a, TaggedComponent[] that)
✳	public		**MultipleComponentProfileHelper** ()
△	public static	TaggedComponent[]	**read** (org.omg.CORBA.portable.InputStream istream)
△	public static synchronized	org.omg.CORBA.TypeCode	**type** ()
△	public static	void	**write** (org.omg.CORBA.portable.OutputStream ostream, TaggedComponent[] value)

Class *Interface* —extends ---implements ○ abstract ● final △ static ▲ static final ✳ constructor × x—inherited × **x**—declared **x x**—overridden
εn—examples of usage ⌐has subclass package—see other volume

648

MultipleComponentProfileHolder
org.omg.IOP

Object
1.4 ● └MultipleComponentProfileHolder ----------- *org.omg.CORBA.portable.Streamable* [1]

1	public	void	**_read** (org.omg.CORBA.portable.InputStream i)
1	public		**_type** ()
	. org.omg.CORBA.TypeCode		
1	public	void	**_write** (org.omg.CORBA.portable.OutputStream o)
*	public		**MultipleComponentProfileHolder** ()
*	public		**MultipleComponentProfileHolder** (TaggedComponent[] initialValue)
	public	TaggedComponent[]	**value**

Name
javax.naming

1.3 *Name*————————————————*Cloneable*, *java.io.Serializable*

public	*Name*	**add** (String comp) throws InvalidNameException	ε480
public	*Name*	**add** (int posn, String comp) throws InvalidNameException	ε480
public	*Name*	**addAll** (*Name* suffix) throws InvalidNameException
public	*Name*	**addAll** (int posn, *Name* n) throws InvalidNameException
public	Object	**clone** ()
public	int	**compareTo** (Object obj)
public	boolean	**endsWith** (*Name* n)
public	String	**get** (int posn)	ε479
public	*java.util.Enumeration*	**getAll** ()
public	*Name*	**getPrefix** (int posn)
public	*Name*	**getSuffix** (int posn)
public	boolean	**isEmpty** ()
public	Object	**remove** (int posn) throws InvalidNameException	ε480
public	int	**size** ()	ε479
public	boolean	**startsWith** (*Name* n)

NameAlreadyBoundException
javax.naming

Object
└Throwable --------------------------- *java.io.Serializable*
 └Exception
1.3   └NamingException [1]
1.3   └NameAlreadyBoundException

1 *20 inherited members from NamingException not shown*
* public **NameAlreadyBoundException** ()
* public **NameAlreadyBoundException** (String explanation)

NameCallback
javax.security.auth.callback

Object
1.4 └NameCallback ------------------------ *Callback*, *java.io.Serializable*

public	String	**getDefaultName** ()
public	String	**getName** ()
public	String	**getPrompt** ()	ε509
* public		**NameCallback** (String prompt)
* public		**NameCallback** (String prompt, String defaultName)
public	void	**setName** (String name)	ε509

NameClassPair
javax.naming

Object [1]   ε474,496
1.3 └NameClassPair ----------------------- *java.io.Serializable*

public	String	**getClassName** ()
public	String	**getName** ()
public	boolean	**isRelative** ()
* public		**NameClassPair** (String name, String className)
* public		**NameClassPair** (String name, String className, boolean isRelative)
public	void	**setClassName** (String name)
public	void	**setName** (String name)
public	void	**setRelative** (boolean r)

NameClassPair

| | 1 | public................... **String toString** () |

NameComponent

Object
1.2 ● └NameComponent ----------------------- *org.omg.CORBA.portable.IDLEntity* ˎ (*java.io.Serializable*)

	public.....................String	**id**
	public.....................String	**kind**
*	public...........................	**NameComponent** ()
*	public...........................	**NameComponent** (String _id, String _kind)

NameComponentHelper

Object
1.2 ○ └NameComponentHelper

△	public static .NameComponent	**extract** (org.omg.CORBA.Any a)
△	public static ....String	**id** ()
△	public static ....void	**insert** (org.omg.CORBA.Any a, NameComponent that)
1.4 *	public...........................	**NameComponentHelper** ()
△	public static .NameComponent	**read** (org.omg.CORBA.portable.InputStream istream)
△	public static synchronized .... . org.omg.CORBA.TypeCode	**type** ()
△	public static ....void	**write** (org.omg.CORBA.portable.OutputStream ostream, NameComponent value)

NameComponentHolder

Object
1.2 ● └NameComponentHolder ----------------- *org.omg.CORBA.portable.Streamable* ˎ [1]

1	public.......................void	**_read** (org.omg.CORBA.portable.InputStream i)
1	public........................... . org.omg.CORBA.TypeCode	**_type** ()
1	public.......................void	**_write** (org.omg.CORBA.portable.OutputStream o)
*	public...........................	**NameComponentHolder** ()
*	public...........................	**NameComponentHolder** (NameComponent initialValue)
	public........NameComponent	**value**

NamedNodeMap

1.4   *NamedNodeMap*

public.....................int	**getLength** ()	ε528,529,533,536,537
public.....................*Node*	**getNamedItem** (String name)	
public.....................*Node*	**getNamedItemNS** (String namespaceURI, String localName)	
public.....................*Node*	**item** (int index)	ε528,529,533,536,537
public.....................*Node*	**removeNamedItem** (String name) throws DOMException	ε537
public.....................*Node*	**removeNamedItemNS** (String namespaceURI, String localName) throws DOMException	
public.....................*Node*	**setNamedItem** (*Node* arg) throws DOMException	ε533
public.....................*Node*	**setNamedItemNS** (*Node* arg) throws DOMException	

NamedValue

Object
1.2 ○ └NamedValue

○	public abstract ....int	**flags** ()
○	public abstract ....String	**name** ()
*	public...........................	**NamedValue** ()
○	public abstract .... Any	**value** ()

Class *Interface* —extends - - -implements ○ abstract ● final △ static ▲ static final ✳ constructor × x—inherited × **x**—declared **x x**—overridden
ε*n*—examples of usage ˎ—has subclass package—see other volume

NameDynAnyPair | org.omg.DynamicAny

Object
1.4 ● └NameDynAnyPair - *org.omg.CORBA.portable.IDLEntity* ⌐ (*java.io.Serializable*)

	public . . . . String	**id**
*	public	**NameDynAnyPair** ()
*	public	**NameDynAnyPair** (String _id, *DynAny* _value)
	public . . . . *DynAny*	**value**

NameDynAnyPairHelper | org.omg.DynamicAny

Object
1.4 ○ └NameDynAnyPairHelper

△	public static . NameDynAnyPair	**extract** (org.omg.CORBA.Any a)
△	public static . . . . String	**id** ()
△	public static . . . . void	**insert** (org.omg.CORBA.Any a, NameDynAnyPair that)
*	public	**NameDynAnyPairHelper** ()
△	public static . NameDynAnyPair	**read** (org.omg.CORBA.portable.InputStream istream)
△	public static synchronized . . . . . org.omg.CORBA.TypeCode	**type** ()
△	public static . . . . void	**write** (org.omg.CORBA.portable.OutputStream ostream, NameDynAnyPair value)

NameDynAnyPairSeqHelper | org.omg.DynamicAny

Object
1.4 ○ └NameDynAnyPairSeqHelper

△	public static . . . . NameDynAnyPair[]	**extract** (org.omg.CORBA.Any a)
△	public static . . . . String	**id** ()
△	public static . . . . void	**insert** (org.omg.CORBA.Any a, NameDynAnyPair[] that)
*	public	**NameDynAnyPairSeqHelper** ()
△	public static . . . . NameDynAnyPair[]	**read** (org.omg.CORBA.portable.InputStream istream)
△	public static synchronized . . . . . org.omg.CORBA.TypeCode	**type** ()
△	public static . . . . void	**write** (org.omg.CORBA.portable.OutputStream ostream, NameDynAnyPair[] value)

NameHelper | org.omg.CosNaming

Object
1.2 ○ └NameHelper

△	public static . . . . NameComponent[]	**extract** (org.omg.CORBA.Any a)
△	public static . . . . String	**id** ()
△	public static . . . . void	**insert** (org.omg.CORBA.Any a, NameComponent[] that)
1.4 *	public	**NameHelper** ()
△	public static . . . . NameComponent[]	**read** (org.omg.CORBA.portable.InputStream istream)
△	public static synchronized . . . . . org.omg.CORBA.TypeCode	**type** ()
△	public static . . . . void	**write** (org.omg.CORBA.portable.OutputStream ostream, NameComponent[] value)

NameHolder | org.omg.CosNaming

Object
1.2 ● └NameHolder - *org.omg.CORBA.portable.Streamable* ⌐ [1]

1	public . . . . void	**_read** (org.omg.CORBA.portable.InputStream i)
1	public . . . . org.omg.CORBA.TypeCode	**_type** ()
1	public . . . . void	**_write** (org.omg.CORBA.portable.OutputStream o)
*	public	**NameHolder** ()
*	public	**NameHolder** (NameComponent[] initialValue)
	public . . . . . . NameComponent[]	**value**

N

Classes

NameNotFoundException

NameNotFoundException		javax.naming

Object
└Throwable ------------------------- *java.io.Serializable*
  └Exception
1.3   └NamingException [1]
1.3   └NameNotFoundException

  [1] *20 inherited members from NamingException not shown*
✻ public......................... **NameNotFoundException** ()
✻ public......................... **NameNotFoundException** (String explanation)

NameParser		javax.naming

1.3 *NameParser*

  public.....................*Name* **parse** (String name) throws NamingException   ε480

NamespaceChangeListener		javax.naming.event

1.3 *NamespaceChangeListener*————————*NamingListener* [1] *(java.util.EventListener)* ε2,3,333,493,494

  [1] public.......................void namingExceptionThrown (NamingExceptionEvent evt) ε493,494
    public.......................void **objectAdded** (NamingEvent evt) ε493
    public.......................void **objectRemoved** (NamingEvent evt) ε493
    public.......................void **objectRenamed** (NamingEvent evt) ε493

NamespaceSupport		org.xml.sax.helpers

Object
1.4 └NamespaceSupport

  public.................. boolean **declarePrefix** (String prefix, String uri)
  public.... *java.util.Enumeration* **getDeclaredPrefixes** ()
  public.................... String **getPrefix** (String uri)
  public.... *java.util.Enumeration* **getPrefixes** ()
  public.... *java.util.Enumeration* **getPrefixes** (String uri)
  public.................... String **getURI** (String prefix)
✻ public......................... **NamespaceSupport** ()
  public.......................void **popContext** ()
  public.................... String[] **processName** (String qName, String[] parts, boolean isAttribute)
  public.......................void **pushContext** ()
  public.......................void **reset** ()
▲ public static final .... String **XMLNS** = "http://www.w3.org/XML/1998/namespace"

NameValuePair ❶		org.omg.CORBA

Object
1.2 ● └NameValuePair ----------------------- *org.omg.CORBA.portable.IDLEntity* (*java.io.Serializable*)

  public.................... String **id**
✻ public......................... **NameValuePair** ()
✻ public......................... **NameValuePair** (String __id, Any __value)
  public..................... Any **value**

NameValuePair ❷		org.omg.DynamicAny

Object
1.4 ● └NameValuePair ----------------------- *org.omg.CORBA.portable.IDLEntity* (*java.io.Serializable*)

  public.................... String **id**
✻ public......................... **NameValuePair** ()
✻ public......................... **NameValuePair** (String _id, org.omg.CORBA.Any _value)
  public....org.omg.CORBA.Any **value**

Class *Interface* —extends - - -implements ○ abstract ● final △ static ▲ static final ✻ constructor x x—inherited x **x**—declared **x x**—overridden
ε*n*—examples of usage ⌐—has subclass package—see other volume

NameValuePairHelper❶		org.omg.CORBA

	Object	
1.3 O	└NameValuePairHelper	

△	public static ... NameValuePair	**extract** (Any a)
△	public static .... String	**id** ()
△	public static .... void	**insert** (Any a, NameValuePair that)
∗	public.........................	**NameValuePairHelper** ()
△	public static ... NameValuePair	**read** (org.omg.CORBA.portable.InputStream istream)
△	public static synchronized	**type** ()
	.... TypeCode	
△	public static .... void	**write** (org.omg.CORBA.portable.OutputStream ostream, NameValuePair value)

NameValuePairHelper❷		org.omg.DynamicAny

	Object	
1.4 O	└NameValuePairHelper	

△	public static ... NameValuePair	**extract** (org.omg.CORBA.Any a)
△	public static .... String	**id** ()
△	public static .... void	**insert** (org.omg.CORBA.Any a, NameValuePair that)
∗	public.........................	**NameValuePairHelper** ()
△	public static ... NameValuePair	**read** (org.omg.CORBA.portable.InputStream istream)
△	public static synchronized	**type** ()
	. org.omg.CORBA.TypeCode	
△	public static .... void	**write** (org.omg.CORBA.portable.OutputStream ostream, NameValuePair value)

NameValuePairSeqHelper		org.omg.DynamicAny

	Object	
1.4 O	└NameValuePairSeqHelper	

△	public static ..NameValuePair[]	**extract** (org.omg.CORBA.Any a)
△	public static .... String	**id** ()
△	public static .... void	**insert** (org.omg.CORBA.Any a, NameValuePair[] that)
∗	public.........................	**NameValuePairSeqHelper** ()
△	public static ..NameValuePair[]	**read** (org.omg.CORBA.portable.InputStream istream)
△	public static synchronized	**type** ()
	. org.omg.CORBA.TypeCode	
△	public static .... void	**write** (org.omg.CORBA.portable.OutputStream ostream, NameValuePair[] value)

Naming		java.rmi

	Object	
1.1 ●	└Naming	

△	public static .... void	**bind** (String name, *Remote* obj) throws AlreadyBoundException, java.net.MalformedURLException, RemoteException
△	public static .... String[]	**list** (String name) throws RemoteException, java.net.MalformedURLException
△	public static ....*Remote*	**lookup** (String name) throws NotBoundException, java.net.MalformedURLException, RemoteException ε189
△	public static .... void	**rebind** (String name, *Remote* obj) throws RemoteException, java.net.MalformedURLException ε188
△	public static .... void	**unbind** (String name) throws RemoteException, NotBoundException, java.net.MalformedURLException

NamingContext		org.omg.CosNaming

1.2	*NamingContext* ——————————————— *NamingContextOperations* [1], *org.omg.CORBA.Object* [2], *org.omg.CORBA.portable.IDLEntity* (*java.io.Serializable*)	

> 2 *13 inherited members from org.omg.CORBA.Object not shown*
> 1 *10 inherited members from NamingContextOperations not shown*

NamingContextExt · org.omg.CosNaming

1.4	*NamingContextExt*————————————	*NamingContextExtOperations* [1] (*NamingContextOperations* [2]), *NamingContext* (*NamingContextOperations* [2], *org.omg.CORBA.Object* [3], *org.omg.CORBA.portable.IDLEntity* (*java.io.Serializable*)), *org.omg.CORBA.portable.IDLEntity* (*java.io.Serializable*)

      [3] *13 inherited members from org.omg.CORBA.Object not shown*
      [2] *10 inherited members from NamingContextOperations not shown*
      [1] *4 inherited members from NamingContextExtOperations not shown*

NamingContextExtHelper · org.omg.CosNaming

Object
1.4 ○ └NamingContextExtHelper

△	public static *NamingContextExt*	**extract** (org.omg.CORBA.Any a)
△	public static .... String	**id** ()
△	public static .... void	**insert** (org.omg.CORBA.Any a, *NamingContextExt* that)
✳	public.........................	**NamingContextExtHelper** ()
△	public static *NamingContextExt*	**narrow** (*org.omg.CORBA.Object* obj)
△	public static *NamingContextExt*	**read** (org.omg.CORBA.portable.InputStream istream)
△	public static synchronized .... . org.omg.CORBA.TypeCode	**type** ()
△	public static ....void	**write** (org.omg.CORBA.portable.OutputStream ostream, *NamingContextExt* value)

NamingContextExtHolder · org.omg.CosNaming

Object
1.4 ● └NamingContextExtHolder - - - - - - - - - - - - - - - - *org.omg.CORBA.portable.Streamable* [1]

[1]	public.......................void	**_read** (org.omg.CORBA.portable.InputStream i)
[1]	public......................... . org.omg.CORBA.TypeCode	**_type** ()
[1]	public.......................void	**_write** (org.omg.CORBA.portable.OutputStream o)
✳	public.........................	**NamingContextExtHolder** ()
✳	public.........................	**NamingContextExtHolder** (*NamingContextExt* initialValue)
	public....... *NamingContextExt*	**value**

NamingContextExtOperations · org.omg.CosNaming

1.4	*NamingContextExtOperations*————————	*NamingContextOperations* [1]

     [1] *10 inherited members from NamingContextOperations not shown*

	public *org.omg.CORBA.Object*	**resolve_str** (String sn) throws org.omg.CosNaming.NamingContextPackage ↵ .NotFound, org.omg.CosNaming.NamingContextPackage.CannotProceed, org.omg.CosNaming.NamingContextPackage.InvalidName
	public...... NameComponent[]	**to_name** (String sn) throws org.omg.CosNaming.NamingContextPackage ↵ .InvalidName
	public................... String	**to_string** (NameComponent[] n) throws org.omg.CosNaming ↵ .NamingContextPackage.InvalidName
	public................... String	**to_url** (String addr, String sn) throws org.omg.CosNaming ↵ .NamingContextExtPackage.InvalidAddress, org.omg.CosNaming ↵ .NamingContextPackage.InvalidName

NamingContextExtPOA · org.omg.CosNaming

Object
1.4 ○ └org.omg.PortableServer.Servant [1]
1.4 ○   └NamingContextExtPOA - - - - - - - - - - - - - - - - *NamingContextExtOperations* (*NamingContextOperations*), *org.omg.CORBA.portable.InvokeHandler* [2]

     [1] *11 inherited members from org.omg.PortableServer.Servant not shown*
     [1] public................. **String[] _all_interfaces** (*org.omg.PortableServer.POA* poa, byte[] objectId)

Class   *Interface*   —extends   - - -implements   ○ abstract   ● final   △ static   ▲ static final   ✳ constructor   x x—inherited   x **x**—declared   **x x**—overridden
ε*n*—examples of usage   ⌐—has subclass   package—see other volume

```
  2  public...... org.omg.CORBA ↵  _invoke (String $method, org.omg.CORBA.portable.InputStream in,
         .portable.OutputStream     org.omg.CORBA.portable.ResponseHandler $rh)
     public.......NamingContextExt  _this ()
     public.......NamingContextExt  _this (org.omg.CORBA.ORB orb)
  *  public..........................  NamingContextExtPOA ()
```

NamingContextHelper org.omg.CosNaming

```
       Object
1.2 ○   └─NamingContextHelper
```

```
  △  public static ... NamingContext extract (org.omg.CORBA.Any a)
  △  public static ..............String id ()
  △  public static ................void insert (org.omg.CORBA.Any a, NamingContext that)
1.4 *  public..........................  NamingContextHelper ()
  △  public static ... NamingContext narrow (org.omg.CORBA.Object obj)
  △  public static ... NamingContext read (org.omg.CORBA.portable.InputStream istream)
  △  public static synchronized .... type ()
     . org.omg.CORBA.TypeCode
  △  public static ................void write (org.omg.CORBA.portable.OutputStream ostream, NamingContext value)
```

NamingContextHolder org.omg.CosNaming   **N**

```
       Object
1.2 ●   └─NamingContextHolder - - - - - - - - - - - - - - - - - - - org.omg.CORBA.portable.Streamable ⌐¹
```

```
  1  public..........................void _read (org.omg.CORBA.portable.InputStream i)
  1  public..........................  _type ()
     . org.omg.CORBA.TypeCode
  1  public..........................void _write (org.omg.CORBA.portable.OutputStream o)
  *  public..........................  NamingContextHolder ()
  *  public..........................  NamingContextHolder (NamingContext initialValue)
     public.......... NamingContext value
```

NamingContextOperations org.omg.CosNaming

```
1.3    NamingContextOperations ⌐
- - - - - - - - - - - - - - - - - - - - - - - - - - - - - - - - - - - - - - - - - - - - - - - - - - -
     public......................void bind (NameComponent[] n, org.omg.CORBA.Object obj)
                              throws org.omg.CosNaming.NamingContextPackage.NotFound,
                              org.omg.CosNaming.NamingContextPackage.CannotProceed,
                              org.omg.CosNaming.NamingContextPackage.InvalidName,
                              org.omg.CosNaming.NamingContextPackage.AlreadyBound
     public......................void bind_context (NameComponent[] n, NamingContext nc)
                              throws org.omg.CosNaming.NamingContextPackage.NotFound,
                              org.omg.CosNaming.NamingContextPackage.CannotProceed,
                              org.omg.CosNaming.NamingContextPackage.InvalidName,
                              org.omg.CosNaming.NamingContextPackage.AlreadyBound
     public.......... NamingContext bind_new_context (NameComponent[] n) throws
                              org.omg.CosNaming.NamingContextPackage.NotFound,
                              org.omg.CosNaming.NamingContextPackage.AlreadyBound,
                              org.omg.CosNaming.NamingContextPackage.CannotProceed,
                              org.omg.CosNaming.NamingContextPackage.InvalidName
     public......................void destroy () throws org.omg.CosNaming.NamingContextPackage.NotEmpty
     public......................void list (int how_many, BindingListHolder bl, BindingIteratorHolder bi)
     public.......... NamingContext new_context ()
     public......................void rebind (NameComponent[] n, org.omg.CORBA.Object obj)
                              throws org.omg.CosNaming.NamingContextPackage.NotFound,
                              org.omg.CosNaming.NamingContextPackage.CannotProceed,
                              org.omg.CosNaming.NamingContextPackage.InvalidName
     public......................void rebind_context (NameComponent[] n, NamingContext nc)
                              throws org.omg.CosNaming.NamingContextPackage.NotFound,
                              org.omg.CosNaming.NamingContextPackage.CannotProceed,
                              org.omg.CosNaming.NamingContextPackage.InvalidName
     public org.omg.CORBA.Object resolve (NameComponent[] n) throws org.omg ↵
                              .CosNaming.NamingContextPackage.NotFound, org ↵
                              .omg.CosNaming.NamingContextPackage.CannotProceed,
                              org.omg.CosNaming.NamingContextPackage.InvalidName
```

Classes

```
public.....................void  unbind (NameComponent[] n) throws org.omg ←
                              .CosNaming.NamingContextPackage.NotFound, org ←
                              .omg.CosNaming.NamingContextPackage.CannotProceed,
                              org.omg.CosNaming.NamingContextPackage.InvalidName
```

NamingContextPOA   org.omg.CosNaming

```
            Object
1.4 ○       └org.omg.PortableServer.Servant [1]
1.4 ○        └NamingContextPOA - - - - - - - - - - - - - - - - - - NamingContextOperations, org.omg.CORBA.portable ←
                                                                   .InvokeHandler [2]
```

1	*11 inherited members from org.omg.PortableServer.Servant not shown*		
1	public.................. **String[]**	**_all_interfaces** (*org.omg.PortableServer.POA* poa, byte[] objectId)	
2	public......org.omg.CORBA ←	**_invoke** (String $method, org.omg.CORBA.InputStream in,	
	.portable.OutputStream	*org.omg.CORBA.portable.ResponseHandler* $rh)	
	public.......... *NamingContext*	**_this** ()	
	public.......... *NamingContext*	**_this** (org.omg.CORBA.ORB orb)	
✳	public.........................	**NamingContextPOA** ()	

NamingEnumeration   javax.naming

```
1.3     NamingEnumeration──────────────────java.util.Enumeration [1]
```

	public.....................void	**close** () throws NamingException	ε489
	public..................boolean	**hasMore** () throws NamingException	ε474,482,486,487,488
1	public..................boolean	hasMoreElements ()	ε454,88,208,217,218
	public...................Object	**next** () throws NamingException	ε474,482,486,487,488
1	public...................Object	nextElement ()	ε454,88,208,217,218

NamingEvent   javax.naming.event

```
            Object                                                              ε333
1.1         └java.util.EventObject [1] - - - - - - - - - - - - - - - - - - - java.io.Serializable
1.3          └NamingEvent
```

	protected...............Object	**changeInfo**	
	public.....................void	**dispatch** (*NamingListener* listener)	
	public...................Object	**getChangeInfo** ()	
	public........... *EventContext*	**getEventContext** ()	
	public... javax.naming.Binding	**getNewBinding** ()	ε493,494
	public... javax.naming.Binding	**getOldBinding** ()	ε493,494
1	public...................Object	getSource ()	
	public.......................int	**getType** ()	
✳	public.........................	**NamingEvent** (*EventContext* source, int type, javax.naming.Binding newBd,	
		javax.naming.Binding oldBd, Object changeInfo)	
	protected.....................	**newBinding**	
	.... javax.naming.Binding		
▲	public static final............int	**OBJECT_ADDED** = 0	
▲	public static final............int	**OBJECT_CHANGED** = 3	
▲	public static final............int	**OBJECT_REMOVED** = 1	
▲	public static final............int	**OBJECT_RENAMED** = 2	
	protected.....................	**oldBinding**	
	.... javax.naming.Binding		
1	protected transient......Object	source	
1	public.....................String	toString ()	
	protected.....................int	**type**	

NamingException   javax.naming

```
            Object                                                   ε472,473,474,475,476
            └Throwable [1] - - - - - - - - - - - - - - - - - - - - - - - java.io.Serializable
             └Exception
1.3           └NamingException
```

public.....................void	**appendRemainingComponent** (String name)	
public.....................void	**appendRemainingName** (*Name* name)	

Class *Interface* ──extends - - -implements ○ abstract ● final △ static ▲ static final ✳ constructor x x─inherited x **x**─declared **x x**─overridden
ε*n*─examples of usage ╷─has subclass package─see other volume

```
        public ..................... String  getExplanation ()
        public ..................... Name    getRemainingName ()
        public ..................... Name    getResolvedName ()
        public ..................... Object  getResolvedObj ()
        public ................... Throwable getRootCause ()
  *     public .............................  NamingException ()
  *     public .............................  NamingException (String explanation)
  1     public ..................... void     printStackTrace ()
  1     public ..................... void     printStackTrace (java.io.PrintStream ps)
  1     public ..................... void     printStackTrace (java.io.PrintWriter pw)
        protected ................. Name     remainingName
        protected ................. Name     resolvedName
        protected ................. Object   resolvedObj
        protected ............... Throwable  rootException
        public ..................... void    setRemainingName (Name name)
        public ..................... void    setResolvedName (Name name)
        public ..................... void    setResolvedObj (Object obj)
        public ..................... void    setRootCause (Throwable e)
  1     public ..................... String   toString ()
        public ..................... String   toString (boolean detail)
```

NamingExceptionEvent — javax.naming.event

```
        Object                                                            ε333
  1.1   └java.util.EventObject¹ ------------------- java.io.Serializable.
  1.3      └NamingExceptionEvent
```

```
        public ..................... void         dispatch (NamingListener listener)
        public ............. EventContext          getEventContext ()
        public ..................... javax↵        getException ()                    ε493,494
              .naming.NamingException
  1     public ..................... Object       getSource ()
  *     public .............................        NamingExceptionEvent (EventContext source, javax.naming.NamingException
                                                    exc)
  1     protected transient ...... Object         source
  1     public ..................... String       toString ()
```

NamingListener — javax.naming.event

```
  1.3   NamingListener ─────────────────────java.util.EventListener.          ε493,494,2,3,333
  - - - - - - - - - - - - - - - - - - - - - - - - - - - - - - - - - - - - - - - - - - - - - -
        public ..................... void  namingExceptionThrown (NamingExceptionEvent evt)   ε493,494
```

NamingManager — javax.naming.spi

```
        Object
  1.3   └NamingManager.
```

```
  ▲     public static final ........ String  CPE = "java.naming.spi.CannotProceedException"
  △     public static ...................     getContinuationContext (javax.naming.CannotProceedException cpe)
              ........ javax.naming.Context      throws javax.naming.NamingException
  △     public static ...................     getInitialContext (java.util.Hashtable env) throws javax.naming.NamingException
              ........ javax.naming.Context
  △     public static ............. Object    getObjectInstance (Object refInfo, javax.naming.Name name, javax.naming↵
                                                .Context nameCtx, java.util.Hashtable environment) throws Exception
  △     public static ............. Object    getStateToBind (Object obj, javax.naming.Name name, javax.naming.Context
                                                nameCtx, java.util.Hashtable environment) throws javax.naming.NamingException
  △     public static ...................     getURLContext (String scheme, java.util.Hashtable environment)
              ........ javax.naming.Context      throws javax.naming.NamingException
  △     public static .......... boolean      hasInitialContextFactoryBuilder ()
  △     public static synchronized void       setInitialContextFactoryBuilder (InitialContextFactoryBuilder builder)
                                                throws javax.naming.NamingException
  △     public static synchronized void       setObjectFactoryBuilder (ObjectFactoryBuilder builder)
                                                throws javax.naming.NamingException
```

Classes

NamingSecurityException

		NamingSecurityException	javax.naming

```
        Object
        └Throwable ------------------------- java.io.Serializable.
          └Exception
1.3         └NamingException¹
1.3 O         └NamingSecurityException.
```

	1	*20 inherited members from NamingException not shown*	
✳		public......................... **NamingSecurityException** ()	
✳		public......................... **NamingSecurityException** (String explanation)	

		NegativeArraySizeException	java.lang

```
        Object
        └Throwable ------------------------- java.io.Serializable.
          └Exception
            └RuntimeException
              └NegativeArraySizeException
```

✳	public......................... **NegativeArraySizeException** ()
✳	public......................... **NegativeArraySizeException** (String s)

N

		NetPermission	java.net
			ε217,218

```
        Object
1.2 O   └java.security.Permission¹ --------------- java.security.Guard, java.io.Serializable.
1.2 O     └java.security.BasicPermission²
1.2 ●       └NetPermission
```

	1	public......................void	checkGuard (Object object) throws SecurityException	
	2	public................. boolean	equals (Object obj)	ε215
	2	public.....................String	getActions ()	ε215
●	1	public final ....String	getName ()	
	2	public.........................int	hashCode ()	ε215
	2	public................. boolean	implies (java.security.Permission p)	ε214,215
✳		public.........................	**NetPermission** (String name)	
✳		public.........................	**NetPermission** (String name, String actions)	
	2	public..........java.security↵	newPermissionCollection ()	
		.PermissionCollection		
	1	public....................String	toString ()	

		NetworkInterface	java.net

```
        Object¹
1.4 ●   └NetworkInterface
```

	1	public................. **boolean**	**equals** (Object obj)
△		public static native.............	**getByInetAddress** (InetAddress addr) throws SocketException
		.... NetworkInterface	
△		public static native.............	**getByName** (String name) throws SocketException
		.... NetworkInterface	
		public.....................String	**getDisplayName** ()
		public.... *java.util.Enumeration*	**getInetAddresses** ()
		public.....................String	**getName** ()
△		public static	**getNetworkInterfaces** () throws SocketException
		.... *java.util.Enumeration*	
	1	public......................... **int**	**hashCode** ()
	1	public................. **String**	**toString** ()

Class *Interface* —extends - - -implements O abstract ● final △ static ▲ static final ✳ constructor x x—inherited x **x**—declared **x x**—overridden
ε*n*—examples of usage .—has subclass package—see other volume

	NO_IMPLEMENT	org.omg.CORBA

```
Object
 └Throwable ---------------------------- java.io.Serializable
   └Exception
     └RuntimeException
       └SystemException 1
         └NO_IMPLEMENT
```

1.2 ○
1.2 ●

	1	*3 inherited members from SystemException not shown*
*	public.........................	**NO_IMPLEMENT** ()
*	public.........................	**NO_IMPLEMENT** (String s)
*	public.........................	**NO_IMPLEMENT** (int minor, CompletionStatus completed)
*	public.........................	**NO_IMPLEMENT** (String s, int minor, CompletionStatus completed)

	NO_MEMORY	org.omg.CORBA

```
Object
 └Throwable ---------------------------- java.io.Serializable
   └Exception
     └RuntimeException
       └SystemException 1
         └NO_MEMORY
```

1.2 ○
1.2 ●

	1	*3 inherited members from SystemException not shown*
*	public.........................	**NO_MEMORY** ()
*	public.........................	**NO_MEMORY** (String s)
*	public.........................	**NO_MEMORY** (int minor, CompletionStatus completed)
*	public.........................	**NO_MEMORY** (String s, int minor, CompletionStatus completed)

N

	NO_PERMISSION	org.omg.CORBA

```
Object
 └Throwable ---------------------------- java.io.Serializable
   └Exception
     └RuntimeException
       └SystemException 1
         └NO_PERMISSION
```

1.2 ○
1.2 ●

	1	*3 inherited members from SystemException not shown*
*	public.........................	**NO_PERMISSION** ()
*	public.........................	**NO_PERMISSION** (String s)
*	public.........................	**NO_PERMISSION** (int minor, CompletionStatus completed)
*	public.........................	**NO_PERMISSION** (String s, int minor, CompletionStatus completed)

	NO_RESOURCES	org.omg.CORBA

```
Object
 └Throwable ---------------------------- java.io.Serializable
   └Exception
     └RuntimeException
       └SystemException 1
         └NO_RESOURCES
```

1.2 ○
1.2 ●

	1	*3 inherited members from SystemException not shown*
*	public.........................	**NO_RESOURCES** ()
*	public.........................	**NO_RESOURCES** (String s)
*	public.........................	**NO_RESOURCES** (int minor, CompletionStatus completed)
*	public.........................	**NO_RESOURCES** (String s, int minor, CompletionStatus completed)

Classes

	NO_RESPONSE	org.omg.CORBA

```
Object
 └Throwable ---------------------------- java.io.Serializable
   └Exception
     └RuntimeException
       └SystemException 1
         └NO_RESPONSE
```

1.2 ○
1.2 ●

NO_RESPONSE

NoClassDefFoundError   java.lang

```
Object
 └Throwable ---------------------------- java.io.Serializable
    └Error
       └LinkageError
          └NoClassDefFoundError
```

NoConnectionPendingException   java.nio.channels

```
Object
 └Throwable ---------------------------- java.io.Serializable
    └Exception
       └RuntimeException
          └IllegalStateException
             └NoConnectionPendingException
```
1.1
1.4

NoContext   org.omg.PortableServer.CurrentPackage

```
Object
 └Throwable ---------------------------- java.io.Serializable
    └Exception
1.2 ○    └org.omg.CORBA.UserException ------- org.omg.CORBA.portable.IDLEntity (java.io.Serializable)
1.4 ●       └NoContext
```

NoContextHelper   org.omg.PortableServer.CurrentPackage

```
Object
1.4 ○ └NoContextHelper
```

Node   org.w3c.dom

Class *Interface* —extends - - -implements ○ abstract ● final △ static ▲ static final ※ constructor x x—inherited x **x**—declared **x x**—overridden
ε*n*—examples of usage ⌣—has subclass package—see other volume

▲	public static final	short	**ELEMENT_NODE** = 1	ε544
▲	public static final	short	**ENTITY_NODE** = 6	
▲	public static final	short	**ENTITY_REFERENCE_NODE** = 5	
	public	*NamedNodeMap*	**getAttributes** ()	ε533,536,537
	public	*NodeList*	**getChildNodes** ()	ε524,527,529,544
	public	*Node*	**getFirstChild** ()	ε527,512
	public	*Node*	**getLastChild** ()	ε527
	public	String	**getLocalName** ()	
	public	String	**getNamespaceURI** ()	
	public	*Node*	**getNextSibling** ()	ε527,530,539
	public	String	**getNodeName** ()	ε529,537,544
	public	short	**getNodeType** ()	ε544
	public	String	**getNodeValue** () throws DOMException	ε536,541
	public	*Document*	**getOwnerDocument** ()	
	public	*Node*	**getParentNode** ()	ε527,544
	public	String	**getPrefix** ()	
	public	*Node*	**getPreviousSibling** ()	ε527
	public	boolean	**hasAttributes** ()	
	public	boolean	**hasChildNodes** ()	ε512
	public	*Node*	**insertBefore** (*Node* newChild, *Node* refChild) throws DOMException	
				ε525,539,541,542,547
	public	boolean	**isSupported** (String feature, String version)	
	public	void	**normalize** ()	ε547
▲	public static final	short	**NOTATION_NODE** = 12	
▲	public static final	short	**PROCESSING_INSTRUCTION_NODE** = 7	
	public	*Node*	**removeChild** (*Node* oldChild) throws DOMException	ε544,547,512
	public	*Node*	**replaceChild** (*Node* newChild, *Node* oldChild) throws DOMException	
				ε533
	public	void	**setNodeValue** (String nodeValue) throws DOMException	
	public	void	**setPrefix** (String prefix) throws DOMException	
▲	public static final	short	**TEXT_NODE** = 3	

NodeChangeEvent — java.util.prefs

```
       Object                                                      ε333
1.1    └java.util.EventObject¹ ------------------- java.io.Serializable⌐
1.4        └NodeChangeEvent
```

	public	Preferences	**getChild** ()	ε422
	public	Preferences	**getParent** ()	ε422
1	public	Object	getSource ()	
*	public		**NodeChangeEvent** (Preferences parent, Preferences child)	
1	protected transient	Object	source	
1	public	String	toString ()	

NodeChangeListener — java.util.prefs

```
1.4    NodeChangeListener——————————————java.util.EventListener⌐    ε2,3,333,493,494
```

	public	void	**childAdded** (NodeChangeEvent evt)	ε422
	public	void	**childRemoved** (NodeChangeEvent evt)	ε422

NodeList — org.w3c.dom

```
1.4    NodeList                                                    ε527
```

	public	int	**getLength** ()	ε524,529,532,541,542
	public	*Node*	**item** (int index)	ε524,525,526,529,532

NoInitialContextException — javax.naming

```
       Object
       └Throwable -------------------------- java.io.Serializable⌐
           └Exception
1.3            └NamingException¹
1.3                └NoInitialContextException
```

1	*20 inherited members from NamingException not shown*		
*	public	**NoInitialContextException** ()	
*	public	**NoInitialContextException** (String explanation)	

NonReadableChannelException

		java.nio.channels

Object
└Throwable - *java.io.Serializable*
  └Exception
    └RuntimeException
1.1   └IllegalStateException
1.4   └NonReadableChannelException

✳	public..........................	**NonReadableChannelException** ()

NonWritableChannelException

		java.nio.channels

Object
└Throwable - *java.io.Serializable*
  └Exception
    └RuntimeException
1.1   └IllegalStateException
1.4   └NonWritableChannelException

✳	public..........................	**NonWritableChannelException** ()

N

NoPermissionException

		javax.naming

Object
└Throwable - *java.io.Serializable*
  └Exception
1.3   └NamingException[1]
1.3 O   └NamingSecurityException
1.3   └NoPermissionException

[1]	*20 inherited members from NamingException not shown*
✳	public.......................... **NoPermissionException** ()
✳	public.......................... **NoPermissionException** (String explanation)

NoRouteToHostException

		java.net

Object
└Throwable - *java.io.Serializable*
  └Exception
    └java.io.IOException
      └SocketException
1.1   └NoRouteToHostException

✳	public..........................	**NoRouteToHostException** ()
✳	public..........................	**NoRouteToHostException** (String msg)

NoServant

		org.omg.PortableServer.POAPackage

Object
└Throwable - *java.io.Serializable*
  └Exception
1.2 O   └org.omg.CORBA.UserException - - - - - - *org.omg.CORBA.portable.IDLEntity* (*java.io.Serializable*)
1.4 ●   └NoServant

✳	public..........................	**NoServant** ()
✳	public..........................	**NoServant** (String $reason)

NoServantHelper

		org.omg.PortableServer.POAPackage

Object
1.4 O└NoServantHelper

△	public static ....NoServant **extract** (org.omg.CORBA.Any a)
△	public static ....String **id** ()

Class *Interface* —extends - - -implements O abstract ● final △ static ▲ static final ✳ constructor x x—inherited x **x**—declared **x x**—overridden
εn—examples of usage —has subclass package—see other volume

662

△	public static ....void	**insert** (org.omg.CORBA.Any a, NoServant that)
✳	public...........................	**NoServantHelper** ()
△	public static ....NoServant	**read** (org.omg.CORBA.portable.InputStream istream)
△	public static synchronized .... . org.omg.CORBA.TypeCode	**type** ()
△	public static ....void	**write** (org.omg.CORBA.portable.OutputStream ostream, NoServant value)

NoSuchAlgorithmException •   java.security

     Object   ε196,198,199,200,201

     └Throwable -------------------------- *java.io.Serializable*⌄

       └Exception

1.2   └GeneralSecurityException

1.1   └NoSuchAlgorithmException

✳	public...........................	**NoSuchAlgorithmException** ()
✳	public...........................	**NoSuchAlgorithmException** (String msg)

NoSuchAttributeException   javax.naming.directory

     Object

     └Throwable -------------------------- *java.io.Serializable*⌄

       └Exception

1.3   └javax.naming.NamingException[1]

1.3   └NoSuchAttributeException

	[1]	*20 inherited members from javax.naming.NamingException not shown*
✳	public...........................	**NoSuchAttributeException** ()
✳	public...........................	**NoSuchAttributeException** (String explanation)

NoSuchElementException   java.util

     Object

     └Throwable -------------------------- *java.io.Serializable*⌄

       └Exception

         └RuntimeException

           └NoSuchElementException

✳	public...........................	**NoSuchElementException** ()
✳	public...........................	**NoSuchElementException** (String s)

NoSuchFieldError   java.lang

     Object

     └Throwable -------------------------- *java.io.Serializable*⌄

       └Error

         └LinkageError

           └IncompatibleClassChangeError

              └NoSuchFieldError

✳	public...........................	**NoSuchFieldError** ()
✳	public...........................	**NoSuchFieldError** (String s)

NoSuchFieldException   java.lang

     Object   ε114

     └Throwable -------------------------- *java.io.Serializable*⌄

       └Exception

1.1   └NoSuchFieldException

✳	public...........................	**NoSuchFieldException** ()
✳	public...........................	**NoSuchFieldException** (String s)

N

Classes

NoSuchMethodError   java.lang

```
Object
└Throwable ----------------------------- java.io.Serializable
  └Error
    └LinkageError
      └IncompatibleClassChangeError
        └NoSuchMethodError
```

✱	public........................	**NoSuchMethodError** ()
✱	public........................	**NoSuchMethodError** (String s)

NoSuchMethodException   java.lang

ε116,118

```
Object
└Throwable ----------------------------- java.io.Serializable
  └Exception
    └NoSuchMethodException
```

✱	public........................	**NoSuchMethodException** ()
✱	public........................	**NoSuchMethodException** (String s)

N

NoSuchObjectException   java.rmi

```
Object
└Throwable ----------------------------- java.io.Serializable
  └Exception
    └java.io.IOException
      └RemoteException 1
        └NoSuchObjectException
```

	1	public...............	Throwable	detail
1.4	1	public...............	Throwable	getCause ()
	1	public...................	String	getMessage ()
✱		public........................		**NoSuchObjectException** (String s)

NoSuchPaddingException   javax.crypto

ε462,463,464,466

```
Object
└Throwable ----------------------------- java.io.Serializable
  └Exception
    └java.security.GeneralSecurityException
      └NoSuchPaddingException
```

1.2
1.4

✱	public........................	**NoSuchPaddingException** ()
✱	public........................	**NoSuchPaddingException** (String msg)

NoSuchProviderException   java.security

```
Object
└Throwable ----------------------------- java.io.Serializable
  └Exception
    └GeneralSecurityException
      └NoSuchProviderException
```

1.2
1.1

✱	public........................	**NoSuchProviderException** ()
✱	public........................	**NoSuchProviderException** (String msg)

Class   *Interface*   —extends   - - -implements   ○ abstract   ● final   △ static   ▲ static final   ✱ constructor   x x—inherited   x **x**—declared   **x x**—overridden
ε*n*—examples of usage   ⌣—has subclass   package—see other volume

	NotActiveException			java.io

```
      Object
      └Throwable ---------------------------- Serializable.
        └Exception
          └IOException
1.1 ○       └ObjectStreamException
1.1           └NotActiveException
```

*	public.........................	**NotActiveException** ()	
*	public.........................	**NotActiveException** (String reason)	

	Notation		org.w3c.dom
1.4	*Notation*————————————*Node*. [1]		ε524,526,529,530,532

	[1] *36 inherited members from Node not shown*			
	[1] public....................String	getNodeName ()		ε528,529,536,537,544
	public....................String	**getPublicId** ()		ε528
	public....................String	**getSystemId** ()		ε528

	NotBoundException		java.rmi

```
                                                        ε189
      Object
      └Throwable ---------------------------- java.io.Serializable.
        └Exception
1.1       └NotBoundException
```

*	public.........................	**NotBoundException** ()	
*	public.........................	**NotBoundException** (String s)	

	NotContextException		javax.naming

```
      Object
      └Throwable ---------------------------- java.io.Serializable.
        └Exception
1.3       └NamingException [1]
1.3         └NotContextException
```

	[1] *20 inherited members from NamingException not shown*		
*	public.........................	**NotContextException** ()	
*	public.........................	**NotContextException** (String explanation)	

	NotEmpty	org.omg.CosNaming.NamingContextPackage

```
      Object
      └Throwable ---------------------------- java.io.Serializable.
        └Exception
1.2 ○     └org.omg.CORBA.UserException ------- org.omg.CORBA.portable.IDLEntity. (java.io.Serializable)
1.2 ●       └NotEmpty
```

*	public.........................	**NotEmpty** ()	
1.4 *	public.........................	**NotEmpty** (String $reason)	

	NotEmptyHelper	org.omg.CosNaming.NamingContextPackage

```
      Object
1.2 ○ └NotEmptyHelper
```

△	public static .... NotEmpty	**extract** (org.omg.CORBA.Any a)	
△	public static ....String	**id** ()	
△	public static ....void	**insert** (org.omg.CORBA.Any a, NotEmpty that)	
1.4 *	public.........................	**NotEmptyHelper** ()	
△	public static .... NotEmpty	**read** (org.omg.CORBA.portable.InputStream istream)	
△	public static synchronized .... . org.omg.CORBA.TypeCode	**type** ()	
△	public static ....void	**write** (org.omg.CORBA.portable.OutputStream ostream, NotEmpty value)	

NotEmptyHolder	org.omg.CosNaming.NamingContextPackage

Object
1.2 ● └NotEmptyHolder ----------------------- *org.omg.CORBA.portable.Streamable* ⌐ [1]

1	public......................void	**_read** (org.omg.CORBA.portable.InputStream i)	
1	public..........................	**_type** ()	
	. org.omg.CORBA.TypeCode		
1	public......................void	**_write** (org.omg.CORBA.portable.OutputStream o)	
∗	public..........................	**NotEmptyHolder** ()	
∗	public..........................	**NotEmptyHolder** (NotEmpty initialValue)	
	public............... NotEmpty	**value**	

NotFound	org.omg.CosNaming.NamingContextPackage

Object
└Throwable -------------------------- *java.io.Serializable* ⌐
  └Exception
1.2 ○   └org.omg.CORBA.UserException ------- *org.omg.CORBA.portable.IDLEntity* ⌐ (*java.io.Serializable*)
1.2 ●   └NotFound

∗	public..........................	**NotFound** ()
∗	public..........................	**NotFound** (NotFoundReason _why, org.omg.CosNaming.NameComponent[] _rest_of_name)
1.4 ∗	public..........................	**NotFound** (String $reason, NotFoundReason _why, org.omg.CosNaming.NameComponent[] _rest_of_name)
	public . org.omg.CosNaming ↵ .NameComponent[]	**rest_of_name**
	public........ NotFoundReason	**why**

NotFoundHelper	org.omg.CosNaming.NamingContextPackage

Object
1.2 ○ └NotFoundHelper

△	public static .... NotFound	**extract** (org.omg.CORBA.Any a)	
△	public static ....String	**id** ()	
△	public static ....void	**insert** (org.omg.CORBA.Any a, NotFound that)	
1.4 ∗	public..........................	**NotFoundHelper** ()	
△	public static .... NotFound	**read** (org.omg.CORBA.portable.InputStream istream)	
△	public static synchronized .... . org.omg.CORBA.TypeCode	**type** ()	
△	public static ....void	**write** (org.omg.CORBA.portable.OutputStream ostream, NotFound value)	

NotFoundHolder	org.omg.CosNaming.NamingContextPackage

Object
1.2 ● └NotFoundHolder ----------------------- *org.omg.CORBA.portable.Streamable* ⌐ [1]

1	public......................void	**_read** (org.omg.CORBA.portable.InputStream i)	
1	public..........................	**_type** ()	
	. org.omg.CORBA.TypeCode		
1	public......................void	**_write** (org.omg.CORBA.portable.OutputStream o)	
∗	public..........................	**NotFoundHolder** ()	
∗	public..........................	**NotFoundHolder** (NotFound initialValue)	
	public............... NotFound	**value**	

NotFoundReason	org.omg.CosNaming.NamingContextPackage

Object
1.2 └NotFoundReason ---------------------- *org.omg.CORBA.portable.IDLEntity* ⌐ (*java.io.Serializable*)

▲	public static final.............int	**_missing_node** = 0	
▲	public static final.............int	**_not_context** = 1	
▲	public static final.............int	**_not_object** = 2	
△	public static . NotFoundReason	**from_int** (int value)	

Class *Interface* —extends - - -implements ○ abstract ● final △ static ▲ static final ∗ constructor x x—inherited x **x**—declared **x x**—overridden
ε*n*—examples of usage ⌐—has subclass package—see other volume

▲	public static final	**missing_node**
	. . . . NotFoundReason	
▲	public static final	**not_context**
	. . . . NotFoundReason	
▲	public static final	**not_object**
	. . . . NotFoundReason	
1.4 ✳	protected	**NotFoundReason** (int value)
	public . . . . int	**value** ()

NotFoundReasonHelper		org.omg.CosNaming.NamingContextPackage

	Object	
1.2 ○	└NotFoundReasonHelper	
△	public static . NotFoundReason	**extract** (org.omg.CORBA.Any a)
△	public static . . . . String	**id** ()
△	public static . . . . void	**insert** (org.omg.CORBA.Any a, NotFoundReason that)
1.4 ✳	public	**NotFoundReasonHelper** ()
△	public static . NotFoundReason	**read** (org.omg.CORBA.portable.InputStream istream)
△	public static synchronized	**type** ()
	. org.omg.CORBA.TypeCode	
△	public static . . . . void	**write** (org.omg.CORBA.portable.OutputStream ostream, NotFoundReason value)

NotFoundReasonHolder		org.omg.CosNaming.NamingContextPackage

	Object	
1.2 ●	└NotFoundReasonHolder - - - - - - - - - - - - - - - - - *org.omg.CORBA.portable.Streamable* [1]	
1	public . . . . void	**_read** (org.omg.CORBA.portable.InputStream i)
1	public	**_type** ()
	. org.omg.CORBA.TypeCode	
1	public . . . . void	**_write** (org.omg.CORBA.portable.OutputStream o)
✳	public	**NotFoundReasonHolder** ()
✳	public	**NotFoundReasonHolder** (NotFoundReason initialValue)
	public . . . . NotFoundReason	**value**

NotOwnerException	java.security.acl

	Object	
	└Throwable - *java.io.Serializable* ˯	
	└Exception	
1.1	└NotOwnerException	
✳	public	**NotOwnerException** ()

NotSerializableException	java.io

	Object	
	└Throwable - *Serializable* ˯	
	└Exception	
	└IOException	
1.1 ○	└ObjectStreamException	
1.1	└NotSerializableException	
✳	public	**NotSerializableException** ()
✳	public	**NotSerializableException** (String classname)

NotYetBoundException	java.nio.channels

	Object	
	└Throwable - *java.io.Serializable* ˯	
	└Exception	
	└RuntimeException	
1.1	└IllegalStateException	
1.4	└NotYetBoundException	
✳	public	**NotYetBoundException** ()

N

Classes

NotYetConnectedException

		java.nio.channels

```
Object
└Throwable ------------------------- java.io.Serializable ⌄
  └Exception
    └RuntimeException
```
1.1   └IllegalStateException
1.4   └NotYetConnectedException

✳	public.......................... **NotYetConnectedException** ()	

NullCipher

		javax.crypto

		ε461

```
        Object
1.4     └Cipher 1
1.4       └NullCipher
```

	1 *37 inherited members from Cipher not shown*	
✳	public.......................... **NullCipher** ()	

NullPointerException

		java.lang

```
Object
└Throwable ------------------------- java.io.Serializable ⌄
  └Exception
    └RuntimeException
      └NullPointerException
```

✳	public.......................... **NullPointerException** ()	
✳	public.......................... **NullPointerException** (String s)	

Number

		java.lang

		ε312,314,315

```
        Object
O       └Number ⌄ ------------------------- java.io.Serializable ⌄
```

1.1	public..................... byte **byteValue** ()	ε58
O	public abstract ....double **doubleValue** ()	ε58
O	public abstract ....float **floatValue** ()	ε58
O	public abstract.............int **intValue** ()	ε58,6,346
O	public abstract .... long **longValue** ()	ε58
✳	public.......................... **Number** ()	
1.1	public.....................short **shortValue** ()	ε58

NumberFormat

		java.text

```
          Object 1
1.1 O     └Format 2 ------------------------- java.io.Serializable ⌄, Cloneable ⌄
1.1 O       └NumberFormat ⌄
```

	2	public..................**Object** **clone** ()	
	1	public..................**boolean** **equals** (Object obj)	
●		public final ....String **format** (double number)	ε311,312,313,314,315
●	2	public final ....String format (Object obj)	ε316,320
●		public final ....String **format** (long number)	ε311
O		public abstract .... StringBuffer **format** (double number, StringBuffer toAppendTo, FieldPosition pos)	
●	2	public final ....**StringBuffer** format (Object number, StringBuffer toAppendTo, FieldPosition pos)	
O		public abstract .... StringBuffer **format** (long number, StringBuffer toAppendTo, FieldPosition pos)	
1.4	2	public........................... formatToCharacterIterator (Object obj)	
		.. *AttributedCharacterIterator*	
▲		public static final.............int **FRACTION_FIELD** = 1	
△		public static .. java.util.Locale[] **getAvailableLocales** ()	
1.4		public........ java.util.Currency **getCurrency** ()	
▲		public static final.............. **getCurrencyInstance** ()	
		...............NumberFormat	
△		public static ....NumberFormat **getCurrencyInstance** (java.util.Locale inLocale)	ε314

Class   *Interface*   —extends   - - -implements   O abstract   ● final   △ static   ▲ static final   ✳ constructor   x x—inherited   x **x**—declared   **x x**—overridden
ε*n*—examples of usage   ⌄—has subclass   package—see other volume

▲		public static final . . . . NumberFormat	**getInstance** ()	
	△	public static . . . . NumberFormat	**getInstance** (java.util.Locale inLocale)	
1.4	▲	public static final . . . . NumberFormat	**getIntegerInstance** ()	
1.4	△	public static . . . . NumberFormat	**getIntegerInstance** (java.util.Locale inLocale)	
		public . . . . int	**getMaximumFractionDigits** ()	
		public . . . . int	**getMaximumIntegerDigits** ()	
		public . . . . int	**getMinimumFractionDigits** ()	
		public . . . . int	**getMinimumIntegerDigits** ()	
▲		public static final . . . . NumberFormat	**getNumberInstance** ()	ε312
	△	public static . . . . NumberFormat	**getNumberInstance** (java.util.Locale inLocale)	ε312
▲		public static final . . . . NumberFormat	**getPercentInstance** ()	
	△	public static . . . . NumberFormat	**getPercentInstance** (java.util.Locale inLocale)	ε315
	1	public . . . . **int**	**hashCode** ()	
▲		public static final . . . . int	**INTEGER_FIELD** = 0	
		public . . . . boolean	**isGroupingUsed** ()	
		public . . . . boolean	**isParseIntegerOnly** ()	
*		public	**NumberFormat** ()	
		public . . . . Number	**parse** (String source) throws ParseException	ε312,314,315
○		public abstract . . . . Number	**parse** (String source, ParsePosition parsePosition)	
	2	public . . . . Object	parseObject (String source) throws ParseException	
●	2	public final . . . . **Object**	**parseObject** (String source, ParsePosition pos)	
1.4		public . . . . void	**setCurrency** (java.util.Currency currency)	
		public . . . . void	**setGroupingUsed** (boolean newValue)	
		public . . . . void	**setMaximumFractionDigits** (int newValue)	
		public . . . . void	**setMaximumIntegerDigits** (int newValue)	
		public . . . . void	**setMinimumFractionDigits** (int newValue)	
		public . . . . void	**setMinimumIntegerDigits** (int newValue)	
		public . . . . void	**setParseIntegerOnly** (boolean value)	

N

NumberFormat.Field   java.text

```
     Object
1.2  └─AttributedCharacterIterator.Attribute¹ - - - - - - - java.io.Serializable ↵
1.4     └─Format.Field
1.4        └─NumberFormat.Field
```

▲		public static final . . . . NumberFormat.Field	**CURRENCY**	
▲		public static final . . . . NumberFormat.Field	**DECIMAL_SEPARATOR**	
●	1	public final . . . . boolean	equals (Object obj)	
▲		public static final . . . . NumberFormat.Field	**EXPONENT**	
▲		public static final . . . . NumberFormat.Field	**EXPONENT_SIGN**	
▲		public static final . . . . NumberFormat.Field	**EXPONENT_SYMBOL**	
*		protected	**NumberFormat.Field** (String name)	
▲		public static final . . . . NumberFormat.Field	**FRACTION**	
	1	protected . . . . String	getName ()	
▲		public static final . . . . NumberFormat.Field	**GROUPING_SEPARATOR**	
●	1	public final . . . . int	hashCode ()	
▲		public static final . . . . NumberFormat.Field	**INTEGER**	
▲		public static final . . . . NumberFormat.Field	**PERCENT**	
▲		public static final . . . . NumberFormat.Field	**PERMILLE**	
	1	protected . . . . **Object**	**readResolve** () throws java.io.InvalidObjectException	
▲		public static final . . . . NumberFormat.Field	**SIGN**	
	1	public . . . . String	toString ()	

Classes

NumberFormatException			java.lang

```
Object
└ Throwable ------------------------------ java.io.Serializable.
  └ Exception
    └ RuntimeException
      └ IllegalArgumentException
        └ NumberFormatException
```

✳	public.........................	**NumberFormatException** ()	
✳	public.........................	**NumberFormatException** (String s)	

NVList		org.omg.CORBA

```
      Object
1.2 O └ NVList
```

O	public abstract ... NamedValue	**add** (int flags)	
O	public abstract ... NamedValue	**add_item** (String item_name, int flags)	
O	public abstract ... NamedValue	**add_value** (String item_name, Any val, int flags)	
O	public abstract .... int	**count** ()	
O	public abstract ... NamedValue	**item** (int index) throws Bounds	
✳	public.........................	**NVList** ()	
O	public abstract .... void	**remove** (int index) throws Bounds	

OBJ_ADAPTER		org.omg.CORBA

```
      Object
      └ Throwable ------------------------------ java.io.Serializable.
        └ Exception
          └ RuntimeException
1.2 O       └ SystemException [1]
1.2 ●         └ OBJ_ADAPTER
```

	1	*3 inherited members from SystemException not shown*	
✳	public.........................	**OBJ_ADAPTER** ()	
✳	public.........................	**OBJ_ADAPTER** (String s)	
✳	public.........................	**OBJ_ADAPTER** (int minor, CompletionStatus completed)	
✳	public.........................	**OBJ_ADAPTER** (String s, int minor, CompletionStatus completed)	

Object❶		java.lang
Object.		ε53,63,100,106,111

	protected native .... Object	**clone** () throws CloneNotSupportedException	ε56
	public................. boolean	**equals** (Object obj)	ε199,417,460
	protected .... void	**finalize** () throws Throwable	
●	public final native .... Class	**getClass** ()	ε59,62,67,120,121
	public native .... int	**hashCode** ()	
●	public final native .... void	**notify** ()	ε96,102
●	public final native .... void	**notifyAll** ()	
✳	public.........................	**Object** ()	ε62,97
	public.................... String	**toString** ()	
●	public final .... void	**wait** () throws InterruptedException	ε96,102
●	public final native .... void	**wait** (long timeout) throws InterruptedException	
●	public final .... void	**wait** (long timeout, int nanos) throws InterruptedException	

Object❷		org.omg.CORBA
1.2	*Object.*	

public................. Request	**_create_request** (Context ctx, String operation, NVList arg_list, NamedValue result)	
public................. Request	**_create_request** (Context ctx, String operation, NVList arg_list, NamedValue result, ExceptionList exclist, ContextList ctxlist)	
public.................... Object	**_duplicate** ()	
public....... DomainManager[]	**_get_domain_managers** ()	

Class *Interface* —extends - - -implements O abstract ● final △ static ▲ static final ✳ constructor x x—inherited x **x**—declared **x x**—overridden
ε*n*—examples of usage .—has subclass package—see other volume

public	Object	**_get_interface_def** ()
public	Policy	**_get_policy** (int policy_type)
public	int	**_hash** (int maximum)
public	boolean	**_is_a** (String repositoryIdentifier)
public	boolean	**_is_equivalent** (*Object* other)
public	boolean	**_non_existent** ()
public	void	**_release** ()
public	Request	**_request** (String operation)
public	Object	**_set_policy_override** (*Policy[]* policies, SetOverrideType set_add)

OBJECT_NOT_EXIST — org.omg.CORBA

```
Object
└Throwable ------------------------------ java.io.Serializable ┐
   └Exception
      └RuntimeException
1.2 ○        └SystemException¹
1.2 ●           └OBJECT_NOT_EXIST
```

	1	*3 inherited members from SystemException not shown*	
*	public	**OBJECT_NOT_EXIST** ()
*	public	**OBJECT_NOT_EXIST** (String s)
*	public	**OBJECT_NOT_EXIST** (int minor, CompletionStatus completed)
*	public	**OBJECT_NOT_EXIST** (String s, int minor, CompletionStatus completed)

O

ObjectAlreadyActive — org.omg.PortableServer.POAPackage

```
Object
└Throwable ------------------------------ java.io.Serializable ┐
   └Exception
1.2 ○     └org.omg.CORBA.UserException ------ org.omg.CORBA.portable.IDLEntity ┐ (java.io.Serializable)
1.4 ●        └ObjectAlreadyActive
```

*	public	**ObjectAlreadyActive** ()
*	public	**ObjectAlreadyActive** (String $reason)

ObjectAlreadyActiveHelper — org.omg.PortableServer.POAPackage

```
Object
1.4 ○ └ObjectAlreadyActiveHelper
```

△	public static ObjectAlreadyActive	**extract** (org.omg.CORBA.Any a)
△	public static String	**id** ()
△	public static void	**insert** (org.omg.CORBA.Any a, ObjectAlreadyActive that)
*	public	**ObjectAlreadyActiveHelper** ()
△	public static ObjectAlreadyActive	**read** (org.omg.CORBA.portable.InputStream istream)
△	public static synchronized org.omg.CORBA.TypeCode	**type** ()
△	public static void	**write** (org.omg.CORBA.portable.OutputStream ostream, ObjectAlreadyActive value)

Classes

ObjectChangeListener — javax.naming.event

1.3	*ObjectChangeListener*————————*NamingListener*¹ (*java.util.EventListener*)	ε2,3,333,493,494
1	public void namingExceptionThrown (NamingExceptionEvent evt)	ε494,493
	public void **objectChanged** (NamingEvent evt)	ε494

ObjectFactory — javax.naming.spi

1.3	*ObjectFactory* ┐	
	public Object **getObjectInstance** (Object obj, *javax.naming.Name* name, *javax.naming.Context* nameCtx, java.util.Hashtable environment) throws Exception	

ObjectFactoryBuilder			javax.naming.spi

1.3 | *ObjectFactoryBuilder*

public.......... *ObjectFactory* **createObjectFactory** (Object obj, java.util.Hashtable environment)
throws javax.naming.NamingException

ObjectHelper	org.omg.CORBA

Object
1.3 ○ └ObjectHelper

△	public static .... *Object* **extract** (Any a)
△	public static ....String **id** ()
△	public static ....void **insert** (Any a, *Object* that)
✳	public........................ **ObjectHelper** ()
△	public static .... *Object* **read** (org.omg.CORBA.portable.InputStream istream)
△	public static synchronized .... **type** ()
	.... TypeCode
△	public static ....void **write** (org.omg.CORBA.portable.OutputStream ostream, *Object* value)

ObjectHolder	org.omg.CORBA

Object
1.2 ● └ObjectHolder --------------------------- *org.omg.CORBA.portable.Streamable* ˬ[1]

1	public.....................void **_read** (org.omg.CORBA.portable.InputStream input)
1	public...............TypeCode **_type** ()
1	public.....................void **_write** (org.omg.CORBA.portable.OutputStream output)
✳	public........................ **ObjectHolder** ()
✳	public........................ **ObjectHolder** (*Object* initial)
	public................. *Object* **value**

ObjectIdHelper	org.omg.PortableInterceptor.ORBInitInfoPackage

Object
1.4 ○ └ObjectIdHelper

△	public static ....String **extract** (org.omg.CORBA.Any a)
△	public static ....String **id** ()
△	public static ....void **insert** (org.omg.CORBA.Any a, String that)
✳	public........................ **ObjectIdHelper** ()
△	public static ....String **read** (org.omg.CORBA.portable.InputStream istream)
△	public static synchronized .... **type** ()
	. org.omg.CORBA.TypeCode
△	public static ....void **write** (org.omg.CORBA.portable.OutputStream ostream, String value)

ObjectImpl ❶	org.omg.CORBA.portable

Object[1]
1.2 ○ └ObjectImpl ˬ --------------------------- *org.omg.CORBA.Object* ˬ[2]

2	public........................ **_create_request** (org.omg.CORBA.Context ctx, String operation,
	....org.omg.CORBA.Request org.omg.CORBA.NVList arg_list, org.omg.CORBA.NamedValue result)
2	public........................ **_create_request** (org.omg.CORBA.Context ctx, String operation,
	....org.omg.CORBA.Request org.omg.CORBA.NVList arg_list, org.omg.CORBA.NamedValue result, org↵
	.omg.CORBA.ExceptionList exceptions, org.omg.CORBA.ContextList contexts)
2	public *org.omg.CORBA.Object* **_duplicate** ()
	public............... Delegate **_get_delegate** ()
2	public.............. *org.omg*↵ **_get_domain_managers** ()
	.CORBA.DomainManager[]
2	public *org.omg.CORBA.Object* **_get_interface_def** ()
2	public. *org.omg.CORBA.Policy* **_get_policy** (int policy_type)
2	public........................int **_hash** (int maximum)
○	public abstract .... String[] **_ids** ()
	public............... InputStream **_invoke** (OutputStream output) throws ApplicationException, RemarshalException
2	public................. boolean **_is_a** (String repository_id)

Class *Interface* —extends - - -implements ○ abstract ● final △ static ▲ static final ✳ constructor x x—inherited x **x**—declared **x x**—overridden
εn—examples of usage ˬ—has subclass package—see other volume

2	public	boolean	**_is_equivalent** (*org.omg.CORBA.Object* that)	
	public	boolean	**_is_local** ()	
2	public	boolean	**_non_existent** ()	
	public	org.omg.CORBA.ORB	**_orb** ()	
2	public	void	**_release** ()	
	public	void	**_releaseReply** (InputStream input)	
2	public		**_request** (String operation)	
	....org.omg.CORBA.Request			
	public	OutputStream	**_request** (String operation, boolean responseExpected)	
	public	void	**_servant_postinvoke** (ServantObject servant)	
	public	ServantObject	**_servant_preinvoke** (String operation, Class expectedType)	
	public	void	**_set_delegate** (Delegate delegate)	
2	public *org.omg.CORBA.Object*		**_set_policy_override** (*org.omg.CORBA.Policy[]* policies,	
			org.omg.CORBA.SetOverrideType set_add)	
1	public	**boolean equals** (Object obj)		
1	public	**int hashCode** ()		
*	public	**ObjectImpl** ()		
1	public	**String toString** ()		

Object
1.2 ○ └org.omg.CORBA.portable.ObjectImpl [1] - - - - - - *org.omg.CORBA.Object* ⌐
1.3 ○   └ObjectImpl ⌐

1	*26 inherited members from org.omg.CORBA.portable.ObjectImpl not shown*		
	public	String	**_get_codebase** ()
*	public		**ObjectImpl** ()

O

1.1   *ObjectInput*————————————————— *DataInput* ⌐ [1]

	public	int	**available** () throws IOException	
	public	void	**close** () throws IOException	
	public	int	**read** () throws IOException	
	public	int	**read** (byte[] b) throws IOException	
	public	int	**read** (byte[] b, int off, int len) throws IOException	
1	public	boolean	readBoolean () throws IOException	
1	public	byte	readByte () throws IOException	
1	public	char	readChar () throws IOException	ε39
1	public	double	readDouble () throws IOException	
1	public	float	readFloat () throws IOException	
1	public	void	readFully (byte[] b) throws IOException	
1	public	void	readFully (byte[] b, int off, int len) throws IOException	
1	public	int	readInt () throws IOException	
1	public	String	readLine () throws IOException	
1	public	long	readLong () throws IOException	
	public	Object	**readObject** () throws ClassNotFoundException, IOException	ε45
1	public	short	readShort () throws IOException	
1	public	int	readUnsignedByte () throws IOException	
1	public	int	readUnsignedShort () throws IOException	
1	public	String	readUTF () throws IOException	
	public	long	**skip** (long n) throws IOException	
1	public	int	skipBytes (int n) throws IOException	

Object   ε252,382,418
○ └InputStream [1]
1.1   └ObjectInputStream - - - - - - - - - - - - - - - - - - *ObjectInput* [2] (*DataInput* [3]), *ObjectStreamConstants*

1	public	**int**	**available** () throws IOException	
1	public	**void**	**close** () throws IOException	ε45,14,36,452,455
	public	void	**defaultReadObject** () throws IOException, ClassNotFoundException	
	protected	boolean	**enableResolveObject** (boolean enable) throws SecurityException	
	public synchronized	void	mark (int readlimit)	
1	public	boolean	markSupported ()	
1.2 *	protected		**ObjectInputStream** () throws IOException, SecurityException	
*	public		**ObjectInputStream** (InputStream in) throws IOException	ε45
1	public	**int**	**read** () throws IOException	ε90,184,256

ObjectInputStream

	1	public	int	read (byte[] b) throws IOException	*ε*452,455,457,170,451
	1	public	**int**	**read** (byte[] buf, int off, int len) throws IOException	*ε*36
	3	public	boolean	**readBoolean** () throws IOException	
	3	public	byte	**readByte** () throws IOException	
	3	public	char	**readChar** () throws IOException	*ε*39
1.3		protected	ObjectStreamClass	**readClassDescriptor** () throws IOException, ClassNotFoundException	
	3	public	double	**readDouble** () throws IOException	
1.2		public		**readFields** () throws IOException, ClassNotFoundException	
		. ObjectInputStream.GetField			
	3	public	float	**readFloat** () throws IOException	
	3	public	void	**readFully** (byte[] buf) throws IOException	
	3	public	void	**readFully** (byte[] buf, int off, int len) throws IOException	
	3	public	int	**readInt** () throws IOException	
D	3	public	String	**readLine** () throws IOException	
	3	public	long	**readLong** () throws IOException	
●	2	public final	Object	**readObject** () throws IOException, ClassNotFoundException	*ε*45
1.2		protected	Object	**readObjectOverride** () throws IOException, ClassNotFoundException	
	3	public	short	**readShort** () throws IOException	
		protected	void	**readStreamHeader** () throws IOException, StreamCorruptedException	
1.4		public	Object	**readUnshared** () throws IOException, ClassNotFoundException	
	3	public	int	**readUnsignedByte** () throws IOException	
	3	public	int	**readUnsignedShort** () throws IOException	
	3	public	String	**readUTF** () throws IOException	
		public	void	**registerValidation** (*ObjectInputValidation* obj, int prio)	
				throws NotActiveException, InvalidObjectException	
	1	public synchronized	void	reset () throws IOException	
		protected	Class	**resolveClass** (ObjectStreamClass desc) throws IOException,	
				ClassNotFoundException	
		protected	Object	**resolveObject** (Object obj) throws IOException	
1.3		protected	Class	**resolveProxyClass** (String[] interfaces) throws IOException,	
				ClassNotFoundException	
	1	public	long	skip (long n) throws IOException	
	3	public	int	**skipBytes** (int len) throws IOException	

ObjectInputStream.GetField   java.io

Object
└ObjectInputStream.GetField

1.2 ○

○	public abstract	boolean	**defaulted** (String name) throws IOException
○	public abstract	int	**get** (String name, int val) throws IOException
○	public abstract	float	**get** (String name, float val) throws IOException
○	public abstract	short	**get** (String name, short val) throws IOException
○	public abstract	char	**get** (String name, char val) throws IOException
○	public abstract	Object	**get** (String name, Object val) throws IOException
○	public abstract	boolean	**get** (String name, boolean val) throws IOException
○	public abstract	byte	**get** (String name, byte val) throws IOException
○	public abstract	double	**get** (String name, double val) throws IOException
○	public abstract	long	**get** (String name, long val) throws IOException
✳	public		**ObjectInputStream.GetField** ()
○	public abstract		**getObjectStreamClass** ()
		ObjectStreamClass	

ObjectInputValidation   java.io

1.1 *ObjectInputValidation*

	public	void	**validateObject** () throws InvalidObjectException

---

ObjectNotActive   org.omg.PortableServer.POAPackage

Object
└Throwable - *java.io.Serializable* ⌐
  └Exception
    └org.omg.CORBA.UserException - - - - - - *org.omg.CORBA.portable.IDLEntity* ⌐ (*java.io.Serializable*)
      └ObjectNotActive

1.2 ○
1.4 ●

Class *Interface* —extends - - -implements ○ abstract ● final △ static ▲ static final ✳ constructor x x—inherited x **x**—declared **x x**—overridden
εn—examples of usage ⌐—has subclass package—see other volume

*	public.........................	**ObjectNotActive** ()
*	public.........................	**ObjectNotActive** (String $reason)

ObjectNotActiveHelper

Object
1.4 O └ObjectNotActiveHelper

△	public static .. ObjectNotActive	**extract** (org.omg.CORBA.Any a)
△	public static ....String	**id** ()
△	public static ....void	**insert** (org.omg.CORBA.Any a, ObjectNotActive that)
*	public.........................	**ObjectNotActiveHelper** ()
△	public static .. ObjectNotActive	**read** (org.omg.CORBA.portable.InputStream istream)
△	public static synchronized	**type** ()
	. org.omg.CORBA.TypeCode	
△	public static ....void	**write** (org.omg.CORBA.portable.OutputStream ostream, ObjectNotActive value)

ObjectOutput

1.1 *ObjectOutput──────────────────── DataOutput* [1]

	public......................void	**close** () throws IOException		ε44
	public......................void	**flush** () throws IOException		
1	public...................... **void**	**write** (byte[] b) throws IOException		
1	public...................... **void**	**write** (int b) throws IOException		
1	public...................... **void**	**write** (byte[] b, int off, int len) throws IOException		
1	public......................void	writeBoolean (boolean v) throws IOException		
1	public......................void	writeByte (int v) throws IOException		
1	public......................void	writeBytes (String s) throws IOException		
1	public......................void	writeChar (int v) throws IOException		
1	public......................void	writeChars (String s) throws IOException		ε39
1	public......................void	writeDouble (double v) throws IOException		
1	public......................void	writeFloat (float v) throws IOException		
1	public......................void	writeInt (int v) throws IOException		
1	public......................void	writeLong (long v) throws IOException		
	public......................void	**writeObject** (Object obj) throws IOException		ε44
1	public......................void	writeShort (int v) throws IOException		
1	public......................void	writeUTF (String str) throws IOException		

ObjectOutputStream

Object   ε183
O └OutputStream [1]
1.1 └ObjectOutputStream ----------------- *ObjectOutput* [2] (*DataOutput* [3]), *ObjectStreamConstants*

	protected ....void	**annotateClass** (Class cl) throws IOException		
1.3	protected ....void	**annotateProxyClass** (Class cl) throws IOException		
1	public...................... **void**	**close** () throws IOException		ε451,453,91,211,224
	public......................void	**defaultWriteObject** () throws IOException		
	protected ....void	**drain** () throws IOException		
	protected .... boolean	**enableReplaceObject** (boolean enable) throws SecurityException		
1	public...................... **void**	**flush** () throws IOException		ε27,54
1.2 *	protected	**ObjectOutputStream** () throws IOException, SecurityException		
*	public.........................	**ObjectOutputStream** (OutputStream out) throws IOException		ε44
1.2	public.. ObjectOutputStream ↵	**putFields** () throws IOException		
	.PutField			
	protected ....Object	**replaceObject** (Object obj) throws IOException		
	public......................void	**reset** () throws IOException		
1.2	public......................void	**useProtocolVersion** (int version) throws IOException		
1	public...................... **void**	**write** (byte[] buf) throws IOException		ε27,91,224
1	public...................... **void**	**write** (int val) throws IOException		ε184
1	public...................... **void**	**write** (byte[] buf, int off, int len) throws IOException		ε451,453,54,449,450
3	public......................void	**writeBoolean** (boolean val) throws IOException		
3	public......................void	**writeByte** (int val) throws IOException		
3	public......................void	**writeBytes** (String str) throws IOException		
3	public......................void	**writeChar** (int val) throws IOException		
3	public......................void	**writeChars** (String str) throws IOException		ε39
1.3	protected ....void	**writeClassDescriptor** (ObjectStreamClass desc) throws IOException		
3	public......................void	**writeDouble** (double val) throws IOException		
1.2	public......................void	**writeFields** () throws IOException		
3	public......................void	**writeFloat** (float val) throws IOException		

O

Classes

ObjectOutputStream

	3	public.....................void	**writeInt** (int val) throws IOException		
	3	public.....................void	**writeLong** (long val) throws IOException		
●	2	public final ....void	**writeObject** (Object obj) throws IOException		ε44
1.2		protected..................void	**writeObjectOverride** (Object obj) throws IOException		
	3	public.....................void	**writeShort** (int val) throws IOException		
		protected..................void	**writeStreamHeader** () throws IOException		
1.4		public.....................void	**writeUnshared** (Object obj) throws IOException		
	3	public.....................void	**writeUTF** (String str) throws IOException		

ObjectOutputStream.PutField   java.io

Object
1.2 ○   └ObjectOutputStream.PutField

○	public abstract ....void	**put** (String name, boolean val)
○	public abstract ....void	**put** (String name, long val)
○	public abstract ....void	**put** (String name, int val)
○	public abstract ....void	**put** (String name, Object val)
○	public abstract ....void	**put** (String name, float val)
○	public abstract ....void	**put** (String name, char val)
○	public abstract ....void	**put** (String name, short val)
○	public abstract ....void	**put** (String name, double val)
○	public abstract ....void	**put** (String name, byte val)
✳	public...........................	**ObjectOutputStream.PutField** ()
D ○	public abstract ....void	**write** (*ObjectOutput* out) throws IOException

---

ObjectStreamClass   java.io

Object[1]
1.1   └ObjectStreamClass - *Serializable*⌄

	public.................... Class	**forClass** ()
1.2	public.......ObjectStreamField	**getField** (String name)
1.2	public..... ObjectStreamField[]	**getFields** ()
	public....................String	**getName** ()
	public..................... long	**getSerialVersionUID** ()
△	public static	**lookup** (Class cl)
	.... ObjectStreamClass	
1.2 ▲	public static final..............	**NO_FIELDS**
	.... ObjectStreamField[]	
1	public.................. **String**	**toString** ()

ObjectStreamConstants   java.io

1.2   *ObjectStreamConstants*
- -

▲	public static final.............int	**baseWireHandle** = 8257536
▲	public static final.............int	**PROTOCOL_VERSION_1** = 1
▲	public static final.............int	**PROTOCOL_VERSION_2** = 2
▲	public static final......... byte	**SC_BLOCK_DATA** = 8
▲	public static final......... byte	**SC_EXTERNALIZABLE** = 4
▲	public static final......... byte	**SC_SERIALIZABLE** = 2
▲	public static final......... byte	**SC_WRITE_METHOD** = 1
▲	public static final.........short	**STREAM_MAGIC** = -21267
▲	public static final.........short	**STREAM_VERSION** = 5
▲	public static final..............	**SUBCLASS_IMPLEMENTATION_PERMISSION**
	.... SerializablePermission	
▲	public static final..............	**SUBSTITUTION_PERMISSION**
	.... SerializablePermission	
▲	public static final......... byte	**TC_ARRAY** = 117
▲	public static final......... byte	**TC_BASE** = 112
▲	public static final......... byte	**TC_BLOCKDATA** = 119
▲	public static final......... byte	**TC_BLOCKDATALONG** = 122
▲	public static final......... byte	**TC_CLASS** = 118
▲	public static final......... byte	**TC_CLASSDESC** = 114
▲	public static final......... byte	**TC_ENDBLOCKDATA** = 120
▲	public static final......... byte	**TC_EXCEPTION** = 123
1.3 ▲	public static final......... byte	**TC_LONGSTRING** = 124

Class *Interface* —extends - - -implements ○ abstract ● final △ static ▲ static final ✳ constructor x x—inherited x **x**—declared **x x**—overridden
ε*n*—examples of usage ⌄—has subclass package—see other volume

▲	public static final	byte	**TC_MAX**	= 125
▲	public static final	byte	**TC_NULL**	= 112
▲	public static final	byte	**TC_OBJECT**	= 115
1.3 ▲	public static final	byte	**TC_PROXYCLASSDESC**	= 125
▲	public static final	byte	**TC_REFERENCE**	= 113
▲	public static final	byte	**TC_RESET**	= 121
▲	public static final	byte	**TC_STRING**	= 116

ObjectStreamException — java.io

```
Object
└Throwable ---------------------------- Serializable
   └Exception
      └IOException
```
1.1 ○ `        └ObjectStreamException`

✳	protected	**ObjectStreamException** ()
✳	protected	**ObjectStreamException** (String classname)

ObjectStreamField — java.io

```
Object¹
```
1.2 `└ObjectStreamField --------------------- Comparable²`

2	public	int	**compareTo** (Object obj)	ε53
	public	String	**getName** ()	
	public	int	**getOffset** ()	
	public	Class	**getType** ()	
	public	char	**getTypeCode** ()	
	public	String	**getTypeString** ()	
	public	boolean	**isPrimitive** ()	
1.4	public	boolean	**isUnshared** ()	
✳	public		**ObjectStreamField** (String name, Class type)	
1.4 ✳	public		**ObjectStreamField** (String name, Class type, boolean unshared)	
	protected	void	**setOffset** (int offset)	
1	public	String	**toString** ()	

ObjID — java.rmi.server

```
Object¹
```
1.1 ● `└ObjID ------------------------------ java.io.Serializable`

1.2 ▲	public static final	int	**ACTIVATOR_ID** = 1	
▲	public static final	int	**DGC_ID** = 2	
1	public	boolean	**equals** (Object obj)	
1	public	int	**hashCode** ()	
✳	public		**ObjID** ()	
✳	public		**ObjID** (int objNum)	
△	public static	ObjID	**read** (java.io.ObjectInput in) throws java.io.IOException	
▲	public static final	int	**REGISTRY_ID** = 0	
1	public	String	**toString** ()	
	public	void	**write** (java.io.ObjectOutput out) throws java.io.IOException	

Observable — java.util

```
Object
└Observable
```

	public synchronized	void	**addObserver** (Observer o)	
	protected synchronized	void	**clearChanged** ()	
	public synchronized	int	**countObservers** ()	
	public synchronized	void	**deleteObserver** (Observer o)	
	public synchronized	void	**deleteObservers** ()	
	public synchronized	boolean	**hasChanged** ()	
	public	void	**notifyObservers** ()	
	public	void	**notifyObservers** (Object arg)	
✳	public		**Observable** ()	
	protected synchronized	void	**setChanged** ()	ε334

O

Classes

677

Observer
		java.util
	Observer	
	public....................void **update** (Observable o, Object arg)	*ε*334

OctetSeqHelper
		org.omg.CORBA
	Object	
1.3 ○	└OctetSeqHelper	
△	public static ....byte[] **extract** (Any a)	
△	public static ....String **id** ()	
△	public static ....void **insert** (Any a, byte[] that)	
✳	public.......................... **OctetSeqHelper** ()	
△	public static ....byte[] **read** (org.omg.CORBA.portable.InputStream istream)	
△	public static synchronized .... **type** ()	
	...................TypeCode	
△	public static ....void **write** (org.omg.CORBA.portable.OutputStream ostream, byte[] value)	

OctetSeqHolder
		org.omg.CORBA
	Object	
1.3 ●	└OctetSeqHolder ------------------------- *org.omg.CORBA.portable.Streamable* ⌐[1]	
1	public.......................void **_read** (org.omg.CORBA.portable.InputStream i)	
1	public................TypeCode **_type** ()	
1	public.......................void **_write** (org.omg.CORBA.portable.OutputStream o)	
✳	public........................... **OctetSeqHolder** ()	
✳	public........................... **OctetSeqHolder** (byte[] initialValue)	
	public...................byte[] **value**	

Oid
		org.ietf.jgss
	Object [1]	
1.4	└Oid	
	public................. boolean **containedIn** (Oid[] oids)	
1	public.................**boolean equals** (Object other)	
	public....................byte[] **getDER** () throws GSSException	
1	public.................... **int hashCode** ()	
✳	public........................... **Oid** (byte[] data) throws GSSException	
✳	public........................... **Oid** (java.io.InputStream derOid) throws GSSException	
✳	public........................... **Oid** (String strOid) throws GSSException	
1	public.................. **String toString** ()	

OMGVMCID
		org.omg.CORBA
1.3	*OMGVMCID*	
▲	public static final ....int **value** = 1330446336	

Operation
		java.rmi.server
	Object [1]	
D	└Operation	
D	public.....................String **getOperation** ()	
D ✳	public.......................... **Operation** (String op)	
D 1	public.................. **String toString** ()	

Class *Interface* —extends - - -implements ○ abstract ● final △ static ▲ static final ✳ constructor x x—inherited x **x**—declared **x x**—overridden
εn—examples of usage ⌐—has subclass package—see other volume

OperationNotSupportedException	javax.naming

```
Object
 └Throwable ---------------------------- java.io.Serializable
   └Exception
1.3    └NamingException¹
1.3      └OperationNotSupportedException
```

	1	*20 inherited members from NamingException not shown*
*	public.........................	**OperationNotSupportedException** ()
*	public.........................	**OperationNotSupportedException** (String explanation)

OptionalDataException	java.io

```
Object
 └Throwable ---------------------------- Serializable
   └Exception
     └IOException
1.1 ○      └ObjectStreamException
1.1        └OptionalDataException
```

public................ boolean **eof**
public........................int **length**

O

ORB❶	org.omg.CORBA

```
       Object
1.2 ○   └ORB
```

Classes

	public.......................void	**connect** (*Object* obj)
	public.............. TypeCode	**create_abstract_interface_tc** (String id, String name)
○	public abstract...... TypeCode	**create_alias_tc** (String id, String name, TypeCode original_type)
○	public abstract............. Any	**create_any** ()
○	public abstract...... TypeCode	**create_array_tc** (int length, TypeCode element_type)
	public................*DynAny*	**create_basic_dyn_any** (TypeCode type) throws org.omg.CORBA.ORBPackage↵ .InconsistentTypeCode
○	public abstract..... ContextList	**create_context_list** ()
	public................*DynAny*	**create_dyn_any** (Any value)
	public................ *DynArray*	**create_dyn_array** (TypeCode type) throws org.omg.CORBA.ORBPackage↵ .InconsistentTypeCode
	public.............. *DynEnum*	**create_dyn_enum** (TypeCode type) throws org.omg.CORBA.ORBPackage↵ .InconsistentTypeCode
	public...........*DynSequence*	**create_dyn_sequence** (TypeCode type) throws org.omg.CORBA.ORBPackage↵ .InconsistentTypeCode
	public.............. *DynStruct*	**create_dyn_struct** (TypeCode type) throws org.omg.CORBA.ORBPackage↵ .InconsistentTypeCode
	public................ *DynUnion*	**create_dyn_union** (TypeCode type) throws org.omg.CORBA.ORBPackage↵ .InconsistentTypeCode
○	public abstract...... TypeCode	**create_enum_tc** (String id, String name, String[] members)
○	public abstract... Environment	**create_environment** ()
○	public abstract.. ExceptionList	**create_exception_list** ()
○	public abstract...... TypeCode	**create_exception_tc** (String id, String name, StructMember[] members)
	public.............. TypeCode	**create_fixed_tc** (short digits, short scale)
○	public abstract...... TypeCode	**create_interface_tc** (String id, String name)
○	public abstract.......... NVList	**create_list** (int count)
○	public abstract... NamedValue	**create_named_value** (String s, Any any, int flags)
	public................. TypeCode	**create_native_tc** (String id, String name)
	public................... NVList	**create_operation_list** (*Object* oper)
○	public abstract................. ....org.omg.CORBA↵ .portable.OutputStream	**create_output_stream** ()
	public...................*Policy*	**create_policy** (int type, Any val) throws PolicyError
D ○	public abstract...... TypeCode	**create_recursive_sequence_tc** (int bound, int offset)
	public.............. TypeCode	**create_recursive_tc** (String id)
○	public abstract...... TypeCode	**create_sequence_tc** (int bound, TypeCode element_type)
○	public abstract...... TypeCode	**create_string_tc** (int bound)
○	public abstract...... TypeCode	**create_struct_tc** (String id, String name, StructMember[] members)
○	public abstract...... TypeCode	**create_union_tc** (String id, String name, TypeCode discriminator_type, UnionMember[] members)
	public............... TypeCode	**create_value_box_tc** (String id, String name, TypeCode boxed_type)

ORB❶

	public	TypeCode	**create_value_tc** (String id, String name, short type_modifier, TypeCode concrete_base, ValueMember[] members)
O	public abstract	TypeCode	**create_wstring_tc** (int bound)
1.3	public	void	**destroy** ()
	public	void	**disconnect** (*Object* obj)
D	public	*Current*	**get_current** ()
O	public abstract	Context	**get_default_context** ()
O	public abstract	Request	**get_next_response** () throws WrongTransaction
O	public abstract	TypeCode	**get_primitive_tc** (TCKind tcKind)
	public	boolean	**get_service_information** (short service_type, ServiceInformationHolder service_info)
△	public static	ORB	**init** ()
△	public static	ORB	**init** (java.applet.Applet app, java.util.Properties props)
△	public static	ORB	**init** (String[] args, java.util.Properties props)
O	public abstract	String[]	**list_initial_services** ()
O	public abstract	String	**object_to_string** (*Object* obj)
✳	public		**ORB** ()
	public	void	**perform_work** ()
O	public abstract	boolean	**poll_next_response** ()
O	public abstract	*Object*	**resolve_initial_references** (String object_name) throws org.omg.CORBA.ORBPackage.InvalidName
	public	void	**run** ()
O	public abstract	void	**send_multiple_requests_deferred** (Request[] req)
O	public abstract	void	**send_multiple_requests_oneway** (Request[] req)
O	protected abstract	void	**set_parameters** (java.applet.Applet app, java.util.Properties props)
O	protected abstract	void	**set_parameters** (String[] args, java.util.Properties props)
	public	void	**shutdown** (boolean wait_for_completion)
O	public abstract	*Object*	**string_to_object** (String str)
	public	boolean	**work_pending** ()

ORB❷ — org.omg.CORBA_2_3

```
Object
1.2 O └org.omg.CORBA.ORB¹
1.3 O    └ORB
```

1	57 inherited members from org.omg.CORBA.ORB not shown		
	public *org.omg.CORBA.Object*		**get_value_def** (String repid) throws org.omg.CORBA.BAD_PARAM
	public *org.omg.CORBA↵ .portable.ValueFactory*		**lookup_value_factory** (String id)
✳	public		**ORB** ()
	public *org.omg.CORBA↵ .portable.ValueFactory*		**register_value_factory** (String id, *org.omg.CORBA.portable.ValueFactory* factory)
	public	void	**set_delegate** (Object wrapper)
	public	void	**unregister_value_factory** (String id)

ORBInitializer — org.omg.PortableInterceptor

```
1.4   ORBInitializer ──────────── ORBInitializerOperations⌄¹, org.omg.CORBA.Object⌄², org.omg.CORBA.portable.IDLEntity⌄ (java.io.Serializable)
```

2	13 inherited members from org.omg.CORBA.Object not shown		
1	2 inherited members from ORBInitializerOperations not shown		

ORBInitializerOperations — org.omg.PortableInterceptor

```
1.4   ORBInitializerOperations⌄
```

	public	void	**post_init** (*ORBInitInfo* info)
	public	void	**pre_init** (*ORBInitInfo* info)

Class *Interface* —extends - - -implements ○ abstract ● final △ static ▲ static final ✳ constructor x x—inherited x **x**—declared **x x**—overridden
ε*n*—examples of usage ⌄—has subclass package—see other volume

ORBInitInfo		org.omg.PortableInterceptor

1.4   *ORBInitInfo*————————————————— *ORBInitInfoOperations*↲ [1], *org.omg.CORBA.Object*↲ [2],
                                                 org.omg.CORBA.portable.IDLEntity↲ (*java.io.Serializable*)

- -

    2   *13 inherited members from org.omg.CORBA.Object not shown*
    1   *10 inherited members from ORBInitInfoOperations not shown*

- -

ORBInitInfoOperations	org.omg.PortableInterceptor

1.4   *ORBInitInfoOperations*↲

- -

public......................void **add_client_request_interceptor** (*ClientRequestInterceptor* interceptor)
                    throws org.omg.PortableInterceptor.ORBInitInfoPackage.DuplicateName
public......................void **add_ior_interceptor** (*IORInterceptor* interceptor) throws
                    org.omg.PortableInterceptor.ORBInitInfoPackage.DuplicateName
public......................void **add_server_request_interceptor** (*ServerRequestInterceptor* interceptor)
                    throws org.omg.PortableInterceptor.ORBInitInfoPackage.DuplicateName
public..........................int **allocate_slot_id** ()
public................. String[] **arguments** ()
public........................... **codec_factory** ()
   ..*org.omg.IOP.CodecFactory*
public....................String **orb_id** ()
public......................void **register_initial_reference** (String id, *org.omg.CORBA.Object* obj)
                    throws org.omg.PortableInterceptor.ORBInitInfoPackage.InvalidName
public......................void **register_policy_factory** (int type, *PolicyFactory* policy_factory)
public *org.omg.CORBA.Object* **resolve_initial_references** (String id) throws org.omg.PortableInterceptor↲
                    .ORBInitInfoPackage.InvalidName

- -

OutOfMemoryError	java.lang

    Object
    └Throwable - *java.io.Serializable*↲
      └Error
○   └VirtualMachineError
         └OutOfMemoryError

✳   public.......................... **OutOfMemoryError** ()
✳   public.......................... **OutOfMemoryError** (String s)

OutputKeys	javax.xml.transform

    Object
1.4   └OutputKeys

▲   public static final........String **CDATA_SECTION_ELEMENTS** = "cdata-section-elements"
▲   public static final........String **DOCTYPE_PUBLIC** = "doctype-public"   ε519
▲   public static final........String **DOCTYPE_SYSTEM** = "doctype-system"   ε519
▲   public static final........String **ENCODING** = "encoding"
▲   public static final........String **INDENT** = "indent"
▲   public static final........String **MEDIA_TYPE** = "media-type"
▲   public static final........String **METHOD** = "method"   ε520
▲   public static final........String **OMIT_XML_DECLARATION** = "omit-xml-declaration"
▲   public static final........String **STANDALONE** = "standalone"
▲   public static final........String **VERSION** = "version"

OutputStream❶	java.io

    Object   ε183
○   └OutputStream↲

    public......................void **close** () throws IOException   ε91,383,452,455,463
    public......................void **flush** () throws IOException   ε27,54
✳   public.......................... **OutputStream** ()   ε184
    public......................void **write** (byte[] b) throws IOException   ε91
○   public abstract.............void **write** (int b) throws IOException   ε184
    public......................void **write** (byte[] b, int off, int len) throws IOException   ε452,455,463

		OutputStream ❷	org.omg.CORBA.portable

Object

   O   └java.io.OutputStream [1]   ε183

1.2 O   └OutputStream ˛

1	*4 inherited members from java.io.OutputStream not shown*
O	public abstract .... InputStream **create_input_stream** ()
	public ... org.omg.CORBA.ORB **orb** ()
✳	public .... **OutputStream** ()
1	public .... **void** **write** (int b) throws java.io.IOException ε184
O	public abstract .... void **write_any** (org.omg.CORBA.Any value)
O	public abstract .... void **write_boolean** (boolean value)
O	public abstract .... void **write_boolean_array** (boolean[] value, int offset, int length)
O	public abstract .... void **write_char** (char value)
O	public abstract .... void **write_char_array** (char[] value, int offset, int length)
	public .... void **write_Context** (org.omg.CORBA.Context ctx, org.omg.CORBA.ContextList contexts)
O	public abstract .... void **write_double** (double value)
O	public abstract .... void **write_double_array** (double[] value, int offset, int length)
	public .... void **write_fixed** (java.math.BigDecimal value)
O	public abstract .... void **write_float** (float value)
O	public abstract .... void **write_float_array** (float[] value, int offset, int length)
O	public abstract .... void **write_long** (int value)
O	public abstract .... void **write_long_array** (int[] value, int offset, int length)
O	public abstract .... void **write_longlong** (long value)
O	public abstract .... void **write_longlong_array** (long[] value, int offset, int length)
O	public abstract .... void **write_Object** (*org.omg.CORBA.Object* value)
O	public abstract .... void **write_octet** (byte value)
O	public abstract .... void **write_octet_array** (byte[] value, int offset, int length)
D	public .... void **write_Principal** (org.omg.CORBA.Principal value)
O	public abstract .... void **write_short** (short value)
O	public abstract .... void **write_short_array** (short[] value, int offset, int length)
O	public abstract .... void **write_string** (String value)
O	public abstract .... void **write_TypeCode** (org.omg.CORBA.TypeCode value)
O	public abstract .... void **write_ulong** (int value)
O	public abstract .... void **write_ulong_array** (int[] value, int offset, int length)
O	public abstract .... void **write_ulonglong** (long value)
O	public abstract .... void **write_ulonglong_array** (long[] value, int offset, int length)
O	public abstract .... void **write_ushort** (short value)
O	public abstract .... void **write_ushort_array** (short[] value, int offset, int length)
O	public abstract .... void **write_wchar** (char value)
O	public abstract .... void **write_wchar_array** (char[] value, int offset, int length)
O	public abstract .... void **write_wstring** (String value)

		OutputStream ❸	org.omg.CORBA_2_3.portable

Object

   O   └java.io.OutputStream [1]   ε183

1.2 O   └org.omg.CORBA.portable.OutputStream [2]

1.3 O   └OutputStream

1	*4 inherited members from java.io.OutputStream not shown*
2	*35 inherited members from org.omg.CORBA.portable.OutputStream not shown*
✳	public .... **OutputStream** ()
	public .... void **write_abstract_interface** (Object obj)
	public .... void **write_value** (*java.io.Serializable* value)
	public .... void **write_value** (*java.io.Serializable* value, Class clz)
	public .... void **write_value** (*java.io.Serializable* value, String repository_id)
	public .... void **write_value** (*java.io.Serializable* value, *org.omg.CORBA.portable* ↵ *.BoxedValueHelper* factory)

		OutputStreamWriter	java.io

Object

1.1 O   └Writer [1]

1.1   └OutputStreamWriter ˛

Class *Interface* —extends - - -implements O abstract ● final △ static ▲ static final ✳ constructor x x—inherited x **x**—declared **x x**—overridden
ε*n*—examples of usage ˛—has subclass package—see other volume

	1	public.....................**void** **close** () throws IOException		ε135,23,37,38,41
	1	public.....................**void** **flush** () throws IOException		ε135,150,224
		public.....................String **getEncoding** ()		
	1	protected ....Object lock		
*		public.....................**OutputStreamWriter** (OutputStream out)		ε135,150
1.4 *		public.....................**OutputStreamWriter** (OutputStream out, java.nio.charset.CharsetEncoder enc)		
*		public.....................**OutputStreamWriter** (OutputStream out, String charsetName)		
		throws UnsupportedEncodingException		ε41,43
1.4 *		public.........................**OutputStreamWriter** (OutputStream out, java.nio.charset.Charset cs)		
				ε224
	1	public.....................void write (char[] cbuf) throws IOException		
	1	public.....................**void** **write** (int c) throws IOException		
	1	public.....................void write (String str) throws IOException		ε135,23,37,38,41
	1	public.....................**void** **write** (char[] cbuf, int off, int len) throws IOException		
	1	public.....................**void** **write** (String str, int off, int len) throws IOException		

OverlappingFileLockException			java.nio.channels
	Object		ε181,182
	└Throwable - *java.io.Serializable* ˅		
	└Exception		
	└RuntimeException		
1.1	└IllegalStateException		
1.4	└OverlappingFileLockException		

*	public.........................**OverlappingFileLockException** ()	

Owner		java.security.acl
1.1	*Owner* ˅	

	public.................boolean **addOwner** (*java.security.Principal* caller, *java.security.Principal* owner)	
	throws NotOwnerException	
	public.................boolean **deleteOwner** (*java.security.Principal* caller, *java.security.Principal* owner)	
	throws NotOwnerException, LastOwnerException	
	public.................boolean **isOwner** (*java.security.Principal* owner)	

Package		java.lang
	Object[1]	
1.2	└Package	

	public.....................String **getImplementationTitle** ()		
	public.....................String **getImplementationVendor** ()		
	public.....................String **getImplementationVersion** ()		
	public.....................String **getName** ()		ε66,109
△	public static ....Package **getPackage** (String name)		
△	public static ....Package[] **getPackages** ()		
	public.....................String **getSpecificationTitle** ()		
	public.....................String **getSpecificationVendor** ()		
	public.....................String **getSpecificationVersion** ()		
1	public.........................**int** **hashCode** ()		
	public.....................boolean **isCompatibleWith** (String desired) throws NumberFormatException		
	public.....................boolean **isSealed** ()		
	public.....................boolean **isSealed** (java.net.URL url)		
1	public.....................**String** **toString** ()		

Parameter		org.omg.Dynamic
	Object	
1.4 ●	└Parameter - *org.omg.CORBA.portable.IDLEntity* ˅ (*java.io.Serializable*)	

	public....org.omg.CORBA.Any **argument**	
	public...............org.omg↵ **mode**	
	.CORBA.ParameterMode	
*	public.........................**Parameter** ()	
*	public.........................**Parameter** (org.omg.CORBA.Any _argument, org.omg.CORBA.ParameterMode	
	_mode)	

P

Classes

ParameterDescriptor

					java.beans
		Object			
1.1		└FeatureDescriptor[1]			
1.1		└ParameterDescriptor			

	1	public.... *java.util.Enumeration*	attributeNames ()		
	1	public....................String	getDisplayName ()		
	1	public....................String	getName ()		ε5,9
	1	public....................String	getShortDescription ()		
	1	public....................Object	getValue (String attributeName)		
	1	public................. boolean	isExpert ()		
	1	public................. boolean	isHidden ()		
1.2	1	public................. boolean	isPreferred ()		
✳		public...........................	**ParameterDescriptor** ()		
	1	public....................void	setDisplayName (String displayName)		
	1	public....................void	setExpert (boolean expert)		
	1	public....................void	setHidden (boolean hidden)		
	1	public....................void	setName (String name)		
1.2	1	public....................void	setPreferred (boolean preferred)		
	1	public....................void	setShortDescription (String text)		
	1	public....................void	setValue (String attributeName, Object value)		ε9

ParameterMetaData

					java.sql
1.4		*ParameterMetaData*			

	public....................String	**getParameterClassName** (int param) throws SQLException	
	public........................int	**getParameterCount** () throws SQLException	
	public........................int	**getParameterMode** (int param) throws SQLException	
	public........................int	**getParameterType** (int param) throws SQLException	
	public....................String	**getParameterTypeName** (int param) throws SQLException	
	public........................int	**getPrecision** (int param) throws SQLException	
	public........................int	**getScale** (int param) throws SQLException	
	public........................int	**isNullable** (int param) throws SQLException	
	public................. boolean	**isSigned** (int param) throws SQLException	
▲	public static final..........int	**parameterModeIn** = 1	
▲	public static final..........int	**parameterModeInOut** = 2	
▲	public static final..........int	**parameterModeOut** = 4	
▲	public static final..........int	**parameterModeUnknown** = 0	
▲	public static final..........int	**parameterNoNulls** = 0	
▲	public static final..........int	**parameterNullable** = 1	
▲	public static final..........int	**parameterNullableUnknown** = 2	

ParameterMode

					org.omg.CORBA
		Object			
1.4		└ParameterMode - *org.omg.CORBA.portable.IDLEntity* ˌ (*java.io.Serializable*)			

▲	public static final..........int	**_PARAM_IN** = 0	
▲	public static final..........int	**_PARAM_INOUT** = 2	
▲	public static final..........int	**_PARAM_OUT** = 1	
△	public static .. ParameterMode	**from_int** (int value)	
▲	public static final..............	**PARAM_IN**	
	.... ParameterMode		
▲	public static final..............	**PARAM_INOUT**	
	.... ParameterMode		
▲	public static final..............	**PARAM_OUT**	
	.... ParameterMode		
✳	protected......................	**ParameterMode** (int value)	
	public........................int	**value** ()	

ParameterModeHelper

			org.omg.CORBA
		Object	
1.4 ○		└ParameterModeHelper	

Class *Interface* —extends - - -implements ○ abstract ● final △ static ▲ static final ✳ constructor x x—inherited x **x**—declared **x x**—overridden
ε*n*—examples of usage ˌ—has subclass package—see other volume

△	public static .. ParameterMode	**extract** (Any a)	
△	public static ....String	**id** ()	
△	public static ....void	**insert** (Any a, ParameterMode that)	
✳	public..........................	**ParameterModeHelper** ()	
△	public static .. ParameterMode	**read** (org.omg.CORBA.portable.InputStream istream)	
△	public static synchronized	**type** ()	
	....................TypeCode		
△	public static ....void	**write** (org.omg.CORBA.portable.OutputStream ostream, ParameterMode value)	

ParameterModeHolder | org.omg.CORBA

Object
└ParameterModeHolder - - - - - - - - - - - - - - - - - - *org.omg.CORBA.portable.Streamable* [1]

1.4 ●

1	public....................void	**_read** (org.omg.CORBA.portable.InputStream i)	
1	public...............TypeCode	**_type** ()	
1	public....................void	**_write** (org.omg.CORBA.portable.OutputStream o)	
✳	public..........................	**ParameterModeHolder** ()	
✳	public..........................	**ParameterModeHolder** (ParameterMode initialValue)	
	public........ ParameterMode	**value**	

ParseException | java.text

Object
└Throwable - *java.io.Serializable*
  └Exception
    └ParseException

1.1

ε312,314,315,317,318

	public........................int	**getErrorOffset** ()	
✳	public..........................	**ParseException** (String s, int errorOffset)	

ParsePosition | java.text

Object [1]
└ParsePosition

1.1

1	public.................**boolean**	**equals** (Object obj)	
1.2	public........................int	**getErrorIndex** ()	
	public........................int	**getIndex** ()	
1	public........................ **int**	**hashCode** ()	
✳	public..........................	**ParsePosition** (int index)	
1.2	public....................void	**setErrorIndex** (int ei)	
	public....................void	**setIndex** (int index)	
1	public.................. **String**	**toString** ()	

Parser ❷ | org.xml.sax

D *Parser*

- -

D	public....................void	**parse** (String systemId) throws SAXException, java.io.IOException	
D	public....................void	**parse** (InputSource source) throws SAXException, java.io.IOException	
D	public....................void	**setDocumentHandler** (*DocumentHandler* handler)	
D	public....................void	**setDTDHandler** (*DTDHandler* handler)	
D	public....................void	**setEntityResolver** (*EntityResolver* resolver)	
D	public....................void	**setErrorHandler** (*ErrorHandler* handler)	
D	public....................void	**setLocale** (java.util.Locale locale) throws SAXException	

- -

ParserAdapter | org.xml.sax.helpers

Object
└ParserAdapter - *org.xml.sax.XMLReader* [1], *org.xml.sax.DocumentHandler* [2]

1.4

2	public....................void	**characters** (char[] ch, int start, int length) throws org.xml.sax.SAXException	
2	public....................void	**endDocument** () throws org.xml.sax.SAXException	
2	public....................void	**endElement** (String qName) throws org.xml.sax.SAXException	
1	public..........................	**getContentHandler** ()	
	. *org.xml.sax.ContentHandler*		
1	public..........................	**getDTDHandler** ()	
	..... *org.xml.sax.DTDHandler*		

P

Classes

ParserAdapter

1	public		**getEntityResolver** ()
		... *org.xml.sax.EntityResolver*	
1	public		**getErrorHandler** ()
		..... *org.xml.sax.ErrorHandler*	
1	public	boolean	**getFeature** (String name) throws org.xml.sax.SAXNotRecognizedException, org.xml.sax.SAXNotSupportedException
1	public	Object	**getProperty** (String name) throws org.xml.sax.SAXNotRecognizedException, org.xml.sax.SAXNotSupportedException
2	public	void	**ignorableWhitespace** (char[] ch, int start, int length) throws org.xml.sax.SAXException
1	public	void	**parse** (String systemId) throws java.io.IOException, org.xml.sax.SAXException
1	public	void	**parse** (org.xml.sax.InputSource input) throws java.io.IOException, org.xml.sax.SAXException
✱	public		**ParserAdapter** () throws org.xml.sax.SAXException
✱	public		**ParserAdapter** (*org.xml.sax.Parser* parser)
2	public	void	**processingInstruction** (String target, String data) throws org.xml.sax.SAXException
1	public	void	**setContentHandler** (*org.xml.sax.ContentHandler* handler)
2	public	void	**setDocumentLocator** (*org.xml.sax.Locator* locator)
1	public	void	**setDTDHandler** (*org.xml.sax.DTDHandler* handler)
1	public	void	**setEntityResolver** (*org.xml.sax.EntityResolver* resolver)
1	public	void	**setErrorHandler** (*org.xml.sax.ErrorHandler* handler)
1	public	void	**setFeature** (String name, boolean state) throws org.xml.sax↵.SAXNotRecognizedException, org.xml.sax.SAXNotSupportedException
1	public	void	**setProperty** (String name, Object value) throws org.xml.sax↵.SAXNotRecognizedException, org.xml.sax.SAXNotSupportedException
2	public	void	**startDocument** () throws org.xml.sax.SAXException
2	public	void	**startElement** (String qName, *org.xml.sax.AttributeList* qAtts) throws org.xml.sax.SAXException

---

ParserConfigurationException   `javax.xml.parsers`

ε510,511,512,513,514

```
Object
└Throwable¹ -------------------------- java.io.Serializable
  └Exception
```
1.4   `    └ParserConfigurationException`

✱	public		**ParserConfigurationException** ()
✱	public		**ParserConfigurationException** (String msg)
1	public	void	printStackTrace ()

ParserFactory   `org.xml.sax.helpers`

```
Object
└ParserFactory
```

D	△	public static *org.xml.sax.Parser* **makeParser** () throws ClassNotFoundException, IllegalAccessException, InstantiationException, NullPointerException, ClassCastException
D	△	public static *org.xml.sax.Parser* **makeParser** (String className) throws ClassNotFoundException, IllegalAccessException, InstantiationException, ClassCastException

---

PartialResultException   `javax.naming`

```
Object
└ Throwable -------------------------- java.io.Serializable
  └Exception
```
1.3   `    └NamingException¹`
1.3   `      └PartialResultException`

1		*20 inherited members from NamingException not shown*
✱	public	**PartialResultException** ()
✱	public	**PartialResultException** (String explanation)

Class   *Interface*   —extends   - - -implements   ○ abstract   ● final   △ static   ▲ static final   ✱ constructor   x x—inherited   x **x**—declared   **x x**—overridden
εn—examples of usage   ˻—has subclass   package—see other volume

PasswordAuthentication · java.net

1.2 ●	Object └PasswordAuthentication		
	public	char[]	**getPassword** ()
	public	String	**getUserName** ()
*	public		**PasswordAuthentication** (String userName, char[] password) ε139

PasswordCallback · javax.security.auth.callback

1.4	Object └PasswordCallback - *Callback, java.io.Serializable*		
	public	void	**clearPassword** ()
	public	char[]	**getPassword** ()
	public	String	**getPrompt** () ε509
	public	boolean	**isEchoOn** ()
*	public		**PasswordCallback** (String prompt, boolean echoOn)
	public	void	**setPassword** (char[] password) ε509

Pattern · java.util.regex

1.4 ●	Object └Pattern - *java.io.Serializable*		
▲	public static final	int	**CANON_EQ** = 128
▲	public static final	int	**CASE_INSENSITIVE** = 2 ε433,435
▲	public static final	int	**COMMENTS** = 4 ε434
△	public static	Pattern	**compile** (String regex) ε423,424,425,426,427
△	public static	Pattern	**compile** (String regex, int flags) ε433,434,435,443,444
▲	public static final	int	**DOTALL** = 32 ε444
	public	int	**flags** ()
	public	Matcher	**matcher** (*CharSequence* input) ε423,424,425,426,427
△	public static	boolean	**matches** (String regex, *CharSequence* input) ε428,433,434,443,444
▲	public static final	int	**MULTILINE** = 8 ε435,443,445,447,448
	public	String	**pattern** ()
	public	String[]	**split** (*CharSequence* input) ε448
	public	String[]	**split** (*CharSequence* input, int limit)
▲	public static final	int	**UNICODE_CASE** = 64
▲	public static final	int	**UNIX_LINES** = 1

PatternSyntaxException · java.util.regex

1.4	Object
	└Throwable [1] - *java.io.Serializable*
	  └Exception
	    └RuntimeException
	      └IllegalArgumentException
	        └PatternSyntaxException		

	public	String	**getDescription** ()
	public	int	**getIndex** ()
1	public	**String**	**getMessage** ()
	public	String	**getPattern** ()
*	public		**PatternSyntaxException** (String desc, String regex, int index)

PBEKey · javax.crypto.interfaces

1.4	*PBEKey* - *javax.crypto.SecretKey (java.security.Key [1] (java.io.Serializable))* ε198,201,210,459,462		
1	public	String	getAlgorithm () ε203,204,205,464,469
1	public	byte[]	getEncoded () ε199,460,471,471
1	public	String	getFormat () ε199
	public	int	**getIterationCount** ()
	public	char[]	**getPassword** ()
	public	byte[]	**getSalt** ()

PBEKeySpec

	PBEKeySpec				javax.crypto.spec

	Object	
1.4	└PBEKeySpec ------------------------- *java.security.spec.KeySpec*	

●	public final ....void	**clearPassword** ()	
●	public final ....int	**getIterationCount** ()	
●	public final ....int	**getKeyLength** ()	
●	public final ....char[]	**getPassword** ()	
●	public final ....byte[]	**getSalt** ()	
✳	public..........................	**PBEKeySpec** (char[] password)	
✳	public..........................	**PBEKeySpec** (char[] password, byte[] salt, int iterationCount)	ε464
✳	public..........................	**PBEKeySpec** (char[] password, byte[] salt, int iterationCount, int keyLength)	

	PBEParameterSpec				javax.crypto.spec

	Object	
1.4	└PBEParameterSpec -------------------- *java.security.spec.AlgorithmParameterSpec*	

	public.......................int	**getIterationCount** ()	
	public...................byte[]	**getSalt** ()	
✳	public..........................	**PBEParameterSpec** (byte[] salt, int iterationCount)	ε464

	*Permission*❶				java.security.acl

1.1	*Permission*	

	public.................. boolean	**equals** (Object another)
	public...................String	**toString** ()

	*Permission*❷				java.security

	Object[1]		ε217,218
1.2 ○	└Permission⌄ -------------------------- *Guard*[2], *java.io.Serializable*⌄		

	2 public.....................void	**checkGuard** (Object object) throws SecurityException		
○	1 public abstract ....**boolean**	**equals** (Object obj)		ε215
○	public abstract ....String	**getActions** ()		ε215
●	public final ....String	**getName** ()		
○	1 public abstract ....**int**	**hashCode** ()		ε215
○	public abstract .... boolean	**implies** (Permission permission)		ε214,215
	public.... PermissionCollection	**newPermissionCollection** ()		
✳	public..........................	**Permission** (String name)		
	1 public.................. **String**	**toString** ()		

	PermissionCollection				java.security

	Object[1]	
1.2 ○	└PermissionCollection⌄ -------------------- *java.io.Serializable*⌄	

○	public abstract ....void	**add** (Permission permission)	
○	public abstract	**elements** ()	ε217,218
	.... *java.util.Enumeration*		
○	public abstract .... boolean	**implies** (Permission permission)	
	public.................. boolean	**isReadOnly** ()	
✳	public..........................	**PermissionCollection** ()	
	public.....................void	**setReadOnly** ()	
	1 public.................. **String**	**toString** ()	

	Permissions				java.security

	Object	
1.2 ○	└PermissionCollection[1] -------------------- *java.io.Serializable*⌄	
1.2 ●	└Permissions	

Class   *Interface*   —extends   - - -implements   ○ abstract   ● final   △ static   ▲ static final   ✳ constructor   x x—inherited   x **x**—declared   **x x**—overridden
ε*n*—examples of usage   ⌄—has subclass   package—see other volume

1	public	**void**	**add** (Permission permission)	
1	public..	**java.util.Enumeration**	**elements** ()	ε217,218
1	public	**boolean**	**implies** (Permission permission)	
1	public	boolean	isReadOnly ()	
*	public		**Permissions** ()	
1	public	void	setReadOnly ()	
1	public	String	toString ()	

PERSIST_STORE · org.omg.CORBA

```
Object
└Throwable ----------------------------- java.io.Serializable
   └Exception
      └RuntimeException
         └SystemException¹
            └PERSIST_STORE
```
1.2 ○
1.2 ●

1	*3 inherited members from SystemException not shown*		
*	public	**PERSIST_STORE** ()	
*	public	**PERSIST_STORE** (String s)	
*	public	**PERSIST_STORE** (int minor, CompletionStatus completed)	
*	public	**PERSIST_STORE** (String s, int minor, CompletionStatus completed)	

P

PersistenceDelegate · java.beans

```
Object
└PersistenceDelegate
```
1.4 ○

	protected	void	**initialize** (Class type, Object oldInstance, Object newInstance, Encoder out)
○	protected abstract .	Expression	**instantiate** (Object oldInstance, Encoder out)
	protected	boolean	**mutatesTo** (Object oldInstance, Object newInstance)
*	public		**PersistenceDelegate** ()
	public	void	**writeObject** (Object oldInstance, Encoder out)

PhantomReference · java.lang.ref

```
Object                                                      ε107
└Reference¹
   └PhantomReference
```
1.2 ○
1.2

1	public	void	clear ()	
1	public	boolean	enqueue ()	
1	public	**Object**	**get** ()	ε106,357
1	public	boolean	isEnqueued ()	
*	public		**PhantomReference** (Object referent, ReferenceQueue q)	ε108

ε108

Classes

Pipe · java.nio.channels

```
Object
└Pipe
```
1.4 ○

△	public static	Pipe	**open** () throws java.io.IOException
*	protected		**Pipe** ()
○	public abstract	Pipe.SinkChannel	**sink** ()
○	public abstract	Pipe.SourceChannel	**source** ()

Pipe.SinkChannel

				java.nio.channels

ε178,183

```
        Object
1.4 ○   └java.nio.channels.spi←------------------- Channel ˅, InterruptibleChannel (Channel)
          .AbstractInterruptibleChannel¹
1.4 ○     └SelectableChannel²
1.4 ○       └java.nio.channels.spi←
              .AbstractSelectableChannel³
1.4 ○         └Pipe.SinkChannel ---------------- WritableByteChannel ˅ (Channel), GatheringByteChannel
                                                    (WritableByteChannel (Channel))
```

●	1	protected final..............void	begin ()	
●	3	public final ....Object	blockingLock ()	
●	1	public final ....void	close () throws java.io.IOException	ε167,170,171,172,174
●	3	public final SelectableChannel	configureBlocking (boolean block) throws java.io.IOException	ε173,177,179
●	1	protected final..............void	end (boolean completed) throws AsynchronousCloseException	
●	3	protected final..............void	implCloseChannel () throws java.io.IOException	
○	3	protected abstract ....void	implCloseSelectableChannel () throws java.io.IOException	
○	3	protected abstract ....void	implConfigureBlocking (boolean block) throws java.io.IOException	
●	3	public final .... boolean	isBlocking ()	
●	1	public final .... boolean	isOpen ()	
●	3	public final .... boolean	isRegistered ()	
●	3	public final ....SelectionKey	keyFor (Selector sel)	
●	3	public final java.nio.channels← .spi.SelectorProvider	provider ()	
●	2	public final ....SelectionKey	register (Selector sel, int ops) throws ClosedChannelException	ε176,179
●	3	public final ....SelectionKey	register (Selector sel, int ops, Object att) throws ClosedChannelException	
✳		protected	**Pipe.SinkChannel** (java.nio.channels.spi.SelectorProvider provider)	
●	2	public final .... **int**	**validOps** ()	ε176

Pipe.SourceChannel

				java.nio.channels

ε178,183

```
        Object
1.4 ○   └java.nio.channels.spi←------------------- Channel ˅, InterruptibleChannel (Channel)
          .AbstractInterruptibleChannel¹
1.4 ○     └SelectableChannel²
1.4 ○       └java.nio.channels.spi←
              .AbstractSelectableChannel³
1.4 ○         └Pipe.SourceChannel -------------- ReadableByteChannel ˅ (Channel), ScatteringByteChannel
                                                    (ReadableByteChannel (Channel))
```

●	1	protected final..............void	begin ()	
●	3	public final ....Object	blockingLock ()	
●	1	public final ....void	close () throws java.io.IOException	ε167,170,171,172,174
●	3	public final SelectableChannel	configureBlocking (boolean block) throws java.io.IOException	ε173,177,179
●	1	protected final..............void	end (boolean completed) throws AsynchronousCloseException	
●	3	protected final..............void	implCloseChannel () throws java.io.IOException	
○	3	protected abstract ....void	implCloseSelectableChannel () throws java.io.IOException	
○	3	protected abstract ....void	implConfigureBlocking (boolean block) throws java.io.IOException	
●	3	public final .... boolean	isBlocking ()	
●	1	public final .... boolean	isOpen ()	
●	3	public final .... boolean	isRegistered ()	
●	3	public final ....SelectionKey	keyFor (Selector sel)	
●	3	public final java.nio.channels← .spi.SelectorProvider	provider ()	
●	2	public final ....SelectionKey	register (Selector sel, int ops) throws ClosedChannelException	ε176,179
●	3	public final ....SelectionKey	register (Selector sel, int ops, Object att) throws ClosedChannelException	
✳		protected	**Pipe.SourceChannel** (java.nio.channels.spi.SelectorProvider provider)	
●	2	public final .... **int**	**validOps** ()	ε176

PipedInputStream

				java.io

ε252,382,418

```
        Object
○       └InputStream¹
          └PipedInputStream
```

	1	public synchronized .... **int available** () throws IOException	
1.1		protected ....byte[] **buffer**	

Class *Interface* —extends - - -implements ○ abstract ● final △ static ▲ static final ✳ constructor x x—inherited x **x**—declared **x x**—overridden
ε*n*—examples of usage ˅—has subclass package —see other volume

	1	public	**void**	**close** () throws IOException	ε14,36,45,452,455
		public	void	**connect** (PipedOutputStream src) throws IOException	
1.1		protected	int	**in**	
	1	public synchronized	void	mark (int readlimit)	
	1	public	boolean	markSupported ()	
1.1		protected	int	**out**	
1.1 ▲		protected static final	int	**PIPE_SIZE**	
*		public		**PipedInputStream** ()	
*		public		**PipedInputStream** (PipedOutputStream src) throws IOException	
	1	public synchronized	**int**	**read** () throws IOException	ε90,184,256
	1	public	int	read (byte[] b) throws IOException	ε452,455,457,170,451
	1	public synchronized	**int**	**read** (byte[] b, int off, int len) throws IOException	ε36
1.1		protected synchronized	void	**receive** (int b) throws IOException	
	1	public synchronized	void	reset () throws IOException	
	1	public	long	skip (long n) throws IOException	

PipedOutputStream

java.io

Object
ε183
○ └OutputStream [1]
 └PipedOutputStream

	1	public	**void**	**close** () throws IOException	ε451,453,91,211,224
		public synchronized	void	**connect** (PipedInputStream snk) throws IOException	
	1	public synchronized	**void**	**flush** () throws IOException	ε27,54
*		public		**PipedOutputStream** ()	
*		public		**PipedOutputStream** (PipedInputStream snk) throws IOException	
	1	public	void	write (byte[] b) throws IOException	ε27,91,224
	1	public	**void**	**write** (int b) throws IOException	ε184
	1	public	**void**	**write** (byte[] b, int off, int len) throws IOException	ε451,453,54,449,450

PipedReader

java.io

Object
1.1 ○ └Reader [1]
1.1 └PipedReader

	1	public	**void**	**close** () throws IOException	ε35,47,135,136,139
		public	void	**connect** (PipedWriter src) throws IOException	
	1	protected	Object	lock	
	1	public	void	mark (int readAheadLimit) throws IOException	
	1	public	boolean	markSupported ()	ε442
*		public		**PipedReader** ()	
*		public		**PipedReader** (PipedWriter src) throws IOException	
	1	public synchronized	**int**	**read** () throws IOException	
	1	public	int	read (char[] cbuf) throws IOException	ε434
	1	public synchronized	**int**	**read** (char[] cbuf, int off, int len) throws IOException	
	1	public synchronized	**boolean**	**ready** () throws IOException	ε442
	1	public	void	reset () throws IOException	
	1	public	long	skip (long n) throws IOException	

PipedWriter

java.io

Object
1.1 ○ └Writer [1]
1.1 └PipedWriter

	1	public	**void**	**close** () throws IOException	ε23,37,38,41,43
		public synchronized	void	**connect** (PipedReader snk) throws IOException	
	1	public synchronized	**void**	**flush** () throws IOException	ε135,150,224
	1	protected	Object	lock	
*		public		**PipedWriter** ()	
*		public		**PipedWriter** (PipedReader snk) throws IOException	
	1	public	void	write (char[] cbuf) throws IOException	
	1	public	**void**	**write** (int c) throws IOException	
	1	public	void	write (String str) throws IOException	ε23,37,38,41,43
	1	public	**void**	**write** (char[] cbuf, int off, int len) throws IOException	
	1	public	void	write (String str, int off, int len) throws IOException	

P

Classes

PKCS8EncodedKeySpec
java.security.spec

Object
ε199

1.2 O └EncodedKeySpec[1] - *KeySpec*
1.2   └PKCS8EncodedKeySpec

	1	public	**byte[]**	**getEncoded** ()	
●	1	public final	**String**	**getFormat** ()	
*		public		**PKCS8EncodedKeySpec** (byte[] encodedKey)	ε199

PKIXBuilderParameters
java.security.cert

Object

1.4 └PKIXParameters[1] - *CertPathParameters* (*Cloneable*)
1.4   └PKIXBuilderParameters

	1	*27 inherited members from PKIXParameters not shown*
		public......................int **getMaxPathLength** ()
*		public.......................... **PKIXBuilderParameters** (java.security.KeyStore keystore, *CertSelector* targetConstraints) throws java.security.KeyStoreException, java.security.InvalidAlgorithmParameterException
*		public.......................... **PKIXBuilderParameters** (*java.util.Set* trustAnchors, *CertSelector* targetConstraints) throws java.security.InvalidAlgorithmParameterException
		public......................void **setMaxPathLength** (int maxPathLength)
	1	public................... **String** **toString** ()

PKIXCertPathBuilderResult
java.security.cert

Object

1.4 └PKIXCertPathValidatorResult[1] - - - - - - - - - - - - - *CertPathValidatorResult* (*Cloneable*)
1.4   └PKIXCertPathBuilderResult - - - - - - - - - - - - *CertPathBuilderResult*[2] (*Cloneable*)

	1	public...................Object clone ()	
	2	public....................CertPath **getCertPath** ()	
	1	public............... *PolicyNode* getPolicyTree ()	
	1	public. *java.security.PublicKey* getPublicKey ()	
	1	public............. TrustAnchor getTrustAnchor ()	ε231
*		public.......................... **PKIXCertPathBuilderResult** (CertPath certPath, TrustAnchor trustAnchor, *PolicyNode* policyTree, *java.security.PublicKey* subjectPublicKey)	
	1	public................... **String** **toString** ()	

PKIXCertPathChecker
java.security.cert

Object[1]

1.4 O └PKIXCertPathChecker - - - - - - - - - - - - - - - - - - *Cloneable*

O		public abstract............void **check** (Certificate cert, *java.util.Collection* unresolvedCritExts) throws CertPathValidatorException
	1	public................... **Object** **clone** ()
O		public abstract..... *java.util.Set* **getSupportedExtensions** ()
O		public abstract............void **init** (boolean forward) throws CertPathValidatorException
O		public abstract........ boolean **isForwardCheckingSupported** ()
*		protected...................... **PKIXCertPathChecker** ()

PKIXCertPathValidatorResult
java.security.cert

Object[1]

1.4 └PKIXCertPathValidatorResult - - - - - - - - - - - - - *CertPathValidatorResult* (*Cloneable*)

	1	public.................... **Object** **clone** ()	
		public............... *PolicyNode* **getPolicyTree** ()	
		public. *java.security.PublicKey* **getPublicKey** ()	
		public............. TrustAnchor **getTrustAnchor** ()	ε231
*		public.......................... **PKIXCertPathValidatorResult** (TrustAnchor trustAnchor, *PolicyNode* policyTree, *java.security.PublicKey* subjectPublicKey)	

Class   *Interface*   —extends   - - -implements   O abstract   ● final   △ static   ▲ static final   * constructor   x x—inherited   x **x**—declared   **x x**—overridden
ε*n*—examples of usage   —has subclass   package—see other volume

1	public	.... **String toString** ()	

PKIXParameters
java.security.cert

Object[1]
1.4 └PKIXParameters ----------------------- *CertPathParameters* (*Cloneable*)

	public	.................void	**addCertPathChecker** (PKIXCertPathChecker checker)
	public	.................void	**addCertStore** (CertStore store)
1	public	...............**Object**	**clone** ()
	public	.............*java.util.List*	**getCertPathCheckers** ()
	public	.............*java.util.List*	**getCertStores** ()
	public	............java.util.Date	**getDate** ()
	public	.............*java.util.Set*	**getInitialPolicies** ()
	public	................boolean	**getPolicyQualifiersRejected** ()
	public	.................String	**getSigProvider** ()
	public	...........*CertSelector*	**getTargetCertConstraints** ()
	public	.............*java.util.Set*	**getTrustAnchors** ()	ε230
	public	................boolean	**isAnyPolicyInhibited** ()
	public	................boolean	**isExplicitPolicyRequired** ()
	public	................boolean	**isPolicyMappingInhibited** ()
	public	................boolean	**isRevocationEnabled** ()
*	public	....	**PKIXParameters** (java.security.KeyStore keystore) throws java.security↵ .KeyStoreException, java.security.InvalidAlgorithmParameterException	ε230,231
*	public	....	**PKIXParameters** (*java.util.Set* trustAnchors) throws java.security.InvalidAlgorithmParameterException
	public	.................void	**setAnyPolicyInhibited** (boolean val)
	public	.................void	**setCertPathCheckers** (*java.util.List* checkers)
	public	.................void	**setCertStores** (*java.util.List* stores)
	public	.................void	**setDate** (java.util.Date date)
	public	.................void	**setExplicitPolicyRequired** (boolean val)
	public	.................void	**setInitialPolicies** (*java.util.Set* initialPolicies)
	public	.................void	**setPolicyMappingInhibited** (boolean val)
	public	.................void	**setPolicyQualifiersRejected** (boolean qualifiersRejected)
	public	.................void	**setRevocationEnabled** (boolean val)	ε231
	public	.................void	**setSigProvider** (String sigProvider)
	public	.................void	**setTargetCertConstraints** (*CertSelector* selector)
	public	.................void	**setTrustAnchors** (*java.util.Set* trustAnchors) throws java.security.InvalidAlgorithmParameterException
1	public	.... **String toString** ()

POA
org.omg.PortableServer

1.4 *POA*————————————— *POAOperations*[1], *org.omg.CORBA.Object*[2], *org.omg.CORBA.portable.IDLEntity* (*java.io.Serializable*)

1 *32 inherited members from POAOperations not shown*
2 *13 inherited members from org.omg.CORBA.Object not shown*

POAHelper
org.omg.PortableServer

Object
1.4 ○ └POAHelper

△	public static	.... *POA*	**extract** (org.omg.CORBA.Any a)
△	public static	...........String	**id** ()
△	public static	...........void	**insert** (org.omg.CORBA.Any a, *POA* that)
△	public static	.... *POA*	**narrow** (*org.omg.CORBA.Object* obj)
*	public	....	**POAHelper** ()
△	public static	.... *POA*	**read** (org.omg.CORBA.portable.InputStream istream)
△	public static synchronized	.... **type** () org.omg.CORBA.TypeCode	
△	public static	...........void	**write** (org.omg.CORBA.portable.OutputStream ostream, *POA* value)

POAManager	org.omg.PortableServer

1.4 POAManager————————————————*POAManagerOperations*,[1], *org.omg.CORBA.Object*,[2],
org.omg.CORBA.portable.IDLEntity, (*java.io.Serializable*)

> 1 5 inherited members from POAManagerOperations not shown
> 2 13 inherited members from org.omg.CORBA.Object not shown

POAManagerOperations	org.omg.PortableServer

1.4 *POAManagerOperations*,

public.....................void **activate** () throws org.omg.PortableServer.POAManagerPackage.AdapterInactive
public.....................void **deactivate** (boolean etherealize_objects, boolean wait_for_completion)
        throws org.omg.PortableServer.POAManagerPackage.AdapterInactive
public.....................void **discard_requests** (boolean wait_for_completion) throws
        org.omg.PortableServer.POAManagerPackage.AdapterInactive
public.......................... **get_state** ()
... org.omg.PortableServer ↵
.POAManagerPackage.State
public.....................void **hold_requests** (boolean wait_for_completion) throws
        org.omg.PortableServer.POAManagerPackage.AdapterInactive

POAOperations	org.omg.PortableServer

1.4 *POAOperations*,

public.....................byte[] **activate_object** (Servant p_servant) throws org↵
        .omg.PortableServer.POAPackage.ServantAlreadyActive,
        org.omg.PortableServer.POAPackage.WrongPolicy
public.....................void **activate_object_with_id** (byte[] id, Servant p_servant)
        throws org.omg.PortableServer.POAPackage.ServantAlreadyActive,
        org.omg.PortableServer.POAPackage.ObjectAlreadyActive,
        org.omg.PortableServer.POAPackage.WrongPolicy
public..... *IdAssignmentPolicy* **create_id_assignment_policy** (IdAssignmentPolicyValue value)
public..... *IdUniquenessPolicy* **create_id_uniqueness_policy** (IdUniquenessPolicyValue value)
public.. *ImplicitActivationPolicy* **create_implicit_activation_policy** (ImplicitActivationPolicyValue value)
public........... *LifespanPolicy* **create_lifespan_policy** (LifespanPolicyValue value)
public..................... *POA* **create_POA** (String adapter_name, *POAManager* a_POAManager, *org.omg*↵
        .CORBA.Policy[] policies) throws org.omg.PortableServer.POAPackage↵
        .AdapterAlreadyExists, org.omg.PortableServer.POAPackage.InvalidPolicy
public *org.omg.CORBA.Object* **create_reference** (String intf) throws org.omg.PortableServer.POAPackage↵
        .WrongPolicy
public *org.omg.CORBA.Object* **create_reference_with_id** (byte[] oid, String intf)
public.............................. **create_request_processing_policy** (RequestProcessingPolicyValue value)
.... *RequestProcessingPolicy*
public.. *ServantRetentionPolicy* **create_servant_retention_policy** (ServantRetentionPolicyValue value)
public............. *ThreadPolicy* **create_thread_policy** (ThreadPolicyValue value)
public.....................void **deactivate_object** (byte[] oid) throws org.omg.PortableServer.POAPackage↵
        .ObjectNotActive, org.omg.PortableServer.POAPackage.WrongPolicy
public.....................void **destroy** (boolean etherealize_objects, boolean wait_for_completion)
public..................... *POA* **find_POA** (String adapter_name, boolean activate_it)
        throws org.omg.PortableServer.POAPackage.AdapterNonExistent
public................... Servant **get_servant** () throws org.omg.PortableServer.POAPackage.NoServant,
        org.omg.PortableServer.POAPackage.WrongPolicy
public......... *ServantManager* **get_servant_manager** () throws org.omg.PortableServer.POAPackage↵
        .WrongPolicy
public.....................byte[] **id** ()
public *org.omg.CORBA.Object* **id_to_reference** (byte[] oid) throws org.omg.PortableServer.POAPackage↵
        .ObjectNotActive, org.omg.PortableServer.POAPackage.WrongPolicy
public................... Servant **id_to_servant** (byte[] oid) throws org.omg.PortableServer.POAPackage↵
        .ObjectNotActive, org.omg.PortableServer.POAPackage.WrongPolicy
public.....................byte[] **reference_to_id** (*org.omg.CORBA.Object* reference)
        throws org.omg.PortableServer.POAPackage.WrongAdapter,
        org.omg.PortableServer.POAPackage.WrongPolicy

Class *Interface* —extends - - -implements ○ abstract ● final △ static ▲ static final ✳ constructor x x—inherited x **x**—declared **x x**—overridden
ε*n*—examples of usage ,—has subclass package—see other volume

public	Servant	**reference_to_servant** (*org.omg.CORBA.Object* reference)
		throws org.omg.PortableServer.POAPackage.ObjectNotActive,
		org.omg.PortableServer.POAPackage.WrongPolicy,
		org.omg.PortableServer.POAPackage.WrongAdapter
public	byte[]	**servant_to_id** (Servant p_servant) throws org.omg.PortableServer.POAPackage ↵
		.ServantNotActive, org.omg.PortableServer.POAPackage.WrongPolicy
public *org.omg.CORBA.Object*		**servant_to_reference** (Servant p_servant) throws
		org.omg.PortableServer.POAPackage.ServantNotActive,
		org.omg.PortableServer.POAPackage.WrongPolicy
public	void	**set_servant** (Servant p_servant) throws org.omg.PortableServer.POAPackage ↵
		.WrongPolicy
public	void	**set_servant_manager** (*ServantManager* imgr) throws
		org.omg.PortableServer.POAPackage.WrongPolicy
public	*AdapterActivator*	**the_activator** ()
public	void	**the_activator** (*AdapterActivator* newThe_activator)
public	*POA[]*	**the_children** ()
public	String	**the_name** ()
public	*POA*	**the_parent** ()
public	*POAManager*	**the_POAManager** ()

Policy❶   java.security

	Object	
1.2 ○	└Policy	

○	public abstract	**getPermissions** (CodeSource codesource)	ε218
	PermissionCollection		
1.4	public PermissionCollection	**getPermissions** (ProtectionDomain domain)	ε217
△	public static Policy	**getPolicy** ()	ε217,218
1.4	public boolean	**implies** (ProtectionDomain domain, Permission permission)	
*	public	**Policy** ()	
○	public abstract void	**refresh** ()	
△	public static void	**setPolicy** (Policy policy)	

Policy❷   javax.security.auth

		Object	
D	○	└Policy	

D	○	public abstract .java.security ↵	**getPermissions** (Subject subject, java.security.CodeSource cs)
		.PermissionCollection	
D	△	public static Policy	**getPolicy** ()
D	*	protected	**Policy** ()
D	○	public abstract void	**refresh** ()
D	△	public static void	**setPolicy** (Policy policy)

Policy❸   org.omg.CORBA

1.2	*Policy* ———————————————— *PolicyOperations*◟[1], *Object*◟[2], *org.omg.CORBA.portable.IDLEntity*◟
	(*java.io.Serializable*)

> [2] *13 inherited members from Object not shown*
> [1] *3 inherited members from PolicyOperations not shown*

PolicyError   org.omg.CORBA

	Object	
	└Throwable ----------------------------- *java.io.Serializable*◟	
	└Exception	
1.2 ○	└UserException -------------------- *org.omg.CORBA.portable.IDLEntity*◟ (*java.io.Serializable*)	
1.2 ●	└PolicyError	

*	public	**PolicyError** ()
*	public	**PolicyError** (short __reason)
*	public	**PolicyError** (String reason_string, short __reason)
	public short	**reason**

	PolicyErrorCodeHelper	org.omg.CORBA

	Object	
1.4 O	└ PolicyErrorCodeHelper	

△	public static .... short	**extract** (Any a)
△	public static .... String	**id** ()
△	public static .... void	**insert** (Any a, short that)
✳	public.........................	**PolicyErrorCodeHelper** ()
△	public static .... short	**read** (org.omg.CORBA.portable.InputStream istream)
△	public static synchronized .... TypeCode	**type** ()
△	public static .... void	**write** (org.omg.CORBA.portable.OutputStream ostream, short value)

	PolicyErrorHelper	org.omg.CORBA

	Object	
1.4 O	└ PolicyErrorHelper	

△	public static .... PolicyError	**extract** (Any a)
△	public static .... String	**id** ()
△	public static .... void	**insert** (Any a, PolicyError that)
✳	public.........................	**PolicyErrorHelper** ()
△	public static .... PolicyError	**read** (org.omg.CORBA.portable.InputStream istream)
△	public static synchronized .... TypeCode	**type** ()
△	public static .... void	**write** (org.omg.CORBA.portable.OutputStream ostream, PolicyError value)

P

	PolicyErrorHolder	org.omg.CORBA

	Object	
1.4 ●	└ PolicyErrorHolder --------------------- *org.omg.CORBA.portable.Streamable*⌐ [1]	

1	public...................... void	**_read** (org.omg.CORBA.portable.InputStream i)
1	public................ TypeCode	**_type** ()
1	public...................... void	**_write** (org.omg.CORBA.portable.OutputStream o)
✳	public...........................	**PolicyErrorHolder** ()
✳	public...........................	**PolicyErrorHolder** (PolicyError initialValue)
	public.............. PolicyError	**value**

	PolicyFactory	org.omg.PortableInterceptor

1.4	*PolicyFactory*————————————— *PolicyFactoryOperations*⌐ [1], *org.omg.CORBA.Object*⌐ [2], *org.omg.CORBA.portable.IDLEntity*⌐ (*java.io.Serializable*)

2	*13 inherited members from org.omg.CORBA.Object not shown*
1	public. *org.omg.CORBA.Policy* create_policy (int type, org.omg.CORBA.Any value) throws org.omg.CORBA.PolicyError

	PolicyFactoryOperations	org.omg.PortableInterceptor

1.4	*PolicyFactoryOperations*⌐

	public. *org.omg.CORBA.Policy* **create_policy** (int type, org.omg.CORBA.Any value) throws org.omg.CORBA.PolicyError

	PolicyHelper	org.omg.CORBA

	Object	
1.3 O	└ PolicyHelper	

△	public static .... *Policy*	**extract** (Any a)
△	public static .... String	**id** ()
△	public static .... void	**insert** (Any a, *Policy* that)
△	public static .... *Policy*	**narrow** (*Object* obj)
✳	public...........................	**PolicyHelper** ()

Class *Interface* —extends - - -implements O abstract ● final △ static ▲ static final ✳ constructor x x—inherited x **x**—declared **x x**—overridden
ε*n*—examples of usage ⌐—has subclass package—see other volume

△	public static	*Policy*	**read** (org.omg.CORBA.portable.InputStream istream)
△	public static synchronized		**type** ()
	....	TypeCode	
△	public static	void	**write** (org.omg.CORBA.portable.OutputStream ostream, *Policy* value)

PolicyHolder `org.omg.CORBA`

Object
1.3 ● └PolicyHolder - *org.omg.CORBA.portable.Streamable* ⌐[1]

1	public......................	void	**_read** (org.omg.CORBA.portable.InputStream i)
1	public...............	TypeCode	**_type** ()
1	public......................	void	**_write** (org.omg.CORBA.portable.OutputStream o)
✳	public.........................		**PolicyHolder** ()
✳	public.........................		**PolicyHolder** (*Policy* initialValue)
	public.................	*Policy*	**value**

PolicyListHelper `org.omg.CORBA`

Object
1.3 ○ └PolicyListHelper

△	public static	*Policy[]*	**extract** (Any a)
△	public static	String	**id** ()
△	public static	void	**insert** (Any a, *Policy[]* that)
✳	public.........................		**PolicyListHelper** ()
△	public static	*Policy[]*	**read** (org.omg.CORBA.portable.InputStream istream)
△	public static synchronized		**type** ()
	....	TypeCode	
△	public static	void	**write** (org.omg.CORBA.portable.OutputStream ostream, *Policy[]* value)

PolicyListHolder `org.omg.CORBA`

Object
1.3 ● └PolicyListHolder - *org.omg.CORBA.portable.Streamable* ⌐[1]

1	public......................	void	**_read** (org.omg.CORBA.portable.InputStream i)
1	public...............	TypeCode	**_type** ()
1	public......................	void	**_write** (org.omg.CORBA.portable.OutputStream o)
✳	public.........................		**PolicyListHolder** ()
✳	public.........................		**PolicyListHolder** (*Policy[]* initialValue)
	public.................	*Policy[]*	**value**

PolicyNode `java.security.cert`

1.4 *PolicyNode*

public..........	*java.util.Iterator*	**getChildren** ()
public..........................	int	**getDepth** ()
public..........................	*java.util.Set*	**getExpectedPolicies** ()
public...............	*PolicyNode*	**getParent** ()
public..........................	*java.util.Set*	**getPolicyQualifiers** ()
public......................	String	**getValidPolicy** ()
public.................	boolean	**isCritical** ()

PolicyOperations `org.omg.CORBA`

1.3 *PolicyOperations* ⌐

public......................	*Policy*	**copy** ()
public......................	void	**destroy** ()
public..........................	int	**policy_type** ()

PolicyQualifierInfo `java.security.cert`

Object[1]
1.4 ● └PolicyQualifierInfo

P

Classes

PolicyQualifierInfo

	public	byte[]	**getEncoded** ()
	public	byte[]	**getPolicyQualifier** ()
	public	String	**getPolicyQualifierId** ()
*	public		**PolicyQualifierInfo** (byte[] encoded) throws java.io.IOException
1	public	**String**	**toString** ()

PolicyTypeHelper
org.omg.CORBA

Object
└PolicyTypeHelper

1.3 ○

△	public static	int	**extract** (Any a)
△	public static	String	**id** ()
△	public static	void	**insert** (Any a, int that)
*	public		**PolicyTypeHelper** ()
△	public static	int	**read** (org.omg.CORBA.portable.InputStream istream)
△	public static synchronized	TypeCode	**type** ()
△	public static	void	**write** (org.omg.CORBA.portable.OutputStream ostream, int value)

PooledConnection
javax.sql

1.4 *PooledConnection*

	public	void	**addConnectionEventListener** (*ConnectionEventListener* listener)
	public	void	**close** () throws java.sql.SQLException
	public	*java.sql.Connection*	**getConnection** () throws java.sql.SQLException
	public	void	**removeConnectionEventListener** (*ConnectionEventListener* listener)

PortableRemoteObject
javax.rmi

Object
└PortableRemoteObject

1.3

△	public static	void	**connect** (*java.rmi.Remote* target, *java.rmi.Remote* source) throws java.rmi.RemoteException
△	public static	void	**exportObject** (*java.rmi.Remote* obj) throws java.rmi.RemoteException
△	public static	Object	**narrow** (Object narrowFrom, Class narrowTo) throws ClassCastException
			ε505
*	protected		**PortableRemoteObject** () throws java.rmi.RemoteException
△	public static	*java.rmi.Remote*	**toStub** (*java.rmi.Remote* obj) throws java.rmi.NoSuchObjectException
△	public static	void	**unexportObject** (*java.rmi.Remote* obj) throws java.rmi.NoSuchObjectException

---

PortableRemoteObjectDelegate
javax.rmi.CORBA

1.3 *PortableRemoteObjectDelegate*

	public	void	**connect** (*java.rmi.Remote* target, *java.rmi.Remote* source) throws java.rmi.RemoteException
	public	void	**exportObject** (*java.rmi.Remote* obj) throws java.rmi.RemoteException
	public	Object	**narrow** (Object narrowFrom, Class narrowTo) throws ClassCastException
	public	*java.rmi.Remote*	**toStub** (*java.rmi.Remote* obj) throws java.rmi.NoSuchObjectException
	public	void	**unexportObject** (*java.rmi.Remote* obj) throws java.rmi.NoSuchObjectException

---

PortUnreachableException
java.net

Object
└Throwable -------------------------- *java.io.Serializable*
  └Exception
    └java.io.IOException
      └SocketException
1.4   └PortUnreachableException

*	public		**PortUnreachableException** ()
*	public		**PortUnreachableException** (String msg)

Class *Interface* —extends - - -implements ○ abstract ● final △ static ▲ static final ✳ constructor x x—inherited x **x**—declared **x x**—overridden
ε*n*—examples of usage ˺—has subclass package—see other volume

		PreferenceChangeEvent		java.util.prefs

		Object		ε333
1.1		└java.util.EventObject[1] - - - - - - - - - - - - - - - - - - - *java.io.Serializable*		
1.4		└PreferenceChangeEvent		

		public....................String **getKey** ()		ε421
		public....................String **getNewValue** ()		ε421
		public.............Preferences **getNode** ()		ε421
	1	public....................Object getSource ()		
*		public.......................... **PreferenceChangeEvent** (Preferences node, String key, String newValue)		
	1	protected transient......Object source		
	1	public....................String toString ()		

		PreferenceChangeListener		java.util.prefs

1.4		*PreferenceChangeListener*————————————*java.util.EventListener*		ε2,3,333,493,494
		public......................void **preferenceChange** (PreferenceChangeEvent evt)		ε421

		Preferences		java.util.prefs

		Object[1]		
1.4 ○		└Preferences		

		public abstract...........String **absolutePath** ()		ε411
○		public abstract.............void **addNodeChangeListener** (*NodeChangeListener* ncl)		ε422
○		public abstract.............void **addPreferenceChangeListener** (*PreferenceChangeListener* pcl)		
				ε421
○		public abstract.........String[] **childrenNames** () throws BackingStoreException		ε416,417
○		public abstract.............void **clear** () throws BackingStoreException		ε408
○		public abstract.............void **exportNode** (java.io.OutputStream os) throws java.io.IOException, BackingStoreException		ε419
○		public abstract.............void **exportSubtree** (java.io.OutputStream os) throws java.io.IOException, BackingStoreException		ε420
○		public abstract.............void **flush** () throws BackingStoreException		
○		public abstract...........String **get** (String key, String def)		ε405,406,407,409
○		public abstract........ boolean **getBoolean** (String key, boolean def)		ε409
○		public abstract........byte[] **getByteArray** (String key, byte[] def)		ε409
○		public abstract.........double **getDouble** (String key, double def)		ε409
○		public abstract.............float **getFloat** (String key, float def)		ε409
○		public abstract.................int **getInt** (String key, int def)		ε409
○		public abstract............. long **getLong** (String key, long def)		ε409
△		public static ....void **importPreferences** (java.io.InputStream is) throws java.io.IOException, InvalidPreferencesFormatException		ε418
○		public abstract........ boolean **isUserNode** ()		
○		public abstract.........String[] **keys** () throws BackingStoreException		ε407
▲		public static final.............int **MAX_KEY_LENGTH** = 80		ε410
▲		public static final.............int **MAX_NAME_LENGTH** = 80		
▲		public static final.............int **MAX_VALUE_LENGTH** = 8192		ε410
○		public abstract...........String **name** ()		ε411
○		public abstract....Preferences **node** (String pathName)		ε415,413,414,416,417
○		public abstract........ boolean **nodeExists** (String pathName) throws BackingStoreException		ε414,415
○		public abstract....Preferences **parent** ()		ε411,416,420
*		protected...................... **Preferences** ()		
○		public abstract.............void **put** (String key, String value)		ε405,409,419,420,421
○		public abstract.............void **putBoolean** (String key, boolean value)		ε409,419,420
○		public abstract.............void **putByteArray** (String key, byte[] value)		ε409,419,420
○		public abstract.............void **putDouble** (String key, double value)		ε409,419,420
○		public abstract.............void **putFloat** (String key, float value)		ε409,419,420
○		public abstract.............void **putInt** (String key, int value)		ε409,419,420
○		public abstract.............void **putLong** (String key, long value)		ε409,419,420
○		public abstract.............void **remove** (String key)		ε408,421
○		public abstract.............void **removeNode** () throws BackingStoreException		ε414,415,422
○		public abstract.............void **removeNodeChangeListener** (*NodeChangeListener* ncl)		
○		public abstract.............void **removePreferenceChangeListener** (*PreferenceChangeListener* pcl)		
○		public abstract.............void **sync** () throws BackingStoreException		
△		public static ...... Preferences **systemNodeForPackage** (Class c)		ε413
△		public static .... Preferences **systemRoot** ()		ε411,413
○	1	public abstract........... **String** **toString** ()		
△		public static ...... Preferences **userNodeForPackage** (Class c)		ε405,408,409,413,416
△		public static .... Preferences **userRoot** ()		ε411,413,414,415,417

PreferencesFactory

PreferencesFactory			java.util.prefs

1.4	*PreferencesFactory*		
	public.............Preferences **systemRoot** ()		
	public.............Preferences **userRoot** ()		

PreparedStatement			java.sql

1.1	*PreparedStatement* ——————————— *Statement* ꜀*1*	*ε*267

1 43 inherited members from Statement not shown

1.2	public.....................void **addBatch** () throws SQLException	*ε*265
	public.....................void **clearParameters** () throws SQLException	
1	public.....................void close () throws SQLException	*ε*260
	public............... boolean **execute** () throws SQLException	*ε*298,303
	public...............*ResultSet* **executeQuery** () throws SQLException	
	public.......................int **executeUpdate** () throws SQLException	*ε*259,260,262
1.2	public...... *ResultSetMetaData* **getMetaData** () throws SQLException	
1.4	public..... *ParameterMetaData* **getParameterMetaData** () throws SQLException	
1.2	public.....................void **setArray** (int i, *Array* x) throws SQLException	
	public.....................void **setAsciiStream** (int parameterIndex, java.io.InputStream x, int length)	
	throws SQLException	*ε*259
	public.....................void **setBigDecimal** (int parameterIndex, java.math.BigDecimal x) throws SQLException	
		*ε*259
	public.....................void **setBinaryStream** (int parameterIndex, java.io.InputStream x, int length)	
	throws SQLException	*ε*259
1.2	public.....................void **setBlob** (int i, *Blob* x) throws SQLException	
	public.....................void **setBoolean** (int parameterIndex, boolean x) throws SQLException	
		*ε*259
	public.....................void **setByte** (int parameterIndex, byte x) throws SQLException	*ε*259
	public.....................void **setBytes** (int parameterIndex, byte[] x) throws SQLException	*ε*260
1.2	public.....................void **setCharacterStream** (int parameterIndex, java.io.Reader reader, int length)	
	throws SQLException	
	public.....................void **setClob** (int i, *Clob* x) throws SQLException	
	public.....................void **setDate** (int parameterIndex, Date x) throws SQLException	*ε*259
1.2	public.....................void **setDate** (int parameterIndex, Date x, java.util.Calendar cal) throws SQLException	
	public.....................void **setDouble** (int parameterIndex, double x) throws SQLException	*ε*259
	public.....................void **setFloat** (int parameterIndex, float x) throws SQLException	*ε*259
	public.....................void **setInt** (int parameterIndex, int x) throws SQLException	*ε*259,298
	public.....................void **setLong** (int parameterIndex, long x) throws SQLException	*ε*259
	public.....................void **setNull** (int parameterIndex, int sqlType) throws SQLException	
1.2	public.....................void **setNull** (int paramIndex, int sqlType, String typeName) throws SQLException	
	public.....................void **setObject** (int parameterIndex, Object x) throws SQLException *ε*298	
	public.....................void **setObject** (int parameterIndex, Object x, int targetSqlType) throws SQLException	
	public.....................void **setObject** (int parameterIndex, Object x, int targetSqlType, int scale)	
	throws SQLException	
1.2	public.....................void **setRef** (int i, *Ref* x) throws SQLException	
	public.....................void **setShort** (int parameterIndex, short x) throws SQLException	*ε*259
	public.....................void **setString** (int parameterIndex, String x) throws SQLException	*ε*259,262,265
	public.....................void **setTime** (int parameterIndex, Time x) throws SQLException	*ε*259
1.2	public.....................void **setTime** (int parameterIndex, Time x, java.util.Calendar cal) throws SQLException	
	public.....................void **setTimestamp** (int parameterIndex, Timestamp x) throws SQLException	
		*ε*259
1.2	public.....................void **setTimestamp** (int parameterIndex, Timestamp x, java.util.Calendar cal)	
	throws SQLException	
D	public.....................void **setUnicodeStream** (int parameterIndex, java.io.InputStream x, int length)	
	throws SQLException	
1.4	public.....................void **setURL** (int parameterIndex, java.net.URL x) throws SQLException	

Principal ❶			java.security

1.1	*Principal* ꜀	
	public.................. boolean **equals** (Object another)	
	public.....................String **getName** ()	*ε*227,508
	public.........................int **hashCode** ()	
	public.....................String **toString** ()	

Class *Interface* —extends - - -implements ○ abstract ● final △ static ▲ static final ✳ constructor x x—inherited x **x**—declared **x x**—overridden
εn—examples of usage ꜀—has subclass package—see other volume

		Principal❷	org.omg.CORBA

```
      Object
D     └Principal
```

D	public....................byte[]	**name** ()	
D	public.....................void	**name** (byte[] value)	
D ✳	public.........................	**Principal** ()	

		PrincipalHolder	org.omg.CORBA

```
      Object
D ●   └PrincipalHolder ----------------------- org.omg.CORBA.portable.Streamable [1]
```

D	1	public.....................void	**_read** (org.omg.CORBA.portable.InputStream input)
D	1	public.................TypeCode	**_type** ()
D	1	public.....................void	**_write** (org.omg.CORBA.portable.OutputStream output)
D ✳		public.........................	**PrincipalHolder** ()
D ✳		public.........................	**PrincipalHolder** (Principal initial)
D		public.................Principal	**value**

		PrintStream	java.io

```
                                                         ε183
      Object
O     └OutputStream
         └FilterOutputStream [1]
            └PrintStream↲
```

		public.................. boolean	**checkError** ()	
	1	public..................... **void**	**close** ()	ε211,501,451,453,91
	1	public..................... **void**	**flush** ()	ε54,27
	1	protected .... OutputStream	out	
		public.....................void	**print** (boolean b)	
		public.....................void	**print** (char c)	
		public.....................void	**print** (char[] s)	
		public.....................void	**print** (double d)	
		public.....................void	**print** (float f)	
		public.....................void	**print** (int i)	
		public.....................void	**print** (Object obj)	ε34
		public.....................void	**print** (String s)	ε34
		public.....................void	**print** (long l)	
		public.....................void	**println** ()	
		public.....................void	**println** (boolean x)	
		public.....................void	**println** (char x)	
		public.....................void	**println** (char[] x)	
		public.....................void	**println** (double x)	
		public.....................void	**println** (float x)	
		public.....................void	**println** (int x)	ε262
		public.....................void	**println** (Object x)	ε69
		public.....................void	**println** (String x)	ε54,69,262
		public.....................void	**println** (long x)	
✳		public.........................	**PrintStream** (OutputStream out)	ε54
✳		public.........................	**PrintStream** (OutputStream out, boolean autoFlush)	
1.4 ✳		public.........................	**PrintStream** (OutputStream out, boolean autoFlush, String encoding)	
			throws UnsupportedEncodingException	
1.1		protected ....void	**setError** ()	
	1	public.....................void	write (byte[] b) throws IOException	ε27,91,224
	1	public..................... **void**	**write** (int b)	ε184
	1	public..................... **void**	**write** (byte[] buf, int off, int len)	ε54,451,453,449,450

		PrintWriter	java.io

```
         Object
1.1 O    └Writer [1]
1.1         └PrintWriter
```

		public.................. boolean	**checkError** ()	
	1	public..................... **void**	**close** ()	ε23,37,38,41,43
	1	public..................... **void**	**flush** ()	ε135,150,224
	1	protected ....Object	lock	

P

Classes

PrintWriter

1.2	protected . . . . Writer	**out**	
	public . . . . void	**print** (boolean b)	
	public . . . . void	**print** (char c)	
	public . . . . void	**print** (char[] s)	
	public . . . . void	**print** (double d)	
	public . . . . void	**print** (float f)	
	public . . . . void	**print** (int i)	
	public . . . . void	**print** (Object obj)	
	public . . . . void	**print** (String s)	
	public . . . . void	**print** (long l)	
	public . . . . void	**println** ()	
	public . . . . void	**println** (boolean x)	
	public . . . . void	**println** (char x)	
	public . . . . void	**println** (char[] x)	
	public . . . . void	**println** (double x)	
	public . . . . void	**println** (float x)	
	public . . . . void	**println** (int x)	
	public . . . . void	**println** (Object x)	
	public . . . . void	**println** (String x)	
	public . . . . void	**println** (long x)	
✳	public	**PrintWriter** (OutputStream out)	
✳	public	**PrintWriter** (Writer out)	
✳	public	**PrintWriter** (OutputStream out, boolean autoFlush)	
✳	public	**PrintWriter** (Writer out, boolean autoFlush)	
	protected . . . . void	**setError** ()	
1	public . . . . **void**	**write** (char[] buf)	
1	public . . . . **void**	**write** (int c)	
1	public . . . . **void**	**write** (String s)	ε23,37,38,41,43
1	public . . . . **void**	**write** (char[] buf, int off, int len)	
1	public . . . . **void**	**write** (String s, int off, int len)	

PRIVATE_MEMBER org.omg.CORBA

1.2	*PRIVATE_MEMBER*		
▲	public static final . . . . short	**value** = 0	

PrivateCredentialPermission javax.security.auth

Object   ε217,218

| 1.2 ○ | └ java.security.Permission[1] - - - - - - - - - - - - - - - *java.security.Guard*, *java.io.Serializable* ⌐ |
| 1.4 ● | └ PrivateCredentialPermission |

1	public . . . . void	checkGuard (Object object) throws SecurityException	
1	public . . . . **boolean**	**equals** (Object obj)	ε215
1	public . . . . **String**	**getActions** ()	ε215
	public . . . . String	**getCredentialClass** ()	
● 1	public final . . . . String	getName ()	
	public . . . . String[][]	**getPrincipals** ()	
1	public . . . . **int**	**hashCode** ()	ε215
1	public . . . . **boolean**	**implies** (java.security.Permission p)	ε214,215
1	public . . . . **java.security** ↩	**newPermissionCollection** ()	
	.PermissionCollection		
✳	public	**PrivateCredentialPermission** (String name, String actions)	
1	public . . . . String	toString ()	

PrivateKey java.security

| 1.1 | *PrivateKey* ⸺⸺⸺⸺⸺⸺⸺⸺ *Key* ⌐ [1] (*java.io.Serializable*) | ε198,201,210,471,459 |

1	public . . . . String	getAlgorithm ()	ε203,204,205,464,469
1	public . . . . byte[]	getEncoded ()	ε199,460,471,471
1	public . . . . String	getFormat ()	ε199
1.2 ▲ 1	public static final . . . . **long**	**serialVersionUID** = 6034044314589513430	

Class   *Interface*   ⸺extends   - - -implements   ○ abstract   ● final   △ static   ▲ static final   ✳ constructor   x x⸺inherited   x **x**⸺declared   **x x**⸺overridden
ε*n*⸺examples of usage   ⌐⸺has subclass   package⸺see other volume

PrivilegedAction	java.security

| 1.2 | *PrivilegedAction* |
| | public .... Object **run** () |

PrivilegedActionException	java.security

```
Object
 └Throwable 1 --------------------------- java.io.Serializable
   └Exception
     └PrivilegedActionException
```

1.4	1	public .... **Throwable** **getCause** ()
		public .... Exception **getException** ()
	*	public .... **PrivilegedActionException** (Exception exception)
	1	public .... **String** **toString** ()

PrivilegedExceptionAction	java.security

| 1.2 | *PrivilegedExceptionAction* |
| | public .... Object **run** () throws Exception |

P

Process	java.lang

```
Object                                            ε89
 └Process
```

O	public abstract .... void **destroy** ()
O	public abstract .... int **exitValue** ()
O	public abstract .... **getErrorStream** ()
	.... java.io.InputStream
O	public abstract .... **getInputStream** () ε90
	.... java.io.InputStream
O	public abstract .... **getOutputStream** () ε91
	.... java.io.OutputStream
*	public .... **Process** ()
O	public abstract .... int **waitFor** () throws InterruptedException

ProcessingInstruction	org.w3c.dom

1.4	*ProcessingInstruction——————— Node 1* ε542,524,526,529,530
	1 *37 inherited members from Node not shown*
	public .... String **getData** ()
	public .... String **getTarget** ()
	public .... void **setData** (String data) throws DOMException

ProfileIdHelper	org.omg.IOP

```
Object
 └ProfileIdHelper
```
1.4 O

△	public static .... int **extract** (org.omg.CORBA.Any a)
△	public static .... String **id** ()
△	public static .... void **insert** (org.omg.CORBA.Any a, int that)
*	public .... **ProfileIdHelper** ()
△	public static .... int **read** (org.omg.CORBA.portable.InputStream istream)
△	public static synchronized .... **type** ()
	. org.omg.CORBA.TypeCode
△	public static .... void **write** (org.omg.CORBA.portable.OutputStream ostream, int value)

Properties

			java.util
		Properties	

```
        Object
  ○     └ Dictionary
              └ Hashtable¹ - - - - - - - - - - - - - - - - - - - - - - - Map⌄, Cloneable⌄, java.io.Serializable⌄
                   └ Properties⌄
```

	1	public synchronized .... void	clear ()		
	1	public synchronized .... Object	clone ()		
	1	public synchronized .. boolean	contains (Object value)		
	1	public synchronized .. boolean	containsKey (Object key)		
1.2	1	public.................. boolean	containsValue (Object value)		ε344
		protected .... Properties	**defaults**		
	1	public synchronized	elements ()		
		.... Enumeration			
1.2	1	public..................... Set	entrySet ()		ε345
	1	public synchronized .. boolean	equals (Object o)		
	1	public synchronized .... Object	get (Object key)		ε88
		public................... String	**getProperty** (String key)		ε366
		public................... String	**getProperty** (String key, String defaultValue)		
	1	public synchronized .... int	hashCode ()		
	1	public synchronized .. boolean	isEmpty ()		
	1	public synchronized	keys ()		
		.... Enumeration			
1.2	1	public..................... Set	keySet ()		ε194,340,345,355,356
		public..................... void	**list** (java.io.PrintStream out)		
1.1		public..................... void	**list** (java.io.PrintWriter out)		
		public synchronized .... void	**load** (java.io.InputStream inStream) throws java.io.IOException		ε365
*		public.........................	**Properties** ()		ε365
*		public.........................	**Properties** (Properties defaults)		
		public............. Enumeration	**propertyNames** ()		ε88
	1	public synchronized .... Object	put (Object key, Object value)		ε472,481,484,485,486
1.2	1	public synchronized .... void	putAll (*Map* t)		
	1	protected .... void	rehash ()		
	1	public synchronized .... Object	remove (Object key)		
D		public synchronized .... void	**save** (java.io.OutputStream out, String header)		
1.2		public synchronized .... Object	**setProperty** (String key, String value)		ε366
	1	public synchronized .... int	size ()		
1.2		public synchronized .... void	**store** (java.io.OutputStream out, String header) throws java.io.IOException		
					ε365
	1	public synchronized ..... String	toString ()		
1.2	1	public............... Collection	values ()		ε340,345,355

		java.beans
PropertyChangeEvent		

```
        Object                                                              ε333
  1.1   └ java.util.EventObject¹ - - - - - - - - - - - - - - - - - - - java.io.Serializable⌄
  1.1        └ PropertyChangeEvent
```

		public.................... Object	**getNewValue** ()		ε11,12
		public.................... Object	**getOldValue** ()		ε11,12,404
		public.................... Object	**getPropagationId** ()		
		public.................... String	**getPropertyName** ()		ε404
	1	public.................... Object	getSource ()		
*		public.........................	**PropertyChangeEvent** (Object source, String propertyName, Object oldValue,		
			Object newValue)		
		public..................... void	**setPropagationId** (Object propagationId)		
	1	protected transient...... Object	source		
	1	public.................... String	toString ()		

		java.beans
PropertyChangeListener		

1.1	*PropertyChangeListener*————————*java.util.EventListener*⌄			ε2,3,333,493,494
	public....................... void **propertyChange** (PropertyChangeEvent evt)			ε11,404

Class *Interface* —extends - - -implements ○ abstract ● final △ static ▲ static final ✳ constructor x x—inherited x **x**—declared **x x**—overridden
ε*n*—examples of usage ⌄—has subclass package—see other volume

	PropertyChangeListenerProxy		java.beans

Object
1.4 ○ └java.util.EventListenerProxy[1] - - - - - - - - - - - - - *java.util.EventListener*⌄
1.4   └PropertyChangeListenerProxy - - - - - - - - - - *PropertyChangeListener*[2] (*java.util.EventListener*)

	1	public... *java.util.EventListener*	getListener ()	
		public...................String	**getPropertyName** ()	
	2	public.......................void	**propertyChange** (PropertyChangeEvent evt)	ε11,404
*		public...........................	**PropertyChangeListenerProxy** (String propertyName, *PropertyChangeListener* listener)	

	PropertyChangeSupport		java.beans

Object
1.1 └PropertyChangeSupport⌄ - - - - - - - - - - - - - - - - *java.io.Serializable*⌄

	public synchronized ....void	**addPropertyChangeListener** (*PropertyChangeListener* listener)	ε2
1.2	public synchronized ....void	**addPropertyChangeListener** (String propertyName, *PropertyChangeListener* listener)	
1.2	public.......................void	**firePropertyChange** (PropertyChangeEvent evt)	
1.2	public.......................void	**firePropertyChange** (String propertyName, boolean oldValue, boolean newValue)	
1.2	public.......................void	**firePropertyChange** (String propertyName, int oldValue, int newValue)	
	public.......................void	**firePropertyChange** (String propertyName, Object oldValue, Object newValue)	ε2
1.4	public synchronized ....*PropertyChangeListener[]*	**getPropertyChangeListeners** ()	
1.4	public synchronized ....*PropertyChangeListener[]*	**getPropertyChangeListeners** (String propertyName)	
1.2	public synchronized .. boolean	**hasListeners** (String propertyName)	
*	public...........................	**PropertyChangeSupport** (Object sourceBean)	ε2
	public synchronized ....void	**removePropertyChangeListener** (*PropertyChangeListener* listener)	ε2
1.2	public synchronized ....void	**removePropertyChangeListener** (String propertyName, *PropertyChangeListener* listener)	

	PropertyDescriptor	.	java.beans

Object[1]
1.1 └FeatureDescriptor[2]
1.1   └PropertyDescriptor⌄

	2	public.... *java.util.Enumeration*	attributeNames ()	
	1	public.................**boolean**	**equals** (Object obj)	
	2	public...................String	getDisplayName ()	
	2	public...................String	getName ()	ε5,9
		public....................Class	**getPropertyEditorClass** ()	
		public....................Class	**getPropertyType** ()	
		public.java.lang.reflect.Method	**getReadMethod** ()	
	2	public...................String	getShortDescription ()	
	2	public....................Object	getValue (String attributeName)	
		public.java.lang.reflect.Method	**getWriteMethod** ()	
		public.................. boolean	**isBound** ()	
		public.................. boolean	**isConstrained** ()	
	2	public.................. boolean	isExpert ()	
	2	public.................. boolean	isHidden ()	
1.2	2	public.................. boolean	isPreferred ()	
*		public...........................	**PropertyDescriptor** (String propertyName, Class beanClass) throws IntrospectionException	
*		public...........................	**PropertyDescriptor** (String propertyName, java.lang.reflect.Method getter, java.lang.reflect.Method setter) throws IntrospectionException	
*		public...........................	**PropertyDescriptor** (String propertyName, Class beanClass, String getterName, String setterName) throws IntrospectionException	
		public.......................void	**setBound** (boolean bound)	
		public.......................void	**setConstrained** (boolean constrained)	
	2	public.......................void	setDisplayName (String displayName)	
	2	public.......................void	setExpert (boolean expert)	
	2	public.......................void	setHidden (boolean hidden)	
	2	public.......................void	setName (String name)	
1.2	2	public.......................void	setPreferred (boolean preferred)	

P

Classes

PropertyDescriptor

	public......................	void	**setPropertyEditorClass** (Class propertyEditorClass)	
1.2	public......................	void	**setReadMethod** (java.lang.reflect.Method getter) throws IntrospectionException	
2	public......................	void	setShortDescription (String text)	
2	public......................	void	setValue (String attributeName, Object value)	ε9
1.2	public......................	void	**setWriteMethod** (java.lang.reflect.Method setter) throws IntrospectionException	

PropertyEditor   java.beans

1.1   *PropertyEditor*

	public......................	void	**addPropertyChangeListener** (*PropertyChangeListener* listener)
	public......................	String	**getAsText** ()
	public....	java.awt.Component	**getCustomEditor** ()
	public......................	String	**getJavaInitializationString** ()
	public......................	String[]	**getTags** ()
	public......................	Object	**getValue** ()
	public......................	boolean	**isPaintable** ()
	public......................	void	**paintValue** (java.awt.Graphics gfx, java.awt.Rectangle box)
	public......................	void	**removePropertyChangeListener** (*PropertyChangeListener* listener)
	public......................	void	**setAsText** (String text) throws IllegalArgumentException
	public......................	void	**setValue** (Object value)
	public......................	boolean	**supportsCustomEditor** ()

PropertyEditorManager   java.beans

Object
└PropertyEditorManager

1.1			
△	public static synchronized .... *PropertyEditor*	**findEditor** (Class targetType)
△	public static synchronized .... String[]	**getEditorSearchPath** ()
✳	public......................	**PropertyEditorManager** ()
△	public static .... void	**registerEditor** (Class targetType, Class editorClass)
△	public static synchronized void	**setEditorSearchPath** (String[] path)

PropertyEditorSupport   java.beans

Object
1.1   └PropertyEditorSupport ------------------ *PropertyEditor* [1]

1	public synchronized	void	**addPropertyChangeListener** (*PropertyChangeListener* listener)
	public......................	void	**firePropertyChange** ()
1	public......................	String	**getAsText** ()
1	public....	java.awt.Component	**getCustomEditor** ()
1	public......................	String	**getJavaInitializationString** ()
1	public......................	String[]	**getTags** ()
1	public......................	Object	**getValue** ()
1	public......................	boolean	**isPaintable** ()
1	public......................	void	**paintValue** (java.awt.Graphics gfx, java.awt.Rectangle box)
✳	protected......................		**PropertyEditorSupport** ()
✳	protected......................		**PropertyEditorSupport** (Object source)
1	public synchronized	void	**removePropertyChangeListener** (*PropertyChangeListener* listener)
1	public......................	void	**setAsText** (String text) throws IllegalArgumentException
1	public......................	void	**setValue** (Object value)
1	public......................	boolean	**supportsCustomEditor** ()

PropertyPermission   java.util

		Object	ε217,218
1.2	O	└java.security.Permission [1] ----------------- *java.security.Guard*, *java.io.Serializable*	
1.2	O	└java.security.BasicPermission [2]	
1.2	●	└PropertyPermission	

1	public......................	void	checkGuard (Object object) throws SecurityException	
2	public...................	**boolean**	**equals** (Object obj)	ε215
2	public...................	**String**	**getActions** ()	ε215

Class *Interface* —extends - - -implements O abstract ● final △ static ▲ static final ✳ constructor x x—inherited x **x**—declared **x x**—overridden
ε*n*—examples of usage   ⌐—has subclass   package—see other volume

●	1	public final .... String	getName ()	
	2	public......................... **int**	**hashCode** ()	ε215
	2	public........................**boolean**	**implies** (java.security.Permission p)	ε214,215
	2	public.........**java.security** ↵	**newPermissionCollection** ()	
		.PermissionCollection		
✻		public.........................	**PropertyPermission** (String name, String actions)	ε216
	1	public................... String	toString ()	

PropertyResourceBundle — java.util

```
Object
1.1 ○  └ResourceBundle 1
1.1       └PropertyResourceBundle
```

▲	1	public static final .... ResourceBundle	getBundle (String baseName)	ε310
▲	1	public static final .... ResourceBundle	getBundle (String baseName, Locale locale)	ε310
1.2 △	1	public static .. ResourceBundle	getBundle (String baseName, Locale locale, ClassLoader loader)	
	1	public............ **Enumeration**	**getKeys** ()	
1.2	1	public................... Locale	getLocale ()	
●	1	public final .... Object	getObject (String key)	
●	1	public final .... String	getString (String key)	ε310
●	1	public final .... String[]	getStringArray (String key)	
	1	public...................**Object**	**handleGetObject** (String key)	
	1	protected ..... ResourceBundle	parent	
✻		public.........................	**PropertyResourceBundle** (java.io.InputStream stream) throws java.io.IOException	
	1	protected ....void	setParent (ResourceBundle parent)	

P

PropertyVetoException — java.beans

```
Object                                              ε3
└Throwable - - - - - - - - - - - - - - - - - - - - - - - - - - java.io.Serializable
   └Exception
1.1       └PropertyVetoException
```

	public... PropertyChangeEvent	**getPropertyChangeEvent** ()	
✻	public.........................	**PropertyVetoException** (String mess, PropertyChangeEvent evt)	
			ε12

ProtectionDomain — java.security

```
Object 1                                            ε217
1.2  └ProtectionDomain
```

1.4 ●		public final .... ClassLoader	**getClassLoader** ()	
●		public final .... CodeSource	**getCodeSource** ()	ε67
●		public final .... PermissionCollection	**getPermissions** ()	
1.4 ●		public final .... *Principal[]*	**getPrincipals** ()	
		public................. boolean	**implies** (Permission permission)	
✻		public.........................	**ProtectionDomain** (CodeSource codesource, PermissionCollection permissions)	
1.4 ✻		public.........................	**ProtectionDomain** (CodeSource codesource, PermissionCollection permissions, ClassLoader classloader, *Principal[]* principals)	
	1	public................. **String**	**toString** ()	

ProtocolException — java.net

```
Object
└Throwable - - - - - - - - - - - - - - - - - - - - - - - - - - java.io.Serializable
   └Exception
      └java.io.IOException
         └ProtocolException
```

✻	public.........................	**ProtocolException** ()
✻	public.........................	**ProtocolException** (String host)

Classes

Provider

				java.security

```
      Object
  ○   └java.util.Dictionary
         └java.util.Hashtable¹ - - - - - - - - - - - - - - - - - - - java.util.Map˅, Cloneable˅, java.io.Serializable˅
            └java.util.Properties²
1.1 ○          └Provider
```

	1	public synchronized ...... **void**	**clear** ()	
	1	public synchronized ....Object	clone ()	
	1	public synchronized .. boolean	contains (Object value)	
	1	public synchronized .. boolean	containsKey (Object key)	
1.2	1	public................. boolean	containsValue (Object value)	ε344
	2	protected ... java.util.Properties	defaults	
	1	public synchronized	elements ()	
		.... *java.util.Enumeration*		
1.2	1	public synchronized	**entrySet** ()	ε345
		.................*java.util.Set*		
	1	public synchronized .. boolean	equals (Object o)	
	1	public synchronized ....Object	get (Object key)	ε88
		public....................String	**getInfo** ()	
		public....................String	**getName** ()	
	2	public....................String	getProperty (String key)	ε366
	2	public....................String	getProperty (String key, String defaultValue)	
		public...................double	**getVersion** ()	
	1	public synchronized ....int	hashCode ()	
	1	public synchronized .. boolean	isEmpty ()	
	1	public synchronized	keys ()	
		.... *java.util.Enumeration*		
1.2	1	public..............*java.util.Set*	**keySet** ()	ε194,340,345,355,356
	2	public.......................void	list (java.io.PrintStream out)	
	2	public.......................void	list (java.io.PrintWriter out)	
	2	public synchronized ...... **void**	**load** (java.io.InputStream inStream) throws java.io.IOException	ε365
	2	public.... *java.util.Enumeration*	propertyNames ()	ε88
*		protected......................	**Provider** (String name, double version, String info)	
	1	public synchronized ....**Object**	**put** (Object key, Object value)	ε472,481,484,485,486
1.2	1	public synchronized ...... **void**	**putAll** (*java.util.Map* t)	
	1	protected ....void	rehash ()	
	1	public synchronized ....**Object**	**remove** (Object key)	
1.2	2	public synchronized ....Object	setProperty (String key, String value)	ε366
	1	public synchronized ....int	size ()	
1.2	2	public synchronized ......void	store (java.io.OutputStream out, String header) throws java.io.IOException	
				ε365
	1	public....................**String**	**toString** ()	
1.2	1	public.....*java.util.Collection*	values ()	ε340,345,355

		java.security

```
      Object
  └Throwable - - - - - - - - - - - - - - - - - - - - - - - - - - java.io.Serializable˅
     └Exception
        └RuntimeException
1.1        └ProviderException
```

*	public...........................	**ProviderException** ()	
*	public...........................	**ProviderException** (String s)	

		java.lang.reflect

```
      Object
1.3   └Proxy - - - - - - - - - - - - - - - - - - - - - - - - - - java.io.Serializable˅
```

△	public static *InvocationHandler*	**getInvocationHandler** (Object proxy) throws IllegalArgumentException	
△	public static .... Class	**getProxyClass** (ClassLoader loader, Class[] interfaces)	
		throws IllegalArgumentException	
	protected ... *InvocationHandler*	**h**	
△	public static .... boolean	**isProxyClass** (Class cl)	

Class *Interface* —extends - - -implements ○ abstract ● final △ static ▲ static final ✳ constructor x x—inherited x **x**—declared **x x**—overridden
ε*n*—examples of usage ˍ—has subclass package—see other volume

△	public static .... Object **newProxyInstance** (ClassLoader loader, Class[] interfaces, *InvocationHandler* h)	
	throws IllegalArgumentException	ε111
✳	protected .... **Proxy** (*InvocationHandler* h)	

PSSParameterSpec

java.security.spec

Object
└PSSParameterSpec - - - - - - - - - - - - - - - - - - - *AlgorithmParameterSpec*

1.4

	public...........................int **getSaltLength** ()	
✳	public........................... **PSSParameterSpec** (int saltLen)	

PUBLIC_MEMBER

org.omg.CORBA

1.2 *PUBLIC_MEMBER*

- -

▲ public static final ....short **value** = 1

- -

PublicKey

java.security

1.1 *PublicKey* ─────────────── *Key* [1] (*java.io.Serializable*)   ε198,201,210,459,462

1	public.....................String getAlgorithm ()		ε204,205,203,464,469
1	public.....................byte[] getEncoded ()		ε199,471,460,471
1	public.....................String getFormat ()		ε199
1.2 ▲ 1	public static final .... **long serialVersionUID** = 7187392471159151072		

- -

P

PushbackInputStream

java.io

ε252,382,418

Object
○ └InputStream
    └FilterInputStream [1]
       └PushbackInputStream

1	public........................ **int available** () throws IOException		
1.1	protected.................byte[] **buf**		
1	public synchronized ...... **void close** () throws IOException		ε14,36,45,452,455
1	protected ....InputStream **in**		
1	public synchronized ....void mark (int readlimit)		
1	public.................**boolean markSupported** ()		
1.1	protected ....int **pos**		
✳	public........................... **PushbackInputStream** (InputStream in)		
1.1 ✳	public........................... **PushbackInputStream** (InputStream in, int size)		
1	public.....................**int read** () throws IOException		ε90,184,256
1	public.....................int read (byte[] b) throws IOException		ε452,455,457,170,451
1	public.....................**int read** (byte[] b, int off, int len) throws IOException		ε36
1	public synchronized ....void reset () throws IOException		
1	public.....................**long skip** (long n) throws IOException		
1.1	public.......................void **unread** (byte[] b) throws IOException		
	public.......................void **unread** (int b) throws IOException		
1.1	public.......................void **unread** (byte[] b, int off, int len) throws IOException		

Classes

PushbackReader

java.io

Object
1.1 ○ └Reader [1]
1.1 ○   └FilterReader [2]
1.1   └PushbackReader

2	public..................... **void close** () throws IOException		ε35,47,135,136,139
2	protected ....Reader **in**		
1	protected ....Object **lock**		
2	public..................... **void mark** (int readAheadLimit) throws IOException		
2	public.................**boolean markSupported** ()		ε442
✳	public........................... **PushbackReader** (Reader in)		
✳	public........................... **PushbackReader** (Reader in, int size)		
2	public..................... **int read** () throws IOException		
1	public.......................int read (char[] cbuf) throws IOException		ε434
2	public..................... **int read** (char[] cbuf, int off, int len) throws IOException		

PushbackReader

2	public	**boolean**	**ready** () throws IOException	ε442
2	public	**void**	**reset** () throws IOException	
2	public	long	skip (long n) throws IOException	
	public	void	**unread** (char[] cbuf) throws IOException	
	public	void	**unread** (int c) throws IOException	
	public	void	**unread** (char[] cbuf, int off, int len) throws IOException	

Random   java.util

Object
└─Random ------------------------------- *java.io.Serializable*   ε195

1.1	protected synchronized	int	**next** (int bits)	
1.2	public	boolean	**nextBoolean** ()	ε331
1.1	public	void	**nextBytes** (byte[] bytes)	ε331
	public	double	**nextDouble** ()	ε331
	public	float	**nextFloat** ()	ε331
	public synchronized	double	**nextGaussian** ()	
	public	int	**nextInt** ()	ε331
1.2	public	int	**nextInt** (int n)	ε331
	public	long	**nextLong** ()	ε331
✳	public		**Random** ()	ε331
✳	public		**Random** (long seed)	ε331
	public synchronized	void	**setSeed** (long seed)	

RandomAccess   java.util

1.4	*RandomAccess*

RandomAccessFile   java.io

Object
└─RandomAccessFile --------------------- *DataOutput*,[1], *DataInput*,[2]

	public native	void	**close** () throws IOException	ε39
1.4 ●	public final	java↵	**getChannel** ()	ε166,167,181,182,183
		.nio.channels.FileChannel		
●	public final	FileDescriptor	**getFD** () throws IOException	
	public native	long	**getFilePointer** () throws IOException	
	public native	long	**length** () throws IOException	
✳	public		**RandomAccessFile** (File file, String mode) throws FileNotFoundException	ε39,166,167,181,182
✳	public		**RandomAccessFile** (String name, String mode) throws FileNotFoundException	
	public native	int	**read** () throws IOException	
	public	int	**read** (byte[] b) throws IOException	
	public	int	**read** (byte[] b, int off, int len) throws IOException	
● 2	public final	boolean	**readBoolean** () throws IOException	
● 2	public final	byte	**readByte** () throws IOException	
● 2	public final	char	**readChar** () throws IOException	ε39
● 2	public final	double	**readDouble** () throws IOException	
● 2	public final	float	**readFloat** () throws IOException	
● 2	public final	void	**readFully** (byte[] b) throws IOException	
● 2	public final	void	**readFully** (byte[] b, int off, int len) throws IOException	
● 2	public final	int	**readInt** () throws IOException	
● 2	public final	String	**readLine** () throws IOException	
● 2	public final	long	**readLong** () throws IOException	
● 2	public final	short	**readShort** () throws IOException	
● 2	public final	int	**readUnsignedByte** () throws IOException	
● 2	public final	int	**readUnsignedShort** () throws IOException	
● 2	public final	String	**readUTF** () throws IOException	
	public native	void	**seek** (long pos) throws IOException	ε39
1.2	public native	void	**setLength** (long newLength) throws IOException	
2	public	int	**skipBytes** (int n) throws IOException	
1	public	void	**write** (byte[] b) throws IOException	
1	public native	void	**write** (int b) throws IOException	
1	public	void	**write** (byte[] b, int off, int len) throws IOException	
● 1	public final	void	**writeBoolean** (boolean v) throws IOException	
● 1	public final	void	**writeByte** (int v) throws IOException	

Class   *Interface*   —extends   - - -implements   ○ abstract   ● final   △ static   ▲ static final   ✳ constructor   x x—inherited   x **x**—declared   **x x**—overridden
ε*n*—examples of usage   ‿—has subclass   package—see other volume

P

●	1	public final	.................void	**writeBytes** (String s) throws IOException	
●	1	public final	.................void	**writeChar** (int v) throws IOException	
●	1	public final	.................void	**writeChars** (String s) throws IOException	ε39
●	1	public final	.................void	**writeDouble** (double v) throws IOException	
●	1	public final	.................void	**writeFloat** (float v) throws IOException	
●	1	public final	.................void	**writeInt** (int v) throws IOException	
●	1	public final	.................void	**writeLong** (long v) throws IOException	
●	1	public final	.................void	**writeShort** (int v) throws IOException	
●	1	public final	.................void	**writeUTF** (String str) throws IOException	

RC2ParameterSpec — javax.crypto.spec

Object[1]
1.4 └RC2ParameterSpec - *java.security.spec.AlgorithmParameterSpec*

	1	public	...............**boolean**	**equals** (Object obj)
		public	.......................int	**getEffectiveKeyBits** ()
		public	...................byte[]	**getIV** ()
	1	public	...............**int**	**hashCode** ()
*		public	....	**RC2ParameterSpec** (int effectiveKeyBits)
*		public	....	**RC2ParameterSpec** (int effectiveKeyBits, byte[] iv)
*		public	....	**RC2ParameterSpec** (int effectiveKeyBits, byte[] iv, int offset)

RC5ParameterSpec — javax.crypto.spec

Object[1]
1.4 └RC5ParameterSpec - *java.security.spec.AlgorithmParameterSpec*

R

	1	public	...............**boolean**	**equals** (Object obj)
		public	...................byte[]	**getIV** ()
		public	.......................int	**getRounds** ()
		public	.......................int	**getVersion** ()
		public	.......................int	**getWordSize** ()
	1	public	...............**int**	**hashCode** ()
*		public	....	**RC5ParameterSpec** (int version, int rounds, int wordSize)
*		public	....	**RC5ParameterSpec** (int version, int rounds, int wordSize, byte[] iv)
*		public	....	**RC5ParameterSpec** (int version, int rounds, int wordSize, byte[] iv, int offset)

ReadableByteChannel — java.nio.channels

1.4 *ReadableByteChannel* ─────────────────── *Channel*[1]

1	public	.......................void	close () throws java.io.IOException	ε167,170,171,172,174
1	public	.... boolean	isOpen ()	
	public	.......................int	**read** (java.nio.ByteBuffer dst) throws java.io.IOException	ε169

Reader — java.io

Object
1.1 ○ └Reader

○	public abstract	.............void	**close** () throws IOException	ε35,47,135,136,139
	protected	...............Object	**lock**	
	public	.......................void	**mark** (int readAheadLimit) throws IOException	
	public	.... boolean	**markSupported** ()	ε442
	public	.......................int	**read** () throws IOException	
	public	.......................int	**read** (char[] cbuf) throws IOException	ε434
○	public abstract	...............int	**read** (char[] cbuf, int off, int len) throws IOException	
*	protected	....	**Reader** ()	
*	protected	....	**Reader** (Object lock)	
	public	.... boolean	**ready** () throws IOException	ε442
	public	.......................void	**reset** () throws IOException	
	public	.... long	**skip** (long n) throws IOException	

ReadOnlyBufferException

ReadOnlyBufferException			java.nio

```
        Object
        └Throwable ------------------------- java.io.Serializable
          └Exception
            └RuntimeException
1.2           └UnsupportedOperationException
1.4             └ReadOnlyBufferException
```

∗	public.	**ReadOnlyBufferException** ()

Ref		java.sql

```
1.2     Ref
```

	public. . . . . String	**getBaseTypeName** () throws SQLException	
1.4	public. . . . . Object	**getObject** () throws SQLException	
1.4	public. . . . . Object	**getObject** (*java.util.Map* map) throws SQLException	
1.4	public. . . . . void	**setObject** (Object value) throws SQLException	

RefAddr			javax.naming

```
        Object¹
1.3 ○   └RefAddr ------------------------- java.io.Serializable
```

	protected . . . . String	**addrType**	
1	public. . . . . **boolean**	**equals** (Object obj)	
○	public abstract . . . . Object	**getContent** ()	
	public. String	**getType** ()	
1	public. . . . . **int**	**hashCode** ()	
∗	protected	**RefAddr** (String addrType)	
1	public. . . . . **String**	**toString** ()	

Reference❶			java.lang.ref

```
        Object                                              ε107
1.2 ○   └Reference
```

	public. . . . . void	**clear** ()	ε108
	public. . . . . boolean	**enqueue** ()	
	public. . . . . Object	**get** ()	ε106,357
	public. . . . . boolean	**isEnqueued** ()	

Reference❷			javax.naming

```
        Object¹
1.3     └Reference ------------------------- Cloneable, java.io.Serializable
```

	public. . . . . void	**add** (RefAddr addr)	
	public. . . . . void	**add** (int posn, RefAddr addr)	
	protected . . . . java.util.Vector	**addrs**	
	protected . . . . String	**classFactory**	
	protected . . . . String	**classFactoryLocation**	
	protected . . . . String	**className**	
	public. . . . . void	**clear** ()	
1	public. . . . . **Object**	**clone** ()	
1	public. . . . . **boolean**	**equals** (Object obj)	
	public. . . . . RefAddr	**get** (int posn)	
	public. . . . . RefAddr	**get** (String addrType)	
	public. . . . *java.util.Enumeration*	**getAll** ()	
	public. String	**getClassName** ()	
	public. String	**getFactoryClassLocation** ()	
	public. String	**getFactoryClassName** ()	
1	public. . . . . **int**	**hashCode** ()	
∗	public.	**Reference** (String className)	
∗	public.	**Reference** (String className, RefAddr addr)	
∗	public.	**Reference** (String className, String factory, String factoryLocation)	

Class *Interface* —extends - - -implements ○ abstract ● final △ static ▲ static final ∗ constructor x x—inherited x **x**—declared **x x**—overridden
ε*n*—examples of usage —has subclass package —see other volume

*	public..........................	**Reference** (String className, RefAddr addr, String factory, String factoryLocation)	
	public..................... Object	**remove** (int posn)	
	public........................int	**size** ()	
1	public.................. String	**toString** ()	

Referenceable
javax.naming

1.3   *Referenceable*

   public............... Reference **getReference** () throws NamingException

---

ReferenceQueue
java.lang.ref

Object
1.2 └ReferenceQueue

	public............... Reference	**poll** ()	
*	public..........................	**ReferenceQueue** ()	ε107,108
	public............... Reference	**remove** () throws InterruptedException	ε107,108
	public............... Reference	**remove** (long timeout) throws IllegalArgumentException, InterruptedException	

ReferralException
javax.naming

Object
 └Throwable -------------------------- *java.io.Serializable*
  └Exception
1.3   └NamingException[1]
1.3 ○   └ReferralException

R

	1	*20 inherited members from NamingException not shown*	
○	public abstract .... *Context*	**getReferralContext** () throws NamingException	
○	public abstract .... *Context*	**getReferralContext** (java.util.Hashtable env) throws NamingException	
○	public abstract .... Object	**getReferralInfo** ()	
*	protected	**ReferralException** ()	
*	protected	**ReferralException** (String explanation)	
○	public abstract ....void	**retryReferral** ()	
○	public abstract .... boolean	**skipReferral** ()	

ReflectPermission
java.lang.reflect

ε217,218

Object
1.2 ○ └java.security.Permission[1] ---------------- *java.security.Guard*, *java.io.Serializable*
1.2 ○   └java.security.BasicPermission[2]
1.2 ●   └ReflectPermission

	1	public......................void	checkGuard (Object object) throws SecurityException	
	2	public................. boolean	equals (Object obj)	ε215
	2	public................. String	getActions ()	ε215
●	1	public final .... String	getName ()	
	2	public....................int	hashCode ()	ε215
	2	public................. boolean	implies (java.security.Permission p)	ε214,215
	2	public.......java.security↩	newPermissionCollection ()	
		.PermissionCollection		
*		public..........................	**ReflectPermission** (String name)	
*		public..........................	**ReflectPermission** (String name, String actions)	
	1	public.................. String	toString ()	

Refreshable
javax.security.auth

1.4   *Refreshable*

   public................. boolean **isCurrent** ()
   public......................void **refresh** () throws RefreshFailedException

Classes

RefreshFailedException

RefreshFailedException				javax.security.auth

```
        Object
        └Throwable - - - - - - - - - - - - - - - - - - - - - - - - - - java.io.Serializable �置
          └Exception
1.4        └RefreshFailedException
```

✳	public.......................	**RefreshFailedException** ()
✳	public.......................	**RefreshFailedException** (String msg)

Registry	java.rmi.registry

```
1.1     Registry────────────────────────────java.rmi.Remote˻
```

public.....................void	**bind** (String name, *java.rmi.Remote* obj) throws java.rmi.RemoteException, java.rmi.AlreadyBoundException, java.rmi.AccessException
public..................String[]	**list** () throws java.rmi.RemoteException, java.rmi.AccessException
public.........*java.rmi.Remote*	**lookup** (String name) throws java.rmi.RemoteException, java.rmi.NotBoundException, java.rmi.AccessException
public.....................void	**rebind** (String name, *java.rmi.Remote* obj) throws java.rmi.RemoteException, java.rmi.AccessException
▲ public static final.............int	**REGISTRY_PORT** = 1099
public.....................void	**unbind** (String name) throws java.rmi.RemoteException, java.rmi.NotBoundException, java.rmi.AccessException

---

RegistryHandler	java.rmi.registry

```
D     RegistryHandler
```

D	public...................*Registry*	**registryImpl** (int port) throws java.rmi.RemoteException
D	public...................*Registry*	**registryStub** (String host, int port) throws java.rmi.RemoteException, java.rmi.UnknownHostException

---

RemarshalException	org.omg.CORBA.portable

```
        Object
        └Throwable - - - - - - - - - - - - - - - - - - - - - - - - - - java.io.Serializable ˻
          └Exception
1.2 ●      └RemarshalException
```

✳	public..........................	**RemarshalException** ()

Remote	java.rmi

```
1.1     Remote˻                                              ε188
```

RemoteCall	java.rmi.server

```
D     RemoteCall
```

D	public.....................void	**done** () throws java.io.IOException
D	public.....................void	**executeCall** () throws Exception
D	public......*java.io.ObjectInput*	**getInputStream** () throws java.io.IOException
D	public....*java.io.ObjectOutput*	**getOutputStream** () throws java.io.IOException
D	public....*java.io.ObjectOutput*	**getResultStream** (boolean success) throws java.io.IOException, java.io.StreamCorruptedException
D	public.....................void	**releaseInputStream** () throws java.io.IOException
D	public.....................void	**releaseOutputStream** () throws java.io.IOException

---

Class   *Interface*   —extends   - - -implements   ○ abstract   ● final   △ static   ▲ static final   ✳ constructor   x x—inherited   x **x**—declared   **x x**—overridden
ε*n*—examples of usage   ˻—has subclass   package—see other volume

RemoteException				java.rmi

Object
  └Throwable[1] -------------------------- *java.io.Serializable*⌄
    └Exception
      └java.io.IOException

*ε*188,189,504,505

1.1   └RemoteException⌄

1.4		public.............Throwable	**detail**
1.4	1	public.............**Throwable**	**getCause** ()
	1	public.................**String**	**getMessage** ()
	*	public............................	**RemoteException** ()
	*	public............................	**RemoteException** (String s)
	*	public............................	**RemoteException** (String s, Throwable ex)

RemoteObject				java.rmi.server

Object[1]

*ε*188

1.1 ○ └RemoteObject⌄ ------------------------ *java.rmi.Remote*⌄, *java.io.Serializable*⌄

	1	public..................**boolean**	**equals** (Object obj)
1.2		public...............*RemoteRef*	**getRef** ()
	1	public.........................**int**	**hashCode** ()
		protected transient. *RemoteRef*	**ref**
	*	protected........................	**RemoteObject** ()
	*	protected........................	**RemoteObject** (*RemoteRef* newref)
	1	public....................**String**	**toString** ()
1.2	△	public static .. *java.rmi.Remote*	**toStub** (*java.rmi.Remote* obj) throws java.rmi.NoSuchObjectException

R

RemoteRef				java.rmi.server

1.1   *RemoteRef*⌄ ————————————————————*java.io.Externalizable*⌄[1] (*java.io.Serializable*)

D		public............................void	**done** (*RemoteCall* call) throws java.rmi.RemoteException
		public............................String	**getRefClass** (*java.io.ObjectOutput* out)
D		public............................void	**invoke** (*RemoteCall* call) throws Exception
1.2		public........................Object	**invoke** (*java.rmi.Remote* obj, java.lang.reflect.Method method, Object[] params, long opnum) throws Exception
D		public..............*RemoteCall*	**newCall** (RemoteObject obj, Operation[] op, int opnum, long hash) throws java.rmi.RemoteException
▲		public static final.........String	**packagePrefix** = "sun.rmi.server"
	1	public............................void	readExternal (*java.io.ObjectInput* in) throws java.io.IOException, ClassNotFoundException
		public..................boolean	**remoteEquals** (*RemoteRef* obj)
		public.........................int	**remoteHashCode** ()
		public....................String	**remoteToString** ()
1.2	▲	public static final..........long	**serialVersionUID** = 3632638527362204081
	1	public............................void	writeExternal (*java.io.ObjectOutput* out) throws java.io.IOException

Classes

RemoteServer				java.rmi.server

Object

*ε*188

1.1 ○ └RemoteObject[1] ------------------------ *java.rmi.Remote*⌄, *java.io.Serializable*⌄
1.1 ○   └RemoteServer⌄

	1	public.................. boolean	equals (Object obj)
	△	public static ....String	**getClientHost** () throws ServerNotActiveException
	△	public static java.io.PrintStream	**getLog** ()
1.2	1	public...............*RemoteRef*	getRef ()
	1	public.........................int	hashCode ()
	1	protected transient. *RemoteRef*	ref
	*	protected........................	**RemoteServer** ()
	*	protected........................	**RemoteServer** (*RemoteRef* ref)
	△	public static ....void	**setLog** (java.io.OutputStream out)
	1	public....................String	toString ()
1.2	△ 1	public static .. *java.rmi.Remote*	toStub (*java.rmi.Remote* obj) throws java.rmi.NoSuchObjectException

RemoteStub

				java.rmi.server
		RemoteStub		

Object   ε188
1.1 ○ └─RemoteObject [1] ------------------------ *java.rmi.Remote* ‿, *java.io.Serializable* ‿
1.1 ○   └─RemoteStub ‿

	1	public................. boolean	equals (Object obj)
1.2	1	public.............. *RemoteRef*	getRef ()
	1	public........................int	hashCode ()
	1	protected transient. *RemoteRef*	ref
✳		protected.....................	**RemoteStub** ()
✳		protected.....................	**RemoteStub** (*RemoteRef* ref)
D △		protected static ....void	**setRef** (RemoteStub stub, *RemoteRef* ref)
	1	public.....................String	toString ()
1.2 △	1	public static .. *java.rmi.Remote*	toStub (*java.rmi.Remote* obj) throws java.rmi.NoSuchObjectException

RepositoryIdHelper

	org.omg.CORBA
RepositoryIdHelper	

Object
1.3 ○ └─RepositoryIdHelper

△	public static ....String	**extract** (Any a)
△	public static ....String	**id** ()
△	public static ....void	**insert** (Any a, String that)
△	public static ....String	**read** (org.omg.CORBA.portable.InputStream istream)
✳	public............................	**RepositoryIdHelper** ()
△	public static synchronized	**type** ()
	....................TypeCode	
△	public static ....void	**write** (org.omg.CORBA.portable.OutputStream ostream, String value)

R

Request

	org.omg.CORBA
Request	

Object
1.2 ○ └─Request

○	public abstract .... Any	**add_in_arg** ()
○	public abstract .... Any	**add_inout_arg** ()
○	public abstract .... Any	**add_named_in_arg** (String name)
○	public abstract .... Any	**add_named_inout_arg** (String name)
○	public abstract .... Any	**add_named_out_arg** (String name)
○	public abstract .... Any	**add_out_arg** ()
○	public abstract .... NVList	**arguments** ()
○	public abstract .....ContextList	**contexts** ()
○	public abstract ....Context	**ctx** ()
○	public abstract ....void	**ctx** (Context c)
○	public abstract ... Environment	**env** ()
○	public abstract .. ExceptionList	**exceptions** ()
○	public abstract ....void	**get_response** () throws WrongTransaction
○	public abstract ....void	**invoke** ()
○	public abstract ....String	**operation** ()
○	public abstract .... boolean	**poll_response** ()
✳	public............................	**Request** ()
○	public abstract ... NamedValue	**result** ()
○	public abstract .... Any	**return_value** ()
○	public abstract ....void	**send_deferred** ()
○	public abstract ....void	**send_oneway** ()
○	public abstract ....void	**set_return_type** (TypeCode tc)
○	public abstract .... *Object*	**target** ()

REQUEST_PROCESSING_POLICY_ID

	org.omg.PortableServer
REQUEST_PROCESSING_POLICY_ID	

1.4   *REQUEST_PROCESSING_POLICY_ID*
▲   public static final.............int **value** = 22

Class *Interface* —extends - - -implements ○ abstract ● final △ static ▲ static final ✳ constructor x x—inherited x **x**—declared **x x**—overridden
ε*n*—examples of usage ‿—has subclass package—see other volume

RequestInfo	org.omg.PortableInterceptor

1.4	*RequestInfo* ———————————————— *RequestInfoOperations* [1], *org.omg.CORBA.Object* [2], *org.omg.CORBA.portable.IDLEntity* (java.io.Serializable)

   2 *13 inherited members from org.omg.CORBA.Object not shown*
   1 *14 inherited members from RequestInfoOperations not shown*

RequestInfoOperations	org.omg.PortableInterceptor

1.4	*RequestInfoOperations*

public....................org⤸ **arguments** ()
   .omg.Dynamic.Parameter[]
public................... String[] **contexts** ()
public....................org⤸ **exceptions** ()
   .omg.CORBA.TypeCode[]
public *org.omg.CORBA.Object* **forward_reference** ()
public........................... **get_reply_service_context** (int id)
   .org.omg.IOP.ServiceContext
public........................... **get_request_service_context** (int id)
   .org.omg.IOP.ServiceContext
public....org.omg.CORBA.Any **get_slot** (int id) throws InvalidSlot
public................... String **operation** ()
public................... String[] **operation_context** ()
public....................short **reply_status** ()
public..........................int **request_id** ()
public.................. boolean **response_expected** ()
public....org.omg.CORBA.Any **result** ()
public....................short **sync_scope** ()

RequestProcessingPolicy	org.omg.PortableServer

1.4	*RequestProcessingPolicy*————————— *RequestProcessingPolicyOperations* [1] (*org.omg.CORBA.PolicyOperations* [2]), *org.omg.CORBA.Policy* (*org.omg.CORBA.PolicyOperations* [2], *org.omg.CORBA.Object* [3], *org.omg.CORBA.portable.IDLEntity* (java.io.Serializable)), *org.omg.CORBA.portable.IDLEntity* (java.io.Serializable)

   3 *13 inherited members from org.omg.CORBA.Object not shown*
   2 *3 inherited members from org.omg.CORBA.PolicyOperations not shown*
   1 public................. Request- **value** ()
     ProcessingPolicyValue

RequestProcessingPolicyOperations	org.omg.PortableServer

1.4	*RequestProcessingPolicyOperations* ——————— *org.omg.CORBA.PolicyOperations* [1]

   1 *3 inherited members from org.omg.CORBA.PolicyOperations not shown*
     public................. Request- **value** ()
     ProcessingPolicyValue

RequestProcessingPolicyValue	org.omg.PortableServer

1.4	Object └RequestProcessingPolicyValue - - - - - - - - - - - *org.omg.CORBA.portable.IDLEntity* (java.io.Serializable)

▲ public static final.............int **_USE_ACTIVE_OBJECT_MAP_ONLY** = 0
▲ public static final.............int **_USE_DEFAULT_SERVANT** = 1
▲ public static final.............int **_USE_SERVANT_MANAGER** = 2
△ public static .... Request- **from_int** (int value)
     ProcessingPolicyValue
* protected..................... **RequestProcessingPolicyValue** (int value)
▲ public static final..... Request- **USE_ACTIVE_OBJECT_MAP_ONLY**
     ProcessingPolicyValue
▲ public static final..... Request- **USE_DEFAULT_SERVANT**
     ProcessingPolicyValue
▲ public static final..... Request- **USE_SERVANT_MANAGER**
     ProcessingPolicyValue
  public..........................int **value** ()

R

Classes

Resolver | javax.naming.spi

	Resolver
1.3	

```
public............ResolveResult resolveToClass (String name, Class contextType)
                               throws javax.naming.NamingException
public............ResolveResult resolveToClass (javax.naming.Name name, Class contextType)
                               throws javax.naming.NamingException
```

ResolveResult | javax.naming.spi

Object
└ ResolveResult - *java.io.Serializable*

1.3

```
    public.......................void appendRemainingComponent (String name)
    public.......................void appendRemainingName (javax.naming.Name name)
    public..... javax.naming.Name getRemainingName ()
    public....................Object getResolvedObj ()
    protected . javax.naming.Name remainingName
    protected............Object resolvedObj
*   protected..................... ResolveResult ()
*   public......................... ResolveResult (Object robj, javax.naming.Name rname)
*   public......................... ResolveResult (Object robj, String rcomp)
    public.......................void setRemainingName (javax.naming.Name name)
    public.......................void setResolvedObj (Object obj)
```

ResourceBundle | java.util

R

Object
└ ResourceBundle

1.1 O

▲	public static final .... ResourceBundle	getBundle (String baseName)	ε310
▲	public static final .... ResourceBundle	getBundle (String baseName, Locale locale)	ε310
1.2 △	public static .. ResourceBundle	getBundle (String baseName, Locale locale, ClassLoader loader)	
O	public abstract ... *Enumeration*	getKeys ()	
1.2	public....................Locale	getLocale ()	
●	public final ....Object	getObject (String key)	
●	public final ....String	getString (String key)	ε310
●	public final .... String[]	getStringArray (String key)	
O	protected abstract ......Object	handleGetObject (String key)	
	protected .....ResourceBundle	parent	
*	public.........................	ResourceBundle ()	
	protected ....void	setParent (ResourceBundle parent)	

ResponseHandler | org.omg.CORBA.portable

	ResponseHandler
1.2	

```
public............ OutputStream createExceptionReply ()
public............ OutputStream createReply ()
```

Result | javax.xml.transform

	Result	ε518,519,520,521,522
1.4		

	public....................String getSystemId ()	
▲	public static final ....String **PI_DISABLE_OUTPUT_ESCAPING** = "javax.xml.transform.disable-output-escaping"	
▲	public static final ....String **PI_ENABLE_OUTPUT_ESCAPING** = "javax.xml.transform.enable-output-escaping"	
	public.......................void setSystemId (String systemId)	

Class *Interface* —extends - - -implements O abstract ● final △ static ▲ static final ✱ constructor x x—inherited x **x**—declared **x x**—overridden
ε*n*—examples of usage ‿—has subclass package—see other volume

ResultSet				java.sql

R

Classes

ResultSet

	public . . . . Timestamp	**getTimestamp** (int columnIndex) throws SQLException	
	public . . . . Timestamp	**getTimestamp** (String columnName) throws SQLException	ε252
1.2	public . . . . Timestamp	**getTimestamp** (int columnIndex, java.util.Calendar cal) throws SQLException	
1.2	public . . . . Timestamp	**getTimestamp** (String columnName, java.util.Calendar cal) throws SQLException	
1.2	public . . . . int	**getType** () throws SQLException	ε268
D	public . . . . . . java.io.InputStream	**getUnicodeStream** (int columnIndex) throws SQLException	
D	public . . . . . . java.io.InputStream	**getUnicodeStream** (String columnName) throws SQLException	
1.4	public . . . . java.net.URL	**getURL** (int columnIndex) throws SQLException	
1.4	public . . . . java.net.URL	**getURL** (String columnName) throws SQLException	
	public . . . . SQLWarning	**getWarnings** () throws SQLException	ε242
1.4 ▲	public static final . . . . int	**HOLD_CURSORS_OVER_COMMIT** = 1	
1.2	public . . . . void	**insertRow** () throws SQLException	ε277
1.2	public . . . . boolean	**isAfterLast** () throws SQLException	ε270
1.2	public . . . . boolean	**isBeforeFirst** () throws SQLException	ε270
1.2	public . . . . boolean	**isFirst** () throws SQLException	ε270
1.2	public . . . . boolean	**isLast** () throws SQLException	ε270
1.2	public . . . . boolean	**last** () throws SQLException	ε269,270,271
1.2	public . . . . void	**moveToCurrentRow** () throws SQLException	
1.2	public . . . . void	**moveToInsertRow** () throws SQLException	ε277
	public . . . . boolean	**next** () throws SQLException	ε252,242,247,253,255
1.2	public . . . . boolean	**previous** () throws SQLException	ε269
1.2	public . . . . void	**refreshRow** () throws SQLException	ε279
1.2	public . . . . boolean	**relative** (int rows) throws SQLException	ε269
1.2	public . . . . boolean	**rowDeleted** () throws SQLException	
1.2	public . . . . boolean	**rowInserted** () throws SQLException	
1.2	public . . . . boolean	**rowUpdated** () throws SQLException	
1.2	public . . . . void	**setFetchDirection** (int direction) throws SQLException	
1.2	public . . . . void	**setFetchSize** (int rows) throws SQLException	
1.2 ▲	public static final . . . . int	**TYPE_FORWARD_ONLY** = 1003	ε272
1.2 ▲	public static final . . . . int	**TYPE_SCROLL_INSENSITIVE** = 1004	ε266,267,268,269,270
1.2 ▲	public static final . . . . int	**TYPE_SCROLL_SENSITIVE** = 1005	ε266,267,268,273,275
1.4	public . . . . void	**updateArray** (int columnIndex, *Array* x) throws SQLException	
1.4	public . . . . void	**updateArray** (String columnName, *Array* x) throws SQLException	
1.2	public . . . . void	**updateAsciiStream** (int columnIndex, java.io.InputStream x, int length) throws SQLException	
1.2	public . . . . void	**updateAsciiStream** (String columnName, java.io.InputStream x, int length) throws SQLException	
1.2	public . . . . void	**updateBigDecimal** (int columnIndex, java.math.BigDecimal x) throws SQLException	
1.2	public . . . . void	**updateBigDecimal** (String columnName, java.math.BigDecimal x) throws SQLException	
1.2	public . . . . void	**updateBinaryStream** (int columnIndex, java.io.InputStream x, int length) throws SQLException	
1.2	public . . . . void	**updateBinaryStream** (String columnName, java.io.InputStream x, int length) throws SQLException	
1.4	public . . . . void	**updateBlob** (int columnIndex, *Blob* x) throws SQLException	
1.4	public . . . . void	**updateBlob** (String columnName, *Blob* x) throws SQLException	
1.2	public . . . . void	**updateBoolean** (int columnIndex, boolean x) throws SQLException	
1.2	public . . . . void	**updateBoolean** (String columnName, boolean x) throws SQLException	
1.2	public . . . . void	**updateByte** (int columnIndex, byte x) throws SQLException	
1.2	public . . . . void	**updateByte** (String columnName, byte x) throws SQLException	
1.2	public . . . . void	**updateBytes** (int columnIndex, byte[] x) throws SQLException	
1.2	public . . . . void	**updateBytes** (String columnName, byte[] x) throws SQLException	
1.2	public . . . . void	**updateCharacterStream** (int columnIndex, java.io.Reader x, int length) throws SQLException	
1.2	public . . . . void	**updateCharacterStream** (String columnName, java.io.Reader reader, int length) throws SQLException	
1.4	public . . . . void	**updateClob** (int columnIndex, *Clob* x) throws SQLException	
1.4	public . . . . void	**updateClob** (String columnName, *Clob* x) throws SQLException	
1.2	public . . . . void	**updateDate** (int columnIndex, Date x) throws SQLException	
1.2	public . . . . void	**updateDate** (String columnName, Date x) throws SQLException	
1.2	public . . . . void	**updateDouble** (int columnIndex, double x) throws SQLException	
1.2	public . . . . void	**updateDouble** (String columnName, double x) throws SQLException	
1.2	public . . . . void	**updateFloat** (int columnIndex, float x) throws SQLException	
1.2	public . . . . void	**updateFloat** (String columnName, float x) throws SQLException	
1.2	public . . . . void	**updateInt** (int columnIndex, int x) throws SQLException	
1.2	public . . . . void	**updateInt** (String columnName, int x) throws SQLException	
1.2	public . . . . void	**updateLong** (int columnIndex, long x) throws SQLException	
1.2	public . . . . void	**updateLong** (String columnName, long x) throws SQLException	
1.2	public . . . . void	**updateNull** (int columnIndex) throws SQLException	
1.2	public . . . . void	**updateNull** (String columnName) throws SQLException	
1.2	public . . . . void	**updateObject** (int columnIndex, Object x) throws SQLException	

R

Class   *Interface*   —extends   - - implements   ○ abstract   ● final   △ static   ▲ static final   ✳ constructor   x x—inherited   x **x**—declared   **x x**—overridden
ε*n*—examples of usage   ⌐has subclass   package—see other volume

1.2	public.....................void	**updateObject** (String columnName, Object x) throws SQLException	
1.2	public.....................void	**updateObject** (int columnIndex, Object x, int scale) throws SQLException	
1.2	public.....................void	**updateObject** (String columnName, Object x, int scale) throws SQLException	
1.4	public.....................void	**updateRef** (int columnIndex, *Ref* x) throws SQLException	
1.4	public.....................void	**updateRef** (String columnName, *Ref* x) throws SQLException	
1.2	public.....................void	**updateRow** () throws SQLException	ε275
1.2	public.....................void	**updateShort** (int columnIndex, short x) throws SQLException	
1.2	public.....................void	**updateShort** (String columnName, short x) throws SQLException	
1.2	public.....................void	**updateString** (int columnIndex, String x) throws SQLException	
1.2	public.....................void	**updateString** (String columnName, String x) throws SQLException	ε275,276,277
1.2	public.....................void	**updateTime** (int columnIndex, Time x) throws SQLException	
1.2	public.....................void	**updateTime** (String columnName, Time x) throws SQLException	
1.2	public.....................void	**updateTimestamp** (int columnIndex, Timestamp x) throws SQLException	
1.2	public.....................void	**updateTimestamp** (String columnName, Timestamp x) throws SQLException	
	public.....................boolean	**wasNull** () throws SQLException	

ResultSetMetaData | java.sql

1.1   *ResultSetMetaData*

▲	public static final..............int	**columnNoNulls** = 0	
▲	public static final..............int	**columnNullable** = 1	
▲	public static final..............int	**columnNullableUnknown** = 2	
	public.....................String	**getCatalogName** (int column) throws SQLException	
1.2	public.....................String	**getColumnClassName** (int column) throws SQLException	
	public.....................int	**getColumnCount** () throws SQLException	ε254
	public.....................int	**getColumnDisplaySize** (int column) throws SQLException	
	public.....................String	**getColumnLabel** (int column) throws SQLException	
	public.....................String	**getColumnName** (int column) throws SQLException	ε254
	public.....................int	**getColumnType** (int column) throws SQLException	
	public.....................String	**getColumnTypeName** (int column) throws SQLException	
	public.....................int	**getPrecision** (int column) throws SQLException	
	public.....................int	**getScale** (int column) throws SQLException	
	public.....................String	**getSchemaName** (int column) throws SQLException	
	public.....................String	**getTableName** (int column) throws SQLException	ε254
	public.....................boolean	**isAutoIncrement** (int column) throws SQLException	
	public.....................boolean	**isCaseSensitive** (int column) throws SQLException	
	public.....................boolean	**isCurrency** (int column) throws SQLException	
	public.....................boolean	**isDefinitelyWritable** (int column) throws SQLException	
	public.....................int	**isNullable** (int column) throws SQLException	
	public.....................boolean	**isReadOnly** (int column) throws SQLException	
	public.....................boolean	**isSearchable** (int column) throws SQLException	
	public.....................boolean	**isSigned** (int column) throws SQLException	
	public.....................boolean	**isWritable** (int column) throws SQLException	

R

RMIClassLoader | java.rmi.server

    Object
1.1   └RMIClassLoader

1.2 △	public static ....String	**getClassAnnotation** (Class cl)	
1.3 △	public static ...... ClassLoader	**getClassLoader** (String codebase) throws java.net.MalformedURLException, SecurityException	
1.4 △	public static .... RMIClassLoaderSpi	**getDefaultProviderInstance** ()	
D △	public static ....Object	**getSecurityContext** (ClassLoader loader)	
D △	public static ....Class	**loadClass** (String name) throws java.net.MalformedURLException, ClassNotFoundException	
1.2 △	public static ....Class	**loadClass** (String codebase, String name) throws java.net.MalformedURLException, ClassNotFoundException	
△	public static ....Class	**loadClass** (java.net.URL codebase, String name) throws java.net.MalformedURLException, ClassNotFoundException	
1.4 △	public static ....Class	**loadClass** (String codebase, String name, ClassLoader defaultLoader) throws java.net.MalformedURLException, ClassNotFoundException	
1.4 △	public static ....Class	**loadProxyClass** (String codebase, String[] interfaces, ClassLoader defaultLoader) throws ClassNotFoundException, java.net.MalformedURLException	

Classes

RMIClassLoaderSpi	java.rmi.server

```
      Object
1.4 ○  └RMIClassLoaderSpi
```

○	public abstract . . . . String	**getClassAnnotation** (Class cl)
○	public abstract . . . ClassLoader	**getClassLoader** (String codebase) throws java.net.MalformedURLException
○	public abstract . . . . Class	**loadClass** (String codebase, String name, ClassLoader defaultLoader)
		throws java.net.MalformedURLException, ClassNotFoundException
○	public abstract . . . . Class	**loadProxyClass** (String codebase, String[] interfaces, ClassLoader defaultLoader)
		throws java.net.MalformedURLException, ClassNotFoundException
✳	public.	**RMIClassLoaderSpi** ()

RMIClientSocketFactory	java.rmi.server

```
1.2    RMIClientSocketFactory
```

public. . . . . java.net.Socket	**createSocket** (String host, int port) throws java.io.IOException

RMIFailureHandler	java.rmi.server

```
1.1    RMIFailureHandler
```

public. . . . . boolean	**failure** (Exception ex)

RMISecurityException	java.rmi

```
      Object
      └Throwable - - - - - - - - - - - - - - - - - - - - - - - - - - java.io.Serializable ⌄
        └Exception
          └RuntimeException
            └SecurityException
D             └RMISecurityException
```

D	✳	public.	**RMISecurityException** (String name)
D	✳	public.	**RMISecurityException** (String name, String arg)

RMISecurityManager	java.rmi

```
      Object
      └SecurityManager 1
1.1     └RMISecurityManager
```

	1	*42 inherited members from SecurityManager not shown*
✳		public. . . . . **RMISecurityManager** ()

RMIServerSocketFactory	java.rmi.server

```
1.2    RMIServerSocketFactory
```

public. . . java.net.ServerSocket	**createServerSocket** (int port) throws java.io.IOException

RMISocketFactory	java.rmi.server

```
      Object
1.1 ○  └RMISocketFactory - - - - - - - - - - - - - - - - - - - - - - RMIClientSocketFactory 1, RMIServerSocketFactory 2
```

○	2	public abstract	**createServerSocket** (int port) throws java.io.IOException
		. . . . java.net.ServerSocket	
○	1	public abstract java.net.Socket	**createSocket** (String host, int port) throws java.io.IOException
1.2 △		public static synchronized	**getDefaultSocketFactory** ()
		. . . . RMISocketFactory	
△		public static synchronized	**getFailureHandler** ()
		. . . . *RMIFailureHandler*	

Class *Interface* —extends - - -implements ○ abstract ● final △ static ▲ static final ✳ constructor x x—inherited x **x**—declared **x x**—overridden
ε*n*—examples of usage ⌄—has subclass package—see other volume

△ public static synchronized .... **getSocketFactory** ()
.... RMISocketFactory
* public.......................... **RMISocketFactory** ()
△ public static synchronized void **setFailureHandler** (*RMIFailureHandler* fh)
△ public static synchronized void **setSocketFactory** (RMISocketFactory fac) throws java.io.IOException

RowSet	javax.sql

1.4   RowSet————————————————*java.sql.ResultSet* [1]   ε251,257

1 *149 inherited members from java.sql.ResultSet not shown*
public......................void **addRowSetListener** (*RowSetListener* listener)
public......................void **clearParameters** () throws java.sql.SQLException
public......................void **execute** () throws java.sql.SQLException
public...................String **getCommand** ()
public...................String **getDataSourceName** ()
public.................boolean **getEscapeProcessing** () throws java.sql.SQLException
public....................int **getMaxFieldSize** () throws java.sql.SQLException
public....................int **getMaxRows** () throws java.sql.SQLException
public...................String **getPassword** ()
public....................int **getQueryTimeout** () throws java.sql.SQLException
public....................int **getTransactionIsolation** ()
public............. *java.util.Map* **getTypeMap** () throws java.sql.SQLException
public...................String **getUrl** () throws java.sql.SQLException
public...................String **getUsername** ()
public.................boolean **isReadOnly** ()
public......................void **removeRowSetListener** (*RowSetListener* listener)
public......................void **setArray** (int i, *java.sql.Array* x) throws java.sql.SQLException
public......................void **setAsciiStream** (int parameterIndex, java.io.InputStream x, int length)
throws java.sql.SQLException
public......................void **setBigDecimal** (int parameterIndex, java.math.BigDecimal x)
throws java.sql.SQLException
public......................void **setBinaryStream** (int parameterIndex, java.io.InputStream x, int length)
throws java.sql.SQLException
public......................void **setBlob** (int i, *java.sql.Blob* x) throws java.sql.SQLException
public......................void **setBoolean** (int parameterIndex, boolean x) throws java.sql.SQLException
public......................void **setByte** (int parameterIndex, byte x) throws java.sql.SQLException
public......................void **setBytes** (int parameterIndex, byte[] x) throws java.sql.SQLException
public......................void **setCharacterStream** (int parameterIndex, java.io.Reader reader, int length)
throws java.sql.SQLException
public......................void **setClob** (int i, *java.sql.Clob* x) throws java.sql.SQLException
public......................void **setCommand** (String cmd) throws java.sql.SQLException
public......................void **setConcurrency** (int concurrency) throws java.sql.SQLException
public......................void **setDataSourceName** (String name) throws java.sql.SQLException
public......................void **setDate** (int parameterIndex, java.sql.Date x) throws java.sql.SQLException
public......................void **setDate** (int parameterIndex, java.sql.Date x, java.util.Calendar cal)
throws java.sql.SQLException
public......................void **setDouble** (int parameterIndex, double x) throws java.sql.SQLException
public......................void **setEscapeProcessing** (boolean enable) throws java.sql.SQLException
public......................void **setFloat** (int parameterIndex, float x) throws java.sql.SQLException
public......................void **setInt** (int parameterIndex, int x) throws java.sql.SQLException
public......................void **setLong** (int parameterIndex, long x) throws java.sql.SQLException
public......................void **setMaxFieldSize** (int max) throws java.sql.SQLException
public......................void **setMaxRows** (int max) throws java.sql.SQLException
public......................void **setNull** (int parameterIndex, int sqlType) throws java.sql.SQLException
public......................void **setNull** (int paramIndex, int sqlType, String typeName)
throws java.sql.SQLException
public......................void **setObject** (int parameterIndex, Object x) throws java.sql.SQLException
public......................void **setObject** (int parameterIndex, Object x, int targetSqlType)
throws java.sql.SQLException
public......................void **setObject** (int parameterIndex, Object x, int targetSqlType, int scale)
throws java.sql.SQLException
public......................void **setPassword** (String password) throws java.sql.SQLException
public......................void **setQueryTimeout** (int seconds) throws java.sql.SQLException
public......................void **setReadOnly** (boolean value) throws java.sql.SQLException
public......................void **setRef** (int i, *java.sql.Ref* x) throws java.sql.SQLException
public......................void **setShort** (int parameterIndex, short x) throws java.sql.SQLException
public......................void **setString** (int parameterIndex, String x) throws java.sql.SQLException
public......................void **setTime** (int parameterIndex, java.sql.Time x) throws java.sql.SQLException
public......................void **setTime** (int parameterIndex, java.sql.Time x, java.util.Calendar cal)
throws java.sql.SQLException
public......................void **setTimestamp** (int parameterIndex, java.sql.Timestamp x)
throws java.sql.SQLException

R

Classes

RowSet

```
public.....................void  setTimestamp (int parameterIndex, java.sql.Timestamp x, java.util.Calendar cal)
                                     throws java.sql.SQLException
public.....................void  setTransactionIsolation (int level) throws java.sql.SQLException
public.....................void  setType (int type) throws java.sql.SQLException
public.....................void  setTypeMap (java.util.Map map) throws java.sql.SQLException
public.....................void  setUrl (String url) throws java.sql.SQLException
public.....................void  setUsername (String name) throws java.sql.SQLException
```

RowSetEvent   javax.sql

ε333

```
       Object
1.1    └─java.util.EventObject 1 - - - - - - - - - - - - - - - - - - java.io.Serializable ⌄
1.4        └─RowSetEvent
```

```
 *  1  public.....................Object  getSource ()
    1  public.....................        RowSetEvent (RowSet source)
    1  protected transient......Object   source
    1  public.....................String  toString ()
```

RowSetInternal   javax.sql

```
1.4    RowSetInternal
```

```
public..... java.sql.Connection  getConnection () throws java.sql.SQLException
public........java.sql.ResultSet  getOriginal () throws java.sql.SQLException
public........java.sql.ResultSet  getOriginalRow () throws java.sql.SQLException
public.................Object[]   getParams () throws java.sql.SQLException
public.....................void   setMetaData (RowSetMetaData md) throws java.sql.SQLException
```

R

RowSetListener   javax.sql

```
1.4    RowSetListener─────────────────java.util.EventListener ⌄              ε2,3,333,493,494
```

```
public.....................void  cursorMoved (RowSetEvent event)
public.....................void  rowChanged (RowSetEvent event)
public.....................void  rowSetChanged (RowSetEvent event)
```

RowSetMetaData   javax.sql

```
1.4    RowSetMetaData───────────────java.sql.ResultSetMetaData ⌄ 1
```

```
 1  public.....................String  getCatalogName (int column) throws java.sql.SQLException
 1  public.....................String  getColumnClassName (int column) throws java.sql.SQLException
 1  public.....................int     getColumnCount () throws java.sql.SQLException                ε254
 1  public.....................int     getColumnDisplaySize (int column) throws java.sql.SQLException
 1  public.....................String  getColumnLabel (int column) throws java.sql.SQLException
 1  public.....................String  getColumnName (int column) throws java.sql.SQLException       ε254
 1  public.....................int     getColumnType (int column) throws java.sql.SQLException
 1  public.....................String  getColumnTypeName (int column) throws java.sql.SQLException
 1  public.....................int     getPrecision (int column) throws java.sql.SQLException
 1  public.....................int     getScale (int column) throws java.sql.SQLException
 1  public.....................String  getSchemaName (int column) throws java.sql.SQLException
 1  public.....................String  getTableName (int column) throws java.sql.SQLException        ε254
 1  public.....................boolean isAutoIncrement (int column) throws java.sql.SQLException
 1  public.....................boolean isCaseSensitive (int column) throws java.sql.SQLException
 1  public.....................boolean isCurrency (int column) throws java.sql.SQLException
 1  public.....................boolean isDefinitelyWritable (int column) throws java.sql.SQLException
 1  public.....................int     isNullable (int column) throws java.sql.SQLException
 1  public.....................boolean isReadOnly (int column) throws java.sql.SQLException
 1  public.....................boolean isSearchable (int column) throws java.sql.SQLException
 1  public.....................boolean isSigned (int column) throws java.sql.SQLException
 1  public.....................boolean isWritable (int column) throws java.sql.SQLException
    public.....................void    setAutoIncrement (int columnIndex, boolean property)
                                          throws java.sql.SQLException
    public.....................void    setCaseSensitive (int columnIndex, boolean property)
                                          throws java.sql.SQLException
    public.....................void    setCatalogName (int columnIndex, String catalogName)
                                          throws java.sql.SQLException
```

Class   *Interface*   —extends   - - -implements   ○ abstract   ● final   △ static   ▲ static final   ✳ constructor   x x—inherited   x **x**—declared   **x x**—overridden
εn—examples of usage   ⌄—has subclass   package—see other volume

public	void	**setColumnCount** (int columnCount) throws java.sql.SQLException	
public	void	**setColumnDisplaySize** (int columnIndex, int size) throws java.sql.SQLException	
public	void	**setColumnLabel** (int columnIndex, String label) throws java.sql.SQLException	
public	void	**setColumnName** (int columnIndex, String columnName) throws java.sql.SQLException	
public	void	**setColumnType** (int columnIndex, int SQLType) throws java.sql.SQLException	
public	void	**setColumnTypeName** (int columnIndex, String typeName) throws java.sql.SQLException	
public	void	**setCurrency** (int columnIndex, boolean property) throws java.sql.SQLException	
public	void	**setNullable** (int columnIndex, int property) throws java.sql.SQLException	
public	void	**setPrecision** (int columnIndex, int precision) throws java.sql.SQLException	
public	void	**setScale** (int columnIndex, int scale) throws java.sql.SQLException	
public	void	**setSchemaName** (int columnIndex, String schemaName) throws java.sql.SQLException	
public	void	**setSearchable** (int columnIndex, boolean property) throws java.sql.SQLException	
public	void	**setSigned** (int columnIndex, boolean property) throws java.sql.SQLException	
public	void	**setTableName** (int columnIndex, String tableName) throws java.sql.SQLException	

RowSetReader   javax.sql

1.4   *RowSetReader*

public .... void **readData** (*RowSetInternal* caller) throws java.sql.SQLException

---

RowSetWriter   javax.sql

1.4   *RowSetWriter*

public .... boolean **writeData** (*RowSetInternal* caller) throws java.sql.SQLException

---

RSAKey   java.security.interfaces

1.3   *RSAKey*

public .... java.math.BigInteger **getModulus** ()

RSAKeyGenParameterSpec   java.security.spec

Object
1.3   └RSAKeyGenParameterSpec -------------- *AlgorithmParameterSpec*

▲   public static final **F0**
     .... java.math.BigInteger
▲   public static final **F4**
     .... java.math.BigInteger
     public ....int **getKeysize** ()
     public .... java.math.BigInteger **getPublicExponent** ()
*   public .... **RSAKeyGenParameterSpec** (int keysize, java.math.BigInteger publicExponent)

RSAMultiPrimePrivateCrtKey   java.security.interfaces

1.4   *RSAMultiPrimePrivateCrtKey*——————— *RSAPrivateKey* [1] (*java.security.PrivateKey* (*java.security.Key* [2]
                                            (*java.io.Serializable*)), *RSAKey* [3])

[2]	public .... String	getAlgorithm ()	ε203,204,205,464,469
	public .... java.math.BigInteger	**getCrtCoefficient** ()	
[2]	public .... byte[]	getEncoded ()	ε199,460,471,471
[2]	public .... String	getFormat ()	ε199
[3]	public .... java.math.BigInteger	getModulus ()	
	public ....java.security ↵	**getOtherPrimeInfo** ()	
	.spec.RSAOtherPrimeInfo[]		
	public .... java.math.BigInteger	**getPrimeExponentP** ()	
	public .... java.math.BigInteger	**getPrimeExponentQ** ()	
	public .... java.math.BigInteger	**getPrimeP** ()	
	public .... java.math.BigInteger	**getPrimeQ** ()	
[1]	public .... java.math.BigInteger	getPrivateExponent ()	
	public .... java.math.BigInteger	**getPublicExponent** ()	

RSAMultiPrimePrivateCrtKeySpec	java.security.spec

```
       Object
1.2    └─RSAPrivateKeySpec 1 ------------------ KeySpec
1.4       └─RSAMultiPrimePrivateCrtKeySpec
```

		public....	java.math.BigInteger	**getCrtCoefficient** ()
	1	public....	java.math.BigInteger	getModulus ()
		public....	RSAOtherPrimeInfo[]	**getOtherPrimeInfo** ()
		public....	java.math.BigInteger	**getPrimeExponentP** ()
		public....	java.math.BigInteger	**getPrimeExponentQ** ()
		public....	java.math.BigInteger	**getPrimeP** ()
		public....	java.math.BigInteger	**getPrimeQ** ()
	1	public....	java.math.BigInteger	getPrivateExponent ()
		public....	java.math.BigInteger	**getPublicExponent** ()
*		public..........................		**RSAMultiPrimePrivateCrtKeySpec** (java.math.BigInteger modulus, java.math.BigInteger publicExponent, java.math.BigInteger privateExponent, java.math.BigInteger primeP, java.math.BigInteger primeQ, java.math.BigInteger primeExponentP, java.math.BigInteger primeExponentQ, java.math.BigInteger crtCoefficient, RSAOtherPrimeInfo[] otherPrimeInfo)

RSAOtherPrimeInfo	java.security.spec

```
       Object
1.4    └─RSAOtherPrimeInfo
```

●	public final	**getCrtCoefficient** ()
	.... java.math.BigInteger	
●	public final	**getExponent** ()
	.... java.math.BigInteger	
●	public final	**getPrime** ()
	.... java.math.BigInteger	
*	public..........................	**RSAOtherPrimeInfo** (java.math.BigInteger prime, java.math.BigInteger primeExponent, java.math.BigInteger crtCoefficient)

RSAPrivateCrtKey	java.security.interfaces

```
1.2    RSAPrivateCrtKey──────────────── RSAPrivateKey 1 (java.security.PrivateKey (java.security.Key 2
                                       (java.io.Serializable)), RSAKey 3)
```

	2	public..................... String	getAlgorithm ()	ε203,204,205,464,469
		public.... java.math.BigInteger	**getCrtCoefficient** ()	
	2	public..................... byte[]	getEncoded ()	ε199,460,471,471
	2	public..................... String	getFormat ()	ε199
1.3	3	public.... java.math.BigInteger	getModulus ()	
		public.... java.math.BigInteger	**getPrimeExponentP** ()	
		public.... java.math.BigInteger	**getPrimeExponentQ** ()	
		public.... java.math.BigInteger	**getPrimeP** ()	
		public.... java.math.BigInteger	**getPrimeQ** ()	
	1	public.... java.math.BigInteger	getPrivateExponent ()	
		public.... java.math.BigInteger	**getPublicExponent** ()	

RSAPrivateCrtKeySpec	java.security.spec

```
       Object
1.2    └─RSAPrivateKeySpec 1 ----------------- KeySpec
1.2       └─RSAPrivateCrtKeySpec
```

		public.... java.math.BigInteger	**getCrtCoefficient** ()
	1	public.... java.math.BigInteger	getModulus ()
		public.... java.math.BigInteger	**getPrimeExponentP** ()
		public.... java.math.BigInteger	**getPrimeExponentQ** ()
		public.... java.math.BigInteger	**getPrimeP** ()
		public.... java.math.BigInteger	**getPrimeQ** ()
	1	public.... java.math.BigInteger	getPrivateExponent ()
		public.... java.math.BigInteger	**getPublicExponent** ()

*	public.........................	**RSAPrivateCrtKeySpec** (java.math.BigInteger modulus, java.math.BigInteger publicExponent, java.math.BigInteger privateExponent, java.math.BigInteger primeP, java.math.BigInteger primeQ, java.math.BigInteger primeExponentP, java.math.BigInteger primeExponentQ, java.math.BigInteger crtCoefficient)

RSAPrivateKey — java.security.interfaces

1.2   *RSAPrivateKey* ——————————————— *java.security.PrivateKey* (*java.security.Key* [1] (*java.io.Serializable*)), *RSAKey* [2]

	1	public....................String	getAlgorithm ()	ε203,204,205,464,469
	1	public....................byte[]	getEncoded ()	ε199,460,471,471
	1	public....................String	getFormat ()	ε199
1.3	2	public.... java.math.BigInteger	getModulus ()	
		public.... java.math.BigInteger	**getPrivateExponent** ()	

RSAPrivateKeySpec — java.security.spec

    Object
1.2   └RSAPrivateKeySpec - - - - - - - - - - - - - - - - - - - *KeySpec*

	public.... java.math.BigInteger	**getModulus** ()
	public.... java.math.BigInteger	**getPrivateExponent** ()
*	public.........................	**RSAPrivateKeySpec** (java.math.BigInteger modulus, java.math.BigInteger privateExponent)

RSAPublicKey — java.security.interfaces

1.2   *RSAPublicKey* ——————————————— *java.security.PublicKey* (*java.security.Key* [1] (*java.io.Serializable*)), *RSAKey* [2]

	1	public....................String	getAlgorithm ()	ε203,204,205,464,469
	1	public....................byte[]	getEncoded ()	ε199,460,471,471
	1	public....................String	getFormat ()	ε199
1.3	2	public.... java.math.BigInteger	getModulus ()	
		public.... java.math.BigInteger	**getPublicExponent** ()	

R

RSAPublicKeySpec — java.security.spec

    Object
1.2   └RSAPublicKeySpec - - - - - - - - - - - - - - - - - - - *KeySpec*

	public.... java.math.BigInteger	**getModulus** ()
	public.... java.math.BigInteger	**getPublicExponent** ()
*	public.........................	**RSAPublicKeySpec** (java.math.BigInteger modulus, java.math.BigInteger publicExponent)

RuleBasedCollator — java.text

    Object
1.1 ○ └Collator[1] - *java.util.Comparator*, *Cloneable*
1.1   └RuleBasedCollator

	1	public....................**Object**	**clone** ()	
1.2	1	public.........................int	compare (Object o1, Object o2)	
	1	public synchronized .... **int**	**compare** (String source, String target)	ε306
	1	public.................**boolean**	**equals** (Object obj)	
	1	public..................boolean	equals (String source, String target)	
△	1	public static synchronized .... java.util.Locale[]	getAvailableLocales ()	
		public. CollationElementIterator	**getCollationElementIterator** (String source)	
1.2		public. CollationElementIterator	**getCollationElementIterator** (*CharacterIterator* source)	
	1	public synchronized .... **CollationKey**	**getCollationKey** (String source)	
	1	public synchronized ....int	getDecomposition ()	
△	1	public static synchronized ....Collator	getInstance ()	
△	1	public static synchronized ....Collator	getInstance (java.util.Locale desiredLocale)	ε306

Classes

RuleBasedCollator

	public.....................String	**getRules** ()
1	public synchronized ....int	getStrength ()
1	public..........................**int**	**hashCode** ()
*	public............................	**RuleBasedCollator** (String rules) throws ParseException
1	public synchronized ......void	setDecomposition (int decompositionMode)
1	public synchronized ......void	setStrength (int newStrength)

Runnable   java.lang

Runnable

- -

public.......................void **run** () ε92,62

Runtime   java.lang

Object
└Runtime

1.3	public.......................void	**addShutdownHook** (Thread hook)	ε50
1.4	public native ....int	**availableProcessors** ()	
	public................Process	**exec** (String command) throws java.io.IOException	ε89,90,91
	public................Process	**exec** (String[] cmdarray) throws java.io.IOException	
	public................Process	**exec** (String cmd, String[] envp) throws java.io.IOException	
	public................Process	**exec** (String[] cmdarray, String[] envp) throws java.io.IOException	
1.3	public................Process	**exec** (String command, String[] envp, java.io.File dir) throws java.io.IOException	
1.3	public................Process	**exec** (String[] cmdarray, String[] envp, java.io.File dir) throws java.io.IOException	
	public.......................void	**exit** (int status)	
	public native .... long	**freeMemory** ()	ε55
	public native ....void	**gc** ()	
D	public...... java.io.InputStream	**getLocalizedInputStream** (java.io.InputStream in)	
D	public.... java.io.OutputStream	**getLocalizedOutputStream** (java.io.OutputStream out)	
△	public static ....Runtime	**getRuntime** ()	ε50,55,89,90,91
1.3	public.......................void	**halt** (int status)	
	public.......................void	**load** (String filename)	
	public.......................void	**loadLibrary** (String libname)	
1.4	public native .... long	**maxMemory** ()	ε55
1.3	public.................boolean	**removeShutdownHook** (Thread hook)	
	public.......................void	**runFinalization** ()	
D △	public static ....void	**runFinalizersOnExit** (boolean value)	
	public native .... long	**totalMemory** ()	ε55
	public native ....void	**traceInstructions** (boolean on)	
	public native ....void	**traceMethodCalls** (boolean on)	

RunTime   org.omg.SendingContext

1.3	*RunTime* ───────────────────	*RunTimeOperations* , org.omg.CORBA.Object [1], org.omg.CORBA.portable.IDLEntity (java.io.Serializable)

- -

    1   *13 inherited members from org.omg.CORBA.Object not shown*

RuntimeException   java.lang

Object
└Throwable - *java.io.Serializable*
  └Exception
    └RuntimeException

*	public..........................	**RuntimeException** ()
*	public..........................	**RuntimeException** (String message)
1.4 *	public..........................	**RuntimeException** (Throwable cause)
1.4 *	public..........................	**RuntimeException** (String message, Throwable cause)

RunTimeOperations   org.omg.SendingContext

1.3   *RunTimeOperations*

- -

Class   *Interface* —extends - - -implements ○ abstract ● final △ static ▲ static final ✳ constructor x x—inherited x **x**—declared **x x**—overridden
ε*n*—examples of usage   —has subclass package—see other volume

	RuntimePermission	java.lang

| | Object | ε217,218 |

1.2 ○ └java.security.Permission[1] ---------------- *java.security.Guard*, *java.io.Serializable*⌄
1.2 ○ └java.security.BasicPermission[2]
1.2 ● └RuntimePermission

	1	public......................void	checkGuard (Object object) throws SecurityException	
	2	public................. boolean	equals (Object obj)	ε215
	2	public....................String	getActions ()	ε215
●	1	public final ....String	getName ()	
	2	public........................int	hashCode ()	ε215
	2	public................. boolean	implies (java.security.Permission p)	ε214,215
	2	public..........java.security ↩	newPermissionCollection ()	
		.PermissionCollection		
*		public..........................	**RuntimePermission** (String name)	
*		public..........................	**RuntimePermission** (String name, String actions)	
	1	public....................String	toString ()	

	Savepoint	java.sql

1.4 *Savepoint*

public........................int	**getSavepointId** () throws SQLException
public....................String	**getSavepointName** () throws SQLException

	SAXException	org.xml.sax

| | Object | ε548,510,512,513,514 |

└Throwable[1] -------------------------- *java.io.Serializable*⌄
└Exception
1.4 └SAXException⌄

	public............... Exception	**getException** ()
1	public............... **String**	**getMessage** ()
1	public....................void	printStackTrace ()
*	public..........................	**SAXException** (Exception e)
*	public..........................	**SAXException** (String message)
*	public..........................	**SAXException** (String message, Exception e)
1	public................. **String**	**toString** ()

	SAXNotRecognizedException	org.xml.sax

Object
└Throwable -------------------------- *java.io.Serializable*⌄
└Exception
1.4 └SAXException[1]
1.4 └SAXNotRecognizedException

1	public............... Exception	getException ()
1	public....................String	getMessage ()
*	public..........................	**SAXNotRecognizedException** (String message)
1	public....................String	toString ()

	SAXNotSupportedException	org.xml.sax

Object
└Throwable -------------------------- *java.io.Serializable*⌄
└Exception
1.4 └SAXException[1]
1.4 └SAXNotSupportedException

1	public............... Exception	getException ()
1	public....................String	getMessage ()
*	public..........................	**SAXNotSupportedException** (String message)
1	public....................String	toString ()

S

Classes

729

SAXParseException

					org.xml.sax

```
Object
 └Throwable ------------------------------- java.io.Serializable
    └Exception
```
1.4   `└SAXException`[1]
1.4   `└SAXParseException`

	public.........................int	**getColumnNumber** ()		ε513
1	public............... Exception	getException ()		
	public.........................int	**getLineNumber** ()		ε513
1	public...................String	getMessage ()		ε513
	public...................String	**getPublicId** ()		ε513
	public...................String	**getSystemId** ()		ε513
*	public.........................	**SAXParseException** (String message, *Locator* locator)		
*	public.........................	**SAXParseException** (String message, *Locator* locator, Exception e)		
*	public.........................	**SAXParseException** (String message, String publicId, String systemId, int lineNumber, int columnNumber)		
*	public.........................	**SAXParseException** (String message, String publicId, String systemId, int lineNumber, int columnNumber, Exception e)		
1	public...................String	toString ()		

					javax.xml.parsers

SAXParser

```
Object
 └SAXParser
```
1.4 ○

○	public abstract ....org.xml.sax.Parser	**getParser** () throws org.xml.sax.SAXException	
○	public abstract ....Object	**getProperty** (String name) throws org.xml.sax.SAXNotRecognizedException, org.xml.sax.SAXNotSupportedException	
○	public abstract ....org.xml.sax.XMLReader	**getXMLReader** () throws org.xml.sax.SAXException	
○	public abstract .... boolean	**isNamespaceAware** ()	
○	public abstract .... boolean	**isValidating** ()	
	public......................void	**parse** (java.io.File f, org.xml.sax.helpers.DefaultHandler dh) throws org.xml.sax.SAXException, java.io.IOException	ε517
	public......................void	**parse** (java.io.File f, org.xml.sax.HandlerBase hb) throws org.xml.sax.SAXException, java.io.IOException	
	public......................void	**parse** (java.io.InputStream is, org.xml.sax.helpers.DefaultHandler dh) throws org.xml.sax.SAXException, java.io.IOException	
	public......................void	**parse** (java.io.InputStream is, org.xml.sax.HandlerBase hb) throws org.xml.sax.SAXException, java.io.IOException	
	public......................void	**parse** (String uri, org.xml.sax.HandlerBase hb) throws org.xml.sax.SAXException, java.io.IOException	
	public......................void	**parse** (String uri, org.xml.sax.helpers.DefaultHandler dh) throws org.xml.sax.SAXException, java.io.IOException	
	public......................void	**parse** (org.xml.sax.InputSource is, org.xml.sax.HandlerBase hb) throws org.xml.sax.SAXException, java.io.IOException	
	public......................void	**parse** (org.xml.sax.InputSource is, org.xml.sax.helpers.DefaultHandler dh) throws org.xml.sax.SAXException, java.io.IOException	
	public......................void	**parse** (java.io.InputStream is, org.xml.sax.HandlerBase hb, String systemId) throws org.xml.sax.SAXException, java.io.IOException	
	public......................void	**parse** (java.io.InputStream is, org.xml.sax.helpers.DefaultHandler dh, String systemId) throws org.xml.sax.SAXException, java.io.IOException	
*	protected	**SAXParser** ()	
○	public abstract ....void	**setProperty** (String name, Object value) throws org.xml.sax↵ .SAXNotRecognizedException, org.xml.sax.SAXNotSupportedException	

					javax.xml.parsers

SAXParserFactory

```
Object
 └SAXParserFactory
```
1.4 ○

○	public abstract .... boolean	**getFeature** (String name) throws ParserConfigurationException, org.xml.sax↵ .SAXNotRecognizedException, org.xml.sax.SAXNotSupportedException	
	public................. boolean	**isNamespaceAware** ()	
	public................. boolean	**isValidating** ()	

Class   *Interface*   —extends   - - -implements   ○ abstract   ● final   △ static   ▲ static final   ✱ constructor   x x—inherited   x **x**—declared   **x x**—overridden
ε*n*—examples of usage   ⌐—has subclass   package—see other volume

△	public static SAXParserFactory	**newInstance** () throws FactoryConfigurationError	ε517
○	public abstract ..... SAXParser	**newSAXParser** () throws ParserConfigurationException, org.xml.sax.SAXException	
			ε517
*	protected	**SAXParserFactory** ()	
○	public abstract .... void	**setFeature** (String name, boolean value) throws ParserConfigurationException, org.xml.sax.SAXNotRecognizedException, org.xml.sax ↵ .SAXNotSupportedException	
	public...................... void	**setNamespaceAware** (boolean awareness)	
	public...................... void	**setValidating** (boolean validating)	ε517

SAXResult `javax.xml.transform.sax`

Object
1.4 └SAXResult --------------------------- *javax.xml.transform.Result* [1]

▲	public static final .... String	**FEATURE** = "http://javax.xml.transform.sax.SAXResult/feature"	
	public.......................... . org.xml.sax.ContentHandler	**getHandler** ()	
	public.................... org ↵ .xml.sax.ext.LexicalHandler	**getLexicalHandler** ()	
1	public.................... String	**getSystemId** ()	
*	public..........................	**SAXResult** ()	
*	public..........................	**SAXResult** (*org.xml.sax.ContentHandler* handler)	ε523
	public.................... void	**setHandler** (*org.xml.sax.ContentHandler* handler)	
	public.................... void	**setLexicalHandler** (*org.xml.sax.ext.LexicalHandler* handler)	
1	public.................... void	**setSystemId** (String systemId)	

SAXSource `javax.xml.transform.sax`

Object
1.4 └SAXSource -------------------------- *javax.xml.transform.Source* [1]

▲	public static final .... String	**FEATURE** = "http://javax.xml.transform.sax.SAXSource/feature"	
	public org.xml.sax.InputSource	**getInputSource** ()	
1	public.................... String	**getSystemId** ()	
	public . org.xml.sax.XMLReader	**getXMLReader** ()	
*	public..........................	**SAXSource** ()	
*	public..........................	**SAXSource** (org.xml.sax.InputSource inputSource)	
*	public..........................	**SAXSource** (*org.xml.sax.XMLReader* reader, org.xml.sax.InputSource inputSource)	
	public.................... void	**setInputSource** (org.xml.sax.InputSource inputSource)	
1	public.................... void	**setSystemId** (String systemId)	ε523
	public.................... void	**setXMLReader** (*org.xml.sax.XMLReader* reader)	
△	public static .... org.xml.sax.InputSource	**sourceToInputSource** (*javax.xml.transform.Source* source)	

SAXTransformerFactory `javax.xml.transform.sax`

Object
1.4 ○ └javax.xml.transform.TransformerFactory [1]
1.4 ○   └SAXTransformerFactory

▲	public static final .... String	**FEATURE** = "http://javax.xml.transform.sax.SAXTransformerFactory/feature"	
▲	public static final .... String	**FEATURE_XMLFILTER** = "http://javax.xml.transform.sax ↵ .SAXTransformerFactory/feature/xmlfilter"	
○ 1	public abstract .... *javax.xml.transform.Source*	getAssociatedStylesheet (*javax.xml.transform.Source* source, String media, String title, String charset) throws javax.xml.transform.TransformerConfigurationException	
○ 1	public abstract .... Object	getAttribute (String name) throws IllegalArgumentException	
○ 1	public abstract .... *javax* ↵ *.xml.transform.ErrorListener*	getErrorListener ()	
○ 1	public abstract .... boolean	getFeature (String name)	
○ 1	public abstract .... *javax* ↵ *.xml.transform.URIResolver*	getURIResolver ()	
△ 1	public static .... *javax.xml.transform* ↵ *.TransformerFactory*	newInstance () throws javax.xml.transform.TransformerFactoryConfigurationError ε518,519,520,521,522	
○ 1	public abstract .... *javax* ↵ *.xml.transform.Templates*	newTemplates (*javax.xml.transform.Source* source) throws javax.xml.transform.TransformerConfigurationException ε521,522	
○	public abstract .... *TemplatesHandler*	**newTemplatesHandler** () throws javax.xml.transform ↵ .TransformerConfigurationException	

S

Classes

SAXTransformerFactory

O	1	public abstract . . . . javax ↵ .xml.transform.Transformer	newTransformer () throws javax.xml.transform.TransformerConfigurationException	ε518,519,520,523
O	1	public abstract . . . . javax ↵ .xml.transform.Transformer	newTransformer (*javax.xml.transform.Source* source) throws javax.xml.transform.TransformerConfigurationException	
O		public abstract . . . . *TransformerHandler*	**newTransformerHandler** () throws javax.xml.transform ↵ .TransformerConfigurationException	
O		public abstract . . . . *TransformerHandler*	**newTransformerHandler** (*javax.xml.transform.Source* src) throws javax.xml.transform.TransformerConfigurationException	
O		public abstract . . . . *TransformerHandler*	**newTransformerHandler** (*javax.xml.transform.Templates* templates) throws javax.xml.transform.TransformerConfigurationException	
O		public abstract . . . . *org.xml.sax.XMLFilter*	**newXMLFilter** (*javax.xml.transform.Source* src) throws javax.xml.transform.TransformerConfigurationException	
O		public abstract . . . . *org.xml.sax.XMLFilter*	**newXMLFilter** (*javax.xml.transform.Templates* templates) throws javax.xml.transform.TransformerConfigurationException	
*		protected	**SAXTransformerFactory** ()	
O	1	public abstract . . . . void	setAttribute (String name, Object value) throws IllegalArgumentException	
O	1	public abstract . . . . void	setErrorListener (*javax.xml.transform.ErrorListener* listener) throws IllegalArgumentException	
O	1	public abstract . . . . void	setURIResolver (*javax.xml.transform.URIResolver* resolver)	

ScatteringByteChannel
java.nio.channels

1.4	*ScatteringByteChannel* ———————— *ReadableByteChannel* [1] (*Channel* [2])		

	2	public . . . . void	close () throws java.io.IOException	ε167,170,171,172,174
	2	public . . . . boolean	isOpen ()	
	1	public . . . . int	read (java.nio.ByteBuffer dst) throws java.io.IOException	ε180,169,174
		public . . . . long	**read** (java.nio.ByteBuffer[] dsts) throws java.io.IOException	
		public . . . . long	**read** (java.nio.ByteBuffer[] dsts, int offset, int length) throws java.io.IOException	

SchemaViolationException
javax.naming.directory

Object
└Throwable - *java.io.Serializable*
  └Exception
1.3   └javax.naming.NamingException [1]
1.3   └SchemaViolationException

	1	*20 inherited members from javax.naming.NamingException not shown*	
*		public	**SchemaViolationException** ()
*		public	**SchemaViolationException** (String explanation)

SealedObject
javax.crypto

Object
└SealedObject - *java.io.Serializable*

	protected . . . . byte[]	**encodedParams**	
●	public final . . . . String	**getAlgorithm** ()	ε466
●	public final . . . . Object	**getObject** (*java.security.Key* key) throws java.io.IOException, ClassNotFoundException, java.security.NoSuchAlgorithmException, java.security.InvalidKeyException	
●	public final . . . . Object	**getObject** (Cipher c) throws java.io.IOException, ClassNotFoundException, IllegalBlockSizeException, BadPaddingException	ε466
●	public final . . . . Object	**getObject** (*java.security.Key* key, String provider) throws java.io.IOException, ClassNotFoundException, java.security.NoSuchAlgorithmException, java.security.NoSuchProviderException, java.security.InvalidKeyException	
*	protected	**SealedObject** (SealedObject so)	
*	public	**SealedObject** (*java.io.Serializable* object, Cipher c) throws java.io.IOException, IllegalBlockSizeException	ε466

SearchControls
javax.naming.directory

Object
└SearchControls - *java.io.Serializable*
1.3

Class   *Interface*   —extends   - - -implements   O abstract   ● final   △ static   ▲ static final   ✳ constructor   x x—inherited   x **x**—declared   **x x**—overridden
ε*n*—examples of usage   ⌐has subclass   package—see other volume

	public	long	**getCountLimit** ()	
	public	boolean	**getDerefLinkFlag** ()	
	public	String[]	**getReturningAttributes** ()	
	public	boolean	**getReturningObjFlag** ()	
	public	int	**getSearchScope** ()	
	public	int	**getTimeLimit** ()	
▲	public static final	int	**OBJECT_SCOPE** = 0	
▲	public static final	int	**ONELEVEL_SCOPE** = 1	
*	public		**SearchControls** ()	ε487,488,494
*	public		**SearchControls** (int scope, long countlim, int timelim, String[] attrs, boolean retobj, boolean deref)	
	public	void	**setCountLimit** (long limit)	
	public	void	**setDerefLinkFlag** (boolean on)	
	public	void	**setReturningAttributes** (String[] attrs)	ε487
	public	void	**setReturningObjFlag** (boolean on)	
	public	void	**setSearchScope** (int scope)	ε488,494
	public	void	**setTimeLimit** (int ms)	
▲	public static final	int	**SUBTREE_SCOPE** = 2	ε488,494

SearchResult		javax.naming.directory

		ε486,487,488,489,497

Object
1.3	└javax.naming.NameClassPair[1] ----------- *java.io.Serializable*
1.3	└javax.naming.Binding[2]
1.3	└SearchResult

	public	*Attributes*	**getAttributes** ()	
2	public	String	getClassName ()	
1	public	String	getName ()	
2	public	Object	getObject ()	
1	public	boolean	isRelative ()	
*	public		**SearchResult** (String name, Object obj, *Attributes* attrs)	
*	public		**SearchResult** (String name, Object obj, *Attributes* attrs, boolean isRelative)	
*	public		**SearchResult** (String name, String className, Object obj, *Attributes* attrs)	
*	public		**SearchResult** (String name, String className, Object obj, *Attributes* attrs, boolean isRelative)	
	public	void	**setAttributes** (*Attributes* attrs)	
1	public	void	setClassName (String name)	
1	public	void	setName (String name)	
2	public	void	setObject (Object obj)	
1	public	void	setRelative (boolean r)	
2	public	String	**toString** ()	

SecretKey		javax.crypto

1.4	*SecretKey* ——————————— *java.security.Key*[1] (*java.io.Serializable*)	ε459,462,463,465,466	

1	public	String	getAlgorithm ()	ε464,469,203,204,205
1	public	byte[]	getEncoded ()	ε460,471,199,471
1	public	String	getFormat ()	ε199

SecretKeyFactory		javax.crypto

Object
1.4	└SecretKeyFactory

●	public final	*SecretKey*	**generateSecret** (*java.security.spec.KeySpec* keySpec) throws java.security.spec.InvalidKeySpecException	ε464
●	public final	String	**getAlgorithm** ()	
▲	public static final ....SecretKeyFactory		**getInstance** (String algorithm) throws java.security.NoSuchAlgorithmException	ε464
▲	public static final ....SecretKeyFactory		**getInstance** (String algorithm, String provider) throws java.security↵ .NoSuchAlgorithmException, java.security.NoSuchProviderException	
▲	public static final ....SecretKeyFactory		**getInstance** (String algorithm, java.security.Provider provider) throws java.security.NoSuchAlgorithmException	
●	public final . *java.security.spec.KeySpec*		**getKeySpec** (*SecretKey* key, Class keySpec) throws java.security.spec.InvalidKeySpecException	
●	public final .... java.security.Provider		**getProvider** ()	
*	protected		**SecretKeyFactory** (SecretKeyFactorySpi keyFacSpi, java.security.Provider provider, String algorithm)	

S

Classes

SecretKeyFactory

●	public final .... *SecretKey* **translateKey** (*SecretKey* key) throws java.security.InvalidKeyException	

SecretKeyFactorySpi

javax.crypto

Object
1.4 ○ └SecretKeyFactorySpi

○	protected abstract .. *SecretKey* **engineGenerateSecret** (*java.security.spec.KeySpec* keySpec)	
	throws java.security.spec.InvalidKeySpecException	
○	protected abstract .... **engineGetKeySpec** (*SecretKey* key, Class keySpec)	
	. *java.security.spec.KeySpec* throws java.security.spec.InvalidKeySpecException	
○	protected abstract .. *SecretKey* **engineTranslateKey** (*SecretKey* key) throws java.security.InvalidKeyException	
＊	public.......................... **SecretKeyFactorySpi** ()	

SecretKeySpec

javax.crypto.spec

Object[1]
1.4 └SecretKeySpec ----------------------- *java.security.spec.KeySpec*, *javax.crypto.SecretKey*
(*java.security.Key* [2] (*java.io.Serializable*))

1	public.................. **boolean equals** (Object obj)	
2	public.....................String **getAlgorithm** ()	ε203,204,205,464,469
2	public.....................byte[] **getEncoded** ()	ε199,460,471,471
2	public.....................String **getFormat** ()	ε199
1	public.................. **int hashCode** ()	
＊	public..................... **SecretKeySpec** (byte[] key, String algorithm)	ε460,465
＊	public..................... **SecretKeySpec** (byte[] key, int offset, int len, String algorithm)	

SecureClassLoader

java.security

Object
○ └ClassLoader[1]
1.2   └SecureClassLoader

	1	*28 inherited members from ClassLoader not shown*
●	protected final............ Class **defineClass** (String name, byte[] b, int off, int len, CodeSource cs)
	protected PermissionCollection **getPermissions** (CodeSource codesource)
＊	protected...................... **SecureClassLoader** ()
＊	protected...................... **SecureClassLoader** (ClassLoader parent)

SecureRandom

java.security

Object	ε195
└java.util.Random[1] ----------------------- *java.io.Serializable*	
1.1 └SecureRandom	

1.2		public....................byte[] **generateSeed** (int numBytes)	ε196
1.2	△	public static ... SecureRandom **getInstance** (String algorithm) throws NoSuchAlgorithmException	
			ε196
1.2	△	public static ... SecureRandom **getInstance** (String algorithm, String provider) throws NoSuchAlgorithmException,	
		NoSuchProviderException	
1.4	△	public static ... SecureRandom **getInstance** (String algorithm, Provider provider) throws NoSuchAlgorithmException	
1.2	●	public final .... Provider **getProvider** ()	
	△	public static ....byte[] **getSeed** (int numBytes)	
●	1	protected final.............. **int next** (int numBits)	
1.2	1	public.................... boolean nextBoolean ()	ε331
	1	public synchronized ...... **void nextBytes** (byte[] bytes)	ε196,331
	1	public....................double nextDouble ()	ε331
	1	public.....................float nextFloat ()	ε331
	1	public synchronized ....double nextGaussian ()	
	1	public.......................int nextInt ()	ε331
1.2	1	public.......................int nextInt (int n)	ε331
	1	public..................... long nextLong ()	ε331
＊		public..................... **SecureRandom** ()	ε502
＊		public..................... **SecureRandom** (byte[] seed)	
1.2	＊	protected...................... **SecureRandom** (SecureRandomSpi secureRandomSpi, Provider provider)	

Class *Interface* —extends - - -implements ○ abstract ● final △ static ▲ static final ＊ constructor x x—inherited x **x**—declared **x x**—overridden
ε*n*—examples of usage —has subclass package —see other volume

public synchronized ....void	**setSeed** (byte[] seed)	ε196
1 public..................... **void**	**setSeed** (long seed)	

SecureRandomSpi java.security

Object
1.2 ○ └SecureRandomSpi - *java.io.Serializable*

○	protected abstract ....byte[]	**engineGenerateSeed** (int numBytes)
○	protected abstract ....void	**engineNextBytes** (byte[] bytes)
○	protected abstract ....void	**engineSetSeed** (byte[] seed)
✳	public.........................	**SecureRandomSpi** ()

Security java.security

Object
1.1 ● └Security

D	△	public static ....int	**addProvider** (Provider provider)
	△	public static ....String	**getAlgorithmProperty** (String algName, String propName)
1.4	△	public static ....*java.util.Set*	**getAlgorithms** (String serviceName)
	△	public static ....String	**getProperty** (String key)
	△	public static synchronized .... Provider	**getProvider** (String name)
	△	public static synchronized .... Provider[]	**getProviders** ()
1.3	△	public static .... Provider[]	**getProviders** (String filter)
1.3	△	public static .... Provider[]	**getProviders** (*java.util.Map* filter)
	△	public static synchronized ..int	**insertProviderAt** (Provider provider, int position)
	△	public static synchronized void	**removeProvider** (String name)
	△	public static ....void	**setProperty** (String key, String datum)

ε194 (aligned with getProviders ())

SecurityException java.lang

Object
└Throwable - *java.io.Serializable*
　└Exception
　　└RuntimeException
　　　└SecurityException

ε212,213

✳	public.........................	**SecurityException** ()
✳	public.........................	**SecurityException** (String s)

SecurityManager java.lang

Object
└SecurityManager

	public.....................void	**checkAccept** (String host, int port)
	public.....................void	**checkAccess** (Thread t)
	public.....................void	**checkAccess** (ThreadGroup g)
1.1	public.....................void	**checkAwtEventQueueAccess** ()
	public.....................void	**checkConnect** (String host, int port)
	public.....................void	**checkConnect** (String host, int port, Object context)
	public.....................void	**checkCreateClassLoader** ()
	public.....................void	**checkDelete** (String file)
	public.....................void	**checkExec** (String cmd)
	public.....................void	**checkExit** (int status)
	public.....................void	**checkLink** (String lib)
	public.....................void	**checkListen** (int port)
1.1	public.....................void	**checkMemberAccess** (Class clazz, int which)
1.1	public.....................void	**checkMulticast** (java.net.InetAddress maddr)
D	public.....................void	**checkMulticast** (java.net.InetAddress maddr, byte ttl)
	public.....................void	**checkPackageAccess** (String pkg)
	public.....................void	**checkPackageDefinition** (String pkg)
1.2	public.....................void	**checkPermission** (java.security.Permission perm)
1.2	public.....................void	**checkPermission** (java.security.Permission perm, Object context)
1.1	public.....................void	**checkPrintJobAccess** ()
	public.....................void	**checkPropertiesAccess** ()
	public.....................void	**checkPropertyAccess** (String key)

S

Classes

SecurityManager

	public	void	**checkRead** (java.io.FileDescriptor fd)	
	public	void	**checkRead** (String file)	
	public	void	**checkRead** (String file, Object context)	
1.1	public	void	**checkSecurityAccess** (String target)	
	public	void	**checkSetFactory** ()	
1.1	public	void	**checkSystemClipboardAccess** ()	
	public	boolean	**checkTopLevelWindow** (Object window)	
	public	void	**checkWrite** (java.io.FileDescriptor fd)	
	public	void	**checkWrite** (String file)	
D	protected native	int	**classDepth** (String name)	
D	protected	int	**classLoaderDepth** ()	
D	protected	ClassLoader	**currentClassLoader** ()	
D	protected	Class	**currentLoadedClass** ()	
	protected native	Class[]	**getClassContext** ()	
D	public	boolean	**getInCheck** ()	
	public	Object	**getSecurityContext** ()	
1.1	public	ThreadGroup	**getThreadGroup** ()	
D	protected	boolean	**inCheck**	
D	protected	boolean	**inClass** (String name)	
D	protected	boolean	**inClassLoader** ()	
*	public		**SecurityManager** ()	ε212

SecurityPermission   java.security

	Object			ε217,218
1.2 ○	└Permission [1] ---------------------------- Guard, java.io.Serializable ⌐			
1.2 ○	└BasicPermission [2]			
1.2 ●	└SecurityPermission			

1	public	void	checkGuard (Object object) throws SecurityException	
2	public	boolean	equals (Object obj)	ε215
2	public	String	getActions ()	ε215
● 1	public final	String	getName ()	
2	public	int	hashCode ()	ε215
2	public	boolean	implies (Permission p)	ε214,215
2	public	PermissionCollection	newPermissionCollection ()	
*	public		**SecurityPermission** (String name)	
*	public		**SecurityPermission** (String name, String actions)	
1	public	String	toString ()	

SelectableChannel   java.nio.channels

	Object			ε178,183
1.4 ○	└java.nio.channels.spi↩ -------------------- Channel ⌐, InterruptibleChannel (Channel)			
	│ .AbstractInterruptibleChannel [1]			
1.4 ○	└SelectableChannel ⌐			

● 1	protected final	void	begin ()	
○	public abstract	Object	**blockingLock** ()	
● 1	public final	void	close () throws java.io.IOException	ε167,170,171,172,174
○	public abstract		**configureBlocking** (boolean block) throws java.io.IOException ε173,177,179	
		SelectableChannel		
● 1	protected final	void	end (boolean completed) throws AsynchronousCloseException	
○ 1	protected abstract	void	implCloseChannel () throws java.io.IOException	
○	public abstract	boolean	**isBlocking** ()	
● 1	public final	boolean	isOpen ()	
○	public abstract	boolean	**isRegistered** ()	
○	public abstract	SelectionKey	**keyFor** (Selector sel)	
○	public abstract		**provider** ()	
		java.nio.channels↩		
		.spi.SelectorProvider		
●	public final	SelectionKey	**register** (Selector sel, int ops) throws ClosedChannelException ε176,179	
○	public abstract	SelectionKey	**register** (Selector sel, int ops, Object att) throws ClosedChannelException	
*	protected		**SelectableChannel** ()	
○	public abstract	int	**validOps** ()	ε176

Class *Interface* —extends - - -implements ○ abstract ● final △ static ▲ static final ✳ constructor x x—inherited x **x**—declared **x x**—overridden
ε*n*—examples of usage ⌐—has subclass package—see other volume

SelectionKey — java.nio.channels

	Object	
1.4 O	└ SelectionKey␣	

●	public final .... Object	**attach** (Object ob)	
●	public final .... Object	**attachment** ()	
O	public abstract .... void	**cancel** ()	ε176
O	public abstract	**channel** ()	ε176,179
	.... SelectableChannel		
O	public abstract .... int	**interestOps** ()	
O	public abstract ... SelectionKey	**interestOps** (int ops)	
●	public final .... boolean	**isAcceptable** ()	ε179
●	public final .... boolean	**isConnectable** ()	ε176
●	public final .... boolean	**isReadable** ()	ε176
O	public abstract .... boolean	**isValid** ()	ε176
●	public final .... boolean	**isWritable** ()	ε176
▲	public static final .... int	**OP_ACCEPT** = 16	ε179
▲	public static final .... int	**OP_CONNECT** = 8	
▲	public static final .... int	**OP_READ** = 1	
▲	public static final .... int	**OP_WRITE** = 4	
O	public abstract .... int	**readyOps** ()	
✳	protected	**SelectionKey** ()	
O	public abstract .... Selector	**selector** ()	

Selector — java.nio.channels

	Object	
1.4 O	└ Selector␣	

O	public abstract .... void	**close** () throws java.io.IOException	
O	public abstract .... boolean	**isOpen** ()	
O	public abstract ..... *java.util.Set*	**keys** ()	
△	public static .... Selector	**open** () throws java.io.IOException	ε176,179
O	public abstract	**provider** ()	
	.... java.nio.channels ↩		
	.spi.SelectorProvider		
O	public abstract .... int	**select** () throws java.io.IOException	ε176,179
O	public abstract .... int	**select** (long timeout) throws java.io.IOException	
O	public abstract ..... *java.util.Set*	**selectedKeys** ()	ε176,179
O	public abstract .... int	**selectNow** () throws java.io.IOException	
✳	protected	**Selector** ()	
O	public abstract .... Selector	**wakeup** ()	

SelectorProvider — java.nio.channels.spi

	Object	
1.4 O	└ SelectorProvider	

O	public abstract ...... java.nio ↩	**openDatagramChannel** () throws java.io.IOException
	.channels.DatagramChannel	
O	public abstract	**openPipe** () throws java.io.IOException
	.... java.nio.channels.Pipe	
O	public abstract	**openSelector** () throws java.io.IOException
	.... AbstractSelector	
O	public abstract	**openServerSocketChannel** () throws java.io.IOException
	.... java.nio.channels ↩	
	.ServerSocketChannel	
O	public abstract ...... java.nio ↩	**openSocketChannel** () throws java.io.IOException
	.channels.SocketChannel	
△	public static .. SelectorProvider	**provider** ()
✳	protected	**SelectorProvider** ()

SequenceInputStream — java.io

ε252,382,418

	Object
O	└ InputStream [1]
	└ SequenceInputStream

SequenceInputStream

	1	public.......................... **int available** () throws IOException	
	1	public.......................... **void close** () throws IOException	ε14,36,45,452,455
	1	public synchronized ....void mark (int readlimit)	
	1	public.......................... boolean markSupported ()	
	1	public.......................... **int read** () throws IOException	ε90,184,256
	1	public..........................int read (byte[] b) throws IOException	ε452,455,457,170,451
	1	public.......................... **int read** (byte[] b, int off, int len) throws IOException	ε36
	1	public synchronized ....void reset () throws IOException	
*		public.......................... **SequenceInputStream** (*java.util.Enumeration* e)	
*		public.......................... **SequenceInputStream** (InputStream s1, InputStream s2)	
	1	public.................... long skip (long n) throws IOException	

Serializable   java.io

1.1	*Serializable*	ε46,1,205,215,466

SerializablePermission   java.io

	Object	ε217,218
1.2 ○	└*java.security.Permission* [1] ---------------- *java.security.Guard, Serializable*	
1.2 ○	└*java.security.BasicPermission* [2]	
1.2 ●	└SerializablePermission	

	1	public..........................void checkGuard (Object object) throws SecurityException	
	2	public.................. boolean equals (Object obj)	ε215
	2	public..........................String getActions ()	ε215
●	1	public final ....String getName ()	
	2	public..........................int hashCode ()	ε215
	2	public.................. boolean implies (*java.security.Permission* p)	ε214,215
	2	public...........*java.security*↵ newPermissionCollection () .PermissionCollection	
*		public.......................... **SerializablePermission** (String name)	
*		public.......................... **SerializablePermission** (String name, String actions)	
	1	public....................String toString ()	

Servant   org.omg.PortableServer

	Object
1.4 ○	└Servant

○	public abstract .... String[] **_all_interfaces** (*POA* poa, byte[] objectId)	
	public..................... *POA* **_default_POA** ()	
●	public final .... **_get_delegate** () ... *org.omg.PortableServer*↵ .portable.Delegate	
	public *org.omg.CORBA.Object* **_get_interface_def** ()	
	public.................. boolean **_is_a** (String repository_id)	
	public.................. boolean **_non_existent** ()	
●	public final ....byte[] **_object_id** ()	
●	public final .... **_orb** () ....org.omg.CORBA.ORB	
●	public final .... *POA* **_poa** ()	
●	public final ....void **_set_delegate** (*org.omg.PortableServer.portable.Delegate* delegate)	
●	public final .... **_this_object** () ..... *org.omg.CORBA.Object*	
●	public final .... **_this_object** (org.omg.CORBA.ORB orb) ..... *org.omg.CORBA.Object*	
*	public.......................... **Servant** ()	

SERVANT_RETENTION_POLICY_ID   org.omg.PortableServer

1.4	*SERVANT_RETENTION_POLICY_ID*	
▲	public static final.............int **value** = 21	

Class   *Interface*   —extends   - - -implements   ○ abstract   ● final   △ static   ▲ static final   ✳ constructor   x x—inherited   x **x**—declared   **x x**—overridden
ε*n*—examples of usage   —has subclass   package—see other volume

ServantActivator		org.omg.PortableServer

1.4	*ServantActivator* ————————	*ServantActivatorOperations* ₎[1] (*ServantManagerOperations*), *ServantManager* ₎ (*ServantManagerOperations*, *org.omg.CORBA.Object* [2], *org.omg.CORBA.portable.IDLEntity* (*java.io.Serializable*)), *org.omg.CORBA.portable.IDLEntity* ₎ (*java.io.Serializable*)

- [2] *13 inherited members from org.omg.CORBA.Object not shown*
- [1] *2 inherited members from ServantActivatorOperations not shown*

ServantActivatorHelper		org.omg.PortableServer

Object
  └ ServantActivatorHelper

1.4 ○		
△	public static .. *ServantActivator*	**extract** (org.omg.CORBA.Any a)
△	public static ....String	**id** ()
△	public static ....void	**insert** (org.omg.CORBA.Any a, *ServantActivator* that)
△	public static .. *ServantActivator*	**narrow** (*org.omg.CORBA.Object* obj)
△	public static .. *ServantActivator*	**read** (org.omg.CORBA.portable.InputStream istream)
✳	public..........................	**ServantActivatorHelper** ()
△	public static synchronized .... . org.omg.CORBA.TypeCode	**type** ()
△	public static ....void	**write** (org.omg.CORBA.portable.OutputStream ostream, *ServantActivator* value)

ServantActivatorOperations		org.omg.PortableServer

1.4	*ServantActivatorOperations* ₎ ————————	*ServantManagerOperations* ₎

public.......................void	**etherealize** (byte[] oid, *POA* adapter, Servant serv, boolean cleanup_in_progress, boolean remaining_activations)	
public.................... Servant	**incarnate** (byte[] oid, *POA* adapter) throws ForwardRequest	

ServantActivatorPOA		org.omg.PortableServer

Object
  └ Servant[1]
    └ ServantActivatorPOA - - - - - - - - - - - - - - - - - *ServantActivatorOperations* ₎ (*ServantManagerOperations*), *org.omg.CORBA.portable.InvokeHandler* ₎[2]

1.4 ○		
1.4 ○		
[1]	*11 inherited members from Servant not shown*	
[1]	public................. **String[]**	**_all_interfaces** (*POA* poa, byte[] objectId)
[2]	public...... org.omg.CORBA ↵ .portable.OutputStream	**_invoke** (String $method, org.omg.CORBA.portable.InputStream in, *org.omg.CORBA.portable.ResponseHandler* $rh)
	public......... *ServantActivator*	**_this** ()
	public......... *ServantActivator*	**_this** (org.omg.CORBA.ORB orb)
✳	public........................	**ServantActivatorPOA** ()

ServantAlreadyActive		org.omg.PortableServer.POAPackage

Object
  └ Throwable - *java.io.Serializable* ₎
    └ Exception
      └ org.omg.CORBA.UserException - - - - - - - *org.omg.CORBA.portable.IDLEntity* ₎ (*java.io.Serializable*)
        └ ServantAlreadyActive

1.2 ○		
1.4 ●		
✳	public..........................	**ServantAlreadyActive** ()
✳	public..........................	**ServantAlreadyActive** (String $reason)

ServantAlreadyActiveHelper		org.omg.PortableServer.POAPackage

Object
  └ ServantAlreadyActiveHelper

1.4 ○		
△	public static .... ServantAlreadyActive	**extract** (org.omg.CORBA.Any a)
△	public static ....String	**id** ()

S

Classes

ServantAlreadyActiveHelper

△	public static ....void	**insert** (org.omg.CORBA.Any a, ServantAlreadyActive that)
△	public static .... ServantAlreadyActive	**read** (org.omg.CORBA.portable.InputStream istream)
✳	public............................	**ServantAlreadyActiveHelper** ()
△	public static synchronized .... . org.omg.CORBA.TypeCode	**type** ()
△	public static ....void	**write** (org.omg.CORBA.portable.OutputStream ostream, ServantAlreadyActive value)

ServantLocator	org.omg.PortableServer

1.4 *ServantLocator*──────────────── *ServantLocatorOperations* [1] (*ServantManagerOperations*), *ServantManager* (*ServantManagerOperations*, org.omg.CORBA.Object [2], org.omg.CORBA.portable.IDLEntity (java.io.Serializable)), org.omg.CORBA.portable.IDLEntity (java.io.Serializable)

2 *13 inherited members from org.omg.CORBA.Object not shown*
1 *2 inherited members from ServantLocatorOperations not shown*

ServantLocatorHelper	org.omg.PortableServer

Object
1.4 ○ └ ServantLocatorHelper

△	public static ... *ServantLocator*	**extract** (org.omg.CORBA.Any a)
△	public static ....String	**id** ()
△	public static ....void	**insert** (org.omg.CORBA.Any a, *ServantLocator* that)
△	public static ... *ServantLocator*	**narrow** (*org.omg.CORBA.Object* obj)
△	public static ... *ServantLocator*	**read** (org.omg.CORBA.portable.InputStream istream)
✳	public...........................	**ServantLocatorHelper** ()
△	public static synchronized .... . org.omg.CORBA.TypeCode	**type** ()
△	public static ....void	**write** (org.omg.CORBA.portable.OutputStream ostream, *ServantLocator* value)

ServantLocatorOperations	org.omg.PortableServer

1.4 *ServantLocatorOperations* ───────────── *ServantManagerOperations*

	public.......................void	**postinvoke** (byte[] oid, *POA* adapter, String operation, Object the_cookie, Servant the_servant)
	public..................Servant	**preinvoke** (byte[] oid, *POA* adapter, String operation, org.omg.PortableServer↩ .ServantLocatorPackage.CookieHolder the_cookie) throws ForwardRequest

---

ServantLocatorPOA	org.omg.PortableServer

Object
1.4 ○ └ Servant [1]
1.4 ○ └ ServantLocatorPOA - - - - - - - - - - - - - - - - *ServantLocatorOperations* (*ServantManagerOperations*), org.omg.CORBA.portable.InvokeHandler [2]

1 *11 inherited members from Servant not shown*

1	public.................. **String[]**	**_all_interfaces** (*POA* poa, byte[] objectId)
2	public...... org.omg.CORBA↩ .portable.OutputStream	**_invoke** (String $method, org.omg.CORBA.portable.InputStream in, *org.omg.CORBA.portable.ResponseHandler* $rh)
	public......... *ServantLocator*	**_this** ()
	public......... *ServantLocator*	**_this** (org.omg.CORBA.ORB orb)
✳	public...........................	**ServantLocatorPOA** ()

ServantManager	org.omg.PortableServer

1.4 *ServantManager* ─────────────── *ServantManagerOperations*, org.omg.CORBA.Object [1], org.omg.CORBA.portable.IDLEntity (java.io.Serializable)

1 *13 inherited members from org.omg.CORBA.Object not shown*

Class *Interface* —extends - - -implements ○ abstract ● final △ static ▲ static final ✳ constructor x x—inherited x **x**—declared **x x**—overridden
εn—examples of usage —has subclass package—see other volume

ServantManagerOperations		org.omg.PortableServer

1.4   *ServantManagerOperations*

- -

ServantNotActive		org.omg.PortableServer.POAPackage

Object
  └ Throwable - *java.io.Serializable*
      └ Exception
1.2 ○   └ *org.omg.CORBA.UserException* - - - - - - *org.omg.CORBA.portable.IDLEntity* (*java.io.Serializable*)
1.4 ●   └ ServantNotActive

∗   public . . . . **ServantNotActive** ()
∗   public . . . . **ServantNotActive** (String $reason)

ServantNotActiveHelper		org.omg.PortableServer.POAPackage

Object
1.4 ○   └ ServantNotActiveHelper

△   public static . ServantNotActive **extract** (org.omg.CORBA.Any a)
△   public static . . . . String **id** ()
△   public static . . . . void **insert** (org.omg.CORBA.Any a, ServantNotActive that)
△   public static . ServantNotActive **read** (org.omg.CORBA.portable.InputStream istream)
∗   public . . . . **ServantNotActiveHelper** ()
△   public static synchronized . . . . **type** ()
    . org.omg.CORBA.TypeCode
△   public static . . . . void **write** (org.omg.CORBA.portable.OutputStream ostream, ServantNotActive value)

ServantObject		org.omg.CORBA.portable

Object
1.2   └ ServantObject

    public . . . . Object **servant**
∗   public . . . . **ServantObject** ()

ServantRetentionPolicy		org.omg.PortableServer

1.4   *ServantRetentionPolicy* —————————— *ServantRetentionPolicyOperations* [1]
                                       (*org.omg.CORBA.PolicyOperations* [2]), *org.omg.CORBA.Policy*
                                       (*org.omg.CORBA.PolicyOperations* [2], *org.omg.CORBA.Object* [3],
                                       org.omg.CORBA.portable.IDLEntity (*java.io.Serializable*)),
                                         org.omg.CORBA.portable.IDLEntity (*java.io.Serializable*)

- -
   3 *13 inherited members from org.omg.CORBA.Object not shown*
   2 *3 inherited members from org.omg.CORBA.PolicyOperations not shown*
   1 public . . . . value ()
      .ServantRetentionPolicyValue
- -

ServantRetentionPolicyOperations		org.omg.PortableServer

1.4   *ServantRetentionPolicyOperations* ————————— *org.omg.CORBA.PolicyOperations* [1]

- -
   1 *3 inherited members from org.omg.CORBA.PolicyOperations not shown*
     public . . . . **value** ()
      .ServantRetentionPolicyValue
- -

ServantRetentionPolicyValue		org.omg.PortableServer

Object
1.4   └ ServantRetentionPolicyValue - - - - - - - - - - - - - *org.omg.CORBA.portable.IDLEntity* (*java.io.Serializable*)

▲   public static final . . . . int **_NON_RETAIN** = 1
▲   public static final . . . . int **_RETAIN** = 0
△   public static . . . . **from_int** (int value)
    .ServantRetentionPolicyValue

S

Classes

ServantRetentionPolicyValue

▲	public static final .... .ServantRetentionPolicyValue	**NON_RETAIN**
▲	public static final .... .ServantRetentionPolicyValue	**RETAIN**
✳	protected	**ServantRetentionPolicyValue** (int value)
	public ....int	**value** ()

ServerCloneException
java.rmi.server

```
Object
└Throwable 1 - - - - - - - - - - - - - - - - - - - - - java.io.Serializable
    └Exception
        └CloneNotSupportedException
1.1          └ServerCloneException
```

	public .... Exception	**detail**	
1.4	1	public .... **Throwable**	**getCause** ()
	1	public .... **String**	**getMessage** ()
✳		public	**ServerCloneException** (String s)
✳		public	**ServerCloneException** (String s, Exception ex)

ServerError
java.rmi

```
Object
└Throwable - - - - - - - - - - - - - - - - - - - - - - - - - java.io.Serializable
    └Exception
        └java.io.IOException
1.1          └RemoteException 1
1.1              └ServerError
```

	1	public .... Throwable	detail
1.4	1	public .... Throwable	getCause ()
	1	public .... String	getMessage ()
✳		public	**ServerError** (String s, Error err)

ServerException
java.rmi

```
Object
└Throwable - - - - - - - - - - - - - - - - - - - - - - - - - java.io.Serializable
    └Exception
        └java.io.IOException
1.1          └RemoteException 1
1.1          └ServerException
```

	1	public .... Throwable	detail
1.4	1	public .... Throwable	getCause ()
	1	public .... String	getMessage ()
✳		public	**ServerException** (String s)
✳		public	**ServerException** (String s, Exception ex)

ServerNotActiveException
java.rmi.server

```
Object
└Throwable - - - - - - - - - - - - - - - - - - - - - - - - - java.io.Serializable
    └Exception
1.1      └ServerNotActiveException
```

✳	public	**ServerNotActiveException** ()
✳	public	**ServerNotActiveException** (String s)

ServerRef	java.rmi.server

1.1		*ServerRef*————————————— *RemoteRef* ⌄ [1] (*java.io.Externalizable* [2] (*java.io.Serializable*))

		public..............RemoteStub **exportObject** (*java.rmi.Remote* obj, Object data) throws java.rmi.RemoteException
		public....................String **getClientHost** () throws ServerNotActiveException
	1	public....................String getRefClass (*java.io.ObjectOutput* out)
1.2	1	public..................Object **invoke** (*java.rmi.Remote* obj, java.lang.reflect.Method method, Object[] params, long opnum) throws Exception
	2	public.....................void **readExternal** (*java.io.ObjectInput* in) throws java.io.IOException, ClassNotFoundException
	1	public.................boolean **remoteEquals** (*RemoteRef* obj)
	1	public..........................int **remoteHashCode** ()
	1	public....................String **remoteToString** ()
1.2 ▲	1	public static final..........**long** **serialVersionUID** = -4557750989390278438
	2	public.....................void **writeExternal** (*java.io.ObjectOutput* out) throws java.io.IOException

ServerRequest	org.omg.CORBA

1.2 ○	Object └ServerRequest

		public.....................void **arguments** (NVList args)
	○	public abstract ....Context **ctx** ()
D		public.....................void **except** (Any any)
D		public....................String **op_name** ()
		public....................String **operation** ()
D		public.....................void **params** (NVList params)
D		public.....................void **result** (Any any)
	✳	public.......................... **ServerRequest** ()
		public.....................void **set_exception** (Any any)
		public.....................void **set_result** (Any any)

ServerRequestInfo	org.omg.PortableInterceptor

1.4	*ServerRequestInfo*————————————— *ServerRequestInfoOperations* ⌄ [1] (*RequestInfoOperations* [2]), *RequestInfo* ⌄ (*RequestInfoOperations* [2], *org.omg.CORBA.Object* [3], *org.omg.CORBA.portable.IDLEntity* (*java.io.Serializable*)), *org.omg.CORBA.portable.IDLEntity* ⌄ (*java.io.Serializable*)

	3	*13 inherited members from org.omg.CORBA.Object not shown*
	2	*14 inherited members from RequestInfoOperations not shown*
	1	*8 inherited members from ServerRequestInfoOperations not shown*

ServerRequestInfoOperations	org.omg.PortableInterceptor

1.4	*ServerRequestInfoOperations* ⌄ ————————— *RequestInfoOperations* ⌄ [1]

	1	*14 inherited members from RequestInfoOperations not shown*
		public.....................byte[] **adapter_id** ()
		public.....................void **add_reply_service_context** (org.omg.IOP.ServiceContext service_context, boolean replace)
		public. *org.omg.CORBA.Policy* **get_server_policy** (int type)
		public.....................byte[] **object_id** ()
		public....org.omg.CORBA.Any **sending_exception** ()
		public.....................void **set_slot** (int id, org.omg.CORBA.Any data) throws InvalidSlot
		public.................boolean **target_is_a** (String id)
		public....................String **target_most_derived_interface** ()

ServerRequestInterceptor	org.omg.PortableInterceptor

1.4	*ServerRequestInterceptor*————————————— *ServerRequestInterceptorOperations* ⌄ [1] (*InterceptorOperations* [2]), *Interceptor* ⌄ (*InterceptorOperations* [2], *org.omg.CORBA.Object* [3], *org.omg.CORBA.portable.IDLEntity* (*java.io.Serializable*)), *org.omg.CORBA.portable.IDLEntity* ⌄ (*java.io.Serializable*)

	2	*2 inherited members from InterceptorOperations not shown*
	1	*5 inherited members from ServerRequestInterceptorOperations not shown*
	3	*13 inherited members from org.omg.CORBA.Object not shown*

S

Classes

ServerRequestInterceptorOperations

			org.omg.PortableInterceptor
	ServerRequestInterceptorOperations		

1.4   *ServerRequestInterceptorOperations* ────── *InterceptorOperations* [1]

1 2 inherited members from InterceptorOperations not shown

public	.... void	**receive_request** (*ServerRequestInfo* ri) throws ForwardRequest
public	.... void	**receive_request_service_contexts** (*ServerRequestInfo* ri) throws ForwardRequest
public	.... void	**send_exception** (*ServerRequestInfo* ri) throws ForwardRequest
public	.... void	**send_other** (*ServerRequestInfo* ri) throws ForwardRequest
public	.... void	**send_reply** (*ServerRequestInfo* ri)

ServerRuntimeException	java.rmi

```
Object
 └ Throwable ------------------------- java.io.Serializable
     └ Exception
         └ java.io.IOException
1.1          └ RemoteException [1]
D                └ ServerRuntimeException
```

D	1	public	.... Throwable	detail
D	1	public	.... Throwable	getCause ()
D	1	public	.... String	getMessage ()
D	*	public	....	**ServerRuntimeException** (String s, Exception ex)

ServerSocket	java.net

```
Object [1]
 └ ServerSocket
```

	public	.... Socket	**accept** () throws java.io.IOException	ε148,500
1.4	public	.... void	**bind** (SocketAddress endpoint) throws java.io.IOException	ε177,179
1.4	public	.... void	**bind** (SocketAddress endpoint, int backlog) throws java.io.IOException	
	public	.... void	**close** () throws java.io.IOException	
1.4	public	..... java.nio.channels ↵ .ServerSocketChannel	**getChannel** ()	
	public	.... InetAddress	**getInetAddress** ()	
	public	.... int	**getLocalPort** ()	ε178
1.4	public	.... SocketAddress	**getLocalSocketAddress** ()	
1.4	public synchronized	.... int	**getReceiveBufferSize** () throws SocketException	
1.4	public	.... synchronized boolean	**getReuseAddress** () throws SocketException	
1.1	public synchronized	.... int	**getSoTimeout** () throws java.io.IOException	
1.1 ●	protected final	.... void	**implAccept** (Socket s) throws java.io.IOException	
1.4	public	.... boolean	**isBound** ()	
1.4	public	.... boolean	**isClosed** ()	
1.4 *	public	....	**ServerSocket** () throws java.io.IOException	
*	public	....	**ServerSocket** (int port) throws java.io.IOException	ε148
*	public	....	**ServerSocket** (int port, int backlog) throws java.io.IOException	
1.1 *	public	....	**ServerSocket** (int port, int backlog, InetAddress bindAddr) throws java.io.IOException	
1.4	public synchronized	.... void	**setReceiveBufferSize** (int size) throws SocketException	
1.4	public	.... void	**setReuseAddress** (boolean on) throws SocketException	
△	public static synchronized void		**setSocketFactory** (*SocketImplFactory* fac) throws java.io.IOException	
1.1	public synchronized	.... void	**setSoTimeout** (int timeout) throws SocketException	
	1 public	.... String	**toString** ()	

ServerSocketChannel	java.nio.channels

ε178,183

```
     Object
1.4 ○ └ java.nio.channels.spi ↵ --------------- Channel, InterruptibleChannel (Channel)
             .AbstractInterruptibleChannel [1]
1.4 ○   └ SelectableChannel [2]
1.4 ○      └ java.nio.channels.spi ↵
                .AbstractSelectableChannel [3]
1.4 ○         └ ServerSocketChannel
```

○		public abstract SocketChannel	**accept** () throws java.io.IOException	ε178
●	1	protected final	.... void	begin ()

Class   *Interface*   —extends   - - -implements   ○ abstract   ● final   △ static   ▲ static final   ✽ constructor   x x—inherited   x **x**—declared   **x x**—overridden
ε*n*—examples of usage   ‿—has subclass   package—see other volume

●	3	public final	Object	blockingLock ()	
●	1	public final	void	close () throws java.io.IOException	ε167,170,171,172,174
●	3	public final SelectableChannel		configureBlocking (boolean block) throws java.io.IOException	ε177,179,173
●	1	protected final	void	end (boolean completed) throws AsynchronousCloseException	
●	3	protected final	void	implCloseChannel () throws java.io.IOException	
○	3	protected abstract	void	implCloseSelectableChannel () throws java.io.IOException	
○	3	protected abstract	void	implConfigureBlocking (boolean block) throws java.io.IOException	
●	3	public final	boolean	isBlocking ()	
●	1	public final	boolean	isOpen ()	
●	3	public final	boolean	isRegistered ()	
●	3	public final	SelectionKey	keyFor (Selector sel)	
△		public static		**open** () throws java.io.IOException	ε177,179
		ServerSocketChannel			
●	3	public final java.nio.channels ↵		provider ()	
		.spi.SelectorProvider			
●	2	public final	SelectionKey	register (Selector sel, int ops) throws ClosedChannelException	ε179,176
●	3	public final	SelectionKey	register (Selector sel, int ops, Object att) throws ClosedChannelException	
✳		protected		**ServerSocketChannel** (java.nio.channels.spi.SelectorProvider provider)	
○		public abstract		**socket** ()	ε177,178,179
		java.net.ServerSocket			
●	2	public final	**int**	**validOps** ()	ε176

ServerSocketFactory — javax.net

Object
1.4 ○ └ServerSocketFactory

	public... java.net.ServerSocket	**createServerSocket** () throws java.io.IOException	
○	public abstract	**createServerSocket** (int port) throws java.io.IOException	ε500
	java.net.ServerSocket		
○	public abstract	**createServerSocket** (int port, int backlog) throws java.io.IOException	
	java.net.ServerSocket		
○	public abstract	**createServerSocket** (int port, int backlog, java.net.InetAddress ifAddress)	
	java.net.ServerSocket	throws java.io.IOException	
△	public static	**getDefault** ()	ε500
	ServerSocketFactory		
✳	protected	**ServerSocketFactory** ()	

ServiceContext — org.omg.IOP

Object
1.4 ● └ServiceContext ----------------------- *org.omg.CORBA.portable.IDLEntity* (*java.io.Serializable*)

	public	byte[]	**context_data**
	public	int	**context_id**
✳	public	**ServiceContext** ()
✳	public	**ServiceContext** (int _context_id, byte[] _context_data)

ServiceContextHelper — org.omg.IOP

Object
1.4 ○ └ServiceContextHelper

△	public static ... ServiceContext	**extract** (org.omg.CORBA.Any a)
△	public static String	**id** ()
△	public static void	**insert** (org.omg.CORBA.Any a, ServiceContext that)
△	public static ... ServiceContext	**read** (org.omg.CORBA.portable.InputStream istream)
✳	public	**ServiceContextHelper** ()
△	public static synchronized	**type** ()
	. org.omg.CORBA.TypeCode	
△	public static void	**write** (org.omg.CORBA.portable.OutputStream ostream, ServiceContext value)

ServiceContextHolder — org.omg.IOP

Object
1.4 ● └ServiceContextHolder ------------------- *org.omg.CORBA.portable.Streamable* [1]

ServiceContextHolder

1	public	void	**_read** (org.omg.CORBA.portable.InputStream i)
1	public		**_type** ()
	. org.omg.CORBA.TypeCode		
1	public	void	**_write** (org.omg.CORBA.portable.OutputStream o)
*	public		**ServiceContextHolder** ()
*	public		**ServiceContextHolder** (ServiceContext initialValue)
	public	ServiceContext	**value**

ServiceContextListHelper org.omg.IOP

Object
└ ServiceContextListHelper 1.4 ○

△	public static	ServiceContext[]	**extract** (org.omg.CORBA.Any a)
△	public static	String	**id** ()
△	public static	void	**insert** (org.omg.CORBA.Any a, ServiceContext[] that)
△	public static	ServiceContext[]	**read** (org.omg.CORBA.portable.InputStream istream)
*	public		**ServiceContextListHelper** ()
△	public static synchronized		**type** ()
	. org.omg.CORBA.TypeCode		
△	public static	void	**write** (org.omg.CORBA.portable.OutputStream ostream, ServiceContext[] value)

ServiceContextListHolder org.omg.IOP

Object
└ ServiceContextListHolder - - - - - - - - - - - - - - - - - *org.omg.CORBA.portable.Streamable* ⌄ [1] 1.4 ●

1	public	void	**_read** (org.omg.CORBA.portable.InputStream i)
1	public		**_type** ()
	. org.omg.CORBA.TypeCode		
1	public	void	**_write** (org.omg.CORBA.portable.OutputStream o)
*	public		**ServiceContextListHolder** ()
*	public		**ServiceContextListHolder** (ServiceContext[] initialValue)
	public	ServiceContext[]	**value**

ServiceDetail org.omg.CORBA

Object
└ ServiceDetail - *org.omg.CORBA.portable.IDLEntity* ⌄ (*java.io.Serializable*) 1.2 ●

	public	byte[]	**service_detail**
	public	int	**service_detail_type**
*	public		**ServiceDetail** ()
*	public		**ServiceDetail** (int service_detail_type, byte[] service_detail)

ServiceDetailHelper org.omg.CORBA

Object
└ ServiceDetailHelper 1.2 ○

△	public static	ServiceDetail	**extract** (Any a)
△	public static	String	**id** ()
△	public static	void	**insert** (Any a, ServiceDetail that)
△	public static	ServiceDetail	**read** (org.omg.CORBA.portable.InputStream in)
1.4 *	public		**ServiceDetailHelper** ()
△	public static synchronized		**type** ()
		TypeCode	
△	public static	void	**write** (org.omg.CORBA.portable.OutputStream out, ServiceDetail that)

ServiceIdHelper org.omg.IOP

Object
└ ServiceIdHelper 1.4 ○

Class *Interface* —extends - - -implements ○ abstract ● final △ static ▲ static final ✽ constructor x x—inherited x **x**—declared **x x**—overridden
ε*n*—examples of usage ⌄—has subclass package—see other volume

△	public static ....int	**extract** (org.omg.CORBA.Any a)
△	public static ....String	**id** ()
△	public static ....void	**insert** (org.omg.CORBA.Any a, int that)
△	public static ....int	**read** (org.omg.CORBA.portable.InputStream istream)
∗	public...........................	**ServiceIdHelper** ()
△	public static synchronized .... . org.omg.CORBA.TypeCode	**type** ()
△	public static ....void	**write** (org.omg.CORBA.portable.OutputStream ostream, int value)

ServiceInformation org.omg.CORBA

Object
1.2 ● └ServiceInformation - *org.omg.CORBA.portable.IDLEntity﹍ (java.io.Serializable)*

	public........... ServiceDetail[]	**service_details**
	public.....................int[]	**service_options**
∗	public........................	**ServiceInformation** ()
∗	public........................	**ServiceInformation** (int[] __service_options, ServiceDetail[] __service_details)

ServiceInformationHelper org.omg.CORBA

Object
1.2 ○ └ServiceInformationHelper [1]

△	public static ....ServiceInformation	**extract** (Any a)
△	public static ....String	**id** ()
△	public static ....void	**insert** (Any a, ServiceInformation that)
△	public static ....ServiceInformation	**read** (org.omg.CORBA.portable.InputStream in)
1.4 ∗	public........................	**ServiceInformationHelper** ()
△	public static synchronized ....TypeCode	**type** ()
△	public static ....void	**write** (org.omg.CORBA.portable.OutputStream out, ServiceInformation that)

ServiceInformationHolder org.omg.CORBA

Object
1.2 ● └ServiceInformationHolder - - - - - - - - - - - - - - - - *org.omg.CORBA.portable.Streamable﹍ [1]*

1	public.......................void	**_read** (org.omg.CORBA.portable.InputStream in)
1	public................TypeCode	**_type** ()
1	public.......................void	**_write** (org.omg.CORBA.portable.OutputStream out)
∗	public........................	**ServiceInformationHolder** ()
∗	public........................	**ServiceInformationHolder** (ServiceInformation arg)
	public.......ServiceInformation	**value**

ServicePermission javax.security.auth.kerberos

ε217,218
Object
1.2 ○ └java.security.Permission [1] - - - - - - - - - - - - - - - - *java.security.Guard, java.io.Serializable﹍*
1.4 ● └ServicePermission

1	public.......................void	checkGuard (Object object) throws SecurityException	
1	public.................**boolean**	**equals** (Object obj)	ε215
1	public................. **String**	**getActions** ()	ε215
● 1	public final ....String	getName ()	
1	public...................... **int**	**hashCode** ()	ε215
1	public.................**boolean**	**implies** (java.security.Permission p)	ε214,215
1	public..........**java.security** ↩ .**PermissionCollection**	**newPermissionCollection** ()	
∗	public........................	**ServicePermission** (String servicePrinicipal, String action)	
1	public....................String	**toString** ()	

ServiceUnavailableException	javax.naming

Object
└Throwable ---------------------------- *java.io.Serializable*
 └Exception
1.3 └NamingException[1]
1.3 └ServiceUnavailableException

1	*20 inherited members from NamingException not shown*		
✳	public.........................	**ServiceUnavailableException** ()	
✳	public.........................	**ServiceUnavailableException** (String explanation)	

Set	java.util

1.2	*Set*————————————————*Collection*[1]	ε341,347,348,339,350

1	public.................	**boolean**	**add** (Object o)	ε352,354,194,342,349
1	public.................	**boolean**	**addAll** (*Collection* c)	ε353,351
1	public.................	**void**	**clear** ()	ε353,351
1	public.................	**boolean**	**contains** (Object o)	ε352
1	public.................	**boolean**	**containsAll** (*Collection* c)	
1	public.................	**boolean**	**equals** (Object o)	
1	public.................	**int**	**hashCode** ()	
1	public.................	**boolean**	**isEmpty** ()	ε102
1	public.................	*Iterator*	**iterator** ()	ε345,352,354,355,356
1	public.................	**boolean**	**remove** (Object o)	ε352,349
1	public.................	**boolean**	**removeAll** (*Collection* c)	ε353,351
1	public.................	**boolean**	**retainAll** (*Collection* c)	ε353,351
1	public.................	**int**	**size** ()	ε340,352,194,349,351
1	public.................	**Object[]**	**toArray** ()	ε340
1	public.................	**Object[]**	**toArray** (Object[] a)	ε340,352,194,508,358

SetOverrideType	org.omg.CORBA

Object
1.2 └SetOverrideType ---------------------- *org.omg.CORBA.portable.IDLEntity* (*java.io.Serializable*)

▲	public static final.............int	**_ADD_OVERRIDE** = 1	
▲	public static final.............int	**_SET_OVERRIDE** = 0	
▲	public static final..............	**ADD_OVERRIDE**	
	..............SetOverrideType		
△	public static ..SetOverrideType	**from_int** (int i)	
▲	public static final..............	**SET_OVERRIDE**	
	..............SetOverrideType		
✳	protected......................	**SetOverrideType** (int _value)	
	public........................int	**value** ()	

SetOverrideTypeHelper	org.omg.CORBA

Object
1.3 ○ └SetOverrideTypeHelper

△	public static ..SetOverrideType	**extract** (Any a)	
△	public static ....String	**id** ()	
△	public static ....void	**insert** (Any a, SetOverrideType that)	
△	public static ..SetOverrideType	**read** (org.omg.CORBA.portable.InputStream istream)	
✳	public.........................	**SetOverrideTypeHelper** ()	
△	public static synchronized	**type** ()	
	....................TypeCode		
△	public static ....void	**write** (org.omg.CORBA.portable.OutputStream ostream, SetOverrideType value)	

Short	java.lang
	ε200,201,252,299,304

Object[1]
○ └Number[2] ---------------------------- *java.io.Serializable*
1.1 ● └Short ------------------------------- *Comparable*[3]

Class *Interface* —extends - - -implements ○ abstract ● final △ static ▲ static final ✳ constructor x x—inherited x **x**—declared **x x**—overridden
ε*n*—examples of usage ˴—has subclass package—see other volume

	2	public	byte	**byteValue** ()	ε58
1.2	3	public	int	**compareTo** (Object o)	ε53
1.2		public	int	**compareTo** (Short anotherShort)	
△		public static	Short	**decode** (String nm) throws NumberFormatException	
	2	public	double	**doubleValue** ()	ε58
	1	public	boolean	**equals** (Object obj)	
	2	public	float	**floatValue** ()	ε58
	1	public	int	**hashCode** ()	
	2	public	int	**intValue** ()	ε58,6,346
	2	public	long	**longValue** ()	ε58
▲		public static final	short	**MAX_VALUE** = 32767	
▲		public static final	short	**MIN_VALUE** = -32768	
△		public static	short	**parseShort** (String s) throws NumberFormatException	ε82
△		public static	short	**parseShort** (String s, int radix) throws NumberFormatException	
*		public		**Short** (String s) throws NumberFormatException	
*		public		**Short** (short value)	ε58
	2	public	short	**shortValue** ()	ε58
	1	public	String	**toString** ()	
△		public static	String	**toString** (short s)	
▲		public static final	Class	**TYPE**	
△		public static	Short	**valueOf** (String s) throws NumberFormatException	
△		public static	Short	**valueOf** (String s, int radix) throws NumberFormatException	

ShortBuffer — java.nio

		Object[1]		ε163,166,171,425
1.4	○	└Buffer[2]		
1.4	○	└ShortBuffer - - - - Comparable[3]		
△		public static	ShortBuffer	**allocate** (int capacity)
●		public final	short[]	**array** ()
●		public final	int	**arrayOffset** ()
○		public abstract	ShortBuffer	**asReadOnlyBuffer** ()
● 2		public	int	**capacity** () — ε159,160,161
● 2		public final	Buffer	clear () — ε161,170,174
○		public abstract	ShortBuffer	**compact** ()
3		public	int	**compareTo** (Object ob) — ε53
○		public abstract	ShortBuffer	**duplicate** ()
1		public	boolean	**equals** (Object ob)
● 2		public final	Buffer	flip () — ε162,164,170,174,175
○		public abstract	short	**get** ()
○		public abstract	short	**get** (int index)
		public	ShortBuffer	**get** (short[] dst)
		public	ShortBuffer	**get** (short[] dst, int offset, int length)
●		public final	boolean	**hasArray** ()
1		public	int	**hashCode** ()
● 2		public final	boolean	hasRemaining () — ε170,184
○		public abstract	boolean	**isDirect** ()
○ 2		public abstract	boolean	isReadOnly ()
● 2		public final	int	limit ()
● 2		public final	Buffer	limit (int newLimit) — ε159,160
● 2		public final	Buffer	mark ()
○		public abstract	ByteOrder	**order** ()
● 2		public final	int	position () — ε159,160
● 2		public final	Buffer	position (int newPosition) — ε159,160
		public	ShortBuffer	**put** (ShortBuffer src)
○		public abstract	ShortBuffer	**put** (short s)
●		public final	ShortBuffer	**put** (short[] src)
○		public abstract	ShortBuffer	**put** (int index, short s)
		public	ShortBuffer	**put** (short[] src, int offset, int length)
● 2		public final	int	remaining () — ε159,160,161,184
● 2		public final	Buffer	reset ()
● 2		public final	Buffer	rewind () — ε159,160,169
○		public abstract	ShortBuffer	**slice** ()
1		public	String	**toString** ()
△		public static	ShortBuffer	**wrap** (short[] array)
△		public static	ShortBuffer	**wrap** (short[] array, int offset, int length)

ShortBufferException

ShortBufferException			javax.crypto

```
Object
 └─Throwable ----------------------------- java.io.Serializable
    └─Exception
       └─java.security.GeneralSecurityException
          └─ShortBufferException
```
1.2
1.4

✳	public..........................	**ShortBufferException** ()
✳	public..........................	**ShortBufferException** (String msg)

ShortHolder			org.omg.CORBA

```
Object
 └─ShortHolder -------------------------- org.omg.CORBA.portable.Streamable [1]
```
1.2 ●

1	public.......................void	**_read** (org.omg.CORBA.portable.InputStream input)
1	public................TypeCode	**_type** ()
1	public.......................void	**_write** (org.omg.CORBA.portable.OutputStream output)
✳	public..........................	**ShortHolder** ()
✳	public..........................	**ShortHolder** (short initial)
	public.......................short	**value**

ShortSeqHelper			org.omg.CORBA

```
Object
 └─ShortSeqHelper
```
1.3 ○

△	public static .... short[]	**extract** (Any a)
△	public static .... String	**id** ()
△	public static ....void	**insert** (Any a, short[] that)
△	public static .... short[]	**read** (org.omg.CORBA.portable.InputStream istream)
✳	public..........................	**ShortSeqHelper** ()
△	public static synchronized .... TypeCode	**type** ()
△	public static ....void	**write** (org.omg.CORBA.portable.OutputStream ostream, short[] value)

ShortSeqHolder			org.omg.CORBA

```
Object
 └─ShortSeqHolder ----------------------- org.omg.CORBA.portable.Streamable [1]
```
1.3 ●

1	public.....................void	**_read** (org.omg.CORBA.portable.InputStream i)
1	public................TypeCode	**_type** ()
1	public.....................void	**_write** (org.omg.CORBA.portable.OutputStream o)
✳	public..........................	**ShortSeqHolder** ()
✳	public..........................	**ShortSeqHolder** (short[] initialValue)
	public.......................short[]	**value**

Signature			java.security

```
Object [1]                                                    ε202
 └─SignatureSpi [2]
    └─Signature
```
1.2 ○
1.1 ○

1.2	2	protected ...... SecureRandom	appRandom
	2	public.................... **Object**	**clone** () throws CloneNotSupportedException
1.4	2	protected AlgorithmParameters	engineGetParameters ()
1.2 ○	2	protected abstract ....void	engineInitSign (*PrivateKey* privateKey) throws InvalidKeyException
1.2	2	protected ....void	engineInitSign (*PrivateKey* privateKey, SecureRandom random) throws InvalidKeyException
1.2 ○	2	protected abstract ....void	engineInitVerify (*PublicKey* publicKey) throws InvalidKeyException
1.2	2	protected ....void	engineSetParameter (*java.security.spec.AlgorithmParameterSpec* params) throws InvalidAlgorithmParameterException
1.2 ○	2	protected abstract ....byte[]	engineSign () throws SignatureException
1.2	2	protected ....int	engineSign (byte[] outbuf, int offset, int len) throws SignatureException

Class *Interface* —extends - - -implements ○ abstract ● final △ static ▲ static final ✳ constructor x x—inherited x **x**—declared **x x**—overridden
ε*n*—examples of usage —has subclass package—see other volume

S

1.2	○	2	protected abstract	.... void	**engineUpdate** (byte b) throws SignatureException
1.2	○	2	protected abstract	.... void	**engineUpdate** (byte[] b, int off, int len) throws SignatureException
1.2	○	2	protected abstract	.... boolean	**engineVerify** (byte[] sigBytes) throws SignatureException
1.4		2	protected	.... boolean	**engineVerify** (byte[] sigBytes, int offset, int length) throws SignatureException
	●		public final	.... String	**getAlgorithm** ()
	△		public static	.... Signature	**getInstance** (String algorithm) throws NoSuchAlgorithmException
					*ε*203,204,205
	△		public static	.... Signature	**getInstance** (String algorithm, String provider) throws NoSuchAlgorithmException,
					NoSuchProviderException
1.4	△		public static	.... Signature	**getInstance** (String algorithm, Provider provider) throws NoSuchAlgorithmException
D	●		public final	.... Object	**getParameter** (String param) throws InvalidParameterException
1.4	●		public final	....	**getParameters** ()
			.... AlgorithmParameters		
1.2	●		public final	.... Provider	**getProvider** ()
	●		public final	.... void	**initSign** (*PrivateKey* privateKey) throws InvalidKeyException *ε*203
1.2	●		public final	.... void	**initSign** (*PrivateKey* privateKey, SecureRandom random)
					throws InvalidKeyException
1.3	●		public final	.... void	**initVerify** (java.security.cert.Certificate certificate) throws InvalidKeyException
	●		public final	.... void	**initVerify** (*PublicKey* publicKey) throws InvalidKeyException *ε*204
1.2	●		public final	.... void	**setParameter** (*java.security.spec.AlgorithmParameterSpec* params)
					throws InvalidAlgorithmParameterException
D	●		public final	.... void	**setParameter** (String param, Object value) throws InvalidParameterException
	▲		protected static final	.... int	**SIGN**
	●		public final	.... byte[]	**sign** () throws SignatureException *ε*203
1.2	●		public final	.... int	**sign** (byte[] outbuf, int offset, int len) throws SignatureException
	✳		protected	....	**Signature** (String algorithm)
			protected	.... int	**state**
	1		public	.... **String**	**toString** ()
	▲		protected static final	.... int	**UNINITIALIZED**
	●		public final	.... void	**update** (byte b) throws SignatureException
	●		public final	.... void	**update** (byte[] data) throws SignatureException
	●		public final	.... void	**update** (byte[] data, int off, int len) throws SignatureException *ε*203,204
	▲		protected static final	.... int	**VERIFY**
	●		public final	.... boolean	**verify** (byte[] signature) throws SignatureException *ε*204
1.4	●		public final	.... boolean	**verify** (byte[] signature, int offset, int length) throws SignatureException

S

SignatureException java.security

Object
  └─Throwable -------------------------------- *java.io.Serializable*   *ε*203,204,205
  └─Exception
1.2   └─GeneralSecurityException
1.1   └─SignatureException

✳	public	....	**SignatureException** ()
✳	public	....	**SignatureException** (String msg)

SignatureSpi java.security

Object [1]   *ε*202
1.2 ○ └─SignatureSpi

		protected	...... SecureRandom	**appRandom**
	1	public	.... **Object**	**clone** () throws CloneNotSupportedException
D	○	protected abstract	...... Object	**engineGetParameter** (String param) throws InvalidParameterException
1.4		protected AlgorithmParameters		**engineGetParameters** ()
	○	protected abstract	.... void	**engineInitSign** (*PrivateKey* privateKey) throws InvalidKeyException
		protected	.... void	**engineInitSign** (*PrivateKey* privateKey, SecureRandom random)
				throws InvalidKeyException
	○	protected abstract	.... void	**engineInitVerify** (*PublicKey* publicKey) throws InvalidKeyException
		protected	.... void	**engineSetParameter** (*java.security.spec.AlgorithmParameterSpec* params)
				throws InvalidAlgorithmParameterException
D	○	protected abstract	.... void	**engineSetParameter** (String param, Object value)
				throws InvalidParameterException
	○	protected abstract	.... byte[]	**engineSign** () throws SignatureException
		protected	.... int	**engineSign** (byte[] outbuf, int offset, int len) throws SignatureException
	○	protected abstract	.... void	**engineUpdate** (byte b) throws SignatureException
	○	protected abstract	.... void	**engineUpdate** (byte[] b, int off, int len) throws SignatureException
	○	protected abstract	.... boolean	**engineVerify** (byte[] sigBytes) throws SignatureException
1.4		protected	.... boolean	**engineVerify** (byte[] sigBytes, int offset, int length) throws SignatureException
	✳	public	....	**SignatureSpi** ()

			java.security
	SignedObject		

Object
1.2 ● └─SignedObject - *java.io.Serializable*

	public	String	**getAlgorithm** ()
	public	Object	**getObject** () throws java.io.IOException, ClassNotFoundException
			ε205
	public	byte[]	**getSignature** ()
✳	public		**SignedObject** (*java.io.Serializable* object, *PrivateKey* signingKey, Signature signingEngine) throws java.io.IOException, InvalidKeyException, SignatureException *ε205*
	public	boolean	**verify** (*PublicKey* verificationKey, Signature verificationEngine) throws InvalidKeyException, SignatureException *ε205*

			java.security
	Signer		

Object
D ○ └─Identity[1] - *Principal*, java.io.Serializable
D ○   └─Signer

D		1	public	void	addCertificate (*Certificate* certificate) throws KeyManagementException
D		1	public	*Certificate[]*	certificates ()
D	●	1	public final	boolean	equals (Object identity)
D		1	public	String	getInfo ()
D	●	1	public final	String	getName () *ε227,508*
D			public	*PrivateKey*	**getPrivateKey** ()
D		1	public	*PublicKey*	getPublicKey ()
D	●	1	public final	IdentityScope	getScope ()
D		1	public	int	hashCode ()
D		1	protected	boolean	identityEquals (Identity identity)
D		1	public	void	removeCertificate (*Certificate* certificate) throws KeyManagementException
D		1	public	void	setInfo (String info)
D	●		public final	void	**setKeyPair** (KeyPair pair) throws InvalidParameterException, KeyException
D		1	public	void	setPublicKey (*PublicKey* key) throws KeyManagementException
D	✳		protected		**Signer** ()
D	✳		public		**Signer** (String name)
D	✳		public		**Signer** (String name, IdentityScope scope) throws KeyManagementException
D		1	public	String	**toString** ()
D		1	public	String	toString (boolean detailed)

			java.beans
	SimpleBeanInfo		

Object
1.1 └─SimpleBeanInfo - *BeanInfo*[1]

	1	public	*BeanInfo[]*	**getAdditionalBeanInfo** ()
	1	public	BeanDescriptor	**getBeanDescriptor** ()
	1	public	int	**getDefaultEventIndex** ()
	1	public	int	**getDefaultPropertyIndex** ()
	1	public	EventSetDescriptor[]	**getEventSetDescriptors** ()
	1	public	java.awt.Image	**getIcon** (int iconKind)
	1	public	MethodDescriptor[]	**getMethodDescriptors** ()
	1	public	PropertyDescriptor[]	**getPropertyDescriptors** () *ε5,9*
		public	java.awt.Image	**loadImage** (String resourceName)
✳		public		**SimpleBeanInfo** ()

			java.text
	SimpleDateFormat		

Object
1.1 ○ └─Format[1] - *java.io.Serializable*, Cloneable
1.1 ○   └─DateFormat[2]
1.1   └─SimpleDateFormat

	2	*47 inherited members from DateFormat not shown*	
		public	void	**applyLocalizedPattern** (String pattern)
		public	void	**applyPattern** (String pattern)

Class   *Interface* —extends - - -implements ○ abstract ● final △ static ▲ static final ✳ constructor x x—inherited x **x**—declared **x x**—overridden
εn—examples of usage —has subclass package—see other volume

752

	2	public	**Object**	**clone** ()	
	2	public	**boolean**	**equals** (Object obj)	
●	1	public final	String	format (Object obj)	ε316,320
	2	public	**StringBuffer**	**format** (java.util.Date date, StringBuffer toAppendTo, FieldPosition pos)	
1.4	1	public		**formatToCharacterIterator** (Object obj)	
		AttributedCharacterIterator			
1.2		public	java.util.Date	**get2DigitYearStart** ()	
		public	DateFormatSymbols	**getDateFormatSymbols** ()	
	2	public	**int**	**hashCode** ()	
	2	public	java.util.Date	parse (String source) throws ParseException	ε317,318,319,321,322
	2	public	**java.util.Date**	**parse** (String text, ParsePosition pos)	
	1	public	Object	parseObject (String source) throws ParseException	
1.2		public	void	**set2DigitYearStart** (java.util.Date startDate)	
		public	void	**setDateFormatSymbols** (DateFormatSymbols newFormatSymbols)	
∗		public		**SimpleDateFormat** ()	
∗		public		**SimpleDateFormat** (String pattern)	ε316,317,320,321
∗		public		**SimpleDateFormat** (String pattern, java.util.Locale locale)	ε319,323
∗		public		**SimpleDateFormat** (String pattern, DateFormatSymbols formatSymbols)	
		public	String	**toLocalizedPattern** ()	
		public	String	**toPattern** ()	

SimpleFormatter | java.util.logging

```
Object
1.4 ○  └Formatter1
1.4         └SimpleFormatter
```

	1	public synchronized	**String**	**format** (LogRecord record)	ε400
	1	public synchronized	String	formatMessage (LogRecord record)	
	1	public	String	getHead (Handler h)	ε400
	1	public	String	getTail (Handler h)	ε400
∗		public		**SimpleFormatter** ()	ε399

S

SimpleTimeZone | java.util

```
Object1
1.1 ○  └TimeZone2 -------------------------- java.io.Serializable, Cloneable
1.1         └SimpleTimeZone
```

	2	public	**Object**	**clone** ()	
	1	public	**boolean**	**equals** (Object obj)	
△	2	public static synchronized	String[]	getAvailableIDs ()	ε371
△	2	public static synchronized	String[]	getAvailableIDs (int rawOffset)	
△	2	public static synchronized	TimeZone	getDefault ()	ε370
1.2 ●	2	public final	String	getDisplayName ()	
1.2 ●	2	public final	String	getDisplayName (Locale locale)	
1.2 ●	2	public final	String	getDisplayName (boolean daylight, int style)	ε371
1.2	2	public	String	getDisplayName (boolean daylight, int style, Locale locale)	
1.2	2	public	**int**	**getDSTSavings** ()	
	2	public	String	getID ()	
1.4	2	public	**int**	**getOffset** (long date)	
	2	public	**int**	**getOffset** (int era, int year, int month, int day, int dayOfWeek, int millis)	
	2	public	**int**	**getRawOffset** ()	ε371
△	2	public static synchronized	TimeZone	getTimeZone (String ID)	ε370,371,372
	1	public synchronized	**int**	**hashCode** ()	
1.2	2	public	**boolean**	**hasSameRules** (TimeZone other)	
	2	public	**boolean**	**inDaylightTime** (Date date)	ε371
△	2	public static synchronized	void	setDefault (TimeZone zone)	
1.2	2	public	void	**setDSTSavings** (int millisSavedDuringDST)	
1.2		public	void	**setEndRule** (int endMonth, int endDay, int endTime)	
		public	void	**setEndRule** (int endMonth, int endDay, int endDayOfWeek, int endTime)	
1.2		public	void	**setEndRule** (int endMonth, int endDay, int endDayOfWeek, int endTime, boolean after)	
	2	public	void	setID (String ID)	
	2	public	**void**	**setRawOffset** (int offsetMillis)	
1.2		public	void	**setStartRule** (int startMonth, int startDay, int startTime)	
		public	void	**setStartRule** (int startMonth, int startDay, int startDayOfWeek, int startTime)	

Classes

SimpleTimeZone

1.2		public............................void	**setStartRule** (int startMonth, int startDay, int startDayOfWeek, int startTime, boolean after)
		public............................void	**setStartYear** (int year)
✳		public...........................	**SimpleTimeZone** (int rawOffset, String ID)
✳		public...........................	**SimpleTimeZone** (int rawOffset, String ID, int startMonth, int startDay, int startDayOfWeek, int startTime, int endMonth, int endDay, int endDayOfWeek, int endTime)
1.2 ✳		public...........................	**SimpleTimeZone** (int rawOffset, String ID, int startMonth, int startDay, int startDayOfWeek, int startTime, int endMonth, int endDay, int endDayOfWeek, int endTime, int dstSavings)
1.4 ✳		public...........................	**SimpleTimeZone** (int rawOffset, String ID, int startMonth, int startDay, int startDayOfWeek, int startTime, int startTimeMode, int endMonth, int endDay, int endDayOfWeek, int endTime, int endTimeMode, int dstSavings)
1.4 ▲		public static final.............int	**STANDARD_TIME** = 1
	1	public..................String	**toString** ()
	2	public........................**boolean**	**useDaylightTime** () ε371
1.4 ▲		public static final.............int	**UTC_TIME** = 2
1.4 ▲		public static final.............int	**WALL_TIME** = 0

SizeLimitExceededException · javax.naming

```
Object
 └Throwable ---------------------------- java.io.Serializable⌐
   └Exception
1.3    └NamingException [1]
1.3      └LimitExceededException
1.3        └SizeLimitExceededException
```

	1	*20 inherited members from NamingException not shown*	
✳		public...........................	**SizeLimitExceededException** ()
✳		public...........................	**SizeLimitExceededException** (String explanation)

S

Skeleton · java.rmi.server

D		*Skeleton*	
D		public............................void	**dispatch** (*java.rmi.Remote* obj, *RemoteCall* theCall, int opnum, long hash) throws Exception
D		public...............Operation[]	**getOperations** ()

SkeletonMismatchException · java.rmi.server

```
Object
 └Throwable ---------------------------- java.io.Serializable⌐
   └Exception
     └java.io.IOException
1.1      └java.rmi.RemoteException [1]
D          └SkeletonMismatchException
```

D	1	public...............Throwable	detail
D	1	public...............Throwable	getCause ()
D	1	public......................String	getMessage ()
D ✳		public...........................	**SkeletonMismatchException** (String s)

SkeletonNotFoundException · java.rmi.server

```
Object
 └Throwable ---------------------------- java.io.Serializable⌐
   └Exception
     └java.io.IOException
1.1      └java.rmi.RemoteException [1]
D          └SkeletonNotFoundException
```

D	1	public...............Throwable	detail
D	1	public...............Throwable	getCause ()
D	1	public......................String	getMessage ()

Class *Interface* —extends - - -implements ○ abstract ● final △ static ▲ static final ✳ constructor x x—inherited x **x**—declared **x x**—overridden
εn—examples of usage ⌐—has subclass package—see other volume

D	✳	public.........................	**SkeletonNotFoundException** (String s)	
D	✳	public.........................	**SkeletonNotFoundException** (String s, Exception ex)	

Socket			java.net

Object[1]
└─Socket┘   ε148

1.4	public.........................void	**bind** (SocketAddress bindpoint) throws java.io.IOException	
	public synchronized ....void	**close** () throws java.io.IOException	ε149
1.4	public.........................void	**connect** (SocketAddress endpoint) throws java.io.IOException	
1.4	public.........................void	**connect** (SocketAddress endpoint, int timeout) throws java.io.IOException	
			ε147
1.4	public...............java.nio ↩	**getChannel** ()	
	.channels.SocketChannel		
	public..............InetAddress	**getInetAddress** ()	
	public......java.io.InputStream	**getInputStream** () throws java.io.IOException	ε149,499,500
1.3	public..................boolean	**getKeepAlive** () throws SocketException	
1.1	public..............InetAddress	**getLocalAddress** ()	
	public..........................int	**getLocalPort** ()	
1.4	public......... SocketAddress	**getLocalSocketAddress** ()	
1.4	public..................boolean	**getOOBInline** () throws SocketException	
	public....java.io.OutputStream	**getOutputStream** () throws java.io.IOException	ε150,499,500
	public..........................int	**getPort** ()	
1.2	public synchronized ....int	**getReceiveBufferSize** () throws SocketException	
1.4	public......... SocketAddress	**getRemoteSocketAddress** ()	
1.4	public..................boolean	**getReuseAddress** () throws SocketException	
1.2	public synchronized ....int	**getSendBufferSize** () throws SocketException	
1.1	public..........................int	**getSoLinger** () throws SocketException	
1.1	public synchronized ....int	**getSoTimeout** () throws SocketException	
1.1	public..................boolean	**getTcpNoDelay** () throws SocketException	
1.4	public..........................int	**getTrafficClass** () throws SocketException	
1.4	public..................boolean	**isBound** ()	
1.4	public..................boolean	**isClosed** ()	
1.4	public..................boolean	**isConnected** ()	
1.4	public..................boolean	**isInputShutdown** ()	
1.4	public..................boolean	**isOutputShutdown** ()	
1.4	public.........................void	**sendUrgentData** (int data) throws java.io.IOException	
1.3	public.........................void	**setKeepAlive** (boolean on) throws SocketException	
1.4	public.........................void	**setOOBInline** (boolean on) throws SocketException	
1.2	public synchronized ....void	**setReceiveBufferSize** (int size) throws SocketException	
1.4	public.........................void	**setReuseAddress** (boolean on) throws SocketException	
1.2	public synchronized ....void	**setSendBufferSize** (int size) throws SocketException	
△	public static synchronized void	**setSocketImplFactory** (*SocketImplFactory* fac) throws java.io.IOException	
1.1	public.........................void	**setSoLinger** (boolean on, int linger) throws SocketException	
1.1	public synchronized ....void	**setSoTimeout** (int timeout) throws SocketException	
1.1	public.........................void	**setTcpNoDelay** (boolean on) throws SocketException	
1.4	public.........................void	**setTrafficClass** (int tc) throws SocketException	
1.3	public.........................void	**shutdownInput** () throws java.io.IOException	
1.3	public.........................void	**shutdownOutput** () throws java.io.IOException	
1.1 ✳	public.........................	**Socket** ()	ε147
1.1 ✳	protected......................	**Socket** (SocketImpl impl) throws SocketException	
✳	public.........................	**Socket** (String host, int port) throws UnknownHostException, java.io.IOException	
✳	public.........................	**Socket** (InetAddress address, int port) throws java.io.IOException	
			ε147
D ✳	public.........................	**Socket** (String host, int port, boolean stream) throws java.io.IOException	
D ✳	public.........................	**Socket** (InetAddress host, int port, boolean stream) throws java.io.IOException	
1.1 ✳	public.........................	**Socket** (String host, int port, InetAddress localAddr, int localPort) throws java.io.IOException	
1.1 ✳	public.........................	**Socket** (InetAddress address, int port, InetAddress localAddr, int localPort) throws java.io.IOException	
1	public....................String	**toString** ()	

SocketAddress			java.net

Object   ε147
1.4 ○ └─SocketAddress┘ - *java.io.Serializable*┘

✳	public.........................	**SocketAddress** ()

S

Classes

SocketChannel

				java.nio.channels

ε178,183

```
        Object
1.4 O   └java.nio.channels.spi←------------------- Channel˵, InterruptibleChannel (Channel)
            │.AbstractInterruptibleChannel¹
1.4 O       └SelectableChannel²
1.4 O         └java.nio.channels.spi←
                │.AbstractSelectableChannel³
1.4 O           └SocketChannel ------------------- ByteChannel (ReadableByteChannel⁴ (Channel),
                                                   WritableByteChannel⁵ (Channel)), ScatteringByteChannel⁶
                                                   (ReadableByteChannel⁴ (Channel)), GatheringByteChannel⁷
                                                   (WritableByteChannel⁵ (Channel))
```

● 1	protected final.............void	begin ()	
● 3	public final ....Object	blockingLock ()	
● 1	public final ....void	close () throws java.io.IOException	ε174,180,167,170,171
● 3	public final SelectableChannel	configureBlocking (boolean block) throws java.io.IOException	ε173,177,179
O	public abstract .... boolean	**connect** (java.net.SocketAddress remote) throws java.io.IOException	
			ε173
● 1	protected final..............void	end (boolean completed) throws AsynchronousCloseException	
O	public abstract .... boolean	**finishConnect** () throws java.io.IOException	ε173,176
● 3	protected final..............void	implCloseChannel () throws java.io.IOException	
O 3	protected abstract ....void	implCloseSelectableChannel () throws java.io.IOException	
O 3	protected abstract ....void	implConfigureBlocking (boolean block) throws java.io.IOException	
● 3	public final .... boolean	isBlocking ()	
O	public abstract .... boolean	**isConnected** ()	
O	public abstract .... boolean	**isConnectionPending** ()	
● 1	public final .... boolean	isOpen ()	
● 3	public final .... boolean	isRegistered ()	
● 3	public final ....SelectionKey	keyFor (Selector sel)	
△	public static ... SocketChannel	**open** () throws java.io.IOException	ε173
△	public static ... SocketChannel	**open** (java.net.SocketAddress remote) throws java.io.IOException	
● 3	public final java.nio.channels←	provider ()	
	.spi.SelectorProvider		
O 4	public abstract ....int	**read** (java.nio.ByteBuffer dst) throws java.io.IOException	ε180,174,169
● 6	public final .... long	**read** (java.nio.ByteBuffer[] dsts) throws java.io.IOException	
O 6	public abstract .... long	**read** (java.nio.ByteBuffer[] dsts, int offset, int length) throws java.io.IOException	
● 2	public final ....SelectionKey	register (Selector sel, int ops) throws ClosedChannelException ε176,179	
● 3	public final ....SelectionKey	register (Selector sel, int ops, Object att) throws ClosedChannelException	
O	public abstract java.net.Socket	**socket** ()	
✳	protected	**SocketChannel** (java.nio.channels.spi.SelectorProvider provider)	
● 2	public final .... int	**validOps** ()	ε176
O 5	public abstract ....int	**write** (java.nio.ByteBuffer src) throws java.io.IOException	ε180,175,170,171
● 7	public final .... long	**write** (java.nio.ByteBuffer[] srcs) throws java.io.IOException	
O 7	public abstract .... long	**write** (java.nio.ByteBuffer[] srcs, int offset, int length) throws java.io.IOException	

SocketException

			java.net

ε151,152

```
        Object
        └Throwable --------------------------- java.io.Serializable˵
          └Exception
            └java.io.IOException
              └SocketException˵
```

✳	public.........................	**SocketException** ()
✳	public.........................	**SocketException** (String msg)

SocketFactory

			javax.net

```
        Object
1.4 O   └SocketFactory˵
```

	public.......... java.net.Socket	**createSocket** () throws java.io.IOException
O	public abstract java.net.Socket	**createSocket** (String host, int port) throws java.io.IOException,
		java.net.UnknownHostException ε499
O	public abstract java.net.Socket	**createSocket** (java.net.InetAddress host, int port) throws java.io.IOException
O	public abstract java.net.Socket	**createSocket** (String host, int port, java.net.InetAddress localHost, int localPort)
		throws java.io.IOException, java.net.UnknownHostException

Class *Interface* —extends - - -implements O abstract ● final △ static ▲ static final ✳ constructor x x—inherited x **x**—declared **x x**—overridden
ε*n*—examples of usage ˵—has subclass package—see other volume

○	public abstract java.net.Socket	**createSocket** (java.net.InetAddress address, int port,	
		java.net.InetAddress localAddress, int localPort) throws java.io.IOException	
△	public static .... SocketFactory	**getDefault** ()	ε499
✳	protected	**SocketFactory** ()	

SocketHandler
java.util.logging

	Object		ε400
1.4 ○	└Handler[1]		
1.4	└StreamHandler[2]		
1.4	└SocketHandler		

2	public synchronized	**void**	**close** () throws SecurityException	
2	public synchronized	void	flush ()	
1	public.....................	String	getEncoding ()	
1	public...........	ErrorManager	getErrorManager ()	
1	public.................	*Filter*	getFilter ()	
1	public.................	Formatter	getFormatter ()	
1	public synchronized	Level	getLevel ()	
2	public.................	boolean	isLoggable (LogRecord record)	
2	public synchronized	**void**	**publish** (LogRecord record)	ε393
1	protected	void	reportError (String msg, Exception ex, int code)	
2	public.....................	void	setEncoding (String encoding) throws SecurityException,	
			java.io.UnsupportedEncodingException	
1	public.....................	void	setErrorManager (ErrorManager em)	
1	public.....................	void	setFilter (*Filter* newFilter) throws SecurityException	ε394
1	public.....................	void	setFormatter (Formatter newFormatter) throws SecurityException	
				ε399,400
1	public synchronized	void	setLevel (Level newLevel) throws SecurityException	
2	protected synchronized ...	void	setOutputStream (java.io.OutputStream out) throws SecurityException	
✳	public.........................		**SocketHandler** () throws java.io.IOException	
✳	public.........................		**SocketHandler** (String host, int port) throws java.io.IOException	

S

SocketImpl
java.net

	Object[1]		
○	└SocketImpl - *SocketOptions*		

○	protected abstract ....void	**accept** (SocketImpl s) throws java.io.IOException	
	protected .... InetAddress	**address**	
○	protected abstract ....int	**available** () throws java.io.IOException	
○	protected abstract ....void	**bind** (InetAddress host, int port) throws java.io.IOException	
○	protected abstract ....void	**close** () throws java.io.IOException	
○	protected abstract ....void	**connect** (String host, int port) throws java.io.IOException	
○	protected abstract ....void	**connect** (InetAddress address, int port) throws java.io.IOException	
1.4 ○	protected abstract ....void	**connect** (SocketAddress address, int timeout) throws java.io.IOException	
○	protected abstract ....void	**create** (boolean stream) throws java.io.IOException	
	protected java.io.FileDescriptor	**fd**	
	protected java.io.FileDescriptor	**getFileDescriptor** ()	
	protected .... InetAddress	**getInetAddress** ()	
○	protected abstract	**getInputStream** () throws java.io.IOException	
	.... java.io.InputStream		
	protected.....................int	**getLocalPort** ()	
○	protected abstract	**getOutputStream** () throws java.io.IOException	
	.... java.io.OutputStream		
	protected.....................int	**getPort** ()	
○	protected abstract ....void	**listen** (int backlog) throws java.io.IOException	
	protected.....................int	**localport**	
	protected.....................int	**port**	
1.4 ○	protected abstract ....void	**sendUrgentData** (int data) throws java.io.IOException	
1.3	protected ....void	**shutdownInput** () throws java.io.IOException	
1.3	protected ....void	**shutdownOutput** () throws java.io.IOException	
✳	public.........................	**SocketImpl** ()	
1.4	protected .... boolean	**supportsUrgentData** ()	
1	public................. String	**toString** ()	

Classes

SocketImplFactory
java.net

SocketImplFactory

public..............SocketImpl **createSocketImpl** ()

SocketOptions
java.net

1.2   *SocketOptions*

	public....................Object	**getOption** (int optID) throws SocketException
▲	public static final.............int	**IP_MULTICAST_IF** = 16
1.4 ▲	public static final.............int	**IP_MULTICAST_IF2** = 31
1.4 ▲	public static final.............int	**IP_MULTICAST_LOOP** = 18
1.4 ▲	public static final.............int	**IP_TOS** = 3
	public....................void	**setOption** (int optID, Object value) throws SocketException
▲	public static final.............int	**SO_BINDADDR** = 15
1.4 ▲	public static final.............int	**SO_BROADCAST** = 32
1.3 ▲	public static final.............int	**SO_KEEPALIVE** = 8
▲	public static final.............int	**SO_LINGER** = 128
1.4 ▲	public static final.............int	**SO_OOBINLINE** = 4099
▲	public static final.............int	**SO_RCVBUF** = 4098
▲	public static final.............int	**SO_REUSEADDR** = 4
▲	public static final.............int	**SO_SNDBUF** = 4097
▲	public static final.............int	**SO_TIMEOUT** = 4102
▲	public static final.............int	**TCP_NODELAY** = 1

SocketPermission
java.net

Object   ε217,218
1.2 ○   └java.security.Permission[1] ---------------- *java.security.Guard, java.io.Serializable*⌄
1.2 ●   └SocketPermission

	1	public....................void	checkGuard (Object object) throws SecurityException
	1	public...............**boolean**	**equals** (Object obj)	ε215
	1	public....................**String**	**getActions** ()	ε215
●	1	public final ....String	getName ()
	1	public....................**int**	**hashCode** ()	ε215
	1	public...............**boolean**	**implies** (java.security.Permission p)	ε214,215
	1	public.........**java.security** ↵ .**PermissionCollection**	**newPermissionCollection** ()
✱		public.........................	**SocketPermission** (String host, String action)
	1	public....................String	toString ()

SocketSecurityException
java.rmi.server

Object
└Throwable -------------------------- *java.io.Serializable*⌄
  └Exception
    └java.io.IOException
1.1   └java.rmi.RemoteException[1]
1.1   └ExportException
1.1   └SocketSecurityException

	1	public...............Throwable	detail
1.4	1	public...............Throwable	getCause ()
	1	public....................String	getMessage ()
✱		public.........................	**SocketSecurityException** (String s)
✱		public.........................	**SocketSecurityException** (String s, Exception ex)

Class *Interface* —extends - - -implements ○ abstract ● final △ static ▲ static final ✱ constructor x x—inherited x **x**—declared **x x**—overridden
ε*n*—examples of usage ⌐—has subclass package—see other volume

SocketTimeoutException | java.net

ε147

```
Object
└Throwable ------------------------- java.io.Serializable┘
   └Exception
      └java.io.IOException
         └java.io.InterruptedIOException 1
1.4         └SocketTimeoutException
```

1	public	int	bytesTransferred
*	public		**SocketTimeoutException** ()
*	public		**SocketTimeoutException** (String msg)

SoftReference | java.lang.ref

ε107

```
      Object
1.2 O └Reference 1
1.2      └SoftReference
```

1	public	void	clear ()	ε108
1	public	boolean	enqueue ()	
1	public	**Object**	**get** ()	ε106,357
1	public	boolean	isEnqueued ()	
*	public		**SoftReference** (Object referent)	ε106
*	public		**SoftReference** (Object referent, ReferenceQueue q)	

SortedMap | java.util

1.2	*SortedMap*————————— *Map*┘1			ε347,348
1	public	void	clear ()	
	public	*Comparator*	**comparator** ()	
1	public	boolean	containsKey (Object key)	ε344
1	public	boolean	containsValue (Object value)	
1	public	*Set*	entrySet ()	ε345
1	public	boolean	equals (Object o)	
	public	Object	**firstKey** ()	
1	public	Object	get (Object key)	ε337,344,346,356,357
1	public	int	hashCode ()	
	public	*SortedMap*	**headMap** (Object toKey)	
1	public	boolean	isEmpty ()	
1	public	*Set*	keySet ()	ε194,340,345,355,356
1	public	Object	**lastKey** ()	
1	public	Object	put (Object key, Object value)	ε337,344,346,355,356
1	public	void	putAll (*Map* t)	
1	public	Object	remove (Object key)	ε355
1	public	int	size ()	ε355
	public	*SortedMap*	**subMap** (Object fromKey, Object toKey)	
	public	*SortedMap*	**tailMap** (Object fromKey)	
1	public	*Collection*	values ()	ε340,345,355

SortedSet | java.util

1.2	*SortedSet*————————— *Set*┘1 (*Collection*)			ε339,341,347,348,350
1	public	boolean	add (Object o)	ε358,342,349,352,354
1	public	boolean	addAll (*Collection* c)	ε351,353
1	public	void	clear ()	ε351,353
	public	*Comparator*	**comparator** ()	
1	public	boolean	contains (Object o)	ε352
1	public	boolean	containsAll (*Collection* c)	
1	public	boolean	equals (Object o)	
	public	Object	**first** ()	
1	public	int	hashCode ()	
	public	*SortedSet*	**headSet** (Object toElement)	
1	public	boolean	isEmpty ()	ε102
1	public	*Iterator*	iterator ()	ε358,345,352,354,355
	public	Object	**last** ()	
1	public	boolean	remove (Object o)	ε349,352
1	public	boolean	removeAll (*Collection* c)	ε351,353
1	public	boolean	retainAll (*Collection* c)	ε351,353

S

Classes

SortedSet

1	public	int	size ()	ε358,340,349,351,352
	public	SortedSet	**subSet** (Object fromElement, Object toElement)	
	public	SortedSet	**tailSet** (Object fromElement)	
1	public	Object[]	toArray ()	ε340
1	public	Object[]	toArray (Object[] a)	ε358,340,352,194,508

Source — javax.xml.transform

1.4	*Source*			ε518,519,520,521,522
	public	String	**getSystemId** ()	
	public	void	**setSystemId** (String systemId)	ε523

SourceLocator — javax.xml.transform

1.4	*SourceLocator* ⌄			
	public	int	**getColumnNumber** ()	ε521
	public	int	**getLineNumber** ()	ε521
	public	String	**getPublicId** ()	ε521
	public	String	**getSystemId** ()	ε521

SQLData — java.sql

1.2	*SQLData*		
	public	String	**getSQLTypeName** () throws SQLException
	public	void	**readSQL** (*SQLInput* stream, String typeName) throws SQLException
	public	void	**writeSQL** (*SQLOutput* stream) throws SQLException

---

SQLException — java.sql

Object
└Throwable [1] - *java.io.Serializable* ⌄
 └Exception
1.1 └SQLException ⌄

ε235,236,237,238,239

	public	int	**getErrorCode** ()	ε241,242
1	public	String	getMessage ()	ε241,242,262
	public	SQLException	**getNextException** ()	ε241
	public	String	**getSQLState** ()	ε241,242
	public synchronized	void	**setNextException** (SQLException ex)	
*	public		**SQLException** ()	
*	public		**SQLException** (String reason)	
*	public		**SQLException** (String reason, String SQLState)	
*	public		**SQLException** (String reason, String SQLState, int vendorCode)	

SQLInput — java.sql

1.2	*SQLInput*		
	public	Array	**readArray** () throws SQLException
	public	java.io.InputStream	**readAsciiStream** () throws SQLException
	public	java.math.BigDecimal	**readBigDecimal** () throws SQLException
	public	java.io.InputStream	**readBinaryStream** () throws SQLException
	public	Blob	**readBlob** () throws SQLException
	public	boolean	**readBoolean** () throws SQLException
	public	byte	**readByte** () throws SQLException
	public	byte[]	**readBytes** () throws SQLException
	public	java.io.Reader	**readCharacterStream** () throws SQLException
	public	Clob	**readClob** () throws SQLException
	public	Date	**readDate** () throws SQLException
	public	double	**readDouble** () throws SQLException
	public	float	**readFloat** () throws SQLException
	public	int	**readInt** () throws SQLException
	public	long	**readLong** () throws SQLException
	public	Object	**readObject** () throws SQLException

Class *Interface* —extends - - -implements ○ abstract ● final △ static ▲ static final ✳ constructor x x—inherited x **x**—declared **x x**—overridden
ε*n*—examples of usage ⌄—has subclass package—see other volume

```
       public........................Ref readRef () throws SQLException
       public......................short readShort () throws SQLException
       public.....................String readString () throws SQLException
       public.......................Time readTime () throws SQLException
       public................Timestamp readTimestamp () throws SQLException
1.4    public...............java.net.URL readURL () throws SQLException
       public..................boolean wasNull () throws SQLException
```

SQLOutput   java.sql

```
1.2    SQLOutput
```

```
       public........................void writeArray (Array x) throws SQLException
       public........................void writeAsciiStream (java.io.InputStream x) throws SQLException
       public........................void writeBigDecimal (java.math.BigDecimal x) throws SQLException
       public........................void writeBinaryStream (java.io.InputStream x) throws SQLException
       public........................void writeBlob (Blob x) throws SQLException
       public........................void writeBoolean (boolean x) throws SQLException
       public........................void writeByte (byte x) throws SQLException
       public........................void writeBytes (byte[] x) throws SQLException
       public........................void writeCharacterStream (java.io.Reader x) throws SQLException
       public........................void writeClob (Clob x) throws SQLException
       public........................void writeDate (Date x) throws SQLException
       public........................void writeDouble (double x) throws SQLException
       public........................void writeFloat (float x) throws SQLException
       public........................void writeInt (int x) throws SQLException
       public........................void writeLong (long x) throws SQLException
       public........................void writeObject (SQLData x) throws SQLException
       public........................void writeRef (Ref x) throws SQLException
       public........................void writeShort (short x) throws SQLException
       public........................void writeString (String x) throws SQLException
       public........................void writeStruct (Struct x) throws SQLException
       public........................void writeTime (Time x) throws SQLException
       public........................void writeTimestamp (Timestamp x) throws SQLException
1.4    public........................void writeURL (java.net.URL x) throws SQLException
```

SQLPermission   java.sql

```
       Object                                                                   ε217,218
1.2 O  └java.security.Permission 1 ----------------- java.security.Guard, java.io.Serializable
1.2 O     └java.security.BasicPermission 2
1.3 ●        └SQLPermission
```

```
    1  public........................void checkGuard (Object object) throws SecurityException
    2  public...................boolean equals (Object obj)                       ε215
    2  public....................String getActions ()                             ε215
 ●  1  public final ...............String getName ()
    2  public.......................int hashCode ()                               ε215
    2  public...................boolean implies (java.security.Permission p)       ε214,215
    2  public...........java.security↵ newPermissionCollection ()
           .PermissionCollection
 *     public........................ SQLPermission (String name)
 *     public........................ SQLPermission (String name, String actions)
    1  public....................String toString ()
```

SQLWarning   java.sql

```
       Object
       └Throwable -------------------------- java.io.Serializable
          └Exception
1.1         └SQLException 1
1.1            └SQLWarning
```

```
    1  public........................int getErrorCode ()                          ε242
    1  public........... SQLException getNextException ()
       public........... SQLWarning getNextWarning ()                            ε242
    1  public....................String getSQLState ()                           ε242
    1  public synchronized .......void setNextException (SQLException ex)
       public........................void setNextWarning (SQLWarning w)
 *     public........................ SQLWarning ()
 *     public........................ SQLWarning (String reason)
```

SQLWarning

✻	public..........................	**SQLWarning** (String reason, String SQLstate)
✻	public..........................	**SQLWarning** (String reason, String SQLstate, int vendorCode)

SSLContext		javax.net.ssl

Object
  └SSLContext

1.4

●	public final *SSLSessionContext*	**getClientSessionContext** ()
△	public static .... SSLContext	**getInstance** (String protocol) throws java.security.NoSuchAlgorithmException
		ε502
△	public static .... SSLContext	**getInstance** (String protocol, java.security.Provider provider)
		throws java.security.NoSuchAlgorithmException
△	public static .... SSLContext	**getInstance** (String protocol, String provider) throws java.security↩
		.NoSuchAlgorithmException, java.security.NoSuchProviderException
●	public final ....String	**getProtocol** ()
●	public final	**getProvider** ()
	.... java.security.Provider	
●	public final *SSLSessionContext*	**getServerSessionContext** ()
●	public final	**getServerSocketFactory** ()
	.....SSLServerSocketFactory	
●	public final . SSLSocketFactory	**getSocketFactory** () ε502
●	public final ....void	**init** (*KeyManager[]* km, *TrustManager[]* tm, java.security.SecureRandom random)
		throws java.security.KeyManagementException ε502
✻	protected	**SSLContext** (SSLContextSpi contextSpi, java.security.Provider provider,
		String protocol)

SSLContextSpi		javax.net.ssl

Object
  └SSLContextSpi

1.4 ○

○	protected abstract	**engineGetClientSessionContext** ()
	...........*SSLSessionContext*	
○	protected abstract	**engineGetServerSessionContext** ()
	...........*SSLSessionContext*	
○	protected abstract	**engineGetServerSocketFactory** ()
	.....SSLServerSocketFactory	
○	protected abstract	**engineGetSocketFactory** ()
	...........SSLSocketFactory	
○	protected abstract ....void	**engineInit** (*KeyManager[]* km, *TrustManager[]* tm, java.security.SecureRandom sr)
		throws java.security.KeyManagementException
✻	public..........................	**SSLContextSpi** ()

SSLException		javax.net.ssl

Object
  └Throwable --------------------------- *java.io.Serializable*⌐
    └Exception
      └java.io.IOException
1.4   └SSLException⌐

✻	public..........................	**SSLException** (String reason)

SSLHandshakeException		javax.net.ssl

Object
  └Throwable --------------------------- *java.io.Serializable*⌐
    └Exception
      └java.io.IOException
1.4   └SSLException
1.4   └SSLHandshakeException

✻	public..........................	**SSLHandshakeException** (String reason)

Class *Interface* —extends - - -implements ○ abstract ● final △ static ▲ static final ✻ constructor x x—inherited x **x**—declared **x x**—overridden
ε*n*—examples of usage ⌐—has subclass package—see other volume

	SSLKeyException	javax.net.ssl

```
      Object
      └Throwable ------------------------- java.io.Serializable
        └Exception
          └java.io.IOException
1.4         └SSLException
1.4           └SSLKeyException
```

*	public........................	**SSLKeyException** (String reason)

	SSLPeerUnverifiedException	javax.net.ssl

ε501

```
      Object
      └Throwable ------------------------- java.io.Serializable
        └Exception
          └java.io.IOException
1.4         └SSLException
1.4           └SSLPeerUnverifiedException
```

*	public........................	**SSLPeerUnverifiedException** (String reason)

	SSLPermission	javax.net.ssl

ε217,218

```
        Object
1.2 ○   └java.security.Permission1 ---------------- java.security.Guard, java.io.Serializable
1.2 ○     └java.security.BasicPermission2
1.4 ●       └SSLPermission
```

	1	public......................void	checkGuard (Object object) throws SecurityException	
	2	public.................. boolean	equals (Object obj)	ε215
	2	public....................String	getActions ()	ε215
●	1	public final ....String	getName ()	
	2	public........................int	hashCode ()	ε215
	2	public.................. boolean	implies (java.security.Permission p)	ε214,215
	2	public...........java.security ↵ .PermissionCollection	newPermissionCollection ()	
*		public........................	**SSLPermission** (String name)	
*		public........................	**SSLPermission** (String name, String actions)	
	1	public....................String	toString ()	

	SSLProtocolException	javax.net.ssl

```
      Object
      └Throwable ------------------------- java.io.Serializable
        └Exception
          └java.io.IOException
1.4         └SSLException
1.4           └SSLProtocolException
```

*	public........................	**SSLProtocolException** (String reason)

	SSLServerSocket	javax.net.ssl

```
        Object
        └java.net.ServerSocket1
1.4 ○     └SSLServerSocket
```

	1	public.......... java.net.Socket	accept () throws java.io.IOException	ε148,500
	1	public......................void	bind (java.net.SocketAddress endpoint) throws java.io.IOException	ε177,179
	1	public......................void	bind (java.net.SocketAddress endpoint, int backlog) throws java.io.IOException	
	1	public......................void	close () throws java.io.IOException	
	1	public..... java.nio.channels ↵ .ServerSocketChannel	getChannel ()	
○		public abstract .... String[]	**getEnabledCipherSuites** ()	
○		public abstract .... String[]	**getEnabledProtocols** ()	
○		public abstract .... boolean	**getEnableSessionCreation** ()	
	1	public.... java.net.InetAddress	getInetAddress ()	

SSLServerSocket

	1	public	int	getLocalPort ()	ε178
	1	public . java.net.SocketAddress		getLocalSocketAddress ()	
O		public abstract	boolean	**getNeedClientAuth** ()	
	1	public synchronized	int	getReceiveBufferSize () throws java.net.SocketException	
	1	public	boolean	getReuseAddress () throws java.net.SocketException	
	1	public synchronized	int	getSoTimeout () throws java.io.IOException	
O		public abstract	String[]	**getSupportedCipherSuites** ()	
O		public abstract	String[]	**getSupportedProtocols** ()	
O		public abstract	boolean	**getUseClientMode** ()	
O		public abstract	boolean	**getWantClientAuth** ()	
●	1	protected final	void	implAccept (java.net.Socket s) throws java.io.IOException	
	1	public	boolean	isBound ()	
	1	public	boolean	isClosed ()	
O		public abstract	void	**setEnabledCipherSuites** (String[] suites)	
O		public abstract	void	**setEnabledProtocols** (String[] protocols)	
O		public abstract	void	**setEnableSessionCreation** (boolean flag)	
O		public abstract	void	**setNeedClientAuth** (boolean flag)	
	1	public synchronized	void	setReceiveBufferSize (int size) throws java.net.SocketException	
	1	public	void	setReuseAddress (boolean on) throws java.net.SocketException	
△	1	public static synchronized void		setSocketFactory (*java.net.SocketImplFactory* fac) throws java.io.IOException	
	1	public synchronized	void	setSoTimeout (int timeout) throws java.net.SocketException	
O		public abstract	void	**setUseClientMode** (boolean flag)	
O		public abstract	void	**setWantClientAuth** (boolean flag)	
✳		protected		**SSLServerSocket** () throws java.io.IOException	
✳		protected		**SSLServerSocket** (int port) throws java.io.IOException	
✳		protected		**SSLServerSocket** (int port, int backlog) throws java.io.IOException	
✳		protected		**SSLServerSocket** (int port, int backlog, java.net.InetAddress address) throws java.io.IOException	
	1	public	String	toString ()	

SSLServerSocketFactory — javax.net.ssl

```
Object
1.4 O └─javax.net.ServerSocketFactory ¹
1.4 O     └─SSLServerSocketFactory
```

	1	public... java.net.ServerSocket		createServerSocket () throws java.io.IOException	
O	1	public abstract java.net.ServerSocket		createServerSocket (int port) throws java.io.IOException	ε500
O	1	public abstract java.net.ServerSocket		createServerSocket (int port, int backlog) throws java.io.IOException	
O	1	public abstract java.net.ServerSocket		createServerSocket (int port, int backlog, java.net.InetAddress ifAddress) throws java.io.IOException	
△	1	public static synchronized **javax ↵ .net.ServerSocketFactory**		**getDefault** ()	ε500
O		public abstract	String[]	**getDefaultCipherSuites** ()	
O		public abstract	String[]	**getSupportedCipherSuites** ()	
✳		protected		**SSLServerSocketFactory** ()	

SSLSession — javax.net.ssl

```
1.4   SSLSession
```

	public	String	**getCipherSuite** ()	
	public	long	**getCreationTime** ()	
	public	byte[]	**getId** ()	
	public	long	**getLastAccessedTime** ()	
	public	java ↵ .security.cert.Certificate[]	**getLocalCertificates** ()	
	public	javax.security ↵ .cert.X509Certificate[]	**getPeerCertificateChain** () throws SSLPeerUnverifiedException	
	public	java ↵ .security.cert.Certificate[]	**getPeerCertificates** () throws SSLPeerUnverifiedException	ε501
	public	String	**getPeerHost** ()	
	public	String	**getProtocol** ()	
	public	*SSLSessionContext*	**getSessionContext** ()	
	public	Object	**getValue** (String name)	

Class   *Interface*   —extends   - - -implements   O abstract   ● final   △ static   ▲ static final   ✳ constructor   x x—inherited   x **x**—declared   x **x**—overridden
ε*n*—examples of usage   ⌐—has subclass   package—see other volume

```
        public ................... String[] getValueNames ()
        public ...................... void invalidate ()
        public ...................... void putValue (String name, Object value)
        public ...................... void removeValue (String name)
```

SSLSessionBindingEvent   javax.net.ssl

```
                                                                        ε333
        Object
1.1     └java.util.EventObject¹ ------------------ java.io.Serializable╷
1.4        └SSLSessionBindingEvent
```

```
        public ................... String getName ()
        public ............. SSLSession getSession ()
    1   public ................... Object getSource ()
    1   protected transient ...... Object source
 *      public ......................      SSLSessionBindingEvent (SSLSession session, String name)
    1   public ................... String toString ()
```

SSLSessionBindingListener   javax.net.ssl

```
1.4   SSLSessionBindingListener——————————java.util.EventListener╷        ε2,3,333,493,494
```
```
        public ...................... void valueBound (SSLSessionBindingEvent event)
        public ...................... void valueUnbound (SSLSessionBindingEvent event)
```

SSLSessionContext   javax.net.ssl

```
1.4   SSLSessionContext
```
```
        public .... java.util.Enumeration getIds ()
        public ............. SSLSession getSession (byte[] sessionId)
        public ...................... int getSessionCacheSize ()
        public ...................... int getSessionTimeout ()
        public ...................... void setSessionCacheSize (int size) throws IllegalArgumentException
        public ...................... void setSessionTimeout (int seconds) throws IllegalArgumentException
```

SSLSocket   javax.net.ssl

```
                                                                        ε148
        Object
        └java.net.Socket¹
1.4 ○      └SSLSocket
```

```
    1   41 inherited members from java.net.Socket not shown
 ○      public abstract ............. void addHandshakeCompletedListener (HandshakeCompletedListener listener)
 ○      public abstract ......... String[] getEnabledCipherSuites ()
 ○      public abstract ......... String[] getEnabledProtocols ()
 ○      public abstract ........ boolean getEnableSessionCreation ()
 ○      public abstract ........ boolean getNeedClientAuth ()
 ○      public abstract .... SSLSession getSession ()                    ε501
 ○      public abstract ......... String[] getSupportedCipherSuites ()
 ○      public abstract ......... String[] getSupportedProtocols ()
 ○      public abstract ........ boolean getUseClientMode ()
 ○      public abstract ........ boolean getWantClientAuth ()
 ○      public abstract ...................void removeHandshakeCompletedListener (HandshakeCompletedListener listener)
 ○      public abstract ............. void setEnabledCipherSuites (String[] suites)
 ○      public abstract ............. void setEnabledProtocols (String[] protocols)
 ○      public abstract ............. void setEnableSessionCreation (boolean flag)
 ○      public abstract ............. void setNeedClientAuth (boolean need)
 ○      public abstract ............. void setUseClientMode (boolean mode)
 ○      public abstract ............. void setWantClientAuth (boolean want)
 *      protected ......................      SSLSocket ()
 *      protected ......................      SSLSocket (String host, int port) throws java.io.IOException,
                                                 java.net.UnknownHostException
 *      protected ......................      SSLSocket (java.net.InetAddress address, int port)
                                                 throws java.io.IOException, java.net.UnknownHostException
 *      protected ......................      SSLSocket (String host, int port, java.net.InetAddress clientAddress, int clientPort)
                                                 throws java.io.IOException, java.net.UnknownHostException
 *      protected ......................      SSLSocket (java.net.InetAddress address, int port,
                                                 java.net.InetAddress clientAddress, int clientPort)
                                                 throws java.io.IOException, java.net.UnknownHostException
```

SSLSocket

O	public abstract............void **startHandshake** () throws java.io.IOException	ε501

SSLSocketFactory javax.net.ssl

Object
```
1.4 O  └─javax.net.SocketFactory ¹
1.4 O     └─SSLSocketFactory
```

	1	public.......... java.net.Socket	createSocket () throws java.io.IOException
O	1	public abstract java.net.Socket	createSocket (String host, int port) throws java.io.IOException, java.net.UnknownHostException ε501,499
O	1	public abstract java.net.Socket	createSocket (java.net.InetAddress host, int port) throws java.io.IOException
O	1	public abstract java.net.Socket	createSocket (String host, int port, java.net.InetAddress localHost, int localPort) throws java.io.IOException, java.net.UnknownHostException
O	1	public abstract java.net.Socket	createSocket (java.net.InetAddress address, int port, java.net.InetAddress localAddress, int localPort) throws java.io.IOException
O		public abstract java.net.Socket	**createSocket** (java.net.Socket s, String host, int port, boolean autoClose) throws java.io.IOException
△	1	public static synchronized .... **javax.net.SocketFactory**	**getDefault** () ε499
O		public abstract .... String[]	**getDefaultCipherSuites** ()
O		public abstract .... String[]	**getSupportedCipherSuites** ()
*		public...........................	**SSLSocketFactory** ()

Stack java.util

Object
```
1.2 O  └─AbstractCollection ----------------------- Collection ˎ
1.2 O     └─AbstractList ¹ ---------------------- List (Collection)
            └─Vector ² ------------------------- RandomAccess, Cloneable ˎ, java.io.Serializable ˎ
              └─Stack
```

	2	*45 inherited members from Vector not shown*	
		public.................. boolean	**empty** ()
1.2	1	public................... *Iterator*	iterator () ε345,352,354,355,356
1.2	1	public...............*ListIterator*	listIterator ()
1.2	1	public...............*ListIterator*	listIterator (int index)
1.2	1	protected transient...........int	modCount
		public synchronized .... Object	**peek** ()
		public synchronized .... Object	**pop** ()
		public.................... Object	**push** (Object item)
		public synchronized ....int	**search** (Object o)
*		public...........................	**Stack** ()

StackOverflowError java.lang

Object
```
   └─Throwable --------------------------- java.io.Serializable ˎ
      └─Error
O        └─VirtualMachineError
            └─StackOverflowError
```

*	public...........................	**StackOverflowError** ()
*	public...........................	**StackOverflowError** (String s)

StackTraceElement java.lang

Object ¹
```
1.4 ●  └─StackTraceElement --------------------- java.io.Serializable ˎ
```

	1	public.................. **boolean**	**equals** (Object obj)
		public.................... String	**getClassName** () ε101
		public.................... String	**getFileName** () ε101
		public........................int	**getLineNumber** () ε101
		public.................... String	**getMethodName** () ε101
	1	public...................... **int**	**hashCode** ()

Class   *Interface*   —extends   - - -implements   O abstract   ● final   △ static   ▲ static final   ✳ constructor   x x—inherited   x **x**—declared   **x x**—overridden
ε*n*—examples of usage   ˎ—has subclass   package—see other volume

| | public | boolean | **isNativeMethod** () | | *ε*101 |
| 1 | public | String | **toString** () | | |

StartTlsRequest   javax.naming.ldap

Object
1.4   └StartTlsRequest ----------------------- *ExtendedRequest* [1] (*java.io.Serializable*)

1	public	*ExtendedResponse*	**createExtendedResponse** (String id, byte[] berValue, int offset, int length)
			throws javax.naming.NamingException
1	public	byte[]	**getEncodedValue** ()
1	public	String	**getID** ()
▲	public static final	String	**OID** = "1.3.6.1.4.1.1466.20037"
✳	public		**StartTlsRequest** ()

StartTlsResponse   javax.naming.ldap

Object
1.4 ○ └StartTlsResponse ----------------------- *ExtendedResponse* [1] (*java.io.Serializable*)

○	public abstract	void	**close** () throws java.io.IOException
1	public	byte[]	**getEncodedValue** ()
1	public	String	**getID** ()
○	public abstract		**negotiate** () throws java.io.IOException
	....*javax.net.ssl.SSLSession*		
○	public abstract		**negotiate** (javax.net.ssl.SSLSocketFactory factory) throws java.io.IOException
	....*javax.net.ssl.SSLSession*		
▲	public static final	String	**OID** = "1.3.6.1.4.1.1466.20037"
○	public abstract	void	**setEnabledCipherSuites** (String[] suites)
○	public abstract	void	**setHostnameVerifier** (*javax.net.ssl.HostnameVerifier* verifier)
✳	protected		**StartTlsResponse** ()

S

State   org.omg.PortableServer.POAManagerPackage

Object
1.4   └State ---------------------------------- *org.omg.CORBA.portable.IDLEntity* (*java.io.Serializable*)

▲	public static final	int	**_ACTIVE** = 1
▲	public static final	int	**_DISCARDING** = 2
▲	public static final	int	**_HOLDING** = 0
▲	public static final	int	**_INACTIVE** = 3
▲	public static final	State	**ACTIVE**
▲	public static final	State	**DISCARDING**
△	public static	State	**from_int** (int value)
▲	public static final	State	**HOLDING**
▲	public static final	State	**INACTIVE**
✳	protected		**State** (int value)
	public	int	**value** ()

StateFactory   javax.naming.spi

1.3   *StateFactory*
- -
| | public | Object | **getStateToBind** (Object obj, *javax.naming.Name* name, *javax.naming.Context* |
| | | | nameCtx, java.util.Hashtable environment) throws javax.naming.NamingException |
- -

Classes

Statement❶   java.beans

Object [1]
1.4   └Statement

	public	void	**execute** () throws Exception	*ε*6
	public	Object[]	**getArguments** ()	
	public	String	**getMethodName** ()	
	public	Object	**getTarget** ()	
✳	public		**Statement** (Object target, String methodName, Object[] arguments)	
				*ε*6
1	public	String	**toString** ()	

Statement ❷ — java.sql

1.1	*Statement*ⱼ		ε267
1.2	public......................void	**addBatch** (String sql) throws SQLException	
	public......................void	**cancel** () throws SQLException	
1.2	public......................void	**clearBatch** () throws SQLException	
	public......................void	**clearWarnings** () throws SQLException	
	public......................void	**close** () throws SQLException	ε260
1.4 ▲	public static final.............int	**CLOSE_ALL_RESULTS** = 3	
1.4 ▲	public static final.............int	**CLOSE_CURRENT_RESULT** = 1	
	public.................. boolean	**execute** (String sql) throws SQLException	ε249,296,297,298,300
1.4	public.................. boolean	**execute** (String sql, int autoGeneratedKeys) throws SQLException	
1.4	public.................. boolean	**execute** (String sql, String[] columnNames) throws SQLException	
1.4	public.................. boolean	**execute** (String sql, int[] columnIndexes) throws SQLException	
1.4 ▲	public static final.............int	**EXECUTE_FAILED** = -3	ε265
1.2	public...................... int[]	**executeBatch** () throws SQLException	ε265
	public...................*ResultSet*	**executeQuery** (String sql) throws SQLException	ε273,242,251,252,254
	public........................int	**executeUpdate** (String sql) throws SQLException	ε245,246,248,249,250
1.4	public........................int	**executeUpdate** (String sql, int autoGeneratedKeys) throws SQLException	
1.4	public........................int	**executeUpdate** (String sql, int[] columnIndexes) throws SQLException	
1.4	public........................int	**executeUpdate** (String sql, String[] columnNames) throws SQLException	
1.2	public...............*Connection*	**getConnection** () throws SQLException	
1.2	public........................int	**getFetchDirection** () throws SQLException	
1.2	public........................int	**getFetchSize** () throws SQLException	ε244
1.4	public...................*ResultSet*	**getGeneratedKeys** () throws SQLException	
	public........................int	**getMaxFieldSize** () throws SQLException	
	public........................int	**getMaxRows** () throws SQLException	
	public.................. boolean	**getMoreResults** () throws SQLException	
1.4	public.................. boolean	**getMoreResults** (int current) throws SQLException	
	public........................int	**getQueryTimeout** () throws SQLException	
	public...................*ResultSet*	**getResultSet** () throws SQLException	
1.2	public........................int	**getResultSetConcurrency** () throws SQLException	
1.4	public........................int	**getResultSetHoldability** () throws SQLException	
1.2	public........................int	**getResultSetType** () throws SQLException	
	public........................int	**getUpdateCount** () throws SQLException	
	public............. SQLWarning	**getWarnings** () throws SQLException	ε242
1.4 ▲	public static final.............int	**KEEP_CURRENT_RESULT** = 2	
1.4 ▲	public static final.............int	**NO_GENERATED_KEYS** = 2	
1.4 ▲	public static final.............int	**RETURN_GENERATED_KEYS** = 1	
	public......................void	**setCursorName** (String name) throws SQLException	
	public......................void	**setEscapeProcessing** (boolean enable) throws SQLException	
1.2	public......................void	**setFetchDirection** (int direction) throws SQLException	
1.2	public......................void	**setFetchSize** (int rows) throws SQLException	ε244
	public......................void	**setMaxFieldSize** (int max) throws SQLException	
	public......................void	**setMaxRows** (int max) throws SQLException	
	public......................void	**setQueryTimeout** (int seconds) throws SQLException	
1.4 ▲	public static final.............int	**SUCCESS_NO_INFO** = -2	ε265

S

Streamable — org.omg.CORBA.portable

1.2	*Streamable*ⱼ	
	public......................void	**_read** (InputStream istream)
	public	**_type** ()
	. org.omg.CORBA.TypeCode	
	public......................void	**_write** (OutputStream ostream)

StreamableValue — org.omg.CORBA.portable

1.3	*StreamableValue*————————————*Streamable*ⱼ[1], *ValueBase*ⱼ[2] (IDLEntity (java.io.Serializable))
	[1] *3 inherited members from Streamable not shown*
	[2] public................... String[] **_truncatable_ids** ()

Class *Interface* —extends - - -implements ○ abstract ● final △ static ▲ static final ✳ constructor x x—inherited x **x**—declared **x x**—overridden
ε*n*—examples of usage ⱼ—has subclass package—see other volume

768

StreamCorruptedException | java.io

```
Object
└Throwable ------------------------------ Serializable⌄
  └Exception
    └IOException
1.1 O     └ObjectStreamException
1.1         └StreamCorruptedException
```

*	public.....................	**StreamCorruptedException** ()
*	public.....................	**StreamCorruptedException** (String reason)

StreamHandler | java.util.logging

ε400

```
Object
1.4 O └Handler 1
1.4     └StreamHandler⌄
```

1	public synchronized ...... **void**	**close** () throws SecurityException	
1	public synchronized ...... **void**	**flush** ()	
1	public.....................String	getEncoding ()	
1	public............ErrorManager	getErrorManager ()	
1	public.....................Filter	getFilter ()	
1	public.................Formatter	getFormatter ()	
1	public synchronized ..... Level	getLevel ()	
1	public.................**boolean**	**isLoggable** (LogRecord record)	
1	public synchronized ...... **void**	**publish** (LogRecord record)	ε393
1	protected ....void	reportError (String msg, Exception ex, int code)	
1	public.....................**void**	**setEncoding** (String encoding) throws SecurityException, java.io.UnsupportedEncodingException	
1	public.....................void	setErrorManager (ErrorManager em)	
1	public.....................void	setFilter (Filter newFilter) throws SecurityException	ε394
1	public.....................void	setFormatter (Formatter newFormatter) throws SecurityException	ε399,400
1	public synchronized ....void	setLevel (Level newLevel) throws SecurityException	
	protected synchronized ...void	**setOutputStream** (java.io.OutputStream out) throws SecurityException	
*	public.........................	**StreamHandler** ()	
*	public.........................	**StreamHandler** (java.io.OutputStream out, Formatter formatter)	

StreamResult | javax.xml.transform.stream

```
Object
1.4 └StreamResult ------------------------- javax.xml.transform.Result 1
```

▲	public static final ....String	**FEATURE** = "http://javax.xml.transform.stream.StreamResult/feature"	
	public.... java.io.OutputStream	**getOutputStream** ()	
1	public.....................String	**getSystemId** ()	
	public............. java.io.Writer	**getWriter** ()	
	public.....................void	**setOutputStream** (java.io.OutputStream outputStream)	
	public.....................void	**setSystemId** (java.io.File f)	
1	public.....................void	**setSystemId** (String systemId)	
	public.....................void	**setWriter** (java.io.Writer writer)	
*	public.........................	**StreamResult** ()	
*	public.........................	**StreamResult** (java.io.File f)	ε518,519,520
*	public.........................	**StreamResult** (java.io.OutputStream outputStream)	ε521
*	public.........................	**StreamResult** (java.io.Writer writer)	
*	public.........................	**StreamResult** (String systemId)	

StreamSource | javax.xml.transform.stream

```
Object
1.4 └StreamSource ------------------------- javax.xml.transform.Source 1
```

▲	public static final ....String	**FEATURE** = "http://javax.xml.transform.stream.StreamSource/feature"	
	public...... java.io.InputStream	**getInputStream** ()	
	public.....................String	**getPublicId** ()	
	public............. java.io.Reader	**getReader** ()	
1	public.....................String	**getSystemId** ()	
	public.....................void	**setInputStream** (java.io.InputStream inputStream)	
	public.....................void	**setPublicId** (String publicId)	

S

Classes

StreamSource

	public.....................void	**setReader** (java.io.Reader reader)	
	public.....................void	**setSystemId** (java.io.File f)	
1	public.....................void	**setSystemId** (String systemId)	ε523
✳	public.........................	**StreamSource** ()	
✳	public.........................	**StreamSource** (java.io.File f)	
✳	public.........................	**StreamSource** (java.io.InputStream inputStream)	ε521,522
✳	public.........................	**StreamSource** (java.io.Reader reader)	
✳	public.........................	**StreamSource** (String systemId)	
✳	public.........................	**StreamSource** (java.io.InputStream inputStream, String systemId)	
✳	public.........................	**StreamSource** (java.io.Reader reader, String systemId)	

StreamTokenizer   java.io

Object[1]
└ StreamTokenizer

	public.....................void	**commentChar** (int ch)	
	public.....................void	**eolIsSignificant** (boolean flag)	ε47
	public......................int	**lineno** ()	
	public.....................void	**lowerCaseMode** (boolean fl)	
	public......................int	**nextToken** () throws IOException	ε47
	public...................double	**nval**	ε47
	public.....................void	**ordinaryChar** (int ch)	
	public.....................void	**ordinaryChars** (int low, int hi)	ε47
	public.....................void	**parseNumbers** ()	ε47
	public.....................void	**pushBack** ()	
	public.....................void	**quoteChar** (int ch)	
	public.....................void	**resetSyntax** ()	
	public.....................void	**slashSlashComments** (boolean flag)	ε47
	public.....................void	**slashStarComments** (boolean flag)	ε47
D ✳	public.........................	**StreamTokenizer** (InputStream is)	
1.1 ✳	public.........................	**StreamTokenizer** (Reader r)	ε47
	public...................String	**sval**	ε47
1	public.............**String toString** ()	
▲	public static final............int	**TT_EOF** = -1	ε47
▲	public static final............int	**TT_EOL** = 10	ε47
▲	public static final............int	**TT_NUMBER** = -2	ε47
▲	public static final............int	**TT_WORD** = -3	ε47
	public......................int	**ttype**	ε47
	public.....................void	**whitespaceChars** (int low, int hi)	
	public.....................void	**wordChars** (int low, int hi)	ε47

StrictMath   java.lang

Object
1.3 ● └ StrictMath

△	public static strictfp.....double	**abs** (double a)	
△	public static strictfp........float	**abs** (float a)	
△	public static strictfp..........int	**abs** (int a)	
△	public static strictfp....... long	**abs** (long a)	
△	public static native strictfp ....double	**acos** (double a)	
△	public static native strictfp ....double	**asin** (double a)	
△	public static native strictfp ....double	**atan** (double a)	
△	public static native strictfp ....double	**atan2** (double y, double x)	
△	public static native strictfp ....double	**ceil** (double a)	
△	public static native strictfp ....double	**cos** (double a)	
▲	public static final........double	**E** = 2.718281828459045	
△	public static native strictfp ....double	**exp** (double a)	
△	public static native strictfp ....double	**floor** (double a)	

Class   *Interface* —extends   - - -implements   ○ abstract   ● final   △ static   ▲ static final   ✳ constructor   x x—inherited   x **x**—declared   **x x**—overridden
ε*n*—examples of usage   ⌐—has subclass   package—see other volume

△	public static native strictfp .... double	**IEEEremainder** (double f1, double f2)		
△	public static native strictfp .... double	**log** (double a)		
△	public static strictfp .....double	**max** (double a, double b)		
△	public static strictfp ....float	**max** (float a, float b)		
△	public static strictfp .... int	**max** (int a, int b)		
△	public static strictfp .... long	**max** (long a, long b)		
△	public static strictfp .....double	**min** (double a, double b)		
△	public static strictfp ....float	**min** (float a, float b)		
△	public static strictfp .... int	**min** (int a, int b)		
△	public static strictfp .... long	**min** (long a, long b)		
▲	public static final........double	**PI** = 3.141592653589793		
△	public static native strictfp .... double	**pow** (double a, double b)		
△	public static strictfp .....double	**random** ()		
△	public static native strictfp .... double	**rint** (double a)		
△	public static strictfp .... long	**round** (double a)		
△	public static strictfp ....int	**round** (float a)		
△	public static native strictfp .... double	**sin** (double a)		
△	public static native strictfp .... double	**sqrt** (double a)		
△	public static native strictfp .... double	**tan** (double a)		
△	public static strictfp .....double	**toDegrees** (double angrad)		
△	public static strictfp .....double	**toRadians** (double angdeg)		

String java.lang

	Object[1]		ε59,66,69,70,83
●	└String - *java.io.Serializable*˽, *Comparable*[2], *CharSequence*[3]		

S

1.2 ▲	public static final .... *java.util.Comparator*	**CASE_INSENSITIVE_ORDER**		ε109,350,359
	3 public............ char	**charAt** (int index)		ε81,442
1.2	2 public....................int	**compareTo** (Object o)		ε53
	public....................int	**compareTo** (String anotherString)		ε71
1.2	public....................int	**compareToIgnoreCase** (String str)		ε71
	public....................String	**concat** (String str)		
1.4	public.................. boolean	**contentEquals** (StringBuffer sb)		ε71
△	public static ....String	**copyValueOf** (char[] data)		
△	public static ....String	**copyValueOf** (char[] data, int offset, int count)		
	public.................. boolean	**endsWith** (String suffix)		ε72
	1 public.................. **boolean**	**equals** (Object anObject)		ε71,9,215,241,407
	public.................. boolean	**equalsIgnoreCase** (String anotherString)		ε71,141
1.1	public....................byte[]	**getBytes** ()		ε91,260,449,456
1.1	public....................byte[]	**getBytes** (String charsetName) throws java.io.UnsupportedEncodingException		
				ε79,382,462,464,469
D	public....................void	**getBytes** (int srcBegin, int srcEnd, byte[] dst, int dstBegin)		
	public....................void	**getChars** (int srcBegin, int srcEnd, char[] dst, int dstBegin)		
	1 public.................... **int**	**hashCode** ()		ε215
	public....................int	**indexOf** (int ch)		ε74,141,194
	public....................int	**indexOf** (String str)		ε72,74,541,546
	public....................int	**indexOf** (int ch, int fromIndex)		
	public....................int	**indexOf** (String str, int fromIndex)		ε76
	public native ....String	**intern** ()		
	public....................int	**lastIndexOf** (int ch)		ε60,74
	public....................int	**lastIndexOf** (String str)		ε74
	public....................int	**lastIndexOf** (int ch, int fromIndex)		
	public....................int	**lastIndexOf** (String str, int fromIndex)		
	3 public....................int	**length** ()		ε76,81,109,131,194
1.4	public.................. boolean	**matches** (String regex)		ε72
	public.................. boolean	**regionMatches** (int toffset, String other, int ooffset, int len)		
	public.................. boolean	**regionMatches** (boolean ignoreCase, int toffset, String other, int ooffset, int len)		
	public....................String	**replace** (char oldChar, char newChar)		ε75,60,230,231
1.4	public....................String	**replaceAll** (String regex, String replacement)		
1.4	public....................String	**replaceFirst** (String regex, String replacement)		
1.4	public....................String[]	**split** (String regex)		ε431,141,157,194,215
1.4	public....................String[]	**split** (String regex, int limit)		ε431
	public.................. boolean	**startsWith** (String prefix)		ε72,31,194
	public.................. boolean	**startsWith** (String prefix, int toffset)		

Classes

String

StringBuffer

java.lang

Object[1]
└ StringBuffer - *java.io.Serializable*◡, *CharSequence*[2]

Class   *Interface*   —extends   - - -implements   ○ abstract   ● final   △ static   ▲ static final   ✳ constructor   x x—inherited   x **x**—declared   **x x**—overridden
ε*n*—examples of usage   ◡—has subclass   package—see other volume

772

		public synchronized .... StringBuffer	**insert** (int offset, char c)	
		public synchronized .... StringBuffer	**insert** (int offset, String str)	ε70
		public.............. StringBuffer	**insert** (int offset, double d)	
		public synchronized .... StringBuffer	**insert** (int offset, Object obj)	
		public.............. StringBuffer	**insert** (int offset, float f)	
1.2		public synchronized .... StringBuffer	**insert** (int index, char[] str, int offset, int len)	
1.4		public synchronized ....int	**lastIndexOf** (String str)	
1.4		public synchronized ....int	**lastIndexOf** (String str, int fromIndex)	
	2	public synchronized ....int	**length** ()	ε76,81,109,131,194
1.2		public synchronized .... StringBuffer	**replace** (int start, int end, String str)	ε70
		public synchronized .... StringBuffer	**reverse** ()	
		public synchronized ....void	**setCharAt** (int index, char ch)	ε70
		public synchronized ....void	**setLength** (int newLength)	
*		public.........................	**StringBuffer** ()	ε76,382,400,430
*		public.........................	**StringBuffer** (int length)	ε400
*		public.........................	**StringBuffer** (String str)	ε70,71
1.4	2	public...........*CharSequence*	**subSequence** (int start, int end)	ε164,437
1.2		public synchronized .....String	**substring** (int start)	
1.2		public synchronized .....String	**substring** (int start, int end)	
	1	public.................. **String**	**toString** ()	ε70,76,131,133,382

StringBufferInputStream

		Object		ε252,382,418
○		└InputStream [1]		
D		└StringBufferInputStream		
D	1	public synchronized .... **int**	**available** ()	
D		protected ....String	**buffer**	
D	1	public.....................void	close () throws IOException	ε14,36,45,452,455
D		protected ....int	**count**	
D	1	public synchronized ......void	mark (int readlimit)	
D	1	public................. boolean	markSupported ()	
D		protected ....int	**pos**	
D	1	public synchronized .... **int**	**read** ()	ε90,184,256
D	1	public.......................int	read (byte[] b) throws IOException	ε452,455,457,170,451
D	1	public synchronized .... **int**	**read** (byte[] b, int off, int len)	ε36
D	1	public synchronized ...... **void**	**reset** ()	
D	1	public synchronized ...... **long**	**skip** (long n)	
D	*	public.........................	**StringBufferInputStream** (String s)	

StringCharacterIterator

		Object [1]		
1.1 ●		└StringCharacterIterator ------------------ *CharacterIterator* [2] (*Cloneable*)		
	1	public....................**Object**	**clone** ()	
	2	public..................... char	**current** ()	ε307
	1	public.................**boolean**	**equals** (Object obj)	
	2	public..................... char	**first** ()	ε307
	2	public.....................int	**getBeginIndex** ()	
	2	public.....................int	**getEndIndex** ()	
	2	public.....................int	**getIndex** ()	ε307
	1	public................. **int**	**hashCode** ()	
	2	public..................... char	**last** ()	ε307
	2	public..................... char	**next** ()	ε307
	2	public..................... char	**previous** ()	ε307
	2	public..................... char	**setIndex** (int p)	ε307
1.2		public.....................void	**setText** (String text)	ε307
	*	public.........................	**StringCharacterIterator** (String text)	ε307
	*	public.........................	**StringCharacterIterator** (String text, int pos)	
	*	public.........................	**StringCharacterIterator** (String text, int begin, int end, int pos)	ε307

StringHolder

StringHolder					org.omg.CORBA

Object
└ StringHolder - *org.omg.CORBA.portable.Streamable*⌣ [1]

1.2 ●

1	public.....................void	**_read** (org.omg.CORBA.portable.InputStream input)
1	public...................TypeCode	**_type** ()
1	public.....................void	**_write** (org.omg.CORBA.portable.OutputStream output)
✳	public...........................	**StringHolder** ()
✳	public...........................	**StringHolder** (String initial)
	public....................String	**value**

StringIndexOutOfBoundsException					java.lang

Object
└ Throwable - *java.io.Serializable*⌣
  └ Exception
    └ RuntimeException
      └ IndexOutOfBoundsException
        └ StringIndexOutOfBoundsException

✳	public...........................	**StringIndexOutOfBoundsException** ()
✳	public...........................	**StringIndexOutOfBoundsException** (int index)
✳	public...........................	**StringIndexOutOfBoundsException** (String s)

StringNameHelper				org.omg.CosNaming.NamingContextExtPackage	

Object
└ StringNameHelper

1.4 ○

△	public static ....String	**extract** (org.omg.CORBA.Any a)
△	public static ....String	**id** ()
△	public static ....void	**insert** (org.omg.CORBA.Any a, String that)
△	public static ....String	**read** (org.omg.CORBA.portable.InputStream istream)
✳	public...........................	**StringNameHelper** ()
△	public static synchronized .... . org.omg.CORBA.TypeCode	**type** ()
△	public static ....void	**write** (org.omg.CORBA.portable.OutputStream ostream, String value)

StringReader					java.io

Object
└ Reader [1]
  └ StringReader

1.1 ○
1.1

1	public..................... **void**	**close** ()	ε35,47,135,136,139
1	protected ....Object	lock	
1	public..................... **void**	**mark** (int readAheadLimit) throws IOException	
1	public.................. **boolean**	**markSupported** ()	ε442
1	public..................... **int**	**read** () throws IOException	
1	public.......................int	read (char[] cbuf) throws IOException	ε434
1	public..................... **int**	**read** (char[] cbuf, int off, int len) throws IOException	
1	public.................. **boolean**	**ready** () throws IOException	ε442
1	public..................... **void**	**reset** () throws IOException	
1	public..................... **long**	**skip** (long ns) throws IOException	
✳	public...........................	**StringReader** (String s)	ε512

StringRefAddr					javax.naming

Object
└ RefAddr [1] - *java.io.Serializable*⌣
  └ StringRefAddr

1.3 ○
1.3

1	protected ....String	addrType
1	public.................. boolean	equals (Object obj)
1	public.................. **Object**	**getContent** ()

Class *Interface* —extends - - -implements ○ abstract ● final △ static ▲ static final ✳ constructor x x—inherited x **x**—declared **x x**—overridden
ε*n*—examples of usage ⌣—has subclass package—see other volume

1	public	String	getType ()
1	public	int	hashCode ()
*	public		**StringRefAddr** (String addrType, String addr)
1	public	String	toString ()

StringSeqHelper — org.omg.CORBA

Object
1.4 ○ └StringSeqHelper

△	public static	String[]	**extract** (Any a)
△	public static	String	**id** ()
△	public static	void	**insert** (Any a, String[] that)
△	public static	String[]	**read** (org.omg.CORBA.portable.InputStream istream)
*	public		**StringSeqHelper** ()
△	public static synchronized TypeCode		**type** ()
△	public static	void	**write** (org.omg.CORBA.portable.OutputStream ostream, String[] value)

StringSeqHolder — org.omg.CORBA

Object
1.4 ● └StringSeqHolder ------------------------ *org.omg.CORBA.portable.Streamable* [1]

1	public	void	**_read** (org.omg.CORBA.portable.InputStream i)
1	public	TypeCode	**_type** ()
1	public	void	**_write** (org.omg.CORBA.portable.OutputStream o)
*	public		**StringSeqHolder** ()
*	public		**StringSeqHolder** (String[] initialValue)
	public	String[]	**value**

StringTokenizer — java.util

Object
└StringTokenizer ------------------------ *Enumeration* [1]

	public	int	**countTokens** ()	
1	public	boolean	**hasMoreElements** ()	ε454,88,208,217,218
	public	boolean	**hasMoreTokens** ()	ε332
1	public	Object	**nextElement** ()	ε454,88,208,217,218
	public	String	**nextToken** ()	ε332
	public	String	**nextToken** (String delim)	
*	public		**StringTokenizer** (String str)	ε332
*	public		**StringTokenizer** (String str, String delim)	
*	public		**StringTokenizer** (String str, String delim, boolean returnDelims)	

StringValueHelper — org.omg.CORBA

Object
1.3 └StringValueHelper ---------------------- *org.omg.CORBA.portable.BoxedValueHelper* [1]

△	public static	String	**extract** (Any a)
1	public	String	**get_id** ()
△	public static	String	**id** ()
△	public static	void	**insert** (Any a, String that)
△	public static	String	**read** (org.omg.CORBA.portable.InputStream istream)
1	public	*java.io.Serializable*	**read_value** (org.omg.CORBA.portable.InputStream istream)
*	public		**StringValueHelper** ()
△	public static synchronized TypeCode		**type** ()
△	public static	void	**write** (org.omg.CORBA.portable.OutputStream ostream, String value)
1	public	void	**write_value** (org.omg.CORBA.portable.OutputStream ostream, *java.io.Serializable* value)

S

Classes

StringWriter

StringWriter					java.io

```
      Object¹
1.1 ○  └Writer²
1.1       └StringWriter
```

2	public..................... **void**	**close** () throws IOException		ε23,37,38,41,43
2	public..................... **void**	**flush** ()		ε135,150,224
	public.............. StringBuffer	**getBuffer** ()		
2	protected................Object	lock		
✳	public.........................	**StringWriter** ()		
✳	public.........................	**StringWriter** (int initialSize)		
1	public............... **String**	**toString** ()		
2	public.....................void	write (char[] cbuf) throws IOException		
2	public..................... **void**	**write** (int c)		
2	public..................... **void**	**write** (String str)		ε23,37,38,41,43
2	public..................... **void**	**write** (char[] cbuf, int off, int len)		
2	public..................... **void**	**write** (String str, int off, int len)		

Struct	java.sql

```
1.2   Struct
```

public................. Object[]	**getAttributes** () throws SQLException
public................. Object[]	**getAttributes** (*java.util.Map* map) throws SQLException
public.................String	**getSQLTypeName** () throws SQLException

StructMember	org.omg.CORBA

```
      Object
1.2 ●  └StructMember ------------------------- org.omg.CORBA.portable.IDLEntity ↘ (java.io.Serializable)
```

	public.................... String	**name**
✳	public.........................	**StructMember** ()
✳	public.........................	**StructMember** (String __name, TypeCode __type, *IDLType* __type_def)
	public...............TypeCode	**type**
	public.................*IDLType*	**type_def**

StructMemberHelper	org.omg.CORBA

```
      Object
1.3 ○  └StructMemberHelper
```

△	public static .....StructMember	**extract** (Any a)
△	public static ....String	**id** ()
△	public static ....void	**insert** (Any a, StructMember that)
△	public static .....StructMember	**read** (org.omg.CORBA.portable.InputStream istream)
✳	public.........................	**StructMemberHelper** ()
△	public static synchronized	**type** ()
	.....................TypeCode	
△	public static ....void	**write** (org.omg.CORBA.portable.OutputStream ostream, StructMember value)

Stub	javax.rmi.CORBA

```
      Object
1.2 ○  └org.omg.CORBA.portable.ObjectImpl¹ ------ org.omg.CORBA.Object ↘
1.3 ○    └org.omg.CORBA_2_3.portable.ObjectImpl²
1.3 ○       └Stub ↘ ---------------------------- java.io.Serializable ↘
```

1	public.........................	**_create_request** (org.omg.CORBA.Context ctx, String operation,
	....org.omg.CORBA.Request	org.omg.CORBA.NVList arg_list, org.omg.CORBA.NamedValue result)
1	public.........................	**_create_request** (org.omg.CORBA.Context ctx, String operation,
	....org.omg.CORBA.Request	org.omg.CORBA.NVList arg_list, org.omg.CORBA.NamedValue result, org↵
		.omg.CORBA.ExceptionList exceptions, org.omg.CORBA.ContextList contexts)
1	public *org.omg.CORBA.Object*	**_duplicate** ()
2	public.................... String	**_get_codebase** ()

Class   *Interface* —extends   - - -implements   ○ abstract   ● final   △ static   ▲ static final   ✳ constructor   x x—inherited   x **x**—declared   **x x**—overridden
ε*n*—examples of usage   ↘—has subclass   package—see other volume

S

	1	public . . . . org.omg↵ .CORBA.portable.Delegate	_get_delegate ()
	1	public . . . . *org.omg*↵ *.CORBA.DomainManager[]*	_get_domain_managers ()
	1	public *org.omg.CORBA.Object*	_get_interface_def ()
	1	public . *org.omg.CORBA.Policy*	_get_policy (int policy_type)
	1	public .int	_hash (int maximum)
O	1	public abstract . . . . String[]	_ids ()
	1	public . . . . . . org.omg.CORBA↵ .portable.InputStream	_invoke (org.omg.CORBA.portable.OutputStream output) throws org.omg.CORBA↵ .portable.ApplicationException, org.omg.CORBA.portable.RemarshalException
	1	public . . . . boolean	_is_a (String repository_id)
	1	public . . . . boolean	_is_equivalent (*org.omg.CORBA.Object* that)
	1	public . . . . boolean	_is_local ()
	1	public . . . . boolean	_non_existent ()
	1	public . . .org.omg.CORBA.ORB	_orb ()
	1	public .void	_release ()
	1	public .void	_releaseReply (org.omg.CORBA.portable.InputStream input)
	1	public . . . . .org.omg.CORBA.Request	_request (String operation)
	1	public . . . . org.omg.CORBA↵ .portable.OutputStream	_request (String operation, boolean responseExpected)
	1	public .void	_servant_postinvoke (org.omg.CORBA.portable.ServantObject servant)
	1	public . . . . . . org.omg.CORBA↵ .portable.ServantObject	_servant_preinvoke (String operation, Class expectedType)
	1	public .void	_set_delegate (org.omg.CORBA.portable.Delegate delegate)
	1	public *org.omg.CORBA.Object*	_set_policy_override (*org.omg.CORBA.Policy[]* policies, org.omg.CORBA.SetOverrideType set_add)
		public .void	**connect** (org.omg.CORBA.ORB orb) throws java.rmi.RemoteException
	1	public . . . . **boolean**	**equals** (Object obj)
	1	public . . . . **int**	**hashCode** ()
*		public	**Stub** ()
	1	public . . . . **String**	**toString** ()

StubDelegate   javax.rmi.CORBA

1.3	*StubDelegate*

public. .void	**connect** (Stub self, org.omg.CORBA.ORB orb) throws java.rmi.RemoteException
public. . . . . boolean	**equals** (Stub self, Object obj)
public. . . . . .int	**hashCode** (Stub self)
public. .void	**readObject** (Stub self, java.io.ObjectInputStream s) throws java.io.IOException, ClassNotFoundException
public. . . . . String	**toString** (Stub self)
public. .void	**writeObject** (Stub self, java.io.ObjectOutputStream s) throws java.io.IOException

---

StubNotFoundException   java.rmi

```
Object
└Throwable ------------------------------ java.io.Serializable
    └Exception
        └java.io.IOException
```
1.1	`        └RemoteException`[1]
1.1	`            └StubNotFoundException`

	1	public . . . . Throwable	detail
1.4	1	public . . . . Throwable	getCause ()
	1	public . . . . String	getMessage ()
*		public	**StubNotFoundException** (String s)
*		public	**StubNotFoundException** (String s, Exception ex)

Subject   javax.security.auth

```
Object[1]
```
1.4 ●	`└Subject ------------------------------ java.io.Serializable`

△	public static . . . . Object	**doAs** (Subject subject, *java.security.PrivilegedExceptionAction* action) throws java.security.PrivilegedActionException
△	public static . . . . Object	**doAs** (Subject subject, *java.security.PrivilegedAction* action)
△	public static . . . . Object	**doAsPrivileged** (Subject subject, *java.security.PrivilegedAction* action, java.security.AccessControlContext acc)

Subject

△	public static ....Object	**doAsPrivileged** (Subject subject, *java.security.PrivilegedExceptionAction* action, java.security.AccessControlContext acc) throws java.security.PrivilegedActionException	
1	public.....................**boolean**	**equals** (Object o)	
	public..............*java.util.Set*	**getPrincipals** ()	ε508
	public..............*java.util.Set*	**getPrincipals** (Class c)	
	public..............*java.util.Set*	**getPrivateCredentials** ()	
	public..............*java.util.Set*	**getPrivateCredentials** (Class c)	
	public..............*java.util.Set*	**getPublicCredentials** ()	
	public..............*java.util.Set*	**getPublicCredentials** (Class c)	
△	public static ....Subject	**getSubject** (java.security.AccessControlContext acc)	
1	public.........................**int**	**hashCode** ()	
	public..................boolean	**isReadOnly** ()	
	public.........................void	**setReadOnly** ()	
*	public.............................	**Subject** ()	
*	public.............................	**Subject** (boolean readOnly, *java.util.Set* principals, *java.util.Set* pubCredentials, *java.util.Set* privCredentials)	
1	public...................**String**	**toString** ()	

SubjectDomainCombiner   javax.security.auth

Object
1.4 └ SubjectDomainCombiner - - - - - - - - - - - - - - - - - *java.security.DomainCombiner* [1]

1	public..................... java↩ .security.ProtectionDomain[]	**combine** (java.security.ProtectionDomain[] currentDomains, java.security.ProtectionDomain[] assignedDomains)	
	public...................Subject	**getSubject** ()	
*	public.............................	**SubjectDomainCombiner** (Subject subject)	

SUCCESSFUL   org.omg.PortableInterceptor

1.4   *SUCCESSFUL*

▲	public static final..........short	**value** = 0

SYNC_WITH_TRANSPORT   org.omg.Messaging

1.4   *SYNC_WITH_TRANSPORT*

▲	public static final..........short	**value** = 1

SyncFailedException   java.io

Object
└ Throwable - *Serializable*
  └ Exception
    └ IOException
1.1   └ SyncFailedException

*	public.........................	**SyncFailedException** (String desc)

SyncScopeHelper   org.omg.Messaging

Object
1.4 ○ └ SyncScopeHelper

△	public static ....short	**extract** (org.omg.CORBA.Any a)
△	public static ....String	**id** ()
△	public static ....void	**insert** (org.omg.CORBA.Any a, short that)
△	public static ....short	**read** (org.omg.CORBA.portable.InputStream istream)
*	public.............................	**SyncScopeHelper** ()
△	public static synchronized .... org.omg.CORBA.TypeCode	**type** ()
△	public static ....void	**write** (org.omg.CORBA.portable.OutputStream ostream, short value)

Class   *Interface*   —extends   - - -implements   ○ abstract   ● final   △ static   ▲ static final   * constructor   x x—inherited   x **x**—declared   **x x**—overridden
ε*n*—examples of usage   ˔—has subclass   package—see other volume

System				java.lang

		Object └System		
●			

△	public static native . . . . void	**arraycopy** (Object src, int srcPos, Object dest, int destPos, int length)	ε84,85,124
△	public static native . . . . long	**currentTimeMillis** ()	ε51,26,259,367
▲	public static final . . . . java.io.PrintStream	**err**	ε54
△	public static . . . . void	**exit** (int status)	ε49
△	public static . . . . void	**gc** ()	
D △	public static . . . . String	**getenv** (String name)	
△	public static java.util.Properties	**getProperties** ()	ε88
△	public static . . . . String	**getProperty** (String key)	ε218,69,86,87,28
△	public static . . . . String	**getProperty** (String key, String def)	
△	public static . SecurityManager	**getSecurityManager** ()	
1.1 △	public static native . . . . int	**identityHashCode** (Object x)	ε57
▲	public static final . . . . java.io.InputStream	**in**	ε34
△	public static . . . . void	**load** (String filename)	
△	public static . . . . void	**loadLibrary** (String libname)	ε52
1.2 △	public static native . . . . . . String	**mapLibraryName** (String libname)	
▲	public static final . . . . java.io.PrintStream	**out**	ε54,44,211,499
△	public static . . . . void	**runFinalization** ()	
D △	public static . . . . void	**runFinalizersOnExit** (boolean value)	
1.1 △	public static . . . . void	**setErr** (java.io.PrintStream err)	ε54
1.1 △	public static . . . . void	**setIn** (java.io.InputStream in)	
1.1 △	public static . . . . void	**setOut** (java.io.PrintStream out)	ε54
△	public static . . . . void	**setProperties** (java.util.Properties props)	
1.2 △	public static . . . . String	**setProperty** (String key, String value)	ε86,212
△	public static . . . . void	**setSecurityManager** (SecurityManager s)	ε212

SYSTEM_EXCEPTION		org.omg.PortableInterceptor

1.4	*SYSTEM_EXCEPTION*	
▲	public static final . . . . short **value** = 1	

SystemException		org.omg.CORBA

	Object └Throwable [1] - *java.io.Serializable* 　└Exception 　　└RuntimeException
1.2 ○	└SystemException

	public . . . . CompletionStatus	**completed**	
	public . . . . int	**minor**	
*	protected	**SystemException** (String reason, int minor, CompletionStatus completed)	
1	public . . . . String	**toString** ()	

TAG_ALTERNATE_IIOP_ADDRESS		org.omg.IOP

1.4	*TAG_ALTERNATE_IIOP_ADDRESS*	
▲	public static final . . . . int **value** = 3	

TAG_CODE_SETS		org.omg.IOP

1.4	*TAG_CODE_SETS*	
▲	public static final . . . . int **value** = 1	

T

Classes

TAG_INTERNET_IOP | org.omg.IOP

1.4	*TAG_INTERNET_IOP*
▲	public static final .... int **value** = 0

TAG_JAVA_CODEBASE | org.omg.IOP

1.4	*TAG_JAVA_CODEBASE*
▲	public static final .... int **value** = 25

TAG_MULTIPLE_COMPONENTS | org.omg.IOP

1.4	*TAG_MULTIPLE_COMPONENTS*
▲	public static final .... int **value** = 1

TAG_ORB_TYPE | org.omg.IOP

1.4	*TAG_ORB_TYPE*
▲	public static final .... int **value** = 0

TAG_POLICIES | org.omg.IOP

1.4	*TAG_POLICIES*
▲	public static final .... int **value** = 2

T

TaggedComponent | org.omg.IOP

Object
└ TaggedComponent - *org.omg.CORBA.portable.IDLEntity* ⌐ (*java.io.Serializable*)

1.4 ●		
	public .... byte[]	**component_data**
	public .... int	**tag**
✳	public	**TaggedComponent** ()
✳	public	**TaggedComponent** (int _tag, byte[] _component_data)

TaggedComponentHelper | org.omg.IOP

Object
└ TaggedComponentHelper

1.4 ○		
△	public static	**extract** (org.omg.CORBA.Any a)
	.... TaggedComponent	
△	public static .... String	**id** ()
△	public static .... void	**insert** (org.omg.CORBA.Any a, TaggedComponent that)
△	public static	**read** (org.omg.CORBA.portable.InputStream istream)
	.... TaggedComponent	
✳	public	**TaggedComponentHelper** ()
△	public static synchronized	**type** ()
	. org.omg.CORBA.TypeCode	
△	public static .... void	**write** (org.omg.CORBA.portable.OutputStream ostream, TaggedComponent value)

TaggedComponentHolder | org.omg.IOP

Object
└ TaggedComponentHolder - - - - - - - - - - - - - - - - - *org.omg.CORBA.portable.Streamable* ⌐ [1]

1.4 ●		
1	public .... void	**_read** (org.omg.CORBA.portable.InputStream i)
1	public	**_type** ()
	. org.omg.CORBA.TypeCode	
1	public .... void	**_write** (org.omg.CORBA.portable.OutputStream o)

Class   *Interface*   —extends   - - -implements   ○ abstract   ● final   △ static   ▲ static final   ✳ constructor   x x—inherited   x **x**—declared   **x x**—overridden
εn—examples of usage   ⌐—has subclass   package —see other volume

*	public		**TaggedComponentHolder** ()
*	public		**TaggedComponentHolder** (TaggedComponent initialValue)
	public	TaggedComponent	**value**

TaggedProfile
org.omg.IOP

Object
1.4 ● └TaggedProfile - *org.omg.CORBA.portable.IDLEntity* ، (*java.io.Serializable*)

	public	byte[]	**profile_data**
	public	int	**tag**
*	public		**TaggedProfile** ()
*	public		**TaggedProfile** (int _tag, byte[] _profile_data)

TaggedProfileHelper
org.omg.IOP

Object
1.4 ○ └TaggedProfileHelper

△	public static	TaggedProfile	**extract** (org.omg.CORBA.Any a)
△	public static	String	**id** ()
△	public static	void	**insert** (org.omg.CORBA.Any a, TaggedProfile that)
△	public static	TaggedProfile	**read** (org.omg.CORBA.portable.InputStream istream)
*	public		**TaggedProfileHelper** ()
△	public static synchronized org.omg.CORBA.TypeCode		**type** ()
△	public static	void	**write** (org.omg.CORBA.portable.OutputStream ostream, TaggedProfile value)

TaggedProfileHolder
org.omg.IOP

Object
1.4 ● └TaggedProfileHolder - *org.omg.CORBA.portable.Streamable* ، [1]

1	public	void	**_read** (org.omg.CORBA.portable.InputStream i)
1	public		**_type** ()
	. org.omg.CORBA.TypeCode		
1	public	void	**_write** (org.omg.CORBA.portable.OutputStream o)
*	public		**TaggedProfileHolder** ()
*	public		**TaggedProfileHolder** (TaggedProfile initialValue)
	public	TaggedProfile	**value**

TCKind
org.omg.CORBA

Object
1.2 └TCKind

▲	public static final	int	**_tk_abstract_interface** = 32
▲	public static final	int	**_tk_alias** = 21
▲	public static final	int	**_tk_any** = 11
▲	public static final	int	**_tk_array** = 20
▲	public static final	int	**_tk_boolean** = 8
▲	public static final	int	**_tk_char** = 9
▲	public static final	int	**_tk_double** = 7
▲	public static final	int	**_tk_enum** = 17
▲	public static final	int	**_tk_except** = 22
▲	public static final	int	**_tk_fixed** = 28
▲	public static final	int	**_tk_float** = 6
▲	public static final	int	**_tk_long** = 3
▲	public static final	int	**_tk_longdouble** = 25
▲	public static final	int	**_tk_longlong** = 23
▲	public static final	int	**_tk_native** = 31
▲	public static final	int	**_tk_null** = 0
▲	public static final	int	**_tk_objref** = 14
▲	public static final	int	**_tk_octet** = 10
▲	public static final	int	**_tk_Principal** = 13
▲	public static final	int	**_tk_sequence** = 19
▲	public static final	int	**_tk_short** = 2
▲	public static final	int	**_tk_string** = 18
▲	public static final	int	**_tk_struct** = 15
▲	public static final	int	**_tk_TypeCode** = 12

T

Classes

TCKind

▲	public static final	int	**_tk_ulong**	= 5
▲	public static final	int	**_tk_ulonglong**	= 24
▲	public static final	int	**_tk_union**	= 16
▲	public static final	int	**_tk_ushort**	= 4
▲	public static final	int	**_tk_value**	= 29
▲	public static final	int	**_tk_value_box**	= 30
▲	public static final	int	**_tk_void**	= 1
▲	public static final	int	**_tk_wchar**	= 26
▲	public static final	int	**_tk_wstring**	= 27
△	public static	TCKind	**from_int** (int i)	
D ✳	protected		**TCKind** (int _value)	
▲	public static final	TCKind	**tk_abstract_interface**	
▲	public static final	TCKind	**tk_alias**	
▲	public static final	TCKind	**tk_any**	
▲	public static final	TCKind	**tk_array**	
▲	public static final	TCKind	**tk_boolean**	
▲	public static final	TCKind	**tk_char**	
▲	public static final	TCKind	**tk_double**	
▲	public static final	TCKind	**tk_enum**	
▲	public static final	TCKind	**tk_except**	
▲	public static final	TCKind	**tk_fixed**	
▲	public static final	TCKind	**tk_float**	
▲	public static final	TCKind	**tk_long**	
▲	public static final	TCKind	**tk_longdouble**	
▲	public static final	TCKind	**tk_longlong**	
▲	public static final	TCKind	**tk_native**	
▲	public static final	TCKind	**tk_null**	
▲	public static final	TCKind	**tk_objref**	
▲	public static final	TCKind	**tk_octet**	
▲	public static final	TCKind	**tk_Principal**	
▲	public static final	TCKind	**tk_sequence**	
▲	public static final	TCKind	**tk_short**	
▲	public static final	TCKind	**tk_string**	
▲	public static final	TCKind	**tk_struct**	
▲	public static final	TCKind	**tk_TypeCode**	
▲	public static final	TCKind	**tk_ulong**	
▲	public static final	TCKind	**tk_ulonglong**	
▲	public static final	TCKind	**tk_union**	
▲	public static final	TCKind	**tk_ushort**	
▲	public static final	TCKind	**tk_value**	
▲	public static final	TCKind	**tk_value_box**	
▲	public static final	TCKind	**tk_void**	
▲	public static final	TCKind	**tk_wchar**	
▲	public static final	TCKind	**tk_wstring**	
	public	int	**value** ()	

Templates	javax.xml.transform

1.4   *Templates*

- -

public .... java.util.Properties **getOutputProperties** ()
public .... Transformer **newTransformer** () throws TransformerConfigurationException *ε*521,522

- -

TemplatesHandler	javax.xml.transform.sax

1.4   *TemplatesHandler*————————————*org.xml.sax.ContentHandler* ¸ [1]

- -

1   public .... void   characters (char[] ch, int start, int length) throws org.xml.sax.SAXException
1   public .... void   endDocument () throws org.xml.sax.SAXException
1   public .... void   endElement (String namespaceURI, String localName, String qName)
                    throws org.xml.sax.SAXException
1   public .... void   endPrefixMapping (String prefix) throws org.xml.sax.SAXException
   public .... String   **getSystemId** ()
   public .... *javax*↵   **getTemplates** ()
      .xml.transform.Templates
1   public .... void   ignorableWhitespace (char[] ch, int start, int length)
                    throws org.xml.sax.SAXException
1   public .... void   processingInstruction (String target, String data) throws org.xml.sax.SAXException
1   public .... void   setDocumentLocator (*org.xml.sax.Locator* locator)   *ε*550

Class   *Interface*   —extends   - - -implements   ○ abstract   ● final   △ static   ▲ static final   ✳ constructor   x x—inherited   x **x**—declared   **x x**—overridden
ε n—examples of usage   ˎ—has subclass   package—see other volume

public	void	**setSystemId** (String systemID)
1 public	void	skippedEntity (String name) throws org.xml.sax.SAXException
1 public	void	startDocument () throws org.xml.sax.SAXException
1 public	void	startElement (String namespaceURI, String localName, String qName, *org.xml.sax.Attributes* atts) throws org.xml.sax.SAXException ε549,550
1 public	void	startPrefixMapping (String prefix, String uri) throws org.xml.sax.SAXException

---

Text — org.w3c.dom

1.4	*Text* ———————————— *CharacterData* [1] (*Node* [2])	ε530,543,545,524,526

2	*37 inherited members from Node not shown*		
1	public	void	appendData (String arg) throws DOMException	ε545
1	public	void	deleteData (int offset, int count) throws DOMException	ε545
1	public	String	getData () throws DOMException	ε546
1	public	int	getLength ()	ε545
1	public	void	insertData (int offset, String arg) throws DOMException	ε545
1	public	void	replaceData (int offset, int count, String arg) throws DOMException	ε545
1	public	void	setData (String data) throws DOMException	ε545
	public	*Text*	**splitText** (int offset) throws DOMException	ε546
1	public	String	substringData (int offset, int count) throws DOMException	ε545

TextInputCallback — javax.security.auth.callback

Object
└TextInputCallback ---------------------- *Callback* , *java.io.Serializable*

public	String	**getDefaultText** ()
public	String	**getPrompt** ()
public	String	**getText** ()
public	void	**setText** (String text)
* public		**TextInputCallback** (String prompt)
* public		**TextInputCallback** (String prompt, String defaultText)

TextOutputCallback — javax.security.auth.callback

Object
└TextOutputCallback ---------------------- *Callback* , *java.io.Serializable*

▲	public static final	int	**ERROR** = 2	ε509
	public	String	**getMessage** ()	ε509
	public	int	**getMessageType** ()	ε509
▲	public static final	int	**INFORMATION** = 0	ε509
*	public		**TextOutputCallback** (int messageType, String message)	
▲	public static final	int	**WARNING** = 1	ε509

Thread — java.lang

Object[1]
└Thread ----------------------------- *Runnable* [2]

△	public static	int	**activeCount** ()	
●	public final	void	**checkAccess** ()	
D	public native	int	**countStackFrames** ()	
△	public static native	Thread	**currentThread** ()	ε99
	public	void	**destroy** ()	
△	public static	void	**dumpStack** ()	
△	public static	int	**enumerate** (Thread[] tarray)	
1.2	public	ClassLoader	**getContextClassLoader** ()	
●	public final	String	**getName** ()	
●	public final	int	**getPriority** ()	
●	public final	ThreadGroup	**getThreadGroup** ()	ε99
1.4 △	public static native	boolean	**holdsLock** (Object obj)	ε97
	public	void	**interrupt** ()	
△	public static	boolean	**interrupted** ()	
●	public final native	boolean	**isAlive** ()	ε94
●	public final	boolean	**isDaemon** ()	
	public	boolean	**isInterrupted** ()	
●	public final	void	**join** () throws InterruptedException	ε94

T

Classes

Thread

	●	public final synchronized . . void	**join** (long millis) throws InterruptedException	ε94
	●	public final synchronized . . void	**join** (long millis, int nanos) throws InterruptedException	
	▲	public static final . . . . int	**MAX_PRIORITY** = 10	
	▲	public static final . . . . int	**MIN_PRIORITY** = 1	
	▲	public static final . . . . int	**NORM_PRIORITY** = 5	
D	●	public final . . . . void	**resume** ()	
	2	public . . . . void	**run** ()	ε92,93,50,96,98
1.2		public . . . . void	**setContextClassLoader** (ClassLoader cl)	
	●	public final . . . . void	**setDaemon** (boolean on)	ε98
	●	public final . . . . void	**setName** (String name)	
	●	public final . . . . void	**setPriority** (int newPriority)	
	△	public static native . . . . void	**sleep** (long millis) throws InterruptedException	ε69,95
	△	public static . . . . void	**sleep** (long millis, int nanos) throws InterruptedException	
		public synchronized native . . . void	**start** ()	ε92,94,98
		. . . . void		
D	●	public final . . . . void	**stop** ()	
D	●	public final synchronized . . void	**stop** (Throwable obj)	
D	●	public final . . . . void	**suspend** ()	
	✳	public	**Thread** ()	ε50,92
	✳	public	**Thread** (*Runnable* target)	ε92
	✳	public	**Thread** (String name)	
	✳	public	**Thread** (*Runnable* target, String name)	
	✳	public	**Thread** (ThreadGroup group, String name)	
	✳	public	**Thread** (ThreadGroup group, *Runnable* target)	
	✳	public	**Thread** (ThreadGroup group, *Runnable* target, String name)	
1.4	✳	public	**Thread** (ThreadGroup group, *Runnable* target, String name, long stackSize)	
	1	public . . . . **String**	**toString** ()	
	△	public static native . . . . void	**yield** ()	

THREAD_POLICY_ID		org.omg.PortableServer

1.4		*THREAD_POLICY_ID*
▲	public static final . . . . int	**value** = 16

ThreadDeath	java.lang

```
Object
└Throwable - - - - - - - - - - - - - - - - - - - - - - - - - - -  java.io.Serializable
  └Error
    └ThreadDeath
```

✳	public	**ThreadDeath** ()

ThreadGroup	java.lang

```
Object 1
└ThreadGroup
```

		public . . . . int	**activeCount** ()	ε99
		public . . . . int	**activeGroupCount** ()	ε99
D		public . . . . boolean	**allowThreadSuspension** (boolean b)	
	●	public final . . . . void	**checkAccess** ()	
	●	public final . . . . void	**destroy** ()	
		public . . . . int	**enumerate** (Thread[] list)	
		public . . . . int	**enumerate** (ThreadGroup[] list)	
		public . . . . int	**enumerate** (Thread[] list, boolean recurse)	ε99
		public . . . . int	**enumerate** (ThreadGroup[] list, boolean recurse)	ε99
	●	public final . . . . int	**getMaxPriority** ()	
	●	public final . . . . String	**getName** ()	
	●	public final . . . . . . ThreadGroup	**getParent** ()	ε99
1.2	●	public final . . . . void	**interrupt** ()	
	●	public final . . . . boolean	**isDaemon** ()	
1.1		public synchronized . . boolean	**isDestroyed** ()	
		public . . . . void	**list** ()	
	●	public final . . . . boolean	**parentOf** (ThreadGroup g)	
D	●	public final . . . . void	**resume** ()	
	●	public final . . . . void	**setDaemon** (boolean daemon)	

Class *Interface* —extends - - -implements ○ abstract ● final △ static ▲ static final ✳ constructor x x—inherited x **x**—declared **x x**—overridden
ε*n*—examples of usage ‿—has subclass package—see other volume

	●	public final	................void	**setMaxPriority** (int pri)
D	●	public final	................void	**stop** ()
D	●	public final	................void	**suspend** ()
	✳	public	....	**ThreadGroup** (String name)
	✳	public	....	**ThreadGroup** (ThreadGroup parent, String name)
	1	public	.... **String**	**toString** ()
		public	....................void	**uncaughtException** (Thread t, Throwable e)

ThreadLocal			java.lang

Object
1.2 └─ThreadLocal␣

	public	...................Object	**get** ()	ε100
	protected	...............Object	**initialValue** ()	
	public	......................void	**set** (Object value)	ε100
✳	public	....	**ThreadLocal** ()	ε100

ThreadPolicy	org.omg.PortableServer

1.4 *ThreadPolicy*————————————— *ThreadPolicyOperations␣ [1] (org.omg.CORBA.PolicyOperations [2]),*
org.omg.CORBA.Policy␣ (org.omg.CORBA.PolicyOperations [2],
org.omg.CORBA.Object [3], org.omg.CORBA.portable.IDLEntity
(java.io.Serializable)), org.omg.CORBA.portable.IDLEntity␣
(java.io.Serializable)

- -

   3 *13 inherited members from org.omg.CORBA.Object not shown*
   2 *3 inherited members from org.omg.CORBA.PolicyOperations not shown*
   1 public.......ThreadPolicyValue **value** ()

- -

ThreadPolicyOperations	org.omg.PortableServer

1.4 *ThreadPolicyOperations␣*——————————— *org.omg.CORBA.PolicyOperations␣ [1]*

- -

   1 *3 inherited members from org.omg.CORBA.PolicyOperations not shown*
    public.......ThreadPolicyValue **value** ()

- -

ThreadPolicyValue	org.omg.PortableServer

Object
1.4 └─ThreadPolicyValue - *org.omg.CORBA.portable.IDLEntity␣ (java.io.Serializable)*

▲	public static final	.............int	**_ORB_CTRL_MODEL** = 0
▲	public static final	.............int	**_SINGLE_THREAD_MODEL** = 1
△	public static ThreadPolicyValue		**from_int** (int value)
▲	public static final	....	**ORB_CTRL_MODEL**
	............ThreadPolicyValue		
▲	public static final	....	**SINGLE_THREAD_MODEL**
	............ThreadPolicyValue		
✳	protected	....	**ThreadPolicyValue** (int value)
	public	......................int	**value** ()

Throwable		java.lang

Object[1]   ε111,388
└─Throwable␣ - *java.io.Serializable␣*

		public synchronized native	....	**fillInStackTrace** ()
		....................Throwable		
1.4		public	................Throwable	**getCause** ()
1.1		public	......................String	**getLocalizedMessage** ()
		public	......................String	**getMessage** ()
1.4		public	.... StackTraceElement[]	**getStackTrace** ()	ε101
1.4		public synchronized Throwable		**initCause** (Throwable cause)
		public	......................void	**printStackTrace** ()
		public	......................void	**printStackTrace** (java.io.PrintStream s)
1.1		public	......................void	**printStackTrace** (java.io.PrintWriter s)
1.4		public	......................void	**setStackTrace** (StackTraceElement[] stackTrace)
	✳	public	....	**Throwable** ()

785

Throwable

	*	public........................	**Throwable** (String message)	
1.4	*	public........................	**Throwable** (Throwable cause)	
1.4	*	public........................	**Throwable** (String message, Throwable cause)	
	1	public................. **String**	**toString** ()	

Tie javax.rmi.CORBA

1.3 *Tie*─────────────────────────── *org.omg.CORBA.portable.InvokeHandler* ,[1]

1	public...... org.omg.CORBA ↵ .portable.OutputStream	**_invoke** (String method, org.omg.CORBA.portable.InputStream input, *org.omg.CORBA.portable.ResponseHandler* handler) throws org.omg.CORBA.SystemException	
	public........................void	**deactivate** () throws java.rmi.NoSuchObjectException	
	public... *java.rmi.Remote*	**getTarget** ()	
	public...org.omg.CORBA.ORB	**orb** ()	
	public........................void	**orb** (org.omg.CORBA.ORB orb)	
	public........................void	**setTarget** (*java.rmi.Remote* target)	
	public *org.omg.CORBA.Object*	**thisObject** ()	

Time java.sql

Object ε252,374,317,321
  └java.util.Date[1] ------------------------- *java.io.Serializable* ,, *Cloneable* ,, *Comparable*
1.1   └Time

	1	public.................... boolean	after (java.util.Date when)	
	1	public.................... boolean	before (java.util.Date when)	
	1	public.................... Object	clone ()	
1.2	1	public........................int	compareTo (Object o)	ε53
1.2	1	public........................int	compareTo (java.util.Date anotherDate)	
	1	public.................... boolean	equals (Object obj)	
D	1	public.................... **int getDate** ()		
D	1	public.................... **int getDay** ()		
D	1	public.................... **int getMonth** ()		
	1	public.................... long	getTime ()	
D	1	public.................... **int getYear** ()		
	1	public........................int	hashCode ()	
D	1	public.................... **void setDate** (int i)		
D	1	public.................... **void setMonth** (int i)		
	1	public.................... **void setTime** (long time)		
D	1	public.................... **void setYear** (int i)		
D	*	public........................	**Time** (long time)	ε259
D	*	public........................	**Time** (int hour, int minute, int second)	
	1	public.................. **String toString** ()		
△		public static .... Time	**valueOf** (String s)	

TimeLimitExceededException javax.naming

Object
  └Throwable --------------------------- *java.io.Serializable* ,
    └Exception
1.3   └NamingException[1]
1.3   └LimitExceededException
1.3   └TimeLimitExceededException

	1	*20 inherited members from NamingException not shown*	
*		public........................	**TimeLimitExceededException** ()
*		public........................	**TimeLimitExceededException** (String explanation)

Timer❶ java.util

Object
1.3 └Timer

public........................void	**cancel** ()	
public........................void	**schedule** (TimerTask task, long delay)	
public........................void	**schedule** (TimerTask task, Date time)	ε367

Class *Interface* —extends - - -implements ○ abstract ● final △ static ▲ static final ✱ constructor x x—inherited x **x**—declared **x x**—overridden
εn—examples of usage ,—has subclass package—see other volume

	public	void	**schedule** (TimerTask task, long delay, long period)
	public	void	**schedule** (TimerTask task, Date firstTime, long period)
	public	void	**scheduleAtFixedRate** (TimerTask task, Date firstTime, long period)
	public	void	**scheduleAtFixedRate** (TimerTask task, long delay, long period) ε368
✳	public		**Timer** () ε367,368
✳	public		**Timer** (boolean isDaemon)

TimerTask   java.util

Object
1.3 ○ └TimerTask -------------------------------- *Runnable* [1]

		public	boolean	**cancel** ()
○	1	public abstract	void	**run** () ε367,368,92,93,50
		public	long	**scheduledExecutionTime** ()
✳		protected		**TimerTask** () ε367,368

Timestamp   java.sql

Object   ε252,374,317,321
└java.util.Date [1] ------------------------- *java.io.Serializable◡, Cloneable◡, Comparable*
1.1 └Timestamp

		public	boolean	**after** (Timestamp ts)
	1	public	boolean	after (java.util.Date when)
		public	boolean	**before** (Timestamp ts)
	1	public	boolean	before (java.util.Date when)
	1	public	Object	clone ()
1.2	1	public	int	**compareTo** (Object o) ε53
1.4		public	int	**compareTo** (Timestamp ts)
1.2	1	public	int	compareTo (java.util.Date anotherDate)
	1	public	boolean	**equals** (Object ts)
		public	boolean	**equals** (Timestamp ts)
		public	int	**getNanos** ()
	1	public	long	**getTime** ()
	1	public	int	hashCode ()
		public	void	**setNanos** (int n)
	1	public	void	**setTime** (long time)
✳		public		**Timestamp** (long time) ε259
D ✳		public		**Timestamp** (int year, int month, int date, int hour, int minute, int second, int nano)
	1	public	String	**toString** ()
△		public static	Timestamp	**valueOf** (String s)

TimeZone   java.util

Object [1]
1.1 ○ └TimeZone◡ -------------------------- *java.io.Serializable◡, Cloneable◡*

	1	public	Object	**clone** ()
△		public static synchronized	String[]	**getAvailableIDs** () ε371
△		public static synchronized	String[]	**getAvailableIDs** (int rawOffset)
△		public static synchronized	TimeZone	**getDefault** () ε370
1.2	●	public final	String	**getDisplayName** ()
1.2	●	public final	String	**getDisplayName** (Locale locale)
1.2	●	public final	String	**getDisplayName** (boolean daylight, int style) ε371
1.2		public	String	**getDisplayName** (boolean daylight, int style, Locale locale)
1.4		public	int	**getDSTSavings** ()
		public	String	**getID** ()
1.4		public	int	**getOffset** (long date)
○		public abstract	int	**getOffset** (int era, int year, int month, int day, int dayOfWeek, int milliseconds)
○		public abstract	int	**getRawOffset** () ε371
△		public static synchronized	TimeZone	**getTimeZone** (String ID) ε370,371,372
1.2		public	boolean	**hasSameRules** (TimeZone other)
○		public abstract	boolean	**inDaylightTime** (Date date) ε371
1.2	▲	public static final	int	**LONG** = 1 ε371
△		public static synchronized	void	**setDefault** (TimeZone zone)

T

Classes

TimeZone

		public	void	**setID** (String ID)	
○		public abstract	void	**setRawOffset** (int offsetMillis)	
1.2 ▲		public static final	int	**SHORT** = 0	ε371
✳		public		**TimeZone** ()	
○		public abstract	boolean	**useDaylightTime** ()	ε371

TooManyListenersException — java.util

```
Object
└ Throwable ---------------------------- java.io.Serializable
   └ Exception
      └ TooManyListenersException
```
1.1

✳	public	**TooManyListenersException** ()	
✳	public	**TooManyListenersException** (String s)	

TRANSACTION_REQUIRED — org.omg.CORBA

```
Object
└ Throwable ---------------------------- java.io.Serializable
   └ Exception
      └ RuntimeException
         └ SystemException¹
            └ TRANSACTION_REQUIRED
```
1.2 ○
1.2 ●

	1	*3 inherited members from SystemException not shown*
✳	public	**TRANSACTION_REQUIRED** ()
✳	public	**TRANSACTION_REQUIRED** (String s)
✳	public	**TRANSACTION_REQUIRED** (int minor, CompletionStatus completed)
✳	public	**TRANSACTION_REQUIRED** (String s, int minor, CompletionStatus completed)

TRANSACTION_ROLLEDBACK — org.omg.CORBA

```
Object
└ Throwable ---------------------------- java.io.Serializable
   └ Exception
      └ RuntimeException
         └ SystemException¹
            └ TRANSACTION_ROLLEDBACK
```
1.2 ○
1.2 ●

	1	*3 inherited members from SystemException not shown*
✳	public	**TRANSACTION_ROLLEDBACK** ()
✳	public	**TRANSACTION_ROLLEDBACK** (String s)
✳	public	**TRANSACTION_ROLLEDBACK** (int minor, CompletionStatus completed)
✳	public	**TRANSACTION_ROLLEDBACK** (String s, int minor, CompletionStatus completed)

TransactionRequiredException — javax.transaction

```
Object
└ Throwable ---------------------------- java.io.Serializable
   └ Exception
      └ java.io.IOException
         └ java.rmi.RemoteException¹
            └ TransactionRequiredException
```
1.1
1.3

	1	public	Throwable	detail
1.4	1	public	Throwable	getCause ()
	1	public	String	getMessage ()
✳		public		**TransactionRequiredException** ()
✳		public		**TransactionRequiredException** (String msg)

Class *Interface* —extends - - -implements ○ abstract ● final △ static ▲ static final ✳ constructor x x—inherited x **x**—declared **x x**—overridden
ε*n*—examples of usage ⌐—has subclass package—see other volume

	TransactionRolledbackException	javax.transaction

Object
└ Throwable - *java.io.Serializable*
  └ Exception
    └ java.io.IOException
1.1   └ java.rmi.RemoteException [1]
1.3   └ TransactionRolledbackException

	1	public . . . . Throwable	detail
1.4	1	public . . . . Throwable	getCause ()
	1	public . . . . String	getMessage ()
*		public	**TransactionRolledbackException** ()
*		public	**TransactionRolledbackException** (String msg)

	TransactionService	org.omg.IOP

1.4   *TransactionService*

▲   public static final . . . . int **value** = 0

	Transformer	javax.xml.transform

Object
1.4 ○ └ Transformer

○	public abstract . . . . void	**clearParameters** ()
○	public abstract . . . *ErrorListener*	**getErrorListener** ()
○	public abstract	**getOutputProperties** ()
	. . . . java.util.Properties	
○	public abstract . . . . String	**getOutputProperty** (String name) throws IllegalArgumentException
○	public abstract . . . . Object	**getParameter** (String name)
○	public abstract . . . *URIResolver*	**getURIResolver** ()
○	public abstract . . . . void	**setErrorListener** (*ErrorListener* listener) throws IllegalArgumentException
○	public abstract . . . . void	**setOutputProperties** (java.util.Properties oformat) throws IllegalArgumentException
○	public abstract . . . . void	**setOutputProperty** (String name, String value) throws IllegalArgumentException
		ε519,520
○	public abstract . . . . void	**setParameter** (String name, Object value)
○	public abstract . . . . void	**setURIResolver** (*URIResolver* resolver)
○	public abstract . . . . void	**transform** (*Source* xmlSource, *Result* outputTarget) throws TransformerException
		ε518,519,520,521,522
*	protected	**Transformer** ()

	TransformerConfigurationException	javax.xml.transform

ε518,519,520,521,522

Object
└ Throwable - *java.io.Serializable*
  └ Exception
1.4   └ TransformerException [1]
1.4   └ TransformerConfigurationException

	1	public . . . . Throwable	getCause ()
	1	public . . . . Throwable	getException ()
	1	public . . . . String	getLocationAsString ()
	1	public . . . . *SourceLocator*	getLocator ()
	1	public . . . . String	getMessageAndLocation ()
	1	public synchronized Throwable	initCause (Throwable cause)
	1	public . . . . void	printStackTrace ()
	1	public . . . . void	printStackTrace (java.io.PrintStream s)
	1	public . . . . void	printStackTrace (java.io.PrintWriter s)
	1	public . . . . void	setLocator (*SourceLocator* location)
*		public	**TransformerConfigurationException** ()
*		public	**TransformerConfigurationException** (String msg)
*		public	**TransformerConfigurationException** (Throwable e)
*		public	**TransformerConfigurationException** (String msg, Throwable e)
*		public	**TransformerConfigurationException** (String message, *SourceLocator* locator)
*		public	**TransformerConfigurationException** (String message, *SourceLocator* locator, Throwable e)

T

Classes

TransformerException

				javax.xml.transform
		Object		ε518,519,520,522,523
		└Throwable[1] - *java.io.Serializable*		
		└Exception		
1.4		└TransformerException		

	1	public	**Throwable**	**getCause** ()	
		public	Throwable	**getException** ()	
		public	String	**getLocationAsString** ()	
		public	*SourceLocator*	**getLocator** ()	ε521
		public	String	**getMessageAndLocation** ()	
	1	public synchronized		**initCause** (Throwable cause)	
			Throwable		
	1	public	**void**	**printStackTrace** ()	
	1	public	**void**	**printStackTrace** (java.io.PrintStream s)	
	1	public	**void**	**printStackTrace** (java.io.PrintWriter s)	
		public	void	**setLocator** (*SourceLocator* location)	
✳		public		**TransformerException** (String message)	
✳		public		**TransformerException** (Throwable e)	
✳		public		**TransformerException** (String message, Throwable e)	
✳		public		**TransformerException** (String message, *SourceLocator* locator)	
✳		public		**TransformerException** (String message, *SourceLocator* locator, Throwable e)	

TransformerFactory

				javax.xml.transform
		Object		
1.4 ○		└TransformerFactory		

○		public abstract	*Source*	**getAssociatedStylesheet** (*Source* source, String media, String title, String charset)	
				throws TransformerConfigurationException	
○		public abstract	Object	**getAttribute** (String name) throws IllegalArgumentException	
○		public abstract	*ErrorListener*	**getErrorListener** ()	
○		public abstract	boolean	**getFeature** (String name)	
○		public abstract	*URIResolver*	**getURIResolver** ()	
△		public static		**newInstance** () throws TransformerFactoryConfigurationError	ε518,519,520,521,522
		TransformerFactory			
○		public abstract	*Templates*	**newTemplates** (*Source* source) throws TransformerConfigurationException	
					ε521,522
○		public abstract	Transformer	**newTransformer** () throws TransformerConfigurationException	ε518,519,520,523
○		public abstract	Transformer	**newTransformer** (*Source* source) throws TransformerConfigurationException	
○		public abstract	void	**setAttribute** (String name, Object value) throws IllegalArgumentException	
○		public abstract	void	**setErrorListener** (*ErrorListener* listener) throws IllegalArgumentException	
○		public abstract	void	**setURIResolver** (*URIResolver* resolver)	
✳		protected		**TransformerFactory** ()	

TransformerFactoryConfigurationError

				javax.xml.transform
		Object		
		└Throwable[1] - *java.io.Serializable*		
		└Error		
1.4		└TransformerFactoryConfigurationError		

		public	Exception	**getException** ()
	1	public	**String**	**getMessage** ()
✳		public		**TransformerFactoryConfigurationError** ()
✳		public		**TransformerFactoryConfigurationError** (Exception e)
✳		public		**TransformerFactoryConfigurationError** (String msg)
✳		public		**TransformerFactoryConfigurationError** (Exception e, String msg)

TransformerHandler

			javax.xml.transform.sax
1.4	*TransformerHandler*	org.xml.sax.ContentHandler[1], org.xml.sax.ext.LexicalHandler[2],	
		org.xml.sax.DTDHandler[3]	

	1	public	void	characters (char[] ch, int start, int length) throws org.xml.sax.SAXException
	2	public	void	comment (char[] ch, int start, int length) throws org.xml.sax.SAXException

Class   *Interface*   —extends   - - -implements   ○ abstract   ● final   △ static   ▲ static final   ✳ constructor   x x—inherited   x **x**—declared   **x x**—overridden
ε*n*—examples of usage   ⌄—has subclass   package—see other volume

2	public	void	endCDATA () throws org.xml.sax.SAXException
1	public	void	endDocument () throws org.xml.sax.SAXException
2	public	void	endDTD () throws org.xml.sax.SAXException
1	public	void	endElement (String namespaceURI, String localName, String qName) throws org.xml.sax.SAXException
2	public	void	endEntity (String name) throws org.xml.sax.SAXException
1	public	void	endPrefixMapping (String prefix) throws org.xml.sax.SAXException
	public	String	**getSystemId** ()
	public	javax↵ .xml.transform.Transformer	**getTransformer** ()
1	public	void	ignorableWhitespace (char[] ch, int start, int length) throws org.xml.sax.SAXException
3	public	void	notationDecl (String name, String publicId, String systemId) throws org.xml.sax.SAXException
1	public	void	processingInstruction (String target, String data) throws org.xml.sax.SAXException
1	public	void	setDocumentLocator (*org.xml.sax.Locator* locator) ε550
	public	void	**setResult** (*javax.xml.transform.Result* result) throws IllegalArgumentException
	public	void	**setSystemId** (String systemID)
1	public	void	skippedEntity (String name) throws org.xml.sax.SAXException
2	public	void	startCDATA () throws org.xml.sax.SAXException
1	public	void	startDocument () throws org.xml.sax.SAXException
2	public	void	startDTD (String name, String publicId, String systemId) throws org.xml.sax.SAXException
1	public	void	startElement (String namespaceURI, String localName, String qName, *org.xml.sax.Attributes* atts) throws org.xml.sax.SAXException ε549,550
2	public	void	startEntity (String name) throws org.xml.sax.SAXException
1	public	void	startPrefixMapping (String prefix, String uri) throws org.xml.sax.SAXException
3	public	void	unparsedEntityDecl (String name, String publicId, String systemId, String notationName) throws org.xml.sax.SAXException

TRANSIENT

org.omg.CORBA

```
Object
└Throwable ---------------------------- java.io.Serializable
  └Exception
    └RuntimeException
      └SystemException 1
        └TRANSIENT
```
1.2 ○
1.2 ●

	1	*3 inherited members from SystemException not shown*
✳	public	**TRANSIENT** ()
✳	public	**TRANSIENT** (String s)
✳	public	**TRANSIENT** (int minor, CompletionStatus completed)
✳	public	**TRANSIENT** (String s, int minor, CompletionStatus completed)

TRANSPORT_RETRY

org.omg.PortableInterceptor

1.4 *TRANSPORT_RETRY*

▲ public static final .... short **value** = 4

TreeMap

java.util

```
Object
└AbstractMap 1 ------------------------ Map
  └TreeMap ------------------------ SortedMap 2 (Map), Cloneable, java.io.Serializable
```
1.2 ○
1.2

1	public	**void**	**clear** ()	
1	public	**Object**	**clone** ()	
2	public	*Comparator*	**comparator** ()	
1	public	**boolean**	**containsKey** (Object key)	ε344
1	public	**boolean**	**containsValue** (Object value)	
1	public	*Set*	**entrySet** ()	ε345
1	public	boolean	equals (Object o)	
2	public	Object	**firstKey** ()	
1	public	**Object**	**get** (Object key)	ε337,344,346,356,357
1	public	int	hashCode ()	
2	public	*SortedMap*	**headMap** (Object toKey)	
1	public	boolean	isEmpty ()	
1	public	*Set*	**keySet** ()	ε194,340,345,355,356
2	public	Object	**lastKey** ()	

T

Classes

TreeMap

1	public	**Object**	**put** (Object key, Object value)	ε337,344,346,355,356
1	public	**void**	**putAll** (*Map* map)	
1	public	**Object**	**remove** (Object key)	ε355
1	public	**int**	**size** ()	ε355
2	public	*SortedMap*	**subMap** (Object fromKey, Object toKey)	
2	public	*SortedMap*	**tailMap** (Object fromKey)	
1	public	String	toString ()	
*	public		**TreeMap** ()	ε355
*	public		**TreeMap** (*Comparator* c)	
*	public		**TreeMap** (*Map* m)	ε347
*	public		**TreeMap** (*SortedMap* m)	
1	public	**Collection**	**values** ()	ε340,345,355

TreeSet java.util

Object [1]
└ AbstractCollection [2] - Collection ⌣   1.2 ○
  └ AbstractSet [3] - Set ⌣ (Collection)   1.2 ○
   └ TreeSet - SortedSet [4] (Set (Collection)), Cloneable ⌣, java.io.Serializable ⌣   1.2

2	public	**boolean**	**add** (Object o)	ε342,349,352,354,358
2	public	**boolean**	**addAll** (*Collection* c)	ε351,353
2	public	**void**	**clear** ()	ε351,353
1	public	**Object**	**clone** ()	
4	public	*Comparator*	**comparator** ()	
2	public	**boolean**	**contains** (Object o)	ε352
2	public	boolean	containsAll (*Collection* c)	
3	public	boolean	equals (Object o)	
4	public	Object	**first** ()	
3	public	int	hashCode ()	
4	public	*SortedSet*	**headSet** (Object toElement)	
2	public	**boolean**	**isEmpty** ()	ε102
2	public	*Iterator*	**iterator** ()	ε345,352,354,355,356
4	public	Object	**last** ()	
2	public	**boolean**	**remove** (Object o)	ε349,352
3	public	boolean	removeAll (*Collection* c)	ε351,353
2	public	boolean	retainAll (*Collection* c)	ε351,353
2	public	**int**	**size** ()	ε340,349,351,352,358
4	public	*SortedSet*	**subSet** (Object fromElement, Object toElement)	
4	public	*SortedSet*	**tailSet** (Object fromElement)	
2	public	Object[]	toArray ()	ε340
2	public	Object[]	toArray (Object[] a)	ε340,352,358,194,508
2	public	String	toString ()	
*	public		**TreeSet** ()	ε358
*	public		**TreeSet** (*Collection* c)	ε347
*	public		**TreeSet** (*Comparator* c)	
*	public		**TreeSet** (*SortedSet* s)	

TrustAnchor java.security.cert

Object [1]
└ TrustAnchor   1.4

●	public final	String	**getCAName** ()	
●	public final		**getCAPublicKey** ()	
		java.security.PublicKey		
●	public final	byte[]	**getNameConstraints** ()	
●	public final	X509Certificate	**getTrustedCert** ()	ε230,231
1	public	**String**	**toString** ()	
*	public		**TrustAnchor** (X509Certificate trustedCert, byte[] nameConstraints)	
*	public		**TrustAnchor** (String caName, *java.security.PublicKey* pubKey, byte[] nameConstraints)	

TrustManager javax.net.ssl

TrustManager ⌣   1.4   ε502
- -

Class *Interface* —extends - - -implements ○ abstract ● final △ static ▲ static final ✳ constructor x x—inherited x **x**—declared **x x**—overridden
ε*n*—examples of usage ⌣—has subclass package—see other volume

	TrustManagerFactory	javax.net.ssl

Object
1.4 └TrustManagerFactory

●	public final ....String	**getAlgorithm** ()
▲	public static final.........String	**getDefaultAlgorithm** ()
▲	public static final.............. ....TrustManagerFactory	**getInstance** (String algorithm) throws java.security.NoSuchAlgorithmException
▲	public static final.............. ....TrustManagerFactory	**getInstance** (String algorithm, java.security.Provider provider) throws java.security.NoSuchAlgorithmException
▲	public static final.............. ....TrustManagerFactory	**getInstance** (String algorithm, String provider) throws java.security↵ .NoSuchAlgorithmException, java.security.NoSuchProviderException
●	public final ....java.security.Provider	**getProvider** ()
●	public final .... *TrustManager[]*	**getTrustManagers** ()
●	public final ....void	**init** (java.security.KeyStore ks) throws java.security.KeyStoreException
●	public final ....void	**init** (*ManagerFactoryParameters* spec) throws java.security↵ .InvalidAlgorithmParameterException
*	protected	**TrustManagerFactory** (TrustManagerFactorySpi factorySpi, java.security.Provider provider, String algorithm)

	TrustManagerFactorySpi	javax.net.ssl

Object
1.4 ○ └TrustManagerFactorySpi

○	protected abstract ....*TrustManager[]*	**engineGetTrustManagers** ()
○	protected abstract ....void	**engineInit** (java.security.KeyStore ks) throws java.security.KeyStoreException
○	protected abstract ....void	**engineInit** (*ManagerFactoryParameters* spec) throws java.security.InvalidAlgorithmParameterException
*	public........................	**TrustManagerFactorySpi** ()

T

	TypeCode	org.omg.CORBA

Object
1.2 ○ └TypeCode - *org.omg.CORBA.portable.IDLEntity* (*java.io.Serializable*)

○	public abstract ......TypeCode	**concrete_base_type** () throws org.omg.CORBA.TypeCodePackage.BadKind
○	public abstract ......TypeCode	**content_type** () throws org.omg.CORBA.TypeCodePackage.BadKind
○	public abstract ....int	**default_index** () throws org.omg.CORBA.TypeCodePackage.BadKind
○	public abstract ......TypeCode	**discriminator_type** () throws org.omg.CORBA.TypeCodePackage.BadKind
○	public abstract ....boolean	**equal** (TypeCode tc)
○	public abstract ....boolean	**equivalent** (TypeCode tc)
○	public abstract ....short	**fixed_digits** () throws org.omg.CORBA.TypeCodePackage.BadKind
○	public abstract ....short	**fixed_scale** () throws org.omg.CORBA.TypeCodePackage.BadKind
○	public abstract ......TypeCode	**get_compact_typecode** ()
○	public abstract ....String	**id** () throws org.omg.CORBA.TypeCodePackage.BadKind
○	public abstract ....TCKind	**kind** ()
○	public abstract ....int	**length** () throws org.omg.CORBA.TypeCodePackage.BadKind
○	public abstract ....int	**member_count** () throws org.omg.CORBA.TypeCodePackage.BadKind
○	public abstract ....Any	**member_label** (int index) throws org.omg.CORBA.TypeCodePackage.BadKind, org.omg.CORBA.TypeCodePackage.Bounds
○	public abstract ....String	**member_name** (int index) throws org.omg.CORBA.TypeCodePackage.BadKind, org.omg.CORBA.TypeCodePackage.Bounds
○	public abstract ......TypeCode	**member_type** (int index) throws org.omg.CORBA.TypeCodePackage.BadKind, org.omg.CORBA.TypeCodePackage.Bounds
○	public abstract ....short	**member_visibility** (int index) throws org.omg.CORBA.TypeCodePackage.BadKind, org.omg.CORBA.TypeCodePackage.Bounds
○	public abstract ....String	**name** () throws org.omg.CORBA.TypeCodePackage.BadKind
○	public abstract ....short	**type_modifier** () throws org.omg.CORBA.TypeCodePackage.BadKind
*	public........................	**TypeCode** ()

	TypeCodeHolder	org.omg.CORBA

Object
1.2 ● └TypeCodeHolder - *org.omg.CORBA.portable.Streamable* [1]

Classes

TypeCodeHolder

1	public................................void	**_read** (org.omg.CORBA.portable.InputStream input)
1	public................................TypeCode	**_type** ()
1	public................................void	**_write** (org.omg.CORBA.portable.OutputStream output)
*	public...........................	**TypeCodeHolder** ()
*	public...........................	**TypeCodeHolder** (TypeCode initial)
	public...............TypeCode	**value**

TypeMismatch❶   org.omg.CORBA.DynAnyPackage

```
Object
└Throwable - - - - - - - - - - - - - - - - - - - - - - - - - java.io.Serializable˛
    └Exception
```
| 1.2 ○ | └org.omg.CORBA.UserException - - - - - - org.omg.CORBA.portable.IDLEntity˛ (java.io.Serializable) |
| 1.2 ● | └TypeMismatch |

*	public...........................	**TypeMismatch** ()
*	public...........................	**TypeMismatch** (String reason)

TypeMismatch❷   org.omg.DynamicAny.DynAnyPackage

```
Object
└Throwable - - - - - - - - - - - - - - - - - - - - - - - - - java.io.Serializable˛
    └Exception
```
| 1.2 ○ | └org.omg.CORBA.UserException - - - - - - org.omg.CORBA.portable.IDLEntity˛ (java.io.Serializable) |
| 1.4 ● | └TypeMismatch |

*	public...........................	**TypeMismatch** ()
*	public...........................	**TypeMismatch** (String $reason)

TypeMismatch❸   org.omg.IOP.CodecPackage

```
Object
└Throwable - - - - - - - - - - - - - - - - - - - - - - - - - java.io.Serializable˛
    └Exception
```
| 1.2 ○ | └org.omg.CORBA.UserException - - - - - - org.omg.CORBA.portable.IDLEntity˛ (java.io.Serializable) |
| 1.4 ● | └TypeMismatch |

*	public...........................	**TypeMismatch** ()
*	public...........................	**TypeMismatch** (String $reason)

TypeMismatchHelper❶   org.omg.DynamicAny.DynAnyPackage

```
Object
└TypeMismatchHelper
```
1.4 ○

△	public static .... TypeMismatch	**extract** (org.omg.CORBA.Any a)
△	public static ....String	**id** ()
△	public static ....void	**insert** (org.omg.CORBA.Any a, TypeMismatch that)
△	public static .... TypeMismatch	**read** (org.omg.CORBA.portable.InputStream istream)
△	public static synchronized .... . org.omg.CORBA.TypeCode	**type** ()
*	public...........................	**TypeMismatchHelper** ()
△	public static ....void	**write** (org.omg.CORBA.portable.OutputStream ostream, TypeMismatch value)

TypeMismatchHelper❷   org.omg.IOP.CodecPackage

```
Object
└TypeMismatchHelper
```
1.4 ○

△	public static .... TypeMismatch	**extract** (org.omg.CORBA.Any a)
△	public static ....String	**id** ()
△	public static ....void	**insert** (org.omg.CORBA.Any a, TypeMismatch that)
△	public static .... TypeMismatch	**read** (org.omg.CORBA.portable.InputStream istream)
△	public static synchronized .... . org.omg.CORBA.TypeCode	**type** ()

Class *Interface* —extends - - -implements ○ abstract ● final △ static ▲ static final ✳ constructor x x—inherited x **x**—declared **x x**—overridden
εn—examples of usage ˛—has subclass package—see other volume

✳	public		**TypeMismatchHelper** ()
△	public static	void	**write** (org.omg.CORBA.portable.OutputStream ostream, TypeMismatch value)

Types   java.sql

Object
1.1 └Types

1.2 ▲	public static final	int	**ARRAY** = 2003
▲	public static final	int	**BIGINT** = -5
▲	public static final	int	**BINARY** = -2
▲	public static final	int	**BIT** = -7
1.2 ▲	public static final	int	**BLOB** = 2004
1.4 ▲	public static final	int	**BOOLEAN** = 16
▲	public static final	int	**CHAR** = 1
1.2 ▲	public static final	int	**CLOB** = 2005
1.4 ▲	public static final	int	**DATALINK** = 70
▲	public static final	int	**DATE** = 91
▲	public static final	int	**DECIMAL** = 3
1.2 ▲	public static final	int	**DISTINCT** = 2001
▲	public static final	int	**DOUBLE** = 8
▲	public static final	int	**FLOAT** = 6
▲	public static final	int	**INTEGER** = 4
1.2 ▲	public static final	int	**JAVA_OBJECT** = 2000
▲	public static final	int	**LONGVARBINARY** = -4
▲	public static final	int	**LONGVARCHAR** = -1
▲	public static final	int	**NULL** = 0
▲	public static final	int	**NUMERIC** = 2
▲	public static final	int	**OTHER** = 1111
▲	public static final	int	**REAL** = 7
1.2 ▲	public static final	int	**REF** = 2006
▲	public static final	int	**SMALLINT** = 5
1.2 ▲	public static final	int	**STRUCT** = 2002
▲	public static final	int	**TIME** = 92
▲	public static final	int	**TIMESTAMP** = 93
▲	public static final	int	**TINYINT** = -6
▲	public static final	int	**VARBINARY** = -3
▲	public static final	int	**VARCHAR** = 12

ε281,282

UID   java.rmi.server

Object[1]
1.1 ● └UID - *java.io.Serializable*

1	public	boolean	**equals** (Object obj)
1	public	int	**hashCode** ()
△	public static	UID	**read** (*java.io.DataInput* in) throws java.io.IOException
1	public	String	**toString** ()
✳	public		**UID** ()
✳	public		**UID** (short num)
	public	void	**write** (*java.io.DataOutput* out) throws java.io.IOException

---

ULongLongSeqHelper   org.omg.CORBA

Object
1.3 ○ └ULongLongSeqHelper

△	public static	long[]	**extract** (Any a)
△	public static	String	**id** ()
△	public static	void	**insert** (Any a, long[] that)
△	public static	long[]	**read** (org.omg.CORBA.portable.InputStream istream)
△	public static synchronized	TypeCode	**type** ()
✳	public		**ULongLongSeqHelper** ()
△	public static	void	**write** (org.omg.CORBA.portable.OutputStream ostream, long[] value)

U

Classes

ULongLongSeqHolder

ULongLongSeqHolder				org.omg.CORBA

Object
1.3 ● └ULongLongSeqHolder - - - - - - - - - - - - - - - - - *org.omg.CORBA.portable.Streamable* ⌐ [1]

	[1]	public.....................void	**_read** (org.omg.CORBA.portable.InputStream i)	
	[1]	public.....................TypeCode	**_type** ()	
	[1]	public.....................void	**_write** (org.omg.CORBA.portable.OutputStream o)	
✳		public...........................	**ULongLongSeqHolder** ()	
✳		public...........................	**ULongLongSeqHolder** (long[] initialValue)	
		public.....................long[]	**value**	

ULongSeqHelper				org.omg.CORBA

Object
1.3 ○ └ULongSeqHelper

△	public static ....int[]	**extract** (Any a)
△	public static ....String	**id** ()
△	public static ....void	**insert** (Any a, int[] that)
△	public static ....int[]	**read** (org.omg.CORBA.portable.InputStream istream)
△	public static synchronized .... TypeCode	**type** ()
✳	public...........................	**ULongSeqHelper** ()
△	public static ....void	**write** (org.omg.CORBA.portable.OutputStream ostream, int[] value)

ULongSeqHolder				org.omg.CORBA

Object
1.3 ● └ULongSeqHolder - *org.omg.CORBA.portable.Streamable* ⌐ [1]

	[1]	public.....................void	**_read** (org.omg.CORBA.portable.InputStream i)
	[1]	public.....................TypeCode	**_type** ()
	[1]	public.....................void	**_write** (org.omg.CORBA.portable.OutputStream o)
✳		public...........................	**ULongSeqHolder** ()
✳		public...........................	**ULongSeqHolder** (int[] initialValue)
		public.....................int[]	**value**

UndeclaredThrowableException				java.lang.reflect

Object
└Throwable [1] - *java.io.Serializable* ⌐
  └Exception
    └RuntimeException
1.3   └UndeclaredThrowableException

1.4	[1]	public............... **Throwable**	**getCause** ()
		public...............Throwable	**getUndeclaredThrowable** ()
✳		public...........................	**UndeclaredThrowableException** (Throwable undeclaredThrowable)
✳		public...........................	**UndeclaredThrowableException** (Throwable undeclaredThrowable, String s)

UnexpectedException				java.rmi

Object
└Throwable - *java.io.Serializable* ⌐
  └Exception
    └java.io.IOException
1.1   └RemoteException [1]
1.1   └UnexpectedException

	[1]	public...............Throwable	detail
1.4	[1]	public...............Throwable	getCause ()
	[1]	public.....................String	getMessage ()
✳		public...........................	**UnexpectedException** (String s)
✳		public...........................	**UnexpectedException** (String s, Exception ex)

Class *Interface* —extends - - -implements ○ abstract ● final △ static ▲ static final ✳ constructor x x—inherited x **x**—declared **x x**—overridden
εn—examples of usage ⌐—has subclass package—see other volume

UnicastRemoteObject

ε188

Object [1]
1.1 ○ └RemoteObject [2] - *java.rmi.Remote*, *java.io.Serializable*
1.1 ○   └RemoteServer [3]
1.1   └UnicastRemoteObject

	1	public . . . . **Object clone** () throws CloneNotSupportedException	
	2	public . . . . boolean equals (Object obj)	
△		public static . . . . . . RemoteStub **exportObject** (*java.rmi.Remote* obj) throws java.rmi.RemoteException	
1.2 △		public static . . *java.rmi.Remote* **exportObject** (*java.rmi.Remote* obj, int port) throws java.rmi.RemoteException	
1.2 △		public static . . *java.rmi.Remote* **exportObject** (*java.rmi.Remote* obj, int port, *RMIClientSocketFactory* csf, *RMIServerSocketFactory* ssf) throws java.rmi.RemoteException	
△	3	public static . . . . String getClientHost () throws ServerNotActiveException	
△	3	public static java.io.PrintStream getLog ()	
1.2	2	public . . . . *RemoteRef* getRef ()	
	2	public . . . . int hashCode ()	
	2	protected transient . *RemoteRef* ref	
△	3	public static . . . . void setLog (java.io.OutputStream out)	
	2	public . . . . String toString ()	
1.2 △	2	public static . . *java.rmi.Remote* **toStub** (*java.rmi.Remote* obj) throws java.rmi.NoSuchObjectException	
1.2 △		public static . . . . boolean **unexportObject** (*java.rmi.Remote* obj, boolean force) throws java.rmi.NoSuchObjectException	
∗		protected . . . . **UnicastRemoteObject** () throws java.rmi.RemoteException	
1.2 ∗		protected . . . . **UnicastRemoteObject** (int port) throws java.rmi.RemoteException	
1.2 ∗		protected . . . . **UnicastRemoteObject** (int port, *RMIClientSocketFactory* csf, *RMIServerSocketFactory* ssf) throws java.rmi.RemoteException	

UnionMember

Object
1.2 ● └UnionMember - *org.omg.CORBA.portable.IDLEntity* (*java.io.Serializable*)

	public . . . . Any **label**
	public . . . . String **name**
	public . . . . TypeCode **type**
	public . . . . *IDLType* **type_def**
∗	public . . . . **UnionMember** ()
∗	public . . . . **UnionMember** (String __name, Any __label, TypeCode __type, *IDLType* __type_def)

UnionMemberHelper

Object
1.3 ○ └UnionMemberHelper

△	public static . . . . . UnionMember **extract** (Any a)
△	public static . . . . String **id** ()
△	public static . . . . void **insert** (Any a, UnionMember that)
△	public static . . . . . UnionMember **read** (org.omg.CORBA.portable.InputStream istream)
△	public static synchronized . . . . **type** () . . . . TypeCode
∗	public . . . . **UnionMemberHelper** ()
△	public static . . . . void **write** (org.omg.CORBA.portable.OutputStream ostream, UnionMember value)

UNKNOWN

Object
└Throwable - *java.io.Serializable*
  └Exception
    └RuntimeException
1.2 ○   └SystemException [1]
1.2 ●   └UNKNOWN

	1	*3 inherited members from SystemException not shown*
∗		public . . . . **UNKNOWN** ()
∗		public . . . . **UNKNOWN** (String s)
∗		public . . . . **UNKNOWN** (int minor, CompletionStatus completed)
∗		public . . . . **UNKNOWN** (String s, int minor, CompletionStatus completed)

U

Classes

UnknownEncoding	org.omg.IOP.CodecFactoryPackage

```
        Object
        └Throwable ------------------------------- java.io.Serializable ⌄
          └Exception
1.2 ○       └org.omg.CORBA.UserException ------- org.omg.CORBA.portable.IDLEntity ⌄ (java.io.Serializable)
1.4 ●         └UnknownEncoding
```

| ✳ | public......................... | **UnknownEncoding** () |
| ✳ | public......................... | **UnknownEncoding** (String $reason) |

UnknownEncodingHelper	org.omg.IOP.CodecFactoryPackage

```
        Object
1.4 ○   └UnknownEncodingHelper
```

△	public static.................... UnknownEncoding	**extract** (org.omg.CORBA.Any a)
△	public static.............String	**id** ()
△	public static.................void	**insert** (org.omg.CORBA.Any a, UnknownEncoding that)
△	public static.................... UnknownEncoding	**read** (org.omg.CORBA.portable.InputStream istream)
△	public static synchronized .... org.omg.CORBA.TypeCode	**type** ()
✳	public.........................	**UnknownEncodingHelper** ()
△	public static...............void	**write** (org.omg.CORBA.portable.OutputStream ostream, UnknownEncoding value)

UnknownError	java.lang

```
        Object
        └Throwable ------------------------------- java.io.Serializable ⌄
          └Error
  ○         └VirtualMachineError
              └UnknownError
```

| ✳ | public......................... | **UnknownError** () |
| ✳ | public......................... | **UnknownError** (String s) |

UnknownException	org.omg.CORBA.portable

```
        Object
        └Throwable ------------------------------- java.io.Serializable ⌄
          └Exception
            └RuntimeException
1.2 ○         └org.omg.CORBA.SystemException [1]
1.3             └UnknownException
```

[1]	*3 inherited members from org.omg.CORBA.SystemException not shown*	
	public...............Throwable	**originalEx**
✳	public.........................	**UnknownException** (Throwable ex)

UnknownGroupException	java.rmi.activation

```
        Object
        └Throwable ------------------------------- java.io.Serializable ⌄
          └Exception
1.2         └ActivationException [1]
1.2           └UnknownGroupException
```

	[1]	public...............Throwable	detail
1.4	[1]	public...............Throwable	getCause ()
	[1]	public.....................String	getMessage ()
✳		public.........................	**UnknownGroupException** (String s)

UnknownHostException❶   java.net

ε144,145,146,147

```
Object
 └Throwable -------------------------------- java.io.Serializable
    └Exception
       └java.io.IOException
          └UnknownHostException
```

✳	public...........................	**UnknownHostException** ()
✳	public...........................	**UnknownHostException** (String host)

UnknownHostException❷   java.rmi

ε188,189

```
       Object
        └Throwable -------------------------------- java.io.Serializable
           └Exception
              └java.io.IOException
1.1           └RemoteException 1
1.1              └UnknownHostException
```

	1	public...............Throwable	detail
1.4	1	public...............Throwable	getCause ()
	1	public.....................String	getMessage ()
✳		public...........................	**UnknownHostException** (String s)
✳		public...........................	**UnknownHostException** (String s, Exception ex)

UnknownObjectException   java.rmi.activation

```
       Object
        └Throwable -------------------------------- java.io.Serializable
           └Exception
1.2           └ActivationException 1
1.2              └UnknownObjectException
```

	1	public...............Throwable	detail
1.4	1	public...............Throwable	getCause ()
	1	public.....................String	getMessage ()
✳		public...........................	**UnknownObjectException** (String s)

UnknownServiceException   java.net

```
Object
 └Throwable -------------------------------- java.io.Serializable
    └Exception
       └java.io.IOException
          └UnknownServiceException
```

✳	public...........................	**UnknownServiceException** ()
✳	public...........................	**UnknownServiceException** (String msg)

UnknownUserException   org.omg.CORBA

```
       Object
        └Throwable -------------------------------- java.io.Serializable
           └Exception
1.2 ○         └UserException --------------------- org.omg.CORBA.portable.IDLEntity (java.io.Serializable)
1.2 ●            └UnknownUserException
```

	public.....................Any	**except**
✳	public...........................	**UnknownUserException** ()
✳	public...........................	**UnknownUserException** (Any a)

UnknownUserExceptionHelper   org.omg.CORBA

```
       Object
1.4 ○  └UnknownUserExceptionHelper
```

U

UnknownUserExceptionHelper

△	public static	**extract** (Any a)	
	......UnknownUserException		
△	public static ....String	**id** ()	
△	public static ....void	**insert** (Any a, UnknownUserException that)	
△	public static	**read** (org.omg.CORBA.portable.InputStream istream)	
	......UnknownUserException		
△	public static synchronized	**type** ()	
	......................TypeCode		
✳	public..............................	**UnknownUserExceptionHelper** ()	
△	public static ....void	**write** (org.omg.CORBA.portable.OutputStream ostream,	
		UnknownUserException value)	

UnknownUserExceptionHolder
org.omg.CORBA

```
       Object
1.4 ●  └UnknownUserExceptionHolder ----------- org.omg.CORBA.portable.Streamable ˌ 1
```

	1	public.......................void	**_read** (org.omg.CORBA.portable.InputStream i)
	1	public...............TypeCode	**_type** ()
	1	public.......................void	**_write** (org.omg.CORBA.portable.OutputStream o)
✳		public..............................	**UnknownUserExceptionHolder** ()
✳		public..............................	**UnknownUserExceptionHolder** (UnknownUserException initialValue)
		public . UnknownUserException	**value**

UnmappableCharacterException
java.nio.charset

```
       Object
       └Throwable 1 --------------------------- java.io.Serializable ˌ
         └Exception
           └java.io.IOException
1.4          └CharacterCodingException
1.4            └UnmappableCharacterException
```

		public.........................int	**getInputLength** ()
	1	public...................**String**	**getMessage** ()
✳		public..............................	**UnmappableCharacterException** (int inputLength)

UnmarshalException
java.rmi

```
       Object
       └Throwable --------------------------- java.io.Serializable ˌ
         └Exception
           └java.io.IOException
1.1          └RemoteException 1
1.1            └UnmarshalException
```

	1	public...............Throwable	detail
1.4	1	public...............Throwable	getCause ()
	1	public...................String	getMessage ()
✳		public..............................	**UnmarshalException** (String s)
✳		public..............................	**UnmarshalException** (String s, Exception ex)

UnrecoverableKeyException
java.security

```
       Object                                            ε210
       └Throwable --------------------------- java.io.Serializable ˌ
         └Exception
1.2        └GeneralSecurityException
1.2          └UnrecoverableKeyException
```

✳	public..............................	**UnrecoverableKeyException** ()	
✳	public..............................	**UnrecoverableKeyException** (String msg)	

Class *Interface* —extends - - -implements ○ abstract ● final △ static ▲ static final ✳ constructor x x—inherited x **x**—declared **x x**—overridden
ε*n*—examples of usage ˌ—has subclass package—see other volume

Unreferenced | java.rmi.server

1.1   *Unreferenced*
- -
     public........................void **unreferenced** ()

UnresolvedAddressException | java.nio.channels

```
Object
 └Throwable ------------------------------- java.io.Serializable
   └Exception
     └RuntimeException
       └IllegalArgumentException
1.4       └UnresolvedAddressException
```

※   public........................... **UnresolvedAddressException** ()

UnresolvedPermission | java.security

ε217,218

```
Object
1.2 ○  └Permission 1 ------------------------- Guard, java.io.Serializable
1.2 ●    └UnresolvedPermission
```

1	public	void	checkGuard (Object object) throws SecurityException
1	public	boolean	**equals** (Object obj)	ε215
1	public	String	**getActions** ()	ε215
● 1	public final	String	getName ()	
1	public	int	**hashCode** ()	ε215
1	public	boolean	**implies** (Permission p)	ε214,215
1	public	PermissionCollection	**newPermissionCollection** ()	
1	public	String	**toString** ()	
※	public		**UnresolvedPermission** (String type, String name, String actions, java.security.cert.Certificate[] certs)	

UnsatisfiedLinkError | java.lang

```
Object
 └Throwable ------------------------- java.io.Serializable
   └Error
     └LinkageError
       └UnsatisfiedLinkError
```

※   public........................... **UnsatisfiedLinkError** ()
※   public........................... **UnsatisfiedLinkError** (String s)

UnsolicitedNotification | javax.naming.ldap

1.3   *UnsolicitedNotification*————————— *ExtendedResponse*1 (java.io.Serializable), *HasControls*2

2	public	Control[]	getControls () throws javax.naming.NamingException	ε497
1	public	byte[]	getEncodedValue ()	
	public	javax↵	**getException** ()	
	.naming.NamingException			
1	public	String	getID ()	
	public	String[]	**getReferrals** ()	

UnsolicitedNotificationEvent | javax.naming.ldap

ε333

```
Object
1.1  └java.util.EventObject 1 ------------------- java.io.Serializable
1.3    └UnsolicitedNotificationEvent
```

	public	void	**dispatch** (*UnsolicitedNotificationListener* listener)
	public	*UnsolicitedNotification*	**getNotification** ()
1	public	Object	getSource ()
1	protected transient	Object	source
1	public	String	toString ()
※	public		**UnsolicitedNotificationEvent** (Object src, *UnsolicitedNotification* notice)

UnsolicitedNotificationListener	javax.naming.ldap

1.3	*UnsolicitedNotificationListener*————————*javax.naming.event.NamingListener*⌄[1] (*java.util.EventListener*)	ε2,3,333,493,494

1	public.....................void namingExceptionThrown (javax.naming.event.NamingExceptionEvent evt)	
		ε493,494
	public.....................void **notificationReceived** (UnsolicitedNotificationEvent evt)	

UNSUPPORTED_POLICY	org.omg.CORBA

1.2	*UNSUPPORTED_POLICY*
▲	public static final..........short **value** = 1

UNSUPPORTED_POLICY_VALUE	org.omg.CORBA

1.2	*UNSUPPORTED_POLICY_VALUE*
▲	public static final..........short **value** = 4

UnsupportedAddressTypeException	java.nio.channels

```
Object
└Throwable ------------------------- java.io.Serializable⌄
  └Exception
    └RuntimeException
      └IllegalArgumentException
```
1.4	└UnsupportedAddressTypeException
✳	public...........................**UnsupportedAddressTypeException** ()

UnsupportedCallbackException	javax.security.auth.callback

```
Object
└Throwable ------------------------- java.io.Serializable⌄
  └Exception
```
1.4	└UnsupportedCallbackException
	public................. *Callback* **getCallback** ()
✳	public...........................**UnsupportedCallbackException** (*Callback* callback)
✳	public...........................**UnsupportedCallbackException** (*Callback* callback, String msg)
		ε509

UnsupportedCharsetException	java.nio.charset

```
Object
└Throwable ------------------------- java.io.Serializable⌄
  └Exception
    └RuntimeException
      └IllegalArgumentException
```
1.4	└UnsupportedCharsetException
	public.....................String **getCharsetName** ()
✳	public...........................**UnsupportedCharsetException** (String charsetName)

UnsupportedClassVersionError	java.lang

```
Object
└Throwable ------------------------- java.io.Serializable⌄
  └Error
    └LinkageError
      └ClassFormatError
```
1.2	└UnsupportedClassVersionError

Class *Interface* —extends - - -implements ○ abstract ● final △ static ▲ static final ✳ constructor x x—inherited x **x**—declared **x x**—overridden
ε*n*—examples of usage ⌄—has subclass package—see other volume

U

*	public.........................		**UnsupportedClassVersionError** ()	
*	public.........................		**UnsupportedClassVersionError** (String s)	

UnsupportedEncodingException	java.io

Object   ε40,41,42,43,79
  └Throwable - *Serializable*⌄
    └Exception
      └IOException
1.1   └UnsupportedEncodingException

*	public.........................	**UnsupportedEncodingException** ()	
*	public.........................	**UnsupportedEncodingException** (String s)	

UnsupportedOperationException	java.lang

Object   ε348
  └Throwable - *java.io.Serializable*⌄
    └Exception
      └RuntimeException
1.2   └UnsupportedOperationException⌄

*	public.........................	**UnsupportedOperationException** ()	
*	public.........................	**UnsupportedOperationException** (String message)	

URI	java.net

Object[1]
1.4 ● └URI - *Comparable*[2], *java.io.Serializable*⌄

	2	public.........................int	**compareTo** (Object ob)	ε53	
△		public static ....URI	**create** (String str)		
	1	public..................**boolean**	**equals** (Object ob)		
		public....................String	**getAuthority** ()		
		public....................String	**getFragment** ()		
		public....................String	**getHost** ()		
		public....................String	**getPath** ()		
		public.......................int	**getPort** ()		
		public....................String	**getQuery** ()		
		public....................String	**getRawAuthority** ()		
		public....................String	**getRawFragment** ()		
		public....................String	**getRawPath** ()		
		public....................String	**getRawQuery** ()		
		public....................String	**getRawSchemeSpecificPart** ()		
		public....................String	**getRawUserInfo** ()		
		public....................String	**getScheme** ()	ε548	
		public....................String	**getSchemeSpecificPart** ()	ε548	
		public....................String	**getUserInfo** ()		
	1	public.......................**int**	**hashCode** ()		
		public..................boolean	**isAbsolute** ()		
		public..................boolean	**isOpaque** ()		
		public.......................URI	**normalize** ()		
		public.......................URI	**parseServerAuthority** () throws URISyntaxException		
		public.......................URI	**relativize** (URI uri)		
		public.......................URI	**resolve** (String str)		
		public.......................URI	**resolve** (URI uri)		
		public....................String	**toASCIIString** ()		
	1	public.....................**String**	**toString** ()	ε523	
		public.......................URL	**toURL** () throws MalformedURLException	ε133	
*		public.........................	**URI** (String str) throws URISyntaxException	ε133,548	
*		public.........................	**URI** (String scheme, String ssp, String fragment) throws URISyntaxException		
*		public.........................	**URI** (String scheme, String host, String path, String fragment) throws URISyntaxException		
*		public.........................	**URI** (String scheme, String authority, String path, String query, String fragment) throws URISyntaxException		
*		public.........................	**URI** (String scheme, String userInfo, String host, int port, String path, String query, String fragment) throws URISyntaxException		

U

Classes

URIResolver				javax.xml.transform

1.4	*URIResolver*		
	public	*Source* **resolve** (String href, String base) throws TransformerException	

URISyntaxException	java.net

Object
└Throwable [1] - *java.io.Serializable*
　└Exception
1.4　　└URISyntaxException

ε133,548

	public	int **getIndex** ()	
	public	String **getInput** ()	
1	public	**String getMessage** ()	
	public	String **getReason** ()	
*	public	**URISyntaxException** (String input, String reason)	
*	public	**URISyntaxException** (String input, String reason, int index)	

URL	java.net

Object [1]
●　└URL - *java.io.Serializable*

ε67,68,69

1	public	**boolean equals** (Object obj)	
1.3	public	String **getAuthority** ()	
●	public final	Object **getContent** () throws java.io.IOException	
1.3 ●	public final	Object **getContent** (Class[] classes) throws java.io.IOException	
1.4	public	int **getDefaultPort** ()	
	public	String **getFile** ()	ε134,14
	public	String **getHost** ()	ε134
1.3	public	String **getPath** ()	
	public	int **getPort** ()	ε134
	public	String **getProtocol** ()	ε134
1.3	public	String **getQuery** ()	
	public	String **getRef** ()	ε134
1.3	public	String **getUserInfo** ()	
1	public synchronized	int **hashCode** ()	
	public	URLConnection **openConnection** () throws java.io.IOException	ε135,138,140,141,142
●	public final java.io.InputStream	**openStream** () throws java.io.IOException	ε136,139,14
	public	boolean **sameFile** (URL other)	
	protected	void **set** (String protocol, String host, int port, String file, String ref)	
1.3	protected	void **set** (String protocol, String host, int port, String authority, String userInfo, String path, String query, String ref)	
△	public static	void **setURLStreamHandlerFactory** (*URLStreamHandlerFactory* fac)	
	public	String **toExternalForm** ()	
1	public	**String toString** ()	ε133
*	public	**URL** (String spec) throws MalformedURLException	ε132,134,135,136,137
*	public	**URL** (URL context, String spec) throws MalformedURLException	
*	public	**URL** (String protocol, String host, String file) throws MalformedURLException	
1.2 *	public	**URL** (URL context, String spec, URLStreamHandler handler) throws MalformedURLException	
*	public	**URL** (String protocol, String host, int port, String file) throws MalformedURLException	ε132
1.2 *	public	**URL** (String protocol, String host, int port, String file, URLStreamHandler handler) throws MalformedURLException	

URLClassLoader	java.net

Object
○　└ClassLoader [1]
1.2　　└java.security.SecureClassLoader [2]
1.2　　　└URLClassLoader

1	*25 inherited members from ClassLoader not shown*	
	protected	void **addURL** (URL url)

Class　*Interface*　—extends　- - -implements　○ abstract　● final　△ static　▲ static final　* constructor　x x—inherited　x **x**—declared　**x x**—overridden
ε*n*—examples of usage　‿—has subclass　package—see other volume

U

● 2	protected final............	Class	**defineClass** (String name, byte[] b, int off, int len, java.security.CodeSource cs)
	protected	Package	**definePackage** (String name, java.util.jar.Manifest man, URL url)
			throws IllegalArgumentException
1	protected	**Class**	**findClass** (String name) throws ClassNotFoundException
1	public.....................	**URL**	**findResource** (String name)
1	public..	*java.util.Enumeration*	**findResources** (String name) throws java.io.IOException
2	protected......	**java.security ↵**	**getPermissions** (java.security.CodeSource codesource)
		.PermissionCollection	
	public....................	URL[]	**getURLs** ()
△	public static . URLClassLoader		**newInstance** (URL[] urls)
△	public static . URLClassLoader		**newInstance** (URL[] urls, ClassLoader parent)
✳	public...........................		**URLClassLoader** (URL[] urls) ε68,69
✳	public...........................		**URLClassLoader** (URL[] urls, ClassLoader parent)
✳	public...........................		**URLClassLoader** (URL[] urls, ClassLoader parent, *URLStreamHandlerFactory* factory)

URLConnection java.net

Object[1]
└URLConnection

1.4	public......................void	**addRequestProperty** (String key, String value)
	protected .... boolean	**allowUserInteraction**
○	public abstract.............void	**connect** () throws java.io.IOException ε142,143
	protected .... boolean	**connected**
	protected .... boolean	**doInput**
	protected .... boolean	**doOutput**
	public .... boolean	**getAllowUserInteraction** ()
	public .... Object	**getContent** () throws java.io.IOException
1.3	public .... Object	**getContent** (Class[] classes) throws java.io.IOException
	public.................... String	**getContentEncoding** ()
	public......................int	**getContentLength** ()
	public.................... String	**getContentType** ()
	public...................... long	**getDate** ()
△	public static .... boolean	**getDefaultAllowUserInteraction** ()
D △	public static .... String	**getDefaultRequestProperty** (String key)
	public .... boolean	**getDefaultUseCaches** ()
	public .... boolean	**getDoInput** ()
	public .... boolean	**getDoOutput** ()
	public .... long	**getExpiration** ()
1.2 △	public static synchronized .... *FileNameMap*	**getFileNameMap** ()
	public.................... String	**getHeaderField** (int n) ε140,141
	public.................... String	**getHeaderField** (String name)
	public .... long	**getHeaderFieldDate** (String name, long Default)
	public......................int	**getHeaderFieldInt** (String name, int Default)
	public.................... String	**getHeaderFieldKey** (int n) ε140,141
1.4	public .... *java.util.Map*	**getHeaderFields** ()
	public .... long	**getIfModifiedSince** ()
	public ...... java.io.InputStream	**getInputStream** () throws java.io.IOException ε135
	public .... long	**getLastModified** ()
	public .... java.io.OutputStream	**getOutputStream** () throws java.io.IOException ε135
1.2	public java.security.Permission	**getPermission** () throws java.io.IOException
1.4	public .... *java.util.Map*	**getRequestProperties** ()
	public.................... String	**getRequestProperty** (String key)
	public .... URL	**getURL** ()
	public .... boolean	**getUseCaches** ()
△	public static .... String	**guessContentTypeFromName** (String fname)
△	public static .... String	**guessContentTypeFromStream** (java.io.InputStream is) throws java.io.IOException
	protected .... long	**ifModifiedSince**
	public......................void	**setAllowUserInteraction** (boolean allowuserinteraction)
△	public static synchronized void	**setContentHandlerFactory** (*ContentHandlerFactory* fac)
△	public static ....void	**setDefaultAllowUserInteraction** (boolean defaultallowuserinteraction)
D △	public static ....void	**setDefaultRequestProperty** (String key, String value)
	public......................void	**setDefaultUseCaches** (boolean defaultusecaches)
	public......................void	**setDoInput** (boolean doinput)
	public......................void	**setDoOutput** (boolean dooutput) ε135
1.2 △	public static ....void	**setFileNameMap** (*FileNameMap* map)
	public......................void	**setIfModifiedSince** (long ifmodifiedsince)
	public......................void	**setRequestProperty** (String key, String value) ε142
	public......................void	**setUseCaches** (boolean usecaches)
1	public .... **String**	**toString** ()
	protected .... URL	**url**

U

Classes

URLConnection

*	protected	**URLConnection** (URL url)
	protected . . . . boolean	**useCaches**

URLDecoder
java.net

Object
└URLDecoder *(1.2)*

D	△	public static . . . . String	**decode** (String s)
1.4	△	public static . . . . String	**decode** (String s, String enc) throws java.io.UnsupportedEncodingException
			ε157
*		public	**URLDecoder** ()

URLEncoder
java.net

Object
└URLEncoder

D	△	public static . . . . String	**encode** (String s)
1.4	△	public static . . . . String	**encode** (String s, String enc) throws java.io.UnsupportedEncodingException
			ε135,157

URLStreamHandler
java.net

Object
└URLStreamHandler ○

1.3	protected . . . . boolean	**equals** (URL u1, URL u2)
1.3	protected . . . . int	**getDefaultPort** ()
1.3	protected synchronized	**getHostAddress** (URL u)
	. . . . InetAddress	
1.3	protected . . . . int	**hashCode** (URL u)
1.3	protected . . . . boolean	**hostsEqual** (URL u1, URL u2)
○	protected abstract	**openConnection** (URL u) throws java.io.IOException
	. . . . URLConnection	
	protected . . . . void	**parseURL** (URL u, String spec, int start, int limit)
1.3	protected . . . . boolean	**sameFile** (URL u1, URL u2)
D	protected . . . . void	**setURL** (URL u, String protocol, String host, int port, String file, String ref)
1.3	protected . . . . void	**setURL** (URL u, String protocol, String host, int port, String authority, String userInfo, String path, String query, String ref)
	protected . . . . String	**toExternalForm** (URL u)
*	public	**URLStreamHandler** ()

URLStreamHandlerFactory
java.net

URLStreamHandlerFactory

	public . . . . . . URLStreamHandler	**createURLStreamHandler** (String protocol)

URLStringHelper
org.omg.CosNaming.NamingContextExtPackage

Object
└URLStringHelper *(1.4 ○)*

△	public static . . . . String	**extract** (org.omg.CORBA.Any a)
△	public static . . . . String	**id** ()
△	public static . . . . void	**insert** (org.omg.CORBA.Any a, String that)
△	public static . . . . String	**read** (org.omg.CORBA.portable.InputStream istream)
△	public static synchronized	**type** ()
	. org.omg.CORBA.TypeCode	
*	public	**URLStringHelper** ()
△	public static . . . . void	**write** (org.omg.CORBA.portable.OutputStream ostream, String value)

Class   *Interface*   —extends   - - -implements   ○ abstract   ● final   △ static   ▲ static final   * constructor   x x—inherited   x **x**—declared   **x x**—overridden
εn—examples of usage   ‿—has subclass   package—see other volume

USER_EXCEPTION	org.omg.PortableInterceptor

1.4   *USER_EXCEPTION*

▲   public static final .... short **value** = 2

UserException	org.omg.CORBA

Object
└Throwable --------------------------- *java.io.Serializable*⌟
  └Exception
1.2 O   └UserException⌟ -------------------- *org.omg.CORBA.portable.IDLEntity*⌟ (*java.io.Serializable*)

∗   protected .... **UserException** ()
∗   protected .... **UserException** (String reason)

UShortSeqHelper	org.omg.CORBA

Object
1.3 O └UShortSeqHelper

△   public static .... short[] **extract** (Any a)
△   public static ....String **id** ()
△   public static ....void **insert** (Any a, short[] that)
△   public static .... short[] **read** (org.omg.CORBA.portable.InputStream istream)
△   public static synchronized .... **type** ()
     .... TypeCode
∗   public........................... **UShortSeqHelper** ()
△   public static ....void **write** (org.omg.CORBA.portable.OutputStream ostream, short[] value)

UShortSeqHolder	org.omg.CORBA

Object
1.3 ● └UShortSeqHolder --------------------- *org.omg.CORBA.portable.Streamable*⌟[1]

1   public......................void **_read** (org.omg.CORBA.portable.InputStream i)
1   public............... TypeCode **_type** ()
1   public......................void **_write** (org.omg.CORBA.portable.OutputStream o)
∗   public........................... **UShortSeqHolder** ()
∗   public........................... **UShortSeqHolder** (short[] initialValue)
    public.................. short[] **value**

UTFDataFormatException ∘	java.io

Object
└Throwable --------------------------- *Serializable*⌟
  └Exception
    └IOException
      └UTFDataFormatException

∗   public........................... **UTFDataFormatException** ()
∗   public........................... **UTFDataFormatException** (String s)

Util	javax.rmi.CORBA

Object
1.3 └Util

△   public static .... Object **copyObject** (Object obj, org.omg.CORBA.ORB orb)
        throws java.rmi.RemoteException
△   public static .... Object[] **copyObjects** (Object[] obj, org.omg.CORBA.ORB orb)
        throws java.rmi.RemoteException
△   public static ..... *ValueHandler* **createValueHandler** ()
△   public static .... String **getCodebase** (Class clz)
△   public static .... *Tie* **getTie** (*java.rmi.Remote* target)
△   public static .... boolean **isLocal** (Stub stub) throws java.rmi.RemoteException
△   public static .... Class **loadClass** (String className, String remoteCodebase, ClassLoader loader)
        throws ClassNotFoundException

U

Util

△	public static . . . . java.rmi.RemoteException	**mapSystemException** (org.omg.CORBA.SystemException ex)	
△	public static . . . . Object	**readAny** (org.omg.CORBA.portable.InputStream in)	
△	public static . . . . void	**registerTarget** (*Tie* tie, *java.rmi.Remote* target)	
△	public static . . . . void	**unexportObject** (*java.rmi.Remote* target) throws java.rmi.NoSuchObjectException	
△	public static . . . . java.rmi.RemoteException	**wrapException** (Throwable orig)	
△	public static . . . . void	**writeAbstractObject** (org.omg.CORBA.portable.OutputStream out, Object obj)	
△	public static . . . . void	**writeAny** (org.omg.CORBA.portable.OutputStream out, Object obj)	
△	public static . . . . void	**writeRemoteObject** (org.omg.CORBA.portable.OutputStream out, Object obj)	

UtilDelegate   javax.rmi.CORBA

1.3   *UtilDelegate*

public. . . . . Object	**copyObject** (Object obj, org.omg.CORBA.ORB orb) throws java.rmi.RemoteException	
public. . . . . Object[]	**copyObjects** (Object[] obj, org.omg.CORBA.ORB orb) throws java.rmi.RemoteException	
public. . . . . *ValueHandler*	**createValueHandler** ()	
public. . . . . String	**getCodebase** (Class clz)	
public. . . . . *Tie*	**getTie** (*java.rmi.Remote* target)	
public. . . . . boolean	**isLocal** (Stub stub) throws java.rmi.RemoteException	
public. . . . . Class	**loadClass** (String className, String remoteCodebase, ClassLoader loader) throws ClassNotFoundException	
public. . . . . java.rmi.RemoteException	**mapSystemException** (org.omg.CORBA.SystemException ex)	
public. . . . . Object	**readAny** (org.omg.CORBA.portable.InputStream in)	
public. . . . . void	**registerTarget** (*Tie* tie, *java.rmi.Remote* target)	
public. . . . . void	**unexportObject** (*java.rmi.Remote* target) throws java.rmi.NoSuchObjectException	
public. . . . . java.rmi.RemoteException	**wrapException** (Throwable obj)	
public. . . . . void	**writeAbstractObject** (org.omg.CORBA.portable.OutputStream out, Object obj)	
public. . . . . void	**writeAny** (org.omg.CORBA.portable.OutputStream out, Object obj)	
public. . . . . void	**writeRemoteObject** (org.omg.CORBA.portable.OutputStream out, Object obj)	

U

ValueBase   org.omg.CORBA.portable

1.3   *ValueBase* ———————————————— *IDLEntity* ⌄ (*java.io.Serializable*)

public. . . . . String[]	**_truncatable_ids** ()

ValueBaseHelper   org.omg.CORBA

Object
└ ValueBaseHelper

1.3 ○

△	public static *java.io.Serializable*	**extract** (Any a)
△	public static . . . . String	**id** ()
△	public static . . . . void	**insert** (Any a, *java.io.Serializable* that)
△	public static *java.io.Serializable*	**read** (org.omg.CORBA.portable.InputStream istream)
△	public static synchronized . . . . TypeCode	**type** ()
✳	public.	**ValueBaseHelper** ()
△	public static . . . . void	**write** (org.omg.CORBA.portable.OutputStream ostream, *java.io.Serializable* value)

ValueBaseHolder   org.omg.CORBA

Object
└ ValueBaseHolder - *org.omg.CORBA.portable.Streamable* ⌄ [1]

1.3 ●

[1]	public. . . . . void	**_read** (org.omg.CORBA.portable.InputStream input)
[1]	public. . . . . TypeCode	**_type** ()
[1]	public. . . . . void	**_write** (org.omg.CORBA.portable.OutputStream output)
	public. . . . . . . *java.io.Serializable*	**value**
✳	public.	**ValueBaseHolder** ()
✳	public.	**ValueBaseHolder** (*java.io.Serializable* initial)

Class   *Interface*   —extends   - - -implements   ○ abstract   ● final   △ static   ▲ static final   ✳ constructor   x x—inherited   x **x**—declared   **x x**—overridden
εn—examples of usage   ⌄—has subclass   package—see other volume

ValueFactory | org.omg.CORBA.portable

1.3 | *ValueFactory*

public ....*java.io.Serializable* **read_value** (org.omg.CORBA_2_3.portable.InputStream is)

ValueHandler | javax.rmi.CORBA

1.3 | *ValueHandler*

public .... String **getRMIRepositoryID** (Class clz)
public .... *org.omg* ↵ **getRunTimeCodeBase** ()
    .SendingContext.RunTime
public .... boolean **isCustomMarshaled** (Class clz)
public ....*java.io.Serializable* **readValue** (org.omg.CORBA.portable.InputStream in, int offset, Class clz,
    String repositoryID, *org.omg.SendingContext.RunTime* sender)
public ....*java.io.Serializable* **writeReplace** (*java.io.Serializable* value)
public .... void **writeValue** (org.omg.CORBA.portable.OutputStream out, *java.io.Serializable* value)

ValueMember | org.omg.CORBA

Object
1.2 ● └ ValueMember ------------------------- *org.omg.CORBA.portable.IDLEntity* (*java.io.Serializable*)

public .... short **access**
public .... String **defined_in**
public .... String **id**
public .... String **name**
public .... TypeCode **type**
public .... *IDLType* **type_def**
* public .... **ValueMember** ()
* public .... **ValueMember** (String __name, String __id, String __defined_in, String __version,
    TypeCode __type, *IDLType* __type_def, short __access)
public .... String **version**

ValueMemberHelper | org.omg.CORBA

Object
1.3 ○ └ ValueMemberHelper

△ public static ..... ValueMember **extract** (Any a)
△ public static .... String **id** ()
△ public static .... void **insert** (Any a, ValueMember that)
△ public static ..... ValueMember **read** (org.omg.CORBA.portable.InputStream istream)
△ public static synchronized .... **type** ()
    .... TypeCode
* public .... **ValueMemberHelper** ()
△ public static .... void **write** (org.omg.CORBA.portable.OutputStream ostream, ValueMember value)

Vector | java.util

Object[1]
1.2 ○ └ AbstractCollection[2] --------------------- *Collection*
1.2 ○   └ AbstractList[3] --------------------- *List* (*Collection*)
        └ Vector ------------------------- *RandomAccess, Cloneable, java.io.Serializable*

1.2	3	public synchronized .. **boolean add** (Object o)		ε342,349,352,354,358
1.2	3	public .... **void add** (int index, Object element)		ε349,362
1.2	2	public synchronized .. **boolean addAll** (*Collection* c)		ε351,353
1.2	3	public synchronized .. **boolean addAll** (int index, *Collection* c)		
		public synchronized ....void **addElement** (Object obj)		
		public synchronized ....int **capacity** ()		
		protected .... int **capacityIncrement**		
1.2	3	public .... **void clear** ()		ε351,353
	1	public synchronized .... **Object clone** ()		
	2	public .... **boolean contains** (Object elem)		ε352
1.2	2	public synchronized .. **boolean containsAll** (*Collection* c)		
		public synchronized ....void **copyInto** (Object[] anArray)		
		public synchronized .... Object **elementAt** (int index)		
		protected .... int **elementCount**		

V

Classes

Vector

		protected .... Object[]	**elementData**		
		public .... *Enumeration*	**elements** ()		
		public synchronized ......void	**ensureCapacity** (int minCapacity)		
	3	public synchronized ..**boolean**	**equals** (Object o)		
	3	public synchronized ....Object	**firstElement** ()		
1.2	3	public synchronized ..**Object**	**get** (int index)		ε349,234
	3	public synchronized .... **int**	**hashCode** ()		
	3	public........................ **int**	**indexOf** (Object elem)		
		public synchronized ....int	**indexOf** (Object elem, int index)		
		public synchronized .....void	**insertElementAt** (Object obj, int index)		
	2	public synchronized ..**boolean**	**isEmpty** ()		ε102
1.2	3	public................... *Iterator*	iterator ()		ε345,352,354,355,356
		public synchronized ....Object	**lastElement** ()		
	3	public synchronized ... **int**	**lastIndexOf** (Object elem)		
		public synchronized ....int	**lastIndexOf** (Object elem, int index)		
1.2	3	public...............*ListIterator*	listIterator ()		
1.2	3	public...............*ListIterator*	listIterator (int index)		
1.2	3	protected transient...........int	modCount		
1.2	3	public synchronized ....**Object**	**remove** (int index)		ε349
1.2	2	public................**boolean**	**remove** (Object o)		ε349,352
1.2	2	public synchronized ..**boolean**	**removeAll** (*Collection* c)		ε351,353
		public synchronized ....void	**removeAllElements** ()		
		public synchronized .. boolean	**removeElement** (Object obj)		
		public synchronized ......void	**removeElementAt** (int index)		
1.2	3	protected.................. **void**	**removeRange** (int fromIndex, int toIndex)		
1.2	2	public synchronized ..**boolean**	**retainAll** (*Collection* c)		ε351,353
1.2	3	public synchronized ....**Object**	**set** (int index, Object element)		ε348
		public synchronized ......void	**setElementAt** (Object obj, int index)		
		public synchronized ......void	**setSize** (int newSize)		
	2	public synchronized .... **int**	**size** ()		ε340,349,351,352,358
1.2	3	public synchronized .. *List*	**subList** (int fromIndex, int toIndex)		ε351
1.2	2	public synchronized ..**Object[]**	**toArray** ()		ε340
1.2	2	public synchronized ..**Object[]**	**toArray** (Object[] a)		ε340,352,358,194,508
	2	public synchronized .... **String**	**toString** ()		
		public synchronized ....void	**trimToSize** ()		
	✳	public........................	**Vector** ()		
	✳	public........................	**Vector** (int initialCapacity)		
1.2	✳	public........................	**Vector** (*Collection* c)		
	✳	public........................	**Vector** (int initialCapacity, int capacityIncrement)		

V

VerifyError java.lang

```
Object
└ Throwable - - - - - - - - - - - - - - - - - - - - - - - - - - - java.io.Serializable ⌐
  └ Error
    └ LinkageError
      └ VerifyError
```

✳	public.........................	**VerifyError** ()
✳	public.........................	**VerifyError** (String s)

VersionSpecHelper org.omg.CORBA

```
Object
└ VersionSpecHelper
```
1.3 ○

△	public static ....String	**extract** (Any a)
△	public static ....String	**id** ()
△	public static ....void	**insert** (Any a, String that)
△	public static ....String	**read** (org.omg.CORBA.portable.InputStream istream)
△	public static synchronized	**type** ()
	.... TypeCode	
✳	public.........................	**VersionSpecHelper** ()
△	public static ....void	**write** (org.omg.CORBA.portable.OutputStream ostream, String value)

Class   *Interface*   —extends   - - -implements   ○ abstract   ● final   △ static   ▲ static final   ✳ constructor   x x—inherited   x **x**—declared   **x x**—overridden
ε*n*—examples of usage   ⌐—has subclass   package—see other volume

VetoableChangeListener — java.beans

1.1	*VetoableChangeListener*————————*java.util.EventListener* ˎ	ε3,2,333,493,494

public......................void **vetoableChange** (PropertyChangeEvent evt) throws PropertyVetoException
ε12

VetoableChangeListenerProxy — java.beans

Object
1.4 O └java.util.EventListenerProxy [1] - - - - - - - - - - - - - *java.util.EventListener* ˎ
1.4 └VetoableChangeListenerProxy - - - - - - - - - - *VetoableChangeListener* [2] (*java.util.EventListener*)

1 public... *java.util.EventListener* getListener ()
  public.....................String **getPropertyName** ()
2 public......................void **vetoableChange** (PropertyChangeEvent evt) throws PropertyVetoException
                                                      ε12
* public.........................**VetoableChangeListenerProxy** (String propertyName,
                            VetoableChangeListener listener)

VetoableChangeSupport — java.beans

Object
1.1 └VetoableChangeSupport - - - - - - - - - - - - - - - - - *java.io.Serializable* ˎ

  public synchronized ....void **addVetoableChangeListener** (*VetoableChangeListener* listener)
                                                ε3
1.2 public synchronized ....void **addVetoableChangeListener** (String propertyName,
                              VetoableChangeListener listener)
1.2 public......................void **fireVetoableChange** (PropertyChangeEvent evt) throws PropertyVetoException
1.2 public......................void **fireVetoableChange** (String propertyName, boolean oldValue, boolean newValue)
                              throws PropertyVetoException
1.2 public......................void **fireVetoableChange** (String propertyName, int oldValue, int newValue)
                              throws PropertyVetoException
  public......................void **fireVetoableChange** (String propertyName, Object oldValue, Object newValue)
                              throws PropertyVetoException   ε3
1.4 public synchronized .... **getVetoableChangeListeners** ()
  ... *VetoableChangeListener[]*
1.4 public synchronized .... **getVetoableChangeListeners** (String propertyName)
  ... *VetoableChangeListener[]*
1.2 public synchronized .. boolean **hasListeners** (String propertyName)
  public synchronized ....void **removeVetoableChangeListener** (*VetoableChangeListener* listener)
                                                ε3
1.2 public synchronized ....void **removeVetoableChangeListener** (String propertyName,
                              VetoableChangeListener listener)
* public......................... **VetoableChangeSupport** (Object sourceBean)   ε3

VirtualMachineError — java.lang

Object
└Throwable - *java.io.Serializable* ˎ
 └Error
O   └VirtualMachineError ˎ

* public......................... **VirtualMachineError** ()
* public......................... **VirtualMachineError** (String s)

Visibility — java.beans

1.1	*Visibility* ˎ	

public.................. boolean **avoidingGui** ()
public.....................void **dontUseGui** ()
public.................. boolean **needsGui** ()
public.....................void **okToUseGui** ()

V

Classes

VisibilityHelper | org.omg.CORBA

```
        Object
1.3 ○   └ VisibilityHelper
```

△	public static ....short **extract** (Any a)
△	public static ....String **id** ()
△	public static ....void **insert** (Any a, short that)
△	public static ....short **read** (org.omg.CORBA.portable.InputStream istream)
△	public static synchronized .... **type** ()
	.... TypeCode
✳	public......................... **VisibilityHelper** ()
△	public static ....void **write** (org.omg.CORBA.portable.OutputStream ostream, short value)

VM_ABSTRACT | org.omg.CORBA

```
1.2   VM_ABSTRACT
```

▲	public static final ....short **value** = 2

VM_CUSTOM | org.omg.CORBA

```
1.2   VM_CUSTOM
```

▲	public static final ....short **value** = 1

VM_NONE | org.omg.CORBA

```
1.2   VM_NONE
```

▲	public static final ....short **value** = 0

VM_TRUNCATABLE | org.omg.CORBA

```
1.2   VM_TRUNCATABLE
```

▲	public static final ....short **value** = 3

VMID | java.rmi.dgc

```
        Object[1]
1.1 ●   └ VMID - - - - - - - - - - - - - - - - - - - - - - - - - - - - - - - *java.io.Serializable*
```

	1	public.................. **boolean equals** (Object obj)
	1	public...................... **int hashCode** ()
D △		public static .... boolean **isUnique** ()
	1	public.................... **String toString** ()
✳		public......................... **VMID** ()

Void | java.lang

```
        Object
1.1 ●   └ Void
```

▲	public static final .... Class **TYPE**	ε60

WCharSeqHelper | org.omg.CORBA

```
        Object
1.3 ○   └ WCharSeqHelper
```

△	public static ....char[] **extract** (Any a)
△	public static ....String **id** ()
△	public static ....void **insert** (Any a, char[] that)
△	public static ....char[] **read** (org.omg.CORBA.portable.InputStream istream)

Class *Interface* —extends - - -implements ○ abstract ● final △ static ▲ static final ✳ constructor x x—inherited x **x**—declared **x x**—overridden
εn—examples of usage ⌐—has subclass package—see other volume

△	public static synchronized .... TypeCode	**type** ()	
*	public...........................	**WCharSeqHelper** ()	
△	public static ....void	**write** (org.omg.CORBA.portable.OutputStream ostream, char[] value)	

WCharSeqHolder — org.omg.CORBA

Object
1.3 ● └WCharSeqHolder ---------------------- *org.omg.CORBA.portable.Streamable*⌣ [1]

1	public....................void	**_read** (org.omg.CORBA.portable.InputStream i)	
1	public...............TypeCode	**_type** ()	
1	public....................void	**_write** (org.omg.CORBA.portable.OutputStream o)	
	public...................char[]	**value**	
*	public.........................	**WCharSeqHolder** ()	
*	public.........................	**WCharSeqHolder** (char[] initialValue)	

WeakHashMap — java.util

Object
1.2 ○ └AbstractMap [1] ------------------------ *Map*⌣
1.2   └WeakHashMap

1	public.................... **void**	**clear** ()	
1	protected ....Object	clone () throws CloneNotSupportedException	
1	public.................**boolean**	**containsKey** (Object key)	ε344
1	public.................**boolean**	**containsValue** (Object value)	
1	public..................... ***Set***	**entrySet** ()	ε345
1	public................. boolean	equals (Object o)	
1	public..................**Object**	**get** (Object key)	ε337,344,346,356,357
1	public....................int	hashCode ()	
1	public.................**boolean**	**isEmpty** ()	
1	public..................... ***Set***	**keySet** ()	ε194,340,345,355,356
1	public..................**Object**	**put** (Object key, Object value)	ε337,344,346,355,356
1	public.................... **void**	**putAll** (*Map* t)	
1	public..................**Object**	**remove** (Object key)	ε355
1	public................... **int**	**size** ()	ε355
1	public.................String	toString ()	
1	public............. ***Collection***	**values** ()	ε340,345,355
*	public.........................	**WeakHashMap** ()	ε357
*	public.........................	**WeakHashMap** (int initialCapacity)	
1.3 *	public.........................	**WeakHashMap** (*Map* t)	
*	public.........................	**WeakHashMap** (int initialCapacity, float loadFactor)	

W

WeakReference — java.lang.ref

Object ε107
1.2 ○ └Reference [1]
1.2   └WeakReference

1	public....................void	clear ()	ε108
1	public.................boolean	enqueue ()	
1	public.................Object	get ()	ε357,106
1	public.................boolean	isEnqueued ()	
*	public.........................	**WeakReference** (Object referent)	ε357
*	public.........................	**WeakReference** (Object referent, ReferenceQueue q)	ε107

Classes

WritableByteChannel — java.nio.channels

1.4   *WritableByteChannel*⌣ ——————— *Channel*⌣ [1]

1	public....................void	close () throws java.io.IOException	ε170,167,171,172,174
1	public.................boolean	isOpen ()	
	public.......................int	**write** (java.nio.ByteBuffer src) throws java.io.IOException	ε170

WriteAbortedException

WriteAbortedException				java.io

```
        Object
        └Throwable¹ - - - - - - - - - - - - - - - - - - - - - - - - - - Serializable⌐
          └Exception
            └IOException
1.1 ○         └ObjectStreamException
1.1             └WriteAbortedException
```

	public	Exception	**detail**	
1.4	1 public	**Throwable**	**getCause** ()	
	1 public	**String**	**getMessage** ()	
✳	public		**WriteAbortedException** (String s, Exception ex)	

Writer		java.io

```
        Object
1.1 ○   └Writer⌐
```

○	public abstract	void	**close** () throws IOException	ε41,43
○	public abstract	void	**flush** () throws IOException	ε224
	protected	Object	**lock**	
	public	void	**write** (char[] cbuf) throws IOException	
	public	void	**write** (int c) throws IOException	
	public	void	**write** (String str) throws IOException	ε41,43,224
○	public abstract	void	**write** (char[] cbuf, int off, int len) throws IOException	
	public	void	**write** (String str, int off, int len) throws IOException	
✳	protected		**Writer** ()	
✳	protected		**Writer** (Object lock)	

WrongAdapter		org.omg.PortableServer.POAPackage

```
        Object
        └Throwable - - - - - - - - - - - - - - - - - - - - - - - - - java.io.Serializable⌐
          └Exception
1.2 ○       └org.omg.CORBA.UserException - - - - - - org.omg.CORBA.portable.IDLEntity⌐ (java.io.Serializable)
1.4 ●         └WrongAdapter
```

✳	public	**WrongAdapter** ()	
✳	public	**WrongAdapter** (String $reason)	

WrongAdapterHelper		org.omg.PortableServer.POAPackage

```
        Object
1.4 ○   └WrongAdapterHelper
```

△	public static	WrongAdapter	**extract** (org.omg.CORBA.Any a)	
△	public static	String	**id** ()	
△	public static	void	**insert** (org.omg.CORBA.Any a, WrongAdapter that)	
△	public static	WrongAdapter	**read** (org.omg.CORBA.portable.InputStream istream)	
△	public static synchronized		**type** ()	
	. org.omg.CORBA.TypeCode			
△	public static	void	**write** (org.omg.CORBA.portable.OutputStream ostream, WrongAdapter value)	
✳	public		**WrongAdapterHelper** ()	

WrongPolicy		org.omg.PortableServer.POAPackage

```
        Object
        └Throwable - - - - - - - - - - - - - - - - - - - - - - - - - java.io.Serializable⌐
          └Exception
1.2 ○       └org.omg.CORBA.UserException - - - - - - org.omg.CORBA.portable.IDLEntity⌐ (java.io.Serializable)
1.4 ●         └WrongPolicy
```

✳	public	**WrongPolicy** ()	
✳	public	**WrongPolicy** (String $reason)	

Class *Interface* —extends - - -implements ○ abstract ● final △ static ▲ static final ✳ constructor x x—inherited x **x**—declared **x x**—overridden
εn—examples of usage ⌐—has subclass package—see other volume

W

WrongPolicyHelper org.omg.PortableServer.POAPackage

```
       Object
1.4 ○  └WrongPolicyHelper
```

△	public static ...... WrongPolicy	**extract** (org.omg.CORBA.Any a)
△	public static .... String	**id** ()
△	public static ....void	**insert** (org.omg.CORBA.Any a, WrongPolicy that)
△	public static ...... WrongPolicy	**read** (org.omg.CORBA.portable.InputStream istream)
△	public static synchronized .... . org.omg.CORBA.TypeCode	**type** ()
△	public static ....void	**write** (org.omg.CORBA.portable.OutputStream ostream, WrongPolicy value)
*	public..........................	**WrongPolicyHelper** ()

WrongTransaction org.omg.CORBA

```
       Object
       └Throwable - - - - - - - - - - - - - - - - - - - - - - - - - - - - java.io.Serializable⌄
         └Exception
1.2 ○      └UserException - - - - - - - - - - - - - - - - - - - - - org.omg.CORBA.portable.IDLEntity⌄ (java.io.Serializable)
1.2 ●        └WrongTransaction
```

*	public..........................	**WrongTransaction** ()
*	public..........................	**WrongTransaction** (String reason)

WrongTransactionHelper org.omg.CORBA

```
       Object
1.4 ○  └WrongTransactionHelper
```

△	public static WrongTransaction	**extract** (Any a)
△	public static .... String	**id** ()
△	public static ....void	**insert** (Any a, WrongTransaction that)
△	public static WrongTransaction	**read** (org.omg.CORBA.portable.InputStream istream)
△	public static synchronized .... TypeCode	**type** ()
△	public static ....void	**write** (org.omg.CORBA.portable.OutputStream ostream, WrongTransaction value)
*	public..........................	**WrongTransactionHelper** ()

W

WrongTransactionHolder org.omg.CORBA

```
       Object
1.4 ●  └WrongTransactionHolder - - - - - - - - - - - - - - - - org.omg.CORBA.portable.Streamable⌄[1]
```

[1]	public......................void	**_read** (org.omg.CORBA.portable.InputStream i)
[1]	public............... TypeCode	**_type** ()
[1]	public......................void	**_write** (org.omg.CORBA.portable.OutputStream o)
	public....... WrongTransaction	**value**
*	public..........................	**WrongTransactionHolder** ()
*	public..........................	**WrongTransactionHolder** (WrongTransaction initialValue)

Classes

WStringSeqHelper org.omg.CORBA

```
       Object
1.4 ○  └WStringSeqHelper
```

△	public static .... String[]	**extract** (Any a)
△	public static .... String	**id** ()
△	public static ....void	**insert** (Any a, String[] that)
△	public static .... String[]	**read** (org.omg.CORBA.portable.InputStream istream)
△	public static synchronized .... TypeCode	**type** ()
△	public static ....void	**write** (org.omg.CORBA.portable.OutputStream ostream, String[] value)
*	public..........................	**WStringSeqHelper** ()

WStringSeqHolder

WStringSeqHolder				org.omg.CORBA

		Object	
1.4 ●		└WStringSeqHolder - *org.omg.CORBA.portable.Streamable*⌐ [1]	

	1	public.....................void	**_read** (org.omg.CORBA.portable.InputStream i)
	1	public................TypeCode	**_type** ()
	1	public.....................void	**_write** (org.omg.CORBA.portable.OutputStream o)
		public...................String[]	**value**
✳		public..................	**WStringSeqHolder** ()
✳		public..................	**WStringSeqHolder** (String[] initialValue)

WStringValueHelper			org.omg.CORBA

		Object	
1.3		└WStringValueHelper - - - - - - - - - - - - - - - - - - - *org.omg.CORBA.portable.BoxedValueHelper* [1]	

△		public static ....String	**extract** (Any a)
	1	public.....................String	**get_id** ()
△		public static ....String	**id** ()
△		public static ....void	**insert** (Any a, String that)
△		public static ....String	**read** (org.omg.CORBA.portable.InputStream istream)
	1	public.......*java.io.Serializable*	**read_value** (org.omg.CORBA.portable.InputStream istream)
△		public static synchronized ....TypeCode	**type** ()
△		public static ....void	**write** (org.omg.CORBA.portable.OutputStream ostream, String value)
	1	public.....................void	**write_value** (org.omg.CORBA.portable.OutputStream ostream, *java.io.Serializable* value)
✳		public..................	**WStringValueHelper** ()

X500Principal			javax.security.auth.x500

		Object [1]		
1.4 ●		└X500Principal - *java.security.Principal*⌐ [2], *java.io.Serializable*⌐		

▲		public static final ....String	**CANONICAL** = "CANONICAL"	
	1	public................**boolean**	**equals** (Object o)	
		public................byte[]	**getEncoded** ()	
	2	public.....................String	**getName** ()	ε227,508
		public.....................String	**getName** (String format)	
	1	public................**int**	**hashCode** ()	
▲		public static final ....String	**RFC1779** = "RFC1779"	
▲		public static final ....String	**RFC2253** = "RFC2253"	
	1	public................**String**	**toString** ()	
✳		public..................	**X500Principal** (byte[] name)	
✳		public..................	**X500Principal** (java.io.InputStream is)	
✳		public..................	**X500Principal** (String name)	

X500PrivateCredential			javax.security.auth.x500

		Object	
1.4 ●		└X500PrivateCredential - - - - - - - - - - - - - - - - - - *javax.security.auth.Destroyable* [1]	

	1	public.....................void	**destroy** ()
		public.....................String	**getAlias** ()
		public.................java↵ .security.cert.X509Certificate	**getCertificate** ()
		public. *java.security.PrivateKey*	**getPrivateKey** ()
	1	public.................. boolean	**isDestroyed** ()
✳		public..................	**X500PrivateCredential** (java.security.cert.X509Certificate cert, *java.security.PrivateKey* key)
✳		public..................	**X500PrivateCredential** (java.security.cert.X509Certificate cert, *java.security.PrivateKey* key, String alias)

Class *Interface* —extends - - -implements ○ abstract ● final △ static ▲ static final ✳ constructor x x—inherited x **x**—declared **x x**—overridden
ε*n*—examples of usage ⌐—has subclass package—see other volume

X509Certificate❶   java.security.cert

Object
  ε230,231,225,227,229
1.2 ○ └─Certificate [1] - *java.io.Serializable*‿
1.2 ○   └─X509Certificate - *X509Extension*

○	public abstract............void	**checkValidity** () throws CertificateExpiredException, CertificateNotYetValidException	
○	public abstract............void	**checkValidity** (java.util.Date date) throws CertificateExpiredException, CertificateNotYetValidException	
1	public................ boolean	equals (Object other)	
○	public abstract................int	**getBasicConstraints** ()	
○ 1	public abstract..........byte[]	getEncoded () throws CertificateEncodingException	ε506,224
1.4	public............. *java.util.List*	**getExtendedKeyUsage** () throws CertificateParsingException	
1.4	public....... *java.util.Collection*	**getIssuerAlternativeNames** () throws CertificateParsingException	
○	public abstract................ *java.security.Principal*	**getIssuerDN** ()	ε227
○	public abstract......boolean[]	**getIssuerUniqueID** ()	
1.4	public......... javax.security ↵ .auth.x500.X500Principal	**getIssuerX500Principal** ()	
○	public abstract......boolean[]	**getKeyUsage** ()	
○	public abstract... java.util.Date	**getNotAfter** ()	
○	public abstract... java.util.Date	**getNotBefore** ()	
○ 1	public abstract................ *java.security.PublicKey*	getPublicKey ()	ε210
○	public abstract................ *java.math.BigInteger*	**getSerialNumber** ()	
○	public abstract..........String	**getSigAlgName** ()	
○	public abstract..........String	**getSigAlgOID** ()	
○	public abstract..........byte[]	**getSigAlgParams** ()	
○	public abstract..........byte[]	**getSignature** ()	
1.4	public....... *java.util.Collection*	**getSubjectAlternativeNames** () throws CertificateParsingException	
○	public abstract................ *java.security.Principal*	**getSubjectDN** ()	ε227
○	public abstract......boolean[]	**getSubjectUniqueID** ()	
1.4	public......... javax.security ↵ .auth.x500.X500Principal	**getSubjectX500Principal** ()	
○	public abstract..........byte[]	**getTBSCertificate** () throws CertificateEncodingException	
● 1	public final ....String	getType ()	
○	public abstract...............int	**getVersion** ()	
1	public........................int	hashCode ()	
○ 1	public abstract...........String	toString ()	
○ 1	public abstract............void	verify (*java.security.PublicKey* key) throws CertificateException, java.security.NoSuchAlgorithmException, java.security.InvalidKeyException, java.security.NoSuchProviderException, java.security.SignatureException	
○ 1	public abstract............void	verify (*java.security.PublicKey* key, String sigProvider) throws CertificateException, java.security.NoSuchAlgorithmException, java.security.InvalidKeyException, java.security.NoSuchProviderException, java.security.SignatureException	
1.3 1	protected ....Object	writeReplace () throws java.io.ObjectStreamException	
*	protected	**X509Certificate** ()	

X509Certificate❷   javax.security.cert

Object
1.4 ○ └─Certificate [1]
1.4 ○   └─X509Certificate

○	public abstract............void	**checkValidity** () throws CertificateExpiredException, CertificateNotYetValidException	
○	public abstract............void	**checkValidity** (java.util.Date date) throws CertificateExpiredException, CertificateNotYetValidException	
1	public................ boolean	equals (Object other)	
○ 1	public abstract..........byte[]	getEncoded () throws CertificateEncodingException	ε506
▲	public static final.............. X509Certificate	**getInstance** (byte[] certData) throws CertificateException	ε506
▲	public static final.............. X509Certificate	**getInstance** (java.io.InputStream inStream) throws CertificateException	
○	public abstract................ *java.security.Principal*	**getIssuerDN** ()	
○	public abstract... java.util.Date	**getNotAfter** ()	
○	public abstract... java.util.Date	**getNotBefore** ()	

X509Certificate ❷

○	1	public abstract .... *java.security.PublicKey*	getPublicKey ()
○		public abstract .... *java.math.BigInteger*	**getSerialNumber** ()
○		public abstract .... String	**getSigAlgName** ()
○		public abstract .... String	**getSigAlgOID** ()
○		public abstract .... byte[]	**getSigAlgParams** ()
○		public abstract .... *java.security.Principal*	**getSubjectDN** ()
○		public abstract .... int	**getVersion** ()
	1	public.......................... int	hashCode ()
○	1	public abstract .... String	toString ()
○	1	public abstract .... void	verify (*java.security.PublicKey* key) throws CertificateException, java.security.NoSuchAlgorithmException, java.security.InvalidKeyException, java.security.NoSuchProviderException, java.security.SignatureException
○	1	public abstract .... void	verify (*java.security.PublicKey* key, String sigProvider) throws CertificateException, java.security.NoSuchAlgorithmException, java.security.InvalidKeyException, java.security.NoSuchProviderException, java.security.SignatureException
∗		public.........................	**X509Certificate** ()

X509CertSelector		java.security.cert

Object[1]
1.4 └─X509CertSelector - *CertSelector*[2] (*Cloneable*)

		public.......................void	**addPathToName** (int type, String name) throws java.io.IOException
		public.......................void	**addPathToName** (int type, byte[] name) throws java.io.IOException
		public.......................void	**addSubjectAlternativeName** (int type, String name) throws java.io.IOException
		public.......................void	**addSubjectAlternativeName** (int type, byte[] name) throws java.io.IOException
	1	public....................**Object**	**clone** ()
		public......................byte[]	**getAuthorityKeyIdentifier** ()
		public..........................int	**getBasicConstraints** ()
		public.......... X509Certificate	**getCertificate** ()
		public.............. java.util.Date	**getCertificateValid** ()
		public..............*java.util.Set*	**getExtendedKeyUsage** ()
		public......................byte[]	**getIssuerAsBytes** () throws java.io.IOException
		public.......................String	**getIssuerAsString** ()
		public.....................boolean[]	**getKeyUsage** ()
		public..................... boolean	**getMatchAllSubjectAltNames** ()
		public......................byte[]	**getNameConstraints** ()
		public....... *java.util.Collection*	**getPathToNames** ()
		public...............*java.util.Set*	**getPolicy** ()
		public.............java.util.Date	**getPrivateKeyValid** ()
		public.... java.math.BigInteger	**getSerialNumber** ()
		public..... *java.util.Collection*	**getSubjectAlternativeNames** ()
		public......................byte[]	**getSubjectAsBytes** () throws java.io.IOException
		public.......................String	**getSubjectAsString** ()
		public......................byte[]	**getSubjectKeyIdentifier** ()
		public. *java.security.PublicKey*	**getSubjectPublicKey** ()
		public.......................String	**getSubjectPublicKeyAlgID** ()
	2	public..................... boolean	**match** (Certificate cert)
		public.......................void	**setAuthorityKeyIdentifier** (byte[] authorityKeyID)
		public.......................void	**setBasicConstraints** (int minMaxPathLen)
		public.......................void	**setCertificate** (X509Certificate cert)
		public.......................void	**setCertificateValid** (java.util.Date certValid)
		public.......................void	**setExtendedKeyUsage** (*java.util.Set* keyPurposeSet) throws java.io.IOException
		public.......................void	**setIssuer** (byte[] issuerDN) throws java.io.IOException
		public.......................void	**setIssuer** (String issuerDN) throws java.io.IOException
		public.......................void	**setKeyUsage** (boolean[] keyUsage)
		public.......................void	**setMatchAllSubjectAltNames** (boolean matchAllNames)
		public.......................void	**setNameConstraints** (byte[] bytes) throws java.io.IOException
		public.......................void	**setPathToNames** (*java.util.Collection* names) throws java.io.IOException
		public.......................void	**setPolicy** (*java.util.Set* certPolicySet) throws java.io.IOException
		public.......................void	**setPrivateKeyValid** (java.util.Date privateKeyValid)
		public.......................void	**setSerialNumber** (java.math.BigInteger serial)
		public.......................void	**setSubject** (byte[] subjectDN) throws java.io.IOException
		public.......................void	**setSubject** (String subjectDN) throws java.io.IOException
		public.......................void	**setSubjectAlternativeNames** (*java.util.Collection* names) throws java.io.IOException

X

Class *Interface* —extends - - -implements ○ abstract ● final △ static ▲ static final ∗ constructor x x—inherited x **x**—declared **x x**—overridden
εn—examples of usage ⌐—has subclass package—see other volume

```
public..................void  setSubjectKeyIdentifier (byte[] subjectKeyID)
public..................void  setSubjectPublicKey (byte[] key) throws java.io.IOException
public..................void  setSubjectPublicKey (java.security.PublicKey key)
public..................void  setSubjectPublicKeyAlgID (String oid) throws java.io.IOException
```
1   `public..................String  toString ()`
*   `public..................  X509CertSelector ()`

X509CRL   java.security.cert

```
Object 1
1.2 O  └CRL 2
1.2 O     └X509CRL -------------------------- X509Extension
```

	1	public..................boolean	equals (Object other)
	O	public abstract..........byte[]	getEncoded () throws CRLException
	O	public abstract..............	getIssuerDN ()
		........java.security.Principal	
1.4		public......... javax.security ↵	getIssuerX500Principal ()
		.auth.x500.X500Principal	
	O	public abstract ... java.util.Date	getNextUpdate ()
	O	public abstract . X509CRLEntry	getRevokedCertificate (java.math.BigInteger serialNumber)
	O	public abstract .....java.util.Set	getRevokedCertificates ()
	O	public abstract ....String	getSigAlgName ()
	O	public abstract ....String	getSigAlgOID ()
	O	public abstract ....byte[]	getSigAlgParams ()
	O	public abstract ....byte[]	getSignature ()
	O	public abstract ....byte[]	getTBSCertList () throws CRLException
	O	public abstract ... java.util.Date	getThisUpdate ()
●	2	public final ....String	getType ()
	O	public abstract ....int	getVersion ()
	1	public..................int	hashCode ()
O	2	public abstract .... boolean	isRevoked (Certificate cert)
O	2	public abstract ....String	toString ()
	O	public abstract ....void	verify (java.security.PublicKey key) throws CRLException,
			java.security.NoSuchAlgorithmException, java.security.InvalidKeyException,
			java.security.NoSuchProviderException, java.security.SignatureException
	O	public abstract ....void	verify (java.security.PublicKey key, String sigProvider) throws CRLException,
			java.security.NoSuchAlgorithmException, java.security.InvalidKeyException,
			java.security.NoSuchProviderException, java.security.SignatureException
*		protected	X509CRL ()

X509CRLEntry   java.security.cert

```
Object 1
1.2 O  └X509CRLEntry ------------------------ X509Extension
```

	1	public..................boolean	equals (Object other)
	O	public abstract ....byte[]	getEncoded () throws CRLException
	O	public abstract ... java.util.Date	getRevocationDate ()
	O	public abstract	getSerialNumber ()
		.... java.math.BigInteger	
	O	public abstract .... boolean	hasExtensions ()
	1	public..................int	hashCode ()
O	1	public abstract ....String	toString ()
*		public......................	X509CRLEntry ()

X509CRLSelector   java.security.cert

```
Object 1
1.4  └X509CRLSelector ---------------------- CRLSelector 2 (Cloneable)
```

		public..................void	addIssuerName (byte[] name) throws java.io.IOException
		public..................void	addIssuerName (String name) throws java.io.IOException
	1	public..................Object	clone ()
		public.......... X509Certificate	getCertificateChecking ()
		public............ java.util.Date	getDateAndTime ()
		public.... java.util.Collection	getIssuerNames ()
		public.... java.math.BigInteger	getMaxCRL ()
		public.... java.math.BigInteger	getMinCRL ()
	2	public.................. boolean	match (CRL crl)

X

Classes

X509CRLSelector

	public	void	**setCertificateChecking** (X509Certificate cert)
	public	void	**setDateAndTime** (java.util.Date dateAndTime)
	public	void	**setIssuerNames** (*java.util.Collection* names) throws java.io.IOException
	public	void	**setMaxCRLNumber** (java.math.BigInteger maxCRL)
	public	void	**setMinCRLNumber** (java.math.BigInteger minCRL)
1	public	**String**	**toString** ()
*	public		**X509CRLSelector** ()

X509EncodedKeySpec java.security.spec

```
       Object                                                    ε199
1.2 O  └ EncodedKeySpec¹ - - - - - - - - - - - - - - - - - - - - KeySpec
1.2       └ X509EncodedKeySpec
```

1	public	**byte[]**	**getEncoded** ()	
● 1	public final	**String**	**getFormat** ()	
*	public		**X509EncodedKeySpec** (byte[] encodedKey)	ε199,471

X509Extension java.security.cert

```
1.2    X509Extension
```

	public	*java.util.Set*	**getCriticalExtensionOIDs** ()
	public	byte[]	**getExtensionValue** (String oid)
	public	*java.util.Set*	**getNonCriticalExtensionOIDs** ()
	public	boolean	**hasUnsupportedCriticalExtension** ()

X509KeyManager javax.net.ssl

```
1.4    X509KeyManager ──────────────── KeyManager
```

	public	String	**chooseClientAlias** (String[] keyType, *java.security.Principal[]* issuers, java.net.Socket socket)
	public	String	**chooseServerAlias** (String keyType, *java.security.Principal[]* issuers, java.net.Socket socket)
	public	java.security↩.cert.X509Certificate[]	**getCertificateChain** (String alias)
	public	String[]	**getClientAliases** (String keyType, *java.security.Principal[]* issuers)
	public	*java.security.PrivateKey*	**getPrivateKey** (String alias)
	public	String[]	**getServerAliases** (String keyType, *java.security.Principal[]* issuers)

X509TrustManager javax.net.ssl

```
1.4    X509TrustManager ──────────────── TrustManager          ε502
```

	public	void	**checkClientTrusted** (java.security.cert.X509Certificate[] chain, String authType)	ε502
			throws java.security.cert.CertificateException	ε502
	public	void	**checkServerTrusted** (java.security.cert.X509Certificate[] chain, String authType)	ε502
			throws java.security.cert.CertificateException	ε502
	public	java.security↩.cert.X509Certificate[]	**getAcceptedIssuers** ()	ε502

XAConnection javax.sql

```
1.4    XAConnection ──────────────── PooledConnection ¹
```

1	public	void	addConnectionEventListener (*ConnectionEventListener* listener)
1	public	void	close () throws java.sql.SQLException
1	public	*java.sql.Connection*	getConnection () throws java.sql.SQLException
	public	*javax↩.transaction.xa.XAResource*	**getXAResource** () throws java.sql.SQLException
1	public	void	removeConnectionEventListener (*ConnectionEventListener* listener)

Class *Interface* —extends - - -implements O abstract ● final △ static ▲ static final ✳ constructor x x—inherited x **x**—declared **x x**—overridden
ε*n*—examples of usage ╷—has subclass package—see other volume

XADataSource

1.4   *XADataSource*

public	int	**getLoginTimeout** () throws java.sql.SQLException
public	java.io.PrintWriter	**getLogWriter** () throws java.sql.SQLException
public	*XAConnection*	**getXAConnection** () throws java.sql.SQLException
public	*XAConnection*	**getXAConnection** (String user, String password) throws java.sql.SQLException
public	void	**setLoginTimeout** (int seconds) throws java.sql.SQLException
public	void	**setLogWriter** (java.io.PrintWriter out) throws java.sql.SQLException

XAException

Object
└Throwable ------------------------------ *java.io.Serializable*
  └Exception
1.4   └XAException

	public	int	**errorCode**
▲	public static final	int	**XA_HEURCOM** = 7
▲	public static final	int	**XA_HEURHAZ** = 8
▲	public static final	int	**XA_HEURMIX** = 5
▲	public static final	int	**XA_HEURRB** = 6
▲	public static final	int	**XA_NOMIGRATE** = 9
▲	public static final	int	**XA_RBBASE** = 100
▲	public static final	int	**XA_RBCOMMFAIL** = 101
▲	public static final	int	**XA_RBDEADLOCK** = 102
▲	public static final	int	**XA_RBEND** = 107
▲	public static final	int	**XA_RBINTEGRITY** = 103
▲	public static final	int	**XA_RBOTHER** = 104
▲	public static final	int	**XA_RBPROTO** = 105
▲	public static final	int	**XA_RBROLLBACK** = 100
▲	public static final	int	**XA_RBTIMEOUT** = 106
▲	public static final	int	**XA_RBTRANSIENT** = 107
▲	public static final	int	**XA_RDONLY** = 3
▲	public static final	int	**XA_RETRY** = 4
▲	public static final	int	**XAER_ASYNC** = -2
▲	public static final	int	**XAER_DUPID** = -8
▲	public static final	int	**XAER_INVAL** = -5
▲	public static final	int	**XAER_NOTA** = -4
▲	public static final	int	**XAER_OUTSIDE** = -9
▲	public static final	int	**XAER_PROTO** = -6
▲	public static final	int	**XAER_RMERR** = -3
▲	public static final	int	**XAER_RMFAIL** = -7
✳	public		**XAException** ()
✳	public		**XAException** (int errcode)
✳	public		**XAException** (String s)

XAResource

1.4   *XAResource*

	public	void	**commit** (*Xid* xid, boolean onePhase) throws XAException
	public	void	**end** (*Xid* xid, int flags) throws XAException
	public	void	**forget** (*Xid* xid) throws XAException
	public	int	**getTransactionTimeout** () throws XAException
	public	boolean	**isSameRM** (*XAResource* xares) throws XAException
	public	int	**prepare** (*Xid* xid) throws XAException
	public	*Xid[]*	**recover** (int flag) throws XAException
	public	void	**rollback** (*Xid* xid) throws XAException
	public	boolean	**setTransactionTimeout** (int seconds) throws XAException
	public	void	**start** (*Xid* xid, int flags) throws XAException
▲	public static final	int	**TMENDRSCAN** = 8388608
▲	public static final	int	**TMFAIL** = 536870912
▲	public static final	int	**TMJOIN** = 2097152
▲	public static final	int	**TMNOFLAGS** = 0
▲	public static final	int	**TMONEPHASE** = 1073741824
▲	public static final	int	**TMRESUME** = 134217728
▲	public static final	int	**TMSTARTRSCAN** = 16777216
▲	public static final	int	**TMSUCCESS** = 67108864
▲	public static final	int	**TMSUSPEND** = 33554432
▲	public static final	int	**XA_OK** = 0

X

Classes

XAResource

Xid   javax.transaction.xa

1.4   *Xid*

```
    public...................byte[] getBranchQualifier ()
    public.......................int getFormatId ()
    public...................byte[] getGlobalTransactionId ()
▲   public static final.............int MAXBQUALSIZE = 64
▲   public static final.............int MAXGTRIDSIZE = 64
```

XMLDecoder   java.beans

Object
1.4   └XMLDecoder

```
    public.....................void close ()                                          ε8
    public.......ExceptionListener getExceptionListener ()
    public...................Object getOwner ()
    public...................Object readObject ()                                     ε8
    public.....................void setExceptionListener (ExceptionListener exceptionListener)
    public.....................void setOwner (Object owner)
*   public........................ XMLDecoder (java.io.InputStream in)                ε8
*   public........................ XMLDecoder (java.io.InputStream in, Object owner)
*   public........................ XMLDecoder (java.io.InputStream in, Object owner,
                                          ExceptionListener exceptionListener)
```

XMLEncoder   java.beans

Object
1.4   └Encoder [1]
1.4   └XMLEncoder

```
    public.....................void close ()                                          ε7,9,10
    public.....................void flush ()
1   public...................Object get (Object oldInstance)
1   public.......ExceptionListener getExceptionListener ()
1   public...................Object getOwner ()
1   public.... PersistenceDelegate getPersistenceDelegate (Class type)
1   public...................Object remove (Object oldInstance)
1   public.....................void setExceptionListener (ExceptionListener exceptionListener)
    public.....................void setOwner (Object owner)
1   public.....................void setPersistenceDelegate (Class type, PersistenceDelegate persistenceDelegate)
                                                                                      ε10
1   public..................... void writeExpression (Expression oldExp)
1   public..................... void writeObject (Object o)                           ε7,9,10
1   public..................... void writeStatement (Statement oldStm)
*   public........................ XMLEncoder (java.io.OutputStream out)              ε7,9,10
```

```
X
```

XMLFilter   org.xml.sax

1.4   *XMLFilter*────────────────────*XMLReader* [1]

```
1   public..........ContentHandler getContentHandler ()
1   public.............DTDHandler getDTDHandler ()
1   public.........EntityResolver getEntityResolver ()
1   public............ErrorHandler getErrorHandler ()
1   public.................. boolean getFeature (String name) throws SAXNotRecognizedException,
                                          SAXNotSupportedException
    public............. XMLReader getParent ()
1   public...................Object getProperty (String name) throws SAXNotRecognizedException,
                                          SAXNotSupportedException
1   public.....................void parse (String systemId) throws java.io.IOException, SAXException
1   public.....................void parse (InputSource input) throws java.io.IOException, SAXException
1   public.....................void setContentHandler (ContentHandler handler)
1   public.....................void setDTDHandler (DTDHandler handler)
```

Class   *Interface*   ──extends   - - -implements   ○ abstract   ● final   △ static   ▲ static final   ✳ constructor   x x──inherited   x **x**──declared   **x x**──overridden
ε*n*──examples of usage   ⌐──has subclass   package──see other volume

822

1	public	void	setEntityResolver (*EntityResolver* resolver)
1	public	void	setErrorHandler (*ErrorHandler* handler)
1	public	void	setFeature (String name, boolean value) throws SAXNotRecognizedException, SAXNotSupportedException
	public	void	**setParent** (*XMLReader* parent)
1	public	void	setProperty (String name, Object value) throws SAXNotRecognizedException, SAXNotSupportedException

- -

XMLFilterImpl   org.xml.sax.helpers

Object
1.4   └XMLFilterImpl - *org.xml.sax.XMLFilter* [1] (*org.xml.sax.XMLReader* [2]),
org.xml.sax.EntityResolver [3], *org.xml.sax.DTDHandler* [4],
org.xml.sax.ContentHandler [5], *org.xml.sax.ErrorHandler* [6]

5	public	void	**characters** (char[] ch, int start, int length) throws org.xml.sax.SAXException
5	public	void	**endDocument** () throws org.xml.sax.SAXException
5	public	void	**endElement** (String uri, String localName, String qName) throws org.xml.sax.SAXException
5	public	void	**endPrefixMapping** (String prefix) throws org.xml.sax.SAXException
6	public	void	**error** (org.xml.sax.SAXParseException e) throws org.xml.sax.SAXException
			ε513
6	public	void	**fatalError** (org.xml.sax.SAXParseException e) throws org.xml.sax.SAXException
			ε513
2	public . org.xml.sax.ContentHandler		**getContentHandler** ()
2	public ..... org.xml.sax.DTDHandler		**getDTDHandler** ()
2	public ... org.xml.sax.EntityResolver		**getEntityResolver** ()
2	public ..... org.xml.sax.ErrorHandler		**getErrorHandler** ()
2	public	boolean	**getFeature** (String name) throws org.xml.sax.SAXNotRecognizedException, org.xml.sax.SAXNotSupportedException
1	public . org.xml.sax.XMLReader		**getParent** ()
2	public	Object	**getProperty** (String name) throws org.xml.sax.SAXNotRecognizedException, org.xml.sax.SAXNotSupportedException
5	public	void	**ignorableWhitespace** (char[] ch, int start, int length) throws org.xml.sax.SAXException
4	public	void	**notationDecl** (String name, String publicId, String systemId) throws org.xml.sax.SAXException
2	public	void	**parse** (String systemId) throws org.xml.sax.SAXException, java.io.IOException
2	public	void	**parse** (org.xml.sax.InputSource input) throws org.xml.sax.SAXException, java.io.IOException
5	public	void	**processingInstruction** (String target, String data) throws org.xml.sax.SAXException
3	public org.xml.sax.InputSource		**resolveEntity** (String publicId, String systemId) throws org.xml.sax.SAXException, java.io.IOException ε548
2	public	void	**setContentHandler** (*org.xml.sax.ContentHandler* handler)
5	public	void	**setDocumentLocator** (*org.xml.sax.Locator* locator) ε550
2	public	void	**setDTDHandler** (*org.xml.sax.DTDHandler* handler)
2	public	void	**setEntityResolver** (*org.xml.sax.EntityResolver* resolver)
2	public	void	**setErrorHandler** (*org.xml.sax.ErrorHandler* handler)
2	public	void	**setFeature** (String name, boolean state) throws org.xml.sax ↵ .SAXNotRecognizedException, org.xml.sax.SAXNotSupportedException
1	public	void	**setParent** (*org.xml.sax.XMLReader* parent)
2	public	void	**setProperty** (String name, Object value) throws org.xml.sax ↵ .SAXNotRecognizedException, org.xml.sax.SAXNotSupportedException
5	public	void	**skippedEntity** (String name) throws org.xml.sax.SAXException
5	public	void	**startDocument** () throws org.xml.sax.SAXException
5	public	void	**startElement** (String uri, String localName, String qName, *org.xml.sax.Attributes* atts) throws org.xml.sax.SAXException ε549,550
5	public	void	**startPrefixMapping** (String prefix, String uri) throws org.xml.sax.SAXException
4	public	void	**unparsedEntityDecl** (String name, String publicId, String systemId, String notationName) throws org.xml.sax.SAXException
6	public	void	**warning** (org.xml.sax.SAXParseException e) throws org.xml.sax.SAXException
			ε513
*	public		**XMLFilterImpl** ()
*	public		**XMLFilterImpl** (*org.xml.sax.XMLReader* parent)

X

Classes

XMLFormatter

XMLFormatter	java.util.logging

Object
1.4 ○ └Formatter[1]
1.4   └XMLFormatter

1	public	**String**	**format** (LogRecord record)	ε400
1	public synchronized	String	formatMessage (LogRecord record)	
1	public	**String**	**getHead** (Handler h)	ε400
1	public	**String**	**getTail** (Handler h)	ε400
✳	public		**XMLFormatter** ()	ε399

XMLReader	org.xml.sax

1.4   *XMLReader*

public	*ContentHandler*	**getContentHandler** ()
public	*DTDHandler*	**getDTDHandler** ()
public	*EntityResolver*	**getEntityResolver** ()
public	*ErrorHandler*	**getErrorHandler** ()
public	boolean	**getFeature** (String name) throws SAXNotRecognizedException, SAXNotSupportedException
public	Object	**getProperty** (String name) throws SAXNotRecognizedException, SAXNotSupportedException
public	void	**parse** (String systemId) throws java.io.IOException, SAXException
public	void	**parse** (InputSource input) throws java.io.IOException, SAXException
public	void	**setContentHandler** (*ContentHandler* handler)
public	void	**setDTDHandler** (*DTDHandler* handler)
public	void	**setEntityResolver** (*EntityResolver* resolver)
public	void	**setErrorHandler** (*ErrorHandler* handler)
public	void	**setFeature** (String name, boolean value) throws SAXNotRecognizedException, SAXNotSupportedException
public	void	**setProperty** (String name, Object value) throws SAXNotRecognizedException, SAXNotSupportedException

XMLReaderAdapter	org.xml.sax.helpers

X

Object
1.4   └XMLReaderAdapter - *org.xml.sax.Parser* [1], *org.xml.sax.ContentHandler* [2]

2	public	void	**characters** (char[] ch, int start, int length) throws org.xml.sax.SAXException
2	public	void	**endDocument** () throws org.xml.sax.SAXException
2	public	void	**endElement** (String uri, String localName, String qName) throws org.xml.sax.SAXException
2	public	void	**endPrefixMapping** (String prefix)
2	public	void	**ignorableWhitespace** (char[] ch, int start, int length) throws org.xml.sax.SAXException
1	public	void	**parse** (String systemId) throws java.io.IOException, org.xml.sax.SAXException
1	public	void	**parse** (org.xml.sax.InputSource input) throws java.io.IOException, org.xml.sax.SAXException
2	public	void	**processingInstruction** (String target, String data) throws org.xml.sax.SAXException
1	public	void	**setDocumentHandler** (*org.xml.sax.DocumentHandler* handler)
2	public	void	**setDocumentLocator** (*org.xml.sax.Locator* locator) ε550
1	public	void	**setDTDHandler** (*org.xml.sax.DTDHandler* handler)
1	public	void	**setEntityResolver** (*org.xml.sax.EntityResolver* resolver)
1	public	void	**setErrorHandler** (*org.xml.sax.ErrorHandler* handler)
1	public	void	**setLocale** (java.util.Locale locale) throws org.xml.sax.SAXException
2	public	void	**skippedEntity** (String name) throws org.xml.sax.SAXException
2	public	void	**startDocument** () throws org.xml.sax.SAXException
2	public	void	**startElement** (String uri, String localName, String qName, *org.xml.sax.Attributes* atts) throws org.xml.sax.SAXException ε549,550
2	public	void	**startPrefixMapping** (String prefix, String uri)
✳	public		**XMLReaderAdapter** () throws org.xml.sax.SAXException
✳	public		**XMLReaderAdapter** (*org.xml.sax.XMLReader* xmlReader)

Class   *Interface*   —extends   - - -implements   ○ abstract   ● final   △ static   ▲ static final   ✳ constructor   x x—inherited   x **x**—declared   **x x**—overridden
ε*n*—examples of usage   ‿—has subclass   package—see other volume

	XMLReaderFactory		org.xml.sax.helpers

		Object	
1.4 ●		└XMLReaderFactory	
△	public static	**createXMLReader** () throws org.xml.sax.SAXException	
	......*org.xml.sax.XMLReader*		
△	public static	**createXMLReader** (String className) throws org.xml.sax.SAXException	
	......*org.xml.sax.XMLReader*		

	ZipEntry		java.util.zip

| | | Object[1] | ε455 |
| 1.1 | | └ZipEntry - java.util.zip.ZipConstants, *Cloneable* | |

	1	public...................**Object** **clone** ()	
▲		public static final.............int **DEFLATED** = 8	
		public...................String **getComment** ()	
		public.................... long **getCompressedSize** ()	
		public.................... long **getCrc** ()	
		public....................byte[] **getExtra** ()	
		public......................int **getMethod** ()	
		public...................String **getName** ()	ε454
		public.................... long **getSize** ()	
		public.................... long **getTime** ()	
	1	public...................... **int hashCode** ()	
		public................... boolean **isDirectory** ()	
		public....................void **setComment** (String comment)	
1.2		public....................void **setCompressedSize** (long csize)	
		public....................void **setCrc** (long crc)	
		public....................void **setExtra** (byte[] extra)	
		public....................void **setMethod** (int method)	
		public....................void **setSize** (long size)	
		public....................void **setTime** (long time)	
▲		public static final.............int **STORED** = 0	
	1	public...................**String** **toString** ()	
＊		public........................ **ZipEntry** (String name)	ε453
1.2 ＊		public........................ **ZipEntry** (ZipEntry e)	

	ZipException		java.util.zip

	Object	
	└Throwable - *java.io.Serializable*	
	└Exception	
	└java.io.IOException	
1.1	└ZipException	

＊	public......................... **ZipException** ()
＊	public......................... **ZipException** (String s)

	ZipFile		java.util.zip

| | | Object[1] | ε138 |
| 1.1 | | └ZipFile - java.util.zip.ZipConstants | |

		public.......................void **close** () throws java.io.IOException	
		public.... *java.util.Enumeration* **entries** ()	ε454
	1	protected.................. **void** **finalize** () throws java.io.IOException	
		public...................ZipEntry **getEntry** (String name)	
		public......java.io.InputStream **getInputStream** (ZipEntry entry) throws java.io.IOException	
		public...................String **getName** ()	
1.3 ▲		public static final.............int **OPEN_DELETE** = 4	
1.3 ▲		public static final.............int **OPEN_READ** = 1	
1.2		public......................int **size** ()	
＊		public......................... **ZipFile** (java.io.File file) throws ZipException, java.io.IOException	
＊		public......................... **ZipFile** (String name) throws java.io.IOException	ε454
1.3 ＊		public......................... **ZipFile** (java.io.File file, int mode) throws java.io.IOException	

Z

Classes

ZipInputStream

ZipInputStream		java.util.zip

o	Object └java.io.InputStream └java.io.FilterInputStream [1]	ε252,382,418
1.1	└InflaterInputStream [2]	
1.1	└ZipInputStream - - - - - - - - - - - - - - - - - java.util.zip.ZipConstants	

2	public.................... **int available** () throws java.io.IOException	
2	protected................byte[] buf	
2	public.................... **void close** () throws java.io.IOException	ε455,14,36,45,452
	public....................void **closeEntry** () throws java.io.IOException	
1.2	protected.............ZipEntry **createZipEntry** (String name)	
2	protected..................void fill () throws java.io.IOException	
	public.................ZipEntry **getNextEntry** () throws java.io.IOException	ε455
1	protected .. java.io.InputStream in	
2	protected....................Inflater inf	
2	protected....................int len	
1	public synchronized ....void mark (int readlimit)	
1	public................. boolean markSupported ()	
2	public....................int read () throws java.io.IOException	ε90,184,256
1	public....................int read (byte[] b) throws java.io.IOException	ε455,452,457,170,451
2	public.................... **int read** (byte[] b, int off, int len) throws java.io.IOException	ε36
1	public synchronized ....void reset () throws java.io.IOException	
2	public.................... **long skip** (long n) throws java.io.IOException	
✻	public........................ **ZipInputStream** (java.io.InputStream in)	ε455

ZipOutputStream		java.util.zip

o	Object └java.io.OutputStream └java.io.FilterOutputStream [1]	ε183
1.1	└DeflaterOutputStream [2]	
1.1	└ZipOutputStream - - - - - - - - - - - - - - - - java.util.zip.ZipConstants	

2	protected................byte[] buf	
2	public.................... **void close** () throws java.io.IOException	ε453,451,91,211,224
	public....................void **closeEntry** () throws java.io.IOException	ε453
2	protected................Deflater def	
2	protected..................void deflate () throws java.io.IOException	
▲	public static final.............int **DEFLATED** = 8	
2	public.................... **void finish** () throws java.io.IOException	ε451
1	public....................void flush () throws java.io.IOException	ε27,54
1	protected java.io.OutputStream out	
	public....................void **putNextEntry** (ZipEntry e) throws java.io.IOException	ε453
	public....................void **setComment** (String comment)	
	public....................void **setLevel** (int level)	
	public....................void **setMethod** (int method)	
▲	public static final.............int **STORED** = 0	
1	public....................void write (byte[] b) throws java.io.IOException	ε27,91,224
2	public....................void write (int b) throws java.io.IOException	ε184
2	public synchronized ...... **void write** (byte[] b, int off, int len) throws java.io.IOException	ε453,451,54,449,450
✻	public........................ **ZipOutputStream** (java.io.OutputStream out)	ε453

Z

Class *Interface* —extends - - -implements O abstract ● final △ static ▲ static final ✻ constructor x x—inherited x **x**—declared **x x**—overridden
ε*n*—examples of usage └—has subclass package—see other volume

Part 3
TOPICS

This part contains information about each major release of the Java APIs.

Contents

Statistics

Packages	8	**Members**	2125
		Fields	261
Classes and Interfaces	212	static	3
Classes	172	static final	167
abstract	21	protected	50
final	20	Constructors	319
Interfaces	40	protected	6
		Methods	1545
		abstract	102
		static	149
		final	140
		static final	1
		protected	78

Packages

Package	Classes	Members	Interfaces	Members
java.applet	1	22	3	16
java.awt	44	732	2	8
java.awt.image	9	94	3	30
java.awt.peer	0	0	22	84
java.io	28	310	3	30
java.lang	62	504	2	1
java.net	16	145	3	3
java.util	12	143	2	3

Exceptions and Errors

This is a complete listing of all the exceptions and errors in this version of Java. The "*" indicates a checked exception or error; these must be declared in the throws clause.

java.lang	AbstractMethodError		java.lang	IllegalMonitorStateException
java.lang	ArithmeticException		java.lang	IllegalThreadStateException
java.lang	ArrayIndexOutOfBoundsException		java.lang	IncompatibleClassChangeError
java.lang	ArrayStoreException		java.lang	IndexOutOfBoundsException
java.awt	AWTError		java.lang	InstantiationError
java.awt	*AWTException		java.lang	*InstantiationException
java.lang	ClassCastException		java.lang	InternalError
java.lang	ClassCircularityError		java.lang	*InterruptedException
java.lang	ClassFormatError		java.io	*InterruptedIOException
java.lang	*ClassNotFoundException		java.io	*IOException
java.lang	*CloneNotSupportedException		java.lang	LinkageError
java.util	EmptyStackException		java.net	*MalformedURLException
java.io	*EOFException		java.lang	NegativeArraySizeException
java.lang	Error		java.lang	NoClassDefFoundError
java.lang	*Exception		java.util	NoSuchElementException
java.io	*FileNotFoundException		java.lang	NoSuchFieldError
java.lang	IllegalAccessError		java.lang	NoSuchMethodError
java.lang	*IllegalAccessException		java.lang	*NoSuchMethodException
java.lang	IllegalArgumentException		java.lang	NullPointerException

java.lang	NumberFormatException	java.lang	*Throwable
java.lang	OutOfMemoryError	java.lang	UnknownError
java.net	*ProtocolException	java.net	*UnknownHostException
java.lang	RuntimeException	java.net	*UnknownServiceException
java.lang	SecurityException	java.lang	UnsatisfiedLinkError
java.net	*SocketException	java.io	*UTFDataFormatException
java.lang	StackOverflowError	java.lang	VerifyError
java.lang	StringIndexOutOfBoundsException	java.lang	VirtualMachineError
java.lang	ThreadDeath		

Statistics

Packages		23
Classes and Interfaces		504
Classes		391
abstract		58
final		38
Interfaces		113

Members		5478
Fields		926
static		4
final		2
static final		764
protected		111
Constructors		701
protected		43
Methods		3851
abstract		202
static		360
final		207
static final		24
protected		191

Packages

New	Package	Classes	Members	Interfaces	Members
	java.applet	1	1	3	0
	java.awt	54	16	7	0
•	java.awt.datatransfer	4	0	2	0
•	java.awt.event	19	4	11	0
	java.awt.image	11	3	3	1
	java.awt.peer	0	0	27	0
•	java.beans	17	2	6	2
	java.io	61	5	8	0
	java.lang	67	8	2	0
•	java.lang.reflect	6	0	1	0
•	java.math	2	3	0	0
	java.net	22	1	4	0
•	java.rmi	18	1	1	0
•	java.rmi.dgc	2	0	1	0
•	java.rmi.registry	1	0	2	0
•	java.rmi.server	16	1	7	0
•	java.security	21	1	5	1
•	java.security.acl	3	0	5	1
•	java.security.interfaces	0	0	5	0
•	java.sql	9	1	8	7
•	java.text	18	3	1	0
	java.util	23	1	3	0
•	java.util.zip	16	1	1	0

New Classes in Existing Packages

java.awt
Adjustable, AWTEvent, AWTEventMulticaster, Cursor, EventQueue, IllegalComponentStateException, *ItemSelectable*, *LayoutManager2*, MenuShortcut,

PopupMenu, *PrintGraphics*, PrintJob, ScrollPane, *Shape*, SystemColor
java.awt.image
AreaAveragingScaleFilter, ReplicateScaleFilter

Topics

java.awt.peer
    ActiveEvent, *FontPeer*, *LightweightPeer*,
    PopupMenuPeer, *ScrollPanePeer*

java.io
    BufferedReader, BufferedWriter, CharArrayReader,
    CharArrayWriter, CharConversionException,
    Externalizable, FileReader, FileWriter, FilterReader,
    FilterWriter, InputStreamReader, InvalidClassException,
    InvalidObjectException, LineNumberReader,
    NotActiveException, NotSerializableException,
    ObjectInput, ObjectInputStream, *ObjectInputValidation*,
    ObjectOutput, ObjectOutputStream, ObjectStreamClass,
    ObjectStreamException, OptionalDataException,
    OutputStreamWriter, PipedReader, PipedWriter,
    PrintWriter, PushbackReader, Reader, *Serializable*,
    StreamCorruptedException, StringReader, StringWriter,

SyncFailedException, UnsupportedEncodingException,
WriteAbortedException, Writer

java.lang
    Byte, ExceptionInInitializerError, IllegalStateException,
    NoSuchFieldException, Short, Void

java.net
    BindException, ConnectException,
    DatagramSocketImpl, *FileNameMap*,
    HttpURLConnection, MulticastSocket,
    NoRouteToHostException

java.util
    Calendar, *EventListener*, EventObject,
    GregorianCalendar, ListResourceBundle, Locale,
    MissingResourceException, PropertyResourceBundle,
    ResourceBundle, SimpleTimeZone, TimeZone,
    TooManyListenersException

New Members in Existing Classes

java.awt
    Component
      list( )
    Container
      processEvent( )

    Menu
      getItemCount( )

java.lang
    Character
      MATH_SYMBOL, UPPERCASE_LETTER

Removed Classes

java.lang
    Win32Process

Removed Members

java.awt.peer
    ComponentPeer
      handleEvent( ), nextFocus( )
    FramePeer
      setCursor( )
    ScrollbarPeer
      setValue( )

java.io
    PushbackInputStream
      pushBack
java.lang
    SecurityManager
      checkPropertyAccess( )
java.net
    DatagramSocket
      finalize( )

Modified Classes and Members

These tables show all the classes and members whose signatures were modified from the previous version. "+" indicates an added keyword; "-" indicates a removed keyword.

Class Modifier Changes

java.awt
    Color   - final

Class Modifier Changes

java.net
ServerSocket, Socket | - final

Implements Changes

java.awt

BorderLayout, CardLayout, GridBagLayout
- java.awt.LayoutManager,
  + java.awt.LayoutManager2,
  + java.io.Serializable

Checkbox, CheckboxMenuItem, Choice, List | + java.awt.ItemSelectable
CheckboxGroup, Color, Dimension, Event, FlowLayout, Font, FontMetrics, GridBagConstraints, GridLayout, Insets, MediaTracker, MenuComponent, Point | + java.io.Serializable

Component
+ java.awt.MenuContainer,
  + java.io.Serializable

Polygon, Rectangle | + java.awt.Shape, + java.io.Serializable
Scrollbar | + java.awt.Adjustable

java.io
File | + java.io.Serializable

java.lang
Boolean, Character, Class, Number, String, StringBuffer, Throwable | + java.io.Serializable

java.net
InetAddress, URL | + java.io.Serializable
SocketImpl | + java.net.SocketOptions

java.util
BitSet, Hashtable, Random, Vector | + java.io.Serializable
Date | + java.io.Serializable, + java.lang.Cloneable

Member Modifier Changes

java.awt
MediaTracker
    checkAll( ) | - synchronized

Newly Deprecated Classes

java.io
LineNumberInputStream, StringBufferInputStream

Newly Deprecated Members

java.awt
BorderLayout
addLayoutComponent( )
CardLayout
addLayoutComponent( )
CheckboxGroup
getCurrent( ), setCurrent( )
Choice
countItems( )
Component
action( ), bounds( ), deliverEvent( ), disable( ),
enable( ), getPeer( ), gotFocus( ), handleEvent( ),
hide( ), inside( ), keyDown( ), keyUp( ), layout( ),
locate( ), location( ), lostFocus( ), minimumSize( ),
mouseDown( ), mouseDrag( ), mouseEnter( ),
mouseExit( ), mouseMove( ), mouseUp( ), move( ),
nextFocus( ), postEvent( ), preferredSize( ),
reshape( ), resize( ), show( ), size( )
Container
countComponents( ), deliverEvent( ), insets( ),
layout( ), locate( ), minimumSize( ), preferredSize( )
FontMetrics
getMaxDecent( )
Frame
getCursorType( ), setCursor( )
Graphics
getClipRect( )
List
allowsMultipleSelections( ), clear( ), countItems( ),
delItems( ), isSelected( ), minimumSize( ),
preferredSize( ), setMultipleSelections( )
Menu
countItems( )

Topics

833

MenuBar
   countMenus( )
MenuComponent
   getPeer( ), postEvent( )
MenuContainer
   postEvent( )
MenuItem
   disable( ), enable( )
Polygon
   getBoundingBox( ), inside( )
Rectangle
   inside( ), move( ), reshape( ), resize( )
ScrollPane
   layout( )
Scrollbar
   getLineIncrement( ), getPageIncrement( ),
   getVisible( ), setLineIncrement( ),
   setPageIncrement( )
TextArea
   appendText( ), insertText( ), minimumSize( ),
   preferredSize( ), replaceText( )
TextField
   minimumSize( ), preferredSize( ), setEchoCharacter( )
Window
   postEvent( )

java.awt.event
KeyEvent
   setModifiers( )

java.io
ByteArrayOutputStream
   toString( )
DataInputStream
   readLine( )
PrintStream
   PrintStream( )
StreamTokenizer
   StreamTokenizer( )

java.lang
Character
   isJavaLetter( ), isJavaLetterOrDigit( ), isSpace( )
ClassLoader
   defineClass( )
Runtime
   getLocalizedInputStream( ),
   getLocalizedOutputStream( )
String
   getBytes( ), String( )
System
   getenv( )

java.net
Socket
   Socket( )

java.util
Date
   Date( ), getDate( ), getDay( ), getHours( ),
   getMinutes( ), getMonth( ), getSeconds( ),
   getTimezoneOffset( ), getYear( ), parse( ),
   setDate( ), setHours( ), setMinutes( ), setMonth( ),
   setSeconds( ), setYear( ), toGMTString( ),
   toLocaleString( ), UTC( )

Statistics

Packages		60
Classes and Interfaces		1781
Classes		1462
abstract		206
final		173
protected		125
abstract protected		1
Interfaces		319

Members		20935
Fields		3538
static		22
final		31
static final		2346
protected		972
Constructors		2337
protected		232
Methods		15060
abstract		915
static		1126
final		417
static final		55
protected		1672

Packages

New	Package	Classes	Members	Interfaces	Members
	java.applet	1	24	3	16
	java.awt	67	1666	14	57
•	java.awt.color	7	180	0	0
	java.awt.datatransfer	5	56	3	6
•	java.awt.dnd	17	182	4	13
	java.awt.event	21	376	13	32
•	java.awt.font	14	224	2	64
•	java.awt.geom	32	645	1	12
•	java.awt.im	3	27	1	7
	java.awt.image	40	685	8	70
•	java.awt.image.renderable	4	80	3	19
	java.awt.peer	0	0	26	123
•	java.awt.print	7	57	3	8
	java.beans	17	140	8	38
•	java.beans.beancontext	12	156	11	32
	java.io	66	680	10	73
	java.lang	75	815	3	2
•	java.lang.ref	5	15	0	0
	java.lang.reflect	8	104	1	5
	java.math	2	91	0	0
	java.net	29	320	5	14
	java.rmi	19	46	1	0
•	java.rmi.activation	12	70	4	16
	java.rmi.dgc	2	8	1	2
	java.rmi.registry	1	7	2	8
	java.rmi.server	16	85	9	30
	java.security	54	369	8	20
	java.security.acl	3	3	5	27
•	java.security.cert	13	94	1	4
	java.security.interfaces	0	0	8	20
•	java.security.spec	11	40	2	0
	java.sql	10	107	16	550
	java.text	21	361	2	20

New	Package	Classes	Members	Interfaces	Members
	java.util	39	697	13	103
•	java.util.jar	8	77	0	0
	java.util.zip	16	156	1	4
•	javax.accessibility	7	136	7	59
•	javax.swing	158	3436	23	175
•	javax.swing.border	9	135	1	3
•	javax.swing.colorchooser	3	22	1	4
•	javax.swing.event	23	140	23	60
•	javax.swing.filechooser	3	20	0	0
•	javax.swing.plaf	42	123	1	0
•	javax.swing.plaf.basic	184	1926	1	8
•	javax.swing.plaf.metal	61	531	0	0
•	javax.swing.plaf.multi	29	443	0	0
•	javax.swing.table	9	238	4	30
•	javax.swing.text	75	1036	21	121
•	javax.swing.text.html	41	483	0	0
•	javax.swing.text.html.parser	9	142	1	35
•	javax.swing.text.rtf	1	7	0	0
•	javax.swing.tree	13	319	7	54
•	javax.swing.undo	7	84	2	14
•	org.omg.CORBA	76	607	29	109
•	org.omg.CORBA.DynAnyPackage	4	8	0	0
•	org.omg.CORBA.ORBPackage	2	4	0	0
•	org.omg.CORBA.TypeCodePackage	2	4	0	0
•	org.omg.CORBA.portable	7	129	4	6
•	org.omg.CosNaming	22	142	2	13
•	org.omg.CosNaming.NamingContextPackage	18	91	0	0

New Classes in Existing Packages

java.awt
ActiveEvent, AlphaComposite, AWTPermission, BasicStroke, ComponentOrientation, *Composite*, *CompositeContext*, GradientPaint, Graphics2D, GraphicsConfigTemplate, GraphicsConfiguration, GraphicsDevice, GraphicsEnvironment, *Paint*, *PaintContext*, RenderingHints, RenderingHints.Key, *Stroke*, TexturePaint, *Transparency*

java.awt.datatransfer
FlavorMap, SystemFlavorMap

java.awt.event
AWTEventListener, InputMethodEvent, *InputMethodListener*, InvocationEvent

java.awt.image
AffineTransformOp, BandCombineOp, BandedSampleModel, BufferedImage, BufferedImageFilter, *BufferedImageOp*, ByteLookupTable, ColorConvertOp, ComponentColorModel, ComponentSampleModel, ConvolveOp, DataBuffer, DataBufferByte, DataBufferInt, DataBufferShort, DataBufferUShort, ImagingOpException, Kernel, LookupOp, LookupTable, MultiPixelPackedSampleModel, PackedColorModel, PixelInterleavedSampleModel, Raster, RasterFormatException, *RasterOp*, *RenderedImage*, RescaleOp, SampleModel, ShortLookupTable, SinglePixelPackedSampleModel, *TileObserver*, WritableRaster, *WritableRenderedImage*

java.beans
AppletInitializer, *DesignMode*

java.io
FileFilter, FilePermission, ObjectInputStream.GetField, ObjectOutputStream.PutField, *ObjectStreamConstants*, ObjectStreamField, SerializablePermission

java.lang
Character.Subset, Character.UnicodeBlock, *Comparable*, InheritableThreadLocal, Package, RuntimePermission, ThreadLocal, UnsupportedClassVersionError, UnsupportedOperationException

java.lang.reflect
AccessibleObject, ReflectPermission

java.net
Authenticator, JarURLConnection, NetPermission, PasswordAuthentication, *SocketOptions*, SocketPermission, URLClassLoader, URLDecoder

java.rmi
MarshalledObject

java.rmi.server
RMIClientSocketFactory, *RMIServerSocketFactory*

java.security
AccessControlContext, AccessControlException, AccessController, AlgorithmParameterGenerator, AlgorithmParameterGeneratorSpi, AlgorithmParameters, AlgorithmParametersSpi, AllPermission, BasicPermission, CodeSource, GeneralSecurityException, *Guard*, GuardedObject,

InvalidAlgorithmParameterException, KeyFactory, KeyFactorySpi, KeyPairGeneratorSpi, KeyStore, KeyStoreException, KeyStoreSpi, MessageDigestSpi, Permission, PermissionCollection, Permissions, Policy, *PrivilegedAction*, PrivilegedActionException, *PrivilegedExceptionAction*, ProtectionDomain, SecureClassLoader, SecureRandomSpi, SecurityPermission, SignatureSpi, SignedObject, UnrecoverableKeyException, UnresolvedPermission

java.security.interfaces
RSAPrivateCrtKey, *RSAPrivateKey*, *RSAPublicKey*

java.sql
Array, BatchUpdateException, *Blob*, *Clob*, *Ref*, *SQLData*, *SQLInput*, *SQLOutput*, *Struct*

java.text
Annotation, *AttributedCharacterIterator*, AttributedCharacterIterator.Attribute, AttributedString

java.util
AbstractCollection, AbstractList, AbstractMap, AbstractSequentialList, AbstractSet, ArrayList, Arrays, *Collection*, Collections, *Comparator*, ConcurrentModificationException, HashMap, HashSet, *Iterator*, LinkedList, *List*, *ListIterator*, *Map*, *Map.Entry*, PropertyPermission, *Set*, *SortedMap*, *SortedSet*, TreeMap, TreeSet, WeakHashMap

New Members in Existing Classes

java.applet
Applet
newAudioClip( )

java.awt
AWTEvent
finalize( ), INPUT_METHOD_EVENT_MASK
AWTEventMulticaster
add( ), caretPositionChanged( ),
inputMethodTextChanged( ), remove( )
BorderLayout
AFTER_LAST_LINE, AFTER_LINE_ENDS,
BEFORE_FIRST_LINE, BEFORE_LINE_BEGINS
Canvas
Canvas( )
Color
Color( ), createContext( ), getAlpha( ),
getColorComponents( ), getColorSpace( ),
getComponents( ), getRGBColorComponents( ),
getRGBComponents( ), getTransparency( )
Component
addInputMethodListener( ),
addPropertyChangeListener( ), coalesceEvents( ),
enableInputMethods( ), firePropertyChange( ),
getBounds( ), getComponentOrientation( ),
getDropTarget( ), getHeight( ), getInputContext( ),
getInputMethodRequests( ), getLocation( ),
getSize( ), getWidth( ), getX( ), getY( ), hasFocus( ),
isDisplayable( ), isDoubleBuffered( ), isLightweight( ),
isOpaque( ), processInputMethodEvent( ),
removeInputMethodListener( ),
removePropertyChangeListener( ),
setComponentOrientation( ), setDropTarget( )
Container
findComponentAt( ), setFont( )
Cursor
Cursor( ), CUSTOM_CURSOR, getName( ),
getSystemCustomCursor( ), name, toString( )
Dialog
Dialog( )
Dimension
getHeight( ), getWidth( ), setSize( )
EventQueue
dispatchEvent( ), invokeAndWait( ), invokeLater( ),
isDispatchThread( ), pop( ), push( )
FlowLayout
LEADING, TRAILING

Font
canDisplay( ), canDisplayUpTo( ),
CENTER_BASELINE, createGlyphVector( ),
deriveFont( ), finalize( ), Font( ), getAttributes( ),
getAvailableAttributes( ), getBaselineFor( ),
getFamily( ), getFont( ), getFontName( ),
getItalicAngle( ), getLineMetrics( ),
getMaxCharBounds( ), getMissingGlyphCode( ),
getNumGlyphs( ), getPSName( ), getSize2D( ),
getStringBounds( ), getTransform( ),
HANGING_BASELINE, hasUniformLineMetrics( ),
pointSize, ROMAN_BASELINE
FontMetrics
getLineMetrics( ), getMaxCharBounds( ),
getStringBounds( ), hasUniformLineMetrics( )
Frame
finalize( ), getFrames( ), getState( ), ICONIFIED,
NORMAL, removeNotify( ), setState( )
Graphics
drawString( ), getClipBounds( ), hitClip( )
GridBagConstraints
GridBagConstraints( )
MenuComponent
getTreeLock( )
MenuShortcut
equals( ), hashCode( )
Point
getX( ), getY( ), setLocation( )
Polygon
contains( ), getBounds2D( ), getPathIterator( ),
intersects( )
Rectangle
contains( ), createIntersection( ), createUnion( ),
getBounds2D( ), getHeight( ), getWidth( ), getX( ),
getY( ), outcode( ), setRect( )
Shape
contains( ), getBounds2D( ), getPathIterator( ),
intersects( )
SystemColor
createContext( )
TextField
setText( )
Toolkit
addAWTEventListener( ),
addPropertyChangeListener( ),
createCustomCursor( ),

Topics

createDragGestureRecognizer( ),
createDragSourceContextPeer( ),
createImage( ), desktopProperties,
desktopPropsSupport, getBestCursorSize( ),
getDesktopProperty( ), getMaximumCursorColors( ),
initializeDesktopProperties( ),
lazilyLoadDesktopProperty( ),
removeAWTEventListener( ),
removePropertyChangeListener( ),
setDesktopProperty( )
Window
applyResourceBundle( ), finalize( ),
getInputContext( ), getOwnedWindows( ),
getOwner( ), Window( )

java.awt.datatransfer
DataFlavor
clone( ), DataFlavor( ), equals( ),
getParameter( ), getPrimaryType( ),
getSubType( ), isFlavorJavaFileListType( ),
isFlavorRemoteObjectType( ),
isFlavorSerializedObjectType( ),
isMimeTypeSerializedObject( ),
isRepresentationClassInputStream( ),
isRepresentationClassRemote( ),
isRepresentationClassSerializable( ),
javaFileListFlavor, javaJVMLocalObjectMimeType,
javaRemoteObjectMimeType,
javaSerializedObjectMimeType, readExternal( ),
tryToLoadClass( ), writeExternal( )

java.awt.event
InputEvent
ALT_GRAPH_MASK, isAltGraphDown( )
KeyEvent
VK_AGAIN, VK_ALL_CANDIDATES,
VK_ALPHANUMERIC, VK_ALT_GRAPH,
VK_AMPERSAND, VK_ASTERISK, VK_AT,
VK_BRACELEFT, VK_BRACERIGHT,
VK_CIRCUMFLEX, VK_CODE_INPUT,
VK_COLON, VK_COMPOSE, VK_COPY, VK_CUT,
VK_DEAD_ABOVEDOT, VK_DEAD_ABOVERING,
VK_DEAD_ACUTE, VK_DEAD_BREVE,
VK_DEAD_CARON, VK_DEAD_CEDILLA,
VK_DEAD_CIRCUMFLEX, VK_DEAD_DIAERESIS,
VK_DEAD_DOUBLEACUTE,
VK_DEAD_GRAVE, VK_DEAD_IOTA,
VK_DEAD_MACRON, VK_DEAD_OGONEK,
VK_DEAD_SEMIVOICED_SOUND,
VK_DEAD_TILDE, VK_DEAD_VOICED_SOUND,
VK_DOLLAR, VK_EURO_SIGN,
VK_EXCLAMATION_MARK, VK_F13, VK_F14,
VK_F15, VK_F16, VK_F17, VK_F18, VK_F19,
VK_F20, VK_F21, VK_F22, VK_F23, VK_F24,
VK_FIND, VK_FULL_WIDTH, VK_GREATER,
VK_HALF_WIDTH, VK_HIRAGANA,
VK_INVERTED_EXCLAMATION_MARK,
VK_JAPANESE_HIRAGANA,
VK_JAPANESE_KATAKANA,
VK_JAPANESE_ROMAN, VK_KATAKANA,
VK_KP_DOWN, VK_KP_LEFT,
VK_KP_RIGHT, VK_KP_UP,
VK_LEFT_PARENTHESIS, VK_LESS, VK_MINUS,
VK_NUMBER_SIGN, VK_PASTE, VK_PLUS,
VK_PREVIOUS_CANDIDATE, VK_PROPS,
VK_QUOTEDBL, VK_RIGHT_PARENTHESIS,
VK_ROMAN_CHARACTERS, VK_STOP,
VK_UNDERSCORE, VK_UNDO

java.awt.image
ColorModel
coerceData( ), ColorModel( ),
createCompatibleSampleModel( ),
createCompatibleWritableRaster( ), equals( ),
getAlpha( ), getAlphaRaster( ), getBlue( ),
getColorSpace( ), getComponents( ),
getComponentSize( ), getDataElement( ),
getDataElements( ), getGreen( ),
getNormalizedComponents( ),
getNumColorComponents( ), getNumComponents( ),
getRed( ), getRGB( ), getTransparency( ),
getUnnormalizedComponents( ), hasAlpha( ),
isAlphaPremultiplied( ), isCompatibleRaster( ),
isCompatibleSampleModel( ), toString( ),
transferType
DirectColorModel
coerceData( ), createCompatibleWritableRaster( ),
DirectColorModel( ), getAlpha( ), getBlue( ),
getComponents( ), getDataElement( ),
getDataElements( ), getGreen( ), getRed( ),
getRGB( ), isCompatibleRaster( ), toString( )
IndexColorModel
convertToIntDiscrete( ),
createCompatibleSampleModel( ),
createCompatibleWritableRaster( ), finalize( ),
getComponents( ), getComponentSize( ),
getDataElement( ), getDataElements( ),
getRGBs( ), getTransparency( ), IndexColorModel( ),
isCompatibleRaster( ), isCompatibleSampleModel( ),
toString( )

java.awt.peer
FramePeer
getState( ), setState( )
WindowPeer
CONSUME_EVENT, FOCUS_NEXT,
FOCUS_PREVIOUS, handleFocusTraversalEvent( ),
IGNORE_EVENT

java.beans
Beans
instantiate( )
FeatureDescriptor
isPreferred( ), setPreferred( )
IndexedPropertyDescriptor
setIndexedReadMethod( ), setIndexedWriteMethod( )
Introspector
flushCaches( ), flushFromCaches( ),
getBeanInfo( ), IGNORE_ALL_BEANINFO,
IGNORE_IMMEDIATE_BEANINFO,
USE_ALL_BEANINFO
PropertyChangeSupport
addPropertyChangeListener( ), firePropertyChange( ),
hasListeners( ), removePropertyChangeListener( )
PropertyDescriptor
setReadMethod( ), setWriteMethod( )
VetoableChangeSupport
addVetoableChangeListener( ),
fireVetoableChange( ), hasListeners( ),
removeVetoableChangeListener( )

java.io
BufferedInputStream
close( )
ByteArrayInputStream
close( )
ByteArrayOutputStream
close( )

File
  compareTo( ), createNewFile( ), createTempFile( ),
  deleteOnExit( ), getAbsoluteFile( ),
  getCanonicalFile( ), getParentFile( ), isHidden( ),
  listFiles( ), listRoots( ), setLastModified( ),
  setReadOnly( ), toURL( )
ObjectInputStream
  ObjectInputStream( ), readFields( ),
  readObjectOverride( )
ObjectOutputStream
  ObjectOutputStream( ), putFields( ),
  useProtocolVersion( ), writeFields( ),
  writeObjectOverride( )
ObjectStreamClass
  getField( ), getFields( ), NO_FIELDS
PipedReader
  read( ), ready( )
PipedWriter
  write( )
PrintWriter
  out
PushbackInputStream
  close( ), skip( )
PushbackReader
  mark( ), reset( )
RandomAccessFile
  setLength( )
Serializable
  serialVersionUID
java.lang
Byte
  compareTo( )
Character
  compareTo( )
Class
  forName( ), getPackage( ), getProtectionDomain( )
ClassLoader
  ClassLoader( ), defineClass( ), definePackage( ),
  findClass( ), findLibrary( ), findResource( ),
  findResources( ), getPackage( ),
  getPackages( ), getParent( ), getResources( ),
  getSystemClassLoader( ), getSystemResources( )
ClassNotFoundException
  ClassNotFoundException( ), getException( ),
  printStackTrace( )
Double
  compareTo( ), parseDouble( )
ExceptionInInitializerError
  printStackTrace( )
Float
  compareTo( ), parseFloat( )
Integer
  compareTo( )
Long
  compareTo( ), decode( )
Math
  toDegrees( ), toRadians( )
SecurityManager
  checkPermission( )
Short
  compareTo( )
String
  CASE_INSENSITIVE_ORDER, compareTo( ),
  compareToIgnoreCase( )

StringBuffer
  delete( ), deleteCharAt( ), insert( ), replace( ),
  substring( )
System
  mapLibraryName( ), setProperty( )
Thread
  getContextClassLoader( ), setContextClassLoader( )
ThreadGroup
  interrupt( )
java.lang.reflect
InvocationTargetException
  printStackTrace( )
Modifier
  isStrict( ), STRICT
java.math
BigDecimal
  compareTo( ), unscaledValue( )
BigInteger
  compareTo( ), ONE, ZERO
java.net
DatagramPacket
  DatagramPacket( ), getOffset( ), setData( )
DatagramSocket
  connect( ), disconnect( ), getInetAddress( ),
  getPort( ), getReceiveBufferSize( ),
  getSendBufferSize( ), setReceiveBufferSize( ),
  setSendBufferSize( )
DatagramSocketImpl
  getTimeToLive( ), setTimeToLive( )
HttpURLConnection
  getErrorStream( ), getPermission( )
MulticastSocket
  getTimeToLive( ), setTimeToLive( )
Socket
  getReceiveBufferSize( ), getSendBufferSize( ),
  setReceiveBufferSize( ), setSendBufferSize( )
URL
  URL( )
URLConnection
  getFileNameMap( ), getPermission( ),
  setFileNameMap( )
java.rmi
RemoteException
  printStackTrace( )
java.rmi.registry
LocateRegistry
  createRegistry( ), getRegistry( )
java.rmi.server
ObjID
  ACTIVATOR_ID
RMIClassLoader
  getClassAnnotation( ), loadClass( )
RMISocketFactory
  getDefaultSocketFactory( )
RemoteObject
  getRef( ), toStub( )
RemoteRef
  invoke( ), serialVersionUID
ServerCloneException
  printStackTrace( )
ServerRef
  serialVersionUID
UnicastRemoteObject
  exportObject( ), unexportObject( ),
  UnicastRemoteObject( )

Topics

Java 1.2
New Members in Existing Classes

java.security
  Key
    serialVersionUID
  KeyPairGenerator
    genKeyPair( ), getProvider( ), initialize( )
  MessageDigest
    digest( ), getDigestLength( ), getProvider( )
  PrivateKey
    serialVersionUID
  Provider
    clear( ), entrySet( ), keySet( ), load( ), put( ), putAll( ),
    remove( ), values( )
  PublicKey
    serialVersionUID
  SecureRandom
    generateSeed( ), getInstance( ), getProvider( ),
    SecureRandom( )
  Signature
    getProvider( ), initSign( ), setParameter( ), sign( )

java.security.interfaces
  DSAPrivateKey
    serialVersionUID
  DSAPublicKey
    serialVersionUID

java.sql
  CallableStatement
    getArray( ), getBigDecimal( ), getBlob( ), getClob( ),
    getDate( ), getObject( ), getRef( ), getTime( ),
    getTimestamp( ), registerOutParameter( )
  Connection
    createStatement( ), getTypeMap( ), prepareCall( ),
    prepareStatement( ), setTypeMap( )
  DatabaseMetaData
    deletesAreDetected( ), getConnection( ),
    getUDTs( ), insertsAreDetected( ),
    othersDeletesAreVisible( ), othersInsertsAreVisible( ),
    othersUpdatesAreVisible( ),
    ownDeletesAreVisible( ), ownInsertsAreVisible( ),
    ownUpdatesAreVisible( ), supportsBatchUpdates( ),
    supportsResultSetConcurrency( ),
    supportsResultSetType( ), updatesAreDetected( )
  DriverManager
    getLogWriter( ), setLogWriter( )
  PreparedStatement
    addBatch( ), getMetaData( ), setArray( ), setBlob( ),
    setCharacterStream( ), setClob( ), setDate( ),
    setNull( ), setRef( ), setTime( ), setTimestamp( )
  ResultSet
    absolute( ), afterLast( ), beforeFirst( ),
    cancelRowUpdates( ), CONCUR_READ_ONLY,
    CONCUR_UPDATABLE, deleteRow( ),
    FETCH_FORWARD, FETCH_REVERSE,
    FETCH_UNKNOWN, first( ), getArray( ),
    getBigDecimal( ), getBlob( ), getCharacterStream( ),
    getClob( ), getConcurrency( ), getDate( ),
    getFetchDirection( ), getFetchSize( ), getObject( ),
    getRef( ), getRow( ), getStatement( ), getTime( ),
    getTimestamp( ), getType( ), insertRow( ),
    isAfterLast( ), isBeforeFirst( ), isFirst( ), isLast( ),
    last( ), moveToCurrentRow( ), moveToInsertRow( ),
    previous( ), refreshRow( ), relative( ), rowDeleted( ),
    rowInserted( ), rowUpdated( ), setFetchDirection( ),
    setFetchSize( ), TYPE_FORWARD_ONLY,
    TYPE_SCROLL_INSENSITIVE,
    TYPE_SCROLL_SENSITIVE, updateAsciiStream( ),
    updateBigDecimal( ), updateBinaryStream( ),

    updateBoolean( ), updateByte( ), updateBytes( ),
    updateCharacterStream( ), updateDate( ),
    updateDouble( ), updateFloat( ), updateInt( ),
    updateLong( ), updateNull( ), updateObject( ),
    updateRow( ), updateShort( ), updateString( ),
    updateTime( ), updateTimestamp( )
  ResultSetMetaData
    getColumnClassName( )
  Statement
    addBatch( ), clearBatch( ), executeBatch( ),
    getConnection( ), getFetchDirection( ),
    getFetchSize( ), getResultSetConcurrency( ),
    getResultSetType( ), setFetchDirection( ),
    setFetchSize( )
  Timestamp
    equals( )
  Types
    ARRAY, BLOB, CLOB, DISTINCT, JAVA_OBJECT,
    REF, STRUCT

java.text
  BreakIterator
    isBoundary( ), preceding( )
  CollationElementIterator
    getMaxExpansion( ), getOffset( ), previous( ),
    setOffset( ), setText( )
  CollationKey
    compareTo( )
  Collator
    compare( )
  DecimalFormat
    setMaximumFractionDigits( ),
    setMaximumIntegerDigits( ),
    setMinimumFractionDigits( ),
    setMinimumIntegerDigits( )
  DecimalFormatSymbols
    getCurrencySymbol( ),
    getInternationalCurrencySymbol( ),
    getMonetaryDecimalSeparator( ),
    setCurrencySymbol( ),
    setInternationalCurrencySymbol( ),
    setMonetaryDecimalSeparator( )
  FieldPosition
    equals( ), hashCode( ), setBeginIndex( ),
    setEndIndex( ), toString( )
  ParsePosition
    equals( ), getErrorIndex( ), hashCode( ),
    setErrorIndex( ), toString( )
  RuleBasedCollator
    getCollationElementIterator( )
  SimpleDateFormat
    get2DigitYearStart( ), set2DigitYearStart( )
  StringCharacterIterator
    setText( )

java.util
  BitSet
    andNot( ), length( )
  Calendar
    getActualMaximum( ), getActualMinimum( ),
    hashCode( ), roll( ), toString( )
  Date
    clone( ), compareTo( )
  GregorianCalendar
    getActualMaximum( ), getActualMinimum( ), roll( )
  Hashtable
    containsValue( ), entrySet( ), equals( ), hashCode( ),
    Hashtable( ), keySet( ), putAll( ), values( )

Locale
  getAvailableLocales( ), getISOCountries( ),
  getISOLanguages( )
Properties
  setProperty( ), store( )
Random
  nextBoolean( ), nextInt( )
ResourceBundle
  getBundle( ), getLocale( )
SimpleTimeZone
  getDSTSavings( ), hasSameRules( ),
  setDSTSavings( ), setEndRule( ), setStartRule( ),
  SimpleTimeZone( ), toString( )
TimeZone
  getDisplayName( ), hasSameRules( ), LONG,
  SHORT

Vector
  add( ), addAll( ), clear( ), containsAll( ), equals( ),
  get( ), hashCode( ), remove( ), removeAll( ),
  removeRange( ), retainAll( ), set( ), subList( ),
  toArray( ), Vector( )
java.util.zip
InflaterInputStream
  available( ), close( )
ZipEntry
  clone( ), hashCode( ), setCompressedSize( ),
  ZipEntry( )
ZipFile
  size( )
ZipInputStream
  available( ), createZipEntry( )

Removed Classes

java.awt.peer
  ActiveEvent

Removed Members

java.awt
  Frame
    dispose( )
  Point
    hashCode( )
  Rectangle
    hashCode( )
java.rmi
  RMISecurityManager
    checkAccept( ), checkAccess( ),
    checkAwtEventQueueAccess( ), checkConnect( ),
    checkCreateClassLoader( ), checkDelete( ),
    checkExec( ), checkExit( ), checkLink( ),
    checkListen( ), checkMemberAccess( ),
    checkMulticast( ), checkPackageDefinition( ),
    checkPrintJobAccess( ), checkPropertiesAccess( ),
    checkPropertyAccess( ), checkRead( ),

    checkSecurityAccess( ), checkSetFactory( ),
    checkSystemClipboardAccess( ),
    checkTopLevelWindow( ), checkWrite( ),
    getSecurityContext( )
java.security
  KeyPairGenerator
    generateKeyPair( )
  MessageDigest
    engineDigest( ), engineReset( ), engineUpdate( )
  Signature
    engineGetParameter( ), engineInitSign( ),
    engineInitVerify( ), engineSetParameter( ),
    engineSign( ), engineUpdate( ), engineVerify( )
java.util
  GregorianCalendar
    after( ), before( )

Modified Classes and Members

These tables show all the classes and members whose signatures were modified from the previous version.
"+" indicates an added keyword; "-" indicates a removed keyword.

Class Modifier Changes

java.awt
  Container   - abstract
java.lang
  SecurityManager   - abstract

Topics

Modified Classes and Members

Class Modifier Changes

java.util
  BitSet   - final

Extends Changes

java.awt
  Dimension   - java.lang.Object,
                                             + java.awt.geom.Dimension2D
  Point   - java.lang.Object, + java.awt.geom.Point2D
  Rectangle   - java.lang.Object,
                                             + java.awt.geom.Rectangle2D

java.awt.image
  DirectColorModel   - java.awt.image.ColorModel,
                                           + java.awt.image.PackedColorModel

java.lang.reflect
  Constructor, Field, Method   - java.lang.Object,
                                           + java.lang.reflect.AccessibleObject

java.security
  DigestException, KeyException, NoSuchAlgorithmException,   - java.lang.Exception,
    NoSuchProviderException, SignatureException   + java.security.GeneralSecurityException
  KeyPairGenerator   - java.lang.Object,
                                           + java.security.KeyPairGeneratorSpi
  MessageDigest   - java.lang.Object,
                                           + java.security.MessageDigestSpi
  Signature   - java.lang.Object,
                                         + java.security.SignatureSpi

java.util
  Vector   - java.lang.Object, + java.util.AbstractList

Implements Changes

java.awt
  AWTEventMulticaster   + java.awt.event.InputMethodListener
  Color   + java.awt.Paint
java.awt.datatransfer
  DataFlavor   + java.io.Externalizable,
                                         + java.lang.Cloneable

java.awt.image
  ColorModel   + java.awt.Transparency
java.io
  File   + java.lang.Comparable
java.lang
  Byte, Character, Double, Float, Integer, Long, Short, String   + java.lang.Comparable
java.math
  BigDecimal, BigInteger   + java.lang.Comparable
java.rmi.server
  RMISocketFactory   + java.rmi.server.RMIClientSocketFactory,
                                         + java.rmi.server.RMIServerSocketFactory

java.security
  KeyPair   + java.io.Serializable
java.text
  BreakIterator   - java.io.Serializable
  CollationKey   + java.lang.Comparable
  Collator   - java.io.Serializable, + java.util.Comparator
java.util
  Date   + java.lang.Comparable
  Hashtable   + java.util.Map
  Vector   + java.util.List
java.util.zip
  ZipEntry   + java.lang.Cloneable

Member Modifier Changes

java.awt
  Button
    setLabel( ) — synchronized
  Checkbox
    setLabel( ) — synchronized
  Choice
    addItem( ), insert( ), remove( ), removeAll( ) — synchronized
    select( ) + synchronized
  Container
    Container( ) — protected, + public
  Dialog
    setResizable( ) — synchronized
  Frame
    setResizable( ) — synchronized
  Label
    setText( ) — synchronized

java.beans
  Introspector
    getBeanInfoSearchPath( ), setBeanInfoSearchPath( ) + synchronized
  PropertyEditorManager
    findEditor( ), getEditorSearchPath( ), setEditorSearchPath( ) + synchronized

java.io
  File
    isAbsolute( ) — native
  FileDescriptor
    valid( ) — native
  ObjectInputStream
    defaultReadObject( ), enableResolveObject( ) — final
  ObjectOutputStream
    defaultWriteObject( ), enableReplaceObject( ) — final
  PipedOutputStream
    connect( ) + synchronized
  PipedReader
    read( ) + synchronized
  PipedWriter
    connect( ), flush( ) + synchronized
  StringWriter
    StringWriter( ) — protected, + public

java.lang
  Class
    forName( ), getClassLoader( ), newInstance( ) — native
    getDeclaringClass( ) + native
  ClassLoader
    findLoadedClass( ) + native
    getSystemResource( ), getSystemResourceAsStream( ) — final
    loadClass( ) — abstract, + synchronized

java.lang.reflect
  Constructor
    getModifiers( ) — native
  Field
    getModifiers( ) — native
  Method
    getModifiers( ) — native

java.lang
  Runtime
    load( ), loadLibrary( ) — synchronized
    runFinalization( ) — native
  SecurityManager
    SecurityManager( ) — protected, + public

Topics

Member Modifier Changes

---

classLoaderDepth( ), currentClassLoader( )	- native
System	
setSecurityManager( )	+ synchronized
Thread	
checkAccess( )	+ final
java.net	
InetAddress	
getLocalHost( )	+ synchronized
MulticastSocket	
send( )	- synchronized
URL	
hashCode( )	+ synchronized
java.rmi	
RMISecurityManager	
checkPackageAccess( )	- synchronized
java.rmi.server	
RMISocketFactory	
getFailureHandler( ), getSocketFactory( ), setFailureHandler( ), setSocketFactory( )	+ synchronized
java.security	
KeyPairGenerator	
initialize( )	- abstract
java.sql	
DriverManager	
deregisterDriver( ), getDriver( ), getDrivers( ), println( ), setLogStream( )	+ synchronized
java.util	
Calendar	
after( ), before( ), equals( )	- abstract
GregorianCalendar	
hashCode( )	- synchronized
Vector	
addElement( ), capacity( ), contains( ), copyInto( ), elementAt( ), ensureCapacity( ), firstElement( ), indexOf( ), insertElementAt( ), isEmpty( ), lastElement( ), lastIndexOf( ), removeAllElements( ), removeElement( ), removeElementAt( ), setElementAt( ), setSize( ), size( ), toString( ), trimToSize( )	- final
elements( )	- final, - synchronized
java.util.zip	
Adler32	
update( )	- native
CRC32	
update( )	- native
Deflater	
deflate( ), end( ), getAdler( ), getTotalIn( ), getTotalOut( ), reset( ), setDictionary( )	- native
Inflater	
end( ), getAdler( ), getTotalIn( ), getTotalOut( ), inflate( ), reset( ), setDictionary( )	- native

---

Throws Changes

---

java.io

FileOutputStream	
FileOutputStream( )	- java.io.IOException, + java.io.FileNotFoundException
RandomAccessFile	
RandomAccessFile( )	- java.io.IOException, + java.io.FileNotFoundException

Throws Changes

StringReader	
ready( )	+ java.io.IOException
StringWriter	
close( )	+ java.io.IOException
java.lang	
ClassLoader	
defineClass( )	+ java.lang.ClassFormatError
java.math	
BigDecimal	
BigDecimal( ), valueOf( )	- java.lang.NumberFormatException
divide( ), setScale( )	- java.lang.ArithmeticException,
	- java.lang.IllegalArgumentException
BigInteger	
BigInteger( )	- java.lang.NumberFormatException
BigInteger( )	- java.lang.IllegalArgumentException
add( ), clearBit( ), divide( ), divideAndRemainder( ), flipBit( ), modInverse( ), pow( ), remainder( ), setBit( ), testBit( )	- java.lang.ArithmeticException
java.rmi	
Naming	
bind( ), list( ), lookup( ), rebind( ), unbind( )	- java.rmi.UnknownHostException
java.rmi.registry	
LocateRegistry	
getRegistry( )	- java.rmi.UnknownHostException

Newly Deprecated Classes

java.rmi
RMISecurityException, ServerRuntimeException
java.rmi.registry
RegistryHandler
java.rmi.server
LoaderHandler, LogStream, Operation, *RemoteCall*, *Skeleton*, SkeletonMismatchException, SkeletonNotFoundException

java.security
Certificate, Identity, IdentityScope, Signer
javax.swing.text
DefaultTextUI
org.omg.CORBA
Principal, PrincipalHolder

Newly Deprecated Members

java.awt
Font
getPeer( )
Frame
CROSSHAIR_CURSOR, DEFAULT_CURSOR,
E_RESIZE_CURSOR, HAND_CURSOR,
MOVE_CURSOR, N_RESIZE_CURSOR,
NE_RESIZE_CURSOR, NW_RESIZE_CURSOR,
S_RESIZE_CURSOR, SE_RESIZE_CURSOR,
SW_RESIZE_CURSOR, TEXT_CURSOR,
W_RESIZE_CURSOR, WAIT_CURSOR
List
addItem( ), delItem( )
Toolkit
getFontList( ), getFontMetrics( ), getFontPeer( )
java.awt.datatransfer
DataFlavor
normalizeMimeType( ),
normalizeMimeTypeParameter( )

java.io
ObjectInputStream
readLine( )
java.lang
Runtime
runFinalizersOnExit( )
SecurityManager
classDepth( ), classLoaderDepth( ),
currentClassLoader( ), currentLoadedClass( ),
getInCheck( ), inCheck, inClass( ), inClassLoader( )
System
runFinalizersOnExit( )
Thread
countStackFrames( ), resume( ), stop( ), suspend( )
ThreadGroup
allowThreadSuspension( ), resume( ), stop( ),
suspend( )
java.net
DatagramSocketImpl
getTTL( ), setTTL( )

Topics

MulticastSocket
getTTL( ), setTTL( )

java.rmi

RMISecurityException
RMISecurityException( )
ServerRuntimeException
ServerRuntimeException( )

java.rmi.registry

RegistryHandler
registryImpl( ), registryStub( )

java.rmi.server

LoaderHandler
getSecurityContext( ), loadClass( )
LogStream
getDefaultStream( ), getOutputStream( ),
log( ), parseLevel( ), setDefaultStream( ),
setOutputStream( ), toString( ), write( )
Operation
getOperation( ), Operation( ), toString( )
RMIClassLoader
getSecurityContext( ), loadClass( )
RemoteCall
done( ), executeCall( ), getInputStream( ),
getOutputStream( ), getResultStream( ),
releaseInputStream( ), releaseOutputStream( )
RemoteRef
done( ), invoke( ), newCall( )
RemoteStub
setRef( )
Skeleton
dispatch( ), getOperations( )
SkeletonMismatchException
SkeletonMismatchException( )

java.security

Security
getAlgorithmProperty( )
Signature
getParameter( ), setParameter( )
SignatureSpi
engineGetParameter( ), engineSetParameter( )

java.sql

CallableStatement
getBigDecimal( )
Date
Date( ), getHours( ), getMinutes( ), getSeconds( ),
setHours( ), setMinutes( ), setSeconds( )
DriverManager
getLogStream( ), setLogStream( )

PreparedStatement
setUnicodeStream( )
ResultSet
getBigDecimal( ), getUnicodeStream( )
Time
getDate( ), getDay( ), getMonth( ), getYear( ),
setDate( ), setMonth( ), setYear( )
Timestamp
Timestamp( )

java.util

Properties
save( )

javax.swing

AbstractButton
getLabel( ), setLabel( )
JInternalFrame
getMenuBar( ), setMenuBar( )
JPasswordField
getText( )
JRootPane
getMenuBar( ), setMenuBar( )
JTable
createScrollPaneForTable( ), sizeColumnsToFit( )
KeyStroke
getKeyStroke( )
ScrollPaneLayout
getViewportBorderBounds( )
ToolTipManager
setLightWeightPopupEnabled( )

javax.swing.text

View
modelToView( ), viewToModel( )

org.omg.CORBA

Any
extract_Principal( ), insert_Principal( )
ORB
create_recursive_sequence_tc( ), get_current( )
Principal
name( )
ServerRequest
except( ), op_name( ), params( ), result( )

org.omg.CORBA.portable

InputStream
read_Principal( )
OutputStream
write_Principal( )

Exceptions and Errors

This is a complete listing of all the exceptions and errors in this version of Java. The "*" indicates a checked exception or error; these must be declared in the throws clause.

java.lang	AbstractMethodError
java.security	AccessControlException
java.rmi	*AccessException
java.security.acl	*AclNotFoundException
java.rmi.activation	*ActivateFailedException
java.rmi.activation	*ActivationException
org.omg.CosNaming.NamingContextPackage	*AlreadyBound
java.rmi	*AlreadyBoundException

org.omg.CORBA.portable	*ApplicationException
java.lang	ArithmeticException
java.lang	ArrayIndexOutOfBoundsException
java.lang	ArrayStoreException
java.awt	AWTError
java.awt	*AWTException
org.omg.CORBA	BAD_CONTEXT
org.omg.CORBA	BAD_INV_ORDER
org.omg.CORBA	BAD_OPERATION
org.omg.CORBA	BAD_PARAM
org.omg.CORBA	BAD_TYPECODE
org.omg.CORBA.TypeCodePackage	*BadKind
javax.swing.text	*BadLocationException
java.sql	*BatchUpdateException
java.net	*BindException
org.omg.CORBA	*Bounds
org.omg.CORBA.TypeCodePackage	*Bounds
org.omg.CosNaming.NamingContextPackage	*CannotProceed
javax.swing.undo	CannotRedoException
javax.swing.undo	CannotUndoException
java.security.cert	*CertificateEncodingException
java.security.cert	*CertificateException
java.security.cert	*CertificateExpiredException
java.security.cert	*CertificateNotYetValidException
java.security.cert	*CertificateParsingException
javax.swing.text	*ChangedCharSetException
java.io	*CharConversionException
java.lang	ClassCastException
java.lang	ClassCircularityError
java.lang	ClassFormatError
java.lang	*ClassNotFoundException
java.lang	*CloneNotSupportedException
java.awt.color	CMMException
org.omg.CORBA	COMM_FAILURE
java.util	ConcurrentModificationException
java.net	*ConnectException
java.rmi	*ConnectException
java.rmi	*ConnectIOException
java.security.cert	*CRLException
org.omg.CORBA	DATA_CONVERSION
java.util.zip	*DataFormatException
java.sql	*DataTruncation
java.security	*DigestException
java.util	EmptyStackException
java.io	*EOFException
java.lang	Error
java.lang	*Exception
java.lang	ExceptionInInitializerError
javax.swing.tree	*ExpandVetoException
java.rmi.server	*ExportException
java.io	*FileNotFoundException
org.omg.CORBA	FREE_MEM
java.security	*GeneralSecurityException
java.lang	IllegalAccessError
java.lang	*IllegalAccessException
java.lang	IllegalArgumentException
java.awt	IllegalComponentStateException

Topics

java.lang	IllegalMonitorStateException
java.awt.geom	IllegalPathStateException
java.lang	IllegalStateException
java.lang	IllegalThreadStateException
java.awt.image	ImagingOpException
org.omg.CORBA	IMP_LIMIT
java.lang	IncompatibleClassChangeError
org.omg.CORBA.ORBPackage	*InconsistentTypeCode
java.lang	IndexOutOfBoundsException
org.omg.CORBA	INITIALIZE
java.lang	InstantiationError
java.lang	*InstantiationException
org.omg.CORBA	INTERNAL
java.lang	InternalError
java.lang	*InterruptedException
java.io	*InterruptedIOException
org.omg.CORBA	INTF_REPOS
java.beans	*IntrospectionException
org.omg.CORBA	INV_FLAG
org.omg.CORBA	INV_IDENT
org.omg.CORBA	INV_OBJREF
org.omg.CORBA	INV_POLICY
org.omg.CORBA.DynAnyPackage	*Invalid
org.omg.CORBA	INVALID_TRANSACTION
java.security	*InvalidAlgorithmParameterException
java.io	*InvalidClassException
java.awt.dnd	InvalidDnDOperationException
java.security	*InvalidKeyException
java.security.spec	*InvalidKeySpecException
org.omg.CORBA.ORBPackage	*InvalidName
org.omg.CosNaming.NamingContextPackage	*InvalidName
java.io	*InvalidObjectException
java.security	InvalidParameterException
java.security.spec	*InvalidParameterSpecException
org.omg.CORBA.DynAnyPackage	*InvalidSeq
org.omg.CORBA.DynAnyPackage	*InvalidValue
java.lang.reflect	*InvocationTargetException
java.io	*IOException
java.util.jar	*JarException
java.security	*KeyException
java.security	*KeyManagementException
java.security	*KeyStoreException
java.security.acl	*LastOwnerException
java.lang	LinkageError
java.net	*MalformedURLException
org.omg.CORBA	MARSHAL
java.rmi	*MarshalException
java.util	MissingResourceException
java.lang	NegativeArraySizeException
org.omg.CORBA	NO_IMPLEMENT
org.omg.CORBA	NO_MEMORY
org.omg.CORBA	NO_PERMISSION
org.omg.CORBA	NO_RESOURCES
org.omg.CORBA	NO_RESPONSE
java.lang	NoClassDefFoundError
java.awt.geom	*NoninvertibleTransformException
java.net	*NoRouteToHostException

java.security	*NoSuchAlgorithmException
java.util	NoSuchElementException
java.lang	NoSuchFieldError
java.lang	*NoSuchFieldException
java.lang	NoSuchMethodError
java.lang	*NoSuchMethodException
java.rmi	*NoSuchObjectException
java.security	*NoSuchProviderException
java.io	*NotActiveException
java.rmi	*NotBoundException
org.omg.CosNaming.NamingContextPackage	*NotEmpty
org.omg.CosNaming.NamingContextPackage	*NotFound
java.security.acl	*NotOwnerException
java.io	*NotSerializableException
java.lang	NullPointerException
java.lang	NumberFormatException
org.omg.CORBA	OBJ_ADAPTER
org.omg.CORBA	OBJECT_NOT_EXIST
java.io	*ObjectStreamException
java.io	*OptionalDataException
java.lang	OutOfMemoryError
java.text	*ParseException
org.omg.CORBA	PERSIST_STORE
org.omg.CORBA	*PolicyError
java.awt.print	*PrinterAbortException
java.awt.print	*PrinterException
java.awt.print	*PrinterIOException
java.security	*PrivilegedActionException
java.awt.color	ProfileDataException
java.beans	*PropertyVetoException
java.net	*ProtocolException
java.security	ProviderException
java.awt.image	RasterFormatException
org.omg.CORBA.portable	*RemarshalException
java.rmi	*RemoteException
java.rmi	RMISecurityException
java.lang	RuntimeException
java.lang	SecurityException
java.rmi.server	*ServerCloneException
java.rmi	*ServerError
java.rmi	*ServerException
java.rmi.server	*ServerNotActiveException
java.rmi	*ServerRuntimeException
java.security	*SignatureException
java.rmi.server	*SkeletonMismatchException
java.rmi.server	*SkeletonNotFoundException
java.net	*SocketException
java.rmi.server	*SocketSecurityException
java.sql	*SQLException
java.sql	*SQLWarning
java.lang	StackOverflowError
java.io	*StreamCorruptedException
java.lang	StringIndexOutOfBoundsException
java.rmi	*StubNotFoundException
java.io	*SyncFailedException
org.omg.CORBA	SystemException
java.lang	ThreadDeath

Topics

java.lang	*Throwable
java.util	*TooManyListenersException
org.omg.CORBA	TRANSACTION_REQUIRED
org.omg.CORBA	TRANSACTION_ROLLEDBACK
org.omg.CORBA	TRANSIENT
org.omg.CORBA.DynAnyPackage	*TypeMismatch
java.rmi	*UnexpectedException
org.omg.CORBA	UNKNOWN
java.lang	UnknownError
java.rmi.activation	*UnknownGroupException
java.rmi	*UnknownHostException
java.net	*UnknownHostException
java.rmi.activation	*UnknownObjectException
java.net	*UnknownServiceException
org.omg.CORBA	*UnknownUserException
java.rmi	*UnmarshalException
java.security	*UnrecoverableKeyException
java.lang	UnsatisfiedLinkError
java.lang	UnsupportedClassVersionError
java.io	*UnsupportedEncodingException
java.awt.datatransfer	*UnsupportedFlavorException
javax.swing	*UnsupportedLookAndFeelException
java.lang	UnsupportedOperationException
org.omg.CORBA	*UserException
java.io	*UTFDataFormatException
java.lang	VerifyError
java.lang	VirtualMachineError
java.io	*WriteAbortedException
org.omg.CORBA	*WrongTransaction
java.util.zip	*ZipException

Statistics

Packages 77	**Members** 23901
	Fields 4006
Classes and Interfaces 2130	static 24
Classes 1730	final 27
abstract 261	static final 2713
final 221	protected 1050
protected 157	Constructors 2737
abstract protected 3	protected 299
Interfaces 400	Methods 17158
	abstract 968
	static 1496
	final 460
	static final 57
	protected 1803

Packages

New	Package	Classes	Members	Interfaces	Members
	java.applet	2	28	3	16
	java.awt	108	2253	14	57
	java.awt.color	7	185	0	0
	java.awt.datatransfer	6	66	3	6
	java.awt.dnd	17	182	4	13
	java.awt.event	23	397	15	35
	java.awt.font	15	236	2	64
	java.awt.geom	32	647	1	12
	java.awt.im	3	35	1	7
•	java.awt.im.spi	0	0	3	24
	java.awt.image	40	699	8	70
	java.awt.image.renderable	4	82	3	19
	java.awt.peer	0	0	27	136
	java.awt.print	7	57	3	8
	java.beans	17	140	8	38
	java.beans.beancontext	12	156	11	32
	java.io	66	684	10	74
	java.lang	76	858	3	2
	java.lang.ref	5	15	0	0
	java.lang.reflect	10	116	2	6
	java.math	2	91	0	0
	java.net	29	347	6	16
	java.rmi	19	45	1	0
	java.rmi.activation	12	70	4	16
	java.rmi.dgc	2	8	1	2
	java.rmi.registry	1	7	2	8
	java.rmi.server	16	86	9	30
	java.security	54	376	9	21
	java.security.acl	3	3	5	27
	java.security.cert	14	97	1	4
	java.security.interfaces	0	0	9	19
	java.security.spec	12	45	2	0
	java.sql	11	109	16	550

Topics

New	Package	Classes	Members	Interfaces	Members
	java.text	21	361	2	20
	java.util	41	715	13	103
	java.util.jar	8	83	0	0
	java.util.zip	16	160	1	4
	javax.accessibility	9	179	10	93
•	javax.naming	36	243	5	64
•	javax.naming.directory	15	120	3	55
•	javax.naming.event	2	19	5	16
•	javax.naming.ldap	4	20	7	22
•	javax.naming.spi	4	26	8	9
•	javax.rmi	1	6	0	0
•	javax.rmi.CORBA	3	21	5	38
•	javax.sound.midi	17	150	9	101
•	javax.sound.midi.spi	4	22	0	0
•	javax.sound.sampled	26	199	8	50
•	javax.sound.sampled.spi	4	29	0	0
	javax.swing	168	3443	23	182
	javax.swing.border	9	152	1	3
	javax.swing.colorchooser	3	22	1	4
	javax.swing.event	23	143	23	60
	javax.swing.filechooser	3	20	0	0
	javax.swing.plaf	46	128	1	0
	javax.swing.plaf.basic	187	1968	1	8
	javax.swing.plaf.metal	67	573	0	0
	javax.swing.plaf.multi	29	443	0	0
	javax.swing.table	9	251	4	30
	javax.swing.text	84	1202	21	121
	javax.swing.text.html	41	533	0	0
	javax.swing.text.html.parser	9	142	1	35
	javax.swing.text.rtf	1	7	0	0
	javax.swing.tree	13	336	7	54
	javax.swing.undo	7	84	2	14
•	javax.transaction	3	6	0	0
	org.omg.CORBA	129	969	38	176
	org.omg.CORBA.DynAnyPackage	4	8	0	0
	org.omg.CORBA.ORBPackage	2	4	0	0
	org.omg.CORBA.TypeCodePackage	2	4	0	0
	org.omg.CORBA.portable	9	133	9	11
•	org.omg.CORBA_2_3	1	6	0	0
•	org.omg.CORBA_2_3.portable	4	18	0	0
	org.omg.CosNaming	22	142	4	13
	org.omg.CosNaming.NamingContextPackage	18	91	0	0
•	org.omg.SendingContext	0	0	2	0
•	org.omg.stub.java.rmi	1	2	0	0

New Classes in Existing Packages

java.applet
Applet.AccessibleApplet
java.awt
Button.AccessibleAWTButton, Canvas ↵
.AccessibleAWTCanvas, Checkbox ↵
.AccessibleAWTCheckbox, CheckboxMenuItem ↵
.AccessibleAWTCheckboxMenuItem, Choice ↵
.AccessibleAWTChoice, Component ↵
.AccessibleAWTComponent, Component ↵
.AccessibleAWTComponent ↵
.AccessibleAWTComponentHandler,

Component.AccessibleAWTComponent ↵
.AccessibleAWTFocusHandler, Container ↵
.AccessibleAWTContainer, Container ↵
.AccessibleAWTContainer.AccessibleContainerHandler,
Dialog.AccessibleAWTDialog, FontFormatException,
Frame.AccessibleAWTFrame, JobAttributes,
JobAttributes.DefaultSelectionType, JobAttributes ↵
.DestinationType, JobAttributes.DialogType,
JobAttributes.MultipleDocumentHandlingType,
JobAttributes.SidesType, Label.AccessibleAWTLabel,
List.AccessibleAWTList, List.AccessibleAWTList ↵

.AccessibleAWTListChild, Menu.AccessibleAWTMenu,
MenuBar.AccessibleAWTMenuBar, MenuComponent ↵
.AccessibleAWTMenuComponent, MenuItem ↵
.AccessibleAWTMenuItem, PageAttributes,
PageAttributes.ColorType, PageAttributes ↵
.MediaType, PageAttributes.OrientationRequestedType,
PageAttributes.OriginType, PageAttributes ↵
.PrintQualityType, Panel.AccessibleAWTPanel,
PopupMenu.AccessibleAWTPopupMenu, Robot,
Scrollbar.AccessibleAWTScrollBar, ScrollPane ↵
.AccessibleAWTScrollPane, TextArea ↵
.AccessibleAWTTextArea, TextComponent ↵
.AccessibleAWTTextComponent, TextField ↵
.AccessibleAWTTextField, Window ↵
.AccessibleAWTWindow

java.awt.datatransfer
MimeTypeParseException

java.awt.event
HierarchyBoundsAdapter, *HierarchyBoundsListener*,
HierarchyEvent, *HierarchyListener*

java.awt.font
TextMeasurer

java.awt.peer
RobotPeer

java.lang
StrictMath

java.lang.reflect
InvocationHandler, Proxy,
UndeclaredThrowableException

java.net
DatagramSocketImplFactory

java.security
DomainCombiner

java.security.cert
Certificate.CertificateRep

java.security.interfaces
RSAKey

java.security.spec
RSAKeyGenParameterSpec

java.sql
SQLPermission

java.util
Timer, TimerTask

javax.accessibility
AccessibleIcon, AccessibleRelation,
AccessibleRelationSet, *AccessibleTable*,
AccessibleTableModelChange

javax.swing
AbstractCellEditor, ActionMap, ComponentInputMap,
ImageIcon.AccessibleImageIcon, InputMap,
InputVerifier, JComponent.AccessibleJComponent ↵
.AccessibleFocusHandler, JTable.AccessibleJTable ↵

.AccessibleJTableModelChange, SizeSequence,
UIDefaults.LazyInputMap, UIDefaults.ProxyLazyValue

javax.swing.plaf
ActionMapUIResource,
ComponentInputMapUIResource, InputMapUIResource,
RootPaneUI

javax.swing.plaf.basic
BasicDesktopPaneUI.OpenAction, BasicHTML,
BasicRootPaneUI

javax.swing.plaf.metal
MetalBorders.OptionDialogBorder, MetalBorders ↵
.PaletteBorder, MetalBorders.TableHeaderBorder,
MetalBorders.ToggleButtonBorder, MetalIconFactory ↵
.PaletteCloseIcon, MetalInternalFrameTitlePane

javax.swing.text
AsyncBoxView, AsyncBoxView.ChildLocator,
AsyncBoxView.ChildState, FlowView, FlowView ↵
.FlowStrategy, GlyphView, GlyphView.GlyphPainter,
LayoutQueue, ZoneView

org.omg.CORBA
_IDLTypeStub, _PolicyStub, AnySeqHelper,
AnySeqHolder, BooleanSeqHelper,
BooleanSeqHolder, CharSeqHelper, CharSeqHolder,
CompletionStatusHelper, CurrentHelper, CurrentHolder,
CurrentOperations, *CustomMarshal*, *DataInputStream*,
DataOutputStream, DefinitionKindHelper,
DomainManagerOperations, DoubleSeqHelper,
DoubleSeqHolder, FieldNameHelper, FloatSeqHelper,
FloatSeqHolder, IdentifierHelper, IDLTypeHelper,
IDLTypeOperations, *IRObjectOperations*,
LongLongSeqHelper, LongLongSeqHolder,
LongSeqHelper, LongSeqHolder, NameValuePairHelper,
ObjectHelper, OctetSeqHelper, OctetSeqHolder,
OMGVMCID, PolicyHelper, PolicyHolder,
PolicyListHelper, PolicyListHolder, *PolicyOperations*,
PolicyTypeHelper, RepositoryIdHelper,
SetOverrideTypeHelper, ShortSeqHelper,
ShortSeqHolder, StringValueHelper,
StructMemberHelper, ULongLongSeqHelper,
ULongLongSeqHolder, ULongSeqHelper,
ULongSeqHolder, UnionMemberHelper,
UShortSeqHelper, UShortSeqHolder, ValueBaseHelper,
ValueBaseHolder, ValueMemberHelper,
VersionSpecHelper, VisibilityHelper, WCharSeqHelper,
WCharSeqHolder, WStringValueHelper

org.omg.CORBA.portable
BoxedValueHelper, *CustomValue*, IndirectionException,
StreamableValue, UnknownException, *ValueBase*,
ValueFactory

org.omg.CosNaming
BindingIteratorOperations, *NamingContextOperations*

New Members in Existing Classes

If a new member overrides an existing member, it is included in this listing.

java.applet
Applet
    getAccessibleContext( )

java.awt
AWTEvent
    HIERARCHY_BOUNDS_EVENT_MASK,
    HIERARCHY_EVENT_MASK, INVOCATION ↵
    _EVENT_MASK, PAINT_EVENT_MASK

AWTEventMulticaster
  add( ), ancestorMoved( ), ancestorResized( ),
  hierarchyChanged( ), remove( )
Button
  getAccessibleContext( ), getListeners( )
Canvas
  getAccessibleContext( )
Checkbox
  getAccessibleContext( ), getListeners( )
CheckboxMenuItem
  getAccessibleContext( ), getListeners( )
Choice
  getAccessibleContext( ), getListeners( )
Component
  addHierarchyBoundsListener( ),
  addHierarchyListener( ), getAccessibleContext( ),
  getGraphicsConfiguration( ), getListeners( ),
  processHierarchyBoundsEvent( ),
  processHierarchyEvent( ),
  removeHierarchyBoundsListener( ),
  removeHierarchyListener( )
Container
  getListeners( )
Cursor
  finalize( )
Dialog
  dispose( ), getAccessibleContext( ), hide( )
Dimension
  hashCode( )
Font
  createFont( ), TRUETYPE_FONT
Frame
  Frame( ), getAccessibleContext( )
GraphicsConfiguration
  getBounds( )
Insets
  hashCode( )
Label
  getAccessibleContext( )
List
  getAccessibleContext( ), getListeners( )
Menu
  getAccessibleContext( )
MenuBar
  getAccessibleContext( )
MenuComponent
  getAccessibleContext( )
MenuItem
  getAccessibleContext( ), getListeners( )
Panel
  getAccessibleContext( )
PopupMenu
  getAccessibleContext( )
RenderingHints
  KEY_STROKE_CONTROL, VALUE_STROKE↵
  _DEFAULT, VALUE_STROKE_NORMALIZE,
  VALUE_STROKE_PURE
ScrollPane
  getAccessibleContext( )
Scrollbar
  getAccessibleContext( ), getListeners( )
TextArea
  getAccessibleContext( )
TextComponent
  getAccessibleContext( ), getBackground( ),
  getListeners( ), setBackground( )

TextField
  getAccessibleContext( ), getListeners( )
Toolkit
  getLockingKeyState( ), getPrintJob( ),
  mapInputMethodHighlight( ), setLockingKeyState( )
Window
  getAccessibleContext( ), getGraphicsConfiguration( ),
  getListeners( ), hide( ), setCursor( ), Window( )
java.awt.color
ICC_Profile
  icSigChromaticityTag, icSigCrdInfoTag,
  icSigDeviceSettingsTag, icSigOutputResponseTag,
  readResolve( )
java.awt.datatransfer
DataFlavor
  getDefaultRepresentationClass( ),
  getDefaultRepresentationClassAsString( ),
  getReaderForText( ), getTextPlainUnicodeFlavor( ),
  hashCode( ), match( ), selectBestTextFlavor( ),
  toString( )
java.awt.event
KeyEvent
  setSource( ), VK_INPUT_METHOD_ON_OFF,
  VK_KANA_LOCK
java.awt.font
TextAttribute
  INPUT_METHOD_UNDERLINE, UNDERLINE↵
  _LOW_DASHED, UNDERLINE_LOW_DOTTED,
  UNDERLINE_LOW_GRAY, UNDERLINE_LOW↵
  _ONE_PIXEL, UNDERLINE_LOW_TWO_PIXEL
java.awt.geom
CubicCurve2D
  solveCubic( )
QuadCurve2D
  solveQuadratic( )
java.awt.im
InputContext
  getLocale( ), isCompositionEnabled( ), reconvert( ),
  setCompositionEnabled( )
InputMethodHighlight
  getStyle( ), InputMethodHighlight( )
InputSubset
  FULLWIDTH_DIGITS, FULLWIDTH_LATIN
java.awt.image
BandedSampleModel
  getSampleDouble( ), getSampleFloat( ), setSample( )
ColorModel
  getTransferType( ), hashCode( )
ComponentSampleModel
  getSampleDouble( ), getSampleFloat( ), setSample( )
IndexColorModel
  getValidPixels( ), IndexColorModel( ), isValid( )
java.awt.image.renderable
RenderContext
  concatenateTransform( ), preConcatenateTransform( )
java.awt.peer
ChoicePeer
  removeAll( )
ComponentPeer
  coalescePaintEvent( ), getGraphicsConfiguration( )
TextComponentPeer
  filterEvents( ), getCharacterBounds( ),
  getIndexAtPoint( )
java.io
ObjectInputStream
  readClassDescriptor( ), resolveProxyClass( )

ObjectOutputStream
  annotateProxyClass( ), writeClassDescriptor( )
ObjectStreamConstants
  TC_LONGSTRING, TC_PROXYCLASSDESC
java.lang
Double
  doubleToRawLongBits( )
Float
  floatToRawIntBits( )
InheritableThreadLocal
  get( ), set( )
Runtime
  addShutdownHook( ), exec( ), halt( ),
  removeShutdownHook( )
java.net
ContentHandler
  getContent( )
DatagramSocket
  setDatagramSocketImplFactory( )
HttpURLConnection
  getHeaderFieldDate( ), getInstanceFollowRedirects( ),
  HTTP_NOT_IMPLEMENTED,
  instanceFollowRedirects,
  setInstanceFollowRedirects( )
Socket
  getKeepAlive( ), setKeepAlive( ), shutdownInput( ),
  shutdownOutput( )
SocketImpl
  shutdownInput( ), shutdownOutput( )
SocketOptions
  SO_KEEPALIVE
URL
  getAuthority( ), getContent( ), getPath( ), getQuery( ),
  getUserInfo( ), set( )
URLConnection
  getContent( )
URLStreamHandler
  equals( ), getDefaultPort( ), getHostAddress( ),
  hashCode( ), hostsEqual( ), sameFile( ), setURL( )
java.rmi.server
RMIClassLoader
  getClassLoader( )
java.security
AccessControlContext
  AccessControlContext( ), getDomainCombiner( )
KeyPairGenerator
  generateKeyPair( )
PrivilegedActionException
  toString( )
Security
  getProviders( )
Signature
  initVerify( )
java.security.cert
Certificate
  writeReplace( )
java.util
AbstractSet
  removeAll( )
Collections
  EMPTY_MAP, singletonList( ), singletonMap( )
WeakHashMap
  WeakHashMap( )

java.util.jar
Attributes.Name
  EXTENSION_INSTALLATION, EXTENSION_LIST,
  EXTENSION_NAME, IMPLEMENTATION_URL,
  IMPLEMENTATION_VENDOR_ID
JarFile
  JarFile( )
java.util.zip
ZipFile
  finalize( ), OPEN_DELETE, OPEN_READ, ZipFile( )
javax.accessibility
AccessibleContext
  ACCESSIBLE_ACTION_PROPERTY,
  ACCESSIBLE_TABLE_CAPTION_CHANGED,
  ACCESSIBLE_TABLE_COLUMN_DESCRIPTION↵
  _CHANGED, ACCESSIBLE_TABLE_COLUMN↵
  _HEADER_CHANGED, ACCESSIBLE↵
  _TABLE_MODEL_CHANGED, ACCESSIBLE↵
  _TABLE_ROW_DESCRIPTION_CHANGED,
  ACCESSIBLE_TABLE_ROW_HEADER_CHANGED,
  ACCESSIBLE_TABLE_SUMMARY_CHANGED,
  getAccessibleIcon( ), getAccessibleRelationSet( ),
  getAccessibleTable( )
AccessibleRole
  CANVAS, ICON, LIST_ITEM
javax.swing
AbstractAction
  getKeys( )
AbstractButton
  configurePropertiesFromAction( ),
  createActionPropertyChangeListener( ), getAction( ),
  imageUpdate( ), isFocusTraversable( ), setAction( )
AbstractButton.AccessibleAbstractButton
  getAccessibleIcon( ), getAccessibleRelationSet( ),
  getAccessibleText( ), getAfterIndex( ), getAtIndex( ),
  getBeforeIndex( ), getCaretPosition( ),
  getCharacterAttribute( ), getCharacterBounds( ),
  getCharCount( ), getIndexAtPoint( ),
  getSelectedText( ), getSelectionEnd( ),
  getSelectionStart( )
AbstractListModel
  getListeners( )
Action
  ACCELERATOR_KEY, ACTION_COMMAND_KEY,
  MNEMONIC_KEY
BorderFactory
  createEtchedBorder( )
ButtonGroup
  getButtonCount( )
DefaultBoundedRangeModel
  getListeners( )
DefaultButtonModel
  getGroup( ), getListeners( )
DefaultCellEditor.EditorDelegate
  shouldSelectCell( )
DefaultListCellRenderer
  firePropertyChange( ), repaint( ), revalidate( ),
  validate( )
DefaultListSelectionModel
  getListeners( )
DefaultSingleSelectionModel
  getListeners( )
ImageIcon
  getAccessibleContext( ), toString( )
JApplet
  remove( )

JButton
    configurePropertiesFromAction( ), JButton( ),
    removeNotify( )
JCheckBox
    BORDER_PAINTED_FLAT_CHANGED↵
    _PROPERTY, configurePropertiesFromAction( ),
    createActionPropertyChangeListener( ),
    isBorderPaintedFlat( ), JCheckBox( ),
    setBorderPaintedFlat( )
JCheckBoxMenuItem
    JCheckBoxMenuItem( )
JComboBox
    configurePropertiesFromAction( ),
    createActionPropertyChangeListener( ), getAction( ),
    setAction( )
JComboBox.AccessibleJComboBox
    addAccessibleSelection( ),
    clearAccessibleSelection( ), getAccessibleChild( ),
    getAccessibleChildrenCount( ),
    getAccessibleSelection( ),
    getAccessibleSelectionCount( ),
    isAccessibleChildSelected( ),
    removeAccessibleSelection( ),
    selectAllAccessibleSelection( )
JComponent
    addPropertyChangeListener( ), disable( ), enable( ),
    getActionMap( ), getInputMap( ), getInputVerifier( ),
    getListeners( ), getVerifyInputWhenFocusTarget( ),
    hide( ), isMaximumSizeSet( ), isMinimumSizeSet( ),
    isPreferredSizeSet( ), print( ), printAll( ),
    printBorder( ), printChildren( ),
    printComponent( ), processKeyBinding( ),
    removePropertyChangeListener( ),
    setActionMap( ), setInputMap( ), setInputVerifier( ),
    setVerifyInputWhenFocusTarget( )
JComponent.AccessibleJComponent
    accessibleFocusHandler
JDesktopPane
    getDragMode( ), getSelectedFrame( ), LIVE↵
    _DRAG_MODE, OUTLINE_DRAG_MODE,
    setDragMode( ), setSelectedFrame( )
JDialog
    processKeyEvent( ), remove( )
JEditorPane
    getEditorKitClassNameForContentType( ),
    isFocusCycleRoot( ), processKeyEvent( )
JFileChooser
    ACCEPT_ALL_FILE_FILTER_USED↵
    _CHANGED_PROPERTY, CONTROL↵
    _BUTTONS_ARE_SHOWN_CHANGED↵
    _PROPERTY, getControlButtonsAreShown( ),
    isAcceptAllFileFilterUsed( ),
    setAcceptAllFileFilterUsed( ),
    setControlButtonsAreShown( )
JFrame
    EXIT_ON_CLOSE, JFrame( ), remove( )
JInternalFrame
    doDefaultCloseAction( ), getFocusOwner( ),
    getNormalBounds( ), paintComponent( ), remove( ),
    restoreSubcomponentFocus( ), setLayer( ),
    setNormalBounds( )
JLabel
    imageUpdate( )
JLabel.AccessibleJLabel
    getAccessibleIcon( ), getAccessibleRelationSet( ),
    getAccessibleText( ), getAfterIndex( ), getAtIndex( ),

getBeforeIndex( ), getCaretPosition( ),
    getCharacterAttribute( ), getCharacterBounds( ),
    getCharCount( ), getIndexAtPoint( ),
    getSelectedText( ), getSelectionEnd( ),
    getSelectionStart( )
JMenu
    add( ), createActionComponent( ),
    getPopupMenuOrigin( ), JMenu( )
JMenuBar
    processKeyBinding( )
JMenuItem
    configurePropertiesFromAction( ),
    createActionPropertyChangeListener( ), JMenuItem( )
JPopupMenu
    createActionComponent( ), isPopupTrigger( ),
    remove( )
JRadioButton
    configurePropertiesFromAction( ),
    createActionPropertyChangeListener( ),
    JRadioButton( )
JRadioButtonMenuItem
    JRadioButtonMenuItem( )
JRootPane
    getUI( ), getUIClassID( ),
    isOptimizedDrawingEnabled( ), setUI( ), updateUI( )
JScrollBar
    isFocusTraversable( )
JScrollPane
    setComponentOrientation( )
JSplitPane
    DIVIDER_LOCATION_PROPERTY,
    getResizeWeight( ), isValidateRoot( ), RESIZE↵
    _WEIGHT_PROPERTY, setResizeWeight( )
JTabbedPane
    getToolTipTextAt( ), remove( ), setToolTipTextAt( )
JTable
    changeSelection( ), doLayout( ), getRowHeight( ),
    isFocusTraversable( ), processKeyBinding( ),
    removeNotify( ), setRowHeight( ),
    unconfigureEnclosingScrollPane( )
JTable.AccessibleJTable
    getAccessibleAt( ), getAccessibleCaption( ),
    getAccessibleColumnAtIndex( ),
    getAccessibleColumnCount( ),
    getAccessibleColumnDescription( ),
    getAccessibleColumnExtentAt( ),
    getAccessibleColumnHeader( ),
    getAccessibleIndexAt( ), getAccessibleRowAtIndex( ),
    getAccessibleRowCount( ),
    getAccessibleRowDescription( ),
    getAccessibleRowExtentAt( ),
    getAccessibleRowHeader( ),
    getAccessibleSummary( ), getAccessibleTable( ),
    getSelectedAccessibleColumns( ),
    getSelectedAccessibleRows( ),
    isAccessibleColumnSelected( ),
    isAccessibleRowSelected( ),
    isAccessibleSelected( ), setAccessibleCaption( ),
    setAccessibleColumnDescription( ),
    setAccessibleColumnHeader( ),
    setAccessibleRowDescription( ),
    setAccessibleRowHeader( ),
    setAccessibleSummary( )
JTextArea
    processKeyEvent( )

JTextField
    configurePropertiesFromAction( ),
    createActionPropertyChangeListener( ), getAction( ),
    setAction( )
JToggleButton
    JToggleButton( )
JToolBar
    createActionComponent( ), JToolBar( )
JTree
    ANCHOR_SELECTION_PATH_PROPERTY,
    EXPANDS_SELECTED_PATHS ↵
    _PROPERTY, getAnchorSelectionPath( ),
    getExpandsSelectedPaths( ), getToggleClickCount( ),
    LEAD_SELECTION_PATH_PROPERTY,
    removeDescendantSelectedPaths( ),
    setAnchorSelectionPath( ),
    setExpandsSelectedPaths( ),
    setLeadSelectionPath( ), setToggleClickCount( ),
    TOGGLE_CLICK_COUNT_PROPERTY
JViewport
    BACKINGSTORE_SCROLL_MODE, BLIT ↵
    _SCROLL_MODE, firePropertyChange( ),
    getScrollMode( ), getUI( ), getUIClassID( ),
    setScrollMode( ), setUI( ), SIMPLE_SCROLL_MODE,
    updateUI( )
JWindow
    JWindow( ), remove( )
KeyStroke
    getKeyStroke( )
LookAndFeel
    loadKeyBindings( ), makeComponentInputMap( ),
    makeInputMap( )
ScrollPaneConstants
    LOWER_LEADING_CORNER, LOWER ↵
    _TRAILING_CORNER, UPPER_LEADING ↵
    _CORNER, UPPER_TRAILING_CORNER
SwingUtilities
    getUIActionMap( ), getUIInputMap( ),
    getWindowAncestor( ), notifyAction( ),
    replaceUIActionMap( ), replaceUIInputMap( )
Timer
    getListeners( )

javax.swing.border
BevelBorder
    getHighlightInnerColor( ), getHighlightOuterColor( ),
    getShadowInnerColor( ), getShadowOuterColor( )
EmptyBorder
    getBorderInsets( )
EtchedBorder
    getHighlightColor( ), getShadowColor( )
LineBorder
    getRoundedCorners( ), LineBorder( )
MatteBorder
    getBorderInsets( ), getMatteColor( ), getTileIcon( ),
    MatteBorder( )
TitledBorder
    LEADING, TRAILING

javax.swing.event
EventListenerList
    getListeners( )
InternalFrameEvent
    getInternalFrame( )
TreeSelectionEvent
    isAddedPath( )

javax.swing.plaf
PopupMenuUI
    isPopupTrigger( )
javax.swing.plaf.basic
BasicBorders
    getButtonBorder( ), getInternalFrameBorder( ),
    getMenuBarBorder( ), getProgressBarBorder( ),
    getRadioButtonBorder( ), getSplitPaneBorder( ),
    getSplitPaneDividerBorder( ), getTextFieldBorder( ),
    getToggleButtonBorder( )
BasicComboBoxRenderer
    getPreferredSize( )
BasicEditorPaneUI
    installKeyboardActions( ), propertyChange( )
BasicInternalFrameTitlePane
    addNotify( ), removeNotify( ), uninstallListeners( )
BasicMenuItemUI
    installComponents( ), uninstallComponents( )
BasicPopupMenuUI
    isPopupTrigger( )
BasicSliderUI
    drawInverted( ), leftToRightCache,
    recalculateIfOrientationChanged( )
BasicSplitPaneDivider
    getBorder( ), getInsets( ), getMinimumSize( ),
    setBorder( )
BasicTextFieldUI
    propertyChange( )
BasicTextUI
    update( )
javax.swing.plaf.metal
MetalBorders
    getButtonBorder( ), getDesktopIconBorder( ),
    getTextBorder( ), getTextFieldBorder( ),
    getToggleButtonBorder( )
MetalFileChooserUI
    addControlButtons( ), createActionMap( ),
    getActionMap( ), getBottomPanel( ),
    getButtonPanel( ), installListeners( ), installUI( ),
    removeControlButtons( ), uninstallComponents( )
MetalIconFactory
    getCheckBoxIcon( )
javax.swing.table
AbstractTableModel
    getListeners( )
DefaultTableCellRenderer
    firePropertyChange( ), repaint( ), revalidate( ),
    validate( )
DefaultTableColumnModel
    getListeners( )
DefaultTableModel
    setColumnCount( ), setRowCount( )
JTableHeader
    createDefaultRenderer( ), getDefaultRenderer( ),
    setDefaultRenderer( )
javax.swing.text
AbstractDocument
    getListeners( )
AbstractWriter
    getCanWrapLines( ), getCurrentLineLength( ),
    getEndOffset( ), getIndentLevel( ),
    getIndentSpace( ), getLineLength( ),
    getLineSeparator( ), getStartOffset( ), getWriter( ),
    isLineEmpty( ), output( ), setCanWrapLines( ),
    setCurrentLineLength( ), setLineSeparator( ), write( ),
    writeLineSeparator( )

Topics

BoxView
forwardUpdate( ), getAxis( ), getChildAllocation( ),
layoutChanged( ), setAxis( )
CompositeView
getViewIndex( )
DefaultCaret
equals( ), getListeners( )
JTextComponent
addInputMethodListener( )
LabelView
getBackground( ), getForeground( ),
isStrikeThrough( ), isSubscript( ), isSuperscript( ),
isUnderline( )
ParagraphView
createRow( ), getFlowSpan( ), getFlowStart( )
Segment
clone( ), current( ), first( ), getBeginIndex( ),
getEndIndex( ), getIndex( ), last( ), next( ),
previous( ), setIndex( )
StyleContext.NamedStyle
getListeners( )
TableView
forwardUpdate( ), replace( )
TableView.TableRow
replace( )
View
append( ), forwardUpdate( ), forwardUpdateToView( ),
getGraphics( ), getViewIndex( ), insert( ), remove( ),
removeAll( ), replace( ), updateChildren( ),
updateLayout( )

javax.swing.text.html
BlockView
calculateMajorAxisRequirements( ),
calculateMinorAxisRequirements( ),
changedUpdate( ), layoutMinorAxis( ), setParent( )
HTML.Tag
SPAN, Tag( )
HTMLDocument
fireChangedUpdate( ), fireUndoableEditUpdate( ),
getElement( ), getParser( ), insertAfterEnd( ),
insertAfterStart( ), insertBeforeEnd( ),
insertBeforeStart( ), setInnerHTML( ),

setOuterHTML( ), setParagraphAttributes( ),
setParser( )
HTMLDocument.HTMLReader
handleEndOfLineString( )
HTMLEditorKit
getDefaultCursor( ), getInputAttributes( ),
getLinkCursor( ), setDefaultCursor( ), setLinkCursor( )
HTMLEditorKit.InsertHTMLTextAction
insertAtBoundary( )
HTMLEditorKit.LinkController
mouseDragged( ), mouseMoved( )
HTMLEditorKit.ParserCallback
handleEndOfLineString( ), IMPLIED
HTMLWriter
output( ), writeLineSeparator( )
InlineView
changedUpdate( ), getBreakWeight( )
ListView
setPropertiesFromAttributes( )
ParagraphView
paint( )
StyleSheet
addAttribute( ), addAttributes( ), addCSSAttribute( ),
addCSSAttributeFromHTML( ), addStyleSheet( ),
createLargeAttributeSet( ), createSmallAttributeSet( ),
getBase( ), getStyleSheets( ), importStyleSheet( ),
removeAttribute( ), removeAttributes( ),
removeStyle( ), removeStyleSheet( ), setBase( )

javax.swing.tree
DefaultTreeCellRenderer
firePropertyChange( ), hasFocus, repaint( ),
revalidate( ), validate( )
DefaultTreeModel
getListeners( )
DefaultTreeSelectionModel
getListeners( )
VariableHeightLayoutCache
getPreferredHeight( )

org.omg.CORBA
ORB
destroy( )

Removed Classes

javax.swing
JPopupMenu.WindowPopup.AccessibleWindowPopup

Removed Members

java.io
Serializable
serialVersionUID
java.rmi
RMISecurityManager
checkPackageAccess( )
java.security.interfaces
RSAPrivateKey
getModulus( )
RSAPublicKey
getModulus( )

javax.swing
Box.AccessibleBox
addFocusListener( ), contains( ), getAccessibleAt( ),
getAccessibleChild( ), getAccessibleChildrenCount( ),
getAccessibleComponent( ),
getAccessibleIndexInParent( ),
getAccessibleParent( ), getAccessibleStateSet( ),
getBackground( ), getBounds( ), getCursor( ),
getFont( ), getFontMetrics( ), getForeground( ),
getLocale( ), getLocation( ), getLocationOnScreen( ),
getSize( ), isEnabled( ), isFocusTraversable( ),

isShowing( ), isVisible( ), removeFocusListener( ),
requestFocus( ), setBackground( ), setBounds( ),
setCursor( ), setEnabled( ), setFont( ),
setForeground( ), setLocation( ), setSize( ),
setVisible( )

Box.Filler.AccessibleBoxFiller
addFocusListener( ), contains( ), getAccessibleAt( ),
getAccessibleChild( ), getAccessibleChildrenCount( ),
getAccessibleComponent( ),
getAccessibleIndexInParent( ),
getAccessibleParent( ), getAccessibleStateSet( ),
getBackground( ), getBounds( ), getCursor( ),
getFont( ), getFontMetrics( ), getForeground( ),
getLocale( ), getLocation( ), getLocationOnScreen( ),
getSize( ), isEnabled( ), isFocusTraversable( ),
isShowing( ), isVisible( ), removeFocusListener( ),
requestFocus( ), setBackground( ), setBounds( ),
setCursor( ), setEnabled( ), setFont( ),
setForeground( ), setLocation( ), setSize( ),
setVisible( )

CellRendererPane.AccessibleCellRendererPane
addFocusListener( ), contains( ), getAccessibleAt( ),
getAccessibleChild( ), getAccessibleChildrenCount( ),
getAccessibleComponent( ),
getAccessibleIndexInParent( ),
getAccessibleParent( ), getAccessibleStateSet( ),
getBackground( ), getBounds( ), getCursor( ),
getFont( ), getFontMetrics( ), getForeground( ),
getLocale( ), getLocation( ), getLocationOnScreen( ),
getSize( ), isEnabled( ), isFocusTraversable( ),
isShowing( ), isVisible( ), removeFocusListener( ),
requestFocus( ), setBackground( ), setBounds( ),
setCursor( ), setEnabled( ), setFont( ),
setForeground( ), setLocation( ), setSize( ),
setVisible( )

DefaultCellEditor
addCellEditorListener( ), changeEvent,
fireEditingCanceled( ), fireEditingStopped( ),
listenerList, removeCellEditorListener( )

JApplet.AccessibleJApplet
addFocusListener( ), contains( ), getAccessibleAt( ),
getAccessibleChild( ), getAccessibleChildrenCount( ),
getAccessibleComponent( ),
getAccessibleIndexInParent( ),
getAccessibleParent( ), getAccessibleRole( ),
getAccessibleStateSet( ), getBackground( ),
getBounds( ), getCursor( ), getFont( ),
getFontMetrics( ), getForeground( ), getLocale( ),
getLocation( ), getLocationOnScreen( ), getSize( ),
isEnabled( ), isFocusTraversable( ), isShowing( ),
isVisible( ), removeFocusListener( ), requestFocus( ),
setBackground( ), setBounds( ), setCursor( ),
setEnabled( ), setFont( ), setForeground( ),
setLocation( ), setSize( ), setVisible( )

JCheckBoxMenuItem
init( ), updateUI( )

JComponent.AccessibleJComponent
addFocusListener( ), contains( ),
getAccessibleAt( ), getAccessibleComponent( ),
getAccessibleIndexInParent( ),
getAccessibleParent( ), getBackground( ),
getBounds( ), getCursor( ), getFont( ),
getFontMetrics( ), getForeground( ), getLocale( ),
getLocation( ), getLocationOnScreen( ), getSize( ),
isEnabled( ), isFocusTraversable( ), isShowing( ),

isVisible( ), removeFocusListener( ), requestFocus( ),
setBackground( ), setBounds( ), setCursor( ),
setEnabled( ), setFont( ), setForeground( ),
setLocation( ), setSize( ), setVisible( )

JDialog.AccessibleJDialog
addFocusListener( ), contains( ), getAccessibleAt( ),
getAccessibleChild( ), getAccessibleChildrenCount( ),
getAccessibleComponent( ),
getAccessibleIndexInParent( ),
getAccessibleParent( ), getAccessibleRole( ),
getBackground( ), getBounds( ), getCursor( ),
getFont( ), getFontMetrics( ), getForeground( ),
getLocale( ), getLocation( ), getLocationOnScreen( ),
getSize( ), isEnabled( ), isFocusTraversable( ),
isShowing( ), isVisible( ), removeFocusListener( ),
requestFocus( ), setBackground( ), setBounds( ),
setCursor( ), setEnabled( ), setFont( ),
setForeground( ), setLocation( ), setSize( ),
setVisible( )

JFrame.AccessibleJFrame
addFocusListener( ), contains( ), getAccessibleAt( ),
getAccessibleChild( ), getAccessibleChildrenCount( ),
getAccessibleComponent( ),
getAccessibleIndexInParent( ),
getAccessibleParent( ), getAccessibleRole( ),
getBackground( ), getBounds( ), getCursor( ),
getFont( ), getFontMetrics( ), getForeground( ),
getLocale( ), getLocation( ), getLocationOnScreen( ),
getSize( ), isEnabled( ), isFocusTraversable( ),
isShowing( ), isVisible( ), removeFocusListener( ),
requestFocus( ), setBackground( ), setBounds( ),
setCursor( ), setEnabled( ), setFont( ),
setForeground( ), setLocation( ), setSize( ),
setVisible( )

JInternalFrame
getBackground( ), getForeground( ),
setBackground( ), setForeground( ), setVisible( )

JPopupMenu
remove( )

JRadioButtonMenuItem
init( ), updateUI( )

JScrollPane
isOpaque( )

JTable
reshape( )

JTextArea
processComponentKeyEvent( )

JTextPane
getScrollableTracksViewportWidth( )

JToolBar
remove( )

JWindow.AccessibleJWindow
addFocusListener( ), contains( ), getAccessibleAt( ),
getAccessibleChild( ), getAccessibleChildrenCount( ),
getAccessibleComponent( ),
getAccessibleIndexInParent( ),
getAccessibleParent( ), getAccessibleRole( ),
getAccessibleStateSet( ), getBackground( ),
getBounds( ), getCursor( ), getFont( ),
getFontMetrics( ), getForeground( ), getLocale( ),
getLocation( ), getLocationOnScreen( ), getSize( ),
isEnabled( ), isFocusTraversable( ), isShowing( ),
isVisible( ), removeFocusListener( ), requestFocus( ),
setBackground( ), setBounds( ), setCursor( ),
setEnabled( ), setFont( ), setForeground( ),
setLocation( ), setSize( ), setVisible( )

Topics

859

javax.swing.plaf.basic
 BasicSplitPaneUI.BasicVerticalLayoutManager
  getAvailableSize( ), getInitialLocation( ),
  getPreferredSizeOfComponent( ),
  getSizeOfComponent( ), minimumLayoutSize( ),
  preferredLayoutSize( ), setComponentToSize( )
javax.swing.plaf.metal
 MetalComboBoxUI
  installKeyboardActions( ), uninstallKeyboardActions( )
 MetalInternalFrameUI
  replacePane( )
javax.swing.text
 BoxView
  changedUpdate( ), insertUpdate( ), removeUpdate( )
 CompositeView
  append( ), insert( ), removeAll( )
 DefaultEditorKit
  clone( )
 JTextComponent
  isOpaque( ), processComponentKeyEvent( ),
  setEnabled( ), setOpaque( )
 LabelView
  breakView( ), createFragment( ), getAlignment( ),
  getBreakWeight( ), getNextVisualPositionFrom( ),
  getPreferredSpan( ), insertUpdate( ), modelToView( ),
  paint( ), removeUpdate( ), toString( ), viewToModel( )
 ParagraphView
  calculateMinorAxisRequirements( ),
  getViewAtPosition( ), getViewIndexAtPosition( ),
  insertUpdate( ), layout( ), loadChildren( ),
  removeUpdate( )

 PlainView
  preferenceChanged( )
 TableView
  loadChildren( )
 TableView.TableCell
  getPreferredSpan( )
 TableView.TableRow
  loadChildren( )
javax.swing.text.html
 HTMLWriter
  write( )
 InlineView
  isVisible( )
 ParagraphView
  changedUpdate( )
org.omg.CORBA
 DomainManager
  get_domain_policy( )
 IDLType
  type( )
 IRObject
  def_kind( ), destroy( )
 Policy
  copy( ), destroy( ), policy_type( )
org.omg.CosNaming
 BindingIterator
  destroy( ), next_n( ), next_one( )
 NamingContext
  bind( ), bind_context( ), bind_new_context( ),
  destroy( ), list( ), new_context( ), rebind( ), rebind ↵
  _context( ), resolve( ), unbind( )

Modified Classes and Members

These tables show all the classes and members whose signatures were modified from the previous version. "+" indicates an added keyword; "-" indicates a removed keyword.

Extends Changes

javax.swing
 Box.AccessibleBox,
 CellRendererPane.AccessibleCellRendererPane,
 JComponent.AccessibleJComponent
   - javax.accessibility.AccessibleContext,
   + java.awt.Container.AccessibleAWTContainer
 Box.Filler.AccessibleBoxFiller
   - javax.accessibility.AccessibleContext,
   + java.awt.Component.AccessibleAWTComponent
 DefaultCellEditor
   - java.lang.Object, + javax.swing.AbstractCellEditor
 JApplet.AccessibleJApplet
   - javax.accessibility.AccessibleContext,
   + java.applet.Applet.AccessibleApplet
 JDialog.AccessibleJDialog
   - javax.accessibility.AccessibleContext,
   + java.awt.Dialog.AccessibleAWTDialog
 JFrame.AccessibleJFrame
   - javax.accessibility.AccessibleContext,
   + java.awt.Frame.AccessibleAWTFrame
 JWindow.AccessibleJWindow
   - javax.accessibility.AccessibleContext,
   + java.awt.Window.AccessibleAWTWindow

javax.swing.text
 LabelView
   - javax.swing.text.View, + javax.swing.text.GlyphView
 ParagraphView
   - javax.swing.text.BoxView, + javax.swing.text.FlowView

Implements Changes

java.awt
 AWTEventMulticaster
   + java.awt.event.HierarchyBoundsListener,
   + java.awt.event.HierarchyListener

Implements Changes

Button, Canvas, Checkbox, CheckboxMenuItem, Choice, Label, List, Menu, MenuBar, MenuItem, Panel, Scrollbar, ScrollPane, TextComponent, Window	+ javax.accessibility.Accessible
java.awt.color	
ColorSpace, ICC_Profile	+ java.io.Serializable
java.security.cert	
Certificate	+ java.io.Serializable
java.security.interfaces	
RSAPrivateKey	- java.security.PrivateKey, + java.security.interfaces.RSAKey, + java.security.PrivateKey
RSAPublicKey	- java.security.PublicKey, + java.security.interfaces.RSAKey, + java.security.PublicKey
javax.swing	
AbstractButton.AccessibleAbstractButton, JLabel.AccessibleJLabel	+ javax.accessibility.AccessibleText
DefaultCellEditor	- java.io.Serializable
ImageIcon	+ javax.accessibility.Accessible
JComboBox.AccessibleJComboBox	+ javax.accessibility.AccessibleSelection
JTable.AccessibleJTable	+ javax.accessibility.AccessibleTable
javax.swing.text	
LabelView	+ javax.swing.text.TabableView
Segment	+ java.lang.Cloneable, + java.text.CharacterIterator
javax.swing.text.html	
CSS	+ java.io.Serializable
HTMLEditorKit.LinkController	+ java.awt.event.MouseMotionListener
javax.swing.text.html.parser	
ParserDelegator	+ java.io.Serializable
org.omg.CORBA	
Current	+ org.omg.CORBA.CurrentOperations, + org.omg.CORBA.portable.IDLEntity
DomainManager	+ org.omg.CORBA.DomainManagerOperations, + org.omg.CORBA.portable.IDLEntity
IDLType	- org.omg.CORBA.Object, + org.omg.CORBA.IDLTypeOperations
IRObject	+ org.omg.CORBA.IRObjectOperations
Policy	+ org.omg.CORBA.PolicyOperations, + org.omg.CORBA.portable.IDLEntity
org.omg.CosNaming	
BindingIterator	+ org.omg.CosNaming.BindingIteratorOperations
NamingContext	+ org.omg.CosNaming.NamingContextOperations

Member Modifier Changes

java.awt	
Component	
setCursor( )	- synchronized
java.awt.datatransfer	
StringSelection	
getTransferData( ), getTransferDataFlavors( )	- synchronized
java.awt	
EventQueue	
postEvent( )	- synchronized
Frame	
setCursor( )	- synchronized
GraphicsEnvironment	
getLocalGraphicsEnvironment( )	+ synchronized

Topics

Member Modifier Changes

java.awt.im	
InputContext	
dispatchEvent( ), endComposition( )	- synchronized
java.awt.image	
IndexColorModel	
getDataElements( )	+ synchronized
java.awt	
Scrollbar	
setValues( )	- synchronized
Toolkit	
setDesktopProperty( )	- synchronized
java.io	
BufferedInputStream	
close( )	- synchronized
java.lang	
Math	
abs( ), max( ), min( ), round( ), toDegrees( ), toRadians( )	+ strictfp
acos( ), asin( ), atan( ), atan2( ), ceil( ), cos( ), exp( ), floor( ), IEEEremainder( ), log( ), pow( ), rint( ), sin( ), sqrt( ), tan( )	- native, + strictfp
random( )	- synchronized, + strictfp
System	
setSecurityManager( )	- synchronized
java.net	
URL	
setURLStreamHandlerFactory( )	- synchronized
URLConnection	
getFileNameMap( )	+ synchronized
java.security	
Provider	
entrySet( )	+ synchronized
Security	
getProvider( ), getProviders( ), insertProviderAt( ), removeProvider( )	+ synchronized
java.text	
RuleBasedCollator	
compare( ), getCollationKey( )	+ synchronized
javax.swing	
AbstractAction	
putValue( ), setEnabled( )	- synchronized
AbstractButton	
getSelectedObjects( )	- synchronized
javax.swing.filechooser	
FileView	
getDescription( ), getIcon( ), getName( ), getTypeDescription( ), isTraversable( )	- abstract
javax.swing	
JCheckBoxMenuItem	
getSelectedObjects( )	- synchronized
JEditorPane	
getEditorKit( )	- final
javax.swing.plaf.basic	
BasicSliderUI	
MAX_SCROLL, MIN_SCROLL, NEGATIVE_SCROLL, POSITIVE_SCROLL	+ static
javax.swing.text	
BoxView	
getHeight( ), getOffset( ), getSpan( ), getWidth( )	- final

Member Modifier Changes

CompositeView
    getBottomInset( ), getLeftInset( ), getRightInset( ),   - final
        getTopInset( ), setInsets( ), setParagraphInsets( )
EditorKit
    clone( )   - abstract
LabelView
    getFont( )   - protected, + public
javax.swing
    UIManager
        addPropertyChangeListener( ),   - synchronized
            removePropertyChangeListener( )

Throws Changes

java.io
    FileOutputStream
        FileOutputStream( )   - java.io.IOException, + java.io.FileNotFoundException
    RandomAccessFile
        RandomAccessFile( )   - java.io.IOException, + java.io.FileNotFoundException
java.net
    URLDecoder
        decode( )   - java.lang.Exception
org.omg.CORBA
    TypeCode
        member_visibility( )   - org.omg.CORBA.Bounds,
                                     + org.omg.CORBA.TypeCodePackage.Bounds

Newly Deprecated Classes

javax.swing.text
    TableView.TableCell

Newly Deprecated Members

java.awt.datatransfer
    DataFlavor
        equals( ), plainTextFlavor
java.awt.image.renderable
    RenderContext
        concetenateTransform( ), preConcetenateTransform( )
java.net
    HttpURLConnection
        HTTP_SERVER_ERROR
    URLConnection
        getDefaultRequestProperty( ),
        setDefaultRequestProperty( )
    URLStreamHandler
        setURL( )
java.rmi.dgc
    VMID
        isUnique( )
java.sql
    Time
        Time( )
javax.swing
    JComponent
        hide( )

JMenuBar
    getComponentAtIndex( )
JPopupMenu
    getComponentAtIndex( )
JRootPane
    defaultPressAction, defaultReleaseAction
JViewport
    backingStore, isBackingStoreEnabled( ),
    setBackingStoreEnabled( )
javax.swing.plaf.basic
    BasicDesktopPaneUI
        closeKey, maximizeKey, minimizeKey, navigateKey,
        navigateKey2
    BasicInternalFrameUI
        openMenuKey
    BasicSplitPaneUI
        createKeyboardDownRightListener( ),
        createKeyboardEndListener( ),
        createKeyboardHomeListener( ),
        createKeyboardResizeToggleListener( ),
        createKeyboardUpLeftListener( ),
        dividerResizeToggleKey, downKey,
        endKey, getDividerBorderSize( ),
        homeKey, keyboardDownRightListener,

Topics

863

keyboardEndListener, keyboardHomeListener,
keyboardResizeToggleListener,
keyboardUpLeftListener, leftKey, rightKey, upKey
BasicTabbedPaneUI
downKey, leftKey, rightKey, upKey
BasicToolBarUI
downKey, leftKey, rightKey, upKey
javax.swing.table
TableColumn
disableResizedPosting( ), enableResizedPosting( ),
resizedPostingDisableCount

javax.swing.text
LabelView
getFontMetrics( )
TableView
createTableCell( )
javax.swing.text.html
FormView
RESET, SUBMIT
HTMLEditorKit.InsertHTMLTextAction
insertAtBoundry( )
org.omg.CORBA
TCKind
TCKind( )

Exceptions and Errors

This is a complete listing of all the exceptions and errors in this version of Java. The "*" indicates a checked exception or error; these must be declared in the throws clause.

java.lang	AbstractMethodError
java.security	AccessControlException
java.rmi	*AccessException
java.security.acl	*AclNotFoundException
java.rmi.activation	*ActivateFailedException
java.rmi.activation	*ActivationException
org.omg.CosNaming.NamingContextPackage	*AlreadyBound
java.rmi	*AlreadyBoundException
org.omg.CORBA.portable	*ApplicationException
java.lang	ArithmeticException
java.lang	ArrayIndexOutOfBoundsException
java.lang	ArrayStoreException
javax.naming.directory	*AttributeInUseException
javax.naming.directory	*AttributeModificationException
javax.naming	*AuthenticationException
javax.naming	*AuthenticationNotSupportedException
java.awt	AWTError
java.awt	*AWTException
org.omg.CORBA	BAD_CONTEXT
org.omg.CORBA	BAD_INV_ORDER
org.omg.CORBA	BAD_OPERATION
org.omg.CORBA	BAD_PARAM
org.omg.CORBA	BAD_TYPECODE
org.omg.CORBA.TypeCodePackage	*BadKind
javax.swing.text	*BadLocationException
java.sql	*BatchUpdateException
java.net	*BindException
org.omg.CORBA	*Bounds
org.omg.CORBA.TypeCodePackage	*Bounds
org.omg.CosNaming.NamingContextPackage	*CannotProceed
javax.naming	*CannotProceedException
javax.swing.undo	CannotRedoException
javax.swing.undo	CannotUndoException
java.security.cert	*CertificateEncodingException
java.security.cert	*CertificateException
java.security.cert	*CertificateExpiredException
java.security.cert	*CertificateNotYetValidException
java.security.cert	*CertificateParsingException

javax.swing.text	*ChangedCharSetException
java.io	*CharConversionException
java.lang	ClassCastException
java.lang	ClassCircularityError
java.lang	ClassFormatError
java.lang	*ClassNotFoundException
java.lang	*CloneNotSupportedException
java.awt.color	CMMException
org.omg.CORBA	COMM_FAILURE
javax.naming	*CommunicationException
java.util	ConcurrentModificationException
javax.naming	*ConfigurationException
java.rmi	*ConnectException
java.net	*ConnectException
java.rmi	*ConnectIOException
javax.naming	*ContextNotEmptyException
java.security.cert	*CRLException
org.omg.CORBA	DATA_CONVERSION
java.util.zip	*DataFormatException
java.sql	*DataTruncation
java.security	*DigestException
java.util	EmptyStackException
java.io	*EOFException
java.lang	Error
java.lang	*Exception
java.lang	ExceptionInInitializerError
javax.swing.tree	*ExpandVetoException
java.rmi.server	*ExportException
java.io	*FileNotFoundException
java.awt	*FontFormatException
org.omg.CORBA	FREE_MEM
java.security	*GeneralSecurityException
java.lang	IllegalAccessError
java.lang	*IllegalAccessException
java.lang	IllegalArgumentException
java.awt	IllegalComponentStateException
java.lang	IllegalMonitorStateException
java.awt.geom	IllegalPathStateException
java.lang	IllegalStateException
java.lang	IllegalThreadStateException
java.awt.image	ImagingOpException
org.omg.CORBA	IMP_LIMIT
java.lang	IncompatibleClassChangeError
org.omg.CORBA.ORBPackage	*InconsistentTypeCode
java.lang	IndexOutOfBoundsException
org.omg.CORBA.portable	IndirectionException
org.omg.CORBA	INITIALIZE
java.lang	InstantiationError
java.lang	*InstantiationException
javax.naming	*InsufficientResourcesException
org.omg.CORBA	INTERNAL
java.lang	InternalError
java.lang	*InterruptedException
java.io	*InterruptedIOException
javax.naming	*InterruptedNamingException
org.omg.CORBA	INTF_REPOS
java.beans	*IntrospectionException

Topics

865

org.omg.CORBA	INV_FLAG
org.omg.CORBA	INV_IDENT
org.omg.CORBA	INV_OBJREF
org.omg.CORBA	INV_POLICY
org.omg.CORBA.DynAnyPackage	*Invalid
org.omg.CORBA	INVALID_TRANSACTION
java.security	*InvalidAlgorithmParameterException
javax.naming.directory	*InvalidAttributeIdentifierException
javax.naming.directory	*InvalidAttributesException
javax.naming.directory	*InvalidAttributeValueException
java.io	*InvalidClassException
java.awt.dnd	InvalidDnDOperationException
java.security	*InvalidKeyException
java.security.spec	*InvalidKeySpecException
javax.sound.midi	*InvalidMidiDataException
org.omg.CosNaming.NamingContextPackage	*InvalidName
org.omg.CORBA.ORBPackage	*InvalidName
javax.naming	*InvalidNameException
java.io	*InvalidObjectException
java.security	InvalidParameterException
java.security.spec	*InvalidParameterSpecException
javax.naming.directory	*InvalidSearchControlsException
javax.naming.directory	*InvalidSearchFilterException
org.omg.CORBA.DynAnyPackage	*InvalidSeq
javax.transaction	*InvalidTransactionException
org.omg.CORBA.DynAnyPackage	*InvalidValue
java.lang.reflect	*InvocationTargetException
java.io	*IOException
java.util.jar	*JarException
java.security	*KeyException
java.security	*KeyManagementException
java.security	*KeyStoreException
java.security.acl	*LastOwnerException
javax.naming.ldap	*LdapReferralException
javax.naming	*LimitExceededException
javax.sound.sampled	*LineUnavailableException
java.lang	LinkageError
javax.naming	*LinkException
javax.naming	*LinkLoopException
javax.naming	*MalformedLinkException
java.net	*MalformedURLException
org.omg.CORBA	MARSHAL
java.rmi	*MarshalException
javax.sound.midi	*MidiUnavailableException
java.awt.datatransfer	*MimeTypeParseException
java.util	MissingResourceException
javax.naming	*NameAlreadyBoundException
javax.naming	*NameNotFoundException
javax.naming	*NamingException
javax.naming	*NamingSecurityException
java.lang	NegativeArraySizeException
org.omg.CORBA	NO_IMPLEMENT
org.omg.CORBA	NO_MEMORY
org.omg.CORBA	NO_PERMISSION
org.omg.CORBA	NO_RESOURCES
org.omg.CORBA	NO_RESPONSE
java.lang	NoClassDefFoundError

javax.naming	*NoInitialContextException
java.awt.geom	*NoninvertibleTransformException
javax.naming	*NoPermissionException
java.net	*NoRouteToHostException
java.security	*NoSuchAlgorithmException
javax.naming.directory	*NoSuchAttributeException
java.util	NoSuchElementException
java.lang	NoSuchFieldError
java.lang	*NoSuchFieldException
java.lang	NoSuchMethodError
java.lang	*NoSuchMethodException
java.rmi	*NoSuchObjectException
java.security	*NoSuchProviderException
java.io	*NotActiveException
java.rmi	*NotBoundException
javax.naming	*NotContextException
org.omg.CosNaming.NamingContextPackage	*NotEmpty
org.omg.CosNaming.NamingContextPackage	*NotFound
java.security.acl	*NotOwnerException
java.io	*NotSerializableException
java.lang	NullPointerException
java.lang	NumberFormatException
org.omg.CORBA	OBJ_ADAPTER
org.omg.CORBA	OBJECT_NOT_EXIST
java.io	*ObjectStreamException
javax.naming	*OperationNotSupportedException
java.io	*OptionalDataException
java.lang	OutOfMemoryError
java.text	*ParseException
javax.naming	*PartialResultException
org.omg.CORBA	PERSIST_STORE
org.omg.CORBA	*PolicyError
java.awt.print	*PrinterAbortException
java.awt.print	*PrinterException
java.awt.print	*PrinterIOException
java.security	*PrivilegedActionException
java.awt.color	ProfileDataException
java.beans	*PropertyVetoException
java.net	*ProtocolException
java.security	ProviderException
java.awt.image	RasterFormatException
javax.naming	*ReferralException
org.omg.CORBA.portable	*RemarshalException
java.rmi	*RemoteException
java.rmi	RMISecurityException
java.lang	RuntimeException
javax.naming.directory	*SchemaViolationException
java.lang	SecurityException
java.rmi.server	*ServerCloneException
java.rmi	*ServerError
java.rmi	*ServerException
java.rmi.server	*ServerNotActiveException
java.rmi	*ServerRuntimeException
javax.naming	*ServiceUnavailableException
java.security	*SignatureException
javax.naming	*SizeLimitExceededException
java.rmi.server	*SkeletonMismatchException

Topics

java.rmi.server	*SkeletonNotFoundException
java.net	*SocketException
java.rmi.server	*SocketSecurityException
java.sql	*SQLException
java.sql	*SQLWarning
java.lang	StackOverflowError
java.io	*StreamCorruptedException
java.lang	StringIndexOutOfBoundsException
java.rmi	*StubNotFoundException
java.io	*SyncFailedException
org.omg.CORBA	SystemException
java.lang	ThreadDeath
java.lang	*Throwable
javax.naming	*TimeLimitExceededException
java.util	*TooManyListenersException
org.omg.CORBA	TRANSACTION_REQUIRED
org.omg.CORBA	TRANSACTION_ROLLEDBACK
javax.transaction	*TransactionRequiredException
javax.transaction	*TransactionRolledbackException
org.omg.CORBA	TRANSIENT
org.omg.CORBA.DynAnyPackage	*TypeMismatch
java.lang.reflect	UndeclaredThrowableException
java.rmi	*UnexpectedException
org.omg.CORBA	UNKNOWN
java.lang	UnknownError
org.omg.CORBA.portable	UnknownException
java.rmi.activation	*UnknownGroupException
java.rmi	*UnknownHostException
java.net	*UnknownHostException
java.rmi.activation	*UnknownObjectException
java.net	*UnknownServiceException
org.omg.CORBA	*UnknownUserException
java.rmi	*UnmarshalException
java.security	*UnrecoverableKeyException
java.lang	UnsatisfiedLinkError
javax.sound.sampled	*UnsupportedAudioFileException
java.lang	UnsupportedClassVersionError
java.io	*UnsupportedEncodingException
java.awt.datatransfer	*UnsupportedFlavorException
javax.swing	*UnsupportedLookAndFeelException
java.lang	UnsupportedOperationException
org.omg.CORBA	*UserException
java.io	*UTFDataFormatException
java.lang	VerifyError
java.lang	VirtualMachineError
java.io	*WriteAbortedException
org.omg.CORBA	*WrongTransaction
java.util.zip	*ZipException

Statistics

Packages	136	**Members**	32138	

Classes and Interfaces	3020
Classes	2367
abstract	477
final	345
protected	162
abstract protected	3
Interfaces	653

Members	32138
Fields	5136
static	23
final	28
static final	3692
protected	1164
Constructors	3736
protected	444
Methods	23266
abstract	1436
static	2213
final	908
static final	91
protected	2172

Packages

New	Package	Classes	Members	Interfaces	Members
	java.applet	2	28	3	19
	java.awt	123	2646	16	60
	java.awt.color	7	189	0	0
	java.awt.datatransfer	6	77	4	8
	java.awt.dnd	19	210	5	14
	java.awt.event	25	454	18	39
	java.awt.font	16	286	2	64
	java.awt.geom	32	639	1	12
	java.awt.im	3	35	1	7
	java.awt.im.spi	0	0	3	25
	java.awt.image	44	778	8	70
	java.awt.image.renderable	4	82	3	19
	java.awt.peer	0	0	27	144
	java.awt.print	7	65	3	8
	java.beans	27	212	9	39
	java.beans.beancontext	12	156	11	32
	java.io	66	701	10	74
	java.lang	78	950	4	6
	java.lang.ref	5	15	0	0
	java.lang.reflect	10	112	2	6
	java.math	2	92	0	0
	java.net	38	520	6	21
•	java.nio	14	238	0	0
•	java.nio.channels	31	142	7	9
•	java.nio.channels.spi	5	37	0	0
•	java.nio.charset	11	95	0	0
•	java.nio.charset.spi	1	3	0	0
	java.rmi	19	43	1	0
	java.rmi.activation	12	67	4	16
	java.rmi.dgc	2	8	1	2
	java.rmi.registry	1	7	2	8
	java.rmi.server	17	92	9	30
	java.security	54	392	9	21

Topics

New	Package	Classes	Members	Interfaces	Members
	java.security.acl	3	3	5	27
	java.security.cert	36	317	8	20
	java.security.interfaces	0	0	10	26
	java.security.spec	15	59	2	0
	java.sql	11	115	18	697
	java.text	26	441	2	20
	java.util	46	787	14	103
	java.util.jar	8	83	0	0
•	java.util.logging	15	170	1	1
•	java.util.prefs	6	104	3	5
•	java.util.regex	3	38	0	0
	java.util.zip	16	159	1	4
	javax.accessibility	9	187	14	110
•	javax.crypto	22	195	1	0
•	javax.crypto.interfaces	0	0	4	6
•	javax.crypto.spec	12	64	0	0
•	javax.imageio	9	328	2	3
•	javax.imageio.event	0	0	5	24
•	javax.imageio.metadata	4	131	2	49
•	javax.imageio.plugins.jpeg	4	36	0	0
•	javax.imageio.spi	9	102	2	3
•	javax.imageio.stream	9	137	2	68
	javax.naming	36	243	5	64
	javax.naming.directory	15	120	3	55
	javax.naming.event	2	19	5	16
	javax.naming.ldap	6	34	7	22
	javax.naming.spi	4	26	8	9
•	javax.net	2	13	0	0
•	javax.net.ssl	19	125	10	34
•	javax.print	15	126	10	42
•	javax.print.attribute	15	120	11	23
•	javax.print.attribute.standard	74	648	0	0
•	javax.print.event	5	24	3	8
	javax.rmi	1	6	0	0
	javax.rmi.CORBA	3	21	5	38
•	javax.security.auth	7	40	2	4
•	javax.security.auth.callback	8	60	2	1
•	javax.security.auth.kerberos	5	61	0	0
•	javax.security.auth.login	8	29	0	0
•	javax.security.auth.spi	0	0	1	5
•	javax.security.auth.x500	2	19	0	0
•	javax.security.cert	7	32	0	0
	javax.sound.midi	17	150	9	101
	javax.sound.midi.spi	4	22	0	0
	javax.sound.sampled	26	199	8	50
	javax.sound.sampled.spi	4	29	0	0
•	javax.sql	2	4	12	110
	javax.swing	189	3799	24	191
	javax.swing.border	9	153	1	3
	javax.swing.colorchooser	3	25	1	4
	javax.swing.event	23	148	23	60
	javax.swing.filechooser	3	33	0	0
	javax.swing.plaf	47	131	1	0
	javax.swing.plaf.basic	192	2059	1	8
	javax.swing.plaf.metal	68	587	0	0
	javax.swing.plaf.multi	31	474	0	0
	javax.swing.table	9	252	4	30
	javax.swing.text	95	1330	21	121

New	Package	Classes	Members	Interfaces	Members
	javax.swing.text.html	42	557	0	0
	javax.swing.text.html.parser	9	142	1	35
	javax.swing.text.rtf	1	6	0	0
	javax.swing.tree	13	342	7	54
	javax.swing.undo	7	85	2	14
	javax.transaction	3	6	0	0
•	javax.transaction.xa	1	29	2	26
•	javax.xml.parsers	6	63	0	0
•	javax.xml.transform	6	63	6	16
•	javax.xml.transform.dom	2	16	1	1
•	javax.xml.transform.sax	3	29	2	7
•	javax.xml.transform.stream	2	30	0	0
•	org.ietf.jgss	5	76	3	74
	org.omg.CORBA	144	1091	38	176
	org.omg.CORBA.DynAnyPackage	4	8	0	0
	org.omg.CORBA.ORBPackage	2	4	0	0
	org.omg.CORBA.TypeCodePackage	2	4	0	0
	org.omg.CORBA.portable	9	133	9	11
	org.omg.CORBA_2_3	1	6	0	0
	org.omg.CORBA_2_3.portable	4	18	0	0
	org.omg.CosNaming	28	183	6	17
•	org.omg.CosNaming.NamingContextExtPackage	6	36	0	0
	org.omg.CosNaming.NamingContextPackage	18	103	0	0
•	org.omg.Dynamic	1	4	0	0
•	org.omg.DynamicAny	27	598	22	96
•	org.omg.DynamicAny.DynAnyFactoryPackage	2	9	0	0
•	org.omg.DynamicAny.DynAnyPackage	4	18	0	0
•	org.omg.IOP	21	128	14	15
•	org.omg.IOP.CodecFactoryPackage	2	9	0	0
•	org.omg.IOP.CodecPackage	6	27	0	0
•	org.omg.Messaging	1	7	1	1
•	org.omg.PortableInterceptor	5	28	29	67
•	org.omg.PortableInterceptor.ORBInitInfoPackage	5	27	0	0
•	org.omg.PortableServer	19	129	35	58
•	org.omg.PortableServer.CurrentPackage	2	9	0	0
•	org.omg.PortableServer.POAManagerPackage	3	20	0	0
•	org.omg.PortableServer.POAPackage	20	92	0	0
•	org.omg.PortableServer.ServantLocatorPackage	1	6	0	0
•	org.omg.PortableServer.portable	0	0	1	8
	org.omg.SendingContext	0	0	2	0
	org.omg.stub.java.rmi	1	2	0	0
•	org.w3c.dom	1	17	17	111
•	org.xml.sax	6	45	11	70
•	org.xml.sax.ext	0	0	2	11
•	org.xml.sax.helpers	10	159	0	0

New Classes in Existing Packages

java.awt
AttributeValue, AWTKeyStroke, BufferCapabilities,
BufferCapabilities.FlipContents, Component↵
.BltBufferStrategy, Component.FlipBufferStrategy,
ContainerOrderFocusTraversalPolicy,
DefaultFocusTraversalPolicy,
DefaultKeyboardFocusManager, DisplayMode,
FocusTraversalPolicy, HeadlessException,
ImageCapabilities, KeyboardFocusManager,
KeyEventDispatcher, KeyEventPostProcessor,
ScrollPaneAdjustable

java.awt.datatransfer
FlavorTable

java.awt.dnd
DragSourceAdapter, DragSourceMotionListener,
DropTargetAdapter

java.awt.event
AWTEventListenerProxy, MouseWheelEvent, *MouseWheelListener*, *WindowFocusListener*, *WindowStateListener*

java.awt.font
NumericShaper

java.awt.image
BufferStrategy, DataBufferDouble, DataBufferFloat, VolatileImage

java.beans
DefaultPersistenceDelegate, Encoder, EventHandler, *ExceptionListener*, Expression, PersistenceDelegate, PropertyChangeListenerProxy, Statement, VetoableChangeListenerProxy, XMLDecoder, XMLEncoder

java.lang
AssertionError, *CharSequence*, StackTraceElement

java.net
Inet4Address, Inet6Address, InetSocketAddress, NetworkInterface, PortUnreachableException, SocketAddress, SocketTimeoutException, URI, URISyntaxException

java.rmi.server
RMIClassLoaderSpi

java.security.cert
CertPath, CertPath.CertPathRep, CertPathBuilder, CertPathBuilderException, *CertPathBuilderResult*, CertPathBuilderSpi, *CertPathParameters*, CertPathValidator, CertPathValidatorException, *CertPathValidatorResult*, CertPathValidatorSpi, *CertSelector*, CertStore, CertStoreException, *CertStoreParameters*, CertStoreSpi, CollectionCertStoreParameters, *CRLSelector*, LDAPCertStoreParameters, PKIXBuilderParameters, PKIXCertPathBuilderResult, PKIXCertPathChecker, PKIXCertPathValidatorResult, PKIXParameters, *PolicyNode*, PolicyQualifierInfo, TrustAnchor, X509CertSelector, X509CRLSelector

java.security.interfaces
RSAMultiPrimePrivateCrtKey

java.security.spec
PSSParameterSpec, RSAMultiPrimePrivateCrtKeySpec, RSAOtherPrimeInfo

java.sql
ParameterMetaData, Savepoint

java.text
Bidi, DateFormat.Field, Format.Field, MessageFormat.Field, NumberFormat.Field

java.util
Currency, EventListenerProxy, IdentityHashMap, LinkedHashMap, LinkedHashSet, *RandomAccess*

javax.accessibility
AccessibleEditableText, *AccessibleExtendedComponent*, *AccessibleExtendedTable*, *AccessibleKeyBinding*

javax.naming.ldap
StartTlsRequest, StartTlsResponse

javax.swing
AbstractSpinnerModel, InternalFrameFocusTraversalPolicy, JFormattedTextField, JFormattedTextField.AbstractFormatter, JFormattedTextField.AbstractFormatterFactory, JSpinner, JSpinner.DateEditor, JSpinner.DefaultEditor, JSpinner.ListEditor, JSpinner.NumberEditor, LayoutFocusTraversalPolicy, Popup, PopupFactory, SortingFocusTraversalPolicy, SpinnerDateModel, SpinnerListModel, *SpinnerModel*, SpinnerNumberModel, Spring, SpringLayout, SpringLayout.Constraints, TransferHandler

javax.swing.plaf
SpinnerUI

javax.swing.plaf.basic
BasicBorders.RolloverButtonBorder, BasicFormattedTextFieldUI, BasicMenuUI ↵ .MouseInputHandler, BasicScrollPaneUI ↵ .MouseWheelHandler, BasicSpinnerUI

javax.swing.plaf.metal
MetalRootPaneUI

javax.swing.plaf.multi
MultiRootPaneUI, MultiSpinnerUI

javax.swing.text
DateFormatter, DefaultFormatter, DefaultFormatterFactory, DocumentFilter, DocumentFilter.FilterBypass, InternationalFormatter, MaskFormatter, NavigationFilter, NavigationFilter ↵ .FilterBypass, NumberFormatter

javax.swing.text.html
ImageView

org.omg.CORBA
LocalObject, ParameterMode, ParameterModeHelper, ParameterModeHolder, PolicyErrorCodeHelper, PolicyErrorHelper, PolicyErrorHolder, StringSeqHelper, StringSeqHolder, UnknownUserExceptionHelper, UnknownUserExceptionHolder, WrongTransactionHelper, WrongTransactionHolder, WStringSeqHelper, WStringSeqHolder

org.omg.CosNaming
_NamingContextExtStub, BindingIteratorPOA, *NamingContextExt*, NamingContextExtHelper, NamingContextExtHolder, *NamingContextExtOperations*, NamingContextExtPOA, NamingContextPOA

New Members in Existing Classes

If a new member overrides an existing member, it is included in this listing.

java.applet
AppletContext
getStream( ), getStreamKeys( ), setStream( )

java.awt
Adjustable
NO_ORIENTATION

AlphaComposite
Dst, DST, DST_ATOP, DstAtop, SRC_ATOP, SrcAtop, Xor, XOR

AWTEvent
MOUSE_WHEEL_EVENT_MASK, setSource( ), WINDOW_FOCUS_EVENT_MASK, WINDOW ↵ _STATE_EVENT_MASK

AWTEventMulticaster
add( ), getListeners( ), mouseWheelMoved( ),
remove( ), windowGainedFocus( ),
windowLostFocus( ), windowStateChanged( )

BorderLayout
LINE_END, LINE_START, PAGE_END, PAGE↵
_START

Button
getActionListeners( )

Canvas
createBufferStrategy( ), getBufferStrategy( ), update( )

Checkbox
getItemListeners( )

CheckboxMenuItem
getItemListeners( )

Choice
getItemListeners( )

Color
BLACK, BLUE, CYAN, DARK_GRAY, GRAY,
GREEN, LIGHT_GRAY, MAGENTA, ORANGE,
PINK, RED, WHITE, YELLOW

Component
addMouseWheelListener( ),
applyComponentOrientation( ),
areFocusTraversalKeysSet( ), createVolatileImage( ),
firePropertyChange( ), getComponentListeners( ),
getFocusCycleRootAncestor( ),
getFocusListeners( ), getFocusTraversalKeys( ),
getFocusTraversalKeysEnabled( ),
getHierarchyBoundsListeners( ),
getHierarchyListeners( ), getIgnoreRepaint( ),
getInputMethodListeners( ), getKeyListeners( ),
getMouseListeners( ), getMouseMotionListeners( ),
getMouseWheelListeners( ),
getPropertyChangeListeners( ),
isBackgroundSet( ), isCursorSet( ), isFocusable( ),
isFocusCycleRoot( ), isFocusOwner( ), isFontSet( ),
isForegroundSet( ), processMouseWheelEvent( ),
removeMouseWheelListener( ),
requestFocus( ), requestFocusInWindow( ),
setFocusable( ), setFocusTraversalKeys( ),
setFocusTraversalKeysEnabled( ),
setIgnoreRepaint( ), transferFocusBackward( ),
transferFocusUpCycle( )

Container
addPropertyChangeListener( ),
applyComponentOrientation( ),
areFocusTraversalKeysSet( ),
getContainerListeners( ), getFocusTraversalKeys( ),
getFocusTraversalPolicy( ), isFocusCycleRoot( ),
isFocusTraversalPolicySet( ), setFocusCycleRoot( ),
setFocusTraversalKeys( ), setFocusTraversalPolicy( ),
transferFocusBackward( ), transferFocusDownCycle( )

Dialog
Dialog( ), isUndecorated( ), setUndecorated( )

EventQueue
getCurrentEvent( ), getMostRecentEventTime( )

Font
isTransformed( ), LAYOUT_LEFT_TO_RIGHT,
LAYOUT_NO_LIMIT_CONTEXT, LAYOUT_NO↵
_START_CONTEXT, LAYOUT_RIGHT_TO_LEFT,
layoutGlyphVector( )

Frame
getExtendedState( ), getMaximizedBounds( ),
isUndecorated( ), MAXIMIZED_BOTH,
MAXIMIZED_HORIZ, MAXIMIZED_VERT,

setExtendedState( ), setMaximizedBounds( ),
setUndecorated( )

GraphicsConfiguration
createCompatibleVolatileImage( ),
getBufferCapabilities( ), getImageCapabilities( )

GraphicsDevice
getAvailableAcceleratedMemory( ),
getDisplayMode( ), getDisplayModes( ),
getFullScreenWindow( ),
isDisplayChangeSupported( ),
isFullScreenSupported( ), setDisplayMode( ),
setFullScreenWindow( )

GraphicsEnvironment
getCenterPoint( ), getMaximumWindowBounds( ),
isHeadless( ), isHeadlessInstance( )

GridBagConstraints
FIRST_LINE_END, FIRST_LINE_START, LAST↵
_LINE_END, LAST_LINE_START, LINE_END,
LINE_START, PAGE_END, PAGE_START

GridBagLayout
adjustForGravity( ), arrangeGrid( ), getLayoutInfo( ),
getMinSize( )

List
getActionListeners( ), getItemListeners( )

MenuItem
getActionListeners( )

Polygon
invalidate( ), reset( )

Robot
mouseWheel( )

Scrollbar
getAdjustmentListeners( ), getValueIsAdjusting( ),
setValueIsAdjusting( )

ScrollPane
eventTypeEnabled( ), isWheelScrollingEnabled( ),
processMouseWheelEvent( ),
setWheelScrollingEnabled( )

TextComponent
addNotify( ), enableInputMethods( ),
getTextListeners( )

TextField
getActionListeners( )

Toolkit
getAWTEventListeners( ),
getPropertyChangeListeners( ), getScreenInsets( ),
getSystemSelection( ), isDynamicLayoutActive( ),
isDynamicLayoutSet( ), isFrameStateSupported( ),
setDynamicLayout( )

Window
addPropertyChangeListener( ),
addWindowFocusListener( ),
addWindowStateListener( ), createBufferStrategy( ),
getBufferStrategy( ), getFocusableWindowState( ),
getFocusCycleRootAncestor( ),
getFocusTraversalKeys( ),
getMostRecentFocusOwner( ),
getWindowFocusListeners( ), getWindowListeners( ),
getWindowStateListeners( ), isActive( ),
isFocusableWindow( ), isFocusCycleRoot( ),
isFocused( ), processWindowFocusEvent( ),
processWindowStateEvent( ),
removeWindowFocusListener( ),
removeWindowStateListener( ),
setFocusableWindowState( ), setFocusCycleRoot( ),
setLocationRelativeTo( )

Topics

java.awt.color
ColorSpace
getMaxValue( ), getMinValue( )
ICC_ColorSpace
getMaxValue( ), getMinValue( )
java.awt.datatransfer
DataFlavor
imageFlavor, isFlavorTextType( ),
isRepresentationClassByteBuffer( ),
isRepresentationClassCharBuffer( ),
isRepresentationClassReader( )
SystemFlavorMap
addFlavorForUnencodedNative( ),
addUnencodedNativeForFlavor( ),
getFlavorsForNative( ), getNativesForFlavor( ),
setFlavorsForNative( ), setNativesForFlavor( )
java.awt.dnd
DragGestureEvent
startDrag( )
DragSource
addDragSourceListener( ),
addDragSourceMotionListener( ),
getDragSourceListeners( ),
getDragSourceMotionListeners( ),
getListeners( ), removeDragSourceListener( ),
removeDragSourceMotionListener( )
DragSourceContext
dragMouseMoved( )
DragSourceDragEvent
DragSourceDragEvent( ), getGestureModifiersEx( )
DragSourceDropEvent
DragSourceDropEvent( )
DragSourceEvent
DragSourceEvent( ), getLocation( ), getX( ), getY( )
java.awt.event
ActionEvent
ActionEvent( ), getWhen( )
AdjustmentEvent
AdjustmentEvent( ), getValueIsAdjusting( )
FocusEvent
FocusEvent( ), getOppositeComponent( )
InputEvent
ALT_DOWN_MASK, ALT_GRAPH_DOWN↵
_MASK, BUTTON1_DOWN_MASK, BUTTON2↵
_DOWN_MASK, BUTTON3_DOWN_MASK,
CTRL_DOWN_MASK, getModifiersEx( ),
getModifiersExText( ), META_DOWN_MASK,
SHIFT_DOWN_MASK
InputMethodEvent
getWhen( ), InputMethodEvent( )
InvocationEvent
getWhen( )
KeyEvent
getKeyLocation( ), KEY_LOCATION_LEFT, KEY↵
_LOCATION_NUMPAD, KEY_LOCATION_RIGHT,
KEY_LOCATION_STANDARD, KEY_LOCATION↵
_UNKNOWN, KeyEvent( ), VK_SEPARATOR
MouseEvent
BUTTON1, BUTTON2, BUTTON3, getButton( ),
getMouseModifiersText( ), MOUSE_WHEEL,
MouseEvent( ), NOBUTTON
WindowAdapter
windowGainedFocus( ), windowLostFocus( ),
windowStateChanged( )

WindowEvent
getNewState( ), getOldState( ),
getOppositeWindow( ), WINDOW_GAINED_FOCUS,
WINDOW_LOST_FOCUS, WINDOW_STATE↵
_CHANGED, WindowEvent( )
java.awt.font
FontRenderContext
equals( ), hashCode( )
GlyphMetrics
getAdvanceX( ), getAdvanceY( ), GlyphMetrics( )
GlyphVector
FLAG_COMPLEX_GLYPHS, FLAG_HAS↵
_POSITION_ADJUSTMENTS, FLAG_HAS↵
_TRANSFORMS, FLAG_MASK, FLAG_RUN_RTL,
getGlyphCharIndex( ), getGlyphCharIndices( ),
getGlyphOutline( ), getGlyphPixelBounds( ),
getLayoutFlags( ), getPixelBounds( )
TextAttribute
NUMERIC_SHAPING
TextMeasurer
clone( )
TransformAttribute
isIdentity( )
java.awt.im.spi
InputMethodContext
createInputMethodJFrame( )
java.awt.image
BandedSampleModel
hashCode( )
ColorModel
getDataElement( ), getDataElements( ),
getNormalizedComponents( )
ComponentColorModel
ComponentColorModel( ), getDataElement( ),
getDataElements( ), getNormalizedComponents( ),
getUnnormalizedComponents( )
ComponentSampleModel
equals( ), hashCode( )
MultiPixelPackedSampleModel
equals( ), hashCode( )
PixelInterleavedSampleModel
hashCode( )
SinglePixelPackedSampleModel
equals( ), hashCode( )
java.awt.peer
ComponentPeer
canDetermineObscurity( ), createBuffers( ),
createVolatileImage( ), destroyBuffers( ), flip( ),
getBackBuffer( ), handlesWheelScrolling( ),
isFocusable( ), isObscured( ), requestFocus( ),
updateCursorImmediately( )
ContainerPeer
beginLayout( ), endLayout( ), isPaintPending( )
FramePeer
setMaximizedBounds( )
RobotPeer
mouseWheel( )
java.awt.print
PrinterIOException
getCause( )
PrinterJob
getPrintService( ), lookupPrintServices( ),
lookupStreamPrintServices( ), pageDialog( ),
print( ), printDialog( ), setPrintService( )

java.beans
  EventSetDescriptor
    EventSetDescriptor( ), getGetListenerMethod( )
  IndexedPropertyDescriptor
    equals( )
  PropertyChangeSupport
    getPropertyChangeListeners( )
  PropertyDescriptor
    equals( )
  VetoableChangeSupport
    getVetoableChangeListeners( )
java.io
  File
    File( ), toURI( )
  FileInputStream
    getChannel( )
  FileOutputStream
    FileOutputStream( ), getChannel( )
  FileWriter
    FileWriter( )
  InputStreamReader
    InputStreamReader( )
  ObjectInputStream
    readUnshared( )
  ObjectOutputStream
    writeUnshared( )
  ObjectStreamField
    isUnshared( ), ObjectStreamField( )
  OutputStreamWriter
    OutputStreamWriter( )
  PrintStream
    PrintStream( )
  RandomAccessFile
    getChannel( )
  WriteAbortedException
    getCause( )
java.lang
  Boolean
    toString( ), valueOf( )
  Character
    DIRECTIONALITY_ARABIC_NUMBER,
    DIRECTIONALITY_BOUNDARY_NEUTRAL,
    DIRECTIONALITY_COMMON_NUMBER↵
    _SEPARATOR, DIRECTIONALITY_EUROPEAN↵
    _NUMBER, DIRECTIONALITY_EUROPEAN↵
    _NUMBER_SEPARATOR, DIRECTIONALITY↵
    _EUROPEAN_NUMBER_TERMINATOR,
    DIRECTIONALITY_LEFT_TO_RIGHT,
    DIRECTIONALITY_LEFT_TO_RIGHT_EMBEDDING,
    DIRECTIONALITY_LEFT_TO_RIGHT_OVERRIDE,
    DIRECTIONALITY_NONSPACING_MARK,
    DIRECTIONALITY_OTHER_NEUTRALS,
    DIRECTIONALITY_PARAGRAPH_SEPARATOR,
    DIRECTIONALITY_POP_DIRECTIONAL↵
    _FORMAT, DIRECTIONALITY_RIGHT_TO_LEFT,
    DIRECTIONALITY_RIGHT_TO_LEFT_ARABIC,
    DIRECTIONALITY_RIGHT_TO_LEFT_EMBEDDING,
    DIRECTIONALITY_RIGHT_TO_LEFT↵
    _OVERRIDE, DIRECTIONALITY_SEGMENT↵
    _SEPARATOR, DIRECTIONALITY_UNDEFINED,
    DIRECTIONALITY_WHITESPACE, FINAL↵
    _QUOTE_PUNCTUATION, getDirectionality( ),
    INITIAL_QUOTE_PUNCTUATION, isMirrored( ),
    toString( )

Character.UnicodeBlock
    BOPOMOFO_EXTENDED, BRAILLE_PATTERNS,
    CHEROKEE, CJK_RADICALS_SUPPLEMENT,
    CJK_UNIFIED_IDEOGRAPHS_EXTENSION_A,
    ETHIOPIC, IDEOGRAPHIC_DESCRIPTION↵
    _CHARACTERS, KANGXI_RADICALS, KHMER,
    MONGOLIAN, MYANMAR, OGHAM, RUNIC,
    SINHALA, SYRIAC, THAANA, UNIFIED↵
    _CANADIAN_ABORIGINAL_SYLLABICS, YI↵
    _RADICALS, YI_SYLLABLES
  Class
    desiredAssertionStatus( )
  ClassLoader
    clearAssertionStatus( ), setClassAssertionStatus( ),
    setDefaultAssertionStatus( ),
    setPackageAssertionStatus( )
  ClassNotFoundException
    getCause( )
  Double
    compare( )
  Error
    Error( )
  Exception
    Exception( )
  ExceptionInInitializerError
    getCause( )
  Float
    compare( )
  Runtime
    availableProcessors( ), maxMemory( )
  RuntimeException
    RuntimeException( )
  String
    contentEquals( ), matches( ), replaceAll( ),
    replaceFirst( ), split( ), subSequence( )
  StringBuffer
    append( ), indexOf( ), lastIndexOf( ), subSequence( )
  Thread
    holdsLock( ), Thread( )
  Throwable
    getCause( ), getStackTrace( ), initCause( ),
    setStackTrace( ), Throwable( )
java.lang.reflect
  InvocationTargetException
    getCause( )
  UndeclaredThrowableException
    getCause( )
java.math
  BigInteger
    probablePrime( )
java.net
  Authenticator
    getRequestingHost( ),
    requestPasswordAuthentication( )
  DatagramPacket
    DatagramPacket( ), getSocketAddress( ),
    setSocketAddress( )
  DatagramSocket
    bind( ), connect( ), DatagramSocket( ),
    getBroadcast( ), getChannel( ),
    getLocalSocketAddress( ),
    getRemoteSocketAddress( ), getReuseAddress( ),
    getTrafficClass( ), isBound( ), isClosed( ),
    isConnected( ), setBroadcast( ), setReuseAddress( ),
    setTrafficClass( )

Topics

DatagramSocketImpl
connect( ), disconnect( ), joinGroup( ), leaveGroup( ),
peekData( )
InetAddress
getByAddress( ), getCanonicalHostName( ),
isAnyLocalAddress( ), isLinkLocalAddress( ),
isLoopbackAddress( ), isMCGlobal( ),
isMCLinkLocal( ), isMCNodeLocal( ),
isMCOrgLocal( ), isMCSiteLocal( ),
isSiteLocalAddress( )
MulticastSocket
getLoopbackMode( ), getNetworkInterface( ),
joinGroup( ), leaveGroup( ), MulticastSocket( ),
setLoopbackMode( ), setNetworkInterface( )
ServerSocket
bind( ), getChannel( ), getLocalSocketAddress( ),
getReceiveBufferSize( ), getReuseAddress( ),
isBound( ), isClosed( ), ServerSocket( ),
setReceiveBufferSize( ), setReuseAddress( )
Socket
bind( ), connect( ), getChannel( ),
getLocalSocketAddress( ), getOOBInline( ),
getRemoteSocketAddress( ), getReuseAddress( ),
getTrafficClass( ), isBound( ), isClosed( ),
isConnected( ), isInputShutdown( ),
isOutputShutdown( ), sendUrgentData( ),
setOOBInline( ), setReuseAddress( ),
setTrafficClass( )
SocketImpl
connect( ), sendUrgentData( ), supportsUrgentData( )
SocketOptions
IP_MULTICAST_IF2, IP_MULTICAST_LOOP,
IP_TOS, SO_BROADCAST, SO_OOBINLINE
URL
getDefaultPort( )
URLConnection
addRequestProperty( ), getHeaderFields( ),
getRequestProperties( )
URLDecoder
decode( )
URLEncoder
encode( )
java.rmi
RemoteException
getCause( )
java.rmi.activation
ActivationException
getCause( )
java.rmi.server
RMIClassLoader
getDefaultProviderInstance( ), loadClass( ),
loadProxyClass( )
ServerCloneException
getCause( )
java.security
AlgorithmParameterGenerator
getInstance( )
AlgorithmParameters
getInstance( )
KeyFactory
getInstance( )
KeyPairGenerator
getInstance( )
KeyStore
getInstance( )

MessageDigest
getInstance( )
Policy
getPermissions( ), implies( )
PrivilegedActionException
getCause( )
ProtectionDomain
getClassLoader( ), getPrincipals( ),
ProtectionDomain( )
SecureRandom
getInstance( )
Security
getAlgorithms( )
Signature
getInstance( ), getParameters( ), verify( )
SignatureSpi
engineGetParameters( ), engineVerify( )
java.security.cert
CertificateFactory
generateCertPath( ), getCertPathEncodings( ),
getInstance( )
CertificateFactorySpi
engineGenerateCertPath( ),
engineGetCertPathEncodings( )
X509Certificate
getExtendedKeyUsage( ),
getIssuerAlternativeNames( ),
getIssuerX500Principal( ),
getSubjectAlternativeNames( ),
getSubjectX500Principal( )
X509CRL
getIssuerX500Principal( )
java.sql
Blob
setBinaryStream( ), setBytes( ), truncate( )
CallableStatement
getArray( ), getBigDecimal( ), getBlob( ),
getBoolean( ), getByte( ), getBytes( ), getClob( ),
getDate( ), getDouble( ), getFloat( ), getInt( ),
getLong( ), getObject( ), getRef( ), getShort( ),
getString( ), getTime( ), getTimestamp( ), getURL( ),
registerOutParameter( ), setAsciiStream( ),
setBigDecimal( ), setBinaryStream( ), setBoolean( ),
setByte( ), setBytes( ), setCharacterStream( ),
setDate( ), setDouble( ), setFloat( ), setInt( ),
setLong( ), setNull( ), setObject( ), setShort( ),
setString( ), setTime( ), setTimestamp( ), setURL( )
Clob
setAsciiStream( ), setCharacterStream( ), setString( ),
truncate( )
Connection
createStatement( ), getHoldability( ), prepareCall( ),
prepareStatement( ), releaseSavepoint( ), rollback( ),
setHoldability( ), setSavepoint( )
DatabaseMetaData
attributeNoNulls, attributeNullable,
attributeNullableUnknown, getAttributes( ),
getDatabaseMajorVersion( ),
getDatabaseMinorVersion( ),
getJDBCMajorVersion( ), getJDBCMinorVersion( ),
getResultSetHoldability( ), getSQLStateType( ),
getSuperTables( ), getSuperTypes( ),
locatorsUpdateCopy( ), sqlStateSQL99,
sqlStateXOpen, supportsGetGeneratedKeys( ),
supportsMultipleOpenResults( ),
supportsNamedParameters( ),

supportsResultSetHoldability( ),
supportsSavepoints( ), supportsStatementPooling( )
PreparedStatement
getParameterMetaData( ), setURL( )
Ref
getObject( ), setObject( )
ResultSet
CLOSE_CURSORS_AT_COMMIT, getURL( ),
HOLD_CURSORS_OVER_COMMIT, updateArray( ),
updateBlob( ), updateClob( ), updateRef( )
SQLInput
readURL( )
SQLOutput
writeURL( )
Statement
CLOSE_ALL_RESULTS, CLOSE_CURRENT↵
_RESULT, execute( ), EXECUTE_FAILED,
executeUpdate( ), getGeneratedKeys( ),
getMoreResults( ), getResultSetHoldability( ),
KEEP_CURRENT_RESULT, NO_GENERATED↵
_KEYS, RETURN_GENERATED_KEYS,
SUCCESS_NO_INFO
Timestamp
compareTo( ), getTime( ), setTime( )
Types
BOOLEAN, DATALINK
java.text
DecimalFormat
formatToCharacterIterator( ), getCurrency( ),
setCurrency( )
DecimalFormatSymbols
getCurrency( ), setCurrency( )
FieldPosition
FieldPosition( ), getFieldAttribute( )
Format
formatToCharacterIterator( )
MessageFormat
formatToCharacterIterator( ),
getFormatsByArgumentIndex( ),
MessageFormat( ), setFormatByArgumentIndex( ),
setFormatsByArgumentIndex( )
NumberFormat
getCurrency( ), getIntegerInstance( ), setCurrency( )
SimpleDateFormat
formatToCharacterIterator( )
java.util
AbstractMap
clone( )
BitSet
cardinality( ), clear( ), flip( ), get( ), intersects( ),
isEmpty( ), nextClearBit( ), nextSetBit( ), set( )
Collections
indexOfSubList( ), lastIndexOfSubList( ), list( ),
replaceAll( ), rotate( ), swap( )
Locale
Locale( )
SimpleTimeZone
getOffset( ), SimpleTimeZone( ), STANDARD_TIME,
UTC_TIME, WALL_TIME
TimeZone
getDSTSavings( ), getOffset( )
WeakHashMap
containsValue( ), keySet( ), putAll( ), values( )

javax.accessibility
AccessibleContext
ACCESSIBLE_HYPERTEXT_OFFSET,
getAccessibleEditableText( )
AccessibleRole
DATE_EDITOR, FONT_CHOOSER, GROUP_BOX,
HYPERLINK, SPIN_BOX, STATUS_BAR
javax.swing
AbstractAction
getPropertyChangeListeners( )
AbstractButton
getActionListeners( ), getChangeListeners( ),
getDisplayedMnemonicIndex( ), getIconTextGap( ),
getItemListeners( ), getMultiClickThreshhold( ),
setDisplayedMnemonicIndex( ), setIconTextGap( ),
setMultiClickThreshhold( )
AbstractButton.AccessibleAbstractButton
getAccessibleKeyBinding( ), getTitledBorderText( ),
getToolTipText( )
AbstractCellEditor
getCellEditorListeners( )
AbstractListModel
getListDataListeners( )
BoxLayout
LINE_AXIS, PAGE_AXIS
DefaultBoundedRangeModel
getChangeListeners( )
DefaultButtonModel
getActionListeners( ), getChangeListeners( ),
getItemListeners( )
DefaultListSelectionModel
getListSelectionListeners( )
DefaultSingleSelectionModel
getChangeListeners( )
JColorChooser
getDragEnabled( ), setDragEnabled( )
JComboBox
addPopupMenuListener( ),
firePopupMenuCanceled( ),
firePopupMenuWillBecomeInvisible( ),
firePopupMenuWillBecomeVisible( ),
getActionListeners( ), getItemListeners( ),
getPopupMenuListeners( ),
getPrototypeDisplayValue( ),
removePopupMenuListener( ),
setPrototypeDisplayValue( )
JComponent
getAncestorListeners( ), getDefaultLocale( ),
getPropertyChangeListeners( ), getTransferHandler( ),
getVetoableChangeListeners( ), requestFocus( ),
requestFocusInWindow( ), setDefaultLocale( ),
setTransferHandler( )
JComponent.AccessibleJComponent
getAccessibleKeyBinding( ), getTitledBorderText( ),
getToolTipText( )
JDialog
isDefaultLookAndFeelDecorated( ), JDialog( ),
setDefaultLookAndFeelDecorated( )
JEditorPane
getHyperlinkListeners( )
JEditorPane.AccessibleJEditorPaneHTML
getAccessibleAt( ), getAccessibleChild( ),
getAccessibleChildrenCount( )
JFileChooser
createDialog( ), getActionListeners( ),
getDragEnabled( ), setDragEnabled( )

Topics

JFrame
  isDefaultLookAndFeelDecorated( ),
  setDefaultLookAndFeelDecorated( )
JInternalFrame
  getFocusCycleRootAncestor( ),
  getInternalFrameListeners( ),
  getMostRecentFocusOwner( ), isFocusCycleRoot( ),
  setFocusCycleRoot( )
JLabel
  getDisplayedMnemonicIndex( ),
  setDisplayedMnemonicIndex( )
JLabel.AccessibleJLabel
  getAccessibleKeyBinding( ), getTitledBorderText( ),
  getToolTipText( )
JList
  getDragEnabled( ), getLayoutOrientation( ),
  getListSelectionListeners( ), getNextMatch( ),
  getToolTipText( ), HORIZONTAL_WRAP,
  setDragEnabled( ), setLayoutOrientation( ),
  VERTICAL, VERTICAL_WRAP
JMenu
  applyComponentOrientation( ),
  configurePropertiesFromAction( ),
  getMenuListeners( ), setComponentOrientation( )
JMenuItem
  getMenuDragMouseListeners( ),
  getMenuKeyListeners( )
JOptionPane
  showInputDialog( )
JPanel
  getUI( ), setUI( )
JPopupMenu
  getPopupMenuListeners( ), processFocusEvent( ),
  processKeyEvent( )
JProgressBar
  getChangeListeners( ), isIndeterminate( ),
  setIndeterminate( )
JRootPane
  COLOR_CHOOSER_DIALOG, ERROR←↵
  _DIALOG, FILE_CHOOSER_DIALOG, FRAME,
  getWindowDecorationStyle( ), INFORMATION←↵
  _DIALOG, NONE, PLAIN_DIALOG, QUESTION←↵
  _DIALOG, setWindowDecorationStyle( ),
  WARNING_DIALOG
JScrollBar
  getAdjustmentListeners( ), setUI( )
JScrollPane
  isWheelScrollingEnabled( ),
  setWheelScrollingEnabled( )
JSlider
  getChangeListeners( )
JTabbedPane
  getChangeListeners( ),
  getDisplayedMnemonicIndexAt( ), getMnemonicAt( ),
  getTabLayoutPolicy( ), indexAtLocation( ),
  JTabbedPane( ), SCROLL_TAB_LAYOUT,
  setDisplayedMnemonicIndexAt( ), setMnemonicAt( ),
  setTabLayoutPolicy( ), WRAP_TAB_LAYOUT
JTable
  getDragEnabled( ),
  getSurrendersFocusOnKeystroke( ),
  setDragEnabled( ),
  setSurrendersFocusOnKeystroke( )
JTable.AccessibleJTable
  getAccessibleColumn( ), getAccessibleIndex( ),
  getAccessibleRow( )

JTextField
  getActionListeners( ), setDocument( )
JToolBar
  isRollover( ), setLayout( ), setRollover( )
JTree
  getDragEnabled( ), getNextMatch( ),
  getTreeExpansionListeners( ),
  getTreeSelectionListeners( ),
  getTreeWillExpandListeners( ), setDragEnabled( )
JViewport
  getChangeListeners( )
JWindow
  update( )
LookAndFeel
  getDesktopPropertyValue( ),
  getSupportsWindowDecorations( ),
  provideErrorFeedback( )
MenuSelectionManager
  getChangeListeners( )
RepaintManager
  getVolatileOffscreenBuffer( )
SizeRequirements
  calculateAlignedPositions( ), calculateTiledPositions( )
SwingConstants
  NEXT, PREVIOUS
SwingUtilities
  calculateInnerArea( ), processKeyBindings( )
Timer
  getActionListeners( )
UIDefaults
  addResourceBundle( ), get( ), getBoolean( ),
  getBorder( ), getColor( ), getDefaultLocale( ),
  getDimension( ), getFont( ), getIcon( ), getInsets( ),
  getInt( ), getPropertyChangeListeners( ), getString( ),
  removeResourceBundle( ), setDefaultLocale( )
UIManager
  get( ), getBoolean( ), getBorder( ), getColor( ),
  getDimension( ), getFont( ), getIcon( ), getInsets( ),
  getInt( ), getPropertyChangeListeners( ), getString( )
WindowConstants
  EXIT_ON_CLOSE
javax.swing.border
SoftBevelBorder
  getBorderInsets( )
javax.swing.colorchooser
AbstractColorChooserPanel
  getDisplayedMnemonicIndex( ), getMnemonic( )
DefaultColorSelectionModel
  getChangeListeners( )
javax.swing.event
HyperlinkEvent
  getSourceElement( ), HyperlinkEvent( )
ListDataEvent
  toString( )
SwingPropertyChangeSupport
  getPropertyChangeListeners( )
javax.swing.filechooser
FileSystemView
  createFileSystemRoot( ), getChild( ),
  getDefaultDirectory( ), getSystemDisplayName( ),
  getSystemIcon( ), getSystemTypeDescription( ),
  isComputerNode( ), isDrive( ), isFileSystem( ),
  isFileSystemRoot( ), isFloppyDrive( ), isParent( ),
  isTraversable( )

javax.swing.plaf
PopupMenuUI
    getPopup( )
TextUI
    getToolTipText( )
javax.swing.plaf.basic
BasicArrowButton
    BasicArrowButton( )
BasicBorders.ButtonBorder
    getBorderInsets( )
BasicBorders.FieldBorder
    getBorderInsets( )
BasicBorders.MarginBorder
    getBorderInsets( )
BasicBorders.MenuBarBorder
    getBorderInsets( )
BasicBorders.RadioButtonBorder
    getBorderInsets( )
BasicBorders.ToggleButtonBorder
    getBorderInsets( )
BasicButtonUI
    paintText( )
BasicComboPopup
    firePopupMenuCanceled( ),
    firePopupMenuWillBecomeInvisible( ),
    firePopupMenuWillBecomeVisible( )
BasicDirectoryModel
    renameFile( )
BasicFileChooserUI
    directoryOpenButtonMnemonic,
    directoryOpenButtonText,
    directoryOpenButtonToolTipText, getDirectory( ),
    isDirectorySelected( ), setDirectory( ),
    setDirectorySelected( )
BasicFileChooserUI.DoubleClickListener
    mouseEntered( )
BasicGraphicsUtils
    drawStringUnderlineCharAt( )
BasicInternalFrameTitlePane
    getTitle( ), paintTitleBackground( )
BasicLookAndFeel
    createAudioAction( ), getAudioActionMap( ),
    playSound( )
BasicMenuItemUI
    doClick( ), paintBackground( ), paintText( )
BasicProgressBarUI
    getAnimationIndex( ), getBox( ),
    incrementAnimationIndex( ), paintDeterminate( ),
    paintIndeterminate( ), setAnimationIndex( ),
    startAnimationTimer( ), stopAnimationTimer( )
BasicScrollPaneUI
    createMouseWheelListener( )
BasicSplitPaneUI.FocusHandler
    focusGained( )
BasicTabbedPaneUI
    calcRect, getNextTabIndexInRun( ),
    getNextTabRun( ), getPreviousTabIndexInRun( ),
    getPreviousTabRun( ), getTabBounds( ),
    getTextViewForTab( ), installComponents( ),
    paintTabArea( ), selectNextTabInRun( ),
    selectPreviousTabInRun( ), uninstallComponents( )
BasicTextFieldUI
    installUI( )
BasicTextPaneUI
    installUI( )

BasicTextUI
    getToolTipText( )
BasicToggleButtonUI
    getTextShiftOffset( )
BasicToolBarUI
    constraintBeforeFloating, createFloatingWindow( ),
    createNonRolloverBorder( ), createRolloverBorder( ),
    installNonRolloverBorders( ), installNormalBorders( ),
    installRolloverBorders( ), isRolloverBorders( ),
    setBorderToNonRollover( ), setBorderToNormal( ),
    setBorderToRollover( ), setRolloverBorders( )
BasicTreeUI.KeyHandler
    keyTyped( )
BasicTreeUI.MouseHandler
    mouseDragged( ), mouseMoved( ),
    mouseReleased( )
DefaultMenuLayout
    preferredLayoutSize( )
javax.swing.plaf.metal
MetalBorders.ButtonBorder
    getBorderInsets( )
MetalBorders.Flush3DBorder
    getBorderInsets( )
MetalBorders.InternalFrameBorder
    getBorderInsets( )
MetalBorders.MenuBarBorder
    getBorderInsets( )
MetalBorders.MenuItemBorder
    getBorderInsets( )
MetalBorders.OptionDialogBorder
    getBorderInsets( )
MetalBorders.PaletteBorder
    getBorderInsets( )
MetalBorders.PopupMenuBorder
    getBorderInsets( )
MetalBorders.ToolBarBorder
    getBorderInsets( )
MetalDesktopIconUI
    getMaximumSize( ), getMinimumSize( ),
    installListeners( ), uninstallListeners( )
MetalFileChooserUI
    createDetailsView( ), createListSelectionListener( ),
    setDirectorySelected( )
MetalFileChooserUI.DirectoryComboBoxModel
    getDepth( )
MetalInternalFrameTitlePane
    addNotify( ), uninstallDefaults( )
MetalInternalFrameUI
    installListeners( ), uninstallComponents( ),
    uninstallListeners( )
MetalLookAndFeel
    getSupportsWindowDecorations( ),
    provideErrorFeedback( )
MetalProgressBarUI
    paintDeterminate( ), paintIndeterminate( )
MetalToolBarUI
    createNonRolloverBorder( ), createRolloverBorder( )
MetalToolTipUI
    isAcceleratorHidden( ), uninstallUI( )
javax.swing.plaf.multi
MultiPopupMenuUI
    getPopup( ), isPopupTrigger( )
MultiTextUI
    getToolTipText( )

Topics

javax.swing.table
  AbstractTableModel
    getTableModelListeners( )
  DefaultTableCellRenderer
    isOpaque( )
  DefaultTableColumnModel
    getColumnModelListeners( )
  TableColumn
    getPropertyChangeListeners( )
javax.swing.text
  AbstractDocument
    getDocumentFilter( ), getDocumentListeners( ),
    getUndoableEditListeners( ), replace( ),
    setDocumentFilter( )
  AsyncBoxView
    getEstimatedMajorSpan( ), getInsetSpan( ),
    getNextVisualPositionFrom( ),
    setEstimatedMajorSpan( )
  BoxView
    isLayoutValid( )
  DefaultCaret
    getChangeListeners( )
  JTextComponent
    getCaretListeners( ), getDragEnabled( ),
    getNavigationFilter( ), getToolTipText( ),
    setComponentOrientation( ), setDragEnabled( ),
    setNavigationFilter( )
  JTextComponent.AccessibleJTextComponent
    cut( ), delete( ), doAccessibleAction( ),
    getAccessibleAction( ), getAccessibleActionCount( ),
    getAccessibleActionDescription( ),
    getAccessibleEditableText( ), getTextRange( ),
    insertTextAtIndex( ), paste( ), replaceText( ),
    selectText( ), setAttributes( ), setTextContents( )
  PasswordView
    getPreferredSpan( )
  PlainDocument
    insertString( )
  PlainView
    damageLineRange( ), lineToRect( ), setSize( ),
    updateDamage( ), updateMetrics( )
  Segment
    isPartialReturn( ), setPartialReturn( )
  StyleContext
    getChangeListeners( )
  StyleContext.NamedStyle
    getChangeListeners( )
  View
    getToolTipText( ), getViewIndex( )
javax.swing.text.html
  BlockView
    getMaximumSpan( ), getMinimumSpan( ),
    getPreferredSpan( )
  FormView
    getMaximumSpan( )
  HTMLEditorKit
    getAccessibleContext( )
javax.swing.tree
  DefaultTreeCellEditor
    getCellEditorListeners( )
  DefaultTreeCellEditor.DefaultTextField
    setBorder( )
  DefaultTreeCellRenderer
    getFont( )
  DefaultTreeModel
    getTreeModelListeners( )

  DefaultTreeSelectionModel
    getPropertyChangeListeners( ),
    getTreeSelectionListeners( )
javax.swing.undo
  UndoableEditSupport
    getUndoableEditListeners( )
org.omg.CORBA
  Any
    extract_Streamable( )
  DefinitionKind
    _dk_AbstractInterface, dk_AbstractInterface
  DynamicImplementation
    _ids( )
  ServiceDetailHelper
    ServiceDetailHelper( )
  ServiceInformationHelper
    ServiceInformationHelper( )
org.omg.CosNaming
  _BindingIteratorStub
    _BindingIteratorStub( )
  _NamingContextStub
    _NamingContextStub( )
  BindingHelper
    BindingHelper( )
  BindingIteratorHelper
    BindingIteratorHelper( )
  BindingListHelper
    BindingListHelper( )
  BindingType
    BindingType( )
  BindingTypeHelper
    BindingTypeHelper( )
  IstringHelper
    IstringHelper( )
  NameComponentHelper
    NameComponentHelper( )
  NameHelper
    NameHelper( )
  NamingContextHelper
    NamingContextHelper( )
org.omg.CosNaming.NamingContextPackage
  AlreadyBound
    AlreadyBound( )
  AlreadyBoundHelper
    AlreadyBoundHelper( )
  CannotProceed
    CannotProceed( )
  CannotProceedHelper
    CannotProceedHelper( )
  InvalidName
    InvalidName( )
  InvalidNameHelper
    InvalidNameHelper( )
  NotEmpty
    NotEmpty( )
  NotEmptyHelper
    NotEmptyHelper( )
  NotFound
    NotFound( )
  NotFoundHelper
    NotFoundHelper( )
  NotFoundReason
    NotFoundReason( )
  NotFoundReasonHelper
    NotFoundReasonHelper( )

Removed Members

java.awt
AWTEvent
finalize( )
java.awt.event
KeyEvent
setSource( )
java.awt.geom
CubicCurve2D
getBounds2D( )
Line2D
getBounds2D( )
QuadCurve2D
getBounds2D( )
RectangularShape
contains( ), getBounds2D( ), getPathIterator( ),
intersects( )
java.awt.peer
ComponentPeer
isFocusTraversable( ), requestFocus( ), setCursor( )
WindowPeer
CONSUME_EVENT, FOCUS_NEXT, FOCUS↩
_PREVIOUS, handleFocusTraversalEvent( ),
IGNORE_EVENT
java.lang
ClassNotFoundException
printStackTrace( )
ExceptionInInitializerError
printStackTrace( )
InheritableThreadLocal
get( ), set( )
java.lang.reflect
InvocationTargetException
printStackTrace( )
UndeclaredThrowableException
printStackTrace( )
java.net
DatagramSocketImpl
getOption( ), setOption( )
SocketImpl
getOption( ), setOption( )
java.rmi
RemoteException
printStackTrace( )
java.rmi.activation
ActivationException
printStackTrace( )
ActivationGroup
newInstance( )
java.rmi.server
ServerCloneException
printStackTrace( )
java.security
PrivilegedActionException
printStackTrace( )
java.security.cert
X509Certificate
getCriticalExtensionOIDs( ), getExtensionValue( ),
getNonCriticalExtensionOIDs( ),
hasUnsupportedCriticalExtension( )

X509CRL
getCriticalExtensionOIDs( ), getExtensionValue( ),
getNonCriticalExtensionOIDs( ),
hasUnsupportedCriticalExtension( )
X509CRLEntry
getCriticalExtensionOIDs( ), getExtensionValue( ),
getNonCriticalExtensionOIDs( ),
hasUnsupportedCriticalExtension( )
java.util.zip
GZIPOutputStream
close( )
javax.swing
AbstractAction
actionPerformed( )
AbstractButton
isFocusTraversable( )
AbstractCellEditor
getCellEditorValue( )
AbstractListModel
getElementAt( ), getSize( )
DefaultFocusManager
focusNextComponent( ), focusPreviousComponent( ),
processKeyEvent( )
FocusManager
focusNextComponent( ), focusPreviousComponent( ),
processKeyEvent( )
JApplet
processKeyEvent( )
JCheckBoxMenuItem
requestFocus( )
JComboBox
isFocusTraversable( )
JComponent
hasFocus( ), hide( ), isFocusCycleRoot( ),
isFocusTraversable( ), processFocusEvent( )
JDialog
processKeyEvent( ), setLocationRelativeTo( )
JEditorPane
isFocusCycleRoot( ), isManagingFocus( ),
processComponentKeyEvent( ), processKeyEvent( )
JFrame
processKeyEvent( )
JMenuBar
isManagingFocus( )
JRadioButtonMenuItem
requestFocus( )
JRootPane
isFocusCycleRoot( )
JScrollBar
isFocusTraversable( )
JSeparator
isFocusTraversable( )
JTable
isFocusTraversable( ), isManagingFocus( )
JTextArea
isManagingFocus( ), processKeyEvent( )
KeyStroke
equals( ), getKeyChar( ), getKeyCode( ),
getModifiers( ), hashCode( ), isOnKeyRelease( ),
toString( )

Topics

javax.swing.plaf.basic
  BasicCheckBoxMenuItemUI
    installDefaults( )
  BasicEditorPaneUI
    installKeyboardActions( )
  BasicFileChooserUI.BasicFileView
    isTraversable( )
  BasicInternalFrameTitlePane
    addNotify( ), removeNotify( )
  BasicRadioButtonMenuItemUI
    installDefaults( )
  BasicTextFieldUI
    createCaret( )
  BasicTextPaneUI
    getEditorKit( )
  BasicToggleButtonUI
    paintButtonPressed( ), paintFocus( ), paintText( )

javax.swing.plaf.metal
  MetalComboBoxUI
    configureArrowButton( ), installListeners( ),
    installUI( ), isFocusTraversable( ),
    selectNextPossibleValue( ),
    selectPreviousPossibleValue( ),
    unconfigureArrowButton( ), uninstallListeners( ),
    uninstallUI( )
  MetalProgressBarUI
    paint( )
  MetalTextFieldUI
    installUI( )
  MetalToolBarUI
    installNonRolloverBorders( ), installNormalBorders( ),
    installRolloverBorders( ), isRolloverBorders( ),
    setBorderToNormal( ), setBorderToRollover( ),
    setRolloverBorders( )
  MetalToolBarUI.MetalContainerListener
    componentAdded( ), componentRemoved( )
  MetalToolBarUI.MetalRolloverListener
    propertyChange( )

javax.swing.table
  AbstractTableModel
    getColumnCount( ), getRowCount( ), getValueAt( )

javax.swing.text
  ComponentView
    setSize( )
  IconView
    setSize( )
  JTextComponent
    isFocusTraversable( )
  LayeredHighlighter
    addHighlight( ), changeHighlight( ),
    deinstall( ), getHighlights( ), install( ), paint( ),
    removeAllHighlights( ), removeHighlight( )
  LayeredHighlighter.LayerPainter
    paint( )

javax.swing.text.html
  HTMLFrameHyperlinkEvent
    getSourceElement( )

javax.swing.text.rtf
  RTFEditorKit
    clone( )

org.omg.CORBA
  CompletionStatus
    CompletionStatus( )

org.omg.CosNaming
  _BindingIteratorImplBase
    destroy( ), next_n( ), next_one( )
  _BindingIteratorStub
    _BindingIteratorStub( )
  _NamingContextImplBase
    bind( ), bind_context( ), bind_new_context( ),
    destroy( ), list( ), new_context( ), rebind( ), rebind ↵
    _context( ), resolve( ), unbind( )
  _NamingContextStub
    _NamingContextStub( )

Modified Classes and Members

These tables show all the classes and members whose signatures were modified from the previous version. "+" indicates an added keyword; "-" indicates a removed keyword.

Class Modifier Changes

java.net
  InetAddress   - final

org.omg.CORBA
  AnySeqHelper, BooleanSeqHelper, CharSeqHelper,   - final, + abstract
    DoubleSeqHelper, FloatSeqHelper, LongLongSeqHelper,
    LongSeqHelper, OctetSeqHelper, ShortSeqHelper,
    ULongLongSeqHelper, ULongSeqHelper,
    UShortSeqHelper, WCharSeqHelper
  CompletionStatus, INV_POLICY, WrongTransaction   + final
  DynamicImplementation, Principal   - abstract
  ServiceDetailHelper, ServiceInformationHelper   + abstract
  StringValueHelper, WStringValueHelper   - final

org.omg.CORBA.ORBPackage
  InvalidName   + final

Class Modifier Changes

org.omg.CosNaming

BindingHelper, BindingIteratorHelper, BindingListHelper, BindingTypeHelper, IstringHelper, NameComponentHelper, NameHelper, NamingContextHelper	+ abstract
BindingType	- final

org.omg.CosNaming.NamingContextPackage

AlreadyBoundHelper, CannotProceedHelper, InvalidNameHelper, NotEmptyHelper, NotFoundHelper, NotFoundReasonHelper	+ abstract
NotFoundReason	- final

Extends Changes

javax.swing

Box	- java.awt.Container, + javax.swing.JComponent
Box.Filler	- java.awt.Component, + javax.swing.JComponent
FocusManager	- java.lang.Object, + java.awt.DefaultKeyboardFocusManager
KeyStroke	- java.lang.Object, + java.awt.AWTKeyStroke

javax.swing.plaf.metal

MetalToolBarUI.MetalContainerListener	- java.lang.Object, + javax.swing.plaf.basic.BasicToolBarUI.ToolBarContListener
MetalToolBarUI.MetalRolloverListener	- java.lang.Object, + javax.swing.plaf.basic.BasicToolBarUI.PropertyListener

Implements Changes

java.awt

AWTEventMulticaster	+ java.awt.event.MouseWheelListener, + java.awt.event.WindowFocusListener, + java.awt.event.WindowStateListener

java.awt.datatransfer

SystemFlavorMap	+ java.awt.datatransfer.FlavorTable

java.awt.dnd

DragGestureRecognizer, DragSource, DropTargetContext	+ java.io.Serializable
DragSourceContext	+ java.awt.dnd.DragSourceMotionListener, + java.io.Serializable

java.awt.event

WindowAdapter	+ java.awt.event.WindowFocusListener, + java.awt.event.WindowStateListener

java.awt.font

TextMeasurer	+ java.lang.Cloneable

java.lang

String, StringBuffer	+ java.lang.CharSequence

java.util

ArrayList, Vector	+ java.util.RandomAccess

javax.swing

AbstractButton.AccessibleAbstractButton, JComponent.AccessibleJComponent, JLabel.AccessibleJLabel	+ javax.accessibility.AccessibleExtendedComponent
JTable.AccessibleJTable	- javax.accessibility.AccessibleTable, + javax.accessibility.AccessibleExtendedTable

javax.swing.plaf.basic

BasicTreeUI.MouseHandler	+ java.awt.event.MouseMotionListener

javax.swing.text

JTextComponent.AccessibleJTextComponent	+ javax.accessibility.AccessibleAction, + javax.accessibility.AccessibleEditableText

Topics

Java 1.4
Modified Classes and Members

Implements Changes

javax.swing.text.html
    HTMLEditorKit   + javax.accessibility.Accessible

Member Modifier Changes

java.awt
  Cursor
    finalize( )   - native
  Dialog
    setTitle( )   - synchronized

java.awt.dnd
  DragGestureRecognizer
    dragGestureListener   + transient
  DragSourceContext
    dragDropEnd( ), dragEnter( ), dragExit( ), dragOver( ),   - synchronized
       dropActionChanged( )
    setCursor( ), updateCurrentCursor( )   + synchronized
  DropTarget
    dropActionChanged( )   + synchronized
    getDefaultActions( ), isActive( ), setDefaultActions( )   - synchronized
  DropTargetContext
    addNotify( ), getTransferable( ), removeNotify( )   - synchronized
  DropTargetContext.TransferableProxy
    getTransferData( ), getTransferDataFlavors( ),   - synchronized
       isDataFlavorSupported( )

java.awt
  EventQueue
    getNextEvent( )   - synchronized
  Frame
    setTitle( )   - synchronized

java.io
  ByteArrayInputStream
    close( )   - synchronized
  ByteArrayOutputStream
    close( )   - native
  FileInputStream
    close( )   - native
  FileOutputStream
    close( )   - native
  ObjectInputStream
    registerValidation( )   - synchronized

java.lang.reflect
  Constructor
    newInstance( )   - native
  Field
    get( ), getBoolean( ), getByte( ), getChar( ), getDouble( ),   - native
       getFloat( ), getInt( ), getLong( ), getShort( ), set( ),
       setBoolean( ), setByte( ), setChar( ), setDouble( ),
       setFloat( ), setInt( ), setLong( ), setShort( )
  Method
    invoke( )   - native

java.lang
  StringBuffer
    capacity( ), length( ), substring( )   + synchronized
  Throwable
    fillInStackTrace( )   + synchronized

java.net
  Socket
    Socket( )   - protected, + public

Member Modifier Changes

URLConnection
    guessContentTypeFromName( )   - protected, + public

java.sql
  DriverManager
    println( ), setLogWriter( )   - synchronized

java.util
  Calendar
    get( ), set( )   - final
    getInstance( )   - synchronized
    getTimeInMillis( ), setTimeInMillis( )   - protected, + public
  Hashtable
    isEmpty( ), size( )   + synchronized
  Vector
    capacity( ), isEmpty( ), lastIndexOf( ), size( ), subList( )   + synchronized

javax.rmi.CORBA
  Stub
    Stub( )   - protected, + public

javax.swing
  BoxLayout
    getLayoutAlignmentX( ), getLayoutAlignmentY( ),   + synchronized
        invalidateLayout( )

javax.swing.filechooser
  FileSystemView
    getRoots( ), isHiddenFile( ), isRoot( )   - abstract

javax.swing
  JEditorPane
    scrollToReference( )   - protected, + public

javax.swing.text
  AsyncBoxView
    flushRequirementChanges( )   - synchronized
  DefaultHighlighter
    DefaultPainter   + final
  PlainDocument
    PlainDocument( )   - protected, + public

org.omg.CORBA
  Any
    extract_Principal( ), insert_Principal( ), insert_Streamable( ) - abstract
    extract_Value( ), insert_Value( )   + abstract
  DynamicImplementation
    invoke( )   - abstract

org.omg.CORBA.portable
  Delegate
    get_interface_def( )   + abstract
  InputStream
    read_Principal( )   - abstract
  OutputStream
    write_Principal( )   - abstract

org.omg.CORBA
  Principal
    name( )   - abstract
  TypeCode
    concrete_base_type( ), equivalent( ), fixed_digits( ),   + abstract
        fixed_scale( ), get_compact_typecode( ),
        member_visibility( ), type_modifier( )

org.omg.CosNaming
  BindingType
    from_int( )   - final

Topics

Member Modifier Changes

org.omg.CosNaming.NamingContextPackage
NotFoundReason
    from_int( )   - final

Throws Changes

java.applet
Applet
    Applet( )   + java.awt.HeadlessException
java.awt
Button
    Button( )   + java.awt.HeadlessException
Checkbox
    Checkbox( )   + java.awt.HeadlessException
CheckboxMenuItem
    CheckboxMenuItem( )   + java.awt.HeadlessException
Choice
    Choice( )   + java.awt.HeadlessException
Cursor
    getSystemCustomCursor( )   + java.awt.HeadlessException
java.awt.dnd
DragSource
    DragSource( )   + java.awt.HeadlessException
DropTarget
    DropTarget( )   + java.awt.HeadlessException
java.awt
Frame
    Frame( )   + java.awt.HeadlessException
GraphicsEnvironment
    getDefaultScreenDevice( ), getScreenDevices( ) + java.awt.HeadlessException
Label
    Label( )   + java.awt.HeadlessException
List
    List( )   + java.awt.HeadlessException
Menu
    Menu( )   + java.awt.HeadlessException
MenuBar
    MenuBar( )   + java.awt.HeadlessException
MenuComponent
    MenuComponent( )   + java.awt.HeadlessException
MenuItem
    MenuItem( )   + java.awt.HeadlessException
PopupMenu
    PopupMenu( )   + java.awt.HeadlessException
java.awt.print
PrinterJob
    pageDialog( ), printDialog( )   + java.awt.HeadlessException
java.awt
Scrollbar
    Scrollbar( )   + java.awt.HeadlessException
ScrollPane
    ScrollPane( )   + java.awt.HeadlessException
TextArea
    TextArea( )   + java.awt.HeadlessException
TextField
    TextField( )   + java.awt.HeadlessException

Throws Changes

Toolkit
    createButton( ), createCheckbox( ),   + java.awt.HeadlessException
        createCheckboxMenuItem( ), createChoice( ),
        createCustomCursor( ), createDialog( ),
        createFileDialog( ), createFrame( ), createLabel( ),
        createList( ), createMenu( ), createMenuBar( ),
        createMenuItem( ), createPopupMenu( ),
        createScrollbar( ), createScrollPane( ),
        createTextArea( ), createTextField( ),
        createWindow( ), getBestCursorSize( ),
        getColorModel( ), getMaximumCursorColors( ),
        getMenuShortcutKeyMask( ), getScreenResolution( ),
        getScreenSize( ), getSystemClipboard( ),
        loadSystemColors( ), mapInputMethodHighlight( )
    getLockingKeyState( ), setLockingKeyState( )   + java.lang.UnsupportedOperationException

java.io
ObjectInputStream
    ObjectInputStream( )   – java.io.StreamCorruptedException
    defaultReadObject( ), readFields( )   – java.io.NotActiveException
ObjectInputStream.GetField
    defaulted( ), get( )   – java.lang.IllegalArgumentException
ObjectInputStream
    readObject( ), readObjectOverride( )   – java.io.OptionalDataException

java.rmi.activation
ActivationGroup_Stub
    newInstance( )   – java.rmi.RemoteException
                                                java.rmi.activation.ActivationException,
                                         + java.rmi.activation.ActivationException,
                                       + java.rmi.RemoteException

java.util
ResourceBundle
    getBundle( ), getObject( ), getString( ), getStringArray( ),   – java.util.MissingResourceException
        handleGetObject( )

javax.rmi.CORBA
Tie
    deactivate( )   + java.rmi.NoSuchObjectException
Util
    unexportObject( )   + java.rmi.NoSuchObjectException
UtilDelegate
    unexportObject( )   + java.rmi.NoSuchObjectException

javax.swing
FocusManager
    setCurrentManager( )   + java.lang.SecurityException
JApplet
    JApplet( )   + java.awt.HeadlessException
JColorChooser
    createDialog( ), showDialog( )   + java.awt.HeadlessException
JDialog
    JDialog( )   + java.awt.HeadlessException
JFileChooser
    showDialog( ), showOpenDialog( ), showSaveDialog( ) + java.awt.HeadlessException
JFrame
    JFrame( )   + java.awt.HeadlessException
JOptionPane
    createDialog( ), getFrameForComponent( ),   + java.awt.HeadlessException
        getRootFrame( ), showConfirmDialog( ),
        showInputDialog( ), showMessageDialog( ),
        showOptionDialog( )

Topics

Throws Changes

org.omg.CORBA
Any
insert_fixed( )   + org.omg.CORBA.BAD_INV_ORDER
insert_Object( )   - org.omg.CORBA.BAD_OPERATION,
                 + org.omg.CORBA.BAD_PARAM

CompletionStatus
from_int( )   - org.omg.CORBA.BAD_PARAM
DefinitionKind
from_int( )   - org.omg.CORBA.BAD_PARAM
SetOverrideType
from_int( )   - org.omg.CORBA.BAD_PARAM
TCKind
from_int( )   - org.omg.CORBA.BAD_PARAM
org.omg.CosNaming
BindingIteratorHelper
narrow( )   - org.omg.CORBA.BAD_PARAM
BindingType
from_int( )   - org.omg.CORBA.BAD_PARAM
NamingContextHelper
narrow( )   - org.omg.CORBA.BAD_PARAM
org.omg.CosNaming.NamingContextPackage
NotFoundReason
from_int( )   - org.omg.CORBA.BAD_PARAM

Newly Deprecated Classes

javax.accessibility
AccessibleResourceBundle
javax.security.auth
Policy
javax.swing.plaf.metal
MetalComboBoxUI.MetalComboPopup

org.omg.CORBA
DynamicImplementation
org.xml.sax
AttributeList, *DocumentHandler*, HandlerBase, *Parser*
org.xml.sax.helpers
AttributeListImpl, ParserFactory

Newly Deprecated Members

java.awt
Component
isFocusTraversable( )
ComponentOrientation
getOrientation( )
Window
applyResourceBundle( )
java.io
ObjectOutputStream.PutField
write( )
java.lang
SecurityManager
checkMulticast( )
java.net
MulticastSocket
send( )
URLDecoder
decode( )

URLEncoder
encode( )
javax.swing
FocusManager
disableSwingFocusManager( ),
isFocusManagerEnabled( )
JComponent
getNextFocusableComponent( ),
isManagingFocus( ), requestDefaultFocus( ),
setNextFocusableComponent( )
SwingUtilities
findFocusOwner( )
javax.swing.plaf.metal
MetalComboBoxUI
editablePropertyChanged( ), removeListeners( )
org.omg.CORBA
DynamicImplementation
invoke( )

Exceptions and Errors

This is a complete listing of all the exceptions and errors in this version of Java. The "*" indicates a checked exception or error; these must be declared in the throws clause.

java.lang	AbstractMethodError
java.security	AccessControlException
java.rmi	*AccessException
javax.security.auth.login	*AccountExpiredException
java.security.acl	*AclNotFoundException
java.rmi.activation	*ActivateFailedException
java.rmi.activation	*ActivationException
org.omg.PortableServer.POAPackage	*AdapterAlreadyExists
org.omg.PortableServer.POAManagerPackage	*AdapterInactive
org.omg.PortableServer.POAPackage	*AdapterNonExistent
org.omg.CosNaming.NamingContextPackage	*AlreadyBound
java.rmi	*AlreadyBoundException
java.nio.channels	AlreadyConnectedException
org.omg.CORBA.portable	*ApplicationException
java.lang	ArithmeticException
java.lang	ArrayIndexOutOfBoundsException
java.lang	ArrayStoreException
java.lang	AssertionError
java.nio.channels	*AsynchronousCloseException
javax.naming.directory	*AttributeInUseException
javax.naming.directory	*AttributeModificationException
javax.naming	*AuthenticationException
javax.naming	*AuthenticationNotSupportedException
java.awt	AWTError
java.awt	*AWTException
java.util.prefs	*BackingStoreException
org.omg.CORBA	BAD_CONTEXT
org.omg.CORBA	BAD_INV_ORDER
org.omg.CORBA	BAD_OPERATION
org.omg.CORBA	BAD_PARAM
org.omg.CORBA	BAD_TYPECODE
org.omg.CORBA.TypeCodePackage	*BadKind
javax.swing.text	*BadLocationException
javax.crypto	*BadPaddingException
java.sql	*BatchUpdateException
java.net	*BindException
org.omg.CORBA	*Bounds
org.omg.CORBA.TypeCodePackage	*Bounds
java.nio	BufferOverflowException
java.nio	BufferUnderflowException
java.nio.channels	CancelledKeyException
org.omg.CosNaming.NamingContextPackage	*CannotProceed
javax.naming	*CannotProceedException
javax.swing.undo	CannotRedoException
javax.swing.undo	CannotUndoException
java.security.cert	*CertificateEncodingException
javax.security.cert	*CertificateEncodingException
java.security.cert	*CertificateException
javax.security.cert	*CertificateException
java.security.cert	*CertificateExpiredException

Topics

javax.security.cert	*CertificateExpiredException
java.security.cert	*CertificateNotYetValidException
javax.security.cert	*CertificateNotYetValidException
java.security.cert	*CertificateParsingException
javax.security.cert	*CertificateParsingException
java.security.cert	*CertPathBuilderException
java.security.cert	*CertPathValidatorException
java.security.cert	*CertStoreException
javax.swing.text	*ChangedCharSetException
java.nio.charset	*CharacterCodingException
java.io	*CharConversionException
java.lang	ClassCastException
java.lang	ClassCircularityError
java.lang	ClassFormatError
java.lang	*ClassNotFoundException
java.lang	*CloneNotSupportedException
java.nio.channels	*ClosedByInterruptException
java.nio.channels	*ClosedChannelException
java.nio.channels	ClosedSelectorException
java.awt.color	CMMException
java.nio.charset	CoderMalfunctionError
org.omg.CORBA	COMM_FAILURE
javax.naming	*CommunicationException
java.util	ConcurrentModificationException
javax.naming	*ConfigurationException
java.net	*ConnectException
java.rmi	*ConnectException
java.rmi	*ConnectIOException
java.nio.channels	ConnectionPendingException
javax.naming	*ContextNotEmptyException
javax.security.auth.login	*CredentialExpiredException
java.security.cert	*CRLException
org.omg.CORBA	DATA_CONVERSION
java.util.zip	*DataFormatException
java.sql	*DataTruncation
javax.security.auth	*DestroyFailedException
java.security	*DigestException
org.w3c.dom	DOMException
org.omg.PortableInterceptor.ORBInitInfoPackage	*DuplicateName
java.util	EmptyStackException
java.io	*EOFException
java.lang	Error
java.lang	*Exception
java.lang	ExceptionInInitializerError
javax.crypto	*ExemptionMechanismException
javax.swing.tree	*ExpandVetoException
java.rmi.server	*ExportException
javax.xml.parsers	FactoryConfigurationError
javax.security.auth.login	*FailedLoginException
java.nio.channels	*FileLockInterruptionException
java.io	*FileNotFoundException
java.awt	*FontFormatException
org.omg.IOP.CodecPackage	*FormatMismatch
org.omg.PortableInterceptor	*ForwardRequest
org.omg.PortableServer	*ForwardRequest
org.omg.CORBA	FREE_MEM
java.security	*GeneralSecurityException

org.ietf.jgss	*GSSException
java.awt	HeadlessException
javax.imageio	*IIOException
javax.imageio.metadata	*IIOInvalidTreeException
java.lang	IllegalAccessError
java.lang	*IllegalAccessException
java.lang	IllegalArgumentException
java.nio.channels	IllegalBlockingModeException
javax.crypto	*IllegalBlockSizeException
java.nio.charset	IllegalCharsetNameException
java.awt	IllegalComponentStateException
java.lang	IllegalMonitorStateException
java.awt.geom	IllegalPathStateException
java.nio.channels	IllegalSelectorException
java.lang	IllegalStateException
java.lang	IllegalThreadStateException
java.awt.image	ImagingOpException
org.omg.CORBA	IMP_LIMIT
java.lang	IncompatibleClassChangeError
org.omg.CORBA.ORBPackage	*InconsistentTypeCode
org.omg.DynamicAny.DynAnyFactoryPackage	*InconsistentTypeCode
java.lang	IndexOutOfBoundsException
org.omg.CORBA.portable	IndirectionException
org.omg.CORBA	INITIALIZE
java.lang	InstantiationError
java.lang	*InstantiationException
javax.naming	*InsufficientResourcesException
org.omg.CORBA	INTERNAL
java.lang	InternalError
java.lang	*InterruptedException
java.io	*InterruptedIOException
javax.naming	*InterruptedNamingException
org.omg.CORBA	INTF_REPOS
java.beans	*IntrospectionException
org.omg.CORBA	INV_FLAG
org.omg.CORBA	INV_IDENT
org.omg.CORBA	INV_OBJREF
org.omg.CORBA	INV_POLICY
org.omg.CORBA.DynAnyPackage	*Invalid
org.omg.CORBA	INVALID_TRANSACTION
org.omg.CosNaming.NamingContextExtPackage	*InvalidAddress
java.security	*InvalidAlgorithmParameterException
javax.naming.directory	*InvalidAttributeIdentifierException
javax.naming.directory	*InvalidAttributesException
javax.naming.directory	*InvalidAttributeValueException
java.io	*InvalidClassException
java.awt.dnd	InvalidDnDOperationException
java.security	*InvalidKeyException
java.security.spec	*InvalidKeySpecException
java.nio	InvalidMarkException
javax.sound.midi	*InvalidMidiDataException
org.omg.CORBA.ORBPackage	*InvalidName
org.omg.CosNaming.NamingContextPackage	*InvalidName
org.omg.PortableInterceptor.ORBInitInfoPackage	*InvalidName
javax.naming	*InvalidNameException
java.io	*InvalidObjectException
java.security	InvalidParameterException

Topics

java.security.spec	*InvalidParameterSpecException
org.omg.PortableServer.POAPackage	*InvalidPolicy
java.util.prefs	*InvalidPreferencesFormatException
javax.naming.directory	*InvalidSearchControlsException
javax.naming.directory	*InvalidSearchFilterException
org.omg.CORBA.DynAnyPackage	*InvalidSeq
org.omg.PortableInterceptor	*InvalidSlot
javax.transaction	*InvalidTransactionException
org.omg.IOP.CodecPackage	*InvalidTypeForEncoding
org.omg.CORBA.DynAnyPackage	*InvalidValue
org.omg.DynamicAny.DynAnyPackage	*InvalidValue
java.lang.reflect	*InvocationTargetException
java.io	*IOException
java.util.jar	*JarException
java.security	*KeyException
java.security	*KeyManagementException
java.security	*KeyStoreException
java.security.acl	*LastOwnerException
javax.naming.ldap	*LdapReferralException
javax.naming	*LimitExceededException
javax.sound.sampled	*LineUnavailableException
java.lang	LinkageError
javax.naming	*LinkException
javax.naming	*LinkLoopException
javax.security.auth.login	*LoginException
java.nio.charset	*MalformedInputException
javax.naming	*MalformedLinkException
java.net	*MalformedURLException
org.omg.CORBA	MARSHAL
java.rmi	*MarshalException
javax.sound.midi	*MidiUnavailableException
java.awt.datatransfer	*MimeTypeParseException
java.util	MissingResourceException
javax.naming	*NameAlreadyBoundException
javax.naming	*NameNotFoundException
javax.naming	*NamingException
javax.naming	*NamingSecurityException
java.lang	NegativeArraySizeException
org.omg.CORBA	NO_IMPLEMENT
org.omg.CORBA	NO_MEMORY
org.omg.CORBA	NO_PERMISSION
org.omg.CORBA	NO_RESOURCES
org.omg.CORBA	NO_RESPONSE
java.lang	NoClassDefFoundError
java.nio.channels	NoConnectionPendingException
org.omg.PortableServer.CurrentPackage	*NoContext
javax.naming	*NoInitialContextException
java.awt.geom	*NoninvertibleTransformException
java.nio.channels	NonReadableChannelException
java.nio.channels	NonWritableChannelException
javax.naming	*NoPermissionException
java.net	*NoRouteToHostException
org.omg.PortableServer.POAPackage	*NoServant
java.security	*NoSuchAlgorithmException
javax.naming.directory	*NoSuchAttributeException
java.util	NoSuchElementException
java.lang	NoSuchFieldError

java.lang	*NoSuchFieldException
java.lang	NoSuchMethodError
java.lang	*NoSuchMethodException
java.rmi	*NoSuchObjectException
javax.crypto	*NoSuchPaddingException
java.security	*NoSuchProviderException
java.io	*NotActiveException
java.rmi	*NotBoundException
javax.naming	*NotContextException
org.omg.CosNaming.NamingContextPackage	*NotEmpty
org.omg.CosNaming.NamingContextPackage	*NotFound
java.security.acl	*NotOwnerException
java.io	*NotSerializableException
java.nio.channels	NotYetBoundException
java.nio.channels	NotYetConnectedException
java.lang	NullPointerException
java.lang	NumberFormatException
org.omg.CORBA	OBJ_ADAPTER
org.omg.CORBA	OBJECT_NOT_EXIST
org.omg.PortableServer.POAPackage	*ObjectAlreadyActive
org.omg.PortableServer.POAPackage	*ObjectNotActive
java.io	*ObjectStreamException
javax.naming	*OperationNotSupportedException
java.io	*OptionalDataException
java.lang	OutOfMemoryError
java.nio.channels	OverlappingFileLockException
java.text	*ParseException
javax.xml.parsers	*ParserConfigurationException
javax.naming	*PartialResultException
java.util.regex	PatternSyntaxException
org.omg.CORBA	PERSIST_STORE
org.omg.CORBA	*PolicyError
java.net	*PortUnreachableException
java.awt.print	*PrinterAbortException
java.awt.print	*PrinterException
java.awt.print	*PrinterIOException
javax.print	*PrintException
java.security	*PrivilegedActionException
java.awt.color	ProfileDataException
java.beans	*PropertyVetoException
java.net	*ProtocolException
java.security	ProviderException
java.awt.image	RasterFormatException
java.nio	ReadOnlyBufferException
javax.naming	*ReferralException
javax.security.auth	*RefreshFailedException
org.omg.CORBA.portable	*RemarshalException
java.rmi	*RemoteException
java.rmi	RMISecurityException
java.lang	RuntimeException
org.xml.sax	*SAXException
org.xml.sax	*SAXNotRecognizedException
org.xml.sax	*SAXNotSupportedException
org.xml.sax	*SAXParseException
javax.naming.directory	*SchemaViolationException
java.lang	SecurityException
org.omg.PortableServer.POAPackage	*ServantAlreadyActive

Topics

org.omg.PortableServer.POAPackage	*ServantNotActive
java.rmi.server	*ServerCloneException
java.rmi	*ServerError
java.rmi	*ServerException ˙
java.rmi.server	*ServerNotActiveException
java.rmi	*ServerRuntimeException
javax.naming	*ServiceUnavailableException
javax.crypto	*ShortBufferException
java.security	*SignatureException
javax.naming	*SizeLimitExceededException
java.rmi.server	*SkeletonMismatchException
java.rmi.server	*SkeletonNotFoundException
java.net	*SocketException
java.rmi.server	*SocketSecurityException
java.net	*SocketTimeoutException
java.sql	*SQLException
java.sql	*SQLWarning
javax.net.ssl	*SSLException
javax.net.ssl	*SSLHandshakeException
javax.net.ssl	*SSLKeyException
javax.net.ssl	*SSLPeerUnverifiedException
javax.net.ssl	*SSLProtocolException
java.lang	StackOverflowError
java.io	*StreamCorruptedException
java.lang	StringIndexOutOfBoundsException
java.rmi	*StubNotFoundException
java.io	*SyncFailedException
org.omg.CORBA	SystemException
java.lang	ThreadDeath
java.lang	*Throwable
javax.naming	*TimeLimitExceededException
java.util	*TooManyListenersException
org.omg.CORBA	TRANSACTION_REQUIRED
org.omg.CORBA	TRANSACTION_ROLLEDBACK
javax.transaction	*TransactionRequiredException
javax.transaction	*TransactionRolledbackException
javax.xml.transform	*TransformerConfigurationException
javax.xml.transform	*TransformerException
javax.xml.transform	TransformerFactoryConfigurationError
org.omg.CORBA	TRANSIENT
org.omg.CORBA.DynAnyPackage	*TypeMismatch
org.omg.DynamicAny.DynAnyPackage	*TypeMismatch
org.omg.IOP.CodecPackage	*TypeMismatch
java.lang.reflect	UndeclaredThrowableException
java.rmi	*UnexpectedException
org.omg.CORBA	UNKNOWN
org.omg.IOP.CodecFactoryPackage	*UnknownEncoding
java.lang	UnknownError
org.omg.CORBA.portable	UnknownException
java.rmi.activation	*UnknownGroupException
java.net	*UnknownHostException
java.rmi	*UnknownHostException
java.rmi.activation	*UnknownObjectException
java.net	*UnknownServiceException
org.omg.CORBA	*UnknownUserException
java.nio.charset	*UnmappableCharacterException
java.rmi	*UnmarshalException

javax.print.attribute	UnmodifiableSetException
java.security	*UnrecoverableKeyException
java.nio.channels	UnresolvedAddressException
java.lang	UnsatisfiedLinkError
java.nio.channels	UnsupportedAddressTypeException
javax.sound.sampled	*UnsupportedAudioFileException
javax.security.auth.callback	*UnsupportedCallbackException
java.nio.charset	UnsupportedCharsetException
java.lang	UnsupportedClassVersionError
java.io	*UnsupportedEncodingException
java.awt.datatransfer	*UnsupportedFlavorException
javax.swing	*UnsupportedLookAndFeelException
java.lang	UnsupportedOperationException
java.net	*URISyntaxException
org.omg.CORBA	*UserException
java.io	*UTFDataFormatException
java.lang	VerifyError
java.lang	VirtualMachineError
java.io	*WriteAbortedException
org.omg.PortableServer.POAPackage	*WrongAdapter
org.omg.PortableServer.POAPackage	*WrongPolicy
org.omg.CORBA	*WrongTransaction
javax.transaction.xa	*XAException
java.util.zip	*ZipException

Topics

Part 4

CROSS-REFERENCE

This part contains a cross-reference of all of the 1.4 Java classes and interfaces of the packages included in this volume. To save space, there are no cross-reference entries for primitive types, constructors, `java.lang.Object`, or `java.lang.String`.

The cross-reference consists of entries and subentries. An entry is displayed in bold type and shows a class, interface, or member name. If the entry is a class or interface, the package containing the class or interface is shown on the right. If the entry is a member name, all classes or interfaces that have a member with that name are listed to the right. Member names are shown in a condensed font to conserve space.

A class or interface may be followed by an up-arrow (ˆ) or a down-arrow (ˬ). The up-arrow inidicates that the class has a superclass other than `Error`, `Exception`, `Object`, or `RuntimeException`. In the case of an interface, it indicates that the interface extends from another interface. The down-arrow indicates that the class has a subclass. In the case of an interface, it indicates that the interface is extended by another interface.

An entry may be followed by subentries that contain more information about that class, interface, or member. For example, the "returned by" subentry for a class lists all members that return an instance of the class. Following is a list of the set of subentries.It's important to note that this cross-reference does not include any overridden methods. For example, if `C.m()` overrides `A.m()`, the entry "m" shows `A` but not `C`. To discover all classes that inherit `m()` and possibly implement `m()`, look up the "A" entry and there you will find all the classes that are descendents of `A`.

Subentry	Description
descendents	Shows the entire list of descendents (except for the ones that already appear in "subclasses") of this class or interface.
extended by	Shows all interfaces that extend this interface.
fields	Shows all fields of this type.
implemented by	Shows all classes that implement this interface.
passed to	Shows each method and constructor whose parameter list includes at least one parameter of this type.
returned by	Shows all methods that return an object of this type.
subclasses	Shows all subclasses of this class.
thrown by	Shows all methods and constructors that throw this exception.

add_value( ): NVList
addAll( ): AbstractCollection˽ BeanContextSupport˄
   Collection˽ CompositeName CompoundName Name˄
addAttribute( ): AttributedString AttributeListImpl
   AttributesImpl
addAttributes( ): AttributedString
addBatch( ): java.sql.Statement˽
addBeanContextMembershipListener( ): BeanContext˄
   BeanContextSupport˄
addBeanContextServicesListener( ): BeanContextServices˄
   BeanContextServicesSupport˄
addCertificate( ): Identity˽
addCertPathChecker( ): PKIXParameters˽
addCertStore( ): PKIXParameters˽
addConnectionEventListener( ): PooledConnection˽
addElement( ): Vector˄
addEntry( ): Acl˄
addFirst( ): LinkedList˄
addHandler( ): Logger
addHandshakeCompletedListener( ): SSLSocket˄
addIdentity( ): IdentityScope˄
addIssuerName( ): X509CRLSelector
addLast( ): LinkedList˄
addLogger( ): LogManager
addMember( ): Group˄
addNamingListener( ): EventContext˄
addNodeChangeListener( ): Preferences˽
addObserver( ): Observable
addOwner( ): Owner˽
addPathToName( ): X509CertSelector
addPermission( ): AclEntry˄
addPreferenceChangeListener( ): Preferences˽
addPropertyChangeListener( ): BeanContextChild˽
   BeanContextChildSupport˽ Customizer LogManager
   PropertyChangeSupport˽ PropertyEditor
   PropertyEditorSupport
addProvider( ): Security
addProviderAtEnd( ): GSSManager
addProviderAtFront( ): GSSManager
addRequestProperty( ): URLConnection˽
address: SocketImpl˽
AddressHelper:
   org.omg.CosNaming.NamingContextExtPackage
addRowSetListener( ): RowSet˄
addrs: javax.naming.Reference˽
addrType: RefAddr˽
addService( ): BeanContextServices˄
   BeanContextServicesSupport˄
addShutdownHook( ): Runtime
addSubjectAlternativeName( ): X509CertSelector
addToEnvironment( ): javax.naming.Context˽ InitialContext˽
addURL( ): URLClassLoader˽
addVetoableChangeListener( ): BeanContextChild˽
   BeanContextChildSupport˽ VetoableChangeSupport
Adler32: java.util.zip
after( ): Calendar˽ java.util.Date˽
afterLast( ): ResultSet˽
AlgorithmParameterGenerator: java.security
  —returned by: AlgorithmParameterGenerator.getInstance( )
AlgorithmParameterGeneratorSpi: java.security
  —passed to: AlgorithmParameterGenerator( )
AlgorithmParameters: java.security
  —passed to: Cipher˽.init( ) CipherSpi.engineInit( )
    EncryptedPrivateKeyInfo( ) ExemptionMechanism.init( )
    ExemptionMechanismSpi.engineInit( )
  —returned by: AlgorithmParameterGenerator.generateParameters( )
    AlgorithmParameterGeneratorSpi.engineGenerateParameters( )
    AlgorithmParameters.getInstance( )
    Cipher˽.getParameters( ) CipherSpi.engineGetParameters( )
    EncryptedPrivateKeyInfo.getAlgParameters( )
    Signature˄.getParameters( )
    SignatureSpi˽.engineGetParameters( )

AlgorithmParameterSpec: java.security.spec
  —passed to: AlgorithmParameterGenerator.init( )
    AlgorithmParameterGeneratorSpi.engineInit( )
    AlgorithmParameters.init( )
    AlgorithmParametersSpi.engineInit( ) Cipher˽.init( )
    CipherSpi.engineInit( ) ExemptionMechanism.init( )
    ExemptionMechanismSpi.engineInit( ) KeyAgreement.init( )
    KeyAgreementSpi.engineInit( ) KeyGenerator.init( )
    KeyGeneratorSpi.engineInit( ) KeyPairGenerator˄.initialize( )
    KeyPairGeneratorSpi˽.initialize( ) Mac.init( )
    MacSpi.engineInit( ) Signature˄.setParameter( )
    SignatureSpi˽.engineSetParameter( )
  —returned by: AlgorithmParameters.getParameterSpec( )
    AlgorithmParametersSpi.engineGetParameterSpec( )
  —implemented by: DHGenParameterSpec DHParameterSpec
    DSAParameterSpec IvParameterSpec PBEParameterSpec
    PSSParameterSpec RC2ParameterSpec
    RC5ParameterSpec RSAKeyGenParameterSpec
AlgorithmParametersSpi: java.security
  —passed to: AlgorithmParameters( )
aliases( ): Charset KeyStore
ALL: Level
allocate( ): ByteBuffer˄ CharBuffer˄ DoubleBuffer˄
   FloatBuffer˄ IntBuffer˄ LongBuffer˄ ShortBuffer˄
allocate_slot_id( ): ORBInitInfoOperations˽
allocateDirect( ): ByteBuffer˄
allowMultipleSelections( ): ChoiceCallback
allowThreadSuspension( ): ThreadGroup
allowUserInteraction: URLConnection˽
AllPermission˄: java.security
allProceduresAreCallable( ): DatabaseMetaData
allTablesAreSelectable( ): DatabaseMetaData
ALPHABETIC_PRESENTATION_FORMS:
   Character.UnicodeBlock˄
AlreadyBound˄: org.omg.CosNaming.NamingContextPackage
  —passed to: AlreadyBoundHelper < insert( ), write( ) >
    AlreadyBoundHolder( )
  —returned by: AlreadyBoundHelper < extract( ), read( ) >
  —thrown by: _NamingContextExtStub˄ < bind( ), bind_context( ),
    bind_new_context( ) > _NamingContextStub˄
    < bind( ), bind_context( ), bind_new_context( ) >
    NamingContextOperations˽ < bind( ), bind_context( ),
    bind_new_context( ) >
  —fields: AlreadyBoundHolder.value
AlreadyBoundException: java.rmi
  —thrown by: Naming.bind( ) Registry˄.bind( )
AlreadyBoundHelper:
   org.omg.CosNaming.NamingContextPackage
AlreadyBoundHolder:
   org.omg.CosNaming.NamingContextPackage
AlreadyConnectedException˄: java.nio.channels
altName: CannotProceedException˄
altNameCtx: CannotProceedException˄
AM: Calendar˽
AM_PM: Calendar˽ DateFormat.Field˄
AM_PM_FIELD: DateFormat˄
and( ): BigInteger˄ BitSet
andNot( ): BigInteger˄ BitSet
annotateClass( ): ObjectOutputStream˄
annotateProxyClass( ): ObjectOutputStream˄
Annotation: java.text
Any: org.omg.CORBA
  —passed to: _DynAnyFactoryStub˄.create_dyn_any( )
    _DynAnyStub˄ < from_any( ), insert_any( ) > _DynArrayStub˄
    < from_any( ), insert_any( ), set_elements( ) > _DynEnumStub˄
    < from_any( ), insert_any( ) > _DynFixedStub˄
    < from_any( ), insert_any( ) > _DynSequenceStub˄
    < from_any( ), insert_any( ), set_elements( ) > _DynStructStub˄
    < from_any( ), insert_any( ) > _DynUnionStub˄ < from_any( ),
    insert_any( ) > _DynValueStub˄ < from_any( ),
    insert_any( ) > AdapterAlreadyExistsHelper < extract( ),
    insert( ) > AdapterInactiveHelper < extract( ), insert( ) >

AdapterNonExistentHelper < extract( ), insert( ) >
AddressHelper < extract( ), insert( ) > **A**lreadyBoundHelper
< extract( ), insert( ) > **A**ny < equal( ), insert_any( ) >
AnyHolder( ) org.omg.CORBA.**A**nySeqHelper.extract( )
org.omg.DynamicAny.**A**nySeqHelper.extract( )
org.omg.CORBA.**A**nySeqHelper.insert( )
org.omg.DynamicAny.**A**nySeqHelper.insert( )
org.omg.CORBA.**A**nySeqHelper.write( )
org.omg.DynamicAny.**A**nySeqHelper.write( )
AnySeqHolder( ) **B**indingHelper < extract( ), insert( ) >
BindingIteratorHelper < extract( ), insert( ) >
BindingListHelper < extract( ), insert( ) > **B**indingTypeHelper
< extract( ), insert( ) > **B**ooleanSeqHelper < extract( ),
insert( ) > **C**annotProceedHelper < extract( ), insert( ) >
CharSeqHelper < extract( ), insert( ) > **C**odecFactoryHelper
< extract( ), insert( ) > *CodecOperations* < encode( ),
encode_value( ) > **C**ompletionStatusHelper < extract( ),
insert( ) > **C**omponentIdHelper < extract( ),
insert( ) > org.omg.CORBA.**C**ontext.set_one_value( )
org.omg.CORBA.**C**urrentHelper.extract( )
org.omg.PortableInterceptor.**C**urrentHelper.extract( )
org.omg.PortableServer.**C**urrentHelper.extract( )
org.omg.CORBA.**C**urrentHelper.insert( )
org.omg.PortableInterceptor.**C**urrentHelper.insert( )
org.omg.PortableServer.**C**urrentHelper.insert( )
org.omg.PortableInterceptor.CurrentOperations^.set_slot( )
org.omg.CORBA.DataOutputStream^ < write_any( ),
write_any_array( ) > **D**efinitionKindHelper < extract( ),
insert( ) > **D**oubleSeqHelper < extract( ), insert( ) >
DuplicateNameHelper < extract( ), insert( ) >
org.omg.CORBA.DynAny^ < from_any( ), insert_any( ) >
DynAnyFactoryHelper < extract( ), insert( ) >
DynAnyFactoryOperations.create_dyn_any( ) **D**ynAnyHelper
< extract( ), insert( ) > *DynAnyOperations* < from_any( ),
insert_any( ) > **D**ynAnySeqHelper < extract( ),
insert( ) > *org.omg.CORBA.DynArray*^.set_elements( )
DynArrayHelper < extract( ), insert( ) >
DynArrayOperations^.set_elements( ) **D**ynEnumHelper
< extract( ), insert( ) > **D**ynFixedHelper < extract( ),
insert( ) > *org.omg.CORBA.DynSequence*^.set_elements( )
DynSequenceHelper < extract( ), insert( ) >
DynSequenceOperations^.set_elements( ) **D**ynStructHelper
< extract( ), insert( ) > **D**ynUnionHelper < extract( ),
insert( ) > *DynValueBoxOperations*^.set_boxed_value( )
DynValueHelper < extract( ), insert( ) >
org.omg.CORBA.**F**ieldNameHelper.extract( )
org.omg.DynamicAny.**F**ieldNameHelper.extract( )
org.omg.CORBA.**F**ieldNameHelper.insert( )
org.omg.DynamicAny.**F**ieldNameHelper.insert( )
FloatSeqHelper < extract( ), insert( ) >
FormatMismatchHelper < extract( ), insert( ) >
org.omg.PortableInterceptor.**F**orwardRequestHelper.extract( )
org.omg.PortableServer.**F**orwardRequestHelper.extract( )
org.omg.PortableInterceptor.**F**orwardRequestHelper.insert( )
org.omg.PortableServer.**F**orwardRequestHelper.insert( )
IdentifierHelper < extract( ), insert( ) > **I**DLTypeHelper
< extract( ), insert( ) > **I**nconsistentTypeCodeHelper
< extract( ), insert( ) > **I**nvalidAddressHelper
< extract( ), insert( ) > org.omg.CosNaming↵
.NamingContextPackage.**I**nvalidNameHelper.extract( )
org.omg.PortableInterceptor.ORBInitInfoPackage↵
.**I**nvalidNameHelper.extract( ) org.omg.CosNaming↵
.NamingContextPackage.**I**nvalidNameHelper.insert( )
org.omg.PortableInterceptor.ORBInitInfoPackage↵
.**I**nvalidNameHelper.insert( ) **I**nvalidPolicyHelper < extract( ),
insert( ) > **I**nvalidSlotHelper < extract( ), insert( ) >
InvalidTypeForEncodingHelper < extract( ), insert( ) >
InvalidValueHelper < extract( ), insert( ) > **I**ORHelper
< extract( ), insert( ) > **I**stringHelper < extract( ), insert( ) >
LongLongSeqHelper < extract( ), insert( ) > **L**ongSeqHelper
< extract( ), insert( ) > **M**ultipleComponentProfileHelper
< extract( ), insert( ) > **N**ameComponentHelper

< extract( ), insert( ) > **N**ameDynAnyPairHelper
< extract( ), insert( ) > **N**ameDynAnyPairSeqHelper
< extract( ), insert( ) > **N**ameHelper < extract( ),
insert( ) > org.omg.CORBA.**N**ameValuePair( )
org.omg.DynamicAny.**N**ameValuePair( )
org.omg.CORBA.**N**ameValuePairHelper.extract( )
org.omg.DynamicAny.**N**ameValuePairHelper.extract( )
org.omg.CORBA.**N**ameValuePairHelper.insert( )
org.omg.DynamicAny.**N**ameValuePairHelper.insert( )
NameValuePairSeqHelper < extract( ), insert( ) >
NamingContextExtHelper < extract( ), insert( ) >
NamingContextHelper < extract( ), insert( ) >
NoContextHelper < extract( ), insert( ) > **N**oServantHelper
< extract( ), insert( ) > **N**otEmptyHelper < extract( ),
insert( ) > **N**otFoundHelper < extract( ), insert( ) >
NotFoundReasonHelper < extract( ), insert( ) >
NVList.add_value( ) **O**bjectAlreadyActiveHelper < extract( ),
insert( ) > **O**bjectHelper < extract( ), insert( ) >
ObjectIdHelper < extract( ), insert( ) > **O**bjectNotActiveHelper
< extract( ), insert( ) > **O**ctetSeqHelper
< extract( ), insert( ) > org.omg.CORBA.**O**RB
< create_dyn_any( ), create_named_value( ), create_policy( ) >
org.omg.CORBA.portable.**O**utputStream^.write_any( )
Parameter( ) **P**arameterModeHelper < extract( ), insert( ) >
POAHelper < extract( ), insert( ) > **P**olicyErrorCodeHelper
< extract( ), insert( ) > **P**olicyErrorHelper < extract( ), insert( ) >
PolicyFactoryOperations.create_policy( ) **P**olicyHelper
< extract( ), insert( ) > **P**olicyListHelper < extract( ),
insert( ) > **P**olicyTypeHelper < extract( ), insert( ) >
ProfileIdHelper < extract( ), insert( ) > **R**epositoryIdHelper
< extract( ), insert( ) > **S**ervantActivatorHelper < extract( ),
insert( ) > **S**ervantAlreadyActiveHelper < extract( ),
insert( ) > **S**ervantLocatorHelper < extract( ), insert( ) >
ServantNotActiveHelper < extract( ), insert( ) >
ServerRequest < except( ), result( ), set_exception( ),
set_result( ) > *ServerRequestInfoOperations*^.set_slot( )
ServiceContextHelper < extract( ), insert( ) >
ServiceContextListHelper < extract( ), insert( ) >
ServiceDetailHelper < extract( ), insert( ) > **S**erviceIdHelper
< extract( ), insert( ) > **S**erviceInformationHelper < extract( ),
insert( ) > **S**etOverrideTypeHelper < extract( ), insert( ) >
ShortSeqHelper < extract( ), insert( ) > **S**tringNameHelper
< extract( ), insert( ) > **S**tringSeqHelper < extract( ), insert( ) >
StringValueHelper < extract( ), insert( ) > **S**tructMemberHelper
< extract( ), insert( ) > **S**yncScopeHelper < extract( ),
insert( ) > **T**aggedComponentHelper < extract( ), insert( ) >
TaggedProfileHelper < extract( ), insert( ) > org.omg↵
.DynamicAny.DynAnyPackage.**T**ypeMismatchHelper.extract( )
org.omg.IOP.CodecPackage.**T**ypeMismatchHelper.extract( )
org.omg.DynamicAny.DynAnyPackage↵
.**T**ypeMismatchHelper.insert( )
org.omg.IOP.CodecPackage.**T**ypeMismatchHelper.insert( )
ULongLongSeqHelper < extract( ), insert( ) >
ULongSeqHelper < extract( ), insert( ) > **U**nionMember( )
UnionMemberHelper < extract( ), insert( ) >
UnknownEncodingHelper < extract( ), insert( ) >
UnknownUserException( ) **U**nknownUserExceptionHelper
< extract( ), insert( ) > **U**RLStringHelper < extract( ), insert( ) >
UShortSeqHelper < extract( ), insert( ) > **V**alueBaseHelper
< extract( ), insert( ) > **V**alueMemberHelper < extract( ),
insert( ) > **V**ersionSpecHelper < extract( ), insert( ) >
VisibilityHelper < extract( ), insert( ) > **W**CharSeqHelper
< extract( ), insert( ) > **W**rongAdapterHelper < extract( ),
insert( ) > **W**rongPolicyHelper < extract( ), insert( ) >
WrongTransactionHelper < extract( ), insert( ) >
WStringSeqHelper < extract( ), insert( ) > **W**StringValueHelper
< extract( ), insert( ) >

—returned by: _DynAnyStub^ < get_any( ), to_any( ) >
_DynArrayStub^ < get_any( ), get_elements( ), to_any( ) >
_DynEnumStub^ < get_any( ), to_any( ) > _DynFixedStub^
< get_any( ), to_any( ) > _DynSequenceStub^
< get_any( ), get_elements( ), to_any( ) > _DynStructStub^

< get_any(), to_any( ) > _DynUnionStub^ < get_any( ),
to_any( ) > _DynValueStub^ < get_any( ), to_any( ) >
Any.extract_any( ) org.omg.CORBA.**A**nySeqHelper.extract( )
org.omg.DynamicAny.**A**nySeqHelper.extract( )
org.omg.CORBA.**A**nySeqHelper.read( )
org.omg.DynamicAny.**A**nySeqHelper.read( )
*C*lientRequestInfoOperations^.received_exception( )
*C*odecOperations_ < decode( ), decode_value( ) >
org.omg.PortableInterceptor.*C*urrentOperations^.get_slot( )
org.omg.CORBA.*D*ataInputStream^.read_any( )
org.omg.CORBA.*D*ynAny^ < get_any( ), to_any( ) >
*D*ynAnyOperations_ < get_any( ), to_any( ) >
org.omg.CORBA.*D*ynArray^.get_elements( )
*D*ynArrayOperations^.get_elements( )
org.omg.CORBA.*D*ynSequence^.get_elements( )
*D*ynSequenceOperations^.get_elements( )
*D*ynValueBoxOperations^.get_boxed_value( )
org.omg.CORBA.portable.**I**nputStream^.read_any( )
NamedValue.value( ) org.omg.CORBA.**O**RB_.create_any( )
Request < add_in_arg( ), add_inout_arg( ), add_named_in_arg( ),
add_named_inout_arg( ), add_named_out_arg( ), add_out_arg( ),
return_value( ) > *R*equestInfoOperations_ < get_slot( ),
result( ) > *S*erverRequestInfoOperations^.sending_exception( )
TypeCode.member_label( )
—fields: **A**nyHolder.value **A**nySeqHolder.value
org.omg.CORBA.**N**ameValuePair.value
org.omg.DynamicAny.**N**ameValuePair.value
Parameter.argument **U**nionMember.label
UnknownUserException^.except
AnyHolder: org.omg.CORBA
AnySeqHelper: org.omg.CORBA
AnySeqHelper: org.omg.DynamicAny
AnySeqHolder: org.omg.CORBA
—passed to: *org.omg.CORBA.*DataInputStream^.read_any_array( )
AppConfigurationEntry: javax.security.auth.login
—returned by: **C**onfiguration.getAppConfigurationEntry( )
AppConfigurationEntry.LoginModuleControlFlag:
javax.security.auth.login
—passed to: **A**ppConfigurationEntry( )
—returned by: **A**ppConfigurationEntry.getControlFlag( )
—fields: **A**ppConfigurationEntry.LoginModuleControlFlag
< OPTIONAL, REQUIRED, REQUISITE, SUFFICIENT >
append( ): **S**tringBuffer
appendChild( ): *N*ode_
appendData( ): *C*haracterData^
appendRemainingComponent( ): **N**amingException_
ResolveResult
appendRemainingName( ): **N**amingException_ **R**esolveResult
appendReplacement( ): **M**atcher
appendTail( ): **M**atcher
APPLET: *javax.naming.Context*_
Applet^: java.applet
—passed to: *A*ppletInitializer < activate( ), initialize( ) >
org.omg.CORBA.**O**RB_ < init( ), set_parameters( ) >
AppletInitializer: java.beans
—passed to: **B**eans.instantiate( )
ApplicationException: org.omg.CORBA.portable
—thrown by: org.omg.CORBA.portable.**D**elegate_.invoke( )
LocalObject_._invoke( )
org.omg.CORBA.portable.**O**bjectImpl_._invoke( )
applyLocalizedPattern( ): **D**ecimalFormat^ **S**impleDateFormat^
applyPattern( ): **C**hoiceFormat^ **D**ecimalFormat^
MessageFormat^ **S**impleDateFormat^
appRandom: **S**ignatureSpi_
APRIL: **C**alendar_
ARABIC: **C**haracter.UnicodeBlock^
ARABIC_PRESENTATION_FORMS_A:
Character.UnicodeBlock^
ARABIC_PRESENTATION_FORMS_B:
Character.UnicodeBlock^
areFieldsSet: **C**alendar_
ARG_IN: org.omg.CORBA

ARG_INOUT: org.omg.CORBA
ARG_OUT: org.omg.CORBA
ARGUMENT: **M**essageFormat.Field^
argument: **P**arameter
arguments( ): *O*RBInitInfoOperations_ **R**equest
*R*equestInfoOperations_ **S**erverRequest
ArithmeticException: java.lang
ARMENIAN: **C**haracter.UnicodeBlock^
ARRAY: **T**ypes
Array: java.lang.reflect
Array: java.sql
—passed to: *P*reparedStatement^.setArray( )
*R*esultSet^.updateArray( ) *R*owSet^.setArray( )
*S*QLOutput.writeArray( )
—returned by: *C*allableStatement^.getArray( )
*R*esultSet^.getArray( ) *S*QLInput.readArray( )
array( ): **B**yteBuffer^ **C**harBuffer^ **D**oubleBuffer^ **F**loatBuffer^
IntBuffer^ **L**ongBuffer^ **S**hortBuffer^
arraycopy( ): **S**ystem
ArrayIndexOutOfBoundsException^: java.lang
—thrown by: java.lang.reflect.**A**rray < get( ), getBoolean( ),
getByte( ), getChar( ), getDouble( ), getFloat( ), getInt( ),
getLong( ), getShort( ), set( ), setBoolean( ), setByte( ),
setChar( ), setDouble( ), setFloat( ), setInt( ), setLong( ),
setShort( ) > javax.sound.midi.**T**rack.get( )
ArrayList^: java.util
—returned by: **C**ollections.list( )
—fields: **B**eanContextServicesSupport^.bcsListeners
BeanContextSupport^.bcmListeners
java.awt.dnd.**D**ragGestureRecognizer.events
arrayOffset( ): **B**yteBuffer^ **C**harBuffer^ **D**oubleBuffer^
FloatBuffer^ **I**ntBuffer^ **L**ongBuffer^ **S**hortBuffer^
Arrays: java.util
ArrayStoreException: java.lang
ARROWS: **C**haracter.UnicodeBlock^
asCharBuffer( ): **B**yteBuffer^
asDoubleBuffer( ): **B**yteBuffer^
asFloatBuffer( ): **B**yteBuffer^
asin( ): **M**ath **S**trictMath
asIntBuffer( ): **B**yteBuffer^
asList( ): **A**rrays
asLongBuffer( ): **B**yteBuffer^
asReadOnlyBuffer( ): **B**yteBuffer^ **C**harBuffer^ **D**oubleBuffer^
FloatBuffer^ **I**ntBuffer^ **L**ongBuffer^ **S**hortBuffer^
AssertionError: java.lang
asShortBuffer( ): **B**yteBuffer^
assign( ): _DynAnyStub^ _DynArrayStub^
_DynEnumStub^ _DynFixedStub^ _DynSequenceStub^
_DynStructStub^ _DynUnionStub^ _DynValueStub^
org.omg.CORBA.**D**ynAny^ *D*ynAnyOperations_
AsynchronousCloseException^: java.nio.channels
—subclasses: **C**losedByInterruptException^
—thrown by: **A**bstractInterruptibleChannel_.end( )
atan( ): **M**ath **S**trictMath
atan2( ): **M**ath **S**trictMath
attach( ): **S**electionKey_
attachment( ): **S**electionKey_
Attr^: org.w3c.dom
—passed to: *E*lement^ < removeAttributeNode( ),
setAttributeNode( ), setAttributeNodeNS( ) >
javax.imageio.metadata.**I**IOMetadataNode
< removeAttributeNode( ), setAttributeNode( ),
setAttributeNodeNS( ) >
—returned by: *D*ocument^ < createAttribute( ),
createAttributeNS( ) > *E*lement^ < getAttributeNode( ),
getAttributeNodeNS( ), removeAttributeNode( ),
setAttributeNode( ), setAttributeNodeNS( ) >
javax.imageio.metadata.**I**IOMetadataNode
< getAttributeNode( ), getAttributeNodeNS( ),
removeAttributeNode( ), setAttributeNodeNS( ),
setAttributeNodeNS( ) >

Attribute^: javax.naming.directory
—passed to: *javax.naming.directory.Attributes*^.put( )
BasicAttributes.put( ) ModificationItem( )
—returned by: *javax.naming.directory.Attributes* < get( ), put( ),
remove( ) > BasicAttributes < get( ), put( ), remove( ) >
ModificationItem.getAttribute( )
—implemented by: BasicAttribute
ATTRIBUTE_NODE: *Node*
AttributedCharacterIterator^: java.text
—passed to: AttributedString( ) Bidi( )
java.awt.Graphics.drawString( )
java.awt.Graphics2D^.drawString( ) *java.awt.im* ←
.spi.*InputMethodContext*.dispatchInputMethodEvent( )
java.awt.event.InputMethodEvent( )
java.awt.font.LineBreakMeasurer < deleteChar( ), insertChar( ),
LineBreakMeasurer( ) > java.awt.font.TextLayout( )
java.awt.font.TextMeasurer < deleteChar( ), insertChar( ),
TextMeasurer( ) >
—returned by: AttributedString.getIterator( )
Format.formatToCharacterIterator( )
java.awt.event.InputMethodEvent^.getText( )
java.awt.im.InputMethodRequests
< cancelLatestCommittedText( ), getCommittedText( ),
getSelectedText( ) >
AttributedCharacterIterator.Attribute: java.text
—subclasses: Format.Field^ java.awt.font.TextAttribute^
—descendents: DateFormat.Field^ MessageFormat.Field^
NumberFormat.Field^
—passed to: *AttributedCharacterIterator*^
< getAttribute( ), getRunLimit( ), getRunStart( ) >
AttributedString < addAttribute( ), AttributedString( ),
getIterator( ) > *java.awt.im.InputMethodRequests*
< cancelLatestCommittedText( ), getCommittedText( ),
getSelectedText( ) >
—returned by: java.awt.Font.getAvailableAttributes( )
—fields: AttributedCharacterIterator.Attribute
< INPUT_METHOD_SEGMENT, LANGUAGE, READING >
attributeDecl( ): *DeclHandler*
AttributedString: java.text
AttributeInUseException^: javax.naming.directory
AttributeList: org.xml.sax
—passed to: AttributeListImpl < AttributeListImpl( ),
setAttributeList( ) > *DocumentHandler*.startElement( )
HandlerBase.startElement( ) ParserAdapter.startElement( )
—implemented by: AttributeListImpl
AttributeListImpl: org.xml.sax.helpers
AttributeModificationException^: javax.naming.directory
attributeNames( ): *FeatureDescriptor*
attributeNoNulls: *DatabaseMetaData*
attributeNullable: *DatabaseMetaData*
attributeNullableUnknown: *DatabaseMetaData*
Attributes: java.util.jar
—passed to: java.util.jar.Attributes( )
—returned by: JarEntry^.getAttributes( ) JarURLConnection^
< getAttributes( ), getMainAttributes( ) > Manifest
< getAttributes( ), getMainAttributes( ) >
Attributes^: javax.naming.directory
—passed to: *DirContext*^ < bind( ), createSubcontext( ),
modifyAttributes( ), rebind( ), search( ) >
DirectoryManager^ < getObjectInstance( ),
getStateToBind( ) > *DirObjectFactory*^.getObjectInstance( )
DirStateFactory^.getStateToBind( ) DirStateFactory.Result( )
InitialDirContext^ < bind( ), createSubcontext( ),
modifyAttributes( ), rebind( ), search( ) > SearchResult^
< SearchResult( ), setAttributes( ) >
—returned by: *DirContext*^.getAttributes( )
DirStateFactory.Result.getAttributes( )
InitialDirContext^.getAttributes( ) SearchResult^.getAttributes( )
—implemented by: BasicAttributes
Attributes: org.xml.sax

—passed to: AttributesImpl < AttributesImpl( ), setAttributes( ) >
org.xml.sax.*ContentHandler*.startElement( )
DefaultHandler.startElement( ) XMLFilterImpl.startElement( )
XMLReaderAdapter.startElement( )
—implemented by: AttributesImpl
Attributes.Name: java.util.jar
—passed to: java.util.jar.Attributes.getValue( )
—fields: Attributes.Name < CLASS_PATH, CONTENT_TYPE,
EXTENSION_INSTALLATION, EXTENSION_LIST,
EXTENSION_NAME, IMPLEMENTATION_TITLE,
IMPLEMENTATION_URL, IMPLEMENTATION_VENDOR,
IMPLEMENTATION_VENDOR_ID, IMPLEMENTATION_VERSION,
MAIN_CLASS, MANIFEST_VERSION, SEALED,
SIGNATURE_VERSION, SPECIFICATION_TITLE,
SPECIFICATION_VENDOR, SPECIFICATION_VERSION >
AttributesImpl: org.xml.sax.helpers
attrID: BasicAttribute
AUGUST: Calendar
AuthenticationException^: javax.naming
AuthenticationNotSupportedException^: javax.naming
Authenticator: java.net
—passed to: Authenticator.setDefault( )
AUTHORITATIVE: *javax.naming.Context*
AuthPermission^: javax.security.auth
available( ): java.io.InputStream *ObjectInput*^ SocketImpl
availableCharsets( ): Charset
availableProcessors( ): Runtime
averageBytesPerChar( ): CharsetEncoder
averageCharsPerByte( ): CharsetDecoder
avoidingGui( ): BeanContextSupport *Visibility*
BackingStoreException: java.util.prefs
—thrown by: AbstractPreferences^ < childrenNamesSpi( ),
flushSpi( ), getChild( ), keysSpi( ), removeNodeSpi( ),
syncSpi( ) > Preferences < childrenNames( ), clear( ),
exportNode( ), exportSubtree( ), flush( ), keys( ), nodeExists( ),
removeNode( ), sync( ) >
BAD_BINDINGS: GSSException
BAD_CONTEXT^: org.omg.CORBA
BAD_INV_ORDER^: org.omg.CORBA
—thrown by: Any < extract_Streamable( ), insert_fixed( ) >
BAD_MECH: GSSException
BAD_MIC: GSSException
BAD_NAME: GSSException
BAD_NAMETYPE: GSSException
BAD_OPERATION^: org.omg.CORBA
—thrown by: Any < extract_any( ), extract_boolean( ),
extract_char( ), extract_double( ), extract_float( ), extract_long( ),
extract_longlong( ), extract_Object( ), extract_octet( ),
extract_Principal( ), extract_short( ), extract_string( ),
extract_TypeCode( ), extract_ulong( ), extract_ulonglong( ),
extract_ushort( ), extract_Value( ), extract_wchar( ),
extract_wstring( ) >
BAD_PARAM^: org.omg.CORBA
—thrown by: Any.insert_Object( )
org.omg.CORBA_2_3.ORB^.get_value_def( )
BAD_POLICY: org.omg.CORBA
BAD_POLICY_TYPE: org.omg.CORBA
BAD_POLICY_VALUE: org.omg.CORBA
BAD_QOP: GSSException
BAD_STATUS: GSSException
BAD_TYPECODE^: org.omg.CORBA
BadKind^: org.omg.CORBA.TypeCodePackage
—thrown by: TypeCode < concrete_base_type( ), content_type( ),
default_index( ), discriminator_type( ), fixed_digits( ),
fixed_scale( ), id( ), length( ), member_count( ), member_label( ),
member_name( ), member_type( ), member_visibility( ), name( ),
type_modifier( ) >
BadPaddingException^: javax.crypto
—thrown by: Cipher.doFinal( ) CipherSpi.engineDoFinal( )
SealedObject.getObject( )
baseIsLeftToRight( ): Bidi
baseWireHandle: *ObjectStreamConstants*

B

BindingIteratorOperations : org.omg.CosNaming
—extended by: *BindingIterator*^
—implemented by: BindingIteratorPOA^
BindingIteratorPOA^: org.omg.CosNaming
BindingListHelper: org.omg.CosNaming
BindingListHolder: org.omg.CosNaming
—passed to: _BindingIteratorStub^.next_n( )
_NamingContextExtStub^.list( ) _NamingContextStub^.list( )
BindingIteratorOperations .next_n( )
NamingContextOperations .list( )
BindingType: org.omg.CosNaming
—passed to: org.omg.CosNaming.**B**inding( )
BindingTypeHelper < insert( ), write( ) > BindingTypeHolder( )
—returned by: BindingType.from_int( ) BindingTypeHelper
< extract( ), read( ) >
—fields: org.omg.CosNaming.**B**inding.binding_type
BindingType < ncontext, nobject > BindingTypeHolder.value
BindingTypeHelper: org.omg.CosNaming
BindingTypeHolder: org.omg.CosNaming
BIT: **T**ypes
bitCount( ): **B**igInteger^
bitLength( ): **B**igInteger^
BitSet: java.util
—passed to: BitSet < and( ), andNot( ), intersects( ), or( ), xor( ) >
javax.swing.text.html.parser.**D**TD.defineElement( )
—returned by: BitSet.get( )
—fields: javax.swing.text.html.parser.**E**lement < exclusions,
inclusions >
BLOB: **T**ypes
Blob: java.sql
—passed to: *Blob*.position( ) *PreparedStatement*^.setBlob( )
ResultSet .updateBlob( ) *RowSet*^.setBlob( )
SQLOutput.writeBlob( )
—returned by: *CallableStatement*^.getBlob( ) *ResultSet* .getBlob( )
SQLInput.readBlob( )
BLOCK_ELEMENTS: **C**haracter.UnicodeBlock^
blockingLock( ): SelectableChannel^
BOOLEAN: **T**ypes
Boolean: java.lang
—passed to: javax.swing.**D**efaultDesktopManager.setWasIcon( )
—returned by: Boolean.valueOf( )
javax.swing.filechooser.**F**ileSystemView.isTraversable( )
javax.swing.filechooser.**F**ileView.isTraversable( )
—fields: Boolean < FALSE, TRUE > java.awt.font.**T**extAttribute^
< RUN_DIRECTION_LTR, RUN_DIRECTION_RTL,
STRIKETHROUGH_ON, SWAP_COLORS_ON >
BooleanHolder: org.omg.CORBA
BooleanSeqHelper: org.omg.CORBA
BooleanSeqHolder: org.omg.CORBA
—passed
to: *org.omg.CORBA.DataInputStream*^.read_boolean_array( )
booleanValue( ): **B**oolean
BOPOMOFO: **C**haracter.UnicodeBlock^
BOPOMOFO_EXTENDED: **C**haracter.UnicodeBlock^
Bounds: org.omg.CORBA
—thrown by: **C**ontextList < item( ), remove( ) > ExceptionList
< item( ), remove( ) > **N**VList < item( ), remove( ) >
Bounds^: org.omg.CORBA.TypeCodePackage
—thrown by: **T**ypeCode < member_label( ), member_name( ),
member_type( ), member_visibility( ) >
BOX_DRAWING: **C**haracter.UnicodeBlock^
BoxedValueHelper: org.omg.CORBA.portable
—passed
to: org.omg.CORBA_2_3.portable.**I**nputStream^.read_value( )
org.omg.CORBA_2_3.portable.**O**utputStream^.write_value( )
—implemented by: **S**tringValueHelper **W**StringValueHelper
BRAILLE_PATTERNS: **C**haracter.UnicodeBlock^
BreakIterator: java.text
—passed to: java.awt.font.**L**ineBreakMeasurer( )
—returned by: BreakIterator < getCharacterInstance( ),
getLineInstance( ), getSentenceInstance( ), getWordInstance( ) >

BRIEF: LogStream^
buf: **B**ufferedInputStream^ **B**ufferedOutputStream^
ByteArrayInputStream^ **B**yteArrayOutputStream^
CharArrayReader^ **C**harArrayWriter^ **D**eflaterOutputStream^
InflaterInputStream^ **P**ushbackInputStream^
buffer: **P**ipedInputStream^ **S**tringBufferInputStream^
Buffer^: java.nio
—subclasses: **B**yteBuffer^ **C**harBuffer^ **D**oubleBuffer^
FloatBuffer^ **I**ntBuffer^ **L**ongBuffer^ **S**hortBuffer^
—descendents: **M**appedByteBuffer^
—returned by: Buffer < clear( ), flip( ), limit( ), mark( ),
position( ), reset( ), rewind( ) >
BufferedInputStream^: java.io
BufferedOutputStream^: java.io
BufferedReader^: java.io
—subclasses: **L**ineNumberReader^
BufferedWriter^: java.io
BufferOverflowException: java.nio
BufferUnderflowException: java.nio
build( ): **C**ertPathBuilder
Byte^: java.lang
—passed to: Byte^.compareTo( )
—returned by: Byte^ < decode( ), valueOf( ) >
ByteArrayInputStream^: java.io
ByteArrayOutputStream^: java.io
ByteBuffer^: java.nio
—subclasses: **M**appedByteBuffer^
—passed to: ByteBuffer^.put( ) **C**harset.decode( )
CharsetDecoder < decode( ), decodeLoop( ) >
CharsetEncoder < encode( ), encodeLoop( ), flush( ),
implFlush( ) > **D**atagramChannel^ < read( ),
receive( ), send( ), write( ) > **F**ileChannel^
< read( ), write( ) > *GatheringByteChannel*^.write( )
ReadableByteChannel^.read( )
ScatteringByteChannel^.read( ) **S**ocketChannel^ < read( ),
write( ) > *WritableByteChannel*^.write( )
—returned by: ByteBuffer^ < allocate( ), allocateDirect( ),
asReadOnlyBuffer( ), compact( ), duplicate( ), get( ), order( ),
put( ), putChar( ), putDouble( ), putFloat( ), putInt( ),
putLong( ), putShort( ), slice( ), wrap( ) > **C**harset.encode( )
CharsetEncoder.encode( )
ByteChannel^: java.nio.channels
—implemented by: **D**atagramChannel^ **F**ileChannel^
SocketChannel^
ByteHolder: org.omg.CORBA
ByteOrder: java.nio
—passed to: **B**yteBuffer^.order( )
javax.imageio.stream.*ImageInputStream*^.setByteOrder( )
javax.imageio.stream.**I**mageInputStreamImpl.setByteOrder( )
—returned by: ByteBuffer^.order( ) ByteOrder.nativeOrder( )
CharBuffer^.order( ) DoubleBuffer^.order( ) FloatBuffer^.order( )
javax.imageio.stream.*ImageInputStream*^.getByteOrder( )
javax.imageio.stream.**I**mageInputStreamImpl.getByteOrder( )
IntBuffer^.order( ) LongBuffer^.order( ) ShortBuffer^.order( )
—fields: ByteOrder < BIG_ENDIAN, LITTLE_ENDIAN >
javax.imageio.stream.**I**mageInputStreamImpl.byteOrder
bytesTransferred: InterruptedIOException^
byteValue( ): **N**umber
cachedChildren( ): **A**bstractPreferences^
calendar: DateFormat^
Calendar : java.util
—subclasses: **G**regorianCalendar^
—passed to: *CallableStatement*^ < getDate( ), getTime( ),
getTimestamp( ), setDate( ), setTime( ), setTimestamp( ) >
DateFormat^.setCalendar( ) *PreparedStatement* < setDate( ),
setTime( ), setTimestamp( ) > *ResultSet* < getDate( ),
getTime( ), getTimestamp( ) > *RowSet*^ < setDate( ), setTime( ),
setTimestamp( ) >
—returned by: Calendar .getInstance( ) DateFormat^.getCalendar( )
—fields: DateFormat^.calendar
CallableStatement^: java.sql

—returned by: **C**onnection.prepareCall( )
Callback: javax.security.auth.callback
—passed to: *CallbackHandler*.handle( )
   UnsupportedCallbackException( )
—returned by: **U**nsupportedCallbackException.getCallback( )
—implemented by: **C**hoiceCallback **C**onfirmationCallback
   LanguageCallback **N**ameCallback **P**asswordCallback
   TextInputCallback **T**extOutputCallback
CallbackHandler: javax.security.auth.callback
—passed to: **L**oginContext( ) *LoginModule*.initialize( )
CANADA: **L**ocale
CANADA_FRENCH: **L**ocale
CANCEL: **C**onfirmationCallback
cancel( ): **S**electionKey *java.sql.Statement* java.util.**T**imer
   TimerTask
CancelledKeyException^: java.nio.channels
cancelledKeys( ): **A**bstractSelector^
cancelRowUpdates( ): *ResultSet*
canEncode( ): **C**harset **C**harsetEncoder
CannotProceed^: org.omg.CosNaming.NamingContextPackage
—passed to: **C**annotProceedHelper < insert( ), write( ) >
   CannotProceedHolder( )
—returned by: **C**annotProceedHelper < extract( ), read( ) >
—thrown by: _NamingContextExtStub^ < bind( ), bind_context( ),
   bind_new_context( ), rebind( ), rebind_context( ), resolve( ),
   resolve_str( ), unbind( ) > _NamingContextStub^
   < bind( ), bind_context( ), bind_new_context( ),
   rebind( ), rebind_context( ), resolve( ), unbind( ) >
   NamingContextExtOperations^.resolve_str( )
   NamingContextOperations < bind( ), bind_context( ),
   bind_new_context( ), rebind( ), rebind_context( ), resolve( ),
   unbind( ) >
—fields: **C**annotProceedHolder.value
CannotProceedException^: javax.naming
—passed to: **D**irectoryManager^.getContinuationDirContext( )
   NamingManager.getContinuationContext( )
CannotProceedHelper:
   org.omg.CosNaming.NamingContextPackage
CannotProceedHolder:
   org.omg.CosNaming.NamingContextPackage
CANON_EQ: **P**attern
CANONICAL: **X**500Principal
CANONICAL_DECOMPOSITION: **C**ollator
canonicalize( ): *GSSName*
canRead( ): **F**ile
canWrite( ): **F**ile
capacity( ): **B**uffer **S**tringBuffer **V**ector^
capacityIncrement( ): **V**ector^
cardinality( ): **B**itSet
CASE_INSENSITIVE: **P**attern
CASE_INSENSITIVE_ORDER: **S**tring
CDATA_SECTION_ELEMENTS: **O**utputKeys
CDATA_SECTION_NODE: *Node*
CDATASection^: org.w3c.dom
—returned by: *Document*^.createCDATASection( )
ceil( ): **M**ath **S**trictMath
Certificate: java.security
—passed to: **I**dentity < addCertificate( ), removeCertificate( ) >
—returned by: **I**dentity.certificates( )
Certificate: java.security.cert
—subclasses: java.security.cert.**X**509Certificate^
—passed to: *CertSelector*^.match( ) **C**ipher.init( ) **C**odeSource( )
   CRL.isRevoked( ) **K**eyStore < getCertificateAlias( ),
   setCertificateEntry( ), setKeyEntry( ) > **K**eyStoreSpi
   < engineGetCertificateAlias( ), engineSetCertificateEntry( ),
   engineSetKeyEntry( ) > **P**KIXCertPathChecker.check( )
   Signature^.initVerify( ) **U**nresolvedPermission( )
   X509CertSelector.match( )
—returned by: **C**ertificateFactory.generateCertificate( )
   CertificateFactorySpi.engineGenerateCertificate( )
   CodeSource.getCertificates( ) **H**andshakeCompletedEvent^
   < getLocalCertificates( ), getPeerCertificates( ) >

HttpsURLConnection^ < getLocalCertificates( ),
   getServerCertificates( ) > **J**arEntry^.getCertificates( )
   JarURLConnection^.getCertificates( ) **K**eyStore
   < getCertificate( ), getCertificateChain( ) > **K**eyStoreSpi
   < engineGetCertificate( ), engineGetCertificateChain( ) >
   SSLSession < getLocalCertificates( ), getPeerCertificates( ) >
Certificate: javax.security.cert
—subclasses: javax.security.cert.**X**509Certificate^
Certificate.CertificateRep: java.security.cert
CertificateEncodingException^: java.security.cert
—thrown by: java.security.cert.**C**ertificate.getEncoded( )
   CertPath.getEncoded( )
   java.security.cert.**X**509Certificate^.getTBSCertificate( )
CertificateEncodingException^: javax.security.cert
—thrown by: javax.security.cert.**C**ertificate.getEncoded( )
CertificateException^: java.security.cert
—subclasses: java.security.cert.**C**ertificateEncodingException^
   java.security.cert.**C**ertificateExpiredException^
   java.security.cert.**C**ertificateNotYetValidException^
   java.security.cert.**C**ertificateParsingException^
—thrown by: java.security.cert.**C**ertificate.verify( )
   CertificateFactory < generateCertificate( ), generateCertificates( ),
   generateCertPath( ), getInstance( ) > **C**ertificateFactorySpi
   < engineGenerateCertificate( ), engineGenerateCertificates( ),
   engineGenerateCertPath( ) > **K**eyStore < load( ),
   store( ) > **K**eyStoreSpi < engineLoad( ), engineStore( ) >
   X509TrustManager^ < checkClientTrusted( ),
   checkServerTrusted( ) >
CertificateException: javax.security.cert
—subclasses: javax.security.cert.**C**ertificateEncodingException^
   javax.security.cert.**C**ertificateExpiredException^
   javax.security.cert.**C**ertificateNotYetValidException^
   javax.security.cert.**C**ertificateParsingException^
—thrown by: javax.security.cert.**C**ertificate.verify( )
   javax.security.cert.**X**509Certificate^.getInstance( )
CertificateExpiredException^: java.security.cert
—thrown by: java.security.cert.**X**509Certificate^.checkValidity( )
CertificateExpiredException^: javax.security.cert
—thrown by: javax.security.cert.**X**509Certificate^.checkValidity( )
CertificateFactory: java.security.cert
—returned by: **C**ertificateFactory.getInstance( )
CertificateFactorySpi: java.security.cert
—passed to: **C**ertificateFactory( )
CertificateNotYetValidException^: java.security.cert
—thrown by: java.security.cert.**X**509Certificate^.checkValidity( )
CertificateNotYetValidException^: javax.security.cert
—thrown by: javax.security.cert.**X**509Certificate^.checkValidity( )
CertificateParsingException^: java.security.cert
—thrown by: java.security.cert.**X**509Certificate^
   < getExtendedKeyUsage( ), getIssuerAlternativeNames( ),
   getSubjectAlternativeNames( ) >
CertificateParsingException^: javax.security.cert
certificates( ): **I**dentity
CertPath: java.security.cert
—passed to: **C**ertPathValidator.validate( )
   CertPathValidatorException( )
   CertPathValidatorSpi.engineValidate( )
   PKIXCertPathBuilderResult( )
—returned by: **C**ertificateFactory.generateCertPath( )
   CertificateFactorySpi.engineGenerateCertPath( )
   CertPathBuilderResult^.getCertPath( )
   CertPathValidatorException^.getCertPath( )
   PKIXCertPathBuilderResult^.getCertPath( )
CertPath.CertPathRep: java.security.cert
CertPathBuilder: java.security.cert
—returned by: **C**ertPathBuilder.getInstance( )
CertPathBuilderException^: java.security.cert
—thrown by: **C**ertPathBuilder.build( )
   CertPathBuilderSpi.engineBuild( )
CertPathBuilderResult^: java.security.cert
—returned by: **C**ertPathBuilder.build( )
   CertPathBuilderSpi.engineBuild( )

— implemented by: **P**KIXCertPathBuilderResult˄
CertPathBuilderSpi: java.security.cert
— passed to: **C**ertPathBuilder( )
CertPathParameters˄: java.security.cert
— passed to: **C**ertPathBuilder.build( )
   CertPathBuilderSpi.engineBuild( )   **C**ertPathValidator.validate( )
   CertPathValidatorSpi.engineValidate( )
— implemented by: **P**KIXParameters˅
CertPathValidator: java.security.cert
— returned by: **C**ertPathValidator.getInstance( )
CertPathValidatorException˄: java.security.cert
— thrown by: **C**ertPathValidator.validate( )
   CertPathValidatorSpi.engineValidate( )   **P**KIXCertPathChecker
   < check( ), init( ) >
CertPathValidatorResult˄: java.security.cert
— returned by: **C**ertPathValidator.validate( )
   CertPathValidatorSpi.engineValidate( )
— implemented by: **P**KIXCertPathValidatorResult˅
CertPathValidatorSpi: java.security.cert
— passed to: **C**ertPathValidator( )
CertSelector˄: java.security.cert
— passed to: **C**ertStore.getCertificates( )
   CertStoreSpi.engineGetCertificates( )   **P**KIXBuilderParameters( )
   PKIXParameters˅.setTargetCertConstraints( )
— returned by: **P**KIXParameters˅.getTargetCertConstraints( )
— implemented by: **X**509CertSelector
CertStore: java.security.cert
— passed to: **P**KIXParameters˅.addCertStore( )
— returned by: **C**ertStore.getInstance( )
CertStoreException˄: java.security.cert
— thrown by: **C**ertStore < getCertificates( ), getCRLs( ) >
   CertStoreSpi < engineGetCertificates( ), engineGetCRLs( ) >
CertStoreParameters˄: java.security.cert
— passed to: **C**ertStore < CertStore( ), getInstance( ) >
   CertStoreSpi( )
— returned by: **C**ertStore.getCertStoreParameters( )
— implemented by: **C**ollectionCertStoreParameters
   LDAPCertStoreParameters
CertStoreSpi: java.security.cert
— passed to: **C**ertStore( )
changeInfo: **N**amingEvent˄
Channel˅: java.nio.channels
— extended by: ***I***nterruptibleChannel˄ ***R***eadableByteChannel˅
   WritableByteChannel˅
— descendents: ***B***yteChannel˄ ***G***atheringByteChannel˄
   ScatteringByteChannel˄
— implemented by: **A**bstractInterruptibleChannel˅
channel( ): **F**ileLock **S**electionKey˅
ChannelBinding: org.ietf.jgss
— passed to: ***G***SSContext.setChannelBinding( )
Channels: java.nio.channels
CHAR: **T**ypes
Character: java.lang
— passed to: java.awt.**A**WTKeyStroke.getAWTKeyStroke( )
   Character.compareTo( ) javax.swing.**K**eyStroke˄.getKeyStroke( )
Character.Subset˅: java.lang
— subclasses: **C**haracter.UnicodeBlock˄
   java.awt.im.**I**nputSubset˄
— passed to: java.awt.im.**I**nputContext.setCharacterSubsets( )
   *java.awt.im.spi.**I**nputMethod.setCharacterSubsets( )*
Character.UnicodeBlock˄: java.lang
— returned by: **C**haracter.UnicodeBlock˄.of( )
— fields: **C**haracter.UnicodeBlock˄
   < ALPHABETIC_PRESENTATION_FORMS,
   ARABIC, ARABIC_PRESENTATION_FORMS_A,
   ARABIC_PRESENTATION_FORMS_B, ARMENIAN,
   ARROWS, BASIC_LATIN, BENGALI, BLOCK_ELEMENTS,
   BOPOMOFO, BOPOMOFO_EXTENDED, BOX_DRAWING,
   BRAILLE_PATTERNS, CHEROKEE, CJK_COMPATIBILITY,
   CJK_COMPATIBILITY_FORMS, CJK_COMPATIBILITY_IDEOGRAPHS,
   CJK_RADICALS_SUPPLEMENT,

   CJK_SYMBOLS_AND_PUNCTUATION, CJK_UNIFIED_IDEOGRAPHS,
   CJK_UNIFIED_IDEOGRAPHS_EXTENSION_A,
   COMBINING_DIACRITICAL_MARKS, COMBINING_HALF_MARKS,
   COMBINING_MARKS_FOR_SYMBOLS, CONTROL_PICTURES,
   CURRENCY_SYMBOLS, CYRILLIC, DEVANAGARI,
   DINGBATS, ENCLOSED_ALPHANUMERICS,
   ENCLOSED_CJK_LETTERS_AND_MONTHS, ETHIOPIC,
   GENERAL_PUNCTUATION, GEOMETRIC_SHAPES,
   GEORGIAN, GREEK, GREEK_EXTENDED, GUJARATI,
   GURMUKHI, HALFWIDTH_AND_FULLWIDTH_FORMS,
   HANGUL_COMPATIBILITY_JAMO, HANGUL_JAMO,
   HANGUL_SYLLABLES, HEBREW, HIRAGANA,
   IDEOGRAPHIC_DESCRIPTION_CHARACTERS, IPA_EXTENSIONS,
   KANBUN, KANGXI_RADICALS, KANNADA,
   KATAKANA, KHMER, LAO, LATIN_1_SUPPLEMENT,
   LATIN_EXTENDED_A, LATIN_EXTENDED_ADDITIONAL,
   LATIN_EXTENDED_B, LETTERLIKE_SYMBOLS,
   MALAYALAM, MATHEMATICAL_OPERATORS,
   MISCELLANEOUS_SYMBOLS, MISCELLANEOUS_TECHNICAL,
   MONGOLIAN, MYANMAR, NUMBER_FORMS,
   OGHAM, OPTICAL_CHARACTER_RECOGNITION,
   ORIYA, PRIVATE_USE_AREA, RUNIC, SINHALA,
   SMALL_FORM_VARIANTS, SPACING_MODIFIER_LETTERS,
   SPECIALS, SUPERSCRIPTS_AND_SUBSCRIPTS,
   SURROGATES_AREA, SYRIAC, TAMIL, TELUGU, THAANA,
   THAI, TIBETAN, UNIFIED_CANADIAN_ABORIGINAL_SYLLABICS,
   YI_RADICALS, YI_SYLLABLES >
CharacterCodingException˄: java.nio.charset
— subclasses: **M**alformedInputException˄
   UnmappableCharacterException˄
— thrown by: **C**harsetDecoder.decode( )
   CharsetEncoder.encode( ) **C**oderResult.throwException( )
CharacterData˅: org.w3c.dom
— extended by: ***C***omment˄ ***T***ext˅
— descendents: ***C***DATASection˄
CharacterIterator˅: java.text
— extended by: ***A***ttributedCharacterIterator˄
— passed to: **B**reakIterator.setText( )
   CollationElementIterator.setText( ) java.awt.**F**ont
   < canDisplayUpTo( ), createGlyphVector( ), getLineMetrics( ),
   getStringBounds( ) > java.awt.**F**ontMetrics
   < getLineMetrics( ), getStringBounds( ) >
   RuleBasedCollator˄.getCollationElementIterator( )
— returned by: **B**reakIterator.getText( )
— implemented by: javax.swing.text.**S**egment
   StringCharacterIterator
characters( ): org.xml.sax.**C**ontentHandler˅ **D**efaultHandler
   DocumentHandler **H**andlerBase **P**arserAdapter
   XMLFilterImpl **X**MLReaderAdapter
CharArrayReader˄: java.io
CharArrayWriter˄: java.io
charAt( ): CharBuffer˄ ***C***harSequence **S**tring **S**tringBuffer
CharBuffer˄: java.nio
— passed to: **C**harBuffer˄.put( ) **C**harset.encode( )
   CharsetDecoder < decode( ), decodeLoop( ), flush( ),
   implFlush( ) > **C**harsetEncoder < encode( ), encodeLoop( ) >
— returned by: **B**yteBuffer˄.asCharBuffer( ) **C**harBuffer˄ < allocate( ),
   asReadOnlyBuffer( ), compact( ), duplicate( ), get( ), put( ),
   slice( ), wrap( ) > **C**harset.decode( ) **C**harsetDecoder.decode( )
CharConversionException˄: java.io
CharHolder: org.omg.CORBA
CharSeqHelper: org.omg.CORBA
CharSeqHolder: org.omg.CORBA
— passed
   to: *org.omg.CORBA.**D**ataInputStream*˄.read_char_array( )
CharSequence: java.lang
— passed to: **C**harBuffer˄.wrap( ) **C**harsetEncoder.canEncode( )
   Matcher.reset( ) **P**attern < matcher( ), matches( ), split( ) >
— returned by: **C**harBuffer˄.subSequence( )
   CharSequence.subSequence( ) **S**tring.subSequence( )
   StringBuffer.subSequence( )
— implemented by: **C**harBuffer˄ **S**tring **S**tringBuffer

Charset: java.nio.charset
—passed to: **C**harset.contains( ) **C**harsetDecoder( )
CharsetEncoder( ) **I**nputStreamReader( )
OutputStreamWriter( )
—returned by: **C**harset.forName( ) **C**harsetDecoder < charset( ),
detectedCharset( ) > **C**harsetEncoder.charset( )
CharsetProvider.charsetForName( )
charset( ): **C**harsetDecoder **C**harsetEncoder
CharsetDecoder: java.nio.charset
—passed to: **C**hannels.newReader( ) **I**nputStreamReader( )
—returned by: **C**harset.newDecoder( ) **C**harsetDecoder
< onMalformedInput( ), onUnmappableCharacter( ), replaceWith( ),
reset( ) >
CharsetEncoder: java.nio.charset
—passed to: **C**hannels.newWriter( ) **O**utputStreamWriter( )
—returned by: **C**harset.newEncoder( ) **C**harsetEncoder
< onMalformedInput( ), onUnmappableCharacter( ), replaceWith( ),
reset( ) >
charsetForName( ): **C**harsetProvider
CharsetProvider: java.nio.charset.spi
charsets( ): **C**harsetProvider
charValue( ): **C**haracter
check( ): **P**KIXCertPathChecker
checkAccept( ): **S**ecurityManager⌄
checkAccess( ): **L**ogManager **S**ecurityManager⌄ **T**hread
ThreadGroup
checkAwtEventQueueAccess( ): **S**ecurityManager⌄
checkClientTrusted( ): *X*509TrustManager^
checkConnect( ): **S**ecurityManager⌄
checkCreateClassLoader( ): **S**ecurityManager⌄
checkDelete( ): **S**ecurityManager⌄
CheckedInputStream^: java.util.zip
CheckedOutputStream^: java.util.zip
checkError( ): **P**rintStream^ **P**rintWriter^
checkExec( ): **S**ecurityManager⌄
checkExit( ): **S**ecurityManager⌄
checkGuard( ): *Guard* java.security.**P**ermission⌄
checkLink( ): **S**ecurityManager⌄
checkListen( ): **S**ecurityManager⌄
checkMemberAccess( ): **S**ecurityManager⌄
checkMulticast( ): **S**ecurityManager⌄
checkPackageAccess( ): **S**ecurityManager⌄
checkPackageDefinition( ): **S**ecurityManager⌄
checkPermission( ): **A**ccessControlContext **A**ccessController
Acl^ *AclEntry*^ **S**ecurityManager⌄
checkPrintJobAccess( ): **S**ecurityManager⌄
checkPropertiesAccess( ): **S**ecurityManager⌄
checkPropertyAccess( ): **S**ecurityManager⌄
checkRead( ): **S**ecurityManager⌄
checkSecurityAccess( ): **S**ecurityManager⌄
checkServerTrusted( ): *X*509TrustManager^
checkSetFactory( ): **S**ecurityManager⌄
Checksum: java.util.zip
—passed to: **C**heckedInputStream( ) **C**heckedOutputStream( )
—returned by: **C**heckedInputStream^.getChecksum( )
CheckedOutputStream^.getChecksum( )
—implemented by: **A**dler32 **C**RC32
checkSystemClipboardAccess( ): **S**ecurityManager⌄
checkTopLevelWindow( ): **S**ecurityManager⌄
checkValidity( ): java.security.cert.**X**509Certificate^
javax.security.cert.**X**509Certificate^
checkWrite( ): **S**ecurityManager⌄
CHEROKEE: **C**haracter.UnicodeBlock^
childAdded( ): *NodeChangeListener*^
childDeserializedHook( ): **B**eanContextSupport⌃
childJustAddedHook( ): **B**eanContextSupport⌃
childJustRemovedHook( ): **B**eanContextSupport⌃
childRemoved( ): *NodeChangeListener*^
children: **B**eanContextMembershipEvent^
BeanContextSupport⌃
childrenAdded( ): *BeanContextMembershipListener*^
childrenNames( ): **P**references⌄

childrenNamesSpi( ): **A**bstractPreferences^
childrenRemoved( ): *BeanContextMembershipListener*^
childSpi( ): **A**bstractPreferences^
childValue( ): **I**nheritableThreadLocal^
CHINA: **L**ocale
CHINESE: **L**ocale
ChoiceCallback: javax.security.auth.callback
ChoiceFormat^: java.text
choices: **D**riverPropertyInfo
chooseClientAlias( ): *X*509KeyManager^
chooseServerAlias( ): *X*509KeyManager^
Cipher⌄: javax.crypto
—subclasses: **N**ullCipher^
—passed to: **C**ipherInputStream( ) **C**ipherOutputStream( )
EncryptedPrivateKeyInfo.getKeySpec( ) **S**ealedObject
< getObject( ), SealedObject( ) >
—returned by: **C**ipher⌄.getInstance( )
CipherInputStream^: javax.crypto
CipherOutputStream^: javax.crypto
CipherSpi: javax.crypto
—passed to: **C**ipher( )
CJK_COMPATIBILITY: **C**haracter.UnicodeBlock^
CJK_COMPATIBILITY_FORMS: **C**haracter.UnicodeBlock^
CJK_COMPATIBILITY_IDEOGRAPHS:
Character.UnicodeBlock^
CJK_RADICALS_SUPPLEMENT: **C**haracter.UnicodeBlock^
CJK_SYMBOLS_AND_PUNCTUATION:
Character.UnicodeBlock^
CJK_UNIFIED_IDEOGRAPHS: **C**haracter.UnicodeBlock^
CJK_UNIFIED_IDEOGRAPHS_EXTENSION_A:
Character.UnicodeBlock^
Class: java.lang
—passed to: javax.swing.text.**A**bstractDocument.getListeners( )
javax.swing.**A**bstractListModel.getListeners( )
javax.swing.**A**bstractSpinnerModel.getListeners( )
javax.swing.table.**A**bstractTableModel.getListeners( )
AlgorithmParameters.getParameterSpec( )
AlgorithmParametersSpi.engineGetParameterSpec( )
java.lang.reflect.**A**rray.newInstance( )
javax.print.attribute.AttributeSet < containsKey( ), get( ),
remove( ) > javax.print.attribute.**A**ttributeSetUtilities
< verifyAttributeCategory( ),
verifyAttributeValue( ), verifyCategoryForValue( ) >
java.awt.**A**WTEventMulticaster.getListeners( )
java.awt.**A**WTKeyStroke.registerSubclass( )
BeanContextServiceAvailableEvent( )
BeanContextServiceProvider < getCurrentServiceSelectors( ),
getService( ) > **B**eanContextServiceRevokedEvent^
< BeanContextServiceRevokedEvent^, isServiceClass( ) >
BeanContextServices^ < addService( ),
getCurrentServiceSelectors( ), getService( ), hasService( ),
revokeService( ) > **B**eanContextServicesSupport^
< addService( ), createBCSSServiceProvider( ), fireServiceAdded( ),
fireServiceRevoked( ), getCurrentServiceSelectors( ),
getService( ), hasService( ), revokeService( ) >
BeanContextServicesSupport.BCSSProxyServiceProvider
< getCurrentServiceSelectors( ), getService( ) >
BeanContextSupport⌃.classEquals( ) **B**eanDescriptor( )
Beans < getInstanceOf( ), isInstanceOf( ) > **C**lass
< getConstructor( ), getDeclaredConstructor( ),
getDeclaredMethod( ), getMethod( ), isAssignableFrom( ) >
ClassLoader⌄ < resolveClass( ), setSigners( ) >
Compiler.compileClass( ) java.awt.**C**omponent.getListeners( )
java.net.**C**ontentHandler.getContent( )
java.awt.datatransfer.**D**ataFlavor( )
javax.sound.sampled.**D**ataLine.Info( )
javax.swing.**D**efaultBoundedRangeModel.getListeners( )
javax.swing.**D**efaultButtonModel.getListeners( )
javax.swing.text.**D**efaultCaret^.getListeners( )
javax.swing.text.**D**efaultFormatter^.setValueClass( )

C

javax.print.attribute.standard.**J**obStateReasons^.getCategory( )
javax.swing.**J**Table^.getColumnClass( )
javax.sound.sampled.**L**ine.Info.getLineClass( )
LoaderHandler.loadClass( )
javax.print.attribute.standard.**M**edia^.getCategory( )   javax ↵
.print.attribute.standard.**M**ediaPrintableArea.getCategory( )
javax.print.attribute.standard.**M**ediaSize^.getCategory( )
Member.getDeclaringClass( )   **M**ethod^ < getDeclaringClass( ),
getExceptionTypes( ),   getParameterTypes( ),   getReturnType( ) >
javax.print.attribute.standard.**M**ultipleDocumentHandling^ ↵
.getCategory( )   javax.print.attribute.standard ↵
.**N**umberOfDocuments^.getCategory( )   javax.print.attribute ↵
.standard.**N**umberOfInterveningJobs^.getCategory( )
javax.print.attribute.standard.**N**umberUp^.getCategory( )
javax.print.attribute.standard.**N**umberUpSupported^ ↵
.getCategory( )   java.lang.**O**bject.getClass( )
ObjectInputStream^ < resolveClass( ),   resolveProxyClass( ) >
ObjectStreamClass.forClass( )   **O**bjectStreamField.getType( )
javax.print.attribute.standard.**O**rientationRequested^ ↵
.getCategory( )   javax.print.attribute ↵
.standard.**O**utputDeviceAssigned^.getCategory( )
javax.print.attribute.standard.**P**ageRanges^.getCategory( )
javax.print.attribute.standard.**P**agesPerMinute^.getCategory( )
javax.print.attribute.standard ↵
.**P**agesPerMinuteColor^.getCategory( )
java.awt.image.renderable.**P**arameterBlock.getParamClasses( )
javax.print.attribute.standard.**P**DLOverrideSupported^ ↵
.getCategory( )   javax.print.attribute ↵
.standard.**P**resentationDirection^.getCategory( )
javax.print.attribute.standard.**P**rinterInfo^.getCategory( )
javax.print.attribute.standard ↵
.**P**rinterIsAcceptingJobs^.getCategory( )
javax.print.attribute.standard.**P**rinterLocation^.getCategory( )
javax.print.attribute.standard.**P**rinterMakeAndModel^ ↵
.getCategory( )   javax.print.attribute.standard ↵
.**P**rinterMessageFromOperator^.getCategory( )
javax.print.attribute.standard.**P**rinterMoreInfo^.getCategory( )
javax.print.attribute.standard ↵
.**P**rinterMoreInfoManufacturer^.getCategory( )
javax.print.attribute.standard.**P**rinterName^.getCategory( )
javax.print.attribute.standard.**P**rinterResolution^.getCategory( )
javax.print.attribute.standard.**P**rinterState^.getCategory( )
javax.print.attribute.standard.**P**rinterStateReason^ ↵
.getCategory( )   javax.print.attribute ↵
.standard.**P**rinterStateReasons^.getCategory( )
javax.print.attribute.standard.**P**rinterURI^.getCategory( )
javax.print.attribute.standard.**P**rintQuality^.getCategory( )
javax.print.**P**rintService.getSupportedAttributeCategories( )
PropertyDescriptor^ < getPropertyEditorClass( ),
getPropertyType( ) >   **P**roxy.getProxyClass( )
javax.print.attribute.standard.**Q**ueuedJobCount^.getCategory( )
javax.print.attribute.standard ↵
.**R**eferenceUriSchemesSupported^.getCategory( )
javax.print.attribute.standard.**R**equestingUserName^ ↵
.getCategory( )   **R**MIClassLoader < loadClass( ),
loadProxyClass( ) >   **R**MIClassLoaderSpi < loadClass( ),
loadProxyClass( ) >   **S**ecureClassLoader^.defineClass( )
SecurityManager < currentLoadedClass( ),   getClassContext( ) >
javax.print.attribute.standard.**S**everity^.getCategory( )
javax.print.attribute.standard.**S**heetCollate^.getCategory( )
javax.print.attribute.standard.**S**ides^.getCategory( )
javax.sound.midi.**S**oundbankResource.getDataClass( )
javax.swing.table.**T**ableModel.getColumnClass( )
javax.swing.**U**IDefaults.getUIClass( )
URLClassLoader^.findClass( )   **U**til.loadClass( )
UtilDelegate.loadClass( )

— fields: _DynAnyFactoryStub^._opsClass
_DynAnyStub^._opsClass   _DynArrayStub^._opsClass
_DynEnumStub^._opsClass   _DynFixedStub^._opsClass
_DynSequenceStub^._opsClass   _DynStructStub^._opsClass
_DynUnionStub^._opsClass   _DynValueStub^._opsClass
_ServantActivatorStub^._opsClass
_ServantLocatorStub^._opsClass
BeanContextServiceAvailableEvent^.serviceClass
BeanContextServiceRevokedEvent^.serviceClass
Boolean.TYPE   **B**yte^.TYPE
Character.TYPE   **D**ouble^.TYPE   **F**loat^.TYPE
javax.imageio.spi.**I**mageInputStreamSpi^.inputClass
javax.imageio.spi.**I**mageOutputStreamSpi^.outputClass
javax.imageio.spi.**I**mageReaderSpi^ < inputTypes,
STANDARD_INPUT_TYPE >   javax.imageio.spi.**I**mageWriterSpi^
< outputTypes,   STANDARD_OUTPUT_TYPE >   **I**nteger^.TYPE
Long^.TYPE   **S**hort^.TYPE   **V**oid.TYPE
CLASS_PATH: **A**ttributes.Name
ClassCastException: java.lang
—thrown by: **P**arserFactory.makeParser( )
PortableRemoteObject.narrow( )
PortableRemoteObjectDelegate.narrow( )
ClassCircularityError^: java.lang
classDepth( ): **S**ecurityManager
ClassDesc: javax.rmi.CORBA
classEquals( ): **B**eanContextSupport^
classFactory: javax.naming.**R**eference
classFactoryLocation: javax.naming.**R**eference
ClassFormatError^: java.lang
—subclasses: **U**nsupportedClassVersionError^
—thrown by: **C**lassLoader.defineClass( )
ClassLoader: java.lang
—subclasses: **S**ecureClassLoader^
—descendents: **U**RLClassLoader^
—passed to: **B**eans.instantiate( )   **C**lass.forName( )
ClassLoader( )   java.awt.datatransfer.**D**ataFlavor
< DataFlavor( ),   tryToLoadClass( ) >
javax.swing.**J**EditorPane^.registerEditorKitForContentType( )
LoaderHandler.getSecurityContext( )
ProtectionDomain( )   **P**roxy < getProxyClass( ),
newProxyInstance( ) >   **R**esourceBundle.getBundle( )
RMIClassLoader < getSecurityContext( ),   loadClass( ),
loadProxyClass( ) >   **R**MIClassLoaderSpi < loadClass( ),
loadProxyClass( ) >   **S**ecureClassLoader( )
javax.imageio.spi.**S**erviceRegistry.lookupProviders( )
Thread.setContextClassLoader( )
javax.swing.**U**IDefaults^.getUIClass( )   **U**RLClassLoader^
< newInstance( ),   URLClassLoader( ) >   **U**til.loadClass( )
UtilDelegate.loadClass( )
—returned by: **C**lass.getClassLoader( )   **C**lassLoader < getParent( ),
getSystemClassLoader( ) >   **P**rotectionDomain.getClassLoader( )
RMIClassLoader.getClassLoader( )
RMIClassLoaderSpi.getClassLoader( )
SecurityManager.currentClassLoader( )
Thread.getContextClassLoader( )
classLoaderDepth( ): **S**ecurityManager
className: javax.naming.**R**eference
classname: **I**nvalidClassException^
ClassNotFoundException: java.lang
—thrown by: *BeanContext*.instantiateChild( )
BeanContextServicesSupport^.bcsPreDeserializationHook( )
BeanContextSupport < bcsPreDeserializationHook( ),
deserialize( ),   instantiateChild( ),   readChildren( ) >
Beans.instantiate( )   **C**lass.forName( )
ClassLoader < findClass^,   findSystemClass( ),
loadClass( ) >   java.awt.datatransfer.**D**ataFlavor
< DataFlavor( ),   readExternal( ),   tryToLoadClass( ) >
Externalizable^.readExternal( )   *LoaderHandler*.loadClass( )
MarshalledObject.get( )   *ObjectInput*^.readObject( )
ObjectInputStream^ < defaultReadObject( ),
readClassDescriptor( ),   readFields( ),   readObject( ),

readObjectOverride( ), readUnshared( ), resolveClass( ),
resolveProxyClass( ) > *ParserFactory*.makeParser( )
RMIClassLoader < loadClass( ), loadProxyClass( ) >
RMIClassLoaderSpi < loadClass( ), loadProxyClass( ) >
SealedObject.getObject( ) **S**ignedObject.getObject( )
StubDelegate.readObject( ) javax.swing.text.**S**tyleContext
< readAttributes( ), readAttributeSet( ) >
java.awt.datatransfer.**S**ystemFlavorMap.decodeDataFlavor( )
javax.swing.**U**IManager.setLookAndFeel( )
URLClassLoader^.findClass( ) **U**til.loadClass( )
UtilDelegate.loadClass( )

clean( ): *DGC*^

clear( ): **A**bstractCollection **A**bstractMap
javax.naming.directory.Attribute^ **A**ttributeListImpl
java.util.jar.**A**ttributes **A**ttributesImpl **B**asicAttribute
BeanContextSupport **B**itSet **B**uffer **C**alendar *Collection*
Environment **H**ashtable^ **M**anifest *Map* **P**references
java.lang.ref.**R**eference javax.naming.**R**eference

clearAssertionStatus( ): **C**lassLoader

clearBatch( ): *java.sql.Statement*

clearBit( ): **B**igInteger^

clearChanged( ): **O**bservable

clearParameters( ): *PreparedStatement*^ *RowSet*^
Transformer

clearPassword( ): **P**asswordCallback **P**BEKeySpec

clearWarnings( ): *Connection* *ResultSet* *java.sql.Statement*

ClientRequestInfo^: org.omg.PortableInterceptor
—passed to: *ClientRequestInterceptorOperations*^
< receive_exception( ), receive_other( ), receive_reply( ),
send_poll( ), send_request( ) >

ClientRequestInfoOperations^: org.omg.PortableInterceptor
—extended by: *ClientRequestInfo*^

ClientRequestInterceptor^: org.omg.PortableInterceptor
—passed
to: *ORBInitInfoOperations*.add_client_request_interceptor( )

ClientRequestInterceptorOperations^:
org.omg.PortableInterceptor
—extended by: *ClientRequestInterceptor*^

CLOB: **T**ypes

Clob: java.sql
—passed to: *Clob*.position( ) *PreparedStatement*^.setClob( )
ResultSet.updateClob( ) *RowSet*^.setClob( )
SQLOutput.writeClob( )
—returned by: *CallableStatement*^.getClob( ) *ResultSet*.getClob( )
SQLInput.readClob( )

clone( ): **A**bstractMap **A**clEntry^ **A**rrayList^
javax.naming.directory.Attribute^ java.util.jar.**A**ttributes
javax.naming.directory.Attributes^ **B**asicAttribute
BasicAttributes **B**itSet **B**reakIterator **C**alendar
CertPathBuilderResult^ *CertPathParameters*^
CertPathValidatorResult^ *CertSelector*^
CertStoreParameters^ *CharacterIterator*^ **C**ollator
CollectionCertStoreParameters **C**ompositeName
CompoundName *CRLSelector*^ java.util.**D**ate
DateFormatSymbols **D**ecimalFormatSymbols **F**ormat
HashSet^ **H**ashtable^ **L**DAPCertStoreParameters
LinkedList^ **L**ocale **M**ac **M**acSpi **M**anifest
MessageDigestSpi *Name*^ java.lang.**O**bject
PKIXCertPathChecker **P**KIXCertPathValidatorResult
PKIXParameters javax.naming.**R**eference **S**ignatureSpi
StringCharacterIterator **T**imeZone **T**reeSet^
UnicastRemoteObject^ **V**ector^ **X**509CertSelector
X509CRLSelector **Z**ipEntry

Cloneable: java.lang
—extended by: *AclEntry*^ *javax.naming.directory.Attribute*^
javax.naming.directory.Attributes^ *CertPathBuilderResult*^
CertPathParameters^ *CertPathValidatorResult*^
CertSelector^ *CertStoreParameters*^ *CharacterIterator*^
CRLSelector^ *GSSCredential* *Name*^
—descendents: *AttributedCharacterIterator*^

—implemented by: javax.swing.**A**bstractAction
java.awt.geom.**A**ffineTransform java.awt.geom.**A**rea
ArrayList^ java.util.jar.**A**ttributes **B**itSet
BreakIterator java.awt.**B**ufferCapabilities
Calendar **C**ollator java.awt.geom.**C**ubicCurve2D
java.awt.datatransfer.**D**ataFlavor java.util.**D**ate
DateFormatSymbols javax.print.attribute.**D**ateTimeSyntax
DecimalFormatSymbols javax.swing.text.**D**efaultFormatter^
javax.swing.**D**efaultListSelectionModel
javax.swing.tree.**D**efaultMutableTreeNode
javax.swing.tree.**D**efaultTreeSelectionModel
java.awt.geom.**D**imension2D java.awt.print.**D**ocFlavor
javax.swing.text.**E**ditorKit javax.swing.text.**E**lementIterator
javax.print.attribute.**E**numSyntax **F**ormat
java.awt.geom.**G**eneralPath java.awt.font.**G**lyphVector
javax.swing.text.**G**lyphView^ java.awt.**G**ridBagConstraints
HashMap^ **H**ashSet^ **H**ashtable^ **I**dentityHashMap^
java.awt.**I**mageCapabilities java.awt.image.**I**mageFilter
java.awt.**I**nsets javax.print.attribute.**I**ntegerSyntax
java.awt.**J**obAttributes java.awt.image.**K**ernel
java.awt.geom.**L**ine2D **L**inkedList **L**ocale **M**ac **M**anifest
javax.sound.midi.**M**idiMessage java.awt.**P**ageAttributes
java.awt.print.**P**ageFormat java.awt.print.**P**aper
java.awt.image.renderable.**P**arameterBlock
PKIXCertPathChecker java.awt.geom.**P**oint2D
java.awt.geom.**Q**uadCurve2D
java.awt.geom.**R**ectangularShape javax.naming.**R**eference
java.awt.image.renderable.**R**enderContext
java.awt.**R**enderingHints
javax.print.attribute.**R**esolutionSyntax
javax.swing.text.**S**egment
javax.print.attribute.**S**etOfIntegerSyntax
javax.swing.text.**S**impleAttributeSet
javax.print.attribute.**S**ize2DSyntax java.awt.font.**T**extLayout
java.awt.font.**T**extMeasurer javax.print.attribute.**T**extSyntax
TimeZone **T**reeMap^ **T**reeSet^
javax.print.attribute.**U**RISyntax **V**ector^ **Z**ipEntry

cloneNode( ): *Node*

CloneNotSupportedException: java.lang
—subclasses: **S**erverCloneException^
—thrown by: javax.swing.**A**bstractAction.clone( )
AbstractMap.clone( )
java.awt.datatransfer.**D**ataFlavor.clone( )
javax.swing.text.**D**efaultFormatter^.clone( )
javax.swing.**D**efaultListSelectionModel.clone( )
javax.swing.tree.**D**efaultTreeSelectionModel.clone( )
javax.swing.**J**FormattedTextField.AbstractFormatter.clone( )
Mac.clone( ) **M**acSpi.clone( ) **M**essageDigestSpi.clone( )
java.lang.**O**bject.clone( ) **S**ignatureSpi.clone( )
UnicastRemoteObject^.clone( )

close( ): **A**bstractInterruptibleChannel *Channel*
Connection javax.naming.*Context* **D**atagramSocket
DatagramSocketImpl **H**andler **I**nitialContext
java.io.**I**nputStream *NamingEnumeration*^ *ObjectInput*^
ObjectOutput^ java.io.**O**utputStream *PooledConnection*
RandomAccessFile **R**eader *ResultSet* **S**elector
ServerSocket **S**ocket **S**ocketImpl **S**tartTlsResponse
java.sql.Statement **W**riter **X**MLDecoder **X**MLEncoder^
ZipFile

CLOSE_ALL_RESULTS: *java.sql.Statement*

CLOSE_CURRENT_RESULT: *java.sql.Statement*

CLOSE_CURSORS_AT_COMMIT: *ResultSet*

CLOSE_FAILURE: **E**rrorManager

ClosedByInterruptException^: java.nio.channels

ClosedChannelException^: java.nio.channels
—subclasses: **A**synchronousCloseException^
—descendents: **C**losedByInterruptException^

—thrown by: **S**electableChannel^.register( )
ClosedSelectorException^: java.nio.channels
closeEntry( ): **Z**ipInputStream^ **Z**ipOutputStream^
code: **D**OMException
Codec^: org.omg.IOP
—returned by: *CodecFactoryOperations*_.create_codec( )
codec_factory( ): *ORBInitInfoOperations*_
CodecFactory^: org.omg.IOP
—passed to: **C**odecFactoryHelper < insert( ), write( ) >
—returned by: **C**odecFactoryHelper < extract( ), narrow( ),
read( ) > *ORBInitInfoOperations*_.codec_factory( )
CodecFactoryHelper: org.omg.IOP
CodecFactoryOperations_: org.omg.IOP
—extended by: *CodecFactory*^
CodecOperations_: org.omg.IOP
—extended by: *Codec*^
CoderMalfunctionError: java.nio.charset
CoderResult: java.nio.charset
—returned by: **C**harsetDecoder < decode( ), decodeLoop( ),
flush( ), implFlush( ) > **C**harsetEncoder < encode( ),
encodeLoop( ), flush( ), implFlush( ) > **C**oderResult
< malformedForLength( ), unmappableForLength( ) >
—fields: **C**oderResult < OVERFLOW, UNDERFLOW >
CodeSets^: org.omg.IOP
CodeSource: java.security
—passed to: **C**odeSource.implies( )
java.security.**P**olicy.getPermissions( )
javax.security.auth.**P**olicy.getPermissions( )
ProtectionDomain( ) **S**ecureClassLoader^ < defineClass( ),
getPermissions( ) > **U**RLClassLoader^.getPermissions( )
—returned by: **P**rotectionDomain.getCodeSource( )
CodingErrorAction: java.nio.charset
—passed to: **C**harsetDecoder < implOnMalformedInput( ),
implOnUnmappableCharacter( ), onMalformedInput( ),
onUnmappableCharacter( ) > **C**harsetEncoder
< implOnMalformedInput( ), implOnUnmappableCharacter( ),
onMalformedInput( ), onUnmappableCharacter( ) >
—returned by: **C**harsetDecoder < malformedInputAction( ),
unmappableCharacterAction( ) > **C**harsetEncoder
< malformedInputAction( ), unmappableCharacterAction( ) >
—fields: **C**odingErrorAction < IGNORE, REPLACE, REPORT >
CollationElementIterator: java.text
—returned by: **R**uleBasedCollator^.getCollationElementIterator( )
CollationKey: java.text
—passed to: **C**ollationKey.compareTo( )
—returned by: **C**ollator_.getCollationKey( )
Collator_: java.text
—subclasses: **R**uleBasedCollator^
—returned by: **C**ollator_.getInstance( )
Collection_: java.util
—extended by: *BeanContext*^ *List*^ *Set*^ *SortedSet*^
—descendents: *BeanContextServices*^ *SortedSet*^
—passed to: **A**bstractCollection < addAll( ), containsAll( ),
removeAll( ), retainAll( ) > **A**bstractList^.addAll( ) **A**rrayList( )
BeanContextMembershipEvent( ) **B**eanContextSupport^
< addAll( ), containsAll( ), deserialize( ), removeAll( ),
retainAll( ), serialize( ) > *Collection*_ < addAll( ), containsAll( ),
removeAll( ), retainAll( ) > **C**ollectionCertStoreParameters( )
Collections < enumeration( ), max( ), min( ),
synchronizedCollection( ), unmodifiableCollection( ) > **H**ashSet( )
javax.print.attribute.standard.**J**obStateReasons( )
LinkedHashSet( ) **L**inkedList( ) *List*^ < addAll( ), containsAll( ),
removeAll( ), retainAll( ) > **P**KIXCertPathChecker.check( )
Set^ < addAll( ), containsAll( ), removeAll( ),
retainAll( ) > **T**reeSet( ) **V**ector( ) **X**509CertSelector
< setPathToNames( ), setSubjectAlternativeNames( ) >
X509CRLSelector.setIssuerNames( )
—returned by: **A**bstractMap_.values( )
java.util.jar.**A**ttributes.values( ) **C**ertificateFactory
< generateCertificates( ), generateCRLs( ) > **C**ertificateFactorySpi
< engineGenerateCertificates( ), engineGenerateCRLs( ) >
CertStore < getCertificates( ), getCRLs( ) > **C**ertStoreSpi

< engineGetCertificates( ), engineGetCRLs( ) >
CollectionCertStoreParameters.getCollection( )
Collections < synchronizedCollection( ),
unmodifiableCollection( ) > **H**ashtable^.values( )
*Map*_.values( ) java.awt.**R**enderingHints.values( )
java.security.cert.**X**509Certificate^
< getIssuerAlternativeNames( ),
getSubjectAlternativeNames( ) > **X**509CertSelector
< getPathToNames( ), getSubjectAlternativeNames( ) >
X509CRLSelector.getIssuerNames( )
—implemented by: **A**bstractCollection
—fields: **B**eanContextMembershipEvent^.children
CollectionCertStoreParameters: java.security.cert
Collections: java.util
columnNoNulls: *DatabaseMetaData* *ResultSetMetaData*_
columnNullable: *DatabaseMetaData* *ResultSetMetaData*_
columnNullableUnknown: *DatabaseMetaData*
*ResultSetMetaData*_
combine( ): *DomainCombiner* **S**ubjectDomainCombiner
COMBINING_DIACRITICAL_MARKS: **C**haracter.UnicodeBlock^
COMBINING_HALF_MARKS: **C**haracter.UnicodeBlock^
COMBINING_MARKS_FOR_SYMBOLS:
Character.UnicodeBlock^
COMBINING_SPACING_MARK: **C**haracter
COMM_FAILURE^: org.omg.CORBA
command( ): **C**ompiler
Comment^: org.w3c.dom
—returned by: *Document*^.createComment( )
comment( ): *LexicalHandler*_
COMMENT_NODE: *Node*_
commentChar( ): **S**treamTokenizer
COMMENTS: **P**attern
commit( ): *Connection* *LoginModule* *XAResource*
CommunicationException^: javax.naming
compact( ): **B**yteBuffer^ **C**harBuffer^ **D**oubleBuffer^
FloatBuffer^ **I**ntBuffer^ **L**ongBuffer^ **S**hortBuffer^
Comparable: java.lang
—passed to: javax.imageio.metadata.**I**IOMetadataFormatImpl ←
.addObjectValue( ) javax.swing.text.**I**nternationalFormatter^
< setMaximum( ), setMinimum( ) >
javax.swing.**S**pinnerDateModel^ < setEnd( ), setStart( ),
SpinnerDateModel( ) > javax.swing.**S**pinnerNumberModel^
< setMaximum( ), setMinimum( ), SpinnerNumberModel( ) >
—returned by: *javax.imageio.metadata.IIOMetadataFormat*
< getObjectMaxValue( ), getObjectMinValue( ) >
javax.imageio.metadata.**I**IOMetadataFormatImpl
< getObjectMaxValue( ), getObjectMinValue( ) >
javax.swing.text.**I**nternationalFormatter^ < getMaximum( ),
getMinimum( ) > javax.swing.**S**pinnerDateModel^ < getEnd( ),
getStart( ) > javax.swing.**S**pinnerNumberModel^
< getMaximum( ), getMinimum( ) >
—implemented by: **B**igDecimal^ **B**igInteger^ **B**yte^ **B**yteBuffer^
Character **C**harBuffer^ **C**harset **C**ollationKey
java.util.**D**ate_ **D**ouble^ **D**oubleBuffer^ **F**ile **F**loat^
FloatBuffer^ **I**ntBuffer^ **I**nteger^ **L**ong^ **L**ongBuffer^
ObjectStreamField **S**hort^ **S**hortBuffer^ **S**tring **U**RI
Comparator: java.util
—passed to: **A**rrays < binarySearch( ), sort( ) >
Collections < binarySearch( ), max( ), min( ), sort( ) >
javax.swing.**S**ortingFocusTraversalPolicy^ < setComparator( ),
SortingFocusTraversalPolicy( ) > **T**reeMap( ) **T**reeSet( )
—returned by: **C**ollections.reverseOrder( )
SortedMap^.comparator( ) *SortedSet*^.comparator( )
javax.swing.**S**ortingFocusTraversalPolicy^.getComparator( )
TreeMap^.comparator( ) **T**reeSet^.comparator( )
—implemented by: **C**ollator_
—fields: **S**tring.CASE_INSENSITIVE_ORDER
comparator( ): *SortedMap*^ *SortedSet*^ **T**reeMap^ **T**reeSet^
compare( ): **C**ollator_ *Comparator* **D**ouble^ **F**loat^

C

C

D

—passed to: *CustomMarshal* .unmarshal( )
DATALINK: Types
DataOutput: java.io
—extended by: *javax.imageio.stream.ImageOutputStream^*
  *ObjectOutput^*
—passed to: **U**ID.write( )
—implemented by: java.io.**D**ataOutputStream^
  RandomAccessFile
DataOutputStream^: java.io
*DataOutputStream^*: org.omg.CORBA
—passed to: *CustomMarshal* .marshal( )
DataSource: javax.sql
DataTruncation^: java.sql
DATE: Calendar Types
Date^: java.sql
—passed to: *CallableStatement^*.setDate( )
  *PreparedStatement^*.setDate( ) *ResultSet* .updateDate( )
  *RowSet^*.setDate( ) *SQLOutput*.writeDate( )
—returned by: *CallableStatement^*.getDate( )
  java.sql.**D**ate^.valueOf( ) *ResultSet* .getDate( )
  SQLInput.readDate( )
Date : java.util
—subclasses: java.sql.**D**ate^ **T**ime^ **T**imestamp^
—passed to: **C**alendar .setTime( ) java.util.**D**ate < after( ),
  before( ), compareTo( ) > **D**ateFormat^.format( )
  javax.print.attribute.standard.**D**ateTimeAtCompleted( )
  javax.print.attribute.standard.**D**ateTimeAtCreation( )
  javax.print.attribute.standard.**D**ateTimeAtProcessing( )
  javax.print.attribute.**D**ateTimeSyntax( )
  GregorianCalendar^.setGregorianChange( )
  javax.print.attribute.standard.**J**obHoldUntil( )
  KerberosTicket( ) **P**KIXParameters .setDate( )
  SimpleDateFormat^.set2DigitYearStart( )
  javax.swing.**S**pinnerDateModel( ) java.util.**T**imer < schedule( ),
  scheduleAtFixedRate( ) > **T**imeZone .inDaylightTime( )
  java.security.cert.**X**509Certificate^.checkValidity( )
  javax.security.cert.**X**509Certificate^.checkValidity( )
  X509CertSelector < setCertificateValid( ), setPrivateKeyValid( ) >
  X509CRLSelector.setDateAndTime( )
—returned by: **C**alendar .getTime( ) **D**ateFormat^.parse( )
  javax.print.attribute.**D**ateTimeSyntax.getValue( )
  GregorianCalendar^.getGregorianChange( ) **K**erberosTicket
  < getAuthTime( ), getEndTime( ), getRenewTill( ),
  getStartTime( ) > **K**eyStore.getCreationDate( )
  KeyStoreSpi.engineGetCreationDate( )
  PKIXParameters .getDate( )
  SimpleDateFormat^.get2DigitYearStart( )
  javax.swing.**S**pinnerDateModel^.getDate( )
  java.security.cert.**X**509Certificate^.getNotAfter( )
  javax.security.cert.**X**509Certificate^.getNotAfter( )
  java.security.cert.**X**509Certificate^.getNotBefore( )
  javax.security.cert.**X**509Certificate^.getNotBefore( )
  X509CertSelector < getCertificateValid( ),
  getPrivateKeyValid( ) > **X**509CRL^ < getNextUpdate( ),
  getThisUpdate( ) > **X**509CRLEntry.getRevocationDate( )
  X509CRLSelector.getDateAndTime( )
DATE_FIELD: **D**ateFormat^
DateFormat^: java.text
—subclasses: **S**impleDateFormat^
—passed to: javax.swing.text.**D**ateFormatter^ < DateFormatter( ),
  setFormat( ) >
—returned by: **D**ateFormat^ < getDateInstance( ),
  getDateTimeInstance( ), getInstance( ), getTimeInstance( ) >
DateFormat.Field^: java.text
—returned by: **D**ateFormat.Field^.ofCalendarField( )
—fields: **D**ateFormat.Field^ < AM_PM, DAY_OF_MONTH,
  DAY_OF_WEEK, DAY_OF_WEEK_IN_MONTH, DAY_OF_YEAR,
  ERA, HOUR0, HOUR1, HOUR_OF_DAY0, HOUR_OF_DAY1,
  MILLISECOND, MINUTE, MONTH, SECOND, TIME_ZONE,
  WEEK_OF_MONTH, WEEK_OF_YEAR, YEAR >
DateFormatSymbols: java.text

—passed to: **S**impleDateFormat^ < setDateFormatSymbols( ),
  SimpleDateFormat( ) >
—returned by: **S**impleDateFormat^.getDateFormatSymbols( )
DAY_OF_MONTH: **C**alendar **D**ateFormat.Field^
DAY_OF_WEEK: **C**alendar **D**ateFormat.Field^
DAY_OF_WEEK_FIELD: **D**ateFormat^
DAY_OF_WEEK_IN_MONTH: **C**alendar **D**ateFormat.Field^
DAY_OF_WEEK_IN_MONTH_FIELD: **D**ateFormat^
DAY_OF_YEAR: **C**alendar **D**ateFormat.Field^
DAY_OF_YEAR_FIELD: **D**ateFormat^
deactivate( ): *POAManagerOperations* *Tie^*
deactivate_object( ): *POAOperations*
decapitalize( ): **I**ntrospector
DECEMBER: **C**alendar
DECIMAL: Types
DECIMAL_DIGIT_NUMBER: **C**haracter
DECIMAL_SEPARATOR: **N**umberFormat.Field^
DecimalFormat^: java.text
—returned by: javax.swing.**J**Spinner.NumberEditor^.getFormat( )
DecimalFormatSymbols: java.text
—passed to: **D**ecimalFormat^ < DecimalFormat( ),
  setDecimalFormatSymbols( ) >
—returned by: **D**ecimalFormat^.getDecimalFormatSymbols( )
DECLARED: *Member*
declarePrefix( ): **N**amespaceSupport
DeclHandler: org.xml.sax.ext
decode( ): **B**yte^ java.security.**C**ertificate **C**harset
  CharsetDecoder *CodecOperations* **I**nteger^ **L**ong^
  Short^ **U**RLDecoder
decode_value( ): *CodecOperations*
decodeLoop( ): **C**harsetDecoder
DECRYPT_MODE: **C**ipher
def: **D**eflaterOutputStream^
def_kind( ): _IDLTypeStub^ *IRObjectOperations*
DEFAULT: **D**ateFormat^
DEFAULT_COMPRESSION: **D**eflater
default_index( ): **T**ypeCode
DEFAULT_LIFETIME: *GSSContext* *GSSCredential^*
default_POA( ): org.omg.PortableServer.portable.**D**elegate
DEFAULT_STRATEGY: **D**eflater
defaulted( ): **O**bjectInputStream.GetField
DefaultHandler: org.xml.sax.helpers
—passed to: **S**AXParser.parse( )
defaultInitCtx: **I**nitialContext
DefaultPersistenceDelegate^: java.beans
defaultReadObject( ): **O**bjectInputStream^
defaults: **P**roperties^
defaultWriteObject( ): **O**bjectOutputStream^
DEFECTIVE_CREDENTIAL: **G**SSException
DEFECTIVE_TOKEN: **G**SSException
defineClass( ): **C**lassLoader
defined_in: **V**alueMember
definePackage( ): **C**lassLoader
DefinitionKind: org.omg.CORBA
—passed to: **D**efinitionKindHelper < insert( ), write( ) >
—returned by: _IDLTypeStub^.def_kind( )
  DefinitionKind.from_int( ) **D**efinitionKindHelper < extract( ),
  read( ) > *IRObjectOperations* .def_kind( )
—fields: **D**efinitionKind < dk_AbstractInterface, dk_Alias, dk_all,
  dk_Array, dk_Attribute, dk_Constant, dk_Enum, dk_Exception,
  dk_Fixed, dk_Interface, dk_Module, dk_Native, dk_none,
  dk_Operation, dk_Primitive, dk_Repository, dk_Sequence,
  dk_String, dk_Struct, dk_Typedef, dk_Union, dk_Value,
  dk_ValueBox, dk_ValueMember, dk_Wstring >
DefinitionKindHelper: org.omg.CORBA
deflate( ): **D**eflater **D**eflaterOutputStream^
DEFLATED: **D**eflater **Z**ipEntry **Z**ipOutputStream^
Deflater: java.util.zip
—passed to: **D**eflaterOutputStream( )
—fields: **D**eflaterOutputStream^.def
DeflaterOutputStream^: java.util.zip
—subclasses: **G**ZIPOutputStream^ **Z**ipOutputStream^

—descendents: **J**arOutputStream^
Delegate: org.omg.CORBA.portable
—subclasses: org.omg.CORBA_2_3.portable.**D**elegate^
—passed to: _IDLTypeStub( ) _PolicyStub( )
org.omg.CORBA.portable.**O**bjectImpl._set_delegate( )
—returned
by: org.omg.CORBA.portable.**O**bjectImpl._get_delegate( )
Delegate: org.omg.CORBA_2_3.portable
Delegate: org.omg.PortableServer.portable
—passed to: **S**ervant._set_delegate( )
—returned by: **S**ervant._get_delegate( )
DelegationPermission^: javax.security.auth.kerberos
delete( ): **F**ile **S**tringBuffer
delete_values( ): org.omg.CORBA.**C**ontext
deleteCharAt( ): **S**tringBuffer
deleteData( ): **C**haracterData^
deleteEntry( ): **K**eyStore
deleteObserver( ): **O**bservable
deleteObservers( ): **O**bservable
deleteOnExit( ): **F**ile
deleteOwner( ): **O**wner
deleteRow( ): **R**esultSet
deletesAreDetected( ): **D**atabaseMetaData
deregister( ): **A**bstractSelector^
deregisterDriver( ): **D**riverManager
DES_EDE_KEY_LEN: **D**ESedeKeySpec
DES_KEY_LEN: **D**ESKeySpec
description: **D**riverPropertyInfo
DESedeKeySpec: javax.crypto.spec
deserialize( ): **B**eanContextSupport^
DesignMode: java.beans
—extended by: **B**eanContext^
—descendents: **B**eanContextServices^
designTime: **B**eanContextSupport^
desiredAssertionStatus( ): **C**lass
DESKeySpec: javax.crypto.spec
destroy( ): _BindingIteratorStub^ _DynAnyStub^
_DynArrayStub^ _DynEnumStub^ _DynFixedStub^
_DynSequenceStub^ _DynStructStub^
_DynUnionStub^ _DynValueStub^ _IDLTypeStub^
_NamingContextExtStub^ _NamingContextStub^
_PolicyStub^ **B**indingIteratorOperations **D**estroyable
org.omg.CORBA.**D**ynAny^ **D**ynAnyOperations
InterceptorOperations **I**RObjectOperations **K**erberosKey
KerberosTicket **N**amingContextOperations
org.omg.CORBA.**O**RB **P**OAOperations **P**olicyOperations
Process **T**hread **T**hreadGroup **X**500PrivateCredential
Destroyable: javax.security.auth
—implemented by: **K**erberosKey **K**erberosTicket
X500PrivateCredential
DestroyFailedException: javax.security.auth
—thrown by: **D**estroyable.destroy( ) **K**erberosKey.destroy( )
KerberosTicket.destroy( )
destroySubcontext( ): javax.naming.**C**ontext InitialContext
detail: **A**ctivationException **R**emoteException^
ServerCloneException^ **W**riteAbortedException^
detectedCharset( ): **C**harsetDecoder
DEVANAGARI: **C**haracter.UnicodeBlock^
DGC^: java.rmi.dgc
DGC_ID: **O**bjID
DHGenParameterSpec: javax.crypto.spec
DHKey: javax.crypto.interfaces
—extended by: **D**HPrivateKey^ **D**HPublicKey^
DHParameterSpec: javax.crypto.spec
—returned by: **D**HKey.getParams( )
DHPrivateKey^: javax.crypto.interfaces
DHPrivateKeySpec: javax.crypto.spec
DHPublicKey^: javax.crypto.interfaces
DHPublicKeySpec: javax.crypto.spec
Dictionary: java.util
—subclasses: **H**ashtable^
—descendents: **P**roperties^ **P**rovider^ javax.swing.**U**IDefaults^

—passed to: javax.swing.text.**A**bstractDocument ↵
.setDocumentProperties( ) javax.swing.**J**Slider^.setLabelTable( )
—returned by: javax.swing.text.**A**bstractDocument ↵
.getDocumentProperties( ) javax.swing.**J**Slider^.getLabelTable( )
digest: **D**igestInputStream^ **D**igestOutputStream^
digest( ): **M**essageDigest^
DigestException^: java.security
—thrown by: **M**essageDigest^.digest( )
MessageDigestSpi^.engineDigest( )
DigestInputStream^: java.security
DigestOutputStream^: java.security
digit( ): **C**haracter
DINGBATS: **C**haracter.UnicodeBlock^
DirContext^: javax.naming.directory
—extended by: **E**ventDirContext^ **L**dapContext^
—returned by: javax.naming.directory.**A**ttribute^
< getAttributeDefinition( ), getAttributeSyntaxDefinition( ) >
BasicAttribute < getAttributeDefinition( ),
getAttributeSyntaxDefinition( ) > **D**irContext^
< createSubcontext( ), getSchema( ), getSchemaClassDefinition( ) >
DirectoryManager^.getContinuationDirContext( )
InitialDirContext < createSubcontext( ), getSchema( ),
getSchemaClassDefinition( ) >
—implemented by: **I**nitialDirContext^
DIRECTION_DEFAULT_LEFT_TO_RIGHT: **B**idi
DIRECTION_DEFAULT_RIGHT_TO_LEFT: **B**idi
DIRECTION_LEFT_TO_RIGHT: **B**idi
DIRECTION_RIGHT_TO_LEFT: **B**idi
DIRECTIONALITY_ARABIC_NUMBER: **C**haracter
DIRECTIONALITY_BOUNDARY_NEUTRAL: **C**haracter
DIRECTIONALITY_COMMON_NUMBER_SEPARATOR:
Character
DIRECTIONALITY_EUROPEAN_NUMBER: **C**haracter
DIRECTIONALITY_EUROPEAN_NUMBER_SEPARATOR:
Character
DIRECTIONALITY_EUROPEAN_NUMBER_TERMINATOR:
Character
DIRECTIONALITY_LEFT_TO_RIGHT: **C**haracter
DIRECTIONALITY_LEFT_TO_RIGHT_EMBEDDING: **C**haracter
DIRECTIONALITY_LEFT_TO_RIGHT_OVERRIDE: **C**haracter
DIRECTIONALITY_NONSPACING_MARK: **C**haracter
DIRECTIONALITY_OTHER_NEUTRALS: **C**haracter
DIRECTIONALITY_PARAGRAPH_SEPARATOR: **C**haracter
DIRECTIONALITY_POP_DIRECTIONAL_FORMAT: **C**haracter
DIRECTIONALITY_RIGHT_TO_LEFT: **C**haracter
DIRECTIONALITY_RIGHT_TO_LEFT_ARABIC: **C**haracter
DIRECTIONALITY_RIGHT_TO_LEFT_EMBEDDING: **C**haracter
DIRECTIONALITY_RIGHT_TO_LEFT_OVERRIDE: **C**haracter
DIRECTIONALITY_SEGMENT_SEPARATOR: **C**haracter
DIRECTIONALITY_UNDEFINED: **C**haracter
DIRECTIONALITY_WHITESPACE: **C**haracter
DirectoryManager^: javax.naming.spi
DirObjectFactory^: javax.naming.spi
DirStateFactory^: javax.naming.spi
DirStateFactory.Result: javax.naming.spi
—returned by: **D**irectoryManager^.getStateToBind( )
DirStateFactory^.getStateToBind( )
dirty( ): **D**GC^
disable( ): **C**ompiler
discard_requests( ): **P**OAManagerOperations
DISCARDING: **S**tate
disconnect( ): **D**atagramChannel^ **D**atagramSocket
DatagramSocketImpl **H**ttpURLConnection^
org.omg.CORBA.**O**RB
discriminator( ): org.omg.CORBA.**D**ynUnion^
discriminator_kind( ): _DynUnionStub^
org.omg.CORBA.**D**ynUnion^ **D**ynUnionOperations^
discriminator_type( ): **T**ypeCode
dispatch( ): **N**amingEvent^ **N**amingExceptionEvent^ **S**keleton
UnsolicitedNotificationEvent^
displayName( ): **C**harset
dispose( ): **G**SSContext **G**SSCredential^

DISTINCT: Types
divide(): BigDecimal^ BigInteger^
divideAndRemainder(): BigInteger^
dk_AbstractInterface: DefinitionKind
dk_Alias: DefinitionKind
dk_all: DefinitionKind
dk_Array: DefinitionKind
dk_Attribute: DefinitionKind
dk_Constant: DefinitionKind
dk_Enum: DefinitionKind
dk_Exception: DefinitionKind
dk_Fixed: DefinitionKind
dk_Interface: DefinitionKind
dk_Module: DefinitionKind
dk_Native: DefinitionKind
dk_none: DefinitionKind
dk_Operation: DefinitionKind
dk_Primitive: DefinitionKind
dk_Repository: DefinitionKind
dk_Sequence: DefinitionKind
dk_String: DefinitionKind
dk_Struct: DefinitionKind
dk_Typedef: DefinitionKind
dk_Union: DefinitionKind
dk_Value: DefinitionKind
dk_ValueBox: DefinitionKind
dk_ValueMember: DefinitionKind
dk_Wstring: DefinitionKind
DNS_URL: *javax.naming.Context*˯
doAs(): Subject
doAsPrivileged(): Subject
DOCTYPE_PUBLIC: OutputKeys
DOCTYPE_SYSTEM: OutputKeys
Document^: org.w3c.dom
—returned by: DocumentBuilder < newDocument( ), parse( ) >
  DOMImplementation.createDocument( ) javax.imageio ↩
  .metadata.IIOMetadataNode.getOwnerDocument( )
  Node˯.getOwnerDocument( )
DOCUMENT_FRAGMENT_NODE: *Node*˯
DOCUMENT_NODE: *Node*˯
DOCUMENT_TYPE_NODE: *Node*˯
DocumentBuilder: javax.xml.parsers
—returned by: DocumentBuilderFactory.newDocumentBuilder( )
DocumentBuilderFactory: javax.xml.parsers
—returned by: DocumentBuilderFactory.newInstance( )
DocumentFragment^: org.w3c.dom
—returned by: *Document*^.createDocumentFragment( )
DocumentHandler˯: org.xml.sax
—passed to: *Parser*.setDocumentHandler( )
  XMLReaderAdapter.setDocumentHandler( )
—implemented by: HandlerBase ParserAdapter
DocumentType^: org.w3c.dom
—passed to: *DOMImplementation*.createDocument( )
—returned by: *Document*^.getDoctype( )
  DOMImplementation.createDocumentType( )
doesMaxRowSizeIncludeBlobs(): *DatabaseMetaData*
doFinal(): Cipher˯ Mac
doInput: URLConnection˯
DomainCombiner˯: java.security
—passed to: AccessControlContext( )
—returned by: AccessControlContext.getDomainCombiner( )
—implemented by: SubjectDomainCombiner
DomainManager˯: org.omg.CORBA
—returned by: org.omg.CORBA.portable.*Delegate*˯ ↩
  .get_domain_managers( ) LocalObject._get_domain_managers( )
  org.omg.CORBA.Object˯._get_domain_managers( ) org ↩
  .omg.CORBA.portable.*ObjectImpl*˯._get_domain_managers( )
DomainManagerOperations˯: org.omg.CORBA
—extended by: *DomainManager*^
DOMException: org.w3c.dom
—thrown by: *Attr*^.setValue( ) *CharacterData*˯
  < appendData( ), deleteData( ), getData( ), insertData( ),

replaceData( ), setData( ), substringData( ) >
  Document^ < createAttribute( ), createAttributeNS( ),
  createCDATASection( ), createElement( ), createElementNS( ),
  createEntityReference( ), createProcessingInstruction( ),
  importNode( ) > *DOMImplementation* < createDocument( ),
  createDocumentType( ) > *Element*^ < removeAttribute( ),
  removeAttributeNode( ), removeAttributeNS( ), setAttribute( ),
  setAttributeNode( ), setAttributeNodeNS( ), setAttributeNS( ) >
  javax.imageio.metadata.IIOMetadataNode
  < getNamespaceURI( ), getNodeValue( ), setAttributeNode( ),
  setNodeValue( ) > *NamedNodeMap* < removeNamedItem( ),
  removeNamedItemNS( ), setNamedItem( ), setNamedItemNS( ) >
  Node˯ < appendChild( ), getNodeValue( ), insertBefore( ),
  removeChild( ), replaceChild( ), setNodeValue( ), setPrefix( ) >
  ProcessingInstruction^.setData( ) *Text*˯.splitText( )
DOMImplementation: org.w3c.dom
—returned by: *Document*^.getImplementation( )
  DocumentBuilder.getDOMImplementation( )
DOMLocator^: javax.xml.transform.dom
DOMResult: javax.xml.transform.dom
DOMSource: javax.xml.transform.dom
DOMSTRING_SIZE_ERR: DOMException
DONE: BreakIterator *CharacterIterator*˯
done(): *RemoteCall* *RemoteRef*˯
dontUseGui(): BeanContextSupport˯ *Visibility*˯
doOutput: URLConnection˯
doPhase(): KeyAgreement
doPrivileged(): AccessController
DOTALL: Pattern
DOUBLE: Types
Double^: java.lang
—passed to: *Double*^.compareTo( )
—returned by: *Double*^.valueOf( )
DoubleBuffer^: java.nio
—passed to: *DoubleBuffer*^.put( )
—returned by: *ByteBuffer*^.asDoubleBuffer( ) *DoubleBuffer*^
  < allocate( ), asReadOnlyBuffer( ), compact( ), duplicate( ), get( ),
  put( ), slice( ), wrap( ) >
DoubleHolder: org.omg.CORBA
DoubleSeqHelper: org.omg.CORBA
DoubleSeqHolder: org.omg.CORBA
—passed
  to: *org.omg.CORBA.DataInputStream*^.read_double_array( )
doubleToLongBits(): Double^
doubleToRawLongBits(): Double^
doubleValue(): Number˯
drain(): ObjectOutputStream^
Driver: java.sql
—passed to: DriverManager < deregisterDriver( ), registerDriver( ) >
—returned by: DriverManager.getDriver( )
DriverManager: java.sql
DriverPropertyInfo: java.sql
—returned by: *Driver*.getPropertyInfo( )
DSAKey˯: java.security.interfaces
—extended by: *DSAPrivateKey*^ *DSAPublicKey*^
DSAKeyPairGenerator: java.security.interfaces
DSAParameterSpec: java.security.spec
DSAParams˯: java.security.interfaces
—passed to: *DSAKeyPairGenerator*.initialize( )
—returned by: *DSAKey*˯.getParams( )
—implemented by: DSAParameterSpec
DSAPrivateKey^: java.security.interfaces
DSAPrivateKeySpec: java.security.spec
DSAPublicKey^: java.security.interfaces
DSAPublicKeySpec: java.security.spec
DST_OFFSET: Calendar˯
DTDHandler˯: org.xml.sax
—extended by: *TransformerHandler*^
—passed to: *Parser*.setDTDHandler( )
  ParserAdapter.setDTDHandler( )
  XMLFilterImpl.setDTDHandler( ) *XMLReader*˯.setDTDHandler( )
  XMLReaderAdapter.setDTDHandler( )

D

Cross-Ref

DynStruct^: org.omg.CORBA
—returned by: org.omg.CORBA.**O**RB‿.create_dyn_struct( )
DynStruct^: org.omg.DynamicAny
—passed to: **D**ynStructHelper < insert( ), write( ) >
—returned by: **D**ynStructHelper < extract( ), narrow( ), read( ) >
—implemented by: _DynStructStub^
DynStructHelper: org.omg.DynamicAny
DynStructOperations^: org.omg.DynamicAny
—extended by: org.omg.DynamicAny.**D**ynStruct^
DynUnion^: org.omg.CORBA
—returned by: org.omg.CORBA.**O**RB‿.create_dyn_union( )
DynUnion^: org.omg.DynamicAny
—passed to: **D**ynUnionHelper < insert( ), write( ) >
—returned by: **D**ynUnionHelper < extract( ), narrow( ), read( ) >
—implemented by: _DynUnionStub^
DynUnionHelper: org.omg.DynamicAny
DynUnionOperations^: org.omg.DynamicAny
—extended by: org.omg.DynamicAny.**D**ynUnion^
DynValue^: org.omg.CORBA
DynValue^: org.omg.DynamicAny
—passed to: **D**ynValueHelper < insert( ), write( ) >
—returned by: **D**ynValueHelper < extract( ), narrow( ), read( ) >
—implemented by: _DynValueStub^
DynValueBox^: org.omg.DynamicAny
DynValueBoxOperations^: org.omg.DynamicAny
—extended by: **D**ynValueBox^
DynValueCommon^: org.omg.DynamicAny
—extended by: org.omg.DynamicAny.**D**ynValue^ **D**ynValueBox^
DynValueCommonOperations^: org.omg.DynamicAny
—extended by: **D**ynValueBoxOperations^ **D**ynValueCommon^
DynValueOperations^
—descendents: org.omg.DynamicAny.**D**ynValue^ **D**ynValueBox^
DynValueHelper: org.omg.DynamicAny
DynValueOperations^: org.omg.DynamicAny
—extended by: org.omg.DynamicAny.**D**ynValue^
E: **M**ath **S**trictMath
effective_profile( ): **C**lientRequestInfoOperations^
effective_target( ): **C**lientRequestInfoOperations^
Element^: org.w3c.dom
—returned by: **A**ttr^.getOwnerElement( ) **D**ocument^
< createElement( ), createElementNS( ), getDocumentElement( ),
getElementById( ) >
—implemented by: javax.imageio.metadata.**I**IOMetadataNode
ELEMENT_NODE: **N**ode‿
elementAt( ): **V**ector^
elementCount: **V**ector^
elementData: **V**ector^
elementDecl( ): **D**eclHandler
elements( ): **D**ictionary‿ **P**ermissionCollection‿ **V**ector^
empty( ): **S**tack^
EMPTY_LIST: **C**ollections
EMPTY_MAP: **C**ollections
EMPTY_SET: **C**ollections
EmptyStackException: java.util
—thrown by: java.awt.**E**ventQueue.pop( )
enable( ): **C**ompiler
enableReplaceObject( ): **O**bjectOutputStream^
enableResolveObject( ): **O**bjectInputStream^
ENCLOSED_ALPHANUMERICS: **C**haracter.UnicodeBlock^
ENCLOSED_CJK_LETTERS_AND_MONTHS:
Character.UnicodeBlock^
ENCLOSING_MARK: **C**haracter
encode( ): java.security.**C**ertificate **C**harset **C**harsetEncoder
CodecOperations‿ **U**RLEncoder
encode_value( ): **C**odecOperations‿
EncodedKeySpec‿: java.security.spec
—subclasses: **P**KCS8EncodedKeySpec^
X509EncodedKeySpec^
encodedParams: **S**ealedObject
encodeLoop( ): **C**harsetEncoder
Encoder‿: java.beans
—subclasses: **X**MLEncoder^

—passed to: **D**efaultPersistenceDelegate^ < initialize( ),
instantiate( ) > **P**ersistenceDelegate‿ < initialize( ), instantiate( ),
writeObject( ) >
ENCODING: **O**utputKeys
Encoding: org.omg.IOP
—passed to: **C**odecFactoryOperations‿.create_codec( )
ENCODING_CDR_ENCAPS: org.omg.IOP
ENCRYPT_MODE: **C**ipher
EncryptedPrivateKeyInfo: javax.crypto
end( ): **A**bstractInterruptibleChannel‿ **A**bstractSelector^
Deflater **I**nflater **M**atcher **X**AResource
END_PUNCTUATION: **C**haracter
endCDATA( ): **L**exicalHandler‿
endDocument( ): org.xml.sax.**C**ontentHandler‿ **D**efaultHandler
DocumentHandler **H**andlerBase **P**arserAdapter
XMLFilterImpl **X**MLReaderAdapter
endDTD( ): **L**exicalHandler‿
endElement( ): org.xml.sax.**C**ontentHandler‿ **D**efaultHandler
DocumentHandler **H**andlerBase **P**arserAdapter
XMLFilterImpl **X**MLReaderAdapter
endEntity( ): **L**exicalHandler‿
endPrefixMapping( ): org.xml.sax.**C**ontentHandler‿
DefaultHandler **X**MLFilterImpl **X**MLReaderAdapter
endsWith( ): **C**ompositeName **C**ompoundName **N**ame^ **S**tring
engineAliases( ): **K**eyStoreSpi
engineBuild( ): **C**ertPathBuilderSpi
engineContainsAlias( ): **K**eyStoreSpi
engineDeleteEntry( ): **K**eyStoreSpi
engineDigest( ): **M**essageDigestSpi‿
engineDoFinal( ): **C**ipherSpi **M**acSpi
engineDoPhase( ): **K**eyAgreementSpi
engineGenerateCertificate( ): **C**ertificateFactorySpi
engineGenerateCertificates( ): **C**ertificateFactorySpi
engineGenerateCertPath( ): **C**ertificateFactorySpi
engineGenerateCRL( ): **C**ertificateFactorySpi
engineGenerateCRLs( ): **C**ertificateFactorySpi
engineGenerateKey( ): **K**eyGeneratorSpi
engineGenerateParameters( ):
AlgorithmParameterGeneratorSpi
engineGeneratePrivate( ): **K**eyFactorySpi
engineGeneratePublic( ): **K**eyFactorySpi
engineGenerateSecret( ): **K**eyAgreementSpi
SecretKeyFactorySpi
engineGenerateSeed( ): **S**ecureRandomSpi
engineGenExemptionBlob( ): **E**xemptionMechanismSpi
engineGetBlockSize( ): **C**ipherSpi
engineGetCertificate( ): **K**eyStoreSpi
engineGetCertificateAlias( ): **K**eyStoreSpi
engineGetCertificateChain( ): **K**eyStoreSpi
engineGetCertificates( ): **C**ertStoreSpi
engineGetCertPathEncodings( ): **C**ertificateFactorySpi
engineGetClientSessionContext( ): **S**SLContextSpi
engineGetCreationDate( ): **K**eyStoreSpi
engineGetCRLs( ): **C**ertStoreSpi
engineGetDigestLength( ): **M**essageDigestSpi‿
engineGetEncoded( ): **A**lgorithmParametersSpi
engineGetIV( ): **C**ipherSpi
engineGetKey( ): **K**eyStoreSpi
engineGetKeyManagers( ): **K**eyManagerFactorySpi
engineGetKeySize( ): **C**ipherSpi
engineGetKeySpec( ): **K**eyFactorySpi **S**ecretKeyFactorySpi
engineGetMacLength( ): **M**acSpi
engineGetOutputSize( ): **C**ipherSpi **E**xemptionMechanismSpi
engineGetParameter( ): **S**ignatureSpi
engineGetParameters( ): **C**ipherSpi **S**ignatureSpi
engineGetParameterSpec( ): **A**lgorithmParametersSpi
engineGetServerSessionContext( ): **S**SLContextSpi
engineGetServerSocketFactory( ): **S**SLContextSpi
engineGetSocketFactory( ): **S**SLContextSpi
engineGetTrustManagers( ): **T**rustManagerFactorySpi
engineInit( ): **A**lgorithmParameterGeneratorSpi
AlgorithmParametersSpi **C**ipherSpi

ExemptionMechanismSpi **K**eyAgreementSpi
KeyGeneratorSpi **K**eyManagerFactorySpi **M**acSpi
SSLContextSpi **T**rustManagerFactorySpi
engineInitSign( ): **S**ignatureSpi␣
engineInitVerify( ): **S**ignatureSpi␣
engineIsCertificateEntry( ): **K**eyStoreSpi
engineIsKeyEntry( ): **K**eyStoreSpi
engineLoad( ): **K**eyStoreSpi
engineNextBytes( ): **S**ecureRandomSpi
engineReset( ): **M**acSpi **M**essageDigestSpi␣
engineSetCertificateEntry( ): **K**eyStoreSpi
engineSetKeyEntry( ): **K**eyStoreSpi
engineSetMode( ): **C**ipherSpi
engineSetPadding( ): **C**ipherSpi
engineSetParameter( ): **S**ignatureSpi␣
engineSetSeed( ): **S**ecureRandomSpi
engineSign( ): **S**ignatureSpi␣
engineSize( ): **K**eyStoreSpi
engineStore( ): **K**eyStoreSpi
engineToString( ): **A**lgorithmParametersSpi
engineTranslateKey( ): **K**eyFactorySpi **S**ecretKeyFactorySpi
engineUnwrap( ): **C**ipherSpi
engineUpdate( ): **C**ipherSpi **M**acSpi **M**essageDigestSpi␣
  SignatureSpi␣
engineValidate( ): **C**ertPathValidatorSpi
engineVerify( ): **S**ignatureSpi␣
engineWrap( ): **C**ipherSpi
ENGLISH: **L**ocale
enqueue( ): java.lang.ref.**R**eference␣
ensureCapacity( ): **A**rrayList^ **S**tringBuffer **V**ector^
entering( ): **L**ogger
*Entity^*: org.w3c.dom
ENTITY_NODE: *Node*␣
ENTITY_REFERENCE_NODE: *Node*␣
*EntityReference^*: org.w3c.dom
  —returned by: *Document^*.createEntityReference( )
EntityResolver: org.xml.sax
  —passed to: **D**ocumentBuilder.setEntityResolver( )
    Parser.setEntityResolver( ) **P**arserAdapter.setEntityResolver( )
    XMLFilterImpl.setEntityResolver( )
    XMLReader␣.setEntityResolver( )
    XMLReaderAdapter.setEntityResolver( )
  —returned by: **P**arserAdapter.getEntityResolver( )
    XMLFilterImpl.getEntityResolver( )
    XMLReader␣.getEntityResolver( )
  —implemented by: **D**efaultHandler **H**andlerBase **X**MLFilterImpl
entries( ): **A**cl^ **Z**ipFile␣
entrySet( ): **A**bstractMap␣ java.util.jar.**A**ttributes **H**ashtable^
  Map␣
enumerate( ): **T**hread **T**hreadGroup
Enumeration␣: java.util
  —extended by: *NamingEnumeration^*
  —passed to: javax.swing.text.**A**bstractDocument↩
    .AbstractElement.removeAttributes( ) *javax.swing.text*↩
    .*AbstractDocument.AttributeContext*.removeAttributes( )
    Collections.list( ) **C**ompositeName( ) **C**ompoundName( )
    javax.swing.**J**Tree^.removeDescendantToggledPaths( )
    *javax.swing.text.MutableAttributeSet^*.removeAttributes( )
    SequenceInputStream( )
    javax.swing.text.**S**impleAttributeSet.removeAttributes( )
    javax.swing.text.**S**tyleContext.removeAttributes( )
    javax.swing.text.**S**tyleContext.NamedStyle.removeAttributes( )
  —returned
    by: javax.swing.text.**A**bstractDocument.AbstractElement
    < children( ),   getAttributeNames( ) >
    javax.swing.tree.**A**bstractLayoutCache.getVisiblePathsFrom( )
    *Acl^* < entries( ),   getPermissions( ) > *AclEntry^*.permissions( )
    java.applet.AppletContext.getApplets( )
    javax.swing.text.html.parser.**A**ttributeList.getValues( )
    javax.swing.text.AttributeSet.getAttributeNames( )
    javax.swing.**B**uttonGroup.getElements( )

ClassLoader␣ < findResources( ), getResources( ),
  getSystemResources( ) > **C**ollections.enumeration( )
  CompositeName.getAll( ) **C**ompoundName.getAll( )
  javax.swing.**D**efaultListModel^.elements( )
  javax.swing.tree.**D**efaultMutableTreeNode
  < breadthFirstEnumeration( ),   children( ),
  depthFirstEnumeration( ), pathFromAncestorEnumeration( ),
  postorderEnumeration( ),   preorderEnumeration( ) >
  javax.swing.text.**D**efaultStyledDocument^.getStyleNames( )
  javax.swing.table.**D**efaultTableColumnModel.getColumns( )
  Dictionary␣ < elements( ), keys( ) > **D**riverManager.getDrivers( )
  FeatureDescriptor␣.attributeNames( )
  *Group^*.members( ) **I**dentityScope^.identities( )
  javax.swing.**J**Tree^ < getDescendantToggledPaths( ),
  getExpandedDescendants( ) > **K**eyStore.aliases( )
  KeyStoreSpi.engineAliases( ) **L**ogManager.getLoggerNames( )
  java.awt.**M**enuBar^.shortcuts( ) *Name^*.getAll( )
  NamespaceSupport < getDeclaredPrefixes( ), getPrefixes( ) >
  NetworkInterface < getInetAddresses( ), getNetworkInterfaces( ) >
  PermissionCollection␣.elements( ) **P**roperties^.propertyNames( )
  javax.naming.**R**eference␣.getAll( ) **R**esourceBundle␣.getKeys( )
  javax.swing.text.**S**impleAttributeSet.getAttributeNames( )
  SSLSessionContext.getIds( )
  javax.swing.text.**S**tyleContext.getStyleNames( )
  javax.swing.text.**S**tyleContext.NamedStyle.getAttributeNames( )
  javax.swing.text.**S**tyleContext↩
  .SmallAttributeSet.getAttributeNames( )
  javax.swing.table.TableColumnModel.getColumns( )
  javax.swing.tree.TreeNode.children( )
  URLClassLoader^.findResources( ) **V**ector^.elements( )
  ZipFile␣.entries( )
  —implemented by: **S**tringTokenizer
  —fields: javax.swing.tree.**D**efaultMutableTreeNode↩
  .EMPTY_ENUMERATION
enumeration( ): **C**ollections
env( ): **R**equest
environment: **C**annotProceedException^
Environment: org.omg.CORBA
  —returned by: org.omg.CORBA.**O**RB␣.create_environment( )
  Request.env( )
eof: **O**ptionalDataException^
EOFException^: java.io
eolIsSignificant( ): **S**treamTokenizer
eos: **G**ZIPInputStream^
equal( ): _**D**ynAnyStub^ _**D**ynArrayStub^ _**D**ynEnumStub^
  _**D**ynFixedStub^ _**D**ynSequenceStub^ _**D**ynStructStub^
  _**D**ynUnionStub^ _**D**ynValueStub^ **A**ny *DynAnyOperations*␣
  TypeCode
equals( ): **A**rrays **C**ollator␣ *Collection*␣ *Comparator*
  org.omg.CORBA.portable.**D**elegate␣ *GSSCredential^*
  GSSName *Map*␣ *Map.Entry* java.lang.**O**bject␣
  java.security.acl.Permission java.security.**P**rincipal␣
  StubDelegate **T**imestamp^ **U**RLStreamHandler
equalsIgnoreCase( ): **S**tring
equivalent( ): **T**ypeCode
ERA: **C**alendar␣ **D**ateFormat.Field^
ERA_FIELD: **D**ateFormat^
err: **F**ileDescriptor **S**ystem
ERROR: **C**onfirmationCallback **T**extOutputCallback
Error^: java.lang
  —subclasses: **A**ssertionError java.awt.**A**WTError
  CoderMalfunctionError **F**actoryConfigurationError
  LinkageError␣ **T**hreadDeath
  TransformerFactoryConfigurationError **V**irtualMachineError␣
  —descendents: **A**bstractMethodError^ **C**lassCircularityError^
  ClassFormatError^ **E**xceptionInInitializerError^
  IllegalAccessError^ **I**ncompatibleClassChangeError^
  InstantiationError^ **I**nternalError^ **N**oClassDefFoundError^
  NoSuchFieldError^ **N**oSuchMethodError^
  OutOfMemoryError^ **S**tackOverflowError^ **U**nknownError^

E

Error / EventObject

javax.swing.event.**H**yperlinkEvent^
javax.sound.sampled.**L**ineEvent^
javax.swing.event.**L**istDataEvent^
javax.swing.event.**L**istSelectionEvent^
javax.swing.event.**M**enuEvent^   **N**amingEvent^
NamingExceptionEvent^   **N**odeChangeEvent^
javax.swing.event.**P**opupMenuEvent^
PreferenceChangeEvent^
javax.print.event.**P**rintEvent^   **P**ropertyChangeEvent^
RowSetEvent^   **S**SLSessionBindingEvent^
javax.swing.event.**T**ableColumnModelEvent^
javax.swing.event.**T**ableModelEvent^
javax.swing.event.**T**reeExpansionEvent^
javax.swing.event.**T**reeModelEvent^
javax.swing.event.**T**reeSelectionEvent^
javax.swing.event.**U**ndoableEditEvent^
UnsolicitedNotificationEvent^
—descendents: java.awt.event.**A**ctionEvent^
java.awt.event.**A**djustmentEvent^
javax.swing.event.**A**ncestorEvent^
BeanContextMembershipEvent^
BeanContextServiceAvailableEvent^
BeanContextServiceRevokedEvent^
java.awt.event.**C**omponentEvent^
java.awt.event.**C**ontainerEvent^
java.awt.dnd.**D**ragSourceDragEvent^
java.awt.dnd.**D**ragSourceDropEvent^
java.awt.dnd.**D**ropTargetDragEvent^
java.awt.dnd.**D**ropTargetDropEvent^
java.awt.event.**F**ocusEvent^   java.awt.event.**H**ierarchyEvent^
javax.swing.text.html.**H**TMLFrameHyperlinkEvent^
java.awt.event.**I**nputEvent^
java.awt.event.**I**nputMethodEvent^
javax.swing.event.**I**nternalFrameEvent^
java.awt.event.**I**nvocationEvent^
java.awt.event.**I**temEvent^   java.awt.event.**K**eyEvent^
javax.swing.event.**M**enuDragMouseEvent^
javax.swing.event.**M**enuKeyEvent^
java.awt.event.**M**ouseEvent^
java.awt.event.**M**ouseWheelEvent^
java.awt.event.**P**aintEvent^
javax.print.event.**P**rintJobAttributeEvent^
javax.print.event.**P**rintJobEvent^
javax.print.event.**P**rintServiceAttributeEvent^
java.awt.event.**T**extEvent^   java.awt.event.**W**indowEvent^
—passed to: javax.swing.**A**bstractCellEditor < isCellEditable( ),
shouldSelectCell( ) >   *javax.swing.CellEditor*
< isCellEditable( ),   shouldSelectCell( ) >
javax.swing.**D**efaultCellEditor.EditorDelegate
< isCellEditable( ),   shouldSelectCell( ),   startCellEditing( ) >
javax.swing.tree.**D**efaultTreeCellEditor < canEditImmediately( ),
isCellEditable( ),   shouldSelectCell( ),   shouldStartEditingTimer( ) >
javax.swing.**J**Table^.editCellAt( )
EventSetDescriptor^: java.beans
—returned by: *BeanInfo*.getEventSetDescriptors( )
SimpleBeanInfo.getEventSetDescriptors( )
except: **U**nknownUserException^
except( ): **S**erverRequest
Exception^: java.lang
—subclasses: **A**clNotFoundException   **A**ctivationException.
AlreadyBoundException   **A**pplicationException
java.awt.**A**WTException   **B**ackingStoreException
javax.swing.text.**B**adLocationException
javax.security.cert.**C**ertificateException.
ClassNotFoundException   **C**loneNotSupportedException.
DataFormatException   **D**estroyFailedException

javax.swing.tree.**E**xpandVetoException
java.awt.**F**ontFormatException
GeneralSecurityException.   **G**SSException
IllegalAccessException   **I**nstantiationException
InterruptedException   **I**ntrospectionException
javax.sound.midi.**I**nvalidMidiDataException
InvalidPreferencesFormatException
InvocationTargetException
IOException.   **L**astOwnerException
javax.sound.sampled.**L**ineUnavailableException
javax.sound.midi.**M**idiUnavailableException
java.awt.datatransfer.**M**imeTypeParseException
NamingException.
java.awt.geom.**N**oninvertibleTransformException
NoSuchFieldException   **N**oSuchMethodException
NotBoundException   **N**otOwnerException
ParseException   **P**arserConfigurationException
java.awt.print.**P**rinterException   javax.print.**P**rintException
PrivilegedActionException   **P**ropertyVetoException
RefreshFailedException   **R**emarshalException
RuntimeException.   **S**AXException.
ServerNotActiveException   **S**QLException.
TooManyListenersException   **T**ransformerException.
javax.sound.sampled.**U**nsupportedAudioFileException
UnsupportedCallbackException
java.awt.datatransfer.**U**nsupportedFlavorException
javax.swing.**U**nsupportedLookAndFeelException
URISyntaxException   **U**serException^   **X**AException
—descendents: **A**ccessControlException^
AccessException^   **A**ccountExpiredException^
ActivateFailedException^   **A**dapterAlreadyExists^
AdapterInactive^   **A**dapterNonExistent^   **A**lreadyBound^
AlreadyConnectedException^   **A**rithmeticException
ArrayIndexOutOfBoundsException^   **A**rrayStoreException
AsynchronousCloseException^   **A**ttributeInUseException^
AttributeModificationException^   **A**uthenticationException^
AuthenticationNotSupportedException^   **B**AD_CONTEXT^
BAD_INV_ORDER^   **B**AD_OPERATION^
BAD_PARAM^   **B**AD_TYPECODE^   **B**adKind^
BadPaddingException^   **B**atchUpdateException^
BindException^   org.omg.CORBA.**B**ounds^
org.omg.CORBA.TypeCodePackage.**B**ounds^
BufferOverflowException   **B**ufferUnderflowException
CancelledKeyException^   **C**annotProceed^
CannotProceedException^
javax.swing.undo.**C**annotRedoException
javax.swing.undo.**C**annotUndoException
java.security.cert.**C**ertificateEncodingException^
java.security.cert.**C**ertificateEncodingException^
java.security.cert.**C**ertificateException^
java.security.cert.**C**ertificateException^
java.security.cert.**C**ertificateExpiredException^
java.security.cert.**C**ertificateExpiredException^
java.security.cert.**C**ertificateNotYetValidException^
java.security.cert.**C**ertificateNotYetValidException^
java.security.cert.**C**ertificateParsingException^
java.security.cert.**C**ertificateParsingException^
CertPathBuilderException^
CertPathValidatorException^   **C**ertStoreException^
javax.swing.text.**C**hangedCharSetException^
CharacterCodingException^   **C**harConversionException^
ClassCastException   **C**losedByInterruptException^
ClosedChannelException^   **C**losedSelectorException^
java.awt.color.**C**MMException^   **C**OMM_FAILURE^
CommunicationException^   **C**oncurrentModificationException
ConfigurationException^   java.net.**C**onnectException^
java.rmi.**C**onnectException^   **C**onnectIOException^
ConnectionPendingException^   **C**ontextNotEmptyException^
CredentialExpiredException^   **C**RLException^
DATA_CONVERSION^   **D**ataTruncation^
DigestException^   **D**OMException   **D**uplicateName^

E

E

Cross-Ref

E

extract_octet( ): Any
extract_Principal( ): Any
extract_short( ): Any
extract_Streamable( ): Any
extract_string( ): Any
extract_TypeCode( ): Any
extract_ulong( ): Any
extract_ulonglong( ): Any
extract_ushort( ): Any
extract_Value( ): Any
extract_wchar( ): Any
extract_wstring( ): Any
F0: RSAKeyGenParameterSpec
F4: RSAKeyGenParameterSpec
FactoryConfigurationError: javax.xml.parsers
—thrown by: DocumentBuilderFactory.newInstance( )
  SAXParserFactory.newInstance( )
FailedLoginException^: javax.security.auth.login
FAILURE: GSSException
failure( ): RMIFailureHandler
FALSE: Boolean
fatalError( ): DefaultHandler ErrorHandler ErrorListener
  HandlerBase XMLFilterImpl
fd: DatagramSocketImpl SocketImpl
FEATURE: DOMResult DOMSource SAXResult SAXSource
  SAXTransformerFactory^ StreamResult StreamSource
FEATURE_XMLFILTER: SAXTransformerFactory^
FeatureDescriptor: java.beans
—subclasses: BeanDescriptor EventSetDescriptor^
  MethodDescriptor^ ParameterDescriptor^
  PropertyDescriptor^
—descendents: IndexedPropertyDescriptor^
FEBRUARY: Calendar
FETCH_FORWARD: ResultSet
FETCH_REVERSE: ResultSet
FETCH_UNKNOWN: ResultSet
Field^: java.lang.reflect
—returned by: Class < getDeclaredField( ), getDeclaredFields( ),
  getField( ), getFields( ) >
FIELD_COUNT: Calendar
FieldNameHelper: org.omg.CORBA
FieldNameHelper: org.omg.DynamicAny
FieldPosition: java.text
—passed to: DateFormat^.format( ) Format.format( )
  MessageFormat^.format( ) NumberFormat^.format( )
fields: Calendar
File: java.io
—passed to: javax.sound.sampled.spi.AudioFileReader
  < getAudioFileFormat( ), getAudioInputStream( ) >
  javax.sound.sampled.spi.AudioFileWriter.write( )
  javax.sound.sampled.AudioSystem < getAudioFileFormat( ),
  getAudioInputStream( ), write( ) > DocumentBuilder.parse( )
  File < compareTo( ), createTempFile( ), File( ), renameTo( ) >
  javax.imageio.stream.FileCacheImageInputStream( )
  javax.imageio.stream.FileCacheImageOutputStream( )
  javax.swing.plaf.FileChooserUI^.ensureFileIsVisible( )
  java.io.FileFilter.accept( )
  javax.swing.filechooser.FileFilter.accept( )
  javax.imageio.stream.FileImageInputStream( )
  javax.imageio.stream.FileImageOutputStream( )
  FileInputStream( ) FilenameFilter.accept( )
  FileOutputStream( ) FileReader( )
  javax.swing.filechooser.FileSystemView < createFileObject( ),
  createFileSystemRoot( ), createNewFolder( ), getChild( ),
  getFiles( ), getParentDirectory( ), getSystemDisplayName( ),
  getSystemIcon( ), getSystemTypeDescription( ), isComputerNode( ),
  isDrive( ), isFileSystem( ), isFileSystemRoot( ), isFloppyDrive( ),
  isHiddenFile( ), isParent( ), isRoot( ), isTraversable( ) >
  javax.swing.filechooser.FileView < getDescription( ),
  getIcon( ), getName( ), getTypeDescription( ), isTraversable( ) >

FileWriter( ) javax.imageio.spi.ImageInputStreamSpi^ ↵
  .createInputStreamInstance( ) javax.imageio.ImageIO < read( ),
  setCacheDirectory( ), write > javax.imageio.spi ↵
  .ImageOutputStreamSpi^.createOutputStreamInstance( )
  JarFile( ) javax.swing.JFileChooser^ < accept( ),
  ensureFileIsVisible( ), getDescription( ), getIcon( ), getName( ),
  getTypeDescription( ), isTraversable( ), JFileChooser( ),
  setCurrentDirectory( ), setSelectedFile( ), setSelectedFiles( ) >
  javax.sound.midi.spi.MidiFileReader < getMidiFileFormat( ),
  getSequence( ) > javax.sound.midi.spi.MidiFileWriter.write( )
  javax.sound.midi.MidiSystem < getMidiFileFormat( ),
  getSequence( ), getSoundbank( ), write( ) >
  RandomAccessFile( ) Runtime.exec( ) SAXParser.parse( )
  javax.sound.midi.spi.SoundbankReader.getSoundbank( )
  StreamResult < setSystemId( ), StreamResult( ) >
  StreamSource < setSystemId( ), StreamSource( ) > ZipFile( )
—returned by: File < createTempFile( ), getAbsoluteFile( ),
  getCanonicalFile( ), getParentFile( ), listFiles( ),
  listRoots( ) > javax.swing.filechooser.FileSystemView
  < createFileObject( ), createFileSystemRoot( ),
  createNewFolder( ), getChild( ), getDefaultDirectory( ),
  getFiles( ), getHomeDirectory( ), getParentDirectory( ),
  getRoots( ) > javax.imageio.ImageIO.getCacheDirectory( )
  javax.swing.JFileChooser^ < getCurrentDirectory( ),
  getSelectedFile( ), getSelectedFiles( ) >
FileChannel^: java.nio.channels
—passed to: FileLock( )
—returned by: FileChannel^ < position( ),
  truncate( ) > FileInputStream^.getChannel( )
  FileLock.channel( ) FileOutputStream^.getChannel( )
  RandomAccessFile.getChannel( )
FileChannel.MapMode: java.nio.channels
—passed to: FileChannel^.map( )
—fields: FileChannel.MapMode < PRIVATE, READ_ONLY,
  READ_WRITE >
FileDescriptor: java.io
—passed to: FileInputStream( ) FileOutputStream( )
  FileReader( ) FileWriter( ) SecurityManager < checkRead( ),
  checkWrite( ) >
—returned by: DatagramSocketImpl.getFileDescriptor( )
  FileInputStream^.getFD( ) FileOutputStream^.getFD( )
  RandomAccessFile.getFD( ) SocketImpl.getFileDescriptor( )
—fields: DatagramSocketImpl.fd FileDescriptor < err, in, out >
  SocketImpl.fd
FileFilter: java.io
—passed to: File.listFiles( )
FileHandler^: java.util.logging
FileInputStream^: java.io
FileLock: java.nio.channels
—returned by: FileChannel^ < lock( ), tryLock( ) >
FileLockInterruptionException^: java.nio.channels
FilenameFilter: java.io
—passed to: File < list( ), listFiles( ) >
  java.awt.FileDialog^.setFilenameFilter( )
  java.awt.peer.FileDialogPeer^.setFilenameFilter( )
—returned by: java.awt.FileDialog^.getFilenameFilter( )
FileNameMap: java.net
—passed to: URLConnection.setFileNameMap( )
—returned by: URLConnection.getFileNameMap( )
FileNotFoundException^: java.io
—thrown by: javax.imageio.stream.FileImageInputStream( )
  javax.imageio.stream.FileImageOutputStream( )
  FileInputStream( ) FileOutputStream( ) FileReader( )
  RandomAccessFile( )
FileOutputStream^: java.io
FilePermission^: java.io
FileReader^: java.io
FileWriter^: java.io
fill( ): Arrays Collections InflaterInputStream^
fillInStackTrace( ): Throwable

Filter: java.util.logging
— passed to: Handler.setFilter() Logger.setFilter()
— returned by: Handler.getFilter() Logger.getFilter()
FILTERED: Deflater
FilterInputStream^: java.io
— subclasses: BufferedInputStream^
CheckedInputStream^ CipherInputStream^
java.io.DataInputStream^ DigestInputStream^
InflaterInputStream^ LineNumberInputStream^
javax.swing.ProgressMonitorInputStream^
PushbackInputStream^
— descendents: GZIPInputStream^ JarInputStream^
ZipInputStream^
FilterOutputStream^: java.io
— subclasses: BufferedOutputStream^ CheckedOutputStream^
CipherOutputStream^ java.io.DataOutputStream^
DeflaterOutputStream^ DigestOutputStream^ PrintStream^
— descendents: GZIPOutputStream^ JarOutputStream^
LogStream^ ZipOutputStream^
FilterReader^: java.io
— subclasses: PushbackReader^
FilterWriter^: java.io
FINAL: Modifier
FINAL_QUOTE_PUNCTUATION: Character
finalize(): Deflater ExemptionMechanism FileInputStream^
FileOutputStream^ Inflater java.lang.Object ZipFile
find(): Matcher
find_POA(): POAOperations
findClass(): ClassLoader
findColumn(): ResultSet
findEditor(): PropertyEditorManager
findLibrary(): ClassLoader
findLoadedClass(): ClassLoader
findResource(): ClassLoader
findResources(): ClassLoader
findSystemClass(): ClassLoader
FINE: Level
fine(): Logger
FINER: Level
finer(): Logger
FINEST: Level
finest(): Logger
finish(): Deflater DeflaterOutputStream^
finishConnect(): SocketChannel^
finished(): Deflater Inflater
fireChildrenAdded(): BeanContextSupport^
fireChildrenRemoved(): BeanContextSupport^
firePropertyChange(): BeanContextChildSupport
PropertyChangeSupport PropertyEditorSupport
fireServiceAdded(): BeanContextServicesSupport^
fireServiceRevoked(): BeanContextServicesSupport^
fireVetoableChange(): BeanContextChildSupport
VetoableChangeSupport
first(): BreakIterator CharacterIterator^ ResultSet
SortedSet^ StringCharacterIterator TreeSet^
firstElement(): Vector^
firstKey(): SortedMap^ TreeMap^
fixed_digits(): TypeCode
fixed_scale(): TypeCode
FixedHolder: org.omg.CORBA
flags(): NamedValue Pattern
flip(): BitSet Buffer
flipBit(): BigInteger^
FLOAT: Types
Float^: java.lang
— passed to: Float^.compareTo()
— returned by: Float^.valueOf()
— fields: java.awt.font.TextAttribute^ < JUSTIFICATION_FULL,
JUSTIFICATION_NONE, POSTURE_OBLIQUE, POSTURE_REGULAR,
WEIGHT_BOLD, WEIGHT_DEMIBOLD, WEIGHT_DEMILIGHT,
WEIGHT_EXTRA_LIGHT, WEIGHT_EXTRABOLD,
WEIGHT_HEAVY, WEIGHT_LIGHT, WEIGHT_MEDIUM,

WEIGHT_REGULAR, WEIGHT_SEMIBOLD, WEIGHT_ULTRABOLD,
WIDTH_CONDENSED, WIDTH_EXTENDED, WIDTH_REGULAR,
WIDTH_SEMI_CONDENSED, WIDTH_SEMI_EXTENDED >
FloatBuffer^: java.nio
— passed to: FloatBuffer^.put()
— returned by: ByteBuffer^.asFloatBuffer() FloatBuffer^
< allocate(), asReadOnlyBuffer(), compact(), duplicate(), get(),
put(), slice(), wrap() >
FloatHolder: org.omg.CORBA
FloatSeqHelper: org.omg.CORBA
FloatSeqHolder: org.omg.CORBA
— passed
to: org.omg.CORBA.DataInputStream^.read_float_array()
floatToIntBits(): Float^
floatToRawIntBits(): Float^
floatValue(): Number
floor(): Math StrictMath
flush(): CharsetDecoder CharsetEncoder Handler
ObjectOutput^ java.io.OutputStream Preferences Writer
XMLEncoder^
FLUSH_FAILURE: ErrorManager
flushCaches(): Introspector
flushFromCaches(): Introspector
flushSpi(): AbstractPreferences^
following(): BreakIterator
force(): FileChannel^ MappedByteBuffer^
forClass(): ObjectStreamClass
forDigit(): Character
forget(): XAResource
format: Encoding
FORMAT: Character
Format: java.text
— subclasses: DateFormat^ MessageFormat^ NumberFormat^
— descendents: ChoiceFormat^ DecimalFormat^
SimpleDateFormat^
— passed to: javax.swing.text.InternationalFormatter^
< InternationalFormatter(), setFormat() >
javax.swing.JFormattedTextField() MessageFormat^
< setFormat(), setFormatByArgumentIndex(), setFormats(),
setFormatsByArgumentIndex() >
— returned
by: javax.swing.text.InternationalFormatter^.getFormat()
MessageFormat^ < getFormats(),
getFormatsByArgumentIndex() >
format(): Format Formatter
Format.Field^: java.text
— subclasses: DateFormat.Field^ MessageFormat.Field^
NumberFormat.Field^
— passed to: FieldPosition()
— returned by: FieldPosition.getFieldAttribute()
javax.swing.text.InternationalFormatter^.getFields()
FORMAT_FAILURE: ErrorManager
formatMessage(): Formatter
FormatMismatch^: org.omg.IOP.CodecPackage
— passed to: FormatMismatchHelper < insert(), write() >
— returned by: FormatMismatchHelper < extract(), read() >
— thrown by: CodecOperations < decode(), decode_value() >
FormatMismatchHelper: org.omg.IOP.CodecPackage
Formatter: java.util.logging
— subclasses: SimpleFormatter^ XMLFormatter^
— passed to: Handler.setFormatter() StreamHandler()
— returned by: Handler.getFormatter()
formatToCharacterIterator(): Format
forName(): Charset Class
forward: org.omg.PortableInterceptor.ForwardRequest^
forward_reference: org.omg.PortableServer.ForwardRequest^
forward_reference(): RequestInfoOperations
ForwardRequest^: org.omg.PortableInterceptor
— passed
to: org.omg.PortableInterceptor.ForwardRequestHelper
< insert(), write() >

—returned
by: org.omg.PortableInterceptor.**F**orwardRequestHelper
< extract( ), read( ) >
—thrown by: *ClientRequestInterceptorOperations*ˇ
< receive_exception( ), receive_other( ), send_request( ) >
*ServerRequestInterceptorOperations*ˇ < receive_request( ),
receive_request_service_contexts( ), send_exception( ),
send_other( ) >
ForwardRequestˆ: org.omg.PortableServer
—passed to: org.omg.PortableServer.**F**orwardRequestHelper
< insert( ), write( ) >
—returned by: org.omg.PortableServer.**F**orwardRequestHelper
< extract( ), read( ) >
—thrown by: _ServantActivatorStubˆ.incarnate( )
_ServantLocatorStubˆ.preinvoke( )
*ServantActivatorOperations*ˇ.incarnate( )
*ServantLocatorOperations*ˇ.preinvoke( )
ForwardRequestHelper: org.omg.PortableInterceptor
ForwardRequestHelper: org.omg.PortableServer
FRACTION: NumberFormat.Fieldˆ
FRACTION_FIELD: NumberFormatˇ
FRANCE: Locale
FREE_MEMˆ: org.omg.CORBA
freeMemory(): Runtime
FRENCH: Locale
FRIDAY: Calendar
from_any(): _DynAnyStubˆ _DynArrayStubˆ
_DynEnumStubˆ _DynFixedStubˆ _DynSequenceStubˆ
_DynStructStubˆ _DynUnionStubˆ _DynValueStubˆ
org.omg.CORBA.**D**ynAnyˇ *D*ynAnyOperations
from_int(): BindingType CompletionStatus
DefinitionKind IdAssignmentPolicyValue
IdUniquenessPolicyValue ImplicitActivationPolicyValue
LifespanPolicyValue NotFoundReason ParameterMode
RequestProcessingPolicyValue ServantRetentionPolicyValue
SetOverrideType State TCKind ThreadPolicyValue
FULL: DateFormatˇ
FULL_DECOMPOSITION: Collator
GAP_TOKEN: GSSException
*GatheringByteChannel*ˆ: java.nio.channels
—implemented by: **D**atagramChannelˆ **F**ileChannelˆ
Pipe.SinkChannelˆ **S**ocketChannelˆ
gc(): Runtime System
gcd(): BigIntegerˆ
GENERAL_PUNCTUATION: Character.UnicodeBlockˆ
GeneralSecurityException: java.security
—subclasses: **B**adPaddingExceptionˆ
java.security.cert.**C**ertificateExceptionˇ
CertPathBuilderExceptionˆ **C**ertPathValidatorExceptionˆ
CertStoreExceptionˆ **C**RLExceptionˆ **D**igestExceptionˆ
ExemptionMechanismExceptionˆ **I**llegalBlockSizeExceptionˆ
InvalidAlgorithmParameterExceptionˆ
InvalidKeySpecExceptionˆ **I**nvalidParameterSpecExceptionˆ
KeyExceptionˇ **K**eyStoreExceptionˆ **L**oginExceptionˇ
NoSuchAlgorithmExceptionˆ **N**oSuchPaddingExceptionˆ
NoSuchProviderExceptionˆ **S**hortBufferExceptionˆ
SignatureExceptionˆ **U**nrecoverableKeyExceptionˆ
—descendents: **A**ccountExpiredExceptionˆ
java.security.cert.**C**ertificateEncodingExceptionˆ
java.security.cert.**C**ertificateExpiredExceptionˆ
java.security.cert.**C**ertificateNotYetValidExceptionˆ
java.security.cert.**C**ertificateParsingExceptionˆ
CredentialExpiredExceptionˆ **F**ailedLoginExceptionˆ
InvalidKeyExceptionˆ **K**eyManagementExceptionˆ
generateCertificate(): CertificateFactory
generateCertificates(): CertificateFactory
generateCertPath(): CertificateFactory
generateCRL(): CertificateFactory
generateCRLs(): CertificateFactory
generateKey(): KeyGenerator
generateKeyPair(): KeyPairGeneratorSpi
generateParameters(): AlgorithmParameterGenerator

generatePrivate(): KeyFactory
generatePublic(): KeyFactory
generateSecret(): KeyAgreement SecretKeyFactory
generateSeed(): SecureRandomˆ
GENERIC_FAILURE: ErrorManager
genExemptionBlob(): ExemptionMechanism
genKeyPair(): KeyPairGenerator
GEOMETRIC_SHAPES: Character.UnicodeBlockˆ
GEORGIAN: Character.UnicodeBlockˆ
GERMAN: Locale
GERMANY: Locale
get(): AbstractListˇ AbstractMap java.lang.reflect.Array
*javax.naming.directory.Attribute*ˆ java.util.jar.Attributes
*javax.naming.directory.Attributes*ˆ **B**asicAttribute
BasicAttributes **B**itSet **B**yteBufferˇ **C**alendar **C**harBuffer
CompositeName **C**ompoundName **D**ictionary
DoubleBuffer **E**ncoder **F**ieldˆ **F**loatBuffer **I**ntBufferˆ
*List*ˆ **L**ongBuffer *Map* **M**arshalledObject
*Name*ˆ **O**bjectInputStream.GetField **P**references
java.lang.ref.**R**eference javax.naming.**R**eference
ShortBuffer **T**hreadLocal
get2DigitYearStart(): SimpleDateFormatˇ
get_any(): _DynAnyStubˆ _DynArrayStubˆ
_DynEnumStubˆ _DynFixedStubˆ _DynSequenceStubˆ
_DynStructStubˆ _DynUnionStubˆ _DynValueStubˆ
org.omg.CORBA.**D**ynAnyˇ *D*ynAnyOperations
get_as_string(): _DynEnumStubˆ *D*ynEnumOperationsˇ
get_as_ulong(): _DynEnumStubˆ *D*ynEnumOperationsˇ
get_boolean(): _DynAnyStubˆ _DynArrayStubˆ
_DynEnumStubˆ _DynFixedStubˆ _DynSequenceStubˆ
_DynStructStubˆ _DynUnionStubˆ _DynValueStubˆ
org.omg.CORBA.**D**ynAnyˇ *D*ynAnyOperations
get_boxed_value(): *D*ynValueBoxOperationsˇ
get_boxed_value_as_dyn_any(): *D*ynValueBoxOperationsˇ
get_char(): _DynAnyStubˆ _DynArrayStubˆ
_DynEnumStubˆ _DynFixedStubˆ _DynSequenceStubˆ
_DynStructStubˆ _DynUnionStubˆ _DynValueStubˆ
org.omg.CORBA.**D**ynAnyˇ *D*ynAnyOperations
get_codebase(): org.omg.CORBA_2_3.portable.**D**elegateˆ
get_compact_typecode(): TypeCode
get_current(): org.omg.CORBA.**O**RB
get_default_context(): org.omg.CORBA.**O**RB
get_discriminator(): _DynUnionStubˆ *D*ynUnionOperationsˇ
get_domain_managers(): org.omg.CORBA.portable.**D**elegate
get_domain_policy(): *D*omainManagerOperations
get_double(): _DynAnyStubˆ _DynArrayStubˆ
_DynEnumStubˆ _DynFixedStubˆ _DynSequenceStubˆ
_DynStructStubˆ _DynUnionStubˆ _DynValueStubˆ
org.omg.CORBA.**D**ynAnyˇ *D*ynAnyOperations
get_dyn_any(): _DynAnyStubˆ _DynArrayStubˆ
_DynEnumStubˆ _DynFixedStubˆ _DynSequenceStubˆ
_DynStructStubˆ _DynUnionStubˆ _DynValueStubˆ
*D*ynAnyOperations
get_effective_component(): *C*lientRequestInfoOperationsˇ
get_effective_components(): *C*lientRequestInfoOperationsˇ
get_effective_policy(): *I*ORInfoOperations
get_elements(): _DynArrayStubˆ _DynSequenceStubˆ
org.omg.CORBA.**D**ynArrayˆ *D*ynArrayOperationsˇ
org.omg.CORBA.**D**ynSequenceˆ *D*ynSequenceOperationsˇ
get_elements_as_dyn_any(): _DynArrayStubˆ
_DynSequenceStubˆ *D*ynArrayOperationsˇ
*D*ynSequenceOperationsˇ
get_float(): _DynAnyStubˆ _DynArrayStubˆ
_DynEnumStubˆ _DynFixedStubˆ _DynSequenceStubˆ
_DynStructStubˆ _DynUnionStubˆ _DynValueStubˆ
org.omg.CORBA.**D**ynAnyˇ *D*ynAnyOperations
get_id(): *B*oxedValueHelper StringValueHelper
WStringValueHelper
get_interface_def(): org.omg.CORBA.portable.**D**elegate
org.omg.PortableServer.portable.**D**elegate
get_length(): _DynSequenceStubˆ *D*ynSequenceOperationsˇ

G

Cross-Ref

getAvailableLocales( ): BreakIterator Calendar. Collator.
    DateFormat. Locale NumberFormat.
getBaseLevel( ): Bidi
getBaseType( ): *java.sql.Array*
getBaseTypeName( ): *java.sql.Array* *Ref*
getBasicConstraints( ): java.security.cert.*X*509Certificate^
    *X*509CertSelector
getBeanClass( ): BeanDescriptor^
getBeanContext( ): *BeanContextChild*.
    BeanContextChildSupport. BeanContextEvent.
getBeanContextChildPeer( ): BeanContextChildSupport.
getBeanContextPeer( ): BeanContextSupport.
getBeanContextProxy( ): *BeanContextProxy*
getBeanContextServicesPeer( ): BeanContextServicesSupport^
getBeanDescriptor( ): *BeanInfo*. SimpleBeanInfo
getBeanInfo( ): Introspector
getBeanInfoSearchPath( ): Introspector
getBeginIndex( ): *CharacterIterator*. FieldPosition
    StringCharacterIterator
getBestRowIdentifier( ): *DatabaseMetaData*
getBigDecimal( ): *CallableStatement*^ *ResultSet*.
getBinaryStream( ): *Blob* *ResultSet*.
getBlob( ): *CallableStatement*^ *ResultSet*.
getBlockSize( ): Cipher.
getBoolean( ): java.lang.reflect.*Array* Boolean
    CallableStatement^ Field^ Preferences. *ResultSet*.
getBranchQualifier( ): *Xid*
getBroadcast( ): DatagramSocket.
getBuffer( ): StringWriter^
getBundle( ): ResourceBundle.
getByAddress( ): InetAddress.
getByInetAddress( ): NetworkInterface
getByName( ): InetAddress. NetworkInterface
getByte( ): java.lang.reflect.*Array* *CallableStatement*^ Field^
    ResultSet.
getByteArray( ): Preferences.
getBytes( ): *Blob* *CallableStatement*^ *ResultSet*. String
getByteStream( ): InputSource
getCalendar( ): DateFormat.
getCalendarField( ): DateFormat.Field^
getCallback( ): UnsupportedCallbackException
getCAName( ): TrustAnchor
getCanonicalFile( ): File
getCanonicalHostName( ): InetAddress.
getCanonicalPath( ): File
getCAPublicKey( ): TrustAnchor
getCatalog( ): *Connection*
getCatalogName( ): *ResultSetMetaData*.
getCatalogs( ): *DatabaseMetaData*
getCatalogSeparator( ): *DatabaseMetaData*
getCatalogTerm( ): *DatabaseMetaData*
getCause( ): Throwable.
getCertificate( ): KeyStore *X*500PrivateCredential
    *X*509CertSelector
getCertificateAlias( ): KeyStore
getCertificateChain( ): KeyStore *X*509KeyManager^
getCertificateChecking( ): *X*509CRLSelector
getCertificates( ): CertPath CertStore CodeSource JarEntry^
    JarURLConnection^
getCertificateValid( ): *X*509CertSelector
getCertPath( ): *CertPathBuilderResult*^
    CertPathValidatorException^ PKIXCertPathBuilderResult^
getCertPathCheckers( ): PKIXParameters.
getCertPathEncodings( ): CertificateFactory
getCertStoreParameters( ): CertStore
getCertStores( ): PKIXParameters.
getChangeInfo( ): NamingEvent^
getChannel( ): DatagramSocket. FileInputStream^
    FileOutputStream^ RandomAccessFile ServerSocket.
    Socket.
getChar( ): java.lang.reflect.*Array* ByteBuffer. Field^
getCharacterInstance( ): BreakIterator

getCharacterStream( ): *Clob* InputSource *ResultSet*.
getChars( ): String StringBuffer
getCharsetName( ): IllegalCharsetNameException^
    UnsupportedCharsetException^
getChecksum( ): CheckedInputStream^
    CheckedOutputStream^
getChild( ): AbstractPreferences^ NodeChangeEvent^
getChildBeanContextChild( ): BeanContextSupport.
getChildBeanContextMembershipListener( ):
    BeanContextSupport.
getChildBeanContextServicesListener( ):
    BeanContextServicesSupport.
getChildNodes( ): *Node*.
getChildPropertyChangeListener( ): BeanContextSupport.
getChildren( ): *PolicyNode*
getChildSerializable( ): BeanContextSupport.
getChildVetoableChangeListener( ): BeanContextSupport.
getChildVisibility( ): BeanContextSupport.
getChoices( ): ChoiceCallback
getCipherSuite( ): HandshakeCompletedEvent^
    HttpsURLConnection^ *SSLSession*
getClass( ): java.lang.Object
getClassAnnotation( ): RMIClassLoader RMIClassLoaderSpi
getClassContext( ): SecurityManager.
getClasses( ): Class
getClassLoader( ): Class ProtectionDomain RMIClassLoader
    RMIClassLoaderSpi
getClassName( ): ActivationDesc ActivationGroupDesc
    MissingResourceException NameClassPair.
    javax.naming.Reference. StackTraceElement
getClient( ): KerberosTicket
getClientAddresses( ): KerberosTicket
getClientAliases( ): *X*509KeyManager^
getClientHost( ): RemoteServer. *ServerRef*^
getClientSessionContext( ): SSLContext
getClob( ): *CallableStatement*^ *ResultSet*.
getCodebase( ): Util *UtilDelegate*
getCodeSource( ): ProtectionDomain
getCollationElementIterator( ): RuleBasedCollator^
getCollationKey( ): Collator.
getCollection( ): CollectionCertStoreParameters
getColumnClassName( ): *ResultSetMetaData*.
getColumnCount( ): *ResultSetMetaData*.
getColumnDisplaySize( ): *ResultSetMetaData*.
getColumnLabel( ): *ResultSetMetaData*.
getColumnName( ): *ResultSetMetaData*.
getColumnNumber( ): *Locator* LocatorImpl
    SAXParseException^ *SourceLocator*.
getColumnPrivileges( ): *DatabaseMetaData*
getColumns( ): *DatabaseMetaData*
getColumnType( ): *ResultSetMetaData*.
getColumnTypeName( ): *ResultSetMetaData*.
getCommand( ): *RowSet*^
getCommandEnvironment( ): ActivationGroupDesc
getCommandOptions( ):
    ActivationGroupDesc.CommandEnvironment
getCommandPath( ):
    ActivationGroupDesc.CommandEnvironment
getComment( ): ZipEntry.
getComponent( ): *BeanContextChildComponentProxy*
getComponentType( ): Class
getCompressedSize( ): ZipEntry.
getConcurrency( ): *ResultSet*.
getConfiguration( ): Configuration
getConfState( ): *GSSContext*
getConnectControls( ): InitialLdapContext^ *LdapContext*^
getConnection( ): *DatabaseMetaData* *DataSource*
    DriverManager *PooledConnection*. *RowSetInternal*
    java.sql.Statement.
getConstructor( ): Class
getConstructors( ): Class
getContainer( ): *BeanContextContainerProxy*

getEncoding(): Handler InputSource InputStreamReader˄
OutputStreamWriter˄
getEncodings(): CertPath
getEncryptedData(): EncryptedPrivateKeyInfo
getEndIndex(): *CharacterIterator*˄ FieldPosition
StringCharacterIterator
getEndTime(): KerberosTicket
getEntities(): DocumentType˄
getEntityResolver(): ParserAdapter XMLFilterImpl
XMLReader˄
getEntries(): Manifest
getEntry(): ZipFile˄
getEntryName(): JarURLConnection˄
getenv(): System
getEnvironment(): CannotProceedException˄
javax.naming.Context˄ InitialContext˄
getEras(): DateFormatSymbols
getErrorCode(): SQLException˄
getErrorHandler(): ParserAdapter XMLFilterImpl *XMLReader*˄
getErrorIndex(): ParsePosition
getErrorListener(): Transformer TransformerFactory˄
getErrorManager(): Handler˄
getErrorOffset(): ParseException
getErrorStream(): HttpURLConnection˄ Process
getEscapeProcessing(): *RowSet*˄
getEventContext(): NamingEvent˄ NamingExceptionEvent˄
getEventPropertyName(): EventHandler
getEventSetDescriptors(): *BeanInfo*˄ SimpleBeanInfo
getException(): ClassNotFoundException
ExceptionInInitializerError˄ FactoryConfigurationError
NamingExceptionEvent˄ PrivilegedActionException
SAXException˄ TransformerException˄
TransformerFactoryConfigurationError
UnsolicitedNotification˄
getExceptionListener(): Encoder˄ XMLDecoder
getExceptionTypes(): Constructor˄ Method˄
getExemptionMechanism(): Cipher˄
getExpectedPolicies(): *PolicyNode*
getExpiration(): URLConnection
getExplanation(): NamingException˄
getExponent(): RSAOtherPrimeInfo
getExponentSize(): DHGenParameterSpec
getExportedKeys(): *DatabaseMetaData*
getExtendedKeyUsage(): java.security.cert.X509Certificate˄
X509CertSelector
getExtensionValue(): *X509Extension*
getExtra(): ZipEntry˄
getExtraNameCharacters(): *DatabaseMetaData*
getFactoryClassLocation(): javax.naming.Reference˄
getFactoryClassName(): javax.naming.Reference˄
getFailureHandler(): RMISocketFactory
getFD(): FileInputStream˄ FileOutputStream˄
RandomAccessFile
getFeature(): ParserAdapter SAXParserFactory
TransformerFactory˄ XMLFilterImpl *XMLReader*˄
getFetchDirection(): *ResultSet*˄ *java.sql.Statement*˄
getFetchSize(): *ResultSet*˄ *java.sql.Statement*˄
getField(): Class FieldPosition ObjectStreamClass
getFieldAttribute(): FieldPosition
getFields(): Class ObjectStreamClass
getFile(): URL
getFileDescriptor(): DatagramSocketImpl SocketImpl
getFileName(): StackTraceElement
getFileNameMap(): URLConnection
getFilePointer(): RandomAccessFile
getFilter(): Handler˄ Logger
getFirst(): LinkedList˄
getFirstChild(): *Node*˄
getFirstDayOfWeek(): Calendar˄
getFlags(): KerberosTicket
getFloat(): java.lang.reflect.Array ByteBuffer˄
CallableStatement˄ Field˄ Preferences˄ *ResultSet*˄

getFollowRedirects(): HttpURLConnection˄
getFormat(): *java.security.Certificate* EncodedKeySpec˄
KerberosKey *Key*˄ SecretKeySpec
getFormatId(): *Xid*
getFormats(): ChoiceFormat˄ MessageFormat˄
getFormatsByArgumentIndex(): MessageFormat˄
getFormatter(): Handler˄
getFragment(): URI
getG(): DHParameterSpec DHPrivateKeySpec
DHPublicKeySpec DSAParameterSpec *DSAParams*
DSAPrivateKeySpec DSAPublicKeySpec
getGeneratedKeys(): *java.sql.Statement*˄
getGetListenerMethod(): EventSetDescriptor˄
getGlobalTransactionId(): *Xid*
getGreatestMinimum(): Calendar˄
getGregorianChange(): GregorianCalendar˄
getGroupID(): ActivationDesc
getGroupingSeparator(): DecimalFormatSymbols
getGroupingSize(): DecimalFormat˄
getGuarantor(): *java.security.Certificate*
getHandler(): SAXResult
getHandlers(): Logger
getHead(): Formatter˄
getHeaderField(): URLConnection˄
getHeaderFieldDate(): URLConnection˄
getHeaderFieldInt(): URLConnection˄
getHeaderFieldKey(): URLConnection˄
getHeaderFields(): URLConnection˄
getHoldability(): *Connection*
getHost(): URI URL
getHostAddress(): InetAddress˄ URLStreamHandler
getHostName(): InetAddress˄ InetSocketAddress˄
getHostnameVerifier(): HttpsURLConnection˄
getHours(): java.util.Date˄
getIcon(): *BeanInfo*˄ SimpleBeanInfo
getId(): ApplicationException *SSLSession*
getID(): Activatable˄ *javax.naming.directory.Attribute*˄
BasicAttribute *javax.naming.ldap.Control*˄
ExtendedRequest˄ *ExtendedResponse*˄ StartTlsRequest
StartTlsResponse TimeZone˄
getIdentifierQuoteString(): *DatabaseMetaData*
getIdentity(): IdentityScope
getIds(): *SSLSessionContext*
getIDs(): *javax.naming.directory.Attributes*˄ BasicAttributes
getIfModifiedSince(): URLConnection˄
getImplementation(): *Document*˄
getImplementationTitle(): Package
getImplementationVendor(): Package
getImplementationVersion(): Package
getImportedKeys(): *DatabaseMetaData*
getInCheck(): SecurityManager˄
getIndex(): *org.xml.sax.Attributes* AttributesImpl
CertPathValidatorException˄ *CharacterIterator*˄
DataTruncation˄ ParsePosition PatternSyntaxException˄
StringCharacterIterator URISyntaxException
getIndexedPropertyType(): IndexedPropertyDescriptor˄
getIndexedReadMethod(): IndexedPropertyDescriptor˄
getIndexedWriteMethod(): IndexedPropertyDescriptor˄
getIndexInfo(): *DatabaseMetaData*
getInetAddress(): DatagramSocket˄ ServerSocket˄ Socket˄
SocketImpl
getInetAddresses(): NetworkInterface
getInfinity(): DecimalFormatSymbols
getInfo(): Identity˄ Provider˄
getInitialContext(): *InitialContextFactory* NamingManager˄
getInitialPolicies(): PKIXParameters
getInitiatorAddress(): ChannelBinding
getInput(): URISyntaxException
getInputLength(): MalformedInputException˄
UnmappableCharacterException˄
getInputSource(): SAXSource

G

Cross-Ref

getParameterMode( ): *ParameterMetaData*
getParameters( ): **C**ipher **L**ogRecord **S**ignature^
getParameterSpec( ): **A**lgorithmParameters
getParameterType( ): *ParameterMetaData*
getParameterTypeName( ): *ParameterMetaData*
getParameterTypes( ): **C**onstructor^ **M**ethod^
getParams( ): *DHKey* *DSAKey* *RowSetInternal*
getParent( ): **C**lassLoader **F**ile **L**ogger **N**odeChangeEvent^
   PolicyNode **T**hreadGroup *XMLFilter*^ **X**MLFilterImpl
getParentFile( ): **F**ile
getParentNode( ): *Node*
getParser( ): **S**AXParser
getPassword( ): **P**asswordAuthentication **P**asswordCallback
   PBEKey **P**BEKeySpec *RowSet*^
getPasswordAuthentication( ): **A**uthenticator
getPath( ): **F**ile **U**RI **U**RL
getPathToNames( ): **X**509CertSelector
getPattern( ): **P**atternSyntaxException^
getPatternSeparator( ): **D**ecimalFormatSymbols
getPeerCertificateChain( ): **H**andshakeCompletedEvent^
   SSLSession
getPeerCertificates( ): **H**andshakeCompletedEvent^
   SSLSession
getPeerHost( ): *SSLSession*
getPercent( ): **D**ecimalFormatSymbols
getPercentInstance( ): **N**umberFormat^
getPerMill( ): **D**ecimalFormatSymbols
getPermission( ): **A**ccessControlException^ **U**RLConnection
getPermissions( ): *Acl*^ java.security.**P**olicy
   javax.security.auth.**P**olicy **P**rotectionDomain
   SecureClassLoader
getPersistenceDelegate( ): **E**ncoder
getPolicy( ): java.security.**P**olicy javax.security.auth.**P**olicy
   X509CertSelector
getPolicyQualifier( ): **P**olicyQualifierInfo
getPolicyQualifierId( ): **P**olicyQualifierInfo
getPolicyQualifiers( ): *PolicyNode*
getPolicyQualifiersRejected( ): **P**KIXParameters
getPolicyTree( ): **P**KIXCertPathValidatorResult
getPooledConnection( ): *ConnectionPoolDataSource*
getPort( ): **D**atagramPacket **D**atagramSocket
   InetSocketAddress^ **L**DAPCertStoreParameters **S**ocket
   SocketImpl **U**RI **U**RL
getPositivePrefix( ): **D**ecimalFormat^
getPositiveSuffix( ): **D**ecimalFormat^
getPrecision( ): *ParameterMetaData* *ResultSetMetaData*
getPrefix( ): **C**ompositeName **C**ompoundName *Name*^
   NamespaceSupport *Node*
getPrefixes( ): **N**amespaceSupport
getPreviousSibling( ): *Node*
getPrimaryKeys( ): *DatabaseMetaData*
getPrime( ): **R**SAOtherPrimeInfo
getPrimeExponentP( ): *RSAMultiPrimePrivateCrtKey*^
   RSAMultiPrimePrivateCrtKeySpec^ *RSAPrivateCrtKey*^
   RSAPrivateCrtKeySpec^
getPrimeExponentQ( ): *RSAMultiPrimePrivateCrtKey*^
   RSAMultiPrimePrivateCrtKeySpec^ *RSAPrivateCrtKey*^
   RSAPrivateCrtKeySpec^
getPrimeP( ): *RSAMultiPrimePrivateCrtKey*^
   RSAMultiPrimePrivateCrtKeySpec^ *RSAPrivateCrtKey*^
   RSAPrivateCrtKeySpec^
getPrimeQ( ): *RSAMultiPrimePrivateCrtKey*^
   RSAMultiPrimePrivateCrtKeySpec^ *RSAPrivateCrtKey*^
   RSAPrivateCrtKeySpec^
getPrimeSize( ): **D**HGenParameterSpec
getPrincipal( ): *AclEntry*^ java.security.*Certificate*
   KerberosKey
getPrincipals( ): **P**rivateCredentialPermission^
   ProtectionDomain **S**ubject
getPriority( ): **T**hread
getPrivacy( ): **M**essageProp
getPrivate( ): **K**eyPair

getPrivateCredentials( ): **S**ubject
getPrivateExponent( ): *RSAPrivateKey*^ **R**SAPrivateKeySpec
getPrivateKey( ): **S**igner^ **X**500PrivateCredential
   X509KeyManager^
getPrivateKeyValid( ): **X**509CertSelector
getProcedureColumns( ): *DatabaseMetaData*
getProcedures( ): *DatabaseMetaData*
getProcedureTerm( ): *DatabaseMetaData*
getPrompt( ): **C**hoiceCallback **C**onfirmationCallback
   NameCallback **P**asswordCallback **T**extInputCallback
getPropagatedFrom( ): **B**eanContextEvent^
getPropagationId( ): **P**ropertyChangeEvent^
getProperties( ): **S**ystem
getProperty( ): **L**ogManager **P**arserAdapter **P**roperties^
   SAXParser **S**ecurity **S**ystem **X**MLFilterImpl *XMLReader*
getPropertyChangeEvent( ): **P**ropertyVetoException
getPropertyChangeListeners( ): **P**ropertyChangeSupport
getPropertyDescriptors( ): *BeanInfo* **S**impleBeanInfo
getPropertyEditorClass( ): **P**ropertyDescriptor^
getPropertyInfo( ): *Driver*
getPropertyName( ): **P**ropertyChangeEvent^
   PropertyChangeListenerProxy^
   VetoableChangeListenerProxy^
getPropertyOverrides( ): **A**ctivationGroupDesc
getPropertyType( ): **P**ropertyDescriptor^
getProtectionDomain( ): **C**lass
getProtocol( ): **S**SLContext *SSLSession* **U**RL
getProvider( ): **A**lgorithmParameterGenerator
   AlgorithmParameters **C**ertificateFactory **C**ertPathBuilder
   CertPathValidator **C**ertStore **C**ipher **E**xemptionMechanism
   KeyAgreement **K**eyFactory **K**eyGenerator
   KeyManagerFactory **K**eyPairGenerator^ **K**eyStore **M**ac
   MessageDigest^ **S**ecretKeyFactory **S**ecureRandom^
   Security **S**ignature^ **S**SLContext **T**rustManagerFactory
getProviders( ): **S**ecurity
getProxyClass( ): **P**roxy
getPublic( ): **K**eyPair
getPublicCredentials( ): **S**ubject
getPublicExponent( ): **R**SAKeyGenParameterSpec
   RSAMultiPrimePrivateCrtKey^
   RSAMultiPrimePrivateCrtKeySpec^ *RSAPrivateCrtKey*^
   RSAPrivateCrtKeySpec^ *RSAPublicKey*^
   RSAPublicKeySpec
getPublicId( ): *DocumentType*^ *Entity*^ **I**nputSource
   Locator **L**ocatorImpl *Notation*^ **S**AXParseException^
   SourceLocator **S**treamSource
getPublicKey( ): java.security.*Certificate*
   java.security.cert.**C**ertificate javax.security.cert.**C**ertificate
   Identity **P**KIXCertPathValidatorResult
getPushLevel( ): **M**emoryHandler^
getQ( ): **D**SAParameterSpec *DSAParams* **D**SAPrivateKeySpec
   DSAPublicKeySpec
getQName( ): *org.xml.sax.Attributes* **A**ttributesImpl
getQOP( ): **M**essageProp
getQuery( ): **U**RI **U**RL
getQueryTimeout( ): *RowSet*^ java.sql.**S**tatement
getRawAuthority( ): **U**RI
getRawFragment( ): **U**RI
getRawOffset( ): **T**imeZone
getRawPath( ): **U**RI
getRawQuery( ): **U**RI
getRawSchemeSpecificPart( ): **U**RI
getRawUserInfo( ): **U**RI
getRead( ): **D**ataTruncation^
getReader( ): **S**treamSource
getReadMethod( ): **P**ropertyDescriptor^
getRealm( ): **K**erberosPrincipal
getReason( ): **U**RISyntaxException
getReceiveBufferSize( ): **D**atagramSocket **S**erverSocket
   Socket
getRef( ): *CallableStatement*^ **R**emoteObject **R**esultSet **U**RL
getRefClass( ): *RemoteRef*^

G

getReference( ): *Referenceable*
getReferralContext( ): ReferralException^
getReferralInfo( ): ReferralException^
getReferrals( ): *UnsolicitedNotification*^
getRegistry( ): LocateRegistry
getRemaining( ): Inflater
getRemainingAcceptLifetime( ): *GSSCredential*^
getRemainingInitLifetime( ): *GSSCredential*^
getRemainingLifetime( ): *GSSCredential*^
getRemainingName( ): NamingException, ResolveResult
getRemainingNewName( ): CannotProceedException^
getRemoteSocketAddress( ): DatagramSocket, Socket,
getRemoveListenerMethod( ): EventSetDescriptor^
getRenewTill( ): KerberosTicket
getReplayDetState( ): *GSSContext*
getRequestControls( ): InitialLdapContext^ *LdapContext*^
getRequestingHost( ): Authenticator
getRequestingPort( ): Authenticator
getRequestingPrompt( ): Authenticator
getRequestingProtocol( ): Authenticator
getRequestingScheme( ): Authenticator
getRequestingSite( ): Authenticator
getRequestMethod( ): HttpURLConnection^
getRequestProperties( ): URLConnection,
getRequestProperty( ): URLConnection,
getResolvedName( ): NamingException,
getResolvedObj( ): NamingException, ResolveResult
getResource( ): *BeanContext*^ BeanContextSupport^ Class
    ClassLoader,
getResourceAsStream( ): *BeanContext*^ BeanContextSupport^
    Class ClassLoader,
getResourceBundle( ): Logger LogRecord
getResourceBundleName( ): Level Logger LogRecord
getResources( ): ClassLoader,
getResponseCode( ): HttpURLConnection^
getResponseControls( ): InitialLdapContext^ *LdapContext*^
getResponseMessage( ): HttpURLConnection^
getRestartMode( ): ActivationDesc
getResultSet( ): *java.sql.Array* *java.sql.Statement*,
getResultSetConcurrency( ): *java.sql.Statement*,
getResultSetHoldability( ): *DatabaseMetaData*
    java.sql.Statement,
getResultSetType( ): *java.sql.Statement*,
getResultStream( ): *RemoteCall*
getReturningAttributes( ): SearchControls
getReturningObjFlag( ): SearchControls
getReturnType( ): Method^
getReuseAddress( ): DatagramSocket, ServerSocket,
    Socket,
getRevocationDate( ): X509CRLEntry
getRevokedCertificate( ): X509CRL^
getRevokedCertificates( ): X509CRL^
getRMIRepositoryID( ): *ValueHandler*
getRootCause( ): NamingException,
getRounds( ): RC5ParameterSpec
getRow( ): *ResultSet*,
getRules( ): RuleBasedCollator^
getRunCount( ): Bidi
getRunLevel( ): Bidi
getRunLimit( ): *AttributedCharacterIterator*^ Bidi
getRunStart( ): *AttributedCharacterIterator*^ Bidi
getRuntime( ): Runtime
getRunTimeCodeBase( ): *ValueHandler*
getSalt( ): *PBEKey*^ PBEKeySpec PBEParameterSpec
getSaltLength( ): PSSParameterSpec
getSavepointId( ): *Savepoint*
getSavepointName( ): *Savepoint*
getScale( ): *ParameterMetaData* *ResultSetMetaData*,
getSchema( ): *DirContext*^ InitialDirContext^
getSchemaClassDefinition( ): *DirContext*^ InitialDirContext^
getSchemaName( ): *ResultSetMetaData*,
getSchemas( ): *DatabaseMetaData*

getSchemaTerm( ): *DatabaseMetaData*
getScheme( ): URI
getSchemeSpecificPart( ): URI
getScope( ): Identity,
getSearchScope( ): SearchControls
getSearchStringEscape( ): *DatabaseMetaData*
getSeconds( ): java.util.Date,
getSecurityContext( ): *LoaderHandler* RMIClassLoader
    SecurityManager,
getSecurityManager( ): System
getSeed( ): SecureRandom^
getSelectedIndex( ): ConfirmationCallback
getSelectedIndexes( ): ChoiceCallback
getSendBufferSize( ): DatagramSocket, Socket,
getSentenceInstance( ): BreakIterator
getSequenceDetState( ): *GSSContext*
getSequenceNumber( ): LogRecord
getSerialNumber( ): java.security.cert.X509Certificate^
    javax.security.cert.X509Certificate^ X509CertSelector
    X509CRLEntry
getSerialVersionUID( ): ObjectStreamClass
getServer( ): KerberosTicket
getServerAliases( ): *X509KeyManager*^
getServerCertificates( ): HttpsURLConnection^
getServerName( ): LDAPCertStoreParameters
getServerSessionContext( ): SSLContext
getServerSocketFactory( ): SSLContext
getService( ): *BeanContextServiceProvider*
    BeanContextServices^ BeanContextServicesSupport^
    BeanContextServicesSupport.BCSSProxyServiceProvider
getServiceClass( ): BeanContextServiceAvailableEvent^
    BeanContextServiceRevokedEvent^
getServiceProvider( ):
    BeanContextServicesSupport.BCSSServiceProvider
getServicesBeanInfo( ): *BeanContextServiceProviderBeanInfo*^
getSession( ): HandshakeCompletedEvent^
    SSLSessionBindingEvent^ *SSLSessionContext* SSLSocket^
getSessionCacheSize( ): *SSLSessionContext*
getSessionContext( ): *SSLSession*
getSessionKey( ): KerberosTicket
getSessionKeyType( ): KerberosTicket
getSessionTimeout( ): *SSLSessionContext*
getShort( ): java.lang.reflect.Array ByteBuffer^
    CallableStatement^ Field^ *ResultSet*,
getShortDescription( ): FeatureDescriptor,
getShortMonths( ): DateFormatSymbols
getShortWeekdays( ): DateFormatSymbols
getSigAlgName( ): java.security.cert.X509Certificate^
    javax.security.cert.X509Certificate^ X509CRL^
getSigAlgOID( ): java.security.cert.X509Certificate^
    javax.security.cert.X509Certificate^ X509CRL^
getSigAlgParams( ): java.security.cert.X509Certificate^
    javax.security.cert.X509Certificate^ X509CRL^
getSignature( ): SignedObject
    java.security.cert.X509Certificate^ X509CRL^
getSigners( ): Class
getSigProvider( ): PKIXParameters,
getSize( ): ZipEntry
getSocket( ): HandshakeCompletedEvent^
getSocketAddress( ): DatagramPacket
getSocketFactory( ): RMISocketFactory SSLContext
getSoLinger( ): Socket,
getSoTimeout( ): DatagramSocket, ServerSocket, Socket,
getSource( ): EventObject,
getSourceAsBeanContextServices( ):
    BeanContextServiceAvailableEvent^
    BeanContextServiceRevokedEvent^
getSourceClassName( ): LogRecord
getSourceMethodName( ): LogRecord
getSourceString( ): CollationKey
getSpecificationTitle( ): Package
getSpecificationVendor( ): Package

getSpecificationVersion(): Package
getSpecified(): *Attr^*
getSpi(): AbstractPreferences^
getSQLException(): ConnectionEvent^
getSQLKeywords(): *DatabaseMetaData*
getSQLState(): SQLException
getSQLStateType(): *DatabaseMetaData*
getSQLTypeName(): *SQLData Struct*
getSrcName(): *GSSContext*
getSSLSocketFactory(): HttpsURLConnection^
getStackTrace(): Throwable
getStartTime(): KerberosTicket
getStatement(): *ResultSet*
getStateToBind(): NamingManager *StateFactory*
getStrength(): Collator
getString(): *CallableStatement^* ResourceBundle *ResultSet*
getStringArray(): ResourceBundle
getStringFunctions(): *DatabaseMetaData*
getStringNameType(): *GSSName*
getSubject(): LoginContext Subject SubjectDomainCombiner
getSubjectAlternativeNames():
    java.security.cert.**X**509Certificate^ X509CertSelector
getSubjectAsBytes(): X509CertSelector
getSubjectAsString(): X509CertSelector
getSubjectDN(): java.security.cert.**X**509Certificate^
    javax.security.cert.**X**509Certificate
getSubjectKeyIdentifier(): X509CertSelector
getSubjectPublicKey(): X509CertSelector
getSubjectPublicKeyAlgID(): X509CertSelector
getSubjectUniqueID(): java.security.cert.**X**509Certificate^
getSubjectX500Principal(): java.security.cert.**X**509Certificate^
getSubString(): *Clob*
getSuffix(): CompositeName CompoundName *Name^*
getSuperclass(): Class
getSuperTables(): *DatabaseMetaData*
getSuperTypes(): *DatabaseMetaData*
getSupportedCipherSuites(): SSLServerSocket^
    SSLServerSocketFactory^ SSLSocket^ SSLSocketFactory^
getSupportedExtensions(): PKIXCertPathChecker
getSupportedProtocols(): SSLServerSocket^ SSLSocket^
getSymbol(): Currency
getSystem(): ActivationGroup^ ActivationGroupID
getSystemClassLoader(): ClassLoader
getSystemFunctions(): *DatabaseMetaData*
getSystemId(): *DocumentType^* DOMResult DOMSource
    *Entity^* InputSource *Locator* LocatorImpl *Notation^*
    Result SAXParseException^ SAXResult SAXSource
    Source SourceLocator StreamResult StreamSource
    *TemplatesHandler^ TransformerHandler^*
getSystemResource(): ClassLoader
getSystemResourceAsStream(): ClassLoader
getSystemResources(): ClassLoader
getSystemScope(): IdentityScope^
getTableName(): *ResultSetMetaData*
getTablePrivileges(): *DatabaseMetaData*
getTables(): *DatabaseMetaData*
getTableTypes(): *DatabaseMetaData*
getTagName(): *Element^*
getTags(): *PropertyEditor* PropertyEditorSupport
getTail(): Formatter
getTarget(): EventHandler *ProcessingInstruction^*
    java.beans.Statement *Tie^*
getTargetCertConstraints(): PKIXParameters
getTargetException(): InvocationTargetException
getTargName(): *GSSContext*
getTBSCertificate(): java.security.cert.**X**509Certificate^
getTBSCertList(): X509CRL^
getTcpNoDelay(): Socket
getTemplates(): *TemplatesHandler^*
getText(): BreakIterator TextInputCallback
getThisUpdate(): X509CRL^
getThreadGroup(): SecurityManager Thread

getThreadID(): LogRecord
getThrown(): LogRecord
getTie(): Util *UtilDelegate*
getTime(): Calendar *CallableStatement^* java.util.**D**ate
    ResultSet ZipEntry
getTimeDateFunctions(): *DatabaseMetaData*
getTimeInMillis(): Calendar
getTimeInstance(): DateFormat^
getTimeLimit(): SearchControls
getTimestamp(): *CallableStatement^ ResultSet*
getTimeToLive(): DatagramSocketImpl MulticastSocket^
getTimeZone(): Calendar *DateFormat^* TimeZone
getTimezoneOffset(): java.util.**D**ate
getTotalIn(): Deflater Inflater
getTotalOut(): Deflater Inflater
getTrafficClass(): DatagramSocket Socket
getTransactionIsolation(): *Connection RowSet^*
getTransactionTimeout(): *XAResource*
getTransferSize(): DataTruncation^
getTransformer(): *TransformerHandler^*
getTrustAnchor(): PKIXCertPathValidatorResult
getTrustAnchors(): PKIXParameters
getTrustedCert(): TrustAnchor
getTrustManagers(): TrustManagerFactory
getTTL(): DatagramSocketImpl MulticastSocket^
getType(): *AttributeList* AttributeListImpl
    *org.xml.sax.**A**ttributes* AttributesImpl
    java.security.cert.**C**ertificate CertificateFactory CertPath
    CertStore Character CRL *Field^* KeyStore
    NamingEvent^ ObjectStreamField RefAddr *ResultSet*
getTypeCode(): ObjectStreamField
getTypeInfo(): *DatabaseMetaData*
getTypeMap(): *Connection RowSet^*
getTypeString(): ObjectStreamField
getUDTs(): *DatabaseMetaData*
getUndeclaredThrowable(): UndeclaredThrowableException
getUnexecutedModifications():
    AttributeModificationException^
getUnicodeStream(): *ResultSet*
getUpdateCount(): java.sql.**S**tatement
getUpdateCounts(): BatchUpdateException^
getURI(): *org.xml.sax.**A**ttributes* AttributesImpl
    NamespaceSupport
getURIResolver(): Transformer TransformerFactory
getUrl(): *RowSet^*
getURL(): *CallableStatement^ DatabaseMetaData ResultSet*
    URLConnection
getURLContext(): NamingManager
getURLOrDefaultInitCtx(): InitialContext
getURLs(): URLClassLoader^
getUsage(): *GSSCredential^*
getUseCaches(): URLConnection
getUseClientMode(): SSLServerSocket^ SSLSocket^
getUseParentHandlers(): Logger
getUserInfo(): URI URL
getUserName(): *DatabaseMetaData* PasswordAuthentication
getUsername(): *RowSet^*
getValidPolicy(): *PolicyNode*
getValue(): Adler32 Annotation *Attr^ AttributeList*
    AttributeListImpl java.util.jar.**A**ttributes
    *org.xml.sax.**A**ttributes* AttributesImpl *Checksum* CRC32
    *Expression^* FeatureDescriptor *Lease Map.Entry*
    PropertyEditor PropertyEditorSupport *SSLSession*
getValueNames(): *SSLSession*
getVariant(): Locale
getVersion(): *Provider* RC5ParameterSpec
    java.security.cert.**X**509Certificate^
    javax.security.cert.**X**509Certificate^ X509CRL^
getVersionColumns(): *DatabaseMetaData*
getVersionNumber(): KerberosKey
getVetoableChangeListeners(): VetoableChangeSupport
getVMID(): *Lease*

G

getWantClientAuth( ): **S**SLServerSocket^ **S**SLSocket^
getWarnings( ): *C*onnection *R*esultSet⌄ *java.sql.***S**tatement⌄
getWeekdays( ): **D**ateFormatSymbols
getWordInstance( ): **B**reakIterator
getWordSize( ): **R**C5ParameterSpec
getWrapSizeLimit( ): *G*SSContext
getWriteMethod( ): **P**ropertyDescriptor⌃
getWriter( ): **S**treamResult
getX( ): *D*HPrivateKey^ **D**HPrivateKeySpec *D*SAPrivateKey^
　　DSAPrivateKeySpec
getXAConnection( ): *X*ADataSource
getXAResource( ): *X*AConnection^
getXMLReader( ): **S**AXParser **S**AXSource
getY( ): *D*HPublicKey^ **D**HPublicKeySpec *D*SAPublicKey^
　　DSAPublicKeySpec
getYear( ): java.util.**D**ate⌄
getZeroDigit( ): **D**ecimalFormatSymbols
getZoneStrings( ): **D**ateFormatSymbols
global: **L**ogger
globalHierarchyLock: *B*eanContext⌃
gotDefault: **I**nitialContext⌄
Graphics: java.awt
　—passed to: *P*ropertyEditor.paintValue( )
　　PropertyEditorSupport.paintValue( )
GREEK: **C**haracter.UnicodeBlock^
GREEK_EXTENDED: **C**haracter.UnicodeBlock^
GregorianCalendar^: java.util
Group^: java.security.acl
group( ): **M**atcher
groupCount( ): **M**atcher
GROUPING_SEPARATOR: **N**umberFormat.Field^
GSSContext: org.ietf.jgss
　—returned by: **G**SSManager.createContext( )
GSSCredential^: org.ietf.jgss
　—passed to: **G**SSManager.createContext( )
　—returned by: *G*SSContext.getDelegCred( )
　　GSSManager.createCredential( )
GSSException: org.ietf.jgss
　—thrown by: *G*SSContext < acceptSecContext( ), dispose( ),
　　export( ), getDelegCred( ), getMech( ), getMIC( ), getSrcName( ),
　　getTargName( ), getWrapSizeLimit( ), initSecContext( ),
　　isInitiator( ), isTransferable( ), requestAnonymity( ), requestConf( ),
　　requestCredDeleg( ), requestInteg( ), requestLifetime( ),
　　requestMutualAuth( ), requestReplayDet( ), requestSequenceDet( ),
　　setChannelBinding( ), unwrap( ), verifyMIC( ), wrap( ) >
　　*G*SSCredential^ < add( ), dispose( ), getMechs( ), getName( ),
　　getRemainingAcceptLifetime( ), getRemainingInitLifetime( ),
　　getRemainingLifetime( ), getUsage( ) > **G**SSManager
　　< addProviderAtEnd( ), addProviderAtFront( ), createContext( ),
　　createCredential( ), createName( ), getNamesForMech( ) >
　　*G*SSName < canonicalize( ), equals( ), export( ),
　　getStringNameType( ) > **O**id < getDER( ), Oid( ) >
GSSManager: org.ietf.jgss
　—returned by: **G**SSManager.getInstance( )
GSSName: org.ietf.jgss
　—passed to: *G*SSCredential^.add( ) **G**SSManager
　　< createContext( ), createCredential( ) > *G*SSName.equals( )
　—returned by: *G*SSContext < getSrcName( ), getTargName( ) >
　　*G*SSCredential^.getName( ) **G**SSManager.createName( )
　　*G*SSName.canonicalize( )
Guard: java.security
　—passed to: **G**uardedObject( )
　—implemented by: java.security.**P**ermission⌄
GuardedObject: java.security
guessContentTypeFromName( ): **U**RLConnection⌄
guessContentTypeFromStream( ): **U**RLConnection⌄
GUJARATI: **C**haracter.UnicodeBlock^
GURMUKHI: **C**haracter.UnicodeBlock^
GZIP_MAGIC: **G**ZIPInputStream^
GZIPInputStream^: java.util.zip
GZIPOutputStream^: java.util.zip
h: **P**roxy

HALFWIDTH_AND_FULLWIDTH_FORMS:
　Character.UnicodeBlock^
halt( ): **R**untime
handle( ): *C*allbackHandler
handleGetObject( ): **R**esourceBundle⌄
Handler⌄: java.util.logging
　—subclasses: **M**emoryHandler^ **S**treamHandler⌃
　—descendents: **C**onsoleHandler^ **F**ileHandler^ **S**ocketHandler^
　—passed to: **F**ormatter⌄ < getHead( ), getTail( ) > **L**ogger
　　< addHandler( ), removeHandler( ) > **M**emoryHandler( )
　—returned by: **L**ogger.getHandlers( )
HandlerBase: org.xml.sax
　—passed to: **S**AXParser.parse( )
handshakeCompleted( ): *H*andshakeCompletedListener^
HandshakeCompletedEvent^: javax.net.ssl
　—passed
　　to: *H*andshakeCompletedListener^.handshakeCompleted( )
HandshakeCompletedListener^: javax.net.ssl
　—passed to: **S**SLSocket^ < addHandshakeCompletedListener( ),
　　removeHandshakeCompletedListener( ) >
HANGUL_COMPATIBILITY_JAMO: **C**haracter.UnicodeBlock^
HANGUL_JAMO: **C**haracter.UnicodeBlock^
HANGUL_SYLLABLES: **C**haracter.UnicodeBlock^
has_no_active_member( ): _DynUnionStub^
　　*D*ynUnionOperations^
hasArray( ): **B**yteBuffer⌃ **C**harBuffer^ **D**oubleBuffer^
　　FloatBuffer^ **I**ntBuffer^ **L**ongBuffer^ **S**hortBuffer^
hasAttribute( ): *E*lement^
hasAttributeNS( ): *E*lement^
hasAttributes( ): *N*ode⌄
hasChanged( ): **O**bservable
hasChildNodes( ): *N*ode⌄
HasControls⌄: javax.naming.ldap
　—extended by: *U*nsolicitedNotification^
hasExtensions( ): **X**509CRLEntry
hasFeature( ): *D*OMImplementation
hash( ): org.omg.CORBA.portable.**D**elegate⌄
hashCode( ): *C*ollection⌄ org.omg.CORBA.portable.**D**elegate⌄
　　*G*SSCredential^ *G*SSName **M**ap⌄ **M**ap.Entry
　　java.lang.**O**bject *java.security.***P**rincipal⌄ *S*tubDelegate
　　URLStreamHandler
HashMap⌃: java.util
　—subclasses: **L**inkedHashMap^
　　javax.print.attribute.standard.**P**rinterStateReasons^
　—fields: **B**eanContextServicesSupport^.services
　　BeanContextSupport⌃.children
HashSet⌃: java.util
　—subclasses: javax.print.attribute.standard.**J**obStateReasons^
　　LinkedHashSet^
Hashtable⌃: java.util
　—subclasses: **P**roperties⌃ javax.swing.**U**IDefaults^
　—descendents: **P**rovider^
　—passed to: java.awt.image.**B**ufferedImage( )
　　CannotProceedException^.setEnvironment( )
　　ControlFactory.getControlInstance( ) **D**irectoryManager^
　　< getObjectInstance( ), getStateToBind( ) >
　　*D*irObjectFactory^.getObjectInstance( )
　　*D*irStateFactory^.getStateToBind( )
　　java.awt.image.*I*mageConsumer.setProperties( )
　　java.awt.image.**I**mageFilter.setProperties( )
　　InitialContext⌄ < init( ), InitialContext( ) >
　　*I*nitialContextFactory.getInitialContext( )
　　*I*nitialContextFactoryBuilder.createInitialContextFactory( )
　　InitialDirContext( ) **I**nitialLdapContext( ) javax.swing.**J**Tree( )
　　LdapReferralException^.getReferralContext( )
　　java.awt.image.**M**emoryImageSource( ) **N**amingManager⌄
　　< getInitialContext( ), getObjectInstance( ), getStateToBind( ),
　　getURLContext( ) > *O*bjectFactory⌄.getObjectInstance( )
　　*O*bjectFactoryBuilder.createObjectFactory( )
　　java.awt.image.**P**ixelGrabber.setProperties( )
　　ReferralException⌃.getReferralContext( )

G

I

inflate( ) / InputStream

inflate( ): Inflater
Inflater: java.util.zip
— passed to: **I**nflaterInputStream( )
— fields: **I**nflaterInputStream^.inf
InflaterInputStream^: java.util.zip
— subclasses: **G**ZIPInputStream^ **Z**ipInputStream⌃
— descendents: **J**arInputStream^
INFO: **L**evel
info( ): **L**ogger
INFORMATION: **C**onfirmationCallback **T**extOutputCallback
InheritableThreadLocal^: java.lang
init( ): **A**lgorithmParameterGenerator **A**lgorithmParameters
Cipher **E**xemptionMechanism **I**nitialContext⌃
KeyAgreement **K**eyGenerator **K**eyManagerFactory **M**ac
org.omg.CORBA.**O**RB⌃ **P**KIXCertPathChecker **S**SLContext
TrustManagerFactory
initCause( ): **T**hrowable⌃
INITIAL_CONTEXT_FACTORY: *javax.naming.*Context⌃
INITIAL_QUOTE_PUNCTUATION: **C**haracter
InitialContext⌃: javax.naming
— subclasses: **I**nitialDirContext⌃
— descendents: **I**nitialLdapContext^
InitialContextFactory: javax.naming.spi
— returned
by: *InitialContextFactoryBuilder*.createInitialContextFactory( )
InitialContextFactoryBuilder: javax.naming.spi
— passed to: **N**amingManager⌃.setInitialContextFactoryBuilder( )
InitialDirContext⌃: javax.naming.directory
— subclasses: **I**nitialLdapContext^
INITIALIZE^: org.omg.CORBA
initialize( ): *A*ppletInitializer **B**eanContextSupport⌃
*D*SAKeyPairGenerator **K**eyPairGeneratorSpi⌃ *LoginModule*
PersistenceDelegate⌃
initializeBeanContextResources( ): **B**eanContextChildSupport⌃
InitialLdapContext^: javax.naming.ldap
initialValue( ): **T**hreadLocal
INITIATE_AND_ACCEPT: *GSSCredential*^
INITIATE_ONLY: *GSSCredential*^
initSecContext( ): *GSSContext*
initSign( ): **S**ignature^
initVerify( ): **S**ignature^
INPUT_METHOD_SEGMENT:
AttributedCharacterIterator.Attribute⌃
InputSource: org.xml.sax
— passed to: **D**ocumentBuilder.parse( ) *Parser*.parse( )
ParserAdapter.parse( ) **S**AXParser.parse( ) **S**AXSource
< SAXSource( ), setInputSource( ) > **X**MLFilterImpl.parse( )
XMLReader⌃.parse( ) **X**MLReaderAdapter.parse( )
— returned by: **D**efaultHandler.resolveEntity( )
EntityResolver.resolveEntity( ) **H**andlerBase.resolveEntity( )
SAXSource < getInputSource( ), sourceToInputSource( ) >
XMLFilterImpl.resolveEntity( )
InputStream⌃: java.io
— subclasses: javax.sound.sampled.**A**udioInputStream^
ByteArrayInputStream^ **F**ileInputStream^ **F**ilterInputStream^
org.omg.CORBA.portable.**I**nputStream⌃ **O**bjectInputStream^
PipedInputStream^ **S**equenceInputStream^
StringBufferInputStream^
— descendents: **B**ufferedInputStream^ **C**heckedInputStream^
CipherInputStream^ java.io.**D**ataInputStream^
DigestInputStream^ **G**ZIPInputStream^ **I**nflaterInputStream^
org.omg.CORBA_2_3.portable.**I**nputStream^
JarInputStream^ **L**ineNumberInputStream^
javax.swing.**P**rogressMonitorInputStream^
PushbackInputStream^ **Z**ipInputStream⌃
— passed to: *java.applet.AppletContext*.setStream( )
javax.sound.sampled.spi.**A**udioFileReader
< getAudioFileFormat( ), getAudioInputStream( ) >
javax.sound.sampled.**A**udioInputStream( )
javax.sound.sampled.**A**udioSystem < getAudioFileFormat( ),
getAudioInputStream( ) > **B**ufferedInputStream( )

CallableStatement^ < setAsciiStream( ), setBinaryStream( ) >
java.security.Certificate.decode( ) **C**ertificateFactory
< generateCertificate( ), generateCertificates( ), generateCertPath( ),
generateCRL( ), generateCRLs( ) > **C**ertificateFactorySpi
< engineGenerateCertificate( ), engineGenerateCertificates( ),
engineGenerateCertPath( ), engineGenerateCRL( ),
engineGenerateCRLs( ) > **C**hannels.newChannel( )
CheckedInputStream( ) **C**ipherInputStream( )
java.io.**D**ataInputStream( ) **D**igestInputStream( )
DocumentBuilder.parse( ) javax.swing.text.**E**ditorKit.read( )
javax.imageio.stream.**F**ileCacheImageInputStream( )
FilterInputStream( ) java.awt.**F**ont.createFont( )
GSSContext < acceptSecContext( ), getMIC( ),
initSecContext( ), unwrap( ), verifyMIC( ), wrap( ) >
GZIPInputStream( ) java.awt.color.**I**CC_Profile.getInstance( )
javax.imageio.**I**mageIO.read( ) **I**nflaterInputStream( )
InputSource < InputSource( ), setByteStream( ) >
InputStreamReader( ) **J**arInputStream( )
javax.swing.**J**EditorPane^.read( ) **K**eyStore.load( )
KeyStoreSpi.engineLoad( ) **L**ineNumberInputStream( )
LogManager.readConfiguration( )
Manifest < Manifest( ), read( ) >
javax.imageio.stream.**M**emoryCacheImageInputStream( )
javax.sound.midi.spi.**M**idiFileReader < getMidiFileFormat( ),
getSequence( ) > javax.sound.midi.**M**idiSystem
< getMidiFileFormat( ), getSequence( ),
getSoundbank( ) > **O**bjectInputStream( ) **O**id( )
Preferences⌃.importPreferences( ) *PreparedStatement*^
< setAsciiStream( ), setBinaryStream( ), setUnicodeStream( ) >
javax.swing.**P**rogressMonitorInputStream( )
Properties^.load( ) **P**ropertyResourceBundle( )
PushbackInputStream( ) *ResultSet*^ < updateAsciiStream( ),
updateBinaryStream( ) > *RowSet*^ < setAsciiStream( ),
setBinaryStream( ) > **R**untime.getLocalizedInputStream( )
SAXParser.parse( ) **S**equenceInputStream( )
javax.sound.midi.Sequencer^.setSequence( )
javax.sound.midi.spi.**S**oundbankReader.getSoundbank( )
SQLOutput < writeAsciiStream( ), writeBinaryStream( ) >
StreamSource < setInputStream( ), StreamSource( ) >
StreamTokenizer( ) **S**ystem.setIn( )
URLConnection⌃.guessContentTypeFromStream( )
X500Principal( )
javax.security.cert.**X**509Certificate^.getInstance( )
XMLDecoder( ) **Z**ipInputStream( )
— returned by: *java.applet.AppletContext*.getStream( )
BeanContext^.getResourceAsStream( )
BeanContextSupport^.getResourceAsStream( )
Blob.getBinaryStream( ) **C**hannels.newInputStream( )
Class.getResourceAsStream( ) **C**lassLoader⌃
< getResourceAsStream( ), getSystemResourceAsStream( ) >
Clob.getAsciiStream( ) javax.print.*Doc*.getStreamForBytes( )
HttpURLConnection⌃.getErrorStream( )
InputSource.getByteStream( )
javax.swing.**J**EditorPane^.getStream( ) **P**rocess
< getErrorStream( ), getInputStream( ) >
ResultSet⌃ < getAsciiStream( ), getBinaryStream( ),
getUnicodeStream( ) > **R**untime.getLocalizedInputStream( )
javax.print.**S**impleDoc.getStreamForBytes( )
Socket⌃.getInputStream( ) **S**ocketImpl.getInputStream( )
SQLInput < readAsciiStream( ), readBinaryStream( ) >
StreamSource.getInputStream( ) **U**RL.openStream( )
URLConnection⌃.getInputStream( ) **Z**ipFile⌃.getInputStream( )
— fields: **F**ilterInputStream^.in **S**ystem.in
InputStream^: org.omg.CORBA.portable
— subclasses: org.omg.CORBA_2_3.portable.**I**nputStream^
— passed to: **A**dapterAlreadyExistsHelper.read( )
AdapterInactiveHelper.read( )
AdapterNonExistentHelper.read( ) **A**ddressHelper.read( )
AlreadyBoundHelper.read( ) **A**lreadyBoundHolder._read( )
Any.read_value( ) **A**nyHolder._read( )

org.omg.CORBA.**A**nySeqHelper.read( )
org.omg.DynamicAny.**A**nySeqHelper.read( )
AnySeqHolder._read( )   **A**pplicationException( )
BindingHelper.read( )   **B**indingHolder._read( )
BindingIteratorHelper.read( )   **B**indingIteratorHolder._read( )
BindingIteratorPOA^._invoke( )   **B**indingListHelper.read( )
BindingListHolder._read( )   **B**indingTypeHelper.read( )
BindingTypeHolder._read( )   **B**ooleanHolder._read( )
BooleanSeqHelper.read( )   **B**ooleanSeqHolder._read( )
BoxedValueHelper.read_value( )   **B**yteHolder._read( )
CannotProceedHelper.read( )   **C**annotProceedHolder._read( )
CharHolder._read( )   **C**harSeqHelper.read( )
CharSeqHolder._read( )   **C**odecFactoryHelper.read( )
CompletionStatusHelper.read( )   **C**omponentIdHelper.read( )
CookieHolder._read( )   org.omg.CORBA.**C**urrentHelper.read( )
org.omg.PortableInterceptor.**C**urrentHelper.read( )
org.omg.PortableServer.**C**urrentHelper.read( )
CurrentHolder._read( )   **D**efinitionKindHelper.read( )
org.omg.CORBA.portable.**D**elegate_.releaseReply( )
DoubleHolder._read( )   **D**oubleSeqHelper.read( )
DoubleSeqHolder._read( )   **D**uplicateNameHelper.read( )
DynAnyFactoryHelper.read( )   **D**ynAnyHelper.read( )
DynAnySeqHelper.read( )   **D**ynArrayHelper.read( )
DynEnumHelper.read( )   **D**ynFixedHelper.read( )
DynSequenceHelper.read( )   **D**ynStructHelper.read( )
DynUnionHelper.read( )   **D**ynValueHelper.read( )
org.omg.CORBA.**F**ieldNameHelper.read( )
org.omg.DynamicAny.**F**ieldNameHelper.read( )
FixedHolder._read( )   **F**loatHolder._read( )
FloatSeqHelper.read( )   **F**loatSeqHolder._read( )
FormatMismatchHelper.read( )
org.omg.PortableInterceptor.**F**orwardRequestHelper.read( )
org.omg.PortableServer.**F**orwardRequestHelper.read( )
IdentifierHelper.read( )   **I**DLTypeHelper.read( )
InconsistentTypeCodeHelper.read( )
IntHolder._read( )   **I**nvalidAddressHelper.read( )
InvalidAddressHolder._read( )   org.omg.CosNaming↵
.NamingContextPackage.**I**nvalidNameHelper.read( )
org.omg.PortableInterceptor.ORBInitInfoPackage↵
.**I**nvalidNameHelper.read( )   **I**nvalidNameHolder._read( )
InvalidPolicyHelper.read( )   **I**nvalidSlotHelper.read( )
InvalidTypeForEncodingHelper.read( )
InvalidValueHelper.read( )   *InvokeHandler*_._invoke( )
IORHelper.read( )   **I**ORHolder._read( )   **I**stringHelper.read( )
LocalObject._releaseReply( )   **L**ongHolder._read( )
LongLongSeqHelper.read( )   **L**ongLongSeqHolder._read( )
LongSeqHelper.read( )   **L**ongSeqHolder._read( )
MultipleComponentProfileHelper.read( )
MultipleComponentProfileHolder._read( )
NameComponentHelper.read( )
NameComponentHolder._read( )
NameDynAnyPairHelper.read( )
NameDynAnyPairSeqHelper.read( )
NameHelper.read( )   **N**ameHolder._read( )
org.omg.CORBA.**N**ameValuePairHelper.read( )
org.omg.DynamicAny.**N**ameValuePairHelper.read( )
NameValuePairSeqHelper.read( )
NamingContextExtHelper.read( )
NamingContextExtHolder._read( )
NamingContextExtPOA^._invoke( )
NamingContextHelper.read( )   **N**amingContextHolder._read( )
NamingContextPOA^._invoke( )   **N**oContextHelper.read( )
NoServantHelper.read( )   **N**otEmptyHelper.read( )
NotEmptyHolder._read( )   **N**otFoundHelper.read( )
NotFoundHolder._read( )   **N**otFoundReasonHelper.read( )
NotFoundReasonHolder._read( )
ObjectAlreadyActiveHelper.read( )   **O**bjectHelper.read( )
ObjectHolder._read( )   **O**bjectIdHelper.read( )
org.omg.CORBA.portable.**O**bjectImpl_._releaseReply( )
ObjectNotActiveHelper.read( )   **O**ctetSeqHelper.read( )
OctetSeqHolder._read( )   **P**arameterModeHelper.read( )
ParameterModeHolder._read( )   **P**OAHelper.read( )

PolicyErrorCodeHelper.read( )   **P**olicyErrorHelper.read( )
PolicyErrorHolder._read( )   **P**olicyHelper.read( )
PolicyHolder._read( )   **P**olicyListHelper.read( )
PolicyListHolder._read( )   **P**olicyTypeHelper.read( )
PrincipalHolder._read( )   **P**rofileIdHelper.read( )
RepositoryIdHelper.read( )   **S**ervantActivatorHelper.read( )
ServantActivatorPOA^._invoke( )
ServantAlreadyActiveHelper.read( )
ServantLocatorHelper.read( )   **S**ervantLocatorPOA^._invoke( )
ServantNotActiveHelper.read( )
ServiceContextHelper.read( )   **S**erviceContextHolder._read( )
ServiceContextListHelper.read( )
ServiceContextListHolder._read( )   **S**erviceDetailHelper.read( )
ServiceIdHelper.read( )   **S**erviceInformationHelper.read( )
ServiceInformationHolder._read( )
SetOverrideTypeHelper.read( )   **S**hortHolder._read( )
ShortSeqHelper.read( )   **S**hortSeqHolder._read( )
*Streamable*_._read( )   **S**tringHolder._read( )
StringNameHelper.read( )   **S**tringSeqHelper.read( )
StringSeqHolder._read( )   **S**tringValueHelper < read( ),
read_value( ) >   **S**tructMemberHelper.read( )
SyncScopeHelper.read( )   **T**aggedComponentHelper.read( )
TaggedComponentHolder._read( )
TaggedProfileHelper.read( )   **T**aggedProfileHolder._read( )
TypeCodeHolder._read( )   org.omg.DynamicAny↵
.DynAnyPackage.**T**ypeMismatchHelper.read( )
org.omg.IOP.CodecPackage.**T**ypeMismatchHelper.read( )
ULongLongSeqHelper.read( )   **U**LongLongSeqHolder._read( )
ULongSeqHelper.read( )   **U**LongSeqHolder._read( )
UnionMemberHelper.read( )   **U**nknownEncodingHelper.read( )
UnknownUserExceptionHelper.read( )
UnknownUserExceptionHolder._read( )
URLStringHelper.read( )   **U**ShortSeqHelper.read( )
UShortSeqHolder._read( )   **U**til.readAny( )
UtilDelegate.readAny( )   **V**alueBaseHelper.read( )
ValueBaseHolder._read( )   *ValueHandler*.readValue( )
ValueMemberHelper.read( )   **V**ersionSpecHelper.read( )
VisibilityHelper.read( )   **W**CharSeqHelper.read( )
WCharSeqHolder._read( )   **W**rongAdapterHelper.read( )
WrongPolicyHelper.read( )   **W**rongTransactionHelper.read( )
WrongTransactionHolder._read( )   **W**StringSeqHelper.read( )
WStringSeqHolder._read( )   **W**StringValueHelper < read( ),
read_value( ) >
— returned by: **A**ny.create_input_stream( )
ApplicationException.getInputStream( )
org.omg.CORBA.portable.**D**elegate_.invoke( )
LocalObject._invoke( )
org.omg.CORBA.portable.**O**bjectImpl_._invoke( )   org.omg↵
.CORBA.portable.**O**utputStream^.create_input_stream( )
InputStream^: org.omg.CORBA_2_3.portable
— passed to: *ValueFactory*.read_value( )
InputStreamReader^: java.io
— subclasses: **F**ileReader^
insert( ): **A**dapterAlreadyExistsHelper **A**dapterInactiveHelper
AdapterNonExistentHelper **A**ddressHelper
AlreadyBoundHelper org.omg.CORBA.**A**nySeqHelper
org.omg.DynamicAny.**A**nySeqHelper **B**indingHelper
BindingIteratorHelper **B**indingListHelper
BindingTypeHelper **B**ooleanSeqHelper
CannotProceedHelper **C**harSeqHelper
CodecFactoryHelper **C**ompletionStatusHelper
ComponentIdHelper org.omg.CORBA.**C**urrentHelper
org.omg.PortableInterceptor.**C**urrentHelper
org.omg.PortableServer.**C**urrentHelper **D**efinitionKindHelper
DoubleSeqHelper **D**uplicateNameHelper
DynAnyFactoryHelper **D**ynAnyHelper **D**ynAnySeqHelper
DynArrayHelper **D**ynEnumHelper **D**ynFixedHelper
DynSequenceHelper **D**ynStructHelper **D**ynUnionHelper
DynValueHelper org.omg.CORBA.**F**ieldNameHelper
org.omg.DynamicAny.**F**ieldNameHelper
FloatSeqHelper **F**ormatMismatchHelper
org.omg.PortableInterceptor.**F**orwardRequestHelper

INTEGER: NumberFormat.Field˅ Types
Integerˆ: java.lang
—passed to: Integerˆ < compareTo( ), getInteger( ) >
javax.swing.JInternalFrameˆ.setLayer( )
—returned by: Integerˆ < decode( ), getInteger( ), valueOf( ) >
javax.swing.JLayeredPaneˆ.getObjectForLayer( )
—fields: javax.swing.JLayeredPaneˆ < DEFAULT_LAYER,
DRAG_LAYER, FRAME_CONTENT_LAYER, MODAL_LAYER,
PALETTE_LAYER, POPUP_LAYER > java.awt.font.TextAttributeˆ
< SUPERSCRIPT_SUB, SUPERSCRIPT_SUPER,
UNDERLINE_LOW_DASHED, UNDERLINE_LOW_DOTTED,
UNDERLINE_LOW_GRAY, UNDERLINE_LOW_ONE_PIXEL,
UNDERLINE_LOW_TWO_PIXEL, UNDERLINE_ON >
INTEGER_FIELD: NumberFormat
Interceptor˅: org.omg.PortableInterceptor
—extended by: ClientRequestInterceptorˆ IORInterceptorˆ
ServerRequestInterceptorˆ
InterceptorOperations˅: org.omg.PortableInterceptor
—extended by: ClientRequestInterceptorOperations˅
Interceptor˅ IORInterceptorOperations˅
ServerRequestInterceptorOperations˅
—descendents: ClientRequestInterceptorˆ IORInterceptorˆ
ServerRequestInterceptorˆ
interestOps( ): SelectionKey˅
INTERFACE: Modifier
intern( ): String
INTERNALˆ: org.omg.CORBA
internalEntityDecl( ): DeclHandler
InternalErrorˆ: java.lang
internalGet( ): Calendar˅
interrupt( ): Thread ThreadGroup
interrupted( ): Thread
InterruptedException: java.lang
—thrown by: java.awt.EventQueue < getNextEvent( ),
invokeAndWait( ) > java.awt.MediaTracker
< waitForAll( ), waitForID( ) > java.lang.Object.wait( )
java.awt.image.PixelGrabber.grabPixels( )
Process.waitFor( ) ReferenceQueue.remove( )
javax.swing.SwingUtilities.invokeAndWait( ) Thread < join( ),
sleep( ) >
InterruptedIOExceptionˆ: java.io
—subclasses: SocketTimeoutExceptionˆ
InterruptedNamingExceptionˆ: javax.naming
InterruptibleChannelˆ: java.nio.channels
—implemented by: AbstractInterruptibleChannel˅
intersects( ): BitSet
INTF_REPOSˆ: org.omg.CORBA
IntHolder: org.omg.CORBA
IntrospectionException: java.beans
—thrown by: EventSetDescriptor( ) IndexedPropertyDescriptorˆ
< IndexedPropertyDescriptor( ), setIndexedReadMethod( ),
setIndexedWriteMethod( ) > Introspector.getBeanInfo( )
PropertyDescriptor˅ < PropertyDescriptor( ), setReadMethod( ),
setWriteMethod( ) >
Introspector: java.beans
intValue( ): Level Number˅
INUSE_ATTRIBUTE_ERR˅: DOMException
INV_FLAGˆ: org.omg.CORBA
INV_IDENTˆ: org.omg.CORBA
INV_OBJREFˆ: org.omg.CORBA
INV_POLICYˆ: org.omg.CORBA
Invalidˆ: org.omg.CORBA.DynAnyPackage
—thrown by: org.omg.CORBA.DynAny˅ < assign( ), from_any( ),
to_any( ) >
INVALID_ACCESS_ERR: DOMException
INVALID_CHARACTER_ERR: DOMException
INVALID_MODIFICATION_ERR: DOMException
INVALID_STATE_ERR: DOMException
INVALID_TRANSACTIONˆ: org.omg.CORBA
InvalidAddressˆ:
org.omg.CosNaming.NamingContextExtPackage

—passed to: InvalidAddressHelper < insert( ), write( ) >
InvalidAddressHolder( )
—returned by: InvalidAddressHelper < extract( ), read( ) >
—thrown by: _NamingContextExtStubˆ.to_url( )
NamingContextExtOperations˅.to_url( )
—fields: InvalidAddressHolder.value
InvalidAddressHelper:
org.omg.CosNaming.NamingContextExtPackage
InvalidAddressHolder:
org.omg.CosNaming.NamingContextExtPackage
InvalidAlgorithmParameterExceptionˆ: java.security
—thrown by: AlgorithmParameterGenerator.init( )
AlgorithmParameterGeneratorSpi.engineInit( )
CertPathBuilder.build( ) CertPathBuilderSpi.engineBuild( )
CertPathValidator.validate( )
CertPathValidatorSpi.engineValidate( )
CertStore.getInstance( ) CertStoreSpi( ) Cipher˅.init( )
CipherSpi.engineInit( ) ExemptionMechanism.init( )
ExemptionMechanismSpi.engineInit( ) KeyAgreement.init( )
KeyAgreementSpi.engineInit( ) KeyGenerator.init( )
KeyGeneratorSpi.engineInit( ) KeyManagerFactory.init( )
KeyManagerFactorySpi.engineInit( )
KeyPairGeneratorˆ.initialize( ) KeyPairGeneratorSpi˅.initialize( )
Mac.init( ) MacSpi.engineInit( ) PKIXBuilderParameters( )
PKIXParameters˅ < PKIXParameters( ), setTrustAnchors( ) >
Signatureˆ.setParameter( ) SignatureSpi˅.engineSetParameter( )
TrustManagerFactory.init( )
TrustManagerFactorySpi.engineInit( )
invalidate( ): SSLSession
InvalidAttributeIdentifierExceptionˆ: javax.naming.directory
InvalidAttributesExceptionˆ: javax.naming.directory
InvalidAttributeValueExceptionˆ: javax.naming.directory
InvalidClassExceptionˆ: java.io
InvalidKeyExceptionˆ: java.security
—thrown by: java.security.cert.Certificate˅.verify( )
javax.security.cert.Certificate˅.verify( ) Cipher˅ < init( ),
unwrap( ), wrap( ) > CipherSpi < engineGetKeySize( ),
engineInit( ), engineUnwrap( ), engineWrap( ) >
DESedeKeySpec < DESedeKeySpec( ), isParityAdjusted( ) >
DESKeySpec < DESKeySpec( ), isParityAdjusted( ),
isWeak( ) > ExemptionMechanism.init( )
ExemptionMechanismSpi.engineInit( ) KeyAgreement
< doPhase( ), generateSecret( ), init( ) > KeyAgreementSpi
< engineDoPhase( ), engineGenerateSecret( ), engineInit( ) >
KeyFactory.translateKey( ) KeyFactorySpi.engineTranslateKey( )
Mac.init( ) MacSpi.engineInit( ) SealedObject.getObject( )
SecretKeyFactory.translateKey( )
SecretKeyFactorySpi.engineTranslateKey( ) Signatureˆ
< initSign( ), initVerify( ) > SignatureSpi˅ < engineInitSign( ),
engineInitVerify( ) > SignedObject < SignedObject( ), verify( ) >
X509CRLˆ.verify( )
InvalidKeySpecExceptionˆ: java.security.spec
—thrown by: EncryptedPrivateKeyInfo.getKeySpec( )
KeyFactory < generatePrivate( ), generatePublic( ),
getKeySpec( ) > KeyFactorySpi < engineGeneratePrivate( ),
engineGeneratePublic( ), engineGetKeySpec( ) >
SecretKeyFactory < generateSecret( ), getKeySpec( ) >
SecretKeyFactorySpi < engineGenerateSecret( ),
engineGetKeySpec( ) >
InvalidMarkExceptionˆ: java.nio
InvalidNameˆ: org.omg.CORBA.ORBPackage
—thrown by: org.omg.CORBA.ORB˅.resolve_initial_references( )
InvalidNameˆ: org.omg.CosNaming.NamingContextPackage
—passed to: org.omg.CosNaming.NamingContextPackage↩
.InvalidNameHelper < insert( ), write( ) > InvalidNameHolder( )
—returned by: org.omg.CosNaming.NamingContextPackage↩
.InvalidNameHelper < extract( ), read( ) >
—thrown by: _NamingContextExtStubˆ < bind( ), bind_context( ),
bind_new_context( ), rebind( ), rebind_context( ), resolve( ),
resolve_str( ), to_name( ), to_string( ), to_url( ), unbind( ) >
_NamingContextStubˆ < bind( ), bind_context( ),
bind_new_context( ), rebind( ), rebind_context( ), resolve( ),

I

unbind( ) > *NamingContextExtOperations*ˆˬ < resolve_str( ), to_name( ), to_string( ), to_url( ) > *NamingContextOperations*ˬ < bind( ), bind_context( ), bind_new_context( ), rebind( ), rebind_context( ), resolve( ), unbind( ) >
—fields: InvalidNameHolder.value

InvalidNameˆ: org.omg.PortableInterceptor.ORBInitInfoPackage
—passed to: org.omg.PortableInterceptor↵ .ORBInitInfoPackage.InvalidNameHelper < insert( ), write( ) >
—returned by: org.omg.PortableInterceptor↵ .ORBInitInfoPackage.InvalidNameHelper < extract( ), read( ) >
—thrown by: *ORBInitInfoOperations*ˬ < register_initial_reference( ), resolve_initial_references( ) >

InvalidNameExceptionˆ: javax.naming
—thrown by: CompositeName < add( ), addAll( ), CompositeName( ), remove( ) > CompoundName < add( ), addAll( ), CompoundName( ), remove( ) > *Name*ˆ < add( ), addAll( ), remove( ) >

InvalidNameHelper: org.omg.CosNaming.NamingContextPackage

InvalidNameHelper: org.omg.PortableInterceptor.ORBInitInfoPackage

InvalidNameHolder: org.omg.CosNaming.NamingContextPackage

InvalidObjectExceptionˆ: java.io
—thrown by: AttributedCharacterIterator.Attributeˬ.readResolve( ) DateFormat.Fieldˆ.readResolve( ) MessageFormat.Fieldˆ.readResolve( ) NumberFormat.Fieldˆ.readResolve( ) ObjectInputStreamˆ.registerValidation( ) *ObjectInputValidation*.validateObject( ) java.awt.font.TextAttributeˆ.readResolve( )

InvalidParameterExceptionˆ: java.security
—thrown by: *DSAKeyPairGenerator*.initialize( ) Signatureˆ < getParameter( ), setParameter( ) > SignatureSpiˬ < engineGetParameter( ), engineSetParameter( ) > Signerˆ.setKeyPair( )

InvalidParameterSpecExceptionˆ: java.security.spec
—thrown by: AlgorithmParameters < getParameterSpec( ), init( ) > AlgorithmParametersSpi < engineGetParameterSpec( ), engineInit( ) >

InvalidPolicyˆ: org.omg.PortableServer.POAPackage
—passed to: InvalidPolicyHelper < insert( ), write( ) >
—returned by: InvalidPolicyHelper < extract( ), read( ) >
—thrown by: *POAOperations*ˬ.create_POA( )

InvalidPolicyHelper: org.omg.PortableServer.POAPackage

InvalidPreferencesFormatException: java.util.prefs
—thrown by: Preferencesˬ.importPreferences( )

InvalidSearchControlsExceptionˆ: javax.naming.directory

InvalidSearchFilterExceptionˆ: javax.naming.directory

InvalidSeqˆ: org.omg.CORBA.DynAnyPackage
—thrown by: *org.omg.CORBA.DynArray*ˆ.set_elements( ) *org.omg.CORBA.DynSequence*ˆ.set_elements( ) *org.omg.CORBA.DynStruct*ˆ.set_members( ) *org.omg.CORBA.DynValue*ˆ.set_members( )

InvalidSlotˆ: org.omg.PortableInterceptor
—passed to: InvalidSlotHelper < insert( ), write( ) >
—returned by: InvalidSlotHelper < extract( ), read( ) >
—thrown by: *org.omg.PortableInterceptor.CurrentOperations*ˆˬ < get_slot( ), set_slot( ) > *RequestInfoOperations*ˬ.get_slot( ) *ServerRequestInfoOperations*ˆˬ.set_slot( )

InvalidSlotHelper: org.omg.PortableInterceptor

InvalidTransactionExceptionˆ: javax.transaction

InvalidTypeForEncodingˆ: org.omg.IOP.CodecPackage
—passed to: InvalidTypeForEncodingHelper < insert( ), write( ) >
—returned by: InvalidTypeForEncodingHelper < extract( ), read( ) >
—thrown by: *CodecOperations*ˬ < encode( ), encode_value( ) >

InvalidTypeForEncodingHelper: org.omg.IOP.CodecPackage

InvalidValueˆ: org.omg.CORBA.DynAnyPackage
—thrown by: *org.omg.CORBA.DynAny*ˆˬ < insert_any( ), insert_boolean( ), insert_char( ), insert_double( ), insert_float( ), insert_long( ), insert_longlong( ), insert_octet( ), insert_reference( ), insert_short( ), insert_string( ), insert_typecode( ), insert_ulong( ), insert_ulonglong( ), insert_ushort( ), insert_val( ), insert_wchar( ), insert_wstring( ) > *org.omg.CORBA.DynFixed*ˆ.set_value( )

InvalidValueˆ: org.omg.DynamicAny.DynAnyPackage
—passed to: InvalidValueHelper < insert( ), write( ) >
—returned by: InvalidValueHelper < extract( ), read( ) >
—thrown by: _DynAnyStubˆ < from_any( ), get_any( ), get_boolean( ), get_char( ), get_double( ), get_dyn_any( ), get_float( ), get_long( ), get_longlong( ), get_octet( ), get_reference( ), get_short( ), get_string( ), get_typecode( ), get_ulong( ), get_ulonglong( ), get_ushort( ), get_val( ), get_wchar( ), get_wstring( ), insert_any( ), insert_boolean( ), insert_char( ), insert_double( ), insert_dyn_any( ), insert_float( ), insert_long( ), insert_longlong( ), insert_octet( ), insert_reference( ), insert_short( ), insert_string( ), insert_typecode( ), insert_ulong( ), insert_ulonglong( ), insert_ushort( ), insert_val( ), insert_wchar( ), insert_wstring( ) > _DynArrayStubˆ < from_any( ), get_any( ), get_boolean( ), get_char( ), get_double( ), get_dyn_any( ), get_float( ), get_long( ), get_longlong( ), get_octet( ), get_reference( ), get_short( ), get_string( ), get_typecode( ), get_ulong( ), get_ulonglong( ), get_ushort( ), get_val( ), get_wchar( ), get_wstring( ), insert_any( ), insert_boolean( ), insert_char( ), insert_double( ), insert_dyn_any( ), insert_float( ), insert_long( ), insert_longlong( ), insert_octet( ), insert_reference( ), insert_short( ), insert_string( ), insert_typecode( ), insert_ulong( ), insert_ulonglong( ), insert_ushort( ), insert_val( ), insert_wchar( ), insert_wstring( ), set_elements( ), set_elements_as_dyn_any( ) > _DynEnumStubˆ < from_any( ), get_any( ), get_boolean( ), get_char( ), get_double( ), get_dyn_any( ), get_float( ), get_long( ), get_longlong( ), get_octet( ), get_reference( ), get_short( ), get_string( ), get_typecode( ), get_ulong( ), get_ulonglong( ), get_ushort( ), get_val( ), get_wchar( ), get_wstring( ), insert_any( ), insert_boolean( ), insert_char( ), insert_double( ), insert_dyn_any( ), insert_float( ), insert_long( ), insert_longlong( ), insert_octet( ), insert_reference( ), insert_short( ), insert_string( ), insert_typecode( ), insert_ulong( ), insert_ulonglong( ), insert_ushort( ), insert_val( ), insert_wchar( ), insert_wstring( ), set_as_string( ), set_as_ulong( ) > _DynFixedStubˆ < from_any( ), get_any( ), get_boolean( ), get_char( ), get_double( ), get_dyn_any( ), get_float( ), get_long( ), get_longlong( ), get_octet( ), get_reference( ), get_short( ), get_string( ), get_typecode( ), get_ulong( ), get_ulonglong( ), get_ushort( ), get_val( ), get_wchar( ), get_wstring( ), insert_any( ), insert_boolean( ), insert_char( ), insert_double( ), insert_dyn_any( ), insert_float( ), insert_long( ), insert_longlong( ), insert_octet( ), insert_reference( ), insert_short( ), insert_string( ), insert_typecode( ), insert_ulong( ), insert_ulonglong( ), insert_ushort( ), insert_val( ), insert_wchar( ), insert_wstring( ), set_value( ) > _DynSequenceStubˆ < from_any( ), get_any( ), get_boolean( ), get_char( ), get_double( ), get_dyn_any( ), get_float( ), get_long( ), get_longlong( ), get_octet( ), get_reference( ), get_short( ), get_string( ), get_typecode( ), get_ulong( ), get_ulonglong( ), get_ushort( ), get_val( ), get_wchar( ), get_wstring( ), insert_any( ), insert_boolean( ), insert_char( ), insert_double( ), insert_dyn_any( ), insert_float( ), insert_long( ), insert_longlong( ), insert_octet( ), insert_reference( ), insert_short( ), insert_string( ), insert_typecode( ), insert_ulong( ), insert_ulonglong( ), insert_ushort( ), insert_val( ), insert_wchar( ), insert_wstring( ), set_elements( ), set_elements_as_dyn_any( ), set_length( ) > _DynStructStubˆ < current_member_kind( ), current_member_name( ), from_any( ), get_any( ), get_boolean( ), get_char( ), get_double( ), get_dyn_any( ), get_float( ), get_long( ), get_longlong( ), get_octet( ), get_reference( ), get_short( ), get_string( ), get_typecode( ), get_ulong( ), get_ulonglong( ), get_ushort( ), get_val( ), get_wchar( ), get_wstring( ), insert_any( ), insert_boolean( ), insert_char( ), insert_double( ), insert_dyn_any( ), insert_float( ), insert_long( ), insert_longlong( ), insert_octet( ), insert_reference( ), insert_short( ), insert_string( ), insert_typecode( ), insert_ulong( ),

< getTimeToLive( ), getTTL( ), join( ), joinGroup( ), leave( ),
leaveGroup( ), peek( ), peekData( ), receive( ), send( ),
setTimeToLive( ), setTTL( ) > *DataInput*⌐ < readBoolean( ),
readByte( ), readChar( ), readDouble( ), readFloat( ), readFully( ),
readInt( ), readLine( ), readLong( ), readShort( ),
readUnsignedByte( ), readUnsignedShort( ), readUTF( ),
skipBytes( ) > java.io.**D**ataInputStream^ < readBoolean( ),
readByte( ), readChar( ), readDouble( ), readFloat( ), readFully( ),
readInt( ), readLine( ), readLong( ), readShort( ),
readUnsignedByte( ), readUnsignedShort( ), readUTF( ),
skipBytes( ) > *DataOutput*⌐ < write( ), writeBoolean( ),
writeByte( ), writeBytes( ), writeChar( ), writeChars( ),
writeDouble( ), writeFloat( ), writeInt( ), writeLong( ), writeShort( ),
writeUTF( ) > java.io.**D**ataOutputStream^ < writeBoolean( ),
writeByte( ), writeBytes( ), writeChar( ), writeChars( ),
writeDouble( ), writeFloat( ), writeInt( ), writeLong( ),
writeShort( ), writeUTF( ) > **D**eflaterOutputStream^ < deflate( ),
finish( ) > *javax.print.Doc* < getPrintData( ), getReaderForText( ),
getStreamForBytes( ) > **D**ocumentBuilder.parse( )
javax.swing.text.html.parser.**D**ocumentParser^.parse( )
java.awt.dnd.**D**ropTargetContext.TransferableProxy ↵
.getTransferData( ) javax.swing.text.html.parser.**D**TD
< getDTD( ), read( ) > javax.swing.text.**E**ditorKit < read( ),
write( ) > **E**ncryptedPrivateKeyInfo < EncryptedPrivateKeyInfo( ),
getEncoded( ) > *EntityResolver*.resolveEntity( ) *Externalizable*⌐
< readExternal( ), writeExternal( ) > **F**ile < createNewFile( ),
createTempFile( ), getCanonicalFile( ), getCanonicalPath( ) >
javax.imageio.stream.**F**ileCacheImageInputStream( )
javax.imageio.stream.**F**ileCacheImageOutputStream( )
FileChannel^ < force( ), lock( ), map( ), position( ),
read( ), size( ), transferFrom( ), transferTo( ),
truncate( ), tryLock( ), write( ) > **F**ileHandler( )
javax.imageio.stream.**F**ileImageInputStream( )
javax.imageio.stream.**F**ileImageOutputStream( )
FileInputStream^ < finalize( ), getFD( ) > **F**ileLock.release( )
FileOutputStream^ < finalize( ), getFD( ) >
javax.swing.filechooser.**F**ileSystemView.createNewFolder( )
FileWriter( ) java.awt.**F**ont.createFont( )
GatheringByteChannel^.write( ) **G**ZIPInputStream( )
GZIPOutputStream( ) javax.swing.text.html.**H**TMLDocument^
< insertAfterEnd( ), insertAfterStart( ), insertBeforeEnd( ),
insertBeforeStart( ), setInnerHTML( ), setOuterHTML( ) >
javax.swing.text.html.**H**TMLEditorKit^.insertHTML( )
javax.swing.text.html.**H**TMLEditorKit.Parser.parse( )
javax.swing.text.html.**H**TMLWriter^
< closeOutUnwantedEmbeddedTags( ), comment( ), emptyTag( ),
endTag( ), output( ), selectContent( ), startTag( ),
text( ), textAreaContent( ), write( ), writeAttributes( ),
writeEmbeddedTags( ), writeLineSeparator( ), writeOption( ) >
HttpsURLConnection( ) **H**ttpURLConnection^
< getResponseCode( ), getResponseMessage( ) >
java.awt.color.**I**CC_Profile < getInstance( ), write( ) >
javax.imageio.stream.ImageInputStream^ < close( ),
flush( ), flushBefore( ), getBitOffset( ), getStreamPosition( ),
length( ), read( ), readBit( ), readBits( ), readBoolean( ),
readByte( ), readBytes( ), readChar( ), readDouble( ),
readFloat( ), readFully( ), readInt( ), readLine( ), readLong( ),
readShort( ), readUnsignedByte( ), readUnsignedInt( ),
readUnsignedShort( ), readUTF( ), reset( ), seek( ), setBitOffset( ),
skipBytes( ) > javax.imageio.stream.**I**mageInputStreamImpl
< checkClosed( ), close( ), flush( ), flushBefore( ), getBitOffset( ),
getStreamPosition( ), read( ), readBit( ), readBits( ),
readBoolean( ), readByte( ), readBytes( ), readChar( ),
readDouble( ), readFloat( ), readFully( ), readInt( ), readLine( ),
readLong( ), readShort( ), readUnsignedByte( ), readUnsignedInt( ),
readUnsignedShort( ), readUTF( ), reset( ), seek( ), setBitOffset( ),
skipBytes( ) > javax.imageio.spi.**I**mageInputStreamSpi^ ↵
.createInputStreamInstance( ) javax.imageio.**I**mageIO
< createImageInputStream( ), createImageOutputStream( ), read( ),

write( ) > *javax.imageio.stream.ImageOutputStream*^
< flushBefore( ), write( ), writeBit( ), writeBits( ),
writeBoolean( ), writeByte( ), writeBytes( ), writeChar( ),
writeChars( ), writeDouble( ), writeDoubles( ), writeFloat( ),
writeFloats( ), writeInt( ), writeInts( ), writeLong( ),
writeLongs( ), writeShort( ), writeShorts( ), writeUTF( ) >
javax.imageio.stream.**I**mageOutputStreamImpl^ < flushBits( ),
write( ), writeBit( ), writeBits( ), writeBoolean( ), writeByte( ),
writeBytes( ), writeChar( ), writeChars( ), writeDouble( ),
writeDoubles( ), writeFloat( ), writeFloats( ), writeInt( ),
writeInts( ), writeLong( ), writeLongs( ), writeShort( ),
writeShorts( ), writeUTF( ) > javax.imageio.spi ↵
.**I**mageOutputStreamSpi^.createOutputStreamInstance( )
javax.imageio.**I**mageReader < getAspectRatio( ),
getFormatName( ), getHeight( ), getImageMetadata( ),
getImageTypes( ), getNumImages( ), getNumThumbnails( ),
getRawImageType( ), getStreamMetadata( ), getThumbnailHeight( ),
getThumbnailWidth( ), getTileGridXOffset( ), getTileGridYOffset( ),
getTileHeight( ), getTileWidth( ), getWidth( ), hasThumbnails( ),
isImageTiled( ), isRandomAccessEasy( ), read( ),
readAll( ), readAsRenderedImage( ), readRaster( ),
readThumbnail( ), readTile( ), readTileRaster( ) >
javax.imageio.spi.**I**mageReaderSpi^ < canDecodeInput( ),
createReaderInstance( ) > javax.imageio.**I**mageWriter
< canInsertEmpty( ), canInsertImage( ),
canRemoveImage( ), canReplaceImageMetadata( ),
canReplacePixels( ), canReplaceStreamMetadata( ),
canWriteEmpty( ), endInsertEmpty( ), endReplacePixels( ),
endWriteEmpty( ), endWriteSequence( ),
prepareInsertEmpty( ), prepareReplacePixels( ),
prepareWriteEmpty( ), prepareWriteSequence( ),
removeImage( ), replaceImageMetadata( ),
replacePixels( ), replaceStreamMetadata( ),
write( ), writeInsert( ), writeToSequence( ) >
javax.imageio.spi.**I**mageWriterSpi^.createWriterInstance( )
InflaterInputStream^.fill( ) java.io.**I**nputStream⌐
< available( ), close( ), read( ), reset( ), skip( ) >
InterruptibleChannel^.close( ) **J**arEntry^.getAttributes( )
JarFile^ < getManifest( ), JarFile( ) > **J**arInputStream^
< getNextJarEntry( ), JarInputStream( ) > **J**arOutputStream^
JarURLConnection^ < getAttributes( ), getCertificates( ),
getJarEntry( ), getJarFile( ), getMainAttributes( ), getManifest( ) >
javax.swing.**J**EditorPane^ < getStream( ), JEditorPane( ),
read( ), setPage( ) > javax.swing.text.**J**TextComponent^
< read( ), write( ) > **K**eyStore < load( ), store( ) >
KeyStoreSpi < engineLoad( ), engineStore( ) >
LogManager.readConfiguration( ) **M**anifest < Manifest( ), read( ),
write( ) > **M**arshalledObject < get( ), MarshalledObject( ) >
javax.sound.midi.**M**idiFileReader < getMidiFileFormat( ),
getSequence( ) > javax.sound.midi.spi.**M**idiFileWriter.write( )
javax.sound.midi.**M**idiSystem < getMidiFileFormat( ),
getSequence( ), getSoundbank( ), write( ) >
javax.swing.text.html.**M**inimalHTMLWriter^ < endFontTag( ),
startFontTag( ), text( ), write( ), writeAttributes( ), writeBody( ),
writeComponent( ), writeContent( ), writeEndParagraph( ),
writeEndTag( ), writeHeader( ), writeHTMLTags( ),
writeImage( ), writeLeaf( ), writeNonHTMLAttributes( ),
writeStartParagraph( ), writeStartTag( ), writeStyles( ) >
MulticastSocket^ < getTimeToLive( ), getTTL( ), joinGroup( ),
leaveGroup( ), MulticastSocket( ), send( ), setTimeToLive( ),
setTTL( ) > *javax.print.MultiDoc* < getDoc( ), next( ) >
ObjectInput^ < available( ), close( ), read( ), readObject( ),
skip( ) > **O**bjectInputStream^ < defaultReadObject( ),
ObjectInputStream( ), readBoolean( ), readByte( ), readChar( ),
readClassDescriptor( ), readDouble( ), readFields( ), readFloat( ),
readFully( ), readInt( ), readLine( ), readLong( ), readObject( ),
readObjectOverride( ), readShort( ), readStreamHeader( ),
readUnshared( ), readUnsignedByte( ), readUnsignedShort( ),
readUTF( ), resolveClass( ), resolveObject( ), resolveProxyClass( ),
skipBytes( ) > **O**bjectInputStream.GetField < defaulted( ),

get( ) > **O**bjectOutput^ < close( ), flush( ), write( ),
writeObject( ) > **O**bjectOutputStream^ < annotateClass( ),
annotateProxyClass( ), defaultWriteObject( ), drain( ),
ObjectOutputStream( ), putFields( ), replaceObject( ), reset( ),
useProtocolVersion( ), writeBoolean( ), writeByte( ), writeBytes( ),
writeChar( ), writeChars( ), writeClassDescriptor( ),
writeDouble( ), writeFields( ), writeFloat( ), writeInt( ),
writeLong( ), writeObject( ), writeObjectOverride( ), writeShort( ),
writeStreamHeader( ), writeUnshared( ), writeUTF( ) >
ObjectOutputStream.PutField.write( ) **O**bjID < read( ),
write( ) > java.io.**O**utputStream, < close( ), flush( ),
write( ) > javax.swing.text.html.parser.**P**arser.parse( )
Parser.parse( ) javax.swing.text.html.parser.**P**arser
< parseDTDMarkup( ), parseMarkupDeclarations( ) >
ParserAdapter.parse( ) Pipe.open( ) **P**ipedInputStream^
< connect( ), PipedInputStream( ), receive( ) >
PipedOutputStream^ < connect( ), PipedOutputStream( ) >
PipedReader^ < connect( ), PipedReader( ) > **P**ipedWriter^
< connect( ), PipedWriter( ) > **P**olicyQualifierInfo( )
Preferences, < exportNode( ), exportSubtree( ),
importPreferences( ) > **P**roperties^ < load( ), store( ) >
PropertyResourceBundle( ) **P**ushbackInputStream^.unread( )
PushbackReader^.unread( ) **R**andomAccessFile < close( ),
getFD( ), getFilePointer( ), length( ), read( ), readBoolean( ),
readByte( ), readChar( ), readDouble( ), readFloat( ), readFully( ),
readInt( ), readLine( ), readLong( ), readShort( ),
readUnsignedByte( ), readUnsignedShort( ), readUTF( ),
seek( ), setLength( ), skipBytes( ), write( ), writeBoolean( ),
writeByte( ), writeBytes( ), writeChar( ), writeChars( ),
writeDouble( ), writeFloat( ), writeInt( ), writeLong( ),
writeShort( ), writeUTF( ) > *ReadableByteChannel*^.read( )
Reader, < close( ), mark( ), read( ), ready( ), reset( ),
skip( ) > *RemoteCall* < done( ), getInputStream( ),
getOutputStream( ), getResultStream( ), releaseInputStream( ),
releaseOutputStream( ) > *RMIClientSocketFactory*.createSocket( )
RMIServerSocketFactory.createServerSocket( )
RMISocketFactory < createServerSocket( ),
createSocket( ), setSocketFactory( ) > **R**untime.exec( )
SAXParser.parse( ) *ScatteringByteChannel*^.read( )
SealedObject < getObject( ), SealedObject( ) >
SelectableChannel^.configureBlocking( ) **S**elector, < close( ),
open( ), select( ), selectNow( ) > **S**electorProvider
< openDatagramChannel( ), openPipe( ), openSelector( ),
openServerSocketChannel( ), openSocketChannel( ) >
javax.sound.midi.*Sequencer*^.setSequence( ) **S**erverSocket,
< accept( ), bind( ), close( ), getSoTimeout( ),
implAccept( ), ServerSocket( ), setSocketFactory( ) >
ServerSocketChannel^ < accept( ), open( ) >
ServerSocketFactory,.createServerSocket( ) **S**ignedObject
< getObject( ), SignedObject( ) > javax.print.**S**impleDoc
< getPrintData( ), getReaderForText( ), getStreamForBytes( ) >
Socket, < bind( ), close( ), connect( ), getInputStream( ),
getOutputStream( ), sendUrgentData( ), setSocketImplFactory( ),
shutdownInput( ), shutdownOutput( ), Socket( ) >
SocketChannel^ < connect( ), finishConnect( ), open( ), read( ),
write( ) > **S**ocketFactory,.createSocket( ) **S**ocketHandler( )
SocketImpl < accept( ), available( ), bind( ), close( ), connect( ),
create( ), getInputStream( ), getOutputStream( ), listen( ),
sendUrgentData( ), shutdownInput( ), shutdownOutput( ) >
javax.sound.midi.spi.**S**oundbankReader.getSoundbank( )
SSLServerSocket( ) **S**SLSocket^
< SSLSocket( ), startHandshake( ) >
SSLSocketFactory^.createSocket( ) **S**tartTlsResponse
< close( ), negotiate( ) > **S**treamTokenizer.nextToken( )
java.awt.datatransfer.**S**tringSelection.getTransferData( )
StubDelegate < readObject( ), writeObject( ) >
javax.swing.text.**S**tyleContext < readAttributes( ),
readAttributeSet( ), writeAttributes( ), writeAttributeSet( ) >
javax.swing.text.html.**S**tyleSheet^.loadRules( )
java.awt.datatransfer.*Transferable*.getTransferData( ) **U**ID

< read( ), write( ) > **U**RL < getContent( ), openConnection( ),
openStream( ) > **U**RLClassLoader^.findResources( )
URLConnection, < connect( ), getContent( ),
getInputStream( ), getOutputStream( ),
getPermission( ), guessContentTypeFromStream( ) >
URLStreamHandler.openConnection( )
WritableByteChannel^.write( ) **W**riter, < close( ), flush( ),
write( ) > **X**509CertSelector < addPathToName( ),
addSubjectAlternativeName( ), getIssuerAsBytes( ),
getSubjectAsBytes( ), setExtendedKeyUsage( ),
setIssuer( ), setNameConstraints( ), setPathToNames( ),
setPolicy( ), setSubject( ), setSubjectAlternativeNames( ),
setSubjectPublicKey( ), setSubjectPublicKeyAlgID( ) >
X509CRLSelector < addIssuerName( ), setIssuerNames( ) >
XMLFilterImpl < parse( ), resolveEntity( ) >
XMLReader,.parse( ) **X**MLReaderAdapter.parse( ) ZipFile,
< close( ), finalize( ), getInputStream( ), ZipFile( ) >
ZipInputStream^ < closeEntry( ), getNextEntry( ) >
ZipOutputStream^ < closeEntry( ), putNextEntry( ) >

IOR: org.omg.IOP
—passed to: **I**ORHelper < insert( ), write( ) > **I**ORHolder( )
—returned by: **I**ORHelper < extract( ), read( ) >
—fields: **I**ORHolder.value

IORHelper: org.omg.IOP

IORHolder: org.omg.IOP

IORInfo^: org.omg.PortableInterceptor
—passed to: *IORInterceptorOperations*^.establish_components( )

IORInfoOperations,: org.omg.PortableInterceptor
—extended by: *IORInfo*^

IORInterceptor^: org.omg.PortableInterceptor
—passed to: *ORBInitInfoOperations*,.add_ior_interceptor( )

IORInterceptorOperations^: org.omg.PortableInterceptor
—extended by: *IORInterceptor*^

IP_MULTICAST_IF: *SocketOptions*

IP_MULTICAST_IF2: *SocketOptions*

IP_MULTICAST_LOOP: *SocketOptions*

IP_TOS: *SocketOptions*

IPA_EXTENSIONS: Character.UnicodeBlock^

IRObject^: org.omg.CORBA
—extended by: *IDLType*^

IRObjectOperations,: org.omg.CORBA
—extended by: *IDLTypeOperations*^, *IRObject*^
—descendents: *IDLType*^

is_a(): org.omg.CORBA.portable.**D**elegate,
org.omg.PortableServer.portable.**D**elegate

is_equivalent(): org.omg.CORBA.portable.**D**elegate,

is_local(): org.omg.CORBA.portable.**D**elegate,

is_null(): _DynValueStub^ *DynValueCommonOperations*^

isAbsolute(): File URI

isAbstract(): **M**odifier

isAcceptable(): **S**electionKey,

isAccessible(): **A**ccessibleObject,

isAfterLast(): *ResultSet*,

isAlive(): Thread

isAnonymous(): *GSSName*,

isAnyLocalAddress(): InetAddress,

isAnyPolicyInhibited(): PKIXParameters,

isArray(): Class

isAssignableFrom(): Class

isAutoDetecting(): CharsetDecoder

isAutoIncrement(): *ResultSetMetaData*,

isBeforeFirst(): *ResultSet*,

isBlocking(): **S**electableChannel^

isBound(): DatagramSocket, PropertyDescriptor^
ServerSocket, Socket,

isBoundary(): BreakIterator

isCaseIgnored(): javax.naming.directory.*Attributes*^
BasicAttributes

isCaseSensitive(): *ResultSetMetaData*,

isCatalogAtStart(): *DatabaseMetaData*,

isCertificateEntry(): KeyStore

isCharsetDetected(): CharsetDecoder

isSigned(): *ParameterMetaData* *ResultSetMetaData*⌣
isSiteLocalAddress(): InetAddress⌣
isSpace(): Character
isSpaceChar(): Character
isStatic(): Modifier
isStrict(): Modifier
isSupported(): Charset *Node*⌣
isSynchronized(): Modifier
isTimeSet: Calendar⌣
isTitleCase(): Character
isTransferable(): *GSSContext*
isTransient(): Modifier
IstringHelper: org.omg.CosNaming
isUnderflow(): CoderResult
isUnicast(): EventSetDescriptor^
isUnicodeIdentifierPart(): Character
isUnicodeIdentifierStart(): Character
isUnique(): VMID
isUnmappable(): CoderResult
isUnresolved(): InetSocketAddress^
isUnseqToken(): MessageProp
isUnshared(): ObjectStreamField
isUpperCase(): Character
isUserNode(): Preferences⌣
isValid(): FileLock SelectionKey⌣
isValidating(): DocumentBuilder DocumentBuilderFactory
 SAXParser SAXParserFactory
isVolatile(): Modifier
isWeak(): DESKeySpec
isWhitespace(): Character
isWritable(): *ResultSetMetaData*⌣ SelectionKey⌣
ITALIAN: Locale
ITALY: Locale
item(): ContextList ExceptionList *NamedNodeMap* NodeList
 NVList
Iterator⌣: java.util
—extended by: *ListIterator*^
—passed to: javax.imageio.ImageReader < getDestination( ),
 readAll( ) > javax.imageio.spi.ServiceRegistry
 < registerServiceProviders( ), ServiceRegistry( ) >
—returned by: AbstractCollection⌣.iterator( )
 java.applet.AppletContext.getStreamKeys( )
 BeanContextMembershipEvent^.iterator( )
 BeanContextServiceAvailableEvent^ ↩
 .getCurrentServiceSelectors( )
 BeanContextServiceProvider.getCurrentServiceSelectors( )
 BeanContextServices^ < getCurrentServiceClasses( ),
 getCurrentServiceSelectors( ) > BeanContextServicesSupport^
 < getCurrentServiceClasses( ), getCurrentServiceSelectors( ) >
 BeanContextServicesSupport ↩
 .BCSSProxyServiceProvider.getCurrentServiceSelectors( )
 BeanContextSupport^ < bcsChildren( ), iterator( ) >
 CertificateFactory.getCertPathEncodings( )
 CertificateFactorySpi.engineGetCertPathEncodings( )
 CertPath.getEncodings( )
 CharsetProvider.charsets( ) *Collection*⌣.iterator( )
 java.awt.dnd.DragGestureEvent^.iterator( )
 javax.imageio.ImageIO < getImageReaders( ),
 getImageReadersByFormatName( ),
 getImageReadersByMIMEType( ), getImageReadersBySuffix( ),
 getImageTranscoders( ), getImageWriters( ),
 getImageWritersByFormatName( ), getImageWritersByMIMEType( ),
 getImageWritersBySuffix( ) > javax.imageio.ImageReader
 < getImageTypes( ), readAll( ) > *List*^.iterator( )
 PolicyNode.getChildren( ) javax.imageio.spi.ServiceRegistry
 < getCategories( ), getServiceProviders( ), lookupProviders( ) >
 Set^.iterator( )
—implemented by: BeanContextSupport.BCSIterator
iterator(): AbstractCollection⌣ BeanContextMembershipEvent^
 BeanContextSupport^ *Collection*⌣
IvParameterSpec: javax.crypto.spec

JANUARY: Calendar⌣
JAPAN: Locale
JAPANESE: Locale
JarEntry^: java.util.jar
—passed to: JarEntry( )
—returned by: JarFile^.getJarEntry( )
 JarInputStream^.getNextJarEntry( )
 JarURLConnection^.getJarEntry( )
JarException^: java.util.jar
JarFile^: java.util.jar
—returned by: JarURLConnection^.getJarFile( )
jarFileURLConnection: JarURLConnection^
JarInputStream^: java.util.jar
JarOutputStream^: java.util.jar
JarURLConnection^: java.net
JAVA_OBJECT: Types
jdbcCompliant(): *Driver*
join(): DatagramSocketImpl Thread
joinGroup(): DatagramSocketImpl MulticastSocket^
JULY: Calendar⌣
JUNE: Calendar⌣
KANBUN: Character.UnicodeBlock^
KANGXI_RADICALS: Character.UnicodeBlock^
KANNADA: Character.UnicodeBlock^
KATAKANA: Character.UnicodeBlock^
KEEP_CURRENT_RESULT: java.sql.*Statement*⌣
KerberosKey: javax.security.auth.kerberos
KerberosPrincipal: javax.security.auth.kerberos
—passed to: KerberosKey( ) KerberosTicket( )
—returned by: KerberosKey.getPrincipal( ) KerberosTicket
 < getClient( ), getServer( ) >
KerberosTicket: javax.security.auth.kerberos
Key^: java.security
—extended by: *PrivateKey*^ *PublicKey*^ *SecretKey*^
—descendents: *DHPrivateKey*^ *DHPublicKey*^ *DSAPrivateKey*^
 DSAPublicKey^ *PBEKey*^ *RSAMultiPrimePrivateCrtKey*^
 RSAPrivateCrtKey^ *RSAPrivateKey*^ *RSAPublicKey*^
—passed to: Cipher < init( ), wrap( ) > CipherSpi
 < engineGetKeySize( ), engineInit( ), engineWrap( ) >
 ExemptionMechanism < init( ), isCryptoAllowed( ) >
 ExemptionMechanismSpi.engineInit( ) KeyAgreement
 < doPhase( ), init( ) > KeyAgreementSpi < engineDoPhase( ),
 engineInit( ) > KeyFactory < getKeySpec( ), translateKey( ) >
 KeyFactorySpi < engineGetKeySpec( ), engineTranslateKey( ) >
 KeyStore.setKeyEntry( ) KeyStoreSpi.engineSetKeyEntry( )
 Mac.init( ) MacSpi.engineInit( ) SealedObject.getObject( )
—returned by: Cipher⌣.unwrap( ) CipherSpi.engineUnwrap( )
 KeyAgreement.doPhase( ) KeyAgreementSpi.engineDoPhase( )
 KeyFactory.translateKey( ) KeyFactorySpi.engineTranslateKey( )
 KeyStore.getKey( ) KeyStoreSpi.engineGetKey( )
KeyAgreement: javax.crypto
—returned by: KeyAgreement.getInstance( )
KeyAgreementSpi: javax.crypto
—passed to: KeyAgreement( )
KeyException^: java.security
—subclasses: InvalidKeyException^
 KeyManagementException^
—thrown by: java.security.*Certificate* < decode( ), encode( ) >
 Signer^.setKeyPair( )
KeyFactory: java.security
—returned by: KeyFactory.getInstance( )
KeyFactorySpi: java.security
—passed to: KeyFactory( )
keyFor(): SelectableChannel⌣
KeyGenerator: javax.crypto
—returned by: KeyGenerator.getInstance( )
KeyGeneratorSpi: javax.crypto
—passed to: KeyGenerator( )
KeyManagementException^: java.security
—thrown by: Identity⌣ < addCertificate( ), Identity( ),
 removeCertificate( ), setPublicKey( ) > IdentityScope^

K

K

LinkedListˆ: java.util
LinkExceptionˆ: javax.naming
　—subclasses: LinkLoopExceptionˆ　**M**alformedLinkExceptionˆ
linkExplanation: **L**inkExceptionˆ
LinkLoopExceptionˆ: javax.naming
LinkRefˆ: javax.naming
linkRemainingName: **L**inkExceptionˆ
linkResolvedName: **L**inkExceptionˆ
linkResolvedObj: **L**inkExceptionˆ
Listˆ: java.util
　—passed to: **C**ertificateFactory.generateCertPath( )
　　CertificateFactorySpi.engineGenerateCertPath( )　**C**ollections
　　< binarySearch( ), copy( ), fill( ), indexOfSubList( ),
　　lastIndexOfSubList( ), replaceAll( ), reverse( ), rotate( ),
　　shuffle( ), sort( ), swap( ), synchronizedList( ),
　　unmodifiableList( ) >　java.awt.dnd.**D**ragGestureEvent( )
　　javax.imageio.**I**IOImage < IIOImage( ), setThumbnails( ) >
　　javax.imageio.metadata.**I**IOMetadataFormatImpl
　　< addAttribute( ), addObjectValue( ) >
　　javax.imageio.**I**mageWriter < prepareInsertEmpty( ),
　　prepareWriteEmpty( ) >　**P**KIXParameters
　　< setCertPathCheckers( ), setCertStores( ) >
　　javax.swing.**S**pinnerListModelˆ < setList( ),
　　SpinnerListModel( ) >
　—returned by: **A**bstractListˆ.subList( )　**A**rrays.asList( )
　　CertPath.getCertificates( )　**C**ollections < nCopies( ),
　　singletonList( ), synchronizedList( ), unmodifiableList( ) >
　　java.awt.dnd.**D**ropTargetContext.getCurrentDataFlavorsAsList( )
　　java.awt.dnd.**D**ropTargetDragEventˆ ↵
　　.getCurrentDataFlavorsAsList( )　java.awt.dnd ↵
　　.**D**ropTargetDropEventˆ.getCurrentDataFlavorsAsList( )
　　java.awt.datatransfer.**F**lavorTableˆ
　　< getFlavorsForNative( ), getNativesForFlavor( ) >
　　javax.imageio.**I**IOImage.getThumbnails( )
　　java.awt.**K**eyboardFocusManager < getKeyEventDispatchers( ),
　　getKeyEventPostProcessors( ) >　**L**istˆ.subList( )
　　PKIXParameters < getCertPathCheckers( ),
　　getCertStores( ) >　javax.swing.**S**pinnerListModelˆ.getList( )
　　java.awt.datatransfer.**S**ystemFlavorMap
　　< getFlavorsForNative( ), getNativesForFlavor( ) >
　　java.security.cert.**X**509Certificateˆ.getExtendedKeyUsage( )
　—implemented by: **A**bstractListˆ
　—fields: **C**ollections.EMPTY_LIST
　　javax.imageio.**I**IOImage.thumbnails
　　javax.imageio.**I**mageReader < progressListeners,
　　updateListeners, warningListeners, warningLocales >
　　javax.imageio.**I**mageWriter < progressListeners,
　　warningListeners, warningLocales >
list( ): _NamingContextExtStubˆ　_NamingContextStubˆ
　　Collections　javax.naming.**C**ontext　**F**ile　**I**nitialContext
　　Naming　**N**amingContextOperations　**P**ropertiesˆ　**R**egistryˆ
　　ThreadGroup
list_initial_services( ): org.omg.CORBA.**O**RB
listBindings( ): javax.naming.**C**ontext　**I**nitialContext
listen( ): **S**ocketImpl
listFiles( ): **F**ile
ListIteratorˆ: java.util
　—returned by: **A**bstractListˆ.listIterator( )　**L**istˆ.listIterator( )
listIterator( ): **A**bstractListˆ　**L**istˆ
ListResourceBundleˆ: java.util
　—subclasses: javax.accessibility.**A**ccessibleResourceBundleˆ
listRoots( ): **F**ile
LITTLE_ENDIAN: **B**yteOrder
load( ): **K**eyStore　**M**appedByteBufferˆ　**P**ropertiesˆ　**R**untime
　　System
loadClass( ): **C**lassLoader　LoaderHandler　**R**MIClassLoader
　　RMIClassLoaderSpi　**U**til　UtilDelegate
LoaderHandler: java.rmi.server
loadImage( ): **S**impleBeanInfo
loadLibrary( ): **R**untime　**S**ystem

loadProxyClass( ): **R**MIClassLoader　**R**MIClassLoaderSpi
locale: **B**eanContextSupportˆ
Locale: java.util
　—passed
　　to: javax.accessibility.**A**ccessibleBundle.toDisplayString( )
　　BeanContextServicesSupport( )　**B**eanContextSupportˆ
　　< BeanContextSupport( ), setLocale( ) >　**B**reakIterator
　　< getCharacterInstance( ), getLineInstance( ),
　　getSentenceInstance( ), getWordInstance( ) >　**C**alendar
　　< Calendar( ), getInstance( ) >　**C**harset.displayName( )
　　Collator.getInstance( )　java.awt.**C**omponent.setLocale( )
　　java.awt.**C**omponentOrientation.getOrientation( )
　　Currency < getInstance( ), getSymbol( ) >　**D**ateFormatˆ
　　< getDateInstance( ), getDateTimeInstance( ), getTimeInstance( ) >
　　DateFormatSymbols( )　**D**ecimalFormatSymbols( )
　　javax.print.attribute.standard.**D**ocumentName( )
　　java.awt.**F**ont < getFamily( ), getFontName( ) >
　　java.awt.**G**raphicsEnvironment.getAvailableFontFamilyNames( )
　　GregorianCalendar( )
　　javax.imageio.metadata.**I**IOMetadataFormat
　　< getAttributeDescription( ), getElementDescription( ) >
　　javax.imageio.metadata.**I**IOMetadataFormatImpl
　　< getAttributeDescription( ), getElementDescription( ) >
　　javax.imageio.spi.**I**IOServiceProvider.getDescription( )
　　javax.imageio.**I**mageReader.setLocale( )
　　javax.imageio.**I**mageWriteParam( )
　　javax.imageio.**I**mageWriter.setLocale( )
　　java.awt.im.**I**nputContext.selectInputMethod( )
　　java.awt.im.spi.**I**nputMethod.setLocale( )
　　java.awt.im.spi.**I**nputMethodDescriptor
　　< getInputMethodDisplayName( ), getInputMethodIcon( ) >
　　javax.swing.**J**Componentˆ.setDefaultLocale( )
　　javax.print.attribute.standard.**J**obMessageFromOperator( )
　　javax.print.attribute.standard.**J**obName( )
　　javax.print.attribute.standard.**J**obOriginatingUserName( )
　　javax.imageio.plugins.jpeg.**J**PEGImageWriteParam( )
　　LanguageCallback.setLocale( )　**L**ocale < getDisplayCountry( ),
　　getDisplayLanguage( ), getDisplayName( ),
　　getDisplayVariant( ), setDefault( ) >　**M**essageFormatˆ
　　< MessageFormat( ), setLocale( ) >　**N**umberFormatˆ
　　< getCurrencyInstance( ), getInstance( ), getIntegerInstance( ),
　　getNumberInstance( ), getPercentInstance( ) >
　　javax.print.attribute.standard.**O**utputDeviceAssigned( )
　　Parser.setLocale( )　javax.print.attribute.standard.**P**rinterInfo( )
　　javax.print.attribute.standard.**P**rinterLocation( )
　　javax.print.attribute.standard.**P**rinterMakeAndModel( )
　　javax.print.attribute.standard.**P**rinterMessageFromOperator( )
　　javax.print.attribute.standard.**P**rinterName( )
　　javax.print.attribute.standard.**R**equestingUserName( )
　　ResourceBundle.getBundle( )　**S**impleDateFormat( )
　　String < toLowerCase( ), toUpperCase( ) >
　　javax.print.attribute.**T**extSyntax( )
　　TimeZone.getDisplayName( )　javax.swing.**U**IDefaultsˆ < get( ),
　　getBoolean( ), getBorder( ), getColor( ), getDimension( ),
　　getFont( ), getIcon( ), getInsets( ), getInt( ), getString( ),
　　setDefaultLocale( ) >　javax.swing.**U**IManager < get( ),
　　getBoolean( ), getBorder( ), getColor( ), getDimension( ),
　　getFont( ), getIcon( ), getInsets( ), getInt( ), getString( ) >
　　XMLReaderAdapter.setLocale( )
　—returned by: javax.accessibility.**A**ccessibleContext.getLocale( )
　　BeanContextSupportˆ.getLocale( )
　　BreakIterator.getAvailableLocales( )
　　Calendar.getAvailableLocales( )　**C**ollator.getAvailableLocales( )
　　java.awt.**C**omponent.getLocale( )
　　DateFormatˆ.getAvailableLocales( )
　　javax.imageio.**I**mageReader < getAvailableLocales( ),
　　getLocale( ) >　javax.imageio.**I**mageWriteParamˆ.getLocale( )

L

javax.imageio.**I**mageWriter < getAvailableLocales( ),
getLocale( ) > java.awt.im.**I**nputContext.getLocale( )
java.awt.im.spi.InputMethod.getLocale( )
java.awt.im.spi.InputMethodDescriptor.getAvailableLocales( )
javax.swing.**J**Component^.getDefaultLocale( )
LanguageCallback.getLocale( ) **L**ocale < getAvailableLocales( ),
getDefault( ) > **M**essageFormat^.getLocale( )
NumberFormat^.getAvailableLocales( )
ResourceBundle .getLocale( )
javax.print.attribute.**T**extSyntax.getLocale( )
javax.swing.**U**IDefaults^.getDefaultLocale( )
—fields: **B**eanContextSupport^.locale
javax.imageio.**I**mageReader < availableLocales,
locale > javax.imageio.**I**mageWriteParam^.locale
javax.imageio.**I**mageWriter < availableLocales, locale > **L**ocale
< CANADA, CANADA_FRENCH, CHINA, CHINESE, ENGLISH,
FRANCE, FRENCH, GERMAN, GERMANY, ITALIAN,
ITALY, JAPAN, JAPANESE, KOREA, KOREAN, PRC,
SIMPLIFIED_CHINESE, TAIWAN, TRADITIONAL_CHINESE, UK,
US >
LocalObject: org.omg.CORBA
localPort: **D**atagramSocketImpl
localport: **S**ocketImpl
LocateRegistry: java.rmi.registry
LOCATION_FORWARD: org.omg.PortableInterceptor
Locator: org.xml.sax
—passed to: *org.xml.sax.**C**ontentHandler* .setDocumentLocator( )
DefaultHandler.setDocumentLocator( )
DocumentHandler.setDocumentLocator( )
HandlerBase.setDocumentLocator( ) **L**ocatorImpl( )
ParserAdapter.setDocumentLocator( ) **S**AXParseException( )
XMLFilterImpl.setDocumentLocator( )
XMLReaderAdapter.setDocumentLocator( )
—implemented by: **L**ocatorImpl
LocatorImpl: org.xml.sax.helpers
locatorsUpdateCopy( ): *DatabaseMetaData*
lock: **A**bstractPreferences^ **R**eader **W**riter
lock( ): **F**ileChannel^
log( ): **L**ogger **L**ogStream^ **M**ath **S**trictMath
Logger: java.util.logging
—passed to: **L**ogger.setParent( ) **L**ogManager.addLogger( )
—returned by: **L**ogger < getAnonymousLogger( ), getLogger( ),
getParent( ) > **L**ogManager.getLogger( )
—fields: **L**ogger.global
LoggingPermission^: java.util.logging
login( ): **L**oginContext *LoginModule*
LoginContext: javax.security.auth.login
LoginException^: javax.security.auth.login
—subclasses: **A**ccountExpiredException^
CredentialExpiredException^ **F**ailedLoginException^
—thrown by: **L**oginContext < login( ), LoginContext( ), logout( ) >
LoginModule < abort( ), commit( ), login( ), logout( ) >
LoginModule: javax.security.auth.spi
LogManager: java.util.logging
—returned by: **L**ogManager.getLogManager( )
logout( ): **L**oginContext *LoginModule*
logp( ): **L**ogger
logrb( ): **L**ogger
LogRecord: java.util.logging
—passed to: *Filter*.isLoggable( ) **F**ormatter < format( ),
formatMessage( ) > **H**andler < isLoggable( ), publish( ) >
Logger.log( )
LogStream^: java.rmi.server
—returned by: **L**ogStream^.log( )
LONG: **D**ateFormat^ **T**imeZone
Long^: java.lang
—passed to: **L**ong^ < compareTo( ), getLong( ) >
—returned by: **L**ong^ < decode( ), getLong( ), valueOf( ) >
longBitsToDouble( ): **D**ouble^
LongBuffer^: java.nio
—passed to: **L**ongBuffer^.put( )

—returned by: **B**yteBuffer^.asLongBuffer( ) **L**ongBuffer^
< allocate( ), asReadOnlyBuffer( ), compact( ), duplicate( ), get( ),
put( ), slice( ), wrap( ) >
LongHolder: org.omg.CORBA
LongLongSeqHelper: org.omg.CORBA
LongLongSeqHolder: org.omg.CORBA
—passed
to: *org.omg.CORBA.**D**ataInputStream*^.read_longlong_array( )
LongSeqHelper: org.omg.CORBA
LongSeqHolder: org.omg.CORBA
—passed
to: *org.omg.CORBA.**D**ataInputStream*^.read_long_array( )
longValue( ): **N**umber
LONGVARBINARY: **T**ypes
LONGVARCHAR: **T**ypes
lookingAt( ): **M**atcher
lookup( ): *javax.naming.**C**ontext* **I**nitialContext **N**aming
ObjectStreamClass *Registry*^
lookup_value_factory( ): org.omg.CORBA_2_3.**O**RB^
lookupLink( ): *javax.naming.**C**ontext* **I**nitialContext
LOWERCASE_LETTER: **C**haracter
lowerCaseMode( ): **S**treamTokenizer
Mac: javax.crypto
—returned by: **M**ac.getInstance( )
MacSpi: javax.crypto
—passed to: **M**ac( )
MAIN_CLASS: **A**ttributes.Name
major_version: **E**ncoding
makeParser( ): **P**arserFactory
MALAYALAM: **C**haracter.UnicodeBlock^
malformedForLength( ): **C**oderResult
malformedInputAction( ): **C**harsetDecoder **C**harsetEncoder
MalformedInputException^: java.nio.charset
MalformedLinkException^: javax.naming
MalformedURLException^: java.net
—thrown by: **F**ile.toURL( ) **J**arURLConnection( )
LoaderHandler.loadClass( ) **N**aming < bind( ), list( ), lookup( ),
rebind( ), unbind( ) > **R**MIClassLoader < getClassLoader( ),
loadClass( ), loadProxyClass( ) > **R**MIClassLoaderSpi
< getClassLoader( ), loadClass( ), loadProxyClass( ) >
URI.toURL( ) **U**RL( )
ManagerFactoryParameters: javax.net.ssl
—passed to: **K**eyManagerFactory.init( )
KeyManagerFactorySpi.engineInit( )
TrustManagerFactory.init( )
TrustManagerFactorySpi.engineInit( )
Manifest: java.util.jar
—passed to: **J**arOutputStream( ) **M**anifest( )
URLClassLoader^.definePackage( )
—returned by: **J**arFile^.getManifest( )
JarInputStream^.getManifest( )
JarURLConnection^.getManifest( )
MANIFEST_NAME: **J**arFile^
MANIFEST_VERSION: **A**ttributes.Name
map: java.util.jar.**A**ttributes
Map: java.util
—extended by: *SortedMap*^
—passed to: **A**bstractMap .putAll( ) **A**ppConfigurationEntry( )
*java.sql.**A**rray* < getArray( ), getResultSet( ) >
AttributedString < addAttributes( ), AttributedString( ) >
java.util.jar.**A**ttributes.putAll( ) *CallableStatement*^.getObject( )
Collections < synchronizedMap( ), unmodifiableMap( ) >
Connection.setTypeMap( ) java.awt.**F**ont < deriveFont( ),
Font( ), getFont( ) > java.awt.**G**raphics2D^
< addRenderingHints( ), setRenderingHints( ) >
HashMap( ) **H**ashtable^ < Hashtable( ), putAll( ) >
IdentityHashMap( ) java.awt.im.**I**nputMethodHighlight( )
LinkedHashMap( ) *LoginModule*.initialize( ) *Map* .putAll( )
javax.print.attribute.standard.**P**rinterStateReasons( )
Ref.getObject( ) java.awt.**R**enderingHints < putAll( ),
RenderingHints( ) > *ResultSet* .getObject( )

RowSet^.setTypeMap( )   **S**ecurity.getProviders( )
Struct.getAttributes( )   java.awt.font.**T**extLayout( )   **T**reeMap( )
WeakHashMap( )
— returned by: **A**ppConfigurationEntry.getOptions( )
AttributedCharacterIterator^.getAttributes( )
Collections < singletonMap( ), synchronizedMap( ),
unmodifiableMap( ) >   *Connection*.getTypeMap( )
java.awt.datatransfer.**F**lavorMap < getFlavorsForNatives( ),
getNativesForFlavors( ) >   java.awt.**F**ont.getAttributes( )
java.awt.im.**I**nputMethodHighlight.getStyle( )
Manifest.getEntries( )   *RowSet*^.getTypeMap( )
java.awt.datatransfer.**S**ystemFlavorMap
< getFlavorsForNatives( ), getNativesForFlavors( ) >
java.awt.**T**oolkit.mapInputMethodHighlight( )   **U**RLConnection
< getHeaderFields( ), getRequestProperties( ) >
— implemented by: **A**bstractMap   java.util.jar.**A**ttributes
Hashtable^   java.awt.**R**enderingHints
— fields: java.util.jar.**A**ttributes.map   **C**ollections.EMPTY_MAP
java.awt.**T**oolkit.desktopProperties
map( ): **F**ileChannel^
Map.Entry: java.util
— passed to: **L**inkedHashMap^.removeEldestEntry( )
mapLibraryName( ): **S**ystem
MappedByteBuffer^: java.nio
— returned by: **F**ileChannel^.map( )   **M**appedByteBuffer^ < force( ),
load( ) >
mapSystemException( ): **U**til   *UtilDelegate*
MARCH: **C**alendar
mark: **B**yteArrayInputStream^
mark( ): **B**uffer   java.io.**I**nputStream   **R**eader
markedPos: **C**harArrayReader^
marklimit: **B**ufferedInputStream^
markpos: **B**ufferedInputStream^
markSupported( ): java.io.**I**nputStream   **R**eader
MARSHAL^: org.omg.CORBA
— thrown by: **A**ny < insert_string( ), insert_Value( ),
insert_wstring( ), read_value( ) >
marshal( ): *CustomMarshal*
MarshalException^: java.rmi
MarshalledObject: java.rmi
— passed to: **A**ctivatable^ < Activatable( ), exportObject( ) >
ActivationDesc( )   **A**ctivationGroup^.activeObject( )
ActivationGroupDesc( )   *ActivationMonitor*^.activeObject( )
— returned by: **A**ctivationDesc.getData( )
ActivationGroup_Stub^.newInstance( )
ActivationGroupDesc.getData( )
ActivationInstantiator^.newInstance( )   *Activator*^.activate( )
match( ): *CertSelector*^   *CRLSelector*^   **X**509CertSelector
X509CRLSelector
Matcher: java.util.regex
— returned by: **M**atcher < appendReplacement( ), reset( ) >
Pattern.matcher( )
matcher( ): **P**attern
matches( ): **M**atcher   **P**attern   **S**tring
Math: java.lang
MATH_SYMBOL: **C**haracter
MATHEMATICAL_OPERATORS: **C**haracter.UnicodeBlock^
max( ): **B**igDecimal^   **B**igInteger^   **C**ollections   **M**ath   **S**trictMath
MAX_KEY_LENGTH: **P**references
MAX_NAME_LENGTH: **P**references
MAX_PRIORITY: **T**hread
MAX_RADIX: **C**haracter
MAX_VALUE: **B**yte^   **C**haracter   **D**ouble^   **F**loat^   **I**nteger^
Long^   **S**hort^
MAX_VALUE_LENGTH: **P**references
MAXBQUALSIZE: *Xid*
maxBytesPerChar( ): **C**harsetEncoder
maxCharsPerByte( ): **C**harsetDecoder
MAXGTRIDSIZE: *Xid*
maxMemory( ): **R**untime
MAY: **C**alendar

MEDIA_TYPE: **O**utputKeys
MEDIUM: **D**ateFormat^
Member: java.lang.reflect
— implemented by: **C**onstructor^   **F**ield^   **M**ethod^
member( ): _DynUnionStub^   org.omg.CORBA.**D**ynUnion^
DynUnionOperations^
member_count( ): **T**ypeCode
member_kind( ): _DynUnionStub^   org.omg.CORBA.**D**ynUnion^
DynUnionOperations^
member_label( ): **T**ypeCode
member_name( ): _DynUnionStub^
org.omg.CORBA.**D**ynUnion^   *DynUnionOperations*^
TypeCode
member_type( ): **T**ypeCode
member_visibility( ): **T**ypeCode
members( ): *Group*^
MemoryHandler^: java.util.logging
MessageDigest^: java.security
— passed to: **D**igestInputStream^ < DigestInputStream( ),
setMessageDigest( ) >   **D**igestOutputStream^
< DigestOutputStream( ), setMessageDigest( ) >
— returned by: **D**igestInputStream^.getMessageDigest( )
DigestOutputStream^.getMessageDigest( )
MessageDigest^.getInstance( )
— fields: **D**igestInputStream^.digest   **D**igestOutputStream^.digest
MessageDigestSpi: java.security
— subclasses: **M**essageDigest^
MessageFormat^: java.text
MessageFormat.Field^: java.text
— fields: **M**essageFormat.Field^.ARGUMENT
MessageProp: org.ietf.jgss
— passed to: *GSSContext* < getMIC( ), unwrap( ), verifyMIC( ),
wrap( ) >
METHOD: **O**utputKeys
method: **H**ttpURLConnection^
Method^: java.lang.reflect
— passed to: **E**ventHandler.invoke( )   **E**ventSetDescriptor( )
IndexedPropertyDescriptor^ < IndexedPropertyDescriptor( ),
setIndexedReadMethod( ), setIndexedWriteMethod( ) >
InvocationHandler.invoke( )   **M**ethodDescriptor( )
PropertyDescriptor^ < PropertyDescriptor( ), setReadMethod( ),
setWriteMethod( ) >   *RemoteRef*^.invoke( )
— returned by: **C**lass < getDeclaredMethod( ), getDeclaredMethods( ),
getMethod( ), getMethods( ) >   **E**ventSetDescriptor^
< getAddListenerMethod( ), getGetListenerMethod( ),
getListenerMethods( ), getRemoveListenerMethod( ) >
IndexedPropertyDescriptor^ < getIndexedReadMethod( ),
getIndexedWriteMethod( ) >   **M**ethodDescriptor^.getMethod( )
PropertyDescriptor^ < getReadMethod( ), getWriteMethod( ) >
MethodDescriptor^: java.beans
— passed to: **E**ventSetDescriptor( )
— returned by: *BeanInfo*.getMethodDescriptors( )
EventSetDescriptor^.getListenerMethodDescriptors( )
SimpleBeanInfo.getMethodDescriptors( )
MILLISECOND: **C**alendar   **D**ateFormat.Field^
MILLISECOND_FIELD: **D**ateFormat^
min( ): **B**igDecimal^   **B**igInteger^   **C**ollections   **M**ath   **S**trictMath
MIN_PRIORITY: **T**hread
MIN_RADIX: **C**haracter
MIN_VALUE: **B**yte^   **C**haracter   **D**ouble^   **F**loat^   **I**nteger^
Long^   **S**hort^
minor: **S**ystemException
minor_version: **E**ncoding
MINUTE: **C**alendar   **D**ateFormat.Field^
MINUTE_FIELD: **D**ateFormat^
MISCELLANEOUS_SYMBOLS: **C**haracter.UnicodeBlock^
MISCELLANEOUS_TECHNICAL: **C**haracter.UnicodeBlock^
missing_node: **N**otFoundReason
MissingResourceException: java.util
— thrown by: **L**ocale < getISO3Country( ), getISO3Language( ) >
mkdir( ): **F**ile
mkdirs( ): **F**ile

M

mod(): **B**igInteger^

modCount: **A**bstractList⌇

mode: **P**arameter

ModificationItem: javax.naming.directory
— passed to: **A**ttributeModificationException^ ↩
 .setUnexecutedModifications( ) *DirContext*⌇.modifyAttributes( )
 InitialDirContext⌇.modifyAttributes( )
— returned by: **A**ttributeModificationException^ ↩
 .getUnexecutedModifications( )

Modifier: java.lang.reflect

MODIFIER_LETTER: **C**haracter

MODIFIER_SYMBOL: **C**haracter

modifyAttributes(): *DirContext*⌇ **I**nitialDirContext⌇

modInverse(): **B**igInteger^

modPow(): **B**igInteger^

MONDAY: **C**alendar⌄

MONGOLIAN: **C**haracter.UnicodeBlock^

MONTH: **C**alendar⌄ **D**ateFormat.Field^

MONTH_FIELD: **D**ateFormat⌇

movePointLeft(): **B**igDecimal^

movePointRight(): **B**igDecimal^

moveToCurrentRow(): *ResultSet*⌄

moveToInsertRow(): *ResultSet*⌄

MulticastSocket^: java.net

MULTILINE: **P**attern

MULTIPLE_ID: **I**dUniquenessPolicyValue

MultipleComponentProfileHelper: org.omg.IOP

MultipleComponentProfileHolder: org.omg.IOP

multiply(): **B**igDecimal^ **B**igInteger^

mutatesTo(): **P**ersistenceDelegate

MYANMAR: **C**haracter.UnicodeBlock^

myProps: **I**nitialContext⌄

mySyntax: **C**ompoundName

name: **D**riverPropertyInfo **D**uplicateName^ **S**tructMember
 UnionMember **V**alueMember

Name^: javax.naming
— passed to: **C**annotProceedException^ < setAltName( ),
 setRemainingNewName( ) > **C**ompositeName < addAll( ),
 endsWith( ), startsWith( ) > **C**ompoundName < addAll( ),
 endsWith( ), startsWith( ) > *javax.naming.Context*⌄ < bind( ),
 composeName( ), createSubcontext( ), destroySubcontext( ),
 getNameParser( ), list( ), listBindings( ), lookup( ), lookupLink( ),
 rebind( ), rename( ), unbind( ) > *DirContext*⌇ < bind( ),
 createSubcontext( ), getAttributes( ), getSchema( ),
 getSchemaClassDefinition( ), modifyAttributes( ), rebind( ),
 search( ) > **D**irectoryManager^ < getObjectInstance( ),
 getStateToBind( ) > *DirObjectFactory*^.getObjectInstance( )
 DirStateFactory^.getStateToBind( )
 EventContext⌇.addNamingListener( )
 EventDirContext^.addNamingListener( ) **I**nitialContext⌄ < bind( ),
 composeName( ), createSubcontext( ), destroySubcontext( ),
 getNameParser( ), getURLOrDefaultInitCtx( ), list( ), listBindings( ),
 lookup( ), lookupLink( ), rebind( ), rename( ), unbind( ) >
 InitialDirContext⌇ < bind( ), createSubcontext( ),
 getAttributes( ), getSchema( ), getSchemaClassDefinition( ),
 modifyAttributes( ), rebind( ), search( ) > **L**inkException⌇
 < setLinkRemainingName( ), setLinkResolvedName( ) >
 LinkRef( ) *Name*^ < addAll( ), endsWith( ), startsWith( ) >
 NamingException⌄ < appendRemainingName( ),
 setRemainingName( ), setResolvedName( ) > **N**amingManager⌄
 < getObjectInstance( ), getStateToBind( ) >
 ObjectFactory⌄.getObjectInstance( ) *Resolver*.resolveToClass( )
 ResolveResult < appendRemainingName( ), ResolveResult( ),
 setRemainingName( ) > *StateFactory*⌄.getStateToBind( )
— returned by: **C**annotProceedException^ < getAltName( ),
 getRemainingNewName( ) > **C**ompositeName
 < add( ), addAll( ), getPrefix( ), getSuffix( ) >
 CompoundName < add( ), addAll( ), getPrefix( ),
 getSuffix( ) > *javax.naming.Context*⌄.composeName( )
 InitialContext⌄.composeName( ) **L**inkException⌇
 < getLinkRemainingName( ), getLinkResolvedName( ) >
 Name^ < add( ), addAll( ), getPrefix( ), getSuffix( ) >

*Name*Parser.parse( ) **N**amingException⌄
 < getRemainingName( ), getResolvedName( ) >
 ResolveResult.getRemainingName( )
— implemented by: **C**ompositeName **C**ompoundName
— fields: **C**annotProceedException^ < altName,
 remainingNewName > **L**inkException⌇ < linkRemainingName,
 linkResolvedName > **N**amingException⌄ < remainingName,
 resolvedName > **R**esolveResult.remainingName

name(): **C**harset *InterceptorOperations*⌄ **N**amedValue
 Preferences⌄ org.omg.CORBA.**P**rincipal **T**ypeCode

NAME_NOT_MN: **G**SSException

NameAlreadyBoundException^: javax.naming

NameCallback: javax.security.auth.callback

NameClassPair⌇: javax.naming
— subclasses: javax.naming.**B**inding⌇
— descendents: **S**earchResult^

NameComponent: org.omg.CosNaming
— passed to: _NamingContextExtStub^ < bind( ), bind_context( ),
 bind_new_context( ), rebind( ), rebind_context( ), resolve( ),
 to_string( ), unbind( ) > _NamingContextStub^
 < bind( ), bind_context( ), bind_new_context( ),
 rebind( ), rebind_context( ), resolve( ), unbind( ) >
 org.omg.CosNaming.**B**inding( ) **C**annotProceed( )
 NameComponentHelper < insert( ), write( ) >
 NameComponentHolder( ) **N**ameHelper < insert( ), write( ) >
 NameHolder( ) *NamingContextExtOperations*⌇.to_string( )
 NamingContextOperations⌄ < bind( ), bind_context( ),
 bind_new_context( ), rebind( ), rebind_context( ), resolve( ),
 unbind( ) > **N**otFound( )
— returned by: _NamingContextExtStub^.to_name( )
 NameComponentHelper < extract( ), read( ) > **N**ameHelper
 < extract( ), read( ) > *NamingContextExtOperations*⌇.to_name( )
— fields: org.omg.CosNaming.**B**inding.binding_name
 CannotProceed^.rest_of_name **N**ameComponentHolder.value
 NameHolder.value **N**otFound^.rest_of_name

NameComponentHelper: org.omg.CosNaming

NameComponentHolder: org.omg.CosNaming

NamedNodeMap: org.w3c.dom
— returned by: *DocumentType*^ < getEntities( ), getNotations( ) >
 javax.imageio.metadata.**I**IOMetadataNode.getAttributes( )
 Node⌄.getAttributes( )

NamedValue: org.omg.CORBA
— passed to: org.omg.CORBA.portable.**D**elegate⌄.create_request( )
 LocalObject⌄.create_request( )
 org.omg.CORBA.Object⌄._create_request( )
 org.omg.CORBA.portable.**O**bjectImpl⌄._create_request( )
— returned by: **N**VList < add( ), add_item( ), add_value( ), item( ) >
 org.omg.CORBA.**O**RB⌄.create_named_value( ) **R**equest.result( )

NameDynAnyPair: org.omg.DynamicAny
— passed to: _DynStructStub^.set_members_as_dyn_any( )
 _DynValueStub^.set_members_as_dyn_any( )
 DynStructOperations⌇.set_members_as_dyn_any( )
 DynValueOperations⌇.set_members_as_dyn_any( )
 NameDynAnyPairHelper < insert( ), write( ) >
 NameDynAnyPairSeqHelper < insert( ), write( ) >
— returned by: _DynStructStub^.get_members_as_dyn_any( )
 _DynValueStub^.get_members_as_dyn_any( )
 DynStructOperations⌇.get_members_as_dyn_any( )
 DynValueOperations⌇.get_members_as_dyn_any( )
 NameDynAnyPairHelper < extract( ), read( ) >
 NameDynAnyPairSeqHelper < extract( ), read( ) >

NameDynAnyPairHelper: org.omg.DynamicAny

NameDynAnyPairSeqHelper: org.omg.DynamicAny

NameHelper: org.omg.CosNaming

NameHolder: org.omg.CosNaming
— fields: **C**ompoundName.impl

NameNotFoundException^: javax.naming

NameParser: javax.naming
— returned by: *javax.naming.Context*⌄.getNameParser( )
 InitialContext⌄.getNameParser( )

NAMESPACE_ERR: **D**OMException

NamespaceChangeListener^: javax.naming.event

NamespaceSupport: org.xml.sax.helpers
NameValuePair: org.omg.CORBA
—passed to: *org.omg.CORBA.DynStruct*^.set_members( )
  org.omg.CORBA.DynValue^.set_members( )
  org.omg.CORBA.**N**ameValuePairHelper < insert( ), write( ) >
—returned by: *org.omg.CORBA.DynStruct*^.get_members( )
  org.omg.CORBA.DynValue^.get_members( )
  org.omg.CORBA.**N**ameValuePairHelper < extract( ), read( ) >
NameValuePair: org.omg.DynamicAny
—passed to: _DynStructStub^.set_members( )
  _DynValueStub^.set_members( )
  DynStructOperations^.set_members( )
  DynValueOperations^.set_members( )
  org.omg.DynamicAny.**N**ameValuePairHelper < insert( ),
  write( ) > **N**ameValuePairSeqHelper < insert( ), write( ) >
—returned by: _DynStructStub^.get_members( )
  _DynValueStub^.get_members( )
  DynStructOperations^.get_members( )
  DynValueOperations^.get_members( )
  org.omg.DynamicAny.**N**ameValuePairHelper < extract( ),
  read( ) > **N**ameValuePairSeqHelper < extract( ), read( ) >
NameValuePairHelper: org.omg.CORBA
NameValuePairHelper: org.omg.DynamicAny
NameValuePairSeqHelper: org.omg.DynamicAny
Naming: java.rmi
NamingContext^: org.omg.CosNaming
—extended by: *NamingContextExt*^
—passed to: _NamingContextExtStub^ < bind_context( ),
  rebind_context( ) > _NamingContextStub^ < bind_context( ),
  rebind_context( ) > **C**annotProceed( ) **N**amingContextHelper
  < insert( ), write( ) > **N**amingContextHolder( )
  NamingContextOperations < bind_context( ),
  rebind_context( ) >
—returned by: _NamingContextExtStub^ < bind_new_context( ),
  new_context( ) > _NamingContextStub^ < bind_new_context( ),
  new_context( ) > **N**amingContextHelper < extract( ), narrow( ),
  read( ) > *NamingContextOperations* < bind_new_context( ),
  new_context( ) > **N**amingContextPOA^._this( )
—implemented by: _NamingContextImplBase^
  _NamingContextStub^
—fields: **C**annotProceed^.cxt **N**amingContextHolder.value
NamingContextExt^: org.omg.CosNaming
—passed to: **N**amingContextExtHelper < insert( ), write( ) >
  NamingContextExtHolder( )
—returned by: **N**amingContextExtHelper < extract( ), narrow( ),
  read( ) > **N**amingContextExtPOA^._this( )
—implemented by: _NamingContextExtStub^
—fields: **N**amingContextExtHolder.value
NamingContextExtHelper: org.omg.CosNaming
NamingContextExtHolder: org.omg.CosNaming
NamingContextExtOperations^: org.omg.CosNaming
—extended by: *NamingContextExt*
—implemented by: **N**amingContextExtPOA^
NamingContextExtPOA^: org.omg.CosNaming
NamingContextHelper: org.omg.CosNaming
NamingContextHolder: org.omg.CosNaming
NamingContextOperations: org.omg.CosNaming
—extended by: *NamingContext* *NamingContextExtOperations*^
—descendents: *NamingContextExt*^
—implemented by: **N**amingContextPOA^
NamingContextPOA^: org.omg.CosNaming
NamingEnumeration^: javax.naming
—returned by: *javax.naming.directory.Attribute*^.getAll( )
  javax.naming.directory.Attributes^ < getAll( ), getIDs( ) >
  BasicAttribute.getAll( ) **B**asicAttributes < getAll( ), getIDs( ) >
  javax.naming.Context < list( ), listBindings( ) >
  DirContext^.search( ) **I**nitialContext < list( ), listBindings( ) >
  InitialDirContext^.search( )
NamingEvent^: javax.naming.event
—passed to: *NamespaceChangeListener*^
  < objectAdded( ), objectRemoved( ), objectRenamed( ) >
  ObjectChangeListener^.objectChanged( )

NamingException: javax.naming
—subclasses: **A**ttributeInUseException^
  AttributeModificationException^
  CannotProceedException^ **C**ommunicationException^
  ConfigurationException^ **C**ontextNotEmptyException^
  InsufficientResourcesException^
  InterruptedNamingException^
  InvalidAttributeIdentifierException^
  InvalidAttributesException^ **I**nvalidAttributeValueException^
  InvalidNameException^ **I**nvalidSearchControlsException^
  InvalidSearchFilterException^ **L**imitExceededException^
  LinkException^ **N**ameAlreadyBoundException^
  NameNotFoundException^ **N**amingSecurityException^
  NoInitialContextException^ **N**oSuchAttributeException^
  NotContextException^ **O**perationNotSupportedException^
  PartialResultException^ **R**eferralException^
  SchemaViolationException^ **S**erviceUnavailableException^
—descendents: **A**uthenticationException^
  AuthenticationNotSupportedException^
  LdapReferralException^ **L**inkLoopException^
  MalformedLinkException^ **N**oPermissionException^
  SizeLimitExceededException^
  TimeLimitExceededException^
—passed to: **N**amingExceptionEvent( )
—returned by: **N**amingExceptionEvent^.getException( )
  UnsolicitedNotification^.getException( )
—thrown by: *javax.naming.directory.Attribute*^ < get( ), getAll( ),
  getAttributeDefinition( ), getAttributeSyntaxDefinition( ) >
  BasicAttribute < get( ), getAll( ), getAttributeDefinition( ),
  getAttributeSyntaxDefinition( ) > *javax.naming.Context*
  < addToEnvironment( ), bind( ), close( ), composeName( ),
  createSubcontext( ), destroySubcontext( ), getEnvironment( ),
  getNameInNamespace( ), getNameParser( ), list( ),
  listBindings( ), lookup( ), lookupLink( ), rebind( ),
  removeFromEnvironment( ), rename( ), unbind( ) >
  ControlFactory.getControlInstance( ) *DirContext*^ < bind( ),
  createSubcontext( ), getAttributes( ), getSchema( ),
  getSchemaClassDefinition( ), modifyAttributes( ), rebind( ),
  search( ) > **D**irectoryManager^.getContinuationDirContext( ),
  getStateToBind( ) > *DirStateFactory*^.getStateToBind( )
  EventContext^ < addNamingListener( ), removeNamingListener( ),
  targetMustExist( ) > *EventDirContext*^.addNamingListener( )
  ExtendedRequest^.createExtendedResponse( )
  HasControls.getControls( ) **I**nitialContext
  < addToEnvironment( ), bind( ), close( ), composeName( ),
  createSubcontext( ), destroySubcontext( ), getDefaultInitCtx( ),
  getEnvironment( ), getNameInNamespace( ), getNameParser( ),
  getURLOrDefaultInitCtx( ), init( ), InitialContext( ),
  list( ), listBindings( ), lookup( ), lookupLink( ),
  rebind( ), removeFromEnvironment( ), rename( ),
  unbind( ) > *InitialContextFactory*.getInitialContext( )
  InitialContextFactoryBuilder.createInitialContextFactory( )
  InitialDirContext < bind( ), createSubcontext( ),
  getAttributes( ), getSchema( ), getSchemaClassDefinition( ),
  InitialDirContext( ), modifyAttributes( ), rebind( ),
  search( ) > **I**nitialLdapContext^ < extendedOperation( ),
  getConnectControls( ), getRequestControls( ),
  getResponseControls( ), InitialLdapContext( ), newInstance( ),
  reconnect( ), setRequestControls( ) > *LdapContext*^
  < extendedOperation( ), getConnectControls( ),
  getRequestControls( ), getResponseControls( ),
  newInstance( ), reconnect( ), setRequestControls( ) >
  LdapReferralException^.getReferralContext( )
  LinkRef^.getLinkName( ) *NameParser*.parse( )
  NamingEnumeration^ < close( ), hasMore( ), next( ) >
  NamingManager < getContinuationContext( ),
  getInitialContext( ), getStateToBind( ), getURLContext( ),
  setInitialContextFactoryBuilder( ), setObjectFactoryBuilder( ) >
  ObjectFactoryBuilder.createObjectFactory( )
  Referenceable.getReference( )
  ReferralException^.getReferralContext( )
  Resolver.resolveToClass( )

N

StartTlsRequest.createExtendedResponse( )
StateFactory.getStateToBind( )
NamingExceptionEvent^: javax.naming.event
— passed to: *NamingListener*^.namingExceptionThrown( )
namingExceptionThrown(): *NamingListener*^
NamingListener^: javax.naming.event
— extended by: *NamespaceChangeListener*^
ObjectChangeListener **U**nsolicitedNotificationListener^
— passed to: *EventContext*^
< addNamingListener( ), removeNamingListener( ) >
EventDirContext^.addNamingListener( )
NamingEvent^.dispatch( ) NamingExceptionEvent^.dispatch( )
NamingManager: javax.naming.spi
— subclasses: DirectoryManager^
NamingSecurityException^: javax.naming
— subclasses: **A**uthenticationException^
AuthenticationNotSupportedException^
NoPermissionException^
NaN: **D**ouble^ **F**loat^
narrow(): **B**indingIteratorHelper **C**odecFactoryHelper
org.omg.CORBA.**C**urrentHelper
org.omg.PortableInterceptor.**C**urrentHelper
org.omg.PortableServer.**C**urrentHelper
DynAnyFactoryHelper **D**ynAnyHelper **D**ynArrayHelper
DynEnumHelper **D**ynFixedHelper **D**ynSequenceHelper
DynStructHelper **D**ynUnionHelper **D**ynValueHelper
IDLTypeHelper **N**amingContextExtHelper
NamingContextHelper **P**OAHelper **P**olicyHelper
PortableRemoteObject *PortableRemoteObjectDelegate*
ServantActivatorHelper **S**ervantLocatorHelper
NATIVE: **M**odifier
nativeOrder(): **B**yteOrder
nativeSQL(): *Connection*
ncontext: **B**indingType
nCopies(): **C**ollections
needsDictionary(): **I**nflater
needsGui(): **B**eanContextSupport^ *Visibility*
needsInput(): **D**eflater **I**nflater
negate(): **B**igDecimal^ **B**igInteger^
NEGATIVE_INFINITY: **D**ouble^ **F**loat^
NegativeArraySizeException: java.lang
— thrown by: java.lang.reflect.**A**rray.newInstance( )
negotiate(): **S**tartTlsResponse
NetPermission^: java.net
NetworkInterface: java.net
— passed to: **D**atagramSocketImpl < joinGroup( ), leaveGroup( ) >
MulticastSocket^ < joinGroup( ), leaveGroup( ),
setNetworkInterface( ) >
— returned by: **M**ulticastSocket^.getNetworkInterface( )
NetworkInterface < getByInetAddress( ), getByName( ) >
new_context(): _NamingContextExtStub^
_NamingContextStub^ *NamingContextOperations*
newBinding: NamingEvent^
newCall(): *RemoteRef*^
newChannel(): Channels
newDecoder(): Charset
newDocument(): DocumentBuilder
newDocumentBuilder(): DocumentBuilderFactory
newEncoder(): Charset
newInputStream(): Channels
newInstance(): **A**ctivationGroup_Stub^ *ActivationInstantiator*^
java.lang.reflect.**A**rray **C**lass **C**onstructor^
DocumentBuilderFactory **I**nitialLdapContext^ *LdapContext*^
SAXParserFactory **T**ransformerFactory **U**RLClassLoader^
newLine(): **B**ufferedWriter^
newNode(): **A**bstractPreferences^
newOutputStream(): Channels
newPermissionCollection(): java.security.**P**ermission
newProxyInstance(): **P**roxy
newReader(): Channels
newSAXParser(): **S**AXParserFactory
newTemplates(): **T**ransformerFactory

newTemplatesHandler(): **S**AXTransformerFactory^
newTransformer(): *Templates* **T**ransformerFactory
newTransformerHandler(): **S**AXTransformerFactory^
newWriter(): Channels
newXMLFilter(): **S**AXTransformerFactory^
next(): _DynAnyStub^ _DynArrayStub^ _DynEnumStub^
_DynFixedStub^ _DynSequenceStub^
_DynStructStub^ _DynUnionStub^ _DynValueStub^
BeanContextSupport.BCSIterator **B**reakIterator
CharacterIterator^ **C**ollationElementIterator
org.omg.CORBA.*DynAny*^ *DynAnyOperations* *Iterator*
NamingEnumeration^ **R**andom *ResultSet*
StringCharacterIterator
next_n(): _BindingIteratorStub^ *BindingIteratorOperations*
next_one(): _BindingIteratorStub^ *BindingIteratorOperations*
nextBoolean(): **R**andom
nextBytes(): **R**andom
nextClearBit(): **B**itSet
nextDouble(): **C**hoiceFormat^ **R**andom
nextElement(): *Enumeration* **S**tringTokenizer
nextFloat(): **R**andom
nextGaussian(): **R**andom
nextIndex(): *ListIterator*
nextInt(): **R**andom
nextLong(): **R**andom
nextSetBit(): **B**itSet
nextToken(): **S**treamTokenizer **S**tringTokenizer
NO: **C**onfirmationCallback
NO_COMPRESSION: **D**eflater
NO_CONTEXT: **G**SSException
NO_CRED: **G**SSException
NO_DATA_ALLOWED_ERR: **D**OMException
NO_DECOMPOSITION: **C**ollator
NO_FIELDS: **O**bjectStreamClass
NO_GENERATED_KEYS: *java.sql.Statement*
NO_IMPLEMENT^: org.omg.CORBA
NO_IMPLICIT_ACTIVATION: **I**mplicitActivationPolicyValue
NO_MEMORY^: org.omg.CORBA
NO_MODIFICATION_ALLOWED_ERR: **D**OMException
NO_PERMISSION^: org.omg.CORBA
NO_RESOURCES^: org.omg.CORBA
NO_RESPONSE^: org.omg.CORBA
nobject: **B**indingType
NoClassDefFoundError^: java.lang
NoConnectionPendingException^: java.nio.channels
NoContext^: org.omg.PortableServer.CurrentPackage
— passed to: **N**oContextHelper < insert( ), write( ) >
— returned by: **N**oContextHelper < extract( ), read( ) >
— thrown by: *org.omg.PortableServer.CurrentOperations*^
< get_object_id( ), get_POA( ) >
NoContextHelper: org.omg.PortableServer.CurrentPackage
Node: org.w3c.dom
— extended by: *Attr*^ *CharacterData*^ *Document*^
DocumentFragment^ *DocumentType*^ *Element*^ *Entity*^
EntityReference^ *Notation*^ *ProcessingInstruction*^
— descendents: *CDATASection*^ *Comment*^ *Text*^
— passed to: *Document*^.importNode( )
DOMResult < DOMResult^, setNode( ) >
DOMSource < DOMSource^, setNode( ) >
javax.imageio.metadata.**I**IOInvalidTreeException( )
javax.imageio.metadata.**I**IOMetadata < mergeTree( ),
setFromTree( ) > javax.imageio.metadata.**I**IOMetadataNode
< appendChild( ), insertBefore( ), removeChild( ), replaceChild( ) >
NamedNodeMap < setNamedItem( ), setNamedItemNS( ) >
Node < appendChild( ), insertBefore( ), removeChild( ),
replaceChild( ) >
— returned by: *Document*^.importNode( )
DOMLocator^.getOriginatingNode( ) DOMResult.getNode( )
DOMSource.getNode( ) javax.imageio.metadata
.**I**IOInvalidTreeException^.getOffendingNode( )
javax.imageio.metadata.**I**IOMetadata.getAsTree( )

javax.imageio.metadata.IIOMetadataNode < appendChild( ),
cloneNode( ), getFirstChild( ), getLastChild( ), getNextSibling( ),
getParentNode( ), getPreviousSibling( ), insertBefore( ),
item( ), removeChild( ), replaceChild( ) > *NamedNodeMap*
< getNamedItem( ), getNamedItemNS( ), item( ),
removeNamedItem( ), removeNamedItemNS( ), setNamedItem( ),
setNamedItemNS( ) > *Node* < appendChild( ), cloneNode( ),
getFirstChild( ), getLastChild( ), getNextSibling( ),
getParentNode( ), getPreviousSibling( ), insertBefore( ),
removeChild( ), replaceChild( ) > *NodeList*.item( )
—fields: javax.imageio.metadata.IIOInvalidTreeException^ ↤
.offendingNode
node( ): Preferences.
NodeChangeEvent^: java.util.prefs
—passed to: *NodeChangeListener*^ < childAdded( ),
childRemoved( ) >
NodeChangeListener^: java.util.prefs
—passed to: Preferences. < addNodeChangeListener( ),
removeNodeChangeListener( ) >
nodeExists( ): Preferences.
NodeList: org.w3c.dom
—returned by: *Document*^ < getElementsByTagName( ),
getElementsByTagNameNS( ) > *Element*^
< getElementsByTagName( ), getElementsByTagNameNS( ) >
javax.imageio.metadata.IIOMetadataNode < getChildNodes( ),
getElementsByTagName( ), getElementsByTagNameNS( ) >
Node.getChildNodes( )
—implemented by: javax.imageio.metadata.IIOMetadataNode
NoInitialContextException^: javax.naming
non_existent( ): org.omg.CORBA.portable.Delegate.
org.omg.PortableServer.portable.Delegate
NON_RETAIN: ServantRetentionPolicyValue
NON_SPACING_MARK: Character
NONCRITICAL: *javax.naming.ldap.Control*^
NonReadableChannelException^: java.nio.channels
NonWritableChannelException^: java.nio.channels
NoPermissionException^: javax.naming
NORM_PRIORITY: Thread
normalize( ): *Node*. URI
NoRouteToHostException^: java.net
NoServant^: org.omg.PortableServer.POAPackage
—passed to: NoServantHelper < insert( ), write( ) >
—returned by: NoServantHelper < extract( ), read( ) >
—thrown by: *POAOperations*.get_servant( )
NoServantHelper: org.omg.PortableServer.POAPackage
NoSuchAlgorithmException^: java.security
—thrown by: AlgorithmParameterGenerator.getInstance( )
AlgorithmParameters.getInstance( )
java.security.cert.Certificate.verify( )
javax.security.cert.Certificate.verify( )
CertPathBuilder.getInstance( ) CertPathValidator.getInstance( )
CertStore.getInstance( ) Cipher. < getInstance( ),
unwrap( ) > CipherSpi < engineSetMode( ),
engineUnwrap( ) > EncryptedPrivateKeyInfo( )
ExemptionMechanism.getInstance( )
KeyAgreement < generateSecret( ), getInstance( ) >
KeyAgreementSpi.engineGenerateSecret( )
KeyFactory.getInstance( ) KeyGenerator.getInstance( )
KeyManagerFactory < getInstance( ), init( ) >
KeyManagerFactorySpi.engineInit( )
KeyPairGenerator^.getInstance( ) KeyStore < getKey( ),
load( ), store( ) > KeyStoreSpi < engineGetKey( ),
engineLoad( ), engineStore( ) > Mac.getInstance( )
MessageDigest^.getInstance( ) SealedObject.getObject( )
SecretKeyFactory.getInstance( ) SecureRandom^.getInstance( )
Signature^.getInstance( ) SSLContext.getInstance( )
TrustManagerFactory.getInstance( ) X509CRL^.verify( )
NoSuchAttributeException^: javax.naming.directory
NoSuchElementException^: java.util
NoSuchFieldError^: java.lang
NoSuchFieldException: java.lang

—thrown by: **C**lass < getDeclaredField( ), getField( ) >
NoSuchMethodError^: java.lang
NoSuchMethodException: java.lang
—thrown by: **C**lass < getConstructor( ), getDeclaredConstructor( ),
getDeclaredMethod( ), getMethod( ) >
NoSuchObjectException^: java.rmi
—thrown by: **A**ctivatable^.unexportObject( )
PortableRemoteObject < toStub( ), unexportObject( ) >
PortableRemoteObjectDelegate < toStub( ),
unexportObject( ) > RemoteObject.toStub( ) *Tie*^.deactivate( )
UnicastRemoteObject^.unexportObject( ) Util.unexportObject( )
UtilDelegate.unexportObject( )
NoSuchPaddingException^: javax.crypto
—thrown by: Cipher.getInstance( ) CipherSpi.engineSetPadding( )
NoSuchProviderException^: java.security
—thrown by: AlgorithmParameterGenerator.getInstance( )
AlgorithmParameters.getInstance( )
java.security.cert.Certificate.verify( )
javax.security.cert.Certificate.verify( )
CertificateFactory.getInstance( ) CertPathBuilder.getInstance( )
CertPathValidator.getInstance( ) CertStore.getInstance( )
Cipher.getInstance( ) ExemptionMechanism.getInstance( )
KeyAgreement.getInstance( ) KeyFactory.getInstance( )
KeyGenerator.getInstance( ) KeyManagerFactory.getInstance( )
KeyPairGenerator^.getInstance( ) KeyStore.getInstance( )
Mac.getInstance( ) MessageDigest.getInstance( )
SealedObject.getObject( ) SecretKeyFactory.getInstance( )
SecureRandom^.getInstance( ) Signature^.getInstance( )
SSLContext.getInstance( ) TrustManagerFactory.getInstance( )
X509CRL^.verify( )
not( ): BigInteger^
not_context: NotFoundReason
NOT_FOUND_ERR: DOMException
not_object: NotFoundReason
NOT_SUPPORTED_ERR: DOMException
NotActiveException^: java.io
—thrown by: ObjectInputStream^.registerValidation( )
Notation^: org.w3c.dom
NOTATION_NODE: *Node*.
notationDecl( ): DefaultHandler *DTDHandler*. HandlerBase
XMLFilterImpl
NotBoundException: java.rmi
—thrown by: Naming < lookup( ), unbind( ) > *Registry*^
< lookup( ), unbind( ) >
NotContextException^: javax.naming
NotEmpty^: org.omg.CosNaming.NamingContextPackage
—passed to: NotEmptyHelper < insert( ), write( ) >
NotEmptyHolder( )
—returned by: NotEmptyHelper < extract( ), read( ) >
—thrown by: _NamingContextExtStub^.destroy( )
_NamingContextStub^.destroy( )
NamingContextOperations.destroy( )
—fields: NotEmptyHolder.value
NotEmptyHelper: org.omg.CosNaming.NamingContextPackage
NotEmptyHolder:
org.omg.CosNaming.NamingContextPackage
NotFound^: org.omg.CosNaming.NamingContextPackage
—passed to: NotFoundHelper < insert( ), write( ) >
NotFoundHolder( )
—returned by: NotFoundHelper < extract( ), read( ) >
—thrown by: _NamingContextExtStub^ < bind( ), bind_context( ),
bind_new_context( ), rebind( ), rebind_context( ), resolve( ),
resolve_str( ), unbind( ) > _NamingContextStub^
< bind( ), bind_context( ), bind_new_context( ),
rebind( ), rebind_context( ), resolve( ), unbind( ) >
NamingContextExtOperations.resolve_str( )
NamingContextOperations. < bind( ), bind_context( ),
bind_new_context( ), rebind( ), rebind_context( ), resolve( ),
unbind( ) >
—fields: NotFoundHolder.value
NotFoundHelper: org.omg.CosNaming.NamingContextPackage

NotFoundHolder:
org.omg.CosNaming.NamingContextPackage
NotFoundReason:
org.omg.CosNaming.NamingContextPackage
—passed to: **N**otFound( ) **N**otFoundReasonHelper < insert( ),
write( ) > **N**otFoundReasonHolder( )
—returned by: **N**otFoundReason.from_int( )
NotFoundReasonHelper < extract( ), read( ) >
—fields: **N**otFound^.why **N**otFoundReason < missing_node,
not_context, not_object > **N**otFoundReasonHolder.value
NotFoundReasonHelper:
org.omg.CosNaming.NamingContextPackage
NotFoundReasonHolder:
org.omg.CosNaming.NamingContextPackage
notificationReceived( ): *UnsolicitedNotificationListener*^
notify( ): java.lang.**O**bject
notifyAll( ): java.lang.**O**bject
notifyObservers( ): **O**bservable
NotOwnerException: java.security.acl
—thrown by: *Acl*^ < addEntry( ), removeEntry( ), setName( ) >
Owner < addOwner( ), deleteOwner( ) >
NotSerializableException^: java.io
NotYetBoundException^: java.nio.channels
NotYetConnectedException^: java.nio.channels
NOVEMBER: **C**alendar
NT_ANONYMOUS: *G*SSName
NT_EXPORT_NAME: *G*SSName
NT_HOSTBASED_SERVICE: *G*SSName
NT_MACHINE_UID_NAME: *G*SSName
NT_STRING_UID_NAME: *G*SSName
NT_USER_NAME: *G*SSName
NULL: **T**ypes
NullCipher^: javax.crypto
NULLORDER: **C**ollationElementIterator
nullPlusNonNullIsNull( ): *DatabaseMetaData*
NullPointerException: java.lang
—thrown by: **P**arserFactory.makeParser( )
java.awt.print.**P**rinterJob.setPageable( )
nullsAreSortedAtEnd( ): *DatabaseMetaData*
nullsAreSortedAtStart( ): *DatabaseMetaData*
nullsAreSortedHigh( ): *DatabaseMetaData*
nullsAreSortedLow( ): *DatabaseMetaData*
Number: java.lang
—subclasses: BigDecimal^ BigInteger^ Byte^ Double^ Float^
Integer^ Long^ Short^
—passed to: javax.swing.**A**bstractButton↵
.AccessibleAbstractButton^.setCurrentAccessibleValue( )
*javax.accessibility.**A**ccessibleValue*↵
.setCurrentAccessibleValue( ) java.awt.**B**utton↵
.AccessibleAWTButton^.setCurrentAccessibleValue( )
java.awt.**C**heckbox.AccessibleAWTCheckbox^ ↵
.setCurrentAccessibleValue( ) javax.swing.**J**InternalFrame↵
.AccessibleJInternalFrame^.setCurrentAccessibleValue( )
javax.swing.**J**InternalFrame.JDesktopIcon↵
.AccessibleJDesktopIcon^.setCurrentAccessibleValue( )
javax.swing.**J**ProgressBar.AccessibleJProgressBar^↵
.setCurrentAccessibleValue( ) javax.swing.**J**ScrollBar↵
.AccessibleJScrollBar^.setCurrentAccessibleValue( )
javax.swing.**J**Slider.AccessibleJSlider^↵
.setCurrentAccessibleValue( ) javax.swing.**J**SplitPane↵
.AccessibleJSplitPane^.setCurrentAccessibleValue( )
java.awt.**M**enuItem.AccessibleAWTMenuItem^↵
.setCurrentAccessibleValue( ) java.awt.**S**crollbar↵
.AccessibleAWTScrollBar^.setCurrentAccessibleValue( )
javax.swing.**S**pinnerNumberModel^ < setStepSize( ),
SpinnerNumberModel( ) >
—returned
by: javax.swing.**A**bstractButton.AccessibleAbstractButton^
< getCurrentAccessibleValue( ), getMaximumAccessibleValue( ),
getMinimumAccessibleValue( ) >

*javax.accessibility.**A**ccessibleValue*
< getCurrentAccessibleValue( ), getMaximumAccessibleValue( ),
getMinimumAccessibleValue( ) >
java.awt.**B**utton.AccessibleAWTButton^
< getCurrentAccessibleValue( ), getMaximumAccessibleValue( ),
getMinimumAccessibleValue( ) >
java.awt.**C**heckbox.AccessibleAWTCheckbox^
< getCurrentAccessibleValue( ), getMaximumAccessibleValue( ),
getMinimumAccessibleValue( ) >
javax.swing.**J**InternalFrame.AccessibleJInternalFrame^
< getCurrentAccessibleValue( ), getMaximumAccessibleValue( ),
getMinimumAccessibleValue( ) > javax.swing↵
.**J**InternalFrame.JDesktopIcon.AccessibleJDesktopIcon^
< getCurrentAccessibleValue( ), getMaximumAccessibleValue( ),
getMinimumAccessibleValue( ) >
javax.swing.**J**ProgressBar.AccessibleJProgressBar^
< getCurrentAccessibleValue( ), getMaximumAccessibleValue( ),
getMinimumAccessibleValue( ) >
javax.swing.**J**ScrollBar.AccessibleJScrollBar^
< getCurrentAccessibleValue( ), getMaximumAccessibleValue( ),
getMinimumAccessibleValue( ) >
javax.swing.**J**Slider.AccessibleJSlider^
< getCurrentAccessibleValue( ), getMaximumAccessibleValue( ),
getMinimumAccessibleValue( ) >
javax.swing.**J**SplitPane.AccessibleJSplitPane^
< getCurrentAccessibleValue( ), getMaximumAccessibleValue( ),
getMinimumAccessibleValue( ) >
java.awt.**M**enuItem.AccessibleAWTMenuItem^
< getCurrentAccessibleValue( ), getMaximumAccessibleValue( ),
getMinimumAccessibleValue( ) > **N**umberFormat^.parse( )
java.awt.**S**crollbar.AccessibleAWTScrollBar^
< getCurrentAccessibleValue( ), getMaximumAccessibleValue( ),
getMinimumAccessibleValue( ) >
javax.swing.**S**pinnerNumberModel^ < getNumber( ),
getStepSize( ) >
NUMBER_FORMS: **C**haracter.UnicodeBlock^
numberFormat: **D**ateFormat^
NumberFormat^: java.text
—subclasses: ChoiceFormat^ DecimalFormat^
—passed to: **D**ateFormat^.setNumberFormat( )
javax.swing.text.**N**umberFormatter( )
—returned by: **D**ateFormat^.getNumberFormat( ) **N**umberFormat^
< getCurrencyInstance( ), getInstance( ), getIntegerInstance( ),
getNumberInstance( ), getPercentInstance( ) >
—fields: **D**ateFormat^.numberFormat
NumberFormat.Field^: java.text
—fields: **N**umberFormat.Field^ < CURRENCY,
DECIMAL_SEPARATOR, EXPONENT, EXPONENT_SIGN,
EXPONENT_SYMBOL, FRACTION, GROUPING_SEPARATOR,
INTEGER, PERCENT, PERMILLE, SIGN >
NumberFormatException^: java.lang
—thrown by: **B**yte^ < Byte( ), decode( ), parseByte( ), valueOf( ) >
java.awt.**C**olor.decode( ) **D**ouble^ < Double( ), parseDouble( ),
valueOf( ) > **F**loat^ < Float( ), parseFloat( ), valueOf( ) >
Integer^ < decode( ), Integer( ), parseInt( ), valueOf( ) >
Long^ < decode( ), Long( ), parseLong( ), valueOf( ) >
Package.isCompatibleWith( ) **S**hort^ < decode( ), parseShort( ),
Short( ), valueOf( ) >
NUMERIC: **T**ypes
nval: **S**treamTokenizer
NVList: org.omg.CORBA
—passed to: org.omg.CORBA.**C**ontext.set_values( )
org.omg.CORBA.portable.**D**elegate.create_request( )
LocalObject._create_request( )
*org.omg.CORBA.**O**bject._create_request( )*
org.omg.CORBA.portable.**O**bjectImpl._create_request( )
ServerRequest < arguments( ), params( ) >
—returned by: org.omg.CORBA.**C**ontext.get_values( )
org.omg.CORBA.**O**RB < create_list( ), create_operation_list( ) >
Request.arguments( )

N

< EnumControl( ), setValue( ) > java.awt.**E**vent( )
*EventDirContext^*.addNamingListener( ) **E**ventHandler
< create( ), EventHandler( ), invoke( ) > **E**ventObject( )
Expression^ < Expression( ), setValue( ) >
FeatureDescriptor‿.setValue( ) Field^ < get( ), getBoolean( ),
getByte( ), getChar( ), getDouble( ), getFloat( ),
getInt( ), getLong( ), getShort( ), set( ), setBoolean( ),
setByte( ), setChar( ), setDouble( ), setFloat( ),
setInt( ), setLong( ), setShort( ) > **F**ile.compareTo( )
Float^.compareTo( ) **F**loatBuffer^.compareTo( )
Format‿ < format( ), formatToCharacterIterator( ) >
javax.swing.text.**G**apVector.replace( )
java.awt.**G**raphics2D^.setRenderingHint( )
java.awt.**G**ridBagLayout.addLayoutComponent( )
*GSSCredential^*.equals( ) *GSSName*.equals( )
Guard.checkGuard( ) **G**uardedObject( )
Hashtable^ < contains( ), containsKey( ),
containsValue( ) > javax.swing.text.*Highlighter*
< changeHighlight( ), removeHighlight( ) >
javax.swing.text.html.**H**TMLDocument^.getElement( )
javax.swing.text.html.**H**TMLFrameHyperlinkEvent( )
javax.swing.event.**H**yperlinkEvent( ) javax.imageio ↩
.metadata.**I**IOMetadataFormatImpl.addObjectValue( )
javax.imageio.metadata.**I**IOMetadataNode.setUserObject( )
javax.imageio.spi.**I**mageInputStreamSpi^ ↩
.createInputStreamInstance( ) javax.imageio.**I**mageIO
< createImageInputStream( ), createImageOutputStream( ),
getImageReaders( ) > javax.imageio.spi ↩
.**I**mageOutputStreamSpi^.createOutputStreamInstance( )
javax.imageio.**I**mageReader.setInput( )
javax.imageio.spi.**I**mageReaderSpi^
< canDecodeInput( ), createReaderInstance( ) >
javax.imageio.**I**mageWriter.setOutput( )
javax.imageio.spi.**I**mageWriterSpi^.createWriterInstance( )
InheritableThreadLocal^.childValue( ) **I**nitialContext‿
< addToEnvironment( ), bind( ), rebind( ) >
InitialDirContext^ < bind( ), rebind( ), search( ) >
javax.swing.**I**nputMap.put( ) **I**ntBuffer^.compareTo( )
Integer^.compareTo( ) java.awt.event.**I**nvocationEvent( )
InvocationHandler.invoke( ) java.awt.event.**I**temEvent( )
javax.swing.**J**Applet^.addImpl( ) javax.swing.**J**ComboBox^
< addItem( ), configureEditor( ), insertItemAt( ),
JComboBox( ), removeItem( ), setPrototypeDisplayValue( ),
setSelectedItem( ) > javax.swing.**J**Component^
< firePropertyChange( ), fireVetoableChange( ), getClientProperty( ),
putClientProperty( ) > javax.swing.**J**Dialog^.addImpl( )
javax.swing.**J**EditorPane^.read( )
javax.swing.**J**FormattedTextField^
< JFormattedTextField( ), setValue( ) >
javax.swing.**J**FormattedTextField.AbstractFormatter ↩
.valueToString( ) javax.swing.**J**Frame^.addImpl( )
javax.swing.**J**InternalFrame^.addImpl( )
javax.swing.**J**LayeredPane^.addImpl( ) javax.swing.**J**List^
< JList( ), setListData( ), setPrototypeCellValue( ),
setSelectedValue( ) > javax.swing.**J**OptionPane^
< JOptionPane( ), setInitialSelectionValue( ), setInitialValue( ),
setInputValue( ), setMessage( ), setOptions( ),
setSelectionValues( ), setValue( ), showConfirmDialog( ),
showInputDialog( ), showInternalConfirmDialog( ),
showInternalInputDialog( ), showInternalMessageDialog( ),
showInternalOptionDialog( ), showMessageDialog( ),
showOptionDialog( ) > javax.swing.**J**RootPane^.addImpl( )
javax.swing.**J**RootPane.RootLayout.addLayoutComponent( )
javax.swing.**J**Spinner^.setValue( )
javax.swing.**J**SplitPane^.addImpl( ) javax.swing.**J**Table^
< getColumn( ), JTable( ), setValueAt( ) >
javax.swing.text.**J**TextComponent^.read( )

javax.swing.**J**ToolBar^.addImpl( ) javax.swing.**J**Tree^
< convertValueToText( ), createTreeModel( ), JTree( ) >
javax.swing.**J**Tree.DynamicUtilTreeNode^
< createChildren( ), JTree.DynamicUtilTreeNode( ) >
javax.swing.**J**Viewport^ < addImpl( ),
firePropertyChange( ) > javax.swing.**J**Window^.addImpl( )
java.awt.**K**eyboardFocusManager
< firePropertyChange( ), fireVetoableChange( ) >
*java.awt.LayoutManager2^*.addLayoutComponent( )
LinkedList^ < addFirst( ), addLast( ) >
LinkException^.setLinkResolvedObj( ) *List^* < add( ), contains( ),
equals( ), indexOf( ), lastIndexOf( ), remove( ), set( ), toArray( ) >
javax.swing.ListCellRenderer.getListCellRendererComponent( )
javax.swing.event.**L**istDataEvent( ) *ListIterator^* < add( ),
set( ) > javax.swing.event.**L**istSelectionEvent( ) **L**ogger
< entering( ), exiting( ), log( ), logp( ), logrb( ) >
LogRecord.setParameters( ) **L**ong^.compareTo( )
LongBuffer^.compareTo( ) javax.swing.**L**ookAndFeel
< getDesktopPropertyValue( ), loadKeyBindings( ),
makeComponentInputMap( ), makeInputMap( ),
makeKeyBindings( ) > *Map‿* < containsKey( ),
containsValue( ), equals( ), get( ), put( ),
remove( ) > *Map.Entry* < equals( ), setValue( ) >
MarshalledObject( ) javax.swing.event.**M**enuEvent( )
MessageFormat^.format( ) **M**ethod^.invoke( )
*javax.swing.text.MutableAttributeSet^* < addAttribute( ),
removeAttribute( ) > *javax.swing.MutableComboBoxModel^*
< addElement( ), insertElementAt( ), removeElement( ) >
*javax.swing.tree.MutableTreeNode^*.setUserObject( )
*Name^*.compareTo( ) **N**amingEvent( )
NamingException‿.setResolvedObj( ) **N**amingManager‿
< getObjectInstance( ), getStateToBind( ) >
java.lang.**O**bject.equals( ) *ObjectFactory‿*.getObjectInstance( )
ObjectFactoryBuilder.createObjectFactory( )
ObjectInputStream^.resolveObject( )
ObjectInputStream.GetField.get( )
*ObjectOutput^*.writeObject( ) **O**bjectOutputStream^
< replaceObject( ), writeObject( ), writeObjectOverride( ),
writeUnshared( ) > **O**bjectOutputStream.PutField.put( )
ObjectStreamField.compareTo( ) **O**bservable.notifyObservers( )
Observer.update( ) org.omg.CORBA_2_3.**O**RB^.set_delegate( )
org.omg.CORBA_2_3.portable ↩
.**O**utputStream^.write_abstract_interface( )
javax.swing.**O**verlayLayout.addLayoutComponent( )
java.awt.image.renderable.**P**arameterBlock < add( ),
addSource( ), set( ), setSource( ) > **P**arserAdapter.setProperty( )
java.security.**P**ermission‿.checkGuard( )
java.security.acl.Permission.equals( ) **P**ersistenceDelegate‿
< initialize( ), instantiate( ), mutatesTo( ), writeObject( ) >
PhantomReference( ) javax.swing.event.**P**opupMenuEvent( )
PortableRemoteObject.narrow( )
PortableRemoteObjectDelegate.narrow( )
*PreparedStatement^*.setObject( )
java.security.Principal‿.equals( )
javax.print.event.**P**rintEvent( )
javax.print.PrintService.equals( ) **P**rintStream^
< print( ), println( ) > **P**rintWriter^ < print( ),
println( ) > javax.swing.**P**rogressMonitor( )
javax.swing.**P**rogressMonitorInputStream( )
PropertyChangeEvent^ < PropertyChangeEvent( ),
setPropagationId( ) > **P**ropertyChangeSupport‿
< firePropertyChange( ), PropertyChangeSupport( ) >
PropertyEditor.setValue( ) **P**ropertyEditorSupport
< PropertyEditorSupport( ), setValue( ) >
Proxy.getInvocationHandler( )
java.awt.image.**R**aster.getDataElements( )
Reader( ) *Ref*.setObject( ) *RemoteRef^*.invoke( )
javax.swing.Renderer.setValue( ) java.awt.**R**enderingHints
< containsKey( ), containsValue( ), get( ),

put( ), remove( ), RenderingHints( ) >
java.awt.**R**enderingHints.Key.isCompatibleValue( )
ResolveResult < ResolveResult( ), setResolvedObj( ) >
*ResultSet*ˆ.updateObject( ) *RowSet*ˆ.setObject( )
java.awt.image.**S**ampleModel < getDataElements( ),
setDataElements( ) > **S**AXParser.setProperty( )
java.awt.**S**crollPaneˆ.addImpl( ) **S**earchResult( )
SecurityManager. < checkConnect( ), checkPermission( ),
checkRead( ), checkTopLevelWindow( ) >
SelectableChannelˆ.register( ) **S**electionKey.attach( )
*ServantLocatorOperations*ˆ.postinvoke( )
*ServerRef*ˆ.exportObject( ) javax.imageio.spi.**S**erviceRegistry
< contains( ), deregisterServiceProvider( ),
registerServiceProvider( ), setOrdering( ), unsetOrdering( ) >
javax.imageio.spi.ServiceRegistry.Filter.filter( )
*Set*ˆ < add( ), contains( ), equals( ), remove( ),
toArray( ) > **S**hortˆ.compareTo( ) **S**hortBufferˆ.compareTo( )
Signatureˆ.setParameter( ) **S**ignatureSpi.engineSetParameter( )
javax.swing.text.**S**impleAttributeSet < addAttribute( ),
containsAttribute( ), getAttribute( ), isDefined( ),
removeAttribute( ) > javax.print.**S**impleDoc( )
SocketOptions.setOption( ) **S**oftReference( ) *SortedMap*ˆ
< headMap( ), subMap( ), tailMap( ) > *SortedSet*ˆ < headSet( ),
subSet( ), tailSet( ) > javax.swing.**S**pinnerListModel( )
javax.swing.SpinnerModel.setValue( )
javax.swing.**S**pringLayout.addLayoutComponent( )
SSLSession.putValue( ) **S**tackˆ < push( ), search( ) >
StateFactory.getStateToBind( ) java.beans.**S**tatement( )
String < compareTo( ), valueOf( ) > **S**tringBuffer
< append( ), insert( ) > *StubDelegate*.equals( )
javax.swing.text.**S**tyleContext < addAttribute( ),
getStaticAttribute( ), getStaticAttributeKey( ),
registerStaticAttributeKey( ), removeAttribute( ) >
javax.swing.text.**S**tyleContext.NamedStyle
< addAttribute( ), containsAttribute( ),
getAttribute( ), isDefined( ), removeAttribute( ) >
javax.swing.text.**S**tyleContext.SmallAttributeSet
< containsAttribute( ), getAttribute( ),
isDefined( ), StyleContext.SmallAttributeSet( ) >
javax.swing.event.**S**wingPropertyChangeSupport( )
javax.swing.**S**wingUtilities.notifyAction( ) **S**ystem < arraycopy( ),
identityHashCode( ) > *javax.swing.table.TableCellEditor*ˆ ←
.getTableCellEditorComponent( ) *javax.swing.table* ←
.*TableCellRenderer*.getTableCellRendererComponent( )
javax.swing.table.**T**ableColumn
< setHeaderValue( ), setIdentifier( ) >
javax.swing.table.TableColumnModel.getColumnIndex( )
javax.swing.table.TableModel.setValueAt( )
java.awt.event.**T**extEvent( ) **T**hread.holdsLock( )
ThreadLocal.set( ) java.awt.**T**oolkit.setDesktopProperty( )
Transformer.setParameter( ) **T**ransformerFactory.setAttribute( )
*javax.swing.tree.TreeCellEditor*ˆ.getTreeCellEditorComponent( )
javax.swing.tree.TreeCellRenderer ←
.getTreeCellRendererComponent( )
javax.swing.event.**T**reeExpansionEvent( )
TreeMapˆ < headMap( ), subMap( ), tailMap( ) >
javax.swing.tree.TreeModel < getChild( ),
getChildCount( ), getIndexOfChild( ), isLeaf( ),
valueForPathChanged( ) > javax.swing.event.**T**reeModelEvent( )
javax.swing.tree.**T**reePath < pathByAddingChild( ),
TreePath( ) > javax.swing.event.**T**reeSelectionEvent( )
< cloneWithSource( ), TreeSelectionEvent( ) > **T**reeSetˆ
< headSet( ), subSet( ), tailSet( ) > javax.swing.**U**IDefaultsˆ
< firePropertyChange( ), get( ), getBoolean( ), getBorder( ),
getColor( ), getDimension( ), getFont( ), getIcon( ),
getInsets( ), getInt( ), getString( ), putDefaults( ),
UIDefaults( ) > javax.swing.**U**IDefaults.LazyInputMap( )
javax.swing.**U**IDefaults.ProxyLazyValue( )

javax.swing.**U**IManager < get( ), getBoolean( ),
getBorder( ), getColor( ), getDimension( ), getFont( ),
getIcon( ), getInsets( ), getInt( ), getString( ),
put( ) > javax.swing.event.**U**ndoableEditEvent( )
javax.swing.undo.**U**ndoableEditSupport( )
UnsolicitedNotificationEvent( ) **U**RI.compareTo( ) **U**til
< copyObject( ), copyObjects( ), writeAbstractObject( ),
writeAny( ), writeRemoteObject( ) > *UtilDelegate*
< copyObject( ), copyObjects( ), writeAbstractObject( ),
writeAny( ), writeRemoteObject( ) > **V**ectorˆ
< addElement( ), copyInto( ), indexOf( ), insertElementAt( ),
lastIndexOf( ), removeElement( ), setElementAt( ) >
VetoableChangeSupport < fireVetoableChange( ),
VetoableChangeSupport( ) > **W**eakReference( )
java.awt.image.**W**ritableRasterˆ.setDataElements( ) **W**riter( )
XMLDecoder < setOwner( ), XMLDecoder( ) > **X**MLEncoderˆ
< setOwner( ), writeObject( ) > **X**MLFilterImpl.setProperty( )
XMLReader.setProperty( )

—returned by: javax.swing.**A**bstractAction < clone( ), getKeys( ),
getValue( ) > javax.swing.**A**bstractButtonˆ.getSelectedObjects( )
AbstractCollection.toArray( )
javax.swing.text.**A**bstractDocument.getProperty( )
javax.swing.text.**A**bstractDocument.AbstractElement ←
.getAttribute( ) **A**bstractListˆ < get( ), remove( ),
set( ) > **A**bstractMap. < clone( ), get( ), put( ),
remove( ) > **A**ccessController.doPrivileged( )
javax.accessibility.**A**ccessibleHyperlink
< getAccessibleActionAnchor( ),
getAccessibleActionObject( ) > *javax.accessibility* ←
.*AccessibleKeyBinding*.getAccessibleKeyBinding( )
javax.accessibility.**A**ccessibleRelationˆ.getTarget( )
javax.accessibility.**A**ccessibleResourceBundleˆ.getContents( )
*AclEntry*ˆ.clone( ) *javax.swing.Action*ˆ.getValue( )
javax.swing.**A**ctionMap < allKeys( ), keys( ) >
java.awt.geom.**A**ffineTransform.clone( )
Annotation.getValue( ) java.awt.geom.**A**rea.clone( )
java.lang.reflect.**A**rray.get( ) *java.sql.Array*.getArray( )
java.lang.reflect.**A**rray.newInstance( ) **A**rrayListˆ.clone( )
*javax.naming.directory.Attribute*ˆ < clone( ), get( ), remove( ),
set( ) > *AttributedCharacterIterator*ˆ.getAttribute( )
AttributedCharacterIterator.Attribute.readResolve( )
java.util.jar.**A**ttributes.clone( )
*javax.naming.directory.Attributes*ˆ.clone( )
java.util.jar.**A**ttributes < get( ), put( ), remove( ) >
javax.swing.text.AttributeSet.getAttribute( )
java.awt.**A**WTKeyStroke.readResolve( ) **B**asicAttribute
< clone( ), get( ), remove( ), set( ) >
BasicAttributes.clone( ) *BeanContext*ˆ.instantiateChild( )
BeanContextMembershipEventˆ.toArray( )
BeanContextServiceProvider.getService( )
*BeanContextServices*ˆ.getService( )
BeanContextServicesSupportˆ.getService( )
BeanContextServicesSupport.BCSSProxyServiceProvider ←
.getService( ) **B**eanContextSupportˆ
< copyChildren( ), instantiateChild( ), toArray( ) >
BeanContextSupport.BCSIterator.next( )
Beans < getInstanceOf( ), instantiate( ) >
javax.naming.**B**indingˆ.getObject( ) **B**itSet.clone( )
BreakIterator.clone( ) java.awt.**B**ufferCapabilities.clone( )
java.awt.image.**B**ufferedImageˆ.getProperty( )
Calendar.clone( ) *CallableStatement*ˆ.getObject( )
javax.swing.CellEditor.getCellEditorValue( )
java.security.cert.**C**ertificate.writeReplace( )
Certificate.CertificateRep.readResolve( )
CertPath.writeReplace( ) **C**ertPath.CertPathRep.readResolve( )
*CertPathBuilderResult*ˆ.clone( ) *CertPathParameters*ˆ.clone( )
*CertPathValidatorResult*ˆ.clone( ) *CertSelector*ˆ.clone( )
*CertStoreParameters*ˆ.clone( ) *CharacterIterator*ˆ.clone( )
java.awt.**C**heckboxˆ.getSelectedObjects( )

O

java.awt.**C**heckboxMenuItem^.getSelectedObjects( )
java.awt.**C**hoice^.getSelectedObjects( )
ChoiceFormat^.getFormats( )　**C**lass < getSigners( ),
newInstance( ) >　**C**ollator ˅.clone( )　*Collection* ˅.toArray( )
CollectionCertStoreParameters.clone( )　**C**ollections < max( ),
min( ) >　java.awt.image.**C**olorModel.getDataElements( )
*javax.swing.**C**omboBoxEditor*.getItem( )
*javax.swing.**C**omboBoxModel*^.getSelectedItem( )
Compiler.command( )　java.awt.**C**omponent.getTreeLock( )
CompositeName < clone( ), remove( ) >　**C**ompoundName
< clone( ), remove( ) >　**C**onstructor^.newInstance( )
java.net.**C**ontentHandler.getContent( )　*javax.naming.**C**ontext* ˅
< addToEnvironment( ), lookup( ), lookupLink( ),
removeFromEnvironment( ) >　*java.awt.image.renderable* ⏎
*.**C**ontextualRenderedImageFactory*^.getProperty( )
CRLSelector^.clone( )　java.awt.geom.**C**ubicCurve2D.clone( )
java.awt.datatransfer.**D**ataFlavor.clone( )
*org.omg.CORBA.**D**ataInputStream*^.read_Abstract( )
java.util.**D**ate ˅.clone( )　**D**ateFormat.Field^.readResolve( )
DateFormatSymbols.clone( )　**D**ecimalFormatSymbols.clone( )
javax.swing.**D**efaultButtonModel.getSelectedObjects( )　javax ⏎
.swing.**D**efaultCellEditor.EditorDelegate.getCellEditorValue( )
javax.swing.**D**efaultComboBoxModel^.getSelectedItem( )
javax.swing.text.**D**efaultFormatter^.clone( )
javax.swing.**D**efaultListModel^ < elementAt( ), firstElement( ),
get( ), lastElement( ), remove( ), set( ), toArray( ) >
javax.swing.**D**efaultListSelectionModel.clone( )
javax.swing.tree.**D**efaultMutableTreeNode
< clone( ), getUserObject( ), getUserObjectPath( ) >
javax.swing.tree.**D**efaultTreeCellEditor.getCellEditorValue( )
javax.swing.tree.**D**efaultTreeModel < getChild( ), getRoot( ) >
javax.swing.tree.**D**efaultTreeSelectionModel.clone( )
Dictionary ˅ < get( ), put( ), remove( ) >
java.awt.geom.**D**imension2D.clone( )
DirectoryManager^.getObjectInstance( )
DirObjectFactory^.getObjectInstance( )
DirStateFactory.Result.getObject( )
*javax.print.**D**oc*.getPrintData( )
*javax.swing.text.**D**ocument*.getProperty( )
DocumentBuilderFactory.getAttribute( )
java.awt.dnd.**D**ragGestureEvent^.toArray( )
java.awt.dnd.**D**ropTargetContext.TransferableProxy ⏎
.getTransferData( )　javax.swing.text.**E**ditorKit.clone( )
javax.swing.text.**E**lementIterator.clone( )　**E**ncoder ˅
< get( ), remove( ) >　javax.sound.sampled.**E**numControl^
< getValue( ), getValues( ) >　*Enumeration* ˅.nextElement( )
javax.print.attribute.**E**numSyntax < clone( ), readResolve( ) >
EventHandler < create( ), getTarget( ), invoke( ) >
javax.swing.event.**E**ventListenerList.getListenerList( )
EventObject ˅.getSource( )　**E**xpression^.getValue( )
FeatureDescriptor ˅.getValue( )　**F**ield^.get( )　**F**ormat ˅ < clone( ),
parseObject( ) >　javax.swing.text.**G**apContent^.allocateArray( )
javax.swing.text.**G**apVector < allocateArray( ),
getArray( ) >　java.awt.geom.**G**eneralPath.clone( )
javax.swing.text.**G**lyphView^.clone( )
java.awt.**G**raphics2D^.getRenderingHint( )
java.awt.**G**ridBagConstraints.clone( )
GuardedObject.getObject( )　**H**ashMap^.clone( )
HashSet^.clone( )　**H**ashtable^.clone( )
*javax.swing.text.**H**ighlighter*.addHighlight( )
java.awt.color.**I**CC_Profile.readResolve( )
IdentityHashMap^.clone( )
*javax.imageio.metadata.**I**IOMetadataFormat*
< getObjectDefaultValue( ), getObjectEnumerations( ) >
javax.imageio.metadata.**I**IOMetadataFormatImpl
< getObjectDefaultValue( ), getObjectEnumerations( ) >
javax.imageio.metadata.**I**IOMetadataNode.getUserObject( )

java.awt.**I**mage.getProperty( )
java.awt.**I**mageCapabilities.clone( )
java.awt.image.**I**mageFilter.clone( )
javax.imageio.**I**mageReader.getInput( )
javax.imageio.**I**mageWriter.getOutput( )
InheritableThreadLocal^.childValue( )
InitialContext ˅ < addToEnvironment( ), lookup( ),
lookupLink( ), removeFromEnvironment( ) >
java.awt.im.**I**nputContext.getInputMethodControlObject( )
javax.swing.**I**nputMap.get( )
*java.awt.im.spi.**I**nputMethod*.getControlObject( )　org.omg ⏎
.CORBA_2_3.portable.**I**nputStream^.read_abstract_interface( )
java.awt.**I**nsets.clone( )　*InvocationHandler*.invoke( )
java.awt.event.**I**temEvent^.getItem( )
*java.awt.**I**temSelectable*.getSelectedObjects( )
Iterator ˅.next( )　javax.swing.**J**ComboBox^
< getItemAt( ), getPrototypeDisplayValue( ),
getSelectedItem( ), getSelectedObjects( ) >
javax.swing.**J**Component^.getClientProperty( )
javax.swing.**J**FormattedTextField^.getValue( )
javax.swing.**J**FormattedTextField.AbstractFormatter < clone( ),
stringToValue( ) >　javax.swing.**J**List^ < getPrototypeCellValue( ),
getSelectedValue( ), getSelectedValues( ) >
java.awt.**J**obAttributes.clone( )　javax.swing.**J**OptionPane^
< getInitialSelectionValue( ), getInitialValue( ), getInputValue( ),
getMessage( ), getOptions( ), getSelectionValues( ), getValue( ),
showInputDialog( ), showInternalInputDialog( ) >
javax.swing.**J**Spinner^ < getNextValue( ), getPreviousValue( ),
getValue( ) >　javax.swing.**J**Table^.getValueAt( )
javax.swing.**J**Tree^.getLastSelectedPathComponent( )
java.awt.image.**K**ernel.clone( )
LDAPCertStoreParameters.clone( )
java.awt.geom.**L**ine2D.clone( )　**L**inkedList^
< clone( ), getFirst( ), getLast( ), removeFirst( ),
removeLast( ) >　**L**inkException^.getLinkResolvedObj( )
List^.get( )　java.awt.**L**ist^.getSelectedObjects( )　*List*^
< remove( ), set( ), toArray( ) >　*ListIterator*^ < next( ),
previous( ) >　*javax.swing.**L**istModel*.getElementAt( )
ListResourceBundle^ < getContents( ), handleGetObject( ) >
LoaderHandler.getSecurityContext( )　**L**ocale.clone( )
LogRecord.getParameters( )　javax.swing.**L**ookAndFeel
< getDesktopPropertyValue( ), makeIcon( ) >　**M**ac.clone( )
MacSpi.clone( )　**M**anifest.clone( )　*Map* ˅
< get( ), put( ), remove( ) >　*Map.Entry* < getKey( ),
getValue( ), setValue( ) >　**M**arshalledObject.get( )
java.awt.**M**ediaTracker < getErrorsAny( ),
getErrorsID( ) >　java.awt.**M**enuComponent.getTreeLock( )
MessageDigestSpi ˅.clone( )　**M**essageFormat^.parse( )
MessageFormat.Field^.readResolve( )　**M**ethod^.invoke( )
javax.sound.midi.**M**idiMessage.clone( )　*Name*^
< clone( ), remove( ) >　*NamingEnumeration*^.next( )
NamingEvent^.getChangeInfo( )
NamingException ˅.getResolvedObj( )　**N**amingManager ˅
< getObjectInstance( ), getStateToBind( ) >
NumberFormat.Field^.readResolve( )
java.lang.**O**bject.clone( )　*ObjectFactory* ˅.getObjectInstance( )
ObjectInput^.readObject( )　**O**bjectInputStream^
< readObject( ), readObjectOverride( ), readUnshared( ),
resolveObject( ) >　**O**bjectInputStream.GetField.get( )
ObjectOutputStream^.replaceObject( )
java.awt.**P**ageAttributes.clone( )
java.awt.print.**P**ageFormat.clone( )
java.awt.print.**P**aper.clone( )
java.awt.image.renderable.**P**arameterBlock
< clone( ), getObjectParameter( ), getSource( ),
shallowClone( ) >　**P**arserAdapter.getProperty( )
java.awt.image.**P**ixelGrabber.getPixels( )
PKIXCertPathChecker.clone( )

O

javax.swing.text.**S**tyleConstants.CharacterConstants^
< Background, BidiLevel, Bold, ComponentAttribute,
Family, Foreground, IconAttribute, Italic, Size,
StrikeThrough, Subscript, Superscript, Underline >
javax.swing.text.**S**tyleConstants.ColorConstants^
< Background, Foreground >
javax.swing.text.**S**tyleConstants.FontConstants^
< Bold, Family, Italic, Size >
javax.swing.text.**S**tyleConstants.ParagraphConstants^
< Alignment, FirstLineIndent, LeftIndent, LineSpacing,
Orientation, RightIndent, SpaceAbove, SpaceBelow, TabSet >
javax.swing.table.**T**ableColumn < headerValue,
identifier > javax.swing.event.**T**reeModelEvent^.children
javax.swing.undo.**U**ndoableEditSupport.realSource
Vector^.elementData **W**riter_.lock

Object_: org.omg.CORBA
— extended by: *AdapterActivator^ BindingIterator^*
*Codec^ CodecFactory^* org.omg.CORBA.*Current*_
*DomainManager^* org.omg.CORBA.*DynAny*_
org.omg.DynamicAny.*DynAny*_ *DynAnyFactory^*
*Interceptor*_ *IRObject^ NamingContext*_
*ORBInitializer*_ *ORBInitInfo^ POA^ POAManager^*
org.omg.CORBA.*Policy*_ *PolicyFactory^ RequestInfo*_
*RunTime*_ *ServantManager^*
— descendents: *ClientRequestInfo^ ClientRequestInterceptor^*
org.omg.PortableInterceptor.*Current^*
org.omg.PortableServer.*Current^*
org.omg.DynamicAny.*DynArray^*
org.omg.DynamicAny.*DynEnum^*
org.omg.DynamicAny.*DynFixed^*
org.omg.DynamicAny.*DynSequence^*
org.omg.DynamicAny.*DynStruct^*
org.omg.DynamicAny.*DynUnion^*
org.omg.DynamicAny.*DynValue^ DynValueBox^*
*DynValueCommon*_ *IdAssignmentPolicy^ IDLType^*
*IdUniquenessPolicy^ ImplicitActivationPolicy^*
*IORInterceptor^ LifespanPolicy^ NamingContextExt^*
*RequestProcessingPolicy^ ServantActivator^*
*ServantLocator^ ServantRetentionPolicy^*
*ServerRequestInfo^ ServerRequestInterceptor^*
*ThreadPolicy^*
— passed to: _DynAnyStub^.insert_reference( )
_DynArrayStub^.insert_reference( )
_DynEnumStub^.insert_reference( )
_DynFixedStub^.insert_reference( )
_DynSequenceStub^.insert_reference( )
_DynStructStub^.insert_reference( )
_DynUnionStub^.insert_reference( )
_DynValueStub^.insert_reference( ) _NamingContextExtStub^
< bind( ), rebind( ) > _NamingContextStub^
< bind( ), rebind( ) > **A**ny.insert_Object( )
BindingIteratorHelper.narrow( ) **C**odecFactoryHelper.narrow( )
org.omg.CORBA.**C**urrentHelper.narrow( )
org.omg.PortableInterceptor.**C**urrentHelper.narrow( )
org.omg.PortableServer.**C**urrentHelper.narrow( )
*org.omg.CORBA.DataOutputStream^*.write_Object( )
org.omg.CORBA.portable.**D**elegate_
< create_request( ), duplicate( ), equals( ) >
org.omg.CORBA_2_3.portable.**D**elegate^.get_codebase( )
org.omg.CORBA.portable.**D**elegate_ < get_domain_managers( ),
get_interface_def( ), get_policy( ), hash( ), hashCode( ), invoke( ),
is_a( ), is_equivalent( ), is_local( ), non_existent( ), orb( ),
release( ), releaseReply( ), request( ), servant_postinvoke( ),
servant_preinvoke( ), set_policy_override( ), toString( ) >
*org.omg.CORBA.DynAny^*.insert_reference( )
DynAnyFactoryHelper.narrow( ) **D**ynAnyHelper.narrow( )
*DynAnyOperations*_.insert_reference( )
DynArrayHelper.narrow( ) **D**ynEnumHelper.narrow( )
DynFixedHelper.narrow( ) **D**ynSequenceHelper.narrow( )
DynStructHelper.narrow( )
DynUnionHelper.narrow( ) **D**ynValueHelper.narrow( )

org.omg.PortableInterceptor.**F**orwardRequest( )
org.omg.PortableServer.**F**orwardRequest( )
IDLTypeHelper.narrow( ) **L**ocalObject._is_equivalent( )
NamingContextExtHelper.narrow( )
NamingContextHelper.narrow( ) *NamingContextOperations*_
< bind( ), rebind( ) > *org.omg.CORBA.Object*_._is_equivalent( )
ObjectHelper < insert( ), write( ) > **O**bjectHolder( )
org.omg.CORBA.portable.**O**bjectImpl._is_equivalent( )
org.omg.CORBA.**O**RB_ < connect( ),
create_operation_list( ), disconnect( ), object_to_string( ) >
*ORBInitInfoOperations*_.register_initial_reference( )
org.omg.CORBA.portable.**O**utputStream^.write_Object( )
POAHelper.narrow( ) *POAOperations*_
< reference_to_id( ), reference_to_servant( ) >
PolicyHelper.narrow( ) **S**ervantActivatorHelper.narrow( )
ServantLocatorHelper.narrow( )
— returned by: _DynAnyStub^.get_reference( )
_DynArrayStub^.get_reference( )
_DynEnumStub^.get_reference( )
_DynFixedStub^.get_reference( )
_DynSequenceStub^.get_reference( )
_DynStructStub^.get_reference( )
_DynUnionStub^.get_reference( )
_DynValueStub^.get_reference( )
_NamingContextExtStub^ < resolve( ), resolve_str( ) >
_NamingContextStub^.resolve( ) **A**ny.extract_Object( )
*ClientRequestInfoOperations*_ < effective_target( ), target( ) >
*org.omg.CORBA.DataInputStream^*.read_Object( )
org.omg.CORBA.portable.**D**elegate_
< duplicate( ), get_interface_def( ) >
org.omg.PortableServer.portable.Delegate.get_interface_def( )
org.omg.CORBA.portable.**D**elegate_.set_policy_override( )
org.omg.PortableServer.portable.Delegate.this_object( )
*org.omg.CORBA.DynAny^*.get_reference( )
*DynAnyOperations*_.get_reference( )
org.omg.CORBA.portable.**I**nputStream^.read_Object( )
LocalObject < _duplicate( ), _get_interface( ),
_get_interface_def( ), _set_policy_override( ) >
*NamingContextExtOperations*_.resolve_str( )
*NamingContextOperations*_.resolve( )
*org.omg.CORBA.Object*_ < _duplicate( ), _get_interface_def( ),
_set_policy_override( ) > **O**bjectHelper < extract( ),
read( ) > org.omg.CORBA.portable.**O**bjectImpl_
< _duplicate( ), _get_interface_def( ), _set_policy_override( ) >
org.omg.CORBA_2_3.**O**RB^.get_value_def( )
org.omg.CORBA.**O**RB_
< resolve_initial_references( ), string_to_object( ) >
*ORBInitInfoOperations*_.resolve_initial_references( )
*POAOperations*_ < create_reference( ),
create_reference_with_id( ), id_to_reference( ),
servant_to_reference( ) > **R**equest.target( )
*RequestInfoOperations*_.forward_reference( ) **S**ervant_
< _get_interface_def( ), _this_object( ) > *Tie^*.thisObject( )
— implemented by: **L**ocalObject
org.omg.CORBA.portable.**O**bjectImpl_
— fields: org.omg.PortableInterceptor.**F**orwardRequest^.forward
org.omg.PortableServer.**F**orwardRequest^.forward_reference
ObjectHolder.value

OBJECT_ADDED: **N**amingEvent^
OBJECT_CHANGED: **N**amingEvent^
OBJECT_FACTORIES: *javax.naming.Context*_
object_id( ): *org.omg.PortableServer.portable.Delegate*
*ServerRequestInfoOperations*_
OBJECT_NOT_EXIST^: org.omg.CORBA
OBJECT_REMOVED: **N**amingEvent^
OBJECT_RENAMED: **N**amingEvent^
OBJECT_SCOPE: *EventContext*_ **S**earchControls
object_to_string( ): org.omg.CORBA.**O**RB_
objectAdded( ): *NamespaceChangeListener^*
ObjectAlreadyActive^: org.omg.PortableServer.POAPackage
— passed to: **O**bjectAlreadyActiveHelper < insert( ), write( ) >
— returned by: **O**bjectAlreadyActiveHelper < extract( ), read( ) >

O

open(): **D**atagramChannel⌐ **P**ipe **S**elector⌐
   ServerSocketChannel^ **S**ocketChannel^
OPEN_DELETE: **Z**ipFile⌐
OPEN_FAILURE: **E**rrorManager
OPEN_READ: **Z**ipFile⌐
openConnection(): **U**RL **U**RLStreamHandler
openDatagramChannel(): **S**electorProvider
openPipe(): **S**electorProvider
openSelector(): **S**electorProvider
openServerSocketChannel(): **S**electorProvider
openSocketChannel(): **S**electorProvider
openStream(): **U**RL
Operation: java.rmi.server
  —passed to: *RemoteRef*^.newCall()
  —returned by: *Skeleton*.getOperations()
operation(): **R**equest *RequestInfoOperations*⌐ **S**erverRequest
operation_context(): *RequestInfoOperations*⌐
OperationNotSupportedException^: javax.naming
OPTICAL_CHARACTER_RECOGNITION:
  Character.UnicodeBlock^
OPTIONAL: **A**ppConfigurationEntry.LoginModuleControlFlag
OptionalDataException^: java.io
or(): **B**igInteger^ **B**itSet
ORB⌐: org.omg.CORBA
  —subclasses: org.omg.CORBA_2_3.**ORB**^
  —passed to: **B**indingIteratorPOA^._this()
  NamingContextExtPOA^._this() **N**amingContextPOA^._this()
  Servant⌐._this_object() **S**ervantActivatorPOA^._this()
  ServantLocatorPOA^._this() **S**tub^.connect()
  StubDelegate.connect() *Tie*^.orb() **U**til < copyObject(),
  copyObjects() > *UtilDelegate* < copyObject(), copyObjects() >
  —returned by: org.omg.CORBA.portable.**D**elegate⌐.orb()
  org.omg.PortableServer.portable.Delegate.orb()
  org.omg.CORBA.portable.**I**nputStream^.orb()
  LocalObject._orb()
  org.omg.CORBA.portable.**O**bjectImpl⌐._orb()
  org.omg.CORBA.**O**RB⌐.init()
  org.omg.CORBA.portable.**O**utputStream^.orb()
  Servant⌐._orb() *Tie*^.orb()
ORB^: org.omg.CORBA_2_3
orb(): org.omg.CORBA.portable.**D**elegate⌐
  org.omg.PortableServer.portable.Delegate
  org.omg.CORBA.portable.**I**nputStream^
  org.omg.CORBA.portable.**O**utputStream^ *Tie*^
ORB_CTRL_MODEL: **T**hreadPolicyValue
orb_id(): *ORBInitInfoOperations*⌐
ORBInitializer^: org.omg.PortableInterceptor
ORBInitializerOperations⌐: org.omg.PortableInterceptor
  —extended by: *ORBInitializer*^
ORBInitInfo^: org.omg.PortableInterceptor
  —passed to: *ORBInitializerOperations*⌐ < post_init(), pre_init() >
ORBInitInfoOperations⌐: org.omg.PortableInterceptor
  —extended by: *ORBInitInfo*^
order(): **B**yteBuffer^ **C**harBuffer^ **D**oubleBuffer^ **F**loatBuffer^
  IntBuffer^ **L**ongBuffer^ **S**hortBuffer^
ordered: **B**asicAttribute
ordinaryChar(): **S**treamTokenizer
ordinaryChars(): **S**treamTokenizer
originalEx: **U**nknownException^
ORIYA: **C**haracter.UnicodeBlock^
OTHER: **T**ypes
OTHER_LETTER: **C**haracter
OTHER_NUMBER: **C**haracter
OTHER_PUNCTUATION: **C**haracter
OTHER_SYMBOL: **C**haracter
othersDeletesAreVisible(): *DatabaseMetaData*
othersInsertsAreVisible(): *DatabaseMetaData*
othersUpdatesAreVisible(): *DatabaseMetaData*
out: **F**ileDescriptor **F**ilterOutputStream⌐ **F**ilterWriter^
  PipedInputStream^ **P**rintWriter^ **S**ystem
OutOfMemoryError^: java.lang
OutputKeys: javax.xml.transform

OutputStream⌐: java.io
  —subclasses: **B**yteArrayOutputStream^ **F**ileOutputStream^
  FilterOutputStream⌐ **O**bjectOutputStream^
  org.omg.CORBA.portable.**O**utputStream⌐
  PipedOutputStream^
  —descendents: **B**ufferedOutputStream^ **C**heckedOutputStream^
  CipherOutputStream^ java.io.**D**ataOutputStream^
  DeflaterOutputStream^ **D**igestOutputStream^
  GZIPOutputStream^ **J**arOutputStream^ **L**ogStream^
  org.omg.CORBA_2_3.portable.**O**utputStream^ **P**rintStream⌐
  ZipOutputStream⌐
  —passed to: javax.sound.sampled.spi.**A**udioFileWriter.write()
  javax.sound.sampled.**A**udioSystem.write()
  BufferedOutputStream^ **B**yteArrayOutputStream^.writeTo()
  java.security.Certificate.encode() **C**hannels.newChannel()
  CheckedOutputStream() **C**ipherOutputStream()
  java.io.**D**ataOutputStream() **D**eflaterOutputStream()
  DigestOutputStream() javax.swing.text.**E**ditorKit.write()
  javax.imageio.stream.**F**ileCacheImageOutputStream()
  FilterOutputStream() *GSSContext* < acceptSecContext(),
  getMIC(), initSecContext(), unwrap(), wrap() >
  GZIPOutputStream() java.awt.color.**I**CC_Profile.write()
  javax.imageio.**I**mageIO.write() **J**arOutputStream()
  KeyStore.store() **K**eyStoreSpi.engineStore()
  LogStream^.setOutputStream() **M**anifest.write()
  javax.imageio.stream.**M**emoryCacheImageOutputStream()
  javax.sound.midi.spi.**M**idiFileWriter.write()
  javax.sound.midi.**M**idiSystem.write() **O**bjectOutputStream()
  OutputStreamWriter() **P**references⌐
  < exportNode(), exportSubtree() > **P**rintStream()
  PrintWriter() **P**roperties⌐ < save(), store() >
  RemoteServer^.setLog() **R**untime.getLocalizedOutputStream()
  StreamHandler⌐ < setOutputStream(),
  StreamHandler() > javax.print.**S**treamPrintService()
  javax.print.**S**treamPrintServiceFactory.getPrintService()
  StreamResult < setOutputStream(), StreamResult() >
  XMLEncoder() **Z**ipOutputStream()
  —returned by: *Blob*.setBinaryStream()
  Channels.newOutputStream() *Clob*.setAsciiStream()
  LogStream^.getOutputStream() **P**rocess.getOutputStream()
  Runtime.getLocalizedOutputStream()
  Socket⌐.getOutputStream() **S**ocketImpl.getOutputStream()
  javax.print.**S**treamPrintService.getOutputStream()
  StreamResult.getOutputStream()
  URLConnection⌐.getOutputStream()
  —fields: **F**ilterOutputStream⌐.out
OutputStream⌐: org.omg.CORBA.portable
  —subclasses: org.omg.CORBA_2_3.portable.**O**utputStream^
  —passed to: **A**dapterAlreadyExistsHelper.write()
  AdapterInactiveHelper.write()
  AdapterNonExistentHelper.write()
  AddressHelper.write() **A**lreadyBoundHelper.write()
  AlreadyBoundHolder._write() **A**ny.write_value()
  AnyHolder._write() org.omg.CORBA.**A**nySeqHelper.write()
  org.omg.DynamicAny.**A**nySeqHelper.write()
  AnySeqHolder._write() **B**indingHelper.write()
  BindingHolder._write() **B**indingIteratorHelper.write()
  BindingIteratorHolder._write() **B**indingListHelper.write()
  BindingListHolder._write() **B**indingTypeHelper.write()
  BindingTypeHolder._write() **B**ooleanHolder._write()
  BooleanSeqHelper.write() **B**ooleanSeqHolder._write()
  BoxedValueHelper.write_value() **B**yteHolder._write()
  CannotProceedHelper.write() **C**annotProceedHolder._write()
  CharHolder._write() **C**harSeqHelper.write()
  CharSeqHolder._write() **C**odecFactoryHelper.write()
  CompletionStatusHelper.write() **C**omponentIdHelper.write()
  CookieHolder._write() org.omg.CORBA.**C**urrentHelper.write()
  org.omg.PortableInterceptor.**C**urrentHelper.write()
  org.omg.PortableServer.**C**urrentHelper.write()
  CurrentHolder._write() **D**efinitionKindHelper.write()

O

org.omg.CORBA.portable.**D**elegate˰.invoke( )
DoubleHolder._write( )　**D**oubleSeqHelper.write( )
DoubleSeqHolder._write( )　**D**uplicateNameHelper.write( )
DynAnyFactoryHelper.write( )　**D**ynAnyHelper.write( )
DynAnySeqHelper.write( )　**D**ynArrayHelper.write( )
DynEnumHelper.write( )　**D**ynFixedHelper.write( )
DynSequenceHelper.write( )　**D**ynStructHelper.write( )
DynUnionHelper.write( )　**D**ynValueHelper.write( )
org.omg.CORBA.**F**ieldNameHelper.write( )
org.omg.DynamicAny.**F**ieldNameHelper.write( )
FixedHolder._write( )　**F**loatHolder._write( )
FloatSeqHelper.write( )　**F**loatSeqHolder._write( )
FormatMismatchHelper.write( )
org.omg.PortableInterceptor.**F**orwardRequestHelper.write( )
org.omg.PortableServer.**F**orwardRequestHelper.write( )
IdentifierHelper.write( )　**I**DLTypeHelper.write( )
InconsistentTypeCodeHelper.write( )
IntHolder._write( )　**I**nvalidAddressHelper.write( )
InvalidAddressHolder._write( )　org.omg.CosNaming ↵
.NamingContextPackage.**I**nvalidNameHelper.write( )
org.omg.PortableInterceptor.ORBInitInfoPackage ↵
.**I**nvalidNameHelper.write( )　**I**nvalidNameHolder._write( )
InvalidPolicyHelper.write( )　**I**nvalidSlotHelper.write( )
InvalidTypeForEncodingHelper.write( )
InvalidValueHelper.write( )　**I**ORHelper.write( )
IORHolder._write( )　**I**stringHelper.write( )
LocalObject._invoke( )　**L**ongHolder._write( )
LongLongSeqHelper.write( )　**L**ongLongSeqHolder._write( )
LongSeqHelper.write( )　**L**ongSeqHolder._write( )
MultipleComponentProfileHelper.write( )
MultipleComponentProfileHolder._write( )
NameComponentHelper.write( )
NameComponentHolder._write( )
NameDynAnyPairHelper.write( )
NameDynAnyPairSeqHelper.write( )
NameHelper.write( )　**N**ameHolder._write( )
org.omg.CORBA.**N**ameValuePairHelper.write( )
org.omg.DynamicAny.**N**ameValuePairHelper.write( )
NameValuePairSeqHelper.write( )
NamingContextExtHelper.write( )
NamingContextExtHolder._write( )
NamingContextHelper.write( )　**N**amingContextHolder._write( )
NoContextHelper.write( )　**N**oServantHelper.write( )
NotEmptyHelper.write( )　**N**otEmptyHolder._write( )
NotFoundHelper.write( )　**N**otFoundHolder._write( )
NotFoundReasonHelper.write( )
NotFoundReasonHolder._write( )
ObjectAlreadyActiveHelper.write( )　**O**bjectHelper.write( )
ObjectHolder._write( )　**O**bjectIdHelper.write( )
org.omg.CORBA.portable.**O**bjectImpl._invoke( )
ObjectNotActiveHelper.write( )　**O**ctetSeqHelper.write( )
OctetSeqHolder._write( )　**P**arameterModeHelper.write( )
ParameterModeHolder._write( )　**P**OAHelper.write( )
PolicyErrorCodeHelper.write( )　**P**olicyErrorHelper.write( )
PolicyErrorHolder._write( )　**P**olicyHelper.write( )
PolicyHolder._write( )　**P**olicyListHelper.write( )
PolicyListHolder._write( )　**P**olicyTypeHelper.write( )
PrincipalHolder._write( )　**P**rofileIdHelper.write( )
RepositoryIdHelper.write( )　**S**ervantActivatorHelper.write( )
ServantAlreadyActiveHelper.write( )
ServantLocatorHelper.write( )　**S**ervantNotActiveHelper.write( )
ServiceContextHelper.write( )　**S**erviceContextHolder._write( )
ServiceContextListHelper.write( )
ServiceContextListHolder._write( )　**S**erviceDetailHelper.write( )
ServiceIdHelper.write( )　**S**erviceInformationHelper.write( )
ServiceInformationHolder._write( )
SetOverrideTypeHelper.write( )　**S**hortHolder._write( )
ShortSeqHelper.write( )　**S**hortSeqHolder._write( )
Streamable˰._write( )　**S**tringHolder._write( )
StringNameHelper.write( )　**S**tringSeqHelper.write( )
StringSeqHolder._write( )　**S**tringValueHelper < write( ),
write_value( ) >　**S**tructMemberHelper.write( )

SyncScopeHelper.write( )　**T**aggedComponentHelper.write( )
TaggedComponentHolder._write( )
TaggedProfileHelper.write( )　**T**aggedProfileHolder._write( )
TypeCodeHolder._write( )　org.omg.DynamicAny ↵
.DynAnyPackage.**T**ypeMismatchHelper.write( )
org.omg.IOP.CodecPackage.**T**ypeMismatchHelper.write( )
ULongLongSeqHelper.write( )　**U**LongLongSeqHolder._write( )
ULongSeqHelper.write( )　**U**LongSeqHolder._write( )
UnionMemberHelper.write( )　**U**nknownEncodingHelper.write( )
UnknownUserExceptionHelper.write( )
UnknownUserExceptionHolder._write( )
URLStringHelper.write( )　**U**ShortSeqHelper.write( )
UShortSeqHolder._write( )　**U**til < writeAbstractObject( ),
writeAny( ),　writeRemoteObject( ) >　*UtilDelegate*
< writeAbstractObject( ),　writeAny( ),
writeRemoteObject( ) > **V**alueBaseHelper.write( )
ValueBaseHolder._write( )　*ValueHandler*.writeValue( )
ValueMemberHelper.write( )　**V**ersionSpecHelper.write( )
VisibilityHelper.write( )　**W**CharSeqHelper.write( )
WCharSeqHolder._write( )　**W**rongAdapterHelper.write( )
WrongPolicyHelper.write( )　**W**rongTransactionHelper.write( )
WrongTransactionHolder._write( )　**W**StringSeqHelper.write( )
WStringSeqHolder._write( )　**W**StringValueHelper < write( ),
write_value( ) >
—returned by: **A**ny.create_output_stream( )
BindingIteratorPOA^._invoke( )
org.omg.CORBA.portable.**D**elegate˰.request( )
InvokeHandler˰._invoke( )　**L**ocalObject._request( )
NamingContextExtPOA^._invoke( )
NamingContextPOA^._invoke( )
org.omg.CORBA.portable.**O**bjectImpl._request( )
org.omg.CORBA.**O**RB˰.create_output_stream( )
ResponseHandler < createExceptionReply( ),
createReply( ) > **S**ervantActivatorPOA^._invoke( )
ServantLocatorPOA^._invoke( )
OutputStream^: org.omg.CORBA_2_3.portable
OutputStreamWriter^: java.io
—subclasses: **F**ileWriter^
OVERFLOW: **C**oderResult
OverlappingFileLockException^: java.nio.channels
overlaps( ): **F**ileLock
ownDeletesAreVisible( ): *DatabaseMetaData*
Owner˰: java.security.acl
—extended by: *Acl*^
ownInsertsAreVisible( ): *DatabaseMetaData*
ownUpdatesAreVisible( ): *DatabaseMetaData*
Package: java.lang
—returned by: **C**lass.getPackage( )　**C**lassLoader˰
< definePackage( ), getPackage( ), getPackages( ) >
Package < getPackage( ),　getPackages( ) >
URLClassLoader^.definePackage( )
packagePrefix: *LoaderHandler*　*RemoteRef*^
paintValue( ): *PropertyEditor*　**P**ropertyEditorSupport
PARAGRAPH_SEPARATOR: **C**haracter
PARAM_IN: **P**arameterMode
PARAM_INOUT: **P**arameterMode
PARAM_OUT: **P**arameterMode
Parameter: org.omg.Dynamic
—returned by: *RequestInfoOperations*˰.arguments( )
ParameterDescriptor^: java.beans
—passed to: **M**ethodDescriptor( )
—returned by: **M**ethodDescriptor^.getParameterDescriptors( )
ParameterMetaData: java.sql
—returned by: *PreparedStatement*^.getParameterMetaData( )
ParameterMode: org.omg.CORBA
—passed to: **P**arameter( )　**P**arameterModeHelper < insert( ),
write( ) > **P**arameterModeHolder( )
—returned by: **P**arameterMode.from_int( )
ParameterModeHelper < extract( ),　read( ) >
—fields: **P**arameter.mode　**P**arameterMode < PARAM_IN,
PARAM_INOUT,　PARAM_OUT > **P**arameterModeHolder.value
ParameterModeHelper: org.omg.CORBA

ParameterModeHolder: org.omg.CORBA
parameterModeIn: *ParameterMetaData*
parameterModeInOut: *ParameterMetaData*
parameterModeOut: *ParameterMetaData*
parameterModeUnknown: *ParameterMetaData*
parameterNoNulls: *ParameterMetaData*
parameterNullable: *ParameterMetaData*
parameterNullableUnknown: *ParameterMetaData*
params( ): **S**erverRequest
parent: **R**esourceBundle
parent( ): org.omg.CORBA.**C**ontext **P**references
parentOf( ): **T**hreadGroup
parse( ): java.util.**D**ate **D**ateFormat^ **D**ocumentBuilder **L**evel
  MessageFormat^ *NameParser* **N**umberFormat^ *Parser*
  ParserAdapter **S**AXParser **X**MLFilterImpl *XMLReader*
  XMLReaderAdapter
parseByte( ): **B**yte^
parseDouble( ): **D**ouble^
ParseException: java.text
—thrown by: **D**ateFormat^.parse( ) **F**ormat.parseObject( )
  javax.swing.**J**FormattedTextField^.commitEdit( )
  javax.swing.**J**FormattedTextField.AbstractFormatter
  < stringToValue( ), valueToString( ) >
  javax.swing.**J**Spinner^.commitEdit( )
  javax.swing.**J**Spinner.DefaultEditor^.commitEdit( )
  javax.swing.text.**M**askFormatter^ < MaskFormatter( ),
  setMask( ) > **M**essageFormat^.parse( ) **N**umberFormat^.parse( )
  RuleBasedCollator( )
parseFloat( ): **F**loat^
parseInt( ): **I**nteger^
parseLevel( ): **L**ogStream^
parseLong( ): **L**ong^
parseNumbers( ): **S**treamTokenizer
parseObject( ): **F**ormat
ParsePosition: java.text
—passed to: **D**ateFormat^.parse( ) **F**ormat.parseObject( )
  MessageFormat^.parse( ) **N**umberFormat^.parse( )
Parser: org.xml.sax
—passed to: **P**arserAdapter( )
—returned by: **P**arserFactory.makeParser( ) **S**AXParser.getParser( )
—implemented by: **X**MLReaderAdapter
ParserAdapter: org.xml.sax.helpers
ParserConfigurationException: javax.xml.parsers
—thrown by: **D**ocumentBuilderFactory.newDocumentBuilder( )
  SAXParserFactory < getFeature( ), newSAXParser( ),
  setFeature( ) >
ParserFactory: org.xml.sax.helpers
parseServerAuthority( ): **U**RI
parseShort( ): **S**hort^
parseURL( ): **U**RLStreamHandler
PartialResultException^: javax.naming
PasswordAuthentication: java.net
—returned by: **A**uthenticator < getPasswordAuthentication( ),
  requestPasswordAuthentication( ) >
PasswordCallback: javax.security.auth.callback
pathSeparator: **F**ile
pathSeparatorChar: **F**ile
Pattern: java.util.regex
—returned by: **M**atcher.pattern( ) **P**attern.compile( )
pattern( ): **M**atcher **P**attern
PatternSyntaxException^: java.util.regex
PBEKey^: javax.crypto.interfaces
PBEKeySpec: javax.crypto.spec
PBEParameterSpec: javax.crypto.spec
pcSupport: **B**eanContextChildSupport
peek( ): **D**atagramSocketImpl **S**tack^
peekData( ): **D**atagramSocketImpl
PERCENT: **N**umberFormat.Field^
perform_work( ): org.omg.CORBA.**O**RB
PERMILLE: **N**umberFormat.Field^
Permission: java.security

—subclasses: **A**llPermission^ **B**asicPermission^ **F**ilePermission^
  PrivateCredentialPermission^ **S**ervicePermission^
  SocketPermission^ **U**nresolvedPermission^
—descendents: javax.sound.sampled.**A**udioPermission^
  AuthPermission^ java.awt.**A**WTPermission^
  DelegationPermission^ **L**oggingPermission^
  NetPermission^ **P**ropertyPermission^ **R**eflectPermission^
  RuntimePermission^ **S**ecurityPermission^
  SerializablePermission^ **S**QLPermission^ **S**SLPermission^
—passed to: **A**ccessControlContext.checkPermission( )
  AccessControlException( )
  AccessController.checkPermission( )
  java.security.**P**ermission.implies( )
  PermissionCollection < add( ), implies( ) >
  java.security.**P**olicy.implies( ) **P**rotectionDomain.implies( )
  SecurityManager.checkPermission( )
—returned by: **A**ccessControlException^.getPermission( )
  URLConnection.getPermission( )
Permission: java.security.acl
—passed to: **A**cl^.checkPermission( ) *AclEntry*^ < addPermission( ),
  checkPermission( ), removePermission( ) >
PermissionCollection: java.security
—subclasses: **P**ermissions^
—passed to: **P**rotectionDomain( )
—returned by: java.security.**P**ermission.newPermissionCollection( )
  java.security.**P**olicy.getPermissions( )
  javax.security.auth.**P**olicy.getPermissions( )
  ProtectionDomain.getPermissions( )
  SecureClassLoader^.getPermissions( )
  URLClassLoader^.getPermissions( )
Permissions^: java.security
permissions( ): *AclEntry*^
PERSIST_STORE^: org.omg.CORBA
PersistenceDelegate: java.beans
—subclasses: **D**efaultPersistenceDelegate^
—passed to: **E**ncoder.setPersistenceDelegate( )
—returned by: **E**ncoder.getPersistenceDelegate( )
PERSISTENT: **L**ifespanPolicyValue
PhantomReference^: java.lang.ref
PI: **M**ath **S**trictMath
PI_DISABLE_OUTPUT_ESCAPING: *Result*
PI_ENABLE_OUTPUT_ESCAPING: *Result*
Pipe: java.nio.channels
—returned by: **P**ipe.open( ) **S**electorProvider.openPipe( )
Pipe.SinkChannel^: java.nio.channels
—returned by: **P**ipe.sink( )
Pipe.SourceChannel^: java.nio.channels
—returned by: **P**ipe.source( )
PIPE_SIZE: **P**ipedInputStream^
PipedInputStream^: java.io
—passed to: **P**ipedOutputStream^ < connect( ),
  PipedOutputStream( ) >
PipedOutputStream^: java.io
—passed to: **P**ipedInputStream^ < connect( ),
  PipedInputStream( ) >
PipedReader^: java.io
—passed to: **P**ipedWriter^ < connect( ), PipedWriter( ) >
PipedWriter^: java.io
—passed to: **P**ipedReader^ < connect( ), PipedReader( ) >
PKCS8EncodedKeySpec^: java.security.spec
—returned by: **E**ncryptedPrivateKeyInfo.getKeySpec( )
PKIXBuilderParameters^: java.security.cert
PKIXCertPathBuilderResult^: java.security.cert
PKIXCertPathChecker: java.security.cert
—passed to: **P**KIXParameters.addCertPathChecker( )
PKIXCertPathValidatorResult: java.security.cert
—subclasses: **P**KIXCertPathBuilderResult^
PKIXParameters: java.security.cert
—subclasses: **P**KIXBuilderParameters^
PM: **C**alendar
POA^: org.omg.PortableServer

P

—passed to: _ServantActivatorStub^ < etherealize( ), incarnate( ) >
_ServantLocatorStub^ < postinvoke( ), preinvoke( ) >
*AdapterActivatorOperations*ₒ.unknown_adapter( ) **POA**Helper
< insert( ), write( ) > **S**ervantₒ._all_interfaces( )
*ServantActivatorOperations*ₒ < etherealize( ), incarnate( ) >
*ServantLocatorOperations*ₒ < postinvoke( ), preinvoke( ) >
—returned
by: *org.omg.PortableServer.CurrentOperations*ₒ.get_POA( )
org.omg.PortableServer.portable.Delegate < default_POA( ),
poa( ) > **POA**Helper < extract( ), narrow( ), read( ) >
POAOperationsₒ < create_POA( ), find_POA( ), the_children( ),
the_parent( ) > **S**ervantₒ < _default_POA( ), _poa( ) >
poa( ): *org.omg.PortableServer.portable.Delegate*
POAHelper: org.omg.PortableServer
POAManager^: org.omg.PortableServer
—passed to: *POAOperations*ₒ.create_POA( )
—returned by: *POAOperations*ₒ.the_POAManager( )
*POAManagerOperations*ₒ: org.omg.PortableServer
—extended by: *POAManager*^
*POAOperations*ₒ: org.omg.PortableServer
—extended by: *POA*^
Policy: java.security
—passed to: java.security.**P**olicy.setPolicy( )
—returned by: java.security.**P**olicy.getPolicy( )
Policy: javax.security.auth
—passed to: javax.security.auth.**P**olicy.setPolicy( )
—returned by: javax.security.auth.**P**olicy.getPolicy( )
Policy^: org.omg.CORBA
—extended by: *IdAssignmentPolicy*^ *IdUniquenessPolicy*^
ImplicitActivationPolicy^ *LifespanPolicy*^
RequestProcessingPolicy^ *ServantRetentionPolicy*^
ThreadPolicy^
—passed
to: org.omg.CORBA.portable.**D**elegateₒ.set_policy_override( )
LocalObject._set_policy_override( )
*org.omg.CORBA.Object*ₒ._set_policy_override( )
org.omg.CORBA.portable.**O**bjectImpl._set_policy_override( )
*POAOperations*ₒ.create_POA( ) **P**olicyHelper < insert( ),
write( ) > **P**olicyHolder( ) **P**olicyListHelper < insert( ),
write( ) > **P**olicyListHolder( )
—returned by: _PolicyStub^.copy( )
*ClientRequestInfoOperations*ₒ.get_request_policy( )
org.omg.CORBA.portable.**D**elegateₒ.get_policy( )
*DomainManagerOperations*ₒ.get_domain_policy( )
*IORInfoOperations*ₒ.get_effective_policy( )
LocalObject._get_policy( )
*org.omg.CORBA.Object*ₒ._get_policy( )
org.omg.CORBA.portable.**O**bjectImpl._get_policy( )
org.omg.CORBA.**O**RBₒ.create_policy( )
*PolicyFactoryOperations*ₒ.create_policy( ) **P**olicyHelper
< extract( ), narrow( ), read( ) > **P**olicyListHelper
< extract( ), read( ) > *PolicyOperations*ₒ.copy( )
ServerRequestInfoOperations^.get_server_policy( )
—implemented by: _PolicyStub^
—fields: **P**olicyHolder.value **P**olicyListHolder.value
policy_type( ): _PolicyStub^ *PolicyOperations*ₒ
PolicyError^: org.omg.CORBA
—passed to: **P**olicyErrorHelper < insert( ), write( ) >
PolicyErrorHolder( )
—returned by: **P**olicyErrorHelper < extract( ), read( ) >
—thrown by: org.omg.CORBA.**O**RBₒ.create_policy( )
*PolicyFactoryOperations*ₒ.create_policy( )
—fields: **P**olicyErrorHolder.value
PolicyErrorCodeHelper: org.omg.CORBA
PolicyErrorHelper: org.omg.CORBA
PolicyErrorHolder: org.omg.CORBA
PolicyFactory^: org.omg.CORBA.PortableInterceptor
—passed to: *ORBInitInfoOperations*ₒ.register_policy_factory( )
*PolicyFactoryOperations*ₒ: org.omg.CORBA.PortableInterceptor
—extended by: *PolicyFactory*^
PolicyHelper: org.omg.CORBA
PolicyHolder: org.omg.CORBA

PolicyListHelper: org.omg.CORBA
PolicyListHolder: org.omg.CORBA
PolicyNode: java.security.cert
—passed to: **P**KIXCertPathBuilderResult( )
PKIXCertPathValidatorResult( )
—returned by: **P**KIXCertPathValidatorResultₒ.getPolicyTree( )
PolicyNode.getParent( )
*PolicyOperations*ₒ: org.omg.CORBA
—extended by: *IdAssignmentPolicyOperations*ₒ
*IdUniquenessPolicyOperations*ₒ
*ImplicitActivationPolicyOperations*ₒ
*LifespanPolicyOperations*ₒ *org.omg.CORBA.Policy*^
*RequestProcessingPolicyOperations*ₒ
*ServantRetentionPolicyOperations*ₒ
*ThreadPolicyOperations*ₒ
—descendents: *IdAssignmentPolicy*^ *IdUniquenessPolicy*^
ImplicitActivationPolicy^ *LifespanPolicy*^
RequestProcessingPolicy^ *ServantRetentionPolicy*^
ThreadPolicy^
PolicyQualifierInfo: java.security.cert
PolicyTypeHelper: org.omg.CORBA
poll( ): **R**eferenceQueue
poll_next_response( ): org.omg.CORBA.**O**RBₒ
poll_response( ): **R**equest
*PooledConnection*ₒ: javax.sql
—extended by: *XAConnection*^
—passed to: **C**onnectionEvent( )
—returned by: *ConnectionPoolDataSource*.getPooledConnection( )
pop( ): **S**tack^
popContext( ): **N**amespaceSupport
port: **S**ocketImpl
PortableRemoteObject: javax.rmi
PortableRemoteObjectDelegate^: javax.rmi.CORBA
PortUnreachableException^: java.net
pos: **B**ufferedInputStream^ **B**yteArrayInputStream^
CharArrayReader^ **P**ushbackInputStream^
StringBufferInputStream^
position( ): *Blob* **B**uffer^ *Clob* **F**ileChannel^ **F**ileLock
POSITIVE_INFINITY: **D**ouble^ **F**loat^
post_init( ): *ORBInitializerOperations*ₒ
postinvoke( ): _ServantLocatorStub^
*ServantLocatorOperations*ₒ
pow( ): **B**igInteger^ **M**ath **S**trictMath
PRC: **L**ocale
pre_init( ): *ORBInitializerOperations*ₒ
preceding( ): **B**reakIterator
preferenceChange( ): *PreferenceChangeListener*^
PreferenceChangeEvent^: java.util.prefs
—passed to: *PreferenceChangeListener*^.preferenceChange( )
PreferenceChangeListener^: java.util.prefs
—passed to: **P**referencesₒ < addPreferenceChangeListener( ),
removePreferenceChangeListener( ) >
Preferencesₒ: java.util.prefs
—subclasses: **A**bstractPreferences^
—passed to: **N**odeChangeEvent( ) **P**referenceChangeEvent( )
—returned by: **N**odeChangeEvent^ < getChild( ), getParent( ) >
PreferenceChangeEvent^.getNode( ) **P**referencesₒ < node( ),
parent( ), systemNodeForPackage( ), systemRoot( ),
userNodeForPackage( ), userRoot( ) > *PreferencesFactory*
< systemRoot( ), userRoot( ) >
PreferencesFactory: java.util.prefs
preinvoke( ): _ServantLocatorStub^ *ServantLocatorOperations*ₒ
prepare( ): *XAResource*
prepareCall( ): **C**onnection
PreparedStatement^: java.sql
—extended by: *CallableStatement*^
—returned by: **C**onnection.prepareStatement( )
prepareStatement( ): **C**onnection
previous( ): **B**reakIterator *CharacterIterator*ₒ
CollationElementIterator *ListIterator*^ **R**esultSetₒ
StringCharacterIterator
previousDouble( ): **C**hoiceFormat^

P

previousIndex( ): *ListIterator*^
PRIMARY: **C**ollator
primaryOrder( ): **C**ollationElementIterator
Principal: java.security
—extended by: ***Group***^
—passed to: ***Acl***^ < addEntry( ), checkPermission( ),
getPermissions( ), removeEntry( ), setName( ) >
AclEntry^.setPrincipal( ) ***Group***^ < addMember( ), isMember( ),
removeMember( ) > **I**dentityScope^.getIdentity( )
Owner < addOwner( ), deleteOwner( ), isOwner( ) >
ProtectionDomain( ) ***X509KeyManager***^ < chooseClientAlias( ),
chooseServerAlias( ), getClientAliases( ), getServerAliases( ) >
—returned by: ***AclEntry***^.getPrincipal( )
*java.security.**C**ertificate* < getGuarantor( ),
getPrincipal( ) > **P**rotectionDomain.getPrincipals( )
java.security.cert.**X**509Certificate^.getIssuerDN( )
javax.security.cert.**X**509Certificate^.getIssuerDN( )
java.security.cert.**X**509Certificate^.getSubjectDN( )
javax.security.cert.**X**509Certificate^.getSubjectDN( )
X509CRL^.getIssuerDN( )
—implemented by: **I**dentity **K**erberosPrincipal **X**500Principal
Principal: org.omg.CORBA
—passed to: **A**ny.insert_Principal( )
org.omg.CORBA.portable.**O**utputStream^.write_Principal( )
PrincipalHolder( )
—returned by: **A**ny.extract_Principal( )
org.omg.CORBA.portable.**I**nputStream^.read_Principal( )
—fields: **P**rincipalHolder.value
PrincipalHolder: org.omg.CORBA
print( ): **P**rintStream^ **P**rintWriter^
println( ): **D**riverManager **P**rintStream^ **P**rintWriter^
printStackTrace( ): **T**hrowable
PrintStream^: java.io
—subclasses: **L**ogStream^
—passed to: javax.swing.text.**A**bstractDocument.dump( )
javax.swing.text.**A**bstractDocument.AbstractElement.dump( )
java.awt.**C**omponent.list( )
javax.swing.**D**ebugGraphics^.setLogStream( )
DriverManager.setLogStream( ) **L**ogStream^.setDefaultStream( )
Properties^.list( ) **S**ystem < setErr( ), setOut( ) >
Throwable.printStackTrace( )
—returned by: javax.swing.**D**ebugGraphics^.logStream( )
DriverManager.getLogStream( ) **L**ogStream^.getDefaultStream( )
RemoteServer^.getLog( )
—fields: **S**ystem < err, out >
PrintWriter^: java.io
—passed to: java.awt.**C**omponent.list( )
ConnectionPoolDataSource.setLogWriter( )
DataSource.setLogWriter( ) **D**riverManager.setLogWriter( )
Properties^.list( ) **T**hrowable.printStackTrace( )
XADataSource.setLogWriter( )
—returned by: ***ConnectionPoolDataSource***.getLogWriter( )
DataSource.getLogWriter( ) **D**riverManager.getLogWriter( )
XADataSource.getLogWriter( )
PRIVATE: **F**ileChannel.MapMode **M**odifier
PRIVATE_KEY: **C**ipher
PRIVATE_MEMBER: org.omg.CORBA
PRIVATE_USE: **C**haracter
PRIVATE_USE_AREA: **C**haracter.UnicodeBlock^
PrivateCredentialPermission^: javax.security.auth
PrivateKey^: java.security
—extended by: ***DHPrivateKey***^ ***DSAPrivateKey***^
RSAPrivateKey^
—descendents: ***RSAMultiPrimePrivateCrtKey***^
RSAPrivateCrtKey^
—passed to: **K**eyPair( ) **S**ignature^.initSign( )
SignatureSpi.engineInitSign( ) **S**ignedObject( )
X500PrivateCredential( )
—returned by: **K**eyFactory.generatePrivate( )
KeyFactorySpi.engineGeneratePrivate( ) **K**eyPair.getPrivate( )

Signer^.getPrivateKey( ) **X**500PrivateCredential.getPrivateKey( )
X509KeyManager^.getPrivateKey( )
PrivilegedAction: java.security
—passed to: **A**ccessController.doPrivileged( ) **S**ubject < doAs( ),
doAsPrivileged( ) >
PrivilegedActionException: java.security
—thrown by: **A**ccessController.doPrivileged( ) **S**ubject < doAs( ),
doAsPrivileged( ) >
PrivilegedExceptionAction: java.security
—passed to: **A**ccessController.doPrivileged( ) **S**ubject < doAs( ),
doAsPrivileged( ) >
probablePrime( ): **B**igInteger^
procedureColumnIn: *DatabaseMetaData*
procedureColumnInOut: *DatabaseMetaData*
procedureColumnOut: *DatabaseMetaData*
procedureColumnResult: *DatabaseMetaData*
procedureColumnReturn: *DatabaseMetaData*
procedureColumnUnknown: *DatabaseMetaData*
procedureNoNulls: *DatabaseMetaData*
procedureNoResult: *DatabaseMetaData*
procedureNullable: *DatabaseMetaData*
procedureNullableUnknown: *DatabaseMetaData*
procedureResultUnknown: *DatabaseMetaData*
procedureReturnsResult: *DatabaseMetaData*
Process: java.lang
—returned by: **R**untime.exec( )
PROCESSING_INSTRUCTION_NODE: *Node*
ProcessingInstruction^: org.w3c.dom
—returned by: *Document*^.createProcessingInstruction( )
processingInstruction( ): *org.xml.sax.ContentHandler*
DefaultHandler **D**ocumentHandler **H**andlerBase
ParserAdapter **X**MLFilterImpl **X**MLReaderAdapter
processName( ): **N**amespaceSupport
profile_data: **T**aggedProfile
ProfileIdHelper: org.omg.IOP
profiles: **I**OR
propagatedFrom: **B**eanContextEvent^
Properties^: java.util
—subclasses: **P**rovider^
—passed to: **A**ctivationGroupDesc( ) **C**ompoundName( )
Driver < connect( ), getPropertyInfo( ) >
DriverManager.getConnection( ) org.omg.CORBA.**O**RB
< init( ), set_parameters( ) > **P**roperties( )
System.setProperties( ) java.awt.**T**oolkit.getPrintJob( )
Transformer.setOutputProperties( )
—returned by: **A**ctivationGroupDesc.getPropertyOverrides( )
System.getProperties( ) *Templates*.getOutputProperties( )
Transformer.getOutputProperties( )
—fields: **C**ompoundName.mySyntax **P**roperties^.defaults
propertyChange( ): **B**eanContextSupport^
PropertyChangeListener^ **P**ropertyChangeListenerProxy^
PropertyChangeEvent^: java.beans
—passed to: **B**eanContextSupport^
< propertyChange( ), vetoableChange( ) >
javax.swing.table.**D**efaultTableColumnModel.propertyChange( )
javax.swing.**J**List.AccessibleJList^.propertyChange( )
javax.swing.**J**Spinner.DefaultEditor^.propertyChange( )
javax.swing.**J**Table.AccessibleJTable^.propertyChange( )
PropertyChangeListener^.propertyChange( )
PropertyChangeListenerProxy^.propertyChange( )
PropertyChangeSupport^.firePropertyChange( )
PropertyVetoException( )
VetoableChangeListener^.vetoableChange( )
VetoableChangeListenerProxy^.vetoableChange( )
VetoableChangeSupport.fireVetoableChange( )
—returned by: **P**ropertyVetoException.getPropertyChangeEvent( )
PropertyChangeListener^: java.beans
—passed to: javax.swing.**A**bstractAction
< addPropertyChangeListener( ), removePropertyChangeListener( ) >
javax.accessibility.**A**ccessibleContext
< addPropertyChangeListener( ), removePropertyChangeListener( ) >

*javax.swing.*A*ction^* < addPropertyChangeListener( ),
removePropertyChangeListener( ) > *B*eanContextChild⌄
< addPropertyChangeListener( ), removePropertyChangeListener( ) >
*B*eanContextChildSupport⌄ < addPropertyChangeListener( ),
removePropertyChangeListener( ) >
*java.awt.*C*omponent* < addPropertyChangeListener( ),
removePropertyChangeListener( ) > *Customizer*
< addPropertyChangeListener( ), removePropertyChangeListener( ) >
*javax.swing.tree.*D*efaultTreeSelectionModel*
< addPropertyChangeListener( ), removePropertyChangeListener( ) >
*java.awt.*K*eyboardFocusManager*
< addPropertyChangeListener( ), removePropertyChangeListener( ) >
*L*ogManager < addPropertyChangeListener( ),
removePropertyChangeListener( ) >
*P*ropertyChangeListenerProxy( ) *P*ropertyChangeSupport⌄
< addPropertyChangeListener( ), removePropertyChangeListener( ) >
PropertyEditor < addPropertyChangeListener( ),
removePropertyChangeListener( ) > *P*ropertyEditorSupport
< addPropertyChangeListener( ), removePropertyChangeListener( ) >
*javax.swing.table.*T*ableColumn* < addPropertyChangeListener( ),
removePropertyChangeListener( ) > *java.awt.*T*oolkit*
< addPropertyChangeListener( ), removePropertyChangeListener( ) >
*javax.swing.tree.*T*reeSelectionModel*
< addPropertyChangeListener( ), removePropertyChangeListener( ) >
*javax.swing.*U*IDefaults^* < addPropertyChangeListener( ),
removePropertyChangeListener( ) >
*javax.swing.*U*IManager* < addPropertyChangeListener( ),
removePropertyChangeListener( ) >
—returned
  by: *javax.swing.*A*bstractAction.getPropertyChangeListeners( )*
  *javax.swing.*A*bstractButton^* ↩
  .createActionPropertyChangeListener( )
  *B*eanContextSupport^.getChildPropertyChangeListener( )
  *java.awt.*C*omponent.getPropertyChangeListeners( )*
  *javax.swing.tree.*D*efaultTreeSelectionModel* ↩
  .getPropertyChangeListeners( )
  *javax.swing.*J*CheckBox^.createActionPropertyChangeListener( )*
  *javax.swing.*J*ComboBox^.createActionPropertyChangeListener( )*
  *javax.swing.*J*Menu^.createActionChangeListener( )*
  *javax.swing.*J*MenuItem^.createActionPropertyChangeListener( )*
  *javax.swing.*J*PopupMenu^.createActionChangeListener( )*
  *javax.swing.*J*RadioButton^.createActionPropertyChangeListener( )*
  *javax.swing.*J*TextField^.createActionPropertyChangeListener( )*
  *javax.swing.*J*ToolBar^.createActionChangeListener( )*
  *java.awt.*K*eyboardFocusManager.getPropertyChangeListeners( )*
  *P*ropertyChangeSupport⌄.getPropertyChangeListeners( )
  *javax.swing.table.*T*ableColumn.getPropertyChangeListeners( )*
  *java.awt.*T*oolkit.getPropertyChangeListeners( )*
  *javax.swing.*U*IDefaults^.getPropertyChangeListeners( )*
  *javax.swing.*U*IManager.getPropertyChangeListeners( )*
—implemented by: *B*eanContextSupport^
  *javax.swing.table.*D*efaultTableColumnModel*
  *javax.swing.*J*List.AccessibleJList^*
  *javax.swing.*J*Spinner.DefaultEditor^*
  *javax.swing.*J*Table.AccessibleJTable^*
  *P*ropertyChangeListenerProxy^
PropertyChangeListenerProxy^: java.beans
PropertyChangeSupport⌄: java.beans
—subclasses: *javax.swing.event.*S*wingPropertyChangeSupport^*
—fields: *B*eanContextChildSupport⌄.pcSupport
  *java.awt.*T*oolkit.desktopPropsSupport*
PropertyDescriptor^: java.beans
—subclasses: *I*ndexedPropertyDescriptor^
—returned by: *BeanInfo*⌄.getPropertyDescriptors( )
  *S*impleBeanInfo.getPropertyDescriptors( )
PropertyEditor: java.beans
—returned by: *P*ropertyEditorManager.findEditor( )
—implemented by: *P*ropertyEditorSupport

PropertyEditorManager: java.beans
PropertyEditorSupport: java.beans
PROPERTYNAME: *DesignMode*⌄
propertyNames( ): *P*roperties^
PropertyPermission^: java.util
PropertyResourceBundle^: java.util
PropertyVetoException: java.beans
—thrown by: *B*eanContextChild⌄.setBeanContext( )
  *B*eanContextChildSupport⌄ < fireVetoableChange( ),
  setBeanContext( ) > *B*eanContextSupport^
  < setLocale( ), vetoableChange( ) >
  *javax.swing.*J*Component^.fireVetoableChange( )*
  *javax.swing.*J*InternalFrame^* < setClosed( ),
  setIcon( ), setMaximum( ), setSelected( ) >
  *java.awt.*K*eyboardFocusManager.fireVetoableChange( )*
  VetoableChangeListener^.vetoableChange( )
  *V*etoableChangeListenerProxy^.vetoableChange( )
  *V*etoableChangeSupport.fireVetoableChange( )
PROTECTED: *M*odifier
ProtectionDomain: java.security
—passed to: *A*ccessControlContext( )
  *C*lassLoader⌄.defineClass( ) *DomainCombiner*.combine( )
  *java.security.*P*olicy* < getPermissions( ), implies( ) >
  *S*ubjectDomainCombiner.combine( )
—returned by: *C*lass.getProtectionDomain( )
  DomainCombiner.combine( )
  *S*ubjectDomainCombiner.combine( )
PROTOCOL_VERSION_1: *ObjectStreamConstants*
PROTOCOL_VERSION_2: *ObjectStreamConstants*
ProtocolException^: java.net
—thrown by: *H*ttpURLConnection^.setRequestMethod( )
Provider^: java.security
—passed to: *A*lgorithmParameterGenerator
  < AlgorithmParameterGenerator( ), getInstance( ) >
  *A*lgorithmParameters < AlgorithmParameters( ), getInstance( ) >
  *C*ertificateFactory < CertificateFactory( ), getInstance( ) >
  *C*ertPathBuilder < CertPathBuilder( ), getInstance( ) >
  *C*ertPathValidator < CertPathValidator( ), getInstance( ) >
  *C*ertStore < CertStore( ), getInstance( ) > *C*ipher⌄
  < Cipher( ), getInstance( ) > *E*xemptionMechanism
  < ExemptionMechanism( ), getInstance( ) > *G*SSManager
  < addProviderAtEnd( ), addProviderAtFront( ) > *K*eyAgreement
  < getInstance( ), KeyAgreement( ) > *K*eyFactory < getInstance( ),
  KeyFactory( ) > *K*eyGenerator < getInstance( ),
  KeyGenerator( ) > *K*eyManagerFactory < getInstance( ),
  KeyManagerFactory( ) > *K*eyPairGenerator^.getInstance( )
  *K*eyStore < getInstance( ), KeyStore( ) > *M*ac < getInstance( ),
  Mac( ) > *M*essageDigest^.getInstance( ) *S*ecretKeyFactory
  < getInstance( ), SecretKeyFactory( ) > *S*ecureRandom^
  < getInstance( ), SecureRandom( ) > *S*ecurity < addProvider( ),
  insertProviderAt( ) > *S*ignature^.getInstance( ) *S*SLContext
  < getInstance( ), SSLContext( ) > *T*rustManagerFactory
  < getInstance( ), TrustManagerFactory( ) >
—returned by: *A*lgorithmParameterGenerator.getProvider( )
  *A*lgorithmParameters.getProvider( )
  *C*ertificateFactory.getProvider( ) *C*ertPathBuilder.getProvider( )
  *C*ertPathValidator.getProvider( ) *C*ertStore.getProvider( )
  *C*ipher⌄.getProvider( ) *E*xemptionMechanism.getProvider( )
  *K*eyAgreement.getProvider( ) *K*eyFactory.getProvider( )
  *K*eyGenerator.getProvider( ) *K*eyManagerFactory.getProvider( )
  *K*eyPairGenerator^.getProvider( ) *K*eyStore.getProvider( )
  *M*ac.getProvider( ) *M*essageDigest^.getProvider( )
  *S*ecretKeyFactory.getProvider( ) *S*ecureRandom^.getProvider( )
  *S*ecurity < getProvider( ), getProviders( ) >
  *S*ignature^.getProvider( ) *S*SLContext.getProvider( )
  *T*rustManagerFactory.getProvider( )
provider( ): *S*electableChannel^ *S*elector⌄ *S*electorProvider
PROVIDER_URL: *javax.naming.*C*ontext*⌄
ProviderException: java.security
proxy: *B*eanContextServicesSupport^
Proxy: java.lang.reflect

P

Cross-Ref

PSSParameterSpec: java.security.spec
PUBLIC: *Member* Modifier
PUBLIC_KEY: **C**ipher
PUBLIC_MEMBER: org.omg.CORBA
*PublicKey*ʾ: java.security
  —extended by: *D*HPublicKeyʾ *D*SAPublicKeyʾ *R*SAPublicKeyʾ
  —passed to: java.security.cert.**C**ertificate .verify( )
    javax.security.cert.**C**ertificate .verify( ) **I**dentity .setPublicKey( )
    IdentityScopeʾ.getIdentity( ) **K**eyPair( )
    PKIXCertPathBuilderResult( ) **P**KIXCertPathValidatorResult( )
    Signatureʾ.initVerify( ) **S**ignatureSpi .engineInitVerify( )
    SignedObject.verify( ) **T**rustAnchor( )
    X509CertSelector.setSubjectPublicKey( ) **X**509CRLʾ.verify( )
  —returned by: java.security.cert.**C**ertificate .getPublicKey( )
    java.security.Certificate.getPublicKey( )
    javax.security.cert.**C**ertificate .getPublicKey( )
    Identity .getPublicKey( ) **K**eyFactory.generatePublic( )
    KeyFactorySpi.engineGeneratePublic( ) **K**eyPair.getPublic( )
    PKIXCertPathValidatorResult .getPublicKey( )
    TrustAnchor.getCAPublicKey( )
    X509CertSelector.getSubjectPublicKey( )
publish( ): **H**andler
push( ): **M**emoryHandlerʾ **S**tackʾ
pushBack( ): **S**treamTokenizer
PushbackInputStreamʾ: java.io
PushbackReaderʾ: java.io
pushContext( ): **N**amespaceSupport
put( ): **A**bstractMap java.util.jar.**A**ttributes
  *javax.naming.directory.Attributes*ʾ **B**asicAttributes
  ByteBufferʾ **C**harBufferʾ **D**ictionary **D**oubleBufferʾ
  FloatBufferʾ **I**ntBufferʾ **L**ongBufferʾ *Map*
  ObjectOutputStream.PutField **P**references **S**hortBufferʾ
putAll( ): **A**bstractMap java.util.jar.**A**ttributes **H**ashtableʾ
  Map
putBoolean( ): **P**references
putByteArray( ): **P**references
putChar( ): **B**yteBufferʾ
putDouble( ): **B**yteBufferʾ **P**references
putFields( ): **O**bjectOutputStreamʾ
putFloat( ): **B**yteBufferʾ **P**references
putInt( ): **B**yteBufferʾ **P**references
putLong( ): **B**yteBufferʾ **P**references
putNextEntry( ): **Z**ipOutputStreamʾ
putShort( ): **B**yteBufferʾ
putSpi( ): **A**bstractPreferencesʾ
putValue( ): java.util.jar.**A**ttributes *SSLSession*
quoteChar( ): **S**treamTokenizer
Random: java.util
  —subclasses: **S**ecureRandomʾ
  —passed to: **B**igIntegerʾ < BigInteger( ), probablePrime( ) >
    Collections.shuffle( )
random( ): **M**ath **S**trictMath
RandomAccess: java.util
  —implemented by: **A**rrayListʾ **V**ectorʾ
RandomAccessFile: java.io
  —passed to: javax.imageio.stream.**F**ileImageInputStream( )
    javax.imageio.stream.**F**ileImageOutputStream( )
RC2ParameterSpec: javax.crypto.spec
RC5ParameterSpec: javax.crypto.spec
read( ): **A**dapterAlreadyExistsHelper **A**dapterInactiveHelper
  AdapterNonExistentHelper **A**ddressHelper
  AlreadyBoundHelper org.omg.CORBA.**A**nySeqHelper
  org.omg.DynamicAny.**A**nySeqHelper **B**indingHelper
  BindingIteratorHelper **B**indingListHelper
  BindingTypeHelper **B**ooleanSeqHelper
  CannotProceedHelper **C**harSeqHelper
  CodecFactoryHelper **C**ompletionStatusHelper
  ComponentIdHelper org.omg.CORBA.**C**urrentHelper
  org.omg.PortableInterceptor.**C**urrentHelper
  org.omg.PortableServer.**C**urrentHelper
  DatagramChannelʾ **D**efinitionKindHelper
  DoubleSeqHelper **D**uplicateNameHelper

DynAnyFactoryHelper **D**ynAnyHelper **D**ynAnySeqHelper
DynArrayHelper **D**ynEnumHelper **D**ynFixedHelper
DynSequenceHelper **D**ynStructHelper **D**ynUnionHelper
DynValueHelper org.omg.CORBA.**F**ieldNameHelper
org.omg.DynamicAny.**F**ieldNameHelper **F**ileChannelʾ
FloatSeqHelper **F**ormatMismatchHelper
org.omg.PortableInterceptor.**F**orwardRequestHelper
org.omg.PortableServer.**F**orwardRequestHelper
IdentifierHelper **I**DLTypeHelper
InconsistentTypeCodeHelper java.io.**I**nputStream
InvalidAddressHelper org.omg.CosNaming ↵
  .NamingContextPackage.**I**nvalidNameHelper
org.omg.PortableInterceptor.ORBInitInfoPackage ↵
  .**I**nvalidNameHelper **I**nvalidPolicyHelper
InvalidSlotHelper **I**nvalidTypeForEncodingHelper
InvalidValueHelper **I**ORHelper **I**stringHelper
LongLongSeqHelper **L**ongSeqHelper **M**anifest
MultipleComponentProfileHelper **N**ameComponentHelper
NameDynAnyPairHelper **N**ameDynAnyPairSeqHelper
NameHelper org.omg.CORBA.**N**ameValuePairHelper
org.omg.DynamicAny.**N**ameValuePairHelper
NameValuePairSeqHelper **N**amingContextExtHelper
NamingContextHelper **N**oContextHelper **N**oServantHelper
NotEmptyHelper **N**otFoundHelper **N**otFoundReasonHelper
ObjectAlreadyActiveHelper **O**bjectHelper **O**bjectIdHelper
*ObjectInput*ʾ **O**bjectNotActiveHelper **O**bjID
OctetSeqHelper **P**arameterModeHelper **P**OAHelper
PolicyErrorCodeHelper **P**olicyErrorHelper **P**olicyHelper
PolicyListHelper **P**olicyTypeHelper **P**rofileIdHelper
RandomAccessFile *ReadableByteChannel*ʾ **R**eader
RepositoryIdHelper **S**ervantActivatorHelper
ServantAlreadyActiveHelper **S**ervantLocatorHelper
ServantNotActiveHelper **S**erviceContextHelper
ServiceContextListHelper **S**erviceDetailHelper
ServiceIdHelper **S**erviceInformationHelper
SetOverrideTypeHelper **S**hortSeqHelper **S**ocketChannelʾ
StringNameHelper **S**tringSeqHelper **S**tringValueHelper
StructMemberHelper **S**yncScopeHelper
TaggedComponentHelper **T**aggedProfileHelper
org.omg.DynamicAny.DynAnyPackage.**T**ypeMismatchHelper
org.omg.IOP.CodecPackage.**T**ypeMismatchHelper
UID **U**LongLongSeqHelper **U**LongSeqHelper
UnionMemberHelper **U**nknownEncodingHelper
UnknownUserExceptionHelper **U**RLStringHelper
UShortSeqHelper **V**alueBaseHelper **V**alueMemberHelper
VersionSpecHelper **V**isibilityHelper **W**CharSeqHelper
WrongAdapterHelper **W**rongPolicyHelper
WrongTransactionHelper **W**StringSeqHelper
WStringValueHelper
read_Abstract( ): *org.omg.CORBA.DataInputStream*ʾ
read_abstract_interface( ):
  org.omg.CORBA_2_3.portable.**I**nputStreamʾ
read_any( ): *org.omg.CORBA.DataInputStream*ʾ
  org.omg.CORBA.portable.**I**nputStreamʾ
read_any_array( ): *org.omg.CORBA.DataInputStream*ʾ
read_boolean( ): *org.omg.CORBA.DataInputStream*ʾ
  org.omg.CORBA.portable.**I**nputStreamʾ
read_boolean_array( ): *org.omg.CORBA.DataInputStream*ʾ
  org.omg.CORBA.portable.**I**nputStreamʾ
read_char( ): *org.omg.CORBA.DataInputStream*ʾ
  org.omg.CORBA.portable.**I**nputStreamʾ
read_char_array( ): *org.omg.CORBA.DataInputStream*ʾ
  org.omg.CORBA.portable.**I**nputStreamʾ
read_Context( ): org.omg.CORBA.portable.**I**nputStreamʾ
read_double( ): *org.omg.CORBA.DataInputStream*ʾ
  org.omg.CORBA.portable.**I**nputStreamʾ
read_double_array( ): *org.omg.CORBA.DataInputStream*ʾ
  org.omg.CORBA.portable.**I**nputStreamʾ
read_fixed( ): org.omg.CORBA.portable.**I**nputStreamʾ
read_float( ): *org.omg.CORBA.DataInputStream*ʾ
  org.omg.CORBA.portable.**I**nputStreamʾ

P

read_float_array(): *org.omg.CORBA.DataInputStream^*
org.omg.CORBA.portable.**I**nputStream°
read_long(): *org.omg.CORBA.DataInputStream^*
org.omg.CORBA.portable.**I**nputStream°
read_long_array(): *org.omg.CORBA.DataInputStream^*
org.omg.CORBA.portable.**I**nputStream°
read_longlong(): *org.omg.CORBA.DataInputStream^*
org.omg.CORBA.portable.**I**nputStream°
read_longlong_array(): *org.omg.CORBA.DataInputStream^*
org.omg.CORBA.portable.**I**nputStream°
read_Object(): *org.omg.CORBA.DataInputStream^*
org.omg.CORBA.portable.**I**nputStream°
read_octet(): *org.omg.CORBA.DataInputStream^*
org.omg.CORBA.portable.**I**nputStream°
read_octet_array(): *org.omg.CORBA.DataInputStream^*
org.omg.CORBA.portable.**I**nputStream°
READ_ONLY: **F**ileChannel.MapMode
read_Principal(): org.omg.CORBA.portable.**I**nputStream°
read_short(): *org.omg.CORBA.DataInputStream^*
org.omg.CORBA.portable.**I**nputStream°
read_short_array(): *org.omg.CORBA.DataInputStream^*
org.omg.CORBA.portable.**I**nputStream°
read_string(): *org.omg.CORBA.DataInputStream^*
org.omg.CORBA.portable.**I**nputStream°
read_TypeCode(): *org.omg.CORBA.DataInputStream^*
org.omg.CORBA.portable.**I**nputStream°
read_ulong(): *org.omg.CORBA.DataInputStream^*
org.omg.CORBA.portable.**I**nputStream°
read_ulong_array(): *org.omg.CORBA.DataInputStream^*
org.omg.CORBA.portable.**I**nputStream°
read_ulonglong(): *org.omg.CORBA.DataInputStream^*
org.omg.CORBA.portable.**I**nputStream°
read_ulonglong_array(): *org.omg.CORBA.DataInputStream^*
org.omg.CORBA.portable.**I**nputStream°
read_ushort(): *org.omg.CORBA.DataInputStream^*
org.omg.CORBA.portable.**I**nputStream°
read_ushort_array(): *org.omg.CORBA.DataInputStream^*
org.omg.CORBA.portable.**I**nputStream°
read_value(): **A**ny *BoxedValueHelper*
org.omg.CORBA_2_3.portable.**I**nputStream^
StringValueHelper *ValueFactory* **W**StringValueHelper
read_Value(): *org.omg.CORBA.DataInputStream^*
org.omg.CORBA.portable.**I**nputStream°
read_wchar(): *org.omg.CORBA.DataInputStream^*
org.omg.CORBA.portable.**I**nputStream°
read_wchar_array(): *org.omg.CORBA.DataInputStream^*
org.omg.CORBA.portable.**I**nputStream°
READ_WRITE: **F**ileChannel.MapMode
read_wstring(): *org.omg.CORBA.DataInputStream^*
org.omg.CORBA.portable.**I**nputStream°
ReadableByteChannel°: java.nio.channels
—extended by: *ByteChannel^* *ScatteringByteChannel^*
—passed to: **C**hannels < newInputStream( ), newReader( ) >
FileChannel^.transferFrom( )
—returned by: **C**hannels.newChannel( )
—implemented by: **P**ipe.SourceChannel^
readAny(): **U**til *UtilDelegate*
readArray(): *SQLInput*
readAsciiStream(): *SQLInput*
readBigDecimal(): *SQLInput*
readBinaryStream(): *SQLInput*
readBlob(): *SQLInput*
readBoolean(): *DataInput* java.io.**D**ataInputStream^
ObjectInputStream^ **R**andomAccessFile *SQLInput*
readByte(): *DataInput* java.io.**D**ataInputStream^
ObjectInputStream^ **R**andomAccessFile *SQLInput*
readBytes(): *SQLInput*
readChar(): *DataInput* java.io.**D**ataInputStream^
ObjectInputStream^ **R**andomAccessFile
readCharacterStream(): *SQLInput*
readChildren(): **B**eanContextSupport°
readClassDescriptor(): **O**bjectInputStream^
readClob(): *SQLInput*

readConfiguration(): **L**ogManager
readData(): *RowSetReader*
readDate(): *SQLInput*
readDouble(): *DataInput* java.io.**D**ataInputStream^
ObjectInputStream^ **R**andomAccessFile *SQLInput*
Reader°: java.io
—subclasses: **B**ufferedReader° **C**harArrayReader^
FilterReader° **I**nputStreamReader° **P**ipedReader^
StringReader^
—descendents: **F**ileReader^ **L**ineNumberReader^
PushbackReader^
—passed to: **B**ufferedReader( )
CallableStatement^.setCharacterStream( )
javax.swing.text.html.parser.**D**ocumentParser^.parse( )
javax.swing.text.**E**ditorKit.read( ) **F**ilterReader( )
javax.swing.text.html.**H**TMLEditorKit.Parser.parse( )
InputSource < InputSource( ), setCharacterStream( ) >
javax.swing.text.**J**TextComponent^.read( )
LineNumberReader( )
javax.swing.text.html.parser.**P**arser.parse( )
PreparedStatement^.setCharacterStream( )
PushbackReader( ) *ResultSet*_.updateCharacterStream( )
RowSet^.setCharacterStream( )
SQLOutput.writeCharacterStream( ) **S**treamSource
< setReader( ), StreamSource( ) > **S**treamTokenizer( )
javax.swing.text.html.**S**tyleSheet^.loadRules( )
—returned by: **C**hannels.newReader( ) *Clob*.getCharacterStream( )
java.awt.datatransfer.**D**ataFlavor.getReaderForText( )
javax.print.Doc.getReaderForText( )
InputSource.getCharacterStream( )
*ResultSet*_.getCharacterStream( )
javax.print.**S**impleDoc.getReaderForText( )
SQLInput.readCharacterStream( ) **S**treamSource.getReader( )
—fields: **F**ilterReader°.in
readExternal(): *Externalizable*°
readFields(): **O**bjectInputStream^
readFloat(): *DataInput* java.io.**D**ataInputStream^
ObjectInputStream^ **R**andomAccessFile *SQLInput*
readFully(): *DataInput* java.io.**D**ataInputStream^
ObjectInputStream^ **R**andomAccessFile
READING: **A**ttributedCharacterIterator.Attribute_
readInt(): *DataInput* java.io.**D**ataInputStream^
ObjectInputStream^ **R**andomAccessFile *SQLInput*
readLine(): **B**ufferedReader° *DataInput*_
java.io.**D**ataInputStream^ **O**bjectInputStream^
RandomAccessFile
readLong(): *DataInput* java.io.**D**ataInputStream^
ObjectInputStream^ **R**andomAccessFile *SQLInput*
readObject(): *ObjectInput*^ **O**bjectInputStream^ *SQLInput*
StubDelegate **X**MLDecoder
readObjectOverride(): **O**bjectInputStream^
ReadOnlyBufferException^: java.nio
readRef(): *SQLInput*
readResolve(): **A**ttributedCharacterIterator.Attribute_
Certificate.CertificateRep **C**ertPath.CertPathRep
readShort(): *DataInput*_ java.io.**D**ataInputStream^
ObjectInputStream^ **R**andomAccessFile *SQLInput*
readSQL(): *SQLData*
readStreamHeader(): **O**bjectInputStream^
readString(): *SQLInput*
readTime(): *SQLInput*
readTimestamp(): *SQLInput*
readUnshared(): **O**bjectInputStream^
readUnsignedByte(): *DataInput*_ java.io.**D**ataInputStream^
ObjectInputStream^ **R**andomAccessFile
readUnsignedShort(): *DataInput*_ java.io.**D**ataInputStream^
ObjectInputStream^ **R**andomAccessFile
readURL(): *SQLInput*
readUTF(): *DataInput*_ java.io.**D**ataInputStream^
ObjectInputStream^ **R**andomAccessFile
readValue(): *ValueHandler*

R

ready(): Reader⌄
readyOps(): SelectionKey⌄
REAL: Types
reason: PolicyError^
rebind(): _NamingContextExtStub^ _NamingContextStub^
  javax.naming.Context⌄ InitialContext⌄ Naming
  NamingContextOperations⌄ *Registry*⌄
rebind_context(): _NamingContextExtStub^
  _NamingContextStub^ *NamingContextOperations*⌄
receive(): DatagramChannel^ DatagramSocket⌄
  DatagramSocketImpl PipedInputStream^
receive_exception(): *ClientRequestInterceptorOperations*⌄
receive_other(): *ClientRequestInterceptorOperations*⌄
receive_reply(): *ClientRequestInterceptorOperations*⌄
receive_request(): *ServerRequestInterceptorOperations*⌄
receive_request_service_contexts():
  ServerRequestInterceptorOperations⌄
received_exception(): *ClientRequestInfoOperations*⌄
received_exception_id(): *ClientRequestInfoOperations*⌄
reconnect(): InitialLdapContext^ *LdapContext*^
recover(): *XAResource*
Rectangle^: java.awt
—passed to: *PropertyEditor*.paintValue()
  PropertyEditorSupport.paintValue()
ref: RemoteObject⌄
REF: Types
Ref: java.sql
—passed to: *PreparedStatement*^.setRef()
  ResultSet⌄.updateRef() *RowSet*^.setRef()
  SQLOutput.writeRef()
—returned by: *CallableStatement*^.getRef() *ResultSet*⌄.getRef()
  SQLInput.readRef()
RefAddr^: javax.naming
—subclasses: BinaryRefAddr^ StringRefAddr^
—passed to: javax.naming.Reference^ < add(), Reference() >
—returned by: javax.naming.Reference^⌄.get()
Reference^: java.lang.ref
—subclasses: PhantomReference^ SoftReference^
  WeakReference^
—returned by: ReferenceQueue < poll(), remove() >
Reference^: javax.naming
—subclasses: LinkRef^
—returned by: *Referenceable*.getReference()
reference_to_id(): *POAOperations*⌄
reference_to_servant(): *POAOperations*⌄
Referenceable: javax.naming
ReferenceQueue: java.lang.ref
—passed to: PhantomReference() SoftReference()
  WeakReference()
REFERRAL: *javax.naming.Context*⌄
ReferralException^: javax.naming
—subclasses: LdapReferralException^
ReflectPermission^: java.lang.reflect
refresh(): Configuration KerberosTicket java.security.Policy
  javax.security.auth.Policy *Refreshable*
Refreshable: javax.security.auth
—implemented by: KerberosTicket
RefreshFailedException: javax.security.auth
—thrown by: KerberosTicket.refresh() *Refreshable*.refresh()
refreshRow(): *ResultSet*⌄
regionMatches(): String
register(): *AbstractSelector*^ *Activatable*^ SelectableChannel^
register_initial_reference(): *ORBInitInfoOperations*⌄
register_policy_factory(): *ORBInitInfoOperations*⌄
register_value_factory(): org.omg.CORBA_2_3.ORB^
registerDriver(): DriverManager
registerEditor(): PropertyEditorManager
registerGroup(): *ActivationSystem*^
registerObject(): *ActivationSystem*^
registerOutParameter(): *CallableStatement*^
registerTarget(): Util *UtilDelegate*
registerValidation(): ObjectInputStream^

Registry^: java.rmi.registry
—returned by: LocateRegistry < createRegistry(), getRegistry() >
  RegistryHandler < registryImpl(), registryStub() >
REGISTRY_ID: ObjID
REGISTRY_PORT: *Registry*^
RegistryHandler: java.rmi.registry
registryImpl(): *RegistryHandler*
registryStub(): *RegistryHandler*
rehash(): Hashtable^
rejectedSetBCOnce: BeanContextChildSupport⌄
relative(): *ResultSet*⌄
relativize(): URI
release(): org.omg.CORBA.portable.*Delegate*⌄ FileLock
releaseBeanContextResources(): BeanContextChildSupport⌄
releaseInputStream(): *RemoteCall*
releaseOutputStream(): *RemoteCall*
releaseReply(): org.omg.CORBA.portable.*Delegate*⌄
releaseSavepoint(): *Connection*
releaseService(): *BeanContextServiceProvider*
  BeanContextServices^ BeanContextServicesSupport^
  BeanContextServicesSupport.BCSSProxyServiceProvider
remainder(): BigInteger^
remaining(): Buffer⌄
remainingName: NamingException⌄ ResolveResult
remainingNewName: CannotProceedException^
RemarshalException: org.omg.CORBA.portable
—thrown by: org.omg.CORBA.portable.*Delegate*⌄.invoke()
  LocalObject._invoke()
  org.omg.CORBA.portable.ObjectImpl⌄._invoke()
Remote⌄: java.rmi
—extended by: *ActivationInstantiator*^ *ActivationMonitor*^
  ActivationSystem^ *Activator*^ *DGC*^ *Registry*^
—passed to: *Activatable*^ < exportObject(), unexportObject() >
  ActivationGroup^.activeObject() Naming < bind(), rebind() >
  PortableRemoteObject < connect(), exportObject(), toStub(),
  unexportObject() > *PortableRemoteObjectDelegate*
  < connect(), exportObject(), toStub(), unexportObject() >
  Registry^ < bind(), rebind() > RemoteObject⌄.toStub()
  RemoteRef^.invoke() *ServerRef*^.exportObject()
  Skeleton.dispatch() *Tie*^.setTarget() UnicastRemoteObject⌄
  < exportObject(), unexportObject() > Util < getTie(),
  registerTarget(), unexportObject() > *UtilDelegate* < getTie(),
  registerTarget(), unexportObject() >
—returned by: *Activatable*^ < exportObject(),
  register() > ActivationID.activate()
  Naming.lookup() PortableRemoteObject.toStub()
  PortableRemoteObjectDelegate.toStub() *Registry*^.lookup()
  RemoteObject⌄.toStub() *Tie*^.getTarget()
  UnicastRemoteObject⌄.exportObject()
—implemented by: _Remote_Stub^ RemoteObject⌄
RemoteCall: java.rmi.server
—passed to: *RemoteRef*^ < done(), invoke() >
  Skeleton.dispatch()
—returned by: *RemoteRef*^.newCall()
remoteEquals(): *RemoteRef*^
RemoteException^: java.rmi
—subclasses: AccessException^ ActivateFailedException^
  java.rmi.ConnectException^ ConnectIOException^
  ExportException^ InvalidTransactionException^
  MarshalException^ NoSuchObjectException^ ServerError^
  ServerException^ ServerRuntimeException^
  SkeletonMismatchException^ SkeletonNotFoundException^
  StubNotFoundException^ TransactionRequiredException^
  TransactionRolledbackException^ UnexpectedException^
  java.rmi.UnknownHostException^ UnmarshalException^
—descendents: SocketSecurityException^
—returned by: Util < mapSystemException(), wrapException() >
  UtilDelegate < mapSystemException(), wrapException() >
—thrown by: *Activatable*^ < Activatable(), exportObject(),
  inactive(), register(), unregister() > ActivationGroup^
  < ActivationGroup(), activeObject(), inactiveGroup(),
  inactiveObject() > ActivationGroup_Stub^.newInstance()

R

R

RequestProcessingPolicyValue: org.omg.PortableServer
—passed to: *POAOperations*⌐.create_request_processing_policy( )
—returned by: *RequestProcessingPolicyOperations*⌐.value( )
RequestProcessingPolicyValue.from_int( )
—fields: RequestProcessingPolicyValue
< USE_ACTIVE_OBJECT_MAP_ONLY, USE_DEFAULT_SERVANT,
USE_SERVANT_MANAGER >
requestReplayDet( ): *GSSContext*
requestSequenceDet( ): *GSSContext*
required: DriverPropertyInfo
REQUIRED: AppConfigurationEntry.LoginModuleControlFlag
requiresBidi( ): Bidi
REQUISITE: AppConfigurationEntry.LoginModuleControlFlag
reset( ): Adler32 Buffer⌐ ByteArrayOutputStream^
CharArrayWriter^ CharsetDecoder CharsetEncoder
Checksum CollationElementIterator CRC32 Deflater
Inflater java.io.InputStream⌐ LogManager Mac Matcher
MessageDigest^ NamespaceSupport ObjectOutputStream^
Reader⌐
resetSyntax( ): StreamTokenizer
resolve( ): _NamingContextExtStub^ _NamingContextStub^
NamingContextOperations⌐ URI *URIResolver*
resolve_initial_references( ): org.omg.CORBA.ORB⌐
ORBInitInfoOperations⌐
resolve_str( ): _NamingContextExtStub^
NamingContextExtOperations⌐
resolveClass( ): ClassLoader⌐ ObjectInputStream^
resolvedName: NamingException⌐
resolvedObj: NamingException⌐ ResolveResult
resolveEntity( ): DefaultHandler *EntityResolver* HandlerBase
XMLFilterImpl
resolveObject( ): ObjectInputStream^
resolveProxyClass( ): ObjectInputStream^
Resolver: javax.naming.spi
ResolveResult: javax.naming.spi
—returned by: *Resolver*.resolveToClass( )
resolveToClass( ): *Resolver*
ResourceBundle⌐: java.util
—subclasses: ListResourceBundle^ PropertyResourceBundle^
—descendents: javax.accessibility.AccessibleResourceBundle^
—passed to: java.awt.ComponentOrientation.getOrientation( )
LogRecord.setResourceBundle( ) ResourceBundle⌐.setParent( )
java.awt.Window^.applyResourceBundle( )
—returned by: Logger.getResourceBundle( )
LogRecord.getResourceBundle( ) ResourceBundle⌐.getBundle( )
—fields: ResourceBundle⌐.parent
response_expected( ): *RequestInfoOperations*⌐
responseCode: HttpURLConnection^
ResponseHandler: org.omg.CORBA.portable
—passed to: BindingIteratorPOA^._invoke( )
InvokeHandler⌐._invoke( ) NamingContextExtPOA^._invoke( )
NamingContextPOA^._invoke( )
ServantActivatorPOA^._invoke( )
ServantLocatorPOA^._invoke( )
responseMessage: HttpURLConnection^
rest_of_name: CannotProceed^ NotFound^
Result: javax.xml.transform
—passed to: Transformer.transform( )
TransformerHandler^.setResult( )
—implemented by: DOMResult SAXResult StreamResult
result( ): Request *RequestInfoOperations*⌐ ServerRequest
ResultSet⌐: java.sql
—extended by: *RowSet*^
—returned by: java.sql.*Array*.getResultSet( ) *DatabaseMetaData*
< getAttributes( ), getBestRowIdentifier( ), getCatalogs( ),
getColumnPrivileges( ), getColumns( ), getCrossReference( ),
getExportedKeys( ), getImportedKeys( ), getIndexInfo( ),
getPrimaryKeys( ), getProcedureColumns( ), getProcedures( ),
getSchemas( ), getSuperTables( ), getSuperTypes( ),
getTablePrivileges( ), getTables( ), getTableTypes( ),
getTypeInfo( ), getUDTs( ), getVersionColumns( ) >
PreparedStatement^.executeQuery( ) *RowSetInternal*

< getOriginal( ), getOriginalRow( ) > java.sql.*Statement*⌐
< executeQuery( ), getGeneratedKeys( ), getResultSet( ) >
ResultSetMetaData⌐: java.sql
—extended by: *RowSetMetaData*^
—returned by: *PreparedStatement*^.getMetaData( )
ResultSet⌐.getMetaData( )
resume( ): Thread ThreadGroup
RETAIN: ServantRetentionPolicyValue
retainAll( ): AbstractCollection⌐ BeanContextSupport^
Collection⌐
retryReferral( ): ReferralException^
RETURN_GENERATED_KEYS: java.sql.*Statement*⌐
return_value( ): Request
reverse( ): Collections StringBuffer
reverseOrder( ): Collections
revokeService( ): *BeanContextServices*^
BeanContextServicesSupport^
rewind( ): _DynAnyStub^ _DynArrayStub^ _DynEnumStub^
_DynFixedStub^ _DynSequenceStub^ _DynStructStub^
_DynUnionStub^ _DynValueStub^ Buffer⌐
org.omg.CORBA.*DynAny*⌐ *DynAnyOperations*⌐
RFC1779: X500Principal
RFC2253: X500Principal
rint( ): Math StrictMath
RMIClassLoader: java.rmi.server
RMIClassLoaderSpi: java.rmi.server
—returned by: RMIClassLoader.getDefaultProviderInstance( )
RMIClientSocketFactory: java.rmi.server
—passed to: Activatable^ < Activatable( ), exportObject( ) >
LocateRegistry < createRegistry( ), getRegistry( ) >
UnicastRemoteObject^ < exportObject( ),
UnicastRemoteObject( ) >
—implemented by: RMISocketFactory
RMIFailureHandler: java.rmi.server
—passed to: RMISocketFactory.setFailureHandler( )
—returned by: RMISocketFactory.getFailureHandler( )
RMISecurityException^: java.rmi
RMISecurityManager^: java.rmi
RMIServerSocketFactory: java.rmi.server
—passed to: Activatable^ < Activatable( ), exportObject( ) >
LocateRegistry.createRegistry( ) UnicastRemoteObject^
< exportObject( ), UnicastRemoteObject( ) >
—implemented by: RMISocketFactory
RMISocketFactory: java.rmi.server
—passed to: RMISocketFactory.setSocketFactory( )
—returned by: RMISocketFactory < getDefaultSocketFactory( ),
getSocketFactory( ) >
roll( ): Calendar⌐
rollback( ): *Connection*⌐ *XAResource*
rootException: NamingException⌐
rotate( ): Collections
round( ): Math StrictMath
ROUND_CEILING: BigDecimal^
ROUND_DOWN: BigDecimal^
ROUND_FLOOR: BigDecimal^
ROUND_HALF_DOWN: BigDecimal^
ROUND_HALF_EVEN: BigDecimal^
ROUND_HALF_UP: BigDecimal^
ROUND_UNNECESSARY: BigDecimal^
ROUND_UP: BigDecimal^
rowChanged( ): *RowSetListener*^
rowDeleted( ): *ResultSet*⌐
rowInserted( ): *ResultSet*⌐
RowSet^: javax.sql
—passed to: RowSetEvent( )
rowSetChanged( ): *RowSetListener*^
RowSetEvent^: javax.sql
—passed to: *RowSetListener*^ < cursorMoved( ), rowChanged( ),
rowSetChanged( ) >
RowSetInternal: javax.sql
—passed to: *RowSetReader*.readData( ) *RowSetWriter*.writeData( )
RowSetListener^: javax.sql

—passed to: ***RowSet***^ < addRowSetListener( ),
removeRowSetListener( ) >
RowSetMetaData^: javax.sql
—passed to: ***RowSetInternal***.setMetaData( )
RowSetReader: javax.sql
RowSetWriter: javax.sql
rowUpdated( ): ResultSet
RSAKey: java.security.interfaces
—extended by: ***RSAPrivateKey***^ ***RSAPublicKey***^
—descendents: ***RSAMultiPrimePrivateCrtKey***^
RSAPrivateCrtKey^
RSAKeyGenParameterSpec: java.security.spec
RSAMultiPrimePrivateCrtKey^: java.security.interfaces
RSAMultiPrimePrivateCrtKeySpec^: java.security.spec
RSAOtherPrimeInfo: java.security.spec
—passed to: ***R***SAMultiPrimePrivateCrtKeySpec( )
—returned by: ***RSAMultiPrimePrivateCrtKey***^.getOtherPrimeInfo( )
RSAMultiPrimePrivateCrtKeySpec^.getOtherPrimeInfo( )
RSAPrivateCrtKey^: java.security.interfaces
RSAPrivateCrtKeySpec^: java.security.spec
RSAPrivateKey^: java.security.interfaces
—extended by: ***RSAMultiPrimePrivateCrtKey***^
RSAPrivateCrtKey^
RSAPrivateKeySpec: java.security.spec
—subclasses: ***R***SAMultiPrimePrivateCrtKeySpec^
RSAPrivateCrtKeySpec^
RSAPublicKey^: java.security.interfaces
RSAPublicKeySpec: java.security.spec
RuleBasedCollator^: java.text
run( ): org.omg.CORBA.**ORB** *PrivilegedAction*
PrivilegedExceptionAction Runnable Thread TimerTask
runFinalization( ): **R**untime **S**ystem
runFinalizersOnExit( ): **R**untime **S**ystem
RUNIC: Character.UnicodeBlock^
Runnable: java.lang
—passed to: javax.swing.text.**A**bstractDocument.render( )
*javax.swing.text.**D**ocument*.render( )
java.awt.**E**ventQueue < invokeAndWait( ),
invokeLater( ) > java.awt.event.**I**nvocationEvent( )
javax.swing.text.**L**ayoutQueue.addTask( )
javax.swing.**S**wingUtilities < invokeAndWait( ), invokeLater( ) >
Thread( )
—returned by: javax.swing.text.**L**ayoutQueue.waitForWork( )
—implemented by: javax.swing.text.**A**syncBoxView.ChildState
java.awt.image.renderable.**R**enderableImageProducer
Thread **T**imerTask
—fields: java.awt.event.**I**nvocationEvent^.runnable
Runtime: java.lang
—returned by: **R**untime.getRuntime( )
RunTime^: org.omg.SendingContext
—passed to: ***ValueHandler***.readValue( )
—returned by: ***ValueHandler***.getRunTimeCodeBase( )
RuntimeException: java.lang
—subclasses: **A**rithmeticException **A**rrayStoreException
BufferOverflowException **B**ufferUnderflowException
javax.swing.undo.**C**annotRedoException
javax.swing.undo.**C**annotUndoException
ClassCastException java.awt.color.**C**MMException
ConcurrentModificationException
DOMException **E**mptyStackException
IllegalArgumentException **I**llegalMonitorStateException
java.awt.geom.**I**llegalPathStateException
IllegalStateException java.awt.image.**I**magingOpException
IndexOutOfBoundsException **M**issingResourceException
NegativeArraySizeException **N**oSuchElementException
NullPointerException java.awt.color.**P**rofileDataException
ProviderException java.awt.image.**R**asterFormatException
SecurityException **S**ystemException
UndeclaredThrowableException

javax.print.attribute.**U**nmodifiableSetException
UnsupportedOperationException
—descendents: **A**ccessControlException^
AlreadyConnectedException^
ArrayIndexOutOfBoundsException^ **B**AD_CONTEXT^
BAD_INV_ORDER^ **B**AD_OPERATION^ **B**AD_PARAM^
BAD_TYPECODE^ **C**ancelledKeyException^
ClosedSelectorException^ **C**OMM_FAILURE^
ConnectionPendingException^ **D**ATA_CONVERSION^
FREE_MEM^ java.awt.**H**eadlessException^
IllegalBlockingModeException^
IllegalCharsetNameException^
java.awt.**I**llegalComponentStateException^
IllegalSelectorException^ **I**llegalThreadStateException^
IMP_LIMIT^ **I**ndirectionException^ **I**NITIALIZE^
INTERNAL^ **I**NTF_REPOS^ **I**NV_FLAG^ **I**NV_IDENT^
INV_OBJREF^ **I**NV_POLICY^ **I**NVALID_TRANSACTION^
java.awt.dnd.**I**nvalidDnDOperationException^
InvalidMarkException^ **I**nvalidParameterException^
MARSHAL^ **N**O_IMPLEMENT^ **N**O_MEMORY^
NO_PERMISSION^ **N**O_RESOURCES^
NO_RESPONSE^ **N**oConnectionPendingException^
NonReadableChannelException^
NonWritableChannelException^ **N**otYetBoundException^
NotYetConnectedException^ **N**umberFormatException^
OBJ_ADAPTER^ **O**BJECT_NOT_EXIST^
OverlappingFileLockException^ **P**atternSyntaxException^
PERSIST_STORE^ **R**eadOnlyBufferException^
RMISecurityException^ **S**tringIndexOutOfBoundsException^
TRANSACTION_REQUIRED^
TRANSACTION_ROLLEDBACK^ **T**RANSIENT^ **U**NKNOWN^
UnknownException^ **U**nresolvedAddressException^
UnsupportedAddressTypeException^
UnsupportedCharsetException^
RunTimeOperations: org.omg.SendingContext
—extended by: ***RunTime***^
RuntimePermission^: java.lang
sameFile( ): **U**RL **U**RLStreamHandler
SATURDAY: **C**alendar
save( ): **P**roperties^
Savepoint: java.sql
—passed to: ***Connection*** < releaseSavepoint( ), rollback( ) >
—returned by: ***Connection***.setSavepoint( )
SAXException: org.xml.sax
—subclasses: **S**AXNotRecognizedException^
SAXNotSupportedException^ **S**AXParseException^
—thrown by: *org.xml.sax.**ContentHandler*** < characters( ),
endDocument( ), endElement( ), endPrefixMapping( ),
ignorableWhitespace( ), processingInstruction( ), skippedEntity( ),
startDocument( ), startElement( ), startPrefixMapping( ) >
DeclHandler < attributeDecl( ), elementDecl( ),
externalEntityDecl( ), internalEntityDecl( ) > **D**efaultHandler
< characters( ), endDocument( ), endElement( ),
endPrefixMapping( ), error( ), fatalError( ), ignorableWhitespace( ),
notationDecl( ), processingInstruction( ), resolveEntity( ),
skippedEntity( ), startDocument( ), startElement( ),
startPrefixMapping( ), warning( ) >
DocumentBuilder.parse( ) *DocumentHandler* < characters( ),
endDocument( ), endElement( ), ignorableWhitespace( ),
processingInstruction( ), startDocument( ), startElement( ) >
DTDHandler < notationDecl( ), unparsedEntityDecl( ) >
EntityResolver.resolveEntity( ) *ErrorHandler* < error( ),
fatalError( ), warning( ) > **H**andlerBase < characters( ),
endDocument( ), endElement( ), error( ), fatalError( ),
ignorableWhitespace( ), processingInstruction( ), resolveEntity( ),
startDocument( ), startElement( ), warning( ) > *LexicalHandler*
< comment( ), endCDATA( ), endDTD( ), endEntity( ),
startCDATA( ), startDTD( ), startEntity( ) > *Parser* < parse( ),
setLocale( ) > **P**arserAdapter < characters( ), endDocument( ),
endElement( ), ignorableWhitespace( ), parse( ), ParserAdapter( ),
processingInstruction( ), startDocument( ), startElement( ) >
SAXParser < getParser( ), getXMLReader( ), parse( ) >

S

SAXParserFactory.newSAXParser( ) **X**MLFilterImpl
< characters( ), endDocument( ), endElement( ),
endPrefixMapping( ), error( ), fatalError( ), ignorableWhitespace( ),
notationDecl( ), parse( ), processingInstruction( ), resolveEntity( ),
skippedEntity( ), startDocument( ), startElement( ),
startPrefixMapping( ), unparsedEntityDecl( ), warning( ) >
XMLReader.parse( ) **X**MLReaderAdapter < characters( ),
endDocument( ), endElement( ), ignorableWhitespace( ), parse( ),
processingInstruction( ), setLocale( ), skippedEntity( ),
startDocument( ), startElement( ), XMLReaderAdapter( ) >
XMLReaderFactory.createXMLReader( )

SAXNotRecognizedException^: org.xml.sax
— thrown by: **P**arserAdapter < getFeature( ), getProperty( ),
setFeature( ), setProperty( ) > **S**AXParser < getProperty( ),
setProperty( ) > **S**AXParserFactory < getFeature( ),
setFeature( ) > **X**MLFilterImpl < getFeature( ), getProperty( ),
setFeature( ), setProperty( ) > *XMLReader* < getFeature( ),
getProperty( ), setFeature( ), setProperty( ) >

SAXNotSupportedException^: org.xml.sax
— thrown by: **P**arserAdapter < getFeature( ), getProperty( ),
setFeature( ), setProperty( ) > **S**AXParser < getProperty( ),
setProperty( ) > **S**AXParserFactory < getFeature( ),
setFeature( ), setProperty( ) > **X**MLFilterImpl < getFeature( ), getProperty( ),
setFeature( ), setProperty( ) > *XMLReader* < getFeature( ),
getProperty( ), setFeature( ), setProperty( ) >

SAXParseException^: org.xml.sax
— passed to: **D**efaultHandler < error( ), fatalError( ), warning( ) >
ErrorHandler < error( ), fatalError( ), warning( ) > **H**andlerBase
< error( ), fatalError( ), warning( ) > **X**MLFilterImpl < error( ),
fatalError( ), warning( ) >

SAXParser: javax.xml.parsers
— returned by: **S**AXParserFactory.newSAXParser( )

SAXParserFactory: javax.xml.parsers
— returned by: **S**AXParserFactory.newInstance( )

SAXResult: javax.xml.transform.sax

SAXSource: javax.xml.transform.sax

SAXTransformerFactory^: javax.xml.transform.sax

SC_BLOCK_DATA: *ObjectStreamConstants*

SC_EXTERNALIZABLE: *ObjectStreamConstants*

SC_SERIALIZABLE: *ObjectStreamConstants*

SC_WRITE_METHOD: *ObjectStreamConstants*

scale( ): **B**igDecimal^

ScatteringByteChannel^: java.nio.channels
— implemented by: **D**atagramChannel^ **F**ileChannel^
Pipe.SourceChannel^ **S**ocketChannel^

schedule( ): java.util.**T**imer

scheduleAtFixedRate( ): java.util.**T**imer

scheduledExecutionTime( ): **T**imerTask

SchemaViolationException^: javax.naming.directory

SEALED: **A**ttributes.Name

SealedObject: javax.crypto
— passed to: **S**ealedObject( )

search( ): *DirContext*^ **I**nitialDirContext^ **S**tack^

SearchControls: javax.naming.directory
— passed to: *DirContext*^.search( )
EventDirContext^.addNamingListener( )
InitialDirContext^.search( )

SearchResult^: javax.naming.directory

SECOND: **C**alendar **D**ateFormat.Field^

SECOND_FIELD: **D**ateFormat^

SECONDARY: **C**ollator^

secondaryOrder( ): **C**ollationElementIterator

SECRET_KEY: **C**ipher

SecretKey^: javax.crypto
— extended by: *PBEKey*^
— passed to: **S**ecretKeyFactory < getKeySpec( ), translateKey( ) >
SecretKeyFactorySpi < engineGetKeySpec( ),
engineTranslateKey( ) >
— returned by: **K**erberosTicket.getSessionKey( )
KeyAgreement.generateSecret( )
KeyAgreementSpi.engineGenerateSecret( )
KeyGenerator.generateKey( )

KeyGeneratorSpi.engineGenerateKey( ) **S**ecretKeyFactory
< generateSecret( ), translateKey( ) > **S**ecretKeyFactorySpi
< engineGenerateSecret( ), engineTranslateKey( ) >
— implemented by: **K**erberosKey **S**ecretKeySpec

SecretKeyFactory: javax.crypto
— returned by: **S**ecretKeyFactory.getInstance( )

SecretKeyFactorySpi: javax.crypto
— passed to: **S**ecretKeyFactory( )

SecretKeySpec: javax.crypto.spec

SecureClassLoader^: java.security
— subclasses: **U**RLClassLoader^

SecureRandom^: java.security
— passed to: **A**lgorithmParameterGenerator.init( )
AlgorithmParameterGeneratorSpi.engineInit( ) **C**ipher.init( )
CipherSpi.engineInit( ) *DSAKeyPairGenerator*.initialize( )
KeyAgreement.init( ) **K**eyAgreementSpi.engineInit( )
KeyGenerator.init( ) **K**eyGeneratorSpi.engineInit( )
KeyPairGeneratorSpi.initialize( ) **S**ignature^.initSign( )
SignatureSpi.engineInitSign( ) **S**SLContext.init( )
SSLContextSpi.engineInit( )
— returned by: **S**ecureRandom^.getInstance( )
— fields: **S**ignatureSpi.appRandom

SecureRandomSpi: java.security
— passed to: **S**ecureRandom( )

Security: java.security

SECURITY_AUTHENTICATION: *javax.naming.Context*

SECURITY_CREDENTIALS: *javax.naming.Context*

SECURITY_PRINCIPAL: *javax.naming.Context*

SECURITY_PROTOCOL: *javax.naming.Context*

SecurityException: java.lang
— subclasses: **A**ccessControlException^ **R**MISecurityException^
— thrown by: **A**ccessibleObject.setAccessible( ) **B**eans
< setDesignTime( ), setGuiAvailable( ) > **C**lass
< getConstructor( ), getConstructors( ), getDeclaredClasses( ),
getDeclaredConstructor( ), getDeclaredConstructors( ),
getDeclaredField( ), getDeclaredFields( ), getDeclaredMethod( ),
getDeclaredMethods( ), getField( ), getFields( ),
getMethod( ), getMethods( ) > **F**ileHandler( )
javax.swing.**F**ocusManager^.setCurrentManager( )
Guard.checkGuard( ) **G**uardedObject.getObject( ) **H**andler
< close( ), setEncoding( ), setFilter( ), setFormatter( ), setLevel( ) >
java.awt.**K**eyboardFocusManager < getGlobalActiveWindow( ),
getGlobalCurrentFocusCycleRoot( ), getGlobalFocusedWindow( ),
getGlobalFocusOwner( ), getGlobalPermanentFocusOwner( ),
setCurrentKeyboardFocusManager( ) > **L**ogger < addHandler( ),
removeHandler( ), setFilter( ), setLevel( ) > **L**ogManager
< addPropertyChangeListener( ), checkAccess( ),
readConfiguration( ), removePropertyChangeListener( ), reset( ) >
MemoryHandler^.setPushLevel( ) **O**bjectInputStream^
< enableResolveObject( ), ObjectInputStream( ) >
ObjectOutputStream^ < enableReplaceObject( ),
ObjectOutputStream( ) > java.security.**P**ermission.checkGuard( )
RMIClassLoader.getClassLoader( )
StreamHandler^.setOutputStream( )
javax.swing.**U**IManager.setInstalledLookAndFeels( )

SecurityManager: java.lang
— subclasses: **R**MISecurityManager^
— passed to: **S**ystem.setSecurityManager( )
— returned by: **S**ystem.getSecurityManager( )

SecurityPermission^: java.security

seek( ): _DynAnyStub^ _DynArrayStub^ _DynEnumStub^
_DynFixedStub^ _DynSequenceStub^
_DynStructStub^ _DynUnionStub^ _DynValueStub^
org.omg.CORBA.DynAny^ *DynAnyOperations*
RandomAccessFile

select( ): **S**elector

SelectableChannel^: java.nio.channels
— subclasses: **A**bstractSelectableChannel^
— descendents: **D**atagramChannel^ **P**ipe.SinkChannel^
Pipe.SourceChannel^ **S**erverSocketChannel^
SocketChannel^

S

S

< entrySet( ), keySet( ) > java.awt.**K**eyboardFocusManager ←
.getDefaultFocusTraversalKeys( ) *Map* < entrySet( ), keySet( ) >
PKIXCertPathChecker.getSupportedExtensions( )
PKIXParameters < getInitialPolicies( ), getTrustAnchors( ) >
PolicyNode < getExpectedPolicies( ), getPolicyQualifiers( ) >
javax.print.attribute.standard.**P**rinterStateReasons^ ←
.printerStateReasonSet( ) java.awt.**R**enderingHints < entrySet( ),
keySet( ) > **S**ecurity.getAlgorithms( ) **S**elector
< keys( ), selectedKeys( ) > **S**ubject < getPrincipals( ),
getPrivateCredentials( ), getPublicCredentials( ) >
X509CertSelector < getExtendedKeyUsage( ), getPolicy( ) >
X509CRL^.getRevokedCertificates( ) *X509Extension*
< getCriticalExtensionOIDs( ), getNonCriticalExtensionOIDs( ) >
—implemented by: **A**bstractSet^
—fields: **C**ollections.EMPTY_SET
set( ): **A**bstractList^ java.lang.reflect.**A**rray
javax.naming.directory.Attribute^ **B**asicAttribute **B**itSet
Calendar **F**ield^ *List*^ *ListIterator*^ **T**hreadLocal **U**RL
set2DigitYearStart( ): **S**impleDateFormat
set_as_default( ): *org.omg.CORBA.DynUnion*^
set_as_string( ): _DynEnumStub^ *DynEnumOperations*^
set_as_ulong( ): _DynEnumStub^ *DynEnumOperations*^
set_boxed_value( ): *DynValueBoxOperations*^
set_boxed_value_as_dyn_any( ): *DynValueBoxOperations*^
set_delegate( ): org.omg.CORBA_2_3.**O**RB^
set_discriminator( ): _DynUnionStub^ *DynUnionOperations*^
set_elements( ): _DynArrayStub^ _DynSequenceStub^
org.omg.CORBA.DynArray^ *DynArrayOperations*^
org.omg.CORBA.DynSequence^ *DynSequenceOperations*^
set_elements_as_dyn_any( ): _DynArrayStub^
_DynSequenceStub^ *DynArrayOperations*^
DynSequenceOperations^
set_exception( ): **S**erverRequest
set_length( ): _DynSequenceStub^ *DynSequenceOperations*^
set_members( ): _DynStructStub^ _DynValueStub^
org.omg.CORBA.DynStruct^ *DynStructOperations*^
org.omg.CORBA.DynValue^ *DynValueOperations*^
set_members_as_dyn_any( ): _DynStructStub^
_DynValueStub^ *DynStructOperations*^
DynValueOperations^
set_one_value( ): org.omg.CORBA.**C**ontext
SET_OVERRIDE: **S**etOverrideType
set_parameters( ): org.omg.CORBA.**O**RB
set_policy_override( ): org.omg.CORBA.portable.**D**elegate
set_result( ): **S**erverRequest
set_return_type( ): **R**equest
set_servant( ): *POAOperations*
set_servant_manager( ): *POAOperations*
set_slot( ): *org.omg.PortableInterceptor.CurrentOperations*^
ServerRequestInfoOperations^
set_to_default_member( ): _DynUnionStub^
DynUnionOperations^
set_to_no_active_member( ): _DynUnionStub^
DynUnionOperations^
set_to_null( ): _DynValueStub^ *DynValueCommonOperations*^
set_to_value( ): _DynValueStub^ *DynValueCommonOperations*^
set_value( ): _DynFixedStub^ *org.omg.CORBA.DynFixed*^
DynFixedOperations^
set_values( ): org.omg.CORBA.**C**ontext
setAccessible( ): **A**ccessibleObject
setActivationDesc( ): *ActivationSystem*^
setActivationGroupDesc( ): *ActivationSystem*^
setAddress( ): **D**atagramPacket
setAllowUserInteraction( ): **U**RLConnection
setAltName( ): **C**annotProceedException^
setAltNameCtx( ): **C**annotProceedException^
setAmPmStrings( ): **D**ateFormatSymbols
setAnyPolicyInhibited( ): **P**KIXParameters
setArray( ): *PreparedStatement*^ *RowSet*^
setAsciiStream( ): *Clob* *PreparedStatement*^ *RowSet*^
setAsText( ): *PropertyEditor* **P**ropertyEditorSupport

setAttribute( ): **A**ttributesImpl **D**ocumentBuilderFactory
Element^ **T**ransformerFactory
setAttributeList( ): **A**ttributeListImpl
setAttributeNode( ): *Element*^
setAttributeNodeNS( ): *Element*^
setAttributeNS( ): *Element*^
setAttributes( ): **A**ttributesImpl **S**earchResult^
setAuthorityKeyIdentifier( ): **X**509CertSelector
setAutoCommit( ): *Connection*
setAutoIncrement( ): *RowSetMetaData*^
setBasicConstraints( ): **X**509CertSelector
setBeanContext( ): *BeanContextChild*
BeanContextChildSupport
setBeanInfoSearchPath( ): **I**ntrospector
setBeginIndex( ): **F**ieldPosition
setBigDecimal( ): *PreparedStatement*^ *RowSet*^
setBinaryStream( ): *Blob* *PreparedStatement*^ *RowSet*^
setBit( ): **B**igInteger^
setBlob( ): *PreparedStatement*^ *RowSet*^
setBoolean( ): java.lang.reflect.**A**rray **F**ield^
PreparedStatement^ *RowSet*^
setBound( ): **P**ropertyDescriptor
setBroadcast( ): **D**atagramSocket
setByte( ): java.lang.reflect.**A**rray **F**ield^ *PreparedStatement*^
RowSet^
setBytes( ): *Blob* *PreparedStatement*^ *RowSet*^
setByteStream( ): **I**nputSource
setCalendar( ): **D**ateFormat
setCaseSensitive( ): *RowSetMetaData*^
setCatalog( ): *Connection*
setCatalogName( ): *RowSetMetaData*^
setCertificate( ): **X**509CertSelector
setCertificateChecking( ): **X**509CRLSelector
setCertificateEntry( ): **K**eyStore
setCertificateValid( ): **X**509CertSelector
setCertPathCheckers( ): **P**KIXParameters
setCertStores( ): **P**KIXParameters
setChanged( ): **O**bservable
setChannelBinding( ): *GSSContext*
setChar( ): java.lang.reflect.**A**rray **F**ield^
setCharacterStream( ): *Clob* **I**nputSource
PreparedStatement^ *RowSet*^
setCharAt( ): **S**tringBuffer
setChoices( ): **C**hoiceFormat^
setClassAssertionStatus( ): **C**lassLoader
setClassName( ): **N**ameClassPair
setClob( ): *PreparedStatement*^ *RowSet*^
setCoalescing( ): **D**ocumentBuilderFactory
setColumnCount( ): *RowSetMetaData*^
setColumnDisplaySize( ): *RowSetMetaData*^
setColumnLabel( ): *RowSetMetaData*^
setColumnName( ): *RowSetMetaData*^
setColumnNumber( ): **L**ocatorImpl
setColumnType( ): *RowSetMetaData*^
setColumnTypeName( ): *RowSetMetaData*^
setCommand( ): *RowSet*^
setComment( ): **Z**ipEntry **Z**ipOutputStream^
setCompressedSize( ): **Z**ipEntry
setConcurrency( ): *RowSet*^
setConfiguration( ): **C**onfiguration
setConstrained( ): **P**ropertyDescriptor^
setContentHandler( ): **P**arserAdapter **X**MLFilterImpl
XMLReader
setContentHandlerFactory( ): **U**RLConnection
setContextClassLoader( ): **T**hread
setCountLimit( ): **S**earchControls
setCrc( ): **Z**ipEntry
setCurrency( ): **D**ecimalFormatSymbols **N**umberFormat^
RowSetMetaData^
setCurrencySymbol( ): **D**ecimalFormatSymbols
setCursorName( ): *java.sql.Statement*
setDaemon( ): **T**hread **T**hreadGroup

setData(): *CharacterData* DatagramPacket
  ProcessingInstruction
setDatagramSocketImplFactory(): DatagramSocket
setDataSourceName(): *RowSet*
setDate(): java.util.Date PKIXParameters
  PreparedStatement *RowSet*
setDateAndTime(): X509CRLSelector
setDateFormatSymbols(): SimpleDateFormat
setDecimalFormatSymbols(): DecimalFormat
setDecimalSeparator(): DecimalFormatSymbols
setDecimalSeparatorAlwaysShown(): DecimalFormat
setDecomposition(): Collator
setDefault(): Authenticator Locale TimeZone
setDefaultAllowUserInteraction(): URLConnection
setDefaultAssertionStatus(): ClassLoader
setDefaultHostnameVerifier(): HttpsURLConnection
setDefaultRequestProperty(): URLConnection
setDefaultSSLSocketFactory(): HttpsURLConnection
setDefaultStream(): LogStream
setDefaultUseCaches(): URLConnection
setDerefLinkFlag(): SearchControls
setDesignTime(): BeanContextSupport Beans *DesignMode*
setDictionary(): Deflater Inflater
setDigit(): DecimalFormatSymbols
setDisplayName(): FeatureDescriptor
setDocumentHandler(): *Parser* XMLReaderAdapter
setDocumentLocator(): org.xml.sax.*ContentHandler*
  DefaultHandler *DocumentHandler* HandlerBase
  ParserAdapter XMLFilterImpl XMLReaderAdapter
setDoInput(): URLConnection
setDoOutput(): URLConnection
setDouble(): java.lang.reflect.Array Field
  PreparedStatement *RowSet*
setDSTSavings(): SimpleTimeZone
setDTDHandler(): *Parser* ParserAdapter XMLFilterImpl
  XMLReader XMLReaderAdapter
setEditorSearchPath(): PropertyEditorManager
setElementAt(): Vector
setEnabledCipherSuites(): SSLServerSocket SSLSocket
  StartTlsResponse
setEnabledProtocols(): SSLServerSocket SSLSocket
setEnableSessionCreation(): SSLServerSocket SSLSocket
setEncoding(): Handler InputSource
setEndIndex(): FieldPosition
setEndRule(): SimpleTimeZone
setEntityResolver(): DocumentBuilder *Parser* ParserAdapter
  XMLFilterImpl *XMLReader* XMLReaderAdapter
setEnvironment(): CannotProceedException
setEras(): DateFormatSymbols
setErr(): System
setError(): PrintStream PrintWriter
setErrorHandler(): DocumentBuilder *Parser* ParserAdapter
  XMLFilterImpl *XMLReader* XMLReaderAdapter
setErrorIndex(): ParsePosition
setErrorListener(): Transformer TransformerFactory
setErrorManager(): Handler
setEscapeProcessing(): *RowSet* java.sql.*Statement*
setExceptionListener(): Encoder XMLDecoder
setExpandEntityReferences(): DocumentBuilderFactory
setExpert(): FeatureDescriptor
setExplicitPolicyRequired(): PKIXParameters
setExtendedKeyUsage(): X509CertSelector
setExtra(): ZipEntry
setFailureHandler(): RMISocketFactory
setFeature(): ParserAdapter SAXParserFactory XMLFilterImpl
  XMLReader
setFetchDirection(): *ResultSet* java.sql.*Statement*
setFetchSize(): *ResultSet* java.sql.*Statement*
setFileNameMap(): URLConnection
setFilter(): Handler Logger
setFirstDayOfWeek(): Calendar

setFloat(): java.lang.reflect.Array Field *PreparedStatement*
  RowSet
setFollowRedirects(): HttpURLConnection
setFormat(): MessageFormat
setFormatByArgumentIndex(): MessageFormat
setFormats(): MessageFormat
setFormatsByArgumentIndex(): MessageFormat
setFormatter(): Handler
setGregorianChange(): GregorianCalendar
setGroupingSeparator(): DecimalFormatSymbols
setGroupingSize(): DecimalFormat
setGroupingUsed(): NumberFormat
setGuiAvailable(): Beans
setHandler(): SAXResult
setHidden(): FeatureDescriptor
setHoldability(): *Connection*
setHostnameVerifier(): HttpsURLConnection
  StartTlsResponse
setHours(): java.util.Date
setID(): TimeZone
setIfModifiedSince(): URLConnection
setIgnoringComments(): DocumentBuilderFactory
setIgnoringElementContentWhitespace():
  DocumentBuilderFactory
setIn(): System
setInDefaultEventSet(): EventSetDescriptor
setIndex(): *CharacterIterator* ParsePosition
  StringCharacterIterator
setIndexedReadMethod(): IndexedPropertyDescriptor
setIndexedWriteMethod(): IndexedPropertyDescriptor
setInfinity(): DecimalFormatSymbols
setInfo(): Identity
setInitialContextFactoryBuilder(): NamingManager
setInitialPolicies(): PKIXParameters
setInput(): Deflater Inflater
setInputSource(): SAXSource
setInputStream(): StreamSource
setInstanceFollowRedirects(): HttpURLConnection
setInt(): java.lang.reflect.Array Field *PreparedStatement*
  RowSet
setInterface(): MulticastSocket
setInternationalCurrencySymbol(): DecimalFormatSymbols
setIssuer(): X509CertSelector
setIssuerNames(): X509CRLSelector
setKeepAlive(): Socket
setKeyEntry(): KeyStore
setKeyPair(): Signer
setKeyUsage(): X509CertSelector
setLastModified(): File
setLength(): DatagramPacket RandomAccessFile
  StringBuffer
setLenient(): Calendar DateFormat
setLevel(): Deflater Handler Logger LogRecord
  ZipOutputStream
setLexicalHandler(): SAXResult
setLineNumber(): LineNumberInputStream
  LineNumberReader LocatorImpl
setLinkExplanation(): LinkException
setLinkRemainingName(): LinkException
setLinkResolvedName(): LinkException
setLinkResolvedObj(): LinkException
setLocale(): BeanContextSupport LanguageCallback
  MessageFormat *Parser* XMLReaderAdapter
setLocalName(): AttributesImpl
setLocalPatternChars(): DateFormatSymbols
setLocator(): TransformerException
setLog(): RemoteServer
setLoggerName(): LogRecord
setLoginTimeout(): *ConnectionPoolDataSource* *DataSource*
  DriverManager *XADataSource*
setLogStream(): DriverManager

S

S

singleton(): **C**ollections
singletonList(): **C**ollections
singletonMap(): **C**ollections
SINHALA: **C**haracter.UnicodeBlock^
sink(): **P**ipe
size(): **A**bstractCollection_ **A**bstractMap_
  javax.naming.directory.Attribute^ java.util.jar.**A**ttributes
  javax.naming.directory.Attributes^ **B**asicAttribute
  BasicAttributes **B**eanContextMembershipEvent^
  BeanContextSupport^ **B**itSet **B**yteArrayOutputStream^
  CharArrayWriter^ *Collection*_ **C**ompositeName
  CompoundName java.io.**D**ataOutputStream^ **D**ictionary_
  FileChannel^ **F**ileLock **I**dentityScope^ **K**eyStore *Map*_
  Name^ javax.naming.**R**eference_ **Z**ipFile_
SizeLimitExceededException^: javax.naming
Skeleton: java.rmi.server
SkeletonMismatchException^: java.rmi.server
SkeletonNotFoundException^: java.rmi.server
skip(): java.io.**I**nputStream_ *ObjectInput*^ **R**eader_
skipBytes(): *DataInput*^ java.io.**D**ataInputStream^
  ObjectInputStream^ **R**andomAccessFile
skippedEntity(): org.xml.sax.*ContentHandler*_ **D**efaultHandler
  XMLFilterImpl **X**MLReaderAdapter
skipReferral(): *ReferralException*^
slashSlashComments(): **S**treamTokenizer
slashStarComments(): **S**treamTokenizer
sleep(): **T**hread
slice(): **B**yteBuffer^ **C**harBuffer^ **D**oubleBuffer^ **F**loatBuffer^
  IntBuffer^ **L**ongBuffer^ **S**hortBuffer^
SMALL_FORM_VARIANTS: **C**haracter.UnicodeBlock^
SMALLINT: **T**ypes
SO_BINDADDR: *SocketOptions*
SO_BROADCAST: *SocketOptions*
SO_KEEPALIVE: *SocketOptions*
SO_LINGER: *SocketOptions*
SO_OOBINLINE: *SocketOptions*
SO_RCVBUF: *SocketOptions*
SO_REUSEADDR: *SocketOptions*
SO_SNDBUF: *SocketOptions*
SO_TIMEOUT: *SocketOptions*
Socket_: java.net
  —subclasses: **S**SLSocket^
  —passed to: **S**erverSocket_.implAccept()
  SSLSocketFactory^.createSocket() *X509KeyManager*^
  < chooseClientAlias(), chooseServerAlias() >
  —returned by: *RMIClientSocketFactory*.createSocket()
  RMISocketFactory.createSocket() **S**erverSocket_.accept()
  SocketChannel^.socket() **S**ocketFactory_.createSocket()
  SSLSocketFactory^.createSocket()
socket(): **D**atagramChannel^ **S**erverSocketChannel^
  SocketChannel^
SocketAddress_: java.net
  —subclasses: **I**netSocketAddress^
  —passed to: **D**atagramChannel^ < connect(), send() >
  DatagramPacket < DatagramPacket(), setSocketAddress() >
  DatagramSocket_ < bind(), connect(), DatagramSocket() >
  DatagramSocketImpl < joinGroup(), leaveGroup() >
  MulticastSocket^ < joinGroup(), leaveGroup(),
  MulticastSocket() > **S**erverSocket_.bind() **S**ocket_ < bind(),
  connect() > **S**ocketChannel^ < connect(), open() >
  SocketImpl.connect()
  —returned by: **D**atagramChannel^.receive()
  DatagramPacket.getSocketAddress() **D**atagramSocket_
  < getLocalSocketAddress(), getRemoteSocketAddress() >
  ServerSocket_.getLocalSocketAddress() **S**ocket_
  < getLocalSocketAddress(), getRemoteSocketAddress() >
SocketChannel^: java.nio.channels
  —returned by: **S**electorProvider.openSocketChannel()
  ServerSocketChannel^.accept() **S**ocket_.getChannel()
  SocketChannel^.open()
SocketException^: java.net

  —subclasses: **B**indException^ java.net.**C**onnectException^
  NoRouteToHostException^ **P**ortUnreachableException^
  —thrown by: **D**atagramPacket() **D**atagramSocket_
  < bind(), connect(), DatagramSocket(), getBroadcast(),
  getReceiveBufferSize(), getReuseAddress(), getSendBufferSize(),
  getSoTimeout(), getTrafficClass(), setBroadcast(),
  setReceiveBufferSize(), setReuseAddress(), setSendBufferSize(),
  setSoTimeout(), setTrafficClass() > **D**atagramSocketImpl
  < bind(), connect(), create() > **M**ulticastSocket^
  < getInterface(), getLoopbackMode(), getNetworkInterface(),
  setInterface(), setLoopbackMode(), setNetworkInterface() >
  NetworkInterface < getByInetAddress(), getByName(),
  getNetworkInterfaces() > **S**erverSocket_ < getReceiveBufferSize(),
  getReuseAddress(), setReceiveBufferSize(), setReuseAddress(),
  setSoTimeout() > **S**ocket_ < getKeepAlive(), getOOBInline(),
  getReceiveBufferSize(), getReuseAddress(), getSendBufferSize(),
  getSoLinger(), getSoTimeout(), getTcpNoDelay(),
  getTrafficClass(), setKeepAlive(), setOOBInline(),
  setReceiveBufferSize(), setReuseAddress(), setSendBufferSize(),
  setSoLinger(), setSoTimeout(), setTcpNoDelay(),
  setTrafficClass(), Socket() > *SocketOptions* < getOption(),
  setOption() >
SocketFactory_: javax.net
  —subclasses: **S**SLSocketFactory^
  —returned by: **S**ocketFactory_.getDefault()
SocketHandler^: java.util.logging
SocketImpl: java.net
  —passed to: **S**ocket() **S**ocketImpl.accept()
  —returned by: *SocketImplFactory*.createSocketImpl()
SocketImplFactory: java.net
  —passed to: **S**erverSocket_.setSocketFactory()
  Socket_.setSocketImplFactory()
SocketOptions: java.net
  —implemented by: **D**atagramSocketImpl **S**ocketImpl
SocketPermission^: java.net
SocketSecurityException^: java.rmi.server
SocketTimeoutException^: java.net
SoftReference^: java.lang.ref
sort(): **A**rrays **C**ollections
SortedMap^: java.util
  —passed to: **C**ollections < synchronizedSortedMap(),
  unmodifiableSortedMap() > **T**reeMap()
  —returned by: **C**harset.availableCharsets() **C**ollections
  < synchronizedSortedMap(), unmodifiableSortedMap() >
  SortedMap^ < headMap(), subMap(), tailMap() > **T**reeMap^
  < headMap(), subMap(), tailMap() >
  —implemented by: **T**reeMap^
SortedSet^: java.util
  —passed to: **C**ollections < synchronizedSortedSet(),
  unmodifiableSortedSet() > **T**reeSet()
  —returned by: **C**ollections < synchronizedSortedSet(),
  unmodifiableSortedSet() > *SortedSet*^ < headSet(), subSet(),
  tailSet() > **T**reeSet^ < headSet(), subSet(), tailSet() >
  —implemented by: **T**reeSet^
source: **E**ventObject_
Source: javax.xml.transform
  —passed to: **S**AXSource.sourceToInputSource()
  SAXTransformerFactory < newTransformerHandler(),
  newXMLFilter() > **T**ransformer.transform()
  TransformerFactory_ < getAssociatedStylesheet(),
  newTemplates(), newTransformer() >
  —returned by: **T**ransformerFactory_.getAssociatedStylesheet()
  URIResolver.resolve()
  —implemented by: **D**OMSource **S**AXSource **S**treamSource
source(): **P**ipe
SourceLocator_: javax.xml.transform
  —extended by: *DOMLocator*^
  —passed to: **T**ransformerConfigurationException()
  TransformerException_ < setLocator(),
  TransformerException() >
  —returned by: **T**ransformerException_.getLocator()
sourceToInputSource(): **S**AXSource

S

setBoolean( ), setByte( ), setBytes( ), setCharacterStream( ), setClob( ), setDate( ), setDouble( ), setFloat( ), setInt( ), setLong( ), setNull( ), setObject( ), setRef( ), setShort( ), setString( ), setTime( ), setTimestamp( ), setUnicodeStream( ), setURL( ) > *Ref* < getBaseTypeName( ), getObject( ), setObject( ) > *ResultSet* ⌣ < absolute( ), afterLast( ), beforeFirst( ), cancelRowUpdates( ), clearWarnings( ), close( ), deleteRow( ), findColumn( ), first( ), getArray( ), getAsciiStream( ), getBigDecimal( ), getBinaryStream( ), getBlob( ), getBoolean( ), getByte( ), getBytes( ), getCharacterStream( ), getClob( ), getConcurrency( ), getCursorName( ), getDate( ), getDouble( ), getFetchDirection( ), getFetchSize( ), getFloat( ), getInt( ), getLong( ), getMetaData( ), getObject( ), getRef( ), getRow( ), getShort( ), getStatement( ), getString( ), getTime( ), getTimestamp( ), getType( ), getUnicodeStream( ), getURL( ), getWarnings( ), insertRow( ), isAfterLast( ), isBeforeFirst( ), isFirst( ), isLast( ), last( ), moveToCurrentRow( ), moveToInsertRow( ), next( ), previous( ), refreshRow( ), relative( ), rowDeleted( ), rowInserted( ), rowUpdated( ), setFetchDirection( ), setFetchSize( ), updateArray( ), updateAsciiStream( ), updateBigDecimal( ), updateBinaryStream( ), updateBlob( ), updateBoolean( ), updateByte( ), updateBytes( ), updateCharacterStream( ), updateClob( ), updateDate( ), updateDouble( ), updateFloat( ), updateInt( ), updateLong( ), updateNull( ), updateObject( ), updateRef( ), updateRow( ), updateShort( ), updateString( ), updateTime( ), updateTimestamp( ), wasNull( ) > *ResultSetMetaData* ⌣ < getCatalogName( ), getColumnClassName( ), getColumnCount( ), getColumnDisplaySize( ), getColumnLabel( ), getColumnName( ), getColumnType( ), getColumnTypeName( ), getPrecision( ), getScale( ), getSchemaName( ), getTableName( ), isAutoIncrement( ), isCaseSensitive( ), isCurrency( ), isDefinitelyWritable( ), isNullable( ), isReadOnly( ), isSearchable( ), isSigned( ), isWritable( ) > *RowSet* ^ < clearParameters( ), execute( ), getEscapeProcessing( ), getMaxFieldSize( ), getMaxRows( ), getQueryTimeout( ), getTypeMap( ), getUrl( ), setArray( ), setAsciiStream( ), setBigDecimal( ), setBinaryStream( ), setBlob( ), setBoolean( ), setByte( ), setBytes( ), setCharacterStream( ), setClob( ), setCommand( ), setConcurrency( ), setDataSourceName( ), setDate( ), setDouble( ), setEscapeProcessing( ), setFloat( ), setInt( ), setLong( ), setMaxFieldSize( ), setMaxRows( ), setNull( ), setObject( ), setPassword( ), setQueryTimeout( ), setReadOnly( ), setRef( ), setShort( ), setString( ), setTime( ), setTimestamp( ), setTransactionIsolation( ), setType( ), setTypeMap( ), setUrl( ), setUsername( ) > *RowSetInternal* < getConnection( ), getOriginal( ), getOriginalRow( ), getParams( ), setMetaData( ) > *RowSetMetaData* ^ < setAutoIncrement( ), setCaseSensitive( ), setCatalogName( ), setColumnCount( ), setColumnDisplaySize( ), setColumnLabel( ), setColumnName( ), setColumnType( ), setColumnTypeName( ), setCurrency( ), setNullable( ), setPrecision( ), setScale( ), setSchemaName( ), setSearchable( ), setSigned( ), setTableName( ) > *RowSetReader*.readData( ) *RowSetWriter*.writeData( ) *Savepoint* < getSavepointId( ), getSavepointName( ) > *SQLData* < getSQLTypeName( ), readSQL( ), writeSQL( ) > *SQLInput* < readArray( ), readAsciiStream( ), readBigDecimal( ), readBinaryStream( ), readBlob( ), readBoolean( ), readByte( ), readBytes( ), readCharacterStream( ), readClob( ), readDate( ), readDouble( ), readFloat( ), readInt( ), readLong( ), readObject( ), readRef( ), readShort( ), readString( ), readTime( ), readTimestamp( ), readURL( ), wasNull( ) > *SQLOutput* < writeArray( ), writeAsciiStream( ), writeBigDecimal( ), writeBinaryStream( ), writeBlob( ), writeBoolean( ), writeByte( ), writeBytes( ), writeCharacterStream( ), writeClob( ), writeDate( ), writeDouble( ), writeFloat( ), writeInt( ), writeLong( ), writeObject( ), writeRef( ), writeShort( ), writeString( ), writeStruct( ), writeTime( ), writeTimestamp( ), writeURL( ) > *java.sql.Statement* ⌣ < addBatch( ), cancel( ), clearBatch( ), clearWarnings( ), close( ), execute( ), executeBatch( ), executeQuery( ), executeUpdate( ), getConnection( ),

getFetchDirection( ), getFetchSize( ), getGeneratedKeys( ), getMaxFieldSize( ), getMaxRows( ), getMoreResults( ), getQueryTimeout( ), getResultSet( ), getResultSetConcurrency( ), getResultSetHoldability( ), getResultSetType( ), getUpdateCount( ), getWarnings( ), setCursorName( ), setEscapeProcessing( ), setFetchDirection( ), setFetchSize( ), setMaxFieldSize( ), setMaxRows( ), setQueryTimeout( ) > *Struct* < getAttributes( ), getSQLTypeName( ) > *XAConnection* ^.getXAResource( ) *XADataSource* < getLoginTimeout( ), getLogWriter( ), getXAConnection( ), setLoginTimeout( ), setLogWriter( ) >

SQLInput: java.sql
— passed to: **S**QLData.readSQL( )

SQLOutput: java.sql
— passed to: **S**QLData.writeSQL( )

SQLPermission ^: java.sql

sqlStateSQL99: *DatabaseMetaData*

sqlStateXOpen: *DatabaseMetaData*

SQLWarning ^: java.sql
— subclasses: **D**ataTruncation ^
— passed to: **S**QLWarning ^.setNextWarning( )
— returned by: **C**onnection.getWarnings( ) *ResultSet* ⌣.getWarnings( ) **S**QLWarning ^.getNextWarning( ) *java.sql.Statement* ⌣.getWarnings( )

sqrt( ): **M**ath **S**trictMath

SSLContext: javax.net.ssl
— returned by: **S**SLContext.getInstance( )

SSLContextSpi: javax.net.ssl
— passed to: **S**SLContext( )

SSLException ^: javax.net.ssl
— subclasses: **S**SLHandshakeException ^ **S**SLKeyException ^ **S**SLPeerUnverifiedException ^ **S**SLProtocolException ^

SSLHandshakeException ^: javax.net.ssl

SSLKeyException ^: javax.net.ssl

SSLPeerUnverifiedException ^: javax.net.ssl
— thrown by: **H**andshakeCompletedEvent ^ < getPeerCertificateChain( ), getPeerCertificates( ) > **H**ttpsURLConnection ^.getServerCertificates( ) *SSLSession* < getPeerCertificateChain( ), getPeerCertificates( ) >

SSLPermission ^: javax.net.ssl

SSLProtocolException ^: javax.net.ssl

SSLServerSocket ^: javax.net.ssl

SSLServerSocketFactory ^: javax.net.ssl
— returned by: **S**SLContext.getServerSocketFactory( ) **S**SLContextSpi.engineGetServerSocketFactory( )

SSLSession: javax.net.ssl
— passed to: **H**andshakeCompletedEvent( ) *HostnameVerifier*.verify( ) **S**SLSessionBindingEvent( )
— returned by: **H**andshakeCompletedEvent ^.getSession( ) **S**SLSessionBindingEvent ^.getSession( ) **S**SLSessionContext.getSession( ) **S**SLSocket ^.getSession( ) **S**tartTlsResponse.negotiate( )

SSLSessionBindingEvent ^: javax.net.ssl
— passed to: **S**SLSessionBindingListener ^ < valueBound( ), valueUnbound( ) >

SSLSessionBindingListener ^: javax.net.ssl

SSLSessionContext: javax.net.ssl
— returned by: **S**SLContext < getClientSessionContext( ), getServerSessionContext( ) > **S**SLContextSpi < engineGetClientSessionContext( ), engineGetServerSessionContext( ) > **S**SLSession.getSessionContext( )

SSLSocket ^: javax.net.ssl
— passed to: **H**andshakeCompletedEvent( )
— returned by: **H**andshakeCompletedEvent ^.getSocket( )

SSLSocketFactory ^: javax.net.ssl
— passed to: **H**ttpsURLConnection ^ < setDefaultSSLSocketFactory( ), setSSLSocketFactory( ) > **S**tartTlsResponse.negotiate( )
— returned by: **H**ttpsURLConnection < getDefaultSSLSocketFactory( ), getSSLSocketFactory( ) > **S**SLContext.getSocketFactory( ) **S**SLContextSpi.engineGetSocketFactory( )

Stack ^: java.util

S

S

MultipleComponentProfileHelper < insert( ),
write( ) > MultipleComponentProfileHolder( )
TaggedComponentHelper < insert( ), write( ) >
TaggedComponentHolder( )
—returned by: *ClientRequestInfoOperations*
< get_effective_component( ), get_effective_components( ) >
MultipleComponentProfileHelper < extract( ), read( ) >
TaggedComponentHelper < extract( ), read( ) >
—fields: MultipleComponentProfileHolder.value
TaggedComponentHolder.value
TaggedComponentHelper: org.omg.IOP
TaggedComponentHolder: org.omg.IOP
TaggedProfile: org.omg.IOP
—passed to: **IOR**( ) TaggedProfileHelper < insert( ), write( ) >
TaggedProfileHolder( )
—returned by: *ClientRequestInfoOperations*.effective_profile( )
TaggedProfileHelper < extract( ), read( ) >
—fields: **IOR**.profiles TaggedProfileHolder.value
TaggedProfileHelper: org.omg.IOP
TaggedProfileHolder: org.omg.IOP
tailMap( ): *SortedMap* TreeMap
tailSet( ): *SortedSet* TreeSet
TAIWAN: Locale
TAMIL: Character.UnicodeBlock
tan( ): Math StrictMath
target( ): *ClientRequestInfoOperations* Request
target_is_a( ): *ServerRequestInfoOperations*
target_most_derived_interface( ):
ServerRequestInfoOperations
targetMustExist( ): *EventContext*
TC_ARRAY: *ObjectStreamConstants*
TC_BASE: *ObjectStreamConstants*
TC_BLOCKDATA: *ObjectStreamConstants*
TC_BLOCKDATALONG: *ObjectStreamConstants*
TC_CLASS: *ObjectStreamConstants*
TC_CLASSDESC: *ObjectStreamConstants*
TC_ENDBLOCKDATA: *ObjectStreamConstants*
TC_EXCEPTION: *ObjectStreamConstants*
TC_LONGSTRING: *ObjectStreamConstants*
TC_MAX: *ObjectStreamConstants*
TC_NULL: *ObjectStreamConstants*
TC_OBJECT: *ObjectStreamConstants*
TC_PROXYCLASSDESC: *ObjectStreamConstants*
TC_REFERENCE: *ObjectStreamConstants*
TC_RESET: *ObjectStreamConstants*
TC_STRING: *ObjectStreamConstants*
TCKind: org.omg.CORBA
—passed to: org.omg.CORBA.**ORB**.get_primitive_tc( )
—returned by: _DynStructStub.current_member_kind( )
_DynUnionStub < discriminator_kind( ), member_kind( ) >
_DynValueStub.current_member_kind( )
org.omg.CORBA.DynStruct.current_member_kind( )
DynStructOperations.current_member_kind( )
org.omg.CORBA.DynUnion < discriminator_kind( ),
member_kind( ) > *DynUnionOperations*
< discriminator_kind( ), member_kind( ) >
org.omg.CORBA.DynValue.current_member_kind( )
DynValueOperations.current_member_kind( )
TCKind.from_int( ) TypeCode.kind( )
—fields: TCKind < tk_abstract_interface, tk_alias, tk_any, tk_array,
tk_boolean, tk_char, tk_double, tk_enum, tk_except, tk_fixed,
tk_float, tk_long, tk_longdouble, tk_longlong, tk_native, tk_null,
tk_objref, tk_octet, tk_Principal, tk_sequence, tk_short,
tk_string, tk_struct, tk_TypeCode, tk_ulong, tk_ulonglong,
tk_union, tk_ushort, tk_value, tk_value_box, tk_void, tk_wchar,
tk_wstring >
TCP_NODELAY: *SocketOptions*
TELUGU: Character.UnicodeBlock
Templates: javax.xml.transform
—passed to: **S**AXTransformerFactory < newTransformerHandler( ),
newXMLFilter( ) >

—returned by: *TemplatesHandler*.getTemplates( )
TransformerFactory.newTemplates( )
TemplatesHandler: javax.xml.transform.sax
—returned by: **S**AXTransformerFactory.newTemplatesHandler( )
TERTIARY: Collator
tertiaryOrder( ): CollationElementIterator
testBit( ): BigInteger
Text: org.w3c.dom
—extended by: CDATASection
—returned by: Document.createTextNode( ) Text.splitText( )
TEXT_NODE: Node
TextInputCallback: javax.security.auth.callback
TextOutputCallback: javax.security.auth.callback
THAANA: Character.UnicodeBlock
THAI: Character.UnicodeBlock
the_activator( ): *POAOperations*
the_children( ): *POAOperations*
the_name( ): *POAOperations*
the_parent( ): *POAOperations*
the_POAManager( ): *POAOperations*
this_object( ): *org.omg.PortableServer.portable.Delegate*
thisObject( ): *Tie*
Thread: java.lang
—passed to: **R**untime < addShutdownHook( ),
removeShutdownHook( ) > SecurityManager.checkAccess( )
Thread.enumerate( ) ThreadGroup < enumerate( ),
uncaughtException( ) >
—returned
by: javax.swing.text.**A**bstractDocument.getCurrentWriter( )
Thread.currentThread( )
THREAD_POLICY_ID: org.omg.PortableServer
ThreadDeath: java.lang
ThreadGroup: java.lang
—passed to: **S**ecurityManager.checkAccess( ) Thread( )
ThreadGroup < enumerate( ), parentOf( ), ThreadGroup( ) >
—returned by: **S**ecurityManager.getThreadGroup( )
Thread.getThreadGroup( ) ThreadGroup.getParent( )
ThreadLocal: java.lang
—subclasses: InheritableThreadLocal
ThreadPolicy: org.omg.PortableServer
—returned by: *POAOperations*.create_thread_policy( )
ThreadPolicyOperations: org.omg.PortableServer
—extended by: *ThreadPolicy*
ThreadPolicyValue: org.omg.PortableServer
—passed to: *POAOperations*.create_thread_policy( )
—returned by: *ThreadPolicyOperations*.value( )
ThreadPolicyValue.from_int( )
—fields: ThreadPolicyValue < ORB_CTRL_MODEL,
SINGLE_THREAD_MODEL >
Throwable: java.lang
—subclasses: Error Exception
—descendents: **A**bstractMethodError AccessControlException
AccessException AccountExpiredException
AclNotFoundException ActivateFailedException
ActivationException AdapterAlreadyExists
AdapterInactive AdapterNonExistent
AlreadyBound AlreadyBoundException
AlreadyConnectedException ApplicationException
ArithmeticException ArrayIndexOutOfBoundsException
ArrayStoreException AssertionError
AsynchronousCloseException AttributeInUseException
AttributeModificationException AuthenticationException
AuthenticationNotSupportedException java.awt.**A**WTError
java.awt.**A**WTException BackingStoreException
BAD_CONTEXT BAD_INV_ORDER BAD_OPERATION
BAD_PARAM BAD_TYPECODE BadKind
javax.swing.text.**B**adLocationException
BadPaddingException BatchUpdateException
BindException org.omg.CORBA.Bounds
org.omg.CORBA.TypeCodePackage.Bounds
BufferOverflowException BufferUnderflowException
CancelledKeyException CannotProceed

SQLException, SQLWarning^ SSLException^
SSLHandshakeException^ SSLKeyException^
SSLPeerUnverifiedException^ SSLProtocolException^
StackOverflowError^ StreamCorruptedException^
StringIndexOutOfBoundsException^
StubNotFoundException^ SyncFailedException^
SystemException, ThreadDeath
TimeLimitExceededException^
TooManyListenersException TRANSACTION_REQUIRED^
TRANSACTION_ROLLEDBACK^
TransactionRequiredException^
TransactionRolledbackException^
TransformerConfigurationException^ TransformerException,
TransformerFactoryConfigurationError TRANSIENT^
org.omg.CORBA.DynAnyPackage.TypeMismatch^
org.omg.DynamicAny.DynAnyPackage.TypeMismatch^
org.omg.IOP.CodecPackage.TypeMismatch^
UndeclaredThrowableException UnexpectedException^
UNKNOWN^ UnknownEncoding^ UnknownError^
UnknownException^ UnknownGroupException^
java.net.UnknownHostException^
java.rmi.UnknownHostException^ UnknownObjectException^
UnknownServiceException^ UnknownUserException^
UnmappableCharacterException^ UnmarshalException^
javax.print.attribute.UnmodifiableSetException
UnrecoverableKeyException^ UnresolvedAddressException^
UnsatisfiedLinkError^ UnsupportedAddressTypeException^
javax.sound.sampled.UnsupportedAudioFileException
UnsupportedCallbackException
UnsupportedCharsetException^
UnsupportedClassVersionError^
UnsupportedEncodingException^
java.awt.datatransfer.UnsupportedFlavorException
javax.swing.UnsupportedLookAndFeelException
UnsupportedOperationException, URISyntaxException
UserException, UTFDataFormatException^ VerifyError^
VirtualMachineError, WriteAbortedException^
WrongAdapter^ WrongPolicy^ WrongTransaction^
XAException ZipException^
—passed to: ActivationException( )
BackingStoreException( ) CertPathBuilderException( )
CertPathValidatorException( ) CertStoreException( )
ClassNotFoundException( ) Error( ) Exception( )
ExceptionInInitializerError( ) javax.imageio.IIOException( )
javax.imageio.metadata.IIOInvalidTreeException( )
InvalidPreferencesFormatException( )
InvocationTargetException( ) Logger < log( ), logp( ),
logrb( ), throwing( ) > LogRecord.setThrown( )
NamingException,.setRootCause( ) RemoteException( )
RuntimeException( ) Thread.stop( )
ThreadGroup.uncaughtException( ) Throwable, < initCause( ),
Throwable( ) > TransformerConfigurationException( )
TransformerException( ) UndeclaredThrowableException( )
UnknownException( ) Util.wrapException( )
UtilDelegate.wrapException( )
—returned by: ClassNotFoundException.getException( )
ExceptionInInitializerError^.getException( )
InvocationTargetException.getTargetException( )
LogRecord.getThrown( ) NamingException,.getRootCause( )
Throwable, < fillInStackTrace( ), getCause( ),
initCause( ) > TransformerException,.getException( )
UndeclaredThrowableException.getUndeclaredThrowable( )
—thrown by: javax.swing.text.AbstractDocument ↵
.AbstractElement.finalize( ) java.awt.Cursor.finalize( )
java.awt.Font.finalize( ) java.awt.Frame^.finalize( )
javax.imageio.stream.ImageInputStreamImpl.finalize( )
InvocationHandler.invoke( ) java.lang.Object.finalize( )
javax.imageio.spi.ServiceRegistry.finalize( )
java.awt.Window^.finalize( )

—fields: ActivationException,.detail
NamingException,.rootException RemoteException^.detail
UnknownException^.originalEx
throwException( ): CoderResult
throwing( ): Logger
THURSDAY: Calendar,
TIBETAN: Character.UnicodeBlock^
Tie^: javax.rmi.CORBA
—passed to: Util.registerTarget( ) *UtilDelegate*.registerTarget( )
—returned by: Util.getTie( ) *UtilDelegate*.getTie( )
time: Calendar,
TIME: Types
Time^: java.sql
—passed to: *CallableStatement*^.setTime( )
PreparedStatement^.setTime( ) *ResultSet*^.updateTime( )
RowSet^.setTime( ) *SQLOutput*.writeTime( )
—returned by: *CallableStatement*^.getTime( )
ResultSet,.getTime( ) *SQLInput*.readTime( ) Time^.valueOf( )
TIME_ZONE: DateFormat.Field^
TimeLimitExceededException^: javax.naming
Timer: java.util
TimerTask: java.util
—passed to: java.util.Timer < schedule( ), scheduleAtFixedRate( ) >
TIMESTAMP: Types
Timestamp^: java.sql
—passed to: *CallableStatement*^.setTimestamp( )
PreparedStatement^.setTimestamp( ) *RowSet*^.setTimestamp( )
ResultSet,.updateTimestamp( ) *RowSet*^.setTimestamp( )
SQLOutput.writeTimestamp( ) Timestamp^ < after( ), before( ),
compareTo( ), equals( ) >
—returned by: *CallableStatement*^.getTimestamp( )
ResultSet,.getTimestamp( ) *SQLInput*.readTimestamp( )
Timestamp^.valueOf( )
TimeZone,: java.util
—subclasses: SimpleTimeZone^
—passed to: Calendar, < Calendar( ), getInstance( ),
setTimeZone( ) > DateFormat^.setTimeZone( )
GregorianCalendar( ) TimeZone, < hasSameRules( ),
setDefault( ) >
—returned by: Calendar,.getTimeZone( )
DateFormat^.getTimeZone( ) TimeZone, < getDefault( ),
getTimeZone( ) >
TIMEZONE_FIELD: DateFormat^
TINYINT: Types
TITLECASE_LETTER: Character
tk_abstract_interface: TCKind
tk_alias: TCKind
tk_any: TCKind
tk_array: TCKind
tk_boolean: TCKind
tk_char: TCKind
tk_double: TCKind
tk_enum: TCKind
tk_except: TCKind
tk_fixed: TCKind
tk_float: TCKind
tk_long: TCKind
tk_longdouble: TCKind
tk_longlong: TCKind
tk_native: TCKind
tk_null: TCKind
tk_objref: TCKind
tk_octet: TCKind
tk_Principal: TCKind
tk_sequence: TCKind
tk_short: TCKind
tk_string: TCKind
tk_struct: TCKind
tk_TypeCode: TCKind
tk_ulong: TCKind
tk_ulonglong: TCKind
tk_union: TCKind

T

InvalidValueHelper.type( ) IORHelper.type( )
IORHolder._type( ) IstringHelper.type( ) LongHolder._type( )
LongLongSeqHelper.type( ) LongLongSeqHolder._type( )
LongSeqHelper.type( ) LongSeqHolder._type( )
MultipleComponentProfileHelper.type( )
MultipleComponentProfileHolder._type( )
NameComponentHelper.type( )
NameComponentHolder._type( )
NameDynAnyPairHelper.type( )
NameDynAnyPairSeqHelper.type( )
NameHelper.type( ) NameHolder._type( )
org.omg.CORBA.NameValuePairHelper.type( )
org.omg.DynamicAny.NameValuePairHelper.type( )
NameValuePairSeqHelper.type( )
NamingContextExtHelper.type( )
NamingContextExtHolder._type( )
NamingContextHelper.type( ) NamingContextHolder._type( )
NoContextHelper.type( ) NoServantHelper.type( )
NotEmptyHelper.type( ) NotEmptyHolder._type( )
NotFoundHelper.type( ) NotFoundHolder._type( )
NotFoundReasonHelper.type( )
NotFoundReasonHolder._type( )
ObjectAlreadyActiveHelper.type( ) ObjectHelper.type( )
ObjectHolder._type( ) ObjectIdHelper.type( )
ObjectNotActiveHelper.type( ) OctetSeqHelper.type( )
OctetSeqHolder._type( ) org.omg.CORBA.ORB
< create_abstract_interface_tc( ), create_alias_tc( ),
create_array_tc( ), create_enum_tc( ), create_exception_tc( ),
create_fixed_tc( ), create_interface_tc( ), create_native_tc( ),
create_recursive_sequence_tc( ), create_recursive_tc( ),
create_sequence_tc( ), create_string_tc( ), create_struct_tc( ),
create_union_tc( ), create_value_box_tc( ), create_value_tc( ),
create_wstring_tc( ), get_primitive_tc( ) >
ParameterModeHelper.type( ) ParameterModeHolder._type( )
POAHelper.type( ) PolicyErrorCodeHelper.type( )
PolicyErrorHelper.type( ) PolicyErrorHolder._type( )
PolicyHelper.type( ) PolicyHolder._type( )
PolicyListHelper.type( ) PolicyListHolder._type( )
PolicyTypeHelper.type( ) PrincipalHolder._type( )
ProfileIdHelper.type( ) RepositoryIdHelper.type( )
RequestInfoOperations .exceptions( )
ServantActivatorHelper.type( )
ServantAlreadyActiveHelper.type( )
ServantLocatorHelper.type( ) ServantNotActiveHelper.type( )
ServiceContextHelper.type( ) ServiceContextHolder._type( )
ServiceContextListHelper.type( )
ServiceContextListHolder._type( ) ServiceDetailHelper.type( )
ServiceIdHelper.type( ) ServiceInformationHelper.type( )
ServiceInformationHolder._type( )
SetOverrideTypeHelper.type( ) ShortHolder._type( )
ShortSeqHelper.type( ) ShortSeqHolder._type( )
Streamable ._type( ) StringHolder._type( )
StringNameHelper.type( ) StringSeqHelper.type( )
StringSeqHolder._type( ) StringValueHelper.type( )
StructMemberHelper.type( ) SyncScopeHelper.type( )
TaggedComponentHelper.type( )
TaggedComponentHolder._type( )
TaggedProfileHelper.type( ) TaggedProfileHolder._type( )
TypeCode < concrete_base_type( ), content_type( ),
discriminator_type( ), get_compact_typecode( ), member_type( ) >
TypeCodeHolder._type( ) org.omg.DynamicAny
.DynAnyPackage.TypeMismatchHelper.type( )
org.omg.IOP.CodecPackage.TypeMismatchHelper.type( )
ULongLongSeqHelper.type( ) ULongLongSeqHolder._type( )
ULongSeqHelper.type( ) ULongSeqHolder._type( )
UnionMemberHelper.type( ) UnknownEncodingHelper.type( )
UnknownUserExceptionHelper.type( )
UnknownUserExceptionHolder._type( )
URLStringHelper.type( ) UShortSeqHelper.type( )
UShortSeqHolder._type( ) ValueBaseHelper.type( )
ValueBaseHolder._type( ) ValueMemberHelper.type( )
VersionSpecHelper.type( ) VisibilityHelper.type( )

WCharSeqHelper.type( ) WCharSeqHolder._type( )
WrongAdapterHelper.type( ) WrongPolicyHelper.type( )
WrongTransactionHelper.type( )
WrongTransactionHolder._type( ) WStringSeqHelper.type( )
WStringSeqHolder._type( ) WStringValueHelper.type( )
—fields: StructMember.type TypeCodeHolder.value
UnionMember.type ValueMember.type
TypeCodeHolder: org.omg.CORBA
TypeMismatch^: org.omg.CORBA.DynAnyPackage
—thrown by: *org.omg.CORBA.DynAny*^ < get_any( ),
get_boolean( ), get_char( ), get_double( ), get_float( ),
get_long( ), get_longlong( ), get_octet( ), get_reference( ),
get_short( ), get_string( ), get_typecode( ), get_ulong( ),
get_ulonglong( ), get_ushort( ), get_val( ), get_wchar( ),
get_wstring( ) >
TypeMismatch^: org.omg.DynamicAny.DynAnyPackage
—passed to: org.omg.DynamicAny.DynAnyPackage↵
.TypeMismatchHelper < insert( ), write( ) >
—returned by: org.omg.DynamicAny.DynAnyPackage↵
.TypeMismatchHelper < extract( ), read( ) >
—thrown by: _DynAnyStub^ < assign( ), current_component( ),
from_any( ), get_any( ), get_boolean( ), get_char( ),
get_double( ), get_dyn_any( ), get_float( ), get_long( ),
get_longlong( ), get_octet( ), get_reference( ), get_short( ),
get_string( ), get_typecode( ), get_ulong( ), get_ulonglong( ),
get_ushort( ), get_val( ), get_wchar( ), get_wstring( ),
insert_any( ), insert_boolean( ), insert_char( ), insert_double( ),
insert_dyn_any( ), insert_float( ), insert_long( ), insert_longlong( ),
insert_octet( ), insert_reference( ), insert_short( ), insert_string( ),
insert_typecode( ), insert_ulong( ), insert_ulonglong( ),
insert_ushort( ), insert_val( ), insert_wchar( ), insert_wstring( ) >
_DynArrayStub^ < assign( ), current_component( ), from_any( ),
get_any( ), get_boolean( ), get_char( ), get_double( ),
get_dyn_any( ), get_float( ), get_long( ), get_longlong( ),
get_octet( ), get_reference( ), get_short( ), get_string( ),
get_typecode( ), get_ulong( ), get_ulonglong( ), get_ushort( ),
get_val( ), get_wchar( ), get_wstring( ), insert_any( ),
insert_boolean( ), insert_char( ), insert_double( ),
insert_dyn_any( ), insert_float( ), insert_long( ), insert_longlong( ),
insert_octet( ), insert_reference( ), insert_short( ), insert_string( ),
insert_typecode( ), insert_ulong( ), insert_ulonglong( ),
insert_ushort( ), insert_val( ), insert_wchar( ), insert_wstring( ),
set_elements( ), set_elements_as_dyn_any( ) > _DynEnumStub^
< assign( ), current_component( ), from_any( ), get_any( ),
get_boolean( ), get_char( ), get_double( ), get_dyn_any( ),
get_float( ), get_long( ), get_longlong( ), get_octet( ),
get_reference( ), get_short( ), get_string( ), get_typecode( ),
get_ulong( ), get_ulonglong( ), get_ushort( ), get_val( ),
get_wchar( ), get_wstring( ), insert_any( ), insert_boolean( ),
insert_char( ), insert_double( ), insert_dyn_any( ), insert_float( ),
insert_long( ), insert_longlong( ), insert_octet( ),
insert_reference( ), insert_short( ), insert_string( ),
insert_typecode( ), insert_ulong( ), insert_ulonglong( ),
insert_ushort( ), insert_val( ), insert_wchar( ), insert_wstring( ) >
_DynFixedStub^ < assign( ), current_component( ), from_any( ),
get_any( ), get_boolean( ), get_char( ), get_double( ),
get_dyn_any( ), get_float( ), get_long( ), get_longlong( ),
get_octet( ), get_reference( ), get_short( ), get_string( ),
get_typecode( ), get_ulong( ), get_ulonglong( ), get_ushort( ),
get_val( ), get_wchar( ), get_wstring( ), insert_any( ),
insert_boolean( ), insert_char( ), insert_double( ),
insert_dyn_any( ), insert_float( ), insert_long( ),
insert_longlong( ), insert_octet( ), insert_reference( ),
insert_short( ), insert_string( ), insert_typecode( ), insert_ulong( ),
insert_ulonglong( ), insert_ushort( ), insert_val( ), insert_wchar( ),
insert_wstring( ), set_value( ) > _DynSequenceStub^
< assign( ), current_component( ), from_any( ), get_any( ),
get_boolean( ), get_char( ), get_double( ), get_dyn_any( ),
get_float( ), get_long( ), get_longlong( ), get_octet( ),
get_reference( ), get_short( ), get_string( ), get_typecode( ),
get_ulong( ), get_ulonglong( ), get_ushort( ), get_val( ),
get_wchar( ), get_wstring( ), insert_any( ), insert_boolean( ),

U

UnknownObjectException^: java.rmi.activation
—thrown by: **A**ctivatable^ < inactive( ), unregister( ) >
ActivationGroup^ < activeObject( ), inactiveObject( ) >
ActivationID.activate( ) *ActivationMonitor*^ < activeObject( ),
inactiveObject( ) > *ActivationSystem*^ < getActivationDesc( ),
setActivationDesc( ), unregisterObject( ) > **A**ctivator^.activate( )
UnknownServiceException^: java.net
UnknownUserException^: org.omg.CORBA
—passed to: **U**nknownUserExceptionHelper < insert( ), write( ) >
UnknownUserExceptionHolder( )
—returned by: **U**nknownUserExceptionHelper < extract( ),
read( ) >
—fields: **U**nknownUserExceptionHolder.value
UnknownUserExceptionHelper: org.omg.CORBA
UnknownUserExceptionHolder: org.omg.CORBA
unmappableCharacterAction( ): **C**harsetDecoder
CharsetEncoder
UnmappableCharacterException^: java.nio.charset
unmappableForLength( ): **C**oderResult
unmarshal( ): *CustomMarshal*
UnmarshalException^: java.rmi
unmodifiableCollection( ): **C**ollections
unmodifiableList( ): **C**ollections
unmodifiableMap( ): **C**ollections
unmodifiableSet( ): **C**ollections
unmodifiableSortedMap( ): **C**ollections
unmodifiableSortedSet( ): **C**ollections
unparsedEntityDecl( ): **D**efaultHandler *DTDHandler*
HandlerBase **X**MLFilterImpl
unread( ): **P**ushbackInputStream^ **P**ushbackReader^
UnrecoverableKeyException^: java.security
—thrown by: **K**eyManagerFactory.init( )
KeyManagerFactorySpi.engineInit( ) **K**eyStore.getKey( )
KeyStoreSpi.engineGetKey( )
Unreferenced: java.rmi.server
unreferenced( ): *Unreferenced*
unregister( ): **A**ctivatable^
unregister_value_factory( ): org.omg.CORBA_2_3.**O**RB^
unregisterGroup( ): *ActivationSystem*^
unregisterObject( ): *ActivationSystem*^
UnresolvedAddressException^: java.nio.channels
UnresolvedPermission^: java.security
UnsatisfiedLinkError^: java.lang
unscaledValue( ): **B**igDecimal^
UNSEQ_TOKEN: **G**SSException
UnsolicitedNotification^: javax.naming.ldap
—passed to: **U**nsolicitedNotificationEvent( )
—returned by: **U**nsolicitedNotificationEvent^.getNotification( )
UnsolicitedNotificationEvent^: javax.naming.ldap
—passed to: *UnsolicitedNotificationListener*^.notificationReceived( )
UnsolicitedNotificationListener^: javax.naming.ldap
—passed to: **U**nsolicitedNotificationEvent^.dispatch( )
UNSPECIFIED_OPTION: **C**onfirmationCallback
UNSUPPORTED_POLICY: org.omg.CORBA
UNSUPPORTED_POLICY_VALUE: org.omg.CORBA
UnsupportedAddressTypeException^: java.nio.channels
UnsupportedCallbackException: javax.security.auth.callback
—thrown by: *CallbackHandler*.handle( )
UnsupportedCharsetException^: java.nio.charset
UnsupportedClassVersionError^: java.lang
UnsupportedEncodingException^: java.io
—thrown by: **B**yteArrayOutputStream^.toString( )
Handler.setEncoding( ) **I**nputStreamReader( )
OutputStreamWriter( ) **P**rintStream( ) **S**tring < getBytes( ),
String( ) > **U**RLDecoder.decode( ) **U**RLEncoder.encode( )
UnsupportedOperationException: java.lang
—subclasses: java.awt.**H**eadlessException^
ReadOnlyBufferException^
—thrown
by: javax.imageio.**I**mageReadParam^.setSourceRenderSize( )
java.awt.**T**oolkit < getLockingKeyState( ), setLockingKeyState( ) >
unwrap( ): **C**ipher *GSSContext*

UNWRAP_MODE: **C**ipher
update( ): **A**dler32 *Checksum* **C**ipher CRC32 **M**ac
MessageDigest^ *Observer* **S**ignature^
updateArray( ): *ResultSet*
updateAsciiStream( ): *ResultSet*
updateBigDecimal( ): *ResultSet*
updateBinaryStream( ): *ResultSet*
updateBlob( ): *ResultSet*
updateBoolean( ): *ResultSet*
updateByte( ): *ResultSet*
updateBytes( ): *ResultSet*
updateCharacterStream( ): *ResultSet*
updateClob( ): *ResultSet*
updateDate( ): *ResultSet*
updateDouble( ): *ResultSet*
updateFloat( ): *ResultSet*
updateInt( ): *ResultSet*
updateLong( ): *ResultSet*
updateNull( ): *ResultSet*
updateObject( ): *ResultSet*
updateRef( ): *ResultSet*
updateRow( ): *ResultSet*
updatesAreDetected( ): *DatabaseMetaData*
updateShort( ): *ResultSet*
updateString( ): *ResultSet*
updateTime( ): *ResultSet*
updateTimestamp( ): *ResultSet*
UPPERCASE_LETTER: **C**haracter
URI: java.net
—passed to: javax.print.attribute.standard.**D**estination( )
File( ) javax.print.attribute.standard.**P**rinterMoreInfo( )
javax.print.attribute.standard.**P**rinterMoreInfoManufacturer( )
javax.print.attribute.standard.**P**rinterURI( ) **U**RI < relativize( ),
resolve( ) > javax.print.attribute.**U**RISyntax( )
—returned by: **F**ile.toURI( ) **U**RI < create( ), normalize( ),
parseServerAuthority( ), relativize( ), resolve( ) >
javax.print.URIException.getUnsupportedURI( )
javax.print.attribute.**U**RISyntax.getURI( )
URIResolver: javax.xml.transform
—passed to: **T**ransformer.setURIResolver( )
TransformerFactory.setURIResolver( )
—returned by: **T**ransformer.getURIResolver( )
TransformerFactory.getURIResolver( )
URISyntaxException: java.net
—thrown by: **U**RI < parseServerAuthority( ), URI( ) >
url: **U**RLConnection
URL: java.net
—passed to: java.applet.**A**pplet^ < getAudioClip( ), getImage( ),
newAudioClip( ), play( ) > *java.applet.AppletContext*
< getAudioClip( ), getImage( ), showDocument( ) >
javax.sound.sampled.spi.**A**udioFileReader
< getAudioFileFormat( ), getAudioInputStream( ) >
javax.sound.sampled.**A**udioSystem < getAudioFileFormat( ),
getAudioInputStream( ) > *CallableStatement*^.setURL( )
ClassLoader.definePackage( ) **C**odeSource( )
javax.swing.text.html.**H**TMLDocument^.setBase( )
javax.swing.text.html.**H**TMLFrameHyperlinkEvent( )
HttpsURLConnection( ) **H**ttpURLConnection( )
javax.swing.event.**H**yperlinkEvent( )
javax.swing.**I**mageIcon( ) javax.imageio.**I**mageIO.read( )
JarURLConnection( ) javax.swing.**J**EditorPane < getStream( ),
JEditorPane( ), setPage( ) > *LoaderHandler*.loadClass( )
javax.sound.midi.spi.**M**idiFileReader
< getMidiFileFormat( ), getSequence( ) >
javax.sound.midi.**M**idiSystem < getMidiFileFormat( ),
getSequence( ), getSoundbank( ) > **P**ackage.isSealed( )
PreparedStatement^.setURL( ) **R**MIClassLoader.loadClass( )
javax.sound.midi.spi.**S**oundbankReader.getSoundbank( )
SQLOutput.writeURL( ) javax.swing.text.html.**S**tyleSheet^

U

< importStyleSheet( ), loadRules( ), setBase( ) > java.awt.Toolkit
< createImage( ), getImage( ) > **U**RL < sameFile( ), URL( ) >
URLClassLoader^ < addURL( ), definePackage( ), newInstance( ),
URLClassLoader( ) > **U**RLConnection( ) **U**RLStreamHandler
< equals( ), getHostAddress( ), hashCode( ), hostsEqual( ),
openConnection( ), parseURL( ), sameFile( ), setURL( ),
toExternalForm( ) >
—returned by: java.applet.**A**pplet < getCodeBase( ),
getDocumentBase( ) > *java.applet.AppletStub* < getCodeBase( ),
getDocumentBase( ) > *BeanContext*^.getResource( )
BeanContextSupport^.getResource( )
CallableStatement^.getURL( ) **C**lass.getResource( )
ClassLoader, < findResource( ), getResource( ),
getSystemResource( ) > **C**odeSource.getLocation( ) **F**ile.toURL( )
javax.swing.text.html.**H**TMLDocument^.getBase( )
javax.swing.event.**H**yperlinkEvent^.getURL( )
javax.swing.text.html.**I**mageView^.getImageURL( )
JarURLConnection^.getJarFileURL( )
javax.swing.**J**EditorPane^.getPage( )
ResultSet,.getURL( ) *SQLInput*.readURL( )
javax.swing.text.html.**S**tyleSheet^.getBase( ) U**R**I.toURL( )
URLClassLoader^ < findResource( ), getURLs( ) >
URLConnection,.getURL( )
—fields: **U**RLConnection,.url
URL_PKG_PREFIXES: *javax.naming.Context*,
URLClassLoader^: java.net
—returned by: **U**RLClassLoader^.newInstance( )
URLConnection,: java.net
—subclasses: **H**ttpURLConnection^ **J**arURLConnection^
—descendents: **H**ttpsURLConnection^
—passed to: java.net.**C**ontentHandler.getContent( )
—returned by: **U**RL.openConnection( )
URLStreamHandler.openConnection( )
—fields: **J**arURLConnection^.jarFileURLConnection
URLDecoder: java.net
URLEncoder: java.net
URLStreamHandler: java.net
—passed to: **U**RL( )
—returned
by: *URLStreamHandlerFactory*.createURLStreamHandler( )
URLStreamHandlerFactory: java.net
—passed to: **U**RL.setURLStreamHandlerFactory( )
URLClassLoader( )
URLStringHelper:
org.omg.CosNaming.NamingContextExtPackage
US: Locale
USE_ACTIVE_OBJECT_MAP_ONLY:
RequestProcessingPolicyValue
USE_ALL_BEANINFO: Introspector
USE_DEFAULT_SERVANT: RequestProcessingPolicyValue
USE_SERVANT_MANAGER: RequestProcessingPolicyValue
useCaches: URLConnection,
useDaylightTime( ): TimeZone,
useProtocolVersion( ): ObjectOutputStream^
USER_EXCEPTION: org.omg.PortableInterceptor
USER_ID: IdAssignmentPolicyValue
UserException,: org.omg.CORBA
—subclasses: **A**dapterAlreadyExists^ **A**dapterInactive^
AdapterNonExistent^ **A**lreadyBound^
BadKind^ org.omg.CORBA.**B**ounds^
org.omg.CORBA.TypeCodePackage.**B**ounds^
CannotProceed^ **D**uplicateName^ **F**ormatMismatch^
org.omg.PortableInterceptor.**F**orwardRequest^
org.omg.PortableServer.**F**orwardRequest^
org.omg.CORBA.ORBPackage.**I**nconsistentTypeCode^
org.omg.DynamicAny.DynAnyFactoryPackage ↵
.InconsistentTypeCode^ **I**nvalid^ **I**nvalidAddress^
org.omg.CORBA.ORBPackage.**I**nvalidName^
org.omg.CosNaming.NamingContextPackage.**I**nvalidName^
org.omg.PortableInterceptor.ORBInitInfoPackage ↵
.InvalidName^ **I**nvalidPolicy^ **I**nvalidSeq^

InvalidSlot^ **I**nvalidTypeForEncoding^
org.omg.CORBA.DynAnyPackage.**I**nvalidValue^
org.omg.DynamicAny.DynAnyPackage.**I**nvalidValue^
NoContext^ **N**oServant^ **N**otEmpty^ **N**otFound^
ObjectAlreadyActive^ **O**bjectNotActive^ **P**olicyError^
ServantAlreadyActive^ **S**ervantNotActive^
org.omg.CORBA.DynAnyPackage.**T**ypeMismatch^
org.omg.DynamicAny.DynAnyPackage.**T**ypeMismatch^
org.omg.IOP.CodecPackage.**T**ypeMismatch^
UnknownEncoding^ **U**nknownUserException^
WrongAdapter^ **W**rongPolicy^ **W**rongTransaction^
userNodeForPackage( ): Preferences,
userRoot( ): Preferences, *PreferencesFactory*
usesLocalFilePerTable( ): *DatabaseMetaData*
usesLocalFiles( ): *DatabaseMetaData*
UShortSeqHelper: org.omg.CORBA
UShortSeqHolder: org.omg.CORBA
—passed
to: *org.omg.CORBA.DataInputStream*^.read_ushort_array( )
usingProxy( ): HttpURLConnection^
UTC( ): java.util.Date,
UTC_TIME: **S**impleTimeZone^
UTFDataFormatException^: java.io
Util: javax.rmi.CORBA
UtilDelegate: javax.rmi.CORBA
valid( ): FileDescriptor
validate( ): CertPathValidator
validate_connection( ): LocalObject
validateObject( ): *ObjectInputValidation*
validatePendingAdd( ): BeanContextSupport^
validatePendingRemove( ): BeanContextSupport^
validatePendingSetBeanContext( ): BeanContextChildSupport,
validOps( ): SelectableChannel^
value: **A**lreadyBoundHolder **A**nyHolder **A**nySeqHolder
ARG_IN ARG_INOUT ARG_OUT BAD_POLICY
BAD_POLICY_TYPE BAD_POLICY_VALUE
BindingHolder **B**indingIteratorHolder
BindingListHolder **B**indingTypeHolder
BooleanHolder **B**ooleanSeqHolder **B**yteHolder
CannotProceedHolder **C**harHolder **C**harSeqHolder
CodeSets **C**ookieHolder *CTX_RESTRICT_SCOPE*
CurrentHolder **D**oubleHolder **D**oubleSeqHolder
DriverPropertyInfo *ENCODING_CDR_ENCAPS*
FixedHolder **F**loatHolder **F**loatSeqHolder
ID_ASSIGNMENT_POLICY_ID ID_UNIQUENESS_POLICY_ID
IMPLICIT_ACTIVATION_POLICY_ID **I**ntHolder
InvalidAddressHolder **I**nvalidNameHolder **I**ORHolder
LIFESPAN_POLICY_ID LOCATION_FORWARD
LongHolder **L**ongLongSeqHolder
LongSeqHolder **M**ultipleComponentProfileHolder
NameComponentHolder **N**ameDynAnyPair
NameHolder org.omg.CORBA.**N**ameValuePair
org.omg.DynamicAny.**N**ameValuePair
NamingContextExtHolder **N**amingContextHolder
NotEmptyHolder **N**otFoundHolder **N**otFoundReasonHolder
ObjectHolder **O**ctetSeqHolder *OMGVMCID*
ParameterModeHolder **P**olicyErrorHolder **P**olicyHolder
PolicyListHolder **P**rincipalHolder *PRIVATE_MEMBER*
PUBLIC_MEMBER REQUEST_PROCESSING_POLICY_ID
SERVANT_RETENTION_POLICY_ID
ServiceContextHolder **S**erviceContextListHolder
ServiceInformationHolder **S**hortHolder **S**hortSeqHolder
StringHolder **S**tringSeqHolder *SUCCESSFUL*
SYNC_WITH_TRANSPORT SYSTEM_EXCEPTION
TAG_ALTERNATE_IIOP_ADDRESS TAG_CODE_SETS
TAG_INTERNET_IIOP TAG_JAVA_CODEBASE
TAG_MULTIPLE_COMPONENTS TAG_ORB_TYPE
TAG_POLICIES **T**aggedComponentHolder
TaggedProfileHolder *THREAD_POLICY_ID*
TransactionService TRANSPORT_RETRY **T**ypeCodeHolder
ULongLongSeqHolder **U**LongSeqHolder
UnknownUserExceptionHolder *UNSUPPORTED_POLICY*

V

—returned by: Lease.getVMID( )
Void: java.lang
VOLATILE: Modifier
wait( ): java.lang.**O**bject
waitFor( ): Process
wakeup( ): Selector
WALL_TIME: SimpleTimeZone^
WARNING: ConfirmationCallback Level TextOutputCallback
warning( ): DefaultHandler *ErrorHandler ErrorListener*
HandlerBase Logger XMLFilterImpl
wasNull( ): *CallableStatement^ ResultSet* SQLInput
WCharSeqHelper: org.omg.CORBA
WCharSeqHolder: org.omg.CORBA
—passed
to: *org.omg.CORBA.DataInputStream^*.read_wchar_array( )
WeakHashMap^: java.util
WeakReference^: java.lang.ref
WEDNESDAY: Calendar
WEEK_OF_MONTH: Calendar DateFormat.Field^
WEEK_OF_MONTH_FIELD: DateFormat^
WEEK_OF_YEAR: Calendar DateFormat.Field^
WEEK_OF_YEAR_FIELD: DateFormat^
whitespaceChars( ): StreamTokenizer
why: NotFound
wordChars( ): StreamTokenizer
work_pending( ): org.omg.CORBA.ORB
wrap( ): ByteBuffer^ CharBuffer^ Cipher DoubleBuffer^
FloatBuffer^ *GSSContext* IntBuffer^ LongBuffer^
ShortBuffer^
WRAP_MODE: Cipher
wrapException( ): Util *UtilDelegate*
WritableByteChannel^: java.nio.channels
—extended by: *ByteChannel^ GatheringByteChannel^*
—passed to: Channels < newOutputStream( ), newWriter( ) >
FileChannel^.transferTo( )
—returned by: Channels.newChannel( )
—implemented by: Pipe.SinkChannel^
write( ): AdapterAlreadyExistsHelper AdapterInactiveHelper
AdapterNonExistentHelper AddressHelper
AlreadyBoundHelper org.omg.CORBA.AnySeqHelper
org.omg.DynamicAny.AnySeqHelper BindingHelper
BindingIteratorHelper BindingListHelper
BindingTypeHelper BooleanSeqHelper
CannotProceedHelper CharSeqHelper
CodecFactoryHelper CompletionStatusHelper
ComponentIdHelper org.omg.CORBA.CurrentHelper
org.omg.PortableInterceptor.CurrentHelper
org.omg.PortableServer.CurrentHelper
DatagramChannel *DataOutput* DefinitionKindHelper
DoubleSeqHelper DuplicateNameHelper
DynAnyFactoryHelper DynAnyHelper DynAnySeqHelper
DynArrayHelper DynEnumHelper DynFixedHelper
DynSequenceHelper DynStructHelper DynUnionHelper
DynValueHelper org.omg.CORBA.FieldNameHelper
org.omg.DynamicAny.FieldNameHelper FileChannel^
FloatSeqHelper FormatMismatchHelper
org.omg.PortableInterceptor.ForwardRequestHelper
org.omg.PortableServer.ForwardRequestHelper
IdentifierHelper IDLTypeHelper
InconsistentTypeCodeHelper InvalidAddressHelper
org.omg.CosNaming.NamingContextPackage↵
.InvalidNameHelper org.omg.PortableInterceptor ↵
.ORBInitInfoPackage.InvalidNameHelper InvalidPolicyHelper
InvalidSlotHelper InvalidTypeForEncodingHelper
InvalidValueHelper IORHelper IstringHelper
LongLongSeqHelper LongSeqHelper Manifest
MultipleComponentProfileHelper NameComponentHelper
NameDynAnyPairHelper NameDynAnyPairSeqHelper
NameHelper org.omg.CORBA.NameValuePairHelper
org.omg.DynamicAny.NameValuePairHelper
NameValuePairSeqHelper NamingContextExtHelper
NamingContextHelper NoContextHelper NoServantHelper

NotEmptyHelper NotFoundHelper NotFoundReasonHelper
ObjectAlreadyActiveHelper ObjectHelper ObjectIdHelper
ObjectNotActiveHelper ObjectOutputStream.PutField
ObjID OctetSeqHelper java.io.OutputStream
ParameterModeHelper POAHelper PolicyErrorCodeHelper
PolicyErrorHelper PolicyHelper PolicyListHelper
PolicyTypeHelper ProfileIdHelper RandomAccessFile
RepositoryIdHelper ServantActivatorHelper
ServantAlreadyActiveHelper ServantLocatorHelper
ServantNotActiveHelper ServiceContextHelper
ServiceContextListHelper ServiceDetailHelper
ServiceIdHelper ServiceInformationHelper
SetOverrideTypeHelper ShortSeqHelper SocketChannel^
StringNameHelper StringSeqHelper StringValueHelper
StructMemberHelper SyncScopeHelper
TaggedComponentHelper TaggedProfileHelper
org.omg.DynamicAny.DynAnyPackage.TypeMismatchHelper
org.omg.IOP.CodecPackage.TypeMismatchHelper
UID ULongLongSeqHelper ULongSeqHelper
UnionMemberHelper UnknownEncodingHelper
UnknownUserExceptionHelper URLStringHelper
UShortSeqHelper ValueBaseHelper ValueMemberHelper
VersionSpecHelper VisibilityHelper WCharSeqHelper
WritableByteChannel^ Writer WrongAdapterHelper
WrongPolicyHelper WrongTransactionHelper
WStringSeqHelper WStringValueHelper
write_Abstract( ): *org.omg.CORBA.DataOutputStream^*
write_abstract_interface( ):
org.omg.CORBA_2_3.portable.OutputStream^
write_any( ): *org.omg.CORBA.DataOutputStream^*
org.omg.CORBA.portable.OutputStream^
write_any_array( ): *org.omg.CORBA.DataOutputStream^*
write_boolean( ): *org.omg.CORBA.DataOutputStream^*
org.omg.CORBA.portable.OutputStream^
write_boolean_array( ): *org.omg.CORBA.DataOutputStream^*
org.omg.CORBA.portable.OutputStream^
write_char( ): *org.omg.CORBA.DataOutputStream^*
org.omg.CORBA.portable.OutputStream^
write_char_array( ): *org.omg.CORBA.DataOutputStream^*
org.omg.CORBA.portable.OutputStream^
write_Context( ): org.omg.CORBA.portable.OutputStream^
write_double( ): *org.omg.CORBA.DataOutputStream^*
org.omg.CORBA.portable.OutputStream^
write_double_array( ): *org.omg.CORBA.DataOutputStream^*
org.omg.CORBA.portable.OutputStream^
WRITE_FAILURE: ErrorManager
write_fixed( ): org.omg.CORBA.portable.OutputStream^
write_float( ): *org.omg.CORBA.DataOutputStream^*
org.omg.CORBA.portable.OutputStream^
write_float_array( ): *org.omg.CORBA.DataOutputStream^*
org.omg.CORBA.portable.OutputStream^
write_long( ): *org.omg.CORBA.DataOutputStream^*
org.omg.CORBA.portable.OutputStream^
write_long_array( ): *org.omg.CORBA.DataOutputStream^*
org.omg.CORBA.portable.OutputStream^
write_longlong( ): *org.omg.CORBA.DataOutputStream^*
org.omg.CORBA.portable.OutputStream^
write_longlong_array( ): *org.omg.CORBA.DataOutputStream^*
org.omg.CORBA.portable.OutputStream^
write_Object( ): *org.omg.CORBA.DataOutputStream^*
org.omg.CORBA.portable.OutputStream^
write_octet( ): *org.omg.CORBA.DataOutputStream^*
org.omg.CORBA.portable.OutputStream^
write_octet_array( ): *org.omg.CORBA.DataOutputStream^*
org.omg.CORBA.portable.OutputStream^
write_Principal( ): org.omg.CORBA.portable.OutputStream^
write_short( ): *org.omg.CORBA.DataOutputStream^*
org.omg.CORBA.portable.OutputStream^
write_short_array( ): *org.omg.CORBA.DataOutputStream^*
org.omg.CORBA.portable.OutputStream^
write_string( ): *org.omg.CORBA.DataOutputStream^*
org.omg.CORBA.portable.OutputStream^

W

write_TypeCode(): *org.omg.CORBA.DataOutputStream*^
org.omg.CORBA.portable.**O**utputStream‿
write_ulong(): *org.omg.CORBA.DataOutputStream*^
org.omg.CORBA.portable.**O**utputStream‿
write_ulong_array(): *org.omg.CORBA.DataOutputStream*^
org.omg.CORBA.portable.**O**utputStream‿
write_ulonglong(): *org.omg.CORBA.DataOutputStream*^
org.omg.CORBA.portable.**O**utputStream‿
write_ulonglong_array(): *org.omg.CORBA.DataOutputStream*^
org.omg.CORBA.portable.**O**utputStream‿
write_ushort(): *org.omg.CORBA.DataOutputStream*^
org.omg.CORBA.portable.**O**utputStream‿
write_ushort_array(): *org.omg.CORBA.DataOutputStream*^
org.omg.CORBA.portable.**O**utputStream‿
write_value(): **A**ny *BoxedValueHelper*
org.omg.CORBA_2_3.portable.**O**utputStream^
StringValueHelper **W**StringValueHelper
write_Value(): *org.omg.CORBA.DataOutputStream*^
write_wchar(): *org.omg.CORBA.DataOutputStream*^
org.omg.CORBA.portable.**O**utputStream‿
write_wchar_array(): *org.omg.CORBA.DataOutputStream*^
org.omg.CORBA.portable.**O**utputStream‿
write_wstring(): *org.omg.CORBA.DataOutputStream*^
org.omg.CORBA.portable.**O**utputStream‿
WriteAbortedException^: java.io
writeAbstractObject(): **U**til *UtilDelegate*
writeAny(): **U**til *UtilDelegate*
writeArray(): *SQLOutput*
writeAsciiStream(): *SQLOutput*
writeBigDecimal(): *SQLOutput*
writeBinaryStream(): *SQLOutput*
writeBlob(): *SQLOutput*
writeBoolean(): *DataOutput*‿ java.io.**D**ataOutputStream^
ObjectOutputStream^ **R**andomAccessFile *SQLOutput*
writeByte(): *DataOutput*‿ java.io.**D**ataOutputStream^
ObjectOutputStream^ **R**andomAccessFile *SQLOutput*
writeBytes(): *DataOutput*‿ java.io.**D**ataOutputStream^
ObjectOutputStream^ **R**andomAccessFile *SQLOutput*
writeChar(): *DataOutput*‿ java.io.**D**ataOutputStream^
ObjectOutputStream^ **R**andomAccessFile
writeCharacterStream(): *SQLOutput*
writeChars(): *DataOutput*‿ java.io.**D**ataOutputStream^
ObjectOutputStream^ **R**andomAccessFile
writeChildren(): **B**eanContextSupport‿
writeClassDescriptor(): **O**bjectOutputStream^
writeClob(): *SQLOutput*
writeData(): *RowSetWriter*
writeDate(): *SQLOutput*
writeDouble(): *DataOutput*‿ java.io.**D**ataOutputStream^
ObjectOutputStream^ **R**andomAccessFile *SQLOutput*
writeExpression(): **E**ncoder‿
writeExternal(): *Externalizable*‿
writeFields(): **O**bjectOutputStream^
writeFloat(): *DataOutput*‿ java.io.**D**ataOutputStream^
ObjectOutputStream^ **R**andomAccessFile *SQLOutput*
writeInt(): *DataOutput*‿ java.io.**D**ataOutputStream^
ObjectOutputStream^ **R**andomAccessFile *SQLOutput*
writeLong(): *DataOutput*‿ java.io.**D**ataOutputStream^
ObjectOutputStream^ **R**andomAccessFile *SQLOutput*
writeObject(): **E**ncoder‿ *ObjectOutput*^ **O**bjectOutputStream^
PersistenceDelegate‿ *SQLOutput* *StubDelegate*
writeObjectOverride(): **O**bjectOutputStream^
Writer‿: java.io
—subclasses: **B**ufferedWriter^ **C**harArrayWriter^ **F**ilterWriter^
OutputStreamWriter‿ **P**ipedWriter^ **P**rintWriter^ **S**tringWriter^
—descendents: **F**ileWriter^
—passed to: javax.swing.text.**A**bstractWriter() **B**ufferedWriter()
CharArrayWriter^.writeTo() javax.swing.text.**E**ditorKit.write()
FilterWriter() javax.swing.text.html.**H**TMLWriter()
javax.swing.text.**J**TextComponent^.write()

javax.swing.text.html.**M**inimalHTMLWriter() **P**rintWriter()
StreamResult < setWriter(), StreamResult() >
—returned by: javax.swing.text.**A**bstractWriter.getWriter()
Channels.newWriter() *Clob*.setCharacterStream()
StreamResult.getWriter()
—fields: **F**ilterWriter^.out **P**rintWriter^.out
writeRef(): *SQLOutput*
writeRemoteObject(): **U**til *UtilDelegate*
writeReplace(): java.security.cert.**C**ertificate‿ **C**ertPath
ValueHandler
writeShort(): *DataOutput*‿ java.io.**D**ataOutputStream^
ObjectOutputStream^ **R**andomAccessFile *SQLOutput*
writeSQL(): *SQLData*
writeStatement(): **E**ncoder‿
writeStreamHeader(): **O**bjectOutputStream^
writeString(): *SQLOutput*
writeStruct(): *SQLOutput*
writeTime(): *SQLOutput*
writeTimestamp(): *SQLOutput*
writeTo(): **B**yteArrayOutputStream^ **C**harArrayWriter^
writeUnshared(): **O**bjectOutputStream^
writeURL(): *SQLOutput*
writeUTF(): *DataOutput*‿ java.io.**D**ataOutputStream^
ObjectOutputStream^ **R**andomAccessFile
writeValue(): *ValueHandler*
written: java.io.**D**ataOutputStream^
WRONG_DOCUMENT_ERR: **D**OMException
WrongAdapter^: org.omg.PortableServer.POAPackage
—passed to: **W**rongAdapterHelper < insert(), write() >
—returned by: **W**rongAdapterHelper < extract(), read() >
—thrown by: *POAOperations*‿ < reference_to_id(),
reference_to_servant() >
WrongAdapterHelper: org.omg.PortableServer.POAPackage
WrongPolicy^: org.omg.PortableServer.POAPackage
—passed to: **W**rongPolicyHelper < insert(), write() >
—returned by: **W**rongPolicyHelper < extract(), read() >
—thrown by: *POAOperations*‿ < activate_object(),
activate_object_with_id(), create_reference(), deactivate_object(),
get_servant(), get_servant_manager(), id_to_reference(),
id_to_servant(), reference_to_id(), reference_to_servant(),
servant_to_id(), servant_to_reference(), set_servant(),
set_servant_manager() >
WrongPolicyHelper: org.omg.PortableServer.POAPackage
WrongTransaction^: org.omg.CORBA
—passed to: **W**rongTransactionHelper < insert(), write() >
WrongTransactionHolder()
—returned by: **W**rongTransactionHelper < extract(), read() >
—thrown by: org.omg.CORBA.**O**RB‿.get_next_response()
Request.get_response()
—fields: **W**rongTransactionHolder.value
WrongTransactionHelper: org.omg.CORBA
WrongTransactionHolder: org.omg.CORBA
WStringSeqHelper: org.omg.CORBA
WStringSeqHolder: org.omg.CORBA
WStringValueHelper: org.omg.CORBA
X500Principal: javax.security.auth.x500
—returned by: java.security.cert.**X**509Certificate^
< getIssuerX500Principal(), getSubjectX500Principal() >
X509CRL^.getIssuerX500Principal()
X500PrivateCredential: javax.security.auth.x500
X509Certificate^: java.security.cert
—passed to: **T**rustAnchor() **X**500PrivateCredential()
X509CertSelector.setCertificate()
X509CRLSelector.setCertificateChecking() *X509TrustManager*^
< checkClientTrusted(), checkServerTrusted() >
—returned by: **T**rustAnchor.getTrustedCert()
X500PrivateCredential.getCertificate()
X509CertSelector.getCertificate()
X509CRLSelector.getCertificateChecking()
X509KeyManager^.getCertificateChain()
X509TrustManager^.getAcceptedIssuers()
X509Certificate^: javax.security.cert

—returned
  by: **H**andshakeCompletedEvent^.getPeerCertificateChain( )
    SSLSession.getPeerCertificateChain( )
    javax.security.cert.**X**509Certificate^.getInstance( )
X509CertSelector: java.security.cert
X509CRL^: java.security.cert
X509CRLEntry: java.security.cert
  —returned by: **X**509CRL^.getRevokedCertificate( )
X509CRLSelector: java.security.cert
X509EncodedKeySpec: java.security.spec
X509Extension: java.security.cert
  —implemented by: java.security.cert.**X**509Certificate^ **X**509CRL^
    X509CRLEntry
X509KeyManager^: javax.net.ssl
X509TrustManager^: javax.net.ssl
XA_HEURCOM: **X**AException
XA_HEURHAZ: **X**AException
XA_HEURMIX: **X**AException
XA_HEURRB: **X**AException
XA_NOMIGRATE: **X**AException
XA_OK: **X**AResource
XA_RBBASE: **X**AException
XA_RBCOMMFAIL: **X**AException
XA_RBDEADLOCK: **X**AException
XA_RBEND: **X**AException
XA_RBINTEGRITY: **X**AException
XA_RBOTHER: **X**AException
XA_RBPROTO: **X**AException
XA_RBROLLBACK: **X**AException
XA_RBTIMEOUT: **X**AException
XA_RBTRANSIENT: **X**AException
XA_RDONLY: **X**AException **X**AResource
XA_RETRY: **X**AException
XAConnection^: javax.sql
  —returned by: **X**ADataSource.getXAConnection( )
XADataSource: javax.sql
XAER_ASYNC: **X**AException
XAER_DUPID: **X**AException
XAER_INVAL: **X**AException
XAER_NOTA: **X**AException
XAER_OUTSIDE: **X**AException
XAER_PROTO: **X**AException
XAER_RMERR: **X**AException
XAER_RMFAIL: **X**AException
XAException: javax.transaction.xa
  —thrown by: **X**AResource < commit( ), end( ), forget( ),
    getTransactionTimeout( ), isSameRM( ), prepare( ), recover( ),
    rollback( ), setTransactionTimeout( ), start( ) >
XAResource: javax.transaction.xa
  —passed to: **X**AResource.isSameRM( )
  —returned by: **X**AConnection^.getXAResource( )
Xid: javax.transaction.xa

—passed to: **X**AResource < commit( ), end( ), forget( ), prepare( ),
  rollback( ), start( ) >
—returned by: **X**AResource.recover( )
XMLDecoder: java.beans
XMLEncoder^: java.beans
XMLFilter^: org.xml.sax
  —returned by: **S**AXTransformerFactory^.newXMLFilter( )
  —implemented by: **X**MLFilterImpl
XMLFilterImpl: org.xml.sax.helpers
XMLFormatter: java.util.logging
XMLNS: **N**amespaceSupport
XMLReader: org.xml.sax
  —extended by: **X**MLFilter^
  —passed to: **S**AXSource < SAXSource( ), setXMLReader( ) >
    XMLFilter^.setParent( ) **X**MLFilterImpl < setParent( ),
    XMLFilterImpl( ) > **X**MLReaderAdapter( )
  —returned by: **S**AXParser.getXMLReader( )
    SAXSource.getXMLReader( )
    XMLFilter^.getParent( ) **X**MLFilterImpl.getParent( )
    XMLReaderFactory.createXMLReader( )
  —implemented by: **P**arserAdapter
XMLReaderAdapter: org.xml.sax.helpers
XMLReaderFactory: org.xml.sax.helpers
xor( ): **B**igInteger^ **B**itSet
YEAR: **C**alendar, **D**ateFormat.Field^
YEAR_FIELD: **D**ateFormat^
YES: **C**onfirmationCallback
YES_NO_CANCEL_OPTION: **C**onfirmationCallback
YES_NO_OPTION: **C**onfirmationCallback
YI_RADICALS: **C**haracter.UnicodeBlock^
YI_SYLLABLES: **C**haracter.UnicodeBlock^
yield( ): **T**hread
ZERO: **B**igInteger^
  —implemented by: **Z**ipEntry, **Z**ipFile, **Z**ipInputStream^
    ZipOutputStream^
ZipEntry: java.util.zip
  —subclasses: **J**arEntry^
  —passed to: **J**arEntry( ) **Z**ipEntry( ) **Z**ipFile.getInputStream( )
    ZipOutputStream^.putNextEntry( )
  —returned by: **J**arInputStream^.createZipEntry( ) **Z**ipFile.getEntry( )
    ZipInputStream^ < createZipEntry( ), getNextEntry( ) >
ZipException^: java.util.zip
  —subclasses: **J**arException^
  —thrown by: **Z**ipFile( )
ZipFile: java.util.zip
  —subclasses: **J**arFile^
ZipInputStream^: java.util.zip
  —subclasses: **J**arInputStream^
ZipOutputStream^: java.util.zip
  —subclasses: **J**arOutputStream^
ZONE_OFFSET: **C**alendar,

Z

The Java™ Series

The Java™ Programming
Language
Third Edition

ISBN 0-201-70433-1

Effective Java™
Programming Language Guide

ISBN 0-201-31005-8

The J2EE™ Tutorial

ISBN 0-201-79168-4

The Real-Time
Specification
for Java™

ISBN 0-201-70323-8

The Java™ Tutorial,
Third Edition
A Short Course on the Basics

ISBN 0-201-70393-9

The Java™ Tutorial
Continued
The Rest of the JDK™

ISBN 0-201-48558-3

J2EE™ Technology
in Practice
Building Business Applications with
the Java™ 2 Platform, Enterprise Edition

ISBN 0-201-74622-0

The Java™ Developers
ALMANAC 2000

ISBN 0-201-43299-4

The Java™ Class Libraries
Second Edition, Volume 1
java.io   java.lang
java.net   java.text   java.util

ISBN 0-201-31002-3

The Java™ Class Libraries
Second Edition, Volume 2
java.applet   java.awt   java.beans

ISBN 0-201-31003-1

The Java™ Class Libraries
Second Edition, Volume 1
Supplement for the Java™ 2 Platform
Standard Edition, v1.2

ISBN 0-201-48552-4

Programming Open Service
Gateways with Java Embedded
Server™ Technology

ISBN 0-201-71102-8

Java Card™ Technology
for Smart Cards
Architecture and Programmer's Guide

ISBN 0-201-70329-7

JavaSpaces™ Principles,
Patterns, and Practice

ISBN 0-201-30955-6

Inside Java™ 2
Platform Security
Architecture, API Design,
and Implementation

ISBN 0-201-31000-7

The Java™ Language
Specification, Second
Edition

ISBN 0-201-31008-2

Java™ Message Service
API Tutorial and Reference
Messaging for the J2EE™ Platform

ISBN 0-201-63456-2

The Java™
FAQ

ISBN 0-201-63456-2

Designing Enterprise
Applications with the Java™ 2
Platform, Enterprise Edition

ISBN 0-201-70277-0

Concurrent
Programming in Java™
Second Edition
Design Principles and Patterns

ISBN 0-201-31009-0

JNDI API Tutorial
and Reference
Building Directory-Enabled
Java™ Applications

ISBN 0-201-70502-8

The Java™
Native Interface
Programmer's Guide
and Specification

ISBN 0-201-32577-2

The Java™ Virtual
Machine Specification
Second Edition

ISBN 0-201-43294-3

Applying Enterprise
JavaBeans™
Component-Based Development
for the J2EE Platform

ISBN 0-201-70267-3

Programming Wireless
Devices with the Java™ 2
Platform, Micro Edition

ISBN 0-201-74627-1

Java™ 2 Platform,
Enterprise Edition
Platform and Component
Specifications

ISBN 0-201-70456-0

J2EE™ Connector
Architecture and Enterprise
Application Integration

ISBN 0-201-77580-8

The Java 3D™
API Specification,
Second Edition

ISBN 0-201-71041-2

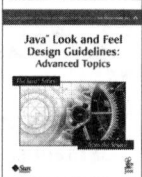

Java™ Look and Feel
Design Guidelines:
Advanced Topics

ISBN 0-201-77582-4

The JFC
Swing Tutorial
A Guide to Constructing GUIs

ISBN 0-201-43321-4

JDBC™ API Tutorial and
Reference, Second Edition
Universal Data Access for
the Java™ 2 Platform

ISBN 0-201-43328-1

Java™ Platform
Performance
Strategies and Tactics

ISBN 0-201-70969-4

The Jini™ Specifications
Second Edition

ISBN 0-201-72617-3

Please see our web site (http://www.awl.com/cseng/javaseries)
for more information on these titles.

Register
Your Book

at www.aw.com/cseng/register

You may be eligible to receive:
- Advance notice of forthcoming editions of the book
- Related book recommendations
- Chapter excerpts and supplements of forthcoming titles
- Information about special contests and promotions throughout the year
- Notices and reminders about author appearances, tradeshows, and online chats with special guests

Contact us

If you are interested in writing a book or reviewing manuscripts prior to publication, please write to us at:

Editorial Department
Addison-Wesley Professional
75 Arlington Street, Suite 300
Boston, MA 02116 USA
Email: AWPro@aw.com

Addison-Wesley

Visit us on the Web: http://www.aw.com/cseng